Contemporary Authors®

NEW REVISION SERIES

Contemporary Authors
was named an
"Outstanding
Reference Source" *by*
the American Library
Association Reference
and Adult Services
Division after its 1962
inception.
In 1985 it was listed by
the same organization
as one of the
twenty-five most
distinguished reference
titles published in the
past twenty-five years.

ISSN 0275-7176

Contemporary Authors®

**A Bio-Bibliographical Guide to
Current Writers in Fiction, General Nonfiction,
Poetry, Journalism, Drama, Motion Pictures,
Television, and Other Fields**

JAMES G. LESNIAK
Editor

NEW REVISION SERIES
volume 37

 **Gale Research Inc.** • DETROIT • LONDON

STAFF

James G. Lesniak, *Editor, New Revision Series*

Elizabeth A. Des Chenes, Kevin S. Hile, Kenneth R. Shepherd, and Thomas Wiloch, *Associate Editors*

Bruce Ching, David Johnson, Margaret Mazurkiewicz, Tom Pendergast,
Susan Reicha, Pamela L. Shelton, and Deborah A. Stanley, *Assistant Editors*

Jean W. Ross, *Interviewer*

Marilyn K. Basel, Anne Janette Johnson, Sharon Malinowski, Diane Telgen, and Michaela Swart Wilson,
Contributing Editors

Hal May, *Senior Editor, Contemporary Authors*

Victoria B. Cariappa, *Research Manager*

Mary Rose Bonk, *Research Supervisor*

Reginald A. Carlton, Clare Collins, Andrew Guy Malonis, and Norma Sawaya, *Editorial Associates*

Mike Avolio, Patricia Bowen, Catherine A. Coulson, Rachel A. Dixon, Shirley Gates,
Sharon McGilvray, and Devra M. Sladics, *Editorial Assistants*

Special acknowledgment is due to members of the
Contemporary Authors Original Volumes staff who assisted in the preparation of this volume.

♾️™ This book is printed on acid-free paper that meets the minimum requirements
of American National Standard for Information Sciences—
Permanence Paper for Printed Library Materials, ANSI Z39.48-1984.

Library of Congress Catalog Card Number 81-640179
ISBN 0-8103-1991-8
ISSN 0275-7176

Printed in the United States of America.

Published simultaneously in the United Kingdom
by Gale Research International Limited
(An affiliated company of Gale Research Inc.)

Contents

Indexing note: All *Contemporary Authors New Revision Series* entries are indexed in the *Contemporary Authors* cumulative index, which is published separately and distributed with even-numbered *Contemporary Authors* original volumes and odd-numbered *Contemporary Authors New Revision Series* volumes.

As always, the most recent *Contemporary Authors* cumulative index continues to be the user's guide to the location of an individual author's listing.

Preface

The *Contemporary Authors New Revision Series* (*CANR*) provides completely updated information on authors listed in earlier volumes of *Contemporary Authors* (*CA*). Entries for individual authors from *any* volume of *CA* may be included in a volume of the *New Revision Series. CANR* updates only those sketches requiring significant change.

Authors are included on the basis of specific criteria that indicate the need for significant revision. These criteria include bibliographical additions, changes in addresses or career, major awards, and personal information such as name changes or death dates. All listings in this volume have been revised or augmented in various ways. Some sketches have been extensively rewritten, and many include informative new sidelights. As always, a *CANR* listing entails no charge or obligation.

How to Get the Most out of *CA* and *CANR:* Use the Index

The key to locating an author's most recent listing is the *CA* cumulative index, which is published separately and distributed with even-numbered original volumes and odd-numbered revision volumes. It provides access to *all* entries in *CA* and *CANR*. Always consult the latest index to find an author's most recent entry.

For the convenience of users, the *CA* cumulative index also includes references to all entries in these related Gale literary series: *Authors and Artists for Young Adults, Authors in the News, Bestsellers, Black Literature Criticism, Black Writers, Children's Literature Review, Concise Dictionary of American Literary Biography, Concise Dictionary of British Literary Biography, Contemporary Authors Autobiography Series, Contemporary Authors Bibliographical Series, Contemporary Literary Criticism, Dictionary of Literary Biography, Drama Criticism, Hispanic Writers, Major 20th Century Writers, Poetry Criticism, Short Story Criticism, Something about the Author, Something about the Author Autobiography Series, Twentieth-Century Literary Criticism, World Literature Criticism,* and *Yesterday's Authors of Books for Children.*

A Sample Index Entry:

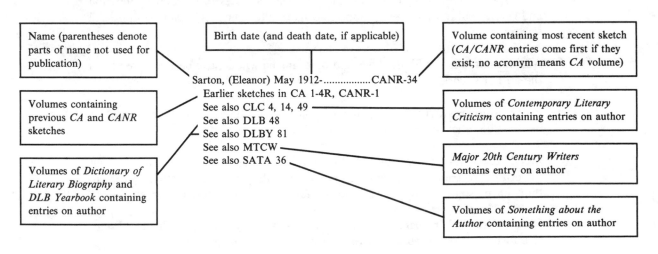

For the most recent *CA* information on Sarton, users should refer to Volume 34 of the *New Revision Series,* as designated by "CANR-34"; if that volume is unavailable, refer to CANR-1. And if CANR-1 is unavailable, refer to CA 1-4R, published in 1967, for Sarton's First Revision entry.

How Are Entries Compiled?

The editors make every effort to secure new information directly from the authors. Copies of all sketches in selected *CA* and *CANR* volumes published several years ago are routinely sent to listees at their last-known addresses, and returns from these authors are then assessed. For deceased writers, or those who fail to reply to requests for data, we consult other reliable biographical sources, such as those indexed in Gale's *Biography and Genealogy Master Index,* and bibliographical sources, such as *National Union Catalog, LC Marc,* and *British National Bibliography.* Further details come from published interviews, feature stories, and book reviews, and often the authors' publishers supply material.

What Kinds of Information Does an Entry Provide?

Sketches in *CANR* contain the following biographical and bibliographical information:

- **Entry heading:** the most complete form of author's name, plus any pseudonyms or name variations used for writing

- **Personal information:** author's date and place of birth, family data, educational background, political and religious affiliations, and hobbies and leisure interests

- **Addresses:** author's home, office, or agent's addresses as available

- **Career summary:** name of employer, position, and dates held for each career post; résumé of other vocational achievements; military service

- **Awards and honors:** military and civic citations, major prizes and nominations, fellowships, grants, and honorary degrees

- **Membership information:** professional, civic, and other association memberships and any official posts held

- **Writings:** a comprehensive list of titles, publishers, dates of original publication and revised editions, and production information for plays, television scripts, and screenplays

- **Adaptations:** a list of films, plays, and other media which have been adapted from the author's work

- **Work in progress:** current or planned projects, with dates of completion and/or publication, and expected publisher, when known

- **Sidelights:** a biographical portrait of the author's development; information about the critical reception of the author's works; revealing comments, often by the author, on personal interests, aspirations, motivations, and thoughts on writing

- **Biographical and critical sources:** a list of books and periodicals in which additional information on an author's life and/or writings appears

Some sketches also feature in-depth interviews that provide exclusive, primary information on writers of special interest. Prepared specifically for *CANR,* the never-before-published conversations give users the opportunity to learn authors' thoughts, in detail, about their craft.

Related Titles in the *CA* Series

Contemporary Authors Autobiography Series complements *CA* original and revised volumes with specially commissioned autobiographical essays by important current authors, illustrated with personal photographs they provide. Common topics include their motivations for writing, the people and experiences that shaped their careers, the rewards they derive from their work, and their impressions of the current literary scene.

Contemporary Authors Bibliographical Series surveys writings by and about important American authors since World War II. Each volume concentrates on a specific genre and features approximately ten writers; entries list works written by and about the author and contain a bibliographical essay discussing the merits and deficiencies of major critical and scholarly studies in detail.

Acknowledgments

The editors wish to thank Judith S. Baughman for her assistance with copy editing.

Suggestions Are Welcome

The editors welcome comments and suggestions from users on any aspects of the *CA* series. If readers would like to suggest authors whose entries should appear in future volumes of the series, they are cordially invited to write: The Editors, *Contemporary Authors,* 835 Penobscot Bldg., Detroit, MI 48226-4094; call toll-free at 1-800-347-GALE; or fax to 1-313-961-6599.

CA Numbering System and Volume Update Chart

Occasionally questions arise about the *CA* numbering system and which volumes, if any, can be discarded. Despite numbers like "29-32R," "97-100" and "136," the entire *CA* series consists of only 100 physical volumes with the publication of *CA New Revision Series* Volume 37. The following chart notes changes in the numbering system and cover design, and indicates which volumes are essential for the most complete, up-to-date coverage.

CA **First Revision**	• 1-4R through 41-44R (11 books) *Cover:* Brown with black and gold trim. There will be no further First Revision volumes because revised entries are now being handled exclusively through the more efficient *New Revision Series* mentioned below.
CA **Original Volumes**	• 45-48 through 97-100 (14 books) *Cover:* Brown with black and gold trim. • 101 through 136 (36 books) *Cover:* Blue and black with orange bands. The same as previous *CA* original volumes but with a new, simplified numbering system and new cover design.
CA **Permanent Series**	• *CAP*-1 and *CAP*-2 (2 books) *Cover:* Brown with red and gold trim. There will be no further *Permanent Series* volumes because revised entries are now being handled exclusively through the more efficient *New Revision Series* mentioned below.
CA **New Revision Series**	• *CANR*-1 through *CANR*-37 (37 books) *Cover:* Blue and black with green bands. Includes only sketches requiring extensive changes; **sketches are taken from any previously published *CA*, *CAP*, or *CANR* volume.**

If You Have:	You May Discard:
CA First Revision Volumes 1-4R through 41-44R **and** *CA Permanent Series* Volumes 1 and 2	*CA* Original Volumes 1, 2, 3, 4 Volumes 5-6 through 23-24 Volumes 25-28 through 41-44
CA Original Volumes 45-48 through 97–100 and 101 through 136	NONE: These volumes will not be superseded by corresponding revised volumes. Individual entries from these and all other volumes appearing in the left column of this chart will be revised and included in the various volumes of the *New Revision Series*.
CA New Revision Series Volumes *CANR*-1 through *CANR*-37	NONE: The *New Revision Series* does not replace any single volume of *CA*. Instead, volumes of *CANR* include entries from many previous *CA* series volumes. All *New Revision Series* volumes must be retained for full coverage.

A Sampling of Authors and Media People Featured in This Volume

John Ashbery
Winner of such prestigious honors as the Pulitzer Prize and the National Book Award, Ashbery is the author of numerous poetry volumes, including *Self-Portrait in a Convex Mirror.*

Judy Blume
Blume is best known for her popular and sometimes controversial novels that examine the problems of modern young people.

Anita Brookner
An accomplished novelist, Brookner has also received international acclaim for her incisive critiques of eighteenth- and nineteenth-century French artists and their work.

Albert Brooks
Comedian Brooks has chronicled the anxieties of modern living in a series of films, including *Lost in America* and the mock documentary *Real Life.*

Agatha Christie
Christie is well known to devotees of mystery and suspense for her ability to blend intricate plots with colorful characters. Among her most famous creations are supersleuths Hercule Poirot and Miss Jane Marple.

William Trevor Cox
Highly acclaimed for his short fictions written under the name William Trevor, the Irish-born author is also an award-winning novelist and playwright whose works often depict ordinary people with tragic, lonely lives. (Entry contains interview.)

Walter Cronkite
Once voted "the most trusted man in America," Cronkite gained widespread respect for both his field reporting and his nineteen-year stint as anchorman of the *CBS Evening News.*

Thomas dePaola
Praised for his inventive picture books for children, dePaola is also well known for his retellings of traditional folktales and fables such as *The Badger and the Magic Fan* and *The Wind and the Sun.*

Northrop Frye
Frye's system of categorizing the various schools of criticism made him one of the most important literary authorities of his generation.

Lynn Hall
Specializing in stories about both animals and young people, Hall often draws on incidents from her childhood for inspiration.

Robert Munsch
Using a combination of humor, repetition, and appealing characters, Munsch excels in entertaining young readers with his storytelling skills.

Reynolds Price
Price often draws on his Southern background to create novels and stories featuring strong characters, intricate plots, and unique settings. (Entry contains interview.)

Gene Roddenberry
Best known for creating the popular "Star Trek" television and movie series, Roddenberry began his career writing scripts for early television programs such as *Four Star Playhouse* and *Have Gun Will Travel.*

Rosemary Sutcliff
A Carnegie Medal-winner, Sutcliff explores the history of England by retelling old legends and stories such as *Beowulf.*

Cynthia Voigt
Voigt is best known for her well-written young-adult narratives that feature both intricate plots and finely honed characters.

T. H. White
Although he first gained fame for his nonfiction works about the English countryside, White was also lauded for such popular fantasy novels as *The Once and Future King* and *The Book of Merlyn.*

Contemporary Authors®

NEW REVISION SERIES

*Indicates that a listing has been compiled from secondary sources believed to be reliable but has not been personally verified for this edition by the author sketched.

ABBENSETTS, Michael 1938-

PERSONAL: Born June 8, 1938, in Georgetown, Guyana; became citizen of England, 1974; son of Neville John (a doctor) and Elaine Abbensetts. *Education:* Attended Queens College (Guyana), 1952-56, Stanstead College (Canada), 1956-58, and Sir George Williams University (Canada), 1960-61.

ADDRESSES: Home—4 Caxton Rd., London W12 8AJ, England. *Agent*—Gil Parker, William Morris Agency, 1350 Avenue of the Americas, New York, NY 10019; and Jane Annakin, William Morris Agency, Ltd., 147-149 Wardour St., London W1V 3TB, England.

CAREER: Playwright. Tower of London, London, England, security attendant, 1963-67; associated with Sir John Soahe Museum, 1968-71; Carnegie Mellon University, Pittsburgh, PA, professor of drama, 1981—. Resident dramatist at Royal Court Theatre, 1974.

AWARDS, HONORS: George Devine Award, Royal Court Theatre, 1973, for *Sweet Talk;* Afro-Caribbean Award, *Afro-Caribbean Post,* 1979, for *Empire Road.*

WRITINGS:

Empire Road (novel), Grenada, 1979.

PLAYS

Sweet Talk (two-act; produced in the West End at Royal Court Theatre, 1973), Methuen, 1974.
Alterations (two-act), produced in the West End at Theatre at New End, 1978.
Samba (two-act), produced in the West End at Tricycle Theatre, 1980.
In the Mood (two-act), produced in the West End at Hampstead Theatre, 1981.
Outlaw, produced at Art's Theatre, 1983.
El Dorado, produced at Theatre Royal, 1984.

TELEVISION PLAYS

Author of *The Museum Attendant,* 1973; *Inner City Blues,* 1974; *Crime and Passion,* 1975; *Roadrunner,* 1977; *Black Christmas,* 1977. Also author of scripts for the series *Empire Road,* 1978-79.

RADIO PLAYS

Sweet Talk, British Broadcasting Corp. Radio (BBC-Radio), 1974.
Home Again, BBC-Radio, 1975.
The Sunny Side of the Street, BBC-Radio, 1977.
Brothers of the Sword, BBC-Radio, 1978.
Alterations, BBC World Service, 1980.
The Fast Lane, Capital Radio, 1980.
The Dark Horse, BBC-Radio, 1981.

WORK IN PROGRESS: Easy Money, a television play; *The Caribbean Lady,* a play for the stage.

SIDELIGHTS: Michael Abbensetts once told *CA:* "When I first started to write for theatre, there were maybe two or three black playwrights living in England. Certainly black novelists wrote plays, but I'm talking about black playwrights. Originally, I, too, wanted to be a novelist. Then I saw a version of John Osborne's play *Look Back in Anger.* It changed my life. After that, all I wanted was to be a playwright. This turned out to be slightly more difficult than I imagined. I knew so little about plays, not only did I have to teach myself to *write* plays, I also had to teach myself to *read* them. I loved reading books, but reading a play was foreign to me.

"The first play I ever wrote was a long one-act, not a full-length play. I no longer remember the title, but the play was about a West Indian adolescent and the mother of a Canadian school friend. When I was about sixteen or seventeen I was sent away to a boarding school in Canada. One summer, a school friend and his mother who was divorced invited me down to their summer cottage. The play is loosely based on what happened during that holiday.

"After I wrote the play I did not know what to do with it. I should add that by then I was living in London, having decided England was the best country for a budding playwright. Anyway, I realized the best thing to do was find myself an agent. I know no agents. None. So I bought a copy of a play by David Mercer and looked to see who his agent was. He was represented by Peggy Ramsay. It was not until later that I discovered that Miss Ramsay was one of the most influential and successful agents in England. So not knowing any of this I just turned up on her doorstep with my play, only to be told by her assistant, 'Oh no, Miss Ramsay never, never accepts a script delivered by hand.' One had to write a letter of introduction first. However, luck was with me that day, because Miss Ramsay's assistant did accept my play. Never underestimate the charm of a Gemini!

"Two weeks later I was still waiting for a reply. So I telephoned to see what had happened about my play. Miss Ramsay herself answered the phone. 'What,' she said, 'you just turned up and left a play here. Come and take it away immediately.' The next day I turned up at her office to take my play away. I discovered that Miss Ramsay had gone to Edinburgh and had taken a pile of plays to read on the train. By accident my play happened to be among the pile. The next day my phone rang. This time it was Peggy Ramsay phoning me. She liked my play. She suggested we meet. So I went around to her office yet again. She talked, I listened. She told me that though she had liked the play, she felt I could do better. She advised me to write another play. A full-length play. 'Tell us,' she said, 'what it feels like to be a Black man in England today.'

"The next day I quit my job and decided this would be my make-or-break play. I began a play about a sweet-talking young man whose weakness was gambling on the horses. In the interest of research, I began to frequent betting parlours to such an extent that I became hooked on gambling. Every morning I would write from 7:30 to 1:00. Then all afternoon I would spend betting on the horses. I couldn't stop myself. I hated Sundays when there was no racing. Yet when the play was finished I lost all interest in gambling. I have never bet again since. The play took me about six months to write. I called it *Sweet Talk*.

"*Sweet Talk* was later performed at the Royal Court Theatre, the same theatre where, years before, Osborne's *Look Back in Anger* started. To date, *Sweet Talk* has been staged in ten different countries. Perhaps the strangest thing of all is that Peggy Ramsay never did become my agent."

BIOGRAPHICAL/CRITICAL SOURCES:

PERIODICALS

Times (London), November 18, 1983; February 6, 1984.*

*   *   *

ABBOTT, R(obert) Tucker 1919-

PERSONAL: Born September 28, 1919, in Watertown, MA; son of Charles Matthew (a paint manufacturer) and Frances (Tucker) Abbott; married Mary M. Sisler, February 18, 1946 (died, 1964); married Sue Sweeney Darwin, January 8, 1966 (died, 1976); married Cecelia White, May 13, 1977; children: (first marriage) Robert Tucker, Jr., Carolyn Tucker, Cynthia Douglas. *Education:* Harvard University, B.S., 1946; George Washington University, M.S., 1953, Ph.D., 1955. *Politics:* Non-partisan. *Religion:* Episcopalian. *Avocational interests:* Photography, vegetable gardening, cliptology (the collecting of paper-clips).

ADDRESSES: Home—2208 South Colonial Dr., Melbourne, FL 32901. *Office*—P.O. Box 2255, Melbourne, FL 32902-2255. *Agent*—Gloria Mosesson, Suite 3501, 20 Exchange Place, New York, NY 10005.

CAREER: U.S. National Museum, Washington, DC, assistant curator, division of mollusks, 1946-49, associate curator, 1949-54; Academy of Natural Sciences of Philadelphia, Philadelphia, PA, research scientist and holder of Pilsbry Chair, 1954-69; Delaware Museum of Natural History, Greenville, assistant director (malacology), 1969-78; currently president, American Malacologists, Inc., Melbourne, FL, and acting director, Bailey-Matthews Shell Museum, Sanibel Island, FL. Adjunct professor, University of Delaware. Member of ten scientific expeditions in search of marine life, in the Philippines, Zanzibar, Thailand, Australia, the Marianas, Hawaii, Bermuda, West Indies, Fiji, and Samoa. Member of board of directors, Natural Sciences Foundation, 1956-63. Member of board of trustees, Bermuda Biological Station. *Military service:* U.S. Navy Reserve, 1942-46; became lieutenant.

MEMBER: American Association for the Advancement of Science (fellow; life member), American Malacological Union (life member; president, 1956-57), Society of Systematic Zoology (secretary, 1960-62), Australian Malacological Society (patron, 1960—), Philadelphia Shell Club (founder; president, 1955-57), Sons of the American Revolution, Harvard Club, Explorers Club (New York), and honorary member of other shell clubs.

AWARDS, HONORS: Smithsonian award for outstanding service, 1954.

WRITINGS:

Handbook of Medically Important Mollusks of the Orient and Western Pacific, Museum of Comparative Zoology, Harvard University, 1948.

(Contributor) *A Manual of Tropical Medicine,* Saunders, 1954.

American Seashells, Van Nostrand, 1954, 2nd edition, 1978.

Introducing Sea Shells: A Colorful Guide for the Beginning Collector, Van Nostrand, 1955.

Shells, National Audubon Society, 1958.

The Marine Mollusks of Grand Cayman Island, British West Indies (monograph), Academy of Natural Sciences (Philadelphia), 1958.

The Genus Strombus in the Indo-Pacific, Academy of Natural Sciences, 1960.

How to Know the American Marine Shells, Signet Books, 1961.

(With Germaine L. Warmke) *Caribbean Seashells,* Livingston, 1961.

Sea Shells of the World, Golden Press, 1962, revised edition, 1985.

(With R. J. L. Wagner) *Van Nostrand's Standard Catalog of Shells,* Van Nostrand, 1964, 3rd edition, 1978.

Shells, Doubleday, 1966.

Venom Apparatus and Geographical Distribution of Conus Gloriamarus (pamphlet), Academy of Natural Sciences, 1967.

Seashells of North America: A Guide to Field Identification, Golden Press, 1968, revised edition, 1986.

(With Hugh and Marguerite Stix) *The Shell: Five Hundred Years of Inspired Design,* Abrams, 1968.

(Editor) *Swainson's Exotic Conchology,* Delaware Museum of Natural History and Van Nostrand, 1968.

Kingdom of the Seashell, Crown, 1972.

Shells in Color, illustrations by K. B. Sandved, Viking, 1973.

(Editor with M. E. Young) *American Malacologists,* American Malacologists, 1973, supplement, 1975.

The Best of the Nautilus: A Bicentennial Anthology of American Conchology, American Malacologists, 1976.

Indexes to the Nautilius: Geographical Volumes 1-90 and Scientific Names Volumes 61-90, American Malacologists, 1979.

(With S. P. Dance) *Compendium of Seashells,* Dutton, 1982.

Collectible Florida Shells, American Malacologists, 1983.

Seashells Photo Postcards, Dover, 1989.

Compendium of Landshells, American Malacologists, 1990.

Seashells of the Northern Hemishpere, Dragon's World (London), 1990.

Register of American Malacologists, American Malacologists, 1991.

Seashells of Southeast Asia, Graham Brash (Singapore), 1991.

Writer of other reports on mollusks issued by Museum of Comparative Zoology, Harvard University, Smithsonian Institution, and Raffles Museum, Singapore. Contributor to *World Book Encyclopedia, Encyclopedia Americana, Grolier's Encyclopedia,* and other encyclopedias. Contributor to *Natural History, Science Digest, Sea Frontiers* and *Science Counselor.* Editor-in-chief, *Nautilus,* 1958-86, and *Monographs of Marine Mollusca,* 1978-85.

WORK IN PROGRESS: Revision of *American Seashells.*

*   *   *

ABEL, Robert H(alsall) 1941-

PERSONAL: Born May 27, 1941, in Painesville, OH; son of Robert H. (a textile worker) and Lora Constance (a school bus driver; maiden name, Logan) Abel; married Joyce Keeler (a budget officer), October 31, 1964; children: Sarah, Charles Robert. *Education:* College of Wooster, B.A. (cum laude), 1964; Kansas State College, M.A., 1967. *Politics:* "Hopeless Utopiast." *Religion:* "Hopeless idealist." *Avocational interests:* Surfcasting, small presses, China.

ADDRESSES: *Home*—27 Stockwell Rd., Hadley, MA 01035. *Agent*—Richard Parks, 138 East 16th St., Apt. 5B, New York, NY 10003.

CAREER: *Painesville Telegraph,* Painesville, OH, reporter, 1964-65; Kansas State University, Pittsburg, instructor in English, 1965-67; affiliated with Flint Community Junior College, Flint, MI, 1967-68; Northern Illinois University, DeKalb, instructor in English, 1968-72; University of Massachusetts, Amherst, creative writing fellow, 1972-75, public affairs writer, 1975-78; free-lance writer. Journalism instructor, Mt. Holyoke College, 1986; visiting writer, Trinity College, 1990-1992. Fiction editor for Lynx House Press. Member of Lake Pleasant Volunteer Fire Department. Instructor at Waubonsee Community Junior College, summer, 1973, and Amherst Senior Center, 1975-76.

MEMBER: Authors Guild, Authors League of America.

AWARDS, HONORS: National Endowment for the Arts fellowship, 1978; O. Henry Festival, Second Place, 1987; Flannery O'Connor Award for Short Fiction, 1989.

WRITINGS:

Skin and Bones (stories), Colorado State Review Press, 1979.

Freedom Dues; or, A Gentleman's Progress in the New World (novel), Dial, 1980.
The Progress of Fire (novel), Simon & Schuster, 1985.
Full-Tilt Boogie (short stories), Lynx House Press, 1989.
Ghost Traps (short stories), University of Georgia Press, 1991.

Also author of *The Preacher's Wife,* a radio play. Work represented in anthologies, including *Great Lakes Anthology II,* edited by Peter Neuramont, Antioch Press, 1965, *The Available Press/PEN Short Story Collection,* 1985, and *O. Henry Festival Stories,* 1987. Contributor of about thirty articles, stories, and reviews to literary magazines, including *Colorado State Review, The Little Magazine, Playgirl, Midwest Quarterly, Explicator, Epoch, Margins,* and *Kansas Quarterly.* Fiction editor, *Lynx,* 1972—.

WORK IN PROGRESS: Novels; stories; research on evolution and new ideas about "human nature."

SIDELIGHTS: Robert H. Abel commented to *CA:* "Fiction should be, at its best, about something that matters. My hope, my gamble is: that fiction can help create a contemporary mythology helpful to the survival of the species, that will make it possible to live in peace. I feel the planet is threatened, that writing should attempt to define and respond to this emergency, not with hysteria, but with some vision of a workable, maybe even beautiful future. Who are we? Where are we going? What are our predicaments, and how do people of this age respond to them?

"I have written some science fiction and a somewhat historical novel, 'experimental' and traditional stories, fantasy and slice-of-life. Stylistics are important, but at the moment it is the subject we are slave to, our survival.

"And in whatever genre what obsesses me is how we are responding to our thermonuclear conditions, whether intelligence, or something like intelligence, or sanity or love or something miraculous will work to save us from ourselves. In such peril, how do we continue to live ordinary lives?"

*   *   *

ABERNATHY, David M(yles) 1933-

PERSONAL: Born June 27, 1933, in Connelly Springs, NC; son of James William and Lorena (Alexander) Abernathy; married Kathryn Lynn Fordham, October 16, 1971; children: Marc Alexander, Chadwick Myles. *Education:* High Point College, A.B., 1955; additional study, University of Maryland, Tokyo Campus, 1956-57; Emory University, M.Div., 1962; Union Theological Seminary, New York City, S.T.M., 1964; RCA Institutes, diplomate,

1964; graduate study at Columbia University and New School for Social Research, 1964-65.

ADDRESSES: Home—935 Bream Ct., N.E., Marietta, GA 30067.

CAREER: University of Maryland, Tokyo Campus, Tokyo, Japan, instructor in English, 1957-59; Atlanta University, Atlanta, GA, visiting instructor in communications, 1965-72, visiting instructor in speech, 1969-72, visiting instructor in speech, 1969-70; Sandpiper Productions (producer of films and radio and television productions), Atlanta, GA, president, 1967—. Instructor in advertising and marketing, Massey College, 1969-70; Beall Memorial Humanities Lecturer, Lon Morris College, 1974. Producer, director, and writer for radio, television, and motion pictures, 1955—; producer and director, *The Protestant Hour,* nationally syndicated radio program, 1959—; producer of television commercials, 1960—. Lieutenant colonel and aide-de-camp, staff of governor of Georgia, 1971-74. Member of board of trustees, CRISIS, Inc.; member of advisory board, Protestant Radio and Television Center. *Military service:* U.S. Air Force, 1956-59; served in Japan.

MEMBER: Authors League of America, National Academy of Television Arts and Sciences, Public Relations Society of America, International Association of Business Communicators, American Academy of Political and Social Sciences, American Society of Composers, Authors, and Publishers, National Education Association, National Academy of Recording Arts and Sciences.

AWARDS, HONORS: Far East Network Gold Mike Award, 1959, for exceptional performance; LL.D. Institute of Communicative Arts, Atlanta, GA, 1970; Litt.D., Rust College, 1974; L.H.D., Texas Wesleyan College, 1980.

WRITINGS:

Hello, Japan, Stars and Stripes Press, 1957.
(Editor with Theodore H. Runyon) *Theology for the Layman,* SLP Publishing Co., 1962.
(Editor with Norman H. Perrin) *The Teaching of Jesus,* CRS Publishing, 1963.
A Child's Guidebook to Rome, Guiseppe Publishing (Rome), 1964.
(Editor) *Reflections,* Massey College Press, 1969.
(With Wayne Knipe) *Ideas, Inventions and Patents: An Introduction to Patent Information,* Pioneer Press (Atlanta), 1973, 2nd edition, 1974.
The Plight of the Independent Inventor in America Today (pamphlet), Pioneer Press, 1974.

Also author of plays, *J.W.,* 1963, *Never Look Up,* 1964, and *The Bridge,* 1972. Author of radio documentary on

Methodism, *Methodism on the Move,* NBC, 1963. Contributor to *Junction* (periodical of Emory University).

WORK IN PROGRESS: Understanding the Teaching of Jesus. *

* * *

ABERNATHY, William J(ackson) 1933-1983

PERSONAL: Born November 21, 1933, in Columbia, TN; died of cancer, December 29, 1983, at the Dana-Farber Cancer Institute in Boston, MA; son of Sidney Guy (an editor) and Estha (a teacher; maiden name Jackson) Abernathy; married Claire St. Arnand, March 7, 1961; children: Evelyn Claire, William J., Jr., Janine Suzanne. *Education:* University of Tennessee, B.S., 1955; Harvard University, M.B.A., 1964, D.B.A., 1967.

CAREER: E. I. DuPont, Columbia, TN, engineer in film division, 1955-56; General Dynamics/Electronics, Rochester, NY, project engineer in electronics systems division, 1959-62; University of California, Los Angeles, assistant professor of business, 1967-68; Stanford University, Stanford, CA, assistant professor of business, 1968-72; Harvard University, Business School, Boston, MA, associate professor, 1972-77, professor of business, 1977-83, William Barclay Harding Professor of Management and Technology, 1982-83. Consultant to government and business. *Military service:* U.S. Air Force Security Service in West Germany.

MEMBER: National Academy of Sciences.

WRITINGS:

(With Alan Sheldon and C. K. Prahalad) *The Management of Health Care: A Technology Perspective,* Ballinger, 1974.
(With Paul W. Marshall and others) *Operations Management: Text and Cases,* Irwin, 1975.
The Productivity Dilemma: Roadblock to Innovation in the Automobile Industry, Johns Hopkins Press, 1978.
(Editor with Douglas Ginsburg) *Government, Technology, and the Future of the Automobile,* McGraw, 1979.
(With Kim B. Clark and Alan M. Kantrow) *Industrial Renaissance: Producing a Competitive Future for America,* Basic Books, 1983.

Contributor to *Harvard Business Review* and academic journals.

SIDELIGHTS: William J. Abernathy once commented: "The management of technology and innovation within firms and the government is a special focus of my work at Harvard Business School. The contribution of science and technology in management decision and in economic planning both in the United States and abroad has been a common theme of my research and publications, and the automobile industry has been a special subject in [later] work. Recent research in Europe is expected to lead to future work on international competition in technology.

"The U.S. automobile industry is in turmoil as a result of high gasoline prices and shortages, government regulation, and the legacy of past decisions. Many problems call for resolution. The book *Government, Technology, and the Future of the Automobile* is the result of a series of conferences and meetings between automotive executives from the United States and abroad, government administrators, consumer advocates, suppliers, labor, and other concerned parties. Held at the Harvard Business School during 1977 and 1978, the purpose was to bring adversarial groups together to better understand one another's points of view and vital concerns with the hope of making a first step toward a resolution of current problems facing the industry, the government, and the public as regards the automobile. The book presents papers written by these participants and comments from the symposium as discussed in the October, 1978, symposium at Harvard."

Abernathy was co-author with Robert Hayes of the *Harvard Business Review* article "Managing Our Way to Economic Decline" that stirred up controversy in the business community. The article said short-sighted management, not labor or Japanese competition, was responsible for the decline of the American auto industry's health during the 1970s and '80s. Improved worker-management cooperation and resistance to seductive short-term profit increases could reverse the trend, Abernathy believed.

OBITUARIES:

PERIODICALS

Chicago Tribune, January 1, 1984.
Los Angeles Times, December 31, 1983.
Newsweek, January 9, 1983.
New York Times, December 30, 1983.
Time, January 9, 1984.
Washington Post, December 31, 1983.*

* * *

ABISH, Walter 1931-

PERSONAL: Born December 24, 1931, in Vienna, Austria; son of Adolph and Frieda (Rubin) Abish; wife's name, Cecile (a sculptor).

ADDRESSES: Home—P.O. Box 485, Cooper Station, New York, NY 10276. *Agent*—Candida Donadio & Associates, 231 West 22nd St., New York, NY 10011.

CAREER: Adjunct professor at State University of New York Empire State College, New York City, 1975; Wheaton College, Norton, MA, writer in residence, spring, 1977; visiting Butler Professor of English at State University of New York at Buffalo, fall, 1977; Columbia University, New York City, lecturer in English, 1979-88. Guest professor, Yale University, New Haven, CT, spring, 1985, and Brown University, Providence, RI, spring, 1986; visiting writer, Cooper Union, New York City, spring, 1984.

MEMBER: International PEN, PEN American Center (executive board, 1982-88), New York Foundation for the Arts (board of governors, 1989—).

AWARDS, HONORS: Fellow of New Jersey State Council for the Arts, 1972; Rose Isabel Williams Foundation grant, 1974, and Ingram Merrill Foundation grant, 1977; fellow of National Endowment for the Arts, 1979 and 1985; Guggenheim fellowship, 1981; CAPS grant, 1981; PEN/Faulkner Award, 1981; D.A.A.D. fellowship, Deutscher Akademischer Austauschdienst, Berlin, Germany, 1987; John D. MacArthur Foundation fellowship, 1987-92; Award of Merit Medal for the Novel, American Academy and Institute of Arts and Letters, 1991.

WRITINGS:

Duel Site (poems), Tibor de Nagy Editions, 1970.
The Alphabetical Africa, New Directions, 1974.
Minds Meet, New Directions, 1975.
In the Future Perfect, New Directions, 1977.
How German Is It, New Directions, 1980.
99: The New Meaning, Burning Deck, 1990.
Destiny: Tomorrow's Truth, Knopf, 1992.
As If (sequel to *How German Is It;* also see below), Knopf, in press.

Work represented in anthologies, including *Individuals: Post-Movement Art in America,* Dutton, 1977, and *Best American Short Stories,* 1981. "Is This Really You," an excerpt from *As If,* appears in *Facing Texts,* edited by Heide Ziegler, Duke University Press, 1988. Contributor to literary journals, including *New Directions in Prose and Poetry, Partisan Review, Antaeus, Conjunctions, Paris Review, Salmagundi* and *Granta. How German Is It* has been published in France, Spain, Germany, Italy, Poland, England, Norway, Sweden, Yugoslavia, Israel, and Holland.

WORK IN PROGRESS: House on Fire, a novel; *Is This Really You?,* a collection of critical texts.

BIOGRAPHICAL/CRITICAL SOURCES:

BOOKS

Caramello, Charles, *Silverless Mirrors: Book, Self and Postmodern American Fiction,* Florida State University, 1983.

Karl, Frederick, *American Fictions, 1940-1980,* Harper, 1983.
Klinkowitz, Jerome, *The Self-Apparent Word,* Southern Illinois Press, 1984.
Klinkowitz, *The Life of Fiction,* University of Illinois Press, 1977.
McHale, Brian, *Postmodernist Fiction,* Methuen, 1987.
Updike, John, *Picked-Up Pieces,* Knopf, 1975.
Varsava, Jerry A., *Contingent Meanings,* Florida State University Press, 1990.

PERIODICALS

Fiction International, Volume 4, no. 3, 1976.
Journal of American Studies, Volume 17, no. 2, 1983.
New Directions in Prose and Poetry, autumn, 1977.
New York Times, February 12, 1981.
Salmagundi, winter/spring, 1990.
Sub-Stance, fall, 1983.
Washington Post, June 16, 1987.
Washington Post Book World, April 17, 1981.

*   *   *

ABRAMSON, Joan   1932-

PERSONAL: Born October 7, 1932, in Los Angeles, CA; daughter of Roman (a photographer) and Katherine (Merkin) Freulich; married Norman Abramson (a professor), July 4, 1954; children: Mark, Caren. *Education:* University of California, Los Angeles, A.B., 1954, M.S., 1955; additional study, Stanford University, 1955-56. *Politics:* Democrat. *Religion:* Jewish.

ADDRESSES: Home and office—3044 Kiele Ave., Honolulu, HI 96815.

CAREER: Palo Alto Times, Palo Alto, CA, reporter, 1955-58; *Revenswood Post,* Menlo Park, CA, editor, 1958; free-lance writer, Woodside, CA, 1958-65; University of Hawaii, Honolulu, instructor in English, 1967-72, assistant director of New College, 1972-73, and chairwoman of faculty senate, 1973; director of federal programs, Hawaii Loa College, 1979-80.

MEMBER: Kappa Tau Alpha.

WRITINGS:

(With father, Roman Freulich) *Hill of Life,* Yoseloff, 1968.
(Author of text) *The Faces of Israel,* photographs by Freulich, A. S. Barnes, 1971.
(Author of text) *Forty Years in Hollywood,* photographs by Freulich, A. S. Barnes, 1972.
The Invisible Woman: Discrimination in the Academic Profession, Jossey-Bass, 1975.

Mark Twain's Letters from the Sandwich Islands, Island Heritage, 1975.

Photographers of Old Hawaii, Island Heritage, 1976.

Old Boys—New Women: The Politics of Sex Discrimination, Praeger, 1979.

Contributor to Time-Life Books, *Frontier States: Alaska and Hawaii, U.S. Overseas, Decades Five,* and *Foods of the Pacific.* Part-time correspondent in Boston, MA, for *Time,* 1965; Hawaii correspondent, Time-Life Books, 1967—.

WORK IN PROGRESS: Down to Earth, an introduction to satellite communications.*

*   *   *

ABRAMSON, Paul R(obert)   1937-

PERSONAL: Born November 28, 1937, in St. Louis, MO; son of Harry B. J. (a printer and businessman) and Hattie (Lewin) Abramson; married Janet Schwartz, September 11, 1966; children: Lee Jacob, Heather Lyn. *Education:* Washington University, St. Louis, MO, B.A., 1959; University of California, Berkeley, M.A., 1961, Ph.D., 1967.

ADDRESSES: Home—2697 Linden Dr., East Lansing, MI 48823. *Office*—Department of Political Science, Michigan State University, East Lansing, MI 48824.

CAREER: Michigan State University, East Lansing, MI, assistant professor, 1967-71, associate professor, 1971-77, professor of political science, 1977—. *Military service:* U.S. Army, 1960-62. U.S. Army Reserve, 1962-64; became captain.

MEMBER: American Political Science Association, American Sociological Association, Phi Beta Kappa.

AWARDS, HONORS: Woodrow Wilson fellow, 1961; Ford Foundation faculty research fellow, 1972-73; Fulbright fellow, Hebrew University of Jerusalem, 1987-88.

WRITINGS:

Generational Change in American Politics, Heath, 1975.

The Political Socialization of Black Americans: A Critical Evaluation of Research on Efficacy and Trust, Free Press, 1977.

(With John H. Aldrich and David W. Rohde) *Change in Continuity in the 1980 Elections,* Congressional Quarterly Press, 1982.

Political Attitudes in America, W. H. Freeman, 1983.

(With Aldrich and Rohde) *Change and Continuity in the 1984 Elections,* Congressional Quarterly Press, 1986.

(With Aldrich and Rohde) *Change and Continuity in the 1988 Elections,* Congressional Quarterly Press, 1990.

WORK IN PROGRESS: Research project on the impact of generational replacement in advanced industrial societies.

*   *   *

ABSHIRE, David M.   1926-

PERSONAL: Born April 11, 1926, in Chattanooga, TN; son of James Ernest (a businessman) and Edith (Patten) Abshire; married Carolyn Lamar Sample, September 7, 1957; children: Lupton, Anna Lamar Bowman, Mary Lee, Phyllis d'Hoop, Caroline. *Education:* U.S. Military Academy, B.S., 1951; Georgetown University, Ph.D. (with honors), 1959. *Politics:* Republican. *Religion:* Episcopalian.

ADDRESSES: Home—311 South St, Asaph St., Alexandria, VA 22314. *Office*—Center for Strategic and International Studies, 1800 K St., Washington, DC 20006.

CAREER: U.S. Army, cadet, 1946-51, regular officer, 1951-55, served as platoon leader, intelligence officer, and company commander, retired as first lieutenant, became captain, U.S. Army Reserve; U.S. House of Representatives, Washington, DC, member of staff, 1959-60; American Enterprise Institute for Public Policy Research, Washington, DC, director of special projects, 1961-62; Georgetown University, Washington, DC, Center for Strategic and International Studies, co-founder, 1962, executive director, 1962-70, chairman, 1973-82, adjunct professor in School of Foreign Service; U.S. Department of State, Washington, DC, assistant secretary of state for congressional relations, 1970-73. Member of congressional committee on Organization of the Government for the Conduct of Foreign Policy, 1974-76; chairman of the U.S. Board for International Broadcasting, 1974-77; director of National Security Group (including Department of State, Department of Defense, and Central Intelligence Agency), 1979-80; member of President's Foreign Intelligence Advisory Board; member of advisory board on Long-Range Planning for Chief of Naval Operations; member of Council on Foreign Relations; Center for Strategic and International Studies, Washington, DC, chairman, 1973-83, president, 1987—; special counsellor to the President (with cabinet rank), 1987; ambassador, U.S. Permanent Representative on the North Atlantic Council (NATO), in Brussels and Belgium, 1983-87; member of President's Task Force on U.S. Government International Broadcasting, 1991—; advisory board member, BP America (Cleveland). Director, Ogden Corp. (New York), and Procter & Gamble (Cincinnati). Former member of Board of National Park Foundation and board of Naval War College; trustee of Baylor Preparatory School (Chattanooga, TN); former vice-chairman of board of Youth for

Understanding; former consultant to *Reader's Digest* and to American International Group, Inc.

MEMBER: International Club (Washington, DC; member of board), Alfalfa Club (Washington, DC), Metropolitan Club (Washington, DC), Alibi Club (Washington, DC), Cosmos Club (Washington, DC), Phi Alpha Theta, Key Society.

AWARDS, HONORS: Military—Bronze Star Medal (twice), Commendation Ribbon, Combat Infantryman Badge (all for service in Korea). Defense Department Distinguished Public Service Medal, Georgetown University John Carroll Award for outstanding service by an alumnus, Gold Medal of the Sons of the American Revolution, Baylor Distinguished Alumni Award, Order of the Crown (Belgium), Medal of the President of the Italian Republic, Seante Parliament and Government and of the Pio Manu Centre (Italy), Commandre de l'Ordre Leopold (Belgium), President's Civilian Service Award, 1989.

WRITINGS:

(Editor with Richard Allen) *National Security: Political, Military and Economic Strategies in the Decade Ahead,* Praeger, 1963.
(Contributor) *Detente: Cold War Strategies in Transition,* Praeger, 1965.
The South Rejects a Prophet: The Life of Senator D. M. Key, 1824-1900, Praeger, 1967.
(Editor with M. Samuels) *Portuguese Africa: A Handbook,* Praeger, 1969.
International Broadcasting: A New Dimension of Western Diplomacy, Sage Publications, 1976.
Foreign Policy Makers: President vs. Congress, Sage Publications, 1979.
(Contributor) Dante B. Fascell, editor, *International News: Freedom Under Attack,* Sage Publications, 1979.
Preventing World War III: A Realistic Grand Strategy, Harper, 1989.

Also editor of *The Growing Power of Congress.* Contributor to the *Annals of the American Academy of Political and Social Science* and to *U.S. Naval Institute Proceedings.* Editor of proceedings of Conference on Plans and Needs for International Strategic Studies, 1969. Contributor of articles to magazines, newspapers, and scholarly journals, including the *New York Times, Times* (London), *Reader's Digest,* and *American Political Science Review.* Founder and editor, *Washington Quarterly: A Journal of Strategic and International Studies.*

BIOGRAPHICAL/CRITICAL SOURCES:

PERIODICALS

New York Times Book Review, January 29, 1989.

Washington Post, January 5, 1989.

*   *   *

ADAM, Michael 1919-

PERSONAL: Born February 27, 1919, in India; married, wife's name, Bea; children: Noah, Michael, Shane Maya. *Education:* "Does not seem very relevant—learned to read and write at some schools and college but not very much else that matters." *Politics:* "None." *Religion:* "None." *Avocational interests:* Painting.

ADDRESSES: Home—Calmynsy-Belmont-Redinnik-Penzance, Cornwall, England TR18 4HY.

CAREER: Art in Industry, Calcutta, India, editor, 1946-49; Dartington Hall, Devon, England, teacher, 1954-55; *Graphis Magazine,* Zurich, Switzerland, associate editor, 1955-59; University of Texas, Austin, 1960-69, became professor of art; Ark Press, Cornwall, England, editor/designer, 1970-83; free-lance book designer, 1984—.

WRITINGS:

A Matter of Death and Life, Ark Press, 1959.
The Labour of Love, Ark Press, 1962.
Man is a Little World, Ark Press, 1969.
The Wild Strange Place, Ark Press, 1971.
Wandering in Eden: Three Ways to the East Within Us, Knopf, 1976.
Womankind: A Celebration, Harper, 1979.
My Wild Love, Quay Books, 1987.

EDITOR

D. H. Lawrence, *The Body of God,* Ark Press, 1970.

Also editor of *The Cry of the Gull: Journals of Elyse Gregory.* Associate editor, *Texas Quarterly.*

WORK IN PROGRESS: The Woman Who Was Merry; As the Lion, As a Day of Spring.

*   *   *

ADAMS, Sexton 1936-

PERSONAL: Born September 4, 1936, in White Oak, TX; son of John Floyd and Jodie (Sexton) Adams; married second wife, Adelaide Griffin (assistant professor of management); children: (first marriage) Elise, Kristin, Julie. *Education:* North Texas State University, B.B.A., 1958, M.B.A., 1961; Louisiana State University, Ph.D., 1965.

ADDRESSES: Home—129 Woodland Hills, Denton, TX 76201. *Office*—North Texas State University, Denton, TX 76203.

CAREER: Texas Technological College (now Texas Tech University), Lubbock, assistant professor, 1965-67, associate professor of management, 1967-68; North Texas State University, Denton, professor of management, 1968—. Public lecturer and consultant to business and professional organizations.

MEMBER: Academy of Management, Society for the Advancement of Management, South Western Academy of Management, Sigma Iota Epsilon.

WRITINGS:

The Corporate Promotables, Gulf Publishing, 1969.
Personnel Management: A Program of Self-Instruction, Grid Publishing, 1971.
Administrative Policy and Strategy: A Casebook, Grid Publishing, 1973, 2nd edition, 1978.
Modern Personnel Management, Gulf Publishing, 1981.

Contributor to professional journals.*

*   *   *

ADAMS, Walter   1922-

PERSONAL: Born August 27, 1922, in Vienna, Austria; son of Edward and Ilona (Schildkraut) Adams; married Pauline Gordon, 1943; children: William James. *Education:* Brooklyn College (now Brooklyn College of the City University of New York), B.A. (magna cum laude), 1942; Yale University, M.A., 1946, Ph.D., 1947.

ADDRESSES: Home—928 Lantern Hill Dr., East Landing, MI 48823. *Office*—Economics Department, Michigan State University, East Lansing, MI 48824.

CAREER: Yale University, New Haven, CT, instructor in economics, 1945-47; Michigan State University, East Lansing, assistant professor, 1947-51, associate professor, 1951-56, professor, 1956-69, distinguished university professor, 1970—, president of university, 1969-70. Visiting professor at Universities of Paris and Grenoble (France), Salzburg Seminar (Austria), and Falkenstein Seminar (Germany). Consultant and economic counsel to U.S. House and Senate Small Business Committees at various times, 1950-56; member of Attorney General's National Committee to Study Antitrust Laws, 1953-55; consultant, U.S. Senate, Judiciary Committee, 1959, 1961-62; has served as expert witness before U.S. House and Senate committees on numerous occasions since 1949. Made evaluation of American university programs in France, Germany, Italy, Switzerland, Denmark, and Turkey under the auspices of the Carnegie Corp., 1957-58; guest lecturer and visiting professor at universities and institutes in France, Austria, and Switzerland, 1958—; official observer, UNESCO East-West Conference of Economists, Bursa, Turkey, 1958. Member of U.S. Advisory Commission on Educational Exchange, 1961-69. *Military service:* U.S. Army, 1943-45; served in European Theatre with 83rd Infantry Division and as aide-de-camp to commanding general of 11th Armored Division; received battlefield commission; became first lieutenant; awarded Bronze Star Medal for heroic conduct.

MEMBER: Association for Social Economics (president, 1980-81), University Professors (president, 1972-74), Midwest Economic Association (president, 1978-79).

WRITINGS:

(With L. E. Trawick) *Readings in Economics,* Macmillan, 1948.
(Editor) *The Structure of American Industry,* Macmillan, 1950, 7th edition, 1986.
(With H. M. Gray) *Monopoly in America: The Government as Promoter,* Macmillan, 1955.
(With J. B. Hendry) *Trucking Mergers, Concentration and Small Business: Analysis of Interstate Commerce Commission Policy, 1950-56,* U.S. Senate, Small Business Committee, 1957.
(With John A. Garraty) *From Main Street to the Left Bank: Students and Scholars Abroad,* Michigan State University Press, 1959.
(With Garraty) *Is the World Our Campus?,* Michigan State University Press, 1960.
(With Garraty) *A Guide to Study Abroad,* introduction by Lyndon B. Johnson, Channel Press, 1962.
On the Strategic Importance of Western Europe, U.S. House of Representatives, 1964.
The Brain Drain, Macmillan, 1968.
The Test, Macmillan, 1971.
(With others) *Tariffs, Quotas, and Trade: Problems of the International Economy,* Institute for Contemporary Issues, 1979.
(With James W. Brock) *The Bigness Complex: Industry, Labor, and Government in the American Economy,* Pantheon, 1986.
(With Brock) *Dangerous Pursuits,* Pantheon, 1989.
(With Brock) *Antitrust Economics on Trial,* Princeton University Press, 1991.

Also author of about thirty journal articles and pamphlets published in the U.S. and Europe.

BIOGRAPHICAL/CRITICAL SOURCES:

PERIODICALS

Business Week, January 19, 1987.
New York Times Book Review, December 17, 1989.
Punch, July 17, 1968.
Saturday Review, August 16, 1969.
Washington Post, October 5, 1971.

ADOFF, Arnold 1935-

PERSONAL: Born July 16, 1935, in New York, NY; son of Aaron Jacob (a pharmacist) and Rebecca (Stein) Adoff; married Virginia Hamilton (a writer), March 19, 1960; children: Leigh Hamilton, Jaime Levi. *Education:* City College of New York (now of the City University of New York), B.A., 1956; attended Columbia University, 1956-58; New School for Social Research, poetry workshops, 1965-67. *Politics:* "Committed to change for full freedom for all Americans." *Religion:* "Freethinking Pragmatist."

ADDRESSES: Home—Yellow Springs, OH. *Office*—Arnold Adoff Agency, P.O. Box 293, Yellow Springs, OH 45387.

CAREER: Board of Education, New York City, teacher in Harlem and upper west side of Manhattan, 1957-69, teaching in most subject areas in most grades, with the latter years spent in working with teenagers with reading difficulties; Arnold Adoff Agency, Yellow Springs, OH, literary agent, 1977—. Instructor in federal projects at New York University, Connecticut College, and other institutions; distinguished visiting professor, Queens College, 1986-87. Lecturer at colleges throughout the country; consultant in children's literature, poetry, and creative writing. Member of planning commission, Yellow Springs; "general agitator" for full equality in education, jobs, and housing. *Military service:* Served with New York National Guard.

AWARDS, HONORS: Children's Book of the Year citation, Child Study Association of America, 1968, for *I Am the Darker Brother: An Anthology of Modern Poems by Negro Americans,* 1969, for *City in All Directions,* and 1986, for *Sports Page;* American Library Association Notable Book awards, 1968, for *I Am the Darker Brother,* 1970, for *Black Out Loud: An Anthology of Modern Poems by Black Americans* and *Malcolm X,* 1971, for *MA nDA LA,* 1972, for *The Poetry of Black America: An Anthology of the 20th Century,* and 1979, for *Celebrations: A New Anthology of Black American Poetry;* Best Children's Book citation, *School Library Journal,* 1971, for *It Is the Poem Singing into Your Eyes: An Anthology of New Young Poets,* and 1973, for *Black Is Brown Is Tan;* Notable Children's Trade Book citation, Children's Book Council/National Council for Social Studies, 1974, and Children's Choice citation, International Reading Association/Children's Book Council, 1985, both for *My Black Me: A Beginning Book of Black Poetry;* Books for the Teen Age citation, New York Public Library, 1980, 1981, and 1982, all for *It Is the Poem Singing into Your Eyes;* special certificate from the Jane Addams Peace Association, 1983, for *All the Colors of the Race;* poetry award, National Council of Teachers of English, 1988.

WRITINGS:

JUVENILE POETRY

Black Is Brown Is Tan, illustrated by McCully, Harper, 1973.
Make a Circle Keep Us In: Poems for a Good Day, illustrated by Ronald Himler, Delacorte, 1975.
Big Sister Tells Me That I'm Black, illustrated by Lorenzo Lynch, Holt, 1976.
Tornado!: Poems, illustrated by Himler, Delacorte, 1977.
Under the Early Morning Trees, illustrated by Himler, Dutton, 1978.
Where Wild Willie, illustrated by McCully, Harper, 1978.
Eats: Poems, illustrated by Susan Russo, Lothrop, 1979.
I Am the Running Girl, illustrated by Himler, Harper, 1979.
Friend Dog, illustrated by Troy Howell, Lippincott, 1980.
OUTside INside Poems, illustrated by John Steptoe, Lothrop, 1981.
Today We Are Brother and Sister, illustrated by Glo Coalson, Lothrop, 1981.
Birds, illustrated by Howell, Lippincott Junior Books, 1982.
All the Colors of the Race, illustrated by Steptoe, Lothrop, 1982.
The Cabbages Are Chasing the Rabbits, illustrated by Janet Stevens, Harcourt, 1985.
Sports Pages, Lippincott Junior Books, 1986.
Flamboyan, illustrated by Karen Barbour, Harcourt, 1988.
Greens, illustrated by Betsy Lewin, Lothrop, 1988.
Chocolate Dreams, illustrated by Turi MacCombie, Lothrop, 1989.
Hard to Be Six, Lothrop, 1990.
In for Winter, Out for Spring, illustrated by Jerry Pinkney, Harcourt, 1991.

EDITOR OF ANTHOLOGIES

I Am the Darker Brother: An Anthology of Modern Poems by Negro Americans, foreword by Charlemae Rollins, drawings by Benny Andrews, Macmillan, 1968.
Black on Black: Commentaries by Negro Americans, Macmillan, 1968.
City in All Directions: An Anthology of Modern Poems, illustrated by Donald Carrick, Macmillan, 1969.
Black Out Loud: An Anthology of Modern Poems by Black Americans (juvenile), illustrated by Alvin Hollingsworth, Macmillan, 1970.
Brothers and Sisters: Modern Stories by Black Americans, Macmillan, 1970.
It Is the Poem Singing into Your Eyes: An Anthology of New Young Poets, Harper, 1971.
The Poetry of Black America: An Anthology of the 20th Century, Harper, 1973.

My Black Me: A Beginning Book of Black Poetry (juvenile), Dutton, 1974.
Celebrations: A New Anthology of Black American Poetry, Follett, 1978.

OTHER

Malcolm X (juvenile biography), illustrated by John Wilson, Crowell, 1970.
MA nDA LA (picture book), illustrated by Emily McCully, Harper, 1971.

Contributor of articles and reviews to periodicals.

SIDELIGHTS: Anthologist and children's poet Arnold Adoff launched his literary career as a teacher in the Harlem district of New York City. Frustrated by the lack of black literature available for teaching his students, he decided to compile and edit his own anthologies of black literature. Adoff is regarded as a thoughtful and, by his own admission, discriminating editor. "The material selected must be the finest in literary terms as well as in content/message/racial vision," he says in *Top of the News.* In an interview with Judith Wagner for the *Cincinnati Enquirer,* Adoff discusses the time and effort involved in publishing one of his anthologies: "Each of the anthologies takes at least a year of hard work and research to put together. Then, I have to find a publisher who believes in what I have done, and artist who can add the black essence and a public who sees the need for reading black literature."

In works like *Black Out Loud: An Anthology of Modern Poems by Black Americans* and *The Poetry of Black America: An Anthology of the 20th Century,* Adoff showcases the poetry of minor writers as well as those of well-known writers such as Gwendolyn Brooks, Robert Hayden, and Langston Hughes. His anthologies, he comments in *Top of the News,* have "been as much directed at raising the literary level of all writing used in classrooms and libraries, as [they have] been to introduce the mass of black American literature neglected in this white mass-culture." Since he is white, Adoff is careful to limit his literary endeavors to those that fall within the realm of his capabilities. He refuses, for instance, to write critical essays or articles on black life or literature because, he explains in the *Cincinnati Enquirer,* "we do not need any more white experts on black anything in this country. . . . I am NOT an expert on black life or culture or even black poetry. I am a continuing student."

In his own poetry for children and young adults, Adoff frequently celebrates black pride and family unity, but he has also dealt with such diverse subjects as natural disasters and the delights of food. Adoff writes in free verse, and his poetry has a musical quality and visual design that is best appreciated when both seen and read aloud. The neglected topic of the interracial family has provided the

theme for two of his poetry books, *Black Is Brown Is Tan* and *All the Colors of the Race.* These books reflect Adoff's experience as the husband of renowned black author Virginia Hamilton and the father of their two children. Both works, writes Margo Alexandre Long in *Interracial Books for Children Bulletin,* are comprised of "beautiful story-poems [that] express the love and good times a family shares."

All the Colors of the Race is told from the perspective of the daughter of a white Jewish father and a black Protestant mother. The book contains forty poems, described by a *Language Arts* reviewer as "contemplative, jubilant, and questioning." Despite the particularity of the book's subject matter, "the themes of the poems," writes Lauralyn Levesque in *School Library Journal,* ". . . are universal, ones that any thoughtful child will be able to relate to." Kate Shackford concludes in *Interracial Books for Children Bulletin:* "Adoff's poems reflect the joys and struggles and hopes of cross-racial families. They . . . demand that we look beyond racism to 'all the colors of the race. Human, of course.'"

BIOGRAPHICAL/CRITICAL SOURCES:

BOOKS

Adoff, Arnold, *All the Colors of the Race,* Lothrop, 1982.
Authors in the News, Volume 1, Gale, 1976.
Children's Literature Review, Volume 7, Gale, 1984.

PERIODICALS

Antioch Review, fall, 1975.
Bulletin of the Center for Children's Books, September, 1970.
Cincinnati Enquirer, January 5, 1975.
Horn Book, June, 1970; February, 1972.
Interracial Books for Children Bulletin, Number 1, 1983; Number 6, 1984.
Kirkus Review, April 15, 1970.
Language Arts, April, 1983.
New York Times Book Review, September 6, 1970.
School Library Journal, March, 1982.
Top of the News, January, 1972.
Tribune Books (Chicago), June 9, 1991, p. 4.
Washington Post Book World, November 11, 1979.*

*   *   *

ADRIAN, Frances
See POLLAND, Madeleine A(ngela Cahill)

AINSWORTH, Ruth (Gallard) 1908-

PERSONAL: Full name Ruth Gallard Ainsworth Gilbert; born October 16, 1908, in Manchester, England; daughter of Percy Clough (a Methodist minister) and Gertrude (Fisk) Ainsworth; married Frank Lathe Gilbert (a managing director of chemical works), March 29, 1935; children: Oliver Lathe, Christopher Gallard, Richard Frank. *Education:* Attended Froebel Training Centre, Leicester, England. *Politics:* Labour.

ADDRESSES: Home—Field End, Corbridge, Northumberland NE45 5JP, England.

CAREER: Writer.

WRITINGS:

CHILDREN'S BOOKS

Tales about Tony, illustrated by Cora E. M. Paterson, Epworth, 1936.

Mr. Popcorn's Friends, Epworth, 1938.

The Gingerbread House, Epworth, 1938.

The Ragamuffins, Epworth, 1939.

Richard's First Term: A School Story, Epworth, 1940.

All Different (poems), illustrated by Linda Bramley, Heinemann, 1947.

Five and a Dog, Epworth, 1949.

"Listen with Mother" Tales (selected from *Listen with Mother* radio program, British Broadcasting Corporation (BBC)), illustrated by Astrid Walford, Heinemann, 1951.

Rufty Tufty the Golliwog, illustrated by Dorothy Craigie, Heinemann, 1952.

The Ruth Ainsworth Readers (contains *The Cottage by the Sea; Little Wife Goody; The Robber; The Wild Boy; A Comfort for Owl; Sugar and Spice; Fun, Fires and Friends; Black Bill; A Pill for Owl; Tortoise in Trouble; The Pirate Ship;* and *Hob the Dwarf*), Heinemann, 1953-55.

Rufty Tufty at the Seaside, illustrated by Craigie, Heinemann, 1954.

Charles Stories, and Others from "Listen with Mother" (selected from *Listen with Mother* program), illustrated by Sheila Hawkins, Heinemann, 1954.

More about Charles, and Other Stories from "Listen with Mother" (selected from *Listen with Mother* program), illustrated by Hawkins, Heinemann, 1954.

Three Little Mushrooms: Four Puppet Plays (contains *Here We Go round the Buttercups, Lob's Silver Spoon, Hide-and-Seek,* and *Hay-Making*), Heinemann, 1955.

More Little Mushrooms: Four Puppet Plays (contains *Three Clever Mushrooms, Tick-Tock, Christmas Eve,* and *The White Stranger*), Heinemann, 1955.

The Snow Bear, illustrated by Rosemary Trew, Heinemann, 1956.

Rufty Tufty Goes Camping, illustrated by Craigie, Heinemann, 1956.

Rufty Tufty Runs Away, illustrated by Craigie, Heinemann, 1957.

Five "Listen with Mother" Tales about Charles (selected from *Listen with Mother* program), illustrated by Matvyn Wright, Adprint, 1957.

Nine Drummers Drumming (stories), illustrated by John Mackay, Heinemann, 1958.

Rufty Tufty Flies High, illustrated by D. G. Valentine, Heinemann, 1959.

Cherry Stones: A Book of Fairy Stories, illustrated by Pat Humphreys, Heinemann, 1960.

Rufty Tufty's Island, illustrated by Valentine, Heinemann, 1960.

Lucky Dip: A Selection of Stories and Verses, illustrated by Geraldine Spence, Penguin, 1961.

Rufty Tufty and Hattie, illustrated by Valentine, Heinemann, 1962.

Far-Away Children, illustrated by Felice Trentin, Heinemann, 1963, Roy, 1968.

The Ten Tales of Shellover, illustrated by Antony Maitland, Deutsch, 1963, Roy, 1968.

The Wolf Who Was Sorry, illustrated by Doritie Kettlewell, Heinemann, 1964, Roy, 1968.

(Editor) James H. Fassett, *Beacon Readers,* Ginn, 1964-65.

Rufty Tufty Makes a House, illustrated by Valentine, Heinemann, 1965.

Jack Frost, illustrated by Jane Paton, Heinemann, 1966.

Daisy the Cow, illustrated by Sarah Garland, Hamish Hamilton, 1966.

Horse on Wheels, illustrated by Janet Duchesne, Hamish Hamilton, 1966.

The Look about You Books, illustrated by Jennie Corbett, Heinemann, Book 1: *In Woods and Fields,* 1967, Book 2: *Down the Lane,* 1967, Book 3: *Beside the Sea,* 1967, Book 4: *By Pond and Stream,* 1969, Book 5: *In Your Garden,* 1969, Book 6: *In the Park,* 1969.

(Reteller) *My Monarch Book of Little Red Riding Hood,* Bancroft & Co., 1967, published as *Little Red Riding Hood,* Purnell, 1977.

(Reteller) *My Monarch Book of Goldilocks and the Three Bears,* Bancroft & Co., 1967, published as *Goldilocks and the Three Bears,* Purnell, 1980.

(Reteller) *My Monarch Book of Cinderella,* Bancroft & Co., 1967, published as *Cinderella,* Purnell, 1980.

Roly the Railway Mouse, illustrated by Leslie Atkinson, Heinemann, 1967, published as *Roly the Railroad Mouse,* F. Watts, 1969.

More Tales of Shellover, illustrated by Maitland, Roy, 1968.

The Aeroplane Who Wanted to See the Sea, Bancroft & Co., 1968.

Boris the Teddy Bear, Bancroft & Co., 1968.

Dougal the Donkey, Bancroft & Co., 1968.

Mungo the Monkey, Bancroft & Co., 1968.

The Old-Fashioned Car, Bancroft & Co., 1968.

The Rabbit and His Shadow, Bancroft & Co., 1968.

The Noah's Ark, illustrated by Elsie Wrigley, Lutterworth, 1969.

The Bicycle Wheel, illustrated by Shirley Hughes, Hamish Hamilton, 1969.

Look, Do and Listen (anthology), illustrated by Bernadette Watts, F. Watts, 1969.

(Reteller) *My Monarch Book of Puss in Boots,* Purnell, 1969, published as *Puss in Boots,* 1977.

(Reteller) *My Monarch Book of Jack and the Beanstalk,* Purnell, 1969, published as *Jack and the Beanstalk,* 1977.

(Reteller) *My Monarch Book of Snow White and the Seven Dwarfs,* Purnell, 1969, published as *Snow White,* 1977.

(Reteller) *My Monarch Book of Beauty and the Beast,* Purnell, 1969, published as *Beauty and the Beast,* 1977.

(Editor) *Book of Colours and Sounds,* Purnell, 1969.

The Ruth Ainsworth Book (stories), illustrated by Hughes, F. Watts, 1970.

The Phantom Cyclist, and Other Stories, illustrated by Maitland, Deutsch, 1971, published in United States as *The Phantom Cyclist, and Other Ghost Stories,* Follett, 1974.

Fairy Gold: Favourite Fairy Tales Retold for the Very Young, illustrated by Barbara Hope Steinberg, Heinemann, 1972.

Another Lucky Dip, illustrated by Hughes, Penguin, 1973.

Three's Company, illustrated by Prudence Seward, Lutterworth, 1974.

Ruth Ainsworth's Bedtime Book, Purnell, 1974.

The Phantom Fisherboy: Tales of Mystery and Magic, illustrated by Hughes, Deutsch, 1974.

Three Bags Full, illustrated by Sally Long, Heinemann, 1975.

The Bear Who Liked Hugging People, and Other Stories, illustrated by Maitland, Heinemann, 1976, Crane Russak, 1978.

(Reteller) *The Sleeping Beauty,* Purnell, 1977.

Up the Airy Mountain: Stories of Magic, illustrated by Eileen Browne, Heinemann, 1977.

The Phantom Roundabout, and Other Ghostly Tales, illustrated by Hughes, Deutsch, 1977, published in United States as *The Phantom Carousel, and Other Ghostly Tales,* Follett, 1978.

Mr. Jumble's Toyshop, illustrated by Paul Wrigley, Lutterworth, 1978.

The Talking Rock, illustrated by Joanna Stubbs, Deutsch, 1979.

(Reteller) *Hansel and Gretel,* Purnell, 1980.

(Reteller) *The Three Little Pigs,* Purnell, 1980.

(Reteller) *The Pied Piper of Hamelin,* Purnell, 1980.

(Reteller) *Rumplestiltskin,* Purnell, 1980.

The Mysterious Baba and Her Magic Caravan: Two Stories, illustrated by Joan Hickson, Deutsch, 1980.

Mermaids' Tales, illustrated by Dandi Palmer, Lutterworth, 1980.

The Pirate Ship and Other Stories, illustrated by Hughes, Heinemann, 1980.

The Little Yellow Taxi and His Friends, illustrated by Gary Inwood, Lutterworth, 1982.

EDUCATIONAL BOOKS WITH RONALD RIDOUT

Look Ahead Readers (eight books, with supplementary readers), illustrated by John Mackay, Heinemann, 1956-58.

Books for Me to Read, Red Series: *Jill and Peter, The House of Hay, Come and Play, A Name of My Own, The Duck That Ran Away,* and *Tim's Hoop,* illustrated by Ingeborg Meyer-Rey, Blue Series: *At the Zoo, What Are They?, Colours, Silly Billy, A Pram and a Bicycle,* and *Pony, Pony,* illustrated by Gwyneth Mamlock, Green Series: *Susan's House, What Can You Hear?, Tim's Kite, Flippy the Frog, Huff the Hedgehog,* and *A House for a Mouse,* illustrated by William Robertshaw, Bancroft & Co., 1965.

Dandy the Donkey, Bancroft & Co., 1971.

The Wild Wood, illustrated by Leslie Orriss, Bancroft & Co., 1971.

OTHER

The Evening Listens (adult poems), Heinemann, 1953.

Also author of plays and stories for television; contributor of stories to BBC programs, including *Listen with Mother* and *English for Schools.*

SIDELIGHTS: British children's author Ruth Ainsworth spent her own childhood by the sea in Suffolk, which accounts for the appearance of lonely beaches, mermaids, and sand dunes in many of her writings. "I am told that I began making up poems when I was three, and wrote an exercise book of fairy tales when I was eight," she recalls. "Throughout my childhood I enjoyed writing, whether diaries, school essays or stories." The numerous warm and gentle stories which fill Ainsworth's works are written primarily for younger readers, falling somewhere between picture books and books for more advanced readers. "It is like coming home, to open a book by Ruth Ainsworth," asserts a *Junior Bookshelf* contributor. "Here is security, an affectionate welcome, and a warm happy tale without surprises or excessive excitement but with plenty of gentle fun."

Ainsworth continued writing throughout her childhood and into her teens, and by the age of fifteen she was published in a national daily. She moved with her family to Leicester two years later, the large library there adding a new dimension to her life. Soon after, her poetry was published in a number of magazines and journals, including *Spectator* and *Country Life,* and when she won a Gold Medal for original work, the publication of more poems ensued as part of the prize. Her first break came when Heinemann published *All Different,* a book of her children's poetry. At the same time, Ainsworth began writing regularly for *Listen with Mother,* a BBC radio program, and Heinemann also published these stories in 1951 as *"Listen with Mother" Tales.* From then on, the books followed steadily.

Many of these books consist of a number of short stories compiled in one volume. *The Ruth Ainsworth Book,* published in 1970, collects a number of Ainsworth's previously published short stories and adds a variety of new selections. The book contains a range of stories, from simple tales for the very young, to longer and more substantial narratives for older children. Everything from realism to fantasy is covered, and a *Bulletin of the Center for Children's Books* contributor maintains that "the collection on the whole has variety and is sturdy enough to be useful for reading aloud, particularly in home collections." In such works as *The Phantom Fisherboy: Tales of Mystery and Magic* and *The Phantom Cyclist, and Other Stories,* Ainsworth delves into the unknown and presents a number of modern ghosts. These spooky spirits appear to various young children, but like Ainsworth's other characters, they are gentle, kind, and even friendly. The stories in *The Phantom Cyclist* are "told in a simple and effective style," describes a *Times Literary Supplement* reviewer. And Catherine Storr concludes in *New Statesman:* "Ainsworth will earn the gratitude of the children who always ask for ghost stories, and of parents who dread the waking and shrieking the following night, with her book of unalarming, but definitely inexplicable eerie tales."

In longer works, such as *The Talking Rock* and *The Mysterious Baba and Her Magic Caravan: Two Stories,* Ainsworth continues to mix elements of fantasy and reality. *The Talking Rock* revolves around six-year-old Jakes and his adventures on a beach in England. Quarantined with the measles, he must remain in England for a short time when his family moves to Nigeria. While staying by the sea with friends of the family, Jakes makes a boy in the sand who magically comes to life. Sand Boy, a young mermaid, and Jakes spend a few wonderful days on the beach until they, along with all the other sea creatures, are threatened by the sea monster Glumper. Jakes must climb to the top of Talking Rock to find out how to fight Glumper, and by the time he rejoins his family all is well. "This is a pleasant fantasy, not epic, but nicely written," remarks *School Library Journal* contributor Janice Giles. With *The*

Talking Rock, asserts a *Junior Bookshelf* reviewer, Ainsworth presents "her most ambitious, and in many ways her most successful, story."

The two stories that make up *The Mysterious Baba and Her Magic Caravan* are set in the Left-Over Land, the place where toys retire when they are not sold. A doll family is among the inhabitants of this land, and they encounter a series of mysteries when they take in Baba, a homeless Russian doll. The other dolls are baffled by the size of some of her clothes and by the amount of food she eats until they find out that she is a Russian nested doll, with six other little Babas inside her. The family accepts Baba and her children, and the second story in the book picks up where the first left off, relating the adventures of the Baba children and their friends. *Baba and Her Magic Caravan* "is an amusing and ingenious story with a satisfying ending," relates Frances Ball in the *British Book News Children's Supplement.* "Warmth and generosity distinguish all the characters, who retain their doll-like qualities along with their human traits," concludes *School Library Journal* contributor Susan Cain.

Ainsworth sees writing as a pleasure, and claims to "write from a top layer of happiness. . . . If I live long enough to write stories for my great-grandchildren," she continues, "I suppose my characters will behave much as they have always done, building sandcastles, making houses, and meaning well, though this sometimes turns out badly. They experience the anguish of separation and disappointment, but there is usually a comforting, solid figure near at hand, an eternal Mrs. Golliwog. Children find magic in the everyday life of play and family. My sources spring from just that. Only children and birds 'Know the sweetness of cherries, / The goodness of bread.' "

BIOGRAPHICAL/CRITICAL SOURCES:

BOOKS

Something about the Author, Volume 7, Gale, 1975, pp. 1-4.

PERIODICALS

British Book News Children's Supplement, autumn, 1980, p. 15.
Bulletin of the Center for Children's Books, March, 1971, p. 101; December, 1979.
Junior Bookshelf, April, 1977, pp. 83-84; December, 1979, pp. 321-322; October, 1980, p. 236.
Library Journal, September 15, 1974, p. 2258.
New Statesman, November 12, 1971, p. 663.
Newsweek, November 9, 1979, p. 729.
Saturday Review, May 27, 1978, p. 60.
School Library Journal, April, 1971, p. 1490; October, 1978, p. 141; January, 1980, p. 64; September, 1980, p. 55; December, 1980, p. 72.

Times Literary Supplement, October 22, 1971, p. 1321; December 2, 1977; November 21, 1980, p. 1325.*

*   *   *

ALDRICH, Ann
See MEAKER, Marijane (Agnes)

*   *   *

ALDRICH, Joseph C(offin) 1940-

PERSONAL: Born November 16, 1940, in Portland, OR; son of Willard and Doris (Coffin) Aldrich; married Ruthe Miles (a housewife), August 18, 1962; children: Stephen, Kristin. *Education:* Multnomah School of the Bible, diploma, 1961; Southern Oregon College (now State College), A.B., 1963; Dallas Theological Seminary, Th.M., 1968, Th.D., 1971.

ADDRESSES: Office—Multnomah School of the Bible, 8435 Northeast Glisan St., Portland, OR 97220.

CAREER: Dallas Theological Seminary, Dallas, TX, instructor, 1969-71; Mariners Church, Newport Beach, CA, pastor, 1971-78; Multnomah School of the Bible, Portland, OR, president, 1978—. Talbot Theological Seminary, Biola University, part-time faculty member, 1973-77; faculty member of Billy Graham School of Evangelism; has been involved in prison ministries at the Oregon State Prison. Has been a speaker/guest on national radio and television broadcasts, at national pastor's conferences, churches, and universities, and in Germany, Switzerland, England, Canada, Hong Kong, Israel, and Egypt.

WRITINGS:

Secrets to Inner Beauty, Vision House, 1977, revised edition, Multnomah, 1984.
Life-Style Evangelism: Crossing Traditional Boundaries to Reach the Unbelieving World, Multnomah, 1982, study guide, 1983.
Self-Worth: How to Become More Loveable, Multnomah, 1982.
Satisfaction: Investing in What Is Important to God, Multnomah, 1983.
Conscience: God's Provision for Your Success, Multnomah, 1983.

Life-Style Evangelism is being translated into nine languages.

ADAPTATIONS: A four-part film has been produced based on *Life-Style Evangelism: Crossing Traditional Boundaries to Reach the Unbelieving World.*

SIDELIGHTS: Joseph C. Aldrich once told *CA:* "Nudging folks towards God, the only infinite reference point capable of illuminating the particulars of life, is the compelling force of my life. Separated from him, life is at best a joke, that [is] 'told by an idiot.' Man's eternal heartache cannot be eased by temporal bicarbonates.

"I believe the pen, skillfully used, can redirect the lives, the eternities of men. Words have always fascinated me. Undergirded by truth, they call the searcher on a pilgrimage towards beauty."

*   *   *

ALSTON, William P(ayne) 1921-

PERSONAL: Born November 29, 1921, in Shreveport, LA; son of William Payne (a salesman) and Eunice (Schoolfield) Alston; married Mary Frances Collins, August 15, 1943 (divorced, 1963); married Valerie Tibbetts, July 3, 1963; children: (first marriage) Frances Ellen. *Education:* Centenary College of Louisiana, B.M., 1942; University of Chicago, Ph.D., 1951. *Avocational interests:* Music (plays piano, sings regularly with a madrigal group), history, psychology.

ADDRESSES: Home—4 Bittersweet Lane, Fayetteville, NY 13066. *Office*—Department of Philosophy, Syracuse University, Syracuse, NY 13244-1170.

CAREER: University of Michigan, Ann Arbor, instructor, 1949-52, assistant professor, 1952-56, associate professor, 1956-61, professor of philosophy, 1961-71; Rutgers University, New Brunswick, NJ, professor of philosophy, 1971-76; University of Illinois at Urbana-Champaign, professor, 1976-80; Syracuse University, Syracuse, NY, professor of philosophy, 1980—. Visiting assistant professor, University of California, Los Angeles, 1952-53; visiting lecturer, Harvard University, 1955-56; fellow, Center for Advanced Study in the Behavioral Sciences, 1965-66. *Military service:* U.S. Army, 1942-46.

MEMBER: American Philosophical Association (president of western division, 1978-79), Society for Philosophy and Psychology (president, 1978-79), Society of Christian Philosophers (president, 1979-81), Michigan Academy of Arts and Sciences (chairman of philosophy section, 1954).

AWARDS, HONORS: Rackham summer research fellow, 1954, 1957; American Philosophical Association fellow, 1955-56; Ford Foundation fellow in behavioral science, 1962; D.H.L., Church Divinity School of the Pacific, 1988; National Endowment for the Humanities fellow, 1988-89.

WRITINGS:

(Editor) *Religious Belief and Philosophical Thought: Readings in the Philosophy of Religion,* Harcourt, 1963.

(Editor with George Nakhnikian) *Readings in Twentieth Century Philosophy,* Free Press of Glencoe, 1963.

Philosophy of Language, Prentice-Hall, 1964.

(Translator with Nakhnikian) Edmund Husserl, *The Idea of Phenomenology,* Nijhoff, 1964.

(With R. B. Brandt) *The Problems of Philosophy,* Allyn & Bacon, 1967, 3rd edition, 1978.

Divine Nature and Human Language, Cornell University Press, 1989.

Epistemic Justification, Cornell University Press, 1989.

Perceiving God, Cornell University Press, 1991.

Contributor to books including *Faith and the Philosophers,* St. Martin's, 1964; *Philosophical Interrogations,* Holt, 1964; *The Philosophy of Psychology,* Macmillan, 1974; and *Values and Morals,* Reidel, 1978. Also contributor to philosophical journals.

WORK IN PROGRESS: Research on epistemology, religious experience, philosophical theology, religious language, and speech acts.

SIDELIGHTS: William P. Alston wrote *CA:* "I have long been interested both in philosophy and psychology and in their interplay. I feel that psychology in this country, in its (commendable) drive to be empirical, has neglected the critical examination of its basic concepts, and that it would profit from such examination, of the sort philosophers are trained to carry on. I have done some of this and hope to do more."

*   *   *

ANDERSCH, Alfred 1914-1980

PERSONAL: Born February 4, 1914, in Munich, Germany; immigrated to Switzerland, 1958; naturalized Swiss citizen, 1973; died February 21, 1980, in Berzona, Switzerland; son of Alfred A. and Hedwig (Watzek) Andersch; married Gisela Dichgans (a painter), 1950; children: Michael, Martin, Annette. *Education:* Attended Wittelsbacher Gymnasium, Munich.

ADDRESSES: Home—6611 Berzona, Ticino, Switzerland.

CAREER: Writer of novels, essays, short stories, radio scripts, and travel books. Member of the youth organization of Communist Party. Worked in a Munich publishing house as a young man to learn book trade; because of his involvement in the Communist youth organization, in 1933 he spent six months in the Dachau Concentration Camp; after release worked in publishing industry; following World War II was a newspaper editor, working on *Der Ruf* and later on *Texte und Zeichen;* radio broadcaster, 1948-60; leader of an Arctic expedition for German television, 1965. Co-founder with Heinrich Boll and Gunter Grass of Gruppe 47. *Military service:* Drafted into the German Army, 1940; deserted in 1944 on the Italian Front and became an American prisoner of war.

MEMBER: Deutsche Akademie fuer Sprache und Dichtkunst, Bayerische Akademie der Schoenen Kuenste, PEN.

AWARDS, HONORS: Deutscher Kritiker-Preis, 1958, for *Sansibar;* Nelly Sachs-Preis, 1968; Prix Charles Veillon, 1968, for *Efraim;* Literaturpreis der Bayerischen Academie der Schoenen Kuenste.

WRITINGS:

Deutsche Literatur in der Entscheidung (essays), Volk & Zeit, 1948.

(Editor) *Europaeische Avantgarde* (anthology), Verlag der Frankfurter Hefte, 1949.

Kirschen der Freiheit: Ein Bericht (autobiographical), Frankfurter Verlagsanstalt, 1952.

Piazza San Gaetano: Suite (narrative), Walter-Verlag, 1957.

Sansibar: oder, der letzte Grund (novel), Walter-Verlag, 1957, translation by Michael Bullock published as *Flight to Afar,* Coward, 1958, edition in German with introduction and notes by Walter G. Hesse, published in England under original title, Harrap, 1964.

Geister und Leute, Walter-Verlag, 1958, translation by Christa Armstrong published as *The Night of the Giraffe and Other Stories,* Random House, 1964.

Fahrerflucht (radio play), Hans Bredow-Institut, 1958, published with three other radio plays under same title, Deutcher Taschenbuch Verlag, 1956, and published singly in *Deutsche Lektuere,* edited by Paul G. Krauss, Holt, 1969.

Die Rote (novel), Walter-Verlag, 1960, translation by Bullock published as *The Redhead,* Pantheon, 1961.

Der Tod des James Dean (radio play; text adapted from John Dos Passos and others), Tschudy, 1960.

Paris ist eine ernste Stadt (narrative), Olten, 1961.

Wanderungen im Norden (travel narrative), illustrated with color pictures by wife, Gisela Andersch, Walter-Verlag, 1962.

Ein Liebhaber des Halbschattens (stories), Walter-Verlag, 1963.

Die Blindheit des Kunstwerks und andere Aufsaetze (essays and other writings), Suhrkamp, 1965.

Bericht, Roman, Erzaehlungen (collection with bibliography of Andersch's works), Walter-Verlag, 1965.

Aus Einem roemischen Winter (travel narrative), Walter-Verlag, 1966.

Efraim (novel), Diogenes Verlag, 1967, translation by Ralph Manheim published as *Efraim's Book,* Doubleday, 1970.

(Contributor) Wolfgang Tschechne, editor, *Geliebte Staedte,* Fackeltraeger-Verlag, 1967.

Ein Auftrag fuer Lord Glouster (collection), Signal-Verlag, 1968.

Hohe Breitengrade (travel narrative on Arctic expedition), Diogenes Verlag, 1968.

Mein Verschwinden in Providence (nine stories), Diogenes Verlag, 1971, translation by Manheim published as *My Disappearance in Providence,* Doubleday, 1978.

Norden, Sueden, rechis and links (essays), Diogenes Verlag, 1972.

Winterspelt, translation by Clara Winston and Richard Winston, Doubleday, 1978, published as *Winterspelt: A Novel about the Last Days of World War II,* Dufour, 1980.

Also author of numerous unpublished radio scripts, including *Strahlende Melancholie,* 1953, *Synnoeves Halsband,* 1958, *Von Ratten und Evangelisten,* 1960, and *Russisches Roulette,* 1961.

ADAPTATIONS: Die Rote was made into a film in Germany.

SIDELIGHTS: Until his death in 1980, Alfred Andersch was recognized as one of Europe's most influential spokespersons of his generation. Involved at an early age in political causes, Andersch expressed his various opinions, including his early opposition to the Nazi Regime, in several formats. Andersch was a very determined speaker and writer on what he considered was his generation's moral responsibilities in post-war Germany. As editor of two respected periodicals, *Der Ruf* and *Texte und Zeichen,* writer of numerous novels such as *Sansibar; oder, Der letze Grung* (*Flight to Afar*) and *Efraim* (*Efraim's Book*), and radio broadcaster, Andersch reached millions of people worldwide.

Not only did he freely express his ideas concerning what he believed was morally correct and ethical, Andersch bravely lived his convictions and beliefs as well. Andersch was so adamant concerning his hatred of Adolph Hitler and of his policies that after he was drafted into the German Army Andersch deserted his post on the Italian Front. He then surrendered to American soldiers, becoming a prisoner of war.

While all of his works were written in his native German, several of Andersch's books have been translated into English and released in the United States. Of these books *Flight to Afar, Efraim's Book,* and *Winterspelt: A Novel about the Last Days of World War II* were the most widely reprinted of his works.

In a *Times Literary Supplement* article Colin Russ discussed the historical and timeless value of Andersch's writings. Russ noted: "Andersch died in 1980. It is good to be reminded . . . of his psychological insight, his mastery of natural description, and his ability to show that great historical processes of politics and war, far from being 'impersonal,' are very personal indeed."

Agreeing that Andersch was indeed a gifted writer whose work greatly impacted his readers, Michael Winkler stated in *Dictionary of Literary Biography* that Andersch was indeed "an accomplished storyteller whose best work shows a subtle ability to capture human frailty and to portray the complicated situations in which thinking people have to make decisions." Winkler continued: "Flight into freedom and withdrawal into the world of artistic creation are dominant themes in all of Andersch's works, and his personal experiences, re-created with intellectual honesty, are the source of inspiration for his fiction."

Andersch's *Flight to Afar* is a fascinating and complex study of four people as they deal with a profound challenge involving freedom—each handling it in their own way. Richard Plant stated in the *New York Times* that in *Flight to Afar* Andersch "has created a gripping drama of four interwoven stories, every step inexorably leading to the next. Each character is illuminated through an inner monologue until all the strands have merged. The climaxes, though growing from minute incidents, still deliver their shattering impact. . . . Mr. Andersch has marvelously succeeded in fulfilling the age-old properties Aristotle assigned to true tragedy; he has aroused awe and pity."

In his *New York Herald Tribune Book Review* article on *Flight to Afar* C. S. Kilby wrote that "Andersch pours more meaning into this thin novel than one usually finds in a large book. . . . The sad thing about freedom endlessly enjoyed is that it tends to lose its reality. This is a novel that lets one feel the wealth contained in simple liberty."

Efraim's Book is yet another interesting look at the human spirit and the power of freedom. The novel follows a Jewish journalist as he searches through Europe for his friend's daughter, who disappeared during World War II. In his review of Andersch's *Efraim's Book,* Charles Markmann remarked in the *Nation:* "It is not always easy to follow, but it is an impressively convincing synthesis of the simultaneous levels of his narrator so that past and present and even future and potential, desired and hated and feared, are elements that in every successful work of art strikes one as inevitable."

Still another complex study of characters, morality, and freedom is Andersch's *Winterspelt.* In *Winterspelt* Andersch explored, according to Michael Bulter in the *Times*

Literary Supplement, "intensely private patterns of behaviour in an ironic dialectic of fact and fiction." Bulter went on to state that "*Winterspelt* remains Andersch's most complex novel: Its ambitious narrative scope and patent honesty of purpose command respect."

Ernest Pawel commented in the *New York Times Book Review* that "because real freedom necessitates choices, it is scary. And the nature of these choices, the moral responsibility of the individual for what he does or fails to do, has been the unifying theme in all of Mr. Andersch's by now substantial body of work." Pawel continued: "But [Andersch's] real strength lies in creating complex, convincingly human beings who struggle not only to survive but also to remain human. Mr. Andersch is one of Europe's most significant and consistently original figures."

BIOGRAPHICAL/CRITICAL SOURCES:

BOOKS

Dictionary of Literary Biography, Volume 69: *Contemporary German Fiction Writers, First Series,* Gale, 1988.

PERIODICALS

Nation, December 13, 1971.
New York Herald Tribune Book Review, October 19, 1958.
New York Times, September 28, 1958; May 6, 1978; July 4, 1978.
New York Times Book Review, July 30, 1978.
Times Literary Supplement, February 5, 1982.

OBITUARIES:

PERIODICALS

New York Times, February 23, 1980.
Times (London), March 10, 1980.*

*   *   *

ANDERSON, Gerald Dwight   1944-

PERSONAL: Born November 18, 1944, in Hitterdal, MN; son of Wilfred Dean (a farmer) and Violet Caria Maria (Heigg) Anderson; married Barbara Thill (an artist), May 13, 1978; children: Carmen Nell, Karl August, Paul Martin. *Education:* Concordia College, Moorhead, MN, B.A., 1965; North Dakota State University, M.A., 1966; University of Iowa, Ph.D., 1973. *Politics:* Democrat. *Religion:* Lutheran.

ADDRESSES: Home—1320 Fifth St. S., Moorhead, MN 56560. *Office*—Department of History, North Dakota State University, Fargo, ND 58105.

CAREER: Waldorf College, Forest City, IA, assistant professor of history, 1966-70; Drake University, Des Moines, IA, assistant professor of history, 1973; Iowa Wesleyan College, Mount Pleasant, assistant professor of history, 1974; Austin Community College, Austin, MN, instructor in history, 1975; rector of Northwest Minnesota Regional History Center, 1976-77; Minnesota State Senate, St. Paul, research aide, 1977-79; Luther College, Decorah, IA, associate professor of history, 1979-85, director of Nottingham Program, 1983-85; North Dakota State University, Fargo, associate professor of history, 1985—. Member of New Minowa Players theatre group.

MEMBER: American Historical Association, Pi Gamma Mu (president of Iota chapter, 1964-65), Phi Alpha Theta.

WRITINGS:

Fascists, Communists, and the National Government: Civil Liberties in Great Britain, University of Missouri Press, 1983.
The Uffda Trial (historical novel), Martin House, 1992.

WORK IN PROGRESS: Prairie Voices: An Oral History of Scandinavian Immigrants in the Upper Midwest.

SIDELIGHTS: Gerald Dwight Anderson told *CA:* "In 1983-84 I spent a year in England living in a communal setting with sixteen of my Luther College students. While they attended the University of Nottingham, I had the opportunity to observe the subjects of so many of my studies. I first became interested in British civil liberties when, as an undergraduate, I discovered that there had actually been a Fascist party in England during the 1930s. Why was fascism successful in gaining power in so much of Europe while fascism in Britain remained such a well-kept secret? At the time, it was obvious that Britain had never experienced a real threat from the communists. Why had the British government been so successful in keeping such challenges to parliamentary democracy to a minimum? While my studies proved that there was a potential for the abuse of traditional civil liberties in Britain during the interwar years, those civil liberties were never seriously threatened. It seemed that British soil was a poor seed-bed for extremist politics.

"While living in Britain in the midst of the 1984 coal strike, this impression was only partly confirmed—there was then considerable extremism in a part of the Labour party. Nevertheless, there remains in the British psyche a deep respect for tradition, proper public behavior, and moderation.

"For the past few years I have also studied the history and impact of Scandinavian immigration to America. This interest has led to the writing of an historical novel based on the experiences of Scandinavian-Americans in Minnesota. It has also led to my current work in progress, the collection and editing of an oral history of Scandinavian-Americans.

"Such observations will, I hope, improve my teaching. Teaching is my life and career; writing is merely an outgrowth of that. This attitude is reflected in my writing, for I believe that even as a teacher's words must come alive in the classroom, so too must the written word reflect the living, human aspects of people moving through time."

* * *

ANDREWS, Elton V.
See POHL, Frederik

* * *

ANDREWS, Kenneth R(ichmond) 1916-

PERSONAL: Born May 24, 1916, in New London, CT; son of William John and Myrtle (Richmond) Andrews; married Edith May Platt, April 29, 1945 (divorced, 1969); married Carolyn Erskine Hall, February 14, 1970; children: (first marriage) Kenneth R. Jr., Carolyn. *Education:* Wesleyan University, B.A., 1936, M.A., 1937; University of Illinois at Urbana-Champaign, Ph.D., 1948.

ADDRESSES: Home—49 Irving St., No. 1, Cambridge, MA 02138. *Office*—Soldier's Field, Boston, MA 02163.

CAREER: University of Illinois at Urbana-Champaign, instructor, 1937-41; Harvard University, Graduate School of Business Administration, Boston, MA, assistant professor, 1946-51, associate professor, 1952-57, professor 1957-65, Donald K. David Professor, 1965-86, Emeritus, 1986. Faculty chairman of Advanced Management Program, 1967-70, master of Leverett House, 1971-81. Leave of absence, 1958-59, as professor of business policy and general management, IMEDE Institute for Management Development, Lausanne, Switzerland. Formerly director, Temple, Barker, Sloane, Price Brothers, Inc., Duriron, Inc., Reed & Barton, Harvard University Press, and Xerox Corp. Trustee, Wesleyan University, 1955-72. Consultant in executive development, management training, and organization problems in industry. *Military service:* U.S. Air Force, 1941-46, commanded 35th Statistical Control Unit, headquarters, U.S. Strategic Air Forces (Pacific Theater). Lieutenant colonel, Air Force Reserve, 1945-56.

MEMBER: Phi Beta Kappa, Phi Nu Theta, Harvard Clubs (Boston and New York).

AWARDS, HONORS: M.A., Harvard University, 1957; Academy of Management Book Award, 1966, for *The Effectiveness of University Management Development Programs;* McKinsey Foundation Book Award, 1971, for *The Concept of Corporate Strategy;* Distinguished Alumnus Award, Wesleyan University, 1986; Harvard Medal, Harvard University, 1986; Distinguished Service Award, Harvard Business School, 1990.

WRITINGS:

Nook Farm: Mark Twain's Hartford Circle, Harvard University Press, 1950, reprinted, University of Washington Press, 1969.
(Editor) *The Case Method of Teaching Human Relations,* Harvard University Press, 1953.
(Contributor) Malcom P. McNair, editor, *The Case Method at the Harvard Business School,* McGraw, 1954.
(Contributor) Frank Pierson, editor, *The Education of American Business,* McGraw, 1959.
(With Edmund P. Learned and C. Roland Christensen) *Problems of General Management: Business Policy,* Irwin, 1961.
(With Learned, Christensen, and William D. Guth) *Business Policy: Text and Cases,* Irwin, 1965, 7th edition, 1987.
The Effectiveness of University Management Development Programs, Division of Research, Harvard Business School, 1966.
The Concept of Corporate Strategy, Dow Jones-Irwin, 1971, revised edition, 1987.
(Editor) *Ethics in Practice,* Harvard Business School Press, 1990.

Contributor of articles to professional journals. *Harvard Business Review,* member of editorial board, 1951-57, chairman of editorial board, 1972-79, editor-in-chief, 1979-85.

* * *

ANTHONY, C. L.
See SMITH, Dorothy Gladys

* * *

APPS, Jerold W(illard) 1934-
(Jerry Apps)

PERSONAL: Born July 25, 1934, in Wild Rose, WI; son of Herman E.(a farmer) and Eleanor (Witt) Apps; married Ruth E. Olson (a home economist), May 20, 1961; children: Susan, Steven, Jeffrey. *Education:* University of Wisconsin, B.S., 1955, M.S. 1957, Ph.D. 1967. *Politics:* Independent. *Religion:* Lutheran. *Avocational Interests:* Wildflower study, bird study, nature photography, hiking, camping, canoeing, fishing, farming.

ADDRESSES: Home—522 Togstad Glen, Madison, WI 53711. *Office*—Department of Continuing and Vocational

Education, University of Wisconsin, 276 Teacher Education Bldg., 225 North Mills St., Madison, WI 53706.

CAREER: County extension agent in Wisconsin, 1957-62; University of Wisconsin—Madison, associate professor, 1967-70, professor of adult education, 1970—, chairman of department of continuing and vocational education, 1977-79, 1982-87. Teacher of creative writing at Rhinelander School of Arts, 1971—, and The Clearing, 1990—. University of Alberta, distinguished visiting professor, 1988. McGraw-Hill, consulting editor, 1976-83. National Extension Leadership Development Program, coordinator, 1990—. Assistant state 4-H leader in Wisconsin, 1962-64. *Military Service:* U.S. Army Reserve, 1956-66; active duty in Transportation Corps, 1956; became captain.

MEMBER: Adult Education Association, Commission of Professors of Adult Education (past president), Authors Guild, Authors League of America, Adult Education Association of Wisconsin (past president), Wisconsin Academy of Sciences, Arts, and Letters (past president), Gamma Sigma Delta (past president), Phi Kappa Phi.

AWARDS, HONORS: Award for best nonfiction book by a Wisconsin author from Wisconsin Council for Writers, 1977, and Nonfiction Book Award of Merit from Wisconsin Historical Society, 1978, both for *Barns of Wisconsin;* Research to Practice Award, Adult Education Association, 1982, for *Problems in Continuing Education* and *Toward a Working Philosophy of Adult Education;* Scholarly Book Award, Wisconsin Council for Writers, 1989; Teaching Excellence Award, School of Arts of Rhinelander, 1990; Lansdowne Scholar, University of Victoria, 1991.

WRITINGS:

(Under name Jerry Apps) *The Land Still Lives,* Wisconsin House, 1970.
(Under name Jerry Apps) *Cabin in the Country,* Argus, 1972.
How to Improve Adult Education in Your Church, Augsburg, 1972.
Toward a Working Philosophy of Adult Education, Syracuse University Press, 1973.
Tips for Article Writers, Wisconsin Regional Writers, 1973.
(Under name Jerry Apps) *Village of Roses,* Wild Rose Historical Society, 1973.
Ideas for Better Church Meetings, Augsburg, 1975.
Barns of Wisconsin, Tamarack Press, 1977.
Study Skills: For Those Adults Returning to School, McGraw, 1978.
Problems in Continuing Education, McGraw, 1979.
Mills of the Midwest, Tamarack Press, 1980.

(Editor with Robert Boyd) *Redefining the Discipline of Adult Education,* Jossey-Bass, 1980.
The Adult Learner on Campus, Follet, 1981.
Improving Your Writing Skills, Follet, 1982.
Skiing into Wisconsin, Pearl-Win, 1985.
Improving Practice in Continuing Education, Jossey-Bass, 1985.
Higher Education in a Learning Society, Jossey-Bass, 1988,
Study Skills for Today's College Student, McGraw, 1990.
Mastering the Teaching of Adults, Krieger, 1991.

Contributor to books, including *Linking Philosophy and Practice,* edited by Sharon Merriam, Jossey-Bass, 1982; *Lifelong Education for Adults: An International Handbook,* Pergamon Press, 1986; *Effective Teaching Style,* edited by Elisabeth Hayes, Jossey-Bass, 1989. Author of weekly column "Outdoor Notebook" appearing in three Wisconsin newspapers. Contributor of numerous articles to periodicals, including *Life Long Learning, Hospital Progress, Resource, Wisconsin Trails, Outdoor World,* and *Wisconsin Academy Review.* Book editor, *Journal of Adult Education,* 1967-69; editor, *Journal of Extension,* 1969-70; Consulting editor, *Adult Learning,* 1989—.

SIDELIGHTS: Jerold W. Apps once told *CA:* "Each day I learn something new about the art and craft of writing. May it always be so."

*   *   *

APPS, Jerry
    See APPS, Jerold W(illard)

*   *   *

AQUINA, Sister Mary
    See WEINRICH, A(nna) K(atharina) H(ildegard)

*   *   *

ASHBERY, John (Lawrence) 1927-
    (Jonas Berry)

PERSONAL: Born July 28, 1927, in Rochester, NY; son of Chester Frederick (a farmer) and Helen (a biology teacher at time of marriage; maiden name, Lawrence) Ashbery. *Education:* Harvard University, B.A., 1949; Columbia University, M.A., 1951; graduate study at New York University, 1957-58.

ADDRESSES: Agent—Georges Borchardt, Inc., 136 East 57th St., New York, NY 10022.

CAREER: Writer, critic, and editor. Worked as reference librarian for Brooklyn Public Library, Brooklyn, NY; Oxford University Press, New York City, copywriter, 1951-54; McGraw-Hill Book Co., New York City, copywriter, 1954-55; New York University, New York City, instructor in elementary French, 1957-58; *New York Herald Tribune,* European Edition, Paris, France, art critic, 1960-65; *Art News,* New York City, Paris correspondent, 1964-65, executive editor in New York City, 1966-72; Brooklyn College of the City University of New York, Brooklyn, professor of English and co-director of Master of Fine Arts Program in Creative Writing, 1974-90, distinguished professor, 1980-90; Harvard University, Cambridge, MA, Charles Eliot Norton Professor of Poetry, 1989-90; Bard College, Annandale-on-Hudson, NY, Charles P. Stevenson, Jr. Professor of Languages and Literature, 1990—. Art critic for *Art International* (Lugano, Switzerland), 1961-64, *New York,* 1978-80, and *Newsweek,* 1980—. Has read his poetry at the Living Theatre, New York City, and at numerous universities, including Yale University, University of Chicago, and University of Texas.

MEMBER: American Academy and Institute of Arts and Letters, 1980—; Academy of American Poets (chancellor, 1988—).

AWARDS, HONORS: Discovery Prize co-winner, Young Men's Hebrew Association, 1952; Fulbright scholarships to France, 1955-56 and 1956-57; Yale Series of Younger Poets Prize, 1956, for *Some Trees;* Poets' Foundation grants, 1960 and 1964; Ingram-Merrill Foundation grants, 1962 and 1972; Harriet Monroe Poetry Award, *Poetry,* 1963; Union League Civic and Arts Foundation Prize, *Poetry,* 1966; National Book Award nomination, 1966, for *Rivers and Mountains;* Guggenheim fellowships, 1967 and 1973; National Endowment for the Arts grants, 1968 and 1969; National Institute of Arts and Letters Award, 1969; Shelley Memorial Award, Poetry Society of America, 1973, for *Three Poems;* Frank O'Hara Prize, Modern Poetry Association, 1974; Harriet Monroe Poetry Award, University of Chicago, 1975; Pulitzer Prize, National Book Award, and National Book Critics Circle Award, all 1976, for *Self-Portrait in a Convex Mirror;* Levinson Prize, *Poetry,* 1977; Rockefeller Foundation grant in playwriting, 1978; D.Litt., Southampton College of Long Island University, 1979; Phi Beta Kappa Poet, Harvard University, 1979; English-Speaking Union Poetry Award, 1979; American Book Award nomination, 1982, for *Shadow Train;* Academy of American Poets fellowship, 1982; The Mayor's Award of Honor for Arts and Culture, New York City, 1983; Charles Flint Kellogg Award in Arts and Letters, Bard College, 1983; National Book Critics Circle award nomination, and *Los Angeles Times* Book Prize nomination, both 1984, for *A Wave;* co-

winner of Bollingen prize, 1985, for the body of his work; *Los Angeles Times* Book Award nomination, 1986, for *Selected Poems;* Common Wealth Award, 1986; Lenore Marshall award, *Nation,* 1986, for *A Wave;* Creative Arts Award in Poetry, Brandeis University, 1989.

WRITINGS:

Turandot and Other Poems (chapbook), Tibor de Nagy Gallery, 1953.

Some Trees (poems), foreword by W. H. Auden, Yale University Press, 1956, Ecco Press, 1978.

The Poems, Tiber Press (New York), 1960.

The Tennis Court Oath (poems), Wesleyan University Press, 1962.

Rivers and Mountains (poems), Holt, 1966.

Selected Poems, J. Cape, 1967.

Sunrise in Suburbia, Phoenix Bookshop, 1968.

Three Madrigals, Poet's Press, 1969.

(With James Schuyler) *A Nest of Ninnies* (novel), Dutton, 1969.

Fragment (poem; also see below), Black Sparrow Press, 1969.

Evening in the Country, Spanish Main Press, 1970.

The Double Dream of Spring (includes poem "Fragment," originally published in book form), Dutton, 1970.

The New Spirit, Adventures in Poetry, 1970.

(With Lee Hawood and Tom Raworth) *Penguin Modern Poets 19,* Penguin, 1971.

Three Poems, Viking, 1972.

The Serious Doll, privately printed, 1975.

(With Joe Brainard) *The Vermont Notebook* (poems), Black Sparrow Press, 1975.

Self-Portrait in a Convex Mirror (poems), Viking, 1975.

Houseboat Days (poems), Viking, 1977.

Some Trees (poems), Ecco Press, 1978.

As We Know (poems), Viking, 1979.

Shadow Train: Fifty Lyrics, Viking, 1981.

(With others) *R. B. Kitaj: Paintings, Drawings, Pastels,* Smithsonian Institution, 1981, Thames Hudson, 1986.

Fairfield Porter: Realist Painter in an Age of Abstraction, New York Graphic Society, 1983.

A Wave (poems), Viking, 1984.

Selected Poems, Viking, 1985.

April Galleons, Penguin, 1987.

The Ice Storm, Hanuman Books, 1987.

Reported Sightings (art criticism), edited by David Bergman, Knopf, 1989.

Flow Chart (poem), Knopf, 1991.

PLAYS

The Heroes (one-act; also see below), produced Off-Broadway at the Living Theater Playhouse, August

5, 1952, produced in London, 1982, published in *Artists' Theater,* edited by Herbert Machiz, Grove, 1969.

The Compromise (three-act; also see below), produced in Cambridge, MA, at the Poet's Theater, 1956, published in *The Hasty Papers,* Alfred Leslie, 1960.

The Philosopher (one-act; also see below), published in *Art and Literature,* No. 2, 1964.

Three Plays (contains "The Heroes," "The Compromise," and "The Philosopher"), Z Press, 1978.

EDITOR

(With others) *The American Literary Anthology,* Farrar, Straus, 1968.

(With Thomas B. Hess) *Light* (art book), Macmillan, 1969.

(With Hess) *Painters Painting* (art book), Newsweek, 1971.

(With Hess) *Art of the Grand Eccentrics,* Macmillan, 1971.

(With Hess) *Avant-Garde Art,* Macmillan, 1971.

Penguin Modern Poets 24: Ken Ward Elmslie, Kenneth Hoch, James Schuyler, Penguin, 1974.

Richard F. Sknow, *The Funny Place,* O'Hara (Chicago), 1975.

Bruce Marcus, *Muck Arbour,* O'Hara, 1975.

(With David Lehman) *The Best American Poetry, 1988,* Scribner, 1989.

CONTRIBUTOR TO ANTHOLOGIES

New American Poetry, 1945-1960, Grove, 1960.

Paris Leary and Robert Kelly, editors, *A Controversy of Poets,* Doubleday/Anchor, 1964.

L'Avant-Garde aujourd'hui, [Brussels], 1965.

Anthology of New York Poets, Random House, 1969.

N.Y. Amerikansk Poesi, Gyldendal (Copenhagen), 1969.

The Voice That Is Great Within Us: American Poetry of the Twentieth Century, Bantam, 1970.

Contemporary American Poetry, Houghton, 1971.

Louis Untermeyer, editor, *50 Modern American and British Poets, 1920-1970,* McKay, 1973.

Shake the Kaleidoscope: A New Anthology of Modern Poetry, Simon & Schuster, 1973.

Works also represented in other anthologies.

OTHER

(Translator) Jean-Jacques Mayoux, *Melville,* Grove Press, 1960.

(Translator, as Jonas Berry, with Lawrence G. Blochman) *Murder in Montmarte,* Dell, 1960.

(Translator, as Berry, with Blochman) Genevieve Manceron, *The Deadlier Sex,* Dell, 1961.

(Translator) Pierre Martory, *Every Question but One,* The Groundwater Press/InterFlo Editions, 1990.

Collaborator with Joe Brainard on C Comic Books; collaborator with Elliott Carter on the musical setting *Syringa,* first produced in New York at Alice Tully Hall, December, 1979; verse has been set to music by Ned Rorem, Eric Salzman, Paul Reif, and James Dashow. Poetry recordings include *Treasury of 100 Modern American Poets Reading Their Poems,* Volume 17, Spoken Arts, and *Poetry of John Ashbery,* Jeffrey Norton. Translator, from the French, of the works of Raymond Roussel, Andre Breton, Pierre Reverdy, Arthur Cravan, Max Jacob, Alfred Jarry, Antonin Artaud, Noel Vexin, and others. Contributor of poetry to periodicals, including *New York Review of Books, Partisan Review, Harper's,* and *New Yorker;* contributor of art criticism to periodicals, including *Art International* and *Aujourd'hui;* contributor of literary criticism to *New York Review of Books, Saturday Review, Poetry, Bizarre* (Paris), and other periodicals. Co-editor, *One Fourteen,* 1952-53; editor, *Locus Solus* (Lans-en-Vercors, France), 1960-62; co-founder and editor, *Art and Literature* (Paris), 1964-66; poetry editor, *Partisan Review,* 1976-80.

WORK IN PROGRESS: Poems; a play; a translation of the literary works of Belgian surrealist painter Rene Magritte.

SIDELIGHTS: "Stop anywhere you happen to be in the underground and listen: that sound you hear is the sound of Ashbery's poetic voice being mimicked—a hushed, simultaneously 'incomprehensible and intelligent whisper with a weird pulsating rhythm that fluctuates like a wave between peaks of sharp clarity and watery droughts of obscurity and languor," Stephen Koch commented in a 1968 *New York Times Book Review* article. Bryan Appleyard of the London *Times* notes that Ashbery's distinctive voice, unlike other American voices, "is neither the language of crisis nor the poetry of the privileged moment." Poet John Ashbery's style, once considered avant-garde, has since become "so influential that its imitators are legion," Helen Vendler observes in the *New Yorker.* After suffering through a period of critical misunderstanding, Ashbery has entered the mainstream of American poetry, becoming, as James Atlas notes in the *New York Times Sunday Magazine,* "the most widely honored poet of his generation." Ashbery's position in American letters is confirmed by his unprecedented sweep of the literary "triple crown" in 1976, as his *Self-Portrait in a Convex Mirror* won the Pulitzer Prize, the National Book Award, and the National Book Critics Circle Prize. According to Howard Wamsley in *Poetry,* "The chances are very good that he will dominate the last third of the century as Yeats . . . dominated the first."

A key element of Ashbery's success is his openness to change; it is both a characteristic of his development as a writer and an important thematic element in his verse. "It is a thankless and hopeless task to try and keep up with Ashbery, to try and summarize the present state of his art," Raymond Carney writes in the *Dictionary of Literary Biography.* "As [*As We Know*] shows, he will never stand still, even for the space (or time) of one poem. Emerson wrote that 'all poetry is vehicular,' and in the case of Ashbery the reader had better resign himself to a series of unending adjustments and movements. With each subsequent book of poetry we only know that he will never be standing still, for that to him is death." In a *Washington Post Book World* review of *Shadow Train,* David Young notes: "You must enjoy unpredictability if you are to like John Ashbery. . . . We must be ready for anything in reading Ashbery because this eclectic, dazzling, inventive creator of travesties and treaties is ready to and eager to include anything, say anything, go anywhere, in the service of an esthetic dedicated to liberating poetry from predictable conventions and tired traditions." And in the *New York Times Book Review,* J. M. Brinnon observes that *Self-Portrait in a Convex Mirror* is "a collection of poems of breathtaking freshness and adventure in which dazzling orchestrations of language open up whole areas of consciousness no other American poet has even begun to explore. . . . The influence of films now shows in Ashbery's deft control of just those cinematic devices a poet can most usefully appropriate. Crosscut, flashback, montage, close-up, fade-out—he employs them all to generate the kinetic excitement that starts on the first page of his book and continues to the last."

As Brinnon's analysis suggests, Ashbery's verse has taken shape under the influence of films and other art forms. The abstract expressionist movement in modern painting, stressing nonrepresentational methods of picturing reality, is an especially important presence in his work. "Modern art was the first and most powerful influence on Ashbery," Helen McNeil notes in the *Times Literary Supplement.* "When he began to write in the 1950s, American poetry was constrained and formal while American abstract-expressionist art was vigorously taking over the heroic responsibilities of the European avant garde. . . . Ashbery remarks that no one now thinks it odd that Picasso painted faces with eyes and mouth in the wrong place, while the hold of realism in literature is such that the same kind of image in a poem would still be considered shocking."

True to this influence, Ashbery's poems, according to Fred Moramarco, are a "verbal canvas" upon which the poet freely applies the techniques of expressionism. Moramarco, writing in the *Journal of Modern Literature,* finds that Ashbery's verse, maligned by many critics for being excessively obscure, becomes less difficult to understand when examined in relation to modern art. "*The Tennis Court Oath* is still a book that arouses passions in critics

and readers, some of whom have criticized its purposeful obscurity. For me it becomes approachable, explicable, and even down-right lucid when read with some of the esthetic assumptions of Abstract Expressionism in mind. . . . The techniques of juxtaposition developed by the Abstract painters, particularly [Mark] Rothko and [Adolph] Gottlieb, can be related to the verbal juxtaposition we find in *The Tennis Court Oath,* where words clash and interact with one another to invigorate our sense of the creative possibilities of language. . . . What we confront [in the title poem], it seems to me, is constantly shifting verbal perceptions. . . . [Jackson] Pollock's drips, Rothko's haunting, color-drenched, luminous, rectangular shapes, and Gottlieb's spheres and explosive strokes are here, in a sense, paralleled by an imagistic scattering and emotional and intellectual verbal juxtaposition."

In the same article, Moramarco reviews "Self-Portrait in a Convex Mirror," a long poem inspired by a work by the Renaissance painter Francesco Parmigianino, and is "struck by Ashbery's unique ability to explore the verbal implications of painterly space, to capture the verbal nuances of Parmigianino's fixed and distorted image. The poem virtually resonates or extends the painter's meaning. It transforms visual impact to verbal precision. . . . It seems to me Ashbery's intention in 'Self-Portrait' is to record verbally the emotional truth contained in Parmigianino's painting. Visual images do not have to conform to verbal *thinking,* and it is this sort of universe that Ashbery's poetry has consistently evoked." And Jonathan Holden believes that "Ashbery is the first American poet to successfully carry out the possibilities of analogy between poetry and 'abstract expressionist' painting. He has succeeded so well for two reasons: he is the first poet to identify the *correct* correspondences between painting and writing; he is the first poet to explore the analogy who has possessed the *skill* to *produce* a first-rate 'abstract expressionist' poetry, a poetry as beautiful and sturdy as the paintings of William de Kooning." In the *American Poetry Review,* Holden says that "it is Ashbery's genius not only to be able to execute syntax with heft, but to perceive that syntax in writing is the equivalent of 'composition' in painting: it has an intrinsic beauty and authority almost wholly independent of any specific context. Thus, in Ashbery's poetry, the isolation of verse is analogous to the framing of a painting; and each sentence . . . is analogous to a 'brushstroke' . . . recorded in paint on a canvas."

Ashbery's experience as an art critic has strengthened his ties to abstract expressionism and instilled in his poetry a sensitivity to the interrelatedness of artistic mediums. As he once commented in an essay on the American artist and architect Saul Steinberg: "Why shouldn't a painting tell a story, or not tell it, as it sees fit? Why should poetry be intellectual and nonsensory, or the reverse? Our eyes, minds, and feelings do not exist in isolated compartments but are part of each other, constantly crosscutting, consulting and reinforcing each other. An art constructed to the above canons, or any others, will wither away since, having left one or more of the faculties out of account, it will eventually lose the attention of the others." Ashbery's poetry is open-ended and multivarious because life itself is, he told Bryan Appleyard of the London *Times:* "I don't find any direct statements in life. My poetry imitates or reproduces the way knowledge or awareness come to me, which is by fits and starts and by indirection. I don't think poetry arranged in neat patterns would reflect that situation. My poetry is disjunct, but then so is life."

Ashbery's verbal expressionism has attracted a mixed critical response. James Schevill, in a *Saturday Review* article on *The Tennis Court Oath,* writes: "The trouble with Ashbery's work is that he is influenced by modern painting to the point where he tries to apply words to the page as if they were abstract, emotional colors and shapes. . . . Consequently, his work loses coherence. . . . There is little substance to the poems in this book." In the *New York Times Book Review,* X. J. Kennedy praises the book: " 'I attempt to use words abstractly,' [Ashbery] declares, 'as an artist uses paint'. . . . If the reader can shut off that portion of the brain which insists words be related logically, he may dive with pleasure into Ashbery's stream of consciousness." Appleyard relates the view of some critics that "however initially baffling his poetry may seem, it is impossible to deny the extraordinary beauty of its surface, its calm and haunting evocation of a world of fragmentary knowledge." And Moramarco believes Ashbery's technique has an invigorating effect: "We become caught up in the rich, vitalized verbal canvas he has painted for us, transported from the mundane and often tedious realities of our daily lives to this exotic, marvelous world. . . . Literature and art can provide these moments of revitalization for us, and although we must always return to the real world, our esthetic encounters impinge upon our sensibilities and leave us altered."

Many critics have commented on the manner in which Ashbery's fluid style has helped to convey a major concern in his poetry: the refusal to impose an arbitrary order on a world of flux and chaos. In his verse, Ashbery attempts to mirror the stream of perceptions of which human consciousness is composed. His poems move, often without continuity, from one image to the next, prompting some critics to praise his expressionist technique and others to accuse him of producing art which is unintelligible, even meaningless.

"Reality, for Ashbery, is elusive, and things are never what they seem to be. They cannot be separated from one another, isolated into component parts, but overlap, intersect, and finally merge into an enormous and constantly changing whole," Paul Auster writes in *Harper's.* "Ashbery's manner of dealing with this flux is associative rather than logical, and his pessimism about our ever really being able to know anything results, paradoxically, in a poetry that is open to everything. His language is discursive, rhetorical, and even long-winded, a kind of obsessive talking around things, suggesting a reality that refuses to come forth and let itself be known."

In the *American Poetry Review,* W. S. Di Piero states: "Ashbery wonders at the processes of change he sees in people, in the seasons, in language, but his perception of the things about him also persuades him that nothing has ever really changed. If all things, all thought and feeling, are subject to time's revisions, then what can we ever know? What events, what feelings can we ever trust? In exploring questions such as these, Ashbery has experimented with forms of dislocated language as one way of jarring things into order; his notorious twisting of syntax is really an attempt to straighten things out, to clarify the problems at hand." David Kalstone, in his book *Five Temperaments,* comments: "In his images of thwarted nature, of a discontinuity between past and present, Ashbery has tuned his agitation into a principle of composition. From the start he has looked for sentences, diction, a syntax which would make these feelings fully and fluidly available." "Robbed of their solid properties, the smallest and surest of words become part of a new geography," Kalstone writes of *The Double Dream of Spring* in the *New York Times Book Review.* To explore this "new geography," Kalstone notes, the reader must immerse himself in Ashbery's language and "learn something like a new musical scale."

Closely related to Ashbery's use of language as a "new musical scale" is his celebration of the world's various motions and drives. Under the poet's care, the most ordinary aspects of our lives leap into a new reality, a world filled with the joyous and bizarre. In his book *The Poem in Its Skin,* Paul Carroll finds that "one quality most of Ashbery's poems share is something like the peculiar excitement one feels when stepping with Alice behind the Looking Glass into a reality bizarre yet familiar in which the 'marvelous' is as near as one's breakfast coffee cup or one's shoes. His gift is to release everyday objects, experiences and fragments of dreams or hallucinations from stereotypes imposed on them by habit or preconception or belief: he presents the world as if seen for the first time." In a review of *Self-Portrait in a Convex Mirror* for *Harper's,* Paul Auster contends that "few poets today have such an uncanny ability to undermine our certainties, to articulate so fully the ambiguous zones of our consciousness. We are constantly thrown off guard as we read his poems. The ordinary becomes strange, and things that a moment ago seemed clear are cast into doubt. Everything remains in place, and yet nothing is the same." Edmund White, appraising *As We Know* in *Washington Post Book World*, writes: "As David Shapiro has pointed out in his critical study, all [of Ashbery's] long poems tend to end on a joyful note, though one harmonized with doubt and anguish. In [the conclusion of 'Litany'] the poet rejects the equation of life and text in order to acknowledge the rich messiness of experience. Like the familiar example of the bee which is aerodynamically impossible but doesn't know so and flies anyway, the poet—though faced with death, crushed under history and immersed in the fog of daily life—evinces a will to joy and thereby, becomes joyful."

Several critics have suggested that this joyful quality is sometimes contradicted by an intellectualism and obscurity present in Ashbery's verse. Victor Howes, reviewing *Houseboat Days* for the *Christian Science Monitor*, recognizes the rich diversity of the poet's work, but asks, "does he touch the heart? Does he know the passions? My dear. My dear. Really, sometimes you ask too much." J. A. Avant of *Library Journal* argues that in *The Double Dream of Spring* "emotion has been intellectualized to the extent that it is almost nonexistent," while Pearl K. Bell comments in the *New Leader*, "Long stretches of 'Self-Portrait' read like the bland prose of an uninspired scholar, complete with references and quotations. Bleached of feeling and poetic surprise, the words gasp for air, stutter, go dead." In a *New York Review of Books* article on *The Double Dream of Spring*, Robert Mazzocco finds that "in Ashbery there has always been a catlike presence, both in the poems themselves and in the person these poems reveal: tender, curious, cunning, tremendously independent, sweet, guarded. Above all, like a cat, Ashbery is a born hunter: now prowling through deepest Africa; now chasing leaves or scraps of paper, rolling over and over, and then curling up, happily exhausted, beneath a bush. . . . But the one prime act of the cat—to spring, to pounce, to make the miraculous leap—Ashbery, for me, has yet to perform."

In *The Poem in Its Skin*, Carroll examines Ashbery's "Leaving the Atocha Station" and finds that "several close readings fail to offer a suspicion of a clue as to what it might be all about. I . . . feel annoyed: the poem makes me feel stupid. . . . [The] narrative skeleton is fleshed out by skin and features made from meaningless phrases, images and occasional sentences. In this sense, 'Leaving the Atocha Station' out-Dadas Dada: it is totally meaningless. . . . The most obvious trait is the general sense that the reader has wandered into somebody else's dream or hallucination." After suggesting several ways to read the poem, Carroll concludes that "the reader should feel free to do whatever he wants with the words in this poem. . . . I also suspect some readers will respond to Ashbery's invitation that the reader too become a poet as

he rereads [the poem]." As Ashbery explains in an essay on Gertrude Stein in *Poetry*, a poem is "a hymn to possibility," "a general, all-purpose model which each reader can adapt to fit his own set of particulars." In the *New York Review of Books*, Irvin Ehrenpreis comments on Ashbery's assessment of the participatory nature of poetry: "The poem itself must become an exercise in re-examining the world from which the self has become alienated. We must confront its language with the same audacity that we want when confronting the darkened world within us and without. To offer a clear meaning would be to fix the reader in his place, to turn him away from the proper business of poetry by directing him to an apparent subject. . . . The act of reading must become the purpose of the poem. Consequently, the poem must stand by itself as the world stands by itself. It must change as the world changes. It must offer the same challenge as the world."

Carney contends that the possibilities inherent in an Ashbery poem often create confusion rather than interpretative freedom: "Ashbery's poetry is a continuous criticism of all the ways in which literature would tidy up experience and make the world safe for poetry. But it must be admitted that the poetry that results is frequently maddening because of Ashbery's willingness to lose himself in a sea of details and memories even if it means losing the reader. Even [a judicious critic] can be baited into a fit of pique by Ashbery's randomness." In a review of *As We Know* for the *Chicago Tribune Book World*, Joseph Parisi grants that Ashbery's " 'subject matter' remains incomprehensible, to be sure—the whole world of sensible objects, memories, and feelings, in all their profusion, variety, and flux," but nevertheless insists: "As these streams of everyday and extraordinary objects flow past us in no apparent order, but always in wondrously lyrical lines, the poems make their own curious kind of sense. After all, isn't this how we perceive 'reality'? . . . Ashbery's poems imply the improbability of finding ultimate significance amid the evanescence and transience of modern life. If, however, in the process of these poems the old order is lost or irrelevant, the longing for it or some kind of meaning is not." Reflecting upon the critical response to his poem "Litany," Ashbery told a *CA* interviewer, "I'm quite puzzled by my work too, along with a lot of other people. I was always intrigued by it, but at the same time a little apprehensive and sort of embarrassed about annoying the same critics who are always annoyed by my work. I'm kind of sorry that I cause so much grief."

Di Piero describes the reaction of critics to Ashbery's style as "amusing. On the one hand are those who berate him for lacking the Audenesque 'censor' (that little editing machine in a poet's head which deletes all superfluous materials) or who accuse him of simply being willfully and unreasonably perverse. On the other hand are those reviewers who, queerly enough, praise the difficulty of Ashbery's verse as if difficulty were a positive literary value in itself, while ignoring what the poet is saying. I think that Ashbery's 'difficulty' (grammatical ellipses, misapplied substantives, fragmented verb phrases, etc.) is a function of his meaning. . . . Ashbery avoids generalized declarations of his vision of our fragmented, unpredictable world. Instead, he gives us a feel for the elusive processes of change." Vendler offers this summary in the *New Yorker:* "It is Ashbery's style that has obsessed reviewers, as they alternately wrestle with its elusive impermeability and praise its power of linguistic synthesis. There have been able descriptions of its fluid syntax, its insinuating momentum, its generality of reference, its incorporation of vocabulary from all the arts and sciences. But it is popularly believed, with some reason, that the style itself is impenetrable, that it is impossible to say what an Ashbery poem is 'about.' An alternative view says that every Ashbery poem is about poetry."

This alternative view emphasizes Ashbery's concern with the nature of the creative act, particularly as it applies to the writing of poetry. This is, Peter Stitt notes, a major theme of *Houseboat Days,* a volume acclaimed by Marjorie Perloff in *Washington Post Book World* as "the most exciting, most original book of poems to have appeared in the 1970s." Ashbery shares with the abstract expressionists of painting "a preoccupation with the art process itself," Stitt writes in the *Georgia Review.* "Ashbery has come to write, in the poet's most implicitly ironic gesture, almost exclusively about his own poems, the ones he is writing as he writes about them. The artist becomes his own theoretical critic, caught in the critical lens even at the moment of conception." Roger Shattuck makes a similar point in the *New York Review of Books:* "Nearly every poem in *Houseboat Days* shows that Ashbery's phenomenological eye fixes itself not so much on ordinary living and doing as on the specific act of composing a poem. Writing on Frank O'Hara's work, Ashbery defined a poem as 'the chronicle of the creative act that produces it.' Thus every poem becomes an ars poetica of its own condition." Ashbery's examination of creativity, according to Paul Breslin in *Poetry,* is a "prison of self-reference" which detracts from the poet's "lyrical genius." *New Leader*'s Phoebe Pettingell, however, argues that "Ashbery carries the saw that 'poetry does not have subject matter because it is the subject' to its furthest limit. Just as we feel we are beginning to make sense of one of his poems, meaning eludes us again. . . . Still, we are somehow left with a sense that the conclusion is satisfactory, with a wondering delight at what we've heard. And since a primary function of poetry is giving pleasure, Ashbery ranks very high. . . . *Houseboat Days* is evidence of the transcendent power of the imagination, and one of the major works of our time."

Ashbery's poetry, as critics have observed, has evolved under a variety of influences besides modern art, becoming in the end the expression of a voice unmistakably his own. Among the influences that have been discerned in his verse are the Romantic tradition in American poetry that progresses from Whitman to Wallace Stevens, the so-called "New York School of Poets," featuring contemporaries such as Frank O'Hara and Kenneth Koch, and the French surrealist writers with whom Ashbery has dealt in his work as a critic and translator. In *The Fierce Embrace,* Charles Molesworth traces Ashbery's development: "The first few books by John Ashbery contained a large proportion of a poetry of inconsequence. Borrowing freely from the traditions of French surrealism, and from his friends Frank O'Hara and Kenneth Koch, Ashbery tried out a fairly narrow range of voices and subjects. Subject matter, or rather the absence of it, helped form the core of his aesthetic, an aesthetic that refused to maintain a consistent attitude toward any fixed phenomena. The poems tumbled out of a whimsical, detached amusement that mixed with a quizzical melancholy. . . . With the exception of *The Tennis Court Oath,* Ashbery's first four commercially published books . . . included some poems with interpretable meanings and recognizable structures. But reading the first four books together, one is struck by how precious are those poems that do make poetic sense, surrounded as they are by the incessant chatter of the poems of inconsequence. Slowly, however, it appears as if Ashbery was gaining confidence for his true project, and, as his work unfolds, an indulging reader can see how it needed those aggressively bland 'experiments' in nonsense to protect its frailty." Ashbery's "true project," Molesworth believes, is *Self-Portrait in a Convex Mirror.* Many reviewers agree with Molesworth that this volume, especially the long title poem, is Ashbery's "masterpiece."

Essentially a meditation on the painting "Self-Portrait in a Convex Mirror" by Parmigianino, the narrative poem focuses on many of the themes present in Ashbery's work. "I have lived with John Ashbery's 'Self-Portrait in a Convex Mirror' as with a favorite mistress for the past nine months," Laurence Lieberman declares in his book *Unassigned Frequencies.* "Often, for whole days of inhabiting the room of its dream, I have felt that it is the only poem—and Ashbery the only author—in my life. It is what I most want from a poem. Or an author." Lieberman finds that "when I put this poem down I catch myself in the act of seeing objects and events in the world as through different—though amazingly novel other eyes: the brilliantly varied other life of surfaces has been wonderfully revivified, and I take this transformation to be an accurate index of the impact of Ashbery's poetry upon the modus operandi of my perception." Like Molesworth, Lieberman believes that Ashbery's early work, though "unreadable," was an "indispensable detour that precipitated, finally, the elevated vision of Ashbery's recent work. . . . Following his many years of withdrawal and seclusion, a period of slow mellowing, this exactly appointed occasion has been granted to him. A reader feels he can bodily sense an immense weight lifting, as if Ashbery has been relieved, suddenly, of the burden of guilt and bewilderment that two decades of self-imposed ostracism that his choice of direction as an artist . . . had condemned him to, years of lonely waiting to connect with a viable audience, and to expedite human good fellowship with a widespread community of readers."

Like other critics, Lieberman believes that Ashbery was once overly concerned with examining the nature of art and creativity, with escaping into his poems and "producing forms that achieved a semblance of ideal beauty." In "Self-Portrait," Lieberman contends, "Ashbery forecloses irrevocably on the mortgage of an *ars poetica* which conceives the poem as 'exotic refuge,' and advances to an aesthetic which carries a full burden of mirroring the age's ills." Unlike Parmigianino, who retreated into his hermitage, Ashbery ventures out from "the comfortable sanctuary of the dream" to confront the world. "His new art achieves a powerful re-engagement with the human community," Lieberman concludes. "That is his honorable quest."

For an interview with this author see *Contemporary Authors New Revision Series,* Volume 9, Gale, 1983.

BIOGRAPHICAL/CRITICAL SOURCES:

BOOKS

Ashton, Dore, *The New York School: A Cultural Reckoning,* Viking, 1973.

Carroll, Paul, *The Poem in Its Skin,* Follett, 1968.

Contemporary Literary Criticism, Gale, Volume 2, 1974; Volume 3, 1975; Volume 4, 1975; Volume 6, 1976; Volume 9, 1978; Volume 13, 1980; Volume 15, 1980; Volume 25, 1983; Volume 41, 1988.

Contemporary Poets, St. Martins, 1985.

Dictionary of Literary Biography, Gale, Volume 5: *American Poets since World War II,* 1980; *Yearbook: 1981,* 1981.

Howard, Richard, *Alone with America: Essays on the Art of Poetry in the United States since 1950,* Athenuem, 1969.

Kalstone, David, *Five Temperaments: Elizabeth Bishop, Robert Lowell, James Merrill, Adrienne Rich, John Ashbery,* Oxford University Press, 1977.

Kermani, David K., *John Ashbery: A Comprehensive Bibliography,* Garland Publishing, 1976.

Koch, Kenneth, *Rose, Where Did You Get That Red?,* Random House, 1973.

Kostelanetz, Richard, editor, *The New American Arts,* Horizon Press, 1965.

Kostelanetz, *The Old Poetries and the New,* University of Michigan Press, 1979.

Leary, Paris and Robert Kelly, editors, *A Controversy of Poets,* Doubleday, 1965.

Lehman, David, editor, *John Ashbery,* Cornell University Press, 1979.

Lehman, editor, *Beyond Amazement: New Essays on John Ashbery,* Cornell University Press, 1980.

Lieberman, Laurence, *Unassigned Frequencies: American Poetry in Review, 1964-1977,* University of Illinois Press, 1977.

Meyers, John Bernard, editor, *The Poets of the New York School,* University of Pennsylvania Press, 1969.

Molesworth, Charles, *The Fierce Embrace: A Study of Contemporary American Poetry,* University of Missouri Press, 1979.

Packard, William, editor, *The Craft of Poetry,* Doubleday, 1964.

Shapiro, David, *John Ashbery: An Introduction to the Poetry,* Columbia University Press, 1979.

Shaw, Robert B., editor, *American Poetry since 1960: Some Critical Perspectives,* Carcanet Press, 1973.

Stepanchev, Stephen, *American Poetry since 1945: A Critical Survey,* Harper, 1965.

Sutton, Walter, *American Free Verse: The Modern Revolution in Poetry,* New Directions, 1973.

PERIODICALS

American Poetry Review, August 1973; September, 1978; July, 1979; July, 1981.

Booklist, May 1, 1981.

Chicago Tribune Book World, January 27, 1980; July 26, 1981.

Christian Science Monitor, September 6, 1962; March 9, 1970; October 12, 1977; December 3, 1979.

Commentary, February, 1973.

Contemporary Literature, winter, 1968; spring, 1969.

Encounter, April, 1980.

Esquire, January, 1978.

Georgia Review, winter, 1975; winter, 1978; summer, 1980.

Harper's, April, 1970; November, 1975.

Hudson Review, spring, 1970; autumn, 1975; autumn, 1976; spring, 1978; autumn, 1980; winter, 1981.

Journal of Modern Literature, September, 1976.

Library Journal, January 1, 1970.

Listener, August 18, 1977.

Nation, December 12, 1966; April 14, 1969; September 3, 1977; November 11, 1978.

New Leader, May 26, 1975; November 7, 1977; January 29, 1981.

New Republic, June 14, 1975; November 29, 1975; November 26, 1977; December 29, 1979.

New Statesman, June 16, 1967; January 4, 1980; April 24, 1981.

Newsweek, September 26, 1977.

New York Arts Journal, November, 1977.

New Yorker, September 1, 1956; March 24, 1969; March 16, 1981.

New York Quarterly, winter, 1972.

New York Review of Books, April 14, 1966; December 14, 1973; October 16, 1975; March 23, 1978; January 24, 1980; July 16, 1981.

New York Times, April 15, 1956.

New York Times Book Review, July 15, 1962; February 11, 1968; May 4, 1969; June 8, 1969; July 5, 1970; April 9, 1972; August 2, 1975; November 13, 1977; January 6, 1980; September 6, 1981.

New York Times Sunday Magazine, May 23, 1976; February 3, 1980.

Observer, December 9, 1979; December 16, 1979.

Parnassus, fall-winter, 1972; fall-winter, 1977; spring-summer, 1978; fall-winter, 1979.

Partisan Review, fall, 1972, summer, 1976.

Poet and Critic, Volume 11, number 3, 1979.

Poetry, July, 1957; September, 1962; December, 1966; October, 1970; August, 1972; October, 1980.

Saturday Review, June 16, 1956; May 5, 1962; August 8, 1970; July 8, 1972; September 17, 1977.

Sewanee Review, April, 1976; April, 1978; July, 1980.

Southern Review, April, 1978.

Spectator, November 22, 1975.

Time, April 26, 1976.

Times (London), August 23, 1984.

Times Literary Supplement, September 14, 1967; July 25, 1975; September 1, 1978; March 14, 1980; June 5, 1981; October 8, 1982.

Village Voice, January 19, 1976; October 17, 1977; December 26, 1977.

Village Voice Literary Supplement, October, 1981.

Virginia Quarterly Review, autumn, 1970; winter, 1973; spring, 1976; spring, 1979; spring, 1980.

Washington Post Book World, May 11, 1975; October 30, 1977; December 11, 1977; November 25, 1979; June 7, 1981.

Western Humanities Review, winter, 1971.

Yale Review, October, 1969; June, 1970; winter, 1981.

*   *   *

ASHFORD, Douglas E(lliott)   1928-

PERSONAL: Born August 8, 1928, in Lockport, NY; son of Howard and Doris (Saunders) Ashford; married Marguerite Anderson, June, 1954 (divorced, 1971); married Karen Knudson (a nurse), June 8, 1974; children: (first marriage) Elizabeth, Douglas Elliot, Jr., David, Michael; (second marriage) Matthew. *Education:* Brown University, B.A., 1950; Oxford University, M.A., 1952; Princeton University, Ph.D., 1960.

ADDRESSES: Office—Department of Political Science, Forbes Quad, University of Pittsburgh, Pittsburgh, PA 15261.

CAREER: Indiana University, Bloomington, assistant professor of political science, 1959-62; Johns Hopkins University, Baltimore, MD, visiting professor of political science, 1962-63; Cornell University, Ithaca, NY, fellow of Center for International Studies, 1963-64, associate professor, 1964-68, professor of political science, 1968-82; University of Pittsburgh, Pittsburgh, PA, Andrew W. Mellon Professor, 1982—. Lecturer for Foreign Service Institute, 1962-69, and for Peace Corps, 1963; visiting fellow, University of Sussex, 1969-70, Netherlands Institute for Advanced Study, 1977-78, and University of Manchester, 1980-81; visiting professor, University of Bordeaux, 1983-84. *Military service:* U.S. Air Force, 1952-55; became first lieutenant.

MEMBER: International Political Science Association, American Political Science Association, Association Francaise de Science Politique, Tocqueville Society, Oxford Society, Phi Beta Kappa.

AWARDS, HONORS: American Council of Learned Societies-Social Science Research Council fellowships, 1958-60, 1963-64; Rhodes Scholar, 1950-52; Simon fellowship, 1980-81; Guggenheim fellowships, 1982, 1983-84; Fulbright fellowship, 1992.

WRITINGS:

Political Change in Morocco, Princeton University Press, 1961.

Perspectives of a Moroccan Nationalist, Bedminster, 1964.

The Elusiveness of Power: The African Single Party State, Cornell University Center for International Studies, 1965.

National Development and Local Reform: Political Participation in Morocco, Tunisia, and Pakistan, Princeton University Press, 1967.

(With Chandler Morse) *Modernization by Design,* Cornell University Press, 1969.

Ideology and Participation, Sage Publications, 1972.

Politics of Consensus, Cornell Western Societies Program, 1976.

Decentralization, Democracy, and Decisions, Sage Professional Papers, 1976.

(Editor) *Yearbook of Public Policy 1977,* Sage Publications, 1977.

(Editor) *Comparative Policy Studies,* Policy Studies, 1977.

(Co-author) *Comparative Bibliography of Public Policy,* Sage Publications, 1977.

Financing Urban Government in the Welfare State, St. Martin's, 1980.

Policy and Politics in Britain: The Limits of Consensus, Temple University Press, 1981.

Policy and Politics in France: Living with Uncertainty, Temple University Press, 1982.

British Dogmatism and French Pragmatism, Allen & Unwin, 1982.

(Co-author) *Nationalizing Social Security in Europe and America,* JAI Press, 1985.

The Emergence of the Welfare States, Basil Blackwell, 1987.

(Editor) *Discretionary Politics,* JAI Press, 1990.

(Co-author) *Searching for the New France,* Routledge & Kegan Paul, 1991.

Also author of *Morocco-Tunisia: Politics and Planning,* and editor with others of *Comparative Public Policy: A Cross-National Bibliography,* both UMI Publications.

WORK IN PROGRESS: Social Democratic Visions: Interpreting the Postwar Welfare States.

SIDELIGHTS: Douglas E. Ashford told *CA* that his "basic concern has been difficulties of exercising democratic control; more recently in policy process in advanced industrial states."

BIOGRAPHICAL/CRITICAL SOURCES:

PERIODICALS

Times Literary Supplement, June 5, 1987.
Washington Post Book World, March 29, 1981.

* * *

ASTON, James
   See WHITE, T(erence) H(anbury)

* * *

ATKIN, Flora B(lumenthal) 1919-

PERSONAL: Born May 15, 1919, in Baltimore, MD; daughter of Joseph (a lawyer) and Anna (Levy) Blumenthal; married Maurice David Atkin (an economist), December 25, 1941; children: Joseph, Barrie, Jonathan. *Education:* George Washington University, junior certificate (with honors), 1937; Syracuse University, A.B. (cum laude), 1940; graduate study, Bennington College, 1941, and Catholic University of America, 1949-51. *Politics:* Democrat. *Religion:* Jewish.

ADDRESSES: Home and office—5507 Uppingham St., Chevy Chase, MD 20815. *Agent*—Pat Whitton, New Plays, Inc., P.O. Box 5074, Charlottesville, VA 22905.

CAREER: Jewish Community Center, Washington, DC, dance instructor, director of recreational arts department, and founding director of Camp JCC (creative arts day camp), 1940-44, instructor of creative dance, drama, music, and director and choreographer, 1940-68; Adventure Theatre, Glen Echo, MD, founding director and playwright of In-School Players, 1969-79; Jewish Community Center of Greater Washington, Rockville, MD, cultural arts chairperson, 1968-69, instructor in drama, 1979-82. Director, *Matinee Lollipops* (a children's entertainment guide), 1989-91. Instructor, Howard University, 1942-43, Coast Guard Auxiliary, 1967-73, National Park Service, 1973-74; guest lecturer at Hebrew University, 1970 and 1978, University of Maryland, 1972 and 1980, San Francisco State University, 1978, University of Connecticut, 1979, and University of Colombo, Sri Lanka, 1982. Instructor in children's playwriting, Writer's Center, Glen Echo, 1980-81; professional tutor, writing center, University of Maryland, 1986-1990. Adjudicator, little theatre one-act play contest, Alexandria, VA, 1980-81; play reader, Children's Theatre Association of America, 1983-84; adjudicator, Children's Theatre Festival, Southeastern Theatre Conference, 1991. Member of children's grant panel of Maryland Arts Council, 1980-83, and judge, grants panel of Montgomery County (Maryland) Arts Council, 1988-1990. Consultant to Washington, DC, recreation department, 1968, and Jewish Community Council Television Program of Greater Washington, DC, 1968-80; artist consultant to public schools and Humanities Project in Arlington, VA, 1977-80.

MEMBER: International Association of Theatre for Children and Youth, American Alliance for Theatre and Education, American Theatre Association, Children's Theatre Association of America, District of Columbia Federation of Music Clubs (state junior counselor, 1944), Washington Music Teachers Association (secretary, 1945), Washington Modern Dance Society, Writer's Center of Glen Echo Park, Phi Sigma Sigma.

AWARDS, HONORS: Maude Eaton Oak Award, Washington Theatre Alliance, 1970; Eastern States Theatre Association, best director award, 1971, and best production award, 1973; Sybil Baker Award, District of Columbia One-Act Play Tournament, 1973; Charlotte B. Chorpenning Cup, Children's Theatre Association of America, 1977, for writing outstanding plays for children; best original script award, Maryland Theatre Festival, 1978, for *Dig 'N Tel;* grants, Montgomery County Arts Council, 1990 and 1991; special recognition citations from Children's Theatre Association of America, Adventure Theatre, Mid-Atlantic Chapter of American Theatre Association, and Board of Education of Montgomery County.

WRITINGS:

Tarradiddle Tales (one-act play; produced in Kensington, MD, 1969; produced in Washington, DC, at Kennedy Center Opera House, 1969), New Plays, 1970.

Tarradiddle Travels (one-act play; produced in Washington, DC, 1970), New Plays, 1971.

Golliwhoppers! (one-act play; produced in Washington, DC, at Smithsonian Institute Theatre, 1972), New Plays, 1973.

Skupper-Duppers (one-act play; produced at Kennedy Center, 1974), New Plays, 1975.

Dig 'N Tel (one-act play; produced in Washington, DC, at Jewish Community Center Theatre, 1978), New Plays, 1978.

Grampo/Scampo (one-act play; produced in Glen Echo, MD, 1980), New Plays 1981.

"Shoorik and Poofik" (one-act puppet play), produced in Rockville, MD, 1982.

Hold That Tiger (play in ten scenes; produced at University of Connecticut, Mystic, 1983), New Plays, 1984.

Contributor of articles to *Dance Observer, Theatre News, Children's Theatre Review, Children Today, Theatre for Young Audiences Today,* and *Avotaynu.*

WORK IN PROGRESS: A play incorporating the subject of genealogy, intended to raise young people's awareness of cultural heritage (expected 1992-93).

SIDELIGHTS: Flora B. Atkin designs her children's plays for in-school productions. Except for *Hold That Tiger,* a full-length work written for adolescents about a family dealing with a medical crisis, the plays are simple and educational, and can be performed anywhere with a minimum of stage props and costumes. Atkin draws most of her dramatic material from folklore. She explained to a *Children's Theatre Review* interviewer: "Folk stories have excitement, humor, and never-ending variety. They have educational value: human problems are presented, even through animals. A child can identify with these stories and yet not be frightened by them. There are problems of sibling rivalry, death, and parental difficulties, but they are removed from the child's own world." This respect for folk-literature is evident in the plays *Tarradiddle Tales, Tarradiddle Travels, Golliwhoppers!* and *Dig 'N Tel,* all of which derive their subject matter from Jewish, American, and world folklore. Like the stories which inspire her, Atkin's recast folklore pays particular attention to the creative potential of both the audience and the community. Atkin's work succeeds when the artist, the performers, and the audience unite to animate what is often perceived as a lost means of communicating and a dead art.

Atkin's plays take a total theatre approach in which a wide range of dramatic skills are used. She incorporates music, singing, mime, puppetry, narration, dialogue, and dance to give children a taste of the richness of theatre while expanding their knowledge of the adult world. To enhance this goal, Atkin also encourages audience participation: "I want warmth and rapport between the players and the audience. I want the children to feel the production on all levels. Also, the children need a kinesthetic release. Every one of my plays starts with the performers in contact with the children. When children enter the auditorium for *Skupper-Duppers,* they are greeted at the door by the boatswain's 'Welcome aboard! Put your gear on the starboard side and find a deck chair on the port side.' The children's immediate, delighted response is 'We're on a ship,' and they are eager to help swab the decks and pull in the lines. The mood is set."

"In the 1980's," Atkin further commented, "The motivation for my plays has expanded beyond folklore. I find myself drawing upon real life experiences as well as folklore as sources for such themes as Soviet immigrant adjustment, the generation gap, and coping with polio." Atkin later reflected on her experience in a brief summary for *Syracuse University Magazine:* "People fail to take children's theatre seriously. I feel that the quality must be very high. Children deserve better than second-rate food. Give them quality food." In addition to her commitment to substantive children's drama, Atkin emphasizes that dramatic material "must be put into an artistic form. We aren't reproducing raw life. We're giving the child magic and hope. Let us not ignore sensitive issues like death, divorce, and disease. But let us treat them sensitively, gently, from a child's viewpoint."

BIOGRAPHICAL/CRITICAL SOURCES:

PERIODICALS

Children's Theatre Review, spring, 1979.
Syracuse University Magazine, September, 1990, p. 9.
Washington Post, April 20, 1972.

*   *   *

AYMAR, Brandt 1911-

PERSONAL: Born May 8, 1911, in New York, NY; son of Edmund B. and Mabel (Rathbun) Aymar. *Education:* Yale University, A.B., 1933.

ADDRESSES: Home—183 Secatogue Lane, West Islip, Long Island, NY 11795. *Office*—Crown Publishers, Inc., 225 Park Ave. S., New York, NY 10003.

CAREER: Greenberg Co. (publishers), New York City, vice president, 1944-58; Chilton Co. (publishers), Philadelphia, PA, director of sales, publishing manager and editor, 1958-64; Crown Publishers, Inc., New York City, senior editor, 1964—. *Military service:* U.S. Coast Guard Reserve, 1942-44; became lieutenant junior grade.

WRITINGS:

Deck Chair Reader, Greenberg, 1937.

Cruising Is Fun, Greenberg, 1941.

The Complete Cruiser, Greenberg, 1947.

Treasury of Snake Lore, Greenberg, 1955.

(Editor) *The Personality of the Cat,* Crown, 1958.

Guide to Boatmanship, Seamanship and Safe Boat Handling, Chilton, 1960.

Cruising Guide, Chilton, 1962.

(Editor with Edward Sagarin) *The Personality of the Horse,* Crown, 1963.

(Editor with E. Sagarin) *The Personality of the Dog,* Crown, 1964.

(Editor) *The Personality of the Bird,* Crown, 1965.

(With E. Sagarin) *Pictorial History of the World's Great Trials, from Socrates to Eichmann,* Crown, 1967.

A Pictorial Treasury of the Marine Museums of the World, Crown, 1969.

The Young Male Figure, Crown, 1970.

(With E. Sagarin) *Laws and Trials That Created History: A Pictorial History,* Crown, 1974.

(Editor) *Men at Sea,* Crown, 1988.

(Editor) *Men in the Air,* Crown, 1990.

B

BAGBY, Wesley M(arvin) 1922-

PERSONAL: Born June 15, 1922, in Albany, GA; son of Wesley Marvin and Essie (Loven) Bagby; married Janice Marceline, 1969; children: Wesley M. IV, Steven D. *Education:* University of North Carolina, A.B., 1943, M.A., 1945; Columbia University, Ph.D., 1953. *Religion:* Methodist.

ADDRESSES: Home—770 Mountain View Pl., Morgantown, WV 26505. *Office*—Department of History, West Virginia University, Morgantown, WV 26506.

CAREER: Pfeiffer Junior College (now Pfeiffer College), Misenheimer, NC, instructor in history, 1945-46; Wake Forest College (now Wake Forest University), Winston-Salem, NC, instructor in history, 1946-48; University of Tennessee, instructor in history, 1949-51; University of Maryland, College of Special and Continuation Studies, Newfoundland, Canada, assistant professor, 1951-52; Anne Arundel County public schools, Annapolis and Baltimore, MD, social studies teacher, 1952-56; West Virginia University, Morgantown, began as instructor, associate professor, 1956-68, professor of history, 1968—, acting chairman of department, 1962-63. Fulbright-Hays lecturer, Tamkang College, 1975-76, Nankai University, 1982-83. *Dominion News,* Morgantown, paid editorial writer, 1967-69. Member, Morgantown City council, 1963-65. Alternate delegate, Democratic National Convention, Atlantic City, 1964, Chicago, 1968. Lay speaker, United Methodist Church.

MEMBER: American Historical Association (state chairman of committee to collect basic quantitative data of American political history), American Association of University Professors (chapter president, 1962-64), Society for Historians of American Foreign Relations.

WRITINGS:

Road to Normalcy: The Presidential Campaign and Election of 1920, Johns Hopkins Press, 1962, revised edition, 1968.
Contemporary American Problems, Nelson-Hall, 1979.
Contemporary American Economic and Political Problems, Nelson-Hall, 1981.
Contemporary American Social Problems, Nelson-Hall, 1981.
Contemporary International Problems, Nelson-Hall, 1983.
Introduction to Social Science, Nelson-Hall, 1987.
The Eagle-Dragon Alliance: America's Relations with China During World War II, University of Delaware Press, 1991.

Contributor to books, including *History of the First World War,* Volume 8, edited by Peter Young, Purnell, 1971; and *American Studies,* Academy Sinica (Taiwan), 1976. Contributor to *Encyclopedia Americana, Collier's Encyclopedia, Dictionary of American Biography,* Supplement 6, *Historical Dictionary of the Progressive Era,* and to conference proceedings. Contributor to periodicals, including *American Historical Review, Tamkang Journal, Washington Post, Mississippi Valley Historical Review, Morgantown Reporter, China Post,* and *Mountaineer Spirit Magazine.*

*   *   *

BARRON, (Richard) Neil 1934-

PERSONAL: Born March 23, 1934, in Hollywood, CA; son of James C. (in sales) and Dorothy (Terrell) Barron; married Dorothy Weiss, 1966 (marriage ended); married Carolyn Witsell, August 19, 1978; children: Craig R., Felicia A. *Education:* University of California, Riverside,

A.B., 1961; University of California, Berkeley, M.L.S., 1964. *Avocational interests:* Reading, music, travel.

ADDRESSES: Home and office—1149 Lime Place, Vista, CA 92083.

CAREER: U.S. Peace Corps, worked in libraries in Lahore, Tando Jam, and Peshawar, Pakistan, 1962-63; Queens Borough Public Library, Jamaica, NY, librarian, 1964-65; Columbia University Libraries, New York City, assistant to associate director of libraries and manager of chemistry library, 1965-67; California State University Library, Sacramento, assistant librarian for technical services, 1967-70; free-lance writer and editor, 1970—; Baker & Taylor Co., Somerville, NJ, coordinator of library services, 1970-72; University of South Florida, Tampa, assistant director for technical services, 1972-73, educational and other sales, 1973-88, manager of consulting engineers technical library, 1989—. *Military service:* U.S. Army, 1954-56; served in Germany.

MEMBER: Science Fiction Research Association.

AWARDS, HONORS: Outstanding Reference Book Award, American Library Association and *Choice,* 1976, for *Anatomy of Wonder;* Hugo Award nominations, World Science Fiction Society, and *Locus* for best work of nonfiction, both 1981 and 1987, both for second and third editions of *Anatomy of Wonder;* Pilgrim Award, Science Fiction Research Association, 1982, for distinguished contributions to the study of science fiction; World SF President's Award, 1989, for independence of thought in science fiction.

WRITINGS:

(Editor) *Anatomy of Wonder: Science Fiction,* Bowker, 1976, 2nd edition published as *Anatomy of Wonder: A Critical Guide to Science Fiction,* 1981, 3rd edition, 1987.
(Editor) *Horror Literature: A Reader's Guide,* Garland Publishing, 1990.
(Editor) *Fantasy Literature: A Reader's Guide,* Garland Publishing, 1990.
(Editor) *What Do I Read Next,* Gale, Volumes 1 and 2, 1991, Volume 3, 1992.

Contributor to books, including *Science Fiction: Education for Tomorrow,* Jack Williamson, Owlswick, 1980, and *World Book Encyclopedia,* 1989—. Also contributor of articles and reviews to newspapers and magazines, including *Choice.* Editor of *Science Fiction and Fantasy Book Review,* 1979-80, 1981-83, book review editor, 1984-85.

SIDELIGHTS: Neil Barron told *CA:* "My interests in fantastic fiction date from the late 1940s, although I read little of it today. My guides were prepared for anyone desiring to read the best, better or historically important works

in their respective fields and to recognize that the best work is fully equal to the best of traditional fiction, a statement still viewed with suspicion by most critics."

*   *   *

BAYNES, Pauline (Diana) 1922-

PERSONAL: Born September 9, 1922, in Brighton, England; daughter of Frederick William Wilberforce (a Commissioner in the Indian Civil Service) and Jessie Harriet Maude (Cunningham) Baynes; married Fritz Otto Gasch (a garden contractor), March 25, 1961 (deceased). *Education:* Attended Farnham School of Art, 1937, and Slade School of Art, 1939-40.

ADDRESSES: Home and office—Rock Barn Cottage, Dockenfield, Farnham, Surrey GU10 4HH, England.

CAREER: Illustrator, 1941—; art teacher at School in Camberley, England, 1946-47. Work exhibited at the Royal Academy, and in London and surrounding areas. Worker for British Army's Camouflage Development and Training Centre, 1940-42, and Hydrographic Department of British Admiralty, 1942-45.

MEMBER: Chartered Society of Designers, Authors Society.

AWARDS, HONORS: Carole Prize, 1964, for *The Puffin Book of Nursery Rhymes;* Kate Greenaway Medal from the British Library Association, and *Book World*'s Spring Book Festival Award, both 1968, both for *A Dictionary of Chivalry; The Joy of the Court* was selected one of Child Study Association of America's Children's Books of the Year, 1971; Kate Greenaway Medal Commendation, 1972, for *Snail and Caterpillar; The Iron Lion* was selected one of *New York Times* Notable Books, 1984; *The Lion, the Witch, and the Wardrobe* and *The Magician's Nephew* were named Notable Books by the American Library Association.

WRITINGS:

ALL SELF-ILLUSTRATED

Victoria and the Golden Bird, Blackie & Sons, 1947.
How Dog Began, Methuen, 1986, Holt, 1987.
Good King Wenceslas, Lutterworth Press, 1987.
(Editor) *Thanks Be to God: Prayers from Around the World,* Macmillan, 1990.

ILLUSTRATOR

Victoria Stevenson, *Clover Magic,* Country Life, 1944.
Stevenson, *The Magic Footstool,* Country Life, 1946.
J. R. R. Tolkien, *Farmer Giles of Ham,* Allen & Unwin, 1949, Houghton, 1950.
Stevenson, *The Magic Broom,* Country Life, 1950.

W. T. Bebbington, *And It Came to Pass,* Allen & Unwin, 1951.

Henri Pourrat, *A Treasury of French Tales,* Allen & Unwin, 1951, Houghton, 1954.

E. J. S. Lay, *Men and Manners,* Macmillan, 1952.

Marjorie Phillips, *Annabel and Bryony,* Oxford University Press, 1953.

A. Hitchcock and L. J. Hitchcock, *Great People thru' the Ages,* Blackie & Sons, 1954.

Hitchcock and Hitchcock, *The British People,* Blackie & Sons, 1955.

Llewellyn, *China's Court and Concubines,* Allen & Unwin, 1956.

Emmeline Garnett, *The Tudors,* Blackie & Sons, 1956.

Garnett, *Queen Anne,* Blackie & Sons, 1956.

Garnett, *Civil War,* Blackie & Sons, 1956.

Amabel Williams-Ellis, *The Arabian Nights,* S. G. Phillips, 1957.

Rhoda Power, *From the Fury Northmen,* Riverside Press, 1957.

Denton, *Stars and Candles,* Benn, 1958.

Monica Backway, *Hasan of Basorah,* Blackie & Sons, 1958.

Joan Mary Bete, *The Curious Tale of Cloud City,* Blackie & Sons, 1958.

Anne Malcolmson, *Miracle Plays,* Houghton, 1959.

Williams-Ellis, *Fairy Tales from the British Isles,* Blackie, 1960, F. Warne, 1964.

Loretta Burrough, *Sister Clare,* Houghton, 1960.

Dorothy Ensor, *The Adventures of Hakim Tai,* Harrap, 1960, Walck, 1962.

Mary C. Borer, *Don Quixote,* Longmans, Green, 1960.

Edmund Spenser, *Saint George and the Dragon,* Methuen, 1961, Houghton, 1963.

Gladys Hickman and E. G. Hume, *Pilgrim Way Geographies,* four volumes, Blackie & Sons, 1961.

Lynette Muir, *The Unicorn Window,* Abelard, 1961.

James Morris, *The Upstairs Donkey and Other Stolen Stories,* Pantheon, 1961.

Alison Uttley, *The Little Knife That Did All the Work,* Faber, 1962.

Tolkien, *The Adventures of Tom Bombadil,* Allen & Unwin, 1962, Houghton, 1963.

Hans Christian Andersen, *Andersen's Fairy Tales,* Collins, 1963.

Iona Opie and Peter Opie, editors, *The Puffin Book of Nursery Rhymes,* Puffin, 1964.

Allan, *Come into My Castle,* Macmillan, 1964.

K. G. Lethbridge, *The Rout of the Ollafubs,* Faber, 1964.

M. Gail, *Avignon in Flower,* Houghton, 1965.

Borer, "Famous Lives" (series), Longman, 1965.

Uttley, *Recipes from an Old Farmhouse,* Faber, 1966.

Radost Pridham, *A Gift from the Heart: Folk Tales from Bulgaria,* Methuen, 1966, World, 1967.

Abigail Homes, *Education by Uncles,* Houghton, 1966.

Tolkien, *Smith of Wootton Major,* Allen & Unwin, 1967.

Jennifer Westwood, *Medieval Tales,* Hart-Davis, 1967, Coward, 1968.

Grant Uden, *A Dictionary of Chivalry,* Longman Young, 1968, Crowell, 1969.

Joseph W. Krutch, *The Most Wonderful Animals That Never Were,* Houghton, 1968.

Lady Jekyll, *Kitchen Essays,* Collins, 1970.

Richard D. Blackmore, *Lorna Doone,* Collins, 1970.

Constance Hieatt, *The Joy of the Court,* Crowell, 1970.

Naomi Mitchison, *Graeme and the Dragon,* Cambridge University Press, 1970.

Westwood, *Isle of Gramarye: An Anthology of the Poetry of Magic,* Hart-Davis, 1970.

Leonard Clark, *All Along Down Along,* Longman, 1971.

Westwood, *Tales and Legends,* Coward, 1971.

Philippa Pearce, *Stories from Hans Andersen,* Collins, 1972.

Helen Piers, *Snail and Caterpillar,* American Heritage, 1972.

Katie Stewart, *The Times Cookery Book,* Collins, 1972.

Enid Blyton, *Land of Far Beyond,* Methuen, 1973 (Baynes was not associated with the earlier edition).

John Symonds, *Harold,* Dent, 1973.

Piers, *Grasshopper and Butterfly,* McGraw, 1975.

Geoffrey Squire, *The Observer's Book of European Costume,* F. Warne, 1975.

G. Markham, *The Compleat Horseman,* Houghton, 1976.

Eileen Hunter, *Tales from Way Beyond,* Deutsch, 1979.

Richard Barber, *A Companion to World Mythology,* Kestrel, 1979.

Christopher Towers, *Oultre Jourdain,* Weidenfeld & Nicolson, 1980.

Rosemary Harris, *The Enchanted Horse,* Kestrel, 1981.

Piers, *Frog and Shrew,* Kestrel, 1981.

Rumer Godden, *The Dragon of Oq,* Macmillan, 1981.

Mary Norton, *The Borrowers Avenged,* Kestrel, 1982.

Godden, *Four Dolls,* Greenwillow, 1983.

Peter Dickinson, *The Iron Lion,* Blackie & Sons, 1983, Peter Bedrick Books, 1984.

Rudyard Kipling, *How the Whale Got His Throat,* Macmillan, 1983.

Althea Peppin, *National Gallery Children's Book,* National Gallery, 1983.

David Harvey, *Dragon Smoke and Magic Song,* Allen & Unwin (Australia), 1984.

Anna Sewell, *Black Beauty,* Puffin, 1984.

Ursula Moray Williams, *The Further Adventures of Gobbolino and the Little Wooden Horse,* Penguin, 1984.

The Song of the Three Holy Children, Holt, 1986.

Mrs. Alexander, *All Things Bright and Beautiful,* Lutterworth Press, 1986.

George Macbeth, *Daniel,* Lutterworth Press, 1986.

Beatrix Potter, *Country Tales,* Warne, 1987.
Potter, *Wag-by-Wall,* Warne, 1987.
Noah and the Ark, Holt, 1988.
Harris, compiler, *Love and the Merry-Go-Round,* Hamish Hamilton, 1988.
Harris, *Colm of the Islands,* Walker, 1989.
Jenny Koralek, *The Cobweb Curtain,* Holt, 1989.
Brian Sibley, *Land of Narnia: Brian Sibley Explores the World of C. S. Lewis,* HarperCollins, 1990.
Tolkien, *Bilbo's Last Song,* Houghton, 1990.
Let There Be Light, Macmillan, 1991.
Margaret Greaves, *The Naming,* Dent, in press.

"CHRONICLES OF NARNIA" SERIES BY C. S. LEWIS

C. S. Lewis, *The Lion, the Witch, and the Wardrobe,* Bles, 1950, Macmillan, 1951.
Lewis, *Prince Caspian,* Macmillan, 1951.
Lewis, *The Voyage of the "Dawn Treader,"* Macmillan, 1952.
Lewis, *The Silver Chair,* Macmillan, 1953.
Lewis, *The Horse and His Boy,* Macmillan, 1954.
Lewis, *The Magician's Nephew,* Macmillan, 1955.
Lewis, *The Last Battle: A Story for Children,* Macmillan, 1956.

ALL BY CLAUDE NICOLAS; ALL ORIGINALLY PUBLISHED IN FRANCE BY L'ECOLE DES LOISIRS

The Roe Deer, Chambers, 1974.
The Frog, Chambers, 1974.
The Butterfly, Chambers, 1974.
The Duck, Chambers, 1974.
The Bee and the Cherry Tree, Chambers, 1976.
The Salmon, Chambers, 1976.
The Dolphin, Chambers, 1977.

SIDELIGHTS: Best known for her illustrations of the fantasy works of C. S. Lewis and J. R. R. Tolkien, Pauline Baynes has also done drawings for numerous other projects, including cookbooks, fairy tales, and geography and history books. Baynes' interest in drawing dates back to childhood; she once commented, "My only ambition as a school girl was to illustrate books, and my only ambition now is to try to illustrate better."

Though born in Brighton, England, Baynes spent her first years in India, where her father had a job in the Indian Civil Service. Baynes' mother became ill, so she returned with her daughters to England. In an interview with *Something About the Author (SATA)*, the illustrator said of her initial schooling, "I was a thoroughly rebellious five-year-old, unaccustomed to discipline and seemed always to be punished for one thing or another. I remember being made to kneel down in the long gallery in disgrace, and the whole school filed past. I can't imagine what a five-year-old child could have done to merit that sort of punishment, but you don't query things as a child, and it

may have been a first lesson in independence!" Several years later at another school, she was again rebellious: "I was asked to leave twice for being thoroughly impertinent and out of hand. I was always rebelling against any sort of authority and particularly resented older girls telling me what to do. I must have been very tiresome, difficult, and nonconformist. All in all, however, I was happy there and was asked to come back to teach the art class although I had no qualifications, so the headmistress must have seen some good in me."

"My older sister, Angela, was an inspiration in my life and had a great influence on me. She was a splendid artist and I copied everything she did," said Baynes, who also recalled that "Angela left school when she was fifteen and went to Farnham Art School. There were always paints and other art materials around. She was patient and encouraging and would help me do the things she was learning." At age fifteen, Baynes herself enrolled in Farnham Art School, where she specialized in design. When World War II interrupted Baynes' studies she and her sister, who was then at Slade School, did volunteer work until they "went to work full time making demonstration models for instruction courses at the Camouflage Development and Training Centre." The illustrator related that she met many professional artists there and that "it was exciting working with all these established artists whose careers had been momentarily stopped by the war." Following her work at the Camouflage Development and Training Centre, she went to the Hydrographic department of the Admiralty, where she drew naval charts until the end of the war.

Several years after the war, Baynes illustrated C. S. Lewis' "Chronicles of Narnia" series. "My reputation seemed to rest on the Lewis books," she said, "but they were done during a short period right at the beginning of my career." The illustrator recalled that "there were only two things Lewis ever criticized: I drew someone rowing the wrong way and he very gently asked if I could possibly turn him around; his other request was that I pretty the children up a little." Lewis' colleague at Oxford, J. R. R. Tolkien, had already chosen Baynes to illustrate his stories. Commenting on her first Tolkien book, *Farmer Giles of Ham,* Baynes said, "As far as I can remember Tolkien didn't send me any instructions. I was given the brief on how many half-pages and full-pages were needed, and it was common sense to scatter them throughout the book." Tolkien had at first thought of having borders for each page of *The Lord of the Rings,* but because of the book's length, Baynes just drew the cover art. She once told *CA:* "I feel it is very important, as a book illustrator, to work for your writer; that is, to be able to adapt your style to the text. It is the *writing* that is important. The work of the illustrator is to embellish and 'sell' the story."

Early in Baynes' career, the editor of *Country Life* told her that an artist could survive with less than perfect pictures if known for accuracy in his or her work. In the interview with *SATA,* the illustrator said of her early jobs, "I worked terribly hard doing nearly everything that was offered: cookery books, geography books, and a whole series of history books. I learned all the time from them and after I'd done a whole range of 'period work,' I could look at other people's drawings and see if they had the wrong shoe for that period or recognize what they'd lifted out of other pictures."

"I have studied historical and Oriental costume," she told *CA,* "and prefer illustrating 'period' stories, but I also enjoy drawing natural subjects, flowers, animals and so forth. I have a passionate interest in all living creatures (apart from humans), but I am especially fond of dogs." Baynes wrote *How Dog Began,* an imaginative story of the world's first domesticated dog, and illustrated her book in the style of prehistoric cave paintings.

Baynes' husband was a former German prisoner of war who "stayed [in England] on the advice of his parents who were in East Germany, the Russian zone." The illustrator recalled, "We only knew each other a few months before we decided to get married. Meeting Fritz was the best thing that ever happened to me; he was a splendid man and a wonderful husband who was completely tolerant of his wife's obsession to draw!" More recently, Baynes told *CA:* "I owe so much to my sister for her early guidance and to my husband for his understanding, and I have always been incredibly lucky that so much superb writing has been sent to me to illustrate."

BIOGRAPHICAL/CRITICAL SOURCES:

BOOKS

Illustrators of Children's Books, Horn Book, 1978.
Something about the Author, Gale, Volume 19, 1980; Volume 59, 1990.

PERIODICALS

Horn Book, June, 1973.
Signal, May, 1973.
Smithsonian, August, 1975.
Times (London), October 17, 1973.*

* * *

BENSOL, Oscar
   See GILBERT, Willie

BERGIER, Jacques 1912-1978

PERSONAL: Born in 1912 in Odessa, U.S.S.R.; immigrated to France, 1920; died of a cerebral hemorrhage, November 24, 1978, in Paris, France; married Jacqueline Bernardeau. *Education:* Educated in France.

CAREER: Writer and scientist. Created laboratory in Paris with Alfred Eskenazi, 1931, to study chemical and nuclear reactions. Co-founder of *Planete* (France), which also had Spanish, Italian, Brazilian, and German editions. *Military service:* Served in French Underground during World War II; captured by German Gestapo and sent to concentration camp, 1943, released in 1945; received Legion of Honor, Croix de Guerre, and Rosette de la Resistance.

WRITINGS:

Agents secrets contre armes secretes, Arthaud, 1955, reprinted, Editions Famot, 1976.
Mysteres de la vie, Le Centurion, 1957.
L'Energie H., Editions du Cap, 1958.
The Secrets of Living Matter, translation by L. R. Celestin, Barrie & Rockliff, 1959.
Les Murailles invisibles, Del Duca, 1960.
(With Louis Pauwels) *Le Matin des magiciens,* Gallimard, 1960, translation by Rollo Myers published as *The Morning of the Magicians,* Stein & Day, 1963 (translation by Myers published in England as *The Dawn of Magic,* A. Gibbs & Phillips, 1964).
(Editor) *Encyclopedie des sciences et des techniques,* Editions de l'Encyclopedie des sciences, 1961.
(Editor) *Les Meilleures histoires de science-fiction sovietique,* Robert Laffont, 1963.
A l'ecoute des planetes, Fayard, 1963.
Rire avec les savants, Fayard, 1964.
(Co-editor with Jacques Sternberg) *Les Chefs d'oeuvre de l'epouvante,* Editions Planete, 1965.
(Co-editor with Sternberg) *Les Chefs d'oeuvre du rire,* Editions Planete, 1966.
(With Pierre Nord) *L'Actuelle guerre secrete,* Editions Planete, 1967.
(Co-editor with Sternberg) *Les Chefs d'oeuvre du fantastique,* Editions Planete, 1967.
La Guerre secrete du petrole, Denoeel, 1968.
(Compiler) *Lo Mejor de la ciencia ficcion rusa,* Bruguera (Barcelona), 1968.
(Translator) Howard Phillips Lovecraft, *Epouvante et surnaturel en litterature,* Christian Bourgois, 1969.
L'Espionnage industriel (also see below), Hachette, 1969.
Admirations (history and criticism of fantasy-fiction), Christian Bourgois, 1970.
(With Victor Alexandrov) *Guerre secrete sous les oceans,* Editions maritimes et d'outremer, 1970.

(With Pauwels) *L'Homme eternel,* Gallimard, 1970, translation published as *The Eternal Man,* Souvenir Press, 1972, Mayflower, 1973.

Aux limites du connu, Casterman, 1971.

Les Frontieres du possible, Casterman, 1971.

L'Espionnage scientifique (also see below), Hachette, 1971.

(With Pauwels) *Impossible Possibilities,* Stein & Day, 1971.

Vous etes paranormal, Hachette, 1972.

Les Empires de la chimie moderne, A. Michel, 1972.

(Compiler and contributor) *Le Livre de l'inexplicable,* A. Michel, 1972.

Extraterrestrial Visitations from Prehistoric Times to the Present, Regnery, 1973.

L'Espionnage politique, A. Michel, 1973.

(With John Philippe Delaban) *L'Espionnage strategique* (also see below), Hachette, 1973.

(Editor with Bernard le Bovier de Fontenelle), *Entretiens sur la pluralite des mondes,* Editions Gerard, 1973.

(Compiler and contributor) *Extraterrestrial Intervention: The Evidence,* Regnery, 1974.

Visa pour une autre terre, A. Michel, 1974, translation by Nicole Teghert published as *Secret Doors of the Earth,* Regnery, 1975.

Secret Armies: The Growth of Corporate and Industrial Espionage (contains *L'Espionnage industriel, L'Espionnage scientifique,* and *L'Espionnage strategique;* also see above), translation by Harold J. Salemson, Bobbs-Merrill, 1975.

La troisieme guerre mondiale est commencee, A. Michel, 1976.

Je ne suis pas une legende (autobiographical), Retz, 1977.

(With George H. Gallet) *Le Livre des anciens astronautes,* A. Michel, 1977.

La grande conspiration russo-americaine, A. Michel, 1978.

(With Jean Dumur) *Entretiens avec Jacques Bergier, le dernier des magiciens,* Favre, 1979.

Some of Bergier's work has been published in other languages, including Spanish and Italian.

SIDELIGHTS: Jacques Bergier worked extensively with the French Underground during World War II. As a member of the Resistance, he devised a radio network as well as numerous devices used in sabotage. He also organized the group of scientists responsible for discovering the location (later bombed by Allied forces) of the V-2 rocket construction by the German Army. In 1943 Gestapo agents captured Bergier and incarcerated him in a concentration camp, where he refused to cooperate in their interrogations. The effects of the torture he experienced there remained with him throughout his life. He later received recognition for his activities during the war.

Bergier devoted most of his writing to the fields of science and the paranormal. With co-author Louis Pauwels, his *Le Matin des Magiciens* (*The Morning of the Magicians* in English translation) achieved bestseller status for its treatment of magic and black magic in a historical context. In addition, the book played a significant role in the resurgence of the practice of magic in Europe.

BIOGRAPHICAL/CRITICAL SOURCES:

BOOKS

Bergier, Jacques, *Je ne suis pas une legende* (autobiographical), Retz, 1977.

Bergier, J., and Jean Dumur, *Entretiens avec Jacques Bergier, le dernier des magiciens,* Favre, 1979.*

*   *   *

BERKOVITS, Eliezer   1908-

PERSONAL: Born September 8, 1908, in Oradea, Rumania; came to United States in 1950, naturalized in 1956; son of Bernard and Bella (Kosch) Berkovits; married Sali Bickel, January 6, 1933; children: Avraham, Shimshon, Bernard. *Education:* Attended University of Frankfurt, 1928; University of Berlin, M.A., Ph.D., 1933.

ADDRESSES: Home—4 Shimoni St., Jerusalem, Israel.

CAREER: Ordained rabbi, Hildesheimer Rabbinical Seminary, Berlin, Germany; Berlin Jewish Community, Berlin, rabbi, 1936-39; United Hebrew Congregation, Leeds, England, rabbi, 1940-46; Central Synagogue, Sydney, Australia, rabbi, 1946-50; Congregation Adath Jeshurun, Boston, MA, rabbi, 1950-58; Hebrew Theological College, Skokie, IL, chairman of department of Jewish philosophy, beginning 1958.

MEMBER: Rabbinical Council of America.

AWARDS, HONORS: Frank and Ethel S. Cohen Award for a Book on Jewish Thought, Jewish Book Council of the National Jewish Welfare Board Awards, 1975, for *Major Themes in Modern Philosophies of Judaism.*

WRITINGS:

Was ist der Talmud?, Judischer Buch-Verlag, 1938.
Towards Historic Judaism, East and West Library, 1943.
Between Yesterday and Tomorrow, East and West Library, 1945.
Judaism: Fossil or Ferment?, Philosophical Library, 1956.
God, Man and History, Jonathan David, 1959.
A Jewish Critique of the Philosophy of Martin Buber, Yeshiva University Press, 1962.
Prayer, Yeshiva University Press, 1962.
T'nai binsuin ub'get, Mosad Harav Kook (Jerusalem), 1967.

Man and God: Studies in Biblical Theology, Wayne State University Press, 1969.
Faith after the Holocaust, Ktav, 1973.
Major Themes in Modern Philosophies of Judaism, Ktav, 1974.
Crisis and Faith, Sanhedrin Press, 1975.
With God in Hell: Judaism in the Ghettos and Death-camps, Sanhedrin Press, 1979.
Ha'Halaha: Koha V'Tafkida, Mosad Harav Kook, 1981.
Not in Heaven: The Nature and Function of Halakha, Ktav, 1983.
Unity in Judaism, American Jewish Committee, 1986.

Contributor to periodicals, including *Judaism, Tradition, Hadarom,* and *Sinai.*

WORK IN PROGRESS: *Principles of Causation in Jewish Law,* in Hebrew.

*   *   *

BERNER, Carl Walter   1902-

PERSONAL: Born August 19, 1902; son of August George and Clara (Boekenhauer) Berner; married Myrtle Harvey, June 17, 1926; children: James, Robert, Carl, Jr. *Education:* Attended Concordia Junior College, Oakland, CA, Concordia Seminary, St. Louis, 1922-25, and University of Southern California, 1927-34.

ADDRESSES: Home—5332 Bahia Blanca, Laguna Hills, CA 92653.

CAREER: Ordained minister of the Lutheran Church; minister of Faith Lutheran Church, Los Angeles, CA, 1925-68. Special lecturer and faculty member at University of Southern California, Los Angeles, 1939-54.

AWARDS, HONORS: D.D., Concordia Seminary, 1954.

WRITINGS:

Spiritual Power for Your Congregation, Concordia, 1956.
Power of Pure Stewardship, Concordia, 1970.
Why Me, Lord?: Meaning and Comfort in Times of Trouble, Augsburg, 1973.
God's Way to Joyful and Abundant Giving, Graphic, 1978.
Teardrops to Diamonds, Augsburg, 1983.

SIDELIGHTS: Carl Walter Berner's book *Why Me Lord?: Meaning and Comfort in Times of Trouble* was selected by the Library of Congress as a talking book for the blind, and is now available to the public at no cost through public libraries.*

BERRY, Jonas
See ASHBERY, John (Lawrence)

*   *   *

BLAKE, Quentin (Saxby)   1932-

PERSONAL: Born December 16, 1932, in Sidcup, Kent, England; son of William (a civil servant) and Evelyn Blake. *Education:* Downing College, Cambridge, M.A., 1956; University of London Institute of Education, P.G.C.E., 1956-57; attended Chelsea School of Art, 1958-59.

ADDRESSES: Home—Flat 8, 30 Bramham Gardens, London SW5 0HF, England. *Agent*—Georges Borchardt, Inc., 136 East 57th St., New York, NY 10022; and A. P. Watt Ltd., 26-28 Bedford Row, London WC1R 4HL, England.

CAREER: Primarily an illustrator, drawing for *Punch,* beginning 1948, and other British magazines, including *Spectator,* and illustrating children's and educational books; free-lance illustrator, 1957—; Royal College of Art, London, England, tutor in School of Graphic Design, 1965-78, head of Illustration Department, 1978-86, visiting tutor, 1986-89, senior fellow, 1988; visiting professor, 1989—. Has also worked as an English teacher at French Lycee in London, 1962-65. Work has been exhibited at Workshop Gallery, 1972, 1973, 1974, 1976, at the National Theatre, 1984, at the Royal Academy, 1984, 1986, 1987, and at the London Group, England, 1987. *Military service:* Served in the Army Education Corps, 1951-53.

AWARDS, HONORS: Several of Blake's books were named on the list of Child Study Association of America's Children's Books of the Year, including *Put on Your Thinking Cap,* 1969, *Arabel's Raven,* 1974, *Custard and Company,* 1985, and *The Giraffe and the Pelly and Me,* 1986; second prize *Guardian* Award, 1969, for *Patrick; How Tom Beat Captain Najork and His Hired Sportsmen* and *The Witches* were named Notable Books by the American Library Association; *How Tom Beat Captain Najork and His Hired Sportsmen* and *The Wild Washerwomen: A New Folktale* were named to the *Horn Book* honor list; Hans Christian Andersen honor book for illustration from the International Board on Books for Young People, 1976, for *How Tom Beat Captain Najork and His Hired Sportsmen,* and 1982, for *Mister Magnolia; A Near Thing for Captain Najork* was selected one of the *New York Times* Best Illustrated Books of the Year, 1976; Kate Greenaway Medal high commendation from the British Library Association, 1980, for *The Wild Washerwomen;* elected to Royal Designer for Industry, 1980; Kate Greenaway Medal from the British Library Association, and Children's Book Award from the Federation of Children's Book Groups, both 1981, both for *Mister Magnolia;* Children's Book Award from the Federation of Children's Book Groups, 1982, for *The BFG;* Kurt Maschler Award runner-up from the National Book League (England), 1982, for *Rumbelow's Dance,* 1984, for *The Story of the Dancing Frog,* 1985, for *The Giraffe and the Pelly and Me,* and 1986, for *The Rain Door; The Rain Door* and *Cyril Bonhamy and Operation Ping* were exhibited at the Bologna International Children's Book Fair, 1985; awarded the Silver Brush (Holland), 1986; officer, Order of the British Empire, 1988; Kurt Maschler Award from the National Book League, 1990, for *All Join In.*

WRITINGS:

SELF-ILLUSTRATED CHILDREN'S BOOKS

Patrick, J. Cape, 1968, Walck, 1969.
Jack and Nancy, J. Cape, 1969.
A Band of Angels (picture book for adults), Gordon Fraser, 1969.
Angelo, J. Cape, 1970.
Snuff, Lippincott, 1973.
Lester at the Seaside, Collins Picture Lions, 1975.
(Compiler with John Yeoman) *The Puffin Book of Improbable Records,* Puffin, 1975, published as *The Improbable Book of Records,* Atheneum, 1976.
The Adventures of Lester, British Broadcasting Corporation (BBC), 1978.
(Compiler) *Custard and Company: Poems by Ogden Nash,* Kestrel, 1979, Little, Brown, 1980.
Mister Magnolia, Merrimack, 1980.
Quentin Blake's Nursery Rhyme Book, J. Cape, 1983, Harper, 1984.
The Story of the Dancing Frog, J. Cape, 1984, Knopf, 1985.
Mrs. Armitage on Wheels, J. Cape, 1987, Knopf, 1988.
Quentin Blake's ABC, Knopf, 1989.
All Join In, J. Cape, 1990, Little, Brown, 1991.

ILLUSTRATOR

Evan Hunter, *The Wonderful Button,* Abelard, 1961.
Frances Gray Patton, *Good Morning, Miss Dove,* Penguin, 1961.
John Moore, editor, *The Boys' Country Book,* Collins, 1961.
Rosemary Weir, *Albert the Dragon,* Abelard, 1961.
Edward Korel, *Listen and I'll Tell You,* Blackie, 1962, Lippincott, 1964.
John Moreton, *Punky: Mouse for a Day,* Faber, 1962.
Ezo, *My Son-in-Law the Hippopotamus,* Abelard, 1962.
Rupert Croft-Cooke, *Tales of a Wicked Uncle,* J. Cape, 1963.
Richard Schickel, *The Gentle Knight,* Abelard, 1964.
Joan Tate, *The Next-Doors,* Heinemann, 1964.

Weir, *Albert the Dragon and the Centaur,* Abelard, 1964.
Weir, *The Further Adventures of Albert the Dragon,* Abelard, 1964.
Fred Loads, Alan Gemmell, and Bil Sowerbutts, *Gardeners' Question Time,* BBC Publications, 1964, second series, 1966.
Ennis Rees, *Riddles, Riddles Everywhere,* Abelard, 1964.
James Britton, editor, *The Oxford Books of Stories for Juniors,* three volumes, Oxford University Press, 1964-66.
Rees, *Pun Fun,* Abelard, 1965.
Bill Hartley, *Motoring and the Motorist,* BBC, 1965.
Charles Connell, *Aphrodisiacs in Your Garden,* Mayflower, 1965.
Barry Ruth, *Home Economics,* Heinemann Educational, 1966.
Jules Verne, *Around the World in Eighty Days,* Chatto, 1966.
Thomas L. Hirsch, *Puzzles for Pleasure and Leisure,* Abelard, 1966.
Robert Tibber, *Aristide,* Hutchinson, 1966, Dial, 1967.
Marjorie Bilbow and Antony Bilbow, *Give a Dog a Good Name,* Hutchinson, 1967.
Tate, *Bits and Pieces,* Heinemann, 1967.
Rees, *Tiny Tall Tales,* Abelard, 1967.
Tate, *Luke's Garden,* Heinemann, 1967.
Helen J. Fletcher, *Put on Your Thinking Cap,* Abelard, 1968.
G. Broughton, *Listen and Read with Peter and Molly,* BBC, 1968.
Gordon Fraser, editor, *Your Animal Book,* Gordon Fraser, 1969.
H. P. Rickman, *Living with Technology,* Zenith Books, 1969.
Broughton, *Success with English: The Penguin Course,* Penguin, 1969.
Nathan Zimelman, *The First Elephant Comes to Ireland,* Follett, 1969.
James Reeves, *Mr. Horrox and the Gratch,* Abelard, 1969.
Rees, *Gillygaloos and the Gollywhoppers: Tall Tales about Mythical Monsters,* Abelard, 1969.
Gillian Edwards, *Hogmanay and Tiffany: The Names of Feasts and Fasts,* Geoffrey Bles, 1970.
D. Mackay, B. Thompson, and P. Schaub, *The Birthday Party,* Longman, 1970.
Elizabeth Bowen, *The Good Tiger,* J. Cape, 1970.
Fletcher, *Puzzles and Quizzles,* Platt, 1970.
Thomas Corddry, *Kibby's Big Feat,* Follett, 1970.
H. Thomson, *The Witch's Cat,* Addison-Wesley, 1971.
J. B. S. Haldane, *My Friend Mr. Leakey,* Puffin, 1971.
Ruth Craft, *Play School Play Ideas,* Penguin, 1971.
Aristophanes, *The Birds,* translated by Dudley Fitts, Royal College of Art, 1971.

Marcus Cunliffe, *The Ages of Man: From Sav-age to Sew-age,* American Heritage, 1971.

Broughton, *Peter and Molly,* BBC, 1972.

Sid Fleischman, *McBroom's Wonderful One-Acre Farm,* Chatto & Windus, 1972.

Natalie Savage Carlson, *Pigeon of Paris,* Blackie, 1972, Scholastic, 1975.

Norman Hunter, *Wizards Are a Nuisance,* BBC, 1973.

Julia Watson, *The Armada Lion Book of Young Verse,* Collins, 1973.

R. C. Scriven, *The Thingummy-jig,* BBC, 1973.

F. Knowles and B. Thompson, *Eating,* Longman, 1973.

Clement Freud, *Grimble,* Penguin, 1974.

Dr. Seuss (pseudonym of Theodor Seuss Geisel), *Great Day for Up!,* Random House, 1974.

Bronnie Cunningham, editor, *The Puffin Joke Book,* Penguin, 1974.

Willis Hall, *The Incredible Kidnapping,* Heinemann, 1975.

Hall, *Kidnapped at Christmas,* Heinemann Educational, 1975.

Broughton, *Peter and Molly's Revision Book,* BBC, 1975.

Lewis Carroll, *The Hunting of the Snark,* Folio Society, 1976.

Sylvia Plath, *The Bed Book,* Faber, 1976.

Adele De Leeuw, *Horseshoe Harry and the Whale,* Parents Magazine Press, 1976.

Ellen Blance and Ann Cook, *Monster Books,* 24 volumes, Longman, 1976-1978.

Fleischman, *Here Comes McBroom!,* Chatto, 1976.

Margaret Mahy, *The Nonstop Nonsense Book,* Dent, 1977.

Sara Brewton, John E. Brewton, and John B. Blackburn, editors, *Of Quarks, Quasars, and Other Quirks: Quizzical Poems for the Supersonic Age,* Harper, 1977.

Ted Allan, *Willie the Squowse,* McClelland & Stewart, 1977, Hastings House, 1978.

Carole Ward, *Play School Ideas 2,* BBC, 1977.

Stella Gibbons, *Cold Comfort Farm,* Folio Society, 1977.

Cunningham, editor, *Funny Business,* Penguin, 1978.

Helen Young, *What Difference Does It Make, Danny?,* Deutsch, 1980.

Evelyn Waugh, *Black Mischief,* Folio Society, 1981.

Fleischman, *McBroom and the Great Race,* Chatto & Windus, 1981.

Jonathan Gathorne-Hardy, *Cyril Bonhamy v. Madam Big,* J. Cape, 1981.

Tony Lacey, editor, *Up with Skool!,* Kestrel, 1981.

Tim Rice and Andrew Lloyd Webber, *Joseph and the Amazing Technicolor Dreamcoat,* Holt, 1982.

Gathorne-Hardy, *Cyril Bonhamy and the Great Drain Robbery,* J. Cape, 1983.

Waugh, *Scoop,* Folio Society, 1983.

George Orwell, *Animal Farm,* Folio Society, 1984.

Rudyard Kipling, *How the Camel Got His Hump,* Macmillan (England), 1984, Bedrick Books, 1985.

Gathorne-Hardy, *Cyril Bonhamy and Operation Ping,* J. Cape, 1984.

Jeff Brown, *A Lamp for the Lambchops,* Methuen, 1985.

Mahy, *The Great Piratical Rumbustification and the Librarian and the Robbers,* Godine, 1986.

Jan Mark, *Frankie's Hat,* Kestrel, 1986.

Dr. Pete Rowan, *Can You Get Warts from Touching Toads?: Ask Dr. Pete,* Messner, 1986.

ILLUSTRATOR; ALL BY JOAN AIKEN

The Escaped Black Mamba, BBC Publications, 1973.

Tales of Arabel's Raven, J. Cape, 1974, published as *Arabel's Raven,* Doubleday, 1974.

The Bread Bin, BBC Publications, 1974.

Mortimer's Tie, BBC Publications, 1976.

Mortimer and the Sword Excalibur, BBC Publications, 1979.

The Spiral Stair, BBC Publications, 1979.

Arabel and Mortimer (includes *Mortimer's Tie, The Spiral Stair,* and *Mortimer and the Sword Excalibur*), J. Cape/BBC Publications, 1979, Doubleday, 1981.

Mortimer's Portrait on Glass, BBC Publications, 1980.

The Mystery of Mr. Jones's Disappearing Taxi, BBC Publications, 1980.

Mortimer's Cross (Junior Literary Guild selection), J. Cape, 1983, Harper, 1984.

Mortimer Says Nothing, Harper, 1987.

ILLUSTRATOR; ALL BY PATRICK CAMPBELL

Come Here Till I Tell You, Hutchinson, 1960.

Constantly in Pursuit, Hutchinson, 1962.

Brewing Up in the Basement, Hutchinson, 1963.

How to Become a Scratch Golfer, Blond, 1963.

The P-P-Penguin Patrick Campbell, Penguin, 1965.

Rough Husbandry, Hutchinson, 1965.

A Feast of True Fandangles, W. H. Allen, 1979.

ILLUSTRATOR; ALL BY ROALD DAHL

The Enormous Crocodile, Knopf, 1978.

The Twits, Knopf, 1980.

George's Marvellous Medicine, J. Cape, 1981, published in the United States as *George's Marvelous Medicine,* Knopf, 1982.

The BFG, Farrar, Straus, 1982.

Roald Dahl's Revolting Rhymes, J. Cape, 1982, Knopf, 1983.

The Witches, Farrar, Straus, 1983.

The Giraffe and the Pelly and Me, Farrar, Straus, 1985.

Dirty Beasts, J. Cape, 1984, Penguin, 1986.

Matilda, J. Cape, 1988, Cornerstone Books, 1989.

Rhyme Stew, J. Cape, 1989, Viking, 1990.

Esio Trot, Viking, 1990.

The Dahl Diary, Puffin, 1991.

ILLUSTRATOR; ALL BY NILS-OLOF FRANZEN

Agaton Sax and the Diamond Thieves, Deutsch, 1965, translated by Evelyn Ramsden, Delacorte, 1967.
Agaton Sax and the Scotland Yard Mystery, Delacorte, 1969.
Agaton Sax and the Incredible Max Brothers, Delacorte, 1970.
Agaton Sax and the Criminal Doubles, Deutsch, 1971.
Agaton Sax and the Colossus of Rhodes, Deutsch, 1972.
Agaton Sax and the London Computer Plot, Deutsch, 1973.
Agaton Sax and the League of Silent Exploders, Deutsch, 1974.
Agaton Sax and the Haunted House, Deutsch, 1975.
Agaton Sax and the Big Rig, Deutsch, 1976.
Agaton Sax and Lispington's Grandfather Clock, Deutsch, 1978.

ILLUSTRATOR; ALL BY RUSSELL HOBAN

How Tom Beat Captain Najork and His Hired Sportsmen, Atheneum, 1974.
A Near Thing for Captain Najork, J. Cape, 1975, Atheneum, 1976.
The Twenty Elephant Restaurant, J. Cape, 1980.
Ace Dragon Ltd., J. Cape, 1980, Merrimack, 1981.
The Marzipan Pig, Farrar, Straus, 1986.
The Rain Door, Gollancz, 1986, Crowell, 1987.
Monsters, Scholastic, 1990.

ILLUSTRATOR; ALL BY J. P. MARTIN

Uncle, J. Cape, 1964, Coward, 1966.
Uncle Cleans Up, J. Cape, 1965, Coward, 1967.
Uncle and His Detective, J. Cape, 1966.
Uncle and the Treacle Trouble, J. Cape, 1967.
Uncle and Claudius the Camel, J. Cape, 1969.
Uncle and the Battle for Badgertown, J. Cape, 1973.

ILLUSTRATOR; ALL BY MICHAEL ROSEN

Mind Your Own Business, S. G. Phillips, 1974.
Wouldn't You Like to Know?, Deutsch, 1977.
The Bakerloo Flea, Longman, 1979.
You Can't Catch Me!, Deutsch, 1981.
Quick, Let's Get Out of Here, Deutsch, 1984.
Don't Put Mustard in the Custard, Deutsch, 1986.
Under the Bed, Prentice-Hall, 1986.
Smelly Jelly Smelly Fish, Prentice-Hall, 1986.
Hard-Boiled Legs: The Breakfast Book, Prentice-Hall, 1987.
Down at the Doctor's: The Sick Book, Simon & Schuster, 1988.

ILLUSTRATOR; ALL BY JOHN YEOMAN

A Drink of Water and Other Stories, Faber, 1960.
The Boy Who Sprouted Antlers, Faber, 1961, revised edition, Collins, 1977.
The Bear's Winter House, World, 1969.
Alphabet Soup (poem), Faber, 1969, Follett, 1970.
The Bear's Water Picnic, Blackie, 1970, Macmillan, 1971.
Sixes and Sevens, Blackie, 1971, Macmillan, 1972.
Mouse Trouble, Hamish Hamilton, 1972, Macmillan, 1973.
Beatrice and Vanessa, Hamish Hamilton, 1974, Macmillan, 1975.
The Young Performing Horse, Hamish Hamilton, 1977, Parents Magazine Press, 1978.
The Wild Washerwomen: A New Folktale, Greenwillow, 1979.
Rumbelow's Dance, Hamish Hamilton, 1982.
The Hermit and the Bear, Deutsch, 1984.
Our Village (Poems), Walker Books, 1988, Atheneum, 1988.
Old Mother Hubbard's Dog Dresses Up, Houghton, 1990.
Old Mother Hubbard's Dog Learns to Play, Houghton, 1990.
Old Mother Hubbard's Dog Needs a Doctor, Houghton, 1990.
Old Mother Hubbard's Dog Takes up Sport, Houghton, 1990.

OTHER

Also author and illustrator of *A Band of Angels* (picture book for adults), Gordon Fraser, 1969. Illustrator for "Jackanory," BBC-TV. Contributor of illustrations to periodicals, including *Punch* and *Spectator.*

ADAPTATIONS: "Patrick" (filmstrip), Weston Woods, 1973; "Snuff" (filmstrip with record or cassette), Weston Woods, 1975; "Great Day for Up!" (filmstrip), Random House.

WORK IN PROGRESS: The author commented, "I'm working on a book about the creative process of illustration, an autobiographical work which I hope will be interesting to children, adults, and especially to art students."

SIDELIGHTS: Writing in *Times Literary Supplement,* John Mole asserted, "[Quentin Blake's] instantly recognizable combination of sprightly pen and watery brush is a guarantee of frequent delight. . . . His pictures are improvisational, curiously featherweight, and full of a witty pathos spiced with mischief." In an interview with *Something about the Author (SATA),* Blake said that rather than working from models, he draws according to his memory of what things look like. Blake also stated that in illustrating actions, he tries to indicate how they would feel: "I try to identify with the *feeling* of doing something. In this sense illustration is like mime."

In high school, Blake began to submit drawings to the humor magazine *Punch,* which eventually accepted some of his work after two years of rejections. He then spent two years in the Army Education Corps, teaching English and illustrating a reader for illiterate soldiers. Later, Blake studied literature at Cambridge University. He continued to draw for magazines, and became a free-lance illustrator after finishing his studies.

He also became a part-time student at Chelsea College of Art, in order to "learn more about life drawing and painting." Blake said of his art studies, "I attended Chelsea for eighteen months. The experience gained in life drawing and painting was very important, and as a result my drawings became richer. I have always liked economical, reduced drawings. A possible analogy is soup—the more ingredients you add to the broth, the better the taste. So it is with my drawings. It is my diverse background knowledge and experience that has made the simplicity of my drawings possible."

Blake moved into illustrating books because he wanted to work with storylines. He sees his work as a collaboration with text and author: "The first collaboration is with the story. If you're the right illustrator for the text, you get a rush of ideas and feelings from the story itself. Then you can go to the author and confer. If you're not the right illustrator, I don't believe the collaboration will ever be fruitful."

Blake said of his own writing, "Most of the books I've written are really just sequences of drawings with text added for necessary explanations. My urge is to draw, and the story is worked out later. The illustrations are, so to speak, *leading* the story. *The Story of the Dancing Frog* was my only book not written like this. Illustrating it was a bit like working on someone else's manuscript. I'm delighted that I can do both, but if I had to give up one, I would give up writing."

"Working on my own books is often more of a headache. When you illustrate someone else's text, that text is well defined when you start. You get the manuscript, you start, you find the structure, think about the mood, the characters and how to fit them into the illustration. You want to do well by the story, but there are limits. When you work on your own text, however, you can change the pictures, or change the text at will. Everything is up for negotiation. The possibilities are infinite. It's like swimming in mud; all I can think about is, 'Where's the shore?' "

Blake further remarked, "My favorite [award] . . . was the Children's Book Award from the Federation of Children's Book Groups, which is actually awarded by chil-

dren—their vote decides the winner. What you win is not a medal or money, but a book filled with their own writing and drawing, all in response to your books. Quite a marvelous prize indeed!"

BIOGRAPHICAL/CRITICAL SOURCES:

BOOKS

Kingman, Lee, and others, compilers, *Illustrators of Children's Books: 1957-1966,* Horn Book, 1968.
Kingman, Lee, and others, compilers, *Illustrators of Children's Books: 1967-1976,* Horn Book, 1978.
Martin, Douglas, *The Telling Line: Essays on Fifteen Contemporary Book Illustrators,* Julia Macrae Books, 1989, pp. 243-263.
Something about the Author, Volume 52, Gale, 1988.
Ward, Martha E., and Dorothy A. Marquardt, *Illustrators of Books for Young People,* Scarecrow, 1975.

PERIODICALS

Artist's and Illustrator's Magazine, April, 1987, pp. 14-17.
Graphis (children's book edition), September, 1975.
New Statesman, October 31, 1969; November 9, 1973; November 21, 1980.
New York Times Book Review, November 3, 1974; January 15, 1989.
Observer, April 15, 1990.
Signal, January, 1975.
Spectator, December 5, 1970; April 16, 1977.
Times (London), July 29, 1989; April 21, 1990.
Times Educational Supplement, March 28, 1980; October 31, 1980; June 9, 1989, p. B9.
Times Literary Supplement, November 26, 1982, p. 1303; November 9, 1984, p. 1294; May 6, 1988, p. 513; July 7, 1989, p. 757.
Washington Post Book World, October 14, 1990, p. 10.

*   *   *

BLUME, Judy (Sussman)   1938-

PERSONAL: Born February 12, 1938, in Elizabeth, NJ; daughter of Rudolph (a dentist) and Esther (Rosenfeld) Sussman; married John M. Blume (an attorney), August 15, 1959 (divorced, 1975); married third husband, George Cooper (a writer), June 6, 1987; children: (first marriage) Randy Lee (daughter), Lawrence Andrew; (third marriage) Amanda (stepdaughter). *Education:* New York University, B.A., 1960. *Religion:* Jewish.

ADDRESSES: Home—New York, NY. *Agent*—Harold Ober Associates, Inc., 425 Madison Ave., New York, NY 10017.

CAREER: Writer of juvenile and adult fiction. Founder of KIDS Fund, 1981.

MEMBER: Society of Children's Book Writers (member of board), PEN, Authors Guild (member of council), Authors League of America, National Coalition Against Censorship (council of advisors).

AWARDS, HONORS: New York Times best books for children list, 1970, Nene Award, 1975, Young Hoosier Book Award, 1976, and North Dakota Children's Choice Award, 1979, all for *Are You There God? It's Me, Margaret;* Charlie May Swann Children's Book Award, 1972, Young Readers Choice Award, Pacific Northwest Library Association, and Sequoyah Children's Book Award of Oklahoma, both 1975, Massachusetts Children's Book Award, Georgia Children's Book Award, and South Carolina Children's Book Award, all 1977, Rhode Island Library Association Award, 1978, North Dakota Children's Choice Award, and West Australian Young Readers' Book Award, both 1980, United States Army in Europe Kinderbuch Award, and Great Stone Face Award, New Hampshire Library Council, both 1981, all for *Tales of a Fourth Grade Nothing;* Arizona Young Readers Award, and Young Readers Choice Award, Pacific Northwest Library Association, both 1977, and North Dakota Children's Choice Award, 1983, all for *Blubber;* South Carolina Children's Book Award, 1978, for *Otherwise Known as Sheila the Great;* Texas Bluebonnet List, 1980, Michigan Young Reader's Award, and International Reading Association Children's Choice Award, both 1981, First Buckeye Children's Book Award, Nene Award, Sue Hefley Book Award, Louisiana Association of School Libraries, United States Army in Europe Kinderbuch Award, West Australian Young Readers' Book Award, North Dakota Children's Choice Award, Colorado Children's Book Award, Georgia Children's Book Award, Tennessee Children's Choice Book Award, and Utah Children's Book Award, all 1982, Northern Territory Young Readers' Book Award, Young Readers Choice Award, Pacific Northwest Library Association, Garden State Children's Book Award, Iowa Children's Choice Award, Arizona Young Readers' Award, California Young Readers' Medal, and Young Hoosier Book Award, all 1983, all for *Superfudge;* American Book Award nomination, Dorothy Canfield Fisher Children's Book Award, Buckeye Children's Book Award, and California Young Readers Medal, all 1983, all for *Tiger Eyes.*

Golden Archer Award, 1974; Today's Woman Award, 1981; Eleanor Roosevelt Humanitarian Award, Favorite Author—Children's Choice Award, Milner Award, and Jeremiah Ludington Memorial Award, all 1983; Carl Sandburg Freedom to Read Award, Chicago Public Library, 1984; Civil Liberties Award, Atlanta American Civil Liberties Union, and John Rock Award, Center for Population Options, Los Angeles, both 1986; D.H.L., Kean College, 1987; South Australian Youth Media

Award for Best Author, South Australian Association for Media Education, 1988.

WRITINGS:

JUVENILE FICTION

The One in the Middle Is the Green Kangaroo, Reilly & Lee, 1969, revised edition, Bradbury, 1981, new revised edition with new illustrations, 1991.
Iggie's House, Bradbury, 1970.
Are You There God? It's Me, Margaret, Bradbury, 1970.
Then Again, Maybe I Won't, Bradbury, 1971.
Freckle Juice, Four Winds, 1971.
Tales of a Fourth Grade Nothing, Dutton, 1972.
Otherwise Known as Sheila the Great (also see below), Dutton, 1972.
It's Not the End of the World, Bradbury, 1972.
Deenie, Bradbury, 1973.
Blubber, Bradbury, 1974.
Starring Sally J. Freedman As Herself, Bradbury, 1977.
Superfudge, Dutton, 1980.
Tiger Eyes, Bradbury, 1981.
The Pain and the Great One, Bradbury, 1984.
Just As Long As We're Together, Orchard, 1987.
Fudge-a-Mania, Dutton, 1990.

OTHER

Forever . . . (young adult novel), Bradbury, 1975.
Wifey (adult novel), Putnam, 1977.
The Judy Blume Diary (limited edition), Dell, 1981.
Smart Women (adult novel), Putnam, 1984.
Letters to Judy: What Your Kids Wish They Could Tell You (nonfiction), Putnam, 1986.
The Judy Blume Memory Book (limited edition), Dell, 1988.
(And producer with son, Lawrence Blume) *Otherwise Known As Sheila the Great* (screenplay; adapted from her novel), Barr Films, 1988.

Some of Blume's works are housed in the Kerlan Collection at the University of Minnesota.

ADAPTATIONS: Forever . . . was adapted into a television film that aired on CBS-TV, February 6, 1978; *Freckle Juice* was made into an animated film by Barr Films, 1987.

WORK IN PROGRESS: A novel about Rachel Robinson, a character from *Just As Long As We're Together.*

SIDELIGHTS: In the twenty years since she published her first book, Judy Blume has become one of the most popular and controversial authors for children writing today. Her accessible, humorous style and direct, sometimes explicit treatment of youthful concerns have won her many fans—as well as critics who sometimes seek to censor her work. Nevertheless, Blume has continued to produce works that are both entertaining and thought-provoking. "Judy Blume has a knack for knowing what children think about and an honest, highly amusing way of writing about it," Jean Van Leeuwen states in the *New York Times Book Review. Newsweek* likewise reports that Angeline Moscatt, head librarian of the Children's Room of the New York Library, believes Blume "has a way of portraying human foibles in a way kids can relate to. In twenty years, I've never seen such a popular children's author."

Many critics attribute Blume's popularity to her ability to discuss openly, realistically, and compassionately the subjects that concern her readers. Her books for younger children, such as *Tales of a Fourth Grade Nothing, Blubber,* and *Otherwise Known as Sheila the Great,* deal with problems of sibling rivalry, establishing self-confidence, and social ostracism. Books for young adults, such as *Are You There God? It's Me, Margaret, Deenie,* and *Just As Long as We're Together* consider matters of divorce, friendship, family breakups, and sexual development (including menstruation and masturbation), while *Forever . . .* specifically deals with a young woman's first love and first sexual experience. But whatever the situation, Blume's characters confront their feelings of confusion as a start to resolving their problems. In *Are You There God? It's Me, Margaret,* for instance, the young protagonist examines her thoughts about religion and speculates about becoming a woman. The result is a book that uses "sensitivity and humor" in capturing "the joys, fears and uncertainty that surround a young girl approaching adolescence," Lavinia Russ writes in *Publishers Weekly.*

"Blume's books reflect a general cultural concern with feelings about self and body, interpersonal relationships, and family problems," Alice Phoebe Naylor and Carol Wintercorn remark in the *Dictionary of Literary Biography.* But Blume has taken this general concern further, the critics continue, for "her portrayal of feelings of sexuality as normal, and not rightfully subject to punishment, [has] revolutionized realistic fiction for children." Blume's highlighting of sexuality reflects her ability to target the issues that most interest young people; when she first began writing, she "knew intuitively what kids wanted to know because I remembered what I wanted to know," she explained to John Neary of *People.* "I think I write about sexuality because it was uppermost in my mind when I was a kid: the need to know, and not knowing how to find out. My father delivered these little lectures to me, the last one when I was 10, on how babies are made. But questions about what I was feeling, and how my body could feel, I *never* asked my parents."

Nowhere is Blume's insight into character more apparent than in her fiction for adolescents, who are undeniably her most loyal and attentive audience. As Naomi Decter observes in *Commentary,* "there is, indeed, scarcely a literate girl of novel-reading age who has not read one or more Blume books." Not only does Blume address sensitive themes, she "is a careful observer of the everyday details of children's lives and she has a feel for the little power struggles and shifting alliances of their social relationships," R. A. Siegal comments in *The Lion and the Unicorn.* This realism enhances the appeal of her books, as Walter Clemons notes in a *Newsweek* review of *Tiger Eyes:* "No wonder teen-agers love Judy Blume's novels: She's very good. . . . Blume's delicate sense of character, eye for social detail and clear access to feelings touches even a hardened older reader. Her intended younger audience gets a first-rate novel written directly to them."

Blume reflected on her ability to communicate with her readers in a *Publishers Weekly* interview with Sybil Steinberg: "I have a capacity for total recall. That's my talent, if there's a talent involved. I have this gift, this memory, so it's easy to project myself back to certain stages in my life. And I write about what I know is true of kids going through those same stages." In addition, Blume enjoys writing for and about this age group. "When you're 12, you're on the brink of adulthood," the author told Joyce Maynard in the *New York Times Magazine,* "but everything is still in front of you, and you still have the chance to be almost anyone you want. That seemed so appealing to me. I wasn't even 30 when I started writing, but already I didn't feel I had much chance myself." As a result, "whether she is writing about female or male sexual awakening, and whatever other adolescent problems, Judy Blume is on target," Dorothy M. Broderick asserts in the *New York Times Book Review.* "Her understanding of young people is sympathetic and psychologically sound; her skill engages the reader in human drama without melodrama."

Blume's style also plays a major role in her popularity; as Adele Geras remarks in *New Statesman,* Blume's books "are liked because they are accessible, warm hearted, often funny, and because in them her readers can identify with children like themselves in difficult situations, which may seem silly to the world at large but which are nevertheless very real to the sufferer." "It's hard not to like Judy Blume," Carolyn Banks elaborates in the *Washington Post Book World.* "Her style is so open, so honest, so direct. Each of her books reads as though she's not so much writing as kaffeeklatsching with you." In addition, Siegal observes that Blume's works are structured simply, making them easy to follow. "Her plots are loose and episodic: they accumulate rather than develop," the critic states. "They are not complicated or demanding."

Another way in which Blume achieves such a close affinity with her readers is through her consistent use of first-person narratives. As Siegal explains: "Through this technique she succeeds in establishing intimacy and identification between character and audience. All her books read like diaries or journals and the reader is drawn in by the narrator's self-revelations." "Given the sophistication of Miss Blume's material, her style is surprisingly simple," Decter similarly comments. "She writes for the most part in the first person: her vocabulary, grammar, and syntax are colloquial; her tone, consciously or perhaps not, evokes the awkwardness of a fifth grader's diary." In *Just as Long as We're Together,* for instance, the twelve-year-old heroine "tells her story in simple, real kid language," notes Mitzi Myers in the *Los Angeles Times,* "inviting readers to identify with her dilemmas over girlfriends and boyfriends and that most basic of all teen problems: 'Sometimes I feel grown up and other times I feel like a little kid.' "

Although Blume's work is consistently in favor with readers, it has frequently been the target of criticism. Some commentators have charged that the author's readable style, with its focus on mundane detail, lacks the depth to deal with the complex issues that she raises. In a *Times Literary Supplement* review of *Just as Long as We're Together,* for example, Jan Dalley claims that Blume's work "is all very professionally achieved, as one would expect from this highly successful author, but Blume's concoctions are unvaryingly smooth, bland and glutinous." But Beryl Lieff Benderly believes that the author's readability sometimes masks what the critic calls her "enormous skill as a novelist," as she writes in a *Washington Post Book World* review of the same book. "While apparently presenting the bright, slangy, surface details of life in an upper-middle class suburban junior high school, she's really plumbing the meaning of honesty, friendship, loyalty, secrecy, individuality, and the painful, puzzling question of what we owe those we love."

Other reviewers have taken exception to Blume's tendency to avoid resolving her fictional dilemmas in a straightforward fashion, for her protagonists rarely finish dealing with all their difficulties by the end of the book. Many critics, however, think that it is to Blume's credit that she does not settle every problem for her readers. One such critic, Robert Lipsyte of *Nation,* maintains that "Blume explores the feelings of children in a nonjudgmental way. The immediate resolution of a problem is never as important as what the protagonist . . . will learn about herself by confronting her life." Lipsyte explains that "the young reader gains from the emotional adventure story both by observing another youngster in a realistic situation and by finding a reference from which to start a discussion with a friend or parent or teacher. For many children, talking about a Blume story is a way to expose their own fears about menstruation or masturbation or death." Countering other criticisms that by not answering the questions they raise Blume's books fail to educate their readers, Sie-

gal likewise suggests: "It does not seem that Blume's books . . . ought to be discussed and evaluated on the basis of what they teach children about handling specific social or personal problems. Though books of this type may sometimes be useful in giving children a vehicle for recognizing and ventilating their feelings, they are, after all, works of fiction and not self-help manuals."

Even more disturbing to some adults is Blume's treatment of mature issues and her use of frank language. "Menstruation, wet dreams, masturbation, all the things that are whispered about in real school halls" are the subjects of Blume's books, relates interviewer Sandy Rovner in the *Washington Post.* As a result, Blume's works have frequently been the targets of censorship, and Blume herself has become an active crusader for freedom of expression. To answer those who would censor her work for its explicitness, Blume replied: "The way to instill values in children is to talk about difficult issues and bring them out in the open, not to restrict their access to books that may help them deal with their problems and concerns," she said in a Toronto *Globe and Mail* interview with Isabel Vincent. And, as she revealed to Peter Gorner in the *Chicago Tribune,* she never intended her work to inspire protest in the first place: "I wrote these books a long time ago when there wasn't anything near the censorship that there is now," she told Gorner. "I wasn't aware at the time that I was writing anything controversial. I just know what these books would have meant to me when I was a kid."

Others similarly defend Blume's choice of subject matter. For example, Natalie Babbitt asserts in the *New York Times Book Review:* "Some parents and librarians have come down hard on Judy Blume for the occasional vulgarities in her stories. Blume's vulgarities, however, exist in real life and are presented in her books with honesty and full acceptance." And those who focus only on the explicit aspects of Blume's books are missing their essence, Judith M. Goldberger proposes in the *Newsletter on Intellectual Freedom.* "Ironically, concerned parents and critics read Judy Blume out of context, and label the books while children and young adults read the whole books to find out what they are really about and to hear another voice talking about a host of matters with which they are concerned in their daily lives. The grownups, it seems, are the ones who read for the 'good' parts, more so than the children."

Blume, too, realizes that the controversiality of her work receives the most attention, and that causes concern for her beyond any censorship attempts. As the author explained to Maynard: "What I worry about is that an awful lot of people, looking at my example, have gotten the idea that what sells is teenage sex, and they'll exploit it. I don't believe that sex is why kids like my books. The impression I get, from letter after letter [I receive], is that a great many kids don't communicate with their parents. They feel alone in the world. Sometimes, reading books that deal with other kids who feel the same things they do, it makes them feel less alone." The volume of Blume's fan mail seems to reinforce the fact that her readers are looking for contact with an understanding adult. Hundreds of letters arrive each week not only praising her books but also asking her for advice or information. As Blume remarked in *Publishers Weekly*, "I have a wonderful, intimate relationship with kids. It's rare and lovely. They feel that they know me and that I know them."

In 1986 Blume collected a number of these letters from her readers and published them, along with some of her own comments, as *Letters to Judy: What Your Kids Wish They Could Tell You*. The resulting book, aimed at both children and adults, "is an effort to break the silence, to show parents that they can talk without looking foolish, to show children that parents are human and remember what things were like when they were young, and to show everyone that however trivial the problem may seem it's worth trying to sort it out," writes Geras. "If parents and children alike read 'Letters to Judy,' " advice columnist Elizabeth Winship likewise observes in the *New York Times Book Review*, "it might well help them to ease into genuine conversation. The book is not a how-to manual, but one compassionate and popular author's way to help parents see life through their children's eyes, and feel it through their hearts and souls." Blume feels so strongly about the lack of communication between children and their parents that she uses the royalties from *Letters to Judy*, among other projects, to help finance the KIDS Fund, which she established in 1981. Each year, the fund contributes approximately $45,000 to various nonprofit organizations set up to help young people communicate with their parents.

Over the years, Blume's writing has matured and her audience has expanded with each new book. While she at first wrote for younger children, as Blume's audience aged she began writing for adolescents and later for adults. Her first adult novel, *Wifey*, deals with a woman's search for more out of life and marriage; the second, *Smart Women*, finds a divorced woman trying to deal with single motherhood and new relationships. Although these books are directed towards a different audience, they are similar to her juvenile fiction in two characteristics: an empathy for the plights and feelings of her characters and a writing style that is humorous and easy to read. Interestingly enough, even in Blume's adult fiction "the voices of the children ring loudest and clearest," Linda Bird Francke declares in a *New York Times Book Review*, praising Blume's *Smart Women* in particular for its portrayal of "the anger, sadness, confusion and disgust children of divorce can feel."

One reason that children play such a role in Blume's "adult" fiction may be due to the author's reluctance to direct her works solely towards one audience, as she disclosed in her interview with Steinberg: "I hate to categorize books. . . . I wish that older readers would read my books about young people, and I hope that younger readers will grow up to read what I have to say about adult life. I'd like to feel that I write for everybody. I think that my appeal has to do with feelings and with character identification. Things like that don't change from generation to generation. That's what I really know." "I love family life," the author added in her interview with Gorner. "I love kids. I think divorce is a tragedy, traumatic and horribly painful for everybody. That's why I wrote 'Smart Women.' I want kids to read that and to think what life might be like for their parents. And I want parents to think about what life is like for their kids."

Banks commends Blume not only for her honest approach to issues, but for her "artistic integrity": "She's never content to rest on her laurels, writing the same book over and over as so many successful writers do." For instance, *Tiger Eyes*, the story of Davey, a girl whose father is killed in a robbery, is "a lesson on how the conventions of a genre can best be put to use," Lipsyte claims. While the author uses familiar situations and characters, showing Davey dealing with an annoying younger sibling, a move far from home, and a new family situation, "the story deepens, takes turns," the critic continues, particularly when Davey's family moves in with an uncle who works for a nuclear weapons plant. The result, Lipsyte states, is Blume's "finest book—ambitious, absorbing, smoothly written, emotionally engaging and subtly political." And even when Blume returns to familiar characters, as she does in the series starting with *Tales of a Fourth Grade Nothing* and *Superfudge*, her sequels "expand on the original and enrich it, so that [the] stories . . . add up to one long and much more wonderful story," Jean Van Leeuwen remarks in a *New York Times Book Review* article about *Fudge-a-Mania*.

"Judy Blume is concerned to describe characters surviving, finding themselves, growing in understanding, coming to terms with life," John Gough notes in *School Librarian*. While the solutions her characters find and the conclusions they make "may not be original or profound," the critic continues, " . . . neither are they trivial. The high sales of Blume's books are testimony to the fact that what she has to say is said well and is well worth saying." "Many of today's children have found a source of learning in Judy Blume," Goldberger contends. "She speaks to children, and, in spite of loud protests, her voice is clear to them." As Faith McNulty similarly concludes in the *New Yorker*: "I find much in Blume to be thankful for. She writes clean, swift, unadorned prose. She has convinced millions of young people that truth can be found in a book and that reading is fun. At a time that many believe may be the twilight of the written word, those are things to be grateful for."

BIOGRAPHICAL/CRITICAL SOURCES:

BOOKS

Children's Literature Review, Gale, Volume 2, 1976, Volume 15, 1988.

Contemporary Literary Criticism, Gale, Volume 12, 1980, Volume 30, 1984.

Dictionary of Literary Biography, Volume 52: *American Writers for Children since 1960: Fiction,* Gale, 1986.

Fisher, Emma and Justin Wintle, *The Pied Pipers,* Paddington Press, 1975.

Gleasner, Diana, *Breakthrough: Women in Writing,* Walker, 1980.

Lee, Betsey, *Judy Blume's Story,* Dillon Press, 1981.

Weidt, Maryann, *Presenting Judy Blume,* Twayne, 1989.

PERIODICALS

Boston Globe, January 30, 1971.

Chicago Tribune, September 24, 1978; March 15, 1985.

Christian Science Monitor, May 14, 1979; March 14, 1984.

Commentary, March, 1980.

Commonweal, July 4, 1980.

Detroit Free Press, February 26, 1984.

Detroit News, February 15, 1985.

Detroit News Magazine, February 4, 1979.

English Journal, September, 1972; March, 1976.

Globe and Mail (Toronto), November 17, 1990.

The Lion and the Unicorn, fall, 1978.

Los Angeles Times, December 26, 1987.

Los Angeles Times Book Review, October 5, 1980; August 31, 1986.

Nation, November 21, 1981.

Newsletter on Intellectual Freedom, May, 1981.

New Statesman, November 5, 1976; November 14, 1980; October 24, 1986.

Newsweek, October 9, 1978; December 7, 1981; August 23, 1982.

New Yorker, December 5, 1983.

New York Times, October 3, 1982; February 21, 1984.

New York Times Book Review, May 24, 1970; November 8, 1970; December 9, 1970; January 16, 1972; September 3, 1972; November 3, 1974; December 28, 1975; May 25, 1976; May 1, 1977; November 23, 1980; November 15, 1981; February 19, 1984; June 8, 1986; November 11, 1990.

New York Times Magazine, December 3, 1978; August 23, 1982.

People, October 16, 1978; August 16, 1982; March 19, 1984.

Publishers Weekly, January 11, 1971; October 8, 1973; April 17, 1978.

Saturday Review, September 18, 1971.

School Librarian, May, 1987.

Time, August 23, 1982.

Times Literary Supplement, October 1, 1976; April 7, 1978; January 29-February 4, 1988.

Washington Post, November 3, 1981.

Washington Post Book World, August 14, 1977; October 8, 1978; November 9, 1980; September 13, 1981; February 12, 1984; November 8, 1987.

—*Sketch by Diane Telgen*

*   *   *

BOTTING, Douglas (Scott) 1934-

PERSONAL: Born February 22, 1934, in London, England; son of Leslie William (a civil servant) and Bessie (Cruse) Botting; married Louise Young (a financial consultant and broadcaster), August 29, 1964; children: Catherine, Anna. *Education:* St. Edmund Hall, Oxford, M.A. (with honors), 1958. *Avocational interests:* Playing classical guitar.

ADDRESSES: Home and office—21 Park Farm Rd., Kingston-upon-Thames, Surrey KT2 5TQ, England. *Agent*—Andrew Hewson, John Johnson Agency, Clerkenwell House, 45-47 Clerkenwell Green, London EC1R 0HT, England.

CAREER: British Broadcasting Corp. (BBC), London, England, writer and independent producer for television, 1958—; explorer, writer, and photographer. *Military service:* British Army, King's African Rifles, 1952-54; served in East Africa; became lieutenant.

MEMBER: Society of Authors, Royal Geographical Society (fellow), Royal Institute of International Affairs.

WRITINGS:

Island of the Dragon's Blood (travels in Arabia), Funk, 1958.

The Knights of Bornu (travels in Tchad), Hodder & Stoughton, 1961.

One Chilly Siberian Morning (travels in Siberia), Macmillan, 1965.

Humboldt and the Cosmos (biography), Harper, 1973.

Pirates of the Spanish Main (juvenile), Puffin, 1973.

Shadow in the Clouds (juvenile), Puffin, 1974.

Wilderness Europe, Time-Life, 1976.

Rio de Janeiro, Time-Life, 1977.

The Pirates, Time-Life, 1978.

The Second Front, Time-Life, 1979.

The U-Boats, Time-Life, 1980.

The Great Airships, Time-Life, 1980.

The Aftermath: Europe, Time-Life, 1983.

(With Ian Sayer) *Nazi Gold,* Congdon & Weed, 1985.

From the Ruins of the Reich, Crown, 1985.

(With I. Sayer) *America's Secret Army,* Franklin Watts, 1989.

Wild Britain, Ebury Press, 1988.

(With I. Sayer) *Hitler's Last General: The Case against Wilhelm Mohnke,* Bantam, 1989.

SIDELIGHTS: Douglas Botting has traveled in Siberia, the Soviet Arctic, the Amazon, Orinoco, Mato Grosso, the Sahara, Southern Arabia, and many parts of Africa. He has participated in scientific and archaeological expeditions, including a balloon flight over East Africa for a study of game migration. Botting speaks French, Portuguese, German, and Swahili.

BIOGRAPHICAL/CRITICAL SOURCES:

PERIODICALS

Chicago Tribune, February 25, 1981.
Los Angeles Times Book Review, April 19, 1981.
New York Times Book Review, May 5, 1985.

*   *   *

BOWERS, Q(uentin) David   1938-

PERSONAL: Born October 21, 1938, in Honesdale, PA; son of Quentin H. (a civil engineer) and Ruth (Garratt) Bowers; married Mary Masters, June 4, 1960 (divorced, 1973); children: Wynnewood, Leland. *Education:* Pennsylvania State University, B.S., 1960.

ADDRESSES: Office—Box 1224, Wolfeboro, NH 03894.

CAREER: Bowers & Ruddy Galleries, Inc., Hollywood, CA, director, beginning 1969; former director and owner of the Mekanisk Musik Museum, Copenhagen, Denmark; American Auction Association, Hollywood, director, beginning 1971; associated with American Numismatic Association and American International Galleries; Bowers & Merena Galleries, Wolfeboro, NH, director, 1982—.

WRITINGS:

United States Half Cents, 1793-1857, Windsor Research Publications, 1963.

Coins and Collectors, Windsor Research Publications, 1964.

Put Another Nickel In, Vestal, 1966.

(Editor) *A Guidebook of Automatic Musical Instruments,* Volume I, Vestal, 1967.

(With Terry Hathaway) *Automatic Musical Instruments,* [Santa Fe Springs, CA], 1970.

American Car Advertisements, Crown, 1971.

Encyclopedia of Automatic Musical Instruments, Vestal, 1972.

The American Auction Association Presents the Matt Rothert Collection . . . , photographs by Robert Budinger, American Auction Association, 1973.

The American Auction Association Presents the Stanislaw Herstal Collection . . . , American Auction Association, 1974.

High Profits from Rare Coin Investment, Bowers & Ruddy Galleries, 1974, 11th revised edition, Bowers & Merena Galleries, 1988.

Collecting Rare Coins for Profit, Harper, 1975.

A Tune for a Token: A Catalogue of Tokens and Medals Relating to Automatic Musical Instruments, circa 1850-1930, Token and Medal Society (Thiensville, WI), 1975.

The History of the Unites States Coinage as Illustrated by the Garrett Collection, Bowers & Ruddy Galleries, 1979.

(With Mary Martin) *The Postcards of Alphonse Mucha,* Vestal, 1980.

(With Christine Bowers) *Robert Robinson: American Illustrator,* Vestal, 1981.

(With Art Reblitz) *Treasures of Mechanical Music,* Vestal, 1981.

Common Sense Coin Investment, Western Publications, 1982.

The Moxie Encyclopedia, Vestal, 1985.

Nickelodeon Theatres and Their Music, Vestal, 1986.

Muriel Ostriche: Princess of Silent Films, Vestal, 1987.

(With Michael Hodder) *The Norweb Collection: An American Legacy,* Bowers & Merena Galleries, 1987.

Coins and Collectors, Bowers & Merena Galleries, 1988.

The Numismatist's Bedside Companion, Volume 1, Bowers & Merena Galleries, 1988.

The Numismatist's Fireside Companion, Volume 2, Bowers & Merena Galleries, 1988.

United States Three-Cent and Five-Cent Pieces: An Action Guide for the Collector and Investor, Bowers & Merena Galleries, 1988.

United States Coins by Design Types: An Action Guide for the Collector and Investor, revised edition, Bowers & Merena Galleries, 1988.

How to Be a Successful Coin Dealer, Bowers & Merena Galleries, 1988.

(Editor) *The Coin Dealer Newsletter: A Study in Rare Coin Price Performance, 1963-1988,* Bowers & Merena Galleries, 1988.

Buyer's Guide to United States Gold Coins, Bowers & Merena Galleries, 1989.

Also author of *Adventures with Rare Coins,* Bowers & Ruddy Galleries, *A Buyer's Guide to the Rare Coin Market,* 1990, *The American Numismatic Association Centennial History,* 2 volumes, 1991, *Commemorative Coins of the United States: A Complete Encyclopedia,* 1991, *How to Start a Coin Collection, United States Gold Coins: An Illustrated History,* and *Virgil Brand: The Man and His Era,* Bowers & Ruddy Galleries. Also author of introduction to *Official ANA Grading Standards for U.S. Coins.* Also editor of a second volume of *A Guidebook of Automatic Musical Instruments.* Contributor to *Encyclopedia Americana.* Contributor to periodicals, including *Numismatist, Coin World, American Heritage,* and *Reader's Digest.*

*   *   *

BRACEWELL-MILNES, (John) Barry 1931-

PERSONAL: Born December 29, 1931, in Wallington, Surrey, England; son of Henry (an actuary) and Kathleen (Hill) Bracewell-Milnes; married Ann Jacqueline Cowley, June 25, 1977; children: Diane Christina, Timothy James Julian. *Education:* New College, Oxford, B.A., 1956, M.A., 1958; King's College, Cambridge, Ph.D., 1959. *Religion:* Church of England. *Avocational interests:* Music, travel.

ADDRESSES: Home—26 Lancaster Ct., Banstead, Surrey SM7 1RR, England.

CAREER: Iron and Steel Board, London, England, economist, 1960-63; Federation of British Industries, London, economist, 1964-65; Confederation of British Industry, London, assistant economic director, 1965-67, deputy economic director, 1967-68, economic director, 1968-73; writer and consultant, 1973—. Institute of Directors, economic adviser, 1973—; Institute of Economic Affairs, senior research fellow, 1989—. *Military service:* British Army, 1950-51; became lieutenant.

MEMBER: International Fiscal Association, Royal Statistical Society (fellow), Institute of Statisticians (fellow), Mont Pelerin Society, Society of Business Economists (fellow), Society of Authors, Independent Publishers' Guild, Association of Learned and Professional Society Publishers.

WRITINGS:

The Cost of Cutting Taxes, Manchester Statistical Society, 1969.
The Measurement of Fiscal Policy: An Analysis of Tax Systems in Terms of the Political Distinction between "Right" and "Left," Confederation of British Industry, 1971.
Pay and Price Control Guide, Butterworth & Co., 1973.
The Counter-Inflation Act, 1973, Butterworth & Co., 1973.
Is Capital Taxation Fair?, Institute of Directors, 1974.
Eastern and Western Economic Integration, St. Martin's, 1976 (published in England as *Economic Integration in East and West,* Croom Helm, 1976).
The Camel's Back: An International Comparison of Tax Burdens, Centre for Policy Studies, 1976.

(With J. C. L. Huiskamp) *Investment Incentives: A Comparative Analysis of the Systems in the EEC, the USA and Sweden,* Kluwer, 1977.
International Tax Avoidance, Kluwer, Volume 1: *General Report,* 1978, Volume 2: *Country Reports,* 1979.
Tax Avoidance and Evasion: The Individual and Society, Panopticum Press, 1979.
The Economics of International Tax Avoidance: Political Power versus Economic Law, Kluwer, 1980.
The Taxation of Industry: Fiscal Barriers to the Creation of Wealth, Panopticum Press, 1981.
Land and Heritage: The Public Interest in Personal Ownership, Institute of Economic Affairs, 1982.
A Market in Corporation Tax Losses, Institute of Directors, 1983.
Smoking and Personal Choice: The Problem of Tobacco Taxation, Forest, 1985.
The Public Sector Borrowing Requirement: The Scope for Privatising Taxation, Institute of Directors, 1985.
Are Equity Markets Short-Sighted?: "Short-Termism" and Its Critics, Institute of Directors, 1987.
Caring for the Countryside: Public Dependence on Private Interests, Social Affairs Unit, 1987.
Taxes on Spending: The Assault on Personal Responsibility, Forest, 1988.
Capital Gains Tax: Reform through Abolition, Institute of Economic Affairs, 1989.
A Tax on Trade; UK Tax Prejudice against Trading Abroad: The Problem of Surplus ACT and Its Solution, Adam Smith Institute, 1989.
The Wealth of Giving: Every One in His Inheritance, Institute of Economic Affairs, 1989.

Also author of numerous pamphlets on economics and taxation. Contributor to books, including *Taxation: A Radical Approach,* edited by Vito Tanzi and others, Transatlantic, 1970; *Private Foreign Investment and the Developing World,* edited by Peter Ady, Praeger, 1971; *The State of Taxation,* Institute of Economic Affairs, 1977; *Tax Avoision: The Economic, Legal and Moral Interrelationships between Avoidance and Evasion,* Institute of Economic Affairs, 1979; *The Case of Earmarked Taxes: Government Spending and Public Choice,* Institute of Economic Affairs, 1991. Contributor to proceedings and other publications of economic organizations; contributor of articles to journals.

WORK IN PROGRESS: A research project on excise duties on alcohol and tobacco.

SIDELIGHTS: Barry Bracewell-Milnes once told *CA:* "My professional interest is market economics in general and fiscal economics (especially the economics of personal taxation) in particular. I became interested in writing on fiscal and economic policy when I was Economic Director of the Confederation of British Industry and it became clear to me that the lobbying activities of pressure groups had to be grounded on a basis of principle if they were to serve the public interest. As a result of policy differences with the CBI, I was asked to resign in 1973; refusing to do so, I was sacked in a blaze of publicity. The CBI has subsequently moved much, but by no means the whole, of the way from its earlier corporatist/collectivist stance to my libertarian/free market position."

*   *   *

BRADBURY, Bianca (Ryley) 1908-1982
(Jane Wyatt)

PERSONAL: Born December 4, 1908, in Mystic, CT; died May 29, 1982, in New Milford, CT; daughter of Thomas Wheeler (a purchasing agent) and Blanche (Keigwin) Ryley; married Harry Burdette Bradbury (an attorney), August 14, 1930 (died December 3, 1977); children: William Wyatt, Michael Ryley. *Education:* Connecticut College for Women (now Connecticut College), B.A., 1930. *Politics:* Democrat. *Avocational interests:* Jazz, sports cars, travel, numismatics, animal welfare, and gardening.

ADDRESSES: Home—New Milford, CT. *Agent*—McIntosh & Otis, Inc., 475 Fifth Ave., New York, NY 10017.

CAREER: Author, writing primarily for children and young adults. New Milford Board of Education, New Milford, CT, member, 1953-63. New Milford Library, trustee, 1965-82, member of the board, 1965-77. Cofounder of New Milford Animal Welfare Society.

MEMBER: Poetry Society of America, American Literary Guild, Authors League of America, New Milford Historical Society.

AWARDS, HONORS: German Children's Book Prize Honor List, 1968, for the German edition of *Two on an Island; Dogs and More Dogs* was selected one of Child Study Association of America's Children's Books of the Year, 1968, *Andy's Mountain,* 1969, and *Nancy and Her Johnny-O,* 1970.

WRITINGS:

JUVENILE

Muggins, Houghton, 1943.
Five Baby Chicks, Houghton, 1944.
The Antique Cat (Junior Literary Guild Selection), Winston, 1946.
(Under name Jane Wyatt) *Rowdy,* Tell-A-Tale Books, 1946.
Amos Learns to Talk, Rand McNally, 1951.
Brave Fireman, Grosset, 1951.

The Brave Fireman and the Firehouse Cat, Wonder Book, 1951.
One Kitten Too Many, illustrated by M. Nichols, Houghton, 1952.
Tough Guy, Houghton, 1953.
Mutt, Houghton, 1956.
Mike's Island, Putnam, 1958.
Jim and His Monkey, illustrated by V. Guthrie, Houghton, 1958.
Happy Acres, Steck, 1958.
A Flood in Still River, Dial, 1960.
Two on an Island, (American Library Association Notable Book), illustrated by Robert MacLean, Houghton, 1965.
The Circus Punk, Macrae, 1966.
Sam and the Colonels, Macrae, 1966.
The Three Keys, illustrated by MacLean, Houghton, 1967.
Dogs and More Dogs, illustrated by MacLean, Houghton, 1968.
Andy's Mountain, illustrated by MacLean, Houghton, 1969.
The Loner, illustrated by John Gretzer, Houghton, 1970.

YOUNG ADULT NOVELS

Say Hello, Candy, Coward, 1960.
The Amethyst Summer (Junior Literary Guild selection), Washburn, 1963.
Goodness and Mercy Jenkins, Washburn, 1963.
Shoes in September, Washburn, 1963.
Laughter in Our House (Junior Literary Guild selection), Washburn, 1963.
Flight into Spring (Junior Literary Guild selection), Washburn, 1965.
Laurie, Washburn, 1965.
Lucinda, MacDonald, 1965, published as *Lots of Love, Lucinda,* Washburn, 1966.
The Undergrounders, illustrated by Jon Nielsen, Washburn, 1966.
The Blue Year, Washburn, 1968.
Red Sky at Night, Washburn, 1968.
To a Different Tune, Washburn, 1968.
Girl in the Middle, Washburn, 1969.
Nancy and Her Johnny-O, Washburn, 1970.
A New Penny, Houghton, 1971.
Those Traver Kids, illustrated by Marvin Friedman, Houghton, 1972.
My Pretty Girl, illustrated by Charles Robinson, Houghton, 1973.
Boy on the Run, Seabury, 1974.
In Her Father's Footsteps, illustrated by Richard Cuffari, Houghton, 1976.
I'm Vinnie, I'm Me, illustrated by Cuffari, Houghton, 1976.
The Girl Who Wanted Out, Lippincott, 1978.

Where's Jim Now?, Houghton, 1978.
Mixed-Up Summer, Houghton, 1979.
The Dogwalker, Warne, 1979.
The Loving Year, Scholastic, Inc., 1982.

OTHER

Half the Music (poetry), Fine Editions, 1944.
The Curious Wine (novel), Beechhurst, 1948.

Contributor to periodicals, including *Saturday Evening Post, Woman's Day, Colliers, Yankee Magazine, Family Circle, Saturday Review of Literature,* and *New York Herald Tribune.*

SIDELIGHTS: The late Bianca Bradbury was a prolific writer of books for both young children and young adults. With a career spanning almost forty years, and forty-six children's books to her credit, Bradbury has held a place in the libraries of many young readers.

Bianca Bradbury spent the greater part of her life in Connecticut, except for travel abroad. Although her experiences were rooted in a strong, traditionally conservative New England heritage, Bradbury commented, "I think the new generation . . . is the most intelligent, most aware, most concerned, that has ever come down the pike." Bianca Bradbury began her writing career at the kitchen table in the old house she shared with her husband in rural New Milford. As a young housewife, she found a way to fill the time between housecleaning and raising children by writing short verse, articles, and short stories for such periodicals as *Family Circle* and *McCall's.* The mother of two sons, William and Michael, Bradbury quite naturally turned her talents to writing for her own children, beginning with short picture books and graduating to more advanced stories as the boys grew older. She was very prolific, and at one point was publishing two books a year. Such an outpouring of work necessitated disciplined work habits. Bradbury's son Michael recalls the schedule his mother followed during his years at home: "She usually got up around five in the morning when it was quiet in the house. She made herself a cup of coffee, fed her animals, and then sat down at the kitchen counter with her notebooks. She did that every day." He added, "When my brother and I were still young, she would be interrupted by the daily routine of getting us off to school and getting my father off to work. Then she would go back to her writing for a while. But after we left home, she just plugged away at it."

Beginning her career writing stories for her two young sons, Bradbury later branched out into writing for a different audience after the boys left home. Many of her later works dealt with issues of concern and interest to a young adult readership. A source of frustration for her was that publishers shied away from some of the more controver-

sial issues that interested teen readers in favor of a more conservative format. "My mother did not see life as a perfect bubble," recalls Michael, "and felt that children should be made aware of that."

Michael Bradbury has affectionate memories of his mother. "She was quite a character, my mother. She loved life and was very spirited. I remember when she was sixty, she was looking for a new car. She looked at Volvos and Pontiacs, but then she saw this Alpha Romeo sport car and had to have it. It's ridiculous, a little sixty-year-old lady doesn't drive a bright red convertible Alpha Romeo. But, she did. She loved shifting and going fast. She was caught one time drag racing some of the kids downtown after one of her Board of Education meetings."

BIOGRAPHICAL/CRITICAL SOURCES:

PERIODICALS

Horn Book, October, 1969.
Library Journal, June 15, 1970.
Young Reader's Review, June, 1967; June, 1968.

OBITUARIES:

PERIODICALS

New Milford Times (CT), June 3, 1982.
Litchfield County Times (CT), June 4, 1982.*

*   *   *

BRODSKY, Iosif Alexandrovich 1940-
(Joseph Brodsky)

PERSONAL: Born May 24, 1940, in Leningrad, Soviet Union; son of Alexander I. and Maria M. (Volpert) Brodsky; children: Andrei (son). *Education:* Attended schools in Leningrad until 1956.

ADDRESSES: Office—Writing Division, School of the Arts, Columbia University, New York, NY 10027; Department of Russian, Mount Holyoke College, South Hadley, MA 01075.

CAREER: Poet. Worked variously as a stoker, sailor, photographer, geologist's assistant on expedition to Central Asia, coroner's assistant, and farm laborer. Exiled by the Soviet government, he left his homeland in June, 1972, for refuge in America; poet-in-residence at University of Michigan, Ann Arbor, beginning 1972; adjunct professor, Columbia University, New York City; Mount Holyoke College, South Hadley, MA, instructor in Russian language department, 1990—.

MEMBER: Bavarian Academy of Sciences (Munich-corresponding member), American Academy of Arts and Sciences, until 1987.

AWARDS, HONORS: D.Litt., Yale University, 1978; Mondello Prize (Italy), 1979; National Book Critics Circle Award nomination, 1980, for *A Part of Speech,* and award, 1986, for *Less Than One: Selected Essays;* MacArthur fellowship, 1981; Guggenheim fellowship; Nobel Prize, 1987.

WRITINGS:

Stikhotvoreniia i poemy (in Russian; title means "Longer and Shorter Poems"), Inter-Language (Washington), 1965.

"Xol 'mi," translated by Jean-Jacques Marie and published in France as *Collines et autres poemes,* Editions de Seuil, 1966.

Ausgewahlte Gedichte (in German), Bechtle Verlag, 1966.

(Under name Joseph Brodsky) *Elegy to John Donne and Other Poems,* selected, translated, and introduced by Nicholas Bethell, Longmans, Green, 1967.

Velka elegie (in Czech), Edice Svedectvi (Paris), 1968.

Ostanovka v pustyne (in Russian; title means "A Halt in the Wilderness"), Chekhov (New York), 1970.

(Under name Joseph Brodsky) *Poems by Joseph Brodsky,* Ardis, 1972.

(Under name Joseph Brodsky) *Selected Poems, Joseph Brodsky,* translated by George L. Kline, Harper, 1973.

(Contributor) *Three Slavic Poets: Joseph Brodsky, Tymoteusz Karpowicz, Djordie Nikoloc,* edited by John Rezek, Elpenor Books, 1975.

(Editor under name Joseph Brodsky with Carl Proffer) *Modern Russian Poets on Poetry: Blok, Mandelstam, Pasternak, Mayakovsky, Gumilev, Tsvetaeva* (nonfiction), Ardis, 1976.

Konets prekrasnoi epokhi: Stikhotvoreniia, 1964-1971 (in Russian; title means "The End of A Wonderful Era: Poems"), Ardis, 1977.

Chast' rechi: Stikhotvoreniia, 1972-1976 (in Russian; title means "A Part of Speech: Poems"), Ardis, 1977, translation published as *A Part of Speech,* Farrar, Straus, 1980.

V Anglii (in Russian; title means "In England"), Ardis, 1977.

Verses on the Winter Campaign 1980, translation by Alan Meyers, Anvil Press (London), 1981.

Rimskie elegii (in Russian; title means Roman Elegies), [New York], 1982.

Novye stansy k Avguste: Stikhi k M.B., 1962-1982 (in Russian; title means "New Stanzas to Augusta: Poems to M.B."), Ardis, 1983.

Uraniia: Novaia kniga stikhov (in Russian; title means "Urania: A New Book of Poems"), Ardis, 1984, translation published as *To Urania: Selected Poems, 1965-1985,* Farrar, Straus, 1988.

Less than One: Selected Essays, Farrar, Straus, 1984.

Mramor, Ardis, 1984.

Translations of his poems appear in James Scully's *Avenue of the Americas,* University of Massachusetts Press, 1971, and in *New Underground Russian Poets: Poems by Yosif Brodsky [and others].* Poems have been published in anthologies in twelve languages, and in *Russian Review, New York Review of Books, Nouvelle Revue Francaise, Unicorn Journal, Observer Review, Kultura, La Fiera Letteraria, New Yorker, New Leader,* and other journals. He also has done translations of poetry from English and Polish into Russian, and from Russian into Hebrew.

WORK IN PROGRESS: Original poems; translations from English into Russian; an English translation of *Chast' rechi* and a collection of essays, both for Farrar, Straus.

SIDELIGHTS: Inside Russia and out, Nobel Prize winner Joseph Brodsky is considered to be one of the Soviet Union's finest poets, although his work has not yet been published in the U.S.S.R. That and other puzzling aspects of Brodsky's exile have been the subject of wide press coverage since he stopped over in Vienna in June, 1972, en route to the United States. Exile has been difficult for the writer, who was born to middle-class Jewish parents in Leningrad before World War II. In one poem, he describes an exiled writer as one "who survives like a fish in the sand."

In many ways, Brodsky had lived as an exile before leaving his homeland. His father had lost a position of rank in the Russian navy because he was Jewish, and the family lived in poverty. Trying to escape the ever-present images of Lenin, Brodsky quit school and embarked on a self-directed education, reading literary classics and working a variety of unusual jobs, which included assisting a coroner, and a geologist in Central Asia. He learned English and Polish so that he would be able to translate the poems of John Donne and Milosz. His own poetry expressed his independent character with an originality admired by poets such as Anna Akhmatova and condemned by the Russian government.

According to a *Times Literary Supplement* reviewer, Brodsky's poetry "is religious, intimate, depressed, sometimes confused, sometimes martyr-conscious, sometimes elitist in its views, but it does not constitute an attack on Soviet society or ideology unless withdrawal and isolation are deliberately construed as attack: of course they can be, and evidently were." According to *Time,* the poet's expulsion from Russia was "the culmination of an inexplicable secret-police vendetta against him that has been going on for over a decade." Brodsky, who is Jewish, said: "They have simply kicked me out of my country, using the Jewish issue as an excuse." The vendetta first came to a head in a Leningrad trial in 1964, when Brodsky was charged with writing "gibberish" instead of doing honest work; he was sentenced to five years hard labor. Protests from artists and writers helped to secure his release after eighteen months, but his poetry still was banned. Israel invited him to emigrate, and the government encouraged him to go; Brodsky, though, refused, explaining that he did not identify with the Jewish state. Finally, Russian officials insisted that he leave the country. Despite the pressures, Brodsky reportedly wrote to Leonid Brezhnev before leaving Moscow asking for "an opportunity to continue to exist in Russian literature and on Russian soil."

Brodsky's poetry bears the marks of his confrontations with the Russian authorities. "Brodsky is someone who has tasted extremely bitter bread," writes Stephen Spender in *New Statesman,* "and his poetry has the air of being ground out between his teeth. . . . It should not be supposed that he is a liberal, or even a socialist. He deals in unpleasing, hostile truths and is a realist of the least comforting and comfortable kind. Everything nice that you would like him to think, he does not think. But he is utterly truthful, deeply religious, fearless and pure. Loving, as well as hating." Brodsky's "constant theme," relates Philip Howard of the *Times,* "is the contrast between the bleakness of life and the brilliance of language."

Though one might expect Brodsky's poetry to be basically political in nature, this is not the case. "Brodsky's recurrent themes are lyric poets' traditional, indeed timeless concerns—man and nature, love and death, the ineluctability of anguish, the fragility of human achievements and attachments, the preciousness of the privileged moment, the 'unrepeatable.' The tenor of his poetry is not so much apolitical as antipolitical," writes Victor Erlich. "[His] besetting sin was not 'dissent' in the proper sense of the word, but a total, and on the whole quietly undemonstrative, estrangement from the Soviet ethos."

Brodsky elaborates on the relationship between poetry and politics in his Nobel lecture, "Uncommon Visage," published in *Poets & Writers* magazine. Art teaches the writer, he says, "the privateness of the human condition. Being the most ancient as well as the most literal form of private enterprise, it fosters in a man . . . a sense of his uniqueness, of individuality, or separateness—thus turning him from a social animal into an autonomous 'I.' . . . A work of art, of literature especially, and a poem in particular, addresses a man tete-a-tete, entering with him into direct—free of any go-betweens—relations."

In addition, literature points to experience that transcends political limits. He observes, "Language and, presumably, literature are things that are more ancient and inevitable, more durable than any form of social organization. The revulsion, irony, or indifference often expressed by literature toward the state is essentially the reaction of the per-

manent—better yet, the infinite—against the temporary, against the finite. . . . A political system, a form of social organization, like any system in general, is by definition a form of the past tense that aspires to impose itself upon the present (and often on the future as well); and a man whose profession is language is the last one who can afford to forget this. The real danger for a writer is not so much the possibility (and often the certainty) of persecution on the part of the state, as it is the possibility of finding oneself mesmerized by the state's features which, whether monstrous or undergoing changes for the better, are always temporary."

Brodsky goes on to say that creative writing is an essential exercise of individual freedom, since the writer must make many aesthetic judgments and choices during the process of composition. "Aesthetic choice is a highly individual matter, and aesthetic experience is always a private one. Every new aesthetic reality makes one's experience even more private; and this kind of privacy, assuming at times the guise of literary (or some other) taste, can in itself turn out to be, if not a guarantee, then a form of defense, against enslavement. For a man with taste, particularly with literary taste, is less susceptible to the refrains and the rhythmical incantations peculiar to any version of political demagogy."

Brodsky points out, "It is precisely in this . . . sense that we should understand Dostoyevsky's remark that beauty will save the world, or Matthew Arnold's belief that we shall be saved by poetry. It is probably too late for the world, but for the individual man there always remains a chance. An aesthetic instinct develops in man rather rapidly, for even without fully realizing who he is and what he actually requires, a person instinctively knows what he doesn't like and what doesn't suit him. In an anthropological respect, . . . a human being is an aesthetic creature before he is an ethical one. Therefore, it is not that art, particularly literature, is a byproduct of our species' development, but just the reverse. If what distinguishes us from other members of the animal kingdom is speech, then literature—and poetry, in particular, being the highest form of locution—is, to put it bluntly, the goal of our species."

Even more compelling than the relationship between poetry and politics is the relationship between the writer and his language, Brodsky claims. He explains that the first experience the writer has when taking up a pen to write "is . . . the sensation of immediately falling into dependence on [language], on everything that has already been uttered, written, and accomplished in it." But the past accomplishments of a language do not impinge on the writer more than the sense of its vast potential. "While always older than the writer," he explains, "language still possesses the colossal centrifugal energy imparted to it by its temporary potential—that is, by all time lying ahead. And this potential is determined not so much by the quantitative body of the nation that speaks it (though it is determined by that, too), as by the quality of the poem written in it. . . . That which is being created in Russian or English, for example, guarantees the existence of these languages over the course of the next millennium also."

A poet, Brodsky adds, is someone intoxicated by language's capability to extend man's consciousness into the future. He said, "There are times when, by means of a single word, a single rhyme, the writer of a poem manages to find himself where no one has ever been before him, further, perhaps, than he himself would have wished for. The one who writes a poem writes it above all because verse writing is an extraordinary accelerator of consciousness, of thinking, of comprehending the universe. Having experienced this acceleration once, . . . one falls into dependency on this process, the way others fall into dependency on drugs or alcohol."

In keeping with these views, Brodsky's poetry is known for its originality. More than one critic holds the view expressed by Arthur C. Jacobs in *The Jewish Quarterly* that Brodsky is "quite apart from what one thinks of as the main current of Russian verse." A critic in *New Leader* writes: "The noisy rant and attitudinizing rhetoric of public issues are superfluous to Brodsky's moral vision and contradictory to his craft. As with all great lyric poets, Brodsky attends to the immediate, the specific, to what he has internally known and felt, to the lucidities of observation heightened and defined by thought. . . . Poetry of such rare power does not need the sustenance of biography. . . . At the age of thirty-three, he has the unfaltering intellectual authority that poets rarely achieve before middle age."

Though most agree that he is one of the finest living Russian poets, several critics believe that the English translations of his poetry are less impressive. Commenting on George L. Kline's translation of *Selected Poems,* Stephen Spender writes: "These poems are impressive in English, though one is left having to imagine the technical virtuousity of brilliant rhyming [in the originals]. . . . One is never quite allowed to forget that one is reading a second-hand version." F. D. Reeve is somewhat more abrupt: "In *Selected Poems,* the translations and their footnotes seem full of rectitude but lacking poetic rigor. Translating is difficult, I know, and thankless. . . . I think these translations are soupy. . . . How can any of us know who is Joseph Brodsky?" In *A Part of Speech,* Brodsky gathered the work of several translators and made amendments to some of the English versions in an attempt to restore the character of the originals. Brodsky's personal style remains somewhat elusive in that collection due to the subtle effects he achieves in the original Russian, Tom Simmons comments in the *Christian Science Monitor.* Brodsky, he

says, "is a poet of dramatic yet delicate vision—a man with a sense of the increasingly obscured loftiness of human life. But under no circumstances is his poetry dully ethereal. His dramatic power cuts both ways: He can portray a luminous moment or a time of seemingly purposeless suffering with equal clarity." Reeve agrees that "Brodsky is an extremely sensitive, alert, skilled, independent, and suggestive poet" whose Russian poems (as distinguished from their English translations) contain "a dignity, a grandeur, and a sadness deeply reflective of Russian culture and of our own world."

Erlich also feels that some of the lines in *Selected Poems* come out "strained or murky," but that Brodsky at his best has "originality, incisiveness, depth and formal mastery which mark a major poet." Czeslaw Milosz feels that Brodsky's background has allowed him to make a vital contribution to literature. Writing in the *New York Review of Books,* Milosz states, "Behind Brodsky's poetry is the experience of political terror, the experience of the debasement of man and the growth of the totalitarian empire. . . . I find it fascinating to read his poems as part of his larger enterprise, which is no less than an attempt to fortify the place of man in a threatening world." This enterprise connects Brodsky to the literary traditions of other times and cultures. Milosz explains, "An intensity that deserves to be called religious combined with a metaphorical denseness makes Brodsky a true descendant of the English metaphysical poets and it is clear he feels an affinity with them." Erlich concludes an analysis of some of Brodsky's major poems by remarking: "The richness and versatility of his gifts, the liveliness and vigor of his intelligence, and his increasingly intimate bond with the Anglo-American literary tradition, augur well for his survival in exile, indeed for his further creative growth."

Brodsky has prospered economically and artistically since taking up residence in the United States, where he has taught at the University of Michigan, has been widely published and translated, and has won several literary grants and prizes, including the Nobel Prize. At first, he was eager to return to Leningrad to see his parents, but he was not allowed to visit them before they died. More recently, he has expressed a change of heart about returning to Russia, which is itself undergoing rapid change. He told David Remnick of the *Washington Post* that those changes "are devoid of autobiographical interest" for him, and that his allegiance is to his language. In the *Detroit News,* Bob McKelvey cites Brodsky's declaration from a letter to Illich, "I belong to the Russian culture. I feel part of it, its component and no change of place can influence the final consequence of this. A language is a much more ancient and inevitable thing than a state. I belong to the Russian language."

BIOGRAPHICAL/CRITICAL SOURCES:

BOOKS

Authors in the News, Volume 1, Gale, 1973.
Brodsky, Joseph, *A Part of Speech,* Farrar, Straus, 1980.
(Under name Joseph Brodsky) *Contemporary Literary Criticism,* Gale, Volume 4, 1975; Volume 6, 1976; Volume 36, 1986; Volume 50, 1988.

PERIODICALS

Antioch Review, winter, 1985.
Choice, April, 1974; September, 1977.
Christian Century, November 11, 1987.
Christian Science Monitor, August 11, 1980.
Detroit Free Press, September 17, 1972; October 23, 1987.
Jewish Quarterly, winter, 1968-69.
Los Angeles Times, October 23, 1987; February 15, 1989.
Nation, October 4, 1980.
New Leader, December 10, 1973; December 14, 1987.
New Statesman, December 14, 1973.
Newsweek, November 2, 1987.
New York Review, August 14, 1980.
New York Review of Books, August 14, 1980; January 21, 1988.
New York Times, October 31, 1987.
New York Times Book Review, November 8, 1987.
Partisan Review, fall, 1974.
Poetry, October, 1975.
Poets & Writers, March/April, 1988.
Texas Studies in Literature and Language, Number 17, 1975.
Time, June 19, 1972; August 7, 1972; April 7, 1986; November 2, 1987.
Times Literary Supplement, July 20, 1967.
Vogue, February, 1988.
Washington Post, October 23, 1987.
Washington Post Book World, August 24, 1980.

—*Sketch by Marilyn K. Basel*

*   *   *

BRODSKY, Joseph
  See BRODSKY, Iosif Alexandrovich

*   *   *

BROOKNER, Anita   1928-

PERSONAL: Born July 16, 1928, in London, England; daughter of Newson (a company director) and Maude (a singer; maiden name, Schiska) Brookner. *Education:* Received B.A. from King's College, London; received Ph.D. from Courtauld Institute of Art, London.

ADDRESSES: Home—68 Elm Park Gardens, London SW10 9PB, England. *Agent*—A. M. Heath, 40 William IV St., London WC2, England.

CAREER: University of Reading, Reading, England, visiting lecturer in the history of art, 1959-64; Courtauld Institute of Art, London, England, lecturer, 1964-77, reader in the history of art, 1977-87; Cambridge University, Slade Professor of Art, 1967-68, New Hall fellow; writer.

AWARDS, HONORS: Royal Society of Literature fellow, 1983; Booker McConnell Prize, National Book League, 1984, for *Hotel du Lac.*

WRITINGS:

ART HISTORY AND CRITICISM

J. A. Dominique Ingres, Purnell, 1965.
Watteau, Hamlyn, 1968.
The Genius of the Future: Studies in French Art Criticism (based upon Slade lectures, 1967-68), Phaidon, 1971, published as *The Genius of the Future: Essays in French Art Criticism,* Cornell University Press, 1988.
Greuze: The Rise and Fall of an Eighteenth-Century Phenomenon, Elek, 1972, Graphic Society, 1974.
Jacques-Louis David, a Personal Interpretation: Lecture on Aspects of Art (address to members of British Academy, January 30, 1974), Oxford University Press for the British Academy, 1974.
Jacques-Louis David, Chatto & Windus, 1980, Harper, 1981, revised edition, Thames & Hudson, 1987.

Also author of *An Iconography of Cecil Rhodes,* 1956. Translator for Oldbourne Press of *Utrillo* by Waldemar George, 1960, *The Fauves* by Jean-Paul Crespelle, 1962, and *Gauguin* by Maximilien Gauthier, 1962. Contributor of essays on Rigaud, Delacroix, Ingres, and Cezanne to British Broadcasting Corporation production on painters from Duccio through Picasso, 1980, published as *Great Paintings,* edited by Edwin Mullins, St. Martin's, 1981. Also contributor to "The Masters" series, Purnell, 1965-67.

NOVELS

A Start in Life, J. Cape, 1981, published in the United States as *The Debut,* Linden Press, 1981, Vintage Books, 1985.
Providence, J. Cape, 1982, Pantheon, 1984.
Look at Me, Pantheon, 1983.
Hotel du Lac, Pantheon, 1984.
Family and Friends, Pantheon, 1985.
A Misalliance, J. Cape, 1986, published in the United States as *The Misalliance,* Pantheon, 1987.
A Friend From England, Pantheon, 1987.
Latecomers, Random House, 1988.
Lewis Percy, J. Cape, 1989, Pantheon, 1990.

Brief Lives, J. Cape, 1990, Random House, 1991.
A Closed Eye, J. Cape, 1991.

OTHER

(Editor, and author of introduction) *The Stories of Edith Wharton,* Volume 2, Simon & Schuster, 1988.

Also author of introduction for Margaret Kennedy's *Troy Chimneys,* Virago, 1985, Edith Templeton's *The Island of Desire,* 1985, *Summer in the Country,* 1985, and *Living on Yesterday,* 1986, all for Hogarth. Contributor of book reviews and articles to periodicals, including the *Burlington, London Review of Books, London Standard, London Sunday Times, Observer, Spectator, Times Literary Supplement,* and *Writer.* ADAPTATIONS: An adaptation of *Hotel du Lac* was co-produced in 1985 by the British Broadcasting Corp./Arts & Entertainment Network.

SIDELIGHTS: Anita Brookner is internationally acclaimed for her extensive knowledge and incisive explications of eighteenth- and nineteenth-century French artists and their work. She is an accomplished novelist as well—penning ten novels in as many years, including the Booker McConnell prize-winning *Hotel du Lac.* Critical response to her work has increasingly swelled with praise, but Phillip Lopate dispels whatever skepticism a first-time reader might have about the caliber or profusion of Brookner's work in the *New York Times Book Review:* "Yes, she is that good, and she keeps producing quality fiction at a calm, even rate precisely because she knows what she is doing. Each new Brookner novel seems a guarantee of the pleasures of a mature intelligence, felicitous language, quirky humor, intensely believable characters, bittersweet karma and shapely narrative."

Brookner, the first woman to be named Slade Professor of Art at Cambridge University, once referred to herself in a *Saturday Review* interview as a "speculative" art historian rather than a scholar. Her work attempts to position a subject within a larger context. For instance, *The Genius of the Future: Studies in French Art Criticism,* based upon Brookner's Slade lectures during the late 1960s, offers "paradigmatic" presentations of Diderot, Stendhal, Baudelaire, Zola, the Brothers Goncourt, and Huysmans, identifying each artist with a principal idea that becomes a "touchstone for her discussion," writes Robert E. Hosmer, Jr., in the *Dictionary of Literary Biography Yearbook: 1987.* Hosmer considers *The Genius of the Future* "a work of impeccable scholarship, precise, carefully annotated and designed, whose grace and narrative ease enable the discerning reader, whether art historian or layperson, to read it with pleasure and profit." *Greuze: The Rise and Fall of an Eighteenth-Century Phenomenon* grew out of Brookner's doctoral dissertation and sought to restore Jean-Baptiste Greuze to the historical recognition she believes his work warrants, says Hosmer, who calls it "intel-

lectually vital and engagingly written." A *New York Times Book Review* contributor similarly remarks that Brookner's "commanding acquaintance with everything and everybody, minor and major, in art, literature, and philosophy . . . is staggering, and the grace with which she organizes the minutiae to give them an air of spontaneity even more so."

Brookner's *Jacques-Louis David: A Personal Interpretation,* the published version of her address to the British Academy in 1974, submits a biographical profile of the artist and traces the progression of his work. "Clearly a blueprint" for her lengthy study six years later, says Hosmer, the work "testifies to Brookner's powers as a critical scholar and her charms as a lecturer: her text displays learning animated by anecdotal wit." In her subsequent major study, *Jacques-Louis David,* Brookner blends biography, history, and criticism to reveal that the artist's shifts in subject matter and style reflect political changes in France from the Revolution to the restoration of the monarchy twenty-five years later. Calling it "a reciprocal reading," Hosmer explains that Brookner demonstrates "how David was both formed by the socio-political/cultural context and how he helped to shape the forces creating that context." Praised by Richard Cobb in the *Times Literary Supplement* as "an art historian of great sensitivity an understanding," Brookner "provides a superb show of investigative work, a thorough and intelligent probing of the meaning of a man's art," maintains Celia Betsky in the *New Republic.*

The study of literature and art helped define Brookner's personal philosophy as well as the fiction she creates—fiction that critics frequently discuss in terms borrowed from the visual arts. At the age of seven, she was introduced to the writings of Charles Dickens, and she matured with the notion that fiction represented "the great repository of the moral sense," explaining to Amanda Smith in a *Publishers Weekly* interview: "I got so much information from fiction about human behavior and oddness of character and varieties of motive—things I could never have picked up from my friends or my parents or my family because on the whole, in society, people dissimulate, are really quite dishonest about what they're doing." Discussing the general influence of literature and art upon her fiction in a *Paris Review* interview with Shusha Guppy, Brookner credits inspiration from French novelists such as Balzac, Stendhal, and Flaubert. She also cites the influence of lost innocence in French art between the eighteenth and nineteenth centuries: "The eighteenth century believed that Reason could change things for the better, and that all would have the vote in the Republic of Virtue. After the Revolution, people realized that Reason could not change anything, that man is moved not by Reason but by darker forces. . . . And it was discovered that once you no longer were constrained to be good, either by Christianity or by a secular philosophy which for a time was even stronger, namely the Enlightenment, there was no limit to bad behavior. But also to inventive, creative, autobiographical behavior."

Brookner eventually left the academic life to devote more time to writing fiction, but she completed many of her novels with essentially one draft during summer holidays from teaching. "I write quite easily without thinking about the words much but rather about what they want to say," she tells Guppy. Regarding her highly praised style, though, Brookner remarks that she is not consciously aware of having one: "I do think that respect for form is absolutely necessary in any art form—painting, writing, anything. I try to write as lucidly as possible. You might say lucidity is a conscious preoccupation." Finding the process of writing "painful rather than difficult," Brookner elaborates in the *Saturday Review:* "You never know what you will learn until you start writing. Then you discover truths you didn't know existed. These books are accidents of the unconscious. It's like dredging, really, seeing if you can keep it going." Detecting similarities between Brookner's personal life and her fiction, some critics tend to identify her with her characters. Although Brookner thinks such autobiographical interpretations are mistaken, she admits to Smith, "If it's an unconscious process, then a lot of me must be in them. Yes—aspirations, longings, desires. Sadnesses, too." As Sheila Hale points out in the *Saturday Review:* "Brookner's novels are not crudely autobiographical; they are far more devastatingly self-analytical than any straightforward autobiography. Discreet to a fault in her relationships with other people, the woman at their center has revealed herself to her readers with an obsessive honesty that is not rendered less painful by her wit and intelligence."

Hosmer catalogues the principal concerns of Brookner's fiction as: "The plight of the sensitive, solitary woman of middle age who achieves a degree of insight but is unable (or unwilling) to act upon it, and remains bitterly disappointed; the depiction of female characters who represent a number of options for womanhood in contemporary society; a concern with what forms of behavior most become a woman; the twin themes of alienation and exile; and the relationship between literature and life." In a *Harper's* essay, Frances Taliaferro regards Brookner's novels as "oddly timeless, not only because they record such unchanging human situations as the filial quandary and the shifts of friendship, but especially because they move in almost total disregard of feminist expectations. They want so little, these blameless heroines!" Distanced from the feminist perspective, Brookner acknowledges to Smith that although it may have enhanced female friendships, "Women are not automatically good to women. There's

a great pecking order there which is sort of undisclosed. And they don't want to be left behind in the race." Indicating a preference for "the company of men because they teach me things I don't know," Brookner remarks to Guppy, "It is the otherness that fascinates me." And although she admires the energy of women who combine career and family, she contends that the idea of a "self-fulfilled" or "complete" woman is a fantasy: "Besides, a complete woman is probably not a very admirable creature. She is manipulative, uses other people to get her own way, and works within whatever system she is in. The *ideal* woman, on the other hand, is quite different; she lives according to a set of principles and is somehow very rare and always has been."

Published in England as *A Start in Life* and in the United States as *The Debut,* the novel concerns Ruth Weiss, a literary scholar in her forties who tries to escape a suffocating life of studying literature and coping with the childish demands of her aging parents. Warped by literature's notion that patience and virtue will triumph in the end, Ruth embraces the opportunistic view of the world expressed by Balzac; after the romantic affair she plans misfires, she returns home to care for her dying parents, and resigns herself to a lonely middle age. "As well as the arm's length of wit, there is a great deal of precision and perception" in Brookner's rendering of Ruth's story, comments Anne Duchene in the *Times Literary Supplement.* And although Duchene believes that Brookner goes too far in blaming literature "for the festering resentments of filial dutifulness," this "hardly matters, given the confidence of the telling." Art Seidenbaum concurs in a *Los Angeles Times* review: "The art historian who studied portraiture and landscapes also knows the terrain of the heart. Her heroine is almost historic, tethered to responsibility, but her technique is modern, hard-edged and as uneuphemistic as today."

With her second novel, *Providence,* Brookner "effectively claims her territory as a writer," suggests Taliaferro. The story focuses on another academic—Kitty Maule, a reserved, elegantly-dressed professor of Romantic literature at a small, well-funded British college. Never having known her British father, Kitty was raised in the French traditions by her maternal grandparents—French and Russian immigrants, and feels like a foreigner in her native England. She falls in love with a handsome and clever colleague, Maurice Bishop, whose unshakable self-assurance and Catholic faith further impede her desire to assimilate into British culture. The *New York Times'* Michiko Kakutani, who praises Brookner's "sharp eye for the telling detail" and "graceful, economical way with words," pronounces Brookner a "master at creating miniaturist portraits of attenuated lives." However, because Brookner narrates the novel almost exclusively in terms of Kitty and through her perspective alone, says Joyce Kornblatt in the *Washington Post,* the reader does not see her in a larger context—its "very strength—the vivid creation of Kitty Maule—becomes its limitation." Nonetheless, Kornblatt calls the novel "perfectly observed and quietly witty," and praises its craft: "Each expertly paced scene is brought to life through a fastidious accretion of detail, a fine ear for speech, a narrative diction that is always intelligent and often arresting."

In *Look at Me,* Brookner's third novel, Brookner portrays the life of Frances Hinton, a young librarian at a British medical institute. Her dreary job of cataloging and filing pictures of death and disease is relieved only by observing the other staff members who frequent the institute's archives. Upon returning to her hideously decorated apartment, bequeathed by her deceased mother, she spends solitary evenings writing about the day's observations. Nick Fraser, an attractive young doctor at the institute, together with his glamorous wife Alix, befriend Frances and welcome her into their intimate circle of friends. They introduce her to Nick's colleague James, with whom Frances shares a chaste romance; but when Frances and James try to secure some privacy in their relationship, they exclude Alix, who then abandons Frances. Angered, Frances finds release in writing the novel that becomes *Look at Me.* In a *Washington Post Book World* review, Julia Epstein deems the book "a nearly impossible achievement, a novel about emptiness and vacancy." Believing that the protagonist's novel is "not so much self-reflexive as self-digesting, its material imaged and converted into prose even as it unfolds in Frances' life," Epstein concludes that *Look at Me* is "simultaneously a tragedy of solitude and loss, and a triumph of the sharp-tongued controlling self."

Brookner's fourth novel *Hotel du Lac,* won the 1984 Booker McConnell Prize, Britain's most prestigious literary award. Like her three earlier novels, it is about romance and loneliness in the life of a discreet, educated, literary woman with conventional dreams of love and marriage; unlike her earlier novels, it suggests that rewards accompany boldness rather than goodness. The story centers on a thirty-nine-year-old London romance novelist, Edith Hope, who jilts her fiance on her wedding day. Exiled to an off-season Swiss hotel by her family and friends, she spends her time observing the other guests, involving herself in their personal lives, writing letters to her married lover, and working on her latest novel. Edith's popular novels promote the romantic equivalent of Aesop's fable of the tortoise and the hare—that slow and steady wins the race; however, while Edith publicly acknowledges the falsity of the myth, she privately clings to romantic ideals of perfect love. The *New York Times'* John Gross, who considers Brookner "one of the finest novelists of her generation," calls *Hotel du Lac* "a novel about ro-

mance, and reality, and the gap between them and the way the need for romance persists in the full knowledge of that gap." What distinguishes this novel from Brookner's previous novels, says Anne Tyler in the *Washington Post Book World,* is that in *Hotel du Lac,* "the heroine is more philosophical from the outset, more self-reliant, more conscious that a solitary life is not, after all, an unmitigated tragedy."

In *Family and Friends,* "Brookner seems to be making a bid to open out her canvas," observes Kakutani: "Her subject is not one waif-like woman, but an entire family; her focus, not simply the consequences of romantic love, but also the effects of the enduring, changing bonds between parents and their children, sisters and their brothers." The novel focuses upon the Dorns who relocate to London between the World Wars but retain many of their Jewish-European traditions. Sofka, a widow, exercises enormous influence over her children, two of whom resist familial traditions and duties while the other two sacrifice their lives to perpetuate them. Finding it a "fine and heartening book," Jonathan Yardley remarks in the *Washington Post Book World* that the novel "may be in some measure about a family coming apart, but it is also about the loyalties that make it endure." Suggesting that the Dorns could serve as ancestors of other Brookner characters, Caryn James points out in the *New York Times Book Review* that while Brookner "looks backward, she focuses on the breakdown of the old social code and the forces that have led to her contemporary heroines' oddly dated notions of love and decorum." According to Derwent May in the *Listener,* though, the novel "is more like some strange kind of painting, with a group of figures who take on different appearances as you tilt it or rotate it, but are always held in exactly the same pattern, and only give the faintest impression of movement of their own."

A Misalliance returns to a type of character familiar from Brookner's earlier novels—a repressed, intellectual woman who finds herself defined by the man she loves. Rejected by her husband of more than twenty years for his secretary, Blanche Vernon still yearns for his occasional visits and spends time in museums contemplating the two contrasting archetypes of woman she sees in paintings: pleasure-loving nymphs of ancient mythology and dutiful saints who personify emotional martyrdom. According to Kakutani, the character sees herself as the inevitable loser in a contest between women who are "calm, sincere, doting and honest in their dealing with men," and those who are "sly, petulant, manipulative and demanding." Yardley thinks that what distinguishes this protagonist from her predecessors, though, "is that she had her chance at love and, much though she wanted to seize it, failed to do so out of misunderstanding and uncertainty." Critical consensus confirmed that the novel solidified Brookner's status as a master of prose. Yardley believes that "in writing about these lonely women, she has universal business in mind: the peculiarities and uncertainties of love, the relationship between fate and will, the connections—and disconnections—between art and reality." However, in the *New York Times Book Review,* Fernanda Eberstadt lauds what she thinks is the novel's "rather salutary and peculiarly welcome message, namely, that keeping up appearances in hard times is a virtue in itself, that kindness, self-restraint, good housekeeping and a certain cheerful worldliness may after all save the day. To this message, delivered with a lucid and refined intelligence and an invigorating asperity of tone, one can respond only with gratitude and pleasure."

A Friend from England presents a female protagonist who has recovered neither from the loss of her parents nor a disillusioning love affair with a married man. Part owner of a London bookstore, Rachel lives alone in a bleak apartment and becomes increasingly involved in the sumptuous lifestyle of her accountant's family—the Livingstones, recent winners of the football pools. Rachel serves as a companion of sorts to their twenty-seven-year-old daughter Heather. Although not especially fond of her charge, Rachel encourages her into independence; then, fearful of becoming a surrogate daughter to the Livingstones, reverses herself and tries to persuade Heather to return to her family. Describing Rachel as "repellently cold and cerebral," Deborah Singmaster adds in the *Times Literary Supplement* that "she becomes increasingly sinister as the book progresses . . . her blundering insensitivity as she thrusts herself into the disintegrating lives of the Livingstones is mesmerizing." Praising Brookner's "unrivalled eye for the details of appearance and behaviour," Heather Neill adds in *Listener:* "Often she writes like someone describing a painting or a photography. . . . She can take her reader into an environment, conjuring the feel of a place, paying particular attention to light and heat, colour and texture." Although he does not find the novel to be one of Brookner's best books, Michael Gorra notes in the *Washington Post Book World* that the beginning of the novel "is as classically elegant as anything Anita Brookner has written and shows why, in its concentration on the limitations of gentility, hers is one of the most characteristically English voices to emerge in the last decade."

Latecomers, considered by critics to be among Brookner's most poignant novels, focuses upon two male characters. Orphaned during the Holocaust, Thomas Fibich and Thomas Hartmann escape Nazi Germany to become schoolmates, friends, and then successful business partners in England. Each character attempts to reconcile himself to the past in a different way, but both rely heavily on the strength and constancy of familial relationships to establish their place in the present. Brookner's "rich, ut-

terly convincing portrayals of Fibich and Hartmann are likely to go a long way in dispelling any labeling of her as a 'women's writer' and in bolstering her reputation for drawing characters with the scrupulousness of a master draftsman," writes Jocelyn McClurg in the *Los Angeles Times.* Yardley calls it "a book not about romantic love but about love in the real world: about accepting and loving people for what they are rather than what one might wish them to be, about the slow, secret ways in which people work themselves so deeply into each other's hearts that extrication is unimaginable, about the acceptance and even celebration of human imperfection." Suggesting that "few writers can offer better, more specific insight than Anita Brookner," Bonnie Burnard maintains in the Toronto *Globe and Mail:* "Her conclusions seem valid, not arrogantly wise or uptown smart. . . . She is in control and has at her disposal a vast, accessible vocabulary of both spoken words and private thought. She can bring to life, calmly and sharply, place, gesture, attitude, intonation; she has mastered the master strokes." Finding the novel "written with grace and elegance that border on the astonishing," Yardley concludes, "At her own pace and in her own fashion, Anita Brookner works a spell on the reader; being under it is both an education and a delight."

Lewis Percy traces an inhibited young man's quest for tranquillity; or as Carol Shields puts it in her Toronto *Globe and Mail* review, it is "a book about finding an appropriate mode of heroism for our times." Lonely following the death of his mother, Lewis marries Tissy, a library co-worker, in an attempt to rescue her from a stifling life. When she falsely suspects him of sleeping with Emmy, the wife of a library colleague, "Lewis struggles to act honorably and keep his marriage vows, thereby antagonizing both women," writes Lopate. The characterization of Lewis recalls that of Ruth in *A Start in Life,* observes Julian Symons in the *Times Literary Supplement:* "Both are immersed in literature, Ruth an authority on Balzac, Lewis working on a thesis about the concept of heroism in the nineteenth-century novel, which in due time becomes a book and brings him a job in the college library. Both find living a trickier business than reading about it." The novel "bears the clear imprint of a painterly quality of mind," says Tyler: "The plot derives less from a chain of events than from a juxtaposition of portraits, each more detailed than the last. People we'd be unlikely to notice on our own . . . take on texture and dimension, gradually rising right off the page." Although Isabel Raphael considers the novel "less brilliant and distilled" than Brookner's other writings, she adds in her London *Times* review, "but for me, it glowed with a new serenity and reality which gave great pleasure, along with a sense that I will return more happily in future to this tender and sympathetic author."

Brookner's most recent novel, *Brief Lives,* concerns Fay Langdon, a successful but aging businesswoman. After the death of her husband, Fay becomes the mistress of his law partner, thus betraying his wife and her longtime friend, Julia. In recalling the events of her life, Fay begins to question what Nicola Murphy describes in the London *Times* as "her immature and foolish supposition that living would be a happy business." In the *Times Literary Supplement,* Lindsay Duguid describes Fay as "an intelligent narrator, who is sensitive and shrinking but always sure of the superiority of her judgment. . . . We follow Fay's flat, pathetic first-person story with interest, keen to find out if she will find happiness, suspecting that she will not." Praising Brookner's "infallible precision," Murphy judges the novel "a fine, poised and pointed examination of stoicism in a woman too marginal to be missed. *Brief Lives* is beautifully written."

Calling Brookner "a writer of high purpose and broad accomplishment," Yardley suggests that her "novels are miniatures, containing within their brief space worlds of feeling, wisdom and compassion, not to mention quiet, understated wit and seamless prose." However, as Brookner relates to Smith, "I would be pretentious if I thought I was doing anything more important than writing love stories. They still need writing. I'm not apologetic." Brookner's intelligence and smooth writing style elevate her work beyond the genre of the simple love story, though; and in her interview with Guppy, Brookner delineates what she perceives as the difference between Romantic and romance novels: "The true Romantic novel is about delayed happiness, and the pilgrimage you go through to get that imagined happiness. In the genuine Romantic novel there is confrontation with truth and in the 'romance' novel a similar confrontation with a surrogate, plastic version of the truth. . . . To remain pure a novel has to cast a moral puzzle. Anything else is mere negotiation." Brookner suggests to Smith that romance novels console their readers, permitting them happy endings in their less-than-happy real lives: "My books differ in the sense that they're more realistic—things *don't* work out. They're more fragmented. There is no safe conclusion." She tells Guppy that she plans to continue to write about love, Brookner remarks: "What else is there? All the rest is mere literature!"

BIOGRAPHICAL/CRITICAL SOURCES:

BOOKS

Contemporary Literary Criticism, Gale, Volume 32, 1985, Volume 34, 1985, Volume 51, 1989.

PERIODICALS

Atlantic Monthly, March, 1985.
Chicago Tribune, March 30, 1989; March 8, 1990.
Detroit News, June 16, 1991.

Globe and Mail (Toronto), November 8, 1986; April 7, 1990.
Harper's, April, 1981; July, 1983.
London Review of Books, September 6, 1984; September 5, 1985.
Los Angeles Times, March 18, 1981; May 3, 1983; February 8, 1984; December 25, 1989.
Los Angeles Times Book Review, March 25, 1990.
Ms., June, 1985.
New Republic, May 30, 1981
New Statesman, May 22, 1981; September 7, 1984.
New Yorker, March 23, 1981; April 9, 1984; February 18, 1985.
New York Review of Books, January 31, 1985.
New York Times, July 4, 1983; February 1, 1984; January 22, 1985; October 12, 1985; February 24, 1989; February 20, 1990; April 6, 1990.
New York Times Book Review, December 3, 1972; March 29, 1981; May 22, 1983; March 18, 1984; February 3, 1985; April 28, 1985; November 10, 1985; March 20, 1988; April 2, 1989; March 11, 1990.
Publishers Weekly, September 6, 1985.
Saturday Review, March/April, 1985; May/June, 1985.
Time, October 28, 1985.
Times (London), March 21, 1983; March 31, 1983; September 6, 1984; October 20, 1984; August 21, 1986.
Times Literary Supplement, November 26, 1971; January 9, 1981; May 29, 1981; May 28, 1982; March 25, 1983; September 14, 1984; April 26, 1985; September 6, 1985; August 29, 1986; August 21, 1987; August 12, 1988; August 25, 1989; August 24-30, 1990.
Village Voice; July 5, 1983.
Vogue, February, 1985.
Washington Post, April 28, 1981; March 9, 1984.
Washington Post Book World, July 24, 1983; October 13, 1985; February 28, 1988; February 18, 1990.

—Sketch by Sharon Malinowski

*　　　*　　　*

BROOKS, Albert
See EINSTEIN, Albert

*　　　*　　　*

BROWN, George Mackay 1921-

PERSONAL: Born October 17, 1921, in Stromness, Orkney Islands, Scotland; son of John and Mary Jane (Mackay) Brown. *Education:* Attended Newbattle Abbey College, 1951-52, 1956; University of Edinburgh, M.A., 1960, graduate study on the poetry of Gerard Manley Hopkins, 1962-64.

ADDRESSES: *Home*—3 Mayburn Court, Stromness, Orkney Islands KW16 3DH, Scotland.

CAREER: Poet and author.

MEMBER: Royal Society of Literature (fellow).

AWARDS, HONORS: Arts Council of Great Britain award for poetry, 1965; Society of Authors Travel Award, 1967; Scottish Arts Council Prize and Katherine Mansfield-Menton Prize, both 1969, for *A Time to Keep, and Other Stories;* officer, Order of the British Empire, 1974; LL.D., University of Dundee, 1977; D.Litt., University of Glasgow, 1985; M.A., Open University; Fletcher of Saltoun (Saltire) Award, 1991.

WRITINGS:

POETRY

The Storm, and Other Poems, Orkney Herald Press, 1954.
Loaves and Fishes, Hogarth, 1959.
The Year of the Whale, Hogarth, 1965.
The Five Voyages of Arnor, K. D. Duval, 1966.
Twelve Poems, Belfast Festival Publications, 1968.
Fishermen with Ploughs: A Poem Cycle, Hogarth, 1971.
Lifeboat, and Other Poems, Gilbertson, 1971.
Poems New and Selected, Hogarth, 1971, Harcourt, 1973, enlarged edition published as *Selected Poems,* Hogarth, 1977.
(With Iain Crichton Smith and Norman MacCaig) *Penguin Modern Poets 21,* Penguin, 1972.
Winterfold, Chatto & Windus, 1976.
Voyages, Hogarth, 1983.
Christmas Poems, illustrations by John Lawrence, Perpetua Press, 1984.
Stone, photographs by Gunnie Moberg, Duval & Hamilton, 1987.
Tryst on Egilsay, Celtic Cross Press, 1988.
Selected Poems, 1954-1983, J. Murray, 1991.

Contributor with Ted Hughes, Seamus Heaney, and Christopher Fry, to *Four Poets for St. Magnus,* Brockness Press, 1987; contributor to *The Wreck of the Archangel,* J. Murray, 1989.

NOVELS

Greenvoe, Harcourt, 1972.
Magnus, Hogarth, 1973.
Time in a Red Coat, Chatto & Windus, 1984, Vanguard Press, 1985.

SHORT FICTION

A Calendar of Love, Hogarth, 1967, published as *A Calendar of Love, and Other Stories,* Harcourt, 1968.
A Time to Keep, and Other Stories, Hogarth, 1969, Harcourt, 1987.
Hawkfall, and Other Stories, Hogarth, 1974.

The Sun's Net, Hogarth, 1976.
Witch, and Other Stories, Longman, 1977.
Andrina, and Other Stories, Chatto & Windus, 1982.
Christmas Stories, illustrations by John Lawrence, Perpetua Press, 1985.
The Hooded Fisherman: A Story, illustrations by Charles Shearer, Duval & Hamilton, 1985.
Selected Stories, Vanguard Press, 1986.
The Golden Bird: Two Orkney Stories, Vanguard Press, 1987.

JUVENILE FICTION

The Two Fiddlers: Tales from Orkney (also see below), illustrations by Ian MacInnes, Hogarth, 1974.
Pictures in the Cave, illustrations by MacInnes, Chatto & Windus, 1977.
Six Lives of Fankle the Cat, Chatto & Windus, 1980.
Keepers of the House, illustrations by Gillian Martin, Old Stile Press, 1986.

PLAYS

Witch, first produced in Edinburgh, Scotland, 1969.
A Time to Keep (television play based on three stories by Brown), telecast, 1969.
A Spell for Green Corn (radio play; broadcast, 1967; produced in Edinburgh, 1970; adaptation produced at Perth Theatre, 1972), Hogarth, 1970.
Orkney (television play), telecast, 1971.
The Loom of Light (produced in Kirkwall, 1972; also see below), photographs by Gunnie Moberg, illustrations by Simon Fraser, Balnain Books, 1986.
The Storm Watchers, produced in Edinburgh, 1976.
The Martyrdom of St. Magnus (opera libretto; music by Peter Maxwell Davies; adaptation of novel *Magnus* by Brown; produced in Kirkwall, Vienna, and London, 1977; produced in Santa Fe, 1979), Boosey and Hawkes, 1977.
Miss Barraclough (television play), telecast, 1977.
Four Orkney Plays for Schools (television play), telecast, 1978.
The Two Fiddlers (opera libretto; music by Davies; adaptation of story by Brown; produced in London, 1978), Boosey and Hawkes, 1978.
The Well (also see below), produced at St. Magnus Festival, 1981.
The Voyage of Saint Brandon (radio play; also see below), broadcast, 1984.
Andrina (teleplay), telecast, 1984.
Three Plays (contains *The Loom of Light, The Well,* and *The Voyage of Saint Brandon*), Chatto & Windus, 1984.
The Road to Colonus, broadcast by PTE-Dublin, 1989.

Also author of *A Celebration for Magnus,* son-et-lumiere play performed in Firkwall, 1987.

OTHER

Let's See the Orkney Islands, Thomson, 1948.
Stromness Official Guide, Burrow, 1956.
An Orkney Tapestry (essays), Gollancz, 1969.
Letters from Hamnavoe (essays), Gordon Wright Publishing, 1975.
Edwin Muir: A Brief Memoir, Castlelaw Press, 1975.
From Stone to Thorn, Abingdon, 1975.
George Mackay Brown (sound recording), Claddagh, 1977.
Under Brinkie's Brae (essays), photographs by Gordon Wright, Gordon Wright Publishing, 1979.
Portrait of Orkney, photographs by Werner Forman, Hogarth, 1981, photographs by Gunnie Moberg, drawings by Erlend Brown, J. Murray, 1989.
The Scottish Bestiary, illustrations by John Bellany, Steven Campbell, Peter Howson, Jack Knox, Bruce McLean, June Redfern, and Adrian Wiszniewski, Paragon Press, 1986.
(Editor) *Selected Prose of Edwin Muir,* J. Murray, 1987.

Also author of television poem *The Winter Islands,* broadcast in 1966. Also collaborator, with composer Peter Maxwell Davies, of musical works, including a cantata, *Solstice of Light.* Brown's manuscripts are collected at the Scottish National Library at the University of Edinburgh.

ADAPTATIONS: The Two Fiddlers was adapted as *The Two Fiddlers: Opera in Two Acts* by Peter Maxwell Davies, with the libretto by Davies published by Boosey & Hawkes in 1978; the story "Andrina" of *Andrina, and Other Stories* was made into a television film by Bill Forsyth in 1982.

WORK IN PROGRESS: A novel, *Vinland,* three long stories, and three collections of poems.

SIDELIGHTS: George Mackay Brown writes of life and nature in his native Orkney Islands. He has written novels, children's stories, essays, and media pieces, although he is best known as a poet. In an essay in the *Dictionary of Literary Biography,* Thomas J. Starr calls Brown "probably the greatest living Scottish writer." In another essay in the *Dictionary of Literary Biography,* Joseph Reino elaborates: "His successes in poetry and the prose narrative are considerable, and the really surprising thing about him is not so much his extensive talents, but rather that he is not more widely known as one of Britain's outstanding contemporary authors." Similarly, poet Seamus Heaney maintains in the *Listener:* "Mackay Brown's imagination is heraldic and formal; it is stirred by legends of Viking warrior and Christian saint; it solemnises the necessary labour of life into a seasonal liturgy; it consecrates the visible survivals of history, and ruins of time, into altars that are decked with the writings themselves. I have never seen his poetry sufficiently praised."

Brown attempts to capture and re-create the reality of his homeland through his prose and verse, through religious, ritualistic themes, especially relating to Orkney living and his fictional Orkney town, Hamnavoe. "George Mackay Brown is a writer in love with the past and with the Orkney Islands where he finds it still precariously lingering," writes Julia O'Faolain in the *New Review.* A *Times Literary Supplement* reviewer comments that "Brown is a uniquely observant and skilful chronicler of life in his native Orkneys, past and present." Harold Massingham concurs in *Phoenix,* seeing the same approach in Brown's poetry: "His local colour, in fact his total effect, is of a mature distillation and blend by an excellent and unmistakable poet patiently subdued by, and to, the demands of his terrain." Reviewing *Voyages* for the *Times Literary Supplement,* Douglas Dunn maintains that "Brown's idealism is retrospective, fictionalizing a place and its meaning through an affectionate exploration of history which he holds up like a cupped treasure in the hands, and as an offering to the residual innocence of his native Orkney Islands."

According to Reino, "Two aspects of Brown's personal convictions are important to keep in mind: his rejection of nineteenth- and twentieth-century concepts of progress and his personal belief that Scotland . . . is a 'Knox-ruined nation,' that is destroyed by the Calvinist reformer John Knox." Neil Roberts, in a *Cambridge Quarterly* assessment of Brown's work, writes that "he is interested in art, religion and ritual, their relations to each other and to the agricultural basis of civilisation. He is interested in the relation of pagan to Christian religion, and of the World of Christ to the word of the poet."

Brown's work concentrates on traditional values and time-honored ethics. Dunn observes in *Poetry Nation* that "Brown, as a poet of remote island communities and unindustrial, non-urban landscapes, is at odds with the tradition of modern poetry." Dunn continues: "Brown's best poems are . . . full of names and characters, their typical vulnerabilities, and the virtues of the way of life their personalities prove. He celebrates an ideal of community." In the *Times Literary Supplement,* Dunn remarks upon Brown's traditional qualities in prose as well: "Brown has perfected a narrative style of great simplicity, its virtues drawn more from the ancient art of telling tales than from new-fangled methodologies of fiction." "Cleaving to a collective tradition which rests on the work of old oral tale-tellers," says O'Faolain, "his stories make no concession to contemporary taste."

About Brown's efforts in *Andrina, and Other Stories,* Stuart Evans claims in the London *Times* that "this superb teller of tales who, whether he is writing in prose or verse, is always the poet, offers in this book a magical selection." Evans adds, "[The stories'] common strength, apart from

George Mackay Brown's exquisite and unerring way with words, is in their humanity." Dunn also applauds Brown's work in the book, stating in the *Times Literary Supplement,* "In writing so controlled, . . . by a poet perfectly at ease with his imagination and a language natural to it, the effect of that apparent collision of old and new can only be fruitful and challenging, as well as, in this case, profoundly enjoyable."

Calling Brown a "portent," Jo Grimond suggests in the *Spectator* that "there are not so many poets and some have only a little poetry in them. We should be thankful for Mr. Brown and grateful to Orkney that has fed him." Considering *Fishermen with Ploughs: A Poem Cycle* to be "Brown's most impressive poetic effort," Reino describes the work as "a sequence of obscurely connected lyrics based on island 'history' as the author reconceives it." Massingham calls the work "a task indeed . . . which is vividly and quietly accomplished with an interesting range of verse-forms and a marvelous prose chorus at the end." Dunn agrees, stating in *Poetry Nation* that "much of Brown's best writing is to be found in *Fishermen with Ploughs.*" Massingham concludes that "all his work to date has been a persistent devotion, not because he is running in runic circles but digging, rooting deeper."

Noting the affinity between Brown's prose and poetry styles, Starr calls him "a prose stylist with a poetic vision," and finds *Greenvoe,* Brown's novel of an imaginary island town, to be a superb example of his artistry. The novel "describes the destruction of a village by progress in the form of a secret military establishment," writes Neil Roberts in the *Cambridge Quarterly.* "Most of the novel is devoted to an evocation of the life of the village." Starr finds that Brown "successfully weaves all of [his recurring themes] into his own seamless garment." Calling it "the culmination of all of George Mackay Brown's fictional concerns," Starr thinks that it "ranks with *The Great Gatsby, Mrs. Dalloway,* and *The Spire* as among the great prose poems of this century." Although Roberts found the novel somewhat "disappointing," suggesting it was overwritten, Ruth Farwell praises Brown for the "beauty and precision of his style," and remarks in the *Washington Post Book World,* "Novels like this don't come along very often."

Brown doesn't always garner critical praise, however. About *Six Lives of Fankle the Cat,* Charles Causley suggests in the *Times Literary Supplement* that "Brown's relaxed manner and somewhat loosely constructed narrative lack the cutting edge, the dramatic tension, that we have grown to expect from his brilliant creation and re-creation of Orcadian myth and legend, for children and adults." And Dunn remarks in *Poetry Nation* that "unfortunately, Brown has now put forward a quaintly antithetical notion that there is a certain kind of real life for the good men

of the Orkneys, and another kind of life in the cities of the mainland which is so vicious that it brings total punishment." Despite the occasional negative comment, most reviewers admire Brown's work. In the *Times Literary Supplement,* David Profumo writes about the unique qualities of Brown's work: "He has kept faith with the same themes—the saving grace of ceremony, the importance of the cycle of the seasons, the past in relation to the present—yet he constantly turns them to fresh advantage, while maintaining a strong sense of tradition." And in the London *Times,* Peter Tinniswood writes that "if an aspiring writer came to me and asked how to tell a story, plot a book, round a character, make dialogue sing and whisper and bellow, I would say: 'Read George Mackay Brown.'"

In a brief commentary on his own writing, Brown told *CA:* "Since it seems to me that our civilization will possibly destroy itself before too long, I am interested in the labour and lives of the most primitive people of our civilization, the food-getters (crofters and fishermen) since it is those people living close to the sources of life who are most likely to survive and continue the human story; and since even their lives would be meaningless otherwise, I see religion as an illuminating and stabilising force in the life of a community. Out of these things I make my poems, stories, and plays."

Brown also told *CA* he considers the following "a kind of basic credo": "I believe in dedicated work rather than in 'inspiration'; of course on some days, one writes better than on others. I believe writing to be a craft like carpentry, plumbing, or baking; one does the best one can. Much mischief has been caused by a loose word like 'culture,' which separates the crafts into the higher arts like music, writing, sculpture, and the lowlier workaday arts (those, and the many others like them, that I have mentioned above). In 'culture circles,' there is a tendency to look upon artists as the new priesthood of some esoteric religion. Nonsense—and dangerous nonsense moreover—we are all hewers of wood and drawers of water; only let us do it as thoroughly and joyously as we can."

BIOGRAPHICAL/CRITICAL SOURCES:

BOOKS

Bold, Alan, *George Mackay Brown,* Oliver & Boyd, 1978.
Contemporary Authors Autobiography Series, Volume 6, Gale, 1988.
Contemporary Literary Criticism, Gale, Volume 5, 1976, Volume 48, 1988.
Dictionary of Literary Biography, Gale, Volume 14: *British Novelists since 1960,* 1983, Volume 27: *Poets of Great Britain and Ireland, 1945-1960,* 1984.
Hart, Francis Russell, *The Scottish Novel: From Smollett to Spark,* Harvard University Press, 1978.

Smith, Iain Chrichton, *Iain Chrichton Smith, Norman MacCaig, George Mackay Brown,* Penguin Books, 1972.

PERIODICALS

Cambridge Quarterly, Volume 6, number 2, 1973.
Chapman (Edinburgh), 1990 (special Brown issue).
Hudson Review, Volume 26, number 4, 1973-74.
Listener, April 17, 1967; August 21, 1969; January 9, 1975.
London Magazine, December, 1959.
London Review of Books, September 17, 1987; March 22, 1990.
New Review, June, 1976.
New York Times Book Review, April 28, 1968; July 19, 1970; September 9, 1984.
Observer, October 11, 1989.
Phoenix, winter, 1971.
Poetry Australia, October, 1978.
Poetry Nation, number 2, 1974.
Spectator, August 23, 1969.
Stand Magazine, Volume 13, number 1, 1972.
Times (London), February 13, 1983; July 23, 1987; December 31, 1987; June 8, 1989.
Times Literary Supplement, February 16, 1967; April 27, 1967; September 28, 1973; September 27, 1974; August 13, 1976; February 22, 1980; November 21, 1980; April 10, 1981; April 1, 1983; January 20, 1984; June 15, 1984; October 30, 1987; June 30, 1989; May 11-17, 1990.
Washington Post Book World, November 26, 1972.

*   *   *

BRUNNER, John (Kilian Houston) 1934-
(John Loxsmith, Trevor Staines, Keith Woodcott)

PERSONAL: Born September 24, 1934, in Oxfordshire, England; son of Anthony and Felicity (Whittaker) Brunner; married Marjorie Rosamond Sauer, July 12, 1958 (deceased, 1986). *Education:* Attended Cheltenham College, 1948-51.

ADDRESSES: Agent—Jane C. Judd, 81 Belitha Villas, London N1 1PD, England; and William Reiss, John Hawkins & Associates, 71 West 23rd St., New York, NY 10010.

CAREER: Science fiction novelist, songwriter, poet, and free-lance writer, 1958—. Abstractor, Industrial Diamond Information Bureau, 1956; editor, Spring Books Ltd., 1956-58. Campaign for Nuclear Disarmament, Hampstead chairman, 1961, member of London regional council, 1962-63, member of national council, 1964-65. Guest novelist in residence, University of Kansas, Lawrence, 1972. Lecturer on science fiction to universities and professional groups in the United States, England, and Italy. *Military service:* Royal Air Force, 1953-55; became pilot officer.

MEMBER: European Science Fiction Society (past joint president), World SF, Science Fiction Writers of America, Writers' Guild, Society of Authors, Science Fiction Foundation (past vice-president), British Science Fiction Association (past chairman), Herb Society, English Folk Dance & Song Society.

AWARDS, HONORS: British Fantasy Award, 1966; Hugo Award, 1968, for *Stand on Zanzibar;* received two British Science Fiction Awards; Prix Apollo; Bronze Porgie Award, *West Coast Review of Books;* Grand Prix du Festival de l'Insolite (France), Cometa d'Argento (twice); Premio Italia; European SF Convention Special Award as Best Western European SF Writer; Gilgamesh Award for Science Fiction (Spain); Clark Ashton Smith Award for fantasy poetry; elected Knight of Mark Twain (twice).

WRITINGS:

Horses at Home, Spring Books, 1958.
The Brink, Gollancz, 1959.
Echo in the Skull (bound with *Rocket to Limbo* by Alan E. Nourse), Ace Books, 1959, expanded version published as *Give Warning to the World,* DAW, 1974.
The Hundredth Millennium (bound with *Edge of Time* by David Grinnell), Ace Books, 1959, revised and enlarged edition of first title published as *Catch a Falling Star,* Ace Books, 1968, reprinted, Ballantine, 1982.
Threshold of Eternity (bound with *The War of Two Worlds* by Poul Andersen), Ace Books, 1959.
The World Swappers (bound with *The Siege of the Unseen* by A. E. Van Vogt), Ace Books, 1959.
Slavers of Space (bound with *Dr. Futurity* by Philip K. Dick), Ace Books, 1960, revised edition of first title published as *Into the Slave of Nebula,* Lancer Books, 1968, reprinted, Millington, 1980.
The Skynappers (bound with *Vulcan's Hammer* by Dick), Ace Books, 1960.
Sanctuary in the Sky (bound with *The Secret Martians* by Jack Sharkey), Ace Books, 1960.
The Atlantic Abomination (bound with *Martian Missile* by Grinnell), Ace Books, 1960, reprinted, 1976.
Meeting at Infinity (bound with *Beyond the Silver Sky* by Kenneth Bulmer), Ace Books, 1961.
Secret Agent of Terra (bound with *The Rim of Space* by A. B. Chandler), Ace Books, 1962, revised and enlarged edition published as *The Avengers of Carrig,* Dell, 1969.
The Super Barbarians, Ace Books, 1962.

Times without Number (bound with *Destiny's Orbit* by Grinnell), Ace Books, 1962, revised edition, 1969, reprinted, Ballantine, 1983.

No Future in It, and Other Science Fiction Stories, Gollancz, 1962, Doubleday, 1964.

The Dreaming Earth, Pyramid Books, 1963.

The Astronauts Must Not Land [and] *The Space-Time Juggler,* Ace Books, 1963, revised version of first title published as *More Things in Heaven,* Dell, 1973.

The Castaways' World [and] *The Rites of One,* Ace Books, 1963, revised edition of first title published as *Polymath,* DAW Books, 1978.

Listen! The Stars! (bound with *The Rebellers* by James Roberts), Ace Books, 1963, enlarged version published as *The Stardroppers,* DAW, 1972.

The Rites of Ohe, Ace Books, 1963.

Endless Shadow (bound with *The Arsenal of Miracles* by Gardner F. Fox), Ace Books, 1964, expanded version of first title published as *Manshape,* DAW, 1982.

The Crutch of Memory, Barrie & Rockliff, 1964.

To Conquer Chaos, Ace Books, 1964.

The Whole Man, Ballantine, 1964, published in England as *Telepathist,* Faber, 1965.

The Squares of the City, Ballantine, 1965.

The Long Result, Faber, 1965, Ballantine, 1981.

Now Then: Three Stories, Mayflower, 1965, Avon, 1968.

Wear the Butchers' Medal, Pocket Books, 1965.

The Altar on Asconel (bound with *Android Avenger* by Ted White), Ace Books, 1965.

Enigma from Tantalus, Ace Books, 1965.

The Repairmen of Cyclops, Ace Books, 1965.

The Day of the Star Cities, Ace Books, 1965.

A Planet of Your Own (bound with *Beast of Kohl* by John Rackham), Ace Books, 1966.

No Other Gods but Me, Compact Books, 1966.

Out of My Mind, Ballantine, 1967.

The Productions of Time, New American Library, 1967.

Quicksand, Doubleday, 1967.

Born under Mars, Ace Books, 1967.

Bedlam Planet, Ace Books, 1968, Ballantine, 1982.

Catch a Falling Star, Ace Books, 1968.

Into the Slave Nebula, Lancer Books, 1968.

Not before Time, New English Library, 1968.

Stand on Zanzibar, Doubleday, 1968, Ballantine, 1988.

Father of Lies (bound with *Mirror Image* by Bruce Duncan), Belmont Books, 1968.

A Plague on Both Your Causes, Hodder & Stoughton, 1969, published in the United States as *Blacklash,* Pyramid, 1969.

Black Is the Color, Pyramid, 1969.

Double, Double, Ballantine, 1969.

The Evil That Men Do (bound with *The Purloined Planet* by Lin Carter), Belmont-Tower, 1969.

Timescoop, Dell, 1969.

The Jagged Orbit, Ace Books, 1969.

Good Men Do Nothing, Hodder & Stoughton, 1970, Pyramid, 1971.

The Gaudy Shadows, Constable, 1970, Beagle Books, 1971.

The Devil's Work, Norton, 1970.

Honky in the Woodpile: A Max Curfew Thriller, Constable, 1971.

The Wrong End of Time, Doubleday, 1971.

Traveler in Black (short stories), Ace Books, 1971.

The Sheep Look Up, Harper, 1972.

Entry to Elsewhen (short stories), DAW Books, 1972.

From This Day Forward, Doubleday, 1972.

The Dramaturges of Yan, Ace Books, 1972, Ballantine, 1982.

Age of Miracles, Ace Books, 1973, revised version published as *The Crucible of Time,* Ballantine, 1984.

The Stone That Never Came Down, Doubleday, 1973.

Web of Everywhere, Bantam, 1974, published as *The Webs of Everywhere,* Del Rey, 1983.

The Shockwave Rider, Harper, 1975.

Total Eclipse, Weidenfeld & Nicolson, 1975, DAW Books, 1978.

The Book of John Brunner, DAW, 1976.

(Contributor) *The Craft of Science Fiction,* edited by R. Bretnor, Harper, 1976.

Interstellar Empire, DAW Books, 1978.

Tomorrow May Even Be Worse, NESFA Press, 1978.

Foreign Constellations: The Fantastic Worlds of John Brunner (short stories), Everest House, 1979.

The Infinitive of Go, Del Rey Books, 1980.

Players at the Game of People, Ballantine, 1980.

A New Settlement of Old Scores, New England Science Fiction Association, 1983.

The Great Steamboat Race, Ballantine, 1983.

The Tides of Time, Ballantine, 1984.

The Compleat Traveller in Black (short stories), Blue Jay Books, 1986.

The Shift Key, Methuen, 1987.

Children of the Thunder, Ballantine, 1989.

Also author of *The Best of John Brunner,* edited by Joe Haldeman, 1988.

UNDER PSEUDONYM KEITH WOODCOTT

I Speak for Earth (bound with *Wandl the Invader* by Ray Carmings), Ace Books, 1961.

The Ladder in the Sky (bound with *The Darkness before Tomorrow*) Ace Books, 1962, first title published separately, 1965.

The Psionic Menace (bound with *Captives of the Flame* by Samuel R. Delany), Ace Books, 1963.

The Martian Sphinx, Ace Books, 1965.

OTHER

Translator of *The Overlords of War* by Gerard Klein, *Femme Fatale* by Marrianne Leconte, and *Transisters* by Christine Renard; translator of poems by Rilke, George, Ausonius, and others. Stories appear in numerous anthologies including *Sixth Annual of the Year's Best SF, Yet More Penguin Science Fiction, More Adventures on Other Planets, Great Science Fiction Adventures,* and *Alien Worlds.* Also author of film scripts, including *The Terrornauts,* Amicus Productions, 1967; author of songs recorded by Pete Seeger and other performing artists. Contributor to many science fiction magazines, and to *Peace News, Aspects, Reason,* and other journals. Contributing editor, *Sanity,* 1964-73.

SIDELIGHTS: John Brunner has long been considered one of the more important and successful speculative and extrapolative science fiction writers in the world. In his fiction, Brunner projects many of the current sociological trends, such as environmental problems, into the near-future. In Joseph W. De Bolt's *The Happening Worlds of John Brunner,* contributor John R. Pfeiffer feels that "what is remarkable is Brunner's consistent grace and intelligibility in explaining and abstracting civilization just beyond the threshold of the present."

Writing in the same essay collection, Edward L. Lamie and Joe De Bolt both believe that "in the hands of a superior practitioner, the speculative and extrapolative nature of science fiction makes it an unparalleled tool for exploring the fundamental questions raised by the man-computer relationship and its societal consequences. John Brunner, whose works deal extensively with computers and their human effects, is especially well suited to be the focus of such an analysis. Few authors draw such complete and informed pictures of the computer in our future."

In recent years, Brunner has set his stories in the near-future which many reviewers feel is far more successful than his earlier style of setting his fiction in the far-future. One of these reviewers, William Brown, feels that Brunner is successful because he "does not play runaway games with his images of the future. Almost everything about them is closely related to the present. There is no escape into a Buck Rogers future where amazing new techniques influence behavior or where man has been transformed into a different creature. Brunner's plausible scenarios and characters can be taken seriously," Brown comments in *The Happening Worlds of John Brunner.*

Discussing the problems of projecting current trends into the near future, John Brunner told an interviewer for *Writer:* "Naturally, the problem is a tricky one—the moment you set a story even a single generation ahead of your time, you're by definition dealing with people whose prej-

udices and preferences are no longer the same as ours." Brown feels Brunner handles this problem of projection well. As he explains, Brunner's "stories are predicated on the basic condition of mankind as it has always been and, as Brunner projects, it always will be. The characters in Brunner's stories are governed by the basic needs, just as characters throughout history have been. They make human choices in the face of their predicaments, and that is what gives the reader such a high degree of catharsis, of pleasure through vicarious identification. Were Brunner to project a new breed of men into a new set of circumstances, the results would be disastrous."

Stand on Zanzibar, winner of the 1968 Hugo Award, is highly regarded by science fiction writers and is often used to represent the genre in college literature courses. Brunner's books play an important role not only in the field of science fiction, but also in the near-future world which they describe. For example, *The Shockwave Rider,* a 1975 work about a man who tampers with computer networks, gained national attention when a computer virus crashed systems around the country in November, 1988. It came to light that Robert Tappan Morris, the originator of the "virus" that was designed as a problem-solving challenge but somehow got out of hand, had been introduced to the subject of computer viruses by Brunner's book. *Los Angeles Times* reporter Paul Dean cites Brunner's comment following his meeting with Morris that for proving the vulnerability of computer-stored data, Morris "has definitely done a service to the public at large."

Brunner went on to say that the incident "is an awful warning to the people who have assumed blithely that they can run a modern society on the basis of secretive, computerized information." Computers have a two-fold impact on contemporary life, he explained. While they can make us better informed than people of the past, they can also be used to manipulate information in a way that puts us at great risk. As a result, he warns, "not just life and death of the individual, but life or death of the society is at stake."

BIOGRAPHICAL/CRITICAL SOURCES:

BOOKS

Benson, Gordon Jr., *John Kilian Houston Brunner,* Galactic Central, 1985.
Contemporary Authors Autobiography Series, Volume 8, Gale, 1988.
Contemporary Literary Criticism, Gale, Volume 8, 1978, Volume 10, 1979.
De Bolt, Joseph W., editor, *The Happening Worlds of John Brunner,* Kennikat, 1975.
Platt, Charles, *Dream Makers: The Uncommon People Who Write Science Fiction,* Berkley, 1980.

PERIODICALS

Arena Science Fiction, January, 1979 (interview).
Locus, April, 1978 (interview).
Los Angeles Times, November 9, 1988.
Mother Jones, August, 1976.
New Republic, October 30, 1976.
New York Times Book Review, October 27, 1968.
Science Fiction Review, January, 1979 (interview).
Writer, December, 1971.
Yale Review, March, 1973.

*   *   *

BRUST, Steven K. (Zoltan) 1955-

PERSONAL: Born November 23, 1955, in St. Paul, MN; son of William Z. (a professor) and Jean (Tilsen) Brust; married wife, Reen, December 29, 1974; children: Corwin Edward, Aliera Jean and Carolyn Rocza (twins), Antonia Eileen. *Education:* Control Data Institute, Programming Certificate (with honors), 1976; also attended University of Minnesota—Twin Cities. *Avocational interests:* Cooking, Shotokan Karate, fencing, Hungarian culture.

ADDRESSES: Home—3248 Portland Ave. S., Minneapolis, MN 55407. *Agent*—Valerie Smith, Rte. 44-55, RD Box 160, Modena NY 12548.

CAREER: Employed as systems programmer, 1976-86, including Network Systems, New Brighton, MN, 1983-86; full-time writer, 1986—. Former actor for local community theater; rock 'n' roll drummer; drummer for Middle-Eastern and Oriental dancers; folk guitarist, banjoist, singer, and songwriter.

MEMBER: Science Fiction Writers of America, Interstate Writers Workshop, Minnesota Science Fiction Society (executive vice-president), Pre-Joycean Fellowship.

WRITINGS:

FANTASY NOVELS

Jhereg, Ace Books, 1983.
To Rein in Hell, Steel Dragon, 1984.
Yendi, Ace Books, 1984.
Brokedown Palace, Ace Books, 1985.
Teckla, Ace Books, 1986.
The Sun, the Moon, and the Stars, Armadillo Press, 1987.
Taltos, Ace Books, 1988.
Cowboy Feng's Space Bar and Grille, Ace Books, 1990.
Phoenix, Ace Books, 1990.
The Phoenix Guards, Tor Books, 1991.
(With Megan Lindholm) *The Gypsy,* Tor Books, 1992.
Agyar, Tor Books, 1992.

OTHER

Work represented in anthologies, including *Liavek Anthology,* 1985.

WORK IN PROGRESS: Athyra, for Ace Books; *500 Years After,* for Tor Books.

SIDELIGHTS: Steven K. Brust once told *CA:* "It is clear to me that a novelist who is unwilling to tell a story is wasting his own and his reader's time. There is so much more that we, as writers, are able to do—but if we can't entertain we are in the wrong profession.

"It is very easy to cheat when writing fantasy—to say 'this is magic, it just works.' But if one is able to avoid this trap, one has the power to work real magic with the story. For me, magic must be either an alternate set of physical laws, used to express something about how we view our tools, or else a metaphor for Mystery, or the Unknown, or whatever. On the other hand, the metaphor itself can be a dangerous toy. There are many fantasy novels that are thinly disguised Christian metaphors. So I wrote *To Reign in Hell,* which is a Christian metaphor that is really a thinly disguised fantasy novel.

"Major influences in my work have been Mark Twain, Roger Zelazny, and my editor, Terri Windling. I admire writers, such as the above, who are able to write on several levels at once—*without* neglecting the most basic thing— telling a good story. It seems that, today, science fiction is one of the few areas where this is possible." Brust recently added: "There appears to be a split in literature between work with strong story values and nothing else, and work that has depth and power but no story values. The stuff I enjoy reading most can be read as simple entertainment but rewards more intense reading as well. Since I try to write the sort of stories I like to read, that is what I attempt to do in my own work. Science fiction is a category that allows and even encourages this, which is one of the reasons I write it."

*   *   *

BRYAN, Sharon 1943-

PERSONAL: Born February 10, 1943, in Salt Lake City, UT; daughter of Glen and Shirley (Storrs) Allen. *Education:* University of Utah, B.A., 1965; Cornell University, M.A., 1969; University of Iowa, M.F.A., 1977.

ADDRESSES: Home—1815 Overton Park, Memphis, TN 38112. *Office*—Department of English, Memphis State University, Memphis, TN 38152.

CAREER: Marlboro College, Marlboro, VT, member of English faculty, 1977-78; manuscript editor, *Journal of*

Asian Studies, 1978-80; University of Washington, Seattle, assistant professor of English, 1980-87; Memphis State University, associate professor of English, 1987—. Faculty member, Creative Writing Workshop, Fort Warden, WA, 1980, Spectrum Writers Conference, Seattle, 1983, and SUNY/Brockport Summer Writers Conference, 1991.

MEMBER: Poetry Society of America, Modern Language Association, Associated Writing Programs.

AWARDS, HONORS: Academy of American Poets prize, 1976, for "Big Sheep Knocks You About"; Discovery award, *Nation,* 1977; Governor's award, state of Washington, 1985, for *Salt Air;* Arvon Foundation prize, 1986; National Endowment for the Arts fellowship, 1987.

WRITINGS:

Salt Air (poems), Wesleyan University Press, 1983.
(Editor) *Intro 14,* Associated Writing Programs, 1983.
Objects of Affection, Wesleyan University Press, 1987.

Work represented several in anthologies, including *Bumbershoot Anthology,* Red Sky Press, 1984; *Morrow Anthology of Younger American Poets,* edited by Dave Smith and David Bottoms, 1984; *Anthology of Magazine Verse and Yearbook of American Poetry,* edited by Alan F. Pater, 1984; *Spectrum: A Reader,* edited by Ostrom, Garratt, and Turnbull, 1986; *Arvon Foundation 1985 Poetry Competition Anthology,* edited by David Pease, 1987; *University Press Anthology,* edited by Ronald Wallace, 1989; *Selections From University and College Poetry Prizes, 1973-1978,* Academy of American Poets.

Contributor of poems to literary magazines, including *American Poetry Review, Atlantic Monthly, Georgia Review, Ironwood Nation, Iowa Review, Ohio Review, Ploughshares, Poetry Northwest,* and *Seattle Review.*

WORK IN PROGRESS: Belongings, a book of poems.

SIDELIGHTS: Writing in the *New York Times Book Review,* Alan Williamson remarked that "one may be grateful for the cool, clear eye that Sharon Bryan brings to her native Utah in *Salt Air.*" Williamson, who favorably compared Bryan's work with that of late poet Elizabeth Bishop, further noted that Bryan is "a touching poet of light and shade."

BIOGRAPHICAL/CRITICAL SOURCES:

PERIODICALS

New York Times Book Review, November 13, 1983.
Poetry, April, 1984.

BURACK, Elmer H(oward) 1927-

PERSONAL: Born October 21, 1927, in Chicago, IL; son of Charles and Rose (Taerbaum) Burack; married Ruth Goldsmith; children: Charles M., Robert J., Alan J. *Education:* University of Illinois, B.S., 1950; Illinois Institute of Technology, M.S., 1956; Northwestern University, Ph.D., 1964.

ADDRESSES: Home—2755 Marl Oak Dr., Highland Park, IL 60035. *Office*—Department of Management, University of Illinois at Chicago Circle, Chicago, IL 60680.

CAREER: Chicago Molded Products, Chicago, IL, production supervisor, 1950-53; Richardson Co., Melrose Park, IL, production superintendent, 1953-55; Federal Tool Corp., Lincolnwood, IL, production manager, 1955-59; Booz, Allen & Hamilton, Chicago, consultant, 1959-60; Illinois Institute of Technology, Chicago, lecturer, 1960-64, associate professor, 1964-68, professor of management, 1968—, head of department, 1969-71; University of Illinois at Chicago Circle, Chicago, professor of management, 1978—, head of department, 1978-83, director of doctoral studies at College of Business Administration, 1990—. Associate chairman, Governor's Advisory Council on Manpower, 1978-83. *Military service:* U.S. Army Air Forces, 1945-47.

MEMBER: Academy of Management (chairperson, Personnel Division and Health Care Division; president, Personnel/Human Resource Division), Institute of Management Sciences, Personnel Accreditation Institute (founding member), Human Resource Planning Society, Association for Computing Machinery, American Institute of Decision Sciences, Midwest Academy of Management (president, 1971-72), Illinois Management Training Institute (president, 1979-80), Industrial Relations Associates of Chicago (president, 1974-75).

WRITINGS:

(With James Walker) *Manpower Planning and Programming,* Allyn & Bacon, 1972.
Strategies for Manpower Planning and Programming, General Learning, 1972.
Organization Analysis, Dryden, 1975.
(With R. D. Smith) *Personnel Management: A Human Resources Approach,* West Publishing, 1977.
(With A. Negandhi) *Organization Design: Theoretical Perspectives and Empirical Findings,* Kent State University Press, 1978.
Personnel Management: Cases and Exercises, West Publishing, 1978.
(With Florence Torda) *The Manager's Guide to Change,* Brace-Park, 1980.

(With Nicholas J. Mathys) *Human Resource Planning: A Pragmatic Approach to Manpower Staffing and Development,* Brace-Park, 1980, revised edition, 1987.

(With Mathys) *Career Management in Organizations: A Practical Human Resource Planning Approach,* Brace-Park, 1980.

(With others) *Growing: A Woman's Guide to Career Satisfaction,* Van Nostrand, 1980.

Career Planning and Management: A Managerial Summary, Brace-Park, 1983.

Planning for Human Resources: A Managerial Summary, Brace-Park, 1983.

Creative Human Resource Planning and Applications: A Strategic Approach, Prentice-Hall, 1988.

(Co-author) *After the Reckoning,* Jossey-Bass, 1992.

Contributor of papers and reviews to periodicals, including *Academy of Management Journal, Human Resource Planning Journal,* and *Human Resource Development Quarterly.* Consulting editor and member of editorial review boards involving human resource planning, health care administration, and strategic management.

*   *   *

BURKHOLDER, John Richard   1928-

PERSONAL: Born December 19, 1928, in Lancaster, PA; son of Clarence A. (a contractor) and Blanche (a housewife; maiden name, Herr) Burkholder; married Susan Elizabeth Herr (a teacher), June 6, 1952; children: Evelyn Burkholder King, Lissa, Samuel, Rebecca, Peter. *Education:* Goshen College, B.A., 1952, B.D., 1955; Harvard University, Ph.D., 1969.

ADDRESSES: Home—1508 South 14th St., Goshen, IN 46526.

CAREER: Ordained Mennonite minister, 1954; Mennonite missionary and teacher in Goiania, Brazil, 1954-57; church administrator in Philadelphia, PA, 1958-60; Goshen College, Goshen, IN, assistant professor, 1963-67, associate professor, 1969-73, professor of religion, 1973-85, chairman of department of religion, 1975-77, director of peace studies, 1975-85; Associated Mennonite Biblical Seminaries, Elkhart, IN, professor of ethics and director of peace studies, 1988-90; Mennonite Board of Congregational Ministries, Elkhart, coordinator for peace and social concerns, 1991—. Bluffton and Goshen Colleges, C. Henry Smith Lecturer, 1984-85; Dallas Peace Center, director, 1982-84. Consultant in peace issues for Mennonite Central Committee, 1985—.

MEMBER: Society of Christian Ethics, Consortium for Peace Research, Education, and Development, Fellowship of Reconciliation (member of national council, 1965-73).

WRITINGS:

(With John Bender) *Children of Peace,* Herald Press, 1982.

Mennonites in Ecumenical Dialogue on Peace and Justice, Mennonite Central Committee, 1988.

(Editor with Barbara Nelson Gingerich, and contributor) *Mennonite Peace Theology: A Panorama of Types,* Mennonite Central Committee Peace Office, 1991.

Also contributor of chapters to books, 1975-90. Contributor to academic and religion journals.

WORK IN PROGRESS: Research on current issues in religious freedom and church-state conflict, personal transformation and action for social change, and alternatives to violence in social conflict.

*   *   *

BURNETT, Hallie Southgate (Zeisel)

PERSONAL: Born in St. Louis, MO; daughter of John McKnight (a consulting engineer) and Elizabeth (Baker) Southgate; married Whit Burnett (a writer and editor), 1942 (died April 22, 1973); married William Zeisel, 1977 (died, 1981); children: (first marriage) John Southgate, Whitney Ann. *Politics:* Independent. *Religion:* Episcopal.

CAREER: Story Press Books, editor, New York City, 1942-65; *Story* magazine, New York City, co-editor, 1942-70; Book-of-the-Month Club, reader, 1957-59; Prentice-Hall, Inc., Englewood Cliffs, NJ, senior editor, 1959-60; Sarah Lawrence College, Bronxville, NY, associate professor of literature and creative writing, 1960-64. Conductor of fiction workshop at New York City Writer's Conference, Wagner College, 1955-60; instructor in short story writing at Hunter College of the City University of New York, 1959-61; lecturer on creative writing at University of Cincinnati, University of Missouri, and other universities and colleges.

MEMBER: PEN (director, 1951-71), Woman Pays Club, Overseas Press Club.

AWARDS, HONORS: O. Henry Award (third prize), 1942, for "Eighteenth Summer."

WRITINGS:

(Editor with Eleanor Gilchrist) *Welcome to Life!,* Fell, 1948.

A Woman in Possession (novel), Dutton, 1951.

This Heart, This Hunter (novel), Holt, 1953.

The Brain Pickers (novel), Messner, 1957.

(With husband, Whit Burnett) *The Modern Short Story in the Making,* Hawthorn, 1964.

The Watch on the Wall (novel), Morrow, 1965.

The Boarders in the Rue Madame: Nine Gallic Tales, Morrow, 1966.

The Daughter-in-Law Cookbook, Hewitt House, 1969.

The Millionaire's Cookbook, Pyramid Publications, 1973.

(With Burnett) *Fiction Writer's Handbook,* Harper, 1975.

On Writing the Short Story, Harper, 1983.

EDITOR WITH HUSBAND, WHIT BURNETT

Story: The Fiction of the Forties, Dutton, 1949.

Sextet: Six Story Discoveries in the Novella Form, McKay, 1951.

Story, four volumes, McKay, 1951-54.

The Tough Ones: A Collection of Realistic Short Stories, Popular Library, 1954.

19 Tales of Terror, Bantam, 1957.

The Fiction of a Generation, two volumes, MacGibbon & Kee, 1959.

Things with Claws, Ballantine, 1961.

Best College Writing, 1961, Random House, 1962.

Prize College Stories, Random House, 1963.

The Stone Soldier, Fleet Press, 1964.

Story Jubilee: Thirty-Three Years of Story, Doubleday, 1965.

Story: The Yearbook of Discovery (College Creative Awards selections), Four Winds, 1968-71.

OTHER

Contributor of book reviews to *New York Times, Saturday Review,* and *Book of the Month;* contributor of articles and short stories to *Town and Country* and other magazines. Contributing editor, *Junior League* magazine, 1937-42; fiction editor, *Yankee,* 1959-60; has held editorial post on *Reader's Digest Book Club.*

WORK IN PROGRESS: Short stories; an autobiography.

SIDELIGHTS: Hallie Southgate Burnett once told *CA:* "[I] have only one recurring problem: what to put on a passport as occupation. [I] have tried editor, novelist, short story writer, college professor, and housewife and finally settled for the latter, as nobody is very impressed anyway.

"I write hard, look soft, think clear, talk vague, and generally wish I had the exterior of somebody else, preferably thinner. I prefer young people to old, old books to new (although I find young talent the most exciting thing in the world), and I hope I never die—at least until I have made a hundred more trips to Europe and at least one around the world."

Burnett's novel, *The Watch on the Wall,* has been translated into German, Japanese, and Portuguese.*

BUTTERWORTH, Oliver   1915-1990

PERSONAL: Born May 23, 1915, in Hartford, CT; died of cancer, September 17, 1990, in West Hartford, CT; son of Paul McMillan and Clarabel (Smith) Butterworth; married Mariam Brooks, 1940; children: Michael, Timothy, Dan, Kate. *Education:* Dartmouth College, A.B., 1937; graduate study at Harvard University, 1941; Middlebury College, M.A., 1947. *Avocational interests:* Camping, traveling, mountain climbing.

ADDRESSES: Home—81 Sunset Farm Rd., West Hartford, CT 06107. *Office*—Hartford College, 1265 Asylum Ave., Hartford, CT.

CAREER: Educator and author of children's books. Teacher at Kent School, Kent, CT, 1937-47; at Junior School, West Hartford, CT, 1947-49; and teacher of English at Hartford College for Women, Hartford, CT, beginning in 1947 until the late 1980s. Hartford College for Women, trustee; Mark Twain Memorial, trustee, 1958-62.

AWARDS, HONORS: New York Herald Tribune Spring Festival of Books prize, 1960, for *The Trouble with Jenny's Ear;* Lewis Carroll Shelf award, 1970, for *The Enormous Egg.*

WRITINGS:

The Enormous Egg, illustrated by Louis Darling, Little, Brown, 1956.

The Trouble with Jenny's Ear, illustrated by Julian de Miskey, Little Brown, 1960.

The Narrow Passage, illustrated by Erik Blegvad, Little, Brown, 1973.

(And illustrator) *The First Blueberry Pig,* Stone Man Press (Lubec, ME), 1986.

A Visit to the Big House, illustrated by Vinny Collins, Families in Crisis (Hartford, CT), 1987.

Also author of *Orrie's Run.*

ADAPTATIONS: The Enormous Egg was filmed for television.

SIDELIGHTS: An educator his entire life, Oliver Butterworth wrote his first book at the age of forty. At the time, repetition of words was thought to be the best way of introducing children to reading. "They were prefabricated books with phrases like 'Look, look Jane,' in them," he told Maureen M. Gallagher in a *Hartford Courant* interview. "I thought if I could write a book that sounded like a 12-year-old talking, then children would like it. It seemed to work. It came as a great surprise." The book, *The Enormous Egg,* has become a classic in children's literature and tells about a barnyard hen that lays and tends a large egg until it hatches into a tiny dinosaur. When the dinosaur, known as Uncle Beasley, quickly grows and threatens to eat the state of New Hampshire, a publicity-hungry senator proposes turning it into a museum exhibit. According to Gallagher, the book was Butterworth's response to the menace of then Senator Joseph McCarthy and his search for communists in the 1950s. "I saw him as a bully. He was throwing his weight around—getting teachers and books thrown out of school. It finally occurred to me that I had no way to confront him except to write about him."

Butterworth considered writing for children "like talking to yourself and keeping one ear cocked to children," and indicated to Gallagher that this also meant listening to their concerns. When a young girl once asked him about why little girls in his books had things happen to them while the boys were active, Butterworth admitted that in this respect, *The Enormous Egg* was "terrible" and that he was "ashamed of it." But in the estimation of Joan McGrath in *Twentieth-Century Children's Writers*, "Butterworth has earned a lasting place in the hearts of child readers" because of his "rare ability to recall the substance of childhood dreams of glory; finding treasure, making contact with the unreachable past; controlling the omnipresent adult population, and setting it gently but firmly in its (subordinate) place." In the *Fourth Book of Junior Authors and Illustrators,* Butterworth, a lifelong lover of nature and history, outlined his aims of sharing his feelings and ideas, "to tell children (and perhaps grown-ups too) about what's precious to me, about the colors of life, the green freedom of leaves and grass, the gray blue of hills and streams, the bone white color of honesty, the flesh tones of the warm pulse of families together . . . and the true blue of courage to speak up for what you think is right."

BIOGRAPHICAL/CRITICAL SOURCES:

BOOKS

Fourth Book of Junior Authors and Illustrators, edited by Doris de Montreville and Elizabeth D. Crawford, Wilson, 1978.
Twentieth-Century Children's Writers, 3rd edition, St. James Press, 1989.

PERIODICALS

Bulletin of the Center for Children's Books, October, 1973.
Hartford Courant, May 13, 1979, p. E1.
Horn Book, June, 1973.
Publisher's Weekly, March 26, 1973.*

C

CARR, J(ames Joseph) L(loyd) 1912-

PERSONAL: Born May 20, 1912, in Thirsk, England; son of Joseph and Elizabeth (Welbourn) Carr; married Sally Sexton; children: Robert Duane. *Education:* Attended grammar school in Castleford, England.

ADDRESSES: Home—27 Milldale Rd., Kettering, Northamptonshire, England. *Agent*—Quince Tree Press, 27 Milldale Rd., Kettering, Northamptonshire, England.

CAREER: Teacher in Hampshire, England, 1933-35, and Birmingham, England, 1935-40; high school teacher in Huron, SD, 1938-39; teacher of English grammar in South Dakota, 1956-57; writer. *Military service:* Royal Air Force, 1940-46; became flight lieutenant.

AWARDS, HONORS: Guardian Prize for fiction, 1988, for *A Month in the Country: A Month in the Country* and *The Battle of Pollock's Crossing* were named on the Booker Prize short list.

WRITINGS:

NONFICTION

The Old Timers, privately printed, 1957.
Dictionary of Extra-Ordinary Cricketers, Milldale Press, 1977, reprinted as *Carr's Dictionary of Extra-Ordinary Cricketers,* Quartet Books/Solo, 1983.
Carr's Dictionary of English Queens, King's Wives, Celebrated Paramours, Handfast Spouses, and Royal Changelings, Milldale Press, 1977.
Dictionary of English Kings, Milldale Press, 1979.
Sydney Smith: The Smith of Smiths, Milldale Press, 1980.

NOVELS

A Day in Summer, Barrie & Rockliff, 1964, reprinted, Hogarth Press, 1986.
A Season in Sinji, London Magazine Editions, 1967.

The Harpole Report, Secker & Warburg, 1972, Penguin Books, 1984.
How Steeple Sinderby Wanders Won the F.A. Cup, London Magazine Editions, 1975.
A Month in the Country, Harvester Press, 1980, St. Martin's Press, 1980.
The Battle of Pollocks Crossing, Viking, 1985, Penguin Books, 1986.
What Hetty Did, Quince Tree Press, 1988.

JUVENILE

The Red Windcheater, Macmillan, 1970.
Red Foal's Coat, Macmillan, 1973.
The Old Farm Cart, Macmillan, 1973.
An Ear-Ring for Anna Beer, Macmillan, 1976.
The Green Children of the Woods, Longman, 1976.
Gone With the Whirlwind, Macmillan, 1980.

ADAPTATIONS: A Month in the Country was adapted for film by Simon Gray, and released by Orion Classics, 1988.

SIDELIGHTS: J. L. Carr "is a rare and precious specimen," writes Eric Korn in the *Times Literary Supplement.* Choosing to escape the strictures of urban life, Carr has planted himself in the quiet Northants village of Kettering, where he has published a great quantity of material—from architectural and historical county maps to various booklets—all from a back bedroom in his home. After a teaching career spanning two continents, which has provided the basis for much of Carr's quasi-autobiographical fiction, he came to novel-writing while in his forties, composing his original prose within a unique publishing format.

Carr's works have been acclaimed for their quiet illuminations and their expression of the inexpressible nuances of time, history, and human emotion. "[B]ehind the seeming artlessness one is always aware . . . of a highly self-conscious artificer," writes Francis King of *The Spectator;* "and behind the seeming eccentricity one is always aware . . . of someone extremely practical and shrewd. Carr . . . may constantly surprise and disconcert one by doing things, whether in [his] novels or in [his life], in a totally idiosyncratic manner; but [he] usually [does] them more capably than people thought to be far more professional and worldly."

BIOGRAPHICAL/CRITICAL SOURCES:

PERIODICALS

Los Angeles Times, March 25, 1988.
Spectator, February 20, 1988.
Times (London), May 30, 1985.
Times Literary Supplement, August 9, 1985; March 25, 1988.

*   *   *

CARRICK, Carol (Hatfield) 1935-

PERSONAL: Born May 20, 1935, in Queens, NY; daughter of Chauncey L. (a salesman) and Elsa (Schweizer) Hatfield; married Donald Carrick (an artist), March 26, 1965 (died June 26, 1989); children: Christopher, Paul. *Education:* Hofstra University, B.A., 1957.

ADDRESSES: Home—High St., Edgarton, MA 02539.

CAREER: Coronet, New York City, staff artist, 1958-60; H. Allen Lightman (advertising agency), New York City, staff artist, 1960-61; free-lance artist, 1961-65; writer for children, 1965—.

AWARDS, HONORS: Children's Book of the Year award from Library of Congress, 1974, for *Lost in the Storm,* 1980, for *The Climb,* and 1983, for *Patrick's Dinosaurs;* Children's Book of the Year from Child Study Association, 1974, for *Lost in the Storm,* 1975, for *The Blue Lobster,* 1976, for *The Accident,* 1979, for *A Rabbit for Easter* and *Some Friend!,* 1980, for *The Climb,* 1981, for *The Empty Squirrel, The Accident,* and *Ben and the Porcupine,* 1983, for *What a Wimp!* and *Two Coyotes,* 1985, for *Beach Bird* and *Stay Away from Simon!,* and 1987, for *The Foundling;* Children's Book Showcase from the Children's Book Council, 1975, for *Lost in the Storm,* 1976, for *The Blue Lobster: A Life Cycle,* and 1978, for *The Washout;* Outstanding Science Trade Book for Children from the National Science Teachers Association and the Children's Book Council, 1975, for *The Blue Lobster,* and 1980, for *The Crocodiles Still Wait;* New York Academy of Sciences Children's Science Book Award Junior Honor Book, 1975, and one of the Best Children's Books of the Season from *Saturday Review,* 1976, both for *The Blue Lobster;* Children's Choice from the International Reading Associ-

ation and the Children's Book Council, 1975, for *The Blue Lobster,* 1978, for *The Sand Tiger Shark,* 1979, for *Octopus* and *Paul's Christmas Birthday,* and 1982, for *The Empty Squirrel; The Crocodiles Still Wait* was selected one of the *New York Times*'s Best Books of the Year, 1980; New York English-Speaking Union Books-across-the-Sea Ambassador of Honor Book, 1982, for *Ben and the Porcupine; Stay Away from Simon!* was selected one of *School Library Journal*'s Best Books of the Year, 1985, and *What Happened to Patrick's Dinosaurs?,* 1986; *Stay Away from Simon!* was selected one of the New York Public Library's Children's Books, 1985; *What Happened to Patrick's Dinosaurs?* was selected one of the *New York Times*'s Notable Books, 1986; California Young Readers Medal from the California Reading Association, 1989, for *What Happened to Patrick's Dinosaurs?*

WRITINGS:

JUVENILES; ILLUSTRATED BY HUSBAND, DONALD CARRICK

The Old Barn, Bobbs-Merrill, 1966.
The Brook, Macmillan, 1967.
Swamp Spring, Macmillan, 1969.
The Pond, Macmillan, 1970.
The Dirt Road, Macmillan, 1970.
A Clearing in the Forest, Dial, 1970.
The Dragon of Santa Lalia, Bobbs-Merrill, 1971.
Sleep Out, Seabury, 1973.
Beach Bird, Dial, 1973.
Lost in the Storm, Seabury, 1974.
Old Mother Witch, Seabury, 1975.
The Blue Lobster: A Life Cycle, Dial, 1975.
The Accident, Seabury, 1976.
The Sand Tiger Shark, Seabury, 1977.
The Highest Balloon on the Common, Greenwillow, 1977.
The Foundling, Seabury, 1977.
Octopus, Seabury, 1978.
The Washout, Seabury, 1978.
Paul's Christmas Birthday, Greenwillow, 1978.
A Rabbit for Easter, Greenwillow, 1979.
Some Friend!, Houghton, 1979.
What a Wimp!, Clarion Books, 1979.
The Crocodiles Still Wait, Houghton, 1980.
The Climb, Clarion Books, 1980.
Ben and the Porcupine, Clarion Books, 1981.
The Empty Squirrel, Greenwillow, 1981.
The Longest Float in the Parade, Greenwillow, 1982.
Two Coyotes, Clarion Books, 1982.
Patrick's Dinosaurs, Clarion Books, 1983.
Dark and Full of Secrets, Clarion Books, 1984.
Stay Away from Simon, Clarion Books, 1985.
What Happened to Patrick's Dinosaurs?, Clarion Books, 1986.
The Elephant in the Dark, Clarion Books, 1988.
Left Behind, Clarion Books, 1988.

Big Old Bones: A Dinosaur Tale, Clarion Books, 1989.
Aladdin and the Wonderful Lamp, Scholastic Books, Inc., 1989.
In the Moonlight, Waiting, Clarion Books, 1990.

Carrick's books have been translated into Swedish, Finnish, Danish, German, and Japanese; a collection of her manuscripts is kept in the University of Minnesota's Kerlan Collection.

ADAPTATIONS: The Accident (videocassette), Barr Films, 1985; *The Foundling* (videocassette), Grey Haven Films, 1986, (cassette), Houghton, 1990; *Patrick's Dinosaurs* (cassette), Houghton, 1987; *What Happened to Patrick's Dinosaurs?* (cassette), Houghton, 1988; *Old Mother Witch* (videocassette), Phoenix, 1989; *Sleep Out* (cassette), Houghton, 1989; *Lost in the Storm* (cassette), 1990.

WORK IN PROGRESS: Three picture books, *Banana Brew,* depicting what life is like for the child of an alcoholic father, *Norman and the Tooth Fairy,* a humorous look at a child who tries to fool the tooth fairy before he has actually lost his first tooth, and *Whaling Days,* a book about American whaling.

SIDELIGHTS: A winner of numerous children's literature awards, Carol Carrick is the author of fiction and nature books. Although she originally trained to be an artist and has had several years' experience in doing advertising and free-lance art, until recently the illustrations for her books were created by her husband, Donald. Donald Carrick died of cancer in 1989, but despite this personal and professional loss Carrick has continued to write for children.

Carrick grew up in Queens, New York, at a time when ponds and woods could still be found in New York City's suburbs. Her family lived near a pond where she found tadpoles, turtles, and, in the surrounding trees, cocoons, all of which she would often take home and try to raise. It was the happiness she found in walking through this next-door natural setting that inspired her later in life to write her nature books, including her acclaimed work, *The Blue Lobster: A Life Cycle.* When she was a child, however, nature books for children were rare; she could not find any books to tell her how to raise her little pets, so most of them died. "Those early disappointments caused me a lot of grief," Carrick once commented in an interview for *Something about the Author,* "and prompted me to make my nature books as accurate as possible."

The career that Carrick originally chose was not writing. She studied art while in college, working as an artist for several years before meeting her husband. Carol offered to write the text for a children's book Donald had been commissioned to illustrate, even though she had never written a book before. Neither Donald nor Carol had any experience in writing for children, and at first they were not even sure what they were going to write about. But Carol did know that she wanted to do some sort of nature-related book, and so the two collaborators eventually came up with *The Old Barn.* "I don't have a great sense of fantasy, so I never really thought of myself as a writer," she once said. "After our first book I never believed there would be another one. As a matter of fact, I fear that every book is the last book for me."

Carol and Donald were married before they first started work on *The Old Barn,* and by the time they finished they had reached the next milestone in their lives. "We signed our first contract when I was in the hospital having our first baby," Carrick recalls in *Junior Literary Guild.* With the addition of two sons to the family, Carrick's interests in writing subjects began to switch from nature stories to stories about children. They were a good source of inspiration for her writing, and Carrick admits that she stole material from their little day-to-day adventures. "*The Empty Squirrel,* for example, concerns a boy who nurses a fish back to health because his mother didn't want to cook it," relates Carrick in her interview. "That really happened to us."

But when her sons grew older than her characters, Carrick ran out of raw material for her writing. "If I had had a daughter, I probably would have gone into writing a teenage book because she would have rekindled things from my childhood." Instead, Carrick wrote her first historical book, *Stay Away from Simon!,* which is set in the nineteenth century and gave the author an ideal opportunity to exercise the meticulous research skills she had first honed with her nature books.

Carrick's favorite books are *Patrick's Dinosaurs* and *What Happened to Patrick's Dinosaurs?* because their element of fantasy made them the most fun to write. She hopes to write more books like these in the future, as well as more nature books. Without her husband to illustrate them, though, Carrick feels her books will never be quite the same. "Donald was skilled at drawing a wide range of subjects: children, nature, humor. To find somebody else who can do all of those thing," she concludes, "is unlikely."

BIOGRAPHICAL/CRITICAL SOURCES:

BOOKS

Something about the Author, Volume 63, Gale, 1991.

PERIODICALS

Children's Literature in Education, Volume 11, number 3, 1980.
Junior Literary Guild, September, 1979; March, 1981; April/September, 1986; April/September, 1988.

New York Times Book Review, May 4, 1975; July 7, 1977; April 30, 1978; November 13, 1983; April 27, 1986.

*   *   *

CARRICK, Donald (F.)   1929-1989

PERSONAL: Born April 7, 1929, in Dearborn, MI; died of cancer, June 26, 1989, in Edgartown, MA; son of Fay and Blanche (Soper) Carrick; married Carol Hatfield (a writer), March 26, 1965; children: Christopher, Paul. *Education:* Attended Colorado Springs Fine Art Center, 1948-49, Arts Student League, 1950, and Vienna Academy of Fine Arts, 1953-54.

CAREER: Artist; author and illustrator of children's books; once worked as an advertising artist in Detroit, MI, and New York City. Has had his work exhibited at the American Federation of Arts National Traveling Exhibition, 1970, Fleming Museum, Burlington, VT, 1971, and several other one-man shows in the United States and Europe. *Military service:* U.S. Army, 1950-51; served in Germany.

AWARDS, HONORS: Child Study Association of America's Children's Books of the Year, 1969, for *The Buffalo King, Tor,* and *City in All Directions,* 1970, for *The Cuban Revolution,* 1971, for *The Tree* and *Journey to Topaz,* 1973, for *Peter and Mr. Brandon* and *Bear Mouse,* 1974, for *Lost in the Storm,* 1975, for *The Blue Lobster: A Life Cycle* and *Grizzly Bear,* 1976, for *Wind, Sand and Sky, The Deer in the Pasture,* and *The Accident,* 1979, for *The Blue Horse and Other Night Poems, A Rabbit for Easter,* and *Some Friend!,* 1981, for *The Empty Squirrel* and *Ben and the Porcupine,* 1983, for *What a Wimp!,* and 1985, for *Beach Bird* and *Stay Away from Simon!;* New York Society of Illustrators Award, 1970, for *The Pond,* and 1971, for *The Tree; New York* was included in the American Institute of Graphic Arts Children's Book Show, 1970, and *Bear Mouse,* 1973-74; Irma Simonton Black Award from Bank Street College of Education, 1973, for *Bear Mouse,* and 1986, for *Doctor Change;* Children's Book Showcase selection from the Children's Book Council, 1974, for *Bear Mouse,* 1975, for *Lost in the Storm,* 1976, for *The Blue Lobster: A Life Cycle,* and 1978, for *The Washout;* Children's Book of the Year from Library of Congress, 1974, for *Lost in the Storm;* Outstanding Science Trade Book for Children from the National Science Teachers Association and the Children's Book Council, 1975, for *The Blue Lobster: A Life Cycle,* and 1980, for *The Crocodiles Still Wait;* Best of the Season from *Saturday Review,* 1975, for *The Blue Lobster: A Life Cycle;* Children's Choice from the International Reading Association and the Children's Book Council, 1975, for *The Blue Lobster: A Life Cycle,* 1978, for *The Sand Tiger Shark,* 1979, for

Octopus, Paul's Christmas Birthday, and *Tawny,* 1982, for *The Empty Squirrel,* and 1985, for *Secrets of a Small Brother* and *Dark and Full of Secrets;* Children's Science Book Award Junior Honor Book from the New York Academy of Sciences, 1976, for *The Blue Lobster: A Life Cycle; Tawny* was selected one of the *New York Times*'s Outstanding Books of the Year, 1978; *The Crocodiles Still Wait* was selected one of the *New York Times*'s Best Books of the Year, 1980; New York English-Speaking Union Books-across-the-Sea Ambassador of Honor Book, 1982, for *Ben and the Porcupine; Alex Remembers* was selected one of the New York Public Library's Children's Books, 1983, and *Stay Away from Simon!,* 1985; *More Alex and the Cat* was selected one of *School Library Journal*'s Best Books of the Year, 1983, *Stay Away from Simon!,* 1985, and *What Happened to Patrick's Dinosaurs?,* 1986; Christopher Award, 1985, for *Secrets of a Small Brother; What Happened to Patrick's Dinosaurs?* was selected one of the *New York Times*'s Notable Books, 1986; California Young Reader's Medal from the California Reading Association, 1989, for *What Happened to Patrick's Dinosaurs?*

WRITINGS:

SELF-ILLUSTRATED JUVENILES

The Tree, Macmillan, 1971.
Drip Drop, Macmillan, 1973.
The Deer in the Pasture, Greenwillow, 1976.
Harald and the Giant Knight, Clarion, 1982.
Morgan and the Artist, Clarion, 1985.
Milk, Greenwillow, 1985.
Harald and the Great Stag, Clarion, 1988.

ILLUSTRATOR; JUVENILES WRITTEN BY WIFE, CAROL CARRICK

The Old Barn, Bobbs-Merrill, 1966.
The Brook, Macmillan, 1967.
Swamp Spring, Macmillan, 1969.
The Pond, Macmillan, 1970.
The Dirt Road, Macmillan, 1970.
A Clearing in the Forest, Dial, 1970.
The Dragon of Santa Lalia, Bobbs-Merrill, 1971.
Sleep Out, Seabury, 1973.
Beach Bird, Dial, 1973.
Lost in the Storm, Seabury, 1974.
Old Mother Witch, Seabury, 1975.
The Blue Lobster: A Life Cycle, Dial, 1975.
The Accident, Seabury, 1976.
The Sand Tiger Shark, Seabury, 1977.
The Highest Balloon on the Common, Greenwillow, 1977.
The Foundling, Seabury, 1977.
Octopus, Seabury, 1978.
The Washout, Seabury, 1978.
Paul's Christmas Birthday, Greenwillow, 1978.
A Rabbit for Easter, Greenwillow, 1979.

Some Friend!, Houghton, 1979.

What a Wimp!, Clarion Books, 1979.

The Crocodiles Still Wait, Houghton, 1980.

The Climb, Clarion Books, 1980.

Ben and the Porcupine, Clarion Books, 1981.

The Empty Squirrel, Greenwillow, 1981.

The Longest Float in the Parade, Greenwillow, 1982.

Two Coyotes, Clarion Books, 1982.

Patrick's Dinosaurs, Clarion Books, 1983.

Dark and Full of Secrets, Clarion Books, 1984.

Stay Away from Simon!, Clarion Books, 1985.

What Happened to Patrick's Dinosaurs?, Clarion Books, 1986.

The Elephant in the Dark, Clarion Books, 1988.

Left Behind, Clarion Books, 1988.

Big Old Bones: A Dinosaur Tale, Clarion Books, 1989.

Aladdin and the Wonderful Lamp, Scholastic Books, Inc., 1989.

In the Moonlight, Waiting, Clarion Books, 1990.

ILLUSTRATOR

Robert Goldston, *The Civil War in Spain,* Bobbs-Merrill, 1966.

Goldston, *The Russian Revolution,* Bobbs-Merrill, 1966.

Goldston, *The Rise of Red China,* Bobbs-Merrill, 1967.

Goldston, *The Life and Death of Nazi Germany,* Bobbs-Merrill, 1967.

Goldston, *The Great Depression: The United States in the Thirties,* Bobbs-Merrill, 1968.

London: The Civic Spirit, Macmillan, 1969.

Barcelona: The Civic Stage, Macmillan, 1969.

Ernestine Byrd, *Tor: Wyoming Bighorn,* Scribner, 1969.

Arnold Adoff, editor, *City in All Directions: An Anthology of Modern Poems,* Macmillan, 1969.

Goldston, *The Cuban Revolution,* Bobbs-Merrill, 1970.

Goldston, *New York: Civic Exploitation,* Macmillan, 1970.

Goldston, *Suburbia: Civic Denial,* Macmillan, 1970.

Lee McGiffin, *Yankee Doodle Dandies,* Dutton, 1970.

Nancy Veglahn, *The Buffalo King: The Story of Scotty Philip,* Scribner, 1971.

Yoshiko Uchida, *Journey to Topaz,* Scribner, 1971, revised edition, Creative Arts Book Co., 1985.

Berniece Freschet, *Turtle Pond,* Scribner, 1971.

Freschet, *Bear Mouse,* Scribner, 1973.

Eleanor Schick, *Peter and Mr. Brandon,* Macmillan, 1973.

David Budbill, *The Christmas Tree Farm,* Macmillan, 1974.

Freschet, *Grizzly Bear,* Scribner, 1975.

Rebecca Caudill, *Wind, Sand and Sky,* Dutton, 1976.

Nathan Zimelman, *Walls Are to Be Walked,* Dutton, 1977.

Joanne Ryder, *A Wet and Sandy Day,* Harper, 1977.

Chas Carner, *Tawny,* Macmillan, 1978.

Siv Cedering Fox, *The Blue Horse and Other Night Poems,* Seabury, 1979.

Betty Baker, *Latki and the Lightning Lizard,* Macmillan, 1979.

Helen R. Haddad, *Truck and Loader,* Greenwillow, 1982.

Helen V. Griffith, *Alex Remembers,* Greenwillow, 1983.

Griffith, *More Alex and the Cat,* Greenwillow, 1983.

Richard J. Margolis, *Secrets of a Small Brother,* Macmillan, 1984.

Marlene F. Shyer, *Here I Am, an Only Child,* Scribner, 1985.

Johanna Hurwitz, *Yellow Blue Jay,* Morrow, 1986.

Joanna Cole, *Doctor Change,* Morrow, 1986.

Hurwitz, *Bunkmates,* Scholastic, 1987.

Eve Bunting, *Ghost's Hour, Spook's Hour,* Clarion, 1987.

William H. Hooks, *Moss Gown,* Clarion, 1987.

Joan Hewett, *Rosalie,* Lothrop, 1987.

Jim Latimer, *Going the Moose Way Home,* Scribner, 1988.

Steven Kroll, *Big Jeremy,* Holiday House, 1989.

Bunting, *The Wednesday Surprise,* Clarion, 1989.

Latimer, *When Moose Was Young,* Scribner, 1990.

OTHER

Collections of Carrick's work are kept at the Pennsylvania Academy of the Fine Arts in Philadelphia, PA, the Mazda Collection, and the Kerlan Collection at the University of Minnesota.

ADAPTATIONS: The Accident (videocassette), Barr Films, 1985; *The Foundling* (videocassette), Grey Haven Films, 1986, (cassette), Houghton, 1990; *Patrick's Dinosaurs* (cassette), Houghton, 1987; *What Happened to Patrick's Dinosaurs?* (cassette), Houghton, 1988; *Old Mother Witch* (videocassette), Phoenix, 1989; *Sleep Out* (cassette), Houghton, 1989; *Lost in the Storm* (cassette), 1990; *Moss Gown* (cassette), Houghton, 1990; *Ghost's Hour, Spook's Hour* (cassette), Houghton, 1990.

SIDELIGHTS: The illustrator of over eighty books, including thirty-seven by his wife, Carol, and seven of his own stories, Donald Carrick was a prolific artist and winner of numerous awards, including a Christopher Award for *Secrets of a Small Brother.* He was also a noted landscape artist and held several one-man exhibitions of his work in New York City, New England, and Europe.

Carrick began drawing as a child growing up in Dearborn, Michigan, but he first put his creative skills to use as a high school student working as an apprentice sign painter. Traveling around Michigan, he spent his summers and weekends painting billboards. This led him eventually to take a job as an advertising artist in Detroit, and later—after serving in Germany with the U.S. Army—in New York City. The time Carrick spent in Europe kindled his desire to do more creative work, and so he saved enough money to return to Europe, where he practiced painting in Spain, Greece, and the Vienna Academy of Fine Art.

Carrick first became interested in doing illustrations for books when he collaborated with Robert Goldston on *The Civil War in Spain.* It was not long after he completed this book that Carrick and his wife wrote and illustrated the first of many books they would do together, *The Old Barn.* Both Donald and Carol loved nature, so many of their works involve animals and natural settings, including *Swamp Spring, A Clearing in the Forest, The Sand Tiger Shark, The Empty Squirrel,* and the highly-acclaimed *The Blue Lobster: A Life Cycle.*

A dedicated and productive illustrator and painter throughout his career, Carrick continued to work industriously even after he learned he had terminal cancer. His wife once commented in an interview in *Something about the Author,* "After Don was diagnosed with terminal cancer, he worked on Jim Latimer's book, *When Moose Was Young,* and had at least four more books to do at the time of his illness. I think he hoped that he would be able to do them all."

BIOGRAPHICAL/CRITICAL SOURCES:

BOOKS

Kingman, Lee, and others, compilers, *Illustrators of Children's Books: 1967-1976,* Horn Book, 1978.
Something about the Author, Volume 63, Gale, 1991, pp. 13-18.
Ward, Martha E., and Dorothy A. Marquardt, *Illustrators of Books for Young People,* Scarecrow, 1975.

OBITUARIES:

PERIODICALS

Boston Globe, July 4, 1989, p. 17.
Horn Book, September-October, 1989, p. 686.
New York Times, July 3, 1989, p. 11.
Publishers Weekly, July 28, 1989.
School Library Journal, August, 1989, p. 28.
Vineyard Gazette, June 27, 1989, p. 1.

[Sketch verified by wife, Carol Carrick]

*　　*　　*

CARTER, Nick
See SWAIN, Dwight V(reeland)

*　　*　　*

CASTELLS, Manuel 1942-

PERSONAL: Born February 9, 1942, in Hellin, Spain. *Education:* University of Paris, LL.B., M.A., 1966, Ph.D., 1967.

ADDRESSES: Office—Department of City and Regional Planning, University of California, Berkeley, CA 94720.

CAREER: University of Paris, Paris, France, assistant professor of sociology, 1967-70; Sorbonne, University of Paris, associate professor of sociology, 1970-79; University of California, Berkeley, professor of city and regional planning, 1979—; Universidad Autonoma de Madrid, joint professor of sociology and director of Institute for Sociology of New Technologies, 1989—. Visiting professor, University of Chile, 1968, 1970, 1971, and 1972, University of Montreal, 1969, University of Wisconsin-Madison, 1975 and 1977, Boston University, 1976, University of Copenhagen, 1976, University of Mexico, 1976 and 1982, University of Hong Kong, 1983, University of Southern California, Los Angeles, 1984, 1986, and 1987, National University of Singapore, 1987, and Moscow University, 1990 and 1991.

MEMBER: International Sociological Association (president of urban research committee, 1978-82; executive committee, 1990-94), American Planning Association, American Sociological Association.

AWARDS, HONORS: Guggenheim Memorial Fellow, 1982-83; C. Wright Mills Award, 1983, for *The City and the Grassroots.*

WRITINGS:

IN ENGLISH

The City and the Grassroots: A Cross-Cultural Theory of Urban Social Movements, University of California Press, 1983.
The Economic Crisis and American Society, Princeton University Press, 1980.
(Co-author and editor) *High Technology, Space, and Society,* Sage Publications, 1985.
Informational City: Information Technology, Economic Restructuring, and the Urban-Regional Process, Basil Blackwell, 1989.
(With others) *The Shik Kip Mei Syndrome: Economic Development and Public Housing in Hong Kong and Singapore,* Pion, 1990.
(Co-author and editor) *The Informal Economy,* Johns Hopkins University Press, 1991.
(Editor) *Dual City: Restructuring New York,* Russell Sage, 1991.

IN ENGLISH TRANSLATION

The Urban Question: A Marxist Approach, MIT Press, 1977.
City, Class, and Power, St. Martin's, 1978.

OTHER

Co-editor of *International Journal of Urban and Regional Research,* 1978—.

WORK IN PROGRESS: The Informational Society: A Cross-cultural Theory of Social Transformation, expected 1994.

SIDELIGHTS: Sociologist Manuel Castells told *CA:* "My work has been concerned for the last 25 years with the processes of social transformation across cultures and countries. I have personally researched in Western Europe, the United States, Canada, Latin America, China, the Asian Pacific, and Russia, looking for an understanding of social change from the top (government policies) and from the grass roots (social movements). . . . My current work aims at bringing all this together in a theory of the new society that is emerging, ushered in by technological revolution and by the formation of an integrated global economy that is resisted by self-conscious cultural communities throughout the world."

A reviewer for the *Times Higher Education Supplement* called Castell's *Informational City* "a major achievement. . . . Although many other social scientists have been groping their way towards an understanding of the new economy and society, Castells has leap-frogged them all to produce the definitive analysis that will surely stand for years to come."

BIOGRAPHICAL/CRITICAL SOURCES:

PERIODICALS

Times Higher Education Supplement (London), June 22, 1990.

* * *

CHAPPEL, Bernice M(arie) 1910-

PERSONAL: Born June 4, 1910, in Fowlerville, MI; daughter of George L. (a farmer) and Gertrude (Avery) Klein; married Kenneth F. Chappel, December 24, 1929; children: Kenneth F., Jr. *Education:* Eastern Michigan University, B.S., 1956; University of Michigan, M.A., 1961. *Religion:* Methodist. *Avocational interests:* Travel (Mexico, Central and South America, India, Nepal, Siberia, Mongolia, China, South Korea, Japan, Burma, and the Scandinavian countries).

ADDRESSES: Home and office—5946 Alan Dr., Apt. 43, Brighton, MI 48116.

CAREER: Rural school teacher in Perry, MI, 1929-32; elementary school teacher in Brighton, MI, 1944-60; Farmington Public Schools, Farmington, MI, school social worker, 1960-70; writer, 1970—.

WRITINGS:

Harvey Hopper (juvenile), Denison, 1966.
Language Arts Seatwork, Fearon, 1967.
Rudolph, the Rooster (juvenile), Bethany Press, 1969.
Mathematics Seatwork for Primary Grades, Fearon, 1970.
Independent Language Arts Activities, Fearon, 1973.
Listening and Learning, Fearon, 1973.
A Time for Learning, Academic Therapy Publications, 1974.
In the Palm of the Mitten (autobiographical), Great Lakes, 1981.
Bittersweet Trail (historical novel), Great Lakes, 1984.
Lure of the Arctic, Wilderness Adventure Books, 1986.
Reap the Whirlwind, Wilderness Adventure Books, 1987.
Blowing in the Wind, Wilderness Adventure Books, 1990.

WORK IN PROGRESS: Frontier Footprints, a historical novel recounting the experiences of wagontrains bound for California.

SIDELIGHTS: Bernice M. Chappel told *CA:* "In my career, first as a classroom teacher and later as a school social worker, I was impressed with the number of unhappy children in our society. Many of these children had academic learning problems. Some were merely slow 'starters,' rather than slow learners. By the time their maturity was adequate they were far behind their age mates.

"Because of my interest in these children of adequate intelligence, I could see the need for usable teacher-aid material. I knew there was not time for the average teacher to meet the needs of these children in a regular classroom. It was for this reason that I wrote several of my books.

"I endeavor to tie learning to interesting child-centered stories or activities. For example, *Listening and Learning* consists of stories, poems, and games that are followed by correlated pupil learning activities.

"*A Time for Learning* is a self-instruction handbook for parents and teachers of young children. It is intended to help guide the youngsters toward an enjoyment of learning and a satisfactory social life.

"*In the Palm of the Mitten* is an autobiographical memory book of Michigan rural life in the early 1900s. *Bittersweet Trail,* a historical novel, is a four-generation American saga of family life in Michigan between the years of 1836 and 1895. Though the two are companion books, each volume is complete in itself. Through them, the reader will see the clash of different cultures, early transportation through Michigan's wilderness, the disastrous results of inadequate medical knowledge, and the friction between the North and the South which builds to the crescendo of the Civil War. A nostalgic view of family life is carried through both books, which are illustrated with authentic historical photographs of the time."

Chappel adds: "*Lure of the Arctic* portrays the Inuit personality and aids young people in understanding another minority culture. *Reap the Whirlwind* is a documentary of Michigan pioneer life covering the years between 1795 and 1866. The plight of the U. S. government treatment of Michigan Indians and the pioneer's growing resentment of Negro slavery are issues throughout the book.

"*Blowing in the Wind* is the story of two families who migrated from Germany to the U. S. in a sailing boat. Their life in the Minnesota wilderness was interrupted by the Sioux massacre of hundreds of the state's pioneers.

"Originally I wrote for the juvenile and educational market, but in recent years my interests have turned to historical books. It is a challenge to research nearly-forgotten areas and to weave accurate background material into true-to-life fiction of a former period in the history of our country."

BIOGRAPHICAL/CRITICAL SOURCES:

BOOKS

Chappel, Bernice M., *In the Palm of the Mitten* (autobiographical), Great Lakes, 1981.

*   *   *

CHARLES, David
See TAYLOR, Charles D(oonan)

*   *   *

CHING, Julia (Chia-yi) 1934-
(Joyce King)

PERSONAL: Born October 15, 1934, in Shanghai, China; came to the United States, 1951, naturalized citizen, 1974; daughter of William L. K. and Christina C. (Tsao) Ching; married Williard G. Oxtoby. *Education:* College of New Rochelle, B.A., 1958; Catholic University of America, M.A., 1960; Australian National University, Ph.D., 1971. *Politics:* Democrat. *Religion:* Roman Catholic.

ADDRESSES: Office—Victoria College, University of Toronto, Toronto, Ontario, Canada M5S 1K7.

CAREER: Australian National University, Canberra, lecturer in Asian studies, 1970-74; Columbia University, New York City, associate professor of East Asian philosophy, 1974-75; Yale University, New Haven, CT, associate professor of East Asian philosophy, 1975-79; University of Toronto, Victoria College, Toronto, Ontario, associate professor of East Asian philosophy and religion, 1979-81, professor of East Asian philosophy and religion, 1981—.

Trustee, United Board for Christian Higher Education in Asia, 1979-88; co-president, International Congress for Asian and North African Studies, 1990. Consultant to National Endowment for the Humanities.

MEMBER: Association of Asian Studies, Phi Tau Phi.

AWARDS, HONORS: Outstanding academic book award, *Choice* magazine, 1977, for *Confucianism and Christianity*; Royal Society of Canada fellow.

WRITINGS:

(Translator) *Shen-ssu lu* (translation of Pascal's *Pensees*), Kuangchi Press, 1968.
Philosophical Letters of Wang Yang-ming, Australian National University Press, 1972.
To Acquire Wisdom, Columbia University Press, 1976.
Confucianism and Christianity, Kodansha, 1977.
(With Hans Kueng) *Christianity and Chinese Religions,* Doubleday, 1989.
Probing China's Soul, Harper & Row, 1990.

Editor, *Journal of the History of Ideas,* 1976—.

WORK IN PROGRESS: Research studies on comparative scripture.

SIDELIGHTS: Julia Ching told *CA:* "As an expatriate from China, I became absorbed in the study and interpretation of Chinese philosophy and religion. I am also interested in comparative religion."

*   *   *

CHRISTIE, Agatha (Mary Clarissa) 1890-1976
(Agatha Christie Mallowan, Mary Westmacott)

PERSONAL: Born September 15, 1890, in Torquay, Devon, England; died January 12, 1976, in Wallingford, England; daughter of Frederick Alvah and Clarissa Miller; married Archibald Christie (a colonel in Royal Air Corps), December 24, 1914 (divorced, 1928; died, 1962); married Max Edgar Lucien Mallowan (an archaeologist), September 11, 1930 (died, 1978); children: (first marriage) Rosalind. *Education:* Tutored at home by her mother until age 16; later studied singing and piano in Paris.

CAREER: Writer. During World War I, served as Voluntary Aid Detachment (V.A.D.) nurse in a Red Cross Hospital, Torquay, South Devon, England; after divorce in 1928, traveled for several years; after marriage to Max Mallowan, 1930, helped him with tabulations and photography at his excavations in Iraq and Syria; during World War II, worked in dispensary for University College Hospital, London, England; during postwar 1940s, helped her husband with excavation of Assyrian ruins.

MEMBER: Royal Society of Literature (fellow), Detection Club (president).

AWARDS, HONORS: Grand Master Award, Mystery Writers of America, 1954; New York Drama Critics' Circle Award, 1955, for *Witness for the Prosecution*; Commander of the British Empire, 1956; D.Litt., University of Exeter, 1961; Dame Commander, Order of the British Empire, 1971.

WRITINGS:

MYSTERY NOVELS

The Secret Adversary, Dodd, 1922, reprinted, Bantam, 1970.

The Man in the Brown Suit, Dodd, 1924.

The Secret of Chimneys, Dodd, 1925, reprinted, Dell, 1978.

The Seven Dials Mystery, Dodd, 1929, reprinted, Bantam, 1976.

The Murder at Hazelmoor, Dodd, 1931 (published in England as *The Sittaford Mystery,* Collins, 1931).

Why Didn't They Ask Evans?, Collins, 1934, reprinted, Dodd, 1968, published as *The Boomerang Clue,* Dodd, 1935, reprinted, G. K. Hall, 1988.

Easy to Kill, Dodd, 1939 (published in England as *Murder Is Easy,* Collins, 1939), reprinted, Pocket Books, 1984.

Ten Little Niggers (also see below), Collins, 1939, reprinted, 1977, published as *And Then There Were None,* Dodd, 1940, published as *Ten Little Indians,* Pocket Books, 1965, reprinted, Dodd, 1978.

N or M?: A New Mystery, Dodd, 1941, reprinted, 1974.

Death Comes as the End, Dodd, 1944.

Towards Zero (also see below), Dodd, 1944, reprinted, 1974.

Remembered Death, Dodd, 1945, reprinted, Pocket Books, 1975 (published in England as *Sparkling Cyanide,* Collins, 1945).

The Crooked House, Dodd, 1949.

They Came to Baghdad, Dodd, 1951, reprinted, Berkley, 1989.

Destination Unknown, Collins, 1954, reprinted, 1978, published as *So Many Steps to Death,* Dodd, 1955.

Ordeal by Innocence, Collins, 1958, Dodd, 1959.

The Pale Horse, Collins, 1961, Dodd, 1962, reprinted, Pocket Books, 1976.

Endless Night, Collins, 1967, Dodd, 1968.

By the Pricking of My Thumbs, Dodd, 1968.

Passenger to Frankfurt, Dodd, 1970.

Postern of Fate, Dodd, 1973.

Murder on Board, Dodd, 1974.

NOVELS FEATURING HERCULE POIROT

The Mysterious Affair at Styles, Lane, 1920, Dodd, 1927, Bantam, 1983.

The Murder on the Links, Dodd, 1923, reprinted, Triad Panther, 1978.

The Murder of Roger Ackroyd, Dodd, 1926, reprinted, Pocket Books, 1983.

The Big Four, Dodd, 1927.

The Mystery of the Blue Train, Dodd, 1928, reprinted, 1973.

Peril at End House, Dodd, 1932, reprinted, Pocket Books, 1982.

Thirteen at Dinner, Dodd, 1933 (published in England as *Lord Edgware Dies,* Collins, 1933, reprinted, 1977).

Murder in Three Acts, Dodd, 1934, reprinted, Popular Library, 1977 (published in England as *Three Act Tragedy,* Collins, 1935).

Murder on the Calais Coach, Dodd, 1934 (published in England as *Murder on the Orient Express,* Collins, 1934, reprinted, Pocket Books, 1976).

Death in the Air, Dodd, 1935 (published in England as *Death in the Clouds,* Collins, 1935), reprinted, Berkley, 1987.

The A.B.C. Murders, Dodd, 1936, reprinted, Pocket Books, 1976, published as *The Alphabet Murders,* Pocket Books, 1966.

Cards on the Table, Collins, 1936, Dodd, 1937.

Murder in Mesopotamia, Dodd, 1936, reprinted, Dell, 1976.

Poirot Loses a Client, Dodd, 1937 (published in England as *Dumb Witness,* Collins, 1937), reprinted, Berkley, 1985.

Death on the Nile (also see below), Collins, 1937, Dodd, 1938.

Appointment with Death (also see below), Dodd, 1938, reprinted, Berkley, 1988.

Hercule Poirot's Christmas, Collins, 1938, reprinted, 1977, published as *Murder for Christmas,* Dodd, 1939, published as *A Holiday for Murder,* Avon, 1947.

One, Two, Buckle My Shoe, Collins, 1940, published as *The Patriotic Murders,* Dodd, 1941, published as *An Overdose of Death,* Dell, 1953, reprinted as *The Patriotic Murders,* edited by Roger Cooper, Berkley, 1988.

Sad Cypress, Dodd, 1940, reprinted, Dell, 1970.

Evil Under the Sun, Dodd, 1941, reprinted, Pocket Books, 1985.

Murder in Retrospect, Dodd, 1942 (published in England as *Five Little Pigs* [also see below], Collins, 1942).

The Hollow (also see below), Dodd, 1946, published as *Murder After Hours,* Dell, 1954, reprinted, 1978.

There Is a Tide . . . , Dodd, 1948, reprinted, Dell, 1970 (published in England as *Taken at the Flood,* Collins, 1948).

Mrs. McGinty's Dead, Dodd, 1952.

Funerals Are Fatal, Dodd, 1953 (published in England as *After the Funeral,* Collins, 1953; published as *Murder at the Gallop,* Fontana, 1963), reprinted, Pocket Books, 1987.

Hickory, Dickory, Death, Dodd, 1955 (published in England as *Hickory, Dickory, Dock,* Collins, 1955), reprinted, Pocket Books, 1988.

Dead Man's Folly, Dodd, 1956, reprinted, Pocket Books, 1984.

Cat Among the Pigeons, Collins, 1959, Dodd, 1960, reprinted, Pocket Books, 1985.

The Clocks, Collins, 1963, Dodd, 1964.

Third Girl, Collins, 1966, Dodd, 1967.

Hallowe'en Party, Dodd, 1969.

Elephants Can Remember, Dodd, 1972.

Curtain: Hercule Poirot's Last Case, Dodd, 1975.

Hercule Poirot novels also published in various omnibus volumes (see below).

NOVELS FEATURING MISS JANE MARPLE

The Murder at the Vicarage, Dodd, 1930, reprinted, Berkley, 1984.

The Body in the Library, Dodd, 1942, reprinted, Pocket Books, 1983.

The Moving Finger, Dodd, 1942, reprinted, Berkley, 1986.

A Murder Is Announced, Dodd, 1950, reprinted, Pocket Books, 1985.

Murder with Mirrors, Dodd, 1952, reprinted, Pocket Books, 1976 (published in England as *They Do It with Mirrors,* Collins, 1952).

A Pocket Full of Rye, Collins, 1953, Dodd, 1954, reprinted, Pocket Books, 1986.

What Mrs. McGillicudy Saw!, Dodd, 1957, reprinted, Pocket Books, 1976 (published in England as *4:50 from Paddington,* Collins, 1957), published as *Murder She Said,* Pocket Books, 1961.

The Mirror Crack'd from Side to Side, Collins, 1962, published as *The Mirror Crack'd,* Dodd, 1963.

A Caribbean Mystery, Collins, 1964, Dodd, 1965, reprinted, Pocket Books, 1976.

At Bertram's Hotel, Collins, 1965, Dodd, 1966, revised edition, Pocket Books, 1984.

Nemesis, Dodd, 1971.

Sleeping Murder, Dodd, 1976.

Miss Jane Marple novels also published in various omnibus volumes (see below).

SHORT STORY COLLECTIONS

Poirot Investigates, Lane, 1924, Dodd, 1925, reprinted, Bantam, 1983.

Partners in Crime, Dodd, 1929 (abridged edition published in England as *The Sunningdale Mystery,* Collins, 1933).

The Under Dog, and Other Stories, Readers Library, 1929, Dodd, 1951, reprinted, Dell, 1978.

The Mysterious Mr. Quin, Dodd, 1930, reprinted, Dell, 1976, also published as *The Passing of Mr. Quin.*

The Thirteen Problems, Collins, 1932, published as *The Tuesday Club Murders,* Dodd, 1933, reprinted, Dell, 1967, abridged edition published as *The Mystery of the Blue Geraniums, and Other Tuesday Club Murders,* Bantam, 1940.

The Hound of Death, and Other Stories, Odhams Press, 1933.

Mr. Parker Pyne, Detective, Dodd, 1934 (published in England as *Parker Pyne Investigates,* Collins, 1934), reprinted, Berkley, 1986.

The Listerdale Mystery, and Other Stories, Collins, 1934.

Dead Man's Mirror, and Other Stories, Dodd, 1937 (published in England as *Murder in the News, and Other Stories,* Collins, 1937).

The Regatta Mystery, and Other Stories, Dodd, 1939, reprinted, Berkley, 1987.

The Mystery of the Baghdad Chest, Bantam, 1943.

The Mystery of the Crime in Cabin 66, Bantam, 1943 (published in England as *The Crime in Cabin 66,* Vallencey, 1944).

Poirot and the Regatta Mystery, Bantam, 1943.

Poirot on Holiday, Todd, 1943.

Problem at Pollensa Bay [and] Christmas Adventure, Todd, 1943.

The Veiled Lady [and] The Mystery of the Baghdad Chest, Todd, 1944.

Poirot Knows the Murderer, Todd, 1946.

Poirot Lends a Hand, Todd, 1946.

The Labours of Hercules: New Adventures in Crime by Hercule Poirot, Dodd, 1947 (published in England as *Labours of Hercules: Short Stories,* Collins, 1947).

Witness for the Prosecution, and Other Stories, Dodd, 1948, reprinted, 1978.

Three Blind Mice, and Other Stories, Dodd, 1950, reprinted, Dell, 1980.

The Adventure of the Christmas Pudding, and Selection of Entrees, Collins, 1960.

Double Sin, and Other Stories, Dodd, 1961, reprinted, Berkley, 1987.

13 for Luck!: A Selection of Mystery Stories for Young Readers, Dodd, 1961.

Surprise! Surprise!: A Collection of Mystery Stories with Unexpected Endings, Dodd, 1965.

(Under name Agatha Christie Mallowan) *Star Over Bethlehem, and Other Stories,* Dodd, 1965.

13 Clues for Miss Marple, Dodd, 1966.

Selected Stories, Progress Publishers (Moscow), 1969.

The Golden Ball, and Other Stories, Dodd, 1971.

Hercule Poirot's Early Cases, Dodd, 1974.

Miss Marple's Final Cases, and Others, Collins, 1979.

Hercule Poirot's Casebook: Fifty Stories, Putnam, 1984.
Miss Marple, the Complete Short Stories, Putnam, 1985.

Short stories also collected in various other volumes.

OMNIBUS VOLUMES

Agatha Christie Omnibus (contains *The Mysterious Affair at Styles, The Murder on the Links,* and *Poirot Investigates*), Lane, 1931.
The Agatha Christie Omnibus of Crime (contains *The Sittaford Mystery, The Seven Dials Mystery, The Mystery of the Blue Train,* and *The Murder of Roger Ackroyd*), Collins, 1932.
Hercule Poirot, Master Detective (contains *The Murder of Roger Ackroyd, Murder on the Calais Coach,* and *Thirteen at Dinner*), Dodd, 1936, published as *Three Christie Crimes,* Grosset, 1937.
Two Detective Stories in One Volume: The Mysterious Affair at Styles [and] The Murder on the Links, Dodd, 1940.
Triple Threat: Exploits of Three Famous Detectives, Hercule Poirot, Harley Quin and Tuppence (contains *Poirot Investigates, The Mysterious Mr. Quin,* and *Partners in Crime*), Dodd, 1943.
Crime Reader (contains selections from *Poirot Investigates, The Mysterious Mr. Quin,* and *Partners in Crime*), World, 1944.
Perilous Journeys of Hercule Poirot (contains *The Mystery of the Blue Train, Death on the Nile,* and *Murder in Mesopotamia*), Dodd, 1954.
Surprise Ending by Hercule Poirot (contains *The A.B.C. Murders, Murder in Three Acts,* and *Cards on the Table*), Dodd, 1956.
Christie Classics (contains *The Murder of Roger Ackroyd, And Then There Were None, Witness for the Prosecution, Philomel Cottage,* and *Three Blind Mice*), Dodd, 1957.
Murder Preferred (contains *The Patriotic Murders, A Murder Is Announced,* and *Murder in Retrospect*), Dodd, 1960.
Make Mine Murder! (contains *Appointment with Death, Peril at End House,* and *Sad Cypress*), Dodd, 1962.
A Holiday for Murder, Bantam, 1962.
Murder International (contains *So Many Steps to Death, Death Comes as the End,* and *Evil Under the Sun*), Dodd, 1965.
Murder in Our Midst (contains *The Body in the Library, Murder at the Vicarage,* and *The Moving Finger*), Dodd, 1967.
Spies Among Us (contains *They Came to Baghdad, N or M?: A New Mystery,* and *Murder in Mesopotamia*), Dodd, 1968.
The Nursery Rhyme Murders (contains *A Pocket Full of Rye, Hickory, Dickory, Death,* and *The Crooked House*), Dodd, 1970.

Murder-Go-Round (contains *Thirteen at Dinner, The A.B.C. Murders,* and *Funerals Are Fatal*), Dodd, 1972.
Murder on Board (contains *Death in the Air, The Mystery of the Blue Train,* and *What Mrs. McGillicudy Saw!*), Dodd, 1974.
Agatha Christie: Best Loved Sleuths (contains *The Moving Finger, Murder in Three Acts, Murder on the Links,* and *There Is a Tide*), Berkley, 1988.
Agatha Christie: Murder by the Box (includes *The Secret of Chimneys, The Man in the Brown Suit,* and *Partners in Crime*), Berkley, 1988.
Three Puzzles for Poirot, Putnam, 1989.

Works also published in numerous other omnibus volumes.

PLAYS

Black Coffee (first produced on the West End, December 8, 1930), Baker, 1934.
Ten Little Niggers (based on novel of the same title; first produced in London, October 17, 1943; produced as *Ten Little Indians* on Broadway at Broadhurst Theatre, June 27, 1944), Samuel French (London), 1944, published as *Ten Little Indians,* Samuel French (New York), 1946.
Appointment with Death (based on the novel of the same title; first produced on the West End at Piccadilly Theatre, March 31, 1945; also see below), Samuel French, 1945.
Little Horizon (based on the novel *Death on the Nile;* first produced in London at Wimbledon Theatre, 1945), revised version entitled *Murder on the Nile* (first produced on the West End at Ambassadors' Theatre, March 19, 1946; produced on Broadway at Plymouth Theatre, September 19, 1946), Samuel French, 1948.
The Hollow (based on the novel of the same title; first produced on the West End at Fortune Theatre, 1951; produced in Princeton, N.J., 1952; produced in New York, 1978), Samuel French, 1952.
The Mousetrap (based on the radio script *Three Blind Mice;* first produced on the West End at Ambassadors' Theatre, November 25, 1952; produced Off-Broadway at Maidman Playhouse, 1960), Samuel French, 1954.
Witness for the Prosecution (based on the short story of the same title; first produced in London, October 28, 1953; produced in New York, December 16, 1954), Samuel French, 1954.
Spider's Web (first produced on the West End at Savoy Theatre, December 14, 1954; produced in New York, January 15, 1974), Samuel French, 1957.
(With Gerald Verner) *Towards Zero* (based on the novel of the same title; first produced in London, September

4, 1956; produced on Broadway at the St. James Theatre, 1956), Dramatists Play Service, 1957.

The Unexpected Guest (first produced on the West End at Duchess Theatre, August 12, 1958), Samuel French, 1958.

Verdict (first produced on the West End at Strand Theatre, 1958), Samuel French, 1958.

Go Back for Murder (based on the novel *Five Little Pigs;* first produced on the West End at Duchess Theatre, March 23, 1960), Samuel French, 1960.

Rule of Three (contains *Afternoon at the Sea-side* [first produced separately in London, 1962], *The Patient* [first produced separately in New York, 1978], and *The Rats* [first produced separately in New York, 1974]; first produced on the West End, December 20, 1962), Samuel French, 1963.

Fiddlers Three, first produced in Southsea at Kings Theatre, June 7, 1971; produced in London, 1972.

Akhnaton (first produced under title *Akhnaton and Nefertiti* in New York, 1979), Dodd, 1973.

The Mousetrap, and Other Plays (contains *Witness for the Prosecution, Ten Little Indians, Appointment with Death, The Hollow, Towards Zero, Verdict,* and *Go Back for Murder*), with introduction by Ira Levin, Dodd, 1978.

NOVELS UNDER PSEUDONYM MARY WESTMACOTT

Giant's Bread, Doubleday, 1930.

Unfinished Portrait, Doubleday, 1934, reprinted, Arbor House, 1972.

Absent in the Spring, Farrar & Rinehart, 1944.

The Rose and the Yew Tree, Rinehart, 1948.

A Daughter's a Daughter, Heinemann, 1952.

The Burden, Heinemann, 1956.

OTHER

The Road of Dreams (poems), Bles, 1925.

Come, Tell Me How You Live (autobiographical travel book), Dodd, 1946.

Poems, Dodd, 1973.

(Editor with others) *The Times of London Anthology of Detective Stories,* John Day, 1973.

An Autobiography, Dodd, 1977.

ADAPTATIONS: The Murder of Roger Ackroyd was adapted for the stage by Michael Morton and first produced under the title *Alibi* on the West End at Prince of Wales Theatre in 1928; the short story *Philomel Cottage* was adapted for the stage by Frank Vosper and first produced under the title *Love from a Stranger* on the West End at Wyndham's Theatre in 1936; *Peril at End House* was adapted for the stage by Arnold Ridley and first produced on the West End at the Vaudeville Theatre in 1940; *Murder at the Vicarage* was adapted for the stage by Moie Charles and Barbara Toy and first produced in London

at the Playhouse Theatre in 1949; *Towards Zero* was adapted for the stage by Gerald Verner and first produced on Broadway at the St. James Theatre in 1956. The short story *Philomel Cottage* was filmed under the title *Love from a Stranger* by United Artists in 1937, and by Eagle Lion in 1947; *And Then There Were None* was filmed by Twentieth Century-Fox in 1945; *Witness for the Prosecution* was filmed for theatrical release by United Artists in 1957 and for television by Columbia Broadcasting System in 1982; *The Spider's Web* was filmed by United Artists in 1960; *Murder She Said* was filmed by Metro-Goldwyn-Mayer in 1962; *Murder at the Gallop* was filmed by Metro-Goldwyn-Mayer in 1963; *Mrs. McGinty's Dead* was filmed under the title *Murder Most Foul* by Metro-Goldwyn-Mayer in 1965; *Ten Little Indians* was filmed by Associated British & Pathe Film in 1965; *The Alphabet Murders* was filmed by Metro-Goldwyn-Mayer in 1967; *Endless Night* was filmed by British Lion Films in 1971; *Murder on the Orient Express* was filmed by EMI in 1974; *Death on the Nile* was filmed by Paramount in 1978; *The Mirror Crack'd* was filmed by EMI in 1980; *The Seven Dials Mystery* and *Why Didn't They Ask Evans?* were filmed by London Weekend Television in 1980; *Evil Under the Sun* was filmed by Universal in 1982. *Murder Ahoy,* filmed by Metro-Goldwyn-Mayer in 1964, features the character Miss Jane Marple in a story not written by Christie.

SIDELIGHTS: "Oh, I'm an incredible sausage machine," the late mystery writer Agatha Christie once jokingly claimed, speaking of her prolific output of novels, stories, and plays. Christie's many works sold a phenomenal 2 billion copies—a record topped only by the Bible and William Shakespeare—and were translated into 103 languages. Christie books still sell a reported 25 million copies a year. Her play "The Mousetrap," originally written as a birthday gift for Queen Mary, is the longest running play in theatrical history. These staggering statistics testify to the enduring popularity of Christie's work. She remains, according to H. R. F. Keating in his article for the *Dictionary of Literary Biography,* "a towering figure in the history of crime literature."

"I don't enjoy writing detective stories," Christie once told an interviewer. "I enjoy thinking of a detective story, planning it, but when the time comes to write it, it is like going to work every day, like having a job." Christie only began writing on a dare from her sister, who challenged her to "write a good detective story." Christie wrote one, *The Mysterious Affair at Styles,* and in 1920 it was published by the English firm of Lane. Although the book only sold some two thousand copies and earned Christie seventy dollars, the publication encouraged her to continue writing mysteries. Throughout the 1920s she wrote them steadily, building a loyal following among mystery aficionados for her unfailingly clever plots.

It wasn't until the publication of *The Murder of Roger Ackroyd* in 1926 that Christie's talent for deceptive mystery plotting caught the attention of the general reading public. The sheer audacity of the novel's plot resolution—the murderer is revealed as a character traditionally above suspicion in mystery novels—outraged, surprised, and delighted readers everywhere. "*The Murder of Roger Ackroyd*," wrote the *New York Times* reviewer, "cannot be too highly praised for its clean-cut construction, its unusually plausible explanation at the end, and its ability to stimulate the analytical faculties of the reader." "The secret [of this novel] is more than usually original and ingenious," the *Nation* reviewer thought, "and is a device which no other writer could have employed without mishap." William Rose Benet of *Saturday Review* recommended that *The Murder of Roger Ackroyd* "should go on the shelf with the books of first rank in its field. The detective story pure and simple has as definite limitations of form as the sonnet in poetry. Within these limitations, with admirable structured art, Miss Christie has genuinely achieved." Writing in *Murder for Pleasure: The Life and Times of the Detective Story,* Howard Haycraft judged the book "a tour de force in every sense of the word and one of the true classics of the literature."

The Murder of Roger Ackroyd proved to be the first in a long string of superlative and highly original mystery novels that made Christie's name synonymous with the mystery story. Such books as *The A.B.C. Murders, Ten Little Indians,* and *Murder on the Orient Express* have been especially singled out by critics as among the best of Christie's work and, indeed, among the finest novels to have been written in the mystery genre. "These books," Anthony Lejeune of *Spectator* believed, "are famous because each of them turns on a piece of misdirection and a solution which, in their day, were startlingly innovatory."

The best of Christie's novels are intricate puzzles presented in such a way as to misdirect the reader's attention away from the most important clues. The solution of the puzzle is invariably startling, although entirely logical and consistent with the rest of the story. "Agatha Christie at her best," Francis Wyndham of the *Times Literary Supplement* stated, "writes animated algebra. She dares us to solve a basic equation buried beneath a proliferation of irrelevancies. By the last page, everything should have been eliminated except for the motive and identity of the murderer; the elaborate working-out, apparently too complicated to grasp, is suddenly reduced to satisfactory simplicity. The effect is one of comfortable catharsis."

"As the genre's undisputed queen of the maze," a *Time* critic wrote, "Christie laid her tantalizing plots so precisely and dropped her false leads so cunningly that few—if any—readers could guess the identity of the villain." Reviewing *The A.B.C. Murders* for *Spectator*, Nich-

olas Blake expressed a quite common response to a Christie mystery: "One can only chalk up yet another defeat at [Christie's] hands and admit sadly that she has led one up the garden path with her usual blend of duplicity and fairness." Speaking of *Ten Little Indians,* Ralph Partridge of *New Statesman* gave a similar appraisal: "Apart from one little dubious proceeding there is no cheating; the reader is just bamboozled in a straightforward way from first to last. To show her utter superiority over our deductive faculty, from time to time Mrs. Christie even allows us to know what every character present is thinking and still we can't guess!"

Christie's ability to construct a baffling puzzle was, Emma Lathen wrote in *Agatha Christie: First Lady of Crime,* the strongest aspect of her writing. "Friend and foe alike," Lathen stated, "bow to the queen of the puzzle. Every Christie plot resolution had been hailed as a masterpiece of sleight-of-hand; she herself as a virtuoso of subterfuge." Julian Symons echoed this judgment in his contribution to *Agatha Christie: First Lady of Crime:* "Agatha Christie's claim to supremacy among the classical detective story writers of her time rests on her originality in constructing puzzles. This was her supreme skill. . . . Although the detective story is ephemeral literature, the puzzle which it embodies has a permanent appeal. . . . If her work survives it will be because she was the supreme mistress of a magical skill that is a permanent, although often secret, concern of humanity: the construction and the solution of puzzles."

Over the fifty years of Christie's writing career, other factors have been suggested for the phenomenal popularity of her books. Lejeune cited three primary factors: "The texture of her writing; a texture smooth and homely as cream, . . . the ability to buttonhole a reader, to make (as Raymond Chandler put it) 'each page throw the hook for the next,' . . . [and] the quality of cosiness." A *Times Literary Supplement* reviewer offered the view that Christie "never excluded any characters from possible revelation as murderers, not the sweet young girl, the charming youth, the wise old man, not even the dear old lady."

Another important factor in Christie's popularity must lie in her ability to create charming and enduring detective characters. Undoubtedly her most popular detective has been Hercule Poirot, an eccentric and amusingly pompous Belgian detective who Christie described in *The Mysterious Affair at Styles* as "an extraordinary-looking little man. He was hardly more than five feet, four inches, but carried himself with great dignity. His head was exactly the shape of an egg. His moustache was very still and military. The neatness of his attire was almost incredible. I believe a speck of dust would have caused him more pain than a bullet wound."

According to David J. Grossvogel in *Mystery and Its Fictions: From Oedipus to Agatha Christie,* Christie "was aware of the faintly ridiculous figure cut by Poirot when she baptized him. She named him after a vegetable—the leek (*poireau,* which also means a wart, in French)—to which she opposed the (barely) Christian name Hercule, in such a way that each name would cast ridicule on the other." Grossvogel saw this bit of absurdity as essential to Poirot's success as a character. He believed that, in order to maintain the tension in a mystery story, there must be some doubt as to the detective's ability to solve the crime. Because Poirot is often "patronizingly dismissed" by other characters, his eventual solution of the crime is that much more entertaining. "Part of the artificial surprise of the detective story," Grossvogel observed, "is contained within the detective who triumphs, as he brings the action to a close, even over his own shortcomings."

"Few fictional sleuths," wrote Howard Haycraft, "can surpass the amazing little Belgian—with his waxed moustache and egg-shaped head, his inflated confidence in the infallibility of his 'little grey cells,' his murderous attacks on the English language—either for individuality or ingenuity." "Poirot," Lejeune explained, "like a survivor from an almost extinct race of giants, is one of the last of the Great Detectives: and the mention of his name should be enough to remind us of how much pleasure Agatha Christie gave millions of people over the past fifty years."

Poirot's illustrious career came to an end in *Curtain: Hercule Poirot's Last Case,* published shortly before Christie's death. Written just after World War II and secreted in a bank vault, the book was originally intended to be posthumously published, but Christie decided to enjoy the ending of Poirot's career herself and published the book early. "*Curtain,*" wrote Peter Prescott of *Newsweek,* "is one of Christie's most ingenious stories, a tour de force in which the lady who had bent all the rules of the genre before bends them yet again." John Heideury of *Commonweal* expressed the usual bafflement when confronted with a Christie mystery: "On page 35 I had guessed the identity of the murderer, by the next page knew the victim, and on page 112 deduced the motive. (On page 41 I had changed my mind and reversed murderer and victim, but on page 69 returned steadfast to my original position.) . . . I was wrong on all counts at book's end."

Christie's own favorite among her detectives was Miss Jane Marple, a spinster who lives in a small town in the English countryside. "Both Poirot and Miss Marple," wrote Ralph Tyler in *Saturday Review,* "are made a little bit absurd, so that we do not begrudge them their astuteness." In *Agatha Christie: First Lady of Crime,* Julian Symons gave Christie's own views of her two famous detectives: "Miss Marple, she said, was more fun [than Poirot], and like many aunts and grandmothers was 'a splendid

natural detective when it comes to observing human nature.' " In contrast to Poirot, a professional detective who attributes his successes to the use of his "little grey cells," Miss Marple is an amateur crime solver who often "owes her success," Margot Peters and Agate Nesaule Krouse wrote in *Southwest Review,* "to intuition and nosiness. Operating on the theory that human nature is universal, she ferrets out the criminal by his resemblance to someone she has known in her native village of St. Mary Mead, since her knowledge of life extends little farther."

Despite what they see as Christie's sexist portrayal of female characters, Peters and Krouse concluded that "Christie is not as sexist" as some other female mystery writers. Miss Marple, for example, is "self-sufficient, possessing a zest for life depending in no way on a man's support or approval." Some observers compared Miss Marple to Christie herself, but Christie rejected the idea. "I don't have Jane Marple's guilty-till-proven-innocent attitude," she said. "But, like Jane, I don't accept surface appearances."

While her mystery novels featuring Hercule Poirot and Miss Marple have enjoyed tremendous success and established Christie as the most widely-read mystery writer of all time, her relatively small output of plays has set equally impressive records. She is the only playwright to have had three plays running simultaneously on London's West End while another of her plays was running on Broadway. Christie's "The Mousetrap" holds the singular distinction of being the longest-running play in theatrical history. It has been translated into 22 languages, performed in 44 countries, and seen by an estimated eight million people. Despite the success of the work, Christie received no royalties for it. She gave the rights to her 9-year-old grandson when the play first opened in 1952. The grandson, it is estimated, has since earned well over fifteen million pounds from his grandmother's gift.

Any evaluation of Christie's career must take into account the enormous influence she had on the mystery genre. Lejeune pointed out that the secret to Christie's success lies "partly in her plots. . . . If they seem hackneyed or contrived now or even too easily guessable, that is precisely because they left so permanent an impression on the detective story genre." "I strongly suspect," Anthony Boucher declared, "that future scholars of the simon-pure detective novel will hold that its greatest practitioner . . . has been Agatha Christie."

Upon Christie's death in 1976, Max Lowenthal of the *New York Times* offered this summary of her work: "Dame Agatha's forte was supremely adroit plotting and sharp, believable characterization (even the names she used usually rang true). Her style and rhetoric were not remarkable; her writing was almost invariably sound and workmanlike, without pretense or flourish. Her characters were likely to be of the middle-middle class or upper-middle class, and there were certain archetypes, such as the crass American or the stuffy retired army officer now in his anecdotage. However familiar all this might be, the reader would turn the pages mesmerized as unexpected twist piled on unexpected twist until, in the end, he was taken by surprise. There was simply no outguessing Poirot or Miss Marple—or Agatha Christie."

BIOGRAPHICAL/CRITICAL SOURCES:

BOOKS

Authors in the News, Gale, Volume 1, 1976, Volume 2, 1976.

Bargainnier, Earl F., *The Gentle Art of Murder: The Detective Fiction of Agatha Christie,* Bowling Green University Press, 1981.

Barnard, Robert, *A Talent to Deceive: An Appreciation of Agatha Christie,* Dodd, 1980.

Behre, F., *Agatha Christie's Writings,* Adler, 1967.

Contemporary Literary Criticism, Gale, Volume 1, 1973, Volume 6, 1976, Volume 8, 1978, Volume 12, 1980, Volume 39, 1986, Volume 48, 1988.

Christie, Agatha, *Come, Tell Me How You Live,* Dodd, 1946.

Christie, Agatha, *An Autobiography,* Dodd, 1977.

Dictionary of Literary Biography, Gale, Volume 13: *British Dramatists Since World War II,* Gale, 1982, Volume 77: *British Mystery Writers, 1920-1939,* 1989.

Feinman, Jeffrey, *The Mysterious World of Agatha Christie,* Award Books, 1975.

Gill, Gillian, *Agatha Christie: The Woman and Her Mysteries,* Free Press, 1990.

Gregg, Hubert, *Agatha Christie and All That Mousetrap,* William Kimber (London), 1981.

Grossvogel, David I., *Mystery and Its Fictions: From Oedipus to Agatha Christie,* Johns Hopkins University Press, 1979.

Hart, Anne, *The Life and Times of Miss Jane Marple: An Entertaining and Definitive Study of Agatha Christie's Famous Amateur Sleuth,* Dodd, 1985.

Haycraft, Howard, *Murder for Pleasure: The Life and Times of the Detective Story,* Biblo & Tannen, 1969.

Keating, H. R. F., editor, *Agatha Christie: First Lady of Crime,* Holt, 1977.

Maida, Patricia D. and Nicholas B. Spornick, *Murder She Wrote: A Study of Agatha Christie's Detective Fiction,* Bowling Green University, 1982.

Mallowan, Max, *Mallowan's Memoirs,* Dodd, 1977.

Morgan, Janet, *Agatha Christie: A Biography,* J. Cape, 1984.

Morselt, Ben, *An A to Z of the Novels and Short Stories of Agatha Christie,* David & Charles, 1985.

Osborne, Charles, *The Life and Crimes of Agatha Christie,* Holt, 1983.

Ramsey, Gordon C., *Agatha Christie: Mistress of Mystery,* Dodd, 1967.

Riley, Dick, and Pam McAllister, editors, *The Bedside, Bathtub, and Armchair Companion to Agatha Christie,* Ungar, 1979.

Robyns, Gwen, *The Mystery of Agatha Christie,* Doubleday, 1978.

Sanders, Dennis and Len Lovalio, *The Agatha Christie Companion: The Complete Guide to Agatha Christie's Life and Work,* Delacorte, 1984.

Symons, Julian, *Mortal Consequences: A History—From the Detective Story to the Crime Novel,* Harper, 1972.

Symons, Julian, and Tom Adams, *Agatha Christie: The Art of Her Crimes, the Paintings of Tom Adams,* Everest House, 1982.

Toye, Randall, *The Agatha Christie Who's Who,* Holt, 1980.

Wagoner, Mary S., *Agatha Christie,* Twayne, 1986.

Wynne, Nancy Blue, *An Agatha Christie Chronology,* Ace Books, 1976. *periodicals*

Armchair Detective, April, 1978; summer, 1981.

Christian Science Monitor, December 20, 1967.

Commonweal, February 13, 1976.

Detroit News, November 13, 1977.

Globe and Mail (Toronto), September 15, 1990.

Harvard Magazine, October, 1975.

Life, December 1, 1967.

Los Angeles Times, March 8, 1970; December 15, 1974; April 20, 1975; September 13, 1990; November 1, 1990.

McCall's, February, 1969.

Milwaukee Journal, February 1, 1976.

Nation, July 3, 1926.

New Republic, July 31, 1976.

New Statesman, May 10, 1930; December 18, 1937; November 18, 1939.

Newsweek, October 6, 1975.

New Yorker, October 14, 1944; January 30, 1978.

New York Herald Tribune Book Review, March 4, 1934.

New York Review of Books, December 21, 1978.

New York Times, July 18, 1926; November 10, 1977; December 24, 1985.

New York Times Book Review, March 25, 1923; April 20, 1924; September 22, 1929; February 25, 1940; September 25, 1966; March 17, 1968; October 14, 1990.

Pittsburgh Press, March 28, 1976.

Saturday Review, July 24, 1926; October 4, 1975.

Seattle Post-Intelligencer, December 23, 1973.

Southwest Review, spring, 1974.

Spectator, May 31, 1930; February 14, 1936; September 19, 1970.

Times (London), September 19, 1984; September 5, 1990.

Times Literary Supplement, April 3, 1924; June 10, 1926; December 2, 1965; September 26, 1975.

OBITUARIES:

PERIODICALS

AB Bookman's Weekly, April 5, 1976.
Bookseller, January 17, 1976.
Detroit Free Press, January 14, 1976.
Newsweek, January 26, 1976.
New York Times, January 13, 1976.
Publishers Weekly, January 19, 1976.
School Library Journal, February, 1976.
Time, January 26, 1976.
Washington Post, January 13, 1976.*

*   *   *

CHRISTOPHER, John
See YOUD, (Christopher) Samuel

*   *   *

CLAPP, Patricia   1912-

PERSONAL: Born June 9, 1912, in Boston, MA; daughter of Howard (a dentist) and Elizabeth (Blachford) Clapp; married Edward della Torre Cone (a transportation consultant), March 3, 1933; children: Christopher, Patricia (Mrs. Vincent A. DiMauro), Pamela (Mrs. William K. Wakefield). *Education:* Attended Columbia University School of Journalism, 1932; various writing courses. *Religion:* Protestant.

ADDRESSES: Home—83 Beverly Rd., Upper Montclair, NJ 07043.

CAREER: Writer of young adult and children's books and plays.

AWARDS, HONORS: National Book Award runner-up and Lewis Carrol Shelf Award, both 1969, both for *Constance: A Story of Early Plymouth;* Best Young Adult Book citation, American Library Association, 1982, for *Witches' Children.*

WRITINGS:

PLAYS

Peggy's on the Phone (one-act), Dramatic Publishing, 1956.
Smart Enough to Be Dumb (one-act), Dramatic Publishing, 1956.
The Incompleted Pass (three-act), Dramatic Publishing, 1957.
Her Kissin' Cousin (three-act), Heuer Publishing, 1957.

The Girl Out Front (three-act), Dramatic Publishing, 1958.
The Ghost of a Chance (three-act), Heuer Publishing, 1958.
The Curley Tale (three-act), Art Craft, 1958.
Inquire Within (three-act), Row, 1959.
Edie-across-the-Street (three-act), Baker Co., 1960.
The Honeysuckle Hedge (three-act), Eldridge Publishing, 1960.
Never Keep Him Waiting, Dramatic Publishing, 1961.
Red Heels and Roses (one-act), McKay, 1961.
If a Body Meet a Body (three-act), Heuer Publishing, 1963.
Now Hear This (one-act), Eldridge Publishing, 1963.
The Invisible Dragon (one-act with music), Dramatic Publishing, 1971.
A Candle on the Table (one-act; for adults), Baker Co., 1972.
The Retirement (one-act; for adults), Eldridge Publishing, 1972.
A Specially Wonderful Day (one-act; in verse), Encyclopedia Britannica Educational Corp., 1972.
The Toys Take Over Christmas (one-act), Dramatic Publishing, 1977.
Mudcake Princess (one-act), Dramatic Publishing, 1979.
The Truly Remarkable Puss in Boots (one-act), Dramatic Publishing, 1979.

Work represented in anthologies, including *Children's Plays from Favorite Stories,* edited by Sylvia E. Kamerman, Plays Inc., 1959; *Fifty Plays for Junior Actors,* edited by Kamerman, Plays Inc., 1966; *Fifty Plays for Holidays,* edited by Kamerman, Plays Inc., 1969; *100 Plays for Children,* edited by A.S. Burack, Plays Inc., 1970. Contributor of plays to several periodicals, including *Instructor Magazine, Plays Magazine, Grade Teacher Magazine,* and *Yankee Magazine,* 1958-81. Editor of little theatre productions.

OTHER

Constance: A Story of Early Plymouth (juvenile novel), Lothrop, 1968.
Jane-Emily (juvenile novel), Lothrop, 1969.
Popsical Song (children's book; in verse), Encyclopedia Britannica Educational Corp., 1972.
Dr. Elizabeth: The Story of the First Woman Doctor (biography), Lothrop, 1974.
King of the Dollhouse (children's book), illustrated by Judith Gywnn Brown, Lothrop, 1974.
I'm Deborah Sampson: A Soldier in the War of the Revolution (juvenile novel), Lothrop, 1978.
Witches' Children: A Story of Salem (juvenile novel), Lothrop, 1982.
(Contributor) Donna E. Norton editor, *Through the Eyes of the Child* (college textbook), Merrill, 1983.

The Tamarack Tree (juvenile novel), Lothrop, 1986.

Also author of published poetry.

Constance: A Story of Early Plymouth has been translated into French and Danish.

SIDELIGHTS: Patricia Clapp told *CA:* "I am a strong believer in the virtues of conservatism, optimism, good manners, thoughtfulness, kindness, and those outmoded beautiful words 'ladies' and 'gentleman.' Deplore untidiness of any sort, moral, spiritual, or physical . . . Think every younger generation rebels, but some generations do it more gracefully than others. I love London, Cape Cod, Lucerne, part of Connecticut, and Florence. Dislike Rome, California, and the Middle West. Enjoy traveling but prefer staying home."

BIOGRAPHICAL/CRITICAL SOURCES:

PERIODICALS

Book World, May 5, 1968.
Chicago Tribune Book World, April 11, 1982.
Commonweal, May 23, 1969.
New York Times Book Review, August 18, 1968.

*   *   *

CLARK, M. R.
See CLARK, Mavis Thorpe

*   *   *

CLARK, Mavis Thorpe   1909-
(M. R. Clark, Mavis Latham)

PERSONAL: Born in Melbourne, Victoria, Australia, in 1909; daughter of John Thorpe (a building contractor) and Rose Matilda (Stanborough) Clark; married Harold Latham (deceased); children: Beverley Jeanne (Mrs. Ralph Henderson Lewis), Ronda Faye (Mrs. Peter Hall). *Education:* Attended Methodist Ladies' College, Melbourne.

ADDRESSES: Home—1/22 Rochester Rd., Canterbury, Victoria 3126, Australia.

CAREER: Writer.

MEMBER: International PEN (Australia Centre; vice-president of Melbourne branch, 1968, 1971, 1973, 1974; president of Melbourne branch, 1969, 1980, 1981), Australian Society of Authors (member of management committee for fifteen years), National Book Council (member of promotions committee for seven years), Fellowship of Australian Writers (life member, 1990), Children's Book Council of Australia (life member).

AWARDS, HONORS: Commendation from Children's Book Council of Australia for *The Brown Land Was Green,* 1956, and *Blue above the Trees,* 1968, and Book of the Year Award for *The Min-Min,* 1967; *The Min-Min* was chosen as an American Library Association Notable Book, 1969; *Spark of Opal,* 1971, and *Iron Mountain,* 1973, were placed on Deutscher Jugendbuchpreis (German Youth Book Award) list.

WRITINGS:

NOVELS FOR YOUNG TEENS

(Under name M. R. Clark) *Hatherly's First Fifteen,* illustrated by F. E. Hiley, Whitcomb & Tombs, 1930.
Dark Pool Island, Oxford University Press, 1949.
The Twins from Timber Creek, Oxford University Press, 1949.
Home Again at Timber Creek, Oxford University Press, 1950.
Jingaroo, Oxford University Press, 1951.
Missing Gold, Hutchinson, 1951.
The Brown Land Was Green (also see below), illustrated by Harry Hudson, Heinemann, 1956, special school edition, Heinemann, 1957, published with new illustrations, Lansdowne Press, 1967, published as *Kammorra,* Octopus-Heinemann, 1990.
Gully of Gold, illustrated by Anne Graham, Heinemann, 1958, published with new illustrations, Lansdowne Press, 1969.
Pony from Tarella, illustrated by Jean M. Rowe, Heinemann, 1959, published with new illustrations, Lansdowne Press, 1969.
They Came South, illustrated by Joy Murray, Heinemann, 1963, published with new illustrations, Lansdowne Press, 1971.
The Min-Min (also see below), illustrated by Genevieve Melrose, Lansdowne Press, 1966, Macmillan (New York), 1969, published as *Armada Lions,* Collins, 1975.
Blue above the Trees, illustrated by G. Melrose, Lansdowne Press, 1967, Meredith Press, 1969, published with new illustrations, Hodder & Stoughton, 1975.
Spark of Opal, illustrated by G. Melrose, Lansdowne Press, 1968, Macmillan (New York), 1973.
Nowhere to Hide, illustrated by G. Melrose, Lansdowne Press, 1969.
Iron Mountain, illustrated by Ronald Brooks, Lansdowne Press, 1970, Macmillan (New York), 1971, published as *If the Earth Falls In,* Scabury Press, 1975.
New Golden Mountain, Lansdowne Press, 1973.
Wildfire, Hodder & Stoughton, 1973, Macmillan (New York), 1974.

The Sky Is Free, Macmillan, 1976.

The Hundred Islands, illustrated by Astra Lacis, Macmillan, 1977.

The Lilly-Pilly, illustrated by Prue Chammen, Rigby Reading Series, 1979.

A Stranger Came to the Mine, illustrated by Jane Walker, Hutchinson, 1980.

Solomon's Child, Hutchinson, 1981.

The Brown Land Was Green [and] *The Min-Min* (classic edition), John Ferguson, 1982.

Soft Shoe, illustrated by Ziba Westenberg, Bookshelf, 1988.

OTHER

John Batman (adult biography), Oxford University Press, 1962.

(As Mavis Latham) *Fishing* (textbook), illustrated by Joy Murray, Oxford University Press, 1963.

Pastor Doug: The Story of an Aboriginal Leader (adult biography), Lansdowne Press, 1965, revised edition published as *Pastor Doug: The Story of Sir Douglas Nicholls, Aboriginal Leader,* 1972.

The Pack-Tracker (textbook), illustrated by Shirley Turner, Oxford University Press, 1968.

The Opal Miner (textbook), illustrated by Barbara Taylor, Oxford University Press, 1969.

Iron Ore Mining (textbook), illustrated by Jocelyn Bell, Oxford University Press, 1971.

Joan and Betty Rayner: Strolling Players (adult biography), Lansdowne Press, 1972.

Spanish Queen (remedial reader), Hodder & Stoughton, 1977.

The Boy from Cumeroogunga: The Story of Sir Douglas Nicholls, Aboriginal Leader, Hodder & Stoughton, 1979.

Joey (reader), Mount Gravat College of Advanced Education, 1980.

Boo to a Goose (reader), Mount Gravat College of Advanced Education, 1981.

The Thief Who Came Quietly (reader), Mount Gravat College of Advanced Education, 1981.

Young and Brave (collection of true short stories), Hodder & Stoughton, 1984.

No Mean Destiny: The Story of Jessie Mary Vasey and Her Founding of the War Widows' Guild of Australia, Hyland House, 1986.

Also author of radio-script adaptations of *The Brown Land Was Green,* 1961, *Gully of Gold,* 1962, and *They Came South,* 1965, for Australian Broadcasting Commission, each broadcast as fifty-two episode serials. Author of many other radio plays, short stories, ad articles. Contributor to anthologies, including *Australian Bushrangers,* Casell (Australia), 1973; *Australians at War,* Casell (Australia), 1974; *Australian Escape Stories,* Casell (Australia),

1976; and *A Handful of Ghosts,* Hodder & Stoughton, 1976. Contributor to *Cricket* (magazine), 1987.

ADAPTATIONS: In 1976, film and television rights for *The Sky Is Free* were purchased by Walt Disney Productions.

WORK IN PROGRESS: An autobiographical account of the author's wanderings throughout Australia, over many years, with emphasis on people met, places visited and lived-in, and incidents that have figured in her books.

SIDELIGHTS: Mavis Thorpe Clark is one of Australia's premier young adult novelists. In works such as *The Brown Land Was Green, The Min-Min, Blue among the Trees, The Sky Is Free* and *Spark of Opal,* she portrays Australian life, both modern and pioneer, in the harsh beauty of the Australian landscape—ranging from the opal mines and sheep stations of the Outback to the lush jungles of the north to the bird-life of the seashore. "I have travelled thousands of miles in search of material," Clark commented, "criss-crossing this vast country from east to west and north to south. I've travelled to Europe and Asia, too, but the spell of my own wide red land lures me continually and sets me on the lonely dusty outback track."

Clark was born in a suburb of Melbourne, the youngest child of a Scottish-born building contractor and his Australian wife. She showed a talent for story-telling and writing early in life, entertaining her friends at school with anecdotes. "Those stories I told my friends—a tight, loyal gang of five—were the immediate prelude to the written story," Clark writes in her *Something about the Author Autobiography Series* (*SAAS*) entry. "In fact, that began almost at the same time, and was nurtured by my oral weavings. I would lie on my stomach in the seclusion of the lounge room floor with half-a-dozen finely sharpened lead pencils, and an exercise book with a shiny plastic-type cover. My eldest sister, Vi, who was a young adult when I was born, was a secretary; she would take my stories to her office, type them out, and bring them back to me set out like small books, the pages fastened together with blue and yellow striped ribbon."

Clark continued her interest in writing throughout her school years. "I wrote my first full-length manuscript when I was fourteen, while studying for my Intermediate Certificate at the Methodist Ladies' College, Melbourne," she writes in the *Fourth Book of Junior Authors.* "This story was not published in book form, but it did appear in the children's pages of the *Australasian,* an Australian weekly newspaper of that time. My first book in hard covers was published when I was eighteen and was an adventure story of boys." This was *Hatherly's First Fifteen,* a story about blindness and the game of rugby. "For this work I consulted with the local doctor on the subject of blindness, and with a young man, who had played rugby for Scotland, on the fine points of the game," Clark explains in her *SAAS* entry. "The actual games described in the book were played out on the dining-room table using matches for players. This was the beginning, if an unrecognised one, of my interest in the factual background. And an early awareness that I must be familiar with my subject."

Clark married young, but continued writing magazine stories, newspaper articles, radio plays, and children's adventure serials for newspapers. One of these, *Dark Island Pool,* was later published as a book. "It was a typical story of the period; a quick-moving boys' school story—no doubt inspired by my own childhood taste—of a fake headmaster, a treasure of gold in the pool, and four lively teenagers who rescued the real headmaster and saved the treasure," Clark explains in her *SAAS* entry. "This was followed by *The Twins from Timber Creek, Home Again at Timber Creek, Jingaroo, Missing Gold.* These were for the ten year olds, with emphasis on adventure and story."

The Brown Land Was Green, Clark's next book, marked an important change in her writing: it had a historical background (the frontier of Victoria in 1844); it was based in part on the experiences of her Aunt Martha, who had entertained Clark as a child with her stories of pioneer life; and it featured a heroine named Henrietta Webster, who "was untrammelled by being female," Clark writes in her *SAAS* entry. Aunt Martha, she continues, "immersed me, the child, in that district. Through her, too, the land . . . the earth . . . of Australia made its first rendezvous with me, though, at the time, its reaching-out was not recognized. . . . It was the first book—and the forerunner of all the others—to bear the imprint of the land." *The Brown Land Was Green* was followed by *Gully of Gold* and *They Came South,* both novels set in Victoria during pioneer days.

In *The Min-Min,* her most celebrated novel, Clark moved out of settled Australia into the Outback. It is the story of Reg, a troubled young man, and his sister Sylvie, who set off on their own from their isolated camp on the border of the railroad to cross the desert. The book was based in part on a trip she took with Harold Darwin, a retired schoolteacher who organized his own travelling library in an old van and spent his days driving from one isolated homestead or sheep station to another, carrying books to people who could not otherwise get them. Clark actually saw the Min-Min on the trip: a bright light, too low for a star, that appeared just above the horizon, changed color, moved back and forth, and vanished as suddenly as it had appeared. "The whole of that book—the characters, the setting, the happenings—went home with me," Clark wrote in her *SAAS* entry; "and also that pure bright light as a symbolic goal for Sylvie to follow, her walking towards the lure of a better life."

Other travels throughout Australia brought other books. "Now I began to range wide," Clark states in her *SAAS* entry. "My whole country—this Australia—was my oyster. I was fascinated by it, awed by its size, its age—one of the oldest land masses in the world—it strength; bound to it by its colour, its scent, its people, most of all by its people. The urge for that further overseas travel which had prickled since I was thirteen, was overlaid and made dormant by this stronger desire to get closer and closer to my own country." *Blue among the Trees,* her next book, was based on the destruction of the Australian rain forest by cattle and sheep ranchers. *Spark of Opal, The Sky Is Free,* and *A Stranger Came to the Mine* are all set in the famous opal fields of Coober Pedy, while *Iron Mountain* evokes the mining towns of Tom Price and Dampier on the very western edge of the continent.

The geographical and cultural details found in Clark's novels echo the deep love she feels for her native Australia and give insight into that country to those who have never been there. "Here again is the tremendous reward of friends in out-of-the-way places and glimpses of lives that are lived so simply yet so richly with the earth of the world's oldest continent," Clark commented. "These intangible joys are the real reward of the writer."

BIOGRAPHICAL/CRITICAL SOURCES:

BOOKS

Contemporary Literary Criticism, Volume 12, Gale, 1980.
de Montreville, Doris, and Elizabeth D. Crawford, editors, *Fourth Book of Junior Authors and Illustrators,* H. W. Wilson, 1978, pp. 84-86.
Something about the Author Autobiography Series, Volume 5, Gale, 1987.

PERIODICALS

Junior Bookshelf, June, 1967.
Library Journal, December 15, 1969.
New York Times Book Review, January 25, 1970.

*   *   *

CLEVE, John
**   See SWAIN, Dwight V(reeland)**

*   *   *

COBALT, Martin
**   See MAYNE, William (James Carter)**

CONE, Molly Lamken 1918-
(Caroline More)

PERSONAL: Born October 3, 1918, in Tacoma, WA; daughter of Arthur and Frances (Sussman) Lamken; married Gerald J. Cone, September 9, 1939; children: Susan, Gary, Ellen. *Education:* Attended University of Washington, 1936-39. *Politics:* Democrat. *Religion:* Jewish.

ADDRESSES: Home—8003 Sand Point Way N.E., Seattle, WA 98115. *Agent*—McIntosh and Otis, Inc., 310 Madison Ave., New York, NY 10017.

CAREER: Children's book author. Advertising copywriter.

AWARDS, HONORS: Woman of achievement award, Theta Sigma Phi, 1960; one of 100 outstanding books for young readers, *New York Times,* 1962, for *Mishmash;* Governor's Festival of Arts Certificate of Recognition, State of Washington, 1966, 1970; Myrtle Wreath Achievement Award, Hadassah (Seattle chapter), 1967; literary creativity citation, Music and Art Foundation of Seattle, 1968; Matrix Table Award, Theta Sigma Phi, 1968; first place award for juvenile books, Washington Press Women, 1969, for *Annie, Annie,* 1970, for *Simon,* and 1974, for *Dance around the Fire;* Neveh Shalom Centennial Award, 1970; second place award for juvenile books, Washington Press Women, 1971, for *You Can't Make Me If I Don't Want To;* Sugar Plum Award, 1972; Shirley Kravitz Children's Book Award, Association of Jewish Libraries, 1973.

WRITINGS:

Only Jane (Junior Literary Guild selection), Thomas Nelson, 1960.
Too Many Girls, Thomas Nelson, 1960.
The Trouble with Toby, Houghton, 1961.
Reeney, Houghton, 1963.
(Under pseudonym Caroline More, with Margaret Pitcairn Strachan) *Batch of Trouble,* Dial, 1963.
Stories of Jewish Symbols, Bloch Publishing, 1963.
The Real Dream, Houghton, 1964.
A Promise Is a Promise, Houghton, 1964.
Who Knows Ten: Children's Tales of the Ten Commandments, Union of American Hebrew Congregations, 1965, teacher's guide, 1967.
The Sabbath, Crowell, 1966.
Crazy Mary, Houghton, 1966.
Hurry Henrietta, Houghton, 1966.
Jewish New Year, Crowell, 1966.
Purim, Crowell, 1967.
The Other Side of the Fence, Houghton, 1967.
The House in the Tree, Crowell, 1968.
The Green Green Sea, Crowell, 1968.
Annie, Annie, Houghton, 1969.

Leonard Bernstein, Crowell, 1970.
Simon, Houghton, 1970.
The Ringling Brothers, Crowell, 1971.
You Can't Make Me If I Don't Want To, Houghton, 1971.
Number Four, Houghton, 1972.
Dance around the Fire, Houghton, 1974.
Call Me Moose, Houghton, 1978.
The Amazing Memory of Harvey Bean, Houghton, 1980.
Paul Silverman Is a Father, Dutton, 1983.
The Big Squeeze, Houghton, 1984.
Come Back, Salmon, Sierra Club Books for Children, 1992.

Only Jane was recorded by the Library of Congress for the blind. Five stories from *Who Knows Ten: Children's Tales of the Ten Commandments,* as told by Peninnah Schram, were recorded on *A Storyteller's Journey,* POM Records, 1978, and on *A Storyteller's Journey II,* POM Records, 1981.

"MISHMASH" SERIES

Mishmash, Houghton, 1962.
Mishmash and the Substitute Teacher, Houghton, 1963.
Mishmash and the Sauerkraut Mystery, Houghton, 1965.
Mishmash and Uncle Looey, Houghton, 1968.
Mishmash and the Venus Flytrap, Houghton, 1976.
Mishmash and the Robot, Houghton, 1981.
Mishmash and the Big Fat Problem, Houghton, 1982.

"SHEMA" (TITLE MEANS "HEAR O ISRAEL") SERIES

First I Say the Shema, Union of American Hebrew Congregations, 1971.
About Belonging, Union of American Hebrew Congregations, 1972.
About Learning, Union of American Hebrew Congregations, 1972.
About God, Union of American Hebrew Congregations, 1973.
The Mystery of Being Jewish, Union of American Hebrew Congregations, 1989.

OTHER

Contributor to anthologies, including *Bold Journeys,* Macmillan, 1966; *The Young America Basic Reading Program,* Rand McNally, 1972; and *Stories My Grandfather Should Have Told Me,* Bonim Books, 1977. Also contributor to juvenile magazines and anthologies.

SIDELIGHTS: Molly Lamken Cone's humorous "Mishmash" series concerns a mischievous little dog. Cone's inspiration for the series came from her own dog, Tiny, who was so eagerly affectionate that she upset the entire Cone household.

BIOGRAPHICAL/CRITICAL SOURCES:

BOOKS

Something about the Author Autobiography Series, Volume 11, Gale, 1991.

PERIODICALS

Christian Science Monitor, February 1, 1968.
Commonweal, May 26, 1967.
New York Times Book Review, November 5, 1972.
Young Readers' Review, March, 1968.

*   *   *

COOK, Albert S(paulding) 1925-

PERSONAL: Born October 28, 1925, in Exeter, NH; son of Albert Spaulding and Adele (Farrington) Cook; married Carol S. Rubin (a librarian), June 19, 1948; children: David, Daniel, Jonathan. *Education:* Harvard University, A.B., 1946, A.M., 1947. *Religion:* Episcopalian.

ADDRESSES: Home—92 Elmgrove, Providence, RI 02906. *Office*—Department of Comparative Literature, Box E, Brown University, Providence, RI 02912.

CAREER: Harvard University, Cambridge, MA, junior fellow, 1948-51; University of California, Berkeley, assistant professor, 1953-56; Western Reserve University (now Case Western Reserve University), Cleveland, OH, associate professor, 1957-62, professor of English and comparative literature, 1962-63; State University of New York at Buffalo, professor of English and chairman of department, 1963-66; Brown University, Providence, RI, professor of English and comparative literature, 1964-78, founder and director of department of comparative literature, 1964-74. University of Munich, Fulbright research professor, 1956-57; University of Vienna, professor of American literature, 1960-61. *Military service:* U.S. Army, 1943-44.

MEMBER: International Association for Philosophy and Literature, American Philological Association, Modern Language Association of America, American Comparative Literature Association, Modern Poetry Association, American Society for Aesthetics.

AWARDS, HONORS: Fulbright fellow, University of Paris, 1952-53; Center for Advanced Study in the Behavioral Sciences senior fellow, 1966-67; American Council of Learned Societies summer fellow, Athens, Geneva, and Paris, 1968; Fondation Hardt fellow in classical studies, Geneva, 1968, 1975, and 1987; Guggenheim fellow, Paris, 1969-70; International Research and Exchange Board senior fellow, Soviet Ministry of Education, 1972; Camargo Foundation fellow, 1977; Clare Hall visiting fellow, Cambridge, 1982; Rockefeller Study Center fellow, Bellagio, 1989; fellow, American Academy in Rome, 1991.

WRITINGS:

The Dark Voyage and the Golden Mean, Harvard University Press, 1949.
(Translator) Sophocles, *Oedipus Rex,* Houghton, 1957.
The Meaning of Fiction, Wayne State University Press, 1960.
Progressions and Other Poems, University of Arizona Press, 1963.
Oedipus Rex: A Mirror for Greek Drama, Wadsworth, 1963, reprinted, Waveland, 1982.
The Classic Line: A Study of Epic, Indiana University Press, 1966.
(Translator) Homer, *The Odyssey,* Norton, 1967.
Prisms, Indiana University Press, 1967.
The Root of the Thing: A Study of Job and the Song of Songs, Indiana University Press, 1968.
The Charges, Swallow Press, 1970.
Enactment: Greek Tragedy, Swallow Press, 1971.
(With E. Dolin) *Plays for the Greek Theatre,* Bobbs-Merrill, 1972.
The Odyssey: A Critical Edition, Norton, 1972.
Shakespeare's Enactment: The Dynamics of Renaissance Theatre, Swallow Press, 1975.
Myth and Language, Indiana University Press, 1980.
Adapt the Living, Swallow Press, 1980.
French Tragedy: The Power of Enactment, Swallow Press, 1981.
Changing the Signs: The Fifteenth-Century Breakthrough, University of Nebraska Press, 1985.
Figural Choice in Poetry and Art, University Press of New England, 1985.
Thresholds: Studies in the Romantic Experience, University of Wisconsin Press, 1985.
History/Writing, Cambridge University Press, 1989.
Dimensions of the Sign in Art, University Press of New England, 1989.
Soundings, Wayne State University Press, 1991.
(With Pamela Perkins) *Women Poets of Russia,* Garland Publishing, 1992.
Temporalizing Space: The Triumphant Strategies of Piero Della Francesca, Peter Lang, 1992.

Also author of verse plays, some of which have been produced on radio and stage. Editor, *Halcyon,* 1947-48.

WORK IN PROGRESS: Recall, a radio play; *Modes,* a long poem; *The Stance of Plato; The Reach of Poetry.*

BIOGRAPHICAL/CRITICAL SOURCES:

PERIODICALS

Criticism, summer, 1967.
Motive, March, 1968.
Times Literary Supplement, August 25, 1989, p. 926.

COOLE, W. W.
  See KULSKI, Wladyslaw W(szebor)

* * *

COONEY, Barbara 1917-

PERSONAL: Born August 6, 1917, in Brooklyn, NY; daughter of Russell Schenck (a stockbroker) and Mae Evelyn (an artist; maiden name, Bossert) Cooney; married Guy Murchie (a war correspondent and author), December, 1944 (divorced, March, 1947); married Charles Talbot Porter (a physician), July 16, 1949; children: (first marriage) Gretel Goldsmith, Barnaby; (second marriage) Charles Talbot, Jr., Phoebe. *Education:* Smith College, B.A., 1938; also attended Art Students League, 1940. *Politics:* Independent.

CAREER: Free-lance author and illustrator, 1938—. *Military service:* Women's Army Corps, World War II, 1942-43; became second lieutenant.

AWARDS, HONORS: New York Herald Tribune's Children's Spring Book Festival Honor Book, 1943, for *Green Wagons,* and 1952, for *Too Many Pets;* Caldecott Medal from the American Library Association, 1959, for *Chanticleer and the Fox,* and 1980, for *Ox-Cart Man;* American Library Association Notable Book citation, 1948, for *American Folk Songs for Children in Home, School and Nursery School,* 1958, for *Chanticleer and the Fox,* and 1974, for *Squawk to the Moon, Little Goose; Horn Book* honor list, 1961, for *The Little Juggler,* 1961, for *Le Hibou et le Poussiquette,* 1965, for *The Courtship, Merry Marriage, and Feast of Cock Robin and Jenny Wren,* 1970, for *Dionysus and the Pirates,* 1979, for *Ox-Cart Man,* and 1988, for *Island Boy;* Chandler Book Talk Award of Merit, 1964; *Christmas Folk* and *The Owl and the Pussy-Cat* were both selected one of Child Study Association of America's Children's Books of the Year, 1969, *Hermes, Lord of Robbers* and *Book of Princesses,* both 1971, *Down to the Beach,* 1973, *Squawk to the Moon, Little Goose,* 1974, *Lexington and Concord, 1775,* 1975, and *The Story of Holly and Ivy, The Little Fir Tree, Christmas in the Barn,* and *Emma,* all 1986; *Squawk to the Moon, Little Goose* was included on *School Library Journal*'s Book List, 1974; *New York Times* Outstanding Books of the Year, 1974, for *Squawk to the Moon, Little Goose,* 1975, for *When the Sky Is Like Lace,* and 1979, for *Ox-Cart Man;* Silver Medallion from the University of Southern Mississippi, 1975, for Outstanding Contributions in the Field of Children's Books; Medal from Smith College, 1976, for body of work; *Ox-Cart Man* was selected one of *New York Times* Best Illustrated Books of the Year, 1979; *Tortillitas para Mama and Other Nursery Rhymes* was selected a Notable Children's Trade Book in the Field of Social Studies

by the National Council for Social Studies and the Children's Book Council, 1982, and *The Story of Holly and Ivy,* 1986; American Book Award for Hardcover Picture Book from the Association of American Publishers, 1983, and *New York Times* Best Book of the Year, 1983, both for *Miss Rumphius; Spirit Child* was chosen as a Notable Children's Book by the Association for Library Service to Children of the American Library Association, 1984; Ph.D., Fitchburg State College, 1988; Keene State College Children's Literature Festival Award, 1989.

WRITINGS:

JUVENILES; SELF-ILLUSTRATED

The King of Wreck Island, Farrar & Rinehart, 1941.
The Kellyhorns, Farrar & Rinehart, 1942.
Captain Pottle's House, Farrar, 1943.
(Adapter) Geoffrey Chaucer, *Chanticleer and the Fox,* Crowell, 1958.
The Little Juggler: Adapted from an Old French Legend (Junior Literary Guild selection), Hastings House, 1961, new edition, 1982.
Twenty-Five Years A-Graying: The Portrait of a College Graduate, a Pictorial Study of the Class of 1938 at Smith College, Northampton, Massachusetts, Based on Statistics Gathered in 1963 for the Occasion of Its 25th Reunion, Little, Brown, 1963.
(Adapter) *The Courtship, Merry Marriage, and Feast of Cock Robin and Jenny Wren: To Which Is Added the Doleful Death of Cock Robin,* Scribner, 1965.
(Adapter) Jacob Grimm and Wilhelm Grimm, *Snow White and Rose Red,* Delacorte, 1966.
Christmas, Crowell, 1967.
(Editor) *A Little Prayer,* Hastings House, 1967.
A Garland of Games and Other Diversions: An Alphabet Book, Holt, 1969.
Miss Rumphius, Viking, 1982.
(Reteller) J. Grimm, *Little Brother and Little Sister,* Doubleday, 1982.
Island Boy, Viking, 1988.
Hattie and the Wild Waves, Viking, 1990.

ILLUSTRATOR

Carl Malmberg, *Ake and His World,* Farrar & Rinehart, 1940.
Frances M. Frost, *Uncle Snowball,* Farrar & Rinehart, 1940.
Oskar Seidlin and Senta Rypins, *Green Wagons,* Houghton, 1943.
Anne Molloy, *Shooting Star Farm,* Houghton, 1946.
Phyllis Crawford, *The Blot: Little City Cat,* Holt, 1946.
Nancy Hartwell, *Shoestring Theater,* Holt, 1947.
L. L. Bein, *Just Plain Maggie,* Harcourt, 1948.
Lee Kingman, *The Rocky Summer,* Houghton, 1948.

Ruth C. Seeger, *American Folk Songs for Children in Home, School and Nursery School: A Book for Children, Parents and Teachers,* Doubleday, 1948.

Child Study Association of America, *Read Me Another Story,* Crowell, 1949.

Rutherford Montgomery, *Kildee House,* Doubleday, 1949.

L. Kingman, *The Best Christmas,* Doubleday, 1949, reprinted, Peter Smith, 1985.

Phyllis Krasilovsky, *The Man Who Didn't Wash His Dishes,* Doubleday, 1950.

R. C. Seeger, *Animal Folk Songs for Children: Traditional American Songs,* Doubleday, 1950.

Nellie M. Leonard, *Graymouse Family,* Crowell, 1950.

Child Study Association of America, *Read Me More Stories,* Crowell, 1951.

R. Montgomery, *Hill Ranch,* Doubleday, 1951.

Elisabeth C. Lansing, *The Pony That Ran Away,* Crowell, 1951.

L. Kingman, *Quarry Adventure,* Doubleday, 1951, published in England as *Lauri's Surprising Summer,* Constable, 1957.

E. C. Lansing, *The Pony That Kept a Secret,* Crowell, 1952.

Mary M. Aldrich, *Too Many Pets,* Macmillan, 1952.

M. W. Brown, *Where Have You Been?,* Crowell, 1952, reprinted, Scholastic Book Services, 1966.

Barbara Reynolds, *Pepper,* Scribner, 1952.

Miriam E. Mason, *Yours with Love, Kate,* Houghton, 1952.

Margaret W. Brown, *Christmas in the Barn,* Crowell, 1952.

Catherine Marshall, *Let's Keep Christmas,* Whittlesey House, 1953.

R. C. Seeger, *American Folk Songs for Christmas,* Doubleday, 1953.

N. M. Leonard, *Grandfather Whiskers, M. D.: A Graymouse Story,* Crowell, 1953.

L. Kingman, *Peter's Long Walk,* Doubleday, 1953.

E. C. Lansing, *A Pony Worth His Salt,* Crowell, 1953.

Jane Quigg, *Fun for Freddie,* Oxford University Press, 1953.

Margaret Sidney, *The Five Little Peppers,* Doubleday, 1954.

M. W. Brown, *The Little Fir Tree,* Crowell, 1954, reissued, 1985.

Margaret G. Otto, *Pumpkin, Ginger, and Spice,* Holt, 1954.

Helen Kay (pseudonym of Helen C. Goldfrank), *Snow Birthday,* Farrar, Straus, 1955.

Louisa May Alcott, *Little Women; or, Meg, Jo, Beth, and Amy,* Crowell, 1955.

Louise A. Kent, *The Brookline Trunk,* Houghton, 1955.

Catherine S. McEwen, *Away We Go! One-Hundred Poems for the Very Young,* Crowell, 1956.

Catherine Marshall, *Friends with God: Stories and Prayers of the Marshall Family,* Whittlesey House, 1956.

H. Kay, *City Springtime,* Hastings House, 1957.

Neil Anderson (pseudonym of Jerrold Beim), *Freckle Face,* Crowell, 1957.

Henrietta Buckmaster, *Lucy and Loki,* Scribner, 1958.

Harry Behn, *Timmy's Search,* Seabury, 1958.

M. G. Otto, *Little Brown Horse,* Knopf, 1959.

Elizabeth G. Speare, *Seasonal Verses Gathered by Elizabeth George Speare from the Connecticut Almanack for the Year of the Christian Era, 1773,* American Library Association, 1959.

Le Hibou et la Poussiquette (French adaptation of *The Owl and the Pussycat* by Edward Lear), translated by Francis Steegmuller, Little, Brown, 1961.

Walter de la Mare, *Peacock Pie: A Book of Rhymes,* Knopf, 1961.

Noah Webster, *The American Speller: An Adaptation of Noah Webster's Blue-Backed Speller,* Crowell, 1961.

M. G. Otto, *Three Little Dachshunds,* Holt, 1963.

Sarah O. Jewett, *A White Heron: A Story of Maine,* Crowell, 1963.

Virginia Haviland, *Favorite Fairy Tales Told in Spain,* Little, Brown, 1963.

Papillot, Clignot, et Dodo (French adaptation of *Wynken, Blynken, and Nod* by Eugene Field), translated by F. Steegmuller and Norbert Guterman, Farrar, Straus, 1964.

Hugh Latham, translator, *Mother Goose in French,* Crowell, 1964.

A. Molloy, *Shaun and the Boat: An Irish Story* (Junior Literary Guild selection), Hastings House, 1965.

Jane Goodsell, *Katie's Magic Glasses,* Houghton, 1965.

Samuel Morse, *All in a Suitcase,* Little, Brown, 1966.

Aldous Huxley, *Crowns of Pearblossom,* Random House, 1967.

Alastair Reid and Anthony Kerrigan, *Mother Goose in Spanish,* Crowell, 1968.

Edward Lear, *The Owl and the Pussy-Cat,* Little, Brown, 1969.

Natalia M. Belting, *Christmas Folk,* Holt, 1969.

E. Field, *Wynken, Blynken and Nod,* Hastings House, 1970.

William Wise, *The Lazy Young Duke of Dundee,* Rand McNally, 1970.

Homer, *Dionysus and the Pirates: Homeric Hymn Number 7,* translated and adapted by Penelope Proddow, Doubleday, 1970.

Felix Salten (pseudonym of Siegmund Salzman), *Bambi: A Life in the Woods,* Simon & Schuster, 1970.

Book of Princesses, Scholastic Book Services, 1971.

Homer, *Hermes, Lord of Robbers: Homeric Hymn Number Four,* translated and adapted by P. Proddow, Doubleday, 1971.

Homer, *Demeter and Persephone: Homeric Hymn Number Two,* translated and adapted by P. Proddow, Doubleday, 1972.

John Becker, *Seven Little Rabbits,* Walker, 1972.

May Garelick, *Down to the Beach,* Four Winds, 1973.

Robyn Supraner, *Would You Rather Be a Tiger?,* Houghton, 1973.

Dorothy Joan Harris, *The House Mouse,* Warne, 1973.

Edna Mitchell Preston, *Squawk to the Moon, Little Goose* Viking, 1974.

Zora L. Olsen, *Herman the Great,* Scholastic Book Services, 1974.

E. L. Horwitz, *When the Sky Is Like Lace,* Lippincott, 1975.

Jean P. Colby, *Lexington and Concord, 1775: What Really Happened,* Hastings House, 1975.

E. M. Preston, *The Sad Story of the Little Bluebird and the Hungry Cat,* Four Winds, 1975.

Marjorie W. Sharmat, *Burton and Dudley* (Junior Literary Guild selection), Holiday House, 1975.

M. J. Craig, *The Donkey Prince,* Doubleday, 1977.

Aileen Fisher, *Plant Magic,* Bowmar, 1977.

Ellin Greene, compiler, *Midsummer Magic: A Garland of Stories, Charms, and Recipes,* Lothrop, 1977.

Donald Hall, *Ox-Cart Man* (Junior Literary Guild selection), Viking, 1979.

Delmore Schwartz, *I Am Cherry Alive, the Little Girl Sang,* Harper, 1979.

Norma Farber, *How the Hibernators Came to Bethlehem,* Walker, 1980.

Wendy Kesselman, *Emma,* Doubleday, 1980.

Margot C. Griego and others, selectors and translators, *Tortillitas para Mama and Other Nursery Rhymes: Spanish and English,* Holt, 1982.

John Bierhorst, translator, *Spirit Child: A Story of the Nativity,* Morrow, 1984.

Rumer Godden, *The Story of Holly and Ivy,* Viking, 1985.

Toni de Gerez, reteller, *Louhi, Witch of North Farm,* Viking, 1986.

Sergei Prokofiev, *Peter and the Wolf Pop-Up Book,* Viking, 1986.

Elinor L. Horwitz, *When the Sky Is Like Lace,* Lippincott, 1987.

Gloria M. Houston, *The Year of the Perfect Christmas Tree: An Appalachian Tale,* Dial, 1988.

Contributor of illustrations to periodicals.

ADAPTATIONS: Chanticleer and the Fox was adapted as a sound filmstrip by Weston Woods, 1959; *Wynken, Blynken and Nod* was adapted as a sound filmstrip by Weston Woods, 1967; *Owl and the Pussycat* was adapted as a sound filmstrip, 1967; *The Man Who Didn't Wash His Dishes* was adapted as a sound filmstrip by Weston Woods, 1973; *Squawk to the Moon, Little Goose* was adapted as a sound filmstrip by Viking, 1975; *Miss Rumphius* was adapted as a filmstrip with cassette by Live Oak Media, 1984; *Ox-Cart Man* was adapted as a filmstrip with cassette by Random House and as a videocassette by Live Oak Media; *How the Hibernators Came to Bethlehem* was adapted as a filmstrip with cassette by Random House; *American Folksongs for Children* was adapted as a cassette.

SIDELIGHTS: Two-time winner of the Caldecott Medal, once for a book she wrote and once for a book she illustrated, Barbara Cooney has had a long and successful career as a children's writer and illustrator. She began drawing when she was still a young girl. In an interview with *Something About the Author* (SATA), Cooney explains: "I've been drawing pictures for as long as I can remember. It's in the blood. . . . My favorite days were when I had a cold and could stay home from school and draw all day long." Cooney's mother was an artist and so paints, brushes, and other supplies were always available. "I became an artist," Cooney relates in *Horn Book,* "because I had access to materials and pictures, a minimum of instruction, and a stubborn nature."

After graduating from Smith College, and taking classes at the Art Students League in New York, Cooney made the rounds of New York art directors looking for work. She tells *SATA:* "Book illustration, I thought, might be a way to use what little talent I judged I had." With the outbreak of the Second World War, Cooney joined the Women's Army Corps. Marriage and her first pregnancy pushed her into leaving the military and turning to more domestic matters.

While raising her family, Cooney began illustrating and writing children's books. To make her illustrations as realistic as possible, she often visits the actual places in the story. "I often go to great lengths to get authentic backgrounds for my illustrations," she explains in *Horn Book.* "I climbed Mount Olympus to see how things up there looked to Zeus. I went down into the cave where Hermes was born. I slept in Sleeping Beauty's castle."

Cooney often bases her stories on historical events, and she takes great care to get the historical details right. "When creating period costumes and environments," *Juvenile Miscellany* reports, "Cooney is very exacting. She travels to the location of the book setting to conduct extensive research." To do her illustrations for *The Year of the Perfect Christmas Tree,* written by Gloria M. Houston, Cooney "went down to Appalachia and met the author's family," she tells *Publishers Weekly.* "They were a great help in telling me how it was back then when the story takes place (post-World War I) and about the spirit of the place—I couldn't have gotten that without going there."

For her Caldecott-winning book *Chanticleer and the Fox,* Cooney retold and illustrated a story by Geoffrey Chaucer. Her inspiration, she tells *Horn Book,* "is a little embarrassing because the answer is so simple. I just happened to want to draw chickens. . . . For years I have admired the work of Chinese and Japanese artists, in particular, their landscapes and their birds. But I think the actual day that *Chanticleer* was conceived was . . . one autumn day. I had been out in the woods picking witch hazel and was on my way to cook supper. As I came out of the woods I passed a little barn that I had often passed before. But never at that time of day nor when the barn door was wide open. At that hour the sun was getting low and it shone right into the doorway. The inside of the barn was like a golden stage set. At that time of year the loft was full of hay, gold hay. And pecking around the floor of the barn was a most gorgeous and impractical flock of fancy chickens, rust-colored chickens, black ones, white ones, speckled ones and laced ones, some with crests on their heads, some with feathered legs, others with iridescent tails, and all with vermilion-colored wattles and combs."

For her book *Miss Rumphius,* Cooney was inspired by a real-life woman who had traveled the world over planting flower seeds. In Cooney's story, Miss Rumphius is a world traveler who returns to her home town when she is very old because she wants to create something of beauty before she dies. The surprising way she does this is the core of the story. "Of all the books I have done," Cooney once said, "*Miss Rumphius* has been, perhaps, the closest to my heart. There are, of course, many dissimilarities between me and Alice Rumphius, but, as I worked, she gradually seemed to become my *alter ego.* Perhaps she had been that right from the start." *Miss Rumphius* won the American Book Award and was selected as a *New York Times* Best Book of the Year.

Although Cooney writes and illustrates her own books, she has also illustrated over 100 books by other writers. She tells *Publishers Weekly:* "I love doing my own books, but my ideas are slow in germinating. I can't put out a book a year. I like to keep my hand in, so I find new things to work on, and interpreting other people's texts is one of them." Ideas for her own books come slowly to her and they take time to develop. The idea for the *Island Boy* grew from her love of the Maine coastline. When she found an old history of Maine which told of a man who lived on a nearby island his whole life, Cooney knew she had found her story. "I've had a love affair with the area since I was born," she tells *Publishers Weekly.* "I wanted to do it justice. I expect I feel it is heaven on earth."

Cooney's Caldecott-winning book *Ox-Cart Man* tells of a New Hampshire farmer of the nineteenth century who, each year, loads the goods and food his family had produced during the year into an ox-drawn cart and takes them to market. There he sells all the goods and the ox and walks back across New Hampshire to his home. Written by Donald Hall, *Ox-Cart Man* takes place very near to where Cooney lives. Cooney explains to *Horn Book* that although the story takes place near her house, she needed to do extensive research for the proper historical details. "First of all," she relates, "I had to establish *exactly* when the story could have happened. 'When' is very important to an illustrator because the sets (the landscape and architecture) must be accurate; so must the costumes, the props, the hairdos, everything." Cooney's research even extended to determining which buildings would have been standing in Portsmouth, New Hampshire, in 1832—a difficult question because of the frequent fires the town suffered. But the natural landscape remained the same. "When you get into country up our way, it still looks pretty much like the New England that the Ox-Cart Man knew," Cooney states.

In the 1970s, Cooney had a new house constructed along the Maine coastline to use as a studio. Her younger son built it over a three year period. As Constance Reed McClellan relates in *Horn Book,* Cooney "conceived the idea, chose the site, designed and planned the house, watched over and participated in its construction. . . . But the house is now her own—her retreat, her fortress, her castle." Containing Cooney's art studio as well as a photography studio, the new house is within a few feet of the Atlantic Ocean.

BIOGRAPHICAL/CRITICAL SOURCES:

BOOKS

Colby, Jean Poindexter, *Writing, Illustrating, and Editing Children's Books,* Hastings House, 1967.
Field, Elinor W., *Horn Book Reflections,* Horn Book, 1969.
Georgiou, Constantine, *Children and Their Literature,* Prentice-Hall, 1969.
Fuller, Muriel, editor, *More Junior Authors,* H. W. Wilson, 1963, pp. 53-54.
Hurlimann, Bettina, *Picture-Book World,* World Publishing, 1969.
Hopkins, Lee Bennett, *Books Are by People,* Citation Press, 1969.
Klemin, Diana, *The Art of Art for Children's Books,* C. N. Potter, 1966.
Something About the Author, Gale, Volume 59, 1990.

PERIODICALS

American Library Association Bulletin, April, 1959.

Horn Book, August, 1959; February, 1961; October, 1969; August, 1980, pp. 378-387.
Juvenile Miscellany, winter, 1986.
Library Journal, April, 1959.
Los Angeles Times Book Review, November 20, 1988, p. 8.
Maine Sunday Telegram, November 27, 1988.
New York Times Book Review, April 25, 1982, p. 42; November 14, 1982, p. 43; December 4, 1988, p. 40; January 6, 1991, p. 26.
Publishers Weekly, March 23, 1959; July 29, 1988, p. 138; June 29, 1990, p. 68.
Washington Post Book World, May 9, 1982, p. 16; November 6, 1988, p. 14.

*   *   *

COONEY, Caroline B. 1947-

PERSONAL: Born May 10, 1947; daughter of Dexter Mitchell (a purchasing agent) and Martha (a teacher; maiden name, Willerton) Bruce; (divorced); children: Louisa, Sayre, Harold. *Education:* Attended Indiana University, 1965-66, Massachusetts General Hospital School of Nursing, 1966-67, and University of Connecticut, 1968. *Avocational interests:* Playing the piano and organ, singing, directing a choir.

ADDRESSES: Home—Westbrook, CT. *Agent*—Curtis Brown Ltd., 10 Astor Pl., New York, NY 10003.

CAREER: Author, 1978—. Musician (organist).

MEMBER: Authors Guild, Authors League of America, Mystery Writers of America.

AWARDS, HONORS: Award for Juvenile Literature, North Carolina chapter, American Association of University Women, 1980, for *Safe as the Grave;* Romantic Book Award, Teen Romance category, 1985, for her body of work.

WRITINGS:

YOUNG ADULT, EXCEPT AS NOTED

Safe as the Grave (juvenile mystery; Junior Literary Guild selection; illustrated by Gail Owens), Coward, 1979.
Rear View Mirror (adult), Random House, 1980.
The Paper Caper (juvenile mystery; Junior Literary Guild selection; illustrated by G. Owens), Coward, 1981.
An April Love Story, Scholastic, 1981.
Nancy and Nick, Scholastic, 1982.
He Loves Me Not, Scholastic, 1982.
A Stage Set for Love, Archway, 1983.
Holly in Love, Scholastic, 1983.
I'm Not Your Other Half, Putnam, 1984.
Sun, Sea, and Boys, Archway, 1984.

Nice Girls Don't, Scholastic, 1984.
Rumors, Scholastic, 1985.
Trying Out, Scholastic, 1985.
Suntanned Days, Simon & Schuster, 1985.
Racing to Love, Archway, 1985.
The Bad and the Beautiful, Scholastic, 1985.
The Morning After, Scholastic, 1985.
All the Way, Scholastic, 1985.
Saturday Night, Scholastic, 1986.
Don't Blame the Music, Putnam, 1986.
Saying Yes, Scholastic, 1987.
Last Dance, Scholastic, 1987.
The Rah Rah Girl, Scholastic, 1987.
Among Friends, Bantam, 1987.
Camp Boy-Meets-Girl, Bantam, 1988.
New Year's Eve, Scholastic, 1988.
Summer Nights, Scholastic, 1988.
The Girl Who Invented Romance, Bantam, 1988.
Camp Reunion, Bantam, 1988.
Family Reunion, Bantam, 1989.
The Fog, Scholastic, 1989.
The Face on the Milk Carton, Bantam, 1990.
The Snow, Scholastic, 1990.
The Fire, Scholastic, 1990.

Contributor of stories to juvenile and young adult magazines, including *Seventeen, American Girl, Jack and Jill, Humpty Dumpty,* and *Young World.*

ADAPTATIONS: Rear View Mirror was filmed as a television movie, starring Lee Remick, Warner Bros., 1984.

WORK IN PROGRESS: The Party's Over, for Scholastic; *Twenty Pageants Later* for Bantam.

SIDELIGHTS: Caroline B. Cooney began writing when she was a young housewife raising two children. "Sitting home with the babies," she once remarked, "I had to find a way to entertain myself. So I started writing with a pencil, between the children's naps—baby in one arm, notebook in the other." Over several years, she wrote eight novels, all of them adult historical fiction, without a sale. But meanwhile her short stories for young adults sold to magazines like *Seventeen.* "I continued to write for that age group and finally found the type of writing that I could both be successful at and enjoy," she remembers.

Cooney's first published novel, *Safe as the Grave,* is a juvenile mystery in which a young girl encounters a secret in the family cemetery. "Having already written eight books with no luck," Cooney says, "I wasn't interested in wasting my time writing another unpublishable novel. So instead I wrote an outline and mailed it along with my short story resume to a number of publishers, saying, 'Would you be interested in seeing this'—knowing, of course, that they wouldn't. Naturally, when they all said 'yes,' I was stunned; the only thing to do was to quick write the book."

Following publication of *Safe as the Grave,* Cooney wrote an adult suspense novel, *Rear View Mirror,* the story of a young woman who is kidnapped and forced to drive two killers in her car. Michele Slung of the *Washington Post* calls the book "so tightly written, so fast-moving, that it's easy not to realize until the last paragraph is over that one hasn't been breathing all the while." In 1984 *Rear View Mirror* was made into a television movie starring Lee Remick as the kidnapped woman.

Cooney returned to young adult writing with *An April Love Story,* a romance novel published in 1981. Since that time she has written young adult novels exclusively, sometimes creating her own plots and sometimes following the requests of her editors. "*Don't Blame the Music* was based on my (then) Pacer editor's wish for a book about a girl who craves fame to the point of destroying herself," Cooney recalls. Other books have been part of the popular "Cheerleader" and "Chrystal Falls" series. "It is exciting 'to write to order,'" Cooney explains. "It often involves an idea or characters I've never thought about before, and I have to tackle it cold like any other assignment. Editors have such good ideas! I also continue to write my own ideas, like *The Girl Who Invented Romance.* 'Romance' is a board game that Kelly designs and the board game [is] part of the book."

Cooney explains that she once wrote books in a spontaneous way. "I never used to know what was going to happen in the story until I wrote it," she states. "Then I began doing paperbacks for Scholastic and they required outlines, largely just to ensure that two writers didn't waste time and effort on similar ideas. Before, I'd always allowed the story to develop out of the characters, but the outlines demanded that the plot and characters evolve together at the same time. Now I wouldn't do it any other way."

Much of Cooney's inspiration comes from her volunteer work with teenagers. "I do a great deal of volunteer work at the school and church, see a lot of kids' pain, fear, hope, and joy. These children have been a tremendously positive influence on me, because they're the ones I'm writing to, the ones I'm writing for." Cooney finds that today's kids want stories with happy endings. "They want hope, want things to work out, want reassurance that even were they to do something rotten, they and the people around them would still be alright. No matter what it is that they're doing, I don't think they want to have to read about it. Teenagers looking for books to read don't say, 'Oh, good, another book about rotten, depressing drug abuse.' I think they want to read about the nicer, sweeter sides of life; I think they want happy endings."

Cooney provides just that in *Among Friends,* a young adult novel with a unique structure. Six students have been given an assignment to write a journal during a three-month period. The entries from those journals, providing a variety of points of view, make up the novel. This approach, Mitzi Myers states in the *Los Angeles Times,* provides "a more rounded interpretation than any single character could supply." Myers concludes: "It is a pleasure to find a book for young readers that not only individualizes characters through their writing but also has wise words to say about how writing offers very real help in coping with the problems of growing up."

Most of Cooney's books are romances because she believes the genre to be important. "I believe that to love and to be loved," she explains, "are the most fierce desires any of us will ever have, and young girls can never read enough about it. (Girls *my* age can never read enough about it, either!) One of my daughters loves teen romances and memorizes mine; the other daughter wouldn't be caught dead reading a romance; and my son wants to know, when each book is published, does this mean we have enough money to go to Disney World again?"

BIOGRAPHICAL/CRITICAL SOURCES:

PERIODICALS

Bulletin of the Center for Children's Books, July-August, 1986.
Los Angeles Times, February 6, 1988.
Publishers Weekly, June 18, 1979; September 26, 1986; August 25, 1989.
Times Literary Supplement, May 20, 1988.
Washington Post, June 1, 1980.

* * *

COOPER, Kay 1941-

PERSONAL: Born July 26, 1941, in Cleveland, OH; daughter of Jack Edwin (an engineer) and Margaret (Stevens) Cooper; married John James Watt III (a pharmacist), June 20, 1964; children: Anne Michelle, Susan Kathleen. *Education:* University of Michigan, B.A., 1963. *Politics:* Independent. *Religion:* Protestant.

ADDRESSES: Home—222 East Hazel Dell Lane, Springfield, IL 62707.

CAREER: Writer. Reporter, *Indianapolis News,* Indianapolis, IN, 1960, *Freeport Journal-Standard,* Freeport, IL, 1963-64, and *Springfield Sun,* Springfield, IL, 1966-67.

MEMBER: P.E.O. Sisterhood, National Association for Search and Rescue (canine), Springfield Children's Reading Round Table (president, 1976), Kappa Delta (president of Springfield alumnae chapter, 1968-69; vice-president, 1969-70).

AWARDS, HONORS: Outstanding science trade book awards, 1973, 1974, 1976.

WRITINGS:

A Chipmunk's Inside-Outside World, Messner, 1973.
All about Rabbits as Pets, Messner, 1974.
All about Goldfish as Pets, Messner, 1976.
C'mon Ducks!, Messner, 1978.
Journeys on the Mississippi, Messner, 1981.
Who Put the Cannon in the Courthouse Square?: A Guide to Uncovering the Past, Walker & Co., 1984.
Hands-on Geography: Illinois, Nystrom, 1985.
Where Did You Get Those Eyes?: A Guide to Discovering Your Family History, Walker & Co., 1988.
Where in the World Are You?: A Guide to Looking at the World, Walker & Co., 1990.
Why Do You Talk as You Do?: A Guide to World Languages, Walker & Co., 1991.

Contributor to *Voyages,* Level 15 in the "Reading Today and Tomorrow" series, Holt, 1989.

WORK IN PROGRESS: An Index to Finger Plays, Neal-Schuman; *Science Finger Plays,* Scholastic.

*   *   *

COOPER, Susan (Mary) 1935-

PERSONAL: Born May 23, 1935, in Burnham, Buckinghamshire, England; came to United States in 1963; daughter of John Richard and Ethel May (Field) Cooper; married Nicholas J. Grant, August 3, 1963 (divorced, 1983); children: Jonathan, Katharine; stepchildren: Anne, Bill (died, 1986), Peter. *Education:* Somerville College, Oxford, M.A., 1956. *Avocational interests:* Music, islands.

CAREER: Writer. *Sunday Times,* London, England, reporter and feature writer, 1956-63.

MEMBER: Society of Authors (United Kingdom), Authors League of America, Authors Guild, Writers Guild of America.

AWARDS, HONORS: Horn Book Honor List citation for *Over Sea, under Stone; Horn Book* Honor List and American Library Association Notable Book citations, both 1970, both for *Dawn of Fear; Boston Globe-Horn Book* award, American Library Association Notable Book citation, Carnegie Medal runner-up, all 1973, and Newbery Award Honor Book, 1974, all for *The Dark Is Rising;* American Library Notable Book citation, for *Greenwitch; Horn Book* Honor List and American Library Association Notable Book citation, Newbery Medal, Tir na N'og Award (Wales), and commendation for Carnegie Medal, all 1976, for *The Grey King;* Tir na N'og Award for *Silver*

on the Tree; Christopher Award, Humanitas Prize, Writers Guild of America Award, and Emmy Award nomination from Academy of Television Arts and Sciences, all 1984, all for *The Dollmaker;* Emmy Award nomination, 1987, and Writers Guild of America Award, 1988, for teleplay *Foxfire; Horn Book* Honor List citation, 1987, for *The Selkie Girl;* B'nai B'rith Janusz Korczak Award, 1989, for *Seaward.*

WRITINGS:

(Contributor) Michael Sissons and Philip French, editors, *The Age of Austerity: 1945-51,* Hodder & Stoughton, 1963, Penguin, 1965, reprinted, Oxford University Press, 1986.
Mandrake (science-fiction novel), J. Cape, 1964, Penguin, 1966.
Behind the Golden Curtain: A View of the U.S.A. (Book Society Alternative Choice), Hodder & Stoughton, 1965, Scribner, 1966.
(Editor and author of preface) J. B. Priestley, *Essays of Five Decades,* Little, Brown, 1968.
J. B. Priestley: Portrait of an Author, Heinemann, 1970, Harper, 1971.
Dawn of Fear, illustrations by Margery Gill, Harcourt, 1970.
Jethro and the Jumbie, illustrations by Ashley Bryan, Atheneum, 1979.
(With Hume Cronyn) *Foxfire* (play; first produced at Stratford, Ontario, 1980; produced on Broadway at Ethel Barrymore Theatre, November 11, 1982; also see below), Samuel French, 1983.
(Reteller) *The Silver Cow: A Welsh Tale,* illustrations by Warwick Hutton, Atheneum, 1983.
Seaward, Atheneum, 1983.
(With Cronyn) *The Dollmaker* (teleplay; adaptation of novel of the same title by Harriette Arnow), produced by American Broadcasting Companies, Inc. (ABC), May 13, 1984.
(Author of introduction) John and Nancy Langstaff, editors, *The Christmas Revels Songbook: In Celebration of the Winter Solstice,* David R. Godine, 1985.
(Reteller) *The Selkie Girl,* illustrated by Warwick Hutton, Margaret McElderry Books/Macmillan, 1986.
Foxfire (teleplay), produced by Columbia Broadcasting System, Inc. (CBS), December 13, 1987.
Tam Lin, illustrated by Warwick Hutton, Margaret McElderry Books/Macmillan, 1991.
Natthew's Dragon, illustrated by Jos. A. Smith, Margaret McElderry Books/Macmillan, 1991.

Also author of teleplay *Dark Encounter,* 1976; author of teleplay version of Anne Tyler's novel *Dinner at the Homesick Restaurant.* Cooper's manuscripts are held in the Lillian H. Smith collection, Toronto Public Library, Toronto, Ontario, Canada.

"THE DARK IS RISING" SEQUENCE; JUVENILE NOVELS

Over Sea, under Stone, illustrated by Margery Gill, J. Cape, 1965, Harcourt, 1966.

The Dark Is Rising, illustrated by Alan E. Cober, Atheneum, 1973.

Greenwitch, Atheneum, 1974.

The Grey King, illustrated by Michael Heslop, Atheneum, 1975.

Silver on the Tree, Chatto & Windus, 1975, Atheneum, 1977.

ADAPTATIONS: "The Dark Is Rising" (two-cassette recording), Miller-Brody, 1979; "The Silver Cow" (filmstrip), Weston Woods, 1985; "The Silver Cow" (recording), Weston Woods, 1986.

WORK IN PROGRESS: The Boggart, a fantasy novel, publication expected in spring, 1993.

SIDELIGHTS: "Susan Cooper is one of the small and very select company of writers who—somehow, somewhere—have been touched by magic; the gift of creation is theirs, the power to bring to life for ordinary mortals 'the best of symbolic high fantasy,'" writes Margaret K. McElderry in *Horn Book Magazine.* In her works for children, Cooper mixes elements of her own life with myth, legend, and folklore from the Caribbean, Wales, and the English countryside where she grew up. "Music and song, old tales and legends, prose and poetry, theater and reality, imagination and intellect, power and control, a strong sense of place and people both past and present—all are part of the magic that has touched Susan Cooper," McElderry states. "Her journeys add great luster to the world of literature."

Cooper was born in rural England, only twenty-three miles outside of London. Her early years were filled with the sounds of World War II, especially the bombing of London: "I was four years old when the war broke out in Britain, and ten when it ended," she writes in her *Something about the Author Autobiography Series (SAAS)* entry. "I never came face-to-face with death, or with blood drawn by anything worse than broken glass, but it was a noisy war. . . . Once, a German aeroplane swooped low, machine-gunning, as we ran; once, a house fifty yards away was blown to pieces; once, we went to school . . . to find a vast gaping hole in the playground." "Once, when I was about six, and we had come back into the dark house after the reassuring monotone of the 'All Clear' siren," Cooper continues, "my parents pulled back the blackout curtain and ceremonially showed me the eastern sky. In a strange great blur along the horizon, it glowed a dull red. 'That's London, burning,' they said."

Young Susan Cooper had few doubts about her future occupation. "I knew I was a writer; I always had, from the age of about eight," she writes in her *SAAS* entry. "People ask us so often, in this trade, 'How did you become a writer?'—and the only possible answer is, 'It just happened.'" In a publicity release for Atheneum Publishers, she states: "The busiest time of my life as a writer was probably the year I turned ten. I was a shy, spherical child, afraid of the dark but full of professional confidence. I wrote three plays for a puppet theatre built by the boy next door, collaborated on a weekly newspaper with the son of my piano teacher, and wrote and illustrated a very small book." She went to Oxford University, taking a degree in English Language and Literature (and attending the lectures of C. S. Lewis and J. R. R. Tolkien), and becoming the first woman editor of the university newspaper *Cherwell.*

After graduation Cooper went on into journalism, working at first for the *Sunday Times*'s foreign manager, Ian Fleming (the author of the James Bond novels), who also authored a regular column for the paper. "When he gave up his column," Cooper states in *SAAS,* "I became a full-time news reporter, and eventually feature writer." "Like every journalist with a really insistent talent for writing," she continues, "I learned the dissatisfaction that goes with the need for brevity, and I began to write books in my spare time." The first of these to be published was a science fiction novel called *Mandrake;* the second was a children's book called *Over Sea, under Stone.*

Over Sea, under Stone traces the adventures of three English siblings—Simon, Jane, and Barnabas Drew—who discover in the attic of their old Cornish vacation home a clue to an ancient hidden treasure endowed with mystic powers against the Dark, an evil force that has warred with its counterpart, the Light, throughout history. With the help of Merriman Lyon, a college professor and family friend who is in fact a strong agent of the Light, the three Drews recover the treasure and defeat the forces of the Dark. The story, published in 1965, eventually became the first part of a quintet called "The Dark Is Rising," a series of fantasy novels based in part on Arthurian legend. "My sequence belongs to the vanished rural Buckinghamshire in which I lived my first eighteen years; to the Cornwall of childhood holidays; to the part of North Wales in which my grandmother was born and my parents lived their last twenty-five years," Cooper writes in her publicity release. "Haunted places all, true springs of the Matter of Britain. Bronze Age barrows littered our landscapes; Celt and Anglo-Saxon merged in our faces; Arthur filled our daydreams, the Welsh legends our darker dreams at night."

Cooper published several more books—a biography of her personal friend, the British writer J. B. Priestley, and *Dawn of Fear,* a fictionalized account of her childhood war experiences—and married an American college professor and moved to the United States before she continued the quintet. The second volume, *The Dark Is Ris-*

ing—a Newbery Honor Book in 1974—is the story of Will Stanton, youngest son of a Buckinghamshire family, who awakes one morning shortly before the winter solstice to discover that he is no longer entirely human. He is the last of the Old Ones, the agents of the Light, and he is coming into his power. Merriman Lyon, of *Over Sea, under Stone,* reappears in *The Dark Is Rising* as Will's tutor, and he, with the help of the other Old Ones, struggles to prevent the Dark from overwhelming Will as Will learns to control his new powers.

Greenwitch, the third volume of the sequence, brings the Drews and Will to Cornwall. The treasure the Drews had uncovered in *Over Sea, under Stone* has been stolen by an agent of the Dark, and Will, Merriman, and the three children work together to recover it. *The Grey King,* Cooper's Newbery Award-winning fourth volume, takes Will to Wales, where he discovers Bran Davies, the Pendragon—the lost heir of Arthur—and combats the evil mountain spirit called the Grey King. In the final volume, *Silver on the Tree,* Will, Bran, and the Drews unite to combat the final rising of the Dark. "The underlying theme of my 'Dark Is Rising' sequence, and particularly of its fourth volume *The Grey King,*" Cooper explained in her Newbery acceptance speech, reprinted in *Horn Book Magazine,* "is, I suppose, the ancient problem of the duality of human nature. The endless coexistence of kindness and cruelty, love and hate, forgiveness and revenge—as inescapable as the cycle of life and death, day and night, the Light and the Dark."

Since completing the "Dark Is Rising" sequence, Cooper has begun working in other genres. "All my life," she writes in *Horn Book,* "I had been rooted in libraries, both as a reader of other people's books and writer of my own. All my life I had been stagestruck, haunted by the theater. Within a year of finishing *Silver on the Tree,* and my sequence of novels," she continues, she had begun working on stage pieces, including a play called *Foxfire,* coauthored with Hume Cronyn, that played on Broadway with Cronyn and his wife Jessica Tandy in the lead roles. Later Cooper wrote a television adaptation of Harriette Arnow's novel *The Dollmaker,* which was presented on ABC in 1984. Jane Fonda played the lead role and was awarded an Emmy for her performance.

In addition to her stage works, Cooper has continued to publish fantasy stories for children and young adults. *Jethro and the Jumbie* is the story of an encounter between a young boy and a ghost, set in the West Indies, where Cooper and her husband had a vacation home. *The Silver Cow* and *The Selkie Girl* are based on folktales and legends from the British Isles. *Seaward,* a young adult novel, was written just after Cooper's parents died and her marriage broke up, and intertwines themes of love, life, death, and hate. Cally and Westerly are two young people who have lost their parents and are thrown into an ambiguous myth-haunted other world. *Seaward* reintroduces the dualism theme that predominates in the "Dark Is Rising" novels, showing how Cally and Westerly are manipulated by the Old Gods in their journey together.

"Every book is a voyage of discovery," Cooper writes in *Celebrating Children's Books.* "Perhaps I speak only for myself, perhaps it's different for other writers; but for me the making of a fantasy is quite unlike the relatively ordered procedure of writing any other kind of book. . . . Each time, I am striking out into a strange land, listening for the music that will tell me which way to go. And I am always overcome by wonder, and a kind of unfocused gratitude, when I arrive." The author describes herself as "a writer whose work sometimes turns out to belong on the children's list, and sometimes elsewhere. To tell the truth," she concludes, "I don't write for you, whoever you are; I write for me. And 'me' is a complicated word; perhaps I know less about its meaning now than when I was that busy ten-year-old."

BIOGRAPHICAL/CRITICAL SOURCES:

BOOKS

Children's Literature Review, Volume 4, Gale, 1982.
de Montreville, Doris, and Elizabeth D. Crawford, editors, *Fourth Book of Junior Authors and Illustrators,* H. W. Wilson, 1978, pp. 98-99.
Hearne, Betsy, and Marilyn Kaye, *Celebrating Children's Books: Essays on Children's Literature in Honor of Zena Sutherland,* Lothrop, 1981.
Sutherland, Zena, and others, *Children and Books,* Scott, Foresman, 1981.
Something about the Author Autobiography Series, Volume 6, Gale, 1988.

PERIODICALS

American Libraries, December, 1974.
Best Sellers, May 15, 1971.
Books, November, 1970.
Books and Bookmen, October, 1973; January, 1975.
Bookseller, September 19, 1970.
Books for Your Children, spring, 1976.
Children's Book Review, September, 1973; autumn, 1974.
Children's Literature in Education, summer, 1977.
Christian Science Monitor, November 2, 1977.
Globe and Mail (Toronto), May 12, 1984.
Growing Point, September, 1965; January, 1975; December, 1975; March, 1978.
Horn Book Magazine, October, 1975; August, 1976, pp. 367-72; October, 1976; December, 1977; May/June, 1990.
Junior Bookshelf, August, 1965; August, 1972; April, 1978.

Los Angeles Times, February 18, 1983.

New Statesman, June 2, 1972.

New York Times, November 12, 1982; May 11, 1984.

New York Times Book Review, October 27, 1968; November 8, 1970; May 22, 1973; May 5, 1974; September 28, 1975.

School Librarian and School Library Review, December, 1965.

School Library Journal, October, 1975; December, 1977; February, 1980.

Times Educational Supplement, June 20, 1980.

Times Literary Supplement, September 18, 1970; July 14, 1972; June 15, 1973; July 5, 1974; December 5, 1975; December 2, 1977; November 25, 1983.

Washington Post Book World, July 8, 1973.

OTHER

Susan Cooper (publicity release), Atheneum, 1985.

*   *   *

COOVER, Robert (Lowell) 1932-

PERSONAL: Born February 4, 1932, in Charles City, IA; son of Grant Marion and Maxine (Sweet) Coover; married Maria del Pilar Sans-Mallafre, June 3, 1959; children: Diana Nin, Sara Chapin, Roderick Luis. *Education:* Attended Southern Illinois University at Carbondale, 1949-51; Indiana University at Bloomington, B.A., 1953; University of Chicago, M.A., 1965.

ADDRESSES: Home—Providence, RI. *Agent*—Georges Borchardt, Inc., 136 East 57th St., New York, NY 10022.

CAREER: Writer of fiction, plays, essays and poetry. Instructor, Bard College, Annandale-on-Hudson, NY, 1966-67, University of Iowa, Iowa City, 1967-69, Princeton University, Princeton, NJ, 1972-73, Columbia University, New York City, 1972, Virginia Military Institute, Lexington, 1976, Brandeis University, Waltham, MA, 1981, and Brown University, Providence, RI, 1981—. Organized conference on literature, "Unspeakable Practices: A Three-Day Celebration of Iconoclastic American Fiction," Brown University, 1988. Producer and director of film *On a Confrontation in Iowa City,* 1969. *Military service:* U.S. Naval Reserve, 1953-57; became lieutenant.

MEMBER: American Academy of Arts and Letters (1987—).

AWARDS, HONORS: William Faulkner Award for best first novel, 1966, for *The Origin of the Brunists;* Rockefeller Foundation grant, 1969; Guggenheim fellowships, 1971 and 1974; citation in fiction from Brandeis University, 1971; Academy of Arts and Letters award, 1975; National Book Award nomination, 1977, for *The Public*

Burning; National Endowment for the Humanities Award, 1985; Rea Award (short story), Dungannan Foundation, 1987, for *A Night at the Movies;* DAAD fellowship, 1991.

WRITINGS:

The Origin of the Brunists (novel; also see below), Putnam, 1966.

The Universal Baseball Association, Inc., J. Henry Waugh, Prop. (novel), Random House, 1968.

Pricksongs & Descants (collected short fiction), Dutton, 1969.

The Water Power, Bruccoli-Clark, 1972.

(Editor with Kent Dixon) *The Stone Wall Book of Short Fiction,* Stone Wall Press, 1973.

(Editor with Elliott Anderson) *Minute Stories,* Braziller, 1976.

The Public Burning (novel), Viking, 1977.

The Hair o' the Chine, Bruccoli-Clark, 1979.

A Political Fable, Viking, 1980.

After Lazarus: A Filmscript, Bruccoli-Clark, 1980.

Charlie in the House of Rue, Penmaen, 1980.

The Convention, Lord John, 1981.

Spanking the Maid, Bruccoli-Clark, 1981.

In Bed One Night and Other Brief Encounters, Burning Deck, 1983.

Gerald's Party: A Novel, Simon & Schuster, 1986.

Aesop's Forest (bound with *The Plot of the Mice and Other Stories* by Brian Swann), Capra Press, 1986.

A Night at the Movies or You Must Remember This (short stories), Simon & Schuster, 1987.

Whatever Happened to Gloomy Gus of the Chicago Bears?, Simon & Schuster, 1987.

Pinocchio in Venice (novel), Simon & Schuster, 1991.

PLAYS

A Theological Position (contains *A Theological Position* and *Rip Awake* [both produced in Los Angeles, CA, 1975], *The Kid* [produced Off-Broadway, 1972], *Love Scene* [produced in Paris as "Scene d'amour," 1973, produced in New York City, 1974]), Dutton, 1972.

Bridge Hound, produced in Providence, RI, 1981.

OTHER

Work represented in many anthologies, including *New American Review 4,* New American Library, 1968, *New American Review 14,* Simon & Schuster, 1972, and *American Review,* Bantam, 1974. Contributor of short stories, poems, essays, and translations to numerous periodicals, including *Noble Savage, Saturday Review, New York Times Book Review, Granta, Fictiona International,* and *Fiddlehead.* Fiction editor, *Iowa Review,* 1975-77.

ADAPTATIONS: Theatre adaptations of Coover's stories include "The Baby Sitter" and "Spanking the Maid." "Pedestrian Accident" has been made into an opera and "The Leper's Helix" into a chamberwork.

WORK IN PROGRESS: "Several narratives, short and long, in various media."

SIDELIGHTS: Robert Coover's work has generated much attention, especially among college audiences and critics, who contend that Coover, by mixing the actual with illusion, creates another, alternative world. Amazing, fantastic, and magic are among the words used to describe the effect of his fiction. *Time*'s Paul Gray notes that Coover has won a "reputation as an avant-gardist who can do with reality what a magician does with a pack of cards: Shuffle the familiar into unexpected patterns." Coover begins his novels with ordinary subjects and events, then introduces elements of fantasy and fear which, left unhindered, grow to equal, if not surpass, what is real within the situation. Michael Mason of the *Times Literary Supplement* believes that Coover structures his novels around the idea of "an American superstition giving rise to its appropriate imaginary apocalypse."

The Origin of the Brunists, Coover's first and most conventional novel, chronicles the rise and fall of a fictitious religious cult. This cult arises when the sole survivor of a mining disaster, Giovanni Bruno, claims to have been visited by the Virgin Mary and rescued via divine intervention. As the cult grows in numbers and hysteria, it is exploited and inflamed by the local newspaper editor until the situation reaches what Philip Callow of *Books and Bookmen* terms "apocalyptic proportions." Although some critics, such as Callow, find the novel's conclusion disappointing and anticlimactic, others, such as the *New Statesman*'s Miles Burrows, describe the book as being "a major work in the sense that it is long, dense, and alive to a degree that makes life outside the covers almost pallid."

In a *New Republic* review of Coover's second novel, *The Universal Baseball Association, Inc.,* Richard Gilman writes, "What this novel summons to action is our sense . . . of the possible substitution of one world for another, of the way reality implies alternatives." The book's protagonist, Henry Waugh, is bored with his job and his life. To alleviate his boredom, Waugh creates, within his imagination, an entire baseball league, complete with statistics and team and player names and histories. Plays, players, and fates are determined by dice, and Waugh, according to Gilman, presides "over this world of chance with a creator's calm dignity." When the dice rule that a favored player must die during a game, both Waugh's imaginary and real worlds fall apart. Waugh could, of course, choose to ignore the dice's decision, but to do so would be in violation of "the necessary laws that hold the cosmos together," a *Time* reviewer explains. At the novel's end, Waugh disappears from the story, leaving his players to

fashion their own existence, myths, and rituals. The *National Observer*'s Clifford A. Ridley comments: "[This] is a novel about continuity, about order, about reason, about God, and about the relationships between them. Which is to say that it is a parable of human existence, but do not feel put off by that; for it is a parable couched in such head-long, original prose and set down in a microcosms of such consistent fascination that it is far too busy entertaining to stop and instruct." Red Smith, however, disagrees. In a *Book World* review, Smith remarks: "A little fantasy goes a long way, though, and after an imaginary beanball kills an imaginary player the author never finds the strike zone again. It all becomes a smothering bore." Ronald Sukenick of the *New York Review* shares Smith's assessment of the novel's second-half: "Baseball has already been made to carry a heavy cargo in this book but now it gets heavier. With the plausibility of the actual game lost, the philosophical freight begins to take over. Mythy echoes and allusions fall thick as snow."

Pricksongs & Descants, Coover's collection of short fiction pieces, has been widely praised. Coover's experimental forms and techniques produce "extreme verbal magic," according to Christopher Lehmann-Haupt of the *New York Times.* "Nothing in Mr. Coover's writing is quite what it seems to be," the critic continues. "In the pattern of the leaves there is always the smile of the Cheshire Cat." And Marni Jackson in *Critique* explains: "An innocent situation develops a dozen sinister possibilities, sprouting in the readers imagination while they are suspended, open-ended, on the page. . . . Every disturbing twist the story might take is explored; all of them could have happened, or none. . . . Like a good conjurer, even when you recognize his gimmicks, the illusion continues to work."

Reaction to *The Public Burning,* Coover's "factional" account of the conviction and execution in 1953 of alleged spies Julius and Ethel Rosenberg, has been mixed. A satire on the mood and mentality of the nation at the time of the execution, the novel loosely combines fact and fiction. Coover sets the site of the Rosenbergs' electrocutions in Times Square, adds surrealistic parodies of various personalities and events of the era, and provides then-Vice-President Richard Nixon as the narrator-commentator. Most critics admire Coover's effort but criticize the book for being excessive and undisciplined. Piers Brendon of *Books and Bookmen* describes the novel as a "literary photo-montage" and "a paean of American self-hatred, a torrid indictment of the morally bankrupt society where for so long Nixon was the one." Lehmann-Haupt, in a later *New York Times* review, states that he was "shocked and amazed" by the book; he explains: "*The Public Burning* is an astonishing spectacle. It does not invite us to participate. . . . It merely allows us to watch, somewhat warily, as its author performs."

In the *New York Times Book Review,* Thomas R. Edwards notes that "horror and anger are the governing feelings in *The Public Burning.*" He comments: "As a work of literary art, *The Public Burning* suffers from excess. . . . But all vigorous satire is simplistic and excessive, and this book is an extraordinary act of moral passion." Brendon was similarly impressed by the novel's scope and also aware of its ultimate shortcomings: "*The Public Burning* is an ambitious failure. It is a huge, sprawling, brilliant, original excercise in literary photo-montage. It combines fact and fiction, comedy and terror, surrealism and satire, travesty and tragedy. [But it] is too overblown, too undisciplined, too crude, too lurid."

Overall, most critics agree that Coover is among the more notable new writers of the past two decades. Noting Coover's experimental approach to fictional forms and his originality and versatility as a prose stylist, they frequently compare his work to that of John Barth, Donald Barthelme, and Thomas Pynchon. In his review of *Pricksongs & Descants,* Lehmann-Haupt of the *New York Times* calls Coover "among the best we now have writing." And Joyce Carol Oates comments in the *Southern Review:* "Coover . . . exists blatantly and brilliantly in his fiction as an authorial consciousness. . . . He will remind readers of William Gass, of John Barth, of Samuel Beckett. He is as surprising as any of these writers, and as funny as Donald Barthelme; both crude and intellectual, predictable and alarming, he gives the impression of thoroughly enjoying his craft."

BIOGRAPHICAL/CRITICAL SOURCES:

BOOKS

Anderson, R., *Robert Coover,* Twayne, 1981.
Contemporary Literary Criticism, Gale, Volume 3, 1975; Volume 7, 1977; Volume 15, 1980; Volume 32, 1985; Volume 46, 1988.
Cope, Jackson I., *Robert Coover's Fictions,* Johns Hopkins University Press, 1986.
Dictionary of Literary Biography, Volume 2: *American Novelists since World War II,* Gale, 1978.
Dictionary of Literary Biography Yearbook: 1981, Gale, 1982.
Gass, William, *Fiction and the Figures of Life,* Knopf, 1971.
Gordon, L. G., *Robert Coover,* Southern Illinois University Press, 1983.
McCaffery, L., *The Metafictional Muse,* University of Pittsburgh Press, 1982.
McKeon, Z. Karl, *Novels and Arguments,* University of Chicago, 1982.

Schulz, Max, *Black Humor Fiction of the 1960s,* Ohio University Press, 1973.

PERIODICALS

Atlanta Journal & Constitution, March 1, 1987.
Atlantic, November, 1977.
Books and Bookmen, May, 1967; August, 1978.
Book World, July 7, 1968; November 2, 1969.
Critique, Volume 11, number 3, 1969.
Cue, November 25, 1972.
Esquire, December, 1970.
Hollins Critic, April, 1970.
Los Angeles Times, February 6, 1987.
Los Angeles Times Book Review, October 25, 1987; January 27, 1991.
Nation, December 8, 1969.
National Observer, July 29, 1968.
New Republic, August, 17, 1967.
New Statesman, April 14, 1967; June 16, 1978.
Newsweek, December 1, 1969.
New York Review, March 13, 1969.
New York Times, June 13, 1968; October 22, 1969; November 18, 1972; September 7, 1977; December 19, 1985; January 7, 1987; August 22, 1987; January 15, 1991.
New York Times Book Review, July 7, 1968; August 14, 1977; June 27, 1982; February 1, 1987; September 27, 1987; January 27, 1991.
Publishers Weekly, December 26, 1986.
Saturday Review, August 31, 1968.
Southern Review, winter, 1971.
Time, June 28, 1968; August 8, 1977.
Times (London), February 5, 1987; May 2, 1991.
Times Literary Supplement, June 16, 1978; February 13, 1987.
Tribune Books, August 16, 1987; January 27, 1991.
Village Voice, July 30, 1970.
Washington Post Book World, May 11, 1982; March 1, 1987; January 6, 1991.

*   *   *

CORLISS, William R(oger) 1926-

PERSONAL: Born August 28, 1926, in Stamford, CT; son of George Martin (a farmer) and Hazel (Brown) Corliss; married Virginia Odabashian, July 22, 1950; children: Cathleen, Steven, James, Laura. *Education:* Rensselaer Polytechnic Institute, B.S., 1950; University of Colorado, M.S., 1953; University of Wisconsin, graduate study, 1953-54.

ADDRESSES: Home and office—P.O. Box 107, Glen Arm, MD 21057.

CAREER: University of California, Radiation Laboratory, Berkeley, senior accelerator technician, 1951; Pratt & Whitney Aircraft, East Hartford, CT, supervisor of heat transfer and hydrodynamics, 1954-56; General Electric Co., Flight Propulsion Laboratory, Cincinnati, OH, space propulsion systems specialist, 1956-59; Martin Co., Nuclear Division, Baltimore, MD, director of advanced programs, 1959-63; free-lance science writer, 1963—; Sourcebook Project, Glen Arm, MD, director, 1974—. *Military service:* U.S. Navy, 1944-46.

MEMBER: American Association for the Advancement of Science.

WRITINGS:

Propulsion Systems for Space Flight, McGraw, 1960.
(With D. G. Harvey) *Radioisotopic Power Generation,* Prentice-Hall, 1964.
Space Probes and Planetary Exploration, Van Nostrand, 1965.
Scientific Satellites, U.S. Government Printing Office, 1967.
Mysteries of the Universe, Crowell, 1967, revised edition, edited by Patrick Moore, published as *Some Mysteries of the Universe,* A. & C. Black, 1969.
(With E. G. Johnsen) *Teleoperator Controls,* U.S. Government Printing Office, 1968.
(Editor) *Encyclopedia of Satellites and Sounding Rockets,* Goddard Space Flight Center, 1970.
Mysteries beneath the Sea, Crowell, 1970.
(With Johnsen) *Human Factors Applications in Teleoperator Design and Operation,* Wiley, 1971.
History of NASA Sounding Rockets, U.S. Government Printing Office, 1971.
(With Glenn T. Seaborg) *Man and Atom,* Dutton, 1971.
History of the Goddard Networks, Goddard Space Flight Center, 1972.
The Interplanetary Pioneers, three volumes, U.S. Government Printing Office, 1972.
Histories of the Space Tracking and Data Acquisition Network (STADAN), the Manned Space Flight Network (MSFN), and the NASA Communications Network (NASCOM), NASA, 1974.
The Unexplained, Bantam, 1976.
(With D. Baals) *Wind Tunnels of NASA,* NASA, 1981.

PUBLISHED BY SOURCEBOOK PROJECT

Strange Phenomena: A Sourcebook of Unusual Natural Phenomena, two volumes, 1974.
Strange Artifacts: A Sourcebook on Ancient Man, Volume 1, 1974, Volume 2, 1976.
Strange Universe, Volume 1, 1975, Volume 2, 1977.
Strange Planet, Volume 1, 1975, Volume 2, 1978.
Strange Life, 1976.
Strange Minds, 1976.

Handbook of Unusual Natural Phenomena, 1977, revised edition, Doubleday, 1983, reprinted in hardcover, Arlington, 1988.
Ancient Man: A Handbook of Puzzling Artifacts, 1978.
Mysterious Universe: A Handbook of Astronomical Anomalies, 1979.
Unknown Earth: A Handbook of Geological Enigmas, 1980.
Incredible Life: A Handbook of Biological Mysteries, 1981.
The Unfathomed Mind: A Handbook of Unusual Mental Phenomena, 1982.
Lightning, Auroras, Nocturnal Lights, and Related Luminous Phenomena, 1982.
Tornados, Dark Days, Anomalous Precipitation, and Related Weather Phenomena, 1983.
Earthquakes, Tides, Unidentified Sounds, and Related Phenomena, 1983.
Rare Halos, Mirages, Anomalous Rainbows, and Related Electromagnetic Phenomena, 1984.
The Moon and the Planets, 1985.
The Sun and Solar System Debris, 1986.
Stars, Galaxies, Cosmos, 1987.
Carolina Bays, Mima Mounds, Submarine Canyons, 1988.
Anomalies in Geology: Physical, Chemical, Biological, 1989.
Neglected Geological Anomalies, 1990.
Inner Earth: A Search for Anomalies, 1991.

OTHER

Also author of several dozen booklets for the U.S. Government. Consulting editor, *McGraw-Hill Encyclopedia of Science and Technology.* Contributor to periodicals, including *International Science and Technology* and *Mosaic.*

*   *   *

CORNWALL, John 1928-

PERSONAL: Born April 27, 1928, in Spencer, IA; son of Morgan (a lawyer) and Inez (a housewife; maiden name, Lally) Cornwall. *Education:* University of Iowa, B.A., 1950; London School of Economics and Political Science, London, M.Sc., 1952; Harvard University, Ph.D., 1958.

ADDRESSES: Office—Department of Economics, Dalhousie University, Halifax, Nova Scotia, Canada B3H 3J5.

CAREER: Tufts University, Medford, MA, assistant professor, 1959-63, associate professor, 1963-66, professor of economics, 1966-70; Southern Illinois University at Carbondale, professor of economics, 1970-76; Dalhousie University, Halifax, Nova Scotia, McCulloch professor of economics, 1976—.

WRITINGS:

Growth and Stability in a Mature Economy, Wiley, 1972.
Modern Capitalism: Its Growth and Transformation, St. Martin's, 1977.
(With Wendy Maclean) *Economic Recovery for Canada,* Lorimer Press, 1983.
The Conditions for Economic Recovery: A Post-Keynesian Analysis, Basil Blackwell, 1983, M.E. Sharpe, 1984.
(Editor) *After Stagflation: Alternatives to Economic Decline,* Basil Blackwell, 1984.
The Theory of Economic Breakdown: An Institutional-Analytical Approach, Basil Blackwell, 1990.
(Editor) *The Capitalist Economies: Prospects for the 1990s,* Edward Elgar, 1991.
(With Wendy Cornwall) *Modelling Capitalist Development,* Cambridge, in press.

SIDELIGHTS: John Cornwall once told *CA:* "The basic aim of my writings is to explain some of the major developments and problems of the advanced capitalist economies over the past century. In the process, I have tried to show that properly-used macroeconomic theory has powerful explanatory capability, and that it is therefore a sound basis for the development of policies to relieve advanced economies of such problems as economic depression, inflation, and stagnation.

"Given these themes, my writing inevitably includes considerable criticism of 'mainstream' economics. I have increasingly come to believe that the dominant schools of economic thought, based on neoclassical economics, trivialize a respectable social science by sacrificing realism for the appearance of scientific rigor."

* * *

COX, William Trevor 1928-
(William Trevor)

PERSONAL: Born May 24, 1928, in Mitchelstown, County Cork, Ireland; son of James William (a bank official) and Gertrude (Davison) Cox; married Jane Ryan, August 26, 1952; children: Patrick, Dominic. *Education:* Attended St. Columba's College, Dublin, Ireland, 1941-46; Trinity College, Dublin, B.A., 1950. *Politics:* Liberal.

ADDRESSES: c/o Literistic Ltd., 32 West 40th St., No. 5F, New York, NY 10018; and c/o A. D. Peters & Company Ltd., 5th Floor, The Chambers, Chelsea Harbour, London SW10, England.

CAREER: Teacher in County Armagh, Northern Ireland, 1952-53; art teacher at prep school near Rugby, England, 1953-55, and in Somerset, England, 1956-59; while teach-

ing, worked as a church sculptor; advertising copywriter in London, England, 1960-65; writer, 1965—. Has had one-man exhibitions of his artwork in Dublin and Bath, England.

MEMBER: Irish Academy of Letters.

AWARDS, HONORS: Winner of Irish section, "Unknown Political Prisoner" sculpture competition, 1953; second prize, *Transatlantic Review* short story competition, 1964; Hawthornden Prize, Royal Society of Literature, 1965, for *The Old Boys;* Society of Authors' traveling scholarship, 1972; Benson Medal, Royal Society of Literature, 1975, for *Angels at the Ritz, and Other Stories;* Allied Irish Bank Prize for literature, 1976; Whitbread Prize for fiction, 1978, for *The Children of Dynmouth;* honorary Commander, Order of the British Empire, 1979; Giles Cooper award for radio play, 1980, for *Beyond the Pale,* and 1982, for *Autumn Sunshine;* Whitbread Prize for best novel, 1983, for *Fools of Fortune;* D.Litt., University of Exeter, 1984, Trinity College, Dublin, 1986, University of Belfast, 1989, and National University of Ireland, Cork, 1990; recipient of Irish Community Prize.

WRITINGS:

UNDER NAME WILLIAM TREVOR

A Standard of Behavior (novel), Hutchinson, 1958.
The Old Boys (novel; also see below), Viking, 1964.
The Boarding-House (novel), Viking, 1965.
The Elephant's Foot (play), first produced in Nottingham, England, 1966.
The Love Department (novel), Bodley Head, 1966, Viking, 1967.
The Day We Got Drunk on Cake, and Other Stories, Bodley Head, 1967, Viking, 1968.
Mrs. Eckdorf in O'Neill's Hotel (novel), Bodley Head, 1969, Viking, 1970.
The Old Boys (play; adapted from his novel; first produced on the West End at Mermaid Theatre, July 29, 1971), Davis-Poynter, 1971.
Miss Gomez and the Brethren (novel), Bodley Head, 1971.
The Ballroom of Romance, and Other Stories (includes "The Mark-2 Wife," "The Grass Widows," and "O Fat White Woman"; also see below), Viking, 1972.
Going Home (one-act play), first produced in London at King's Head Islington, February 29, 1972.
A Night with Mrs. da Tanka (one-act play), first produced in London, 1972.
Elizabeth Alone (novel), Bodley Head, 1973, Viking, 1974.
A Perfect Relationship (one-act play), first produced in London, 1973.
The 57th Saturday (one-act play), first produced in London, 1973.
Marriages (one-act play), first produced in London, 1973.

Angels at the Ritz, and Other Stories, Bodley Head, 1975, Viking, 1976.

The Children of Dynmouth (novel), Bodley Head, 1976, Viking, 1977.

Old School Ties, Lemon Tree Press, 1976.

Lovers of Their Time, and Other Stories, Viking, 1978.

Other People's Worlds (novel), Bodley Head, 1980, Viking, 1981.

Beyond the Pale (radio play; also see below), first broadcast in England, 1980, televised, 1989.

Scenes from an Album (play), first produced in Dublin at the Abbey Theatre, 1981.

Beyond the Pale, and Other Stories, Bodley Head, 1981, Viking, 1982.

Fools of Fortune (novel), Viking, 1983.

The Stories of William Trevor, Penguin, 1983.

A Writer's Ireland: Landscape in Literature (nonfiction), Viking, 1984.

The News from Ireland, and Other Stories, Viking, 1986.

Nights at the Alexandra (novel), Harper, 1987.

The Silence in the Garden (novel), Viking, 1988.

(Editor) *The Oxford Book of Irish Short Stories,* Oxford University Press, 1989.

Family Sins, and Other Stories, Viking, 1989.

Two Lives (contains the novels *Reading Turgenev* and *My House in Umbria*), Viking, 1991.

Also author of television and radio plays for British Broadcasting Corp. and ITV, including *The Mark-2 Wife, O Fat White Woman, The Grass Widows, The General's Day, Love Affair, Last Wishes, Matilda's England, Secret Orchards, Autumn Sunshine, The Penthouse Apartment, Travellers,* and *Events at Drimaghleen.* Stories anthologized in *Voices 2,* edited by Michael Ratcliffe, M. Joseph, 1964; *Winter's Tales 14,* edited by Kevin Crossley-Holland, Macmillan, 1968; *Splinters: A New Anthology of Modern Macabre Fiction,* edited by Alex Hamilton, Hutchinson, 1968, Walker & Co., 1969; *The Bedside Guardian,* edited by W. L. Webb, Collins, 1969; *The Seventh Ghost Book,* edited by Rosemary Timperley, Barrie & Jenkins, 1972; *Modern Irish Short Stories,* edited by David Marcus, Sphere, 1972; *The Eighth Ghost Book,* edited by Timperley, Barrie & Jenkins, 1973; *Winter's Tales from Ireland 2,* edited by Kevin Casey, Macmillan, 1973; *Modern Irish Love Stories,* edited by Marcus, Sphere, 1974; *The Bodley Head Book of Longer Short Stories,* edited by James Michie, Bodley Head, 1974; *A Book of Contemporary Nightmares,* edited by Giles Gordon, M. Joseph, 1977; *Best for Winter,* edited by A. D. Maclean, Macmillan, 1979; *The Bodley Head Book of Irish Short Stories,* edited by Marcus, Bodley Head, 1980; *Seven Deadly Sins,* Severn House, 1983.

Contributor of short stories to periodicals, including *Transatlantic Review, London Magazine, Town, Queen, Nova, Encounter, Times* (London), *Irish Press, Penguin Modern Stories, Listener, Argosy, Redbook, Atlantic, Observer, New Yorker, Spectator, Antaeus,* and *Antioch Review.*

ADAPTATIONS: The Old Boys was adapted as a BBC television play, 1965; *The Ballroom of Romance* was broadcast on BBC-TV, 1982; *The Children of Dynmouth* was aired on BBC-TV, 1987; a screenplay by Michael Hirst was based on *Fools of Fortune* and directed by Pat O'Connor, 1990; *Elizabeth Alone* was also produced for BBC-TV.

SIDELIGHTS: Short story writer, novelist, and playwright William Trevor Cox is an Irish-born English writer better known to his readers as William Trevor. Highly acclaimed for his short fiction, Trevor has been called "one of the finest living short-story writers in English" by such critics as *Washington Post Book World* contributor Jonathan Yardley. However, he is also a two-time recipient of the Whitbread Prize for his novels and is widely known in England for the British television productions of his novels. Having lived in both Ireland and England, Trevor has written about people in both countries and is especially concerned with the many ordinary people in the world who lead tragic, lonely lives. "I don't really have any heroes or heroines," Trevor remarks in a *Publishers Weekly* interview with Amanda Smith. "I don't seem to go in for them. I think I am interested in people who are not necessarily the victims of other people, but simply the victims of circumstances. . . . I'm very interested in the sadness of fate, the things that just happen to people."

Originally working as a sculptor, Trevor became displeased with the increasingly abstract turn his art was taking, and so he took up writing as a means of better expressing his concern for the human condition. "I think the humanity that isn't in abstract art began to go into [my] short stories," Trevor tells Smith. "The absence of people, I think, was upsetting me. I still don't like pictures without people in them." In order to make a clean break from his sculpting career, Trevor dropped his last name in his published writing. Nevertheless, his background in art influenced his choice to focus primarily on the short story form. "He compares the art of the short story to painting or sculpture," writes Geordie Greig in an *Irish Times* interview. The author explains to Greig, "A short story is like an impressionist painting. You cut down everything enormously and you get the effects from one big splash or explosion. You have to cut to the very edge. What excites me is to go as far as I can." Just as Trevor's short stories attempt to pare unnecessary elements down to a minimum, his "novels have been for the most part short, compact, highly saturated works that explore the consequences of a single event or situation," according to *New York Times Book Review* critic Robert Towers.

In many of Trevor's novels and stories, the events or situations that most affect his characters occur offstage and often years in the past. This interest in the importance of the past is evident from as early as his first successful novel, *The Old Boys,* a tale of how the public school reunion of eight octogenarians causes them to revert back to childish competitive behavior by reminding them of old grudges and rivalries. "For Trevor," observes *Encounter* critic Tom Paulin in a later review of *Lovers in Their Time,* "an obsession with the past is a kind of madness," a notion that is invested in many of the author's stories and novels. But the novel's situation also provides Trevor plenty of opportunities to demonstrate his characteristic use of understated humor.

"In most of his early work," remarks Towers, "Mr. Trevor's comic briskness and the energy with which he invests his villains do much to mitigate any depressing effect that the regular defeat or disappointment of the innocent might otherwise produce." Satire is also prominent in early Trevor books like *The Boarding House* and *The Love Department,* although the situations in which his characters find themselves are often lamentable. However, the critic writes, since "the mid-1970's there has been . . . a subtle change of tone in the stories. The harsh comedy—the gleeful misanthropy—is less in evidence, as is the stance of impartiality; in the later work one can guess rather clearly where the author's sympathies lie."

In what one *Times Literary Supplement* reviewer declares to be "a collection that is never disappointing," *The Ballroom of Romance, and Other Stories* portrays a series of characters who are caught in dreary, barren lives, but are not self-confident enough to change. Instead, they can only reflect upon what might have been, their memories and dreams leaving them isolated and alone. "The stories may be sad, but they have about them the unmistakable ring of truth." It is with these sad stories of ordinary people that the author finds himself repeatedly concerned. They may live unhappy lives because of their unwillingness or inability to give up the past or their illusions of reality, or, as with Trevor's *Elizabeth Alone,* because they are simply victims of fate.

With *Elizabeth Alone* Trevor first proposes a possible reason for people's suffering. Set in a hospital, the author presents a series of ostensibly comic situations while simultaneously probing deeper issues through his sympathetic character portrayals. The title character, Elizabeth Aidallbery, has in one way or another lost everyone in her life that was important to her, and has even begun to lose her sense of identity. She finds the strength to overcome her loneliness and carry on through one of her hospital mates, Miss Samson, whose religious faith has recently been shaken. Miss Samson convinces Elizabeth that the importance of caring for others, even—or perhaps especially—if the world has no God, gives people a purpose in life. A *Times Literary Supplement* critic compliments Trevor on his ability to execute this conclusion convincingly in a seriocomic novel, attributing this success to "the authority he has built up, as a writer, out of the sheer, detailed understanding of the characters he creates. . . . The stance of compassion which is adopted finally in *Elizabeth Alone* can now be seen to be implicit in all Mr. Trevor's best work. It gives him a place as a writer capable of handling the human comedy instead of merely manipulating comic human beings."

Collections such as *Angels at the Ritz, and Other Stories* and *Lovers of Their Time, and Other Stories* that followed *Elizabeth Alone* continue to illustrate Trevor's concern for average people and the importance of the effects of time. "Trevor is especially adept at making the presence of the past, the presence of people offstage, lean upon his characters," says Peter S. Prescott in a *Newsweek* review of *Angels at the Ritz.* Similarly, *New York Times Book Review* contributor Victoria Glendinning comments on the stories in *Lovers of Their Time,* "Nothing very extraordinary happens to [Trevor's] teachers, tradesmen, farmers and shop-assistants; the action is all off-stage, and they are caught and thrown off course by the wash of great and passionate events that happened in another time, another place."

For some critics, the author's understated approach is too dispassionate to be effective. "All too often Trevor settles for a decent, tolerant, middle-brow obviousness . . . ," complains Paulin in his review of *Lovers in Their Time.* "The oddly dated atmosphere of Trevor's stories is the main obstacle to a more complete—and more generous—appreciation of his talent." But V. S. Pritchett points out in a *New York Times Book Review* article that Trevor's aim is to portray people "crucified by the continuity of evil and cruelty in human history, particularly the violent history of, say, the wars and cruelties of the last sixty years of this century. Theirs is a private moral revolt. The point is important, for Trevor has sometimes been thought of as the quiet recorder of 'out of date' lives living tamely on memories of memories, as times change."

With Trevor's *The Children of Dynmouth,* his first Whitbread Prize-winning book, the author takes a different approach to his theme of personal suffering by focusing on an unsympathetic boy named Timothy Gedge. Abandoned by his father and ignored by the rest of his family, Timothy has become a despicable character who has a crude sense of humor and is fascinated by death. Desperate for attention, he becomes convinced that he can find fame by doing an act for the variety television show, "Opportunity Knocks." But to get the props he needs, Timothy blackmails several of the respectable citizens of Dynmouth and "by the novel's end he has come close to destroying several people," writes Joyce Carol Oates in the *New York Times Book Review.* "Timothy's malice arises from his chronic aloneness, so that it isn't possible, as the [character of] the vicar recognizes, to see the boy as evil."

Some critics see Timothy's rescue by the vicar at the novel's conclusion to be a weak solution to an otherwise excellent book. "To imply that sooner or later the shrinks and the socialists will put an end to evil is to drag out an old chestnut indeed," writes *Sewanee Review* contributor Walter Sullivan—"and to negate the fine performance which leads up to this foolishness." But Thomas R. Edwards asserts in the *New York Review of Books* that *The Children of Dynmouth* "succeeds in being funny, frightening, and morally poised and intelligent at once." Oates similarly concludes that it is "a skillfully written novel, a small masterpiece of understatement."

In another Whitbread Prize-winning novel, *Fools of Fortune,* Trevor chronicles the years of lonely isolation of two lovers separated by a tragic turn of fate. A "benchmark novel against which other contemporary novels will have to be measured," in *Washington Post Book World* critic Charles Champlin's assessment, *Fools of Fortune* also reflects the " . . . last seven decades of English-Irish history." The novel relates how British soldiers misguidedly destroy Willie Quinton's family and home in the year 1918, and how Willie's revenge on a British officer leads to his exile from Ireland. Forced to leave his beloved English cousin, Marianne, he is denied the chance to see her or their daughter, Imelda, for years to come. The Quintons, remarks Jonathan Yardley in the *Washington Post Book World,* "are all good, honorable people, but they—like poor Ireland—are victims of mere chance, arbitrary and random." But although *Fools of Fortune* is a somber tale, Trevor still flavors the stew with Irish humor and a conclusion that offers hope for the future. "The ultimate reunion of [Quinton, Marianne, and Imelda] is exquisitely rendered in a brief final chapter that will seal the book in your memory," concludes James Idema in the *Chicago Tribune Book World.*

The problems between Ireland and England are touched upon in a number of Trevor's other short stories and novels, but not with the intention of making a political statement. As Trevor tells Greig, "The troubles are part of the story, rather than the driving force. It is the human qualities rather than the Irish question, as it is called in England, that I am primarily interested in." As with the title story of *Beyond the Pale, and Other Stories,* Trevor at times uses the problems in Ireland to shock his upper-class characters out of delusions that "shield them from truth and its reflections," attests Doris Brett in the *Washington Post Book World.* "He is steadily against the smug and self-righteous," the critic later observes.

With other tales, such as the central story of *The News from Ireland, and Other Stories* and the novel, *The Silence in the Garden,* Trevor relates the struggles in Ireland to the misfortunes of his characters and, as Richard Eder of the *Los Angeles Times* puts it, "the passing of a kind of civility that Yeats celebrated." In the case of *The Silence in the Garden,* the story of how war and terrorism ruin a once happy and prosperous Anglo-Irish family, *Washington Post Book World* critic Gregory A. Schirmer notes that Trevor "has much to say about the attitudes and patterns that lie behind the [British-Irish] violence, and about the ways in which the present is inevitably—and, in Ireland, often tragically—shaped by the past." But, again, as Richard Eder explains in the *Los Angeles Times Book Review,* Trevor's point is not so much social and historical as it is personal. The Anglo-Irish conflict is presented in such a way as to demonstrate the "universal condition," and the decline of the English hegemony "stand[s] for a broader image of human life as a struggle against entropy."

Although Trevor's stories and novels often involve dramatic events, he is mainly concerned with how these events preoccupy and obsess his characters. This inner tension is subtly portrayed through the author's quiet, understated writing style. Michiko Kakutani of the *New York Times* describes Trevor's style in a review of *Fools of Fortune,* as "spare, lilting prose, . . . delineat[ing] these melodramatic events with economy and precision." For some critics, however, Trevor's use of understatement is a drawback in his writing. Anatole Broyard, for one, writes in a *New York Times* review of *Beyond the Pale:* "Though everyone regards [Trevor] as a master of understatement, I wonder whether it isn't conceited in a way to insist on writing such carefully removed stories, so breathlessly poised on the edge of nonexistence." But many others who have studied Trevor's work over the years have admired the author's talent. "Trevor's stories are constructed with unfailing skill and almost unfailing delicacy," declares Eder; and while *Saturday Review* critic Josh Rubins notes that Trevor addresses many common themes in literature, he adds that "rarely have they been invoked with such compact eloquence."

During his career, William Trevor has been compared to such luminaries as Muriel Spark, Anton Chekov, and Andre Malraux, but most often to his Irish predecessor, James Joyce. *New York Times Book Review* critic Ted Solotaroff compared Joyce and Trevor this way: "Both Trevor and the early Joyce are geniuses at presenting a seemingly ordinary life as it is, socially, psychologically, morally, and then revealing the force of these conditions in the threatened individual's moment of resistance to them. This is the deeper realism: accurate observation turning into moral vision." "Yet like Joyce before him," concludes *Washington Post Book World* contributor Howard Frank Mosher, "Trevor is entirely his own writer, with his own uncompromised vision of human limitations made accessible by a rare generosity toward his characters and their blighted lives."

CA INTERVIEW

CA interviewed William Trevor by telephone on July 10, 1990, at his home in Devon, England.

CA: You were a sculptor before you became a writer, and you told Amanda Smith for Publishers Weekly *that the sense of form and shape at work in your sculpture carried over into your fiction. You also worked several years in an advertising agency. Did anything from that experience prove helpful to you as a fiction writer?*

TREVOR: Not at all. Advertising was just a job to make money. It wasn't important, except that in a purely mundane way it did give me a lot of time. I wasn't greatly pressed, and I had a typewriter. In advertising in the 1960s in England they tended to give you a huge amount of time to write one single advertisement. I don't think that is true now, but it was then. In many ways the agency I was at was quite a gentlemanly place, quite leisurely. I put that time to fairly fruitful use; I wrote my first novel in office time.

CA: Many of your characters feel a sense of isolation. Is that a sense you felt early on, with parents from the south and north of Ireland, and having to move about frequently?

TREVOR: I don't think so. I didn't feel particularly isolated as a child. I did belong to that strange little sliver of Irish society which comes some place between the old Ascendancy and De Valera's Ireland, the new republic; because I was a Protestant, I belonged to a tiny minority. But it wasn't an isolating experience. I don't remember any feeling of being out on a limb, as it were. I think that if I understand isolation it would be really through my own personality rather than that particular experience.

CA: And maybe through your keen observation of other people.

TREVOR: Yes, in my case it's a question of observing other people rather than observing one's self. I have no interest whatsoever in myself. That's why I find interviews like this very difficult. I'm far more interested in you as I talk to you. I don't know what you look like; I don't quite know who I'm talking to. Any interview starts an inquisitiveness in me which I think is part of my writing. I write from a standpoint of curiosity about other people, about what other people are like. But I have to qualify this by saying that, of course, all fiction is autobiographical in the sense that, when pain is described, it can only be the

author's own pain. It's another way of saying that we all may not see the same color when we say it's blue.

CA: You live in England, spend a lot of time in Italy, visit Ireland, write about all three (though less about Italy). How does the distance work to your advantage when you're in one place and writing about another?

TREVOR: You have to distance yourself, but not quite in the way you're suggesting. I had to leave Ireland for economic reasons, but had I not left I don't believe I'd ever have been able to write about it. It's necessary to distance yourself from familiarity, but I don't think that spending, say, six months in Italy makes it easier to write about Ireland or England during that period. You distance yourself in a far more general way, by not settling anywhere.

CA: You said in an interview for the Irish Times, *"The main company I keep is with the characters I create. They are with me for ages when I am writing." How does a character begin and develop in your mind?*

TREVOR: I think all art is a pretty untidy business; I don't believe there are any rules. I certainly don't believe there are any rules in the creation of fiction. Therefore I don't think that characters get onto the page through the same channel each time. In the same way, I don't really believe that every short story has the same kind of starting point. Characters arrive from all sorts of areas and places. It's not simply that one meets somebody and takes a bit of that person, then meets somebody else and takes a bit of *that* person—it's not quite so neat and formal. Quite often a character is an absolute invention of my own, not based in any way on anyone I know. On the other hand, other characters are based on aspects of people. I would find it uninteresting simply to write the biography of a person, so I do a considerable amount of what might appear to be disguising, although in fact it's not. In other words, there's a lot of recreating, a lot of speculating, in my search for a starting point. Once you have the starting point, everything else is much easier. Discovering the spring to get you going isn't at all straightforward because it may be found in all sorts of different places.

CA: Do you know a character quite well before you begin to write about him or her, or does the familiarity come as you write?

TREVOR: I think almost always the familiarity comes as the writing is done, as the character develops a life of his or her own and tells you what to put down, as it were. On the other hand, the opposite is also true: some of the time I know exactly what the character is like. Or quite often I know perhaps what the story is like, and the story tells me what the characters are like, one after another. I do really think of it as a much messier business than people sometimes believe the creation of any art is. You begin with a kind of chaos, raw material you have to form and transform in order to communicate.

CA: You write about women with great understanding, as reviewers have noted and I'm sure many readers have appreciated. Do you always feel on sure ground there?

TREVOR: I must confess I never feel on sure ground at all. I think that to feel on sure ground would be death to what I am trying to do. I'm speaking now purely personally; this will not apply to other writers, because writers work in different ways. But for me, there has to be the feeling that I'm experimenting, that I'm trying things out. That's why as a short story writer I am repetitious: I often write the same story in a different form. It's rather like the Renaissance painters painting the virgin and child over and over again in order to get it right. In repeating, I am experimenting again. I don't like the feeling of being certain; I like the feeling of having to write in order to know. I'm an instinctive writer, and if you work with instincts I think you are bound to be like that.

Yes, I do write a great deal about women. I do so, I suppose, because I am not a woman, which comes back to what I said about curiosity: I want to know what it's like to be a woman. When I first began to write, I was much younger than I am now and I wrote about the elderly. Because I was not then elderly, I wanted to know what it felt like as a elderly person to walk across a room, what it felt like when you got rheumatism in your joints, all those things. That was a deliberate pressure I put on myself as a fiction writer. To invent and to imagine and to have hunches: that, for me, is the center of my writing process.

CA: What you've said seems to imply taking a risk.

TREVOR: Yes. There is a considerable amount of risk. This you can do more easily, I think, with short stories than you can with novels. There can be many short stories: you can risk one, you can risk another—rather like betting on horses. With a novel, which takes such a long time, the riskiness is not quite so tempting.

CA: Back to the idea of living with your characters—and perhaps related to the repetition you mentioned earlier—do you ever feel at the end of a story that you aren't quite finished with a character, and so you bring that character back in some other guise in later writing?

TREVOR: I don't think so. I might not be finished with the obsession which is the spring of that story, and I might find myself similarly obsessed again. But I doubt very much that I would consciously bring back the same character. I rather think that, if that happens—and I'm sure it does—it happens for other reasons, not because I want

to do it but because it just occurs, maybe because the character floats in without my even knowing it. It's not a conscious thing.

CA: How does your preference for writings short stories—assuming that still to be true—affect the way you go about shaping your novels?

TREVOR: No one else has said this, I think, but I always maintain that my novels are short stories strung together. It seems to me that you can quite easily break my novels down and find that there are several short stories interwoven there, knitted into a pattern. I am a short story writer, I believe, who also happens to write novels, not the other way around. In the same way that you can tell a novelist's short stories, I think you can tell that my novels are the work of a short-story writer. To analyze that more deeply I think you'd have to do a tremendous amount of unwinding, a kind of academic exercise, and I wouldn't have the patience for it. I distrust analysis where the art of fiction, or any art, is concerned.

CA: Houses are central to some of your stories and novels, and they come very much alive in your descriptions. Are the main houses of your fiction based on real models?

TREVOR: Yes, they're based on real models to some extent. In *The Silence in the Garden* the house and town described are real. I've never been inside the house, but, as a child, I saw it every day of my life for five or six years when I lived in that particular town, and I remember it. That's sometimes how things begin. An image of a house across the water is all you need. You don't need to go into the rooms. If you have more than the image, you're not going to invent, and I am not happy unless I'm inventing. Fiction is nearly always this mixture of reality and invention, which comes back to what I was saying about characters a moment ago. In fact, I am at present putting together a nonfiction book which will be not exactly an autobiography but a book about real places and real people—left behind as a kind of smear or blurred image in my mind over the years.

CA: What a nice idea for a book.

TREVOR: It is, because there are so many people that you meet in a lifetime who don't rate any kind of newspaper obituary, who aren't "important." And there are so many places that are more than places to you personally. It seems a suitable exercise for the storyteller to record the memory of people who have been amusing or villainous or noble, although they might not have been recognized as such at the time or by others. And it also seems right to record houses, hotels, towns, cities which, known for a day or two or just for a moment even, left a mark that has never gone away.

CA: I liked the way you took a literary look at the country in your nonfiction book A Writer's Ireland. *Did you enjoy that work?*

TREVOR: I did, because that's a great change from writing fiction, as I hope this planned one will be. I am fortunate in that I write novels and short stories, which are very different, so that when I get tired of the shorter form, I can spread myself out over a very long period with a novel. And then, of course, I become rather weary of that and it's nice to go back to the short story. But it's an even greater relief to get away from both—simply to go back to reality and to write as the camera sees. Unless you're careful, fiction can absorb you utterly. This is especially so the more you write and the older you get: you can find yourself living—almost—in a fictional world.

CA: Back to houses for a moment. Tell me about Cloverhill, the house in your novella Nights at the Alexandra, *and the doomed movie theater in the same story. Did they both have real-life inspirations?*

TREVOR: Yes. Cloverhill illustrates what I was saying earlier. It is, in fact, a house where my ancestors lived. But I've never seen it. I don't think it even exists anymore. Only the name is real; the rest of the fictional house is invented. And the movie house is real to this extent: When I was a child, the existing cinema in the town of Tipperary was burnt down, to everyone's great dismay. There was no picture house to go to (we called them picture houses in those days). The local bicycle-shop owner decided there was money to be made from a cinema, so he built a magnificent new one, which he called the Excel. I watched it being built, eager that the bricks would fall quickly into place so that we could again see the wonders of Hollywood. One summer's day it was finished, and I think that quite a lot of the description in that novella is actually based on the building of that cinema. I remember, in particular, hanging baskets with flowers in them. I remember the wonder of having such a magnificent cinema as opposed to the rather dirty, mucky ones we were used to in small Irish towns. This was a marvel, and I think it must have been the inspiration for the cinema in *Nights at the Alexandra.*

CA: Gardens are also important in your fiction. Are you a gardener yourself?

TREVOR: My wife is a good gardener, and I do the rough work. I don't know an awful lot about it, but I spend a great deal of my time working outside. I'm very fond of that. I'm a practical person and enjoy practical pursuits.

CA: Some reviewers have noted that Irish storytelling has similarities to storytelling in the southern United States. Do you think that's true to a large extent?

TREVOR: I've heard this too. I happen to like very much the storytelling of the southern states. The only thoughts I've got which are even vaguely related to that are about the position of the Irish short story in general, which sometimes does seem allied to the short story in other countries, and especially the United States—not just the southern states. The short story is particularly sinewy and shows no sign of withering away in Ireland, perhaps because the novel has never been such a challenge to it in Ireland—as it became, for instance, in England.

I'm more or less quoting here from what I said in my introduction to *The Irish Book of Short Stories.* When the novel, in the nineteenth century, broke upon the English public, England was right for it. In a stable, leisurely society there was time both to write novels and to read them. Ireland at that time was a country of considerable disaffection, with two religions, one of them repressed, two languages, one of them repressed. It was not a place with the kind of wealth or ease to be found in what I always think of as the great big mahogany establishment which England was in the nineteenth century. Ireland was the opposite of that, a rough-and-ready place.

I think the communication of the past simply continued, that very rapid communication of people telling stories, not taking time—nor even possessing the education sometimes—to scribble them down. That used to be the case in England also, but it kept going in Ireland, and when this antique story form was turned inside out by Chekhov in Russia and Joyce and Elizabeth Bowen in Ireland, Ireland still had a healthy storytelling tradition. It had gone from England. The short story thrives in countries which aren't quite settled.

CA: You're very favorably reviewed here in widely read review periodicals, and your short stories now often appear in magazines here before they're collected into books. Has your U.S. readership increased considerably over the years?

TREVOR: That's the sort of thing I never dare to ask. I never ask any publisher for sales figures, fearing that they'll be so low. So I don't know, but I think there's a gallant band of people who read short stories in the U.S. and who know all about them, and I suppose that's one of the reasons why I'm read there.

CA: Fools of Fortune *is in the works as a movie, I read not long ago. How does that stand now?*

TREVOR: It's finished. It had a premier about three weeks ago in Dublin and it's showing in London and Dublin at the moment. I think it will open in New York sometime in early autumn.

CA: Are you happy with the movie?

TREVOR: Yes, I am. It's very different from the novel in many ways. I didn't script it, but I'm used to the transformation of my fiction to the screen because many of my stories have become television films over the last twenty-five years. Since I've scripted most of them myself, I'm aware of the difficulties: I know one should never expect to see the printed page on the screen, that prose has to be replaced by images. When large areas of the book aren't there, other people may be upset, but I don't particularly mind. "Fools of Fortune" is a good film. It has been very well made. It's extremely well acted and directed.

CA: What can your readers look forward to next? Will it be the book about some of the real people and places that have informed your fiction?

TREVOR: I don't think so. I think that book will be written between writing fiction and in odd moments. I'm not sure how long it will take. Some of it is written already, because it will include pieces which I have written in the past about visiting certain places and about people, but the greater part of it will be new. I don't think it will be the next published book, though. It's much more likely there will be some more fiction next.

BIOGRAPHICAL/CRITICAL SOURCES:

BOOKS

Contemporary Literary Criticism, Gale, Volume 7, 1977, Volume 9, 1978, Volume 14, 1980, Volume 25, 1983.
Dictionary of Literary Biography, Volume 14: *British Novelists since 1960,* Gale, 1983.
Firchow, Peter, editor, *The Writer's Place: Interviews on the Literary Situation in Contemporary Britain,* University of Minnesota Press, 1974.

PERIODICALS

Atlantic Monthly, August, 1986.
Books and Bookmen, July, 1967.
Chicago Tribune, November 13, 1987; September 30, 1988.
Chicago Tribune Book World, July 29, 1979; March 15, 1981; February 14, 1982; October 30, 1983.
Christian Science Monitor, February 26, 1970.
Encounter, January, 1979.
Globe and Mail (Toronto), December 31, 1983; October 24, 1987; September 17, 1988.
Irish Times, May 22, 1988.
London Magazine, August, 1968.
Los Angeles Times, October 2, 1983; September 29, 1988.
Los Angeles Times Book Review, January 11, 1981; March 11, 1984; May 4, 1986; August 6, 1989.
New Republic, February 4, 1967.
New Statesman, October 15, 1971; July 9, 1976; September 22, 1978.
Newsweek, June 14, 1976; February 22, 1982; October 10, 1983.
New Yorker, July 12, 1976.

New York Review of Books, April 19, 1979; March 19, 1981.
New York Times, September 31, 1972; March 31, 1979; January 17, 1981; February 3, 1982; September 26, 1983; May 14, 1986; August 27, 1988; May 11, 1990.
New York Times Book Review, February 11, 1968; July 11, 1976; April 8, 1979; February 1, 1981; February 21, 1982; October 2, 1983; June 8, 1986; October 9, 1988; September 8, 1991, p. 3.
Observer, June 11, 1980.
Plays and Players, September, 1971.
Publishers Weekly, October 28, 1983.
Spectator, October 11, 1969; May 13, 1972.
Stage, March 9, 1972.
Time, January 26, 1970; October 10, 1983.
Times (London), June 18, 1980; October 15, 1981; April 28, 1983; March 20, 1986; May 30, 1991, p. 12.
Times Literary Supplement, October 26, 1973; June 20, 1980; October 16, 1981; April 29, 1983; August 31, 1984; April 11, 1986; November 5, 1987; June 10, 1988; January 26, 1990; May 31, 1991, p. 21.
Tribune Books (Chicago), September 10, 1989.
Vogue, February 1, 1968.
Washington Post Book World, April 8, 1979; February 1, 1981; February 21, 1982; September 25, 1983; March 4, 1984; May 25, 1986; August 28, 1988.

—Sketch by Kevin S. Hile

—Interview by Jean W. Ross

*   *   *

CRAIG, David 1932-

PERSONAL: Born October 7, 1932, in Aberdeen, Scotland; son of John (a doctor) and Margaret (Simpson) Craig; married Gillian Stephenson (a doctor), 1957 (divorced, 1978); married Anne Spillard (a writer), 1990; children: (first marriage) Marian, Peter, Donald, Neil. *Education:* University of Aberdeen, B.A. (with first class honors), 1954; Cambridge University, Ph.D., 1958. *Politics:* Socialist. *Religion:* None.

ADDRESSES: Home—Hill House, Main St., Burton, Carnforth, Lancashire LA6 1LY, England. *Office*—University of Lancaster, Bailrigg, Lancaster, England.

CAREER: University of Ceylon, Peradeniya, lecturer in English, 1959-61; Workers' Educational Association, Richmond, Yorkshire, England, organizing tutor, 1961-64; University of Lancaster, Lancaster, England, senior lecturer, 1964—, professor of literature and creative writing, 1990—.

WRITINGS:

Scottish Literature and the Scottish People: 1680-1830, Chatto & Windus, 1961.

(Editor) *Moderne Prosa und Lyrik der Britischen Inseln,* Aufbau-Verlag, 1968.

(Editor) Alan Silitoe, *Saturday Night and Sunday Morning,* Longmans, Green, 1968.

(Editor) Charles Dickens, *Hard Times,* Penguin, 1969.

(Editor with John Manson) Hugh MacDiarmid, *Selected Poems,* Penguin, 1970.

The Real Foundations: Literature and Social Change, Chatto & Windus, 1973, Oxford University Press, 1974.

(Editor) *Marxists on Literature,* Penguin, 1975.

(Editor with Margot Heinemann) *Experiments in English Teaching,* Arnold, 1976.

Latest News (poems), Journeyman, 1978.

(With Nigel Gray) *The Rebels and the Hostage* (novel), Journeyman, 1978.

(With Michael Egan) *Extreme Situations,* Macmillan, 1979.

Homing (poems), Platform, 1980.

Native Stones: A Book about Climbing, Secker & Warburg, 1987.

Against Looting (poems), Giant Steps, 1987.

(With Rick Graham) *Buttermere* (climbing guide; bound with *Eastern Crags* by J. Earl, A. Griffiths, and R. Smith), edited by D. Miller, illustrated by A. Phizacklea and D. Lee, Fell & Rock Club of the English Lake District, 1987.

On the Crofter's Trail: In Search of the Clearance Highlanders, Cape, 1990.

(With Chris Culshaw) *Headwork,* Oxford University Press, 1990.

King Cameron (novel), Carcanet Press, 1991.

Contributor to books, including *New Writing and Writers,* Calder, 1979, and *New Stories: An Arts Council Anthology,* Hutchinson, 1980 and 1983. Contributor of poetry to anthologies, including *Young Commonwealth Poets,* edited by P. L. Brent, Heinemann, 1969, and *Doves for the Seventies,* edited by Peter Robins, Corgi, 1969 and 1972. Also contributor to periodicals, including *New Statesman, New York Review of Books, Spectator, Times Literary Supplement, Times Higher Education Supplement, New Left Review, Scotsman, New Poetry, Tribune, Mosaic, Marxism Today, London Review of Books,* and *Essays in Criticism.* Co-founder and editor of *Fireweed,* 1975-78.

SIDELIGHTS: David Craig presents the story of the crofters evicted from the Scottish Highlands during the nineteenth century in his *On the Crofters' Trail: In Search of the Clearance Highlanders.* Alexander Urquhart explains in the *Times Literary Supplement* that "two undisputed truths supply the mainspring for his moving and powerful book; the first is the fact that appallingly brutal evictions took place on a considerable scale, irrespective of their exact extent, and the second, the accessibility of the crofters' ordeals which have passed from generation to generation like a family heirloom." Craig interviewed countless descendants of those cleared off their land; and includes with the interviews his own observations while he travelled to meet these people. "Anybody who can make a stay in a sleazy southern Ontario motel both funny and spiritual is worth reading," claims Don Akenson in the Toronto *Globe and Mail,* adding: "Craig evokes a wonderful personal travelogue through physical space and, more important, through time."

Set in the eighteenth century, Craig's novel *King Cameron* continues to describe the plight of crofters and small farmers in Scotland. The book revolves around Angus Cameron, democratic ruler, who is well aware of the injustices of the system, yet realizes that they cannot simply be eliminated. Craig writes bitterly about poor people being chased and burned out of their homes, or being forced to join the army and fight meaningless wars. "The huge manipulation practised by the landowners," asserts Anne Barnes in the London *Times,* "and the hypocrisy of people in government are set out in harsh and uncompromising detail and left unresolved, drawing the reader in to reflect on the relationship, in any period, between the governors and the governed."

BIOGRAPHICAL/CRITICAL SOURCES:

PERIODICALS

Globe and Mail (Toronto), January 1, 1991, p. C8.
Times (London), May 23, 1991, p. 20.
Times Literary Supplement, July 3, 1987, p. 729; March 1, 1991, p. 8.

*   *   *

CRANE, Robert
See SELLERS, Con(nie Leslie, Jr.)

*   *   *

CRAY, Ed(ward)   1933-

PERSONAL: Born July 3, 1933, in Cleveland, OH; son of Max (a laundry owner) and Sara (a teacher; maiden name, Negin) Cray; married Marjorie Best, 1963 (divorced, 1966); children: Jennifer Hilary. *Education:* University of California, Los Angeles, B.A., 1957, graduate study, 1958-59. *Politics:* "Usually Democratic." *Religion:* "Nominally Jewish." *Avocational interests:* Model trains, photography.

ADDRESSES: Home—10436 Kinnard Ave., Los Angeles, CA 90024. *Office*—10906 Rochester Ave., Los Angeles, CA 90024. *Agent*—Michael Hamilburg, 292 S. La Cienega Blvd., Beverly Hills, CA 90211.

CAREER: University of California, Los Angeles, instructor in folklore and folksong, 1958-60; *Frontier,* Los Angeles, associate editor and business manager, 1961-64; free-lance writer, 1964-65; American Civil Liberties Union of Southern California, Los Angeles, director of publications, 1965-70; Southern California Symphony-Hollywood Bowl Association, Los Angeles, director of publicity and public relations, 1970-71; free-lance writer, 1971—; City News Service, Los Angeles, editor, 1972-73; University of Southern California, Los Angeles, associate professor, 1976-90, professor of journalism, 1991—. *Hollywood Reporter,* copy editor, summer, 1972. Consultant to the President's Commission on the Causes of Violence. *Military service:* U.S. Army, 1952-54.

MEMBER: American Civil Liberties Union.

WRITINGS:

(Editor) *The Anthology of Erotic Restoration Verse,* Brandon House, 1965.
(Editor) *The Fifteen Plagues of Maidenhead, and Other Forbidden Verse,* Brandon House, 1966.
The Big Blue Line: Police Power versus Human Rights, Coward, 1967.
(Editor) *The Erotic Muse,* Oak Publications, 1967, 2nd edition, University of Illinois Press, 1992.
Law Enforcement: The Matter of Redress (monograph), Institute of Modern Legal Thought, 1969.
(Editor) *Bawdy Ballads,* Anthony Bland, 1970.
In Failing Health: The Medical Crisis and the A.M.A., Bobbs-Merrill, 1971.
The Enemy in the Streets, Doubleday, 1972.
Burden of Proof: The Trial of Juan Corona, Macmillan, 1973.
Levi's: The History of Levi Strauss & Co., Houghton, 1978.
Chrome Colossus: General Motors and Its Times, McGraw-Hill, 1981.
General of the Army: George C. Marshall, Soldier and Statesman, Norton, 1990.
(Editor with Jonathan Kotler and Miles Beller) *American Datelines: An Anthology of 150 of the Most Important Pieces in American Journalism from 1700s to the Present,* Facts on File, 1990.

Author of instructional filmscripts, including *All Bottled Up,* 1975, *Teenagers Talk: Getting through Adolescence,* 1976, and *Joey and Me,* 1977. Contributor of articles and reviews to periodicals.

WORK IN PROGRESS: A biography of Chief Justice of the United States Earl Warren, for Simon & Schuster.

SIDELIGHTS: Ed Cray told *CA:* "Informally trained as a reporter, I tend to write books and articles on subjects which are 'news,' that is, which have not appeared in print before. I find it difficult to regurgitate the pioneering work of others. My books are generally in the area of what might be called public affairs with the exception of *The Erotic Muse,* an anthology of American bawdy songs. That work was an outgrowth of a deep and abiding interest in American folklore and folksong stimulated by a remarkable man and teacher at UCLA, Wayland Hand. Even there, however, there was a 'news' element. This was the first open publication of these ribald, sometimes offensive (to some, anyway) songs and the first time they had received serious scholarly annotations."

Cray adds: "Until 1982 when I joined the faculty of the University of Southern California School of Journalism on a full-time basis, I essentially made my living as a writer. I now divide my time between teaching and writing."

In a *Detroit News* review, Bernard A. Weisberger describes Cray's *Chrome Colossus* as "a lively, informative and thought-provoking history of the super-corporation, mostly told through the stories of the men who ran it. It tells the reader practically all he needs to understand what GM is all about. And since that is very much what the United States is all about . . . Cray deserves a wide audience." Weisberger concludes, "His tale provides entertaining hours while raising . . . hard questions as overtones. It gives us a general history of General Motors that we need."

BIOGRAPHICAL/CRITICAL SOURCES:

PERIODICALS

Detroit News, November 2, 1980.
Los Angeles Times Book Review, June 24, 1990, p. 11.
New Yorker, August 6, 1990.
New York Times Book Review, June 17, 1990, p. 14.
Tribune Books (Chicago), June 17, 1990, p. 5.
Washington Post Book World, July 22, 1990, p. 10; December 30, 1990, p. 13.

*   *   *

CRESSWELL, Helen   1934-

PERSONAL: Born July 11, 1934, in Nottinghamshire, England; daughter of J. E. (an electrical engineer) and A. E. (Clarke) Cresswell; married Brian Rowe (in textiles), April 14, 1962; children: Caroline Jane, Candida Lucy. *Education:* Kings College, University of London, B.A. (with honors), 1955. *Religion:* Church of England. *Avocational interests:* Collecting antiques, walking, visiting the seashore, "ticking"—exploring new places, philosophy, gardening, and "collecting coincidences."

ADDRESSES: Home—Old Church Farm, Eakring, Newark, Nottinghamshire NG22 0DA, England. *Agent*—A. M. Heath & Co. Ltd., 40-42 William IV St., London WC2N 4DD, England.

CAREER: Writer, mainly of books for children. Career up to marriage was varied, including periods as literary assistant to a foreign author, fashion buyer, teacher, and television work for British Broadcasting Corp.

MEMBER: International PEN, Society of Authors.

AWARDS, HONORS: Nottingham Poetry Society Award for best poem submitted in annual competition, 1950; runner-up, Carnegie Medal, Library Association, 1967, for *The Piemakers,* 1969, for *The Night-watchmen,* 1971, for *Up the Pier,* and 1973, for *The Bongleweed;* runner-up, *Guardian* Award for children's fiction, 1967, for *The Piemakers,* 1968, for *The Signposters;* runner-up for best children's original television drama, Television Writers Guild of Great Britain, 1972, for "Lizzie Dripping"; *Absolute Zero: Being the Second Part of the Bagthorpe Saga* was named "Best Book" by *School Library Journal,* 1978; *Absolute Zero: Being the Second Part of the Bagthorpe Saga* and *Bagthorpes Unlimited: Being the Third Part of the Bagthorpe Saga* were both selected as "Children's Choice" by the International Reading Association, both 1979; runner-up, Whitbread Literary Award for best children's novel, Booksellers Association of Great Britain and Ireland, 1982, for *The Secret World of Polly Flint;* Phoenix Award, Children's Literature Association, for *The Night-watchmen,* 1988; *Up the Pier, The Winter of the Birds, Ordinary Jack: Being the First Part of the Bagthorpe Saga, Absolute Zero: Being the Second Part of the Bagthorpe Saga,* and *Bagthorpes Unlimited: Being the Third Part of the Bagthorpe Saga* were all named Notable Books by the American Library Association; *Up the Pier, The Winter of the Birds,* and *Ordinary Jack: Being the First Part of the Bagthorpe Saga,* were named to the *Horn Book* honor list.

WRITINGS:

JUVENILE

Sonya-by-the-Shore, illustrated by Robbin Jane Wells, Dent, 1960.

The White Sea Horse (also see below), illustrated by Robin Jacques, Oliver & Boyd, 1964, Lippincott, 1965.

Pietro and the Mule, illustrated by Maureen Eckersley, Oliver & Boyd, 1965, Bobbs-Merrill, 1970.

Where the Wind Blows, illustrated by Peggy Fortnum, Faber, 1966, Funk & Wagnalls, 1968.

The Piemakers, illustrated by V. H. Drummond, Faber, 1967, Lippincott, 1968, new edition illustrated by Judith G. Brown, Macmillan, 1980.

A Day on Big O, illustrated by Shirley Hughes, Benn, 1967, Follett, 1968.

A Tide for the Captain (also see below), illustrated by Jacques, Oliver & Boyd, 1967.

The Signposters, illustrated by Gareth Floyd, Faber, 1968.

The Sea Piper (also see below), illustrated by Jacques, Oliver & Boyd, 1968.

Rug Is a Bear, illustrated by Susanna Gretz, Benn, 1968.

Rug Plays Tricks, illustrated by Gretz, Benn, 1968.

The Barge Children, illustrated by Lynette Hemmant, Brockhampton, 1968.

The Night-Watchmen, illustrated by Floyd, Macmillan, 1969, published in England as *The Night-watchmen,* Faber, 1969.

A Game of Catch, illustrated by Floyd, Oliver & Boyd, 1969, illustrated by Ati Forberg, Macmillan, 1977.

A Gift from Winklesea, illustrated by Janina Ede, Brockhampton Press, 1969.

A House for Jones, illustrated by Margaret Gordon, Benn, 1969.

Rug Plays Ball, illustrated by Gretz, Benn, 1969.

Rug and a Picnic, illustrated by Gretz, Benn, 1969.

The Outlanders, illustrated by Doreen Roberts, Faber, 1970.

Rainbow Pavement, illustrated by Hughes, Benn, 1970.

The Wilkses, illustrated by Floyd, BBC Publications, 1970.

John's First Fish, illustrated by Prudence Seward, Macmillan, 1970.

At the Stroke of Midnight: Traditional Fairy Tales Retold, illustrated by Carolyn Dinan, Collins, 1971.

The Bird Fancier, illustrated by Renate Meyer, Benn, 1971.

Up the Pier, illustrated by Floyd, Faber, 1971, Macmillan, 1972.

The Weather Cat, illustrated by Margery Gill, Benn, 1971.

The Beachcombers, illustrated by Errol Le Cain, Macmillan, 1972.

Bluebirds over Pit Row, illustrated by Richard Kennedy, Benn, 1972.

Jane's Policeman, illustrated by Gill, Benn, 1972.

The Long Day, illustrated by Gill, Benn, 1972.

Roof Fall!, illustrated by Kennedy, Benn, 1972.

Short Back and Sides, illustrated by Kennedy, Benn, 1972.

The White Sea Horse and Other Stories from the Sea (contains *The White Sea Horse, The Sea Piper,* and *A Tide for the Captain*), Chatto & Windus, 1972.

The Beetle Hunt, illustrated by Anne Knight, Longman, 1973.

The Bongleweed, illustrated by Ann Strugnell, Macmillan, 1973.

The Bower Bird, illustrated by Gill, Benn, 1973.

The Key, illustrated by Kennedy, Benn, 1973.

Cheap Day Return, illustrated by Kennedy, Benn, 1974.

The Trap, illustrated by Kennedy, Benn, 1974.
Shady Deal, illustrated by Kennedy, Benn, 1974.
Two Hoots, illustrated by Martine Blanc, Benn, 1974, Crown, 1978.
Two Hoots Go to Sea, illustrated by Blanc, Benn, 1974, Crown, 1978.
Butterfly Chase, illustrated by Gill, Kestrel, 1975.
The Winter of the Birds, Faber, 1975, Macmillan, 1976.
Awful Jack, illustrated by Joannna Stubbs, Hodder & Stoughton, 1977.
Donkey Days, illustrated by Hughes, Benn, 1977.
The Flyaway Kite, illustrated by Bridget Clarke, Kestrel, 1979.
My Aunt Polly by the Sea, illustrated by Margaret Gordon, Wheaton, 1980.
Nearly Goodbye, illustrated by Tony Morris, Macmillan (London), 1980.
Penny for the Guy, illustrated by Nicole Goodwin, Macmillan (London), 1980.
Dear Shrink, Macmillan, 1982.
The Secret World of Polly Flint, illustrated by Shirley Felts, Faber, 1982, Macmillan, 1984.
Ellie and the Hagwitch, illustrated by J. Heap, P. Hardy, 1984.
Petticoat Smuggler, illustrated by Shirley Bellwood, Macmillan, 1985.
Whodunnit, illustrated by Caroline Browne, J. Cape, 1986.
Greedy Alice, illustrated by Martin Honeysett, Deutsch, 1986.
Moondial, Faber, 1987.
Trouble, Gollancz, 1987.
Dragon Ride, illustrated by Liz Roberts, Kestrel, 1987.
Time Out, Lutterworth, 1987.
The Story of Grace Darling, Viking, 1988.
Rosie and the Boredom Eater, Heinemann, 1989.
Whatever Happened in Winklesea?, Lutterworth, 1989.
Almost Goodbye Guzzler, Black, 1990.
Hokey Pokey Did It, Ladybird, 1990.
The Return of the Psammead, BBC Books, in press.

"JUMBO SPENCER" SERIES

Jumbo Spencer, illustrated by Clixby Watson, Brockhampton Press, 1963, Lippincott, 1966.
Jumbo Back to Nature, illustrated by Leslie Wood, Brockhampton Press, 1965.
Jumbo Afloat, illustrated by Wood, Brockhampton Press, 1966.
Jumbo and the Big Dig, illustrated by Wood, Brockhampton Press, 1968.

"LIZZIE DRIPPING" SERIES

Lizzie Dripping, illustrated by Jenny Thorne, BBC Publications, 1972.

Lizzie Dripping by the Sea, illustrated by Faith Jacques, BBC Publications, 1974.
Lizzie Dripping and the Little Angel, illustrated by F. Jacques, BBC Publishing, 1974.
Lizzie Dripping Again, illustrated by F. Jacques, BBC Publications, 1974.
More Lizzie Dripping, illustrated by F. Jacques, BBC Publications, 1974.
Lizzie Dripping and the Witch, BBC Books, 1991.

"TWO HOOTS" SERIES

Two Hoots in the Snow, illustrated by Blanc, Benn, 1975, Crown, 1978.
Two Hoots and the Big Bad Bird, illustrated by Blanc, Benn, 1975, Crown, 1978.
Two Hoots and the King, illustrated by Blanc, Benn, 1977, Crown, 1978.
Two Hoots Play Hide and Seek, illustrated by Blanc, Benn, 1977, Crown, 1978.

"BAGTHORPE" SERIES

Ordinary Jack: Being the First Part of the Bagthorpe Saga, illustrated by J. Bennet, Macmillan, 1977.
Absolute Zero: Being the Second Part of the Bagthorpe Saga, illustrated by Bennet, Macmillan, 1978.
Bagthorpes Unlimited: Being the Third Part of the Bagthorpe Saga, illustrated by Bennet, Macmillan, 1978.
Bagthorpes Versus the World: Being the Fourth Part of the Bagthorpe Saga, illustrated by Bennet, Macmillan, 1979.
Bagthorpes Abroad: Being the Fifth Part of the Bagthorpe Saga, Macmillan, 1984.
Bagthorpes Haunted: Being the Sixth Part of the Bagthorpe Saga, Macmillan, 1985.
Bagthorpes Liberated: Being the Seventh Part of the Bagthorpe Saga, Faber/Macmillan, 1989.
The Bagthorpe Triangle, Faber, in press.

"POSY BATES" SERIES

Meet Posy Bates, Bodley Head, 1990.
Posy Bates, Again!, Bodley Head, 1991.
Posy Bates and the Bag Lady, Bodley Head, in press.

TELEVISION PLAYS

Dick Whittington (based on original fairytale), BBC, 1974.
For Bethlehem Read Little Thraves (adult), BBC, 1976.
Lizzie Dripping and the Witch, BBC, 1977, stage play first produced at Unicorn Theater, London, England, 1979.
The Day Posy Bates Made History, BBC, 1977.
The Haunted School, eight part mini-series, BBC, Revcom (France) and Australian Broadcasting Co., 1986.

OTHER

Also author of a television adaptation of Edith Nesbit's *Five Children and It,* 1991. Contributor to *Winter's Tales for Children 4,* Macmillan (London), 1968; *Winter's Tales,* Macmillan, 1969; *The World of Ballet,* Collins, 1970; *Bad Boys,* Puffin, 1972; *Author's Choice 2,* Hamish Hamilton, 1973, Crowell, 1974; *Bakers Dozen,* Ward, Lock, 1973, Lothrop, 1974; *My England,* Heinnemann, 1973; *Christmas Holiday Book,* Dent, 1973; *Summer Holiday Book,* Dent, 1973; *Cricket's Choice,* Open Court Publishing, 1974; *Birthday Book,* Dent, 1975; *The Cat-Flap and the Apple Pie and Other Funny Stories,* W. H. Allen, 1979; *They Wait,* Pepper Press, 1983; *Over the Rainbow,* St. Michael, 1983; *The Methuen Book of Animal Tales,* Methuen, 1983; *Shades of Dark,* Patrick Hardy Books, 1984; *Shivers in the Dark,* Magnet Books, 1984; *I Like This Story,* Puffin, 1986; *Hidden Turnings,* Greenwillow, 1989. Also contributor of short stories and poetry to *Cornhill Magazine.*

ADAPTATIONS: The following television plays have been made from Cresswell's books: *The Piemakers,* BBC, 1967; *The Signposters,* BBC, 1968; *The Night-watchmen,* BBC, 1969; *The Outlanders,* BBC, 1970; *Lizzie Dripping* (series), BBC, six episodes, 1973, five episodes, 1975; *Jumbo Spencer* (series), five episodes, BBC, 1976; *The Bagthorpe Saga,* BBC, 1981; *The Secret World of Polly Flint* (series), seven episodes, ITV Central Television, 1986; *Moondial* (six-part series), BBC, 1987. *The Return of the Psammead* (six episodes), is scheduled to be produced by BBC in 1993.

SIDELIGHTS: Helen Cresswell, four-time nominee for the prestigious Carnegie Medal, is one of Great Britain's foremost children's authors. Cresswell's popularity stems in part from her ability to appeal to children of all ages; she has written adaptations of fairy stories for pre-schoolers as well as novels for older children. "Helen Cresswell is one of those rare souls who can write angelically well for the child in the child," stated *Spectator* writer Leon Garfield.

Cresswell began writing in childhood by imitating the styles of her favorite poets, such as Edmund Spencer, John Keats, and Gerard Manley Hopkins. She once told *Something about the Author (SATA):* "I began writing at the age of six or seven, in fact don't remember ever *not* writing, and all my earliest work was verse. I had a tremendous output right through my teens and early twenties. I experimented with countless techniques, and altogether think it a very useful apprenticeship. I think the fantasy I now write is an extension of poetry, and that very much the same processes are involved in the writing of them. I still think of myself as a poet rather than a novelist, though certain of my books, e.g. the 'Jumbo Spencer' series, clearly are novels. The main body of my work is fantasy.

It seems to me that a very much deeper level of truth can be reached through fantasy than by any other form of writing (except poetry, of course)."

"There are two main strands in [Cresswell's] work: poetic fantasy and humour," wrote John Rowe Townsend in his *A Sense of Story: Essays on Contemporary Writers for Children.* Among Cresswell's fantasy books, particularly noted by reviewers are *The Piemakers,* which depicts a family's creation of a giant pie to win a contest, and *The Night-Watchmen,* which is concerned with a boy's adventures with a pair of hobos; the comic "Bagthorpe" series, which follows the exploits of a family of impractical geniuses, has also won critical acclaim.

Townsend stated that *"The Signposters* and its successors *The Night-Watchmen* and *The Outlanders* seem increasingly to be expressing an attitude to life: a belief that spontaneity, individualism, creative artistry or craftsmanship, a readiness to move on and to take what life offers are virtues to be prized; rigidity and stuffiness are sins against the human spirit." In an essay for *The Thorny Paradise: Writers on Writing for Children,* Cresswell herself declared her belief in the importance of imagination: "I find the present technocracy alien and humanly barren, and I do not believe in the one-sided development of rationality at the expense of every other aspect of human experience. I look for balance to the shadow side of the psyche, the subjective reality of the individual, the power of the creative imagination."

The division between fantasy and reality in Cresswell's work is not always distinct. *"The Winter of the Birds . . .* more than any other children's book I know of, brings together the words *epic* and *fantasy,"* according to *Horn Book's* Gregory Maguire, who also stated that *"The Bongleweed, The Night- Watchmen,* and *Up the Pier . . .* are fantasies which evoke morality plays, dream journeys, and vacation stories." However, in a *Times Literary Supplement* review of *The Beachcombers,* the critic asked: "Is it fantasy? There are none of the conventional trappings of fantasy, no magic, no bending of natural laws." Another *Times Literary Supplement* reviewer said, *"The Night-watchmen* treads delicately on the brink of Wonderland, yet it is planted in reality, a close and affectionate observation of the ordinariness of backstreets and holes in the ground and the extraordinariness of human beings." *New Statesman* critic Nicholas Tucker declared that *The Piemakers, The Night-Watchmen,* and *The Bongleweed* all show "balance of the surreal and the earthy."

Humor in Cresswell's books ranges from the slapstick and nonsensical, as in the "Bagthorpe" stories, to the whimsical and poignant in such books as *The Night-Watchmen* and *The Piemakers.* Katherine Patterson in *Washington Post Book World* related that while reading *Ordinary Jack:*

Being the First Part of the Bagthorpe Saga, her son "found himself laughing out loud, . . . which was a problem, actually, because he was sneak reading after lights-out and didn't want to be discovered." A *Horn Book* reviewer commented that "seldom, if ever, has there been such consistently funny writing for children as in the Bagthorpe chronicles." A *Times Literary Supplement* reviewer asserted: "[Cresswell is] that rarest of children's writers, a master of high comedy. As in the best comedy, too, there is in [*The Piemakers* and *The Signposters*] a hint of sadness and a vein of genuine poetry."

A few reviewers have criticized Cresswell's comic inventions. For example, in the *New York Times Book Review* Margaret F. O'Connell stated that "whimsey is extravagantly thick" in *The White Sea Horse and Other Stories from the Sea.* However, Townsend declared that "[Cresswell's] humour, often hackneyed and obvious at first, has developed . . . into the comic richness which accompanied the fantasy of *The Piemakers* and *The Night-Watchmen.*" In a review of *The Piemakers*, the *Times Literary Supplement* critic observes that "there is a warmth, a richness of humor, an inner truthfulness in *The Piemakers* which puts this apparently slight tale in the select company of books which make nonsense credible, which make the reader laugh and cry and delight in a job exceedingly well done." "My own favourite book is still *The Piemakers*," Cresswell said in an article appearing in Townsend's *A Sense of Story*, "partly because I think it the most nearly perfect in form (not that it's anywhere near enough) and partly because it marked a turning-point in my writing, and was the first book in which humour and fantasy became fused."

Gillian Cross, writing in *Times Literary Supplement*, stated that Cresswell has "the two great virtues of originality and versatility. Her pen spawns new and unexpected worlds." Commenting on the creation of her stories, Cresswell told *SATA*: "The actual 'trigger' for a book is usually a feeling or atmosphere rather than plot or character. What my books mean, except on the purely narrative level, I often don't realise myself till after they're written." Similarly, in her essay for *The Thorny Paradise*, she stated: "I have said that I write partly in order to find out, and in a sense I do not know what I mean until I have said it. And in the same way as I am operating on this level as a writer, so the reader too is experiencing things which he recognizes but has no words for. This is partly what any kind of reading does. It makes accessible all kinds of floating feelings and attitudes and ideas which probably have never been crystallized before."

BIOGRAPHICAL/CRITICAL SOURCES:

BOOKS

Baskin, Barbara H., and Karen H. Harris, *Books for the Gifted Child,* Bowker, 1980, pp. 117-118.

Blishen, Edward, editor, *The Thorny Paradise: Writers on Writing for Children,* Penguin, 1975, pp. 108-116.

Children's Literature Review, Volume 18, Gale, 1989.

Landsberg, Michele, "Fantasy," in her *Reading for the Love of It: Best Books for Young Readers,* Prentice Hall, 1987, pp. 157-182.

Something about the Author, Volume 1, Gale, 1971.

Swinfen, Ann, "Worlds in Parallel," in her *In Defence of Fantasy: A Study of the Genre in English and American Literature since 1945,* Routledge & Kegan Paul, 1984, pp. 44-74.

Townsend, John Rowe, "Helen Cresswell," *A Sense of Story: Essays on Contemporary Writers for Children,* Lippincott, 1971, pp. 57-67.

PERIODICALS

Books and Bookmen, February, 1973; November, 1975; June, 1980.

Books for Keeps, January, 1987, pp. 12-13.

Chicago Tribune Book World, October 10, 1982.

Children's Literature in Education, March, 1971; July, 1971, pp. 51-59; spring, 1975, pp. 21-30.

Growing Point, April, 1967, pp. 882-883; December, 1975, pp. 2272-2273.

Horn Book, February, 1973, p. 52; October, 1978, p. 514; April, 1981, pp. 215-217.

Junior Bookshelf, June, 1970, pp. 135-139.

Listener, November 10, 1977.

New Statesman, November 9, 1973, p. 704.

New York Times Book Review, January 2, 1966, p. 18; November 8, 1970.

Spectator, October 20, 1973, pp. xii-xiii.

Times Literary Supplement, May 25, 1967, p. 445; June 6, 1968, p. 584; April 4, 1969; June 26, 1969, p. 687; July 2, 1970, p. 714; December 3, 1971, p. 1516; November 3, 1972, p. 1323; November 23, 1973, p. 1428; December 5, 1975, p. 1457; April 7, 1978, p. 378; July 23, 1982, p. 794.

Washington Post Book World, April 9, 1978, p. E4.*

*   *   *

CRONKITE, Walter (Leland, Jr.) 1916-

PERSONAL: Born November 4, 1916, in St. Joseph, MO; son of Walter Leland (a dentist) and Helen Lena (Fritsche) Cronkite; married Mary Elizabeth Simmons Maxwell (a journalist), March 30, 1940; children: Nancy Elizabeth, Mary Kathleen, Walter Leland III. *Education:* Attended

University of Texas, 1933-35. *Politics:* Independent. *Religion:* Episcopalian. *Avocational interests:* Yachting, dancing, golf, tennis, bowling, and reading.

ADDRESSES: Office—CBS News, 51 West 52nd St., New York, NY 10019.

CAREER: Scripps-Howard Bureau, Austin, TX, reporter on state capitol staff, 1933-35; *Houston Press,* Houston, TX, reporter, 1935-36; KCMO-Radio, Kansas City, MO, news and sports editor and broadcaster, 1936-37; United Press International (UPI), organizer of El Paso (TX) bureau, 1937; WKY-Radio, Oklahoma City, OK, football announcer, 1937; Braniff Airways, Kansas City, executive, 1937; UPI, reporter, 1937-48, war correspondent from Germany, North Africa, British Isles, Normandy, and Belgium, 1941-45, established bureaus in Belgium, the Netherlands, and Luxembourg, 1945, chief correspondent from the Nuremberg trials of Nazi war criminals, 1945-46, chief correspondent from the Soviet Union in Moscow, 1946-48; broadcaster, lecturer, and journalist from Washington, D.C., 1948-50; Columbia Broadcasting System (CBS)-News, New York City and Washington, D.C., 1950—, discussion chairman of *Man of the Week,* 1951, anchor of *The Week in Review,* 1951-62, moderator of *Pick the Winner,* 1952, narrator of *You Are There,* 1953-55, host of *It's News to Me,* 1954, coordinator and master of ceremonies of *Morning Show,* 1955, narrator of *The Twentieth Century,* 1957-67, managing editor and anchor of *CBS Evening News with Walter Cronkite,* 1962-81, special correspondent, 1981—.

Writer, editor, and narrator of television specials for CBS, including *The Newsreel Era—Seventy Years of Headlines,* 1972; *Solzhenitsyn,* 1974; *The Rockefellers,* 1974; *Vietnam: A War That Is Finished,* 1975; *The President in China,* 1975; *In Celebration of US,* 1976; *Our Happiest Birthday,* 1977; *Walt Disney. . .One Man's Dream,* 1981; *Walter Cronkite's Universe,* 1981-82; *A Journey of the Mind,* 1983; *1984 Revisited,* 1984; and *Walter Cronkite at Large,* 1986-88.

MEMBER: Overseas Press Club, Overseas Writers Club, National Press Club, Academy of Television Arts and Sciences (president, 1959), Association of Radio News Analysts, Chi Phi, Century Association, Players Club, New York Yacht Club, Edgartown Yacht Club, Cruising Club of America.

AWARDS, HONORS: George Foster Peabody Radio and Television Award, 1962; William Allen White Award of Journalistic Merit, 1969; Emmy Award from Academy of Television Arts and Sciences, 1970; George Polk Memorial Award from Long Island University, 1971; Fourth Estate Award from National Press Club, 1973; Emmy Awards, 1973, for "coverage of shooting of Governor Wallace" and for *The Watergate Affair;* Emmy Awards,

1974, for *The Agnew Resignation, The Rockefellers,* and *Solzhenitsyn;* gold medal from International Radio and Television Society and Freedom Award from John Marshall Law School, both 1974; Alfred I. DuPont-Columbia University Award in Broadcast Journalism, 1978; Governor's Award (special Emmy award), 1979; Jefferson Award, Paul White Award, special George Foster Peabody Award, and Presidential Medal of Freedom, all 1981; Distinguished Service Award from National Association of Broadcasters and Trustees Award from National Academy of Television Arts and Sciences, both 1982. Recipient of numerous honorary degrees, including University of Notre Dame, Harvard University, Northwestern University, University of Massachusetts, Bucknell University, Ohio State University, University of Michigan, Duke University, and Dartmouth College.

WRITINGS:

(Contributor) M. Mirkin Stanford, editor, *Conventions and Elections, 1960: A Complete Handbook,* Channel Press, 1960.
Vietnam Perspective: A CBS News Special Report, Pocket Books, 1965.
Eye on the World, Cowles Book Co., 1971.
The Challenge of Change, Public Affairs Press, 1971.
(Editor) *South by Southeast: Paintings by Ray Ellis,* Oxmoor House, 1983.
North by Northeast, Oxmoor House, 1986.
Westwind, Oxmoor House, 1990.

Also author of *I Can Hear It Now: The Sixties,* 1970.

AUTHOR OF INTRODUCTION

George Orwell, *Nineteen Eighty-Four: Commemorative Edition,* Dutton, 1950.
Steve Weinberg, *Trade Secrets of Washington Journalists: How To Get the Facts about What's Going on in Washington,* Acropolis, 1981.
Kathy Cronkite, *On the Edge of the Spotlight,* Warner Books, 1982.
John Bryson, *The World of Armand Hammer,* Harry N. Abrams, 1985.
Dennis Conner, *Comeback: My Race for the America's Cup,* St. Martin's, 1988.
Roger Tory Peterson, *Save the Birds,* Houghton, 1989.
Register of American Yachts 1988-89: The Yacht Owners Register, Yacht Owners Register, Inc., 1989.
Lorraine Monk, *Photographs That Changed the World,* Doubleday, 1989.
Register of American Yachts, 1990, Yacht Owners Register, Inc., 1990.

SIDELIGHTS: Walter Cronkite was voted "the most trusted man in America" in a 1973 opinion poll, a reflection of the respect he earned as anchorman of the *CBS*

Evening News. Cronkite joined CBS in 1950 and began broadcasting a nightly news show in 1962. He earned numerous Emmy Awards and other citations from his peers before he retired in 1981. According to Maureen Orth in *Vogue,* Cronkite "has not only been the ultimate witness to history, he has also helped shape our perception of that history by virtue of his role in directing the course of television news." In his reassuring, generally unflappable manner, Cronkite told national television audiences of the first man on the moon, of the assassinations of John F. Kennedy, Robert F. Kennedy, and Martin Luther King, Jr., of the failing Vietnam War, and of the resignation of Richard Nixon. An estimated nineteen million viewers tuned in to his broadcasts each night at the dinner hour.

In a *50 Plus* profile, Dalma Heyn called Cronkite "our most reliable world guide; someone so familiar and real to us he might have been a close friend." Heyn also pinpointed the anchorman's popularity, only now diminishing after more than a decade off the air: "As a constant, someone who was thoroughly professional, believable and honest for so many years, he filled a deeply felt need. He seemed to make the bad news a little more palatable." Cronkite prided himself on his unbiased presentation of national and world events—he often pointed out that he was not a commentator, but a reporter who allowed his viewers to form their own opinions. This philosophy contributed to his reputation for integrity in presenting the news, but most Americans appreciated him more for his steady on-air presence. As Michael Gorkin put it in *50 Plus,* Cronkite's "steady and reassuring voice—'And that's the way it is . . .'—provided just the soothing we needed. *He,* at least, believed we would muddle through."

Some critics have observed that Cronkite's standing in Middle America was enhanced by the fact that he comes from Midwestern and middle-class origins himself. He was born in St. Joseph, Missouri, in 1916, the son of a dentist. From an early age he felt tugged toward journalism, and his ambitions were nurtured by his public school teachers. After attending high school in Houston, Texas, he enrolled at the University of Texas, but he spent more time stringing for the *Houston Post* and working as a radio announcer than he did attending classes. After two years of college he dropped out and took a full-time reporting job. Within a year he was working as a correspondent for United Press International.

Prior to World War II, Cronkite held a number of positions as a journalist, radio broadcaster, and bureau organizer. He rejoined UPI as war erupted in Europe, and he was sent to cover the fighting from the front lines. Gorkin claimed that Cronkite's associates found him "one of the most daring war-front reporters. He parachuted into Holland with the 101st Airborne Division, and was with the U.S. Third Army for the Battle of the Bulge. He special-

ized in the personal story with the hometown angle, and nobody worked harder or wrote faster than he did. He was, they say, simply one of the best American reporters to come out of the war."

Cronkite has insisted that he was never extraordinarily courageous during his years as a war correspondent. "I was scared to death all the time," he told *Playboy.* "I did everything possible to avoid getting into combat. . . . But the truth is that I did everything only once. It didn't take any great courage to do it once. If you go back, and do it a second time—knowing how bad it is—that's courage."

After the war Cronkite stayed with UPI, working in Europe, the Soviet Union, and Washington, D.C. He joined CBS in 1950 and began appearing on a number of fledgling television shows, most notably *The Week in Review.* Cronkite told *50 Plus:* "There were better speakers, better interviewers, and better-looking people than me, [but] people sensed that I believe in what I am doing." Cronkite's early career at CBS took some unexpected turns. Beginning in 1953 he hosted *You Are There,* a show that re-created historical events and offered imaginary interviews with such luminaries as Joan of Arc and Julius Caesar.

Cronkite proved himself a serious on-air reporter in 1952, when CBS sent him to provide radio coverage of the presidential nominating conventions in Chicago. In an *Atlantic Monthly* expose on CBS, David Halberstam noted that Cronkite "was thoroughly prepared, knew the weight of each delegation, and was able to bind the coverage together at all times. He was a pro in a field short of professionalism. By the end of the first day . . . the other people in the control booth just looked at each other; they knew they had a winner." Subsequently, CBS expanded Cronkite's duties as an on-site television reporter. He especially enjoyed covering rocket liftoffs at Cape Canaveral and elsewhere—a prelude to his longstanding interest in the nation's space program.

A shuffle of personnel at CBS in 1962 made Cronkite the anchorman of the evening news. Throughout the turbulent 1960s the show gained steadily on its competitors, and in the 1970s it led the ratings by a wide margin every year. Cronkite served as managing editor of the show as well as its anchor, taking great responsibility for the content of each program and the wording of each script. Halberstam observed that Cronkite "was a good synthesizer and clarifier, working hard in the brief time allotted to his program to make the news understandable to millions of people. And his style and character seemed to come through."

"In no small measure," Orth wrote, "Walter Cronkite's success and the esteem in which he is held have helped glamorize television news and invest it with the kind of disturbing power it has today." Eventually Cronkite transcended his role as reporter of the news and began to *make* news himself. After a visit to South Vietnam in 1968, during which he observed the Tet Offensive, Cronkite made a special broadcast and candidly reported that the United States was losing the war. Historians credit that broadcast with helping to turn majority opinion against the effort in Southeast Asia, as well as helping to convince Lyndon Johnson not to seek re-election. In 1977 Cronkite was instrumental in initiating peace talks between Egypt and Israel, when chance comments in an interview led to a live-broadcast dialogue between those countries' leaders.

Cronkite told *Playboy* that he made every effort to remain impartial on every story he reported. "The basic function of the press has to be the presentation of all the facts on which the story is based," he said. "Advocacy is all right in special columns. But how the hell are you going to give people the basis on which to advocate something if you don't present the facts to them? If you go only for advocacy journalism, you're really assuming unto yourself a privilege that was never intended anywhere in the definition of a free press."

Nevertheless, Cronkite's special interest in space exploration and the environment meant that CBS News gave extra precedence to these issues. *Newsweek* contributor Harry F. Waters claimed that Cronkite's "passion for moon shots probably did more to rally the nation behind the U.S. space program than all of NASA's public-relations efforts." Heyn maintained that Cronkite's love of nature "almost certainly helped create the climate for passage of the environmental legislation of the '70s." After retiring from the daily anchor spot in 1981, Cronkite continued to pursue his interests in these fields through a series of specials called *Walter Cronkite's Universe* and *Walter Cronkite at Large.*

Since 1981 Cronkite has remained on the staff at CBS as a consultant and the host of numerous special broadcasts. He has used his spare time to indulge his passion for yachting and other sports and has written several books on boating and its pleasures. Cronkite is still much sought after as a speaker; his positions on broadcast journalism in particular are accorded a great deal of respect. Cronkite told the *Washington Post* that he misses his work as an anchorman, but he relishes the opportunity to enjoy himself. "I've made my contribution over 45 or 50 years of journalism," he said. "I don't know why I shouldn't be entitled to take it easier as well as others. . . . I was tired of the Evening News when I stepped down. I wasn't tired of the job so much as I was tired of the routine. The job I loved. It would be wonderful if I could dip into the Evening News—if I could say, 'Gee, I'm going to go and work this week.' There's no place for individuals with such whimsical ideas."

Arthur Taylor, former corporate president of CBS, told *50 Plus:* "I think Walter will go down in history for having the character not to exploit the power that was his. Had he not had the character to do that, he might have provoked an enormous change in the rules. . . . And I think life would have become very difficult for the broadcast community." Cronkite told *TV Guide* how he managed to keep his perspective over a twenty-year career in front of the camera. "A good journalist doesn't just *know* the public, he *is* the public," Cronkite concluded. "He feels the same things they do."

BIOGRAPHICAL/CRITICAL SOURCES:

BOOKS

Authors in the News, Gale, Volume 1, 1975; Volume 2, 1976.
Contemporary Theatre, Film, and Television, Volume 6, Gale, 1989.
Cronkite, Kathy, *On the Edge of the Spotlight,* Warner Books, 1982.
Wood, Carlyle, *Television Personalities Biographical Sketch Book,* Television Personalities, 1956.

PERIODICALS

Atlantic Monthly, February, 1976.
Broadcasting, October 15, 1973.
Christian Science Monitor, December 26, 1973.
Current, June, 1980.
Esquire, April, 1973; December, 1980.
50 Plus, November, 1979; March, 1985.
Look, August 25, 1964; November 17, 1970; March 26, 1971.
Newsweek, February 9, 1953; March 11, 1968; November 12, 1973; December 5, 1980; March 9, 1981.
New York Post Magazine, March 21, 1954.
New York Times, July 20, 1952; January 18, 1981; April 27, 1988.
People, March 9, 1981; September 22, 1986.
Playboy, June, 1973.
Publishers Weekly, May 3, 1971.
Reader's Digest, December, 1969; June, 1980.
Saturday Evening Post, March 16, 1963.
Saturday Review, November, 1983.
Time, October 14, 1966; November 21, 1969; September 10, 1973; November 11, 1973.
Today's Health, autumn, 1972.
Vogue, April, 1986.
Washington Post, August 28, 1973; November 20, 1983; April 16, 1988; October 25, 1988.

—Sketch by Anne Janette Johnson

D

DAHL, Roald 1916-1990

PERSONAL: Given name is pronounced "Roo-aal"; born September 13, 1916, in Llandaff, South Wales; died November 23, 1990, in Oxford, England; son of Harald (a shipbroker, painter, and horticulturist) and Sofie (Hesselberg) Dahl; married Patricia Neal (an actress), July 2, 1953 (divorced, 1983); married Felicity Ann Crosland, 1983; children: (first marriage) Olivia (deceased), Tessa, Theo, Ophelia, Lucy. *Education:* Graduate of British public schools, 1932.

ADDRESSES: Home—Gipsy House, Great Missenden, Buckinghamshire HP16 0PB, England. *Agent*—Watkins Loomis Agency, 150 East 35th St., New York, NY 10016.

CAREER: Shell Oil Co., London, England, member of eastern staff, 1933-37, member of staff in Dar-es-Salaam, Tanzania, 1937-39; writer. Host of a series of half-hour television dramas, *Way Out,* during early 1960s. *Military service:* Royal Air Force, fighter pilot, 1939-45; became wing commander.

AWARDS, HONORS: Edgar Award, Mystery Writers of America, 1954, 1959, and 1980; New England Round Table of Children's Librarians award, 1972, and Surrey School award, 1973, both for *Charlie and the Chocolate Factory;* Surrey School award, 1975, and Nene award, 1978, both for *Charlie and the Great Glass Elevator;* Surrey School award, 1978, and California Young Reader Medal, 1979, both for *Danny: The Champion of the World;* Federation of Children's Book Groups award, 1982, for *The BFG;* Massachusetts Children's award, 1982, for *James and the Giant Peach; New York Times* Outstanding Books award, 1983, Whitbread Award, 1983, and West Australian award, 1986, all for *The Witches;* World Fantasy Convention Lifetime Achievement Award, and Federation of Children's Book Groups award, both 1983; Maschler award runner-up, 1985, for *The Giraffe and the*

Pelly and Me; Boston Globe/Horn Book nonfiction honor citation, 1985, for *Boy: Tales of Childhood;* International Board on Books for Young People awards for Norwegian and German translations of *The BFG,* both 1986; Smarties Award, 1990, for *Esio Trot.*

WRITINGS:

FOR ADULTS

Sometime Never: A Fable for Supermen (novel), Scribner, 1948.
My Uncle Oswald (novel), M. Joseph, 1979, Knopf, 1980.
Going Solo (autobiography), Farrar, Straus, 1986.

FOR CHILDREN

The Gremlins, illustrations by Walt Disney Productions, Random House, 1943.
James and the Giant Peach: A Children's Story (also see below), illustrations by Nancy Ekholm Burkert, Knopf, 1961, illustrations by Michel Simeon, Allen & Unwin, 1967.
Charlie and the Chocolate Factory (also see below), illustrations by Joseph Schindelman, Knopf, 1964, revised edition, 1973, illustrations by Faith Jaques, Allen & Unwin, 1967.
The Magic Finger (also see below), illustrations by William Pene du Bois, Harper, 1966, illustrations by Pat Marriott, Puffins Books, 1974.
Fantastic Mr. Fox (also see below), illustrations by Donald Chaffin, Knopf, 1970.
Charlie and the Great Glass Elevator: The Further Adventures of Charlie Bucket and Willy Wonka, Chocolate-Maker Extraordinary (also see below), illustrations by J. Schindelman, Knopf, 1972, illustrations by F. Jaques, Allen & Unwin, 1973.

Danny: The Champion of the World, illustrations by Jill Bennett, Knopf, 1975 (collected with *James and the Giant Peach* and *Fantastic Mr. Fox,* Bantam, 1983).

The Enormous Crocodile (also see below), illustrations by Quentin Blake, Knopf, 1978.

The Complete Adventures of Charlie and Mr. Willy Wonka (contains *Charlie and the Chocolate Factory* and *Charlie and the Great Glass Elevator*), illustrations by F. Jaques, Allen & Unwin, 1978.

The Twits, illustrations by Q. Blake, J. Cape, 1980, Knopf, 1981.

George's Marvelous Medicine, illustrations by Q. Blake, J. Cape, 1981, Knopf, 1982.

Roald Dahl's Revolting Rhymes, illustrations by Q. Blake, J. Cape, 1982, Knopf, 1983.

The BFG (also see below), illustrations by Q. Blake, Farrar, Straus, 1982.

Dirty Beasts (verse), illustrations by Rosemary Fawcett, Farrar, Straus, 1983.

The Witches (also see below), illustrations by Q. Blake, Farrar, Straus, 1983.

Boy: Tales of Childhood, Farrar, Straus, 1984.

The Giraffe and Pelly and Me, illustrations by Q. Blake, Farrar, Straus, 1985.

Matilda, illustrations by Q. Blake, Viking Kestrel, 1988.

Roald Dahl: Charlie and the Chocolate Factory, Charlie and the Great Glass Elevator, The BFG (boxed set), Viking, 1989.

Rhyme Stew (comic verse), illustrations by Q. Blake, J. Cape, 1989, Viking, 1990.

Esio Trot, illustrations by Q. Blake, Viking, 1990.

The Dahl Diary, 1992, illustrations by Q. Blake, Puffin Books, 1991.

The Vicar of Nibbleswicke, illustrations by Q. Blake, Viking, 1992.

SHORT FICTION

Over to You: Ten Stories of Flyers and Flying (also see below), Reynal, 1946.

Someone Like You (also see below), Knopf, 1953.

Kiss, Kiss (also see below), Knopf, 1959.

Selected Stories of Roald Dahl, Modern Library, 1968.

Twenty-nine Kisses from Roald Dahl (contains *Someone Like You* and *Kiss, Kiss*), M. Joseph, 1969.

Switch Bitch (also see below), Knopf, 1974.

The Wonderful World of Henry Sugar and Six More, Knopf, 1977 (published in England as *The Wonderful Story of Henry Sugar and Six More,* Cape, 1977).

The Best of Roald Dahl (selections from *Over to You, Someone Like You, Kiss Kiss,* and *Switch Bitch*), introduction by James Cameron, Vintage, 1978.

Roald Dahl's Tales of the Unexpected, Vintage, 1979.

Taste and Other Tales, Longman, 1979.

A Roald Dahl Selection: Nine Short Stories, edited and introduced by Roy Blatchford, photographs by Catherine Shakespeare Lane, Longman, 1980.

More Tales of the Unexpected, Penguin, 1980 (published in England as *More Roald Dahl's Tales of the Unexpected,* Joseph, 1980, and as *Further Tales of the Unexpected,* Chivers, 1981).

(Editor) *Roald Dahl's Book of Ghost Stories,* Farrar, Straus, 1983.

Two Fables (contains "Princess and the Poacher" and "Princess Mammalia"), illustrations by Graham Dean, Viking, 1986.

The Roald Dahl Omnibus, Hippocrene Books, 1987.

A Second Roald Dahl Selection: Eight Short Stories, edited by Helene Fawcett, Longman, 1987.

Ah, Sweet Mystery of Life, illustrations by John Lawrence, J. Cape, 1988, Knopf, 1989.

Contributor of short fiction to *Penguin Modern Stories 12,* 1972.

SCREENPLAYS

"Lamb to the Slaughter" (teleplay), *Alfred Hitchcock Presents,* Columbia Broadcasting System (CBS-TV), 1958.

(With Jack Bloom) *You Only Live Twice,* United Artists, 1967.

(With Ken Hughes) *Chitty Chitty Bang Bang,* United Artists, 1968.

The Night-Digger (based on *Nest in a Falling Tree,* by Joy Crowley), Metro-Goldwyn-Mayer, 1970.

Willie Wonka and the Chocolate Factory (motion picture; adaptation of *Charlie and the Chocolate Factory*), Paramount, 1971.

Also author of screenplays *Oh Death, Where Is Thy Sting-a-Ling-a-Ling?,* United Artists, *The Lightning Bug,* 1971, and *The Road Builder.*

OTHER

The Honeys (play), produced in New York City, 1955.

Dahl has recorded *Charlie and the Chocolate Factory,* Caedmon, 1975, *James and the Giant Peach,* Caedmon, 1977, *Fantastic Mr. Fox,* Caedmon, 1978, and *Roald Dahl Reads His "The Enormous Crocodile" and "The Magic Finger,"* Caedmon, 1980, as well as an interview, *Bedtime Stories to Children's Books,* Center for Cassette Studies, 1973. Contributor to anthologies and to periodicals including *Harper's, New Yorker, Playboy, Collier's, Town and Country, Atlantic, Esquire,* and *Saturday Evening Post.*

ADAPTATIONS:

MOVIES AND FILMSTRIPS

36 Hours (motion picture; adaptation of Dahl's short story "Beware of the Dog"), Metro-Goldwyn-Mayer, 1964.

Delicious Inventions (motion picture; excerpted from film *Willie Wonka and the Chocolate Factory,* Paramount, 1971), Films, Inc., 1976.

Willie Wonka and the Chocolate Factory—Storytime (filmstrip; excerpted from the 1971 Paramount motion picture of the same name), Films, Inc., 1976.

Willie Wonka and the Chocolate Factory—Learning Kit (filmstrip; excerpted from the 1971 Paramount motion picture of the same name), Films, Inc., 1976.

The Witches, screenplay by Allan Scott, Lorimar, 1990.

TELEVISION

Tales of the Unexpected, WNEW-TV, 1979.

PLAYS

George, Richard, *Roald Dahl's Charlie and the Chocolate Factory: A Play,* introduction by Dahl, Knopf, 1976.

George, R., *Roald Dahl's James and the Giant Peach: A Play,* introduction by Dahl, Penguin, 1982.

RECORDINGS

The Great Switcheroo, read by Patricia Neal, Caedmon, 1977.

SIDELIGHTS: Roald Dahl, best known as the author of children's books *Charlie and the Chocolate Factory* and *James and the Giant Peach,* was also noted for his short stories for adults, and his enchanting autobiographical descriptions of growing up in England and flying in World War II. His children's fiction is known for its sudden turns into the fantastic, its wheeling, fast-moving prose, and its decidedly harsh treatment of any adults foolish enough to cause trouble for the young heroes and heroines. Similarly, his adult fiction often relies on a sudden twist that throws light on what has been happening in the story, a trait most evident in *Tales of the Unexpected,* which was made into a television series.

Dahl was born on September 13, 1916, the son of an adventurous shipbroker. He was an energetic and mischievous child and from an early age proved adept at finding trouble. His very earliest memory was of pedalling to school at breakneck speed on his tricycle, his two sisters struggling to keep up as he whizzed around curves on two wheels. In *Boy: Tales of Childhood,* Dahl recounted many of these happy memories from his childhood, remembering most fondly the trips that the entire family took to Norway, which he always considered home. Each summer the family would tramp aboard a steamer for the two-day trip to Oslo, where they were treated to a Norwegian feast with his grandparents, and the next day board a smaller ship for a trip north to what they called "Magic Island." On the island the family whiled away the long summer days swimming and boating.

Though Dahl's father died when the author was four, his mother abided by her husband's wish to have the children attend English schools, which he considered the best in the world. At Llandaff Cathedral School the young Dahl began his career of mischievous adventures and met up with the first of many oppressive, even cruel, adults. One exploit in particular foretold both the author's career in school and the major themes of his adult work. Each day on the way to and from school the seven-year-old Dahl and his friends passed a sweetshop. Unable to resist the lure of "Bootlace Liquorice" and "Gobstoppers"—familiar candy to *Charlie and the Chocolate Factory* fans— the children would pile into the store and buy as much candy as they could with their limited allowances. Day after day the grubby, grouchy storekeeper, Mrs. Pratchett, scolded the children as she dug her dirty hands into the jars of candy; one day the kids had had enough of her abuse, and Dahl hatched the perfect plan to get back at her. The very next day, when she reached into the jar of Gobstoppers she clamped her hand around a very stiff, dead mouse and flung the jar to the ground, scattering Gobstoppers and glass all over the store floor. Mrs. Pratchett knew who to blame, and when the boys went to school the next day she was waiting, along with a very angry Headmaster Coombes. Not only did Coombes give each of the boys a severe beating, but Mrs. Pratchett was there to witness it. "She was bounding up and down with excitement," Dahl remembered in *Boy,* " 'Lay it into 'im!' she was shrieking. 'Let 'im 'ave it! Teach 'im a lesson!' "

Dahl's mother complained about the beating the boys were given, but was told if she didn't like it she could find another school. She did, sending Roald to St. Peters Boarding School the next year, and later to Repton, a renowned private school. Of his time at St. Peters, Dahl said: "Those were days of horrors, of fierce discipline, of not talking in the dormitories, no running in the corridors, no untidiness of any sort, no this or that or the other, just rules, rules and still more rules that had to be obeyed. And the fear of the dreaded cane hung over us like the fear of death all the time."

Dahl received undistinguished marks while attending Repton, and showed little sign of his future prowess as a writer. His end-of-term report from Easter term, 1931, which he saved, declared him "a persistent muddler. Vocabulary negligible, sentences mal-constructed. He reminds me of a camel." Nevertheless, his mother offered him the option of attending Oxford or Cambridge when he finished school. His reply, recorded in *Boy,* was, "No, thank you. I want to go straight from school to work for a company that will send me to wonderful faraway places life Africa or China." He got his wish, for he was soon hired by the Shell Oil Company, and later shipped off to Tanganyika (now Tanzania), where he enjoyed "the roasting heat and the crocodiles and the snakes and the log safaris up-country, selling Shell oil to the men who ran the diamond mines and the sisal plantations. . . . Above all, I learned how to look after myself in a way that no young person can ever do by staying in civilization."

In 1939, Dahl's adventures took on a more dangerous cast as he joined the Royal Air Force training squadron in Nairobi, Kenya. World War II was just beginning, and Dahl would soon make his mark as a fighter pilot combatting the Germans all around the Mediterranean Sea. While strafing a convoy of trucks near Alexandria, Egypt, his plane was hit by machine-gun fire. The plane crashed to the ground and Dahl crawled from the wreckage as the gas tanks exploded. The crash left his skull fractured, his nose crumpled, and his eyes temporarily stuck shut. After six months of recovery he returned to his squadron in Greece and shot down four enemy planes, but frequent blackouts as a result of his earlier injuries eventually rendered him unable to fly.

Dahl was soon transferred to Washington, D.C., to serve as an assistant air attache. One day C. S. Forester interviewed Dahl over lunch for an article he was writing for the *Saturday Evening Post,* but was too engrossed in eating to take notes himself. The notes that Dahl took for him turned out to be a story, which Forester sent to the magazine under Dahl's name. The magazine paid Dahl one thousand dollars for the story, which was titled "Piece of Cake" and later published in *Over to You: Ten Stories of Fliers and Flying.* Soon his stories appeared in *Collier's, Harper's, Ladies' Home Journal, Tomorrow* and *Town and Country.* Dahl indicated in a *New York Times Book Review* profile by Willa Petschek that "as I went on, the stories became less and less realistic and more fantastic. But becoming a writer was pure fluke. Without being asked to, I doubt if I'd ever have thought of it."

In 1943, Dahl wrote his first children's story, and coined a term, with *The Gremlins.* Gremlins were tiny saboteurs who lived on fighter planes and bombers and were responsible for all crashes. Mrs. Roosevelt, the president's wife, read the book to her children and liked it so much that she invited Dahl to dinner, and he and the president soon became friends. Through the 1940s and into the 1950s Dahl continued as a short story writer for adults, establishing his reputation as a writer of macabre tales with an unexpected twist. A *Books and Bookmen* reviewer called Dahl "a master of horror—an intellectual Hitchcock of the writing world." J. D. O'Hara, writing in *New Republic,* labelled him "our Supreme Master of Wickedness," and his

stories earned him three Edgar Allan Poe Awards from the Mystery Writers of America.

In 1953 he married Hollywood actress Patricia Neal, star of such movies as *The Fountainhead* and, later, *Hud,* for which she won an Academy Award. Dahl recalled in *Pat and Roald* that "she wasn't at all movie-starish; no great closets filled with clothes or anything like that. She had a drive to be a great actress, but it was never as strong as it is with some of these nuts. You could turn it aside." Although the marriage did not survive, it produced five children. As soon as the children were old enough, he began making up stories for them each night before they went to bed. These stories became the basis for his career as a children's writer, which began in earnest with the publication of *James and the Giant Peach* in 1961. Dahl insisted that having to invent stories night after night was perfect practice for his trade, telling the *New York Times Book Review:* "Children are a great discipline because they are highly critical. And they lose interest so quickly. You have to keep things ticking along. And if you think a child is getting bored, you must think up something that jolts it back. Something that tickles. You have to know what children like." Sales of Dahl's books certainly attest to his skill: *Charlie and the Chocolate Factory* and *Charlie and the Great Glass Elevator* have sold over one million hardcover copies in America, and *James and the Giant Peach* more than 350,000.

James and the Giant Peach recounts the fantastic tale of a young boy who travels thousands of miles in a house-sized peach with as bizarre an assemblage of companions as can be found in a children's book. After the giant peach crushes his aunts, James crawls into the peach through a worm hole, making friends with a centipede, a silkworm, a spider, a ladybug, and a flock of seagulls that lifts the peach into the air and carries it across the ocean to Central Park. Gerald Haigh, writing in *Times Literary Supplement,* said that Dahl had the ability to "home unerringly in on the very nub of childish delight, with brazen and glorious disregard for what is likely to furrow the adult brow."

One way that Dahl delighted his readers was to exact often vicious revenge on cruel adults who harmed children. In *Matilda,* the Amazonian headmistress Miss Turnbull, who deals with unruly children by grabbing them by the hair and tossing them out windows, is finally banished by the brilliant, triumphant Matilda. *The Witches,* released as a movie in 1990, finds the heroic young character, who has been turned into a mouse, thwarting the hideous and diabolical witches who are planning to kill all the children of England. But even innocent adults receive rough treatment: parents are killed in car crashes in *The Witches,* and eaten by a rhinoceros in *James and the Giant Peach;* aunts are flattened by a giant peach in *James and the Giant*

Peach; and pleasant fathers are murdered in *Matilda.* Many critics have objected to the rough treatment of adults. Eleanor Cameron, for example, in *Children's Literature in Education,* found that "Dahl caters to the streak of sadism in children which they don't even realize is there because they are not fully self-aware and are not experienced enough to understand what sadism is." And in *Now Upon a Time: A Contemporary View of Children's Literature,* Myra Pollack Sadker and David Miller Sadker criticized *Charlie and the Chocolate Factory* for its "ageism": "The message with which we close the book is that the needs and desires and opinions of old people are totally irrelevant and inconsequential."

However, Dahl explained in the *New York Times Book Review* that the children who wrote to him "invariably pick out the most gruesome events as the favorite parts of the books. . . . They don't relate it to life. They enjoy the fantasy. And my nastiness is never gratuitous. It's retribution. Beastly people must be punished." Alasdair Campbell, writing in *School Librarian,* argued that "normal children are bound to take some interest in the darker side of human nature, and books for them should be judged not by picking out separate elements but rather on the basis of their overall balance and effect." He found books such as *James and the Giant Peach, Charlie and the Chocolate Factory,* and *The Magic Finger* "ultimately satisfying, with the principles of justice clearly vindicated."

In *Trust Your Children: Voices Against Censorship in Children's Literature,* Dahl contended that adults may be disturbed by his books "because they are not quite as aware as I am that children are different from adults. Children are much more vulgar than grownups. They have a coarser sense of humor. They are basically more cruel." Dahl often commented that the key to his success with children was that he conspired with them against adults. Vicki Weissman, in her review of *Matilda* in the *New York Times Book Review,* agreed that Dahl's books are aimed to please children rather than adults in a number of ways. She thought that "the truths of death and torture are as distant as when the magician saws the lady in half," and delighted that "anarchic and patently impossible plots romp along with no regard at all for the even faintly likely." Just as children are more vulgar than adults, so too do they have more tolerance for undeveloped characters, loose linking of events, ludicrous word play, and mind-boggling plot twists. Eric Hadley, in his sketch of Dahl in *Twentieth Century Children's Writers,* suggested that the "sense of sharing, of joining with Dahl in a game or plot, is crucial: you admire him and his cleverness, *not* his characters." The result, according to Hadley, is that the audience has the "pleasure of feeling that they are in on a tremendous joke."

"The writer for children must be a jokey sort of a fellow . . . ," Dahl once told *Writer.* "He must like simple tricks and jokes and riddles and other childish things. He must be unconventional and inventive. He must have a really first-class plot." As a writer, Dahl encountered difficulty in developing plots. He filled an old school exercise book with ideas that he had jotted down in pencil, crayon, or whatever was handy, and insisted in *The Wonderful Story of Henry Sugar and Six More* that every story he had ever written, for adults or for children, "started out as a three- or four-line note in this little, much-worn, red-covered volume." And each book was written in a tiny brick hut in the apple orchard about two hundred yards away from his home in Buckinghamshire, England. The little hut was rarely cleaned, and the walls were lined with "ill-fitting sheets of polystyrene, yellow with age and tobacco smoke, and spiders . . . [making] pretty webs in the upper corners," Dahl once declared. "The room itself is of no consequence. It is out of focus, a place for dreaming and floating and whistling in the wind, as soft and silent and murky as a womb."

Looking back on his years as a writer in *Boy,* Dahl contended that "the life of a writer is absolute hell compared with the life of a businessman. The writer has to force himself to go to work. . . . Two hours of writing fiction leaves this particular writer absolutely drained. For those two hours he has been miles away, he has been somewhere else, in a different place with totally different people, and the effort of swimming back into normal surroundings is very great. It is almost a shock. The writer walks out of his workroom in a daze. He wants a drink. He needs it. It happens to be a fact that nearly every writer of fiction in the world drinks more whisky than is good for him. He does it to give himself faith, hope, and courage. A person is a fool to become a writer. His only compensation is absolute freedom. He has no master except his own soul, and that, I am sure, is why he does it."

BIOGRAPHICAL/CRITICAL SOURCES:

BOOKS

Children's Literature Review, Gale, Volume 1, 1976, Volume 7, 1984.

Contemporary Literary Criticism, Gale, Volume 1, 1973, Volume 6, 1976, Volume 18, 1981.

Dahl, Roald, *The Wonderful Story of Henry Sugar and Six More,* Knopf, 1977.

Dahl, Roald, *Boy: Tales of Childhood,* Farrar, Straus, 1984.

Dahl, Roald, *Going Solo,* Farrar, Straus, 1986.

Farrell, Barry, *Pat and Roald,* Random House, 1969.

McCann, Donnarae, and Gloria Woodard, editors, *The Black American in Books for Children: Readings in Racism,* Scarecrow, 1972.

Powling, Chris, *Roald Dahl,* Hamish Hamilton, 1983.
Sadker, Myra Pollack, and David Miller Sadker, *Now Upon a Time: A Contemporary View of Children's Literature,* Harper, 1977.
Twentieth-Century Children's Writers, 3rd edition, St. James Press, 1989, pp. 255-256.
West, Mark I., interview with Roald Dahl in *Trust Your Children: Voices against Censorship in Children's Literature,* Neal-Schuman, 1988, pp. 71-76.
Wintle, Justin, and Emma Fisher, *Pied Pipers: Interviews with the Influential Creators of Children's Literature,* Paddington Press, 1975.

PERIODICALS

Atlantic, December, 1964.
Best Sellers, January, 1978.
Books and Bookmen, January, 1969; May, 1970.
Chicago Sunday Tribune, February 15, 1960; November 12, 1961.
Chicago Tribune, October 21, 1986.
Chicago Tribune Book World, August 10, 1980; May 17, 1981.
Children's Book News, March-April, 1968.
Children's Literature in Education, spring, 1975; summer, 1976, pp. 59-63.
Christian Century, August 31, 1960.
Christian Science Monitor, November 16, 1961.
Commonweal, November 15, 1961.
Horn Book, October, 1972; December, 1972; February, 1973; April, 1973; June, 1973.
Kenyon Review, Volume 31, number 2, 1969.
Library Journal, November 15, 1961.
Life, August 18, 1972.
New Republic, October 19, 1974, p. 23; April 19, 1980.
New Statesman, October 29, 1960; March 5, 1971; November 4, 1977.
New York, December 12, 1988.
New York Herald Tribune Book Review, November 8, 1953; February 7, 1960.
New York Review of Books, December 17, 1970; December 14, 1972.
New York Times, November 8, 1953; April 29, 1980.
New York Times Book Review, February 7, 1960; November 12, 1961; October 25, 1964; November 8, 1970; September 17, 1972; October 27, 1974; October 26, 1975; December 25, 1977, pp. 6, 15; September 30, 1979; April 20, 1980; March 29, 1981; January 9, 1983; January 20, 1985; October 12, 1986; January 15, 1989, p. 31.
People, November 3, 1986; May 9, 1988.
Publishers Weekly, June 6, 1980.
Punch, November 29, 1967; December 6, 1978.
San Francisco Chronicle, February 15, 1960; December 10, 1961.

Saturday Review, December 26, 1953; February 20, 1960; February 17, 1962; November 7, 1964; March 10, 1973.
School Librarian, June, 1981, pp. 108-114.
Sewanee Review, winter, 1975.
Spectator, December, 1977.
Springfield Republican, March 13, 1960.
Times (London), December 22, 1983; April 21, 1990.
Times Educational Supplement, November 19, 1982, p. 35.
Times Literary Supplement, October 28, 1960; December 14, 1967; June 15, 1973; November 15, 1974; November 23, 1979; November 21, 1980; July 24, 1981; July 23, 1982; November 30, 1984; September 12, 1986; May 6, 1988.
Washington Post, October 8, 1986.
Washington Post Book World, November 13, 1977; April 20, 1980; May 8, 1983; January 13, 1985.
Wilson Library Bulletin, February, 1962; February, 1989.
Writer, August, 1976, pp. 18-19.
Young Reader's Review, November, 1966.*

—*Sketch by Tom Pendergast*

* * *

DALY, Maureen 1921-
(Maureen Daly McGivern)

PERSONAL: Born March 15, 1921, in Castlecaufield, County Tyrone, Ulster, Ireland; naturalized American citizen; daughter of Joseph Desmond (a salesman) and Margaret (Mellon-Kelly) Daly; married William P. McGivern (a writer), December 28, 1946 (died, November, 1983); children: Megan (deceased), Patrick. *Education:* Rosary College, B.A., 1942. *Politics:* Democrat.

ADDRESSES: Home—73-305 Ironwood St., Palm Desert, CA 92260. *Agent*—Eleanor Wood, Blassingame, McCauley, and Wood, 432 Park Ave. S., Suite 1205, New York, NY 10016.

CAREER: Writer, 1938—. *Chicago Tribune,* Chicago, IL, reporter and columnist, 1941-44; Chicago City News Bureau, Chicago, reporter, 1941-43; *Ladies' Home Journal,* Philadelphia, PA, associate editor, 1944-49; *Saturday Evening Post,* Philadelphia, consultant to editors, 1960-69; *Desert Sun,* Palm Desert, CA, reporter and columnist, 1987—. Screenwriter for Twentieth Century-Fox. Lecturer on foreign lands and emerging nations.

MEMBER: PEN, Mystery Writers of America, Writers Guild of America (West).

AWARDS, HONORS: Scholastic magazine's short story contest, 1936, third prize for "Fifteen," 1937, first prize for "Sixteen"; O. Henry Memorial Award, 1938, for short story "Sixteen"; Dodd, Mead Intercollegiate Literary Fellowship Novel Award, 1942, and Lewis Carroll Shelf Award, 1969, both for *Seventeenth Summer;* Freedoms Foundation Award, 1952, for "humanity in reporting"; Gimbel Fashion Award, 1962, for contribution to U.S. fashion industry through *Saturday Evening Post* articles; *Acts of Love* was selected one of *Redbook*'s ten great books for teens, 1987.

WRITINGS:

YOUNG ADULT FICTION

Seventeenth Summer, Dodd, 1942, illustrated edition, 1948.
Sixteen and Other Stories, illustrated by Kendall Rossi, Dodd, 1961.
Acts of Love, Scholastic, 1986.
First a Dream, Scholastic, 1990.

YOUNG ADULT NONFICTION

Smarter and Smoother: A Handbook on How to Be That Way, illustrated by Marguerite Bryan, Dodd, 1944.
What's Your P.Q. (Personality Quotient)?, illustrated by Ellie Simmons, Dodd, 1952, revised edition, 1966.
Twelve around the World, illustrated by Frank Kramer, Dodd, 1957.
Spanish Roundabout (travel), Dodd, 1960.
Moroccan Roundabout (travel), Dodd, 1961.

ADULT NONFICTION

The Perfect Hostess: Complete Etiquette and Entertainment for the Home, Dodd, 1950.
(Under name Maureen Daly McGivern; with husband, William P. McGivern) *Mention My Name in Mombasa: The Unscheduled Adventures of an American Family Abroad,* illustrated by Kramer, Dodd, 1958.
(With W. P. McGivern) *A Matter of Honor,* Arbor House, 1984.

JUVENILE

Patrick Visits the Farm (fiction), illustrated by Simmons, Dodd, 1959.
Patrick Takes a Trip (fiction), illustrated by Simmons, Dodd, 1960.
Patrick Visits the Library (fiction), illustrated by Paul Lantz, Dodd, 1961.
Patrick Visits the Zoo (fiction), illustrated by Sam Savitt, Dodd, 1963.
The Ginger Horse (fiction), illustrated by Wesley Dennis, Dodd, 1964.
Spain: Wonderland of Contrasts (nonfiction), Dodd, 1965.
The Small War of Sergeant Donkey (fiction), illustrated by Dennis, Dodd, 1966.
Rosie, the Dancing Elephant (fiction), illustrated by Lorence Bjorklund, Dodd, 1967.

EDITOR

My Favorite Stories (young adult), Dodd, 1948.
Profile of Youth (adult), Lippincott, 1951.
My Favorite Mystery Stories (young adult), Dodd, 1966.
(And author of introduction) *My Favorite Suspense Stories* (young adult), Dodd, 1968.

OTHER

Also author of "High School Career Series," Curtis Publishing Co., 1942-49. Writer with husband of scripts for television series, including "Kojak," and of screenplay, *Brannigan.* Work represented in several textbooks and anthologies. Contributor of over two hundred articles to numerous periodicals, including *Vogue, Mademoiselle, Cosmopolitan, Woman's Day, Scholastic, Woman's Home Companion,* and *Redbook.* Daly's papers are housed in a permanent collection at the University of Oregon Library.

ADAPTATIONS: The film rights to *Seventeenth Summer* were purchased by Warner Bros. in 1949; *The Ginger Horse* was filmed by Walt Disney Studios; Daly's short story, 'You Can't Kiss Caroline,' has also been dramatized.

WORK IN PROGRESS: Indian Summer, a story of a young Hollywood stunt woman and a young man just off the Morongo Reservation outside Palm Springs; *Hollywood People,* an adult novel about contemporary Hollywood based on Daly's experience working there.

SIDELIGHTS: Maureen Daly is an accomplished and prolific writer who throughout her career successfully bridged genres and print mediums making her name recognizable by young and old. In addition to numerous works for young adults, including her bestselling novel, *Seventeenth Summer,* Daly has also written three books of nonfiction for adults and several tales for young children. She has also reported for and penned columns for the *Chicago Tribune* and *Desert Sun,* authored screenplays for films and television, and contributed over two hundred articles to periodicals.

Daly began her writing career at an early age. She was fifteen when a story she entered in *Scholastic* magazine's short story contest won third prize. The next year, her English teacher submitted another work written by Daly to the contest. This time, Daly's "Sixteen," a tale about a boy and a girl who meet at a skating rink, was awarded first prize. Since *Scholastic* first printed Daly's story in 1938, "Sixteen" has been included in over three hundred anthologies and published in twelve different languages. The story is also in Daly's collection *Sixteen and Other Stories.* "Even now, when I get checks from the reprint of 'Sixteen,' it's like seeing an old friend from 1938," Daly comments to an interviewer for *Publishers Weekly.*

The following year, when she was seventeen years old, Daly started working on a story about a small town boy and girl who fall in love. Finally finishing the novel during her senior year at college, Daly sent the manuscript of *Seventeenth Summer* to a publisher who immediately accepted it for publication. The book quickly became a best-seller making Daly a successful author at the age of twenty-one. *Seventeenth Summer* has remained in print for nearly half a century, selling more than a million copies worldwide. Though originally released as a adult title, *Seventeenth Summer* is now credited as one of the first novels to begin defining the genre of young adult literature.

Reviewers praise *Seventeenth Summer* for its sensitive portrayal of the many and varied emotions and facets involved in young, first love. Set in a rural Wisconsin town, *Seventeenth Summer* follows the sweet and innocent romance of two teenagers as they experience all the joys and tribulations that are so commonly felt by most adolescents when they discover love for the first time. "*Seventeenth Summer,* perhaps captures better than any other novel the spirit of adolescence," states Dwight L. Burton in *English Journal.* Burton goes on to note: "More than just a love story of two adolescents, *Seventeenth Summer,* with its introspection and fine mastery of the scene, portrays the adolescent validly in several of his important relationships—with his family, with his age mates, and, very important, with himself. In each of these three aspects, Miss Daly is discerning."

In her review of *Seventeenth Summer,* Edith H. Walton writes in the *New York Times Book Review:* "Lyrically young and breathless, [*Seventeenth Summer*] deals with one of the oldest themes in the world, the theme of first love, and deals with it in a fashion which is so unhackneyed and so fresh that one forgets how often the same story has been told before. . . . Completely up to date in its idiom and its atmosphere, vividly authentic in a warm and homely way, it seems to me to be as unpretentiously good a first novel as any one could ask. . . . Simply, eloquently, Maureen Daly tells one how youth in love really feels—how it felt yesterday and how it feels today."

"My first and most widely published novel, *Seventeenth Summer,* was written in a spurt of creativity and emotion because I was so wildly and vividly happy about love and life at a particular time in my existence," Daly explains to *CA.* "I knew that euphoria and hope could not last (and it didn't) and I wanted to get all that fleeting excitement down on paper before it passed, or I forgot the true feelings. Lucky I did. I have never felt so hopeful since. It was not until the reviews came out (and the royalties came in) that I realized I had recorded universal emotions and joys—and people would want to read about them year after year."

Although *Seventeenth Summer* caused quite a stir in the publishing field, Daly decided to complete her university studies and resolved to pursue a career in journalism. While still a college senior, Daly accepted a job as a reporter covering the police beat for the *Chicago Tribune.* Working as a reporter challenged Daly's writing skills. As she reveals in *Publishers Weekly:* "I had to work really hard to keep all the details straight, when I called from the scene of news stories. I was so afraid they would fire a question at me and I wouldn't have the answer. Often I'd be standing in phone booths with sweat pouring down my back."

In addition to reporting on crime for the *Chicago Tribune,* Daly also reviewed books and wrote an advice column for the paper's Sunday magazine. Aimed at teenagers, Daly's column, *On the Solid Side,* was so popular the paper soon ran the column three times a week. Later, *On the Solid Side* was syndicated to more than a dozen newspapers. A collection of these articles was published as *Smarter and Smoother* in 1944. By the following year, the book had gone into it ninth printing. A critic for *Virginia Kirkus* suggests that "parents should be thankful to Maureen Daly for she gives all the advice and counsel that teenagers think is sermonizing from parents, but that they'll lap up in this form."

Since her first job as a reporter in Chicago, Daly has worked for several respected publications, such as the *Ladies' Home Journal* and the *Saturday Evening Post,* earning awards and a reputation as a talented and thoroughly professional journalist. In addition to her work as a reporter, columnist, and associate editor, Daly has also written hundreds of articles on a wide variety topics. Many of these articles explored one of her favorite subjects—travel and foreign lands.

Daly's interest in travel accelerated in 1949, when she left her job as associate editor for *Ladies' Home Journal,* moved to Europe, and began work as a freelance writer. Accompanied by her husband, William McGivern, and their two-year-old daughter, Megan, Daly spent time in Paris, Rome, Dublin, London, and Spain. She reported on the important issues of the day and interviewed many famous people, including Eleanor Roosevelt and Harry Truman. Her son, Patrick, was born during Daly's early years in Europe. The family returned to the United States to live when Daly's children were teenagers.

Daly's years travelling and living in Europe were the inspiration for her several books on travel, including her own family's personal experiences in *Mention My Name in Mombasa: The Unscheduled Adventures of an American Family Abroad.* Written with her husband, Daly introduces her readers to many of the quaint places and captivating people her family encountered during their travels.

A writer for *Virginia Kirkus* called *Mention My Name in Mombasa* "charming." The critic goes on to comment: "Writing with intelligence, sympathy and humor, interested in people rather than scenery, the authors tell of fishermen and babysitters, flowers and artists, bulls and bull-fighting, friendly servants, food good and bad, palaces and hotels. Lengthy but never dull, neither a guidebook nor a study of social conditions, the book should appeal to all kinds of travelers, those who go to far places and those who dream of them, and to students of social life outside the United States."

While *Mention My Name in Mombasa* is considered adult nonfiction, Daly has also shared many of her travel experiences with young readers in *Spain: Wonderland of Contrasts* and with young adults in *Twelve around the World, Spanish Roundabout,* and *Moroccan Roundabout.* In the *New York Times Book Review,* Lavinia R. Davis states that *Spanish Roundabout* "is not a guide book in the usual sense. It is, rather, a cohesive series of profiles and sketches of Spain drawn from affection, experience and compassion. . . . [The] emphasis is on people in contemporary Spain. Family life, bull-fighting, religious observances, cooking and teenage mores are described so skillfully and with such a complete lack of condescension that the reader cannot help sharing the author's enthusiasm and eager curiosity."

In 1986, Daly returned to the genre of literature that made her a bestselling author when *Acts of Love* was published. Another young adult novel, *First a Dream,* followed in 1990. As in her first novel for young adults, *Seventeenth Summer,* Daly once again provides her readers with a sweet love story that involved many of the experiences and emotions young people realize on their road to maturity. Both these books tell of the wonders and magic that are only known once in a lifetime—when love is discovered for the first time. Describing Daly as "the spiritual grandmother of the young adult novel," Richard Peck notes in the *Los Angeles Times* that "well before the term 'YA' [Young Adult] was coined [Daly] wrote the perennial best-seller, *Seventeenth Summer.* With *Acts of Love* she returns after 44 years to the sort of love story she pioneered when she was herself a YA."

In correspondence with *CA,* Daly shared her thoughts on writing: "I write more than one kind of book. In travel books I try to put down what I see, feel and learn as vividly and memorably as the experiences that have occurred to me. In fiction I am an entertainer but sometimes a sad one. The stories, the fictionalized versions of real life, are often melancholy but sometimes there is a joy, and a relief, in just sharing a human adventure.

"Writing is my kind of freedom, the chance to look outward as well as inward. It is an excellent excuse for curiosity, for travelling, studying, and just staring at other people and other scenes. I am constantly plagued by 'need to know,' not just to stockpile lists of facts and statistics but to have some understanding of what it is like to be someone else, or live somewhere else. So I travel to 'see' and write to 'think' and find out about myself and other people I meet—or invent."

BIOGRAPHICAL/CRITICAL SOURCES:

BOOKS

Contemporary Literary Criticism, Volume 17, Gale, 1981.
Something about the Author Autobiograpy Series, Volume 1, Gale, 1986.

PERIODICALS

Chicago Tribune, September 1, 1986.
English Journal, September, 1951.
Los Angeles Times, October 11, 1986.
New York Times Book Review, May 3, 1942; July 12, 1942; July 24, 1960.
Publishers Weekly, June 27, 1986.
Virginia Kirkus, March 1, 1944; July 15, 1958.

—*Sketch by Margaret Mazurkiewicz*

* * *

DANZIGER, Paula 1944-

PERSONAL: Born August 18, 1944, in Washington, DC; daughter of Samuel (worked in garment district) and Carolyn (a nurse; maiden name, Seigel) Danziger. *Education:* Montclair State College, B.A., 1967, M.A.

ADDRESSES: Home—New York, NY, and Bearsville, NY. *Agent*—Donald C. Farber, 99 Park Ave., New York, NY 10016.

CAREER: Substitute teacher, Edison, NJ, 1967; Title I teacher, Highland Park, NJ, 1967-1968; junior-high school English teacher, Edison, NJ, 1968-1970; Lincoln Junior High School, West Orange, NJ, English teacher, 1977-1978; full-time writer, 1978—. Worked for the Educational Opportunity Program, Montclair State College, until 1977.

AWARDS, HONORS: New Jersey Institute of Technology Award, and Young Reader Medal Nomination, California Reading Association, both 1976, Massachusetts Children's Book Award, first runner-up, 1977, winner, 1979, and Nene Award, Hawaii Association of School Librarians and the Hawaii Library Association, 1980, all for *The Cat Ate My Gymsuit;* Child Study Association of America's Children's Books of the Year citation, 1978, Massachusetts Children's Book Award, Education Department of Salem State College, 1979, Nene Award,

1980, California Young Reader Medal Nomination, 1981, and Arizona Young Reader Award, 1983, all for *The Pistachio Prescription;* Children's Choice Award, International Reading Association and the Children's Book Council, 1979, for *The Pistachio Prescription,* 1980, for *The Cat Ate My Gymsuit* and *Can You Sue Your Parents for Malpractice?,* 1981, for *There's a Bat in Bunk Five,* and 1983, for *The Divorce Express.*

New Jersey Institute of Technology Award, and New York Public Library's Books for the Teen Age citation, both 1980, and Land of Enchantment Book Award, New Mexico Library Association, 1982, all for *Can You Sue Your Parents for Malpractice?;* Read-a-Thon Author of the Year Award, Multiple Sclerosis Society, and Parents' Choice Award for Literature, Parents' Choice Foundation, both 1982, Woodward Park School Annual Book Award, 1983, and South Carolina Young Adult Book Award, South Carolina Association of School Librarians, 1985, all for *The Divorce Express;* CRABbery Award, Prince George's County Memorial Library System (MD), 1982, and Young Readers Medal, 1984, both for *There's a Bat in Bunk Five;* Parents' Choice Award for Literature, Bologna International Children's Book Fair exhibitor, and Child Study Association of America's Children's Books of the Year citation, all 1985, all for *It's an Aardvark-Eat-Turtle World.*

WRITINGS:

YOUNG ADULT NOVELS

The Cat Ate My Gymsuit, Delacorte, 1974.
The Pistachio Prescription, Delacorte, 1978.
Can You Sue Your Parents for Malpractice?, Delacorte, 1979.
There's a Bat in Bunk Five, Delacorte, 1980.
The Divorce Express, Delacorte, 1982.
It's an Aardvark-Eat-Turtle World, Delacorte, 1985.
This Place Has No Atmosphere, Delacorte, 1986.
Remember Me to Harold Square, Delacorte, 1987.
Everyone Else's Parents Said Yes, Delacorte, 1989.
Make Like a Tree and Leave, Delacorte, 1990.

ADAPTATIONS: Cheshire has made a filmstrip and cassette from *The Cat Ate My Gymsuit,* 1985; Listening Library has made cassettes of *The Cat Ate My Gymsuit, The Pistachio Prescription, There's a Bat in Bunk Five, Can You Sue Your Parents for Malpractice?,* and *The Divorce Express,* 1985-86.

SIDELIGHTS: Since the 1974 publication of her first novel *The Cat Ate My Gymsuit,* Paula Danziger has become one of America's most popular authors for young adults. Most of her books "center around young teenage girls faced with the problems of establishing a grownup identity," Alleen Pace Nilsen summarizes in *Twentieth-*

Century Children's Writers. But while Danziger's characters frequently deal with personal and family problems, they do so with humor, wit, and spirit. As a result, Nilsen writes, "teenagers begin to smile at themselves and come away from [Danziger's] books a little more confident that they too will make it."

"My life as an author began as a small child when I realized that was what I wanted to do and started mentally recording a lot of information and observations," Danziger told Marguerite Feitlowitz in an interview for *Authors and Artists for Young Adults* (*AAYA*). "That's also when I started to develop the sense of humor and the sense of perspective that allows me to write the way I do." While in high school, Danziger spent much of her time reading and also wrote for school and town newspapers. Nevertheless, she recalled, "I'd been raised to believe that I was not particularly bright, not college material. . . . Family dynamics were such that I fell into fulfilling their low expectations."

Despite her lackluster performance in school, Danziger was admitted to Montclair State College, where she studied to be a teacher. While in college, she was introduced to John Ciardi, a noted poet and author for children. She secured a semi-regular babysitting job with his family, including several summers when she accompanied the Ciardis to writers' conferences. The poet encouraged Danziger in her studies, and frequently shared his literary knowledge and insight with her, as the author related in her *AAYA* interview: "John Ciardi taught me more than anyone else about poetry and writing. Their house was full of books, and I borrowed liberally from the shelves. . . . It was the best lesson I've ever had in my life. He read the poems and explained them, giving me a sense of language structure."

After her graduation from college in 1967, Danziger began working as a substitute teacher—"an occupation that could have been a punishment in Dante's *Inferno,*" the author commented in *English Journal.* That job led to full-time positions as a junior high school English teacher. Danziger wanted to further her education, however, so she returned to school after three years to pursue a master's degree. But Danziger's studies were interrupted when she was involved in a bizarre series of car accidents. The first mishap was relatively minor, leaving her with a painful case of whiplash. But when she sought treatment several days later, the car she was traveling in was hit head-on by a drunken driver. Danziger hit the windshield of the car, and suffered temporary brain damage that left her unable to read and haunted by nightmares.

To combat her fear and feelings of powerlessness, Danziger began writing a novel about a teenager beset by self-doubt and family troubles. "I felt very out of control," she once explained, and "the last time I felt that way was when I was a kid. When you're a kid, everyone seems to be in charge, to have the right to tell you what to do, how to feel. In hospitals and schools it seemed to be the same way. So I wanted to confront all that." In addition, the author continued, "I really missed teaching my eighth graders . . . . [so] I decided to write a book to talk to them about survival—learning to like oneself, dealing with school systems, and being able to celebrate one's own uniqueness. The result was *The Cat Ate My Gymsuit.*"

"The cat ate my gymsuit" is one of the excuses junior high school student Marcy Lewis gives to her phys ed teacher to avoid dressing for gym class. Uncomfortable with her looks, unhappy with her insensitive and uncommunicative parents, and unsatisfied with a school that stifles individuality, Marcy becomes involved in a student protest over a teacher's firing and learns to have faith in herself and her abilities. The result is "a thoroughly enjoyable, tightly written, funny/sad tale of an unglamorous but plucky girl who is imaginative, believable, and worthy of emulation," a reviewer writes in *Journal of Reading.*

With its "fresh and funny" approach, *The Cat Ate My Gymsuit* "grabbed teenagers' attention because it was so different from the serious realistic novels that adult critics were raving over," Nilsen notes in *Twentieth-Century Children's Writers.* Despite the book's popularity, Danziger returned to teaching after recovering from her accident. Meanwhile, she continued working on a second book, *The Pistachio Prescription.* But eventually "the realization came that it was incredibly hard to be a good creative writer and a good creative teacher" at the same time, the author commented in *English Journal.* "Each was a full-time job. My choice was to write full time. I was never good at taking attendance, doing lesson plans, or getting papers back on time. I sold two ideas to Dell, took the advance money, and hoped for decent royalties."

The success of Danziger's next books allowed her the freedom to remain a full-time writer. *The Pistachio Prescription,* which details how an insecure teenager overcomes health problems and conflicts with her feuding parents, "is unusually well done," Zena Sutherland of the *Bulletin of the Center for Children's Books* comments; "the characterization and dialogue are strong, the relationships depicted with perception, and the writing style vigorous." Sutherland likewise finds that *Can You Sue Your Parents for Malpractice?* "has enough humor and breezy dialogue to make it fun to read, and enough solidity in the characters and relationships to make it thought-provoking." A story of a ninth-grader confused by relationships with stubborn parents and unpredictable boyfriends, the novel has a "skillful balance between humor and pathos" which makes it "yet another to add to [Danziger's] growing list of successful efforts in literature that's particularly appro-

priate for junior high students," Michele Simpson comments in *Journal of Reading.*

While Danziger's readers enjoy the humor and pacing of her books, some critics have faulted them as superficial, containing generic characters and situations. Perry Nodelman of *Children's Literature in Education,* for instance, comments that the "typicality" of books such as *The Cat Ate My Gymsuit* means that "we cannot possibly understand the story unless we fill in its exceedingly vague outlines with knowledge from our own experience. . . . The book demands, not distance, but involvement." Sutherland, on the other hand, believes that *There's a Bat in Bunk Five,* which recounts Marcy Lewis's summer as a camp counselor, "has depth in the relationships and characterizations; and it's written with vigor and humor." While the novel contains elements of familiar camping stories, the critic explains, it "doesn't, however, follow a formula plot."

Against criticisms that her books offer readers familiarity instead of challenges, Danziger countered: "For anyone who has ever felt alone—and who hasn't, in truth—a book can make a very good friend," the author told Feitlowitz in *AAYA.* "Like a good friend, a book can help you see things a little more clearly, help you blow off steam, get you laughing, let you cry." The author continued: "I think there is so much in life that is hard and sad and difficult and that there is so much in life that is . . . joyous and funny. There's also a lot of in between those two extremes. As a writer, I try to take all of those things and put them together. That way people can say 'I know that feeling' and identify with it."

This sense of identification helps make Danziger's books so popular with her readers; as Nilsen and Kenneth L. Donelson state in *Literature for Today's Young Adults,* Danziger's books "remain favorites . . . because they do not talk down to their readers, because they present real issues and real problems facing their readers, and because they do not pretend that there are easy answers to any problems." Danziger's sometimes negative portrayals of adults and quick one-liners "may annoy adults," the critics conclude, "but her humor is exactly what her readers want."

Later Danziger novels have included the humor that delights her fans and yet branched out to include a science-fiction spoof, a biracial protagonist, and two books for preteen readers. *This Place Has No Atmosphere* is set in the year 2057 and follows a teenager whose family moves to a colony on the moon. *The Divorce Express* presents Phoebe, who shuttles between her long-divorced parents. "Mercifully avoiding the . . . gloom and wearisome heart-searching of so many novels on this highly topical subject," Margery Fisher comments in *Growing Point,* "*The Divorce Express* makes its point in an agreeably relaxed and shrewd manner." The book also introduces Rosie, the biracial daughter of a mixed marriage, and in *It's an Aardvark-Eat-Turtle World* Rosie must cope with a new "family" when her mother combines households with her boyfriend. And the novels *Everyone Else's Parents Said Yes* and *Make Like a Tree and Leave,* which follow the adventures of sixth-grader Matthew Martin, continue "to reflect Danziger's awareness of what students of a certain age are like and what appeals to them," Dona Weisman remarks in *School Library Journal.*

Danziger has a good sense of how kids think and what their concerns are; even so, she sometimes considers returning to teach full-time so she can be closer to them, she told Feitlowitz. "I miss working with the kids, but I don't miss the faculty meetings, taking attendance, and grading papers," the author revealed. "I'm also not great about getting papers back in time. My strength as a teacher was that I really cared about kids, books and creativity." So to keep in touch with her audience Danziger travels the country, giving lectures and visiting schools. She also puts in extended visits of several days in length at various schools so that she can talk in depth with students.

"So here I am a full-time writer, a 'grown-up' who chooses to write about kids," Danziger commented. "I've made this choice because I think that kids and adults share a lot of the same feelings and thoughts, that we have to go through a lot of similar situations." And, she explained in her *AAYA* interview, "All writers write from deep experience. For me, that is childhood. From it flow feelings of vulnerability, compassion, and strength. Perhaps it would be better to say that I write 'of' young people rather than 'for' or 'to' them. Writers tell the best stories we possibly can, hopefully in ways that others will like."

BIOGRAPHICAL/CRITICAL SOURCES:

BOOKS

Authors and Artists for Young Adults, Volume 4, Gale, 1990, pp. 73-80.
Children's Literature Review, Volume 20, Gale, 1990.
Contemporary Literary Criticism, Volume 21, Gale, 1982.
Nilsen, Alleen Pace, and Kenneth L. Donelson, *Literature for Today's Young Adults,* 2nd edition, Scott, Foresman, 1985, pp. 335-369.
Twentieth-Century Children's Writers, 3rd edition, St. James Press, 1989, p. 262.

PERIODICALS

Bulletin of the Center for Children's Books, May, 1978, p. 140; June, 1979, pp. 172-173; December, 1980, p. 68.
Children's Literature in Education, winter, 1981, pp. 177-185.
English Journal, November, 1984, pp. 24-27.
Growing Point, September, 1986, pp. 4673-4674.

Journal of Reading, January, 1976, pp. 333-335; February, 1980, p. 473.
New Yorker, December 3, 1979.
New York Times Book Review, January 5, 1975; March 18, 1979, June 17, 1979; November 23, 1980; February 13, 1983.
PEN Newsletter, September, 1988, pp. 16-26.
School Library Journal, September, 1989, p. 249; October, 1990.*

　　　　　　　　　　　　　　—*Sketch by Diane Telgen*

*　　　*　　　*

DARACK, Arthur J. 1918-

PERSONAL: Born January 1, 1918, in Royal Oak, MI; son of Edward Charles and Sonia (Resnikov) Darack; married Jean Claire Puttmyer, May 28, 1942; children: Glenn Arthur, Brenda Lee. *Education:* Cincinnati Conservatory, Mus.M., 1949; Indiana University—Bloomington, Ph.D., 1951. *Avocational interests:* The fine arts; "tinkering" with automobiles.

ADDRESSES: Home and office—1864 Venetian Pt. Dr., Clearwater, FL 34615.

CAREER: Cincinnati Enquirer, Cincinnati, OH, music editor, 1951-61, feature writer and author of column "Offbeat," 1961-62, book and art editor, 1962-67; *Encyclopaedia Britannica,* Chicago, IL, associate editor, 1967-70; senior editor of monthly magazine *Actual Specifying Engineering,* 1971—. University of Cincinnati, College of Music, adjunct associate professor of music. Consumer Group, Inc., president, 1978—. Cincinnati Symphony Orchestra, program annotator, 1952-61. *Military service:* U.S. Army, 1941-45.

MEMBER: Pi Kappa Lambda.

WRITINGS:

Repair Your Own Car for Pennies: It's Easy, Consumers Digest, 1973, 3rd edition, 1976.
Buying Guide to 1974 Cars, Consumers Digest, 1974.
The Eat Right and Live Longer Cookbook, Consumers Digest, 1975.
Which Foods Are Best for You?: Your Food Nutrition Guide, Consumers Digest, 1974.
Outdoor Power Equipment: How It Works, How to Fix It, Stein & Day, 1977.
The Consumers Digest Automobile Repair Book, McGraw, 1978.
(With wife, Jean P. Darack, and Sander Goodman) *The Great Eating, Great Dieting Cookbook,* Crowell, 1978.
The Guide to Home Appliance Repair, McGraw, 1979.
Playboy's Book of Sports Car Repair, Playboy Press, 1980.

Used Cars: How to Avoid Highway Robbery, Prentice-Hall, 1983.

How to Repair and Care for Small Home Appliances, Prentice-Hall, 1983.

Taking Profits from the OEX, Bonus Books, 1988.

Trade the OEX: Cut Risk, Not Profit, Bonus Books, 1990.

Author of columns "Buy Right," for the Des Moines *Register* and the Des Moines *Tribune,* 1977-81, and "The Darack Column," for *Money Letter,* 1979-84. Contributor to *Saturday Review.* Co-founder and editor, *Dimension,* 1963-65; editor, *Consumers Digest,* 1972-78; contributing editor, *Money Letter,* 1979—.

WORK IN PROGRESS: Two novels about Chicago; a book on car repair for woman; a book on investments.

SIDELIGHTS: Arthur J. Darack told *CA:* "My review on consumer-oriented subjects is that the average person finds the cards stacked against informed buying decisions—not because the marketplace is deceptive but because it is difficult. Yet buying decisions control the quality of life, as do investment decisions. Investments ultimately require as much art as science. My consumer writing has been based on digging out the facts and presenting them in a readable, easily understood fashion.

"Journalism became my field and remains so, but I find today's journalism vastly different from what it was when I began in 1951. Investigative journalism, as it applies to consumer subjects, can be very helpful if it goes to the basics of the subject. If investigative journalism is used to support an existing point of view, as too often is the case, it becomes propaganda. In the old days, the propaganda came from the right. Today it comes from the left, but I do not see this as an advance."

*　　*　　*

DAUBER, Kenneth Marc   1945-

PERSONAL: Born April 3, 1945, in Brooklyn, NY; son of Isidore (a businessman) and Beatrice (a teacher; maiden name, Young) Dauber; married Antoinette Butler (a marketing executive), 1968; children: Jonathan, Abigail, Maayan. *Education:* Columbia University, A.B., 1966; Princeton University, M.A., 1968, Ph.D., 1973. *Religion:* Jewish.

ADDRESSES: Home—29 Barberry Ln., Buffalo, NY 14221. *Office*—Department of English, 306 Clemens Hall, State University of New York at Buffalo—Amherst Campus, Buffalo, NY 14260.

CAREER: State University of New York at Buffalo—Amherst Campus, Buffalo, assistant professor, 1970-78,

associate professor, 1978-90, professor of English, 1990—. Lecturer at Hebrew University of Jerusalem, 1981-84.

MEMBER: Modern Language Association of America, American Studies Association, Phi Beta Kappa.

AWARDS, HONORS: Woodrow Wilson fellow; Fulbright fellow.

WRITINGS:

Rediscovering Hawthorne, Princeton University Press, 1977.

Nathaniel Hawthorne, Life Work and Criticism, York Press, 1986.

The Idea of Authorship in America, University of Wisconsin Press, 1990.

SIDELIGHTS: Kenneth Marc Dauber told *CA:* "Writing is hard, but knowing you have good readers makes it easier. We should work to be good readers so that we may write better, too."

*　　*　　*

DAVID, A. R.
See DAVID, A(nn) Rosalie

*　　*　　*

DAVID, A(nn) Rosalie   1946-
(A. R. David, Rosalie David)

PERSONAL: Born May 30, 1946, in Cardiff, Wales; daughter of Idris (a merchant Navy officer) and Edna (a homemaker; maiden name, Jones) David; married Antony E. David (an archaeologist), October 17, 1970. *Education:* University College, London, B.A. (with honors), 1967; University of Liverpool, Ph.D., 1971. *Avocational interests:* Travel (Egypt, Greece, Italy, the United States, Canada, and Australia), languages (Egyptian hieroglyphics, Latin, Greek, French, and Welsh).

ADDRESSES: Home—Franklins, 7 Carr Rd., Hale, Cheshire WA15 8DX, England. *Office*—Manchester Museum, The University, Manchester M13 9PL, England.

CAREER: University of Manchester, Manchester, England, Manchester Museum, 1972—, director of Manchester Museum Egyptian Mummy Research Project, 1973—, honorary lecturer in comparative religion, 1974—, keeper of Egyptology and senior lecturer, 1989—. Guest lecturer on annual cruise in Egypt.

MEMBER: National Decorative and Fine Arts Society (lecturer, 1979—), Egypt Exploration Society (committee member, 1978—; honorary secretary of northern branch, 1978—).

WRITINGS:

Religious Ritual at Abydos c. 1300 B.C., Aris & Phillips, 1973, 2nd revised edition published as *A Guide to Religious Ritual at Abydos,* 1980.
Kingdoms of Egypt, Elsevier, 1975.
(Under name Rosalie David) *Mysteries of the Mummies: The Story of the Unwrapping of a Two-Thousand-Year-Old Mummy by a Team of Experts,* Cassell, 1978, Scribner, 1979.
(Editor under name A. R. David) *The Manchester Egyptian Mummy Research Project,* Manchester Museum, 1979.
(Under name Rosalie David) *Cult of the Sun: Myth and Magic in Ancient Egypt,* Dent, 1980.
The Ancient Egyptians: Religious Beliefs and Practices, Routledge & Kegan Paul, 1982.
(Under name Rosalie David) *A Catalogue of the Macclesfield Collection,* Aris & Phillips, 1982.
Evidence Embalmed, Manchester University Press, 1985.
A Pyramid Workman's Village, Routledge & Kegan Paul, 1985.
(Editor) *Science in Egyptology: The Proceedings of the 1979 and 1984 Symposia,* Manchester University Press, 1986.
Scientific Study of the Mummy Natsef-Amun, Michael O'Mara Books, 1991.

Also author of screenplay of film *Scientific Study of the Mummy Natsef-Amun,* based on her book of the same title, 1991. Contributor to British Broadcasting Corp. (BBC) films on Egyptology, including *Revelations of a Mummy,* 1978, and *Life and Death in Ancient Egypt,* 1983.

SIDELIGHTS: As director of the Manchester Museum Egyptian Mummy Research Project, A. Rosalie David led a team of experts in one of the most thorough examinations ever performed on a collection of mummies. The investigative group included specialists in pharmacognosy (study of crude drugs and medicinal plants), histopathology (study of tissue changes associated with disease), and forensic medicine as well as Egyptology; through a variety of methods the experts determined age, appearance, and state of health of the mummy subjects at the time of death. David recounts the scientific processes in *Mysteries of the Mummies: The Story of the Unwrapping of a Two-Thousand-Year-Old Mummy by a Team of Experts.* In the *Washington Post Book World,* Barbara Mertz describes the work as "a most rewarding book" that "provides a coherent, well-organized introduction" to Egyptian mummies and a "particularly good" summary of mummification methodology. Mertz adds: "The book is a magnificent illustration of the way in which archaeological disciplines can be used to help archaeologists in their studies. But it is more than that. Throughout the detailed, but always

comprehensible descriptions of method, there is a constant awareness of the fact that the withered husks under analysis were once human beings."

In *The Ancient Egyptians: Religious Beliefs and Practices,* David examines chronologically the different historical periods of ancient Egypt, focusing on both religious texts and the religious features which permeated many aspects of Egyptian society. In a *Times Literary Supplement* review, B. J. Kemp notes that David's "brisk and businesslike approach mirrors the way in which modern scholarship, unable to cope with Egyptian religion as a revelatory phenomenon, has retreated to political explanation." Yet the critic acknowledges that the author's traditional analysis may aid in scrutinizing a culture in which "logically consistent arrangement and explanation in the modern sense were not part of [its] thinking." Kemp adds that the book's numerous appendices would prove useful to a novice and concludes, "For the newcomer who wants a sensible and accurate introduction to the basic shapes of Egyptian religion, this book will serve well enough."

David told *CA:* "The motivation behind research projects at the Museum on Egyptology collection (one of the largest in Britain) is to use multi-disciplinary scientific techniques available in the university to augment knowledge of ancient Egypt. This has resulted in worldwide interest."

BIOGRAPHICAL/CRITICAL SOURCES:

PERIODICALS

Times Literary Supplement, April 30, 1976; February 8, 1980; December 12, 1980; December 17, 1982.
Washington Post Book World, August 26, 1979.

*   *   *

DAVID, Rosalie
See DAVID, A(nn) Rosalie

*   *   *

DEAVER, Julie Reece 1953-

PERSONAL: Born March 13, 1953, in Geneva, IL; daughter of Wilds P. (an advertising writer) and Dee Rider Deaver. *Avocational interests:* Cats, "animals of all kinds (except those with more than four legs and less than two), listening to and singing old fashioned love songs" (Gershwin, for instance).

ADDRESSES: Home—618 Sinex, Pacific Grove, CA 93950. *Agent*—c/o Harper & Row Publishers, Inc., 10 East 53rd St., New York, NY 10022.

CAREER: Teacher's aide in special education in Pacific Grove, CA, 1978-88.

Illustrator for *Reader's Digest, New Yorker, Chicago Tribune,* and *McCall's Working Mother.*

MEMBER: Writer's Guild, West.

AWARDS, HONORS: Best Book for Young Adults citation, 1988, for *Say Goodnight, Gracie;* Books for the Teenage recommendation, New York Public Library, *Book List* Young Adult Editors' Choice citation, and Books for Children recommendation, Library of Congress, all 1988; Virginia State Reading Association Young Readers Award, 1991, for *Say Goodnight, Gracie.*

WRITINGS:

Say Goodnight, Gracie, Harper, 1988.
First Wedding, Once Removed, Harper, 1990.

Also author of a screenplay based on *Say Goodnight, Gracie.* Writer for television series *Adam's Rib,* 1973.

WORK IN PROGRESS: *Watch Out for Those Morton Cabs,* for Harper.

SIDELIGHTS: Julie Reece Deaver commented, "I've always been interested in writing. I started out writing puppet plays when I was about six for a captive audience (my family). My parents were both very creative and encouraged me a lot. My father was an advertising writer and an accomplished artist (oil painting and pottery) and my mother was an excellent artist herself (water colors). Because of this encouragement, probably, my older brother (Jeffery Wilds Deaver) and I both grew up to be writers. My brother writes mysteries.

"I also started drawing and painting at an early age. I've enjoyed doing small illustrations for various magazines, like *Reader's Digest* and the *New Yorker,* but primarily I enjoy painting now for my own pleasure. I paint with egg tempera (I use real eggs!). Maybe someday I'll combine my art with my writing, although for right now I'm mostly interested in writing young adult novels, and of course they aren't illustrated!

"One question I get a lot from my readers is: 'Where do you get your ideas?' It's not an easy question to answer. I usually start writing dialogue, and eventually a situation or a story emerges. I don't use an outline when I write, but let the characters take me where they want to go. When a book is finished, there's always a lot of revising to do, but for the most part, I enjoy the polishing of a story.

"With *Say Goodnight, Gracie,* the original version was about twice as long as the published version. My editors guided me and helped me see what to cut out (not as easy as it might seem, because when one thing is cut, it always alters something later on you might not want to cut). I always think of revision as trying to remove a middle card from a house of cards. You try to do it without letting the

whole thing collapse! But somehow With *Say Goodnight, Gracie,* I wanted to show a boy-girl friendship about best friends who were not romantically involved. I was so pleased the first time I got a letter from a girl in Iowa who liked reading about the friendship—that letter was my first feedback on the book. Since then a lot of letters have followed, and I feel very lucky that my readers take the time to sit down and write me. I love hearing about what they think of my books.

"*First Wedding, Once Removed* is a lighter-in-tone book than *Gracie,* but has a few serious moments, too. I originally thought of it as a skinny book for very young readers, but my editors showed me how it was more suited for middle-grade readers, so I expanded it by about a hundred pages. From my initial idea to the time a book is eventually revised can be a long process. *Say Goodnight, Gracie* started out as a short story that *Seventeen Magazine* didn't want, and Harper & Row encouraged me to expand it into novel form. I had never thought of writing young adult novels. At the time Harper first read *Gracie,* I had been trying to break into the short story market (mostly to *Seventeen,* where I had won an honorable mention in their annual fiction contest when I was seventeen). I was collecting hundreds (well, it seemed like hundreds) of rejection slips, so it was really nice to have a publisher interested in my work."

Deaver concluded, "I'm interested in writing books that entertain. I don't like young adult books that try to teach a lesson, so I don't write that way. I'm just interested in telling what I hope will be a good story."

* * *

deBARY, William Theodore 1919-

PERSONAL: Born August 9, 1919, in Bronx, NY; son of William Emil and Mildred (Marquette) deBary; married Fanny Brett, June 16, 1942; children: Mary Brett, Paul Ambrose, Catherine Anne, Mary Beatrice. *Education:* Columbia University, A.B., 1941, A.M., 1948, Ph.D., 1953.

ADDRESSES: *Home*—98 Hickory Hill Rd., Tappan, NY 10983. *Office*—502 Kent, Columbia University, New York, NY 10027.

CAREER: Columbia University, New York City, 1949—, professor of Chinese and Japanese, 1959-66, Horace Walpole Carpentier Professor of Oriental Studies, 1966-78, chairman of department of East Asian languages and cultures, 1960-66, director of East Asian Language and Area Center, 1960-72, executive vice-president for academic affairs and provost, 1971-78, John Mitchell Mason Professor, 1978-90, Mason Professor and Provost Emeritus, 1990—. Ch'ien Mu lecturer, Chinese University of Hong

Kong, 1982; inaugural lecturer, Edwin O. Reischauer Lectureship in East Asian Affairs, Harvard, 1986; guest lecturer, College de France, 1986; Tanner lecturer, University of California, Berkeley, 1987. *Military service:* U.S. Naval Reserve, 1942-46; became lieutenant commander.

MEMBER: American Academy of Arts and Sciences (fellow, 1970—; member of council), Association of Asian Studies (member of board of directors, 1961-64; president, 1969-70), American Council of Learned Societies (fellow, 1947-48; director, 1978-88), China Society, Japan Society of New York (member of board of directors, 1964-66).

AWARDS, HONORS: Fulbright scholarship to China, 1948-49; Watumull Prize from American Historical Association, 1958; Fishburn Prize of Educational Press Association, 1964; Great Teacher Award, Columbia University, 1969; Lionel Trilling Book Award, 1983; Mark Van Doren Award, 1987, Columbia College. D. Litt., St. Lawrence University, 1968; L.H.D., Loyola University, Chicago, 1970.

WRITINGS:

(Translator) *Five Women Who Loved Love,* Tuttle, 1956.
(Editor) *Sources of Indian Tradition,* Columbia University Press, 1958.
(Editor) *Sources of Japanese Tradition,* Columbia University Press, 1958.
(Editor) *Approaches to the Oriental Classics,* Columbia University Press, 1959.
(Editor) *Approaches to Chinese Tradition,* Columbia University Press, 1960.
Sources of Chinese Tradition, Columbia University Press, 1960.
(Editor) *Approaches to Asian Civilizations,* Columbia University Press, 1964.
A Guide to Oriental Classics, Columbia University Press, 1964.
(Editor) *The Hindu Tradition,* Columbia University Press, 1968.
(Compiler) *The Buddhist Tradition in India, China and Japan,* Modern Library, 1969.
(Editor) *Self and Society in Ming Thought,* Columbia University Press, 1970.
Letters from War-Wasted Asia, Kodansha, 1975.
The Unfolding of Neo-Confucianism, Columbia University Press, 1975.
Principle and Practicality: Neo-Confucianism and Practical Learning, Columbia University Press, 1979.
Neo-Confucian Orthodoxy and the Learning of the Mind-and-Heart, Columbia University Press, 1981.
Yuan Thought: Essays on Chinese Thought and Religion under the Mongols, Columbia University Press, 1982.
The Liberal Tradition in China, Columbia University Press, 1983.

The Rise of Neo-Confucianism in Korea, Columbia University Press, 1985.
East Asian Civilizations: A Dialogue in Five Stages, Harvard University Press, 1988.
Approaches to the Asian Classics, Columbia University Press, 1988.
The Message of the Mind in Neo-Confucianism, Columbia University Press, 1988.
Neo-Confucian Education, University of California Press, 1989.
Learning for Oneself, Columbia University Press, 1991.
The Trouble with Confucianism, Harvard University Press, 1991.

BIOGRAPHICAL/CRITICAL SOURCES:

PERIODICALS

New York Times, February 24, 1987.

*   *   *

DEBICKI, Andrew P(eter)   1934-

PERSONAL: Born June 28, 1934, in Warsaw, Poland; son of Roman (a diplomat and professor) and Jadwiga (Dunin) Debicki; married Mary Jo Tidmarsh, December 28, 1959 (died, 1975); married Mary Elizabeth Gwin, May 16, 1987; children: Mary Beth, Margaret. *Education:* Yale University, B.A. (summa cum laude), 1955, Ph.D., 1960. *Religion:* Roman Catholic. *Politics:* Republican.

ADDRESSES: Home—1445 Applegate Ct., Lawrence, KS 66049. *Office*—Hall Center for the Humanities, University of Kansas, Lawrence, KS 66045.

CAREER: Trinity College, Hartford, CT, instructor in Spanish, 1957-60; Grinnell College, Grinnell, IO, assistant professor, 1960-62, associate professor, 1962-66, professor of Spanish, 1968—, University Distinguished Professor, 1976—, director of Hall Center for the Humanities, 1989—. Director, National Endowment for the Humanities summer seminar, 1976, 1978, and 1989.

MEMBER: Modern Language Association (executive council, 1989-92), Phi Beta Kappa.

AWARDS, HONORS: Danforth research award, summer, 1959; American Council of Learned Societies fellow, 1966-67; Fulbright travel grant, 1966; American Philosophical Society grant, 1969; *Hispania* award for best article, Spanish American literature category, 1969-71; Guggenheim fellow, 1971-72 and 1980; University of Kansas teaching award, 1972; Jeffrey research award, 1974; National Humanities Center fellow, 1980.

WRITINGS:

La Poesia de Jose Gorostiza, Ediciones de Andrea, 1962.

Estudios sobre poesia espanola contemporanea: La Generacion de 1924-1925, Editorial Gredos, 1968, new edition, 1981.

Damaso Alonso, Twayne, 1970.

La poesia de Jorge Guillen, Editorial Gredos, 1973.

(Editor) *Pedro Salinas,* Taurus Ediciones, 1976.

(Editor) *Antologia de la poesia mexicana moderna,* Tamesis Books, 1977.

Poetas hispanoamericanos contemporaneos: Punto de vista, perspectiva, experiencia, Editoria Gredos, 1977.

Poetry of Discovery, University Press of Kentucky, 1982.

(Editor) Ruben Dario, *Azul; prosas profanas,* Alhambra, 1985.

Angel Gonzalez, Ediciones Jucar, 1989.

(Editor) *En homenaje a Angel Gonzalez,* Society for Spanish and Spanish American Studies, in press.

Editor of special issue of *Studies in Twentieth Century Literature* on Spanish poetry, winter, 1992. Also contributor of over forty articles to language journals. Associate editor, *Hispania,* 1974-80; member of editorial advisory board, *PMLA,* 1976-80.

WORK IN PROGRESS: A new history of contemporary Spanish poetry.

*   *   *

DeCROW, Karen 1937-

PERSONAL: Born December 18, 1937, in Chicago, IL; daughter of Samuel Meyer (a businessman) and Juliette (a ballet dancer; maiden name, Abt) Lipschultz; married Alexander Kolben, December 15, 1960 (divorced, 1965); married Roger DeCrow, August 27, 1965 (divorced, 1972). *Education:* Northwestern University, B.S., 1959; Syracuse University, graduate study in journalism, 1967-68, J.D., 1972.

ADDRESSES: Home—7599 Brown Gulf Road, Jamesville, NY 13078. *Agent*—Frank J. Weimann, 153 East 32nd Street, New York, NY 10016.

CAREER: Golf Digest, Norwalk, CT, fashion and resorts editor, 1959-60; *Zoning Digest* (monthly magazine of American Society of Planning Officials), Chicago, IL, editor, 1960-61; Center for the Study of Liberal Education of Adults, Chicago, writer and editor, 1961-64; Holt, Rinehart & Winston, Inc., New York City, social studies and adult education editor, 1965; L. W. Singer Co., Inc., New York City, social science editor, 1965-66; Eastern Regional Institute for Education, Syracuse, NY, writer, 1967-69; National Organization for Women, Washington, DC, former Eastern regional director and political chairwoman, national board member, 1968-77, president, 1974-77; admitted to New York State Bar, 1974. Liberal

Party candidate for mayor of Syracuse, 1969; speaker at World Congress of Women, Helsinki, 1969, and Moscow, 1975; national coordinator of Women's Strike for Equality, 1970; co-founder of World Woman Watch, 1988; New York State Women's Bar Association, Central New York chapter president, 1989-90. Columnist for *Syracuse Post-Standard;* consultant on affirmative action, sexism in the law, and images of women and men in media; lecturer throughout the country; guest on "Today Show," "Monitor," and other network television and radio programs; also has been on radio shows in Europe, Japan, and Canada. Elizabeth Cady Stanton Foundation, member of board of trustees; Working Women United, former member of board of advisers; Working Women's Institute, member of board of advisers; American Arbitration Association, member of community disputes panel; National Council on Children's Rights, advisory panel; National Congress for Men, gender issues adviser; New York Bar Association, member of specialization committee; Syracuse University, member of chancellor's affirmative action committee; Onondaga County Bar Association, member of professional ethics committee; Mariposa Education and Research Foundation; council of overseers.

MEMBER: National Women's Political Caucus, Equal Rights for Fathers, Women's Institute for Freedom of the Press, Women in Communications (Theta Sigma Phi), Atlantic States Legal Foundation, The Nature Conservancy, The Wilderness Society, Art Institute of Chicago, Honorary Committee to Save Alice Paul's Birthplace, Yale Political Union (honorary life member), Northwestern University Alumni Association, Syracuse Friends of Chamber Music.

AWARDS, HONORS: Selected by *Time* magazine as one of two hundred future leaders of America, 1974; selected by Newspaper Enterprise Association as one of fifty most influential women in America, 1975; Ralph E. Kharas Award for Distinguished Service in Civil Liberties, American Civil Liberties Union, 1985; Professional Recognition Award, Syracuse Press Club, 1990, for Best Newspaper Column.

WRITINGS:

(With Roger DeCrow) *University Adult Education: A Selected Bibliography,* American Council on Education, 1967.

(Editor) Howard Osofsky, *The Pregnant Teenager,* C. C Thomas, 1968.

The Young Woman's Guide to Liberation, Bobbs-Merrill, 1971.

(Editor) Robert Seidenberg, *Corporate Wives, Corporate Casualties,* American Management Association, 1973.

Sexist Justice, Random House, 1974.

(With Seidenberg) *Women Who Marry Houses: Panic and Protest in Agoraphobia,* McGraw, 1983.
(Contributor) *Social Problems,* Allyn & Bacon, 1988.
(Contributor) *United States of America vs. Sex: How the Meese Commission Lied About Pornography,* Minotaur Press, 1988.

Contributor to periodicals, including *Mademoiselle, Adult Leadership, Judge, Life, Vogue, New York Times, Los Angeles Times,* and *Boston Globe.*

WORK IN PROGRESS: Tales of a Feminist Lawyer, Ending Gender Gridlock (with Robert Seidenberg), both for New American Library.

SIDELIGHTS: A lawyer and a former president of the National Organization for Women, Karen DeCrow has been involved in issues of social change. Her concern for the expansion of women's rights is reflected in such titles as *The Young Woman's Guide to Liberation* and *Sexist Justice.* In a more recent work, *Women Who Marry Houses: Panic and Protest in Agoraphobia,* DeCrow and Robert Seidenberg note that eighty-eight percent of agoraphobics—people who fear going out of their homes—are women, and argue that these women are lashing out against their traditional, home-bound role. Such women "have retaliated by refusing to leave home altogether. They have been 'on strike against the female condition,'" summarizes Brenda Hirsch in a book review for *Psychology Today.* Writing in *Los Angeles Times Book Review,* Lisa Mitchell asserts that DeCrow and Seidenberg do not give immediately practical suggestions for treating agoraphobia: "The authors contend that the state of marriage and the entire *world* must change before women will be able to stop going on strike. That is all well and good, but what does the woman with the cold sweats and depression—the shame that is paralyzing her this morning—*do* until the world changes?" However, Mitchell also gives a more favorable general assessment of *Women Who Marry Houses* when she says that it "fascinates, educates."

BIOGRAPHICAL/CRITICAL SOURCES:

PERIODICALS

Atlantic, March, 1974.
Best Sellers, July 1, 1971.
Los Angeles Times Book Review, March 27, 1983.
Psychology Today, June, 1974; June, 1983.

*   *   *

DELESSERT, Etienne 1941-

PERSONAL: Born January 4, 1941, in Lausanne, Switzerland; son of Ferdinand (a minister) and Berengere (de Mestral) Delessert; married Rita Marshall (a graphic de-

signer and art director), 1985; children: Adrien (son). *Education:* Attended College Classique, Lausanne, 1951-56, and Gymnase Classique, Lausanne, 1957-58. *Religion:* Protestant.

ADDRESSES: Home—Lausanne, Switzerland; and Lakeville, CT.

CAREER: Painter, graphic designer, illustrator, film director, publisher and author. Free-lance graphic designer and illustrator in Lausanne, Switzerland and in Paris, France, 1962-65; author and illustrator of children's books, 1965—; co-founder with Herb Lubalin, Good Book (a publishing house), 1969-74; co-founder with Anne van der Essen, Societe Carabosse (production company of animated films), Lausanne, 1973-1984. Art director, *Record* (children's magazine), Paris, 1975-76; co-founder of Editions Tournesol, 1977. Artwork has shown in one-man exhibitions at Art Alliance Gallery, Philadelphia, PA, 1970; California State College Gallery, 1972; Galerie Delpire, Paris, 1972; Galerie Melisa, Lausanne, 1974; Galerie Marquet, Paris, 1975; Le Musee des Arts decoratifs du Louvre, Paris, 1975; Musee des Arts decoratifs, Lausanne, 1976; Palais de l'Athenee, Geneva, Switzerland, 1976; Le Manoir, Martigny, 1985; Palazzio delle Espozizioni, Rome, 1991; Lustrare Gallery, New York, 1991. Group: Galerie Wolfsberg, Zurich, Switzerland, 1970; Galerie Pauli, Lausanne, 1976; Centre Pompidou, 1985; Art Institute, Boston, MA, 1985.

AWARDS, HONORS: Gold Medal from the Society of Illustrators, 1967, 1972, 1976, and 1978; *Story Number One for Children under Three Years of Age* 1968, and *Just So Stories,* 1972, were named to list of *New York Times* Ten Best Illustrated Books of the Year; *How the Mouse Was Hit on the Head by a Stone and So Discovered the World,* 1971, and *Just So Stories,* 1972 were both chosen one of American Institute of Graphic Arts Fifty Books of the Year, and for the Children's Book Show, 1971-72; Brooklyn Art Books for Children citation, the Brooklyn Museum and the Brooklyn Public Library, 1973, 1974, and 1975, for *How the Mouse Was Hit on the Head by a Stone and So Discovered the World;* Premio Europeo Prize (best European book for children), Trente, Italy, for *Thomas et l'Infini,* 1977; Gold Plaque, Biennale of Illustration of Bratislava, 1979, for both *Les sept familles du lac Pipple-Popple* (*The Seven Families from Lake Pipple-Popple*) and *Die Maus und was ihr bleibt* (*Amelia Mouse and Her Great-Great-Grandchild*), and 1985, for *La Belle et la Bete* (*Beauty and the Beast*); Hans Christian Andersen highly commended illustrator award, 1980, for entire body of work; Prix Loisirs-Jeunes, Paris, 1981, for *Quinze gestes de Jesus;* First Graphic Prize, International Bologna Book Fair, 1981, for the "Yok-Yok" series; First Graphic Prize,

International Bologna Book Fair, 1989, for *A Long Long Song;* Best Book of the Year, Germany, for *Story Number One for Children under Three Years of Age* and *Story Number Two for Children under Three Years of Age;* Prix Loisirs-Jeunes, Paris, for *Story Number One for Children under Three Years of Age, How the Mouse Was Hit on the Head by a Stone and So Discovered the World, Le Roman de Renart,* and *L'eau* (title means "The Water");

WRITINGS:

FOR CHILDREN

(With Eleonore Schmid) *The Endless Party* (self-illustrated; original title, *San Fin la Fete*), Quist, 1967, revised edition, retold by Jeffrey Tabberner, Oxford University Press, 1981.

How the Mouse Was Hit on the Head by a Stone and So Discovered the World (self-illustrated), Doubleday, 1971.

(With Anne van der Essen) *La Souris s'en va-t'en en Guerre,* Gallimard, 1978.

(With Christophe Gallaz) *L'Amour-Petit Croque et Ses Amis* Tournesol-Gallimard, 1982.

(Designed by Rita Marshall) *Happy Birthdays: A Notebook for Everyone's Birthday,* Stewart, Tabori, 1986.

A Long Long Song (self-illustrated), Farrar, Straus, 1988.

Ashes, Ashes (self-illustrated), Stewart, Tabori, 1990.

(With Rita Marshall) *I Hate to Read!,* self-illustrated, Creative Education, 1992.

ILLUSTRATOR; CHILDREN

Eugene Ionesco, *Story Number One for Children under Three Years of Age,* Quist, 1968.

Betty Jean Lifton, *The Secret Seller,* Norton, 1968.

George Mendoza, *A Wart Snake in a Fig Tree,* Dial, 1968.

Ionesco, *Story Number Two for Children under Three Years of Age,* Quist, 1969.

Rudyard Kipling, *Just So Stories* (anniversary edition), Doubleday, 1972.

Gordon Lightfoot, *The Pony Man,* Harper Magazine Press, 1972.

Joseph G. Raposo, *Being Green,* Western, 1973.

Michel Deon, *Thomas et l'Infini* (title means "Thomas and the Infinite"), Gallimard, 1975.

van der Essen, *La souris et les papillons* (title means "The Mouse and the Butterflies"), Gallimard, 1975.

van der Essen, *La souris et les poisons,* Gallimard, 1975, translation published as *The Mouse and the Poisons,* Middelhauve, 1977.

van der Essen, *Die Maus und die Schmetterlinge, Die Maus und die Giftchen,* [and] *Die Maus und der Larm,* Middelhauve, 1975.

van der Essen, *Die Maus und was ihr bleibt,* Middlehauve, 1977, translation published as *Amelia Mouse and Her Great-Great-Grandchild,* Evans, 1978.

Oscar Wilde, *The Happy Prince,* Gallimard, 1977.

Edgar Allan Poe, *The Gold-Bug,* Gallimard, 1978.

Edward Lear, *Les sept familles du lac Pipple-Popple* (translation of *The Seven Families from Lake Pipple-Popple*), Gallimard, 1978.

Andrienne Soutter-Perrot, *Les premiers livres de la nature* (title means "My First Nature Books"), Tournesol-Gallimard, 1979, Book 1: *The Earth,* Book 2: *The Water,* Book 3: *The Air,* Book 4: *The Worm.*

Jacques Prevert, *Paroles,* Gallimard-Rombaldi, 1979.

Pierre-Marie Beaude and Jean Debruyne, *Quinze gestes de Jesus,* Centurion Jeunesse, 1981.

Gallaz, Jean Touvet and Francois Baudier, *Petit Croque et ses amis,* Tournesol, 1982.

Truman Capote, *A Christmas Memory,* Creative Education, 1984.

Marie Catherine D'Aulnoy, *La Belle et la Bete,* Editions Grasset, 1984, published in the United States as *The Beauty and the Beast,* Creative Education, 1985.

Henri Des, *Chanson pour mon chien,* Script (Switzerland), 1986.

Des, *La Petite Charlotte,* Script, 1986.

Des, *On ne verra jamais,* Script, 1986.

Willa Cather, *A Wagner Matinee,* Redpath Press, 1986.

Roald Dahl, *Taste,* Redpath Press, 1986.

A. A. Milne, *The Secret,* Redpath Press, 1986.

William Saroyan, *The Pheasant Hunter: About Fathers & Sons,* Redpath Press, 1986.

Zora Neale Hurston, *The Gilded Six-Bits,* Redpath Press, 1986.

Mark Twain (pseudonym of Samuel Clemens), *Baker's Bluejay Yarn,* Redpath Press, 1986.

Daniel Keyes, *Flowers for Algernon,* Creative Education, 1988.

ILLUSTRATOR FOR "YOK-YOK" SERIES; ALL WRITTEN BY ANNE VAN DER ESSEN

The Caterpillar, Tournesol-Gallimard, 1979, Merrill, 1980.

The Magician, Tournesol-Gallimard, 1979, Merrill, 1980.

The Night, Tournesol-Gallimard, 1979, Merrill, 1980.

The Blackbird, Tournesol-Gallimard, 1979, Merrill, 1980.

The Frog, Tournesol-Gallimard, 1979, Merrill, 1980.

The Rabbit, Tournesol-Gallimard, 1979, Merrill, 1980.

The Shadow, Tournesol-Gallimard, 1981.

The Circus, Tournesol-Gallimard, 1981.

The Cricket, Tournesol-Gallimard, 1981.

The Snow, Tournesol-Gallimard, 1981.

The Violin, Tournesol-Gallimard, 1981.

The Cherry, Tournesol-Gallimard, 1981.

Le grand livre de Yok-Yok, Tournesol-Gallimard, 1981.

ILLUSTRATOR; ADULT

Joel Jakubec, *Kafka contre l'absurde,* Cahiers, 1960.

Maurice Chappaz, *Le Match Valais-Judee,* Cahiers, 1968.

Jacques Chessex, *La confession du Pasteur Burg,* Le Livre du Mois, 1970.

Francois Nourissier, *Le temps,* Le Verseau-Roth & Sauter, 1982.

Chessex, *Des Cinq sens,* Le Verseau-Roth & Sauter, 1982.

Anne Morrow Lindbergh, *Hour of Lead: Sharing Sorrow,* Redpath Pres, 1986.

Maya Angelou, *Mrs. Flowers: A Moment of Friendship,* Redpath Press, 1986.

Woody Allen, *The Lunatic's Tale,* Redpath Press, 1986.

Bob Greene, *Diary of a Newborn Baby,* Redpath Press, 1986.

P. G. Wodehouse, *The Clicking of Cuthbert,* Redpath Press, 1986.

John Updike, *A&P,* Redpath Press, 1986.

Sonoko Kondo, *The Poetical Pursuit of Food,* C. N. Potter, 1986.

Ogden Nash, *Ogden Nash's Zoo* (edited by Roy Finamore), Stewart, Tabori, 1987.

John Cheever, *Angel of the Bridge,* 1987.

Ernest Hemingway, *Christmas on the Roof of the World: A Holiday in the Swiss Alps,* Redpath Press, 1987.

Saki, *The Story-Teller,* Redpath Press, 1987.

Nash, *Ogden Nash's Food* (edited by Finamore), Stewart, Tabori, 1989.

Also author of animated films and children's films. Illustrator of *Le Roman de Renart,* Gallimard, 1977. Contributor of editorial illustrations to magazines, including *Atlantic Monthly, New York Times, Fortune, Rolling Stone, Redbook, McCall's, Fact,* and *Elle.*

ADAPTATIONS: How the Mouse Was Hit on the Head by a Stone and So Discovered the World was adapted by Nathalie Nath into a play that was staged in Geneva, Switzerland, produced by the Amstramgram Theater Group, with Delessert designing the costumes and settings, and the play was filmed by Michel Soutter for Swiss television.

WORK IN PROGRESS: Adult books; editorial work; paintings; watercolors.

SIDELIGHTS: Award-winning Swiss children's writer, illustrator, publisher, and filmmaker Etienne Delessert traces his interest in storytelling to early childhood. He once told *Something about the Author* (*SATA*): "I was raised by my stepmother, who was a great storyteller, and who influenced my creative development tremendously. . . . The stories she told were of her own invention; she was best at dialogue and situation. I'm sure she would have made a fine playwright. We often acted out simple scenarios together which resembled [Samuel] Beckett plays—no sets, no props, no costumes—just long endless monologues in which I would attempt to become a tree or animal. . . . If my stepmother had to stop this activity to run an errand, I would go on for hours by my-

self. It was very good training for my imagination, and as an only child, it taught me how to play by myself."

Later in childhood, Delessert became interested in the fairy tales of Northern and Eastern Europe, which have continued to influence his imagination. "Much like in the northern fables," he remarked, "I have looked into the shadows and the fog for monsters and witches." Delessert worked at recapturing the mood of such stories when he collaborated with Rita Marshall, an American graphic designer and art director whom he later married, to supervise the production of a series of fairy tale books. "Many fairy tales are illustrated and interpreted too sweetly, even when the story itself is quite strong," he said. "I feel it is important to use visuals which are equivalent in strength to the text. Fairy tales usually work to open the reader up, to give him a kind of psychological help; while some images of the tale may be violent or bizarre, by the end, things are resolved and open. These great stories bring out the fears, loneliness and violence that a person must face in order to move into peace and harmony."

Delessert and Marshall recruited a group of artists to illustrate the fairy tale storylines. Commenting on one of the books in the series, Delessert observed that *Little Red Riding Hood* "ends with the girl being eaten by the wolf. I saw no reason to rewrite it, or to use other 'sweeter' versions such as the Brothers Grimm. We used the Perrault original text, and Sarah Moon set the story in Paris in the forties, using very disturbing, black and white photographs." He further asserted that one "should not present children with sugar coated versions of reality. You have to expose them to all kinds of experiences, especially with a sense of humor and a sense of the bizarre with surrealistic situations which open them up to another kind of reality, another point of view. . . . After all, truth is not one sided, not only what you see on T.V. or read in the papers, or what your parents tell you, or what you learn in school: truth is also what *you* see and how you perceive the unknown forces of the world, how you face birth, life, decay and death. That has been, I believe, the essence of my books."

In an attempt to incorporate children's views of the world into his books, Delessert worked with noted Swiss psychologist Jean Piaget, who has investigated stages of children's mental development. Delessert worked into story form some explanations for features of the natural world—such as the sun and moon—that children gave Piaget in interviews held several decades ago. Then Piaget's assistants read Delessert's story to children, checking for comprehension of words and concepts. The resulting finished work, *How the Mouse was Hit on the Head by a Stone and So Discovered the World,* was written and illustrated by Delessert for the cognitive level of five- and six-year old children. Commenting on the process of creating the book, the author stated: "One of the most interesting discoveries was that five- and six-year olds have their own interpretation of how the sun and moon rise and set, interpretations which are somewhat similar to some ancient Mexican and African legends. Big hands, for example, throw the sun into the sky at dawn, and catch it back at sunset. We asked children to make their own drawings illustrating the story we had built together. Without knowing it, the children made drawings very similar to my own."

In addition to writing and illustrating, Delessert has worked in film production. He stated: "I'm a storyteller, and I love to tell stories. I was attracted to children's books because they are a medium in which I can develop a story through text and illustrations on several levels. Picture books are closely related to film, which also play with images and text." In 1973, Delessert and Anne van der Essen founded Carabosse Studios [Carabosse being the fairy who cast a spell on Sleeping Beauty], for the production of animated films. The main project was *Supersaxo,* a film adaptation of a fantasy novel by Swiss writer Maurice Chappaz. Writing in *Phaedrus,* Denise von Stockar observed that "Many French-Swiss illustrators have started their careers at Delessert's studio." Delessert commented to *SATA*: "The positive aspect of having the studio was that it became like a school of illustration. Young illustrators worked with me and slowly created their own styles. Several have become fine artists." But when financial difficulties put an end to the work on *Supersaxo,* Delessert decided to close the studio.

One of Delessert's most popular characters, Yok-Yok, was created at Carabosse, and book adaptations of the "Yok-Yok" films were later printed by Editions Tournesol ["Sunflower"], which Delessert founded with van der Essen in 1977. Van der Essen wrote the texts for the "Yok-Yok" books, while Delessert produced the illustrations. "The 'Yok-Yok' books were based on 150 ten-second animated films," said Delessert. "When I first made the films for Swiss television I wanted to base them on nature. I wanted to answer such questions as 'Why does a woodpecker tap on a tree trunk?' and 'What do frogs eat?' with animation. We did pilots but felt that something was missing and created a character to link all the films." Tournesol has also printed numerous children's books of other authors and illustrators. Noting Delessert's role in establishing Tournesol, von Stockar asserted that Delessert "has become the catalyst for a newly born picture book activity in his homeland [Switzerland's French-speaking region]."

Delessert said of his own illustration work: "I take at least three or four months to do a book. In some ways, I get more pleasure out of conceiving an idea than executing it. I love to make the little thumbnail sketches. But after that,

there is a long period which is simply craft—slowly executing what you intended—which sometimes makes me impatient. The very last part of drawing, the polishing, the 'making it work,' interests me again, but I don't like that in-between, very technical and painstaking stage."

BIOGRAPHICAL/CRITICAL SOURCES:

BOOKS

Catalogue du Musee des Arts decoratifs du Louvre, Paris, 1975.
Chessex, Jacques, *Les dessins d'Etienne Delessert,* Bertil Galland, 1974.
Etienne Delessert (monograph), Gallimard, 1991, Stewart, Tabori, 1992.
Kingman, Lee, and others, compilers, *Illustrators of Children's Books: 1967-1976,* Horn Book, 1978.
Something about the Author, Volume 46, Gale, 1987.

PERIODICALS

Idea (Japan), Number 66, 1965; Number 71, 1965.
Graphis, Number 128, 1967; Number 208, 1979-80; Number 235, 1985.
New York Times, August 22, 1971.
New York Times Book Review, October 23, 1988.
Novum gebrauchs graphik, January 1, 1976.
Phaedrus, 1982, pp. 35-39.
Print, April, 1986.

*   *   *

DEMARAY, Donald E(ugene) 1926-

PERSONAL: Born December 6, 1926, in Adrian, MI; son of C. Dorr and Grace (Vore) Demaray; married Kathleen Bear, 1948; children: Cherith, Elyse, James. *Education:* Azusa Pacific College, B.A., 1946; Asbury Theological Seminary, B.D., 1949; graduate study at University of Southern California, 1949-50, and University of Zurich, 1951; University of Edinburgh, Ph.D., 1952; postdoctoral research at University of Manchester, University of London, Cambridge University, Oxford University, University of Durham, and University of Edinburgh, 1962-89. *Avocational interests:* Collecting books and stamps, jogging, traveling, reading, gardening, tennis.

ADDRESSES: Home—409 Talbot, Wilmore, KY 40390. *Office*—Asbury Theological Seminary, Wilmore, KY 40390.

CAREER: Ordained minister of Free Methodist Church. Seattle Pacific College (now University), Seattle, WA, 1952-66, began as lecturer, became professor of religion, dean of School of Religion, 1959-66; Asbury Theological Seminary, Wilmore, KY, associate professor, 1966-67, professor of preaching and dean of students, 1967-75, Fisher Professor of Preaching, 1975—. Minister of youth, Seattle Pacific College Church, 1952-53.

WRITINGS:

"Amazing Grace!," Light & Life Press, 1957.

(Editor) *Devotions and Prayers of John Wesley,* Baker Book, 1957.

Basic Beliefs: An Introductory Guide to Christian Theology, Baker Book, 1958.

Loyalty to Christ, Baker Book, 1958.

The Book of Acts: A Study Manual, Baker Book, 1959.

(Editor) *A Pulpit Manual,* Baker Book, 1959.

(Editor) *Devotions and Prayers of Charles Spurgeon,* Baker Book, 1960.

Acts A and B, Light & Life Press, 1961.

Questions Youth Ask, Baker Book, 1961.

Cowman Handbook of the Bible, Cowman, 1964, published as *Bible Study Sourcebook,* Zondervan, 1973.

Alive to God through Prayer, Baker Book, 1965, revised edition published as *How Are You Praying?,* Francis Ashbury, 1985.

Preacher Aflame!, Baker Book, 1972.

Pulpit Giants: What Made Them Great, Moody, 1973.

An Introduction to Homiletics, Baker Book, 1974.

The Minister's Ministries, Light & Life Press, 1974.

A Guide to Happiness, Baker Book, 1974.

(Editor) *Blow, Wind of God: Spirit Powered Passages from the Writing and Preaching of Billy Graham,* Baker Book, 1975.

(Editor) *Alive to God through Praise,* Baker Book, 1976.

Near Hurting People: The Pastoral Ministry of Robert Moffat Fine, Light & Life Press, 1978.

Proclaiming the Truth: Guides to Scriptural Preaching, Baker Book, 1979.

(Editor) Thomas A. Kempis, *Imitation of Christ,* Baker Book, 1982.

Watch Out for Burnout, Baker Book, 1985.

Snapshots: The People Called Free Methodist, Light & Life Press, 1985.

Laughter, Joy and Healing, Baker Book, 1986.

The Innovation of John Newton 1725-1807: Synergism of Word and Music in 18th Century Evangelism, Mellen Press, 1988.

Listen to Luther!, Victor, 1989.

Contributor to religion journals and anthologies.

*   *   *

DEON, Michel 1919-

PERSONAL: Born August 4, 1919, in Paris, France; son of Paul and Alice (de Fossey) Deon; married Chantal Re-naudeau d'Arc, March 15, 1963; children: Alice, Alexander. *Education:* University of Paris, Licence de droit, 1940. *Religion:* Roman Catholic. *Avocational interests:* Collecting modern paintings and lead soldiers, shooting, horses, and bibliophily.

ADDRESSES: Home—Old Rectory, Tynagh, County Galway, Ireland; 17 Rue de L'Universite, 75007 Paris, France.

CAREER: Action Francaise (daily newspaper), Paris, France, journalist, 1942-44; *Paris-Match* (weekly), Paris, Journalist, 1954-56; author, 1944—. Literary advisor, Plon, 1956-58, and La Table Ronde, 1961-63. *Military service:* French Army, 1939-42.

AWARDS, HONORS: Prix Interallie, 1970, for *Les Poneys sauvages;* Grand Prix du Roman de l'Academie Francaise, 1973, for *Un Taxi mauve;* named member of Academie Francaise, 1978; Chevalier, Legion d'honneur; Officier des Arts et des Lettres.

WRITINGS:

FICTION

La Princesse de Manfred (short story), Editions Sun (Lyon), 1949.

Je ne veux jamais l'oublier, Plon, 1950.

La Corrida, Plon, 1952.

Des Enfants s'aimaient, Les Oeuvres Libres, 1953.

La Dieu pale, Plon, 1954.

La Tache rose, Les Oeuvres Libres, 1955.

Tout l'amour du monde (prose sketches), Plon, Part I, 1956, Part II, 1960.

Les Gens de la nuit, Plon, 1958.

La Carotte et le Baton, Plon, 1960.

Le Rendezvous de Patmos, Plon, 1965.

Un Parfum de jasmin (short stories), Gallimard, 1967.

Les Poneys sauvages, Gallimard, 1970.

Un Taxi mauve, Gallimard, 1975.

Le Jeune homme vert, Gallimard, 1976.

Les Vingt Ans du jeune homme vert, Gallimard, 1977.

Mes Arches de Noe, La Table Ronde, 1978.

Un Dejeuner de Soleil, Gallimard, 1981, English translation by Julian Evans published as *Where Are You Dying Tonight?,* Hamish Hamilton, 1983.

Je vous ecris d'Italie, Gallimard, 1984.

Le Montee du soir, Gallimard, 1988.

Un Sovenir, Gallimard, 1990.

Les Trompeuses esperances, Gallimard, 1991.

AUTHOR OF TEXT

La Cote d'Azur, photographs by Patrice Moulinard, Editions Mondiales, 1950.

Versailles, Editions Sun, 1951.

Le Cote basque et les Pyrenees, photographs by Moulinard, Editions Mondiales, 1951.

Venise que j'aime, photographs by Jean Imbert, Editions Sun, 1956, translation by Ruth Whipple Fermaud, published as *The Venice I Love,* Tudor, 1957.

Iles Baleares, photographs by Jaques Boulas, Hachette, 1958.

La Grece que j'aime, photographs by Robert Descharnes, Editions Sun, 1961, translation by Fermaud, published as *The Greece I Love,* Tudor, 1961.

Le Portugal que j'aime, Editions Sun, 1963, translation by Fermaud, published as *The Portugal I Love,* Tudor, 1964.

(With Nino Franck) *L'Italie que j'aime,* Editions Sun, 1968, translation by Fermaud, published as *As the Italy I Love,* Tudor, 1968.

Rever dela Grece, Vilo, 1968.

Londre que j'aime, Editions Sun, 1970, translation by Fermaud, published as *The London I Love,* Tudor, 1970.

Haddelsey's Horses, Editions Sun, 1978.

Minnie, illustrated by Baltazar, Nicaise, 1980.

Balinbadour, illustrated by Willie Mucha, Nicaise, 1981.

Turbulences, illustrated by Baltazar, Matarasso, 1981.

Une Jeune Parque, illustrated by Mathieux-Marie, La Palantine, 1982.

Un Barbare au paradis, illustrated by Baltazar, Nicaise, 1987.

Ouest-est, illustrated by Jean Corot, Christiani, 1989.

HU.TU.FU., illustrated by Baltazar, Nicaise, 1991.

Songes, illustrated by Baltazar, Piroir, 1991.

EDITOR

Louis XIV, King of France, *Louis XIV par lui-meme,* Librarie Academique Perrin, 1964.

Salvador Dali, *Journal d'une genie,* La Table Ronde, 1964.

TRANSLATOR

Victor Gollomb, *La Vie ardente d'Albert Schweitzer,* Editions Sun, 1951.

Alarcon, *Le Tricorne,* illustrated by Dali, Editions du Rocher, 1952.

Saul Bellow, *L'Homme de Buridan (Dangling Man),* Plon, 1952.

OTHER

Lettre a un jeune Rastignac (pamphlet), Fasquelle, 1956.

(With Dali) *Historie d'un grand livre: Don Quichotte* (nonfiction), illustrated by Dali, Foret, 1951.

L'Armee d'Algerie et la pacification (nonfiction), Plon, 1959.

Le Balcon de Spetsai (nonfiction), Gallimard, 1961.

(Author of introduction) Honore de Balzac, *Illusions perdues,* Livre de Poche, 1962.

(Contributor) *Prenoms,* Plon, 1967.

Megalonose: Supplement aux "Voyages du Gulliver," (pamphlet), La table Rond, 1967.

(With Yves Boisset) *The Purple Taxi* (screenplay; adaptation of Deon's *Un Taxi mauve*) Quarter/Films Inc., 1977.

Also author of introduction to a book on Marivaux's theatre, Livre De Poche, 1966. Contributor to periodicals.

SIDELIGHTS: Where Are You Dying Tonight?, the English translation of Michel Deon's *Un Dejeuner de Soliel,* is "a clever, witty, beautifully oblique novel," according to Stuart Evans of the London *Times.*

BIOGRAPHICAL/CRITICAL SOURCES:

BOOKS

Cayrol, Regis, *La Droite desabusee et nonchalante,* University Center of Perpignan, 1975.

De Boisdeffre, Pierre, *Une Histoire vivante de la litterature d'aujourd'hui,* Perrin, 1958.

Haedans, Kleber, *Une Histoire de la litterature francaise,* Grasset, 1970.

Vandromme, Pol, *La Droite Buissonniers,* Les Sept Couleurs, 1957.

Vandromme, *Deon, ou le nomade sedentaire,* La Table Rond, 1991.

PERIODICALS

L'Express, September, 1970.

Livres de France, special issue, August-September, 1962.

Matulu, July-August, 1973.

Times (London), November 10, 1983.

*   *   *

dePAOLA, Thomas Anthony   1934-
(Tomie dePaola)

PERSONAL: Some sources cite surname as de Paola; name pronounced "Tommy de-*pow*la"; born September 15, 1934, in Meriden, CT; son of Joseph N. (a union official) and Florence (Downey) dePaola. *Education:* Pratt Institute, B.F.A., 1956; California College of Arts and Crafts, M.F.A., 1969; Lone Mountain College, doctoral equivalency, 1970.

ADDRESSES: c/o The Putnam & Grosset Book Group, 200 Madison Ave., New York, NY 10016.

CAREER: Professional artist and designer, and teacher of art, 1956—; writer and illustrator of juvenile books; creative director of Whitebird Books, his imprint at G. P. Putnam's Sons. Newton College of the Sacred Heart, Newton, MA, instructor, 1962-63, assistant professor of art, 1963-66; San Francisco College for Women (now Lone Mountain College), San Francisco, CA, assistant professor of art, 1967-70; Chamberlayne Junior College, Boston, MA, instructor in art, 1972-73; Colby-Sawyer College, New London, NH, New London, NH, associate professor, designer, and technical director in speech and theater department, writer and set and costume designer for Children's Theatre Project, 1973-76; New England College, Henniker, NH, associate professor of art, 1976-78, artist-in-residence, 1978-79. Painter and muralist, with many of his works done for Catholic churches and monasteries in New England; designer of greeting cards, posters, magazine and catalogue covers, record album covers, and theatre and nightclub sets. Member of board of directors of Society of Children's Book Writers of Los Angeles.

EXHIBITIONS: Work has been shown at one-man shows at the Botolph Group, Inc., Boston, MA, 1961, 1964, 1967; Putnam Art Center, Newton College of the Sacred Heart, Newton, MA, 1971-72, 1975, 1978; Alliance Corporation, Boston, 1972; Library Arts Center, Newport, NH, 1975, 1982, 1984; Rizzoli Gallery, New York City, 1977; Clark County Library, Las Vegas, NV, 1979; Englewood (NJ) Library, 1980; Louisiana Arts and Science Center, Baton Rouge, LA, 1981; University of Minnesota, Minneapolis, 1981; Children's Theatre, Minneapolis, 1981; Yuma City-County (AZ) Library, 1981; Charles Fenton Gallery, Woodstock, VT, 1984; Arts and Science Center, Nashua, NH., 1985, 1986; Bush Galleries, Norwich, VT, 1987; Women's Club, Minneapolis, 1988; Dayton's-Bachman's Annual Flower Show, Minneapolis, 1989.

Work has also been exhibited in group shows at the South Vermont Art Center, Manchester, 1958; Grail Festival of the Arts, Brooklyn, NY, 1959; Botolph Group, Boston, 1962, 1964, 1969; San Francisco College for Women, CA, 1969; Immaculate Heart College, Los Angeles, CA, 1969; Botolph in Cambridge, MA, 1971-74; Library Arts Center, Newport, NH, 1975; "Children's Book Illustrators," Everson Museum, Syracuse, NY, 1977; "Exhibition of Original Pictures of International Children's Picture Books," sponsored by Maruzen Ltd. and Shiko-Sha Ltd., Japan, 1977, 1979, 1981; "Illustrators' Exhibition," Children's Book Fair, Bologna, Italy, 1978; "Art and the Alphabet," Museum of Fine Arts, Houston, TX, 1978; "Book Forms," Dayton (OH) Art Institute, 1978; "Children's Book Illustrators," Brattleboro (VT) Museum and Art Center, 1980; "This Pure Creature: The Unicorn in Art," Wilson Arts Center, Harley School, Rochester, NY, 1980-88; "December Art Exhibit," Port Washington (NY) Public Library, 1981; "A Decade of Original Art of the Best Illustrated Children's Books, 1970-80," University of Connecticut Library, Storrs, CT, 1982; "Annual

Exhibition," Society of Illustrators, New York City, 1982, 1983, 1984, 1985; "Illustrators Exhibition," Metropolitan Museum of Art, New York City, 1982, 1983; "A Peaceable Kingdom: Animals in Art," Museum of Fine Art, Houston, TX, 1982; "D Is for Dog," Dog Museum of America, New York City, 1983; "Once Upon a Time," Boulder (CO) Center for Visual Arts, 1983; "Illustrious: Contemporary New Hampshire Illustrators," University Art Galleries, University of New Hampshire, Durham, 1983; "And Peace Attend Thee," Trustman Art Gallery, Simmons College, Boston, 1984; Bush Galleries, Norwich, VT, 1985; Congress Square Gallery, Portland, ME, 1985; Denver (CO) Public Library, 1986; Colorado Academy, Denver, 1986; "Daffodil Arts Show," New London (NH) Historical Society, 1985, 1986, 1988; Aetna Institute Gallery, Hartford, CT, 1986; "Once Upon a Picture," Miami (FL) Youth Museum, 1986; "New Hampshire Illustrators Exhibit," New Hampshire Historical Society, Concord, 1988. Works are also included in many private collections.

MEMBER: Society of Children's Book Writers (member of board of directors), Authors Guild.

AWARDS, HONORS: Boston Art Directors' Club awards for typography and illustration, 1968; Child Study Association children's book of the year citations, 1968, for *Poetry for Chuckles and Grins,* 1971, for *John Fisher's Magic Book,* 1974, for *David's Window* and *Charlie Needs a Cloak,* and 1975 for *Strega Nona* and *Good Morning to You, Valentine,* 1986 for *Strega Nona's Magic Lessons, Tattie's River Journey, Tomie dePaola's Mother Goose,* and *The Quilt Story,* 1987, for *Teeny Tiny* and *Tomie dePaola's Favorite Nursery Tales;* Franklin Typographers Silver Award for poster design, 1969; three books included in American Institute of Graphic Arts exhibit of outstanding children's books, *The Journey of the Kiss,* 1970, *Who Needs Holes?,* 1973, and *Helga's Dowry,* 1979; two books included on *School Library Journal*'s list of best picture books, *Andy, That's My Name,* 1973, and *Charlie Needs a Cloak,* 1974; Friends of American Writers Award as best illustrator of a children's book, 1973, for *Authorized Autumn Charts of the Upper Red Canoe River Country;* two books chosen as Children's Book Showcase titles, *Authorized Autumn Charts of the Upper Red Canoe River Country,* 1973, and *Charlie Needs a Cloak,* 1975; Brooklyn Art Books for Children Award, Brooklyn Museum and Brooklyn Public Library, 1975, for *Charlie Needs a Cloak,* and 1977, 1978, and 1979, for *Strega Nona,* which also received the Caldecott Honor Book Award, 1976, and the Nakamore Prize (Japan), 1978; *The Quicksand Book* and *Simple Pictures Are Best* were both chosen one of *School Library Journal*'s Best Books for Spring, 1977; Chicago Book Clinic Award, 1979, for *The Christmas Pageant; Helga's Dowry* was chosen a Children's Choice by the International Reading Association and the Children's Book Council, 1978, *The Popcorn Book, Pancakes for Breakfast,*

The Clown of God, Four Scary Stories, Jamie's Tiger, and *Bill and Pete,* all 1979, *Big Anthony and the Magic Ring* and *Oliver Button Is a Sissy,* both 1980, *The Comic Adventures of Old Mother Hubbard and Her Dog,* 1982; *Strega Nona's Magic Lessons,* 1983, *The Carsick Zebra and Other Animal Riddles,* 1984, and *The Mysterious Giant of Barletta,* 1985; Garden State Children's Book Award for Younger Nonfiction, New Jersey Library Association, 1980, for *The Quicksand Book;* Kerlan Award, University of Minnesota, 1981, for "singular attainment in children's literature"; Golden Kite Award for Illustration, Society of Children's Book Writers, 1982, for *Giorgio's Village,* and 1983, for *Marianna May and Nursey; Boston Globe-Horn Book* Award Honor Book for Illustration, 1982, and Critici in Erba commendation from Bologna Biennale, 1983, both for *The Friendly Beasts;* Regina Medal, Catholic Library Association, 1983, for "continued distinguished contribution to children's literature"; *Sing, Pierrot, Sing* was chosen one of *School Library Journal*'s Best Books, 1983; *Mary Had a Little Lamb* was chosen as a Notable Book by the Association of Library Service to Children (American Library Association), 1984; *Clown of God* was selected a Notable Children's Film, 1984; *Sing, Pierrot, Sing* was selected a Notable Children's Trade Book in the Field of Social Studies by the National Council of Social Studies and the Children's Book Council, 1984, and *The Mysterious Giant of Barletta,* 1985; Award from the Bookbuilders West Book Show, 1985, for *Miracle on 34th Street; Redbook* Children's Picturebook Award Honorable Mention, 1986, for *Tomie dePaola's Favorite Nursery Tales; Horn Book* Honor List citation, 1986, for *Tomie dePaola's Mother Goose;* Golden Kite Honor Book for Illustration, 1987, for *What the Mailman Brought; The Art Lesson* was named one of the *New York Times*' best picture books of the year, 1989; American nominee in illustration for the Hans Christian Andersen Award, 1990.

WRITINGS:

AUTHOR; UNDER NAME TOMIE dePAOLA

Criss-Cross, Applesauce, illustrations by B. A. King and his children, Addison House, 1979.

AUTHOR AND ILLUSTRATOR; UNDER NAME TOMIE dePAOLA

The Wonderful Dragon of Timlin, Bobbs-Merrill, 1966.
Fight the Night, Lippincott, 1968.
Joe and the Snow, Hawthorn, 1968.
Parker Pig, Esquire, Hawthorn, 1969.
The Journey of the Kiss, Hawthorn, 1970.
The Monsters' Ball, Hawthorn, 1970.
(Reteller) *The Wind and the Sun,* Ginn, 1972.
Andy, That's My Name, Prentice-Hall, 1973.
Charlie Needs a Cloak (Junior Literary Guild selection), Prentice-Hall, 1973.

Nana Upstairs and Nana Downstairs, Putnam, 1973.
The Unicorn and the Moon, Ginn, 1973.
Watch Out for the Chicken Feet in Your Soup (Junior Literary Guild selection), Prentice-Hall, 1974.
The Cloud Book: Word and Pictures, Holiday House, 1975.
Michael Bird-Boy, Prentice-Hall, 1975.
(Reteller) *Strega Nona: An Old Tale,* Prentice-Hall, 1975, published as *The Magic Pasta Pot,* Hutchinson, 1979.
Things to Make and Do for Valentine's Day, F. Watts, 1976.
When Everyone Was Fast Asleep, Holiday House, 1976.
Four Stories for Four Seasons, Prentice-Hall, 1977.
Helga's Dowry: A Troll Love Story, Harcourt, 1977.
The Quicksand Book, Holiday House, 1977.
Bill and Pete (Junior Literary Guild selection), Putnam, 1978.
The Christmas Pageant, Winston, 1978, published as *The Christmas Pageant Cutout Book,* 1980.
(Adapter) *The Clown of God: An Old Story,* Harcourt, 1978.
Pancakes for Breakfast, Harcourt, 1978.
The Popcorn Book (Junior Literary Guild selection), Holiday House, 1978.
Big Anthony and the Magic Ring, Harcourt, 1979.
Flicks (Junior Literary Guild selection), Harcourt, 1979.
The Kids' Cat Book, Holiday House, 1979.
Oliver Button Is a Sissy, Harcourt, 1979.
Songs of the Fog Maiden, Holiday House, 1979.
The Family Christmas Tree Book, Holiday House, 1980.
The Knight and the Dragon (Junior Literary Guild selection), Putnam, 1980.
The Lady of Guadalupe, Holiday House, 1980.
The Legend of the Old Befana: An Italian Christmas Story, Harcourt, 1980.
(Reteller) *The Prince of the Dolomites: An Old Italian Tale,* Harcourt, 1980.
The Comic Adventures of Old Mother Hubbard and Her Dog (Junior Literary Guild selection), Harcourt, 1981.
(Reteller) *Fin M'Coul, the Giant of Knockmany Hill,* Holiday House, 1981.
The Friendly Beasts: An Old English Christmas Carol, Putnam, 1981.
The Hunter and the Animals: A Wordless Picture Book, Holiday House, 1981.
Now One Foot, Now the Other, Putnam, 1981.
Strega Nona's Magic Lessons, Harcourt, 1982.
Francis, the Poor Man of Assisi, Holiday House, 1982.
Giorgio's Village, Putnam, 1982.
(Adapter) *The Legend of the Bluebonnet: An Old Tale of Texas,* Putnam, 1983.
Marianna May and Nursey, Holiday House, 1983.
Noah and the Ark, Winston, 1983.

Sing, Pierrot, Sing: A Picture Book in Mime, Harcourt, 1983.

(Adapter) *The Story of the Three Wise Kings,* Putnam, 1983.

(Adapter) *David and Goliath,* Winston, 1984.

Esther Saves Her People, Winston, 1984.

The First Christmas, a Festive Pop-Up Book, Putnam, 1984.

(Adapter) *The Mysterious Giant of Barletta: An Italian Folktale,* Harcourt, 1984.

Tomie dePaola's Country Farm, Putnam, 1984.

Tomie dePaola's Mother Goose Story Streamers, Putnam, 1984.

Tomie dePaola's Mother Goose (also see below), Putnam, 1985.

Pajamas for Kit, Simon & Schuster, 1986.

Katie and Kit at the Beach, Simon & Schuster, 1986.

Katie's Good Idea, Simon & Schuster, 1986.

Katie, Kit and Cousin Tom, Simon & Schuster, 1986.

Merry Christmas, Strega Nona, Harcourt, 1986.

(With others) *Once Upon a Time: Celebrating the Magic of Children's Books in Honor of the Twentieth Anniversary of Reading Is Fundamental,* Putnam, 1986.

(Adapter) *Queen Esther,* Winston, 1986, revised edition, Harper, 1987.

Tomie dePaola's Favorite Nursery Tales, Putnam, 1986.

Bill and Pete Go Down the Nile, Putnam, 1987.

An Early American Christmas, Holiday House, 1987.

The Legend of the Indian Paintbrush, Putnam, 1987.

The Miracles of Jesus, Holiday House, 1987.

The Parables of Jesus, Holiday House, 1987.

Tomie dePaola's Book of Christmas Carols, Putnam, 1987.

Tomie dePaola's Diddle, Diddle, Dumpling and Other Poems and Stories from Mother Goose (selections from *Tomie dePaola's Mother Goose*), Methuen, 1987.

Tomie dePaola's Three Little Kittens and Other Poems and Songs from Mother Goose (selections from *Tomie dePaola's Mother Goose*), Methuen, 1987.

Baby's First Christmas, Putnam, 1988.

(Reteller) *Hey Diddle Diddle: And Other Mother Goose Rhymes* (selections from *Tomie dePaola's Mother Goose*), Putnam, 1988.

Tomie dePaola's Book of Poems, Putnam, 1988.

(With others) *The G.O.S.H ABC Book,* Aurum Books for Children, 1988.

The Art Lesson, Putnam, 1989.

Haircuts for the Woolseys, Putnam, 1989.

My First Chanukah, Putnam, 1989.

Tony's Bread: An Italian Folktale, Putnam, 1989.

Too Many Hopkins, Putnam, 1989.

Little Grunt and the Big Egg, Holiday House, 1990.

Tomie dePaola's Book of Bible Stories, Putnam/ Zondervan, 1990.

Bonjour Mr. Satie, Putnam, 1991.

My First Easter, Putnam, 1991.

My First Passover, Putnam, 1991.

My First Halloween, Putnam, 1991.

ILLUSTRATOR; UNDER NAME TOMIE dePAOLA

Lisa Miller (pseudonym of Bernice Kohn Hunt) *Sound,* Coward, 1965.

Pura Belpre, *The Tiger and the Rabbit and Other Tales,* Lippincott, 1965.

L. Miller, *Wheels,* Coward, 1965.

Jeanne B. Hardendorff, editor, *Tricky Peik and Other Picture Tales,* Lippincott, 1967.

Joan M. Lexau, *Finders Keepers, Losers Weepers,* Lippincott, 1967.

Melvin L. Alexenberg, *Sound Science,* Prentice-Hall, 1968.

James A. Eichner, *The Cabinet of the President of the United States,* F. Watts, 1968.

Leland Blair Jacobs, compiler, *Poetry for Chuckles and Grins,* Garrard, 1968.

M. L. Alexenberg, *Light and Sight,* Prentice-Hall, 1969.

Robert Bly, *The Morning Glory,* Kayak, 1969.

Sam and Beryl Epstein, *Take This Hammer,* Hawthorn, 1969.

Mary C. Jane, *The Rocking-Chair Ghost,* Lippincott, 1969.

Nina Schneider, *Hercules, the Gentle Giant,* Hawthorn, 1969.

Eleanor Boylan, *How to Be a Puppeteer,* McCall, 1970.

Duncan Emrich, editor, *The Folklore of Love and Courtship,* American Heritage Press, 1970.

D. Emrich, editor, *The Folklore of Weddings and Marriage,* American Heritage Press, 1970.

S. and B. Epstein, *Who Needs Holes?,* Hawthorn, 1970.

Barbara Rinkoff, *Rutherford T. Finds 21B,* Putnam, 1970.

Philip Balestrino, *Hot as an Ice Cube,* Crowell, 1971.

S. and B. Epstein, *Pick It Up,* Holiday House, 1971.

John Fisher, *John Fisher's Magic Book,* Prentice-Hall, 1971.

William Wise, *Monsters of the Middle Ages,* Putnam, 1971.

Peter Zachary Cohen, *Authorized Autumn Charts of the Upper Red Canoe River Country,* Atheneum, 1972.

Sibyl Hancock, *Mario's Mystery Machine,* Putnam, 1972.

Jean Rosenbaum and Lutie McAuliff, *What Is Fear?,* Prentice-Hall, 1972.

Rubie Saunders, *The Franklin Watts Concise Guide to Babysitting,* F. Watts, 1972, published as *Baby-Sitting: For Fun and Profit,* Archway, 1979.

S. and B. Epstein, *Hold Everything,* Holiday House, 1973.

S. and B. Epstein, *Look in the Mirror,* Holiday House, 1973.

Kathryn F. Ernst, *Danny and His Thumb,* Prentice-Hall, 1973.

Valerie Pitt, *Let's Find Out about Communications,* F. Watts, 1973.

Charles Keller and Richard Baker, compilers, *The Star-Spangled Banana and Other Revolutionary Riddles,* Prentice-Hall, 1974.

Alice Low, *David's Window,* Putnam, 1974.

Mary Calhoun, *Old Man Whickutt's Donkey,* Parents' Magazine Press, 1975.

Norma Farber, *This Is the Ambulance Leaving the Zoo* (Junior Literary Guild selection), Dutton, 1975.

Lee B. Hopkins, compiler, *Good Morning to You, Valentine* (poems), Harcourt, 1975.

Martha and Charles Shapp, *Let's Find Out about Houses,* F. Watts, 1975.

Eleanor Coerr, *The Mixed-Up Mystery Smell,* Putnam, 1976.

John Graham, *I Love You, Mouse,* Harcourt, 1976.

Bernice Kohn Hunt, *The Whatchamacallit Book,* Putnam, 1976.

Steven Kroll, *The Tyrannosaurus Game,* Holiday House, 1976.

M. and C. Shapp, *Let's Find Out about Summer,* F. Watts, 1976.

Barbara Williams, *If He's My Brother,* Harvey House, 1976.

L. B. Hopkins, compiler, *Beat the Drum: Independence Day Has Come* (poems), Harcourt, 1977.

Daniel O'Connor, *Images of Jesus,* Winston, 1977.

Belong, Winston, 1977.

Journey, Winston, 1977.

(With others) N. Farber, *Six Impossible Things before Breakfast,* Addison-Wesley, 1977.

Jean Fritz, *Can't You Make Them Behave, King George?,* Coward, 1977.

Patricia Lee Gauch, *Once upon a Dinkelsbuehl,* Putnam, 1977.

Tony Johnston, *Odd Jobs,* Putnam, 1977, published as *The Dog Wash,* Scholastic, 1977.

S. Kroll, *Santa's Crash-Bang Christmas,* Holiday House, 1977.

Stephen Mooser, *The Ghost with the Halloween Hiccups,* F. Watts, 1977.

Annabelle Prager, *The Surprise Party,* Pantheon, 1977.

Malcolm E. Weiss, *Solomon Grundy, Born on Oneday: A Finite Arithmetic Puzzle,* Crowell, 1977.

Nancy Willard, *Simple Pictures Are Best* (Junior Literary Guild selection), Harcourt, 1977.

Jane Yolen, *The Giants' Farm,* Seabury, 1977.

Sue Alexander, *Marc, the Magnificent,* Pantheon, 1978.

William Cole, compiler, *Oh, Such Foolishness!* (poems), Lippincott, 1978.

T. Johnston, *Four Scary Stories,* Putnam, 1978.

S. Kroll, *Fat Magic,* Holiday House, 1978.

Naomi Panush Salus, *My Daddy's Moustache,* Doubleday, 1978.

Jan Wahl, *Jamie's Tiger,* Harcourt, 1978.

The Cat on the Dovrefell: A Christmas Tale, translated from the Norse by George Webbe Dasent, Putnam, 1979.

L. B. Hopkins, compiler, *Easter Buds Are Springing: Poems for Easter* (poems), Harcourt, 1979.

Anne Rose, *The Triumphs of Fuzzy Fogtop,* Dial, 1979.

Daisy Wallace, compiler, *Ghost Poems,* Holiday House, 1979.

J. Yolen, *The Giants Go Camping* (Junior Literary Guild selection), Seabury, 1979.

P. L. Gauch, *The Little Friar Who Flew,* Putnam, 1980.

Patricia MacLachlan, *Moon, Stars, Frogs, and Friends,* Pantheon, 1980.

Clement Moore, *The Night before Christmas,* Holiday House, 1980.

Daniel M. Pinkwater, *The Wuggie Norple Story,* Four Winds, 1980.

Pauline Watson, *The Walking Coat,* Walker, 1980.

Malcolm Hall, *Edward, Benjamin and Butter,* Coward, 1981.

Michael Jennings, *Robin Goodfellow and the Giant Dwarf,* McGraw, 1981.

S. Mooser, *Funnyman's First Case,* F. Watts, 1981.

A. Prager, *The Spooky Halloween Party,* Pantheon, 1981.

J. Fritz, adapter, *The Good Giants and the Bad Pukwudgies,* Putnam, 1982.

T. Johnston, *Odd Jobs and Friends,* Putnam, 1982.

Ann McGovern, *Nicholas Bentley Stoningpot III,* Holiday House, 1982.

David A. Adler, *The Carsick Zebra and Other Animal Riddles,* Holiday House, 1983.

T. Johnston, *The Vanishing Pumpkin,* Putnam, 1983.

Shirley Rousseau Murphy, *Tattie's River Journey,* Dial, 1983.

Valentine Davies, *Miracle on 34th Street,* Harcourt, 1984.

Sarah Josepha Hale, *Mary Had a Little Lamb,* Holiday House, 1984.

S. Mooser, *Funnyman and the Penny Dodo,* F. Watts, 1984.

T. Johnston, *The Quilt Story,* Putnam, 1985.

(With others) Hans Christian Andersen *The Flying Trunk and Other Stories by Andersen,* new English version by Naiomi Lewis, Andersen Press, 1986.

Jill Bennett, reteller, *Teeny Tiny,* Putnam, 1986.

Tom Yeomans, *For Every Child a Star: A Christmas Story,* Holiday House, 1986.

Sanna Anderson Baker, *Who's a Friend of the Water-Spurting Whale?,* Cook, 1987.

Carolyn Craven, *What the Mailman Brought* (Junior Literary Guild selection), Putnam, 1987.

J. Fritz, *Shh! We're Writing the Constitution,* Putnam, 1987.

Nancy Willard, *The Mountains of Quilt,* Harcourt, 1987.

Elizabeth Winthrop, *Maggie and the Monster,* Holiday House, 1987.

Caryll Houselander, *Petook: An Easter Story,* Holiday House, 1988.

T. Johnston, *Pages of Music,* Putnam, 1988.

Cindy Ward, *Cookie's Week,* Putnam, 1988.

T. Johnston, adapter, *The Badger and the Magic Fan: A Japanese Folktale,* Putnam, 1990.

J. Yolen, *Hark! A Christmas Sampler,* Putnam, 1991.

OTHER; UNDER NAME TOMIE dePAOLA

Conceived, designed, and directed puppet ballet, *A Rainbow Christmas,* at Botolph in Cambridge, Massachusetts, 1971; dePaola's books have been published in many countries, including Denmark, Germany, Netherlands, Sweden, Norway, Japan, Italy, France and South Africa. Work is represented at the Kerlan Collection at the University of Minnesota and at the Osborne Collection, Toronto, Canada.

ADAPTATIONS:

Wind and the Sun (sound filmstrip), Xerox Films/Lumin Films, 1973.

Andy (sound filmstrip), Random House, 1977.

Charlie Needs a Cloak (filmstrip with cassette), Weston Woods, 1977.

Strega Nona (filmstrip with cassette), Weston Woods, 1978, (musical, adapted by Dennis Rosa, based on *Strega Nona, Big Anthony and the Magic Ring,* and *Strega Nona's Magic Lessons*), first produced in Minneapolis, MN, by the Children's Theatre Company, 1987, (videocassette), CC Studios, 1985.

Clown of God (play; adapted by Thomas Olson), first produced in Minneapolis by the Children's Theatre Company, 1981, (16mm film; videocassette), Weston Woods, 1984.

Strega Nona's Magic Lessons and Others Stories (record and cassette; includes *Strega Nona's Magic Lessons, Strega Nona, Big Anthony and the Magic Ring, Helga's Dowry, Oliver Button Is a Sissy, Now One Foot, Now the Other, Nana Upstairs and Nana Downstairs*), read by Tammy Grimes, Caedmon, 1984.

Big Anthony and Helga's Dowry, Children's Radio Theatre, 1984.

The Night before Christmas (cassette) Live Oak Media, 1984.

The Vanishing Pumpkin (filmstrip with cassette), Random House.

The Legend of the Bluebonnet: An Old Tale of Texas (filmstrip with cassette), Random House, 1985.

The Mysterious Giant of Barletta (cassette), Random House, 1985.

Mary Had a Little Lamb (filmstrip with cassette), Weston Woods, 1985.

The Legend of the Indian Paintbrush (filmstrip with cassette), Listening Library, 1988.

Tomie dePaola's Christmas Carols (cassette), Listening Library, 1988.

Merry Christmas, Strega Nona (cassette), Listening Library, (play; adapted by T. Olson), first produced in Minneapolis by the Children's Theatre Company, 1988.

Tomie dePaola's Mother Goose (play; adapted by Constance Congdon), first produced in Minneapolis by the Children's Theatre Company, 1990.

Charlie Needs a Cloak has been adapted into Braille and *Strega Nona* has been produced as a talking book. Filmstrips of *Let's Find Out about Houses, Let's Find Out about Summer, The Surprise Party, Pancakes for Breakfast, Sing, Pierrot, Sing,* and *Tattie's River Journey* have been produced.

SIDELIGHTS: "Tomie dePaola is one of the most popular creators of picture books for children in America today," state Richard F. Abrahamson and Marilyn Colvin in the *Reading Teacher.* Calling dePaola "an artist and writer of seemingly boundless energy," Anne Sherrill notes in an essay for *Dictionary of Literary Biography: American Writers for Children since 1960* that he "has worked in several areas of children's literature." His art illumines the work of dozens of other authors in addition to the scores of books he has written himself. Several critics, such as Abrahamson and Colvin, find that dePaola is at his best, though, "when he both illustrates and writes a picture book," and consider his retold folktales to "represent some of the most beautiful picture storybooks available today."

DePaola was born in 1934, near the end of the Great Depression, to Irish and Italian parents in Meriden, Connecticut. This talented and prolific author and illustrator grew up during World War II, before television deposed radio in American homes, in a family that appreciated books and creativity. "Growing up before television," dePaola once remarked, "I had what I can only consider the good fortune to be exposed to radio and I never missed that wonderful Saturday morning show, 'Let's Pretend.' I have always felt that that particular program, plus the fact that my mother was in love with books and spent many long hours reading aloud to my brother and me, were the prime factors that caused me to announce to my first grade teacher that when I grew up I was going to make books with pictures." He has frequently said that from the age of four, he knew he wanted to be an artist. "I must have been a stubborn child," he once commented, "because I never swayed from that decision."

DePaola recalls that the Christmas of 1943, when he was nine years old, was one of his most memorable holidays: "All my presents were art supplies: paints, brushes, colored pencils, all sorts of instruction books, watercolors and even an easel." Throughout his grade school years, teachers more or less encouraged his art; when he graduated to middle school, though, he was excited to learn that he would actually be able to take entire classes in the subject. By the time he was a sophomore in high school, dePaola knew that he wanted to attend Pratt Institute in New York and wrote to them to find out what classes he should be taking to prepare for his studies there; in 1952 he entered Pratt, earning a degree in 1956.

After graduation from Pratt, dePaola entered a Benedictine Monastery in Vermont where he stayed for six months. He is grateful for the time spent there because it "solidified, not religious, but some deep spiritual values." Moreover, because the Benedictines are involved in the arts, he also learned that "culture was an important thing as well. If you can add to the culture of the race of man, you're doing a really hot number. It certainly gave me time to delve even more into the study of art; I was sort of the resident artist." DePaola maintained his association with the monastery when he returned to the secular life. In addition to crafting liturgical art, he designed fabric for their weaving studio, designed Christmas cards, and started them in a little business. Living in the monastery influenced the subject matter of his writing as well. Several of his children's books draw upon religious stories or themes, often from the perspective of legend. *The Clown of God: An Old Story,* for example, is a retelling of the story about the rise and fall of a juggler and the miracle that occurs at his final astonishing performance before a statue of the Virgin Mary and Christ Child. Sherrill remarks that dePaola's tale "was inspired by Anatole France's version of the legend about a juggler who offers his talent as a gift to the Christ Child. DePaola retells it with an Italian Renaissance setting."

Beginning his career as a teacher of art at Newton College of the Sacred Heart in Massachusetts in 1962, dePaola first illustrated Lisa Miller's science book, *Sound,* in 1965; the following year, he illustrated the first of his own books, *The Wonderful Dragon of Timlin.* In 1967, he travelled west to teach at San Francisco College for Women, which became Lone Mountain College; and while in California, he earned a master of fine arts degree from the California College of Arts and Crafts in 1969, and a doctoral equivalency a year later at Lone Mountain College. "The time

I spent in San Francisco also helped raise my consciousness—about women's issues especially—and to realign my thinking about antiwar and peace organizations," dePaola told Lisa Lane in a *Chicago Tribune* interview. Following his graduate work, he returned to New England where he continued to teach art, adding theatrical writing, technical direction, and set design to his professorial tasks. DePaola has also exhibited his work extensively in numerous one-man and group shows, both nationally and internationally. He is the recipient of numerous awards and honors as well as high praise from reviewers for his appealing retellings of religious and ethnic folktales, realistic fiction with elements of fantasy, and concept books that combine fiction with educational topics. But as Abrahamson and Colvin remark, "Can there be a higher honor for a creator of children's books than to be selected by children as a favorite? In 1978, children across the U.S. chose four of Tomie dePaola's works among their favorites. No other creator of children's books in 1978 was given such an honor."

DePaola's family was a closely connected one and some of his stories for children focus upon relationships among family members. One of dePaola's first books, *Nana Upstairs and Nana Downstairs,* is "based upon the death of his grandmother," notes Lane, adding that he admits that "it was a highly personal and challenging book to write." It is the story of Tommy, whose grandmother and great grandmother both live in the same house with him. When he is very young, his great grandmother dies; several years later, his grandmother passes away also. Remarking that "years later when the grandmother dies, he thinks of them both as Nana Upstairs," Sherrill adds that "though the book deals with the death of loved ones, the focus is on affection and fond memories." The story is about Tommy's adjustment to their deaths. Writing in the *Bulletin of the Center for Children's Books,* Sutherland thinks that this ranks with the "best of stories for very young children that shows the love between a child and a grandparent and pictures the child's adjustment to death." According to Janet Dobbins in the *World of Children's Books,* dePaola "reinforces the conviction that the infirmities which so often accompany old age are a fact of live which need not be feared, ridiculed, or hidden." For instance, during Tommy's visits with his great grandmother, who is tied into her chair so that she will not fall out, he insists on being tied into his chair as well, just for the fun of it. And in the *School Library Journal,* Melinda Schroeder suggests that "children will want to hear this again and again, as they puzzle over what it means to be young and old and very old and, finally to die."

A companion piece to *Nana Upstairs and Nana Downstairs* is *Now One Foot, Now the Other,* which involves young Bobby and his grandfather, Bob, who enjoy doing many things together. When the grandfather suffers a stroke, though, Bobby helps him to learn to walk again. Indicating that the "explanations are forthright and appropriate to readers' level of understanding," Karen Harris adds in *School Library Journal,* "The tone is gentle and low-key and the illustrations are, as usual, first-rate." Natalie Babbitt remarks in the *New York Times Book Review* that although "this is a big and difficult story compressed into a small and simple story," dePaola omits nothing and is able to "present a warm and positive picture of the power of love." She also finds that "the illustrations are exactly right. In calm browns and blues, with figures that are just realistic enough, they reinforce the straightforward tone of the prose."

Sherrill believes that dePaola's work is "particularly strong when it builds upon his Irish and Italian family background." *Watch Out for the Chicken Feet in Your Soup,* for example, is based on his relationship with his own Italian grandmother. "Like Joey's grandmother in the story she pinched my cheeks, talked 'funny,' and made Easter bread dolls that were a highlight in my young life . . . ," reminisced dePaola. "She always put chicken feet in chicken soup, and I was fascinated. It certainly was something to brag about. I could mow down my opponents with 'My Grandma puts chicken feet in the soup!' Da Dah! Stardom." In the story, Joey brings his friend Eugene home to meet his Italian grandmother, who tends to embarrass Joey by her old-world ways. Eugene, however, is amazed by the real chicken feet in the soup; he thinks she is fantastic and even helps her to bake marvelous bread dolls. This upsets a pouting Joey, who eventually learns to appreciate his good fortune in having such a remarkable grandmother. Although Leah Deland Stenson, in a *School Library Journal* review, found the "food-obsessed" grandmother "a humorless cliche," Sherrill believes that "besides showing a boy in a nonstereotypical role, the story provides a good sprinkling of Italian words that make the Italian grandmother memorable and authentic." DePaola includes a recipe for bread dolls at the back of the book, a recipe he recalls his grandmother having used.

Many critics concur with Sherrill that dePaola's greatest achievement has been "in retelling traditional folktales and in writing stories in the folktale tradition." *Strega Nona: An Old Tale,* which was named a Caldecott Honor Book and received the Nakamore Prize in Japan, is a traditional tale about a magic pot that, upon the recitation of a verse, produces food and ceases only with the recitation of another verse. According to Sherrill, dePaola discussed the origin of *Strega Nona* in an interview with Phyllis Boyson in *New Era:* "In doing research for writing a porridge pot story, he found among other variations the rice pot in India but no Italian variant for the well-known tale, so he created one. Porridge became pasta and the

magic character became Strega Nona, his own creation. 'That was when I became aware of the folktale variant,' " dePaola said. In his variation, Strega Nona ("Grandmother Witch") has hired a helper, Anthony, who secretly observes her and believes that he too can make the pot perform magically. What Anthony has missed is that Strega Nona also blows three kisses to the pot to get it to stop. Chaos ensues, threatening the entire town. Strega Nona sets things right and chooses to punish Anthony not by hanging him, as the townspeople suggest, but by forcing him to eat all the pasta he has created—"an ending children will probably enjoy tremendously," remarks Zena Sutherland in *Bulletin of the Center for Children's Books.*

In *Helga's Dowry: A Troll Love Story,* the story of a beautiful but poor troll who accumulates a dowry and attracts the handsome king of the trolls as her suitor but discards him for another of her own choice, dePaola invents his own tale in the folktale tradition. According to Jennifer Dunning in the *New York Times Book Review,* "Mr. dePaola's inspiration often comes from faculty-meeting doodles. 'A troll appeared on the doodle pad,' Mr. dePaola recalled. 'I thought, "Gee, must be a troll story inside me."' So I did a lot of research on trolls and found the women are condemned to wander the face of the earth if they have no dowry.' " DePaola's troll acquires her dowry from doing enormous tasks for others—cows for laundry, land for clearing trees; and, according to Sutherland in *Bulletin of the Center for Children's Books,* "Most of the fun is in Helga's magical despatch of loot-producing tasks."

DePaola also has some very definite ideas about the presence of sexual stereotyping in children's books. Sherrill remarks that dePaola has frequently said that he "consciously tries to avoid presenting sexual stereotypes, and certainly the independent Helga underscores that." He indicated to Dunning: "I feel strongly about stereotyping roles. If the children's book people don't make an effort to avoid them then we're in trouble. My mother always mowed the lawn and my father cooked. I guess I feel that the younger a child can get the proper values, the better. But ultimately it has to be a good story. I don't want to preach."

In *Fin M'Coul: The Giant of Knockmany Hill,* Celtic motifs frame the half-page illustrations and text involving the legendary Irish hero Cu Chulainn. M'Coul is huge and powerful good giant who is afraid of being beaten by Cucullin, who is larger than he is. M'Coul's clever wife comes to his rescue, and he appears dressed as a baby stuffed into a real cradle; Cucullin retreats fearing that if the giant M'Coul could produce a child the size of the baby before him, what must the father be like? "Fin M'Coul comes alive through Tomie dePaola's comic illustrating and retelling of this tale," writes Fellis L. Jordan in *Children's Book Review Service.* "You can almost hear

Fin's Irish brogue as you read the story." "Much as we may admire the sheer cleverness of the book it is the humour that lives longest in the mind," states a reviewer in the *Junior Bookshelf.* "This is the perfect version of the immemorial theme of the triumph of cunning over force, and Mr. dePaola tells it for all it is worth."

DePaola's gently drawn illustrations are hallmarked by bright colors and an almost primitive style that is reminiscent of folk art. "Although colored inks and watercolors on handmade watercolor paper are used most frequently as a base for dePaola's books, he also uses pencil drawings, etchings, charcoal drawings, and other techniques," writes Sherrill, adding that his "interest in theater is evident from pictures that frequently resemble stage sets. . . . Characters in the stories are made distinctive through dePaola's treatment of eyes, facial expressions, noses, hair, and moths. Tousle-haired children have become an identifying characteristic of his work." Considering his use of color "distinctive," dePaola added: "I think my style of illustration has been refined over the years. Style has to do with the kinds of things you are drawn to personally, and I'm drawn to Romanesque and folk art. I think that my style is very close to those—very simple and direct. I simplify."

In *Books for Your Children,* he indicates that he tries not to form images for a book until the story line is set, and the text has been written and edited. "Once the story-line is good and strong (and hopefully appealing) then I can let my pictures not only illustrate the text but amplify it, add to it, and sometimes include a sub-plot told only through the pictures. This, of course is extremely important in a picture-book. My personal definition for a picture-book (as opposed to an illustrated story-book) is that the very young child who may not even know how to decipher words can indeed read the book by actually 'reading the pictures.'" According to Sherrill, "Perhaps the two qualities that consistently emerge from the work of this popular and talented author-illustrator are his keen sense of humor and his love of childhood and children." DePaola says that he enjoys writing and drawing for children not only because it stimulates his own imagination, "but hopefully I will touch at least some children to instill in them the great love I personally have always had for books. Making children's books has literally forced me into an honesty of expression because . . . children demand honesty and recognize false performance."

"The child dePaola once was shines through all his works, captivating readers and enriching the field of children's books," remarks Barbara Elleman in *Twentieth-Century Children's Writers.* "Of all the zillions of things that could be said about Tomie dePaola," says Robert D. Hale in *Horn Book,* "the one that comes most strongly to mind is his exuberance. He is joyful, ebullient. His exhilaration

fills all the spaces around him, wrapping everyone present in rare high spirits. The books he creates radiate this quality of good cheer, even when they have serious messages to impart. . . . Everything Tomie does is done with gusto and zest—which is why his work appeals to all generations. Tomie's softly-colorful illustrations invite tots, while at the other end of the cycle adults appreciate his sharing of feelings." "For me," dePaola once remarked, "my expression is always the sum total of my personal experience with people. Not that it shows consciously or conspicuously, but it is the inner support that makes the terrifying experience of starting a new project less frightening."

BIOGRAPHICAL/CRITICAL SOURCES:

BOOKS

Dictionary of Literary Biography, Volume 61, *American Writers for Children since 1960: Poets, Illustrators, and Nonfiction Authors,* Gale, 1987, pp. 15-26.
Holtze, Sandra Holmes, editor, *Fifth Book of Junior Authors and Illustrators,* H. W. Wilson, 1983.
Kingman, Lee, and others, compilers, *Illustrators of Children's Books: 1957-1966,* Horn Book, 1968.
Kirkpatrick, D. L., editor, *Twentieth-Century Children's Writers,* St. Martin's, 1983.
Marquardt, Dorthy A., and Martha E. Ward, *Illustrators of Books for Young People,* Scarecrow, 1975.
Roginski, Jim, compiler, *Newbery and Caldecott Medalists and Honor Book Winners,* Libraries Unlimited, 1982.
Twentieth-Century Children's Writers, 3rd edition, St. James Press, 1989, pp. 279-281.

PERIODICALS

Books for Your Children, summer, 1980, pp. 2-3.
Bulletin of the Center for Children's Books, October, 1973, pp. 24-25; November, 1975, p. 42.
Chicago Tribune, February 13, 1989.
Children's Book Review Service, May, 1981, p. 81.
Hartford Courant (CN), September 13, 1985.
Horn Book, April, 1974; August, 1975; October, 1975; November/December, 1985, pp. 770-772.
Junior Bookshelf, August, 1981, p. 144.
Language Arts, March, 1979.
New York Times Book Review, November 13, 1977, pp, 42, 45; September 20, 1981, p. 30.
Publishers Weekly, July 19, 1976; July 23, 1982.
Reading Teacher, December, 1979, pp. 264-269.
School Library Journal, September, 1973, p. 56; November, 1974, pp. 46-47; September, 1981, pp. 105-106.
Top of the News, April, 1976.
Wilson Library Bulletin, October, 1977.
World of Children's Books, spring, 1978, pp. 38-39.

—*Sketch by Sharon Malinowski*

dePAOLA, Tomie
  See dePAOLA, Thomas Anthony

                    *   *   *

DETINE, Padre
  See OLSEN, Ib Spang

                    *   *   *

DEVLIN, Diana (Mary) 1941-

PERSONAL: Born April 1, 1941, in Portmadoc, North Wales; daughter of William G. (an actor) and Mary (a musician; maiden name, Casson) Devlin. *Education:* Girton College, Cambridge, B.A., (with honors), 1963, M.A., 1967; University of Minnesota, M.A., 1969, Ph.D., 1972; University of Surrey, diploma, 1989. *Avocational interests:* Opera, history, "gardening for novices."

ADDRESSES: Home—Street Farm Cottage, Frittenden, Cranbrook, Kent TN17 2DD, England. *Agent*—Dinah Wiener, 27 Arlington Rd., London NW1 7ER, England.

CAREER: Inner London Education Authority, London, England, teacher of drama, 1964-67; Goldsmith's College, London, senior lecturer in drama, 1971-79; private teaching, 1983-89; personnel and training manager, Leeds Castle, Maidstone, Kent, England. Part-time or temporary teacher at University of Minnesota, 1973, 1983-85, Open University, 1977, 1978, and 1984—, Colorado College, 1979-82, American Heritage Association, 1980-84, Trinity College of Music, 1982-85, Central School of Speech and Drama, 1984, Royal Academy of the Dramatic Arts, 1984, Lawrence University, 1985, and London Theatre School, 1987-88. International Shakespeare Globe Centre, United Kingdom, member of academic advisory committee, 1981—, member of board of directors, 1982—, chairman of museum committee, 1984—, and administrator, 1985-87; member of board of directors, World Centre for Shakespeare Studies, 1975-82, and Bear Gardens Museum and Arts Centre, 1978-83.

MEMBER: Society of Authors.

AWARDS, HONORS: Fulbright scholarship, 1967-70; graduate actress award, University of Minnesota.

WRITINGS:

(With Douglas Campbell) *Looking ahead to a Career: Theatre,* Dillon, 1970.
(Contributor) Christopher Edwards, editor, *London Theatre Guide: 1576-1642,* Burlington, 1979.
(Contributor) Helen Krich Chinoy and Linda Walsh Jenkins, editors, *Women in the American Theatre,* Crown, 1980.

A Speaking Part: Lewis Casson and the Theatre of His Time (biography of her grandfather), Hodder & Stoughton, 1982.
Macmillan Masterguides: The Winter's Tale by William Shakespeare, Macmillan, 1985.
(Contributor) Linda Cook and Bryan Loughrey, editors, *Critical Essays on Hamlet,* Longman, 1988.
(Contributor) Cook and Loughrey, editors, *Critical Essays on the Tempest,* Longman, 1988.
Mask and Scene: An Introduction to a World View of Theatre, Scarecrow, 1989.
(Contributor) Cook and Loughrey, editors, *Critical Essays on Richard II,* Longman, 1989.
(Contributor) Cook and Loughrey, editors, *Critical Essays on a Midsummer Night's Dream,* Longman, in press.
(Contributor) Cook and Loughrey, editors, *Critical Essays on Measure for Measure,* Longman, in press.

Contributor of articles to *Drama.*

SIDELIGHTS: Diana Devlin's biography *A Speaking Part: Lewis Casson and the Theatre of His Time* chronicles the life of one of the most distinguished members of the British theatre, whose career spanned the years from the turn of the century until after World War II. In the *Times Literary Supplement,* Stephan Wall observes that Devlin, as Casson's granddaughter, "is able to give us an inside picture of the private and family man as well as of a public life of dignity and value."

Devlin told *CA:* "I have expanded my interests to include the heritage field, where I am currently employed. My future writing will reflect this development. I live in London and Kent, and have also resided in the United States."

BIOGRAPHICAL/CRITICAL SOURCES:

PERIODICALS

Times Literary Supplement, December 24, 1982; January 5, 1990.

                    *   *   *

DEVLIN, Harry 1918-

PERSONAL: Born March 22, 1918, in Jersey City, NJ; son of Harry George (general manager of Savarin Co.) and Amelia (Crawford) Devlin; married Dorothy Wende (an artist and writer), August 30, 1941; children: Harry Noel, Wende Elizabeth (Mrs. Geoffrey Gates), Jeffrey Anthony, Alexandra Gail (Mrs. James Eldridge), Brion Phillip, Nicholas Kirk, David Matthew. *Education:* Syracuse University, B.F.A., 1939. *Religion:* Congregationalist.

ADDRESSES: Home and office—443 Hillside Ave., Mountainside, NJ 07092.

CAREER: Artist, 1939—. *Collier's,* New York, NY, editorial cartoonist, 1945-54; Union College, Cranford, NJ, lecturer in history of fine arts and history of American domestic architecture, 1962-64. President, Mountainside Public Library, 1968-69; served as grants chairman and vice-chairman, New Jersey State Council on the Arts, 1970-79; chairman, Advisory Board on the Arts, Union County, NJ, vocational and technical schools, 1972-75; trustee, Morris Museum, Morristown, NJ, 1980—; member, New Jersey Committee for the Humanities, 1984—; founding member, Rutgers University Advisory Council on Children's Literature. One-person art exhibitions, Morris Museum, 1979, World Headquarters, General Electric, Fairfield, CT, 1980, Union League Club, New York City, 1981, World Headquarters, AT&T, 1986, Schering Plough, 1986, and Jane Voorhees Zimmerli Art Museum, Rutgers State University, New Brunswick, NJ, December 9, 1990-February 24, 1991. Works represented in permanent collections, including the Midlantic Bank, Crum & Foster, First Atlantic Bank, and the Corporate Headquarters of City Federal Savings. *Military service:* U.S. Naval Reserve, 1942-46; served as artist; became lieutenant, Office of Naval Intelligence.

MEMBER: Society of Illustrators (life member), National Cartoonists Society (president, 1956-57), Associated Artists of New Jersey (president, 1984-85), Artists Equity Association (New Jersey), Graphic Artists Guild, Dutch Treat Club.

AWARDS, HONORS: Best in Advertising Cartoon Award, National Cartoonists Society, 1956, 1962, 1963, 1977, and 1978; Special Citation for Husband-Wife Writers of Children's Books, New Jersey Institute of Technology, 1969; New Jersey Teachers of English Award, 1970, for *How Fletcher Was Hatched!;* Award of Excellence, Chicago Book Fair, 1974, for *Old Witch Rescues Halloween;* New Jersey Institute of Technology Award, 1976, for *Tales of Thunder and Lightning;* Arents Award for Art and Literature, Syracuse University, 1977; elected to Hall of Fame in Literature, New Jersey Institute of Technology, 1980; Chairman's Award for the painting "House on High Street," Society of Illustrators, 1981; elected to Advertising Hall of Fame, 1983; D.H.L., Kean College, 1985; inducted into New Jersey Literary Hall of Fame, 1987.

WRITINGS:

SELF-ILLUSTRATED JUVENILES

To Grandfather's House We Go: A Roadside Tour of American Homes, Four Winds Press, 1967.
The Walloping Window Blind: An Old Nautical Tale, Van Nostrand, 1968.
What Kind of a House Is That?, Parents' Magazine Press, 1969.

Tales of Thunder and Lightning, Parents' Magazine Press, 1975.

WITH WIFE, WENDE DEVLIN; JUVENILES; SELF-ILLUSTRATED

Old Black Witch, Encyclopaedia Britannica Press, 1963.
The Knobby Boys to the Rescue, Parents' Magazine Press, 1965.
Aunt Agatha, There's a Lion under the Couch, Van Nostrand, 1968.
How Fletcher Was Hatched!, Parents' Magazine Press, 1969.
What's Under My Bed?, Forty Four Sounds, 1970.
A Kiss for a Warthog, Van Nostrand, 1970.
Old Witch and the Polka Dot Ribbon, Parents' Magazine Press, 1970.
Cranberry Thanksgiving, Parents' Magazine Press, 1971.
Old Witch Rescues Halloween, Parents' Magazine Press, 1973.
Hang on Hester!, Forty Four Sounds, 1974.
Cranberry Christmas, Parents' Magazine Press, 1976.
Cranberry Mystery, Macmillan, 1978.
Cranberry Halloween, Macmillan, 1982.
Cranberry Valentine, Macmillan, 1986.
Cranberry Birthday, Macmillan, 1988.
Cranberry Easter, Macmillan, 1990.

OTHER

Portraits of American Architecture (adult nonfiction), East View Editions, 1982, published as *Portraits of American Architecture: Monuments to a Romantic Mood, 1830-1900,* David Godine, 1989.

Also author and host of four films entitled *Fare You Well, Old House,* 1976, 1979, 1980, and 1981, and of films *Houses of the Hackensack,* 1976, and *To Grandfather's House We Go,* 1981, all for New Jersey Public Broadcasting Corp.

ADAPTATIONS: Old Black Witch was filmed by Gerald Herman as *The Winter of the Witch,* starring Hermione Gingold, Parents' Magazine Films, 1972; *How Fletcher Was Hatched!, A Kiss for a Warthog, The Knobby Boys to the Rescue,* and *Aunt Agatha, There's a Lion under the Couch* were adapted as film strips by Spoken Arts, Inc., in 1985; *Cranberry Halloween, Cranberry Thanksgiving, Cranberry Christmas,* and *Cranberry Mystery* were adapted as film strips by Spoken Arts, Inc., in 1986.

SIDELIGHTS: Harry Devlin collaborates on children's books with his wife, Wende Devlin. "Our first book," he once explained, "sold over a million copies, which beguiled us into the belief that we could write." The team has written fifteen books together and earned a Special Citation from the New Jersey Institute of Technology for their work in children's literature. Many of their books have been best-sellers.

Although he had been an artist since 1939, Devlin's career took off just after the Second World War when he became an editorial cartoonist for *Collier's* magazine, a position he held for nine years. His cartoons won him acclaim as a shrewd and clear-headed commentator on the current scene. During this time he also created two short-lived comic strips, *Fullhouse* and *Raggmopp,* the latter comic strip being described by Jerry Robinson in *The Comics* as "stylishly drawn with a tasteful use of white space." Devlin has also done artwork for magazine and newspaper advertising. He has won five awards for his advertising work from the National Cartoonists Society. Devlin has also designed postage stamps for the U. S. Postal Service.

Because of his stature as an artist, Devlin was asked to become a member of the New Jersey State Council on the Arts in 1970. "While a member . . . ," he remembers, "I was able to get funding for the founding of the Rutgers University Collection of Children's Art and Literature, now a thriving entity of the Voorhees Zimmerli Museum of Rutgers University."

Devlin says that the diversity of his work has enabled him to have a long artistic career: "As I have survived as an artist and writer, I can say that diversity is the key to survival. I have illustrated magazines, novels, children's books, painted portraits and murals, and was an editorial cartoonist." His collaboration with his wife utilizes the strengths that each one possesses. "Wende writes more and better than I can," Devlin admits. "I write only about those things that I think may fascinate and pay no heed to trends or styles."

BIOGRAPHICAL/CRITICAL SOURCES:

BOOKS

Gauley, Sherrie, *Harry Devlin: Illustrations for Children's Literature: Essay and Annotated Catalogue,* Jane Voorhees Zimmerli Art Museum, 1990.
Harry Devlin: A Retrospective, Morris Museum, 1991.
Robinson, Jerry, *The Comics: An Illustrated History of Comic Strip Art,* Putnam, 1974.

PERIODICALS

Library Journal, May 15, 1969; May 15, 1970.
New York Times Book Review, May 9, 1965; January 4, 1970.

*   *   *

DEVLIN, (Dorothy) Wende   1918-

PERSONAL: Born April 27, 1918, in Buffalo, NY; daughter of Bernhardt Philip (a veterinarian) and Elizabeth (Buffington) Wende; married Harry Devlin (an artist and writer), August 30, 1941; children Harry Noel, Wende Elizabeth (Mrs. Geoffrey Gates), Jeffrey Anthony, Alexandra Gail (Mrs. James Eldridge), Brion Phillip, Nicholas Kirk, David Matthew. *Education:* Syracuse University, B.F.A., 1940. *Politics:* Independent. *Religion:* Congregationalist.

ADDRESSES: Home and office—443 Hillside Ave., Mountainside, NJ 07092. *Agent*—Dorothy Markinko, McIntosh & Otis, Inc., 475 Fifth Ave., New York, NY 10017 (literary); Swain Gallery, 703 Watchung Ave., Plainfield, NJ (art).

CAREER: Free-lance writer and portrait painter. One-person art exhibitions, Schering Plough, Kenilworth, NJ, 1986, City of Trenton Museum, Trenton, NJ, 1987, and Schering Plough, Madison, NJ, 1988. Works represented in permanent collections, including Midlantic Bank, Edison, NJ, and Central Jersey Trust, Freehold, NJ. Member of Rutgers University advisory council on children's literature.

MEMBER: Authors Guild, Authors League of America, Woman Pays Club.

AWARDS, HONORS: Special Citation for Husband-Wife Writers of Children's Books, New Jersey Institute of Technology, 1969; New Jersey Teachers of English Award, 1970, for *How Fletcher Was Hatched!;* Award of Excellence, Chicago Book Fair, 1974, for *Old Witch Rescues Halloween;* Arents Award for Art and Literature, Syracuse University, 1977; inducted into New Jersey Literary Hall of Fame, 1981; The Michael Award, New Jersey School of Engineering, 1987.

WRITINGS:

WITH HUSBAND, HARRY DEVLIN; JUVENILES

Old Black Witch, Encyclopaedia Britannica Press, 1963.
The Knobby Boys to the Rescue, Parents' Magazine Press, 1965.
Aunt Agatha, There's a Lion under the Couch, Van Nostrand, 1968.
How Fletcher Was Hatched!, Parents' Magazine Press, 1969.
What's Under My Bed?, Forty Four Sounds, 1970.
A Kiss for a Warthog, Van Nostrand, 1970.
Old Witch and the Polka Dot Ribbon, Parents' Magazine Press, 1970.
Cranberry Thanksgiving, Parents' Magazine Press, 1971.
Old Witch Rescues Halloween, Parents' Magazine Press, 1973.
Hang on Hester!, Forty Four Sounds, 1974.
Cranberry Christmas, Parents' Magazine Press, 1976.
Cranberry Mystery, Macmillan, 1978.
Cranberry Halloween, Macmillan, 1982.

Cranberry Valentine, Macmillan, 1986.
Cranberry Birthday, Macmillan, 1988.
Cranberry Easter, Macmillan, 1990.

Author of feature page, "Beat Poems for a Beat Mother," *Good Housekeeping,* 1963-71.

ADAPTATIONS: Old Black Witch was filmed by Gerald Herman as *The Winter of the Witch,* starring Hermione Gingold, Parents' Magazine Films, 1972; *How Fletcher Was Hatched!, A Kiss for a Warthog, The Knobby Boys to the Rescue,* and *Aunt Agatha, There's a Lion under the Couch* were adapted as film strips by Spoken Arts, Inc., in 1985; *Cranberry Halloween, Cranberry Thanksgiving, Cranberry Christmas,* and *Cranberry Mystery* were adapted as film strips by Spoken Arts, Inc., in 1986.

SIDELIGHTS: Wende Devlin collaborates on children's books with her husband, Harry Devlin. "My husband and I became children's book-oriented," she explains, "when we had seven children of our own. We had a built in sounding board for ideas and I can't think of more worthwhile work than pleasing and developing a child's mind and imagination." The team has won a Special Citation from the New Jersey Institute of Technology for their work in children's literature. Many of their books have been best-sellers.

Particularly popular with children are the Devlins' books set in the town of Cranberryport and featuring a girl named Maggie, her grandmother, the local sewing circle, and Mr. Whiskers. Usually set during a holiday celebration, the Cranberry stories emphasize the value of good friends.

BIOGRAPHICAL/CRITICAL SOURCES:

PERIODICALS

Elizabeth (NJ) Daily Journal, August 29, 1968.
Library Journal, May 15, 1969; May 15, 1970.
Newark Star Ledger, June 22, 1988.
New York Times, June 19, 1977.
New York Times Book Review, May 9, 1965; January 4, 1970.

*   *   *

DIXON, Franklin W.
See McFARLANE, Leslie (Charles)

*   *   *

DODGE, Fremont
See GRIMES, Lee

DRABEK, Thomas E(dward) 1940-

PERSONAL: Born February 29, 1940, in Chicago, IL; son of Thomas F. (a salesman) and Glenna (a fashion buyer; maiden name, Martin) Drabek; married Ruth Ann Obduskey, June 10, 1960; children: Deborah Kaye, Russell Ray. *Education:* University of Denver, B.A. (magna cum laude), 1961; Ohio State University, M.A., 1962, Ph.D., 1965.

ADDRESSES: Home—7643 Navarro Pl., Denver, CO 80237. *Office*—Department of Sociology, University of Denver, Denver, CO 80208-0209.

CAREER: Ohio State University, Disaster Research Center, Columbus, research associate, 1963-65; University of Denver, Denver, CO, assistant professor, 1965-69, associate professor, 1969-74, professor of sociology, 1974—, chairperson, 1974-79, 1985-87. Vice-chairman for disaster planning and interorganizational coordinator, Denver Region of American Red Cross, 1970-72; chairman, committee on U.S. emergency preparedness, National Academy of Sciences, 1978-80. Consultant to chairman for disaster planning, Rocky Mountain Division, American Red Cross, 1975-80.

MEMBER: International Sociological Association (president of research committee on disasters, 1991—), American Sociological Association, Western Social Science Association (member of executive council, 1967-70; president, 1971-72), Pacific Sociological Association, Midwest Sociological Society, Phi Beta Kappa.

AWARDS, HONORS: National Institute of Mental Health grants, 1965-67, 1969-72; National Science Foundation grants, 1966-68, 1977-80, 1980-82, 1982-87, 1986-90, 1989—; Air Force Office of Scientific Research grant, 1967-68; Exxon Education Foundation grant, 1975-77.

WRITINGS:

Disaster in Aisle Thirteen, College of Administrative Sciences, Ohio State University, 1968.
(With Gresham M. Sykes) *Law and the Lawless,* Random House, 1969.
Laboratory Simulation of a Police Communication System under Stress, College of Administrative Sciences, Ohio State University, 1969.
(With J. Eugene Haas) *Complex Organizations: A Sociological Perspective,* Macmillan, 1973.
(With Haas) *Understanding Complex Organizations,* W. C. Brown, 1974.
(With Haas and D. Mileti) *Human Systems in Extreme Environments,* Institute of Behavioral Sciences, University of Colorado, 1975.

(With D. Brodie, J. Edgerton, and P. Munson) *The Flood Breakers,* Institute of Behavioral Sciences, University of Colorado, 1979.

(With H. Tamminga, T. Kilijanek, and C. Adams) *Managing Multiorganizational Emergency Responses: Emergent SAR Networks in Natural Disaster and Remote Area Settings,* Institute of Behavioral Sciences, University of Colorado, 1981.

(With Kilijanek and A. Mushkatel) *Earthquake Mitigation Policy: The Experience of Two States,* Institute of Behavioral Sciences, University of Colorado, 1983.

(With W. H. Key) *Conquering Disaster: Family Recovery and Long-Term Consequences,* Irvington, 1984.

Emergency Management: The Human Factor, National Emergency Training Center, 1985.

Human System Responses to Disaster: An Inventory of Sociological Findings, Springer-Verlag, 1986.

The Professional Emergency Manager: Structures and Strategies for Success, Institute of Behavioral Science, University of Colorado, 1987.

The Local Emergency Manager: The Emerging Professional (Part I), National Emergency Training Center, Federal Emergency Management Agency, 1988.

Emergency Management: Strategies for Maintaining Organizational Integrity, Springer-Verlag, 1990.

(With G. Hoetmer) *Emergency Management: Principles and Practice for Local Government,* International City Management Association, 1991.

Microcomputers in Emergency Management: Implementation of Computer Technology, Institute of Behavioral Science, University of Colorado, 1991.

Contributor to *Dynamic Issues in Social Psychology,* edited by Dwight G. Dean, Random House, 1969; and *Social and Psychological Factors in Stress,* edited by Joseph McGrath, Holt, 1970. Also contributor to social science journals.

WORK IN PROGRESS: Research on disaster evacuation decision-making behavior by executives responsible for tourist-oriented firms.

*   *   *

DRUXMAN, Michael Barnett   1941-

PERSONAL: Born February 23, 1941, in Seattle, WA; son of Harry (a jeweler) and Florence (Barnett) Druxman; married Theresa M. Lundy (a park director), March 18, 1966 (divorced, 1979); married Laurie Singer (a school teacher), July 3, 1983 (divorced, 1984); children: (first marriage) David Michael. *Education:* University of Washington, Seattle, B.A., 1963.

ADDRESSES: Home—Calabasas, CA. *Office*—Michael B. Druxman, Public Relations, P.O. Box 8086, Calabasas, CA 91372.

CAREER: Pope & Talbot, Inc., Seattle, WA, real estate salesman, 1963; Retail Credit Co., Los Angeles, CA, credit investigator, 1964-65; Michael B. Druxman (public relations firm), Calabasas, CA, owner, 1965—.

WRITINGS:

Paul Muni: His Life and His Films, A. S. Barnes, 1974.
Basil Rathbone: His Life and His Films, A. S. Barnes, 1975.
Make It Again, Sam: A Survey of Movie Remakes, A. S. Barnes, 1975.
Merv, Award Books, 1976, revised edition, Leisure Books, 1980.
Charlton Heston, Pyramid Books, 1976.
One Good Film Deserves Another: A Survey of Movie Sequels, A. S. Barnes, 1980.
Tracy (play), first produced in Los Angeles, 1984.
Gable (play), first produced in Los Angeles, 1984.
Jolson (play), first produced in Los Angeles, 1988
Keaton's Cop (screenplay), Cannon Pictures, 1990.

Also author of one-person plays about Clara Bow, Errol Flynn, Carole Lombard, and Orson Welles; author of two other plays, *Father and Son* and *Hail on the Chief.*

WORK IN PROGRESS: Dillinger and Capone (screenplay) has been sold to Concorde Pictures for future production; working on various stage plays and screenplays.

*   *   *

DUBOFSKY, Melvyn   1934-

PERSONAL: Born October 25, 1934, in Brooklyn, NY; son of Harry (a projectionist) and Lillian (Schneider) Dubofsky; married Joan S. Klores (a speech pathologist), January 16, 1959; children: David Mark, Lisa Sue. *Education:* Brooklyn College (now Brooklyn College of the City University of New York), B.A., 1955; University of Rochester, Ph.D., 1960.

ADDRESSES: Home—23 Devon Blvd., Binghamton, NY 13903. *Office*—Department of History, State University of New York, Binghamton, NY 13901.

CAREER: Northern Illinois University, DeKalb, assistant professor of history, 1959-67; University of Massachusetts—Amherst, associate professor of history, 1967-69; University of Wisconsin—Milwaukee, professor of history, 1970-71; State University of New York at Binghamton, professor of history, 1971—. Senior lecturer in the history of American labor at the University of Warwick, England, 1969; Fulbright Distinguished Professor of History, University of Salzburg, Austria, 1988-89.

MEMBER: American Historical Association, Organization of American Historians, Labor Historians Society.

AWARDS, HONORS: Grants from American Philosophical Society and American Council of Learned Societies, both 1965; National Endowment for the Humanities senior fellow, 1973-74.

WRITINGS:

When Workers Organize: New York City in the Progressive Era, University of Massachusetts Press, 1968.
We Shall Be All: A History of the Industrial Workers of the World, Quadrangle, 1969.
(Editor) *American Labor since the New Deal,* Quadrangle, 1971.
Industrialism and the American Worker, 1865-1920, Crowell, 1975, 2nd edition, edited by John H. Franklin and Abraham Eisenstadt, Harlan Davidson, 1985.
(With Warren W. Van Tine) *John L. Lewis: A Biography,* Quadrangle, 1977, abridged edition, University of Illinois Press, 1986.
(With Daniel Smith and Athan Theoharis) *The United States in the Twentieth Century,* Prentice-Hall, 1978.
(With Theoharis) *Imperial Democracy: The United States since 1945,* Prentice-Hall, 1983.
(With Foster R. Dulles) *Labor in America: A History,* 4th revised edition (Dubofsky was not associated with earlier editions), Harlan Davidson, 1984.
(Editor) *Technological Change and Worker's Movements,* Sage Publications, 1985.
"Big Bill" Haywood, University of Manchester Press, 1987.
(Editor with Van Tine) *Labor Leaders in America,* University of Illinois Press, 1987.

SIDELIGHTS: Thomas Brooks of the *New York Times Book Review* describes Melvyn Dubofsky's *We Shall Be All: A History of the Industrial Workers of the World* as "the definitive history of the I.W.W. It's a fine fat book that gets behind the romanticism to the gut experience of the men and women who tackled a tough job in tough times."

Progressive reviewer Ward Sinclair also labels Dubofsky's *John L. Lewis: A Biography,* co-authored with Warren W. Van Tine, "definitive." The story of John L. Lewis "has never been told in such detail or with such objectivity before," claims *Newsweek* reviewer Raymond Sokolov. Sinclair concurs that the authors' research "is impressive; their sources in many instances new and previously untapped; their organization skillful." Sokolov explains that Dubofsky and Van Tine "are labor historians who have drawn on hitherto unpublished [United Mine Workers] archives and various oral accounts to produce a vivid history of Lewis's rise from obscurity in a humble Iowa mining town to power and wealth."

A *Best Sellers* critic observes that *John L. Lewis: A Biography* "was clearly intended to be a scholarly effort, seeking

to distinguish fact from the alleged hearsay and gossip of earlier books." The reviewer contends that "there is tedium in the text and documentation (71 pages of footnotes)," yet adds, "let the graduate student wrestle with the infinite detail while the general reader sifts for the romance of the greatest force American labor has ever known." Sinclair concludes that the book "contributes vastly to our understanding of a man who was one of the titanic figures of the American century."

BIOGRAPHICAL/CRITICAL SOURCES:

PERIODICALS

Best Sellers, November, 1977.
Book World, November 9, 1969.
Historian, November, 1979.
Newsweek, August 8, 1977.
New York Times Book Review, November 23, 1969; February 1, 1970.
Progressive, February, 1978.
Times Literary Supplement, July 16, 1970.
Washington Post, November 28, 1969.

*   *   *

DUKE, Will
  See GAULT, William Campbell

*   *   *

DUNCAN, (Sandy) Frances (Mary)   1942-

PERSONAL: Born January 24, 1942, in Vancouver, British Columbia, Canada; married Norman Duncan, 1963; children: Kelly, Kirsten. *Education:* University of British Columbia, B.A., 1962, M.A., 1963. *Avocational interests:* Outdoor activities, travel ("reading and conversation cannot come under this category: they are essentials").

ADDRESSES: Home—Gabriola, British Columbia, Canada. *Office*—Writers Union of Canada, 24 Ryerson Ave., Toronto, Ontario, Canada M5R 1K5.

CAREER: Woodlands School, New Westminster, British Columbia, psychologist, 1963-65; Burnaby Mental Health Centre, Burnaby British Columbia, psychologist, 1965-67; Metropolitan Health Department, Vancouver, British Columbia, psychologist, 1969-73; writer, 1973—.

MEMBER: P.E.N. International, Writers Union of Canada, Canadian Society of Children's Authors, Illustrators and Performers (CANSCAIP), West Coast Women and Words Society, Federation of British Columbia Writers.

WRITINGS:

Cariboo Runaway (juvenile), Burns & MacEachern, 1976, Pacific Edge, 1990.

Kap-Sung Ferris (Children's Book Centre choice), Burns & MacEachern, 1977, Macmillan, 1980.
The Toothpaste Genie (juvenile fantasy; Children's Book Centre choice), Scholastic, Inc., 1981.
Dragonhunt (novel), Women's Educational Press, 1981.
Finding Home (novel), Avon, 1982.
Pattern Makers, Women's Educational Press, 1989.
Listen to Me, Grace Kelly, Kids Can Press, 1990.

Contributor to books, including *New: West Coast* (poems), Intermedia, 1977, *Common Ground* (short fiction), Press Gang, 1980, *Canadian Short Fiction Anthology,* Volume 2, Intermedia, 1982, *Baker's Dozen* (short fiction), Women's Educational Press, 1984, and *Anthology* (short fiction), University of British Columbia Press, 1986. Also contributor of short stories to magazines, including *Makara, Northern Journey,* and *Canadian Fiction Magazine.*

SIDELIGHTS: Sandy Frances Duncan once commented: "I am primarily interested in individuals and how they cope with situations, external crises, and crises of their own making; also in isolation and attempts to overcome it. I am interested in Canadian identity, but within a framework of individual identity which has international applications. When I am writing, I make no distinction between 'juvenile' and 'adult' books, that is, I do not say 'Now I will write a book for children' or 'a story for adults.' I write to tell the protagonist's story and hope that it will be read by whoever is interested in her (usually her) story. I am not particularly concerned about the readers' ages, and think a lot of the categorizations used for writing are gratuitous."

BIOGRAPHICAL/CRITICAL SOURCES:

PERIODICALS

In Review, October, 1979.

*   *   *

DYKES, Jack
    See OWEN, Jack

E

EATON, George L.
See VERRAL, Charles Spain

*   *   *

EHRENREICH, Barbara 1941-

PERSONAL: Born August 26, 1941, in Butte, MT; daughter of Ben Howes and Isabelle Oxley (Isely) Alexander; married John Ehrenreich, August 6, 1966 (marriage ended); married Gary Stevenson, December 10, 1983; children: (first marriage) Rosa, Benjamin. *Education:* Reed College, B.A., 1963; Rockefeller University, Ph.D., 1968. *Politics:* "Socialist and feminist." *Religion:* None.

ADDRESSES: Home—9 Devine Ave., Syosset, NY 11791.

CAREER: Health Policy Advisory Center, New York City, staff member, 1969-71; State University of New York College at Old Westbury, assistant professor of health sciences, 1971-74; writer, 1974—. New York Institute for the Humanities, associate fellow, 1980—; Institute for Policy Studies, fellow, 1982—. Co-chairperson, Democratic Socialists of America, 1983—.

AWARDS, HONORS: National Magazine award, 1980; Ford Foundation award for Humanistic Perspectives on Contemporary Issues, 1981; Guggenheim fellowship, 1987.

WRITINGS:

(With husband, John Ehrenreich) *Long March, Short Spring: The Student Uprising at Home and Abroad,* Monthly Review Press, 1969.
(With J. Ehrenreich) *The American Health Empire: Power, Profits, and Politics, a Report from the Health Policy Advisory Center,* Random House, 1970.

(With Deirdre English) *Witches, Midwives, and Nurses: A History of Women Healers,* Feminist Press, 1972.
(With English) *Complaints and Disorders: The Sexual Politics of Sickness,* Feminist Press, 1973.
(With English) *For Her Own Good: One Hundred Fifty Years of the Experts' Advice to Women,* Doubleday, 1978.
The Hearts of Men: American Dreams and the Flight from Commitment, Doubleday, 1983.
(With Annette Fuentes) *Women in the Global Factory* (pamphlet), South End Press, 1983.
(With Elizabeth Hess and Gloria Jacobs) *Re-making Love: The Feminization of Sex,* Anchor Press/Doubleday, 1986.
(With Fred Block, Richard Cloward, and Frances Fox Piven) *The Mean Season: An Attack on the Welfare State,* Pantheon, 1987.
Fear of Falling: The Inner Life of the Middle Class, Pantheon Books, 1989.
The Worst Years of Our Lives: Irreverent Notes from a Decade of Greed, Pantheon Books, 1990.

Contributor to magazines, including *Radical America, Nation, Esquire, Vogue, New Republic,* and *New York Times Magazine.* Contributing editor, *Ms.,* 1981—, and *Mother Jones,* 1988—.

SIDELIGHTS: An outspoken feminist and socialist party leader, Barbara Ehrenreich crusades for social justice in her books. While working for the Health Policy Advisory Center, she published a scathing critique of the American health "empire," exposing its inefficiency, inhumanity, and self-serving policies. Then, turning from the population in general to women in particular, Ehrenreich and her co-author Deirdre English unveiled the male domination of the female health care system in *Complaints and Disorders: The Sexual Politics of Sickness* and *For Her Own Good: One Hundred Fifty Years of the Experts' Advice to*

Women. In her most controversial book to date, *The Hearts of Men: American Dreams and the Flight from Commitment,* Ehrenreich takes on the whole male establishment, challenging the assumption that feminism is at the root of America's domestic upheaval.

Describing *The Hearts of Men* as a study of "the ideology that shaped the breadwinner ethic," Ehrenreich surveys the three decades between the 1950s and the 1980s, showing how male commitment to home and family collapsed during this time. "The result," according to *New York Times* contributor Eva Hoffman, "is an original work of cultural iconography that supplements—and often stands on its head—much of the analysis of the relations between the sexes that has become the accepted wisdom of recent years." Ehrenreich's interpretation of the evidence led her to the surprising conclusion that anti-feminism evolved not in response to feminism—but to men's abdication of their breadwinner role.

The seeds of male revolt were planted as far back as the 1950s, according to Ehrenreich, when what she calls "the gray flannel dissidents" began to balk at their myriad responsibilities. "The gray flannel nightmare of the commuter train and the constant pressure to support a houseful of consumers caused many men to want to run away from it all," Carol Cleaver writes in the *New Leader.* What held these men in check, says Ehrenreich, was the fear that, as bachelors, they would be associated with homosexuality. Hugh Hefner banished that stigma with the publication of *Playboy,* a magazine whose name alone "defied the convention of hard-won maturity," Ehrenreich says in her book. "The magazine's real message was not eroticism, but escape . . . from the bondage of breadwinning. Sex—or Hefner's Pepsi-clean version of it—was there to legitimize what was truly subversive about *Playboy.* In every issue, every month, there was a Playmate to prove that a playboy didn't have to be a husband to be a man." Around this time, another more openly rebellious group called the Beats came into ascendancy. Rejecting both marriage and job for the glory of the road, Beats like Jack Kerouac embodied a freewheeling lifestyle that appealed to many men, Ehrenreich maintains.

Neither separately nor in conjunction with one another did these dissident groups possess the power to lure large numbers of male breadwinners from their traditional roles. To allow them "comfortable entree into a full-scale male revolt . . . would take the blessing of those high priests of normalcy, psychologists and doctors," writes Judith Levine in the *Village Voice.* "The *deus ex medica*—the 'scientific' justification for a male revolt—was coronary heart disease. The exertion of breadwinning, Ehrenreich writes in the most original section of her book, was allegedly, literally attacking the hearts of men.

In the decades that followed, men's increasing "flight from commitment" was sanctioned by pop psychologists and other affiliates of the Human Potential Movement, who banished guilt and encouraged people to "do their own thing." Unfortunately for women, Ehrenreich concludes that men abandoned the breadwinner role "without overcoming the sexist attitudes that role has perpetuated: on the one hand, the expectation of female nurturance and submissive service as a matter of right; on the other hand a misogynist contempt for women as 'parasites' and entrappers of men." In response to male abdication, women increasingly adopted one of two philosophies: they became feminists, committed to achieving economic and social parity with men, or they became anti-feminists, who tried to keep men at home by binding themselves ever more tightly to them. Despite such efforts, Ehrenreich concludes that women have not fared well, but instead have found themselves increasingly on their own "in a society that never intended to admit us as independent persons, much less as breadwinners for others."

Widely reviewed in both magazines and newspapers, *The Hearts of Men* was hailed for its provocative insights—even as individual sections of the study were soundly criticized. In her *Village Voice* review, for instance, Judith Levine is both appreciative of the work and skeptical of its conclusions: "Barbara Ehrenreich—one of the finest feminist-socialist writers around—has written a witty, intelligent book based on intriguing source material. *The Hearts of Men* says something that needs saying: men have not simply reacted to feminism—skulking away from women and children, hurt, humiliated, feeling cheated of their legal and emotional rights. Men, as Ehrenreich observes, have, as always, done what they want to do. . . . I applaud her on-the-mark readings of *Playboy,* medical dogma, and men's liberation; her insistence that the wage system punishes women and children when families disintegrate; her mordant yet uncynical voice. . . . But I believe *The Hearts of Men* is wrong. When she claims that the glue of families is male volition and the breadwinner ideology—and that a change in that ideology caused the breakup of the family—I am doubtful. The ideology supporting men's abdication of family commitment is not new. It has coexisted belligerently with the breadwinner ethic throughout American history."

Similarly, in a *New York Times Book Review* article, Carol Tarvis describes *The Hearts of Men* as "a pleasure to read, entertaining and imaginative," but goes on to say that "Ehrenreich's analysis falters in its confusion of causes and effects. She continually implies a sequence (first came concerted pressures upon men to conform, then male protest, then scientific legitimation of male protest) when her own evidence shows simultaneity. . . . Further, to suggest that feminism came after the male revolt is to mix what people say with what they do. . . . In arguing that male protest preceded female protest, Miss Ehrenreich succumbs to an unhelpful, unanswerable 'Who started this?' spiral."

While *New York Times* contributor Eva Hoffman echoes Tarvis's concern about the confusion of causes and effects, she points out that "by her own admission, Miss Ehrenreich is more interested in cultural imagery and ideas than in sociological proof; and to this reader, her narrative makes good, if sometimes unexpected sense." *Los Angeles Times* reviewer Lois Timnick reaches a similar conclusion: "One may take issue with her cause-and-effect pairings, her prescription for cure . . . and her rather gloomy view of the '80s. . . . But Ehrenreich needs especially to be read by those who fear that 'women's libbers' will wrest away the values she shows men tossed out long ago, or who still cling to the notion that we could, if we wanted, go back to the mythical 'Ozzie and Harriet' days."

In the 1986 *Re-making Love: The Feminization of Sex,* coauthored with Elizabeth Hess and Gloria Jacobs, Ehrenreich reports and applauds the freer attitudes towards sex that women adopted in the 1970s and 1980s. The authors assert that women have gained the ability to enjoy sex just for the sake of pleasure, separating it from idealistic notions of love and romance. In her review of *Re-making Love* for the *Chicago Tribune,* Joan Beck noted that the book "is an important summing up of what has happened to women and sex in the last two decades and [that it] shows why the sex revolution requires re-evaluation." Beck, however, argued that the authors ignore the "millions of walking wounded"—those affected by sexually transmitted diseases, unwanted pregnancy, or lack of lasting relationships. *Washington Post Book World* contributor Anthony Astrachan also expresses a wish for a deeper analysis, but nevertheless finds *Re-making Love* "full of sharp and sometimes surprising insights that come from looking mass culture full in the face."

Ehrenreich's next work to attract critical notice, *Fear of Falling: The Inner Life of the Middle Class,* examines the American middle class and its attitudes towards people of the working and poorer classes. Jonathan Yardley writes in the *Washington Post* that what Ehrenreich actually focuses on is a class "composed of articulate, influential people. . . . in fact what most of us think of as the upper-middle class." According to Ehrenreich this group perceives itself as threatened, is most concerned with self-preservation, and has isolated itself—feeling little obligation to work for the betterment of society. This attitude, Ehrenreich maintains, is occurring at a time when the disparity in income between classes has reached the greatest point since World War II and has become "almost as perilously skewed as that of India," Joseph Coates quotes *Fear of Falling* in *Tribune Books.*

Globe and Mail contributor Maggie Helwig, though praising the book as "witty, clever, [and] perceptive," describes as unrealistic Ehrenreich's hope for a future when everyone could belong to the professional middle class and hold fulfilling jobs. Similarly, David Rieff remarks in the *Los Angeles Times Book Review* that Ehrenreich's proposed solutions to class polarization are overly optimistic and tend to romanticize the nature of work. "Nonetheless," Rieff concludes, " 'Fear of Falling' is a major accomplishment, a breath of fresh thinking about a subject that very few writers have known how to think about at all." The book elicited even higher praise from Coates, who deems it "a brilliant social analysis and intellectual history, quite possibly the best on this subject since Tocqueville's."

In *The Worst Years of Our Lives: Irreverent Notes from a Decade of Greed,* Ehrenreich discusses in a series of reprinted articles what some consider to be one of the most self-involved and consumeristic decades in American history: the 1980s. Most of these articles first appeared in *Mother Jones,* but some come from such periodicals as *Nation, Atlantic, New York Times,* and *New Republic.* Together, they summarize "what Ms. Ehrenreich sees as the decade's salient features: blathering ignorance, smug hypocrisy, institutionalized fraud and vengeful polarization—all too dangerous to be merely absurd," says H. Jack Geiger in the *New York Times Book Review.* "One of Mrs. Ehrenreich's main themes," observes *New York Times* reviewer Herbert Mitgang, " . . . is that the Reagan Administration, which dominated the last decade, cosmeticized the country and painted over its true condition. The author writes that the poor and middle class are now suffering the results of deliberate neglect."

Several critics have praised *The Worst Years of Our Lives* as a book that, as Michael Eric Dyson avers in *Tribune Books,* "reflect[s] the work of an engaged intellectual for whom mere description of the world, no matter how incisive, will not suffice. Her aim is to change the world, and her persuasive analyses of many of America's most difficult problems makes a valuable contribution toward that end." However, some reviewers have objected to what they see as Ehrenreich's moralistic approach to her subject. Priscilla Painton, a *Time* contributor, comments, "Overall, her observations suffer from a simplistic yearning for a nonexistent era when the poor were not blamed for their poverty, when people did not cram their appointment books and when college graduates pursued ideals instead of salaries." Others like Geiger, however, consider this quality to be a virtue, rather than a flaw. "Ehrenreich is an up-front socialist," Geiger attests, "but—even more centrally—she is an old-fashioned moralist, someone who believes in the sturdy values of truth, honesty, self-knowledge and family, and argues that the really valid moral reference point for the comfortable and affluent is other people's pain."

BIOGRAPHICAL/CRITICAL SOURCES:

BOOKS

Ehrenreich, Barbara, *The Hearts of Men: American Dreams and the Flight from Commitment,* Doubleday, 1983.
Ehrenreich, Barbara, *Fear of Falling: The Inner Life of the Middle Class,* Pantheon, 1989.

PERIODICALS

Chicago Tribune, September 25, 1986.
Globe and Mail (Toronto), August 26, 1986.
Los Angeles Times, July 24, 1983.
Los Angeles Times Book Review, August 20, 1989.
Nation, December 24, 1983.
New Leader, July 11, 1983.
New Republic, July 11, 1983.
New York Review of Books, July 1, 1971.
New York Times, January 20, 1971; August 16, 1983; May 16, 1990.
New York Times Book Review, March 7, 1971; June 5, 1983; August 6, 1989; May 20, 1990.
Time, May 7, 1990.
Times Literary Supplement, July 22, 1977.
Tribune Books (Chicago), November 8, 1987; September 24, 1989; May 13, 1990.
Village Voice, February 5, 1979; August 23, 1983.
Washington Post, August 23, 1989.
Washington Post Book World, August 19, 1979; July 24, 1983; November 9, 1986.*

*   *   *

EINSTEIN, Albert   1947-
(Albert Brooks)

PERSONAL: Known professionally as Albert Brooks; born July 22, 1947, in Los Angeles, CA; son of Harry (a radio comedian) and Thelma (a singer; maiden name, Leeds) Einstein. *Education:* Attended Carnegie Institute of Technology (now Carnegie-Melon University), 1966-67.

ADDRESSES: c/o Gelfand & Rennert, 1880 Century Park E., Los Angeles, CA 90067.

CAREER: Comedian, writer, actor, director of motion pictures. Sportswriter for KMPC-Radio in Los Angeles, CA, 1962-63. Comedy writer for television show *Turn On,* 1968. Comedian appearing on television shows, including *The Ed Sullivan Show, The Steve Allen Show, The Gold Diggers, The Merv Griffin Show, The Tonight Show,* and

Saturday Night Live, 1969—. Actor in motion pictures, including *Taxi Driver,* 1976, *Real Life,* 1979, *Modern Romance,* 1980, *Private Benjamin,* 1980, *Twilight Zone: The Movie,* 1983, *Unfaithfully Yours,* 1984, *Lost in America,* 1985, *Broadcast News,* 1987, and *Defending Your Life,* 1991. Director of motion pictures, including *Real Life,* 1979, *Modern Romance,* 1980, *Lost in America,* 1985, and *Defending Your Life,* 1991.

AWARDS, HONORS: Grammy Award nomination from National Academy of Recording Arts and Sciences, 1975, for album *A Star is Bought;* Academy Award nomination, best supporting actor, 1987, for *Broadcast News.*

WRITINGS:

UNDER PSEUDONYM ALBERT BROOKS

(With Monica Johnson and Harry Shearer; and director) *Real Life,* Paramount, 1979.
(With Johnson; and director) *Modern Romance,* Columbia, 1980.
(With Johnson) *Lost in America,* Geffen, 1985.
Defending Your Life, Warner Brothers, 1991.

Author of short films aired on *Saturday Night Live,* National Broadcasting Co. (NBC-TV), including *Hello from Albert,* 1975, and *The National Audience Research Test.* Recorded comedy albums, *Comedy Minus One,* ABC, 1973, and *A Star is Bought,* Electra-Asylum, 1975. Also contributor to *Esquire* magazine.

SIDELIGHTS: Albert Brooks is well-known for his frequent appearances on the *Tonight Show*—where he is a favorite of host Johnny Carson—and for his short, satiric films featured on *Saturday Night Live.* A *Time* critic once described Brooks as the "smartest, most audacious comic since Lenny Bruce and Woody Allen" and noted that he "traffics not so much in jokes as wild ideas, bits of madhouse theatre." The critic added: "His material offers no snappy punch lines to repeat the next day at the office. Brooks makes comic epiphanies out of the giddy, gruesome excesses of popular culture."

Brooks began performing comedy at an early age. According to *People* reporter Cheryl McCall, "he came into the world a one-liner" when his parents named him Albert Einstein. The son of singer Thelma Leeds and Greek-dialect comedian Harry Einstein (who performed on radio as Parkyarkarkas), Brooks grew up in a household devoted to comedy. "Obviously, there was a lot of shtick going on in our house," he told McCall. "I was the class clown, the school clown, the city clown, the clown of the year. I guess many people thought of me as a clown." By the time he was in the fifth grade Brooks was getting laughs with his interpretive readings of the daily class announcements.

At age fifteen Brooks formed his first comedy act, a brief partnership with comedian Joey Bishop's son Larry. When the duo split up Brooks got a job as a radio sports-writer, but he did not abandon his comedic urge—as *Time* reported, he "made up most of the baseball scores." Brooks next moved to television, writing for the comedy series *Turn On,* and when the show was canceled after the first episode he began performing his own material. "Even when he first started appearing on national TV he displayed startling self-confidence," *Time* stated. "He almost never auditioned any of his material before friends or tried it out, like most other comedians, in small clubs. . . . Even today, Brooks seldom repeats a routine."

Brooks's spontaneity has won the attention of critics such as William Wolfe, who praised the comedian's work for its "freshness and intelligence." Lamenting what he feels is the depressingly low level of comedy today, Wolf placed his hope for the future of comedy on Brooks and other "dedicated comedy-filmmakers who have high aspirations and can bring their vision of what's funny to the screen." Wolf further commented that "based on [his] apparent capacity for artistic growth," Brooks "may answer at least some of our need for laughter."

Brooks is known for a finely honed satiric style, a style evident in his first feature-length film *Real Life.* It parodies the *cinema verite* style of filmmaking typified by the Public Broadcasting Service (PBS) documentary series *An American Family.* (A chronicle of a year in the life of an average American family, the series was widely criticized as an insensitive invasion of privacy.) In *Real Life* Brooks portrays the director of a film crew that moves into a Phoenix household to record the daily interactions of veterinarian William Yaeger and his family. Crew members "pester these people mercilessly, and invade their privacy in a number of colorful ways," noted *New York Times* critic Janet Maslin. Cameramen film "their subjects from odd, unflattering angles and never allow them a moment's peace."

According to *Nation* reviewer Robert Hatch, the underlying thesis of Brooks's *Real Life* is that "anthropological TV, which also has an entertainment ax to grind, not only distorts but disastrously traumatizes the objects of its 'scientific' investigation." Quoted by Gene Siskel of the *Chicago Tribune,* Brooks explained: "I guess the point of the movie is to say that if you let a film crew interview you, you've given up most of your rights. And if you let them into your house, forget it. The idea that a camera can unobtrusively record the truth is absurd."

Although *Real Life* was enthusiastically received by critics, Siskel noted that the film was "much less than a smash" at the box office. "The problem Paramount has," Siskel said, "is explaining Albert Brooks's comic mind.

It's not easy. He is not a hit-yourself-in-the-head-with-a-beer-can comedian." Maslin echoed that view, describing the style of *Real Life* as "deadpan and sly, so sly that some viewers may not find it comic at all." *Time* critic Frank Rich insisted that *Real Life* was not "designed as a hoot." Instead, he called it a "scrupulously honest satire . . . that sacrifices compulsive jokiness in the effort to reveal the nasty truth." Rich praised Brooks for "refusing to pander to the crowd," a quality he feels "puts a healthy distance" between Brooks and many of his filmmaking contemporaries.

Modern Romance, Brooks's second film, details the rocky relationship of a fictitious Los Angeles film editor, Robert Cole, and his girlfriend, Mary Harvard. The film begins with the couple's break-up. Robert (played by Brooks) asks Mary, "You've heard of a no-win situation, haven't you? Vietnam . . . us?" from that point, *Modern Romance* follows Robert through post-break-up depression and his obsession with winning Mary back.

In his review of *Modern Romance,* Siskel pointed out that "the characters . . . will make some people furious. It is difficult to understand how Mary could continue to see Robert, who is so thoroughly annoying." *New York*'s David Denby wrote: "Brooks shows us that Robert is a coercive, self-pitying little whiner; what he doesn't show us is why Mary puts up with this jabbering neurotic for a single minute." Not all critics were as harsh in their assessment of the film. Carrie Rickey's *Village Voice* review of *Modern Romance* lauded Brooks's artful handling of "desultory conversation" and commonplace scenes. "In Brooks's hands," she said, "the ephemera of everyday life is so relentlessly revealed in all its dopey boredom that its laughable—not belly laughs, mind you, but nonstop chortles." She described Robert as having "schleppy appeal" and she noted that "Brooks's on-screen personality is perfectly matched by the straightfaced humor" of the film. William Wolf called *Modern Romance* a "leap forward" from Brooks's *Real Life,* finding the later film better disciplined and more controlled. He wrote that Brooks "subjugates his ego to the needs of a scene" and added that this work in *Modern Romance* indicates Brooks's "obvious potential for directing films in which he does not appear."

Brooks's follow-up to *Modern Romance* was 1985's *Lost in America. Lost in America* chronicles a yuppie couple's mid-life crisis. David and Linda Howard have all the material trappings of success and upward mobility, yet ride an emotional see-saw of apathy and angst. When David is passed over for a much-anticipated promotion, his knee-jerk response is to drop out. He and Linda sell everything, buy a Winnebago, and set off for adventure on the open road to the tune of *Born to Be Wild.* The couple's cross-country odyssey is part farce, part nightmare. After a number of calamities befall them, the Howards discover their dream life to be as frustrating as the fast-paced existence they'd left behind (largely due to the fact their 'executive training' did not prepare them for the baser realities of everyday living).

Brooks elicited praise from critics for his portrayal of a manic over-achiever with nothing left to achieve. "Brooks has created a fine vehicle with which to strut his comic strengths. Whether expressing joy, fury or horror, he always seems on the verge of going a tad too far, and we eagerly await the moment when his respectable-looking character will cross the line into uncontrolled dementia," observed Clay Warnick in the *Washinton Post. Los Angeles Times* critic Patrick Goldstein concurred, noting "Brooks turns his comic energies on his favorite target—himself—painting an agonizingly accurate portrait of a man imprisoned in his own fantasies." A reviewer for the *Washington Post* found the enjoyment of *Lost in America* to be its "sheer reality" where "the funniest stories are the true ones," a sentiment reiterated by *Newsweek* reviewer David Ansen when he wrote of Brooks that "few comics cut so close to the bone of daily life, and that's to be cherished."

Brooks took a break from writing and directing in 1987 to co-star in James Brooks's (no relation) award-winning film *Broadcast News.* On one level a behind-the-scenes look at the daily workings of a Washington network news bureau, the film also examines a professional/romantic triangle involving three newspeople. Brooks plays Aaron Altman, described by Pauline Kael of the *New Yorker* as "the near-genius who doesn't know how to use what he knows." Aaron, an ace writer and researcher, is in love with his best friend, producer Jane Craig. Jane isn't sure how she feels, a situation made even more complicated by the arrival of Tom Grunick, an aspiring anchorman long on looks and short on brains. To Aaron, Tom is little more than a smooth operator, an opportunist both at work and at love. As Tom begins to learn more about the news business (and Jane), Aaron must deal with his own feelings of jealousy, anger, and loneliness.

Director Brooks leaves the resolution of the triangle ambiguous, focussing largely on the trials and tribulations Jane, Tom, and Aaron undergo in the workplace each day and how these experiences are symptomatic of a profession where surface reality is everything. Jane handles the pressures of her job by rigidly scheduling all phases of her day (including solitary crying jags). Tom, good with the camera, must learn how to project a knowledge of events he doesn't have. Aaron, for all his quick wit, intelligence, and desire to be a network anchor, falls apart when finally given the chance to sub on a national news broadcast, causing a technician to exclaim: "This is more than Nixon ever sweated."

Many critics viewed the role of Aaron to be tailor-made for Brooks, an idea the comedian acknowledged when he claimed: "There's a lot of *me* in Aaron Altman." Brad Darrach of *People* magazine noted that "Jim Brooks . . . shaped the character of Aaron the untelegenic to fit Albert like a body stocking. They're both brilliant, loveable, workaholic, funny peculiar, and, above all, funny ha-ha." Kael felt Brooks "gives the picture its bit of soul," and that "when he's at his most desperate, he's funniest." Brooks spent a great deal of time with reporters, researching and preparing for the part. Ansen commended Brooks on his ability to 'flesh out' the role, calling Aaron the "best part of his career . . . [Brooks is] an actor who paints in bold, clean colors—usually to portray grating monomaniacs. Here he shows his full pallette . . . His Aaron is a brainy, competitive bulldog, but behind the zingers lies a sea of insecurity."

The three *Broadcast News* leads garnered Academy Award nominations, Brooks for Best Supporting Actor. At the time, he jested: "If the others had gotten nominated and I didn't, I would have killed myself." Brooks didn't win, but that didn't sour him on the movie business. After *Broadcast News,* Brooks wrote and directed a new film of his own entitled *Defending Your Life.* Ostensibly the story of a Los Angeles ad executive's adventures in the afterlife, *Defending Your Life* also functions as a multi-faceted satire whose targets include idealized love, middle-class comforts, and New Age thinking. In the Brooks universe, death means a trip to Judgement City, a sort of "Club Dead" where the freshly dead wait to defend themselves in wacky court proceedings reminiscent of *This Is Your Life.* Brooks arrives in Judgement City courtesy of an accident between his BMW and a bus. Once there, he finds that his quest to become a "full citizen of the universe" is hampered by the less-than-stellar way in which he led his life.

Stanley Kauffmann of the *New Republic* found *Defending You Life* a disappointment, noting that the film is "an afterlife opus that adds zero to the field. . . . As for Brooks, down to earth, next time I hope. Earthier and funnier." The film fared better with Stuart Klawans of *The Nation.* Klawans termed the film "droll and uproarious." He added: "Brooks wants to send the folks home happy. He still refuses to talk down to the Little Brains in his audience. . . . He can manage to be life-affirming without turning stupid." "Brooks asks us to banish the cha-cha-cha beat of conventional comedy from mind and bend to a slower rhythm," noted Richard Schickel of *Time.* "His pace is not that of a comic standing up at a microphone barking one-liners, but of an intelligent man sitting down by the fire mulling things over. And in this case offering us a large slice of angel food for thought."

Defending Your Life exemplified Brooks's ability to view life (and death) as stressful, complicated, and ultimately very funny. According to Pete Travers of *Rolling Stone,* the prototypal Brooks character "makes anxiety a way of life." Brooks's strength lies in making such characters oddly endearing, if not overly sympathetic. In analyzing Brooks's success, Schickel mused, "Albert Brooks seems to be a very rational fellow. His screen character is typically a man who listens attentively to other people, does not demand too much of them (or life), and is always amenable to compromise should a conflict arrive. No wonder a faint air of depression surrounds his movies. Reasonable behavior is not a quality likely to get you far at this late date in this unreasonable century."

BIOGRAPHICAL/CRITICAL SOURCES:

PERIODICALS

Chicago Tribune, July 23, 1979; April 3, 1981.
Esquire, February, 1971.
Los Angeles Times, March 3, 1985.
Nation, April 22, 1991.
New Republic, March 31, 1979; April 22, 1991.
Newsweek, March 12, 1979; March 30, 1981; February 25, 1985; December 28, 1987.
New Yorker, January 11, 1988.
New York Times, March 2, 1979; March 13, 1981; February 2, 1985.
People, April 16, 1979; February 1, 1988; April 11, 1988.
Rolling Stone, April 30, 1981; April 4, 1991.
Time, August 4, 1975; March 5, 1979; December 14, 1987; March 25, 1991.
Village Voice, March 18, 1981.
Washington Post, March 22, 1985.

*   *   *

ENCEL, Sol
   See ENCEL, Solomon

*   *   *

ENCEL, Solomon 1925-
   (Sol Encel)

PERSONAL: Born in 1925, in Warsaw, Poland; son of G. and Ethel (Kutner) Encel; married Diana Helen Hovev (a research assistant), June 23, 1949; children: Vivien, Deborah, Daniel, Sarah. *Education:* University of Melbourne, B.A., 1949, M.A., 1952, Ph.D., 1960.

ADDRESSES: Office—Department of Sociology, University of New South Wales, P.O. Box 1, Kensington, New South Wales 2033, Australia.

CAREER: University of Melbourne, Parkville, Australia, lecturer in political science, 1952-55; Australian National University, Canberra, senior lecturer, 1956-62, reader in political science, 1962-66; University of New South Wales, Kensington, Australia, professor, 1966-90, professor emeritus of sociology, 1990—. Visiting fellow at Harvard University, 1960, and University of Sussex, 1968, 1973, and 1978. Radio broadcaster. Member of administrative research committee of New South Wales Public Service Board, 1975-78; member of Australian Science and Technology Council, 1975; member of New South Wales Education Commission, 1980-83, and Higher Education Board, 1981-83; member of National Health and Medical Research Council, 1991—; honorary associate, Social Policy Research Centre, University of New South Wales, 1990—; consultant to Telecom Australia and Royal Commission on Australian Government Administration. *Military service:* Royal Australian Air Force, 1944-45.

MEMBER: Sociological Association of Australia and New Zealand (chairman, 1969-70).

WRITINGS:

Cabinet Government in Australia, Melbourne University Press, 1962, revised edition, 1974.
(Editor with A. F. Davies, M. Berry, and L. Bryson, and contributor) *Australian Society: Introductory Essays,* Longman Cheshire, 1965, 4th edition, 1980.
Equality and Authority, Tavistock Press, 1970.
(With M. Cass and C. Bullard) *Librarians: A Survey,* New South Wales University Press, 1972.
(With B. S. Buckley) *The New South Wales Jewish Community,* New South Wales University Press, 1972, revised edition, 1978.
(With N. MacKenzie and M. Tebbutt) *Women and Society,* Longman Cheshire, 1974.
(With P. Marstrand and W. Page) *The Art of Anticipation,* Martin Robertson, 1975.
(Editor with D. Horne and E. Thompson, and contributor; under name Sol Encel) *Change the Rules!,* Penguin, 1977.
(Editor with Colin Bell, and contributor) *Inside the Whale,* Pergamon, 1978.
(With C. Johnston) *Compensation and Rehabilitation,* New South Wales University Press, 1978.
(Editor with J. R. Ronayne) *Science, Technology, and Public Policy,* Pergamon, 1979.
(Editor with P. S. Wilenski and B. B. Schaffer, and contributor) *Decisions,* Longman Cheshire, 1981.
(Editor) *The Ethnic Dimension,* Allen & Unwin, 1981.
Technological Change: Some Case Histories (monograph), University of New South Wales, 1982.
(With N. K. Meaney and T. S. Matthews) *The Japanese Connection,* Longman Cheshire, 1988.

(With Dorothy Campbell) *Out of the Doll's House: Women in the Public Sphere,* Longman Cheshire, 1991.

Contributor to books, including *Automation and Unemployment,* Australian and New Zealand Association for the Advancement of Science, 1979, *The Uses and Abuses of Forecasting,* Macmillan, 1979, *Quarry Australia?,* Oxford University Press (Australia), 1982, *A Nation Apart,* Longman Cheshire, 1983, and *Technology, Work, and Industrial Relations,* Longman Cheshire, 1983. Also contributor to sociology journals.

SIDELIGHTS: Solomon Encel once told *CA:* "In the last six or seven years my main research interest has been the role of work in the life of the individual and the related problems of organizing work in contemporary industrial society. This links up with my interest in the status of women in technological change and in the problems of the future."

BIOGRAPHICAL/CRITICAL SOURCES:

PERIODICALS

Times Literary Supplement, April 9, 1976.

*   *   *

EXCELLENT, Matilda
   See FARSON, Daniel (Negley)

F

FABER, Adele 1928-

PERSONAL: Born January 12, 1928, in New York, NY; daughter of Morris (a furrier) and Betty (Kamay) Meyrowitz; married Leslie Faber (a guidance counselor), August 27, 1950; children: Carl, Joanna, Abram. *Education:* Queens College (now of City University of New York), B.A., 1949; New York University, M.A., 1950.

ADDRESSES: Home—351 I.U. Willets Rd., Roslyn Heights, NY 11577.

CAREER: New York School of Printing, New York City, teacher of speech, 1950-51; high school English teacher, Brooklyn, NY, 1952-58; Long Island University, C.W. Post College, Greenvale, NY, leader of parenting workshops, 1975-83. New School for Social Research, workshop instructor, 1976. Lecturer and consultant.

AWARDS, HONORS: Christopher Book Award, 1975, for *Liberated Parents/Liberated Children.*

WRITINGS:

(With Elaine Mazlish) *Liberated Parents/Liberated Children: Your Guide to a Happier Family,* Grosset, 1974.
(With Mazlish) *Breaking Barriers: A Workshop Series in Human Relations Skills for Teenagers,* Salvation Army, 1976.
(With Mazlish) *How to Talk So Kids Will Listen and Listen So Kids Will Talk,* Rawson Wade Publishers, 1980.
(With Mazlish) *How to Talk So Kids Will Listen* (Group Workshop Kit), Negotiation Institute, 1981.
(With Mazlish) *Siblings Without Rivalry: How to Help Your Children Live Together So You Can Live Too,* Norton, 1987.
(With Mazlish) *Siblings Without Rivalry* (Group Workshop Kit), Negotiation Institute, 1987.

Between Brothers and Sisters: A Celebration of Life's Most Enduring Relationship, Putnam, 1989.
(With Mazlish) *Bobby and the Brockles* (children's book), Avm, 1993.

TELEVISION SCRIPTS

Mr. Sad-Sack, ABC-TV, 1975.
The Princess, American Broadcasting Corp. Television (ABC-TV), 1975.
(With Mazlish) *How To Talk So Kids Will Listen Video Series,* Kentucky Educational Television (KET-TV), 1990.

OTHER

(With Mazlish) *How to Be the Parent You Always Wanted to Be* (audio cassettes and workbook), Hyperion, 1992.

SIDELIGHTS: Adele Faber comments: "As a child I remember wincing at the ways adults spoke to children. It was generally accepted that if you loved your child it was alright to tell him what was wrong with him—loud and often. I knew exactly what doctor Haim Ginott [with whom she studied for ten years] meant when he said,'The children. . . no more scratches on their souls.' Yet as a parent I soon discovered that being 'nice' was not enough. It was the search for another way to live with children that launched me into writing *Liberated Parents/Liberated Children,* my subsequent books, and my present work with parents and teachers. I'm never bored. The question of how people can communicate more honestly and helpfully remains eternally fascinating to me."

FABRE, Michel J(acques) 1933-

PERSONAL: Born October 31, 1933, in Le Puy, France; son of Jean and Marcelle (Mazoyer) Fabre; married Genevieve Moreau (a university professor), July 13, 1960; children: Pierre, Jean-Marc. *Education:* University of London, diploma of international phonetics, 1958; Universite de Paris and Ecole Normale Superieure, licence d'anglais, 1955, D.E.S. d'anglais, 1956, agregation d'anglais, 1959, doctorat d'etudes americaines, 1970, diplome d'etudes approfondies d'anthropologie, 1976.

ADDRESSES: Home—12 Square Montsouris, 75014 Paris, France. *Office*—UER d'Anglais, 5 rue Ecole de Medecine, 75006 Paris, France. *Agent*—Ellen Wright, 20 rue Jacob, 75006 Paris, France.

CAREER: Wellesley College, Wellesley, MA, instructor in French, 1962-63; Harvard University, Cambridge, MA, instructor in French, 1963-64; University of Paris (X), Nanterre, France, assistant professor of English, 1964-69; University of Paris (VIII), Vincennes, France, associate professor of American studies, 1969-70; Universite de la Sorbonne Nouvelle of University of Paris (III), Paris, France, professor of American and Afro-American studies, 1970—, director of Afro-American Studies and Third World Literatures Center, 1973—. Adviser to Center for Southern Culture, University of Mississippi, 1979—. *Military service:* French Navy, 1959-62; interpreter and cipher officer; became lieutenant.

MEMBER: French Association of American Studies (A.F.E.A; secretary, 1969-75), French Association of English Studies, Association des Ecrivains de Langue Francaise, Association des Gens de Lettres, Societe d'Etude des Pays du Commonwealth.

AWARDS, HONORS: Anisfield-Wolf Award in Race Relations, 1973, for *The Unfinished Quest of Richard Wright;* MAWA Distinguished Writer Award; Officier des Palmes Academiques; honorary membership in Modern Language Association.

WRITINGS:

Les Noirs Americains, A. Colin, 1967.
The British Isles (geography text), Europe Editions, 1968.
(With Wife, Genevieve Fabre, and Andre Le Vot) Bernard Poli, editor, *Francis Scott Fitzgerald,* A. Colin, 1969.
Esclaves et planteurs dans le Sud Americain au XIX siecle, Julliard, 1970.
(With Paul Orean) *Harlem, ville noire,* A. Colin, 1971.
(With others) *Guide de l'etudiant d'anglais,* Presses Universitaires de France, 1971.
The Unfinished Quest of Richard Wright, Morrow, 1973.
(Editor with Ellen Wright) *Richard Wright Reader,* Harper, 1978.

(With G. Fabre, William French, And Ameritjit Singh) *Afro-American Poetry and Drama,* Gale, 1979.
Richard Wright: A Primary Bibliography, G. K. Hall, 1983.
(Editor and contributor) *Ralph Ellison,* Universite Paul Valery, 1984.
La Rive Noire, Editions Lieu Commun, 1985.
The World of Richard Wright, University of Mississippi Press, 1985.
Richard Wright: Books and Writers, University of Mississippi Press, 1990.
From Harlem to Paris, University of Illinois Press, 1991.

Also author of introduction and notes for the bilingual edition of Richard Wright's, *L'Homme qui vivait sous terre,* Aubier, 1971. Contributor of reviews to *Le Monde, La Nouvelle Critique, Etudes Anglaises, Presence Africaine,* and to professional journals. Contributing editor of *New Letters,* 1972-75, *World Literature Written in English,* 1978—, *Melus,* 1978-80, *French-American Review,* 1979-83, and *Black Studies Journal,* 1984—.

WORK IN PROGRESS: A biography of Chester Himes; a work on the cultural production of New Orleans Creoles of color.

SIDELIGHTS: In addition to English and French, Michel J. Fabre speaks Spanish, German, and Portuguese. He has travelled throughout Europe, Australia, Africa, and the Caribbean. Fabre once told *CA* that his interest in Richard Wright and Afro-American writers made him "discover cultural relativity and new possibilities in cultural pluralism and world civilization."

*   *   *

FADERMAN, Lillian 1940-

PERSONAL: Born July 18, 1940, in Bronx, NY; daughter of Mary Lifton. *Education:* University of California, Berkeley, A.B., 1962; University of California, Los Angeles, M.A., 1964, Ph.D., 1967.

ADDRESSES: Office—Department of English, California State University, Fresno, CA 93740.

CAREER: California State University, Fresno, 1967—, associate professor, 1971-72, professor of English, 1973—, chairman of department, 1971-72, dean of School of Humanities, 1972-73, assistant vice-president of academic affairs, 1973-76; visiting professor, University of California, Los Angeles, 1989-91.

MEMBER: Modern Language Association of America, American Association of University Women.

WRITINGS:

(With Barbara Bradshaw) *Speaking for Ourselves: American Ethnic Writing,* Scott, Foresman, 1969, 2nd edition, 1975.

(Editor with Luis Omar Salinas) *From the Barrio: A Chicano Anthology,* Canfield Press, 1973.

(With Brigitte Eriksson) *Lesbian-Feminism in Turn-of-the-Century Germany,* Naiad Press, 1980, published as *Lesbians in Germany,* 1990.

Surpassing the Love of Men: Romantic Friendship and Love between Women from the Renaissance to the Present, Morrow, 1981.

Scotch Verdict, Morrow, 1983.

Odd Girls and Twilight Lovers: A History of Lesbian Life in Twentieth Century America, Columbia University Press, 1991.

Contributor of articles to journals, including *Massachusetts Review, New England Quarterly, Journal of Popular Culture, Conditions, Signs, Journal of Homosexuality,* and *Journal of the History of Sexuality.*

SIDELIGHTS: Lillian Faderman's *Surpassing the Love of Men: Romantic Friendship and Love between Women from the Renaissance to the Present* "is a comprehensive and illuminating study of women's struggles to live and love as they please," Phyllis Grosskurth indicates in *New York Review of Books.* Three periods of life and literature are examined in the book, the sixteenth through the eighteenth centuries, the nineteenth century, and the twentieth century, according to Benjamin DeMott in *Atlantic Monthly,* and it concerns both sexual and nonsexual woman-to-woman relationships.

Carolyn G. Heilbrun says in *New York Times Book Review* that, throughout *Surpassing the Love of Men,* Faderman demonstrates that, "except when women preempted male power or tried to pass as men, they were usually, until quite recently, left free to love one another." Faderman's "quite thorough scholarship" indicates that "the Lesbian did not even exist in Europe until the 1880s and in the United States until 1910," Joanna Russ points out in *Washington Post Book World.* "Love between women, which did exist, was unlike Lesbianism in being socially honored, not secretive, and extremely common." Keith Walker says in *Times Literary Supplement* that Faderman "stumbled over this not startlingly original version of events when she was reading Emily Dickinson's love poems and letters to Sue Gilbert," the woman who later became her sister-in-law, "and noticed that Dickinson showed no 'guilt' and moreover that her niece, editing the letters early in this century, felt obliged to bowdlerize them."

Most critics find *Surpassing the Love of Men* praiseworthy. Heilbrun describes the book as "a welcome and

needed history" and states that "its account of women loving women before the 20th century is invaluable." Walker, however, objects to "the cosy glow engendered by the belief that lesbian relationships are finer, more enduring, and more satisfying than heterosexual ones." Grosskurth, in agreement, believes that probably "many such relationships exist, but by investing them all with a romantic coloration, [Faderman] never considers the tensions, irritations, or jealousy engendered by most close relationships." According to Russ, "At times she seems to say that sexism and the segregation of the sexes causes love between women, a confusingly negative view that contradicts her assertion of the normality (statistical and other) of such behavior."

"But despite my deep unease at some of these implicit assumptions," Grosskurth writes, "I think this is an important book; certainly one of the most significant contributions yet made to feminist literature." As DeMott comments, *Surpassing the Love of Men* remains "a work of genuine interest and value. Its pages are filled with vivid portraits of heroes and heroines struggling to lead their contemporaries out of delusion on sex and gender matter, and with astonishingly fresh disclosures about details of sexist feeling from age to age."

BIOGRAPHICAL/CRITICAL SOURCES:

PERIODICALS

Atlantic Monthly, March, 1981.
New York Review of Books, May 28, 1981.
New York Times Book Review, April 5, 1981.
Times Literary Supplement, September 4, 1981; September 23, 1983.
Washington Post Book World, May 3, 1981.

*　　　*　　　*

FARMER, Penelope (Jane) 1939-

PERSONAL: Born June 14, 1939, in Westerham, Kent, England; daughter of Hugh Robert MacDonald and Penelope (Boothby) Farmer; married Michael John Mockridge (a lawyer), August 16, 1962 (divorced, 1977); married Simon Shorvon (a neurologist), January 20, 1984; children: (first marriage) Clare Penelope, Thomas. *Education:* St. Anne's College, Oxford, Degree in History (with second-class honors), 1960; Bedford College, London, Diploma in Social Studies, 1962; doctoral study at Keele University, 1988—. *Politics:* Centre left. *Avocational interests:* Reading, walking, travelling, cinema, listening to music, opera.

ADDRESSES: Home—30 Ravenscourt Rd., London W6 0UG, England. *Agent*—Deborah Owen, 78 Narrow St., London E14, England.

CAREER: Writer. Teacher for London County Council Education Department, 1961-63, sociological researcher, 1985-90.

MEMBER: Society of Authors, PEN.

AWARDS, HONORS: American Library Association notable book, 1962, and Carnegie Medal commendation, 1963, both for *The Summer Birds.*

WRITINGS:

ADULT NOVELS

Standing in the Shadow, Gollancz, 1984.
Eve: Her Story, Gollancz, 1985, Mercury House, 1988.
Away from Home: A Novel in Ten Episodes, Gollancz, 1987.
Glasshouses, Gollancz, 1988, Trafalgar Square, 1989.

CHILDREN'S BOOKS

The China People, illustrated by Pearl Falconer, Hutchinson, 1960.
The Summer Birds, illustrated by James J. Spanfeller, Harcourt, 1962, revised edition, Dell, 1985.
The Magic Stone, illustrated by John Kaufmann, Harcourt, 1964.
The Saturday Shillings, illustrated by Prudence Seward, Hamish Hamilton, 1965, published as *Saturday by Seven,* Penguin, 1978, revised edition, Dell, 1986.
The Seagull, illustrated by Ian Ribbons, Hamish Hamilton, 1965, Harcourt, 1966.
Emma in Winter, illustrated by Spanfeller, Harcourt, 1966.
Charlotte Sometimes, illustrated by Chris Connor, Harcourt, 1969, revised edition, Dell, 1985.
Daedalus and Icarus (picture book), illustrated by Connor, Harcourt, 1971.
Dragonfly Summer, illustrated by Tessa Jordan, Hamish Hamilton, 1971, Scholastic Book Services, 1974.
The Serpent's Teeth: The Story of Cadmus (picture book), illustrated by Connor, Collins, 1971, Harcourt, 1972.
A Castle of Bone, Atheneum, 1972.
The Story of Persephone (picture book), illustrated by Graham McCallum, Collins, 1972, Morrow, 1973.
William and Mary, Atheneum, 1974.
Heracles, illustrated by McCallum, Collins, 1975.
August the Fourth, illustrated by Jael Jordon, Heinemann, 1975, Parnassus, 1976.
Year King (young adult novel), Atheneum, 1977.
The Coal Train, illustrated by William Bird, Heinemann, 1977.
(Editor) *Beginnings: Creation Myths of the World,* illustrated by Antonio Frasconi, Chatto & Windus, 1978, Atheneum, 1979.
(Translator with Amos Oz) Oz, *Soumchi,* illustrated by William Papas, Harper, 1980.

The Runaway Train, illustrated by Bird, Heinemann, 1980.
Thicker Than Water, Walker, 1989.
Stone Croc, Walker, 1991.

OTHER

Also author of short stories and of television and radio scripts, including *The Suburb Cuckoo,* 1961. Contributor of book reviews to the *Times Literary Supplement* and the *New York Times.*

WORK IN PROGRESS: An adult novel.

SIDELIGHTS: Penelope Farmer presents a mixture of fantasy and reality through the settings, moods, and characters which fill her young adult works. She uses dreams and magic to structure her writings and to advance her themes of identity, development, and the nature of reality. Juxtaposed between a world of fantasy and a world of reality, her characters gain important insights which they are able to apply to their everyday lives. In this way, Farmer writes what are known as "introvert" fantasies, for most of the action takes place inside her characters' minds and her novels often have personal origins. In addition to her fantasy novels for adolescents and mythical legends for young readers, Farmer has also created adult novels which present women protagonists struggling to overcome sexual conflicts. Margaret K. McElderry asserts in *Elementary English* that Farmer constructs "books that cannot be predicted, that become part of the living literature of a period, that offer readers new realms of experience and understanding, that reflect life from unexpected angles, illumine fascinating perspectives, and leave the reader with a heightened sense of wonder and expectation." And Linda Brandon maintains in *Books* that Farmer's "writing is both strong and delicate and can be explosive, leaving its shards lodged uncomfortably in the imagination."

Farmer was born in Kent, just outside London, the second of twin girls. "Apart from being a twin, which in most people's eyes makes you slightly freaky, we had a normal English middle-class childhood," recalls Farmer. She progressed from a private prep school to a private boarding school, the only notable event being the six months she spent in bed at the age of eight when she contracted tuberculosis. "I suppose it was there that I started to read as voraciously as I have always done since," suggests Farmer. "In fact," she continues, "I spent the greater part of my childhood alone, indoors and reading, being described variously as solitary or antisocial, according to prejudice or lack of it."

Farmer reveals that she initially wanted to be an artist, and she expressed herself through illustrations rather than words. "But I have always written too," she adds, "beginning with unfinished sagas about rabbits and so forth." While attending college, and after, Farmer tried a variety of jobs, including teaching and waitressing, without much success. Meanwhile, she gave up drawing, but continued writing, and had her first stories published while still in school. *The China People* was published in England in 1960, and it was on the strength of these stories that Harcourt commissioned Farmer to write a children's book. "I've gone on from there," comments Farmer, "the books growing up as I've grown up, painfully. . . . What I'm writing now—or about to write—sits on a line between adult and children's fiction."

The Summer Birds, Farmer's first published novel, came from a short story that had originally been written for inclusion in *The China People*. It involves two sisters, Charlotte and Emma, and an unusual boy who teaches them how to fly. The other children in school are also eventually taught, and they spend their summer secretly enjoying the elation of flight. They do not discover who the boy is until fall is upon them, and when they do, he must leave and the children lose their ability to fly. "The whole book is about the onceness of experience," maintains Hugh Crago in *Signal*, adding that "innocence, the openness to new experience, can only happen once, and it cannot be prolonged." *The Summer Birds* is "a fantasy unusual in sustained mood and quiet style," describes *Bulletin of the Center for Children's Books* reviewer Zena Sutherland; and *New York Times Book Review* contributor Ethna Sheehan agrees, concluding that "it is atmosphere, mood and human reactions that make the story so extraordinarily moving."

The characters of Charlotte and Emma reappear in two of Farmer's subsequent novels, *Emma in Winter* and *Charlotte Sometimes*. "Charlotte and Emma are very much based on my mother and her sister as little girls," explains Farmer. "They were rather in the same situation, with no parents and having to be everything to each other. One of them was very much the responsible one and protected her sister, who was rather difficult. Emma and Charlotte have grown in their own ways and aren't exactly based on my mother and her sister now, but this is where it started."

Emma in Winter is a sequel to *The Summer Birds*, and relates the developing friendship between Emma and Bobby, two minor characters from the first novel. When they discover they are both experiencing the same dream, in which they gradually fly backwards in time, the bond is strengthened and the dreams become the most vibrant part of their lives. Through the dreams, Emma and Bobby eventually reach the beginning of time, where a barrage of images erupt before their eyes, climaxing with phantom replicas of themselves. The children reject the phantoms, and choose to return to reality. "In *Emma in Winter* the

focus is narrow, the development internal," remarks a *Virginia Kirkus' Service* contributor. "The author displays her usual wizardry at evoking sensations, but youngsters are likely to become impatient with the psychological unravelling of Emma and Bobby long before the end." Margery Fisher, though, concludes in *Growing Point* that Farmer "brilliantly" sustains "the emotions of children in a dream-sequence" through her "elegant, rhythmic style."

With *Charlotte Sometimes*, Farmer once again presents a character caught between the everyday world and a world of fantasy, searching for her identity. Charlotte, a main character from *The Summer Birds*, is away at boarding school when she discovers she is able to travel through time and change places with Clare, who lived in 1918. The two girls begin alternating places in their daily lives, and eventually appear to be trapped in the wrong time periods. Charlotte fears that she will soon forget that she is not really Clare, and struggles to keep her identity intact. "The book is well-found in every respect," points out Fisher, adding: "The prose is grave, flexible and rich in texture, the social and domestic detail sharp and fascinating; the moments of terror and affection are given their full value. Above all, here is a dream-allegory which teaches not through statement but through feeling." *Charlotte Sometimes* "is a book of quite exceptional distinction," concludes *Christian Science Monitor* contributor Neil Millar. Farmer "has built a haunting, convincing story which comes close to being a masterpiece of its kind."

Like Farmer's previous novels, *A Castle of Bone* also incorporates many of the conventions of the standard two-world fantasy. Hugh, his sister Jean, Penn, and his sister Anna, discover a magic cupboard—when an object is placed in it, it is reduced to its original form. Thus, matches are turned into a fir tree, and a sweater becomes a bundle of wool. The cupboard also transports the four children to a fantasy world which is dominated by a large castle. Hugh, the owner of the cupboard, is drawn to the castle of bone each night through what he believes are his dreams. In the meantime, Penn is shut in the cupboard by Anna and transformed into an infant, and the other children must learn how to change him back. During Hugh's third trip to the fantasy world, he finds himself inside the castle with Jean. They watch as Anna holds her infant brother over a vessel of fire, and it is only when Jean spurns him with a pin that Hugh chooses to stop Anna. As the tension of the moment fades, the children return to reality through the cupboard and Penn is restored to his normal age.

Throughout *A Castle of Bone* Farmer uses a variety of mythological symbols and images to relate her theme, which is that of an adolescent's first glimmer of mortality. The children are haunted by the realization that the cupboard can provide eternal life, and when Hugh stops Anna from burning Penn he stops her from giving him just this, thus choosing mortality and destroying the magic of the cupboard. "In a most original way the story explores the 'shut-offness' of adolescents, their spasmodic panic at being isolatedly 'themselves,' their reactions to an unforeseeable world. Fantasy rarely probes reality as deeply as this," describes C. S. Hannabuss in *Children's Book Review*. And *New York Times Book Review* contributor Doris Orgel declares that "the story bursts forth like a torrent, sweeping one along. In fact, a rarer category than fantasy or dream novel comes to mind: Necessary writing. What a writer 'must write—or burst,' as C. S. Lewis said; what readers' lives are changed by."

In 1984, Farmer's writing crossed the line between young adult and adult fiction with the publication of *Standing in the Shadow*. Her second novel for adults, *Eve, Her Story*, was published the following year and re-examines the Garden of Eden myth from Eve's point of view. Farmer makes Eve the narrator of the story and endows her with feminist qualities—she chooses to eat the fig of knowledge, well aware of the consequences. *Eve, Her Story* "is original, well-written and clever," remarks Antony Beevor in *Books and Bookmen*. "While in no sense a children's book," concludes *Times Educational Supplement* contributor Nicholas Tucker, "it could well become something of a cult novel drawing as it does on what is surely one of the most haunting stories from our mythological past." With *Glasshouses*, published in 1989, Farmer presents another strong feminist character. A farmer's daughter, Grace rebels when she runs away to London and her future husband, a gifted but careless glassblower. He abandons her, though, when she becomes pregnant, and Grace eventually takes his place and establishes her own glasshouse. She also acquires a lover when a young man, Terry, becomes her apprentice. Soon after, Grace hears the voice of Betsy, a bitter ghost who strengthens Grace's resolve against oppressive and domineering men. "Farmer's skilful blending of magic and realism bewitches us into believing in the myths that haunt her bleak modern parable about sexual politics," comments Brandon. "The most disturbing and also the richest of her novels to date, *Glasshouses* shows her to be an impressive alchemist of style."

Farmer returned to the young adult audience in 1989 with *Thicker Than Water*, continuing her examination of human interaction through another young boy and girl. When Will is orphaned, his Aunt Maggie takes him in, causing numerous problems for his spoiled cousin Becky both at home and at school. The two cousins alternately narrate the story, and the supernatural element enters into it when they are exploring an abandoned lead mine. From that point on, Will is haunted by a voice pleading for help,

which he eventually discovers is the spirit of a young boy left to suffocate in the mines in the nineteenth century. When the bones are found and properly buried, the haunting stops, the whole incident bringing Will and Becky closer together. "The alternation of narrators . . . is skillfully handled with virtually no overlap and no hiatus either. The doubled insight this affords nudges the reader's empathy left and right to maintain and yet balance response," explains a *Junior Bookshelf* contributor. "Intensity of feeling and a sharp description of ordinary places and objects combine in a novel in which the interaction of human personality is enhanced and illuminated by a similar interaction of real and unreal," summarizes a *Growing Point* reviewer.

Farmer prefers writing about the unreal because she finds it more absorbing than the real world, and believes it ultimately uncovers more about human nature. "I think the reactions you describe in fancy are more revealing and interesting—often not only of the characters, but of people in general in an ordinary world—than more realistic situations could ever be, at least any that I could describe; just as, say, a poetic image says far more, often, than a direct statement," she explains. Through her blend, then, of reality and fantasy, Farmer reveals her characters along with her themes. "The world of childhood is made of the inextricable mixture of magic and reality," claims Marion R. Hewitt in *Junior Bookshelf*, "and it is because [Farmer] has captured this so completely and easily, that I feel she will take her place among the finest children's authors writing to-day."

BIOGRAPHICAL/CRITICAL SOURCES:

BOOKS

Arbuthnot, May Hill, and Zena Sutherland, *Children and Books,* 4th edition, Scott, Foresman, 1972.
Baskin, Barbara H., and Karen H. Harris, *Books for the Gifted Child,* Bowker, 1980.
Children's Literature Review, Volume 8, Gale, 1985.
De Montreville, Doris, and Elizabeth D. Crawford, editors, *Fourth Book of Junior Authors and Illustrators,* H. W. Wilson, 1978.
Fisher, Margery, *Who's Who in Children's Books: A Treasury of the Familiar Characters of Childhood,* Holt, 1975.
Moss, Elaine, editor, *Children's Books of the Year: 1974,* Hamish Hamilton, 1975.
Rees, David, *The Marble in the Water: Essays on Contemporary Writers of Fiction for Children and Young Adults,* Horn Book, 1980.
Something about the Author, Volume 40, Gale, 1985.

PERIODICALS

Booklist, June 1, 1976.

Books, July, 1988.
Books and Bookmen, July, 1985.
British Book News, June, 1984; September, 1985.
Bulletin of the Center for Children's Books, April, 1962; December, 1964; September, 1966; March, 1972; July-August, 1974; February, 1975.
Children's Book Review, October, 1972.
Children's Literature in Education, March, 1972; autumn, 1983.
Christian Science Monitor, November 6, 1969.
Elementary English, September, 1974.
Growing Point, September, 1965; November, 1966; November, 1969; December, 1971; September, 1972; January, 1973; January, 1975; May, 1976; May, 1990.
Horn Book, April, 1962; February, 1965; December, 1969; October, 1974; August, 1976; October, 1976.
Junior Bookshelf, December, 1962; January, 1963; August, 1965; April, 1967; December, 1969; August, 1971; February, 1973; December, 1980; February, 1990.
Kirkus Reviews, April 15, 1971; October 1, 1973.
Library Journal, December, 1987.
New Statesman, November 10, 1972.
New York Times Book Review, April 1, 1962; May 1, 1966; May 2, 1971; August 27, 1972; January 21, 1973; February 28, 1988; July 15, 1990.
Observer, April 22, 1984; June 12, 1988.
Publishers Weekly, August 26, 1974; November 13, 1987.
School Librarian, September, 1969; June, 1972.
School Library Journal, May, 1962; December, 1969; September, 1972; September, 1976.
Signal, May, 1975, pp. 81-90.
Times (London), May 5, 1987.
Times Educational Supplement, August 22, 1980; August 9, 1985.
Times Literary Supplement, April 27, 1984; June 21, 1985; July 24, 1987; July 8, 1988; November 24, 1989.
Village Voice, March 15, 1988.
Virginia Kirkus' Service, August 15, 1966.

—*Sketch by Susan M. Reicha*

*   *   *

FARSON, Daniel (Negley) 1927-
(Matilda Excellent)

PERSONAL: Born January 8, 1927, in London, England; son of Negley (a writer and foreign correspondent) and Eve (Stoker) Farson. *Education:* Cambridge University, B.A., 1950.

ADDRESSES: Home—Appledore, North Devonshire, England. *Agent*—Bill Hamilton, A.M. Heath, 79 St. Martin's Ln., London WC2, England.

CAREER: House of Commons, London, England, lobby correspondent, 1945-46; *Picture Post,* London, staff photographer, 1951-53; free-lance writer and photographer, 1954; British Merchant Navy, seaman, 1955; Documentary Television, London, television interviewer, 1956-64, with shows including "Farson's Guide to the British," 1959, "Farson in Australia," 1961, and "Time Gentlemen Please!," 1962; landlord of public house in Waterman's Arms, England, 1962-66; free-lance writer, 1964—. "The Dracula Business," BBC-TV, interviewer, 1974—; has created an art quiz for a local television station. *Military service:* U.S. Army Air Forces, 1947-48.

AWARDS, HONORS: Voted best television interviewer by British critics, 1960.

WRITINGS:

Jack the Ripper (nonfiction), M. Joseph, 1972.
Marie Lloyd and Music Hall, Staley, 1972.
(Editor) *Wanderlust,* White Lion Publishers, 1972.
Out of Step (autobiography), M. Joseph, 1972.
The Man Who Wrote Dracula (biography of his great-uncle, Bram Stoker), St. Martin's, 1975.
Vampires, Zombies, and Monster Men, Doubleday, 1975.
(Editor) *In Praise of Dogs* (stories), Harrap, 1976.
The Dan Farson Black and White Picture Show, Lemon Tree Press, 1976.
A Window on the Sea, M. Joseph, 1977.
The Hamlyn Book of Ghosts (juvenile), Hamlyn, 1978.
The Clifton House Mystery (juvenile), Arrow, 1978.
The Hamlyn Book of Horror, Hamlyn, 1979.
(Under pseudonym Matilda Excellent) *The Dog Who Knew Too Much,* Jay Landesman, 1979.
Curse, Hamlyn, 1980.
Transplant, Hamlyn, 1980.
Henry: An Appreciation of Henry Williamson, M. Joseph, 1982.
The Hamlyn Book of Monsters, Hamlyn, 1984.
A Traveller in Turkey, Routledge & Kegan Paul, 1985.
Turkey: Independent Traveller's Guide, Collins, 1988, revised edition, 1991.
Swansdowne, St. Martin's, 1986.
(Self-illustrated with photographs) *Soho in the Fifties,* M. Joseph, 1987.
(Self-illustrated with photographs) *Sacred Monsters,* Bloomsbury, 1988.
(Self-illustrated with photographs) *Escapades,* Bloomsbury, 1989.
Gallery (based on his Art Tv Quiz for Channel 4), Bloomsbury, 1990.
(Self-illustrated with photographs) *Limehouse Days,* M. Joseph, 1991.
With Gilbert and George in Moscow, Bloomsbury, 1991.

UNPUBLISHED PLAYS

The Frighteners, BBC-TV, 1966.

The Marie Lloyd Story (two-act musical), produced in London at Theatre Royal, 1967.

The Funniest Man in the World (two-act musical), produced at Theatre Royal, 1977.

Clifton House Mystery (serial for children), ITV Britain, 1978.

OTHER

Also author of introduction, Negley Farson, *Caucasian Journey,* Penguin. Contributor to periodicals, including *Daily Telegraph, Telegraph Magazine,* and *Men Only.* Sunday *Mail,* television critic, 1983-84, art correspondent, 1990-91.

WORK IN PROGRESS: An account of his journey through Russia in August, 1991, during the coup, fulfilling the intentions of his father, Negley Farson, who described his own attempt at the same itinerary in 1929 in *Caucasian Journey,* for M. Joseph; *Convict,* "a big historical novel on a family who emigrate, and a convict who is transported, to Van Diemans Land (Tasmania) in the 1840s," for Arrow.

SIDELIGHTS: Daniel Farson told *CA:* "Though I was born in London, my father was an American foreign correspondent, and much of my childhood was spent in traveling abroad. At the age of seventeen I became the youngest-ever lobby correspondent in the House of Commons. I chose British nationality at the age of twenty-one, and went to Cambridge University, where I started my own magazine, *Panorma.* In 1962, an entertainment program, 'Time Gentlemen Please!,' led to my taking over a pub on the Isle of Dogs and started a boom in pub entertainment. At this time I lived on the River Thames at Limehouse, but in 1964 I resigned from television, gave up the pub, and went to live in North Devon to concentrate on writing. Today, I live in the fishing village of Appledore, in an old boat-house overlooking the water."

Farson adds: "After many vicissitudes I seem to have found my pace at last. This began with my series of books which were illustrated by my own photographs, starting with *Soho in the Fifties* which acquired a following and ran to several editions. This was followed by *Sacred Monsters, Escapades,* and *Limehouse Days.* Now my work is on the upturn with more recognition and, better still, grander advances. At last!"

BIOGRAPHICAL/CRITICAL SOURCES:

BOOKS

Farson, Daniel, *Out of Step* (autobiography), M. Joseph, 1972.

PERIODICALS

Times (London), June 10, 1982.
Times Literary Supplement, September 24, 1982.
Washington Post Book World, May 3, 1987, p. 6.

*   *   *

FERRIS, James Cody
    See McFARLANE, Leslie (Charles)

*   *   *

FISCHER, Edward (Adam) 1914-

PERSONAL: Born August 17, 1914, in Louisville, KY; son of Edward (a farmer) and Louise (Steinmetz) Fischer; married Mary Ewaniec (a television producer), April 10, 1939; children: John, Thomas. *Education:* University of Notre Dame, A.B., 1937, M.A., 1961. *Avocational interests:* Horsemanship, painting.

ADDRESSES: Home—1006 St. Vincent, South Bend, IN 46617. *Office*—Department of American Studies, University of Notre Dame, Notre Dame, IN 46656.

CAREER: News Times, South Bend, IN, reporter, 1936-38; *Herald Examiner,* Chicago, IL, reporter, 1938-39; St. Joseph's College, Rensselaer, IN, director of public relations, 1939-42; University of Notre Dame, Notre Dame, IN, faculty member, 1947—, currently professor emeritus of American Studies. *Military service:* U.S. Army, Infantry, 1942-46, 1950-51; became captain.

AWARDS, HONORS: Doctor of Letters (honoris causa), St. Joseph's College.

WRITINGS:

The Screen Arts, Sheed, 1960.
Film as Insight, Fides, 1971.
Why Americans Retire Abroad, Sheed, 1973.
Light in the Far East, Seabury, 1976.
Everybody Steals from God: Communication as Worship, University of Notre Dame Press, 1977.
Mindanao Mission: Archbishop Patrick Cronin's Forty Years in the Philippines, Seabury, 1978.
Mission in Burma: The Columban Fathers' Forty-three Years in Kachin Country, Seabury, 1980.
Fiji Revisited: A Columban Father's Memories of Twenty-eight Years in the Islands, Crossroad Publishing, 1981.
Maybe a Second Spring, Crossroad Publishing, 1983.
Japan Journey: The Columban Fathers in Nippon, Crossroad Publishing, 1984.
Journeys Not Regretted, Crossroad Publishing, 1985.
Life in the Afternoon, Paulist Press, 1987.

Notre Dame Remembered (autobiography), University of Notre Dame Press, 1987.

The Chancy War: China, Burma and India in World War II, Orion Books, 1991.

Also author of filmscripts *Shake Down the Thunder,* 1953, *Life without Germs,* 1956, *War on Gobbledygook,* 1964, *Elements of the Film,* 1965, The *Nature of the Film,* 1965, *Visual Language of Film,* 1965, *Film as Arts,* 1965, and *Poetry of Polymers,* 1967.

WORK IN PROGRESS: Designing a Life.

SIDELIGHTS: Edward Fischer told *CA:* "A half century ago, Professor John M. Cooney said to a class in writing at Notre Dame: 'Have something to say, say it, and be done with it!' He was aware that written words take the place of spoken words. He believed that writing should be more disciplined than speaking but not changed so much that the relationship is lost. He felt that if a piece of writing cannot be read aloud with some grace, it is probably artificial. To give a piece an easy-to-read, easy-to-understand, natural effect, one must rewrite again and again. The process gets harder as we grow older for with the years we become more conscious of what is good."

*　　　*　　　*

FISHER, Aileen (Lucia)　1906-

PERSONAL: Born September 9, 1906, in Iron River, MI; daughter of Nelson E. and Lucia (Milker) Fisher. *Education:* Attended University of Chicago, 1923-25; University of Missouri, B.J., 1927. *Avocational interests:* Woodworking, hiking, mountain climbing.

ADDRESSES: Home and office—505 College Ave., Boulder, CO 80302.

CAREER: Women's National Journalistic Register, Chicago, IL, director, 1928-31; Labor Bureau of the Middle West, Chicago, research assistant, 1931-32; free-lance writer, 1932—.

MEMBER: Women in Communications.

AWARDS, HONORS: Silver Medal from U.S. Treasury Department, World War II; American Library Association Notable Book of the Year, 1960, for *Going Barefoot,* 1961, for *Where Does Everyone Go?,* 1962, for *My Cousin Abe,* 1964, for *Listen, Rabbit,* 1965, for *In the Middle of the Night,* and 1966, for *Valley of the Smallest: The Life Story of a Shrew;* Western Writers of America Award for juvenile nonfiction, 1967, and Hans Christian Andersen Honor Book, 1968, both for *Valley of the Smallest: The Life Story of a Shrew;* award for children's poetry, National Council of Teachers of English, 1978.

WRITINGS:

The Coffee-Pot Face (Junior Literary Guild selection), McBride, 1933.

Inside a Little House, McBride, 1938.

Guess Again! (riddles), McBride, 1941.

Up the Windy Hill: A Book of Merry Verse with Silhouettes, Abelard, 1953.

Runny Days, Sunny Days: Merry Verses, Abelard, 1958.

I Wonder How, I Wonder Why, Abelard, 1962.

Cricket in a Thicket, Scribner, 1963.

In the Woods, in the Meadow, in the Sky, Scribner, 1965.

Out in the Dark and Daylight, Harper, 1980.

Rabbits, Rabbits, Harper, 1983.

My First Hanukkakh Book, Children's Press, 1985.

(With Jane Belk Moncure) *In Summer,* Children's World, 1985.

The House of a Mouse, Harper, 1988.

Wishes, DLM, 1990.

Her We Are Together, DLM, 1990.

Under the Open Sky, DLM, 1990.

Always Wondering, Harper, 1991.

JUVENILE; PUBLISHED BY THOMAS NELSON

That's Why (verse), 1946.

Off to the Gold Fields, 1955, published as *Secret in the Barrel,* Scholastic, 1965.

All on a Mountain Day (Junior Literary Guild selection), 1956, reprinted, Rod & Staff, 1971.

A Lantern in the Window, 1957.

Skip, 1958.

Fisherman of Galilee, 1959.

Summer of Little Rain (Junior Literary Guild selection), 1961.

My Cousin Abe, 1962.

JUVENILE; PUBLISHED BY ALLADIN

Over the Hills to Nugget, 1949.

Trapped by the Mountain Storm, 1950, reprinted, Rod & Staff, 1991.

Homestead of the Free: The Kansas Story, 1953.

Timber!: Logging in Michigan, 1955.

Cherokee Strip: The Race for Land, 1956.

JUVENILE; PUBLISHED BY CROWELL

Going Barefoot, 1960.

Where Does Everyone Go?, 1961.

Like Nothing at All, 1962.

I Like Weather, 1963.

Listen, Rabbit, 1964.

In the Middle of the Night, 1965.

Arbor Day, 1965.

Best Little House, 1966.

Valley of the Smallest: The Life Story of a Shrew, 1966.

(With Rabe) *Human Rights Day,* 1966.

Skip around the Year, 1967.
My Mother and I, 1967.
Easter, 1968, new edition, 1992.
We Went Looking (verse), 1968.
Up, up the Mountain, 1968.
In One Door and Out the Other: A Book of Poems, 1969.
Sing, Little Mouse (verse), 1969.
Clean as a Whistle (verse), 1969.
But Ostriches . . . (verse), 1970.
Jeanne d'Arc, 1970.
Feathered Ones and Furry (verse; Junior Literary Guild selection), 1971.
Do Bears Have Mothers, Too? (verse), 1973.
My Cat Has Eyes of Sapphire Blue (verse), 1975.
Once We Went on a Picnic (verse), 1975.
I Stood Upon a Mountain, 1979.
Anybody Home? (verse), 1980.
When It Comes to Bugs (verse), 1985.

JUVENILE; PUBLISHED BY BOWMAR/NOBLE

Animal Houses, 1972.
Animal Disguises, 1973.
Animal Jackets, 1973.
Now That Days Are Colder, 1973.
Tail Twisters, 1973.
Filling the Bill, 1973.
Going Places, 1973.
Sleepy Heads, 1973.
You Don't Look Like Your Mother, 1973.
No Accounting for Tastes, 1973.
Now That Spring Is Here, 1977.
And a Sunflower Grew, 1977.
Mysteries in the Garden, 1977.
Seeds on the Go, 1977.
Plant Magic, 1977.
Petals Yellow and Petals Red, 1977.
Swords and Daggers, 1977.
Prize Performance, 1977.
A Tree with a Thousand Uses, 1977.
As the Leaves Fall Down, 1977.

JUVENILE PLAYS

The Squanderbug's Christmas Carol, United States Treasury Department, 1943.
The Squanderbug's Mother Goose, United States Treasury Department, 1944.
A Tree to Trim: A Christmas Play, Row, Peterson, 1945.
What Happened in Toyland, Row, Peterson, 1945.
Nine Cheers for Christmas: A Christmas Pageant, Row, Peterson, 1945.
Before and After: A Play about the Community School Lunch Program, War Food Administration, 1945.
All Set for Christmas, Row, Peterson, 1946.

Here Comes Christmas!: A Varied Collection of Christmas Program Materials for Elementary Schools, Row, Peterson, 1947.
Witches, Beware: A Hallowe'en Play, Play Club, 1948.
Set the Stage for Christmas: A Collection of Pantomimes, Skits, Recitations, Readings, Plays and Pageants, Row, Peterson, 1948.
(Author of lyrics) *Christmas in Ninety-Nine Words,* with music by Rebecca Welty Dunn, Row, Peterson, 1949.
The Big Book of Christmas: A Collection of Plays, Songs, Readings, Recitations, Pantomimes, Skits, and Suggestions for Things to Make and Do for Christmas, Row, Peterson, 1951.
Health and Safety Plays and Programs, Plays, 1953.
Holiday Programs for Boys and Girls, Plays, 1953.
(With Rabe) *United Nations Plays and Programs,* Plays, 1954, 2nd edition, 1961.
(With Rabe) *Patriotic Plays and Programs,* Plays, 1956.
Christmas Plays and Programs, Plays, 1960.
Plays about Our Nation's Songs, Plays, 1962.
Bicentennial Plays and Programs, Plays, 1975.
Year-Round Programs for Young Players, Plays, 1985.

OTHER

(With Olive Rabe) *We Dickinsons: The Life of Emily Dickinson as Seen Through the Eyes of Her Brother Austin* (Junior Literary Guild selection), 1965.
(With Rabe) *We Alcotts: The Life of Louisa May Alcott as Seen Through the Eyes of 'Marmee'. . . ,* 1968.

Work appears in *Thirty Plays for Classroom Reading,* edited by Donald D. Durrell, Plays, 1965, and *Fifty Plays for Holidays,* edited by Sylvia E. Kamerman, Plays, 1969. Contributor to periodicals, including *Story Parade, Plays, Jack and Jill,* and *Child Life.*

SIDELIGHTS: The natural world figures prominently in Aileen Fisher's books for children. Her love of plants and animals is most evident in her poetry, where she speaks of the beauty and wonder of nature. Fisher has also written about religious subjects and holidays, as well as two biographies of famous authors.

Fisher was raised on a farm in Michigan's Upper Peninsula. The family house was big and square and set on forty acres. "We called the place High Bank," Fisher recalls, "because it was on a high bank above the river, which was always red with water pumped from the iron mines. Still, the river was good to wade in, swim in, fish in, and skate on in winter. When I was young there was still quite a bit of logging nearby, and my brother and I used to follow the iced logging roads. There was a big landing for the logs on the railroad about a mile from our house. We had all kinds of pets—cows, horses, and chickens. And we had a big garden in summer. I loved it. I have always loved the country."

After graduating from college and working for several years in Chicago, Fisher left the city for Colorado. She wanted to find a place in the country. "My aim in Chicago was to save every cent I was able to so that I could escape back to the country life I loved and missed," Fisher explains. In 1932, she and her friend, Olive Rabe, moved to Colorado and bought a 200-acre ranch in the foothills near Boulder, Colorado. The pair lived there for more than thirty years.

Fisher and Rabe collaborated on several books together, including a biography of poet Emily Dickinson, *We Dickinsons.* "Emily Dickinson has long been our favorite poet," Fisher tells *Junior Literary Guild,* "not only for her wonderful insights about nature, but for the depth of her searching thoughts about life and death, eternity and immortality. Our great devotion to this 'modern' poet of one hundred years ago led to the desire to know as much about her life as possible, and our reading and study in turn led us to want to make Emily Dickinson come alive to others."

Fisher now lives in the city of Boulder, "on a dead-end street at the foot of Flagstaff Mountain," she states. "Except for rabbits, I find more wildlife here at the edge of town than on the ranch; and I still enjoy many of the pleasures of country living, including what my neighbor calls a 'wild' yard. I like an organized life of peace and quiet, and so I avoid crowds, cities, noise, airports, neon lights, and confusion. My first and chief love in writing is writing children's verse."

Speaking to Lee Bennett Hopkins in *Language Arts,* Fisher explains: "I try to be at my desk four hours a day, from 8:00 a.m. to noon. Ideas come to me out of experience and from reading and remembering. I usually do a first draft by hand. I can't imagine writing verse on a typewriter, and for years I wrote nothing but verse so I formed the habit of thinking with a pencil or pen in hand. I usually rework my material, sometimes more, sometimes less. I *never* try out my ideas on children, except on the child I used to know—me! Fortunately I remember pretty well what I used to like to read, think about, and do. I find, even today, that if I write something I like, children are pretty apt to like it too. I guess what it amounts to is that I never grew up."

BIOGRAPHICAL/CRITICAL SOURCES:

BOOKS

Hopkins, Lee Bennett, *Books Are by People,* Citation Press, 1969.
Hopkins, Lee Bennett, *Pass the Poetry, Please,* Citation Press, 1972.

PERIODICALS

Elementary English, October, 1967.
Junior Literary Guild, September, 1965-April, 1966.
Language Arts, October, 1978.
New Yorker, December 14, 1968.
Young Readers' Review, November, 1968.

*   *   *

FISHER, Leonard Everett   1924-

PERSONAL: Born June 24, 1924, in the Bronx, NY; son of Benjamin M. and Ray M. (Shapiro) Fisher; married Margery M. Meskin (a school librarian), 1952; children: Julie Anne, Susan Abby, James Albert. *Education:* Attended Arts Students League, 1941, and Brooklyn College, 1941-42; Yale University, B.F.A., 1949, M.F.A., 1950.

ADDRESSES: Home and office—7 Twin Bridge Acres Rd., Westport, CT 06880.

CAREER: Painter, illustrator, author and educator. Graduate teaching fellow, Yale Art School, 1949-50; Whitney School of Art, New Haven, CT, dean, 1951-53; faculty member, Paier College of Art, 1966-78, academic dean, 1978-82, dean emeritus, 1982—, visiting professor, 1982-87; visiting professor, Case Western Reserve University, 1970; faculty member, Silvermine Guild School of the Arts, 1971; artist-in-residence, Hartford University School of Art, 1976; adjunct, Fairfield University, 1983-84, 1985, consultant, 1984; consultant, University of California, 1984. Designer of U.S. postage stamps for the U.S. Postal Service, 1972-77; design consultant, Postal Agent, Staffa and Bernera Islands, Scotland, 1979-82. Delegate National Association of Trade and Technical Schools Conference, Mexico City, 1978; delegate-at-large, the White House Conference on Library and Information Services, Washington, DC, 1979. Member, Arts Committee, Westport, CT, 1964; director, ex officio, Art Council of Greater New Haven, CT, 1968-70; honorary trustee, Westport Bicentennial Committee, 1975-76; trustee, Westport Historical Society, 1976; member of advisory board, Art Resources of Connecticut, 1977; member of acquisitions committee, Bicentennial Trust for Westport Art, 1977-78; member of Council for Continuing Education, Westport, 1977-79; trustee, Westport Public Library Board of Trustees, 1982-85, vice-president, 1985-86, president, 1986-89. Lecturer and speaker at art institutes, academic seminars, education workshops and children's book programs nationwide. *Military service:* U.S. Army, Corps of Engineers, 1942-46; became technical sergeant; participated in topographic mapping of five major campaigns in European and Pacific theatres.

EXHIBITIONS: One-man shows: Hewitt Gallery, NY; Bevier Gallery, Rochester Institute of Technology, NY; Silvermine Guild, CT; New Britain Museum (24-year retrospective), CT; Free Library of Philadelphia, PA; Rotunda Gallery, PA; Joseloff Gallery, University of Hartford Art School, CT; General Electric Corporation World Headquarters, CT; John Slade Ely House, CT; Mellon Gallery, Choate School, CT; Center for Financial Studies, Fairfield University, CT; Newport Beach Public Library, CA; Everson Museum, University of Syracuse, NY; Bluffton College, OH; New Britain Youth Museum, CT; Kimberly Gallery, New York, NY; Museum of American Illustration, Society of Illustrators (50-year retrospective), New York, NY; Homer Babbidge Library, University of Connecticut (50-year retrospective); and special mini-exhibitions (including Smithsonian Institution, and Fairview Park Library, OH) all from 1952 to the present. *Group shows:* Group exhibitions include Grand Central Galleries, NY; Brooklyn Museum, NY; Rockefeller Center, NY; Seligmann Galleries, NY; Eggleston Galleries, NY; Hewitt Gallery, NY; Whitney Museum, NY; Springfield Museum, MA; Pennsylvania State University, PA; National Academy (Audubon Artists), NY; New York Historical Society, NY; Hartford Art Festival, CT; Slater Memorial Museum, CT; Yale Art Gallery, CT; Hurlbut Gallery, Greenwich Public Library, CT; Wunsch Art Center, Glen Cove, NY; Atwood Library Gallery, Pelham Art Center, NY; Ariel Gallery, New York, NY, and many others, all from 1939 to the present. *Public collections:* Has had work exhibited in public collections throughout the United States.

MEMBER: PEN, Society of Children's Book Writers, Authors Guild, Silvermine Guild of Artists (trustee, 1970-74), New Haven Paint and Clay Club (president, 1968-70; trustee, 1968-74), Westport-Weston Arts Council (founding member; director, 1969-76, vice-president, 1972-73, president, 1973-74, board chairman, 1975-76), Society of Illustrators.

AWARDS, HONORS: William Wirt Winchester traveling fellowship, Yale University, 1949; Joseph Pulitzer scholarship in art, Columbia University and the National Academy of Design, 1950; American Institute of Graphic Arts outstanding textbooks, 1958, outstanding children's books, 1963; Ten Best Illustrated Books Award of *New York Times,* 1964, for *Casey at Bat;* New Haven Paint and Clay Club, Carle J. Blenner Prize for painting, 1968; premio grafico, Fiera di Bologna, 5a Fiera Internazionale del Libro per l'Infanzia e la Gioventu, Italy, 1968, for *The Schoolmasters;* Mayor's Proclamation: Leonard Everett Fisher Day, Fairview Park, OH, opening National Children's Book Week, November 12, 1978; New York Library Association/School Library Media Section Award for Outstanding Contributions in the Fields of Art and

Literature, 1979; Medallion of the University of Southern Mississippi for Distinguished Contributions to Children's Literature, 1979; Christopher Medal for illustration, 1981, for *All Times, All Peoples;* National Jewish Book Award for Children's Literature, and Association of Jewish Libraries Award for Children's Literature, both 1981, both for *A Russian Farewell;* nominee, Utah Children's Informational Book Award, 1987, runner-up, Kentucky Blue Grass Award, nominee, Sequoyah Children's Book Award (OK), nominee, Texas Blue Bonnet Award, nominee, William Allen White Children's Book Award, Emoria State University, all 1988, all for *The Great Wall of China;* Parenting's Reading Magic Award, Time-Life, 1988, for *Monticello;* Children's Book Guild/*Washington Post* Nonfiction Award, 1989; nominee, Orbis Pictus Award for Oustanding Nonfiction for Children, National Council Teachers of English, 1989, for *The White House;* Parents' Choice Award, 1989, for *The Seven Days of Creation;* Regina Medal, Catholic Library Association, 1991, for "lifetime distinguished contributions to children's literature"; Kerlan Award, University of Minnesota, 1991, for "singular attainments in the creation of children's literature."

WRITINGS:

ALL SELF-ILLUSTRATED

Pumpers, Boilers, Hooks and Ladders, Dial, 1961.
Pushers, Spads, Jennies and Jets, Dial, 1961.
A Head Full of Hats, Dial, 1962.
Two If by Sea, Random House, 1970.
Picture Book of Revolutionary War Heroes, Stockpole, 1970.
The Death of Evening Star: The Diary of a Young New England Whaler (ALA Notable Book), Doubleday, 1972.
The Art Experience, F. Watts, 1973.
The Warlock of Westfall, Doubleday, 1974.
Across the Sea and Galway, Four Winds, 1975.
Sweeney's Ghost, Doubleday, 1975.
Leonard Everett Fisher's Liberty Book, Doubleday, 1976.
Letters from Italy, Four Winds, 1977.
Noonan, Doubleday, 1978, Avon, 1981.
Alphabet Art: Thirteen ABCs from Around the World, Four Winds, 1979.
A Russian Farewell, Four Winds, 1980.
Storm at the Jetty, Viking, 1980.
The Seven Days of Creation (ALA Notable Book), Holiday House, 1981.
Number Art: Thirteen 1, 2, 3's from Around the World, Four Winds, 1982.
Star Signs, Holiday House, 1983.
Symbol Art: Thirteen Squares, Circles and Triangles from Around the World, Four Winds, 1984.
Boxes! Boxes!, Viking, 1984.

The Olympians: Great Gods and Goddessess of Ancient Greece, Holiday House, 1984.
The Statue of Liberty, Holiday House, 1985.
The Great Wall of China, Macmillan, 1986.
Ellis Island, Holiday House, 1986.
Calendar Art: Thirteen Days, Weeks, Months and Years from Around the World, Four Winds, 1987.
The Tower of London, Macmillan, 1987.
The Alamo, Holiday House, 1987.
Look Around: A Book about Shapes, Viking, 1987.
Monticello, Holiday House, 1988.
Pyramid of the Sun, Pyramid of the Moon, Macmillan, 1988.
Theseus and the Minotaur, Holiday House, 1988.
The Wailing Wall, Macmillan, 1989.
The White House, Holiday House, 1989.
Prince Henry the Navigator, Macmillan, 1990.
Jason and the Golden Fleece, Holiday House, 1990.
The Oregon Trail, Holiday House, 1990.
The ABC Exhibit, Macmillan, 1991.
Sailboat Lost, Macmillan, 1991.
Cyclops, Holiday House, 1991.
Galileo, Macmillan, 1992.
Tracks Across America: The Story of the American Railroad, 1825-1900, Holiday House, 1992.

THE "COLONIAL AMERICANS" SERIES

The Glassmakers, F. Watts, 1964.
The Silversmiths, F. Watts, 1964.
The Papermakers, F. Watts, 1965, reprinted, David Godine, 1986.
The Printers, F. Watts, 1965.
The Wigmakers, F. Watts, 1965.
The Hatters, F. Watts, 1965.
The Weavers, F. Watts, 1966.
The Cabinet Makers, F. Watts, 1966.
The Tanners, F. Watts, 1966, reprinted, David Godine, 1986.
The Shoemakers, F. Watts, 1967.
The Schoolmasters, F. Watts, 1967, reprinted, David Godine, 1986.
The Peddlers, F. Watts, 1968.
The Doctors, F. Watts, 1968, reprinted, David Godine, 1986.
The Potters, F. Watts, 1969.
The Limners, F. Watts, 1969.
The Architects, F. Watts, 1970.
The Shipbuilders, F. Watts, 1971.
The Homemakers, F. Watts, 1973.
The Blacksmiths, F. Watts, 1976.

"NINETEENTH CENTURY AMERICA" SERIES

The Factories, Holiday House, 1979.
The Railroads, Holiday House, 1979.

The Hospitals, Holiday House, 1980.
The Sports, Holiday House, 1980.
The Newspapers, Holiday House, 1981.
The Unions, Holiday House, 1982.
The Schools, Holiday House, 1983.

ADULT

Masterpieces of American Painting, Bison/Exeter, 1985.
Remington and Russell, W. H. Smith, 1986.

ILLUSTRATOR

Geoffrey Household, *The Exploits of Xenophon,* Random House, 1955, revised edition, Shoestring Press, 1989.
Florence Walton Taylor, *Carrier Boy,* Abelard, 1956.
Manley Wade Wellman, *To Unknown Lands,* Holiday House, 1956.
Roger P. Buliard, *My Eskimos: A Priest in the Arctic,* Farrar, Straus, 1956.
Richard B. Morris, *The First Book of the American Revolution,* F. Watts, 1956, revised edition published as *The American Revolution,* Lerner Publications, 1985.
L. D. Rich, *The First Book of New England,* F. Watts, 1957.
Kenneth S. Giniger, *America, America, America,* F. Watts, 1957.
Henry Steele Commager, *The First Book of American History,* F. Watts, 1957.
James C. Bowman, *Mike Fink,* Little, Brown, 1957.
Robert Payne, *The Splendor of Persia,* Knopf, 1957.
R. B. Morris, *The First Book of the Constitution,* F. Watts, 1958, revised edition published as *The Constitution,* Lerner Publications, 1985.
Jeanette Eaton, *America's Own Mark Twain,* Morrow, 1958.
Harry B. Ellis, *The Arabs,* World, 1958.
Robert Irving, *Energy and Power,* Knopf, 1958.
Estelle Friedman, *Digging into Yesterday,* Putnam, 1958.
E. B. Meyer, *Dynamite and Peace,* Little, Brown, 1958.
E. M. Brown, *Kateri Tekakwitha,* Farrar, Straus, 1958.
C. Edell, *Here Come the Clowns,* Putnam, 1958.
L. H. Kuhn, *The World of Jo Davidson,* Farrar, Straus, 1958.
Catharine Wooley, *David's Campaign Buttons,* Morrow, 1959.
Maurice Dolbier, *Paul Bunyan,* Random House, 1959.
Edith L. Boyd, *Boy Joe Goes to Sea,* Rand McNally, 1959.
Gerald W. Johnson, *America is Born* (ALA Notable Book), Morrow, 1959.
R. B. Morris, *The First Book of Indian Wars,* F. Watts, 1959, revised edition published as *The Indian Wars,* Lerner Publications, 1985.
Elizabeth Abell, editor, *Westward, Westward, Westward,* F. Watts. 1959.
Phillip H. Ault, *This is the Desert,* Dodd, 1959.

R. Irving, *Sound and Ultrasonics,* Knopf, 1959.

G. W. Johnson, *America Moves Forward,* Morrow, 1960.

G. W. Johnson, *America Grows Up,* Morrow, 1960.

R. Irving, *Electromagnetic Waves,* Knopf, 1960.

Declaration of Independence, F. Watts, 1960.

Trevor N. Dupuy, *Military History of Civil War Naval Actions,* F. Watts, 1960.

T. N. Dupuy, *Military History of Civil War Land Battles,* F. Watts, 1960.

Edward E. Hale, *The Man Without a Country,* F. Watts, 1960.

Anico Surnay, *Ride the Cold Wind* (ALA notable Book), Putnam, 1960.

Natalia M. Belting, *Indy and Mrs. Lincoln,* Holt, 1960.

N. M. Belting, *Verity Mullens and the Indian,* Holt, 1960.

R. B. Morris, *The First Book of the War of 1812,* F. Watts, 1961, revised edition published as *The War of 1812,* Lerner Publications, 1985.

Emma G. Sterne, *Vasco Nunez De Balboa,* Knopf, 1961.

James Playsted Wood, *The Queen's Most Honorable Pirate,* Harper, 1961.

Harold W. Felton, *A Horse Named Justin Morgan,* Dodd, 1962.

Charles M. Daugherty, *Great Archaeologists,* Crowell, 1962.

Margery M. Fisher, *But Not Our Daddy,* Dial, 1962.

Robert C. Suggs, *Modern Discoveries in Archaeology,* Crowell, 1962.

Paul Engle, *Golden Child,* Dutton, 1962.

Jean L. Latham, *Man of the Monitor,* Harper, 1962.

G. W. Johnson, *The Supreme Court* (*Horn Book* honor list), Morrow, 1962.

Harold W. Felton, *Sergeant O'Keefe and His Mule, Balaam,* Dodd, 1962.

G. W. Johnson. *The Presidency* (*Horn Book* honor list), Morrow, 1962.

Jack London, *Before Adam,* Macmillan, 1962.

Eric B. Smith and Robert Meredith, *Pilgrim Courage* (*Horn Book* honor list), Little, Brown, 1962.

E. Hubbard, *Message of Garcia,* F. Watts, 1962.

Charles Ferguson, *Getting to Know the U.S.A.,* Coward, 1963.

A. Surany, *Golden Frog,* Putnam, 1963.

G. W. Johnson, *The Congress,* Morrow, 1963.

Margery M. Fisher, *One and One,* Dial, 1963.

Andre Maurois, *The Weigher of Souls,* Macmillan, 1963.

J. London, *Star Rover,* Macmillan, 1963.

Helen Hoke, editor, *Patriotism, Patriotism, Patriotism,* F. Watts, 1963.

Gettysburg Address, F. Watts, 1963.

G. W. Johnson, *Communism: An American's View,* Morrow, 1964.

E. Brooks Smith and R. Meredith, *Coming of the Pilgrims,* Little, Brown, 1964.

Richard Armour, *Our Presidents,* Norton, 1964.

R. Meredith and E. B. Smith, *Riding with Coronado,* Little, Brown, 1964.

Robert C. Suggs, *Alexander the Great, Scientist-King,* Macmillan, 1964.

John F. Kennedy's Inaugural Address, F. Watts, 1964.

R. C. Suggs, *Archaeology of San Francisco,* Crowell, 1965.

Martin Gardner, *Archimedes,* Macmillan, 1965.

Florence Stevenson, *The Story of Aida* (based on the opera by Giuseppe Verdi), Putnam, 1965.

Lois P. Jones, *The First Book of the White House,* F. Watts, 1965.

Ernest L. Thayer, *Casey at the Bat,* F. Watts, 1965.

John Foster, *Rebel Sea Raider,* Morrow, 1965.

A. Surany, *The Burning Mountain,* Holiday House, 1965.

Martha Shapp and Charles Shapp, *Let's Find Out about John Fitzgerald Kennedy,* F. Watts, 1965.

R. C. Suggs, *Archaeology of New York,* Crowell, 1966.

Clifford L. Alderman, *The Story of the Thirteen Colonies,* Random House, 1966.

J. Foster, *Guadalcanal General,* Morrow, 1966.

Robert Silverberg, *Forgotten by Time,* Crowell, 1966.

G. W. Johnson, *The Cabinet,* Morrow, 1966.

Washington Irving, *The Legend of Sleepy Hollow,* F. Watts, 1966.

A. Surany, *Kati and Kormos,* Holiday House, 1966.

A. Surany, *A Jungle Jumble,* Putnam, 1966.

R. K. Meredith and E. B. Smith, *Quest of Columbus,* Little, Brown, 1966.

Madeleine L'Engle, *Journey with Jonah,* Farrar, Straus, 1967.

L. Sprague and Catherine C. De Camp, *The Story of Science in America,* Scribner, 1967.

Nathaniel Hawthorne, *Great Stone Face and Two Other Stories,* F. Watts, 1967.

G. W. Johnson, *Franklin D. Roosevelt,* Morrow, 1967.

George B. Shaw, *The Devil's Disciple,* F. Watts, 1967.

A. Surany, *Covered Bridge,* Holiday House, 1967.

A. Surany, *Monsieur Jolicoeur's Umbrella,* Putnam, 1967.

W. Irving, *Rip Van Winkle,* F. Watts, 1967.

R. B. Morris, *The First Book of the Founding of the Republic,* F. Watts, 1968.

A. Surany, *Malachy's Gold,* Holiday House, 1968.

Bret Harte, *The Luck of Roaring Camp,* F. Watts, 1968.

(With Cynthia Basil) J. Foster, *Napoleon's Marshall,* Morrow, 1968.

Gerald W. Foster, *The British Empire,* Morris, 1969.

R. Meredith and E. B. Smith, *Exploring the Great River,* Little, Brown, 1969.

A. Surany, *Lora Lorita,* Putnam, 1969.

Julian May, *Why the Earth Quakes,* Holiday House, 1969.

Victor B. Scheffer, *The Year of the Whale,* Scribner, 1969.

V. B. Scheffer, *The Year of the Seal,* Scribner, 1970.

Berenice R. Morris, *American Popular Music,* F. Watts, 1970.

V. B. Scheffer, *Little Calf,* Scribner, 1970.

J. May, *The Land Beneath the Sea,* Holiday House, 1971.

Loren Eisely, *The Night Country,* Scribner, 1971.

Isaac B. Singer, *The Wicked City* (ALA Notable Book), Farrar, Straus, 1972.

Jan Wahl, *Juan Diego and the Lady,* Putnam, 1973.

Gladys Conklin, *The Journey of the Gray Whales,* Holiday House, 1974.

James E. Gunn, *Some Dreams are Nightmares,* Scribner, 1974.

The Joy of Crafts, Blue Mountain Crafts Council, 1975.

E. Thompson, *The White Falcon,* Doubleday, 1976.

Milton Meltzer, *All Times, All Peoples: A World History of Slavery,* Harper, 1980.

Myra Cohn Livingston, *A Circle of Seasons* (ALA Notable Book), Holiday House, 1982.

Richard Armour, *Our Presidents,* revised edition, Woodbridge Press, 1983.

M. C. Livingston, *Sky Songs,* Holiday House, 1984.

M. C. Livingston, *Celebrations,* Holiday House, 1985.

M. C. Livingston, *Sea Songs,* Holiday House, 1986.

M. C. Livingston, *Earth Songs,* Holiday House, 1986.

M. C. Livingston, *Space Songs,* Holiday House, 1988.

M. C. Livingston, *Up in the Air,* Holiday House, 1989.

Alice Schertle, *Little Frog's Song,* Harper, 1992.

ILLUSTRATOR OF TEXT BOOKS AND LEARNING MATERIALS

Our Reading Heritage (six volumes), Holt, 1956-58.

Marjorie Wescott Barrows, *Good English through Practice,* Holt, 1956.

M. W. Barrows and E. N. Woods, *Reading Skills,* Holt, 1958.

Don Parker, editor, *The Reading Laboratories* (eight volumes), Science Research Associates, 1957-62.

Dolores Betler, editor, *The Literature Sampler* (two volumes), Learning Materials, Inc., 1962, 1964.

How Things Change, Field Enterprise, 1964.

ILLUSTRATOR OF AUDIO-VISUAL FILM STRIPS

Edgar Allan Poe, *Murders in the Rue Morgue,* Encyclopaedia Britannica, 1978.

Robert Louis Stevenson, *Dr. Jekyll and Mr. Hyde,* Encyclopaedia Britannica, 1978.

Bram Stoker, *The Judge's House,* Encyclopaedia Britannica, 1978.

A. B. Edwards, *Snow* (from *The Phantom Coach*), Encyclopaedia Britannica, 1978.

Poe, *The Tell-Tale Heart,* Encyclopaedia Britannica, 1980.

Also illustrator for *Cricket* and *Lady Bug* magazines. Many of Fisher's manuscripts, illustrations, drawings, and correspondence are housed at the Leonard Everett Fisher Archive, University of Connecticut, Storrs, the Kerlan Collection, University of Minnesota, Minneapolis, the de Grummond Collection, University of Southern Mississippi, Hattiesburg, the library of the University of Oregon, Eugene, and at the Postal History Collection, Smithsonian Institution, Washington, DC.

ADAPTATIONS: Filmstrips, all by Anico Surany and all produced by Random House: *The Golden Frog, The Burning Mountain, A Jungle Jumble, Monsieur Jolicouer's Umbrella, Ride the Cold Wind,* and *Lora Lorita.*

SIDELIGHTS: Leonard Everett Fisher is a prominent illustrator of both children's nonfiction and fiction books, particularly books of American and world history. He credits his father's love of art with his own decision to become an artist. The elder Fisher was a ship designer and draftsman who painted in his spare time. One of his paintings was still on the easel when two-year-old Leonard got hold of some india ink and a paint brush and added his own embellishments to his father's work. The result was an unusable mess. But instead of getting punished, Fisher was given his own little studio—a converted hall closet—complete with work table, crayons, paper and pencils. "I was cozily in business," Fisher recalls in his article for *Something About the Author Autobiography Series (SAAS),* "ensconced in my first studio, lit from the ceiling by a naked bulb and about six steps from the kitchen."

Fisher's early efforts concentrated on scenes of wartime battle, inspired by his uncles' stories of their World War I experiences. Both uncles had fought in the trenches with the American Expeditionary Force, defending Paris from German attack. His mother, he remembers in *SAAS,* "would sit in one of the little studio chairs and read to me from *Mother Goose* or *A Child's Garden of Verses* while I drew battlefield ambulances filled with bleeding heroes."

While in school, Fisher began to win local art competitions, including several prizes sponsored by department stores. One of these was a float design for the Macy Thanksgiving Day parade. A pencil drawing was exhibited with the works of other high school students at the Brooklyn Museum. In addition to his school work, Fisher also took art classes at Moses Soyer's art studio, at the Art Students' League, and at the Heckscher Foundation. His mother made sure he visited the art museums of New York, too.

After graduating from high school at the age of 16, Fisher studied art and geology at Brooklyn College for a time before entering the Army. He enlisted in 1942 and was assigned to become a mapmaker. Shipped overseas, Fisher worked at a base in Algeria drawing battle maps for the Allied campaigns in Italy, and the invasions of Normandy, southern France, and Germany. After a year, he was transferred to Hawaii to work on battle maps for the invasions of the islands of Iwo Jima and Okinawa, and for the never-executed invasion of Japan itself. His first professional writing was done at this time, with Fisher describing his unit's topographical work.

Fisher returned to college after his military service, earning two degrees from Yale University. "The Yale experience," Fisher explains in his *SAAS* article, "was memorable. It prepared me for every artistic eventuality. It was up to me to discover those eventualities." Following graduation, Fisher traveled to Europe using money received from two fellowships. He visited the major art museums of London, Paris, Milan, Florence, Venice, Rome, and elsewhere in Italy. "I saw every painting I came to see and more," he remembers in *SAAS*.

Upon his return to the United States, Fisher became dean of the Whitney School of Art. He had his first New York exhibition at the Edwin C. Hewitt Gallery in 1952. Although not one painting was sold, the critical reviews were favorable and Fisher, encouraged by the response, proposed to Margery Meskin, then a systems service representative with IBM. The couple was married later that year.

Shortly after leaving the Whitney School of Art in 1953, Fisher began to illustrate books for children. His first was *The Exploits of Xenophon,* written by Geoffrey Household. It tells the story of an ancient Greek writer, historian, and military leader. Other projects soon followed, including the six-volume *Our Reading Heritage* and the *Multilevel Reading Laboratory,* an experimental concept in which 150 reading selections were printed with 150 suitable illustrations. Fisher did the illustrations for eight of the "laboratory" packages, more than 3,000 illustrations in all.

In addition to illustrating educational materials, Fisher also illustrated a number of children's picture books, working for Holiday House and Franklin Watts. These books included both fiction and nonfiction titles, particularly American history, a subject close to Fisher's heart. "American history," he explains in *SAAS,* "had a strong presence during my growing years. To my parents, one an immigrant, the other the son of immigrants, the United States was heaven-sent."

Fisher has also written children's books, many of them about historical subjects. His "Nineteenth-Century America" series for Holiday House describes various aspects of American society, such as the growth of the railroads or the nation's most popular leisure-time activities, and is meant to provide a panoramic picture of the development of nineteenth century America. Fisher explains in *SAAS* that the books also "deal with my determination not to disconnect. In a culture like ours, wherein today's material gratification seems to deny any historical link, knowl-

edge of the past is often and mistakenly brushed aside as irrelevant to our present and future values, much less the course of our nation. I try to say otherwise."

The "Colonial Americans" series from Franklin Watts consists of nineteen books describing Colonial crafts, trades, and professions. Each begins with a brief history of the craft, trade, or profession in question and then proceeds to describe the actual techniques used by Colonial craftsmen. Fisher's illustrations for the books were done in a style reminiscent of old-time engravings to give them the proper feeling. The "Colonial Americans" series, according to O. Mell Busbin in the *Dictionary of Literary Biography,* "has received wide use in classrooms throughout the United States, especially in the arts and social sciences." Over 500,000 copies of the series have been sold.

The American experience is also illuminated in Fisher's books about immigrants. *Across the Sea from Galway* tells of a group of Irish immigrants who flee famine and oppression in Ireland only to be shipwrecked off the Massachusetts coast. *Letters from Italy* is the story of several generations of an Italian-American family, beginning with a grandfather who fought with Garibaldi for Italian independence to a grandson who dies in World War II fighting Mussolini. *A Russian Farewell* traces a Jewish- Ukrainian family from their trials under the Czarist government to their decision to leave for America.

Other books were inspired by Fisher's childhood on the seashore. *The Death of Evening Star, Noonan,* and *Storm at the Jetty* are all based on his recollections of living in the family house at Sea Gate in Brooklyn. Situated on the jetty of land where the Atlantic Ocean waters met the waters of Gravesend Bay, the family house had a magnificent view of passing ships, storms at sea, and the local lighthouse. *Storm at the Jetty* is a descriptive story of how a beautiful August afternoon on the seashore gradually transforms into a violent and ugly thunderstorm at sea. *The Death of Evening Star* concerns a nineteenth century whaling ship from New England and the many tribulations of its final voyage.

Although an illustrator and author of children's books, Fisher has also created easel paintings, held exhibitions of his work, and painted murals for such public buildings as the Washington Monument. In the early 1970s he designed a number of postage stamps for the U.S. Postal Service, including a series of four stamps on American craftsmen for the Bicentennial. These stamps were first issued at Williamsburg, Virginia, on July 4, 1972. Fisher also designed the commemorative stamp *The Legend of Sleepy Hollow,* a tribute to Washington Irving's classic story.

In a letter to *CA,* Fisher notes a general tendency among critics to categorize him as an artist of American historical subjects, ignoring the wider range of his work. "I am an artist—painter, illustrator, designer—who happens to have been immersed from time to time in colonial America, Ellis Island, the Statue of Liberty, Monticello, the White House, and the Alamo," Fisher explains. "But I do not wish my effort in this direction to detract from the energies I have devoted to my painted interpretations of poetry, Greek mythology, and world history and the artistic expressions thus generated. The three books I have published in 1991—*The ABC Exhibit, Sailboat Lost,* and *Cyclops*—are more about art and me as an artist than anything else."

Writing in *Horn Book* about the place of art in contemporary children's nonfiction, Fisher offers these observations: "We have a tendency in children's nonfiction to respond only to the desires of curriculum and educators and to ignore the other needs. . . . The qualities of high art are hardly ever a factor for the judgment of nonfiction. What is important about me is the quality of my thinking, what drives me to do what I am doing; not the facts of my life—but the creative impulse behind that life. I am trying to make an artistic statement logically, and a logical statement to children artistically. I think the time has come for a stronger and more artistically expansive view of nonfiction."

BIOGRAPHICAL/CRITICAL SOURCES:

BOOKS

Children's Literature Review, Volume 18, Gale, 1989.
Daugherty, Charles M., *Six Artists Paint a Still Life,* North Light, 1977, pp. 10-29.
Dictionary of Literary Biography, Volume 61: *American Writers for Children since 1960: Poets, Illustrators and Nonfiction Authors,* Gale, 1987, pp. 57-67.
Hopkins, Lee Bennett, *More Books by More People,* Citation, 1971, pp. 159-164, 316.
Munce, Howard, editor, *Magic and Other Realism,* Hastings House, 1979, pp. 56-59.
Something about the Author Autobiography Series, Volume 1, Gale, 1986, pp. 89-113.

PERIODICALS

American Artist, September, 1966, pp. 42-47, 67-70.
Catholic Library World, July-August, 1971.
Horn Book, May-June, 1988, pp. 315-323.
Language Arts, March, 1982, pp. 224-230.
Publishers Weekly, February 26, 1982, pp. 62-63.

*   *   *

FISKE, Sharon
    See HILL, Pamela

FLEISCHMAN, Paul 1952-

PERSONAL: Born September 5, 1952, in Monterey, CA; son of Albert Sidney (a children's author) and Beth (Taylor) Fleischman; married Becky Mojica (a nurse), December 15, 1978; children: Seth, Dana. *Education:* Attended University of California, Berkeley, 1970-72; University of New Mexico, B.A., 1977.

ADDRESSES: Home—855 Marino Pines, Pacific Grove, CA 93950.

CAREER: Author. Worked variously as a bagel baker, bookstore clerk, and proofreader.

MEMBER: Authors Guild, Society of Children's Book Writers.

AWARDS, HONORS: Silver Medal, Commonwealth Club of California, Golden Kite honor book, Society of Children's Book Writers, and *New York Times* outstanding book citation, all 1980, all for *The Half-a-Moon Inn;* Newbery honor book, American Library Association (ALA), 1983, for *Graven Images: Three Stories;* Golden Kite honor book, Society of Children's Book Writers, and Parents' Choice Award, Parents' Choice Foundation, both 1983, both for *Path of the Pale Horse; Boston Globe-Horn Book* Award honor book, best books for young adults nomination, ALA, both 1988, and Newbery Medal, ALA, 1989, all for *Joyful Noise: Poems for Two Voices; Boston Globe-Horn Book* Award honor book, 1990, and ALA notable book, 1991, both for *Saturnalia.*

WRITINGS:

JUVENILE BOOKS

The Birthday Tree, illustrated by Marcia Sewall, Harper, 1979.
The Half-a-Moon Inn, illustrated by Kathy Jacobi, Harper, 1980.
Graven Images: Three Stories, illustrated by Andrew Glass, Harper, 1982.
The Animal Hedge (picture book), illustrated by Lydia Dabcovich, Dutton, 1983.
Path of the Pale Horse, Harper, 1983.
Phoebe Danger, Detective, in the Case of the Two-Minute Cough, illustrated by Margot Apple, Houghton, 1983.
Finzel the Farsighted, illustrated by Sewall, Dutton, 1983.
Coming-and-Going Men: Four Tales, illustrated by Randy Gaul, Harper, 1985.
I Am Phoenix: Poems for Two Voices, illustrated by Ken Nutt, Harper, 1985.
Rear-View Mirrors, Harper, 1986.
Rondo in C, illustrated by Janet Wentworth, Harper, 1988.
Joyful Noise: Poems for Two Voices, illustrated by Eric Beddows, Harper, 1988.

Saturnalia, Harper, 1990.
Shadow Play (picture book), illustrated by Beddows, Harper, 1990.
The Borning Room, HarperCollins, 1991.
Time Train, illustrated by Claire Ewart, HarperCollins, 1991.

OTHER

Contributor to various journals and magazines.

SIDELIGHTS: Paul Fleischman's writings encompass a variety of genres, from picture books and poetry to eerie tales and young adult novels, but all are unified by his intense attention to sound. Claiming he would be a musician if he had talent, Fleischman fills his works with musical words instead. He enhances his historic, mysterious tales and lyrical poetry with his sensual use of language, utilizing such writing techniques as alliteration and rhythm. And out of this language emerge intricate psychological and moral stories in which characters exhibit powerful emotional needs and make revealing discoveries about themselves and each other. "Fleischman establishes a storyteller's hold on his audience; they can put themselves in his hands with the assurance that they won't be disappointed," maintains a *Kirkus Reviews* contributor.

Fleischman first learned the importance of sound in stories from his father, Sid Fleischman, who also writes children's books. While growing up in Santa Monica, California, Fleischman would gather with the rest of his family to hear the chapters of his father's books as he completed them. "As well as being a good writer, he's an excellent reader," explains Fleischman. "The sense of beginning communicated by the rhythm of an opening sentence, the feeling of closing inherent in a chapter's last line were unmistakable. His books brim with the pleasures to be found in the sounds of speech: dialect, forgotten turns of phrase, wonderful names for characters." Music itself became a major influence when Fleischman discovered the classical masters while in high school. He spent hours in the public library listening to such artists as Beethoven, Bach, and Brahms, learning how to shape his writing from what he heard.

Fleischman's fascination with the past, where he often sets his books, was also passed on to him from his father. "Like my father," comments Fleischman, "I'm attracted to the past. From him I learned the joys of research: digging up old names, old words, old facts about how people dressed, what they ate, how they worked." Fleischman's two short story collections, *Graven Images: Three Stories* and *Coming-and-Going Men: Four Tales,* reflect this interest. Linked together by the dominant image of a sculpted figure, the stories in *Graven Images* are powerful and mysterious narratives that include everything from a comical love story to the tale of a sculptor commissioned by a dis-

agreeable ghost. "Unusual in our day," asserts *Horn Book* contributor Ethel L. Heins, Fleischman's "timeless, elegant, figurative prose is fashioned with fluency and skill."

In *Coming-and-Going Men* Fleischman uses a central location, New Canaan, Vermont, to connect his stories of four travelling men. The men are salesmen or showmen, and each, while leaving a lasting impression on at least one of the inhabitants of New Canaan, is deeply affected by their visit to the town. A *Bulletin of the Center for Children's Books* contributor points out, "Period details (the year is 1800) are convincing, the language and the concepts of the characters are appropriate for the time and place, and the writing style is honed and polished in a book that is enjoyable almost as much for its style as for its story." And a *Kirkus Reviews* contributor concludes that "one can easily imagine Fleischman himself a coming-and-going man, fabricating his way through his storybook Early America and enthralling the populace with his illusionist's wordcraft."

Fleischman pays particular attention to the crafting of his words in his two poetry collections, *I Am Phoenix: Poems for Two Voices* and *Joyful Noise: Poems for Two Voices.* Both works are designed to be read aloud by two alternating voices, and Fleischman's celebration of sound is evident throughout. The first collection, *I Am Phoenix,* extols a variety of birds, whereas the second, *Joyful Noise,* focuses on the diverse inhabitants of the insect world. "Fleischman steps imaginatively inside each insect and in fine, free verse gives that creature's own point of view on its unique qualities, life cycle, and habits," describes Carolyn Phelan in *Booklist.* Although Katha Pollitt, writing in the *New York Times Book Review,* maintains that the "words and images" in *Joyful Noise* "are sometimes surprisingly flat and prosaic," Mary M. Burns claims in *Horn Book:* "The imagery throughout the volume is as remarkable as the technique: memorable but never intrusive, again because the words seem exactly right for the particular voice. . . . Each selection is a gem, polished perfection. If Paul Fleischman never wrote another book, his reputation would remain secure with this one."

With *Shadow Play,* a picture book published in 1990, Fleischman continues his rhythmic writing and combines elements of the past and the present. The book tells the story of a young brother and sister at a county fair. Having only a limited amount of money, they decide to exchange it for admission into a small theater where a shadow play of *Beauty and the Beast* is to be presented. The play takes an unexpected turn when a fierce bull storms into the story, but a young girl is able to tame him with her gentleness. After the show is over, the children and the reader are invited backstage and learn that one man alone made all the shadows. "The grittiness of the relatively modern carnival is contrasted with the refined and graceful shadow play, set in an earlier, more elegant time," points out Arthur Yorinks in the *New York Times Book Review.* "This is what a picture book is meant to be—words, pictures, rhythm, pacing, all woven together to tell a complete story."

Although Fleischman sees the actual story being told as the most important element of his work, he derives the most pleasure out of the actual writing of it. "If I can please my readers' ears while telling my tale, such that a listener who knew no English would enjoy it read aloud purely for its music, so much the better," writes Fleischman in *Horn Book.* "Since I think the sense of my stories out in some detail before I put them into words, the spontaneous, joyful, serendipitous, and most satisfying side of writing for me is trying to do exactly that: moving this clause to take advantage of that rhyme, finding a four-syllable word for *slender,* playing with the length of sentences. Giving the sense a sound."

BIOGRAPHICAL/CRITICAL SOURCES:

BOOKS

Chevalier, Tracy, editor, *Twentieth-Century Children's Writers,* 3rd edition, St. James Press, 1989, pp. 349-50.
Children's Literature Review, Volume 20, Gale, 1990, pp. 63-70.
Holtze, Sally Holmes, editor, *Fifth Book of Junior Authors and Illustrators,* H. W. Wilson, 1983, pp. 114-16.

PERIODICALS

Booklist, June 15, 1980, p. 1531; June 1, 1983, p. 1275; February 15, 1988, p. 1000.
Bulletin of the Center for Children's Books, March, 1983, pp. 125-26; January, 1984; September, 1985; October, 1985, p. 26; April, 1986; February, 1988, p. 115.
Horn Book, June, 1980, p. 294; December, 1982, p. 656; June, 1983, p. 289; May-June, 1986, pp. 329-30; September-October, 1986, pp. 551-55; May-June, 1988, pp. 366-67; September-October, 1988, p. 614; July, 1989, pp. 452-55; May-June, 1990, pp. 337-38; January-February, 1991, pp. 63-64.
Kirkus Reviews, May 15, 1979, p. 573; August 15, 1982, p. 937; April 1, 1983, pp. 375-76; September 1, 1983, pp. J147-J148; May 15, 1985, pp. J32-J33; December 15, 1987, p. 1732; September 15, 1988, p. 145.
New York Times, December 3, 1990.
New York Times Book Review, April 27, 1980, pp. 45, 67; November 28, 1982, p. 24; March 4, 1984, p. 31; September 8, 1985, p. 35; March 26, 1989; September 30, 1990, p. 39; November 11, 1990, p. 52.
New York Times Magazine, November 28, 1982.

Publishers Weekly, February 25, 1983, p. 88; September 30, 1988, pp. 67-68; February 1, 1991, p. 81; March 29, 1991, p. 94.
School Library Journal, September, 1979, p. 110; May, 1983, p. 92; December, 1983, p. 65; November, 1985, p. 84; May, 1986, pp. 102-03; February, 1988, p. 79; May, 1988, pp. 48-49; November, 1988, p. 86.
Voice of Youth Advocates, June, 1986, p. 78; August, 1988, p. 145; June, 1990, p. 102.
Washington Post Book World, May 8, 1983, pp. 15, 18; August 12, 1990, p. 8; March 24, 1991, p. 12.

*　　　*　　　*

FLEISCHMAN, (Albert) Sid(ney) 1920- (Carl March)

PERSONAL: Born March 16, 1920, in Brooklyn, NY; son of Reuben and Sadie (Solomon) Fleischman; married Betty Taylor, January 25, 1942; children: Jane, Paul, Anne. *Education:* San Diego State College (now University), B.A., 1949. *Avocational interests:* Magic, astronomy, playing classical guitar.

ADDRESSES: Home and office—305 Tenth St., Santa Monica, CA 90402.

CAREER: Professional magician; screenwriter; author of books for young people. Magician in vaudeville and night clubs, 1938-41; traveled with Mr. Arthur Bull's Francisco Spook Show (magic act), 1939-40; *Daily Journal,* San Diego, CA, reporter and rewrite man, 1949-50; *Point* (magazine), San Diego, associate editor, 1950-51; full-time writer, 1951—. Author of scripts for television show *3-2-1 Contact,* 1979-82. *Military service:* U.S. Naval Reserve, 1941-45; served as yeoman on destroyer escort in the Philippines, Borneo, and China.

MEMBER: Authors Guild, Authors League of America, Writers Guild of America West, Society of Children's Book Writers.

AWARDS, HONORS: New York Herald Tribune's Children's Spring Book Festival Award Honor Book, 1962, for *Mr. Mysterious and Company;* Spur Award from the Western Writers of America, Southern California Council on Literature for Children and Young People Award, and Boys' Clubs of America Junior Book Award, all 1964, George C. Stone Center for Children's Books Recognition of Merit Award, 1972, and Friends of Children and Literature (FOCAL) Award from the Los Angeles Public Library, 1983, all for *By the Great Horn Spoon!;* Commonwealth Club of California Juvenile Book Award, 1966, for *Chancy and the Grand Rascal;* Lewis Carroll Shelf Award, 1969, for *McBroom Tells the Truth; Longbeard the Wizard* was selected one of the American Institute of

Graphic Arts Children's Books, 1970; *Book World*'s Children's Spring Book Festival Award Honor Book, 1971, for *Jingo Django;* Southern California Council on Literature for Children and Young People Award, 1972, for "Comprehensive Contribution of Lasting Value to the Literature for Children and Young People"; Golden Kite Award Honor Book from the Society of Children's Book Writers, 1974, for *McBroom the Rainmaker;* Mark Twain Award from the Missouri Association of School Libraries, and Charlie May Simon Children's Book Award from the Arkansas Elementary School Council, both 1977, and Young Hoosier Award from the Association for Indiana Media Educators, 1979, all for *The Ghost on Saturday Night;* National Book Award finalist, and *Boston Globe-Horn Book* Award for Fiction, both 1979, both for *Humbug Mountain;* Newbery Medal from the American Library Association, and selected one of Child Study Association of America Children's Books of the Year, both 1987, both for *The Whipping Boy;* Paul A. Witty Award from the International Reading Association, and Children's Picturebook Award from *Redbook,* both 1988, both for *The Scarebird.*

WRITINGS:

JUVENILE

Mr. Mysterious and Company (*Horn Book* honor list; Junior Literary Guild selection; illustrated by Eric von Schmidt), Atlantic/Little, Brown, 1962.

By the Great Horn Spoon! (Junior Literary Guild selection; illustrated by E. von Schmidt), Atlantic/Little, Brown, 1963, published as *Bullwhip Griffin,* Avon, 1967.

The Ghost in the Noonday Sun (Junior Literary Guild selection; illustrated by Warren Chappell), Atlantic/Little, Brown, 1965, new edition (illustrated by Peter Sis), Greenwillow, 1989.

McBroom Tells the Truth (illustrated by Kurt Werth), Norton, 1966, new edition (illustrated by W. Lorraine), Atlantic/Little, Brown, 1981.

Chancy and the Grand Rascal (*Horn Book* honor list; illustrated by E. von Schmidt), Atlantic/Little, Brown, 1966.

McBroom and the Big Wind (illustrated by K. Werth), Norton, 1967, new edition (illustrated by W. Lorraine), Atlantic/Little, Brown, 1982.

McBroom's Ear (illustrated by K. Werth), Norton, 1969, new edition (illustrated by W. Lorraine), Atlantic/Little, Brown, 1982.

Longbeard the Wizard (Junior Literary Guild selection; illustrated by Charles Bragg), Atlantic/Little, Brown, 1970.

Jingo Django (ALA Notable Book; Junior Literary Guild selection; illustrated by E. von Schmidt), Atlantic/Little, Brown, 1971.

McBroom's Ghost (illustrated by Robert Frankenberg), Grosset, 1971, new edition (illustrated by W. Lorraine), Atlantic/Little, Brown, 1981.

McBroom's Zoo (illustrated by K. Werth), Grosset, 1972, new edition (illustrated by W. Lorraine), Atlantic/Little, Brown, 1982.

The Wooden Cat Man (illustrated by Jay Yang), Atlantic/Little, Brown, 1972.

McBroom's Wonderful One-Acre Farm (includes *McBroom Tells the Truth, McBroom and the Big Wind,* and *McBroom's Ghost;* illustrated by Quentin Blake), Chatto & Windus, 1972.

McBroom the Rainmaker (illustrated by K. Werth), Grosset, 1973, new edition (illustrated by W. Lorraine), Atlantic/Little, Brown, 1982.

The Ghost on Saturday Night (illustrated by E. von Schmidt), Atlantic/Little, Brown, 1974.

Mr. Mysterious's Secrets of Magic (illustrated by E. von Schmidt), Atlantic/Little, Brown, 1975, published as *Secrets of Magic,* Chatto & Windus, 1976.

McBroom Tells a Lie (Junior Literary Guild selection; illustrated by W. Lorraine), Atlantic/Little, Brown, 1976.

Here Comes McBroom (includes *McBroom Tells a Lie, McBroom the Rainmaker,* and *McBroom's Zoo;* illustrated by Q. Blake), Chatto & Windus, 1976.

Kate's Secret Riddle Book, F. Watts, 1977.

Me and the Man on the Moon-Eyed Horse (Junior Literary Guild selection; illustrated by E. von Schmidt), Atlantic/Little, Brown, 1977, published in England as *The Man on the Moon-Eyed Horse,* Gollancz, 1980.

Humbug Mountain (Junior Literary Guild selection; illustrated by E. von Schmidt), Atlantic/Little, Brown, 1978.

Jim Bridger's Alarm Clock and Other Tall Tales (illustrated by E. von Schmidt), Dutton, 1978.

McBroom and the Beanstalk (Junior Literary Guild selection; illustrated by W. Lorraine), Atlantic/Little, Brown, 1978.

The Hey Hey Man (illustrated by Nadine Bernard Westcott), Atlantic/Little, Brown, 1979.

McBroom and the Great Race (Junior Literary Guild selection; illustrated by W. Lorraine), Atlantic/Little, Brown, 1980.

The Bloodhound Gang in the Case of the Flying Clock (illustrated by William Harmuth), Random House/Children's Television Workshop, 1981.

The Bloodhound Gang in the Case of the Cackling Ghost (illustrated by Anthony Rao), Random House, 1981.

The Bloodhound Gang in the Case of Princess Tomorrow (illustrated by Bill Morrison), Random House, 1981.

The Bloodhound Gang in the Case of the Secret Message (illustrated by W. Harmuth), Random House, 1981.

The Bloodhound Gang's Secret Code Book (illustrated by Bill Morrison), Random House, 1982.

The Bloodhound Gang in the Case of the 264-Pound Burglar (illustrated by B. Morrison), Random House, 1982.

McBroom's Almanac (illustrated by W. Lorraine), Atlantic/Little, Brown, 1984.

The Whipping Boy (illustrated by P. Sis), Greenwillow, 1986.

The Scarebird (*Horn Book* honor list; illustrated by P. Sis), Greenwillow, 1988.

The Ghost in the Noonday Sun, Greenwillow, 1989.

The Midnight Horse, Greenwillow, 1990.

ADULT NOVELS

The Straw Donkey Case, Phoenix Press, 1948.

Murder's No Accident, Phoenix Press, 1949.

Shanghai Flame, Gold Medal, 1951.

Look Behind You, Lady, Gold Medal, 1952, published in England as *Chinese Crimson,* Jenkins, 1962.

Danger in Paradise, Gold Medal, 1953.

Counterspy Express, Ace Books, 1954.

Malay Woman, Gold Medal, 1954, published as *Malaya Manhunt,* Jenkins, 1965.

Blood Alley, Gold Medal, 1955.

Yellowleg, Gold Medal, 1960.

The Venetian Blonde, Gold Medal, 1963.

SCREENPLAYS

Blood Alley, starring John Wayne and Lauren Bacall, Batjac Productions, 1955.

Goodbye, My Lady (based on a novel by James Street), Batjac Productions, 1956.

(With William A. Wellman) *Lafayette Escadrille,* Warner Bros., 1958.

The Deadly Companions (based on his novel *Yellowleg*), starring Maureen O'Hara, Carousel Productions, 1961.

(With Albert Maltz) *Scalawag,* starring Kirk Douglas, Byrna Productions, 1973.

OTHER

Between Cocktails, Abbott Magic Company, 1939.

(Under pseudonym Carl March) *Magic Made Easy,* Croydon, 1953.

(Contributor) Paul Heins, editor, *Crosscurrents of Criticism,* Horn Book, 1977.

ADAPTATIONS: By the Great Horn Spoon! was filmed as *Bullwhip Griffin* by Walt Disney, 1967; *The Ghost in the Noonday Sun,* starring Peter Sellers, was filmed by Cavalcade Films, 1974. Fleischman's books have been translated into fourteen languages.

SIDELIGHTS: Sid Fleischman began his career as a stage magician, and he has displayed the same sleight-of-hand magic in his many books for children and adults. "A sleight-of-hand artist," writes Paul Fleischman of his father in *Horn Book,* "must be skilled at misdirection, keeping his audience's eyes away from the real action. My father is a master at doing the same with words, stealthily slipping in a clue, unnoticed by the reader, that will reappear in the book's climax, just as he used to miraculously pull nickels and dimes out of our ears."

Fleischman's books for children often draw on America's rich folklore and pioneer history for inspiration, although, as he explains in *Horn Book,* "I never plot a story in advance. A notion or two, a character or two and I'm off." Many of his books are tall tales populated by rogues, rascals, and conmen. And all contain humor. "When I sit at the typewriter," Fleischman tells *Publishers Weekly,* "amusing notions come into my head." Emily Rhoads Johnson in *Language Arts* claims that "Fleischman's plots are masterful weavings of mystery, adventure, puzzle, and legend."

Among Fleischman's most popular books is his series about Josh McBroom, an Iowa farmer whose tall tales are as inventively funny as they are unlikely. In *McBroom Tells a Lie,* according to Barbara Elleman in *Booklist,* the reader finds "a conveyance that runs on popcorn power and frozen sunlight, tomatoes that grow overnight, jumping-bean-eating chickens whose eggs flip over when fried, and hens that glow in the dark from consuming too many lightning bugs." In *McBroom's Zoo,* according to *Kirkus Reviews,* one meets "a wrong-legged Sidehill Gouger, a backward-swimming dryland catfish called a Desert Vamooser, and a Great Seventeen-Toed Hairy Prairie Hidebehind."

Another popular series features the Bloodhound Gang, a team of three young detectives who investigate mysterious crimes. Based on Fleischman's scripts for the *3-2-1 Contact* television show, the books are fast-paced, fun-to-solve mysteries for younger readers. In each book, as Judith Goldberger notes in *Booklist,* "a neatly worked out plot is based on simple, believable gimmicks."

"I am a strong advocate of humor in children's books," Fleischman has said, "which in the past has been regarded as something from the wrong side of the literary tracks. I am delighted to see a growing critical acceptance for this genre. It amazes me that I have written eight McBroom tall tales, with a ninth beginning to surface. It was never my intention to go beyond the first book (*McBroom Tells the Truth*), but a new idea seems to crop up every year or so—an irresistible notion. Sequels can be a treacherous enterprise, for the quality and spontaneity of the first may slip away. I feel that I have been uncommonly fortunate in that McBroom's vitality will not be downed and sees him through from book to book. Nevertheless, I tell myself that each new McBroom tale is *positively* the last—until the next irresistible idea makes me a liar."

Fleischman's love of extravagant language is evident in the flamboyant names he gives to his characters, his use of wild metaphors, and the colorful expressions dotting his stories. Johnson explains that Fleischman's "words don't just sit there on the page; they leap and cavort, turn somersaults, and sometimes just hang suspended, like cars teetering at the top of a roller coaster. What marvelous fun to bump into words like *sniggle* and *flamigigs, wrathy, muckworm, buffle-brained,* and *slickens!*"

In 1986, Fleischman won the Newbery Medal for *The Whipping Boy,* a novel set in nineteenth century Europe and telling of a young orphan who runs away with a prince. The book, writes Martha Saxton in the *New York Times Book Review,* "is full of adventure, suspense, humor and lively characters."

It took Fleischman almost ten years to write *The Whipping Boy.* The initial idea came from some historical research during which he discovered that a whipping boy was just that, a boy who took the whipping whenever a young prince misbehaved. A prince was royalty and could not be struck. Fleischman thought he could write the book quickly. But "after about eighteen months," Fleischman recalls in *Horn Book,* "I was still trying to get to the bottom of page five."

Eventually Fleischman worked his way through his writer's "befuddlement" by reevaluating his concept for the story. "My original concept for the story was wrong," he explains in *Horn Book.* "Wrong, at least, for me. I saw *The Whipping Boy* as a picture book story." One day he read over the manuscript and it came to him that the story needed to be much longer: "Once I took the shackles off, the story erupted. Scenes, incidents, and characters came tumbling out of a liberated imagination." When told that the book had won the Newbery Medal, Fleischman was elated. "I don't happen to believe in levitation, unless it's done with mirrors, but for a few days I had to load my pockets with ballast. The Newbery Medal is an enchantment. It's bliss. It should happen to everyone."

BIOGRAPHICAL/CRITICAL SOURCES:

BOOKS

Cameron, Eleanor, *The Green and Burning Tree,* Atlantic/Little, Brown, 1969.
Children's Literature Review, Gale, Volume 1, 1976, Volume 15, 1988.
Huck, Charlotee S. and Doris Young Kuhn, *Children's Literature in the Elementary School,* 2nd edition, Holt, 1968.

Meigs, Cornelia and others, editors, *A Critical History of Children's Literature,* revised edition, Macmillan, 1969.
Sadker, Myra Pollack and David Miller Sadker, *Now Upon a Time: A Contemporary View of Children's Literature,* Harper, 1977.
Townsend, John Rowe, *Written for Children: An Outline of English Language Children's Literature,* revised edition, Lippincott, 1974.

PERIODICALS

Booklist, September 15, 1976; April 15, 1981.
Horn Book, October, 1976; July/August, 1987.
Kirkus Reviews, October 1, 1972.
Language Arts, October, 1982.
New York Times Book Review, October 17, 1971; February 22, 1987.
Publishers Weekly, February 27, 1978.

*   *   *

**FLEUR, Paul
See POHL, Frederik**

*   *   *

FLEXNER, James Thomas   1908-

PERSONAL: Born January 13, 1908, in New York, NY; son of Simon (a medical scientist) and Helen (a teacher of English at Bryn Mawr College, and author; maiden name, Thomas) Flexner; married Beatrice Hudson (a singer), August 2, 1950; children: Helen Hudson. *Education:* Harvard University, B.S. (magna cum laude), 1929.

ADDRESSES: Home and office—530 East 86th St., New York, NY 10028.

CAREER: New York Herald Tribune, New York City, reporter, 1929-31; New York City Department of Health, Noise Abatement Commission, New York City, executive secretary, 1931-32; professional writer, 1932—. Consultant, Colonial Williamsburg, 1956-57, and Amon Carter Museum of Western Art, 1974-75. Honorary trustee, New York Public Library.

MEMBER: American Academy and Institute of Arts and Letters (vice president for literature), PEN (president, American Center, 1954-55), Society of American Historians (president, 1976-77), Authors League of America, Century Association.

AWARDS, HONORS: Library of Congress grant-in-aid for studies in the history of American civilization, 1945; Life in America Prize, 1946, for *First Flowers of Our Wil-*

derness: *American Painting, the Colonial Period;* Guggenheim fellowships, 1953, 1979; Francis Parkman Prize, 1963, for *That Wilder Image: The Native School from Thomas Cole to Winslow Homer;* National Book Award for biography, 1972, for *George Washington: Anguish and Farewell;* special Pulitzer Prize citation, 1972, for George Washington biography; Christopher Award, 1974, for *Washington: The Indispensable Man;* Archives of American Art Award, Smithsonian Institution, 1979, for his services in creating a public interest in American art; American Book Award nomination, 1980, for *Washington: The Indispensable Man;* Peabody Award, 1984, and Emmy Award nomination, for the television miniseries *George Washington;* Gold Medal for Eminence in Biography, American Academy and Institute of Arts and Letters, 1988.

WRITINGS:

Doctors on Horseback: Pioneers of American Medicine, Viking, 1937, reprint of Armed Services Edition (distributed to American military personnel during World War II), Dover, 1991.

America's Old Masters, Viking, 1939, 2nd revised edition, Doubleday, 1980.

(With father, Simon Flexner) *William Henry Welch and the Heroic Age of American Medicine,* Viking, 1941, reprinted, Dover, 1966.

Steamboats Come True, Viking, 1944, reprinted, Little, Brown, 1978, published as *Inventors in Action: The Story of the Steamboat,* Collier Books, 1962, reprinted, Easton Press, 1991.

History of American Painting, Volume 1: *First Flowers of Our Wilderness: American Painting, the Colonial Period,* Houghton, 1947, reprinted, Dover, 1988, Volume 2: *The Light of Distant Skies (1760-1835),* Harcourt, 1954, reprinted, Dover, 1988, Volume 3: *That Wilder Image: The Native School from Thomas Cole to Winslow Homer,* Little, Brown, 1962, reprinted, Dover, 1988.

John Singleton Copley, Houghton, 1947.

A Short History of American Painting, Houghton, 1950, published as *Pocket History of American Painting,* Washington Square Press, 1962.

The Traitor and the Spy: Benedict Arnold and John Andre, Harcourt, 1953, revised edition, Little Brown, 1975, abridged edition published as *The Benedict Arnold Case: Benedict Arnold and John Andre,* Collier Books, 1962, reprinted, Syracuse University Press, 1991.

Gilbert Stuart, Knopf, 1955.

Mohawk Baronet: Sir William Johnson of New York, Harper, 1959, revised edition published as *Lord of the Mohawks: A Biography of Sir William Johnson,* Little, Brown, 1979.

George Washington: A Biography, Little, Brown, Volume 1: *The Forge of Experience, 1732-1775,* 1965, Volume 2: *George Washington in the American Revolution, 1775-1783,* 1968, Volume 3: *George Washington and the New Nation, 1783-1793,* 1970, Volume 4: *Anguish and Farewell, 1793-1799,* 1972.

The World of Winslow Homer, 1836-1910, Time-Life, 1966.

The Double Adventure of John Singleton Copley, Little, Brown, 1969.

Nineteenth Century Painting, Putnam, 1970.

Washington: The Indispensable Man, Little, Brown, 1974.

The Face of Liberty, Clarkson Potter, 1975.

The Young Hamilton, Little, Brown, 1978.

States Dyckman: American Loyalist, Little, Brown, 1980.

Asher B. Durand: An Engraver's and a Farmer's Art, Hudson River, 1983.

An American Saga: The Story of Helen Thomas and Simon Flexner, Little, Brown, 1984.

Poems of the Nineteen Twenties, Stonehouse, 1991.

Also author of television drama, "Treason 1780," CBS-TV, 1954. Contributor of short stories, essays, book reviews, and introductions to various publications.

ADAPTATIONS: Two miniseries were produced from Flexner's four-volume Washington biography. Both starred Barry Bostwick in the title role and featured Patty Duke as Martha Washington: *George Washington,* based on Flexner's first two volumes, aired on CBS-TV, in April, 1984. It has also been aired in England by the BBC and syndicated all over the world. *George Washington: The Forging of a Nation,* based on the last two volumes, aired on CBS-TV, September, 1986. It was rebroadcast by PBS-TV in 1989.

SIDELIGHTS: Throughout his long career, James Thomas Flexner has chronicled American lives. His subjects have included painters, inventors and doctors, loyalists, traitors and spies, people not usually remembered nowadays as well as such luminaries as Alexander Hamilton and George Washington. In his works Flexner presents these people not just as characters who made important contributions to their professions, but as individuals who were intimately involved with American history in the making. Flexner puts these lives in context, reminding his readers of how the things these people accomplished continue to affect modern Americans.

Doctors on Horseback, Flexner's first book, illustrates this intention. The seven short biographies that make up the book draw pictures of men who "fought on two frontiers: riding the wilderness of a new continent, they explored the mysteries of the human body," Flexner explains in his foreword. Dr. Benjamin Rush, one of the signers of the Declaration of Independence, went on to become one of the most influential early American doctors. He also helped found the temperance movement and the first anti-slavery in the United States, and prepared Thomas Paine's *Common Sense* for publication. Ephraim McDowell, the first surgeon to perform an ovariotomy on a living woman, and Daniel Drake, who helped found several of the earliest medical schools in the midwest, both came from poor pioneer families and lived their early lives in the rugged environment of frontier America. Crawford W. Long, a Georgian physician, and William T. G. Morton, a Connecticut dentist, both pioneered the use of nitrous oxide and ether as an anaesthetic in the 1840s and 1850s. The question of who discovered it gained new fervor when the Civil War divided the country, and the question was hotly debated in medical journals long after the war itself ended. Flexner shows how factors from American history shaped these men, and how they in turn influenced it.

George Washington's life has always inspired legend and myth, some of it dating to within a few years of his own lifetime. "Basic to the whole phantasmagoria," Flexner writes in *American Heritage,* "are two roles that Washington has played in the American psyche: first as the father of our country, and second as the human equivalent of the American flag." Because of such conceptions, Flexner continues, views of Washington have changed with the times—when patriotism is high, Washington is celebrated and idolized; when patriotism is low, spurious stories about him circulate, ranging from accusations of financial mismanagement while Washington was commander-in-chief to historian Arnold Toynbee's suggestion that Washington contracted the illness that killed him "while on an illicit visit to an adolescent girl in the slave quarters."

One of the first (and most original) Washington biographers was Mason Locke Weems, a travelling bookseller and Episcopal clergyman. Weems's main interest was in telling a good story—one both exciting and morally correct—and he often was careless with historical facts. In the revised edition of his extremely popular *Life of George Washington,* published in 1808, Weems related many of the stories popularly associated with Washington: the cherry-tree incident, for instance. John Marshall, one of the first Chief Justices of the Supreme Court, also wrote an important five-volume *Life of George Washington* from 1804-07, and Congressman Henry Cabot Lodge composed a two-volume biography that was published in 1889. Until Flexner's work was published, the standard Washington biography was that written by Douglas Southall Freeman, best known for his four-volume biography *R. E. Lee* and the three volumes of *Lee's Lieutenants: A Study in Command.* Freeman began—he died before completing the work—a life of Washington that ran to seven volumes, which John L. Gignilliat, writing in the *Dictionary of Literary Biography,* calls "one of the monumental American

biographies," and which won the Pulitzer Prize in biography in 1958.

Flexner's biography differed from its predecessors in several ways. Weems, intending—according to Ronald W. Howard in the *Dictionary of Literary Biography*—"to inculcate patriotism as well as morality among his young readers," portrayed a superhuman, impossibly saintly Washington. Freeman, on the other hand, drew a picture of Washington that showed "a rather calculating . . . man whose ambition [was] balanced, in moral terms, only by a determination to accept responsibility and to deal fairly with his fellows," says Gignilliat. Flexner, however, portrays the first president as a human being. He writes in the introduction to his single-volume *Washington: The Indispensable Man,* "My continuing effort has been to disentangle the Washington who actually lived from all the symbolic Washingtons, to rescue the man and his deeds from the layers and layers of obscuring legend. . . . I found a fallible human being made of flesh and blood and spirit—not a statue of marble and wood. And inevitably—for that was the fact—I found a great and good man. In all history few men who possessed unassailable power have used that power so gently and self-effacingly for what their best instincts told them was the welfare of their neighbors and all mankind."

Yet, according to Thomas Lask, Flexner shows Washington's fallibilities along with his greatness. "Flexner has softened the marble into flesh and blood, brought the hero down from Olympus, if not to eye level, at least to where we can see him whole and plain," Lask writes in the *New York Times.* "By being candid about his mistakes and his frailties, Mr. Flexner has made Washington even more impressive. . . . The writing is always vigorous and the different parts of the study are in the right proportions. It is not often that a man who knows so much writes so well." A. Bakshian Jr. of the *National Review* calls the third volume of the biography "a well-written, scrupulously documented work, with an admirable reliance on Washington's own written and spoken words, and those of the men and women who knew him. . . . It is the best life of Washington yet written."

In his introduction to *George Washington: Anguish and Farewell,* Flexner wryly observes: "Introductions being commonly written last, these paragraphs end twelve years' labor. Since this is the only extensive biography of Washington in more than a century which the author has lived to finish, my reaction should probably be relief that I am here alive to write these words and ready for future projects. Yet the completion of such a task as this brings sadness as well as jubilation." Flexner continues: "During twelve years, I have on most mornings waked up anticipating association with an endlessly complicated and various individual who, so I became convinced, was one of the great men in all history. This is a privilege hard to relinquish." So hard was it for Flexner to give up writing on Washington that he wrote an original single-volume biography, *Washington: The Indispensable Man*. In this book, W. M. Wallace comments in the *New York Times Book Review*: "[Flexner] writes with greater tautness and verve than in his four volumes, yet without sacrifice of elegance, and he achieves an objectivity that excludes neither sympathy nor criticism. This book deserves a place on every American's bookshelf."

In *An American Saga,* Flexner relates the story of his own family—how Simon Flexner, the son of poor German Jewish immigrants, who left school in the sixth grade, became one of the foremost medical pathologists in America, discovering (among other things) a cure for spinal meningitis. *An American Saga* also tells how Simon Flexner came to marry Helen Thomas, feminist scion of a Maryland Quaker family, whose sister served as president of Bryn Mawr College, and whose correspondants included the famous British philosopher Bertrand Russell. "Perhaps only in America," writes Alice Digilio in the *Washington Post Book World,* "could their paths have converged in marriage." "It takes a scholar and an artist," Digilio continues, "to skillfully plait together the many strands of American history, scientific discovery, family traits, and social customs which came together in the marriage of Helen Thomas and Simon Flexner. Flexner has succeeded with flair and integrity."

CA INTERVIEW

CA interviewed James Thomas Flexner by telephone on May 24, 1990, at his home in New York City.

CA: You've written more than twenty books. One of them that I suspect you have a special fondness for is Doctors on Horseback.

FLEXNER: That book (published when I was twenty-nine) was a turning point in my life. I had considered myself a writer, I delight to say, from before the time I could read and write, and, as a boy and young man, I gained some small reputation as a poet. But *Doctors* was the first book that I really got out into the world, and it was a tremendous success. An unpublished author gets kicked around, but when you have a book that does go a considerable distance, it both encourages you and changes your position in the world as a writer.

CA: Wasn't the book compared to the writing of Sinclair Lewis and Ernest Hemingway?

FLEXNER: It was compared to Lewis and Hemingway, and to Plutarch also; it was published in England, and they went in for Plutarch. Also, during World War II

there was something called the Armed Services Editions, which were distributed as general issue to all the people in the armed forces. *Doctors on Horseback* was sent out everywhere in that form. That had a very great effect on its reputation; people who read the book in very difficult or boring circumstances remembered it. More than fifty years later, I run into people who say, "Oh, you wrote *Doctors on Horseback.*"

CA: So this confirmed your ambition to be a writer?

FLEXNER: I had never in my memory not thought I was going to be a writer. I was encouraged by my mother, and I started out as a poet, as I mentioned earlier. Actually, a little anthology of my early poetry is going to come out in the next few months, selected with an introduction by William Jay Smith, the well-known poet. I've always considered myself a writer, and *Doctors on Horseback* was when I really got away with it.

CA: That book often does read like fiction, as many people have said. Did you ever spare facts in order to tell a better story?

FLEXNER: No, I didn't, and it never got any criticism of that nature. There were one or two places where I had to fill in, but I make what I was doing clear. In connection with the childhood or young days of Ephraim McDowell, who performed the first recorded ovarian surgery in the United States, I acknowledged that, there having been very few facts, I had found it necessary to fill in from what I knew about the period.

CA: Your father was the well-know pathologist Simon Flexner. Did you get any help on the book from him?

FLEXNER: I got advice from him when I got tangled with medical problems, but no particular help on the writing.

CA: In a preface to the Dover edition of Doctors, *you said that Lytton Strachey was a big influence on you. Has he remained a model over the years?*

FLEXNER: I don't think so. His influence was primarily the idea of doing a group of short biographies. I think I've become much more scholarly. Lytton Strachey took three or four Victorian biographies and then used them to make fun of his characters as Victorian. I can't think of any particularly major influence on me; Dickens was more than anybody else, really.

CA: Sainte-Beuve also wrote short, anecdotal sketches, similar in a way to many of the sketches you've done on painters.

FLEXNER: I've never read Sainte-Beuve, so any likeness of my work to his would be a pure coincidence. I've been compared to everybody, including Jane Austen and Balzac.

After the success of *Doctors,* I observed that many important people in America's past hadn't been dealt with biographically, so I thought that I would go on and do books of short biographies of people in other fields. I did painters first. Then I decided I would do inventors, and I quickly discovered that there was one invention that overwhelmed everything else, so I found myself doing a history of the invention of the steamboat. That was the end of my books of short biographies. Of course there were a lot of short biographies in my other books, but they were always interwoven.

CA: Did the painters hold more interest for you than anyone else?

FLEXNER: Up to a point. I did a three-volume history of American painting, and there were various problems with that. Every time I did a volume, I had trouble getting it published, because no one had an interest in those days. So I'd have to do something which would surely sell that I could tie it onto to get it published. For instance, I did my book on Benedict Arnold and John Andre, and with that I was able to sell my next painting book. But next to George Washington and the founding fathers, the painters have been my greatest interest. I might say too that I've always been very anxious to get what I write out to the public. That doesn't mean that I'm trying to get bestsellers, but I do wish to communicate. That separates me from most scholars.

CA: Did you ever have any desire to become a painter yourself?

FLEXNER: No. But I consider myself an artist as a writer. I found interest in dealing with a different art. Also, I got to know Bernard Berenson as a young man, and he influenced me in the direction of art history. His wife was my mother's first cousin. He was in Italy, but I did stay at I Tatti, his villa near Florence. He had considerable influence on me.

CA: Speaking of biography in general, do you think today's biographers have an advantage over earlier biographers in not having to worry so much about the censors? In his Thomas Wolfe biography, David Donald goes rather deeply into Wolfe's sexual life, and I can't imagine his being able to do that a generation ago. Have you wanted to pursue such areas in your biographies more thoroughly than you felt you could do?

FLEXNER: The one time when I might have gotten into trouble was when I wrote about George Washington and Sally Fairfax. But I had no difficulty. I thought that I might get into trouble because I gave a much more human picture of George Washington than had ever been done before; but that, on the whole, worked to the advantage of the book. I thought I might get attacked from the right, but, amusingly enough, I actually got attacked—so far as I was attacked—from the left, who didn't like the idea of making Washington into a human being. They wanted to have a marble image to smash.

CA: Why did you choose Washington as a subject?

FLEXNER: In the various other biographies and books I had written, I kept meeting George Washington in various contexts, and he never fitted the picture of Washington that was in everybody's mind. So I said to myself, When I'm old enough, I will do a biography of Washington. Then Little, Brown came to me and asked if I would write a biography of Washington, so I decided I was old enough. I thought I was going to do a one-volume book, and I very quickly discovered that from my point of view that was impossible, since I wanted to deal with him as a man as well as a historical figure. We ended up with four volumes.

CA: How did you go about the research for the volumes?

FLEXNER: I did a general survey of the material and then did the detailed research volume by volume; so I knew what was going to happen, but as far as going on from day to day, I did it for each volume. The life broke very comfortably into these four sections. Then we published them separately.

CA: You said in the appendix to the first volume of your biography that it could never be done in one volume, but then you did it in one volume after you'd done the four-volume account.

FLEXNER: I knew that the four-volume book was on shelves, so most documentation and argument could be left out of the one-volume life. I was able to go along from high point to high point, knowing that if anybody was going to argue with me, he could go back to the four-volume book and look up the point. I was very much emancipated. It was great fun, because I love to write.

CA: In the preface to your biography you said you tried to eliminate all preconceptions that you had about Washington and start afresh. That must have been rather difficult to do.

FLEXNER: Not really. I was trained by a medical scientist father always to be skeptical about everything until I could prove it to myself. People have regarded my work as a very original interpretation of Washington. What I actually did was get back to the interpretation that existed during his lifetime, by those who knew him, because everything came out of the original sources. That wasn't much of a problem. I'm so used to trying to avoid damnfoolishness in what I write.

CA: Yes. You even said that you wouldn't refer to secondary sources, with the one exception of Douglas Freeman's work.

FLEXNER: Freeman's work is very close to being a primary source. And I didn't follow Freeman's conclusions particularly. The source references in his books were tremendously valuable, a guide to thousands of publications. He had a nice big research team. I was able to borrow it, so to speak.

CA: The one-volume work was published in 1974, more than fifteen years ago. Have you changed any of your opinions since then?

FLEXNER: No. The book went all over the country—as a matter of fact, all over the world—as the basis for a large television miniseries. It ended up as twelve hours, and I was much concerned with that.

CA: Did you think the miniseries was well done?

FLEXNER: Well, I had a great deal to do with it. As an author, I was extremely fortunate in being consulted all down the line. I was pleased with it. I had had previous television experience which had primarily taught me what I didn't know about television, so I was able to cooperate with Richard Fielder, the scriptwriter, who was a very able man who knew how to dramatize things for television and was willing to listen to my ideas as to what he ought to dramatize. We got on well on that basis. Oh, there were some things I wouldn't have wanted, and there were some annoying changes made at the last minute without consulting. But on the whole I was very pleased with it, which is very unusual. Everyone connected with the production got to have an evangelical feeling that they were making a contribution to the American people by giving them back George Washington. As I was the only person around who knew about George Washington, they were willing to accept what I told them.

CA: Some of the illustrations in your book were most interesting. One in particular was the bust of Washington done by the French sculptor Houdon, which was in the possession of Thomas Jefferson. It gives the reader a picture of Washington that isn't usually conveyed.

FLEXNER: It's the best portrait of Washington. For one thing, it was done when he was a relatively young man. Of course Gilbert Stuart got at him when he was quite far along.

CA: We have "Parson" Mason Locke Weems to thank for the cherry tree story and others that were so long a part of the Washington mythology. Was just about everything Weems said inaccurate?

FLEXNER: He made the stories up as he went along, and he probably did more damage to Washington than anybody else. Interestingly enough, there's one note in Wash-

ington's journals that someone had brought along as a guest the Reverend something-or-other Weems; the note didn't proceed any further. It shows that you never know when the nemesis is really after you.

CA: Did the muckrakers do any harm to Washington's reputation in their treatment of him?

FLEXNER: I think there has always been a Freudian image of Washington as a father-figure that you want to get rid of. There was a great deal of satisfaction on many people's parts in putting him down, and there are always iconoclasts. Also, so much of [what was] held against him was stuff that had been manufactured for him, as in the case of Weems. More prayers had been written for him by various preachers of various denominations. Washington never wrote a prayer in his life. So a great deal of what was held against him was based on what was subsequently published and believed. People were likely to pick things up against him out of all this mythology. I have a basic principle for biography which is not followed particularly: it's ridiculous to write about an individual and give a picture of somebody who couldn't have achieved what the individual did achieve. Most of these muckraking biographies of great men present a picture of an individual who couldn't possibly have done what the individual did.

CA: In the introduction to the George Washington life you said, "My labors have persuaded me that George Washington became one of the noblest and greatest men who ever lived." Why do you feel that?

FLEXNER: There were many things. The most conspicuous thing is that he's about the only individual in history who refused absolute power. What happens in revolutions is that everything is torn down. When peace returns, there is nothing on the landscape and anything that's started is likely to be torn down again. The natural tendency was to turn to a man, such as Lenin, Hitler, Napoleon. Washington was the only individual who had the stature. No one else could compete with him. But he was absolutely deaf to all suggestions that he take over power. That is the most obvious thing, though there were many others.

CA: Despite the power he did have, he was always a very gentle man, wasn't he?

FLEXNER: Yes. He was nervous about the exertion of power; he didn't enjoy it. He didn't like to [be] kicked around, but then who does? On the other hand, during the Revolution, two or three times when things looked awfully dark, the Continental Congress would invest him with really dictatorial powers, partly because when Philadelphia was captured, they had to disperse. And Washington was very, very careful about what he did.

CA: Washington was the only one of the founding fathers, you pointed out, who freed his slaves.

FLEXNER: Washington's attitudes towards slavery had been left to me to discover. Scholars were afraid that they would be forced to conclusions that they wouldn't like. I was the first person who investigated the whole question. And I demonstrated that he started out as a conventional slaveholder and gradually became an abolitionist.

CA: You don't think he looked upon whites and blacks as equals at that time, though, do you?

FLEXNER: What he said was that he was worried about freeing slaves bang off, because they hadn't been given an opportunity to learn how to handle themselves and to take responsibility. His theory was that they should be freed and employed on the plantation, and then have the children get the education which they would then be enabled to take. But there's no indication that he thought the blacks were inferior. He thought their position had placed them where they couldn't be expected to walk out of slavery and be ordinary citizens.

CA: In the opening chapters of your book American Saga *you describe your father's not finishing grade school, losing many jobs, seeming to be headed for a dead end. Was his finding the microscope really the main turning point in his life?*

FLEXNER: The real turning point—and he didn't understand this himself—was after all these very unfortunate experiences and being considered the liability in a large family, he came down with typhoid fever and almost died. As a result, during the long period of convalescence he was treated with interest by his family, and particularly by his mother, whom he adored. He was also allowed time to think about things. He sat by himself in the little garden they had, and he didn't read, because they didn't have a public library then in Louisille, Kentucky, which may have been an advantage to him. During that period of time, he sorted himself out. From then on, he went like a rocket.

CA: Reading the American Saga, *I kept wondering why somebody in the family didn't recognize his tremendous potential during those early years.*

FLEXNER: They didn't, and he didn't recognize it himself. His teachers didn't recognize it. I think it probably isn't surprising in the circumstances. He didn't really show it. Also, it was a family on the edge of poverty, and he wasn't considered by any means one of the bright sons. His older brother Jacob and his younger brother Abraham were considered to be the hotshots of the family, and Simon was considered to be the dumb cluck. I tried to describe the amazement of the family when Simon won the gold medal from the College of Pharmacy.

CA: Who has that now?

FLEXNER: I have.

CA: Did you spend a lot of time in Louisville doing research for the book?

FLEXNER: I didn't, because there was no one left there who would have known Father in those days. I had a tremendous amount of other reference material. For one thing, I had a partial autobiography Father had written; and I had interviewed him, because he wanted me to do a biography, so I had my own notes on what he said.

CA: You said earlier that the lack of a public library may have been to your father's advantage. And as a student, he seemed to do everything in his own way. Do you think his academic experience might even have been an impediment?

FLEXNER: It could have been. He always did things his own way, and as a research scientist, of course, as soon as you got moving, you passed beyond the realm where things are known. Father was always very scornful of people who followed tradition.

CA: Did he pass that on to you?

FLEXNER: I think he did.

CA: With all the responsibilities he had as an adult, did he have much time to spend with you as you were growing up?

FLEXNER: Not a great deal. We were much more raised by my mother. She was much concerned with literature, poetry, and so forth. She published an autobiographical book called *A Quaker Childhood*. But I had great respect for my father, and he was a great model.

CA: Did you ever think of going into medical research yourself?

FLEXNER: I had no special interest in science at all. My brother did, but Father, being by then a very famous man, thought it would be awfully foolish for either of his sons to follow in his footsteps. He said we'd never get any credit; people would always say, "Oh, he's Simon Flexner's son." My brother became a mathematician, and I followed my mother's direction and became a writer.

CA: Are you working on a book now?

FLEXNER: I am, but I can't say what it is. That's part of my method.

BIOGRAPHICAL/CRITICAL SOURCES:

BOOKS

Dictionary of Literary Biography, Gale, Volume 17: *Twentieth-Century American Historians*, 1983, Volume 30: *American Historians, 1607-1865*, 1985.

Flexner, James Thomas, *Doctors on Horseback: Pioneers of American Medicine*, Viking, 1937.

FIexner, James Thomas, *George Washington: Anguish and Farewell, 1793-1799,* Little, Brown, 1972.
Flexner, James Thomas, *Washington: The Indispensible Man,* Little, Brown, 1974.
Freeman, Douglas Southall, *George Washington,* Scribners, Volumes 1 and 2: *Young Washington,* 1948, Volume 3: *Planter and Patriot,* 1951, Volume 4: *Leader of the Revolution,* 1951, Volume 5: *Victory with the Help of France,* 1952, Volume 6: *Patriot and President,* 1954, Volume 7: (with John Alexander Carroll and Mary Wells Ashworth) *First in Peace,* 1957.
Weems, Mason Locke, *A History of the Life and Death, Virtues, and Exploits of General George Washington,* Green & English, 1800, enlarged edition published as *The Life of George Washington, with Curious Anecdotes, Equally Honourable to Himself, and Exemplary to His Young Countrymen,* R. Cochran, 1808.

PERIODICALS

Atlantic, April, 1968.
Christian Science Monitor, October 16, 1974; May 10, 1978.
National Review, April 6, 1971.
New Yorker, April 20, 1968; October 17, 1970; March 10, 1973.
New York Review of Books, May 4, 1978.
New York Times, October 24, 1937; April 2, 1968; November 2, 1970; April 15, 1973; March 17, 1978.
New York Times Book Review, November 14, 1965; March 31, 1968; October 25, 1970; November 19, 1972; October 20, 1974; March 26, 1978; March 4, 1984.
Newsweek, November 20, 1972.
Saturday Review, January 15, 1966; May 25, 1968; November 21, 1970; October 23, 1972.
Saturday Review of Literature, October 30, 1937.
Washington Post, April 8, 1984.
Washington Post Book World, August 31, 1980; February 19, 1984.

—*Sketch by Kenneth R. Shepherd*

—*Interview by Walter W. Ross*

*   *   *

FLINT, Lucy
See FLINT-GOHLKE, Lucy

*   *   *

FLINT-GOHLKE, Lucy 1954-
(Lucy Flint)

PERSONAL: Born March 4, 1954, in Madrid, Spain; U.S. citizen born abroad; daughter of Weston (a professor) and Noma (a teacher; maiden name, Clayton), Flint. *Education:* Attended University of Madrid, 1974-75; Wesleyan University, Middletown, CT, B.A., 1976; Columbia University, M.A., 1979.

ADDRESSES: Home—65 Cross St., Ashland, MA 01721.

CAREER: Solomon R. Guggenheim Museum, New York City, research assistant, 1978-79, curatorial assistant, 1980-81, curatorial coordinator, 1981-83; free-lance art historian, 1983-87; Wellesley College Museum, Wellesley, MA, assistant director, 1987—.

AWARDS, HONORS: Award of Merit, American Association of Museums, 1984, for *Handbook: The Peggy Guggenheim Collection.*

WRITINGS:

(Under name Lucy Flint) *Handbook: The Peggy Guggenheim Collection,* Abrams, 1983.
Photo Call: Five Photographers Refigure a Tradition, Wellesley College Museum, 1988.
Duchamp-Villon's Baudelaire: Sources and Transformations, Wellesley College Museum, 1990.
Walker Art Center: Painting and Sculpture from the Collection, Rizzoli, 1991.

Contributor to periodicals, including *Beaux-Arts* and *Hungry Mind Review.*

WORK IN PROGRESS: Davis Museum: Works from the Collection.

SIDELIGHTS: Lucy Flint-Gohlke told *CA,* "In my work I intend to provide information that will be useful and illuminating for the scholar, and yet accessible enough to engage the interested lay person."

*   *   *

FLYNN, Leslie Bruce 1918-

PERSONAL: Born October 3, 1918, in Hamilton, Ontario, Canada; son of James A. and Agnes (Shaver) Flynn; married Bernice L. Carlson, 1945; children: Linnea, Janna, Marilee, Annilee, Donna, Carol, Susan. *Education:* Attended Moody Bible Institute, 1937-40; Wheaton College, A.B., 1942; Eastern Baptist Theological Seminary, B.D., 1944; University of Pennsylvania, A.M., 1946.

ADDRESSES: Home—32 Highview Ave., Nanuet, NY 10954. *Office*—Grace Conservative Baptist Church, 22 Demarest, Nanuet, NY 10954.

CAREER: Bethlehem Baptist Church, St. Clair, PA, pastor, 1944-49; Grace Conservative Baptist Church, Nanuet, NY, pastor, 1949—. Instructor, Nyack College, 1951-72.

MEMBER: Evangelical Theological Society.

AWARDS, HONORS: D.D. from Conservative Baptist Theological Seminary, 1963.

WRITINGS:

Did I Say That?, Broadman, 1959.
Serve Him with Mirth, Zondervan, 1960.
Your God and Your Gold, Zondervan, 1961.
The Power of Christlike Living, Zondervan, 1962.
Did I Say Thanks?, Broadman, 1963.
Christmas Messages, Baker Book, 1964.
Day of Resurrection, Broadman, 1965.
How to Save Time in the Ministry, Broadman, 1966.
Your Influence Is Showing, Broadman, 1967.
You Can Live above Envy, Conservative Baptist Press, 1970.
A Source Book of Humorous Stories, Baker Book, 1973.
It's about Time, Timothy Books, 1974.
Nineteen Gifts of the Spirit, Scripture Press, 1974.
Great Church Fights, Scripture Press, 1976.
Now a Word from Our Creator, Scripture Press, 1976.
Man: Ruined and Restored, Scripture Press, 1978.
(With wife, Bernice Flynn) *God's Will: You Can Know It,* Scripture Press, 1979.
Joseph: God's Man in Egypt, Scripture Press, 1979.
The Gift of Joy, Scripture Press, 1980.
From Clay to Rock, Christian Herald, 1981.
You Don't Have to Go It Alone, Accent, 1981.
Dare to Care Like Jesus, Scripture Press, 1982.
The Twelve, Scripture Press, 1982.
Worship—Together We Celebrate, Scripture Press, 1983.
Your Inner You, Scripture Press, 1984.
The Sustaining Power of Hope, Scripture Press, 1985.
Holy Contradictions, Scripture Press, 1987.
Come Alive with Illustrations, Baker Book, 1988.
The Other Twelve, Scripture Press, 1988.
(With B. Flynn) *Humorous Incidents and Quips for Church Publications,* Baker Book, 1990.
The Miracles of Jesus, Scripture Press, 1990.
How to Survive in the Ministry, Kregel, 1992.

*   *   *

FORD, Hilary
See YOUD, (Christopher) Samuel

*   *   *

FOREST, Dial
See GAULT, William Campbell

FRASCINO, Edward

PERSONAL: Surname is pronounced "Fra-*shee*-no"; born in Bronx, NY; son of Mario (a clothes designer) and Rose (D'Agostino) Frascino. *Education:* Attended Parson's School of Design, 1951. *Avocational interests:* Painting, sculpting, watching old movies, and the New York Mets.

ADDRESSES: Home—Brooklyn, NY. *Office*—c/o *New Yorker,* 25 West 43rd St., New York, NY 10036.

CAREER: Cartoonist, author and illustrator of books for children. Began career as a designer of greeting cards, worked as draftsman for Remington Rand, and in advertising; free-lance cartoonist, 1965—. *Military service:* U.S. Army, 1951-53; served in Korea.

AWARDS, HONORS: Awards for illustrating E. B. White's *The Trumpet of the Swan* include Spring Book Festival Award from *Book World* and American Library Association notable book citation, both 1970, finalist in National Book Award nominations, 1971, honor list of International Board on Books for Young People, 1972, Sequoyah Children's Book Award from Oklahoma Library Association, 1973, William Allen White Children's Book Award from William Allen White Library at Emporia State University, 1973, Sue Hefly Award from Louisiana Association of School Librarians, 1975, and Young Hoosier Book Award from Association for Indiana Media Educators, 1975.

WRITINGS:

FOR CHILDREN; SELF-ILLUSTRATED

Eddie Spaghetti, Harper, 1978.
Eddie Spaghetti on the Home Front, Harper, 1983.
My Cousin the King, Prentice-Hall, 1985.
Nanny Noony and the Magic Spell, Pippin Press, 1988.
Nanny Noony and the Dust Queen, Pippin Press, 1990.

FOR CHILDREN; ILLUSTRATOR

Mary Stolz, *Say Something,* Harper, 1968.
M. Stolz, *The Dragons of the Queen,* Harper, 1969.
M. Stolz, *The Story of a Singular Hen and Her Peculiar Children,* Harper, 1969.
Marjorie W. Sharmat, *Gladys Told Me to Meet Her Here,* Harper, 1970.
E. B. White, *The Trumpet of the Swan,* Harper, 1970.
Hans Christian Andersen, *The Little Mermaid,* translated by Eva Le Gallienne, Harper, 1971.
Gladys Y. Cretan, *A Hole, a Box, and a Stick,* Lothrop, 1972.
Carole Hart, *Delilah,* Harper, 1973.
Robert E. Barry, *Snowman's Secret,* Macmillan, 1975.
Shirley Gordon, *Crystal Is the New Girl,* Harper, 1976.
S. Gordon, *Crystal Is My Friend,* Harper, 1978.

Nancy L. Robison, *UFO Kidnap!,* Lothrop, 1978.

Nigel Gray, *It'll All Come Out in the Wash,* Harper, 1979.

N. Robison, *Space Hijack!,* Lothrop, 1979.

S. Gordon, *Me and the Bad Guys,* Harper, 1980.

N. Robison, *Izoo,* Lothrop, 1980.

S. Gordon, *Happy Birthday, Crystal,* Harper, 1981.

Charles Keller, compiler, *Oh, Brother: And Other Family Jokes,* Prentice-Hall, 1982.

William E. Warren, *The Graveyard and Other Not-So-Scary Stories,* Prentice-Hall, 1984.

W. E. Warren, *The Thing in the Swamp and More Not-So-Scary Stories,* Prentice-Hall, 1984.

W. E. Warren, *Footsteps in the Fog: Still More Not-So-Scary Stories,* Prentice-Hall, 1985.

Rudyard Kipling, *The Elephant's Child,* Prentice-Hall, 1987.

C. Keller, *Count Draculations! Monster Riddles,* Prentice-Hall, 1988.

S. Gordon, *Crystal's Christmas Carol,* Harper, 1989.

C. Keller, compiler, *King Henry the Ape: Animal Jokes,* Pippin Press, 1990.

OTHER

Avocado Is Not Your Color: And Other Scenes of Married Bliss (adult cartoons), Penguin, 1983.

Contributor of cartoons to periodicals and newspapers, including *Punch, Saturday Review, New York Times,* and a regular series in *New Yorker.*

SIDELIGHTS: Edward Frascino, best known for his illustrations of E. B. White's *The Trumpet of the Swan,* is a prolific illustrator and cartoonist. His simple yet vivid drawings have appeared in the works of numerous authors, and in the pages of many magazines. After ten years as an illustrator, Frascino began to write his own stories, some of which tell of his life as a child growing up in New York City during the Second World War. Whether drawing for others or for himself, for adults or for children, Frascino brings a comical touch to his work that consistently delights the reader.

Frascino was born in Bronx, New York, the son of Albanian-Italian parents. He once said that "on Sundays the extended family gathered at my grandmother's, a sweet, gentle, submissive-seeming lady who, I eventually realized, ruled the family." At his grandmother's Frascino was first exposed to the magazines and radio programs which later influenced him to become an artist. He saw the *New Yorker* magazine for the first time there, he recalls in his autobiographical sketch in *Something about the Author Autobiography Series* (*SAAS*), and remembers that "the humor was a bit over my head, but the cartoon drawings fascinated me. Each was a work of art." He also remembers the entire family listening to the comedy shows on the radio in the evening.

Other sources of early joy for Frascino were comic strips and the movies. In the 1940s New York City had eight or nine daily newspapers, most of which published comic strips every day of the week. Frascino commented: "Comic strips were a critical influence on me, not only as a visual artist, but as a storyteller, too. In a certain way, cartoons were for us what television is today." Frascino would copy his favorite comics over and over, and he especially loved the villains—"the more moustache-twirling the better!" His other great love as a child was the movies. "A movie palace was like a cathedral," he remembers in *SAAS,* "and in the images projected on screen the actors' faces seemed to glow from within." Frascino rewrote the endings to movies if he didn't like them, often allowing the villain to win if he didn't like the actor playing the character.

While movies, magazines, comic strips, and radio influenced Frascino to become an artist, other aspects of his childhood appeared in two semi-autobiographical books he has written. *Eddie Spaghetti* and *Eddie Spaghetti on the Home Front* paint vivid pictures of growing up in Yonkers, New York, before and during the Second World War. In the first book, Frascino recreates his beloved trips with his brother and mother to Bronx Park and the reptile house at the Bronx Zoo, trips that instilled in him an abiding love for all animals. The second book describes the adventures of a group of boys caught up in the patriotism and excitement of helping the war effort in their own small ways. A *New York Times Book Review* critic calls the book "an affectionate answer" to a child's questions about the "olden days."

While Frascino enjoyed his childhood, he hated going to school. He once said: "I can still look back and say, 'Nothing was worse than school.' I hated the regimentation, the routine." He had few friends, and recalls getting good grades only in the classes of the few teachers who truly loved their subject and transmitted that enthusiasm to the students. His fondest memories of that time were of starring in a radio play at age eleven and of playing hooky from school to spend the afternoon in the dark fantasy world of the movie theatre.

Frascino was able to major in art in high school however, and after graduation convinced his father to allow him to attend the Parsons School of Design in New York City. There he finally met people who shared his interests and he was able to spend all his time doing what he loved: drawing. Upon graduating from Parsons he was unable to turn that love into employment, though he tried to find jobs with many magazines and advertising agencies. Frustrated, Frascino joined the Army Reserves in 1951 and soon found himself drawing topographical maps in Korea for a colonel whom he once described as "a lunatic—career majors and sergeants quaked in his presence."

After leaving the service, Frascino lived in Los Angeles, where he had hoped to secure a position with Walt Disney's studio; unsuccessful, he returned to New York City where he looked for work as an illustrator. What he found was a job as a waiter, but it brought him in contact with a set of artistic friends whose creativity and belief in their own work encouraged him in his. Finally, he found a job drawing greeting cards, and later a job with an advertising agency that offered little excitement but did allow him time to draw on his own. Frascino began submitting cartoon drawings to *New Yorker* every week; after a series of refusals the prestigious magazine bought first his ideas and then his drawings. At long last Frascino was working for the very magazine he had admired as a child.

Frascino worked as a free-lance cartoonist for about five years before a friend at Harper and Row (a publishing company) suggested that he think about illustrating a children's book. He submitted some drawings and soon did the illustrations for *Say Something,* a picture book by the popular Mary Stolz. With the help of Ursula Nordstrom, an editor at Harper's, Frascino did the drawings for two more Stolz books, and was then contracted to do the illustrations for E. B. White's *The Trumpet of the Swan.* Frascino says in *SAAS:* "I especially like *The Trumpet of the Swan* because it promotes wildlife conservation and, after it was published, many handicapped children wrote letters telling how they were encouraged by the triumph of Louis, a trumpeter born mute."

A number of Frascino's books feature his favorite animal: cats. Frascino discovered the company of cats one day when he returned home from breakfast to find a fat, calico cat sitting on his doorstep. He remembers in *SAAS:* "Her pale green eyes looked at me pleadingly. My love for animals plus an old Albanian superstition about a cat at your door bringing good luck prompted me to invite her inside." The cat, named Elvira, soon delivered a litter of kittens and Frascino learned to work with cats sprawling comfortably on the desk beside him. Before he had cats, Frascino had written a book about a cat that was turned down by a publisher because it lacked focus. Later, thoroughly schooled in feline ways, he wrote and published *My Cousin the King,* "a fable about a stray cat who swells with pride when he learns he is related to the lion, King of Beasts," dedicating the book to Elvira. To this day Frascino takes in stray cats until he is able to find homes for them.

For ten years Frascino did drawings for other people's books, but eventually decided to write his own book. He says in *SAAS:* "The idea of writing a novel for children had never occurred to me, but once I began I found I could make pictures with words." Surprisingly, he found it more difficult to illustrate his own books at first. He recalls that "drawing pictures I had already made with words seemed redundant." Frascino works nearly every day out of his home in Park Slope, a historic landmark section of Brooklyn, New York, and describes his working habits for *SAAS:* "At the same hour every day I sit at my writing table, on which a cat is usually stretched out asleep, and, on a large pad in longhand, I write. To get ideas flowing, I write anything: nonsense, letters to myself, my name. Eventually a story begins to emerge. . . . Much thought and effort and patience is necessary, but this is stimulating and, when the solution arrives, exhilarating." Frascino insists that the most important element of his work is spontaneity, saying "I must work spontaneously or I have trouble working at all. I can't even talk about work in progress. If I give voice to an idea, it's as if I've already realized it and the execution becomes a bore. I make so many exciting discoveries in the course of working. Sometimes ideas just explode. I never want to deny myself the joy of that by letting the energy seep out when it shouldn't."

BIOGRAPHICAL/CRITICAL SOURCES:

BOOKS

Kingman, Lee, and others, compilers, *Illustrators of Children's Books: 1967-1976,* Horn Book, 1978.
Something about the Author Autobiography Series, Volume 9, Gale, 1990, pp. 153-168.
Ward, Martha E., and Dorothy Marquardt, *Illustrators of Books for Young People,* 2nd edition, Scarecrow, 1975.

PERIODICALS

New York Times Book Review, April 16, 1978, p. 26.*

*   *   *

FRITZ, Jean (Guttery) 1915-

PERSONAL: Born November 16, 1915, in Hankow, China; daughter of Arthur Minton (a minister and YMCA missionary) and Myrtle (Chaney) Guttery; married Michael Fritz, November 1, 1941; children: David, Andrea. *Education:* Wheaton College, A.B., 1937; study at Columbia University.

ADDRESSES: Home—50 Bellewood Ave., Dobbs Ferry, NY 10522. *Agent*—Gina MacCoby Literary Agency, 1123 Broadway, Suite 1010, New York, NY 10010.

CAREER: Author of historical biographies and novels for young people. Silver Burdett Co., New York City, research assistant, 1937-41; Dobbs Ferry Library, Dobbs Ferry, NY, children's librarian, 1955-57; Jean Fritz Writers' Workshops, Katonah, NY, founder and instructor, 1962-70; Board of Co-operative Educational Service, Westchester County, NY, teacher, 1971-73; Appalachian

State University, Boone, NC, faculty member, summers, 1980-82. Lecturer.

AWARDS, HONORS: Named *New York Times* outstanding book of the year, 1973, for *And Then What Happened, Paul Revere?*, 1974, for *Why Don't You Get a Horse, Sam Adams?*, 1975, for *Where Was Patrick Henry on the 29th of May?*, 1976, for *What's the Big Idea, Ben Franklin?*, 1981, for *Traitor: The Case of Benedict Arnold,* and 1982, for *Homesick: My Own Story;* named *Boston Globe-Horn Book* honor book, 1974, for *And Then What Happened, Paul Revere?*, 1976, for *Will You Sign Here, John Hancock?*, and 1980, for *Stonewall;* named outstanding Pennsylvania author, Pennsylvania School Library Association, 1978; Honor Award for Nonfiction, Children's Book Guild, 1978, for the "body of her creative writing," and 1979; American Book Award nomination, 1980, for *Where Do You Think You're Going, Christopher Columbus?*, and 1981, for *Traitor: The Case of Benedict Arnold;* LL.D., Washington and Jefferson College, 1982, Wheaton College, 1987; Child Study Award and Christopher Award, both 1982, Newbery Honor Book Award, American Book Award, and named *Boston Globe-Horn Book* honor book, all 1983, all for *Homesick: My Own Story;* *Boston Globe-Horn Book* Nonfiction Award, 1984, for *The Double Life of Pocahontas;* Regina Award, 1985; Laura Ingalls Wilder Award, 1986; Orbis Pictus Award, National Council of English Teachers, 1989, for *The Great Little Madison;* many of Fritz's books have been named notable books by the American Library Association.

WRITINGS:

Bunny Hopwell's First Spring, illustrated by Rachel Dixon, Wonder Books, 1954.

Help Mr. Willy Nilly, illustrated by Jean Tamburine, Treasure Books, 1954.

Fish Head, illustrated by Marc Simont, Coward, 1954.

Hurrah for Jonathan!, illustrated by Violet La Mont, A. Whitman, 1955.

121 Pudding Street, illustrated by Sofia, Coward, 1955.

Growing Up, illustrated by Elizabeth Webbe, Rand McNally, 1956.

The Late Spring, illustrated by Erik Blegvad, Coward, 1957.

The Cabin Faced West, illustrated by Feodor Rojankovsky, Coward, 1958.

(With Tom Club) *Champion Dog, Prince Tom,* illustrated by Ernest Hart, Coward, 1958.

The Animals of Doctor Schweitzer, illustrated by Douglas Howland, Coward, 1958.

How to Read a Rabbit, illustrated by Leonard Shortall, Coward, 1959.

Brady, illustrated by Lynd Ward, Coward, 1960.

Tap, Tap Lion, 1, 2, 3, illustrated by Shortall, Coward, 1962.

San Francisco, illustrated by Emil Weiss, Rand McNally, 1962.

I, Adam, illustrated by Peter Burchard, Coward, 1963.

Magic to Burn, illustrated by Beth Krush and Joe Crush, Coward, 1964.

Surprise Party (reader), illustrated by George Wiggins, Initial Teaching Alphabet Publications, 1965.

The Train (reader), illustrated by Jean Simpson, Grosset, 1965.

Early Thunder, illustrated by Ward, Coward, 1967.

George Washington's Breakfast, illustrated by Paul Galdone, Coward, 1969.

And Then What Happened, Paul Revere?, illustrated by Margot Tomes, Coward, 1973.

Why Don't You Get a Horse, Sam Adams?, illustrated by Trina Schart Hyman, Coward, 1974.

Where Was Patrick Henry on the 29th of May?, illustrated by Tomes, Coward, 1975.

Who's That Stopping on Plymouth Rock?, illustrated by J. B. Handelsman, Coward, 1975.

Will You Sign Here, John Hancock?, illustrated by Hyman, Coward, 1976.

What's the Big Idea, Ben Franklin?, illustrated by Tomes, Coward, 1976.

The Secret Diary of Jeb and Abigail: Growing Up in America, 1776-1783, illustrated by Kenneth Bald and Neil Boyle, Reader's Digest Association, 1976.

Can't You Make Them Behave, King George?, illustrated by Tomie de Paola, Coward, 1977.

Brendan the Navigator, illustrated by Enrico Amo, Coward, 1979.

Stonewall, illustrated by Stephen Gammell, Putnam, 1979.

Where Do You Think You're Going, Christopher Columbus?, illustrated by Tomes, Putnam, 1980.

The Man Who Loved Books, illustrated by Hyman, Putnam, 1981.

Traitor: The Case of Benedict Arnold, illustrated by John Andrew, Putnam, 1981.

Back to Early Cape Cod, Acorn Press, 1981.

The Good Giants and the Bad Pukwudgies (folktales), illustrated by de Paola, Putnam, 1982.

Homesick: My Own Story, illustrated by Tomes, Putnam, 1982.

The Double Life of Pocahontas, illustrated by Ed Young, Putnam, 1983.

China Homecoming, illustrated with photographs by Mike Fritz, Putnam, 1985.

Make Way for Sam Houston!, illustrated by Elise Primavera, Putnam, 1986.

Shh! We're Writing the Constitution, illustrated by de Paola, Putnam, 1987.

China's Long March: 6000 Miles of Danger, illustrated by Yang Zhr Cheng, Putnam, 1988.

The Great Little Madison, Putnam, 1989.
Bully for You, Teddy Roosevelt!, Putnam, 1991.

OTHER

Cast for a Revolution: Some American Friends and Enemies, 1728-1814 (adult biography), Houghton, 1972.
(Contributor) William Zinsser, editor, *Worlds of Childhood: The Art and Craft of Writing for Children,* Houghton, 1990.

Book reviewer, *San Francisco Chronicle,* 1941-43, and *New York Times,* 1970—. Contributor of short stories to periodicals, including *Seventeen, Redbook,* and *New Yorker.*

Fritz's writings have been recorded on audio cassette.

Fritz's papers are housed in a permanent collection in the Children's Literature Collection at the University of Oregon, Eugene, and included in the Kerland Collection at the University of Minnesota, and in a collection at the University of Southern Mississippi.

SIDELIGHTS: Jean Fritz is generally acknowledged as being one of the best authors of historical biographies written for young people. Although many of these biographies are studies of American Revolutionary War figures (including George Washington, Paul Revere, Samuel Adams, and John Hancock), Fritz has also published books on such people as Christopher Columbus, King George the Third, Pochontas, St. Brendan the Navigator, and Thomas Jonathon "Stonewall" Jackson. In 1978, Fritz was given the Children's Book Guild's Honor Award for Nonfiction paying tribute to the "body of her creative writing."

Fritz has attributed her love of writing to the fact that her childhood was most unusual and she needed an outlet to record her thoughts and feelings. Fritz spent the first thirteen years of her life in China because her parents were doing missionary work. An only child, Fritz often felt lonely and out of place in China. Writing became her "private place, where no one could come," she recalls in a *Publishers Weekly* interview.

At an early age, Fritz told her parents she wanted to become a writer and began keeping a journal. According to O. Mell Busbin in *Dictionary of Literary Biography,* this journal "at first consisted primarily of quotes from books and poems she was reading but which soon expanded into more than just a collection of comments on life by great writers; it became a place for her to articulate her feelings about people and life. Years later she drew upon it in her writings for children."

While living in China and separated from their homeland, Fritz's parents spoke glowingly of their memories of the United States. Fritz listened to these stories with intense interest forming strong emotional bonds to America. "I think it is because I was so far away that I developed a homesickness that made me want to embrace not just a given part of America at a given time but the whole of it," Fritz writes in an article for *Horn Book.* "No one is more patriotic than the one separated from his country; no one is as eager to find roots as the person who has been uprooted."

In addition to reminiscing about life in the United States, Fritz's father frequently told her fascinating stories about American heroes, especially his favorite, Woodrow Wilson. In her award winning and critically acclaimed biographies, Fritz seems to combine her keen curiosity with American heroes and her appreciation for this fine country to create books that are both fascinating to read as well as educational.

Critics have marvelled at the fact that a Fritz biography consistently delivers a well-crafted, realistic, thoroughly researched, and frequently witty look at the characters that have shaped and influenced our history. For example, in her *Language Arts* review of *Traitor: The Case of Benedict Arnold,* Ruth M. Stein notes that Fritz's "books exemplify criteria for good biographies—accuracy, interest, relevance to our times, and insight into the person, the period, and contemporaries. . . . However cozy the style and informal the writing, the scholarship is solid, yet unobtrusive. Primary and secondary material are woven so neatly into the narrative, you scarcely notice the internal documentation. . . . She manages to clarify her protagonist and the positions he took, even though she cannot be accused of remaining unbiased." And Georgess McHargue remarks in the *New York Times Book Review* that "Jean Fritz has what amounts to perfect pitch when writing history or biography for young people."

Fritz's talent for making her characters come to life is one of the major reasons for her popularity with readers and critics alike. As Busbin states in *Dictionary of Literary Biography:* "In her biographies Fritz attempts to get at the truth of the individual through his likes, dislikes, worries, joys, successes, failures. In each case she reveals the humanity of the individual, presenting his life as revealed in his diary, letters, and other original sources. Through her humorous style she paints a full, believable picture of each individual, using specific, exact language and precise detail. She refuses to create fictional dialogue for the characters in her biographies; the only conversation found in these books is that which she has discovered in letters, diaries, journals, and other original sources, which she draws upon plentifully." "I like being a detective, a treasure hunter, an eavesdropper," Fritz reveals to Richard Ammon in a profile for *Language Arts.* "I look for personalites whose lives make good stories. I like complicated people, persons who possessed contradictions or who has interesting quirks."

In the *Los Angeles Times Book Review,* Barbara Karlin cites the reasons she feels Fritz's historical character studies as so well-received. Karlin explains in a review of *And Then What Happened, Paul Revere?, What's the Big Idea, Ben Franklin?,* and *Where Was Patrick Henry on the 29th of May?* that Fritz's "style is original for this type of book and is what makes these books so attractive to young readers—a friendly, almost chatty delivery, accessible and human subjects. They have foibles and frailties, neuroses and warts. She includes the kind of personal anecdotes and facts that kids find fascinating. Studying American history was never so much fun." And in an article on Fritz's *Homesick: My Own Story,* James A. Michener reports in the *New York Times Book Review* that what impresses him most is "the felicitous way in which Mrs. Fritz uses children's language and conveys the attitudes of a faraway land and period."

Fritz once shared her thoughts on the reasons behind her books popularity with *CA:* "I think young people of almost any age or ability read biographies for the same reason that adults do—or would if they could find what they what. We all seek insight into the human condition, and it is helpful to find familiar threads running through the lives of others, however famous. We need to know more people in all circumstances and times so we can pursue our private, never-to-be-fulfilled quest to find out what life is all about. In actual experience we are able to see so few lives in the round and to follow them closely from beginning to end. I, for one, need to possess a certain number of relatively whole lives in the long span of history."

Fritz is also widely recognized for her juvenile novels, many of which (like her biographies) are set in colonial America at the time of the Revolutionary War. Most critics find that these books are written in the same clear, easy to read, informative style as her biographies. Fritz's research for these novels has been called extraordinary, and reviewers note that she has a habit of turning up new facts about familiar historical happenings. As a result, her work is often called refreshing and innovative; as Zena Sutherland, writing in the *Bulletin of the Center for Children's Books* observes, "Jean Fritz really has an approach to history that is unique; she makes it fun." And finally, Faith McNulty reflects in the *New Yorker* that "it is a rare writer who can recapture the intense feelings and bittersweet flavor of childhood as honestly and convincingly as Jean Fritz."

Fritz sums up her feelings on writing about America's past in her biographies and novels in this manner: "My interest in writing about American history stemmed originally, I think, from a subconscious desire to find roots. I lived in

China until I was thirteen, hearing constant talk about 'home' (meaning America), but since I had never been 'home,' I felt like a girl without a country. I have put down roots quite firmly by now, but in the process I have discovered the joys of research and am probably hooked. I eavesdrop on the past to satisfy my own curiosity, but if I can surprise children into believing history, I will be happy, especially if they find, as I do, that truth is stranger (and often funnier) than fiction."

BIOGRAPHICAL/CRITICAL SOURCES:

BOOKS

Children's Literature Review, Gale, Volume 2, 1976, Volume 14, 1988. *Dictionary of Literary Biography,* Volume 52: *American Writers for Children since 1960: Fiction,* Gale, 1986.

Hostetler, Elizabeth Ann Rumer, *Jean Fritz: A Critical Biography,* University of Toledo, 1981.

Norton, Donna E., *Through the Eyes of a Child: An Introduction to Children's Literature,* 2nd edition, Merrill, 1987.

Something about the Author, Gale, Volume 1, 1971, Volume 29, 1982.

Something About the Author Autobiography Series, Volume 2, Gale, 1986.

PERIODICALS

Bulletin of the Center for Children's Books, March, 1961; March, 1974; November, 1975; July/August, 1982.

Catholic Library World, July/August, 1985.

Early Years, February, 1982.

Five Owls, May/June, 1987.

Horn Book, October, 1967; January/February, 1985; July/August, 1986.

Language Arts, February, 1977; April, 1980; September, 1982; March, 1983.

Los Angeles Times Book Review, July 25, 1982.

New Yorker, December 6, 1982.

New York Times Book Review, November 9, 1980; November 14, 1982.

Publishers Weekly, July 24, 1981.

San Francisco Chronicel, April 3, 1985.

School Library Journal, November, 1967.

Top of the News, June, 1976.

—*Sketch by Margaret Mazurkiewicz*

*   *   *

FRYE, (Herman) Northrop 1912-1991

PERSONAL: Born July 14, 1912, in Sherbrooke, Quebec, Canada; died of a heart attack, January 22, 1991, in Toronto, Ontario, Canada; son of Herman Edward (a hardware merchant) and Catherine Maud (Howard) Frye; married Helen Kemp, August 24, 1937 (died, 1986); married Elizabeth Brown, 1988. *Education:* University of Toronto, B.A. (philosophy and English; with honors), 1933; Emmanuel College, ordained, 1936; Merton College, Oxford, M.A., 1940. *Religion:* United Church of Canada.

ADDRESSES: Home—127 Clifton Rd., Toronto, Ontario, Canada M4T 2G5. *Office*—Massey College, University of Toronto, Toronto, Ontario, Canada M5S 2E1.

CAREER: Worked as a pastor of a congregation near Shaunavon, Saskatchewan, 1934; University of Toronto, Victoria College, Toronto, Ontario, lecturer in English, 1939-41, assistant professor, 1942-46, associate professor, 1947, professor of English, 1948-91, chairman of department, 1952-59, principal, 1959-67, University Professor, 1967-91. Chancellor, Victoria University, Toronto, 1978-91. Visiting professor at Harvard University, Princeton University, Columbia University, Indiana University, University of Washington, University of British Columbia, Cornell University, University of California, Berkeley, and Oxford University. Andrew D. White Professor-at-Large, Cornell University, 1970-75; Charles Eliot Norton Poetry Professor, Harvard University, 1974-75. Member of board of governors, Ontario Curriculum Institute, 1960-63; chairman of Governor-General's Literary Awards Committee, 1962. Canadian Radio Television and Telecommunications Commission, advisory member, 1968-77.

MEMBER: Modern Language Association of America (executive council member, 1958-62; president, 1976), English Institute (former chairman), Royal Society of Canada (fellow), American Academy of Arts and Sciences (foreign honorary member), British Academy (corresponding fellow), American Philosophical Society (foreign member), American Academy and Institute of Arts and Letters (honorary member).

AWARDS, HONORS: Guggenheim fellow, 1950-51; Lorne Pierce Medal of the Royal Society of Canada, 1958; Canada Council Medal, 1967; Pierre Chauveau Medal of the Royal Society of Canada, 1970; Canada Council Molson Prize, 1971; Companion of the Order of Canada, 1972; honorary fellow, Merton College, Oxford, 1974; Civic Honour, City of Toronto, 1974; Royal Bank Award, 1978; Governor General's Award, 1987. Thirty-six honorary degrees from colleges and universities in Canada and the United States, including Dartmouth College, Harvard University, Princeton University, and University of Manitoba.

WRITINGS:

Fearful Symmetry: A Study of William Blake, Princeton University Press, 1947.

Anatomy of Criticism: Four Essays, Princeton University Press, 1957.

(With others) *The English and Romantic Poets and Essayists: A Review of Research and Criticism,* Modern Language Association of America, 1957.

Culture and the National Will, Carleton University, for Institute of Canadian Studies, 1957.

(With Kluckhohn and Wigglesworth) *Three Lectures,* University of Toronto, 1958.

By Liberal Things, Clarke, Irwin, 1959.

(Editor) William Shakespeare, *The Tempest,* Penguin, 1959.

(Editor) *Design for Learning,* University of Toronto Press, 1962.

(With L. C. Knights and others) *Myth and Symbol: Critical Approaches and Applications,* edited by Bernice Slote, University of Nebraska Press, 1963.

The Developing Imagination (published together with an essay by A. R. MacKinnon), Harvard University Press, 1963.

The Changing Pace of Canadian Education, Sir George Williams University (Montreal), 1963.

The Well-Tempered Critic, Indiana University Press, 1963.

T. S. Eliot: An Introduction, Grove, 1963.

Fables of Identity: Studies in Poetic Mythology, Harcourt, 1963.

(Editor) *Romanticism Reconsidered: Selected Papers from the English Institute,* Columbia University Press, 1963.

The Educated Imagination, Indiana University Press, 1964.

A Natural Perspective: The Development of Shakespearean Comedy and Romance, Columbia University Press, 1965.

The Return of Eden: Five Essays on Milton's Epics, University of Toronto Press, 1965.

(Editor) *Selected Poetry and Prose,* McGraw, 1966.

(Editor) *Blake: A Collection of Critical Essays,* Prentice-Hall, 1966.

Fools of Time: Studies in Shakespearean Tragedy, University of Toronto Press, 1967.

The Modern Century (Whidden Lectures), Oxford University Press, 1967.

A Study of English Romanticism, Random House, 1968.

Silence in the Sea, Memorial University of Newfoundland, 1969.

The Stubborn Structure: Essays on Criticism and Society, Methuen, 1970.

The Bush Garden: Essays on the Canadian Imagination, House of Anansi Press, 1971.

The Critical Path: An Essay on the Social Context of Literary Criticism, Indiana University Press, 1971.

On Teaching Literature, Harcourt, 1972.

The Secular Scripture: A Study of the Structure of Romance, Harvard University Press, 1976.

Spiritus Mundi: Essays on Literature, Myth and Society, Indiana University Press, 1976.

Northrop Frye on Culture and Literature: A Collection of Review Essays, edited by Robert Denham, Chicago University Press, 1978.

Creation and Recreation, University of Toronto Press, 1980.

Criticism as Education, School of Library Service, Columbia University, 1980.

The Great Code: The Bible and Literature, Harcourt, 1982.

Divisions on a Ground: Essays on Canadian Culture, House of Anansi Press, 1982.

The Myth of Deliverance: Reflections on Shakespeare's Problem Comedies, University of Toronto Press, 1982.

(Editor with Sheridan Baker and George W. Perkins) *The Harper Handbook to Literature,* Harper, 1985.

Northrop Frye on Shakespeare, edited by Robert Sandler, Yale University Press, 1986.

(With others) *The Practical Imagination,* Harper, 1987.

On Education, University of Michigan Press, 1988.

Northrop Frye—Myth and Metaphor: Selected Essays, University Press of Virginia, 1990.

Reading the World: Selected Writings, Peter Lang, 1990.

Words with Power: Being a Second Study of "The Bible and Literature," Harcourt, 1990.

Has written educational radio and television programs for the Canadian Broadcasting Co. Work represented in anthologies. Contributor to professional journals. *Canadian Forum,* literary editor, 1947-49, editor, 1949-52.

SIDELIGHTS: Because of the influential theories on literary criticism that he presented in *Anatomy of Criticism: Four Essays* and other books, Northrop Frye was regarded as one of the most important literary critics of his generation. Although Frye made no effort during his life to form a school of criticism based on his ideas, his ability to categorize the different approaches used to analyze literature put the field of criticism as a whole into new perspective. The critic and educator was also once a pastor for the United Church of Canada, and even though he abandoned this career for that of a university professor his religious background led to an interest in the relationship between the Bible and Western literature. Influenced by the poet William Blake, Frye saw the Bible not as something holy in itself, but rather as a text that could lead one to higher spirituality through contact with the Holy Spirit dwelling within each human being. According to Harold Bloom in the *New York Times,* Frye's "true greatness" was his advocacy "of a Protestant and Romantic tradition that has dominated much of British and American literature, the

tradition of the Inner Light, by which each person reads Scripture for himself or herself without yielding to a premature authority imposed by Church or State or School." But for others familiar with Frye's work, like *New York Times Book Review* contributor Robert M. Adams, the critic will be remembered primarily as "one of the bold, inventive—and unhappily rare—schematizers of our literature."

Many of Frye's ideas about literature came from Blake, the eighteenth-century English poet, artist, and critic about whom Frye wrote *Fearful Symmetry: A Study of William Blake.* Before the publication of this book, critics approached Blake's poetry as being "private, mystical, or deranged," according to *Dictionary of Literary Biography* contributor Robert D. Denham. But Frye showed ". . . that Blake's poetry is typical, that he belongs squarely in the tradition of English literature, and that he should be read in imaginative, rather than simply historical, terms." Although Blake's use of symbolism was unique, Frye argued that the basis of this symbolism was universal and could be compared to writings by "Edmund Spenser and John Milton, and especially the Bible." By studying the unity of imagination in Blake's work, Frye extrapolated in *Fearful Symmetry* "that all symbolism in all art and religion is mutually intelligible among all men, and that there is such a thing as the iconography of the imagination."

Frye elaborated upon this theory in *Anatomy of Criticism,* a book that "forced itself" on him when he was trying to write about another subject. After writing *Fearful Symmetry,* Frye was determined at first to apply Blake's principles of literary symbolism and Biblical analysis to the poet Edmund Spenser. But "the introduction to Spenser became an introduction to the theory of allegory, and that theory obstinately adhered to a much larger theoretical structure," Frye explained in *Anatomy's* preface. "The basis of argument became more and more discursive, and less and less historical and Spenserian. I soon found myself entangled in those parts of criticism that have to do with such words as 'myth,' 'symbol,' 'ritual,' and 'archetype'. . . . Eventually, the theoretical and the practical aspects of the task I had begun completely separated." But rather than abandon the project, Frye simply shifted his focus, writing not about Spenser in particular, but about literature in general. When he finished, he had produced four essays of what he calls "pure critical theory." Published together in 1957, these essays comprise *Anatomy of Criticism,* a schematic, non-judgmental theory of literature and the first, according to David Schiller in *Commentary,* "which enables a student to tell where, in the totality of his literary experiences, an individual experience belongs."

Frye believed that the field of literary criticism was an art that was not only misunderstood, but also in disarray, and that setting down a general framework would help to organize all the different theories of criticism. "It is all very well for Blake to say that to generalize is to be an idiot," Frye wrote in his study, "but when we find ourselves in the cultural situation of savages who have words for ash and willow and no word for tree, we wonder if there is not such a thing as being too deficient in the capacity to generalize." To remedy the problem, Frye set out to develop "a coordinating principle, a central hypothesis which, like the theory of evolution in biology, will see the phenomena it deals with as parts of a whole."

His idea was to approach poetry (and by poetry Frye means all literature) the way Aristotle did—"as a biologist [approaching] a system of organisms, picking out its genera and species, formulating the broad laws of literary experience and, in short, writing as though . . . there is a totally intelligible structure of knowledge attainable about poetry which is not poetry itself, or the experience of it, but poetics." To figure out what these "poetics" were, Frye surveyed the whole phenomena of literary experience, isolating each genre, myth and archetypal literary symbol and then relating it to literature as a whole. He organized his findings into categories and came up with the four critical approaches that would eventually form the basis of his essays. They are: historical criticism (theory of modes), ethical criticism (theory of symbols), archetypal criticism (theory of myths), and rhetorical criticism (theory of genres). Although Frye allotted each of these approaches a place in his hypothetical structure, his own particular emphasis was on literary archetypes and how they relate to myths.

When Frye wrote about archetypes, he was referring not to the Jungian concept of a racial consciousness, but to certain "typical" images that recur in poetry. In literature, the repetition of such common images of physical nature as the sea or the forest cannot be explained away as "coincidence," Frye argued. Instead, he asserted that each is an "archetype" or "symbol which connects one poem with another and thereby helps to unify and integrate our literary experience." When we study a masterpiece, Frye explained in his study, the work "draws us to a point at which we seem to see an enormous number of converging patterns of significance. We begin to wonder if we cannot see literature, not only as complicating itself in time, but as spread out in conceptual space from some kind of center that criticism could locate." That center represents the primitive myths from which archetypes spring.

Frye contended that archetypal criticism provides an effective means of deriving the structural principles of literature because it assumes a larger context of literature as a whole. Employing an analogy, Frye compared literature to painting, showing that just as the structural principles of painting are related to plane geometry, so too are the structural principles of literature related to religion and mythology. The Biblical archetypes of the "city" the "garden," and the "sheepfold" are as pervasive in religious writing as gods and demons are in myths, Frye maintained. Thus Frye turned to the symbolism of the Bible and to classical mythology employing both "as a grammar of literary archetypes" to use his words.

Although post-classical literature rarely seems mythic, Frye argued that the myth has simply been "displaced" or covered over with a veneer of realism, making the new work "credible, logically motivated, or morally acceptable" to its audience. In Nathaniel Hawthorne's *The Marble Faun,* for example, there is a girl of singular purity and gentleness who lives in a tower surrounded by doves. Wrote Frye: "The doves are very fond of her; another character calls her his 'dove,' and remarks indicating some special affinity with doves are made about her by both author and characters. If we were to say that [she] is a dove-goddess like Venus . . . we should not be reading the story quite accurately in its own mode; we should be translating it into straight myth." But, Frye claimed, to recognize that Hawthorne employs an archetypal pattern is not irrelevant, or unfair. In fact, he postulated that a person "can get a whole liberal education simply by picking up one conventional poem and following its archetypes as they stretch out into the rest of literature."

One of the most controversial features of Frye's schema is the role it assigns critics. The historical function of criticism, from the time of Samuel Johnson to T. S. Eliot, has been to provide a means of discriminating good writing from bad. But Frye's interest was in what makes works of literature similar to one another, not what makes them different, and he adamantly rejected the notion of critic as judge. It is not, he asserted, the critic's responsibility to evaluate poetry or to say that one poem is better than another because his judgment, while informed, is really nothing more than a reflection of taste. And, "the history of taste is no more a part of the structure of criticism than the Huxley-Wilberforce debate is part of the structure of biological science," Frye wrote. Matters of judgment are best left to book reviewers, not critics, in Frye's point of view.

But W. K. Wimsatt, in an essay in *Northrop Frye in Modern Criticism,* charged Frye with inconsistency: "He can and is willing to distinguish 'ephemeral rubbish,' mediocre works, random and peripheral experience, from the greatest classics, the profound masterpieces in which may be discerned the converging patterns of the primitive formulas. At other moments, however, he says that criticism has nothing whatever to do with either the experience or the judging of literature. The direct experience of literature is central to criticism, yet somehow this center is excluded from it." The effect, Wimsatt concluded, is that the reader remains unsure whether Frye "wishes to discredit all critical valuing whatever, or only the wrong kinds of valuing."

Another important feature of Frye's schema is his view in general and poetry in particular. According to A. Walton Litz, writing in the *Harvard Guide to Contemporary American Writing,* Frye "share[d] with his modern predecessors a poet-Romantic view of the poem as an autonomous organism, which exists independently from the intentions of its creator." And in his study, Frye employed a metaphor that bears out Litz's supposition. "The poet who writes creatively rather than deliberately," Frye said, "is not the father of his poem; he is at best a midwife, or, more accurately still, the womb of Mother Nature herself. . . . The fact that revision is possible, that a poet can make changes in a poem not because he likes them better, but because they are better, shows clearly that the poet has to give birth to the poem as it passes through his mind. He is responsible for delivering it in as uninjured a state as possible, and if the poem is alive, it is equally anxious to be rid of him, and screams to be cut loose from all the navel-strings and feeding-tubes of his ego."

If the poet is the "midwife" of the poem, the critic, according to Frye, may be conceived of as the nurse who presents the creation to the world. And in this role as a describer and classifier of literature, the critic assumes a position that is not subservient, but equal to that of the artist, as Litz explained: "If *Anatomy of Criticism* is a major work of enduring importance, as I believe it to be, then it is the first great work of English or American literary criticism not produced by a practicing artist, and signals a decisive turn toward the continental model. The critic is no longer the servant of the artist but a colleague, with his own special knowledge and powers. . . . [Frye provided] a system which tempts the critic to interpose himself between the artist and the audience as an independent creative force." Despite his admiration for *Anatomy,* Litz said that Frye's system "when manipulated by less subtle minds—tend[s] to homogenize literature and give the critic a spurious authority."

Nor was this the only objection raised against Frye's theory. Some critics charged that Frye's preoccupation with myth and convention isolates literature from its social context, while others accused him of ignoring history and imprisoning literature in a timeless vacuum of archetypal myths. Wimsatt articulated this objection this way: "The Ur-Myth, the Quest Myth, with all its complications, its cycles, acts, scenes, characters, and special symbols, is not a historical fact. And this is so not only in the obvious sense that the stories are not true, but in another sense, which I think we tend to forget and which mythopoeic writing does much to obscure: that such a coherent, cyclic,

and encyclopedic system, such a monomyth, cannot be shown ever to have evolved actually either from ritual, anywhere in the world, or ever anywhere to have been entertained in whole or even in any considerable part. We are talking about the myth of myth. As Frye himself, in his moments of cautionary vision, observe[d], the 'derivation' of the literary genres from the quest myth is 'logical,' not historical. [But,] if we take Frye at his word and attempt to deduce his system 'logically,' we will reject it, for the structure which he shows us is . . . divided between truism and *ad libitum* fantasy."

As a way of countering these charges, Frye, in his subsequent writings, frequently employed subtitles that insist upon the social reference of his criticism, according to Scott Sanders in *Cambridge Review.* Frye's publications, *The Stubborn Structure: Essays on Criticism and Society* and *The Critical Path: An Essay on the Social Context of Literary Criticism* are two such examples. Sanders said that in such publications, however, Frye was "less concerned with the communal sources of literature than he is with the potential role of the humanities, informed by literature, in directing social change." In addition to addressing issues raised by his adversaries, Frye's later writing also elucidates his original theory, and offers some of the practical criticism that was absent in his masterwork. In *A Natural Perspective: The Development of Shakespearean Comedy and Romance,* for instance, Frye turned to Shakespeare to demonstrate his belief that art does not imitate life directly, but instead art imitates art.

With *The Great Code: The Bible and Literature* and its companion study, *Words with Power: Being a Second Study of "The Bible and Literature,"* Frye attempted "his most ambitious literary ascent: a two-volume assault on the central and highest massif in Western civilization," according to John B. Breslin in *Washington Post Book World.* The Bible was for Frye the single most important book upon which the overall structure and mythology behind literature could be based. Indeed, he asserted in *The Great Code* that a "student of English literature who does not know the Bible does not understand a good deal of what is going on in what he reads." Viewing the New and Old Testaments with the eye of a critic rather than a theologian or historian, Frye professed that the Bible could only be fully understood when subjected to systematic literary study.

The Great Code, as the title implies, analyzes the words of the Bible. Frye examined the text typologically, that is, as words representing things, people, and events in the Old Testament that foreshadow those in the New Testament. According to *New York Review of Books* contributor J. M. Cameron, this approach was necessary in Frye's view, "not because this is an interesting pattern after we have given the kaleidoscope a shake, but because this is how the

Biblical authors, in the main, wrote." Viewing the Bible this way, the reader can see the relationship between the Old and New Testaments, such as how the twelve tribes of Israel are reflected in the twelve apostles, how Moses receiving the Ten Commandments is reflected by Jesus's "Sermon on the Mount," and how Israel's defeat of its enemies in Canaan is reflected by the victory of the Resurrection, to give only a few examples.

If the Testaments were written as literary reflections of each other, their historicity might then be brought into question, since this would imply that they are artistic rather than historical works. But Frye was not concerned with proving the historical verity of the Bible in *The Great Code.* Instead, as Rachel Trickett noted in the *Times Literary Supplement,* he "define[d] the linguistic idiom of the Bible as 'kerygma, proclamation,'" meaning that the Bible was written for the primary purpose of proclaiming a message. Frye also asserted that "myth is the linguistic vehicle of *kerygma,* and to . . . 'demythologize' any part of the Bible would be the same thing as to obliterate it." The Bible, in other words, uses myth as a device to proclaim its message of salvation, the importance of which far outweighs any of the specifics behind the stories it relates. As Frye put it, "It is the words themselves that have the authority, not the events they describe." "[The] Bible deliberately blocks off the sense of the referential from itself," Frye later concluded; "it is not a book pointing to a historical presence outside itself, but a book that identifies itself with that presence. At the end the reader, also, is invited to identify himself with the book." By eliminating any preoccupations with the events in the Bible (and thus the necessity for interpretations, either from outside authorities or from any of the reader's preconceived ideas), only the message of salvation remains. Cameron explained that to Frye the Bible's "function is not to point beyond itself, and to summon us to faith, with its conjoined virtues of humility and obedience, but to elevate us beyond faith to the higher life of vision."

The Great Code thus illustrates the imaginative unity of the Bible, and how its use of myths and symbols combine to convey a message (or "theme") of salvation. In Frye's terms, according to W. J. Keith in the *Globe and Mail, The Great Code* is therefore a study of the "'centripetal' coherence" of the Bible. The companion book to *The Great Code,* on the other hand, "moves outward in a 'centrifugal' manner to demonstrate 'the extent to which the canonical unity of the Bible indicates or symbolizes a much wider imaginative unity in secular European literature.'" *New York Times* critic Michiko Kakutani summarized that *Words with Power* "helps the reader recognize some of the recurring myths that connect religious and secular literature, and [Frye] shows how ideological and

social changes can cause changes in the interpretation and emphasis of those myths."

Frye published *Words with Power* just before his death early in 1991, thus completing the last part of "the big book about the Bible" that he had "set out to write as long ago as 1957," but which was set aside for what was to become *Anatomy of Criticism,* according to *New York Times Book Review* contributor Hugh Kenner. As with his other books, Frye set out to study his subject as systematically and scientifically as possible. But a few critics felt that some of Frye's personal beliefs still linger behind his attempted objective analysis. "Frye's career has been devoted unswervingly to the delicate task of placing the Christian religion on a scientific footing," declared Paul H. Fry in the *Yale Review.* "This he has attempted by claiming, first, that his method is indeed scientific, . . . and second, somewhat less candidly, I think, that the object of his discipline is not the Christian revelation, but mythopoetic thinking wherever it appears. It seems to me that Frye is caught in a bind that he cannot acknowledge, one that is perforce more apparent in *The Great Code* than hitherto: he cannot admit the religious basis of his undertaking without admitting that his analytic point of departure . . . is not quite dispassionately chosen." But a number of reviewers have praised Frye's studies of the Bible and its influence in literature. This "is a magnificent book," averred Cameron in his review of *The Great Code,* "a necessary recall to some fundamental principles of Biblical interpretation, and a collection of problems and questions of the first importance for critics, Biblical scholars, and the educated public in general." And *Washington Post Book World* critic Alfred Corn judged *Words with Power* to be "one of the most intelligent and passionate surveys of mythology-and-literature ever written, with Frye's earlier books as its only real competitors."

While Frye's ideas on structuralism have given way to other schools of criticism since the publication of *Anatomy of Criticism,* the critic and his work are still widely admired. "[Frye's] was a hard mind with an intricate and completely assured gift for the patterning of concepts and attitudes," wrote Adams. "[His] wit was concise and dry, his erudition compendious. The first two books [he wrote] expressed exactly the nature of his interests: one was an anatomy, the other laid bare a symmetry. He was always getting down to the bare bones of things while demonstrating the way they could be articulated into larger and larger structures." Nevertheless, Frye's "[d]etractors termed some of his writing turgid and pedantic reworkings of his earlier theories in efforts to rebut critics," according to a *New York Times* obituary by Peter B. Flint. *Sewanee Review* critic Douglas Paschall countered, however, that "Frye has unquestionably earned his right to continuity in his principles, even to his numerous reiterations of them, but less because they have provided a complete universal system than because . . . they have enabled him at best to enliven and inform his readers as few other living critics have done." Novelist Margaret Atwood, who once studied with Frye, praised him in the *Globe and Mail* for making the field of literary criticism available to a nonprofessional audience. As one of only a handful of critics to be read by the general public, Frye "did not lock literature into an ivory tower; instead he emphasized its centrality to the development of a civilized and humane society."

BIOGRAPHICAL/CRITICAL SOURCES:

BOOKS

Ayre, John, *Northrop Frye: A Critical Biography,* General Publishing (Don Mills, Canada), 1988.
Contemporary Literary Criticism, Volume 24, Gale, 1983.
Denham, Robert, *Northrop Frye and Critical Method,* Pennsylvania State University Press, 1978.
Denham, Robert, *Northrop Frye: An Annotated Bibliography of Primary and Secondary Sources,* University of Toronto Press, 1988.
Dictionary of Literary Biography, Gale, Volume 67: *Modern American Critics Since 1955,* 1988, Volume 68: *Canadian Writers, 1920-1959, First Series,* 1988.
Frye, Northrop, *Anatomy of Criticism: Four Essays,* Princeton University Press, 1957.
Frye, Northrop, *The Great Code: The Bible and Literature,* Harcourt, 1982.
Hoffman, Daniel, editor, *Harvard Guide to Contemporary American Writing,* Belknap Press, 1979.
Krieger, Murray, editor, *Northrop Frye in Modern Criticism: Selected Papers from the English Institute,* Columbia University Press, 1966.

PERIODICALS

Book Week, July 19, 1964.
Cambridge Review, May 7, 1971.
Chicago Tribune Book World, May 16, 1982.
Commentary, September, 1968.
Commonweal, September 20, 1957.
Criticism, summer, 1967.
Fiddlehead, summer, 1967.
Globe and Mail (Toronto), October 4, 1986; December 1, 1990.
Nation, February 19, 1968.
New York Review of Books, April 14, 1977; April 15, 1982.
New York Times, April 18, 1976; December 4, 1990.
New York Times Book Review, April 18, 1976; April 11, 1982; November 30, 1986; March 31, 1991.
Partisan Review, winter, 1969.
Sewanee Review, January, 1980.
South Atlantic Quarterly, spring, 1967.
Times Literary Supplement, August 12, 1965; July 2, 1982; February 17, 1984; April 26, 1985.
Washington Post Book World, May 16, 1982.
Yale Review, autumn, 1957; spring, 1964; spring, 1967; March, 1971; summer, 1983.

OBITUARIES:

PERIODICALS

Chicago Tribune, January 24, 1991; January 27, 1991.
Globe and Mail (Toronto), January 24, 1991.
New York Times, January 25, 1991.
Times (London), January 26, 1991.*

—*Sketch by Kevin S. Hile*

G

GALLOWAY, David D(arryl) 1937-

PERSONAL: Born May 5, 1937, in Memphis, TN; son of James Henry (an attorney) and Kathlyn (Snipes) Galloway; married Sally Lee Gantt, August 22, 1959; children: Gantt Perkins. *Education:* Harvard University, B.A. (with honors), 1959; State University of New York, Ph.D., 1962.

ADDRESSES: Home—Wuppertal, Germany; and Forcalquier, France.

CAREER: Calasanctius Preparatory School for Gifted Boys, Buffalo, NY, chairman of department of English, 1961-64; State University of New York at Buffalo, lecturer in English and American studies, 1964-67; University of Hamburg, Hamburg, Germany, professor of American literature, 1967-68; Case Western Reserve University, Cleveland, OH, associate professor of modern literature, 1968-72; Ruhr University, Bochum, Germany, chairman of American studies, beginning 1972. Guest professor in Egypt, Kuwait, England, Germany, Iran, and Ireland; lecturer on tours throughout Europe, Africa, and the Middle East. Guest curator of museum exhibitions in Europe and the Middle East; Tehran Museum of Contemporary Art, chief curator, 1977-78; curator, "artware," 1985-90. Albright-Knox Art Gallery, Buffalo, editor, 1962-64.

MEMBER: Modern Language Association of America, American Studies Association, Royal Society of the Arts (fellow), British Association for American Studies, Harvard Club, Sloane Club.

AWARDS, HONORS: Ford Foundation grant.

WRITINGS:

The Absurd Hero in American Fiction: Updike, Styron, Bellow, Salinger, University of Texas Press, 1966, 2nd revised edition, 1981.

Henry James: "The Portrait of a Lady," Edward Arnold, 1967.

(Editor and author of introduction) Edgar Allan Poe, *Selected Writings,* Penguin, 1967.

(Editor with John Whitley) *Ten Modern American Short Stories,* Methuen, 1968.

Melody Jones (novel), Calder & Boyars, 1976, Riverrun Press, 1980.

A Family Album (novel), Harcourt, 1978.

Edward Lewis Wallant, Twayne, 1979.

(With others) *New Writers Twelve,* Riverrun Press, 1980.

Lamaar Ransom: Private Eye (novel), Riverrun Press, 1981.

(Editor with Christian Sabisch) *Calamus: Male Homosexuality in Twentieth-Century Literature: An International Anthology,* Morrow, 1982.

Tamsen (novel), Harcourt, 1983.

(Editor and author of introduction) Poe, *The Other Poe: Comedies and Satires,* Penguin, 1983.

artware: Kunst und Elektronik, Econ Verlag, 1987.

Art critic, *Herald Tribune,* 1981—. Editor, *Audit Magazine,* 1960-63; corresponding editor, *Art in America,* 1984—.

SIDELIGHTS: David D. Galloway's novel *A Family Album* consists of descriptions of six photographs. Galloway examines the photographs in detail by revealing events and emotions behind each picture. Marilyn Lutz describes the book in a *Library Journal* review as "a provocative investigation into the paradoxical nature of a photograph: on the one hand an image of what appears, on the other, a symbolic report of an event capable of unlocking the secret character of the past."

Reproduced on the dust cover of the book, the photographs depict simple family scenes. In the *New York Times Book Review,* Jonathan Yardley notes that the pictures may come "from Mr. Galloway's own family. . . . Photographically, they are without merit; emotionally, they carry a heavy burden." Galloway expresses this poignant quality in a voice "analytical, controlled [and] lucidly detached from both cheap nostalgia and cheap shots at the negative images [Galloway] considers," observes Thomas LeClair in *New Republic,* adding, "This voice conducts us through the album in an almost offhand manner. . . . The result is a prose that is moving without a trace of sentiment." Reviewer Yardley concludes that the novel succeeds because "Mr. Galloway has taken an odd, quirky structure and made a real story out of it. He makes the reader *care*—care very much, in fact—and that is no small accomplishment."

BIOGRAPHICAL/CRITICAL SOURCES:

PERIODICALS

Antioch Review, fall, 1978.
Christian Science Monitor, April 21, 1978.
Library Journal, April 15, 1978.
Los Angeles Times, February 18, 1981.
Los Angeles Times Book Review, January 17, 1982.
New Republic, May 13, 1978.
New Yorker, May 15, 1978.
New York Times Book Review, April 16, 1978; April 26, 1981.
Observer, July 16, 1978; June 24, 1979.
Saturday Review, September 3, 1966.
Sewanee Review, October, 1978.
Times Literary Supplement, September 8, 1978.
Washington Post, November 17, 1983.

*   *   *

GARRETT, Richard   1920-

PERSONAL: Born January 15, 1920, in London, England; son of Victor (in business) and Gladys (Fisher) Garrett; married Anne Selves, August 20, 1945; children: Anthony, Simon, Jane. *Education:* Attended school in Berkshire, England. *Politics:* "Middle of the road." *Religion:* Christian. *Avocational interests:* Walking, the countryside, watching the sea.

ADDRESSES: Home and office—White Cottage, 27-A Broadwater Down, Tunbridge Wells, Kent TN2 5NL, England.

CAREER: Free-lance writer, 1969—. Worked previously in journalism, public relations, and advertising. Owner of industrial book and magazine publishing company in England, 1958-69. Broadcaster of weekly general interest shows for British Broadcasting Corp. (BBC); guest on radio and television programs. *Military service:* British

Army, 1939-45; served as officer in Norway; prisoner-of-war in Italy and Germany, 1943-45; became captain; staff writer for *Soldier.*

MEMBER: Society of Authors.

WRITINGS:

Fast and Furious: The Story of the World Championship of Drivers, foreword by Graham Hill, Stanley Paul, 1968, Arco, 1969.
The Motor Racing Story, Stanley Paul, 1969, A. S. Barnes, 1970.
Anatomy of a Grand Prix Driver, Arthur Barker, 1970.
The Rally-Go-Round: The Story of International Rallying, Stanley Paul, 1970.
Motoring and the Mighty, Motorbooks International, 1971.
Cross-Channel, Hutchinson, 1972.
The Search for Prosperity: Emigration from Britain, 1815-1930, Wayland, 1973.
Stories of Famous Ships, Arthur Barker, 1974.
General Gordon, Arthur Barker, 1974.
The British Sailor, Wayland, 1974.
General Wolfe, Arthur Barker, 1975.
Famous Characters of the Wild West, Arthur Barker, 1975, St. Martin's, 1977.
Stories of Famous Natural Disasters, Arthur Barker, 1976.
Clash of Arms: The World's Great Land Battles, Weidenfeld & Nicolson, 1976.
Robert Clive, Arthur Barker, 1976.
Submarines, Little, Brown, 1977.
Famous Rescues at Sea, Arthur Barker, 1977.
Scharnhorst and Gneisenau: The Elusive Sisters, Hippocrene, 1977.
Mrs. Simpson, St. Martin's, 1979.
The Raiders, Van Nostrand, 1980.
P.O.W., Hippocrene, 1981.
Royal Travel, Blandford, 1982.
Royal Quiz, Longman, 1985.
Atlantic Disaster: The 'Titanic' and Other Victims of the North Atlantic, Buchan & Enright, 1986.
Flight into Mystery: Reports from the Dark Side of the Sky, Weidenfeld & Nicolson, 1986.
Voyage into Mystery: Reports from the Sinister Side of the Sea, Weidenfeld & Nicolson, 1987.
Great Escapes of World War II, Weidenfeld & Nicolson, 1989.
The Final Betrayal: Armistice 1918 . . . and Afterwards, Buchan & Enright, 1989.
Sky High: Heroic Pilots of the Second World War, Weidenfeld & Nicolson, 1991.

CHILDREN'S BOOKS

Great Sea Mysteries, Piccolo, 1971.
Atlantic Jet, Hutchinson, 1971.

Hoaxes and Swindles, Piccolo, 1972.
True Tales of Detection, Piccolo, 1972.
Narrow Squeaks, Piccolo, 1973.
Heroines, Piccolo, 1974.
Queen Victoria, Hutchinson, 1974.
They Must Have Been Crazy, Piccolo, 1977.
Kaiser Bill, Wayland, 1978.
Dangerous Journeys, Piccolo, 1978.
Great Air Adventures, Piccolo, 1978.
In the Nick of Time, Piccolo, 1979.
File on Spies, Granada, 1981.
File on Forgers, Granada, 1982.
Jailbreakers, Granada, 1983.
Aliens from Outer Space, Piccolo, 1983.
The Story of Britain, Granada, 1983, revised edition, HarperCollins, 1991.

WORK IN PROGRESS: "Currently enjoying a sabbatical (surely reasonable after a large output over a relatively short time). There is, however, an idea that nags and which, one day, may seem to deserve attention".

SIDELIGHTS: Richard Garrett once told *CA:* "I see my writing very much as a job of work. I try to write at least three thousand words a day when I am not carrying out research. Professionalism is, I believe, maintaining a constant and consistent output no matter what the circumstances. 'Not feeling like it' can usually be overcome by doing it.

"My basic aim is to tell a story (I suspect a novelist screaming to get out, but since I have no talent in this area, he remains inside). I attempt to explore history, to experience the feeling of the times, and, in the case of children's books, to pass on this excitement. I suspect that history is taught without much imagination in the schools—there is little attempt to show what tremendous stories history contains. My books concentrate on entertainment—easy to read books which could happily occupy a long train journey."

BIOGRAPHICAL/CRITICAL SOURCES:

PERIODICALS

Times Literary Supplement, January 25, 1980; January 9, 1981.

*   *   *

GAULT, William Campbell 1910-
(Will Duke, Dial Forest, Roney Scott)

PERSONAL: Born March 9, 1910, in Milwaukee, WI; son of John H. and Ella (Hovde) Gault; married Virginia Kaprelian, August 29, 1942; children: William Barry, Shelley Gault Amacher. *Education:* Attended University of Wis-

consin, 1929. *Politics:* "Revolutionary Republican." *Religion:* "Faith in man."

ADDRESSES: Home and Office—482 Vaquero Lane, Santa Barbara, CA 93111. *Agent*—Michael Congdon, Don Congdon Associates, Inc., 177 East 70th St., New York, NY 10021.

CAREER: Free-lance writer. Has worked as a waiter, busboy, shoe sole cutter, hotel manager, and mailman. Secretary, Channel Cities Funeral Society. *Military service:* U.S. Army, 1943-45.

AWARDS, HONORS: Edgar Allan Poe Award from Mystery Writers of America, 1952, for *Don't Cry for Me;* award from Boy's Club of America, 1957, for *Speedway Challenge;* award from Southern California Council on Literature for Children and Young People, 1968; Shamus Award, for best paperback mystery, 1983, and Lifetime Achievement Award, both from Private Eye Writers of America; Bouchercon Award, 1991, for lifetime achievement.

WRITINGS:

MYSTERY NOVELS

Don't Cry for Me, Dutton, 1952.
The Bloody Bokhara, Dutton, 1952.
The Canvas Coffin, Dutton, 1953.
Blood on the Boards, Dutton, 1953.
Run, Killer, Run, Dutton, 1954.
Ring around Rosa, Dutton, 1955.
Day of the Ram, Random House, 1956.
Square in the Middle, Random House, 1956.
The Convertible Hearse, Random House, 1957.
Night Lady, Fawcett, 1959.
(Under pseudonym Will Duke) *Fair Prey,* Boardman, 1958.
Sweet Wild Wench, Fawcett, 1959.
The Wayward Widow, Fawcett, 1959.
Death out of Focus, Random House, 1959.
Come Die with Me, Random House, 1959.
Million Dollar Tramp, Fawcett, 1960.
Vein of Violence, Simon & Schuster, 1961.
The Hundred Dollar Girl, Dutton, 1961.
County Kill, Simon & Schuster, 1962.
Dead Hero, Dutton, 1963.
The Bad Samaritan, Harlequin, 1980.
The Cana Diversion, Raven House, 1982.
Death in Donegal Bay, Walker & Co., 1984.
The Dead Seed, Walker & Co., 1985.
The Chicano War, Walker & Co., 1986.
Cat and Mouse, St. Martin's Press, 1988.

Also author of *Dead Pigeon,* in press. Has also published books under the pseudonyms Dial Forest and Roney Scott.

FOR CHILDREN

Thunder Road, Dutton, 1952.
Mr. Fullback, Dutton, 1953.
Gallant Colt, Dutton, 1954.
Mr. Quarterback, Dutton, 1955.
Speedway Challenge, Dutton, 1956.
Bruce Benedict, Halfback, Dutton, 1957.
Rough Road to Glory, Dutton, 1958.
Dim Thunder, Dutton, 1958.
Drag Strip, Dutton, 1959.
Dirt Track Summer, Dutton, 1961.
Through the Line, Dutton, 1961.
Two Wheeled Thunder, Dutton, 1962.
Road Race Rookie, Dutton, 1962.
Wheels of Fortune: Four Racing Stories, Dutton, 1963.
Little Big Foot, Dutton, 1963.
The Checkered Flag, Dutton, 1964.
The Long Green, Dutton, 1965.
The Karters, Dutton, 1965.
Sunday's Dust, Dutton, 1966.
Backfield Challenge, Dutton, 1967.
The Lonely Mound, Dutton, 1967.
The Oval Playground, Dutton, 1968.
Stubborn Sam, Dutton, 1969.
Quarterback Gamble, Dutton, 1970.
The Last Lap, Dutton, 1972.
Trouble at Second, Dutton, 1973.
Gasoline Cowboy, Dutton, 1974.
Wild Willie, Wide Receiver, Dutton, 1974.
The Underground Skipper, Dutton, 1975.
The Big Stick, Dutton, 1975.
Showboat in the Backcourt, Dutton, 1976.
Cut-Rate Quarterback, Dutton, 1977.
Thin Ice, Dutton, 1978.

OTHER

The Sunday Cycles, Dodd, 1979.
Super Bowl Bound, Dodd, 1980.

Contributor of about three hundred short stories to magazines, including *Grit* and *Saturday Evening Post.*

WORK IN PROGRESS: A mystery novel.

SIDELIGHTS: William Campbell Gault, creator of the popular Brock Callahan series, returned to mystery writing after abandoning the genre for juvenile fiction for nearly twenty years. With publication of his 1982 novel *The Cana Diversion,* Gault put Callahan back into action in what the *Los Angeles Times Book Review* deems a "well-paced, engaging whodunit." In an interview with David Wilson, published in the *Los Angeles Times,* Gault explained the appeal of the hard-boiled detective: "It's the individual man. . . . It's a revolt against the corporate

and the conglomerate man, just one dirty guy doing a seedy job in a miserable world."

Although Callahan is in his fifth decade, the private eye has aged only slightly, maturing from his early thirties to what Gault describes as "around forty. It gets me," he told Wilson. "A guy says, 'Well, how old is he now?' But how old is Little Orphan Annie? She's 112, isn't she? How old is Ellery Queen? Callahan is an able-bodied man. I don't want him to be sixty. He's still looking at the girls in their summer dresses but he's not making a move, see?"

Gault told *CA:* "At the tender age of eighty-one, my writing isn't what it used to be—but I will persist. Writing is the only trade I ever wanted. Bill Pronzini is the man who keeps me happy. He's been a big help to me. He is the writer who corrected *Dead Pigeon* for me. I have no idea why he never won an Edgar."

BIOGRAPHICAL/CRITICAL SOURCES:

PERIODICALS

Los Angeles Times, June 6, 1982.
Los Angeles Times Book Review, December 14, 1984.
Saturday Review, June 28, 1969.

*   *   *

GEGGUS, David Patrick   1949-

PERSONAL: First syllable of surname rhymes with "egg"; born November 19, 1949, in Romford, Essex, England; son of David (a greyhound trainer) and Alice Winifred (Thorne) Geggus; married Pamela Joan Burnard, June 26, 1971 (divorced November, 1977). *Education:* Keble College, Oxford, B.A., 1971, M.A., 1976; University of London, M.A. (with distinction), 1972; University of York, D.Phil., 1979. *Avocational interests:* Foreign travel (Caribbean, Europe, the Middle East).

ADDRESSES: Office—Department of History, University of Florida, Gainesville, FL 32611.

CAREER: Oxford University, Oxford, Oxfordshire, England, junior research fellow at Wolfson College, 1976-80; University of Southampton, Southampton, Hampshire, England, Hartley research fellow, 1980-82; University of Florida, Gainesville, assistant professor, 1983-85, associate professor of history, 1985—. Temporary consultant for the BBC2-TV program *Chronicle,* 1979.

MEMBER: Royal Historical Society (fellow), American Historical Society, Society of Caribbean Studies, Association of Caribbean Historians, Societe haitienne d'histoire, Society for French Historical Studies.

AWARDS, HONORS: Leverhulme Overseas Award, 1974; British Academy fellow, 1979-80; Roger Brew Memorial Prize for Latin American History, Cambridge University Press and St. Antony's College, Oxford, 1980; Guggenheim fellow, 1984-85; Woodrow Wilson Center fellow, 1986-87; National Humanities Center fellow, 1989-90.

WRITINGS:

Slavery, War, and Revolution: The British Occupation of Saint Domingue, 1793-1798, Oxford University Press, 1982.

CONTRIBUTOR

J. Walvin, editor, *Slavery and British Society, 1776-1846,* Macmillan, 1982.
C. Jones, editor, *Conflict, Conspiracy, and Propaganda,* University of Exeter, 1982.
D. Richardson, editor, *Abolition and Its Aftermath,* Cass, 1985.
G. Henman, editor, *Out of the House of Bondage,* Cass, 1986.
E. Knight, editor, *The Modern Caribbean,* University of North Carolina Press, 1989.
Knight, editor, *Atlantic Port Cities,* University of Tennessee Press, 1991.
D. Gaspar, editor, *Black Women and Slavery,* Indiana University Press, 1991.

OTHER

Contributor to "Occasional Papers" series, Latin American and Caribbean Center, Florida International University. Contributor to numerous academic journals. Book review editor, *Hispanic American Historical Review,* 1990-91.

WORK IN PROGRESS: A monograph, *The Saint Domingue Slave Revolt and the Rise of Toussaint Louverture; The Greater Caribbean,* for Indiana University Press; *The French Revolution Research Collection,* Volume 11, number 2, for Pergamon; *Slave Society in Saint Domingue.*

SIDELIGHTS: David Geggus's historical study *Slavery, War, and Revolution: The British Occupation of Saint Domingue, 1793-1798* presents a new view of the 1793 British invasion of Saint Domingue (modern Haiti). As Geggus explains, the British, invited by those French inhabitants of Saint Domingue who opposed the French Revolution, faced an elusive enemy, a volatile and racially complex society, and terrible epidemics. Although Geggus concurs with the widely-accepted assessment of the invasion as a military fiasco, he contends that it was not as detrimental to Britain as many historians generally believe. According to *Times Literary Supplement* critic Piers Mackesy, "It is surprising that David Geggus's book is the first close and scholarly study of an episode which looms so large in British history." Favorably impressed by the

author's prose, Mackesy describes *Slavery, War, and Revolution* as "indispensable" and a "work of scholarly depth and sound judgement."

BIOGRAPHICAL/CRITICAL SOURCES:

PERIODICALS

Hispanic American Historical Review, February, 1983.
Times Literary Supplement, September 24, 1982.
William and Mary Quarterly, April, 1983.

*   *   *

GEORGE, Barbara
See KATZ, Bobbi

*   *   *

GEORGE, Emily
See KATZ, Bobbi

*   *   *

GEORGE, Gail
See KATZ, Bobbi

*   *   *

GILBERT, Willie 1916-1980
(Oscar Bensol, Glenville Mareth, joint pseudonym)

PERSONAL: Born William Gilbert Gomberg, February 24, 1916, in Cleveland, OH; died, December 2, 1980; son of Louis (a grocer) and Jessie (Pollock) Gomberg; married Grace Goldstein, June 7, 1942 (divorced, 1949); married Jane Hutchinson, October 25, 1957; children: (first marriage) Barbara Lynne; (second marriage) Judith Bannard. *Education:* Ohio State University, B.S., 1938. *Avocational interests:* Painting.

ADDRESSES: Home and Office—225 East 70th Street, 7-C, New York, NY 10021.

CAREER: Actor in radio dramas and Off-Broadway productions, 1938-40; performed in a comedy trio with a Major Bowes unit and in night clubs and hotels, 1940-41; free-lance television writer, 1950-61; playwright. *Military service:* U.S. Army, 1943-46; writer, director, and performer in Army camp shows; became technical sergeant.

MEMBER: Dramatists Guild, Authors League of America, Writer's Guild of America(East), American Society of Composers, Authors and Publishers, Societe des Auteurs et Compositeurs (France; honorary member).

AWARDS, HONORS: Pulitzer Prize, Antoinette Perry ("Tony") Award, and New York Drama Critics Circle Award, all in 1962, for *How to Succeed in Business without Really Trying.*

WRITINGS:

PLAYS

(Author of book with Abe Burrows and Jack Weinstock) *How to Succeed in Business without Really Trying* (two-act musical based on the novel by Sheperd Mead; first produced in Philadelphia at the Schubert Theatre, 1961; produced on Broadway, 1961), A. Meyerson, 1961.
(Author of book with Weinstock) *Hot Spot* (two-act musical), produced at the Majestic Theatre, 1963.
(With Weinstock) *Catch Me if You Can* (three-act comedy; based on a play in French by Robert Thomas; first produced at the Schubert Theatre, 1964; produced on Broadway, 1965), Samuel French, 1965.
(With George Haimsohn) *The Big Broadcast of 1944,* first produced in Devon, PA at the Valley Forge Music Fair, 1979.

SCREENPLAYS

(With Weinstock, under joint pseudonym Glenville Mareth) *Santa Claus Conquers the Martians,* Embassy, 1964.

Also author of *A Man Called Rio, Feet of Clay,* and *Run For the Hills.*

OTHER

Also author of more than three thousand produced scripts for television programs, including *The Howdy Doody Show, The Jerry Lester Chesterfield Show, The Jackie Gleason Show,* and *Tom Corbett, Space Cadet,* as well as over seventy animated cartoon programs, some under the pseudonym Oscar Bensol. Writer of material for touring performers, and of industrial shows and films for sales conventions.

ADAPTATIONS: How to Succeed in Business without Really Trying was adapted for film by David Swift and released by United Artists, 1967.

WORK IN PROGRESS: Blizzard, a stage drama.

SIDELIGHTS: How to Succeed in Business Without Really Trying ran for 1417 performances at the 46th Street Theatre on Broadway.

BIOGRAPHICAL/CRITICAL SOURCES:

PERIODICALS

Chicago Tribune, October 10,1985.

*   *   *

GILL, Bartholomew
See McGARRITY, Mark

*   *   *

GILL, Brendan 1914-

PERSONAL: Born October 4, 1914, in Hartford, CT; son of Michael Henry Richard (a physician) and Elizabeth Pauline (Duffy) Gill; married Anne Barnard, June 20, 1936; children: Brenda, Michael, Holly, Madelaine, Rosemary, Kate, Charles. *Education:* Yale University, A.B., 1936.

ADDRESSES: Home—Bronxville, NY. *Office—New Yorker,* 20 West 43rd St., New York, NY 10036.

CAREER: New Yorker, New York, NY, regular contributor, 1936—, film critic, 1960-67, drama critic, 1968-87, author of architecture column, "The Sky Line," 1987—. Chairman of board of directors, October Fund. Member of New York City Commission on Cultural Affairs and Mayor's Committee in the Public Interest. Member of board of directors, Whitney Museum of American Art, Pratt Institute, and MacDowell Colony.

MEMBER: Irish Georgian Society (board member), Institute for Art and Urban Resources (president), Victorian Society (vice-president), New York Landmarks Conservancy (board chairman), Municipal Art Society (board chairman), Film Society of Lincoln Center (vice-president), Coffee House (New York City), Century Association (New York City).

AWARDS, HONORS: National Institute and American Academy of Arts and Letters grant, 1951; National Book Award, 1951, for *The Trouble of One House.*

WRITINGS:

Death in April and Other Poems, Hawthorne House, 1935.
The Trouble of One House (novel), Doubleday, 1950.
The Day the Money Stopped (novel), Doubleday, 1957.
La Belle (play), first produced in Philadelphia, 1962.
(With Robert Kimball) *Cole: A Book of Cole Porter Lyrics and Memorabilia,* Holt, 1971 (published in England as *Cole: A Biographical Essay,* M. Joseph, 1972).
Tallulah, Holt, 1972.
(Author of introduction) *The Portable Dorothy Parker,* Viking, 1973.

The Malcontents, Harcourt, 1973.

(Editor) *Happy Times,* photography by Jerome Zerbe, Harcourt, 1973.

Ways of Loving: Two Novellas and Eighteen Short Stories, Harcourt, 1974.

(Editor) Philip Barry, *States of Grace: Eight Plays,* Harcourt, 1975.

Here at "The New Yorker" (Book-of-the-Month Club alternate selection), Random House, 1975.

The New York Custom House on Bowling Green, New York Landmarks Conservancy, 1976.

Lindbergh Alone, Harcourt, 1977.

Summer Places, photography by Dudley Witney, Stewart & McClelland, 1977.

(Author of introduction) *St. Patrick's Cathedral: A Centennial History,* Quick Fox, 1979.

The Dream Come True: Great Houses of Los Angeles, with photographs by Derry Moore, Lippincott, 1980.

Wooings: Five Poems, Plain Wrapper Press (Verona, Italy), 1980.

(Author of foreword) Gene Schermerhorn, *Letters to Phil: Memories of a New York Boyhood,* New York Bound, 1982.

John F. Kennedy Center for the Performing Arts, Abrams, 1982.

A Fair Land to Build In: The Architecture of the Empire State, Press League of New York State, 1984.

Many Masks: A Life of Frank Lloyd Wright, Putnam, 1987.

A New York Life: Of Friends and Others, Poseidon, 1990.

Contributor to anthologies, including *World's Great Tales of the Sea,* World Publishing, 1944, *The Best American Short Stories, 1945,* Houghton, 1945, *Fireside Book of Yuletide Tales,* Bobbs Merrill, 1948, and *Girls from Esquire,* Random House, 1952. Contributor of short stories to *Saturday Evening Post, New Yorker, Collier's,* and *Virginia Quarterly Review.*

ADAPTATIONS: Gill's novel *The Day the Money Stopped* was adapted as a play by Maxwell Anderson.

SIDELIGHTS: In his book *Here at "The New Yorker,"* Brendan Gill writes fondly of his long career at the magazine: "I started out at the place where I wanted most to be and with much pleasure and very little labor have remained here since." Beginning at the *New Yorker* just after leaving college in 1936, Gill has written a wide range of articles, stories, and columns over the years, serving as both the theatre and architecture critic in his time, and as a frequent writer for the "Talk of the Town" section. Gill has also published several biographies of prominent people and *A New York Life: Of Friends and Others,* a collection of character portraits.

Here at "The New Yorker", published to coincide with the magazine's fiftieth anniversary, is Gill's account of his many years at the popular magazine. His memories of his magazine work, and of those with whom he worked, are combined in *Here at "The New Yorker"* with such things as floor plans of the magazine's offices, humorous memos that made the rounds among staff members, photographs of such famous *New Yorker* writers as James Thurber and John O'Hara, and old cartoons from the magazine itself. As John Leonard remarks in the *New York Times Book Review,* Gill's "memoir is a splendid artichoke of anecdotes, in which not merely the heart and leaves but the thistles as well are edible."

In *A New York Life,* Gill expands his reminiscences to include the many interesting personalities he has met during his magazine career, including such figures as Eleanor Roosevelt, Dorothy Parker, and George Plimpton. Some 47 characters are covered in all. "Many of Mr. Gill's anecdotes," notes Caroline Seebohm in the *New York Times Book Review,* "shed new light on a character." Among Gill's more controversial pronouncements in the book is his charges regarding the late Joseph Campbell, a popular writer on mythology best known for his *The Power of Myth* television series on PBS. Gill characterized Campbell as a racist and anti-semite who "was uttering a vicious message," as Gill tells John Blades in the *Chicago Tribune.* Although Campbell's friends and associates have denied the charges, Gill insists that his characterization is accurate. For the most part, *A New York Life* is "a book of heroes," Gill explains to Blades. The character portraits "give the sense of what it was like to have lived in New York over the last half-century."

Gill has also written several biographies of famous personalities, including Tallulah Bankhead, Charles Lindbergh, Cole Porter, and Frank Lloyd Wright. In *Many Masks: A Life of Frank Lloyd Wright,* Gill portrayed the famous architect of modernism in sometimes unflattering terms. "The Frank Lloyd Wright who emerges . . . ," Michiko Kakutani writes in the *New York Times,* "is an architect of genius, but he's also an arrogant con man—a self-promoter and prevaricator, who uses his gift of gab to seduce women and clients, and enhance his own mythic stature as a visionary artist." More sympathetically, Witold Rybczynski, writing in the Toronto *Globe and Mail,* finds that Gill presents a version of Wright as "the owner of an extraordinary talent" who was "in many ways a very ordinary man—or rather a man with very ordinary impulses."

A diversified writer who has produced novels, short stories, biographies, essays, film and drama reviews, Gill told *CA:* "Fiction is my chief interest, followed by architectural history, followed by literary and dramatic criticism. If these fields were to be closed to me, I would write copy for a bird-seed catalogue. In any event, I would write."

BIOGRAPHICAL/CRITICAL SOURCES:

BOOKS

Gill, Brendan, *Here at "The New Yorker,"* Random House, 1975.

PERIODICALS

Chicago Tribune, October 9, 1990.
Chicago Tribune Book World, December 7, 1980.
Globe and Mail (Toronto), February 6, 1988.
Los Angeles Times, November 29, 1987; December 13, 1987.
Los Angeles Times Book Review, March 22, 1981; September 20, 1987; November 22, 1987; November 29, 1987.
New York Times, September 21, 1979; December 9, 1987.
New York Times Book Review, February 16, 1975; April 24, 1977; December 13, 1987; October 21, 1990.
Saturday Evening Post, August 9, 1941.
Saturday Review of Literature, February 17, 1951.
Time, February 24, 1975.
Times Literary Supplement, November 14, 1980; March 24, 1989.
Tribune Books (Chicago), November 8, 1987; October 7, 1990.
Wall Street Journal, October 22, 1990.
Washington Post, February 24, 1987; April 13, 1987.
Washington Post Book World, November 22, 1987; November 18, 1990.

*   *   *

GODFREY, William
   See YOUD, (Christopher) Samuel

*   *   *

GOODE, Erich   1938-

PERSONAL: Born September 21, 1938, in Austin, TX; son of William Josiah (a university professor) and Josephine (Cannizzo) Goode; married Roberta Buckingham, June 17, 1961 (divorced March 28, 1964); married Alice Neufeld (a college professor), December 28, 1968 (divorced February 9, 1977); married Barbara Weinstein (a university professor), March 23, 1984. *Education:* Oberlin College, A.B., 1960; Columbia University, Ph.D., 1966.

ADDRESSES: Home—108 Willis Ave., Port Jefferson, NY 11777. *Office*—Department of Sociology, Social and Behavioral Sciences Building, State University of New York, Stony Brook, NY 11794-4356.

CAREER: New York University, Washington Square College, New York City, instructor, 1965-66, assistant professor of sociology, 1966-67; State University of New York at Stony Brook, assistant professor, 1967-70, associate professor, 1970-81, professor of sociology, 1981—. Visiting associate professor at Florida Atlantic University, 1974, and University of North Carolina at Chapel Hill, 1977. Consultant to National Commission on Marijuana and Drug Abuse, 1971-72.

MEMBER: American Sociological Association, Society for the Study of Social Problems, American Society of Criminology.

AWARDS, HONORS: National Institute of Mental Health grants, 1968-69, 1976-78; grants from Research Foundation of State University of New York, summers, 1968, 1969, 1975, 1980; Guggenheim fellow, 1975-76.

WRITINGS:

(Editor) *Marijuana,* Atherton Press, 1969.
The Marijuana Smokers, Basic Books, 1970.
Drugs in American Society, Knopf, 1972, 3rd edition, 1989.
The Drug Phenomenon, Bobbs-Merrill, 1973.
(Editor with Harvey A. Farberman) *Social Reality,* Prentice-Hall, 1973.
(Editor with Richard R. Troiden) *Sexual Deviance and Sexual Deviants,* Morrow, 1974.
Deviant Behavior, Prentice-Hall, 1978, 3rd edition, 1990.
Social Class and Church Participation, Arno Press, 1980.
Sociology, Prentice-Hall, 1984, 2nd edition, 1988.
(Editor) *Drugs, Society, and Behavior* (annual edition), Dushkin, 6th edition, 1991, 7th edition, in press.
Collective Behavior, Harcourt, 1992.

Contributor to periodicals, including *Social Problems, Deviant Behavior, Journal of Health and Social Behavior, Psychiatry, The Journal of Sex Research, American Journal of Sociology, Teaching Sociology,* and *International Journal of the Addictions.* Consulting editor, *American Journal of Sociology,* 1975-77; associate editor, *Journal of Health and Social Behavior,* 1977-79; member of editorial policy board, *Deviant Behavior: An Interdisciplinary Journal,* 1978—; member of editorial board, *Social Pharmacology,* 1985-90. *Marijuana* has been translated into Spanish.

WORK IN PROGRESS: Moral Panics; The Personals; Thinking Straight; a fourth edition of *Drugs in American Society.*

SIDELIGHTS: Erich Goode once told *CA:* "I write for three, only slightly overlapping audiences: specialists (in the form of monographs and articles in professional journals), students and instructors (in the form of textbooks), and the general public. To all three, I attempt to communicate the same basic message: the excitement and wonder that comes from examining the experience of life in human society." More recently, he added, "To me, an author has four writing obligations: to be clear, to be interesting, to be ruthlessly honest, and to help bring about human liberation, however the author defines it. Sometimes these obligations contradict one another. On college campuses in particular, there has been something of an uproar over the political implications of intellectual work. I am sympathetic to much of this thrust—oppression has been an ugly fact of human existence for millenia, and future generations are going to ask of ours what we did to help wipe it out—and I do believe its repressive side has been greatly exaggerated by the media. However, I believe that we cannot dismiss, define away, or declare as irrelevant, concrete, real-life happenings—what I call 'videotape reality.' All writers have an obligation to find out *what* is happening before we speculate about the whys, wherefores, and ideological meanings of supposed concrete events. Too often, authors confuse what they wish to be true with this bedrock, videotape reality—in my view, often with repugnant consequences. Challenging one's own cherished views—now, *that* takes courage!"

*   *   *

GORDON-WATSON, Mary 1948-

PERSONAL: Born April 3, 1948, in Cranborne, Dorset, England; daughter of Michael (a farmer and retired military officer) and Thalia (a farmer; maiden name, Gordon) Gordon-Watson. *Education:* Attended St. Clare's Hall, Oxford, 1963-64. *Religion:* Roman Catholic. *Avocational interests:* Travel, reading.

ADDRESSES: Home and office—20 Lochmore House, Cundy St., London SW1, England.

CAREER: Oakham, Rutland, England, horse trainer and competitor, 1972-76; Ridgemead, Windsor Park, England, horse trainer and riding instructor, 1976-82; independent riding teacher in England and the United States, 1982—, and in Africa, 1988—. Member of senior selection committee for British Horse Trial teams, 1976—. Presenter, *Horse Sense* television series, Television South West, 1987.

AWARDS, HONORS: European equestrian champion, 1969, world champion, 1970; member of England's Olympic Gold Medal equestrian team, 1972; member of the Order of the British Empire, 1973.

WRITINGS:

(Contributor) Jane Kidd, editor, *Horses in Competition,* Horseman's Year, 1970.
The Handbook of Riding, Knopf, 1982.
(Editor and primary contributor) *Design and Construction of Cross-Country Courses,* Threshold, 1987.

Horse Sense (television series), Television South West, 1987.
Fields and Fencing, Threshold, 1988.
Make Your Own Jumps, Threshold, 1988.
Beds and Bedding, Threshold, 1988.
Feeds and Feeding, Threshold, 1988.

Contributor to *The Complete Book of the Horse,* edited by Carol Foster, Octopus Books. Contributor to *Riding Annual* and *Pony Annual.* Equestrian correspondent for newspaper *The Independent on Sunday.* Contributor to numerous periodicals, including *Horse and Hound.*

WORK IN PROGRESS: A novel based on the eventing world; *Learn to Ride in a Weekend,* for Dorling Kindersley.

SIDELIGHTS: Mary Gordon-Watson told *CA:* "My family is involved in [horse] racing, both as a business and as a personal interest. I am a local steward for the Jockey Club (flat racing and steeplechasing) at Newbury, Bath, and Salisbury racecourses. I love racing but I also judge dressage and show hunters. In 1987 I was writer and television presenter for a seven-part series, *Horse Sense,* for Television South West, and would like to do more television work."

She adds: "I have ridden since I was a small child, whenever possible. My first horse (after riding ponies) was Cornishman V, on which I achieved all my competitive success. With the help of professional trainers for short spells (two or three days every few months), I trained the horse myself in his early years—so we 'grew up' together and had several setbacks, as well as successes. Our performances became more consistent from 1969 until the horse retired in 1973, after establishing an unequaled international record. The training was arduous, involving dressage work, cross-country (twenty-mile Olympic course), and show jumping. (These three phases constitute the Three Day Event.)

"*The Handbook of Riding* is aimed at *all* thinking riders and is designed to cover the first stages for the beginner all the way up to an advanced level of riding, training a young horse, and jumping. Other aspects included are Western riding, side-saddle riding, showing, gymkhana, and long-distance and endurance riding—so it is a comprehensive book that took two and a half years to write.

"I hope to continue writing. I would like to write novels and children's books, not necessarily related to horses."

*   *   *

GOTTESMAN, S. D.
See POHL, Frederik

GOUGOV, Nikola Delchev 1914-
(Pavel Vezhinov)

PERSONAL: Born November 9, 1914, in Sofia, Bulgaria; son of Delcho Gougov and Ivanka (Lasheva) Loulchev; married Nina Spassova; children: Pavlina, Pavel. *Education:* Attended University of Sofia.

ADDRESSES: Home—Oborishte St. 1 Sofia, Bulgaria. *Office*—Bulgarian Cinematography, Sofia, Bulgaria.

CAREER: Editor of literary magazines and a newspaper in Sofia, Bulgaria; member of scenario committee of the Bulgarian Cinematography, Sofia.

MEMBER: Union of Bulgarian Writers (secretary).

AWARDS, HONORS: Dimitrov Prize.

WRITINGS:

UNDER PSEUDONYM PAVEL VEZHINOV

Za chestta na rodinata (originally published in 1949), Izd-vo na ISK na DKMS, 1981.
Far from the Shore (originally published as *Dalech ot bregovite*, 1958), translation by Gregor Pavlov, Foreign Languages Press (Sofia, Bulgaria), 1967.
V poleto, Bulgarski Pisatel, 1961.
The Boy with the Violin, edited by Pauline Pirinska, translated by Pavlov, Foreign Languages Press, 1965.
Chovekut v siankata (novel; title means "The Man in the Shade"), Narodna Mladezh, 1965.
Dukh no bademi (stories and novelette), Narodna Mladezh, 1966.
Barierata; Beliiat gushter; Izmereniia, Izd-vo Bulgarski Pisatel, 1978.
Sledite ostavat, Izd-vo Otechestvo, 1978.
Noshtem s belite kone, Izd-vo Khristo G. Danov, 1981.
Az sum atomna, Profizdat, 1981.
Vezni, Bulgarski Pisatel, 1982.
Povesti, Bulgarski Pisatel, 1984.
Druzhba zakalialas v boiakh, Lit-ra Artistike, 1985.

Also author of *Dni i vecheri* (title means "Days and Evenings"), 1942; *Meka mebel* (humorous stories), 1948; *Vtora rota* (title means "Second Company"), 1949; *Sukhata ravnina,* 2nd edition, 1957; *Nashata sila,* 1957; *Proizshestive na tikhata ulitsa* (title means "Crime in the Quiet Street"), 1960; *Ravninnyl reld,* 1963; *Izhrani povesti,* 1964; *Mal'chik so skripkol* (short stories), 1964; *Izhrani razkazi,* 1965; *Zvezdit nad nas* (novel; title means "The Stars above Us"), 1966; *Razkazi* (stories), 1969. Also author of motion picture and television scripts. Work represented in *The Peach Thief and Other Bulgarian Stories,* translated by Radost Pridham and Jean Morris, Cassell, 1968.*

GRAAF, Peter
See YOUD, (Christopher) Samuel

*   *   *

GREEN, Harvey 1946-

PERSONAL: Born September 15, 1946, in Buffalo, NY; son of Herman (a farmer and laboratory technician) and Bessie (a homemaker; maiden name, Krassen) Green; married Susan Williams (a historian), June 21, 1980. *Education:* University of Rochester, B.A., 1968; Rutgers University, M.A., 1970, Ph.D., 1976.

ADDRESSES: Home—P.O. Box 244, New Ipswich, NH 03071. *Office*—249 Meserve Hall, Northeastern University, Boston, MA 02115.

CAREER: Margaret Woodbury Strong Museum, Rochester, NY, historian and deputy director for interpretation, 1976-89; Northeastern University, Boston, MA, associate professor of history, 1989—. Adjunct associate professor of history at University of Rochester, 1983-89. Consultant to various historical organizations.

MEMBER: American Association for State and Local History, American Studies Association, Organization of American Historians, American Historical Association.

WRITINGS:

The Light of the Home: An Intimate View of the Lives of Women in Victorian America, Pantheon, 1983.
Fit for America: Health, Fitness, Sport, and American Society, 1830-1940, Pantheon, 1986.
The Uncertainty of Everyday Life, 1915-1945, HarperCollins, 1992.

SIDELIGHTS: Gathering material for his book *The Light of the Home: An Intimate View of the Lives of Women in Victorian America,* historian Harvey Green analyzed thousands of advertisements, diaries, advice columns and manuals, labor-saving gadgets, kitchen tools, and furniture. The result, according to Elizabeth Crow of the *Washington Post Book World,* is a "fascinating, lavishly illustrated, and very disturbing inventory of the means by which 'woman's place' was defined in the years between 1870 and 1910 and by which it has been maintained for the past century." The book, said Crow, "is most grimly compelling" when Green "catalogues the dark side of Victorian housewifery." The critic further stated, "In explaining our past, [Green] has provided insight into our present, especially in his analysis of the economics of a sexually stratified society." A book reviewer for *Time* similarly praised *The Light of the Home*: "Delightfully illustrated with pictures of artifacts from the Margaret Woodbury Strong Museum," the book "illuminates the deadening burden that male supremacy imposed during the 19th century." The reviewer concluded that "Green's hindsight is an education."

In *Fit for America: Health, Fitness, Sport, and American Society, 1830-1940,* Green examines another aspect of American life since the Victorian era. "*Fit for America* investigates the changing ideas, realities, and solutions for problems of health and fitness over the course of a century," said *Washington Post* reviewer John Riddle, who noted Green's attention to detail. "The author researched catalogs, trade journals, diaries, medical books, athletic instruction manuals, advice books and household guides," Riddle said. "By putting them all together, he provides the reader with an understanding of just how the health and fitness craze has evolved."

Green suggests that health products and practices have maintained their popularity because, to Americans at least, success in the pursuit of health and fitness can compensate for failure in other areas. Dr. William Bennett explained in the *New York Times Book Review*: "In America's free-enterprise society, most people, most of the time, are failures. . . . The pursuit of physical (or mental) perfection, or the nearest thing to it, can be a way of salvaging self-esteem in a culture that offers few other consolations to those who have put out their best effort and still lost the game."

BIOGRAPHICAL/CRITICAL SOURCES:

PERIODICALS

Los Angeles Times Book Review, January 1, 1989, p. 10.
Ms., August, 1986.
New York Review of Books, April 12, 1984.
New York Times Book Review, March 23, 1986, p. 32.
Time, July 4, 1983.
Washington Post, November 11, 1986.
Washington Post Book World, August 21, 1983, p. 11; April 20, 1986, p. 3.

*   *   *

GREGOR, Lee
  See POHL, Frederik

*   *   *

GREINER, Donald J(ames) 1940-

PERSONAL: Born June 10, 1940, in Baltimore, MD; son of D. James (a physician) and Katherine (Murphy) Greiner; married Ellen Brunot (a teacher), June 20, 1964; children: Kay, Jim. *Education:* Wofford College, B.A.

(magna cum laude), 1962; University of Virginia, M.A., 1963, Ph.D., 1967.

ADDRESSES: Home—3833 Edinburgh Rd., Columbia, SC 29204. *Office*—Department of English, University of South Carolina at Columbia, Columbia, SC 29208.

CAREER: University of South Carolina at Columbia, assistant professor, 1967-70, associate professor, 1970-74, professor of English, 1974-87, chair professor, 1987—.

MEMBER: Modern Language Association of America, South Atlantic Modern Language Association, Phi Beta Kappa.

WRITINGS:

(Editor with wife, Ellen Greiner) *The Notebook of Stephen Crane,* University Press of Virginia, 1969.
Guide to Robert Frost, C. E. Merrill, 1969.
Checklist of Robert Frost, C. E. Merrill, 1969.
Comic Terror: The Novels of John Hawkes, Memphis State University Press, 1973, revised edition, 1978.
Robert Frost: The Poet and His Critics, American Library Association, 1974.
(Editor) *Dictionary of Literary Biography,* Volume 5: *American Poets since World War II,* two parts, Gale, 1980.
The Other John Updike: Poems, Short Stories, Prose, Play, Ohio University Press, 1981.
John Updike's Novels, Ohio University Press, 1984.
Adultery in the American Novel: Updike, James, and Hawthorne, University of South Carolina Press, 1985.
Understanding John Hawkes, University of South Carolina Press, 1985.
Domestic Particulars: The Novels of Frederick Busch, University of South Carolina Press, 1988.
Women Enter the Wilderness: Male Bonding and the American Novel of the 1980s, University of South Carolina Press, 1991.

Contributor to *Contemporary Literature, Critique, Studies in Modern Fiction, Southwest Review, English Journal, South Carolina Review,* and other professional journals. Editor of *Critique: Studies in Contemporary Fiction,* 1986—.

SIDELIGHTS: Donald J. Greiner told *CA:* "My writing comes from my reading; I find it stimulating to organize my ideas about the authors who give me the greatest pleasure."

*   *   *

GRIM, Patrick 1950-

PERSONAL: Born October 29, 1950, in Pasadena, CA; son of Elgas Shull (an artist) and Dorathy Mae (a potter;

maiden name O'Neal) Grim; married Ellen Louise Forde, 1970 (divorced 1974); married Kriste Taylor, 1977 (divorced 1987). *Education:* University of California at Santa Cruz, A.B. (philosophy and anthropology), 1971; University of St. Andrews, B.Phil., 1975; Boston University, M.A., 1975, Ph.D., 1976.

ADDRESSES: Home—Patchogue, NY. *Office*—Department of Philosophy, State University of New York at Stony Brook, Stony Brook, NY 11794.

CAREER: State University of New York at Stony Brook, visting assistant professor, 1976-77, assistant professor, 1978-84, associate professor of philosophy, 1984—.

MEMBER:: International Association for the Philosophy of Law and Social Philosophy, American Philosophical Association, Association for Symbolic Logic.

AWARDS, HONORS: Fulbright fellow, 1971-72; Mellon Faculty fellow, 1977-78; President's Award for Excellence in Teaching, State University of New York at Stony Brook, 1988; Chancellor's Award for Excellence in Teaching, State University of New York System, 1988.

WRITINGS:

(Contributor) Frederick Elliston, Jane English, and Mary Vetterling-Braggin, editors, *Feminism and Philosophy,* Littlefield, 1977.
(Editor with John T. Sanders and David Boyer) *The Philosophers Annual,* thirteen volumes, Rowman and Littlefield and Ridgeway Press, 1979-92.
(Contributor) Vetterling-Braggin, editor, *Sexist Language,* Littlefield, 1981.
(Contributor) Vetterling-Braggin, editor, *"Femininity", "Masculinity", and "Androgeny": A Modern Philosophical Discussion,* Littlefield, 1982.
(Contributor) Anthony Flew, editor, *Readings in the Philosophical Problems of Parapsychology,* Prometheus, 1987.
(Editor) *Philosophy of Science and the Occult,* State University of New York Press, 1990.
The Incomplete Universe: Totality, Knowledge, and Truth, MIT Press, 1991.
(Contributor) Jonathan Dancy and Ernest Sosa, editors, *Companion to Epistemology,* Blackwell, 1992.

Contributor to philosophy journals, including *Nous, Analysis, Philosophical Studies,* and *American Philosophical Quarterly.*

WORK IN PROGRESS: Philosophical research on chaos and the semantics of paradox.

SIDELIGHTS: Patrick Grim told *CA:* "My work is simply disciplined imagination. Here both parts are crucial: discipline without imagination is pedantry, but imagina-

tion without discipline is sterile. I have a great respect for craft.

"Contemporary analytic philosophy profits immensely from close ties with mathematical logic—though those ties are complicated and far from one-sided—and it is this, I think, that gives it its current vigor. Logic offers a possibility of clear codification and at the same time facilitates a subtlety and sophistication of argument that characterizes philosophical thought at its best. Logic also offers, I think, a freedom for creative imagination, and that freedom has paid off in the last ten to twenty years with new logics and new areas of philosophical exploration based on them.

"*The Incomplete Universe* is an exploration of a family of related logical results, including the liar paradox, applications and extension of Kaplan and Montague's paradox of the Knower, generalizations of Goedel's work on incompleteness, and new uses of Cantorian diagonalization. Taken together, I propose, something philosophically important to teach us: something about knowledge and truth, and something about the logical impossibility of *totalities* of knowledge and truth."

*   *   *

GRIMES, Lee 1920-
(Fremont Dodge)

PERSONAL: Born February 27, 1920, in Fremont, NE; son of George Eichelberger (a newspaper editor and publisher) and Eva Irene (a newspaperwoman; maiden name Miller) Grimes; married Mary Aileen Cochran (an historian), April 29, 1945; children: Robert Lee, Douglas Cochran, Diana Lee. *Education:* Yale College, B.A., 1941; attended Columbia Graduate School of Journalism, 1942.

ADDRESSES: Home—426 Prospect St., New Haven, CT 06511. *Agent*—Harold Ober Associates, 425 Madison Ave., New York, NY 10017.

CAREER: Press-Courier, Oxnard, CA, managing editor, 1946-63, editor, 1963-67; also worked at *Omaha World-Herald* and *New Haven Register.* Chairman, California Editors Conference, 1957.

MEMBER: Authors League, Authors Guild of America.

AWARDS, HONORS: International Press Institute fellowship in Europe, 1958.

WRITINGS:

The Eye of Shiva, Warner, 1974.
The Ax of Atlantis, Warner, 1975.
McIvor's Secret, Berkley, 1976.
Fortune Cookie Castle, Dutton, 1990.

(Editor) *50 Years from '41,* Yale Alumni Records Office, 1991.

Contributor, sometimes under pseudonym of Fremont Dodge, of stories and articles to periodicals.

* * *

GROESCHEL, Benedict J(oseph)   1933-

PERSONAL: Born July 23, 1933, in Jersey City, NJ; son of Edward Joseph (a civil engineer) and Marjulea (a housewife; maiden name, Smith) Groeschel. *Education:* Capuchin Theological Seminary, B.A., 1955; Iona Pastoral Counselors Institute, M.S., 1965; Columbia University, Ed.D., 1972.

ADDRESSES: Home and office—Trinity Retreat, 1 Pryer Manor Rd., Larchmont, NY 10538.

CAREER: Entered Order of Friars Minor Capuchin (Capuchin Franciscan Friars), 1951, ordained Roman Catholic priest, 1959; Children's Village, Dobbs Ferry, NY, chaplain, 1960-73; Roman Catholic Archdiocese of New York, New York City, director of spiritual development, 1974—. Associate professor at Iona Pastoral Counselors Institute, 1971—, St. Joseph's Seminary, Dunwoodie, NY, 1973—, and Maryknoll School of Theology, 1973—. Director of St. Francis House for Homeless Boys, Brooklyn, NY. Postulator of Cause of Beatification of Terence Cardinal Cooke; Superior of Franciscan Friars of the Renewal.

MEMBER: American Psychological Association, National Chaplains Association for Youth Rehabilitation (past president), National Association of Catholic Chaplains.

WRITINGS:

God and Us, St. Paul Editions, 1981.
St. Catherine of Genoa, Paulist Press, 1981.
Spiritual Passages: The Psychology of Spiritual Development, Crossroad/Continuum, 1983.
Listening at Prayer, Paulist Press, 1984.
Courage to be Chaste, Paulist Press, 1985.
Stumbling Blocks and Stepping Stones, Paulist Press, 1987.
Reform of Renewal, Ignatius Press, 1990.
Thy Will Be Done (biography of Terence Cardinal Cooke), Alba House, 1990.
A Still Small Voice, Alba House, 1992.
Psychology of Spiritual Experience, Harper, in press.

SIDELIGHTS: Benedict J. Groeschel once told *CA:* "My principal interest is relating contemporary psychological theory and research to religious experience and spiritual growth. I am also deeply involved in social concerns as the director of a small agency for homeless boys. I usually spend my summer vacation overseas, teaching foreign missionaries, and I have done this on every continent. Another interest is ecumenical relations of various religious denominations, particularly Catholic-Jewish relations."

Groeschel more recently added: "I presently spend half of my time in the South Bronx where our community works with the homeless and destitute."

* * *

GROVE, Fred(erick)   1913-

PERSONAL: Born July 4, 1913, in Hominy, OK; married, 1938; children: William Riley. *Education:* University of Oklahoma, B.A., 1937. *Religion:* Episcopalian.

ADDRESSES: Home—P.O. Box 1248, Silver City, NM 88062.

CAREER: Daily Citizen, Cushing, OK, sports editor, 1938-39; *Morning News,* Shawnee, OK, reporter, 1940-42; *The Star,* Harlingen, TX, sports editor, 1942; *Morning News and Star,* Shawnee, reporter, 1943-44, managing editor, 1944-46; *Oklahoma City Times* and *Daily Oklahoman,* copyreader, 1946-47; University of Oklahoma, Norman, senior assistant in public relations, 1947-54; currently full-time writer.

MEMBER: Western Writers of America, Westerners (Silver City).

AWARDS, HONORS: Wrangler Award, National Cowboy Hall of Fame and Western Heritage Center, 1962, for short story "Comanche Son," and 1969, for novel *The Buffalo Runners;* Spur Award, Western Writers of America, 1963, for short material "Comanche Woman," 1963, for novel *Comanche Captives,* 1969, for short material "When the Caballos Came," 1977, for novel *The Great Horse Race,* and 1982, for novel *Match Race;* Spur Award finalist, 1971, for novel *War Journey,* and 1972, for novel *The Child Stealers.*

WRITINGS:

Flame of the Osage, Pyramid Books, 1958.
Sun Dance, Ballantine, 1958.
No Bugles, No Glory, Ballantine, 1959.
Comanche Captives, Ballantine, 1961.
The Land Seekers, Ballantine, 1963.
Buffalo Spring, Doubleday, 1967.
The Buffalo Runners, Doubleday, 1968.
War Journey, Doubleday, 1971.
The Child Stealers, Doubleday, 1973.
Warrior Road, Doubleday, 1974.
Drums without Warriors, Doubleday, 1976.

The Great Horse Race, Doubleday, 1977.
Bush Track, Doubleday, 1978.
The Running Horses, Doubleday, 1980.
Phantom Warrior, Doubleday, 1981.
Match Race, Doubleday, 1982.
A Far Trumpet, Doubleday, 1985.
Search for the Breed, Doubleday, 1986.
Deception Trail, Doubleday, 1988.
Bitter Trumpet, Doubleday, 1989.

Contributor to books, including *Spurs West,* Doubleday, 1960; *Western Roundup,* Macmillan, 1961; and *The Pick of the Roundup,* Avon, 1963.

SIDELIGHTS: Fred Grove studied under Foster Harris, western author and teacher, and the noted biographer and historian Walter Stanley Campbell at the University of Oklahoma. Grove later studied with Dwight V. Swain, nationally-known teacher and science fiction writer. He is a researcher on the history of the American Southwest and quarter-horse racing.

*   *   *

GUPTA, Shiv K(umar)   1930-

PERSONAL: Born April 6, 1930, in Simla, Punjab, India; son of Jai (a government officer) and Leela (Aggarwal) Narayan; married Elizabeth Coilparampil (in accounting), February, 1952; children: Nirmal, Vinita, Vimal, Kamal, Rita, Anita. *Education:* University of Punjab, B.A., 1950; University of Dayton, M.B.A., 1967. *Religion:* Hindu.

ADDRESSES: Home—310 Fraser St., Findlay, OH 45840. *Office*—Department of Business and Economics, Findlay College, Main St., Findlay, OH 45840.

CAREER: Government of India, New Delhi, chief purchasing officer, 1963-65; University of Dayton, Dayton, OH, instructor in economics, 1967-69; Findlay College, Findlay, OH, assistant professor of business administration, 1969-73, associate professor of marketing, 1973—.

WRITINGS:

(With Ray T. Hamman) *Starting a Small Business: A Simulation Game,* Prentice-Hall, 1974.
(With John M. Cozzolino) *Fundamentals of Operations Research for Management,* Holden-Day, 1975.
An American Business Challenge, Findlay College, 1980.
A Business Challenge: A Simulation Game, Addison-Wesley, 1981.

WORK IN PROGRESS: Franchise Management: A Simulation Game; Consumer Behavior in Market Place.

BIOGRAPHICAL/CRITICAL SOURCES:

PERIODICALS

Ohio Business Teacher, March, 1973; March, 1974.*

*   *   *

GUSTAFSON, James M(oody)   1925-

PERSONAL: Born December 2, 1925, in Norway, MI; son of John O. (a minister) and Edith (Moody) Gustafson; married Louise Roos, September 3, 1947; children: Karl D., Greta L., John Richard, Birgitta Maria. *Education:* Attended North Park College, 1942-44; Northwestern University, B.S., 1948; Chicago Theological Seminary and University of Chicago, B.D., 1951; Yale University, Ph.D., 1955. *Politics:* Democrat.

ADDRESSES: Home—5450 South Ridgewood Ct., Chiacgo, IL 60615. *Office*—Divinity School, Swift Hall, University of Chicago, Chicago, IL 60637.

CAREER: Ordained clergyman of United Church of Christ, 1951; pastor in Northford, CT, 1951-54; assistant director of study of theological education in America, New Haven, CT, 1954-55; Yale University, New Haven, 1955-72, began as instructor, professor of Christian ethics, 1963-72, chairman of department of religious studies, 1964-67; University of Chicago, Chicago, IL, professor of theological ethics, 1972—. *Military service:* U.S. Army, Corps of Engineers, 1944-46; became technical sergeant.

MEMBER: American Academy of Arts and Sciences (fellow), American Society of Christian Ethics (president, 1969), American Theological Society, Phi Beta Kappa.

AWARDS, HONORS: Guggenheim fellowships, 1959-60, 1967-68.

WRITINGS:

(With H. Richard Niebuhr and D. D. Williams) *The Advancement of Theological Education,* Harper, 1957.
Treasure in Earthen Vessels: Church as a Human Community, Harper, 1961, reprinted, 1976.
Christ and the Moral Life, Harper, 1968.
(Editor with James T. Laney) *On Being Responsible: Issues in Personal Ethics,* Harper, 1968.
(Editor with R. D. Lambert) *Sixties: Radical Change in American Religion,* American Academy of Political and Social Science, 1970.
The Church as Moral Decision Maker, Pilgrim Press, 1971.
Christian Ethics and the Community, Pilgrim Press, 1971.
(With others) *Moral Education: Five Lectures,* Harvard University Press, 1971.
(Contributor) John T. Noonan, Jr., editor, *The Morality of Abortion,* Harvard University Press, 1971.

Theology and Christian Ethics, Pilgrim Press, 1974.
Can Ethics Be Christian?, University of Chicago Press, 1975.
The Contributions of Theology to Modern Ethics, Marquette, 1975.
Protestant and Roman Catholic Ethics: Prospects for Rapprochement, University of Chicago Press, 1978.
Ethics from a Theocentric Perspective: Theology and Ethics, University of Chicago Press, Volume 1, 1981, Volume 2, 1984.*

*   *   *

GUSTIN, Lawrence Robert   1937-

PERSONAL: Born May 26, 1937, in Flint, MI; son of Robert Stuart and Doris Mary (Irving) Gustin; married Rose Mary Murphy, July 10, 1965; children: Robert Lawrence, David Martin. *Education:* Michigan State University, B.A., 1959. *Religion:* Presbyterian.

ADDRESSES: Home—1438 Country View Lane, Flint, MI 48504. *Office*—*Flint Journal,* 200 East First St., Flint, MI 48502.

CAREER: United Press International, New York City, capitol correspondent in Lansing, MI, 1959, Michigan sports editor in Detroit, 1960; *Flint Journal,* Flint, MI, 1960-84, automotive editor, 1969-76; political writer, 1976-77; assistant metro editor, 1977-84. Buick Motor Division, manager of news relations, 1984—. Member of acquisitions committee of Sloan Museum. *Military service:* U.S. Army, 1960. U.S. Air Force Reserve, active duty, 1963-66.

MEMBER: MENSA, Detroit Press Club.

AWARDS, HONORS: Award of Merit from Michigan Historical Society, certificate of commendation from American Association for State and Local History, both 1974, and Thomas McKean Memorial Cup from Antique Automobile Club of America, 1975, for *Billy Durant: Creator of General Motors;* shared Detroit Press Club top news writing award, 1980, for news series.

WRITINGS:

Billy Durant: Creator of General Motors, Eerdmans, 1973.
The Flint Journal Picture History of Flint, Eerdmans, 1st and 2nd editions, 1976, 3rd edition, 1977.
(With Terry B. Dunham) *The Buick: A Complete History,* Automobile Quarterly, 1980, 4th edition, in press.

SIDELIGHTS: Lawrence Robert Gustin once told *CA* that while preparing his first prize-winning book, *Billy Durant: Creator of General Motors,* he "was able to find

and make first use of the personal papers of W. C. Durant, founder of General Motors, and also to interview his widow at length shortly before her death." These sources helped him to recognize "that Durant, though almost forgotten, was second only to Henry Ford in auto history importance."

*   *   *

GUTHKE, Karl S(iegfried)   1933-

PERSONAL: Born February 17, 1933, in Lingen, Germany; son of Karl H. (a government official) and Helene (Beekman) Guthke; married Dagmar von Nostitz, April 24, 1965; children: Carl Ricklef. *Education:* Attended University of Heidelberg, 1952, 1953-54; University of Texas at Austin, M.A., 1953; University of Goettingen, Ph.D., 1956. *Avocational interests:* Old maps, nineteenth-century graphics, pre-Columbian archaeology.

ADDRESSES: Home—Hillside Rd., Lincoln, MA 01773. *Office*—Department of German, Harvard University, Cambridge, MA 02138.

CAREER: University of California, Berkeley, instructor, 1956-68, assistant professor, 1958-59, associate professor, 1959-62, professor of German literature, 1962-65; University of Toronto, Toronto, Ontario, Canada, professor of German literature, 1965-68; Harvard University, Cambridge, MA, professor of German literature, 1968-78, Kuno Francke Professor of German Art and Culture, 1978—. Visiting professor at University of Colorado, 1963, and University of Massachusetts, 1967.

AWARDS, HONORS: American Philosophical Society grant, 1961-62; Guggenheim fellowship, 1965; American Council of Learned Societies fellowship, 1973; Walter Channing Cabot prize, 1977; Australian National University Humanities Research fellowship, 1985; Institute for Advanced Studies in the Humanities grants, Edinburgh, 1987 and 1989; Herzog August Bibliothek Research Center fellow in Wolfenbuettel, 1991.

WRITINGS:

Englische Vorromantik und deutscher Sturm und Drang: M. G. Lewis' Stellung in der Geschichte der deutsch-englischen Literaturbeziehungen, Vandenhoeck & Ruprecht, 1958.
(With Hans M. Wolff) *Das Leid im Werke Gerhart Hauptmann: Fuenf Studien,* University of California Press, 1958.
Geschichte und Poetik der deutschen Tragikomoedie, Vandenhoeck & Ruprecht, 1961.
Gerhart Hauptmann: Weltbild im Werk, Vandenhoeck & Ruprecht, 1961.
Haller und die Literatur, Vandenhoeck & Ruprecht, 1962.

Der Stand der Lessing-Forschung: Ein Bericht ueber die Literatur 1932-1962, Metzler, 1965.

Modern Tragi-Comedy: An Investigation into the Nature of the Genre, Random House, 1966.

Wege zur Literatur: Studien zur deutschen Dichtungs-und Geistesgeschichte, A. Francke, 1967.

Gotthold Ephraim Lessing, Metzler, 1967, 3rd edition, 1979.

Die Mythologie der entgoetterten Welt: Ein literarisches Thema von der Aufklaerung bis zur Gegenwart, Vandenhoeck & Ruprecht, 1971.

Das deutsche buergerliche Trauerspiel, Metzler, 1972, 4th edition, 1984.

G. E. Lessing, Metzler, 1973, 3rd edition, 1979.

Literarisches Leben im achtzehnten Jahrhundert in Deutschland und in der Schweiz, A. Francke, 1975.

Das Abenteuer der Literatur: Studien zum literarische Leben der deutschsprachigen Laender von der Aufklaerung bis zum Exil, A. Francke, 1981.

Haller im Halblicht, A. Francke, 1981.

Der Mythos der Neuzeit: Das Thema der Mehrheit der Welten in Literatur und Philosophie van der Kopernikanischen Wende bis zur Science Ficiton, A. Francke, 1982.

Erkundungen: Essays zur Literatur von Milton bis Traven, Herbert Lang, 1983.

"Das Geheimnis um B. Traven entdeckt": und raetselvoller denn je, Buechergilde Gutenberg, 1984.

B. Traven: Biographie eines Raetsels, Buechergilde Gutenberg, 1987, translation by Robert C. Sprung published as *B. Traven: The Life behind the Legends,* Lawrence Hill Books, 1991.

Letzte Worte, C. H. Beck, 1990.

The Last Frontier, Cornell University Press, 1990.

EDITOR

Friedrich Schiller, *Turandot, Prinzessin von China, ein tragikomisches Maerchen nach Gozzi,* Reclam, 1959.

Johann Heinrich Fuessli, *Remarks on the Writings and Conduct of J. J. Rousseau,* Augustan Reprint Society, 1960.

Dichtung und Deutung: Gedaechtnisschrift fuer Hans M. Wolff, A. Francke, 1961.

(And author of introduction) Hans M. Wolff, *Die Weltanschauung der deutschen Aufklaerung in geschichtlicher Entwicklung,* 2nd edition, A. Francke, 1963.

Jacob M. R. Lenz, *Der Hofmeister,* Reclam, 1963.

Gotthold E. Lessing, *D. Faust und die Matrone von Ephesus,* Reclam, 1968.

Gerhart Hauptmann, *Fasching Der Apostel,* Reclam, 1969.

Hallers Literaturkritik, Niemeyer, 1970.

G. E. Lessing, *Werke,* Carl Hanser, Volume 1, 1971, Volume 3, 1973.

F. M. Klinger, *Die Zwillinge,* Reclam, 1972.

Johann Heinrich Fuessli, *Saemtlichte Gedichte,* Orell Fuessli, 1973.

Albrecht von Haller, *Die Alpen,* de Clivo, 1988.

Contributor to books and journals in United States, Germany, and Italy.

* * *

GUTHMAN, William H(arold) 1924-

PERSONAL: Born October 22, 1924, in Chicago, IL; son of Harold Sol (a photographer) and Ethel (Goodman) Guthman; married Elizabeth J. Stillinger (an author, lecturer, and editor), April 9, 1981; children: Pamela, William Scott. *Education:* Northwestern University, B.A., 1951. *Politics:* Republican.

ADDRESSES: Home and office—P.O. Box 392, Westport, CT 06881.

CAREER: Society photographer, 1946-52; purchasing agent, 1952-66; antiquarian, 1966—. *Military service:* U.S. Army Air Forces, 1942-45; served in China theatre; received two bronze battle stars and China War Memorial medal.

MEMBER: American Society of Arms Collectors (director), Company of Military Historians (fellow), Kentucky Rifle Association (past president), Antique Arms Collectors Association of Connecticut.

WRITINGS:

(With John Curtis) *New England Militia Uniforms and Acoutrements,* Old Sturbridge Village, 1971.

March to Massacre: A History of the First Seven Years of the United States Army, 1785-1791, Mcgraw, 1975.

U.S. Army Weapons: 1784-1791, American Society of Arms Collectors, 1975.

(Editor) *Guns and Other Arms,* Main Street Press, 1979.

The Correspondence of Capt. Nathan and Lois Peters, Connecticut Historical Society, 1980.

Contributor to *Antiques.*

WORK IN PROGRESS: Research on carved powder horns as an art form.

* * *

GUTMANN, Joseph 1923-

PERSONAL: Born August 17, 1923, in Wuerzburg, Germany; came to the United States in 1936, naturalized in 1943; son of Henry (a merchant) and Selma (Eisemann) Gutmann; married Marilyn B. Tuckman (a teacher of mathematics), October 8, 1953; children: David, Sharon. *Education:* Temple University, B.S., 1949; New York University, M.A., 1952; Hebrew Union College-Jewish Institute of Religion, Cincinnati, Ph.D., 1960. *Avocational interests:* Travel, reading, tennis.

ADDRESSES: Home—13151 Winchester, Huntington Woods, MI 48070.

CAREER: Ordained rabbi, 1957. Hebrew Union College-Jewish Institute of Religion, Cincinnati, OH, assistant professor, 1960-65, associate professor of art history, 1965-69; Wayne State University, Detroit, MI, professor of art and art history, 1969-89. Adjunct professor, University of Cincinnati, 1961-68, University of Central Florida, 1992; Antioch College, Charles Friedman Visiting Lecturer, 1964; visiting professor, University of Michigan, 1985, Spertus College of Judaica, 1989, University of Windsor, 1990-91. Wayne State University Press, member of board of advisors, 1970-74; Detroit Institute of Arts, adjunct curator, 1971-89. Temple Beth El, Detroit, interim associate rabbi, 1974; Congregation Solel, Brighton, MI, rabbi, 1979-82. *Military service:* U.S. Army Air Forces, 1943-46; interrogator and research analyst, U.S. Strategic Bombing Survey in Europe.

MEMBER: International Center of Medieval Art, World Union of Jewish Studies, Society of Biblical Literature (chairman of art and Bible section, 1970-81), Central Conference of American Rabbis, College Art Association of America, Beta Gamma Sigma.

AWARDS, HONORS: Henry Morgenthau fellowships to Israel, 1957, 1958; Memorial Foundation for Jewish Culture grants, 1959, 1972; American Philosophical Society grant to Europe, 1965; Wayne State University faculty grants, 1971, 1973; American Council of Learned Societies grants, 1973, 1983; honorary Doctor of Divinity, Hebrew Union College-Jewish Institute of Religion, 1984; Gershenson Distinguished Faculty Fellow, Wayne State University, 1986-88.

WRITINGS:

Juedische Zeremonialkunst, Ner-Tamid-Verlag, 1963, translation by Gutmann published as *Jewish Ceremonial Art,* T. Yoseloff, 1964, revised edition, 1968.
Images of the Jewish Past: An Introduction to Medieval Hebrew Miniatures, Society of Jewish Bibliophiles, 1965.
(Editor and contributor) *Beauty in Holiness: Studies in Jewish Customs and Ceremonial Art,* Ktav, 1970.
(Editor and contributor) *No Graven Images: Studies in Art and the Hebrew Bible,* Ktav, 1971.
(With Paul Pieper) *Die Darmstaedter Pessach-Haggadah,* Propylaen Verlag, 1972.

(Editor and contributor) *The Dura-Europos Synagogue: A Re-Evaluation,* Council on the Study of Religion, 1973, revised edition, Scholars Press, 1992.
(With Stanley Chyet) *Moses Jacob Ezekiel: Memoirs from the Bath of Diocletian,* Wayne State University Press, 1975.
(Editor and contributor) *The Synagogue: Origins, Archaeology, and Architecture,* Ktav, 1975.
(Editor and contributor) *The Temple of Solomon: Archaeological Fact and Mediaeval Tradition in Christian, Islamic, and Jewish Art,* Scholars Press, 1976.
(Editor and contributor) *The Image and the Word: Confrontations in Judaism, Christianity, and Islam,* Scholars Press, 1977.
Hebrew Manuscript Painting, Braziller, 1978.
(Editor and contributor) *Ancient Synagogues: The State of Research,* Scholars Press, 1981.
The Jewish Sanctuary, E. J. Brill, 1983.
The Jewish Life Cycle, E. J. Brill, 1987.
Sacred Images: Studies in Jewish Art from Antiquity to the Middle Ages, Variorum Publications, 1979.

Contributor of over one hundred fifty articles, many reprinted separately, to scholarly journals.

Hebrew Manuscript Painting has been published in German, French, and Dutch.

*   *   *

GUTTING, Gary (Michael) 1942-

PERSONAL: Born April 11, 1942, in St. Louis, MO; married, 1965; children: three. *Education:* St. Louis University, B.A., 1964, Ph.D., 1968.

ADDRESSES: Office—Department of Philosophy, University of Notre Dame, Notre Dame, IN 46556.

CAREER: St. Louis University, St. Louis, MO, instructor in philosophy, 1967-68; University of Notre Dame, Notre Dame, IN, assistant professor, 1969-74, associate professor, 1974-82, professor of philosophy, 1982—.

MEMBER: American Philosophical Association, Philosophy of Science Association.

AWARDS, HONORS: Fulbright fellow at Catholic University of Louvain, 1968-69.

WRITINGS:

(With Michael Loux) *The Synoptic Vision: The Philosophy of Wilfrid Sellars,* University of Notre Dame Press, 1977.
(Editor) *Paradigms and Revolutions: Applications and Appraisals of Thomas Kuhn's Philosophy of Science,* University of Notre Dame Press, 1980.

Religious Faith and Religious Skepticism, University of Notre Dame Press, 1982.

Michel Foucault's Archaeology of Scientific Reason, Cambridge University Press, 1989.

Contributor of over twenty articles on various philosophical topics in philosophy of science, religion, and recent Continental philosophy to philosophy journals.

BIOGRAPHICAL/CRITICAL SOURCES:

PERIODICALS

Times Literary Supplement, July 27, 1990.

H

HALL, Lynn   1937-

PERSONAL: Born November 9, 1937, in Lombard, IL; daughter of Raymond Edwin (a city official) and Alice (a high school teacher; maiden name, Seeds) Hall; married Dean W. Green, May 1, 1960 (divorced September, 1961). *Education:* Attended schools in Iowa. *Religion:* Protestant.

ADDRESSES: Home—Touchwood, Route 2, Elkader, IA 52043.

CAREER: Secretary in Fort Worth, TX, 1955-57; secretary and veterinarian's assistant in Des Moines, IA, 1957-66; affiliated with Ambro Advertising Agency, Des Moines, IA, 1966-68; writer, 1968—. Member of Garnavillo Library Board.

MEMBER: Society of Children's Book Writers, Dubuque Kennel Club, Bedlington Terrier Club of America.

AWARDS, HONORS: Book of the year selections from Child Study Association of America include *Ride a Wild Dream,* 1969, *Too Near the Sun,* 1970, *Gently Touch the Milkweed,* 1970, *To Catch a Tartar,* 1973, *Barry, the Bravest St. Bernard,* 1973, *New Day for Dragon,* 1975, *Just One Friend,* 1985, and *Mrs. Portree's Pony,* 1987; Charles W. Follett Award, 1971, for *A Horse Called Dragon;* Best Young Adult Books selections by American Library Association, 1972, for *Sticks and Stones,* 1980, for *The Leaving,* and 1984, for *Uphill All the Way;* Netherlands' Silver Quill Award, 1976, for *Sticks and Stones;* Edgar Allan Poe Award runner up from the Mystery Writers of America, 1980, for *The Whispered Horse; The Leaving* was selected as one of the best young adult books by American Library Association, 1980, received the *Boston Globe-Horn Book* Award for fiction, 1981, and was selected as one of New York Public Library's books for teenagers, 1981 and 1982; Tennessee Children's Choice Award from Tennessee Library Association, 1981, for *Shadows; The Horse Trader* was selected as one of New York Public Library's books for teenagers, 1982; *Uphill All the Way* was selected as one of the best young adult books by American Library Association, 1984; *Tazo and Me* was selected an Outstanding Science Trade Book for Children by the National Science Teachers Association and the Children's Book Council, 1985; Golden Kite Award Honor Book for Fiction from the Society of Children's Book Writers, 1986, for *The Solitary;* Children's Literature Award from the Society of Midland Authors, 1987, for *Mrs. Portree's Pony;* Johnson Brigham Award from the Iowa State Historical Society, 1989, for *The Secret Life of Dagmar Schultz.*

WRITINGS:

JUVENILE FICTION

The Shy Ones, illustrated by Greta Elgaard, Follett, 1967.
The Secret of Stonehouse, illustrated by Joseph Cellini, Follett, 1968.
Ride a Wild Dream, illustrated by George Roth, Follett, 1969.
Too Near the Sun (Junior Literary Guild selection), illustrated by Stefan Martin, Follett, 1970.
Gently Touch the Milkweed (Junior Literary Guild selection), illustrated by Rod Ruth,Follett, 1970.
A Horse Called Dragon (Junior Literary Guild selection), illustrated by Joseph Cellini, Follett, 1971, published as *Wild Mustang,* Scholastic, 1976.
The Famous Battle of Bravery Creek, Garrard, 1972.
The Siege of Silent Henry, Follett, 1972.
Sticks and Stones, Follett, 1972.
Lynn Hall's Dog Stories, Follett, 1972.
Flash, Dog of Old Egypt, Garrard, 1973.
Barry, the Bravest St. Bernard, illustrated by Richard Amundsen, Garrard, 1973.
Riff, Remember, Follett, 1973.

To Catch a Tartar, illustrated by Cellini, Follett, 1973.

The Stray, illustrated by Cellini, Follett, 1974.

Bob, Watchdog of the River, illustrated by Taylor Oughton, Garrard, 1974.

Troublemaker, illustrated by Cellini, Follett, 1974.

New Day for Dragon, illustrated by Cellini, Follett, 1975.

Captain: Canada's Flying Pony, illustrated by Tran Mawicke, Garrard, 1976.

Flowers of Anger, illustrated by Cellini, Follett, 1976.

Owney, the Traveling Dog, Garrard, 1977.

Dragon Defiant, illustrated by Cellini, Follett, 1977.

Shadows, illustrated by Cellini, Follett, 1977.

The Mystery of Pony Hollow, illustrated by Ruth Sanderson, Garrard, 1978.

The Mystery of the Lost and Found Hound, illustrated by Alan Daniel, Garrard, 1979.

The Mystery of the Schoolhouse Dog, illustrated by William Hutchinson, Garrard, 1979.

The Whispered Horse, Follett, 1979.

Dog of the Bondi Castle, Follett, 1979.

The Leaving, Scribner, 1980.

Dragon's Delight, Follett, 1980.

The Mystery of the Stubborn Old Man, illustrated by Herman Vestal, Garrard, 1980.

The Mystery of the Plum Park Pony, illustrated by Daniel, Garrard, 1980.

The Haunting of the Green Bird, Follett, 1980.

The Disappearing Grandad, Follett, 1980.

The Mysterious Moortown Bridge, illustrated by Sanderson, Follett, 1980.

The Ghost of the Great River Inn, illustrated by Allen Davis, Follett, 1981.

The Horse Trader, Scribner, 1981.

The Mystery of the Caramel Cat, illustrated by Sanderson, Garrard, 1981.

Danza!, Scribner, 1981.

Half the Battle, Scribner, 1982.

Tin Can Tucker, Scribner, 1982.

Denison's Daughter, Scribner, 1983.

Megan's Mare, Scribner, 1983.

The Mystery of Pony Hollow Panda, illustrated by Hutchinson, Garrard, 1983.

Nobody's Dog, Scholastic Inc., 1984.

Uphill All the Way, Scribner, 1984.

The Boy in the Off-White Hat, Scribner, 1984.

The Giver, Scribner, 1985.

The Something-Special Horse, illustrated by Sandy Rabinowitz, Scribner, 1985.

Just One Friend, Scribner, 1985.

If Winter Comes, Scribner, 1986.

The Solitary, Scribner, 1986.

Danger Dog, Scribner, 1986.

Mrs. Portree's Pony, Scribner, 1986.

Letting Go, Scribner, 1987.

Flyaway, Scribner, 1987.

In Trouble Again, Zelda Hammersmith?, illustrated by Ray Cruz, Harcourt, 1987.

Ride a Dark Horse, Morrow, 1987.

A Killing Freeze, Morrow, 1988.

Zelda Strikes Again!, Harcourt, 1988.

Murder at the Spaniel Show, Scribner, 1988.

The Secret Life of Dagmar Schultz, Scribner, 1988.

Dagmar Schultz and the Powers of Darkness, Scribner, 1988.

Dagmar Schultz and the Angel Edna, Scribner, 1989.

Here Comes Zelda Claus, and Other Holiday Disasters, Harcourt, 1989.

Where Have All the Tigers Gone?, Scribner, 1989.

The Tormentors, Harcourt, 1990.

Fair Maiden, Scribner, 1990.

Halsey's Pride, Scribner, 1990.

Murder in a Pig's Eye, Harcourt, 1990.

Dagmar Schultz and the Green-Eyed Monster, Scribner, 1991.

Flying Changes, Harcourt, 1991.

The Soul of the Silver Dog, Harcourt, 1992.

Windsong, Scribner, 1992.

JUVENILE NONFICTION

Kids and Dog Shows, Follett, 1975.

Careers for Dog Lovers, Follett, 1978.

Tazo and Me, photographs by Jan Hall, Scribner, 1985.

SIDELIGHTS: "From earliest memory I had been yearning toward the country, toward animals, specifically toward horses and dogs. . . . All of my clearest childhood memories center around animals," said Lynn Hall in *Something about the Author Autobiography Series (SAAS).* Hall has featured dogs and horses in many of her works for children, but she is also known as an author of young adult novels concerned with teenagers facing difficult circumstances.

In her search for a life surrounded by animals, Hall once thought of offering herself to a farm family for adoption. At age seven, she ran away from home hoping to join a pony-ride concession. Throughout her early years, Hall tended to keep to herself. "My nature was to be a loner," she told *Something About the Author (SATA),* "and I did manage to have a lot of time to myself. I wrote plays, went to the little local library, read continually, primarily horse and dog stories—wish fulfillment books. They became the center of my life. I wasn't trying to expand my mind, but merely to get a horse or a dog any way I could."

In childhood, Hall didn't think of becoming a published author. "I thought about drawing the pictures [of children's books], about being an illustrator," she said. "But my conception of someone who wrote books was beyond anything I ever imagined I could be. Writers, I thought, sat at the right hand of God. Henry Gregor Felsen, a children's author, lived in our small town in Iowa. I used to follow him around, not realizing, I'm sure, that on some subliminal level I too wanted to write. We met years later, when I was in my mid-twenties and had written my first book."

The author's family moved several times during her childhood and teenage years. At each new home, Hall sought the company of animals, at one point working in a stable where she was occasionally allowed to ride. At age fourteen, Hall bought her first horse with money earned by babysitting, and she rode daily. A few years later, while a high school student, she had to leave her horse behind when the family moved again. Hall felt out of place in high school, and was not optimistic about her chances of living as she wished. She remarked in her *SAAS* essay: "As the end of high school drew closer, I became more frantic in my search for a future. My dream was strong and definite, but impractical. I wanted to live alone, somewhere with rolling fields and woods and quiet. I wanted my family to be dogs and horses. I wanted, in some unspoken way, to belong to myself."

After graduating from high school, Hall travelled across the country, working at a succession of jobs. The author commented to *SATA*, "The jobs I held ranged from assistant dog trainer to assistant to a veterinarian, from clerk in a blue jeans factory to secretary in a juvenile parole office, from radio station copywriter to ad agency writer. It was a very difficult time for me. It was full of false starts and mislaid directions. I was searching, almost desperately, for a career."

In *SAAS*, Hall related the circumstances of her short-lived marriage: "My jobs were boring, routine office jobs that used only a small fraction of my mind. I felt ready to settle down now, and join the rest of the world. So I picked out a husband and married him. He was a mild, pleasant man, a pharmacist in a small town in southern Iowa. He was stability personified, and I had already outgrown him even before the wedding. . . . The marriage was predictably short. In less than two years I was on the road again, with all my belongings packed in the back of my '57 Chevy, and a blooming sense of freedom inside me. I felt that I had paid my dues to society, now the rest of my life was going to be my way."

Hall told *SATA* she decided to become a writer when she saw a horse book that she thought she could have written better: "In passing a bookstore window one day, I noticed a display for a new horse book by a local author. I went in to investigate. The book was poorly written in my opinion, and showed a laughable lack of knowledge of horses. This was just what I needed. By this time I had enough technical knowledge about horses and dogs to write about

them convincingly. I had the answer I'd been looking for during all those frustrating years. I had my dream."

To prepare for her new career, Hall read novels of the sort she hoped to write. "I read and read and read, and before long the structure of the books became apparent. Even more important, I began to develop the ability to tell the well-written books from the poorly written ones, and to pinpoint in what specific ways they differed," the author wrote in *SAAS*. A writer to whom Hall showed her first manuscript—a story about a dog show—suggested that her writing needed more character development. "Grimly, I went to work on the second book," said Hall. "This, too, was a dog story but with more emphasis on the characters and their relationships. It was a little bit better, I thought hopefully. And it came a little easier than the first book had. There was less self-doubt to battle the second time around." The second manuscript became her first published book, *The Shy Ones*. "I couldn't imagine," Hall related to *SATA*, "that life would hold a higher moment than my first realization that I was a published author. I was instantly vindicated in the eyes of parents who thought I was a hopeless drifter." In *SAAS*, the author said of her subsequent works, "Each book got a little better, a little easier."

Hall once told *CA:* "The loves of my life, horses and dogs, provide the impetus for my writing. The truth is that I write not so much to provide books for children as to relish the sheer fun of a good horse story or a good dog story. When I've read all the horse stories I can find, then there's nothing to do but make up some new ones. I consider myself singularly lucky to have made a life's work out of a life-long love."

Several of Hall's books reflect incidents in her own childhood. For example, *The Stray* tells her story of having wanted to be adopted by a farmer so that she could be with animals. In addition, the author told *SATA* that "Each of the stories [in *Lynn Hall's Dog Stories*] is about a particular dog I owned at one time," and that "*The Horse Trader* is a fictionalized account about my experience of buying my first horse." Hall has also worked history into some of her stories: *A Horse Named Dragon* is based on the life of one of the sires of the Ponies of the Americas breed; the author followed this novel with three more books—*New Day for Dragon*, *Dragon Defiant*, and *Dragon's Delight*—to make a series. Other Hall stories, such as those about ghost animals, are pure fiction.

Aside from her stories about animals, Hall has written books about young adults confronted with perplexing situations. Tom, the protagonist of *Sticks and Stones*, befriends a young man who has been discharged from the military because he is a homosexual. At school, Tom finds that teachers and students believe rumors asserting that he too is homosexual. Writing in *New York Times Book Review,* Judy Blume noted that *Sticks and Stones* focuses on "injustice through the power of gossip." Blume also stated that Hall "has handled a difficult subject with intelligence and understanding."

"Seventeen-year-old Jane's need for solitude derives from her bitter experience of living with relatives after her mother shot her father, who was a wife-beater and child-abuser," a review for the *Bulletin of the Center for Children's Books* said of *The Solitary.* Jane eventually comes to terms with her past, and visits her mother in prison.

The Boy in the Off-White Hat features a babysitter's discovery that her young charge has been sexually molested by the boyfriend of the child's mother. Hall commented to *SATA:* "I'd wanted to write this for a long time because I had suffered a few such incidents in my childhood—nothing serious, but they are still clear memories. There is a lot of guilt attached for the child, which is the most damaging part. It felt good to finally be able to write about this and have my publisher accept *The Boy in the Off-White Hat* without any qualms."

The author currently lives with several dogs and a horse at a rural house which she planned and helped construct. She wrote in *SAAS:* "Sometimes I think about those childish dreams of mine, and I realize that there would probably be more truly happy people in the world if more attention were paid to childhood dreams. They probably hold the keys to our real needs. For me, those needs were country and solitude, hills and woods and a family of horses and dogs; work that was a continual joy and a continual challenge; a sense of belonging to myself."

BIOGRAPHICAL/CRITICAL SOURCES:

BOOKS

Something About the Author, Volume 47, Gale, 1987.
Something About the Author Autobiography Series, Volume 4, Gale, 1987.

PERIODICALS

Booklist, January 15, 1985.
Bulletin of the Center for Children's Books, December, 1986, p. 68.
English Journal, September, 1981, p. 77.
New York Times Book Review, May 28, 1972, p. 8.*

*   *   *

HAMILTON, Virginia 1936-

PERSONAL: Born March 12, 1936, in Yellow Springs, OH; daughter of Kenneth James (a musician) and Etta Belle (Perry) Hamilton; married Arnold Adoff (an anthol-

ogist and poet), March 19, 1960; children: Leigh Hamilton, Jaime Levi. *Education:* Studied at Antioch College, 1952-55, Ohio State University, 1957-58, and New School for Social Research, 1958-60.

ADDRESSES: Agent—Arnold Adoff Agency, Box 293, Yellow Springs, OH 45387.

CAREER: "Every source of occupation imaginable, from singer to bookkeeper."

AWARDS, HONORS: Zeely appeared on the American Library Association's list of notable children's books of 1967 and received the Nancy Block Memorial Award of the Downtown Community School Awards Committee, New York; Edgar Allan Poe Award for best juvenile mystery, 1969, for *The House of Dies Drear;* Ohioana Literary Award, 1969; John Newbery Honor Book Award, 1971, for *The Planet of Junior Brown;* Lewis Carroll Shelf Award, *Boston Globe-Horn Book* Award, 1974, John Newbery Medal and National Book Award, both 1975, and Gustav-Heinemann-Friedinspreis fur kinder und Lugendbucher (Dusseldorf, Germany), 1991, all for *M. C. Higgins, the Great;* John Newbery Honor Book Award, Coretta Scott King Award, *Boston Globe-Horn Book* Award, and American Book Award nomination, all 1983, all for *Sweet Whispers, Brother Rush; Horn Book* Fanfare Award in fiction, 1985, for *A Little Love;* Coretta Scott King Award, *New York Times* Best Illustrated Children's Book Award, Children's Book Bulletin Other Award, and *Horn Book* Honor List selection, all 1986, all for *The People Could Fly: American Black Folktales; Boston Globe-Horn Book* Award, 1988, and Coretta Scott King Award, 1989, both for *Anthony Burns: The Defeat and Triumph of a Fugitive Slave;* John Newbery Honor Book Award, 1989, for *In the Beginning: Creation Stories from around the World;* Honorary Doctor of Humane Letters, Bank St. College, 1990; Catholic Library Association Regina Medal, 1990; Hans Christian Andersen Award U.S. nominee, 1992, for body of work.

WRITINGS:

(Editor) *The Writings of W. E. B. Du Bois,* Crowell, 1975.
(Author of introduction) Martin Greenberg, editor, *The Newbery Award Reader,* Harcourt, 1984.

BIOGRAPHIES FOR CHILDREN

W. E. B. Du Bois: A Biography, Crowell, 1972.
Paul Robeson: The Life and Times of a Free Black Man, Harper, 1974.

FICTION FOR CHILDREN

Zeely, illustrated by Symeon Shimin, Macmillan, 1967.
The House of Dies Drear, illustrated by Eros Keith, Macmillan, 1968.
The Time-Ago Tales of Jahdu, Macmillan, 1969.

The Planet of Junior Brown, Macmillan, 1971.

Time-Ago Lost: More Tales of Jahdu, illustrated by Ray Prather, Macmillan, 1973.

M. C. Higgins, the Great, Macmillan, 1974, published with teacher's guide by Lou Stanek, Dell, 1986.

Arilla Sun Down, Greenwillow, 1976.

Justice and Her Brothers (first novel in the "Justice" trilogy), Greenwillow, 1978.

Jahdu, pictures by Jerry Pinkney, Greenwillow, 1980.

Dustland (second novel in the "Justice" trilogy), Greenwillow, 1980.

The Gathering (third novel in the "Justice" trilogy), Greenwillow, 1981.

Sweet Whispers, Brother Rush, Philomel, 1982.

The Magical Adventures of Pretty Pearl, Harper, 1983.

Willie Bea and the Time the Martians Landed, Greenwillow, 1983.

A Little Love, Philomel, 1984.

Junius over Far, Harper, 1985.

The People Could Fly: American Black Folktales, illustrated by Leo and Diane Dillon, Knopf, 1985, published with cassette, 1987.

The Mystery of Drear House: The Conclusion of the Dies Drear Chronicle, Greenwillow, 1987.

A White Romance, Philomel, 1987.

In the Beginning: Creation Stories from around the World, Harcourt, 1988.

Anthony Burns: The Defeat and Triumph of a Fugitive Slave (an historical reconstruction based on fact), Knopf, 1988.

Bells of Christmas, illustrated by Davis, Harcourt, 1989.

The Dark Way: Stories from the Spirit World, illustrated by Lambert Davis, Harcourt, 1990.

Cousins, Putnam, 1990.

The All Jahdu Storybook, illustrated by Barry Moser, Harcourt, 1991.

Many Thousand Gone, illustrated by L. Dillon and D. Dillon, Knopf, 1992.

ADAPTATIONS: The House of Dies Drear was adapted for the Public Broadcasting Service series "Wonderworks" in 1984.

SIDELIGHTS: Virginia Hamilton is one of the most prolific and influential authors of children's books writing today. Not only have many of her works received awards such as the National Book Award, but her novel, *M. C. Higgins, the Great,* was the first work in history to win both the National Book Award and the Newbery Medal. Hamilton is recognized as a gifted and demanding storyteller. Ethel L. Heins, for example, writes in *Horn Book:* "Few writers of fiction for young people are as daring, inventive, and challenging to read—or to review—as Virginia Hamilton. Frankly making demands on her readers, she nevertheless expresses herself in a style essentially sim-

ple and concise." Hamilton's writing is a mix of realism, history, myth, and folklore, which, according to *Horn Book* contributor Paul Heins, "always [results in] some exterior manifestation—historical and personal—that she has examined in the light of her feelings and her intelligence."

Although Hamilton has been praised for her depiction of contemporary African-American life and its historical and cultural heritage, the author does not see herself in such narrow terms. "There's nothing you can really do about being referred to as a 'minority' or 'black' writer," she tells *Something about the Author (SATA)* interviewer Marguerite Feitlowitz. "For a long time, I tried to fight it, saying I'm a writer, *period.* But in a country like ours, there really is a dominant culture. I prefer the term 'parallel culture.'" Throughout her writing career, Hamilton has struggled "to find a certain form and content to express black literature as American literature and perpetuate a pedigree of American black literature for the young," she explains to Wendy Smith in the *Chicago Tribune Book World.*

Hamilton's vision has been deeply influenced by her background. Her mother's side of the family was descended from a fugitive slave, Levi Perry, who settled in the southern Ohio Miami valley town of Yellow Springs. The Perry family grew and prospered by farming the rich Ohio soil. "I grew up within the warmth of loving aunts and uncles, all reluctant farmers but great storytellers," Hamilton recalls in a *Horn Book* article by Lee Bennett Hopkins. "I remember the tales best of all. My own father, who was an outlander from Illinois, Iowa, and points west, was the finest of the storytellers besides being an exceptional mandolinist. Mother, too, could take a slice of fiction floating around the family and polish it into a saga."

"In the succeeding generation—that is, my generation," Hamilton writes in *Horn Book*—"stories and tall tales were less frequent but were told often enough so that the child I was learned to think and to manage feelings in terms of stories. When it came time for me to attempt my own telling, I found I was good at drawing on the lapses between true memories, which had grown large with the passage of time." While attending Antioch College on a scholarship, Hamilton majored in writing and composed short stories. One of her instructors liked her stories enough to encourage the young student to leave college and test her skills in New York City. Hamilton was eager to experience the excitement of city life, and so in 1955 she began spending her summers in New York working as a bookkeeper. Later, she moved to the city permanently. "I don't have a clear recollection of the day I officially left home to go to New York," she tells Feitlowitz. "My plan was to find a cheap apartment, a part-time job, write and have a good time. And it all came together."

Working various jobs, reading voraciously, and soaking in the artistic atmosphere of Greenwich Village, Hamilton did not place writing on a high priority. "I worked hard at my writing, but wasn't singularly fixed on it. . . . *The New Yorker* wrote me very encouraging letters and tried to help me. But I would never quite fit their mold. I was meeting all kinds of people and having a wonderful time. Seriousness came slowly." While in New York, Hamilton attended the New School where one of her teachers, Atheneum co-founder Hiram Hayden, supported her efforts and tried to get her first novel, a work for adults entitled *Mayo,* published. "Unfortunately, his partners [at Atheneum] didn't agree. If they had, I might never have become a writer of children's books." Instead, at the suggestion of a friend, Hamilton expanded a children's story she had written into the novel, *Zeely.*

An important influence on the creation of *Zeely* came after Hamilton married poet and anthologist Arnold Adoff, whom she met not long after arriving in New York City. The two newlyweds traveled to Spain and then to northern Africa. "Going to Africa had been an enduring dream of Hamilton's," according to *Dictionary of Literary Biography* contributor Jane Ball, "and the land of dark-skinned people had 'a tremendous impression' on her, she said, even though her stay was brief. The impact is apparent on her first book." According to John Rowe Townsend in his *A Sounding of Storytellers: New and Revised Essays on Contemporary Writers for Children, Zeely* exemplifies the type of writing that Hamilton would produce throughout her career: there "is not taint of racism in her books. . . . All through her work runs an awareness of black history, and particularly of black history in America. And there is a difference in the furniture of her writing mind from that of most of her white contemporaries: dream, myth, legend and ancient story can be sensed again and again in the background of naturalistically-described present-day events."

Zeely is about a girl called Geeder who, fascinated by a tall, regal-looking woman she sees tending pigs on a farm, obsessively imagines her to be a Watusi queen. By the end of the tale, Zeely convinces Geeder she is nothing of the sort, "and with the aid of a parable she helps Geeder [accept herself for who she is, too]. She is not a queen; and perhaps there is an implication that for black Americans to look back towards supposed long-lost glories in Africa is unfruitful."

After living in New York City for about fifteen years, Hamilton decided to return to her home state. "I loved the city until the moment I could no longer stand it, which happened one day between four and five in the afternoon," she recalls in Heins's article. "I think what happened was that I had always found it too stimulating. No time to think, only time to recoil or react. I felt no control over my life. I could not initiate or change anything. I had no *effect.*" The city, however, did have some effect on Hamilton's writing in that her books *The Time-Ago Tales of Jahdu* and *The Planet of Junior Brown* take place there.

"Most of my books have some element of fantasy," Hamilton remarks in *Children's Literature Association Quarterly,* "from little Jahdu who was born in an oven and the Night Traveller in *Zeely,* on to the dead James False Face speaking to the child, Arilla, in *Arilla Sun Down,* to the ghost in *Sweet Whispers, Brother Rush* and the divine power of the gods in *The Magical Adventures of Pretty Pearl.*" Hamilton varies the degree of fantasy from book to book. With the "Justice" trilogy, which some critics have classified as science fiction, the author deals with such subjects as clairvoyance, global disaster, and time travel. Hamilton, however, does not consider these books science fiction. Rather, she feels they are fantasy books. "Science fiction is based on scientific fact; fantasy need not be," she explains to Feitlowitz.

In books like the Jahdu tales, including *The Time-Ago Tales of Jahdu, Time-Ago Lost: More Tales of Jahdu, Jahdu,* and *The All Jahdu Storybook,* Hamilton takes an approach that mimics the style of the traditional folk tale. These works tell of the fantastic adventures of Jahdu and his "encounters [with] the allegorical figures Sweetdream, Nightmare, Trouble, Chameleon, and others . . . ," writes Marilyn F. Apseloff in the *Dictionary of Literary Biography.* "These original tales have a timeless quality about them; in addition, they reveal racial pride, as Jahdu discovers in [*The Time-Ago Tales of Jahdu*] that he is happiest when he becomes a part of a black family in Harlem." Similarly, in the collections *The People Could Fly: American Black Folktales, In the Beginning: Creation Stories from around the World,* and *The Dark Way: Stories from the Spirit World* Hamilton retells old myths and folk tales from her own black ancestry—as well as many other cultures—in an attempt to restore pride in this diverse and rich literary heritage.

One ethnic group in particular, American Indians, has influenced Hamilton's writing in books like the Edgar Award-winning *The House of Dies Drear.* "The references to Indians in her books," observes Apseloff, "are probably the result of two factors: Hamilton knew that many Shawnees lived in the Yellow Springs area originally, with Cherokees further south, and her grandmother claimed to be part American Indian." Despite this element in the story, however, *The House of Dies Drear* is a mystery novel centered around the history of the Underground Railroad, the route that fugitive blacks took to escape slavery in the South before the Civil War. It "is a taut mystery, one which youngsters gulp down quickly and find hard to forget," attests Hopkins. "Miss Hamilton remarked, '*The House of Dies Drear* is [one of] my favorite book[s], I think, because it is so full of all the things I love: excitement, mystery, black history, the strong, black family. In it I tried to pay back all those wonderful relatives who gave me so much in the past."

Family is an important theme in all of Hamilton's books, and her strong faith and love of family, along with the fact that she has always considered herself to be a loner, has influenced the characterization in her novels. "I think I'd have to say my characters are for the most part based on me," she tells Hopkins. She later adds, "My characters are the way I see the artist, the *human,* isolated, out of time, in order to reveal himself more clearly. I am tremendously interested in the human as oracle and as spirit isolated." She first tackled this theme of the isolated individual head on in *The Planet of Junior Brown* in which three people, the fat but musically gifted Junior, an eccentric janitor named Mr. Pool, and the street-wise, independent Buddy Clark, find support in each other in a secret room in the school basement. The intensity of Junior's isolation from his parents and the rest of the world is so great that it finally leads to a madness induced by his piano teacher, Miss Peebs. Together, Mr. Pool and Buddy help Junior, and in so doing Buddy also matures. "He realizes that living for himself, his old belief, is not the answer," relates Apseloff: " 'We have to learn to live for each other.' "

Hamilton's *M. C. Higgins, the Great* also emphasizes the importance of family. The story portrays the Higginses, a close-knit family that resides on Sarah's Mountain in southern Ohio. The mountain has special significance to the Higginses, for it has belonged to their family since M. C.'s great-grandmother Sarah, an escaped slave, settled there. The conflict in the story arises when a huge spoil heap, created by strip mining, threatens to engulf their home. M. C. is torn between his love for his home and his concern for his family's safety, and he searches diligently for a solution that will allow him to preserve both. *M. C. Higgins, the Great* was highly praised by critics, including poet Nikki Giovanni, who writes in the *New York Times Book Review:* "Once again Virginia Hamilton creates a world and invites us in. *M. C. Higgins, the Great* is not an adorable book, not a lived-happily-ever-after kind of story. It is warm, humane and hopeful and does what every book should do—creates characters with whom we can identify and for whom we care."

Today, Hamilton lives with her husband on her family's land in Ohio. Her children are now grown and persuing careers in New York. She continues to write books involving family life like *Bells of Christmas* and *Cousins.* Although African-American characters are featured in all her books, and elements of black history form the background for a number of these, Hamilton is first and foremost an author concerned with theme, characterization, and setting. She respects her audiences of children and

young adults, asserting to Feitlowitz that even though "books can, and do help us to live; and some may even change our lives, . . . it is not a good thing to put sociological/didactic considerations before literary ones." "Virginia Hamilton has heightened the standards of children's literature as few others have," concludes Betsy Hearne in *Bookbird.* "She does not address children or the state of children so much as she explores with them, sometimes ahead of them, the full possibilities of boundless imagination."

BIOGRAPHICAL/CRITICAL SOURCES:

BOOKS

Authors in the News, Volume 1, Gale, 1976.
Butler, Francelia, editor, *Children's Literature: Annual of the Modern Language Association Seminar on Children's Literature and the Children's Literature Association,* Volume 4, Temple University Press, 1975.
Children's Literature Review, Gale, Volume 1, 1976, Volume 8, 1985, Volume 11, 1986.
Contemporary Literary Criticism, Volume 26, Gale, 1983.
Dictionary of Literary Biography, Gale, Volume 33: *Afro-American Fiction Writers after 1955,* 1984, Volume 52: *American Writers for Children since 1960: Fiction,* 1986.
Egoff, Sheila A., *Thursday's Child: Trends and Patterns in Contemporary Children's Literature,* American Library Association, 1981, pp. 31-65, 130-158.
Lystad, Mary, *From Dr. Mather to Dr. Seuss: 200 Years of American Books for Children,* Schenkman Books, pp. 179-205.
Rees, David, *Painted Desert, Green Shade: Essays on Contemporary Writers of Fiction for Children and Young Adults,* Horn Book, 1984, pp. 168-184.
Sims, Rudine, *Shadow and Substance: Afro-American Experience in Contemporary Children's Fiction,* National Council of Teachers of English, 1982, pp. 79-102.
Something about the Author, Volume 56, Gale, 1989, pp. 60-70.
Townsend, John Rowe, *A Sounding of Storytellers: New and Revised Essays on Contemporary Writers for Children,* Lippincott, 1979, pp. 97-108.

PERIODICALS

Best Sellers, January, 1983.
Bookbird, December 15, 1980, pp. 22-23.
Booklist, August, 1982, p. 1525; April 1, 1983, pp. 1034-1035; July, 1985, p. 1554.
Bulletin of the Center for Children's Books, September, 1978, p. 9; March, 1981, p. 134; July-August, 1982, p. 207; November, 1983, pp. 50-51; April, 1985, p. 148; June, 1988.
Chicago Tribune Book World, November 10, 1985, pp. 33-34.

Children's Literature Association Quarterly, fall, 1982, pp. 45-48; winter, 1983, pp. 10-14, 25-27; spring, 1983, pp. 17-20.

Children's Literature in Education, winter, 1983; summer, 1987, pp. 67-75.

Christian Science Monitor, May 4, 1972, p. B5; March 12, 1979, p. B4; May 12, 1980, p. B9; March 2, 1984, p. B7; August 3, 1984.

Cincinnati Enquirer, January 5, 1975.

Growing Point, July, 1977, pp. 3147-3148; November, 1985, pp. 4525-4526; January, 1988.

Horn Book, October, 1968, p. 563; February, 1970; February, 1972; October, 1972, p. 476; December, 1972, pp. 563-569; June, 1973; October, 1974, pp. 143-144; April, 1975; August, 1975, pp. 344-348; December, 1976, p. 611; December, 1978, pp. 609-619; June, 1980, p. 305; October, 1982, pp. 505-506; June, 1983; February, 1984, pp. 24-28; September-October, 1984, pp. 597-598; September-October, 1985, pp. 563-564; March-April, 1986, pp. 212-213; January-February, 1988, pp. 105-106; March-April, 1989, pp. 183-185.

Interracial Books for Children Bulletin, Numbers 1 and 2, 1983, p. 32; Number 5, 1984; Volume 15, number 5, 1984, pp. 17-18; Volume 16, number 4, 1985, p. 19.

Kirkus Reviews, July 1, 1974; October 15, 1980, pp. 1354-1355; April 1, 1983; October 1, 1985, pp. 1088-1089.

Kliatt Young Adult Paperback Book Guide, winter, 1982, p. 21.

Library Journal, September 15, 1971.

The Lion and the Unicorn, Volume 9, 1985, pp. 50-57.

Listener, November 6, 1975.

Los Angeles Times Book Review, March 23, 1986; May 22, 1988, p. 11; December 17, 1989, p. 8; November 18, 1990, p. 8.

New York Times Book Review, October 13, 1968, p. 26; October 24, 1971, p. 8; September 22, 1974, p. 8; December 22, 1974, p. 8; October 31, 1976, p. 39; December 17, 1978, p. 27; May 4, 1980, pp. 26, 28; September 27, 1981, p. 36; November 14, 1982, pp. 41, 56; September 4, 1983, p. 14; March 18, 1984, p. 31; April 7, 1985, p. 20; November 10, 1985, p. 38; November 8, 1987, p. 36; October 16, 1988, p. 46; November 13, 1988, p. 52; December 17, 1989, p. 29; November 11, 1990, p. 6.

School Library Journal, December 1968, pp. 53-54; September, 1971, p. 126; December, 1978, p. 60; March, 1980, p. 140; April, 1981, p. 140; April, 1983, p. 123.

Times (London), November 20, 1986.

Times Literary Supplement, May 23, 1975; July 11, 1975, p. 766; March 25, 1977, p. 359; September 19, 1980, p. 1024; November 20, 1981, p. 1362; August 30, 1985, p. 958; February 28, 1986, p. 230; October 30, 1987, p. 1205; November 20, 1987, p. 1286; July 29, 1988, p. 841.

Tribune Books (Chicago), November 13, 1988, p. 6; February 26, 1989, p. 8; November 11, 1990.

Village Voice, December 14, 1975.

Voice of Youth Advocates, August, 1980, pp. 31-32; October, 1983, p. 215.

Washington Post Book World, June 25, 1967, p. 12; November 10, 1974; November 7, 1976, p. G7; November 11, 1979; September 14, 1980, p. 6; November 7, 1982, p. 14; November 10, 1985; July 10, 1988, p. 11; April 8, 1990, p. 8; November 4, 1990, p. 19; December 9, 1990, p. 14.

—*Sketch by Kevin S. Hile*

*   *   *

HARRISON, Mary
See RASH, Nancy

*   *   *

HARTLEY, Keith   1940-

PERSONAL: Born July 14, 1940, in Leeds, England; son of Walter and Ivy (Stead) Hartley; married Winifred Kealy (a teacher), April 12, 1966; children: Adam, Lucy, Cecilia. *Education:* University of Hull, B.Sc. (economics), 1962, Ph.D. 1974. *Religion:* Roman Catholic. *Avocational interests:* Music, sports, angling.

ADDRESSES: Office—Institute for Research in the Social Sciences, University of York, Heslington, York YO1 5DD, England.

CAREER: University of York, Heslington, York, England, lecturer, 1964-72, senior lecturer, 1972-77, reader in economics, 1977—, director of Institute for Research in the Social Sciences, 1982—, director of Centre for Defence Economics, 1990—. Visiting associate professor at University of Illinois, 1974; visiting professor at National University of Malaysia, 1984. Specialist adviser to the House of Commons Select Committee on Defense, 1984-85.

MEMBER: Royal Economic Society.

AWARDS, HONORS: NATO research fellowships, 1977-79, 1986-87.

WRITINGS:

(With Clem Tisdell) *Micro-Economic Policy,* Wiley, 1981.

(With Douglas Dosser and David Gowland) *Collaboration of Nations,* Martin Robertson, 1982.

NATO Arms Co-operation: A Study in Economics and Politics, Allen & Unwin, 1983.

(With N. Hooper) *The Economics of Defence, Disarmament and Peace,* Elgar, 1990.

(Coeditor with Todd Sandler) *The Economics of Defence Spending,* Ron Hedge, 1990.

Economics of Defence Policy, Brassey's Defence Publishers, 1991.

Also coeditor with Todd Sandler of the journal *Defence Economics.*

WORK IN PROGRESS: Work on defense policy, public choice, and industrial policy.

SIDELIGHTS: In *NATO Arms Co-operation: A Study in Economics and Politics,* Keith Hartley investigates ways in which arms procurement could be better facilitated among the participating countries of the North Atlantic Treaty Organization (NATO). The author highlights economics in his examination of the complex factors that affect arms cooperation and development, advocating a laissez-faire, open market where competition will foster reduced costs and improved product capabilities.

While *Times Literary Supplement* reviewer Michael Carver perceived some problems in Hartley's "relentless quest for the best buy," including those of inequity among nations and technical disparity with the Soviets, he commended the author for debunking "many of the facile platitudes which echo round the marble halls of NATO when questions of arms procurement are discussed."

Hartley once told *CA:* "My NATO book analyzes, evaluates, and quantifies the costs and benefits of alternative weapons procurement policies. It provides evidence on the costs of nationalism, of collaboration and co-production. Recognition is given to the role of political factors in public choices."

BIOGRAPHICAL/CRITICAL SOURCES:

PERIODICALS

Times Literary Supplement, July 29, 1983.

*   *   *

HEDREN, Paul L(eslie) 1949-

PERSONAL: Born November 12, 1949, in New Ulm, MN; son of Thomas H. and Muriel M. (Kunz) Hedren; married Janeen Wolcott (a teacher), June 19, 1974; children: Ethne, Whitney (daughters). *Education:* St. Cloud State University, B.A., 1972.

ADDRESSES: Home—Williston, ND. *Office*—Fort Union Trading Post National Historic Site, Buford Route, Williston, ND 58801.

CAREER: National Park Service, Fort Laramie National Historic Site, Fort Laramie, WY, park ranger-historian, 1971-76, Big Hole National Battlefield, Wisdom, MT,

park historian, 1976-78, Golden Spike National Historic Site, Brigham City, UT, chief ranger, 1978-84, Fort Union Trading Post National Historic Site, Williston, ND, superintendent, 1984—.

MEMBER: Company of Military Historians, Western Historical Society, several state historical societies.

WRITINGS:

First Scalp for Custer: The Skirmish at Warbonnet Creek, Nebraska, July 17, 1876, Arthur Clark, 1980.
With Crook in the Black Hills: Stanley J. Morrow's 1976 Photographic Legacy, Pruett, 1985.
Fort Laramie in 1876: Chronicle of a Frontier Post at War, University of Nebraska Press, 1987.
(Editor and contributor) Don Russell, *Campaigning with King: Charles King, Chronicler of the Old Army,* University of Nebraska Press, 1991.

Also author of an anthology on the Great Sioux War, 1991.

SIDELIGHTS: Paul L. Hedren told *CA,* "My publications reflect a continuing interest in military aspects of the Sioux War of 1876, as well as the life and accomplishments of General Charles King, a largely forgotten Indian wars officer-turned-author who became a principal chronicler of the frontier army in the late nineteenth century."

BIOGRAPHICAL/CRITICAL SOURCES:

PERIODICALS

Washington Post Book World, August 11, 1985.

*   *   *

HELBIG, Alethea K. 1928-

PERSONAL: Born June 23, 1928, in Ann Arbor, MI; daughter of Elmer J. (a farmer) and Hilda (Goebel) Kuebler; married Harold R. Helbig (an accountant), June 12, 1948; children: Rick, Reid (deceased). *Education:* University of Michigan, B.A., 1950, M.A., 1953; graduate study at Eastern Michigan University, Fort Hayes State College, University of Michigan, and Temple University. *Politics:* Democrat. *Religion:* United Church of Christ. *Avocational interests:* Reading, sewing, travel.

ADDRESSES: Home—3640 Eli Rd., Ann Arbor, MI 48104. *Office*—Eastern Michigan University, 612-G Pray-Harrold, Ypsilanti, MI 48197.

CAREER: High school teacher of Latin and history, Manchester, MI, 1950-52; high school teacher of Latin and English, Chelsea, MI, 1953-54; elementary school teacher, Ann Arbor, MI, 1966; Eastern Michigan University, Ypsilanti, instructor, 1966-69, assistant professor, 1969-76, associate professor, 1976-81, professor of English, 1981—.

MEMBER: Children's Literature Association (International), National Council of Teachers of English, National Folklore Society, Modern Language Association of America, American Association of University Professors, Assembly on Literature for the Adolescent (founding member), Midwest Modern Language Association, Michigan Academy of Arts and Sciences, Michigan Folklore Society, Michigan Council of Teachers of English, Phi Beta Kappa, Phi Kappa Phi, Alpha Lambda Delta.

WRITINGS:

(Editor with Helen Hill and Agnes Perkins) *Straight on Till Morning: Poems of the Imaginary World* (an anthology of poetry for children), Crowell, 1977.

(Editor with Hill and Perkins) *Dusk to Dawn* (an anthology of poetry for children), Crowell, 1981.

(With Perkins) *Dictionary of American Children's Fiction, 1859-1959: Books of Recognized Merit,* Greenwood Press, 1986.

(With Perkins) *Dictionary of American Children's Fiction, 1960-1984,* Greenwood Press, 1986.

(With Perkins) *Nanabozhoo, Giver of Life,* Green Oak, 1986.

(With Perkins) *Dictionary of British Children's Fiction: Books of Recognized Merit,* Volumes I and II, Greenwood Press, 1989.

(With Perkins) *Dictionary of Children's Fiction from Australia, Canada, India, New Zealand, and Selected African Countries: Books of Recognized Merit,* Greenwood Press, 1992.

Author of "My Views in Reviews" column in *Michigan English Teacher,* 1980-86; contributor of articles and reviews to professional journals.

WORK IN PROGRESS: Heroes and Heroines, retellings of hero tales and a study of the traditional hero; two poetry anthologies for children with Helen Hill and Agnes Perkins; *Dictionary of American Children's Fiction, 1985-89: Books of Recognized Merit.*

SIDELIGHTS: Alethea K. Helbig wrote: "As far back as I can remember, I've wanted to be a teacher. Books and learning have always been important to me, and my parents strongly encouraged me to read and continue my education. Old stories, myths and hero tales, and biblical stories have always enthralled me, and poetry, too, has provided special thrills down through the years.

"My association with Helen Hill and Agnes Perkins began as a professional one, since the three of us teach together. But we have worked together on many projects, and over the years we have become good friends. We share the philosophy that only the best literature is good enough for children and young people. Working on our anthologies has given the three of us a great deal of pleasure. We sit around our dining room or kitchen tables an afternoon a week, munching cheese and crackers, drinking pots of tea, and reading the poems we have found aloud to one another. We enjoy listening to them, arguing about how good they are, re-reading the ones we especially like, and experimenting with ways in which to group them for the most interesting effects. The projects have been a lot of fun."

*   *   *

HERITEAU, Jacqueline 1925-

PERSONAL: Born October 12, 1925, in France; daughter of Marcel (a chef) and Piney (Sutherland) Heriteau; married H. A. Littledale, Jr., April 2, 1955 (divorced, 1961); married David M. Hunter, 1962 (divorced, 1973); married Earl W. Hubbard, 1980; children: (first marriage) Krishna; (second marriage) David S., Holly Brown. *Education:* Attended University of Montreal, 1944, and Sorbonne, University of Paris, 1948, 1950. *Religion:* Christian Science.

ADDRESSES: Home—100 Fifth St. N.E., Washington, DC 20002.

CAREER: Free-lance writer. *Montreal Star,* Montreal, Quebec, member of staff, 1950-55.

AWARDS, HONORS: Garden Communicator's Award, American Association of Nurserymen, 1990; Take Pride in America Award, 1990, for *The National Arboretum Book of Outstanding Garden Plants.*

WRITINGS:

How to Grow and Cook It Book of Vegetables, Herbs, Fruits and Nuts, Hawthorn, 1970.

Oriental Cooking the Fast Wok Way, Hawthorn, 1972.

Potpourri and Other Fragrant Delights, Simon & Schuster, 1973.

Take-It-Along Cookbook, Hawthorn, 1975.

Tomato Gardening and Cooking, Grosset & Dunlap, 1975.

(With Elvin McDonald and Francesca Morris) *Hyponex Handbook of Houseplants,* Wentworth Press, 1975.

Easy Gardening Projects, Popular Library, 1975.

Small Fruit and Vegetable Gardens, Popular Library, 1975.

(With Thalia Erath) *Preserving and Pickling: Putting Foods by in Small Batches,* Western Publishing, 1976.

Clear & Simple Crockery Cooking, Grosset & Dunlap, 1976.

How to Grow and Can It, Hawthorn, 1976.

Home Canning & Freezing, Grosset & Dunlap, 1976.

Growing and Cooking with Herbs, Grosset & Dunlap, 1976.
(Editor) *Budget Recipes,* Winchester Press, 1976.
Hurry Up and Grow Gardens, Popular Library, 1976.
Best of Electric Crockery Cooking, Grosset & Dunlap, 1977.
The Office Gardener, Hawthorn, 1977.
Growing Your Own Houseplants, Western Publishing, 1977.
Small Flower Gardens, Popular Library, 1977.
The Complete Book of Beans, Hawthorn, 1978.
A Feast of Soups, Dial, 1981.
The Cook's Almanac, World Almanac, 1983.
Mad about Mushrooms, Perigee, 1984.
Mad about Raspberries and Strawberries, Perigee, 1984.
Mad about Fish and Seafood, Perigee, 1984.
Mad about Pasta and Cheese, Perigee, 1984.
Fast and Easy Oriental Cooking, New American Library, 1988.
The National Arboretum Book of Outstanding Garden Plants, Simon & Schuster, 1990.
The American Horticultural Society Flower Finder, Simon & Schuster, 1992.

General editor of *Family Creative Workshop* series, Time-Life, *The Good Housekeeping Illustrated Encyclopedia of Gardening,* Hearst, and *Woman Alive,* Doubleday. Contributor to *Family Circle, House Beautiful, House & Garden, New York Times, Christian Science Monitor,* and other magazines.

SIDELIGHTS: Jacqueline Heriteau once told *CA:* "I always found my joy in gardening and cooking. Arranging flowers in the garden and in the vases—making a warm and welcome table with food that delighted the palate and with flowers and candles and pretty things that delighted the eye—had a certain glory. All my books about gardening and cooking were written effortlessly and with remarkable speed because they'd been born in my most relaxed moments. So, when my children look puzzled at the many choices their talents and a contemporary world offer, I say 'follow your love' (quoting the philosopher/painter Earl Hubbard) because what I have loved most has sustained me in every way."

*   *   *

HICKEY, Raymond 1936-

PERSONAL: Born April 21, 1936, in Dublin, Ireland; son of Thomas (a civil servant) and Gladys (McInerney) Hickey. *Education:* Pontifical Gregorian University, Rome, Italy, B.D., 1958, S.T.L., 1960, D.D., 1977. *Politics:* "Christian Socialist."

ADDRESSES: Home—Augustinian Monastery, P.O. Box 1627, Jos, Nigeria.

CAREER: Entered Irish Province of the Order of St. Augustine (Augustinians), 1953, ordained Roman Catholic priest, 1960; Roman Catholic missionary in Borno State, Nigeria, 1960—, secretary to bishop and chancellor of diocese of Maiduguri, 1983-88, secretary of Augustinian Order in Nigeria, 1989—.

WRITINGS:

Africa: The Case for an Auxiliary Priesthood, Geoffrey Chapman, 1980, published as *A Case for an Auxiliary Priesthood,* Orbis, 1982.
Tarihin Ekklesiya Katolika (title means "A History of the Catholic Church"), Augustinian Publications (Jos, Nigeria), 1980.
A History of the Catholic Church in Northern Nigeria, Augustinian Publications, 1981.
(Editor) *Modern Missionary Documents and Africa,* Dominican Publications (Dublin), 1982.
Christianity in Borno State, Diocese of Maiduguri, 1985.
A Married Priesthood in the Catholic Church, LISS (Liverpool), 1986.
The Augustinians in Nigeria, [Jos], 1990.
A History of the Diocese of Yola, [Jos], 1990.

Contributor to European journals in English, Spanish, and Italian.

SIDELIGHTS: Raymond Hickey's *A Case for an Auxiliary Priesthood* argues that the increasing number of Catholics in Africa has necessitated the ordaining of auxiliary priests, including married men, under the church's auspices. J. J. O'Keefe, reviewing Hickey's work in the *National Catholic Reporter,* describes it as a "serious, informative and persuasive book," adding that "what comes across here is not a dry academic study, but the feelings of a man who wants to share his experiences, hopes, and thoughts."

Hickey told *CA:* "The proposal for an auxiliary married priesthood in Africa was the subject of my doctoral dissertation in theology. It formed the basis for *A Case for an Auxiliary Priesthood,* which provoked much comment. All my writing on Africa is motivated by my missionary vocation and seeks to draw attention to the rapid growth of Christianity in Africa, and to the new problems this poses.

"It is estimated that there will be 350 million Christians in Africa by the year 2000 and that half of these will be Roman Catholic. Christianity has never known such rapid growth on this scale. It calls for systematic planning, especially in the area of ministry. I have witnessed the growth in an area largely hostile to Christianity on the fringe of the Sahel region. I have also known the anguish of leaving fledgling Christian communities without the services of a priest for many months. The proposal for an auxiliary married priesthood, under the guidance of a professional seminary-trained priesthood, is above all a practical response to a pressing problem which must be faced up to."

BIOGRAPHICAL/CRITICAL SOURCES:

PERIODICALS

America, October 9, 1982.
National Catholic Reporter, June 4, 1982.

* * *

HIGGINBOTHAM, (Prieur) Jay 1937-

PERSONAL: Born July 16, 1937, in Pascagoula, MS; son of Prieur Jay (a contractor) and Vivian (Perez) Higginbotham; married Alice Louisa Martin, June 27, 1970; children: Jeanne-Felice, Denis Prieur, Robert Findlay. *Education:* University of Mississippi, B.A., 1960; graduate study at Hunter College of the City University of New York and American University.

ADDRESSES: Home—60 North Monterey St., Mobile, AL 36604. *Office*—Mobile Municipal Archives, Mobile, AL.

CAREER: State House of Representatives, Jackson, MS, assistant clerk, 1955-61; Mobile (AL) Public Schools, teacher, 1962-73; Mobile Public Library, head of local history department, 1973-83; Mobile Municipal Archives, director, 1983—. *Military service:* U.S. Army Reserve, 1955-62.

MEMBER: Authors League of America, Franklin Society, Smithsonian Associates.

AWARDS, HONORS: General L. Kemper Williams Prize, Louisiana Historical Association, 1977; award of merit, Mississippi Historical Society, 1978; Alabama Library Association nonfiction award, 1978; Gilbert Chinard Prize, Institut Francais de Washington and Society for French Historical Studies, 1978.

WRITINGS:

The Mobile Indians, Colonial Books, 1966.
Family Biographies, Colonial Books, 1967.
The Pascagoula Indians, Colonial Books, 1967.
Pascagoula: Singing River City, Gill Press, 1968.
Mobile: City by the Bay, Mobile Jaycees, 1968.
The Journal of Sauvole, Colonial Books, 1969.
Fort Maurepas: The Birth of Louisiana, Colonial Books, 1969.
Brother Holyfield, Thomas-Hull, 1972.
A Voyage to Dauphin Island, Museum of the City of Mobile, 1974.

Old Mobile: Fort Louis de la Louisiane, 1702-1711, Museum of the City of Mobile, 1977.
Autumn in Petrishchevo, Progress (Moscow), 1986.
Discovering Russia, Progress, 1989.
Mauvila, Acton, 1990.

Contributor to *Encyclopaedia Britannica* and *Funk & Wagnall's Encyclopaedia*. Also contributor of articles to newspapers, magazines, and journals in the United States and abroad, including *Alabama Review, Journal of Mississippi History, Library Journal, Literaturnaya Gazeta, Louisiana Studies, Novedades de Moscu, Sovietskaya Rossia, XX Century and Peace*, and *Zvezda* (Leningrad).

WORK IN PROGRESS: One novel, six poems, two plays.

SIDELIGHTS: Jay Higginbotham, whose works have been distributed in 128 countries and translated into seventeen languages, including Arabic, Czech, Japanese, Russian, and Hungarian, once told *CA:* "I began writing as a child and have never stopped. I began because I came from a family of lawyers, orators and raconteurs, and I could never get any words in except by writing. I always have been, and always will be, determined to be heard on a wide variety of subjects."

* * *

HILL, Pamela 1920-
(Sharon Fiske)

PERSONAL: Born November 26, 1920, in Nairobi, Kenya; daughter of Harold John Edward (a mining engineer) and Jean Evelyn Napier (Davidson) Hill. *Education:* Glasgow School of Art, D.A., 1943; University of Glasgow, B.Sc. equiv., 1952. *Religion:* Catholic.

ADDRESSES: Home—London, England.

CAREER: Has worked as both a pottery teacher and biology instructor in Glasgow and Edinburgh, Scotland, and in London, England, 1958-74, and as a mink farmer in Galloway, Scotland, 1965-70; novelist.

WRITINGS:

ROMANCE NOVELS

The King's Vixen, Putnam, 1954 (published in England as *Flaming Janet: A Lady of Galloway*, Chatto & Windus, 1954).
The Crown and the Shadow: The Story of Francoise D'Aubigne, Marquise de Maintenon, Putnam, 1955 (published in England as *Shadow of Palaces: The Story of Francoise d'Aubigne, Marquise de Maintenon*, Chatto & Windus, 1955).
Marjorie of Scotland, Putnam, 1956.
Here Lies Margot, Chatto & Windus, 1957, Putnam, 1958.
Maddelena, Cassell, 1963.

Forget Not Ariadne, Cassell, 1965.

Julia, Cassell, 1967.

The Devil of Aske, St. Martin's, 1973.

The Malvie Inheritance, St. Martin's, 1973.

The Incumbent, Hodder & Stoughton, 1974, published as *The Heatherton Heritage,* St. Martin's, 1976.

Whitton's Folly, St. Martin's, 1975.

Norah Stroyan, Hodder & Stoughton, 1976, published as *Norah,* St. Martin's, 1977.

Csar's Woman, R. Hale, 1977, published as *Tsar's Woman,* St. Martin's, 1985.

The Green Salamander, St. Martin's, 1977.

Stranger's Forest, St. Martin's, 1978.

Daneclere, St. Martin's, 1978.

Homage to a Rose, R. Hale, 1979.

Daughter of Midnight, R. Hale, 1980.

Fire Opal, St. Martin's, 1980.

A Place of Ravens, R. Hale, 1980.

Knock at a Star, R. Hale, 1981.

(Under pseudonym Sharon Fiske) *Summer Cypress,* R. Hale, 1981.

This Rough Beginning, R. Hale, 1981.

Dutchess Cain, R. Hale, 1982.

The Fairest One of All, R. Hale, 1982.

The House of Cray, St. Martin's, 1982.

The Copper-Haired Marshall, R. Hale, 1983.

Bride of Ae, St. Martin's, 1983.

Children of Lucifer, R. Hale, 1984.

Still Blooms the Rose, R. Hale, 1984.

The Governess, R. Hale, 1984.

Sable for the Count, R. Hale, 1985.

My Lady Glamis, St. Martin's, 1985.

Digby, R. Hale, 1987.

Venables, R. Hale, 1987.

Jean Urquhart, State Mutual Book, 1988.

The Sisters, G. K. Hall, 1988.

The Woman in the Cloak, St. Martin's, 1988.

The Sutburys, St. Martin's, 1988.

Artemia, R. Hale, 1989, St. Martin's, 1990.

Trevithick, R. Hale, 1989.

A Dark Star Passing, R. Hale, 1990.

Fenfallow, Chivers, 1990.

The Loves of Ginevra, R. Hale, 1990.

Vollands, R. Hale, c. 1990.

The Sword and the Flame, R. Hale, 1991.

The Brocken, R. Hale, c. 1991.

SIDELIGHTS: Pamela Hill treats her vocation as a writer of romance novels with sardonic humor. As she tells *CA,* her writing career began in 1950 as a result of sunstroke. As to what motivates her, Hall replied, "I write because I write because I write!" However, her humorous view of her profession belies the popularity of her books, which have been translated into French, German, and Spanish.

HIRSCHMAN, A. O.
See HIRSCHMAN, Albert O.

*   *   *

HIRSCHMAN, Albert O. 1915-
(A. O. Hirschman)

PERSONAL: Born April 7, 1915, in Berlin, Germany; son of Carl and Hedwig (Marcuse) Hirschmann; married Sarah Chapiro, 1941; children: Catherine Jane, Elisabeth Nicole. *Education:* Ecole des Hautes Etudes Commerciales, Sorbonne, University of Paris, diploma, 1935; attended London School of Economics and Political Science, 1935-36; University of Trieste, Doctor Econ. Sci., 1938.

ADDRESSES: Office—Institute for Advanced Study, Princeton, NJ.

CAREER: Federal Reserve Board, Washington, DC, economist, 1946-52; financial adviser, National Planning Board, and private economic counselor in Bogota, Colombia, 1952-56; Yale University, New Haven, CT, research professor, 1956-58; Columbia University, New York City, professor of international economic relations, 1958-64; Harvard University, Cambridge, MA, professor, 1964-74; Institute for Advanced Study, Princeton, NJ, professor of social science, 1974—. Irving Fisher Research Professor, Yale University, 1956-57; visiting member, Institute for Advanced Study, 1972-73. British Academy corresponding fellow, 1984—. Consultant to governmental agencies and foundations. *Military service:* Office of Strategic Services, 1943-45.

MEMBER: American Economic Association, American Philosophical Society, American Academy of Arts and Sciences, National Academy of Sciences, Council on Foreign Relations.

AWARDS, HONORS: Rockefeller fellow, 1941-43; Ford Foundation faculty research fellow, 1964-65; Center for Advanced Study in the Behavioral Sciences fellow, 1968-69; honorary doctor of laws, Rutgers University, 1978; Frank E. Seidman Distinguished Award in Political Economy, 1980; Talcott Parsons Prize for Social Science, American Academy of Arts and Sciences, 1983; American Economic Association distinguished fellow, 1984; Wissenschaftskolleg zu Berlin fellow, 1990-91.

WRITINGS:

National Power and the Structure of Foreign Trade, University of California Press, 1945, enlarged edition, 1980.

The Strategy of Economic Development, Yale University Press, 1958, reprinted, Norton, 1978.

(Editor and contributor; under name A. O. Hirschman) *Latin American Issues: Essays and Comments,* Twentieth Century Fund, 1961.

Journeys toward Progress: Studies of Economic Policy-Making in Latin America, Twentieth Century Fund, 1963.

Development Projects Observed, Brookings Institution, 1967.

Exit, Voice, and Loyalty: Responses to Decline in Firms, Organizations and States, Harvard University Press, 1970.

A Bias for Hope: Essays on Development and Latin America, Yale University Press, 1971.

The Passions and the Interests: Political Arguments for Capitalism before Its Triumph, Princeton University Press, 1977.

Essays in Trespassing: Economics to Politics and Beyond, Cambridge University Press, 1981.

Shifting Involvements: Private Interest and Public Action, Princeton University Press, 1981.

Getting Ahead Collectively: Grassroots Experiences in Latin America, Pergamon, 1984.

Rival Views of Market Society and Other Recent Essays, Penguin, 1986.

The Rhetoric of Reaction: Perversity, Futility, Jeopardy, Harvard University Press, 1991.

Contributor of chapters to numerous books. Contributor to professional journals. Member of boards of editors of several journals.

BIOGRAPHICAL/CRITICAL SOURCES:

PERIODICALS

New York Times Book Review, May 12, 1991.

*   *   *

HOBAN, Russell (Conwell) 1925-

PERSONAL: Born February 4, 1925, in Lansdale, PA; son of Abram T. (an advertising manager for the *Jewish Daily Forward*) and Jeanette (Dimmerman) Hoban; married Lillian Aberman (an illustrator), January 31, 1944 (divorced, 1975); married Gundula Ahl (a bookseller), 1975; children: (first marriage) Phoebe, Abrom, Esme, Julia; (second marriage) Jachin Boaz, Wieland, Benjamin. *Education:* Attended Philadelphia Museum School of Industrial Art, 1941-43. *Avocational interests:* Stones, short wave listening.

ADDRESSES: Home and office—Fulham, London, England. *Agent*—David Higham Associates Ltd., 5-8 Lower John St., Golden Sq., London WlR 4HA, England.

CAREER: Artist and illustrator for magazine and advertising studios, New York City, 1945-51; Fletcher Smith

Film Studio, New York City, story board artist and character designer, 1951; Batten, Barton, Durstine & Osborn, Inc., New York City, television art director, 1952-57; J. Walter Thompson Co., New York City, television art director, 1956; free-lance illustrator for advertising agencies and magazines, including *Time, Life, Fortune, Saturday Evening Post, True,* 1957-65; Doyle, Dane, Bembach, New York City, copywriter, 1965-67; novelist and author of children's books, 1967—. Art instructor at the Famous Artists Schools, Westport, CT, and School of Visual Arts, New York City. *Military service:* U.S. Army, Infantry, 1943-45; served in Italian campaign; received Bronze Star.

MEMBER: Authors Guild, Authors League of America, Society of Authors, PEN.

AWARDS, HONORS: The Sorely Trying Day, The Mouse and His Child, How Tom Beat Captain Najork and His Hired Sportsmen, and *Dinner at Alberta's* have all been named notable books by the American Library Association; *Bread and Jam for Frances* was selected as a Library of Congress Children's book, 1964; Boys' Club Junior Book Award, 1968, for *Charlie the Tramp; Emmet Otter's Jug-Band Christmas* was selected as one of *School Library Journal's* Best Books, 1971, and received the Lewis Carroll Shelf Award and the Christopher Award, both 1972; Whitbread Literary Award, 1974, and International Board on Books for Young People Honor List, 1976, both for *How Tom Beat Captain Najork and His Hired Sportsmen; A Near Thing for Captain Najork* was selected as one of the best illustrated children's books of the year by the *New York Times,* 1976; *Riddley Walker* received John W. Campbell Memorial Award for the best science fiction novel of the year from Science Fiction Research Association, 1981, and was nominated as the most distinguished book of fiction by National Book Critics Circle and for the Nebula Award by Science Fiction Writers of America, both 1982, and the Australian Science Fiction Achievement Award, 1983; Recognition of Merit, George G. Stone Center for Children's Books, 1982, for his contributions to books for younger children.

WRITINGS:

NOVELS

The Lion of Boaz-Jachin and Jachin-Boaz, Stein & Day, 1973.

Kleinzeit: A Novel, Viking, 1974.

Turtle Diary, J. Cape, 1975, Random House, 1976.

Riddley Walker, J. Cape, 1980, Summit Books, 1981.

Pilgermann, Summit Books, 1983.

The Medusa Frequency, edited by Gary Fisketjohn, Atlantic Monthly, 1987.

CHILDREN'S NONFICTION

What Does It Do and How Does It Work?: Power Shovel, Dump Truck, and Other Heavy Machines, illustrations by the author, Harper, 1959.

The Atomic Submarine: A Practice Combat Patrol under the Sea, illustrations by the author, Harper, 1960.

CHILDREN'S FICTION

Bedtime for Frances, illustrations by Garth Williams, Harper, 1960.

Herman the Loser, illustrations by Lillian Hoban, Harper, 1961.

The Song in My Drum, illustrations by L. Hoban, Harper, 1961.

London Men and English Men, illustrations by L. Hoban, Harper, 1962.

(With L. Hoban) *Some Snow Said Hello,* Harper, 1963.

The Sorely Trying Day, illustrations by L. Hoban, Harper, 1964.

A Baby Sister for Frances, illustrations by L. Hoban, Harper, 1964.

Nothing to Do, illustrations by L. Hoban, Harper, 1964.

Bread and Jam for Frances, illustrations by L. Hoban, Harper, 1964.

Tom and the Two Handles, illustrations by L. Hoban, Harper, 1965.

The Story of Hester Mouse Who Became a Writer and Saved Most of Her Sisters and Brothers and Some of Her Aunts and Uncles from the Owl, illustrations by L. Hoban, Norton, 1965.

What Happened When Jack and Daisy Tried to Fool the Tooth Fairies, illustrations by L. Hoban, Scholastic Book Services, 1965.

Henry and the Monstrous Din, illustrations by L. Hoban, Harper, 1966.

The Little Brute Family, illustrations by L. Hoban, Macmillan, 1966.

(With L. Hoban) *Save My Place,* Norton, 1967.

Charlie the Tramp, illustrations by L. Hoban, Four Winds, 1967, (book and record) Scholastic Book Services, 1970.

The Mouse and His Child (novel), illustrations by L. Hoban, Harper, 1967.

A Birthday for Frances, illustrations by L. Hoban, Harper, 1968.

The Stone Doll of Sister Brute, illustrations by L. Hoban, Macmillan, 1968.

Harvey's Hideout, illustrations by L. Hoban, Parents' Magazine Press, 1969.

Best Friends for Frances, illustrations by L. Hoban, Harper, 1969.

Ugly Bird, illustrations by L. Hoban, Macmillan, 1969.

The Mole Family's Christmas, illustrations by L. Hoban, Parents' Magazine Press, 1969.

A Bargain for Frances, illustrations by L. Hoban, Harper, 1970.

Emmet Otter's Jug-Band Christmas, illustrations by L. Hoban, Parents' Magazine Press, 1971.

The Sea-Thing Child, illustrations by son, Abrom Hoban, Harper, 1972.

Letitia Rabbit's String Song (Junior Literary Guild selection), illustrations by Mary Chalmers, Coward, 1973.

How Tom Beat Captain Najork and His Hired Sportsmen, illustrations by Quentin Blake, Atheneum, 1974.

Ten What?: A Mystery Counting Book, illustrations by Sylvie Selig, J. Cape, 1974, Scribner, 1975.

Crocodile and Pierrot: A See the Story Book, illustrations by S. Selig, J. Cape, 1975, Scribner, 1977.

Dinner at Alberta's, pictures by James Marshall, Crowell, 1975.

A Near Thing for Captain Najork, illustrations by Q. Blake, J. Cape, 1975, Atheneum, 1976.

Arthur's New Power, illustrations by Byron Barton, Crowell, 1978.

The Twenty-Elephant Restaurant, illustrations by Emily Arnold McCully, Atheneum, 1978, published in England with illustrations by Q. Blake, J. Cape, 1980.

La Corona and the Tin Frog (originally published in *Puffin Annual,* 1974), illustrations by Nicola Bayley, J. Cape, 1978, Merrimack Book Service, 1981.

The Dancing Tigers, illustrations by David Gentlemen, J. Cape, 1979, Merrimack Book Service, 1981.

Flat Cat, illustrations by Clive Scruton, Philomel, 1980.

Ace Dragon Ltd., illustrations by Q. Blake, J. Cape, 1980, Merrimack Book Service, 1981.

They Came from Aargh!, illustrations by Colin McNaughton, Philomel, 1981.

The Serpent Tower, illustrations by David Scott, Methuen/Walker, 1981.

The Great Fruit Gum Robbery, illustrations by C. McNaughton, Methuen, 1981, published as *The Great Gum Drop Robbery,* Philomel, 1982.

The Battle of Zormla, illustrations by C. McNaughton, Philomel, 1982.

The Flight of Bembel Rudzuk, illustrations by C. McNaughton, Philomel, 1982.

Big John Turkle, illustrations by Martin Baynton, Walker Books, 1983, Holt, 1984.

Jim Frog, illustrations by M. Baynton, Walker Books, 1983, Holt, 1984.

Lavinia Bat, illustrations by M. Baynton, Holt, 1984.

Charlie Meadows, illustrations by M. Baynton, Holt, 1984.

The Rain Door, illustrations by Q. Blake, J. Cape, 1986, HarperCollins, 1987.

The Marzipan Pig, illustrations by Q. Blake, J. Cape, 1986.

Ponders, illustrations by M. Baynton, Walker Books, 1988.

Monsters, illustrations by Q. Blake, Scholastic, Inc., 1989.
Jim Hedgehog and the Lonesome Tower, illustrations by Betsy Lewin, Clarion Books, 1990.

CHILDREN'S VERSE

Goodnight, illustrations by L. Hoban, Norton, 1966.
The Pedaling Man, and Other Poems, illustrations by L. Hoban, Norton, 1968.
Egg Thoughts, and Other Frances Songs, illustrations by L. Hoban, Harper, 1972.

OTHER

(Illustrator) W. R. Burnett, *The Roar of the Crowd: Conversations with an Ex-Big-Leaguer,* C. N. Potter, 1964.
Come and Find Me (television play), 1980.
The Carrier Frequency (play), first produced in London, 1984.
Riddley Walker (stage adaptation of his novel), first produced in Manchester, 1986.
(Author of introduction) Wilhelm K. Grimm, *Household Tales,* illustrations by Mervyn Peake, Schocken, 1987.

Contributor to *The Thorny Paradise: Writers on Writing for Children,* edited by Edward Blishen, Kestrel, 1975. Also contributor of articles to *Granta, Fiction Magazine,* and *Holiday.* Hoban's papers are included in the Kerlan Collection at the University of Minnesota.

ADAPTATIONS: The Mouse and His Child was made into a feature-length animated film by Fario-Lockhart-Sanrio Productions in 1977 and starred the voices of Cloris Leachman, Andy Devine, and Peter Ustinov (who also read an abridged version of the novel for a Caedmon recording in 1977); Glynnis Johns recorded selections from *Bedtime for Frances, A Baby Sister for Frances, Bread and Jam for Frances,* and *A Birthday for Frances* in a sound recording entitled "Frances," as well as selections from *A Bargain for Frances, Best Friends for Frances,* and *Egg Thoughts, and Other Frances Songs* in a sound recording entitled "A Bargain for Frances and Other Stories," both by Caedmon in 1977; *Turtle Diary* was adapted for the screen by United British Artists/Brittanic in 1986, featuring a screenplay by Harold Pinter and starring Glenda Jackson and Ben Kingsley; *Riddley Walker* was staged by the Manchester Royal Exchange Theatre Company, also in 1986.

SIDELIGHTS: "Russell Hoban is a writer whose genius is expressed with equal brilliance in books both for children and for adults," writes Alida Allison in *Dictionary of Literary Biography.* Largely self-educated, Hoban has moved masterfully from artist and illustrator to the author of children's fables and adult allegorical fiction. Praising his "unerring ear for dialogue," his "memorable depiction of scenes," and his "wise and warm stories notable for de-

lightful plots and originality of language," Allison considers Hoban to be "much more than just a clever and observant writer. His works are permeated with an honest, often painful, and always uncompromising urge toward self-identity." Noting that "this theme of identity becomes more apparent, more complex as Hoban's works have become longer and more penetrating," Allison states, "Indeed, Hoban's writing has leaped and bounded—paralleling upheavals in his own life."

In an interview with Rhonda M. Bunbury in *Children's Literature in Education,* Hoban indicates that as a child he was "good with words and good with drawing. It just happened my parents more or less seized on the drawing and thought that I'd probably end up being a great painter. I did become an illustrator, but I think that the drawing formula was always a little bit poisoned by the expectations that were laid on me, while the writing was allowed to be my own thing." He wrote poetry and short stories in school, and won several prizes. Having attended the Philadelphia Museum School of Industrial Art, Hoban worked as a free-lance illustrator before he began writing children's stories. He would drive throughout Connecticut, occasionally stopping at construction sites and sketching the machinery being used. A friend saw his work and suggested that it might make a good children's book; Hoban's first published work was about construction equipment—*What Does It Do and How Does It Work?: Power Shovel, Dump Truck, and Other Heavy Machines.*

Although Hoban has since originated several well-known characters in children's literature, including Charlie the Tramp, Emmet Otter, the Mouse and his Child, and Manny Rat, he is especially recognized for a series of bedtime books about an anthropomorphic badger named Frances. Reviewers generally concur that these stories depict ordinary family life with much humor, wit, and style. Benjamin DeMott suggests in the *Atlantic Monthly* that "these books are unique, first, because the adults in their pages are usually humorous, precise of speech, and understandingly conversant with general life, and second, because the author confronts—not unfancifully but without kinky secret garden stuff—problems with which ordinary parents and children have to cope." *Bedtime for Frances,* for instance, concerns nighttime fears and is regarded by many as a classic in children's literature; and according to a *Saturday Review* contributor, "The exasperated humor of this book could only derive from actual parental experience, and no doubt parents will enjoy it."

"Hoban has established himself as a writer with a rare understanding of childhood (and parental) psychology, sensitively and humorously portrayed in familiar family situations," writes Allison. He and his first wife, Lillian, also an illustrator and author of books for children, collaborated on many successful works, including several in the Frances series. Allison notes that although their work together was usually well-received, "there were pans as well as paeans." While some books have been faulted for "excessive coziness, for sentimentality, and for stereotyped male-female roles," Allison adds that a more general criticism of their work together is that "it tends toward repetition." However, in their *Children and Books,* May Hill Arbuthnot and Zena Sutherland find that all of Hoban's stories about Frances show "affection for and understanding of children" as well as "contribute to a small child's understanding of himself, his relationships with other people, and the fulfillment of his emotional needs." Further, they say, "These characters are indeed ourselves in fur." Yet as a *Times Literary Supplement* contributor observes, "Excellent as [the Frances books] are, they give no hint that the author had in him such a blockbuster of a book as *The Mouse and His Child.*"

Revered in England as a modern children's classic, *The Mouse and His Child* is described in the *New York Times Book Review* by Barbara Wersba as a story about two wind-up toy mice who are discarded from a toyshop and are then "buffeted from place to place as they seek the lost paradise of their first home—a doll house—and their first 'family,' a toy elephant and seal." Ill-equipped for the baffling, threatening world into which they are tossed, the mouse and his child innocently confront the unknown and its inherent treachery and violence, as well as their own fears. The book explores not only the transience and inconstancy of life but the struggle to persevere also. "Helpless when they are not wound up, unable to stop when they *are,* [the mice] are fated like all mechanical things to breakage, rust and disintegration as humans are to death," writes Margaret Blount in her *Animal Land: The Creatures of Children's Fiction.* "As an adult," says Blount, "it is impossible to read [the book] unmoved." Distressed, however, by the "continuing images of cruelty and decay," Penelope Farmer remarks in *Children's Literature in Education* that *The Mouse and His Child* is "like Beckett for children." But assessing whatever cruelty and decay there is in the novel as the "artful rendering of the facts of life," Allison affirms, "If there is betrayal, there is also self-sacrifice. If there is loss, there is also love. If there is homelessness, there is also destination. The mouse child gets his family in the end; children's literature gets a masterpiece."

"Like the best of books, [*The Mouse and His Child*] is a book from which one can peel layer after layer of meaning," says the *Times Literary Supplement* contributor. Some critics, however, wonder whether it is a children's book at all. Wersba, for instance, feels that "it is the mouse, his child and their search we care about not—metaphysics—and the intellectual trappings of this story

are unnecessary." Hoban responds to such assessments in an essay for *Books for Your Children:* "When I wrote [*The Mouse and His Child*] I didn't think it was [a children's book]. I was writing as much book as I was capable of at the time. No concessions were made in style or content. It was my first novel and . . . it was the fullest response I could make to being alive and in the world." Hoban indicates to Bunbury that the book has become his favorite book for children, the one that has given him the most satisfaction, "Though it may not be the best of my novels, it is the closest to my heart because of that." Believing the book reveals "an absolute respect for its subject—which means its readers as well," Isabel Quigley adds in the *Spectator,* "I'm still not sure just who is going to read it but that hardly seems to matter. . . . It will last." Hoban feels that within its limitations, the book is suitable for children, though. "Its heroes and heroines found out what they were and it wasn't enough, so they found out how to be more," he says in his essay. "That's not a bad thought to be going with."

Nominated as the most distinguished book of fiction by the National Book Critics Circle, and for the Nebula Award by the Science Fiction Writers of America, *Riddley Walker* received the John W. Campbell Memorial Award from the Science Fiction Research Association as the year's best science fiction novel and the Australian Science Fiction Achievement Award. *Riddley Walker* imagines a world and civilization decades after a nuclear holocaust; the story of what remains is narrated in a fragmented, phonetical English by a twelve-year-old boy struggling to comprehend the past so that its magnificence might be recaptured. "Set in a remote future and composed in an English nobody ever spoke or wrote," writes DeMott in the *New York Times,* "this short, swiftly paced tale juxtaposes preliterate fable and Beckettian wit, Boschian monstrosities and a hero with Huck Finn's heart and charm, lighting by El Greco and jokes by Punch and Judy. It is a wrenchingly vivid report on the texture of life after Doomsday."

Detecting similarities in *Riddley Walker* to other contemporary works such as Anthony Burgess's *The Clockwork Orange,* John Gardner's *Grendel,* and the complete works of William Golding, DeMott believes that "in vision and execution, this is an exceptionally original work, and Russell Hoban is actually his own best source." *Riddley Walker* "is not 'like' anything," concurs Victoria Glendinning in the *Listener.* As A. Alverez expresses in the *New York Review of Books,* Hoban has "transformed what might have been just another fantasy of the future into a novel of exceptional depth and originality."

Critically lauded and especially popular in England, *Riddley Walker* has been particularly commended for its inventive language, which Alverez thinks "reflects with extraordinary precision both the narrator's understanding and the desolate landscape he moves through." Reviewing the book in the *Washington Post Book World,* Michael Dirda believes that "what is marvelous in all this is the way Hoban makes us experience the uncanny familiarity of this world, while also making it a strange and animistic place, where words almost have a life of their own." "What Hoban has done," suggests Barbara A. Bannon in a *Publishers Weekly* interview with Hoban, "is to invent a world and a language to go with it, and in doing both he remains a storyteller, which is the most significant achievement of 'Riddley Walker.' "

Alverez calls *Riddley Walker* an "artistic tour deforce in every possible way," but Natalie Maynor and Richard F. Patteson suggest in *Critique* that even more than that, it is "perhaps the most sophisticated work of fiction ever to speculate about man's future on earth and the implications for a potentially destructive technology." Eliot Fremont-Smith maintains in the *Village Voice* that "the reality of the human situation now is so horrendous and bizarre that to get a hold on it requires all our faculties, including the imaginative. We can't do it through plain fact and arms controllers' reasoning alone. . . . Read *Riddley,* too." Although Kelly Cherry refers to the novel in the *Chicago Tribune Book World* as a "philosophical essay in fictional drag," DeMott thinks that Hoban's focus on what has been lost in civilization "summons the reader to dwell anew on that within civilization which is separate from, opposite to, power and its appurtenances, ravages, triumphs." *Riddley Walker,* says DeMott, is "haunting and fiercely imagined and—this matters most—intensely ponderable."

Hoban is the author of nearly sixty books; although most are for children, for whom he continues to write, adults have found much in his books to appreciate as well. The world that Hoban often explores may be a child's world, but it is a world seen in its complexity. "In my books there aren't characters who are simply bad or simply good," Hoban tells Fred Hauptfuhrer in *People.* "Nothing in life is that simple." Writing for adults has added both breadth and depth to Hoban's work; and as his work has grown in complexity, he has commented upon the process by which an idea evolves into a book. As he explains to Bannon: "There always seems to be something in my mind waiting to put something together with some primary thought I will encounter. It's like looking out of the window and listening to the radio at the same time. I am committed to what comes to me, however it links up."

In an essay appearing in *The Thorny Paradise: Writers on Writing for Children,* Hoban addresses what appears to be an intrinsic characteristic of his writing for both children and adults: "If in my meandering I have seemed to offer tangled thinking more than worked-out thoughts, it has

not been through self-indulgence; I have wanted to join the action of my being with that of my readers in a collective being. Collectively we must possess and be repossessed by the past that we alter with our present, must surrender the vanity of personal identity to something more valuable." Underlying the most powerful of Hoban's works, according to Allison, is the idea that "we must struggle for meaning and identity and place against the random element of loss in the attempt to gain 'self-winding.' " She considers Hoban a "great writer because he makes unsentimental reality into art."

BIOGRAPHICAL/CRITICAL SOURCES:

BOOKS

Arbuthnot, May Hill, and Zena Sutherland, *Children and Books,* 4th edition, Scott, Foresman, 1972.
Blishen, Edward, editor, *The Thorny Paradise: Writers on Writing for Children,* Kestrel, 1975.
Blount, Margaret, *Animal Land: The Creatures of Children's Fiction,* Morrow, 1974.
Children's Literature Review, Volume 3, Gale, 1978.
Contemporary Literary Criticism, Gale, Volume 7, 1977, Volume 25, 1983.
Dictionary of Literary Biography, Volume 52: *American Writers for Children since 1960: Fiction,* Gale, 1986, pp. 192-202.
Twentieth-Century Children's Writers, 3rd edition, St. James Press, 1989.

PERIODICALS

American Artist, October, 1961.
Antioch Review, summer, 1982.
Atlantic Monthly, August, 1976, pp. 83-84; December, 1983.
Books for Your Children, winter, 1976, p. 3.
Chicago Tribune Book World, July 12, 1981.
Children's Literature in Education, March, 1972; spring, 1976; fall, 1986, pp. 139-149.
Critique, fall, 1984.
Educational Foundation for Nuclear Science, June, 1982.
Encounter, June, 1981.
Globe and Mail (Toronto), March 29, 1986.
Harper's, April, 1983.
Junior Bookshelf, July, 1963.
Listener, October 30, 1980, p. 589.
Los Angeles Times, February 14, 1986.
New Statesman, May 25, 1973; April 11, 1975.
Newsweek, March 1, 1976; June 29, 1981; December 7, 1981; May 30, 1983; February 17, 1986.
New Yorker, March 22, 1976; July 20, 1981; August 8, 1983.
New York Review of Books, November 19, 1981, pp. 16-18.
New York Times, June 28, 1981, pp. 1, 25; November 1, 1981; June 20, 1983; February 14, 1986.

New York Times Book Review, February 4, 1968; March 21, 1976; June 6, 1982; May 29, 1983; November 27, 1983.

Observer (London), March 13, 1983.

People, August 10, 1981.

Publishers Weekly, May 15, 1981.

Saturday Review, May 7, 1960; May 1, 1976; December, 1981.

Spectator, May 16, 1969, pp. 654-655; April 5, 1975; March 12, 1983.

Time, February 16, 1976; June 22, 1981; May 16, 1983.

Times (London), January 7, 1982; March 24, 1983.

Times Literary Supplement, April 3, 1969, p. 357; March 16, 1973; March 29, 1974; October 31, 1980; March 7, 1986; April 3, 1987; September 4, 1987.

Village Voice, June 15, 1982.

Washington Post, February 28, 1986.

Washington Post Book World, June 7, 1981, pp. 1, 14; June 27, 1982; May 29, 1983; July 12, 1987; October 14, 1990.

Wilton Bulletin (Wilton, CT), September 26, 1962.*

*   *   *

HOLDEN, Jonathan   1941-

PERSONAL: Born July 18, 1941, in Morristown, NJ; son of Alan Nordby (a physicist) and Jaynet (Conselyea) Holden; married Gretchen Weltzheimer, November 16, 1963 (divorced May 20, 1991). *Education:* Oberlin College, B.A., 1963; San Francisco State College (now University), M.A., 1970; University of Colorado, Ph.D., 1974.

ADDRESSES: Home—1731 Fairview, Manhattan, KS 66502. *Office*—Department of English, Kansas State University, Manhattan, KS 66506.

CAREER: Cambridge Book Co., Bronxville, NJ, editorial assistant, 1963-65; high school mathematics teacher in West Orange, NJ, 1965-68; Stephens College, Columbia, MO, poet-in-residence, 1974-78; Kansas State University, Manhattan, poet-in-residence, beginning 1978, currently distinguished professor of English.

AWARDS, HONORS: Devins Award for poetry, 1972, for *Design for a House;* National Endowment for the Humanities grant, 1974; Borestone Mountain poetry award, 1975; Aspen Foundation for the Arts Prize, 1978; *Kansas Quarterly* first award, 1979; Associated Writing Programs award series in poetry, 1982, for *Leverage;* MASUA Honor Lecturer at Kansas State University, 1984-85; National Endowment for the Arts creative writing fellowship, 1984-85; Juniper Prize, 1985, for *The Names of the Rapids;* Thrusten P. Morton chair, Department of English, University of Louisville, 1991.

WRITINGS:

Design for a House (poems), University of Missouri Press, 1972.

The Mark to Turn: A Reading of William Stafford's Poetry, University Press of Kansas, 1976.

The Rhetoric of the Contemporary Lyric, Indiana University Press, 1980.

Leverage (poems), University Press of Virginia, 1984.

Falling from Stardom (poems), Carnegie-Mellon University Press, 1984.

Landscapes of the Self: The Development of Richard Hugo's Poetry, Associated Faculty Press, 1985.

The Names of the Rapids (poems), University of Massachusetts Press, 1985.

Style and Authenticity in Postmodern Poetry, University of Missouri Press, 1986.

Against Paradise (poems), University of Utah Press, 1989.

The Fate of American Poetry, University of Georgia Press, 1991.

American Gothic (poems), University of Georgia Press, 1992.

Contributor of poems and essays to *The American Poetry Review, Poetry, The Kenyon Review,* and other journals. Editorial assistant, *English Language Notes,* 1970.

SIDELIGHTS: Jonathan Holden told *CA:* "My conviction, based on half a lifetime of studying and writing, of teaching and being taught poetry, is that like painting, folk music, tale telling, joke telling, or cinema, like every other art developed to the level of self-conscious sophistication, the 'poem' is a blatantly artificial convention; and that like the conventions which define each of the arts—TV soap opera, for example, or country-and-western music—poetry evolves to serve specialized uses that cannot be as efficiently served by other means, uses which are not merely academic and exegetical."

BIOGRAPHICAL/CRITICAL SOURCES:

PERIODICALS

Times Literary Supplement, June 5, 1981.

*   *   *

HOLLANDS, Roy (Derrick)   1924-

PERSONAL: Born July 20, 1924, in Canterbury, England; son of Albert George and Victoria (a housewife; maiden name, Sawyer) Hollands; married Sarah Carroll (a housewife), April 13, 1945; children: Ann Hollands Nightingale. *Education:* Southampton University, B.Sc., 1951, teacher's certificate, 1953; Sheffield University, certificate in education, 1967; University of Exeter, M.A., 1969; University of Newcastle-upon-Tyne, M.Ed., 1980. *Religion:* Atheist.

ADDRESSES: Home and office—6 Wyde Feld, Aldwick, Bognor Regis, West Sussex PO21 3DH, England.

CAREER: Meteorologist, 1941-43; teacher of mathematics in Altrincham, England, 1952-57, Normanton, England, 1957-61, and head of department in Sheffield, England, 1961-67; College of Education, Totley Hall, Sheffield, England, lecturer in mathematics, 1967-71; College of Education, Dundee, Scotland, lecturer in mathematics and head of department, 1971-79; free-lance writer, 1980—. *Military service:* Royal Air Force, meteorologist and flier, 1943-47; became flight sergeant.

MEMBER: Mensa, College of Preceptors (fellow), Society of Authors (deputy chairman of educational writers group), Mathematical Association, Society for Teachers of Mathematics.

WRITINGS:

Modern Mathematics for Parents and Teachers, Cambridge Aids to Learning, 1971.
Mathematical Games and Activities for First Schools, Chatto & Windus, 1971.
The Unconscious Humour of Children, Cambridge Aids to Learning, 1973.
Mathematics Enrichment Cards, Hart-Davis, 1975.
(With others) *Mathematics for General Education,* Macmillan, 1975.
(With Howell Moses) *Headway Mathematics,* with teacher's supplement, five volumes, Hart-Davis, 1977.
Mathematics Games and Activities, Hart-Davis, 1977.
Puzzle Mathematics, Macmillan, 1977.
Primary Mathematics for Nigeria, with teacher's supplement, five volumes, Longman, 1979.
Dictionary of Mathematics, Longman, 1980.
Foundation of Arithmetic, with answer book, Cambridge University Press, 1980.
Basic Arithmetic, with answer book, Cambridge University Press, 1980.
(With Moses) *Basic Mathematics,* with teacher's supplement, twelve volumes, Hart-Davis, 1981.
Ginn Primary Mathematics, with teacher's supplement and enrichment cards, multi-volume, Ginn, 1982, new edition, 1990.
Development of Mathematics Skill, Basil Blackwell, 1983.
Sum It Up, Cassell, 1983.
Success with Numbers, Macmillan, 1983.
Basic Arithmetic, Macmillan, 1983.
Primary Mathematics for Lesotho, with teacher's supplement, six volumes, Longman, 1985.
Let's Solve Problems, Basil Blackwell, 1985.
Progress Tests in Math, Macmillan, 1986.
Primary Mathematics for Cameroon, Longman, 1987.

Primary Mathematics for the Caribbean, Longman, 1987.

Also author, *Primary Mathematics for Egypt,* Longman, and *Preparatory Mathematics for Egypt,* Longman. Also editor and consultant, *Primary Mathematics for Uganda,* Uganda Publishing House. Contributor of three hundred articles and reviews to mathematics journals.

WORK IN PROGRESS: Finalizing the last books in the "National Curriculum of Ginn Mathematics" series.

SIDELIGHTS: Roy Hollands has planned mathematics education programs which required him to visit Uganda, Nigeria, Lesotho, the Caribbean, Swaziland, Kenya, Cameroon, Egypt, and much of Europe. He explained to *CA* that while mathematics is basically universal in its structure and in its pupils' development, textbooks written for use in foreign countries must be modified to include local elements; to be effective they need to incorporate material such as appropriate place names, goods available, and indigenous culture. Hollands has found that, in addition to his visits to the countries involved, local co-authors provide much of the needed cultural information.

Hollands told *CA:* "My approach is based on wide experience in the classroom; it involves knowing what succeeds for children and what succeeds with teachers. This classroom experience is coupled with a psychological foundation plus educational theory, thus giving a combination of the practical and the theoretical."

*   *   *

HOWARD, Warren F.
  See POHL, Frederik

*   *   *

HUNTER, Mollie   1922-

PERSONAL: Full name is Maureen Mollie Hunter McIlwraith; born June 30, 1922, in Longniddry, East Lothian, Scotland; daughter of William George (a motor mechanic) and Helen Eliza Smeaton (a confectioner; maiden name, Waitt) McVeigh; married Thomas "Michael" McIlwraith (a hospital catering manager), December 23, 1940; children: Quentin Wright, Brian George. *Education:* Attended Preston Lodge School, East Lothian, Scotland. *Politics:* Scottish Nationalist. *Religion:* Episcopalian. *Avocational interests:* Theatre, music, physical exercise, traveling to new places. "Like dogs (useful ones only) and places without people. Company preferred—children."

ADDRESSES: Home—"The Shieling," Milton, near Drumnadrochit, Inverness-shire 1V3 6UA, Scotland.

Agent—A. M. Heath & Co. Ltd., 79 St. Martin's Ln., London WC2N 4AA, England; McIntosh & Otis, Inc., 475 Fifth Ave., New York, NY 10017.

CAREER: Writer, 1953—. May Hill Arbuthnot Lecturer in the United States in 1975, and in 1976 toured New Zealand and Australia lecturing under the joint auspices of the British Council, the International Reading Association and the education authorities for New Zealand and Australia; writer-in-residence, Dalhousie University, Halifax, Nova Scotia, 1980, 1981; organized and taught in writer's workshops for both adults and children; 29th Anne Carroll Moore Spring Lecturer, 1986; teacher of creative writing, Aberlour Summer School for Gifted Children, 1987, 1988. *Wartime service:* Performed volunteer services in a Serviceman's canteen during World War II.

MEMBER: Society of Authors (past chairman, Society of Authors in Scotland).

AWARDS, HONORS: Child Study Association of America's Children's Books of the Year citations, for *The Ferlie*, 1968, *The Walking Stones*, 1970, *The Thirteenth Member*, 1971, *A Sound of Chariots* and *The Haunted Mountain*, both 1972, *The Stronghold*, 1974, *A Stranger Came Ashore*, 1975, *Talent Is Not Enough*, 1976, *A Furl of Fairy Wind*, 1977, and *Cat, Herself*, 1987; *Book World*'s Children's Spring Book Festival honor book citation, 1970, for *The Lothian Run*; *New York Times* Outstanding Book of the Year citations, for *The Haunted Mountain* and *A Sound of Chariots*, both 1972, and *A Stranger Came Ashore*, 1975; Children's Book Award from the Child Study Association of America, 1973, for *A Sound of Chariots;* Scottish Arts Council Award, 1973, for *The Haunted Mountain;* Carnegie Medal for Children's Book of Outstanding Merit, British Library Association, 1974, and Silver Pencil Award (Holland), 1975, both for *The Stronghold; A Stranger Came Ashore* was selected one of *School Library Journal*'s Best Children's Books, 1975, and was a *Boston Globe-Horn Book* Award Honor Book, 1976; *The Wicked One* was selected one of *School Library Journal*'s Best Books for Spring and was selected a Scottish Arts Council Award Book, both 1977; *You Never Knew Her as I Did!* was selected one of the New York Public Library's Books for the Teen Age, and a Notable Children's Trade Book in the Field of Social Studies by the National Council of Social Studies and the Children's Book Council, both 1982; *Cat, Herself* was chosen one of the American Library Association's Best Books for Young Adults, and one of *School Library Journal*'s Best Books for Young Adults, both 1986.

WRITINGS:

A Love-Song for My Lady (one-act play; first produced at Empire Theatre, Inverness, Scotland, 1961), Evans, 1962.

Stay for an Answer (one-act play; first produced at Empire Theatre, Inverness, 1962), French, 1962.

Patrick Kentigern Keenan (fantasy), illustrated by Charles Keeping, Blackie & Son, 1963, published in America as *The Smartest Man in Ireland,* Funk, 1965.

Hi Johnny, illustrated by Drake Brookshaw, Evans, 1964, Funk, 1967, illustrated by M. Christopherson, Byway Books, 1986.

The Spanish Letters (historical novel), illustrated by Elizabeth Grant, Evans, 1964, Funk, 1967.

The Kelpie's Pearls (fantasy), illustrated by C. Keeping, Blackie & Son, 1964, illustrated by Joseph Cellini, Funk, 1966.

A Pistol in Greenyards (historical novel), illustrated by E. Grant, Evans, 1965, Funk, 1968.

The Ghosts of Glencoe (historical novel), Evans, 1966, Funk, 1969.

Thomas and the Warlock (fantasy), illustrated by J. Cellini, Funk, 1967.

The Ferlie (fantasy), illustrated by J. Cellini, Funk, 1968, published as *The Enchanted Whistle,* Methuen, 1985.

The Bodach (fantasy), illustrated by Gareth Floyd, Blackie & Son, 1970, published in America as *The Walking Stones: A Story of Suspense,* illustrated by Trina Schart Hyman, Harper, 1970.

The Lothian Run (historical novel), Funk, 1970.

The Thirteenth Member: A Story of Suspense (historical novel), Harper, 1971.

A Sound of Chariots (young adult novel; also see below), Harper, 1972.

The Haunted Mountain: A Story of Suspense, illustrated by Lazslo Kubinyi, Harper, 1972.

The Stronghold, Harper, 1974.

A Stranger Came Ashore: A Story of Suspense (fantasy), Harper, 1975.

Talent Is Not Enough: Mollie Hunter on Writing for Children, Harper, 1976.

The Wicked One: A Story of Suspense, Harper, 1977.

A Furl of Fairy Wind: Four Stories (includes "A Furl of Fairy Wind," "The Enchanted Boy," "The Brownie," and "Hi Johnny"; also see below), illustrated by S. Gammell, Harper, 1977.

The Third Eye (young adult novel), Harper, 1979.

You Never Knew Her as I Did! (historical novel), Harper, 1981, published as *Escape from Loch Leven,* Canongate (Edinburgh), 1987.

The Knight of the Golden Plain (fantasy; also see below), illustrated by Marc Simont, Harper, 1983.

The Dragonfly Years (young adult novel; sequel to *A Sound of Chariots*), Hamish Hamilton, 1983, published in America as *Hold on to Love,* Harper, 1984.

The Three-Day Enchantment (fantasy; sequel to *The Knight of the Golden Plain*), illustrated by M. Simont, Harper, 1985.

I'll Go My Own Way, Hamish Hamilton, 1985, published in America as *Cat, Herself,* Harper, 1986.

The Brownie, illustrated by M. Christopherson, Byway Books, 1986.

The Enchanted Boy, illustrated by M. Christopherson, Byway Books, 1986.

A Furl of Fairy Wind, illustrated by M. Christopherson, Byway Books, 1986.

Flora MacDonald and Bonnie Prince Charlie, Methuen, 1987.

The Mermaid Summer, Harper, 1988.

The Pied Piper Syndrome, Harper, 1991.

The Day of the Unicorn (fantasy; sequel to *The Three-Day Enchantment*), Harper, in press.

Contributor of articles to numerous newspapers and magazines, including *Scotsman* and *Glasgow Herald;* contributor to anthologies. Mollie Hunter's papers are held in the collection of the National Library of Scotland.

ADAPTATIONS: A number of Hunter's books have been serialized on BBC-Radio programs, including *The Kelpie's Pearls, The Lothian Run,* and *The Enchanted Whistle* (in the U.S., *The Ferlie*). *A Stranger Came Ashore* has been read in serial form on Swedish radio, the four stories in *A Furl of Fairy Wind* are published in cassette form in the U.K., and *The Walking Stones* and *The Wicked One* have been featured in Yorkshire TV's "Book Tower" program.

WORK IN PROGRESS: Continuing research into Scottish history and folklore, with emphasis on Celtic folklore.

SIDELIGHTS: Mollie Hunter, writes Connie C. Epstein in the journal of the *Society of Children's Book Writers,* "is known as Scotland's most gifted storyteller." Her works range from fantasies in the tradition of Celtic fairy-lore (such as *The Kelpie's Pearls, The Bodach* and *The Ferlie*) to historical novels about Scotland's richly colorful past—including *The Ghosts of Glencoe,* based on the massacre of the Macdonalds of Glencoe by the Campbells in 1692, and *You Never Knew Her as I Did!,* a story that deals with the fate of Mary, Queen of Scots. Hunter, writes Peter Hollindale in *Children's Literature in Education,* "is read with pleasure not only in her own country or by the offspring of expatriate Scots, but by legions of young children whose prior knowledge of Celtic legend is nonexistent, and by older readers whose aquaintance with Scots history is at best rudimentary."

Maureen Mollie Hunter McVeigh was born on June 30, 1922, in the village of Longniddry, Scotland—in the historic district of East Lothian in the Lowlands, near the border of Scotland and England. Her father was a war veteran, Irish by birth, and her mother a Scots native. Mollie, the third of five children, was raised with the traditions of Celtic tales and their tellers. "My father was merry and fiery by nature; my mother merry and gentle," Hunter writes in *Third Book of Junior Authors.* "His tongue had a charm to it that could coax a bird out of a bush. She was, like many a Borderer before her, a born storyteller. Together they set the standards that have been the main formative influence on my life."

The McVeighs were a country family, poor in goods but rich in spirit. Often Mollie and her siblings "improvised theatre out of the stories our mother had told us, the songs she had sung, the long poems she had recited from memory," she writes in her *Something about the Author Autobiography Series (SAAS)* entry. "We were all voracious readers, too, with certain favourite books that gave us further splendid material for our acting games. And of course, there were also the dramatised tales of our own weaving, all of these as wildly inventive as our combined imaginations could make them. But such diversions, naturally were still only for the housebound dark of winter evenings. Out of doors, we had for our enjoyment a part of the countryside so beautiful and so fertile that, for centuries past, it has been known as 'the garden of Scotland,' and every free waking moment of other seasons saw us either there or in the village of Longniddry itself.

"Without my having the least awareness of what was happening, in fact, that childhood environment of mine was nurturing a whole range of feelings so essentially part of my nature that they were quite inevitably destined to become also an integral part of my writing. But even so, what I did realise in those childhood years, was that I revelled, literally revelled, in being what I was then—partly a little country savage, but partly also an exalted dreamer finding total fulfillment in a world where (metaphorically speaking, at least) the sun always shone.

"For all of us, however, there was to come a day when the sun went in. That was the day my father died." When Mollie was nine years old, William McVeigh succumbed to wounds he suffered in World War I. "He and my mother had been the great and only love of one another's lives," Hunter explains in *SAAS.* "For her, thereafter, there was to be not only intense grief, but also a struggle against poverty that shortened her own life. I had been the favourite one of his children, the one who delighted him with her high spirits and what he called her 'gift of the gab.' " Mollie, who had already made up her mind to be a writer one day, began to carry a notebook with her in which to record her thoughts. She later used her experiences as the basis of her novels *A Sound of Chariots* and *Hold on to Love.*

Within a few years of William McVeigh's death, the family's poverty forced Mollie to leave school. "I had to leave school at fourteen—the earliest age at which one could legally do so," she writes in her *SAAS* entry. "As my two elder sisters had already done, also, I had to find some kind of a job." She went to work in the Edinburgh flower shops owned by her mother's relatives, but remained determined to complete her education. "There was nightschool, wasn't there? And libraries. I would use them both, and educate myself," she declared in her *SAAS* entry. "Stubbornly then, I followed up my decision with a routine that had me travelling back and forward between home and Edinburgh to work a six-day week in the shop, with nightschool study to follow on four evenings of each week, and the other two evenings spent in research reading at The National Library of Scotland."

It was while reading at the National Library that Hunter first came across records of Scottish folklore and beliefs. "With a feeling of intense excitement, then," she writes in her *SAAS* entry, "I recognised some of the very superstitions that had survived into the time of my own childhood. . . . Now at last I knew them for what they were! All of them, they were simply vestiges of the same belief in the power of magic, vestiges that had survived in folk memory right up to the time of my childhood." "The folk who had carried out such practices were *my* folk," she declares. "I had their blood and bone. Somewhere deep in my brain moved the same fears and longings that had moved for untold generations in theirs." At the same time, Hunter became interested in Scottish history, especially where it involved people accused of practicing magic and prosecuted before the law.

Hunter worked and studied in Edinburgh for four years. When she turned seventeen, she writes in her *SAAS* entry, she "met again someone I had known earlier—the young man who was to become, as my father had been for my mother, the great and only true love of my life." Thomas "Michael" McIlwraith and Mollie McVeigh were married in 1940, shortly after McIlwraith was drafted in the Navy. Hunter spent the war doing volunteer work for servicemen, continued her research, and took to politics, stumping against "the elderly politicians who had for so long tolerated those evils" of Fascism which had brought the war to a head.

When the war was over, Hunter and her husband settled in a cottage in the Scottish Highlands, near Inverness. There she raised two sons and settled down to write. Her first book was written at her children's request. "The book they coaxed from me was expanded from stories I had previously made up for them," Hunter writes in *Talent Is Not Enough: Mollie Hunter on Writing for Children;* "but for me it was also a sustained attempt at a form of language that could ring true only if it hit a particular note—a tradi-

tional note, evolved from many, many past centuries of the music in the storyteller's voice." The resulting book, *Patrick Kentigern Keenan,* was very successful, and remains in print today under the title *The Smartest Man in Ireland.* Hunter also used her interest in Scottish history to produce award-winning historical novels, including *The Spanish Letters, The Thirteenth Member,* and *You Never Knew Her as I Did!*

"The child that was myself was born with a little talent, and I have worked hard, hard, hard, to shape it," Hunter writes in *Talent Is Not Enough.* "Yet even this could not have made me a writer, for there is no book can tell anything worth saying unless life itself has first said it to the person who conceived that book. A philosophy has to be hammered out, a mind shaped, a spirit tempered. This is true for all of the craft. It is the basic process which must happen before literature can be created. It is also the final situation in which the artist is fully fledged; and because of the responsibilities involved, these truths apply most sharply to the writer who aspires to create literature for children.

"Especially for this writer, talent is not enough—no, by God, it is not! Hear this, critics, editors, publishers, parents, teachers, librarians—all you who will shortly pick up a children's book to read it, or even glance idly through it. There must be a person behind that book."

BIOGRAPHICAL/CRITICAL SOURCES:

BOOKS

Author's Choice 2, Crowell, 1974.
Blishen, Edward, editor, *The Thorny Paradise: Writers on Writing for Children,* Kestrel, 1975.
Cameron, Eleanor, *The Green and Burning Tree,* Atlantic-Little, Brown, 1969.
Contemporary Literary Criticism, Volume 21, Gale, 1982.
de Montreville, Doris, and Donna Hill, editors, *Third Book of Junior Authors,* H. W. Wilson, 1972.
Hunter, Mollie, *Talent Is Not Enough: Mollie Hunter on Writing for Children,* Harper, 1976.
Something about the Author Autobiography Series, Volume 7, Gale, 1989.
Ward, Martha E., and Dorothy A. Marquardt, *Authors of Books for Young People,* 2nd edition, Scarecrow, 1971.

PERIODICALS

Children's Literature in Education, autumn, 1977.
Horn Book, June, 1970; February, 1971; December, 1975; June, 1978; August, 1978.
Language Arts, March, 1979.
Society of Children's Book Writers, July/August, 1986.
Times Educational Supplement, January 13, 1984.
Top of the News, June, 1975.

J

JACKINS, Harvey 1916-

PERSONAL: Born June 28, 1916, in Spirit Lake, ID; son of Harvey Wilson (a farmer) and Caroline (a teacher; maiden name, Moland) Jackins; married Dorothy Diehl, September 3, 1939; children: Gordon, Tim, Sarah, Christopher. *Education:* University of Washington, Seattle, B.A., 1960. *Religion:* Methodist.

ADDRESSES: Home—719 Second Ave. N., Seattle, WA 98109. *Office*—Personal Counselors, Inc., 2327 Fourth Ave., Seattle, WA 98121.

CAREER: Personal Counselors, Inc., Seattle, WA, president, 1952—. International reference person for Re-evaluation Counseling Communities, 1971—.

MEMBER: American Association for the Advancement of Science, American Mathematical Society, Mathematical Association of America, American Geophysical Union, Amonii Socii, Phi Beta Kappa, Phi Lambda Upsilon, Pi Mu Epsilon.

WRITINGS:

The Human Side of Human Beings: The Theory of Re-evaluation Counseling, Rational Island, 1965.
The Meaningful Holiday: Poems, Rational Island, 1970.
Fundamentals of Co-Counseling Manual, Rational Island, 1970.
The Human Situation, Rational Island, 1973, revised edition, 1991.
Zest Is Best: Poems, Rational Island, 1973.
Quotes from Harvey Jackins, Rational Island, 1975.
Guidebook for Re-evaluation Counseling, Rational Island, 1975.
Rough Notes from Liberation I and II, Rational Island, 1976.
(With others) *Rough Notes from La Scherpa I,* Rational Island, 1977.

The Upward Trend, Rational Island, 1978.
Rough Notes from Buck Creek I, Rational Island, 1979.
The Benign Reality, Rational Island, 1981.
(With others) *Rough Notes from Calvinwood I,* Rational Island, 1983.
The Reclaiming of Power, Rational Island, 1983.
The Rest of Our Lives, Rational Island, 1985.
The Longest View, Rational Island, 1987.
Start Over Every Morning, Rational Island, 1989.
Counselor's and Client's Notebooks, Rational Island, 1989.

MONOGRAPHS

Communications of Important Ideas, Rational Island, 1963.
Complete Appreciation of Oneself, Rational Island, 1964.
Co-Counseling for Married Couples, Rational Island, 1965.
Flexible Human in the Rigid Society, Rational Island, 1965.
Logic of Being Completely Logical, Rational Island, 1965.
Who's in Charge, Rational Island, 1965.
Nature of the Learning Process, Rational Island, 1966.
Uses of Beauty and Order, Rational Island, 1967.
Multiplied Awareness: The Intermediate Co-Counseling Group, Rational Island, 1969.
Is Death Necessary?, Rational Island, 1970.
Letter to a Respected Psychiatrist, Rational Island, 1970.
Necessity of Long-Range Goals, Rational Island, 1972.
The Distinctive Characteristics of Re-evaluation Counseling, Rational Island, 1973.
A New Kind of Communicator, Rational Island, 1974.
A Rational Theory of Sexuality, Rational Island, 1977.
Where Did God Come From?, Rational Island, 1981.
The Art of Listening, Rational Island, 1981.
The Enjoyment of Leadership, Rational Island, 1987.
Logical Thinking about a Future Society, Rational Island, 1990.

Also author of *The Good and Great Art,* Rational Island.

SIDELIGHTS: Harvey Jackins, whose books have been translated into twenty-six languages, told *CA* that his "writing is about the continually evolving theory and practice of re-evaluation counseling, a body of knowledge and movement to enable people to reach their full potential. It has many additional implications for freedom from all oppression and for social change. At its core, it is people learning to listen well to each other." Jackins added that his writing also includes a "new kind of people's journalism," in which he excerpts and edits portions of his correspondence to produce journals about the practice of re-evaluation counseling. "Many people have been able to have the experience of being published and read in this way," says Jackins.

*   *   *

JACKSON, Guida M.   1930-

PERSONAL: Given name is pronounced "*Guy*-da"; born August 29, 1930, in Amarillo, TX; daughter of James Hurley (a merchant) and Ina (Benson) Miller; married Prentice Lamar Jackson (an anesthesiologist), June 15, 1951 (divorced, 1986); married William H. Laufer (an artist), February 16, 1986; children: (first marriage) Jeffrey Allen, William Andrew, James Tucker, Annabeth. *Education:* Attended Musical Arts Conservatory, Amarillo, 1945-47; Texas Technological College (now Texas Tech University), B.A., 1951; attended University of Houston, 1953; California State University, M.A., 1985; attended Union Graduate School, 1986; International Institute of Advanced Studies, Ph.D., 1990.

ADDRESSES: Home—116 Tree Crest Cir., The Woodlands, TX 77381.

CAREER: English teacher at public high schools in Houston, TX, 1951-54; music teacher and free-lance writer in Houston, 1956-71; Monday Shop (antiques store), Houston, owner, 1971-75; *Texas Country* (magazine), Houston, editor, 1976-78; free-lance writer, 1978—. Lecturer, University of Houston, 1985-90.

MEMBER: International Women's Writing Guild, Dramatists Guild, Women in Communications, Woodlands Writers Guild, Authors UNLTD of Houston, Houston Writers Guild, Houston Novel Writers.

WRITINGS:

Passing Through (novel), Simon & Schuster, 1979.
A Common Valor, Simon & Schuster, 1980.
The Lamentable Affair of the Vicar's Wife (play), I. E. Clark, 1980.
(Contributor) Phyllis Stillwell Prokop, compiler, *The Three-Ingredient Cookbook,* Broadman, 1981.

Heart to Hearth, Prism, 1988.
African Women Write, Touchstone Books, 1990.
Women Who Ruled, American Bibliographical Center-Clio Press, 1990.
Favorite Fables, Prism, 1991.

Contributor to magazines. Editor, *TSA Newsletter,* 1974-82, and *Touchstone Literary Quarterly,* 1976—; contributing editor, *Houston Town and Country,* 1975.

WORK IN PROGRESS: Subtractions, a novel.

SIDELIGHTS: Guida M. Jackson told *CA:* "I consider more carefully, these days, whether or not what I write is worth destroying even one tree in order to publish it. Still, there are stories that beg to be told, lives that need to be chronicled. There are noble and courageous people whose histories are the heritage of our children, stories that will be forgotten if someone doesn't preserve them. Writers are like switchboard operators: we plug cultures together; we plug generations together. When my writing accomplishes this, I figure there will be a tree for me."

BIOGRAPHICAL/CRITICAL SOURCES:

PERIODICALS

Houston Chronicle, December 16, 1979.
Houston Post, November 4, 1979.
Houston Reporter, February 28, 1979.
Texas Monthly, November, 1979.
Washington Post, September 22, 1979.

*   *   *

JACOB, Margaret C(andee)   1943-

PERSONAL: Born June 9, 1943, in New York; daughter of Thomas W. (a mechanic) and Margaret (a maid; maiden name, O'Reilly) Candee; married James R. Jacob (an historian), November 3, 1967 (divorced). *Education:* St. Joseph's College, Brooklyn, NY, B.A., 1964; Cornell University, M.A., 1966, Ph.D., 1969.

ADDRESSES: Office—New School for Social Research, 65 Fifth Ave., New York, NY 10011.

CAREER: University of South Florida, Tampa, assistant professor of history, 1968-69; University of East Anglia, Norwich, England, lecturer in European studies, 1969-71; Bernard M. Baruch College of the City University of New York, New York City, assistant professor, 1971-76, associate professor, 1976-78, professor of history, 1978-85; New School for Social Research, New York City, dean of the College, 1985-88. Coordinating Committee on Women in the Historical Profession, co-chairwoman, 1973-74.

MEMBER: American Historical Association, Past and Present Society.

AWARDS, HONORS: American Council of Learned Societies summer grants, 1973, 1976; National Endowment for the Humanities summer grant, 1975; American Philosophical Society grant, 1976; Guggenheim fellow, 1988-89.

WRITINGS:

The Newtonians and the English Revolution, 1689-1720, Cornell University Press, 1979.
The Radical Enlightenment: Pantheists, Freemasons, and Republicans, Allen & Unwin, 1981.
Living the Enlightenment, Oxford University Press, 1991.

EDITOR

(With husband, James R. Jacob) *Seventeenth-Century Peace Proposals,* Garland Publishing, 1973.
Eighteenth-Century Peace Proposals, Garland Publishing, 1974.
(With J. R. Jacob) *The Origins of Anglo-American Radicalism,* Allen & Unwin, 1983.
(With Margaret Hunt) *Women and the Enlightenment,* Haworth Press, 1984.

OTHER

Contributor of articles and reviews to history journals. History of science editor, *The Eighteenth Century: A Current Bibliography,* 1974-76.

*   *   *

JAMES, Dynely
See MAYNE, William (James Carter)

*   *   *

JAMES, Mary
See MEAKER, Marijane (Agnes)

*   *   *

JOHNSON, A.
See JOHNSON, Annabell (Jones)

*   *   *

JOHNSON, A. E.
See JOHNSON, Annabell (Jones) and
JOHNSON, Edgar (Raymond)

JOHNSON, Annabel
See JOHNSON, Annabell (Jones)

*   *   *

JOHNSON, Annabell (Jones) 1921-
(A. Johnson; Annabel Johnson; A. E. Johnson, joint pseudonym)

PERSONAL: Born June 18, 1921, in Kansas City, MO; daughter of Burnam R. and Mary Estelle (Ball) Jones; married Edgar Raymond Johnson, September 14, 1949 (died December 2, 1990). *Education:* Attended College of William and Mary, 1939-40, and Art Students League. *Avocational interests:* Ceramics, gardening, hand-weaving, trout-fly tying.

ADDRESSES: Home—2925 South Teller, Denver, CO 80227.

CAREER: Worked in publishing houses, as a librarian, legal secretary, and in other secretarial posts prior to 1957; writer, mainly in collaboration with husband, Edgar Raymond Johnson, 1957—.

MEMBER: Gamma Phi Beta.

AWARDS, HONORS: Spring Book Festival Award, 1959, for *The Black Symbol,* and 1960, for *Torrie;* Friends of American Writers Award, 1962, for *The Secret Gift;* Golden Spur Award, Western Writers of America, 1966, for *The Burning Glass;* William Allen White Children's Book Award, 1967, for *The Grizzly.*

WRITINGS:

(Under name A. Johnson) *As a Speckled Bird,* Crowell, 1956.
(Under name Annabel Johnson) *I Am Leaper,* illustrated by Stella Ormai, Galley, 1990.

JUVENILE; WITH HUSBAND, EDGAR JOHNSON

The Big Rock Candy, Crowell, 1957.
The Black Symbol, illustrated by Brian Saunders, Harper, 1959.
Torrie, illustrated by Pearl Falconer, Harper, 1960.
The Bearcat, Harper, 1960.
The Rescued Heart, Harper, 1961.
Pickpocket Run, Harper, 1961.
Wilderness Bride, Harper, 1962.
A Golden Touch, Harper, 1963.
The Grizzly, illustrated by Gilbert Riswold, Harper, 1964.
A Peculiar Magic, illustrated by Lynd Ward, Houghton, 1965.
The Burning Glass, Harper, 1966.
Count Me Gone, Simon & Schuster, 1968.
The Last Knife (short stories), Simon & Schuster, 1971.
Finders, Keepers, Four Winds, 1981.

An Alien Music, Four Winds, 1982.
The Danger Quotient, Harper, 1984.
Prisoner of Psi, Atheneum, 1985.
A Memory of Dragons, Atheneum, 1986.
Gamebuster, illustrated by Stephen Marchesi, Dutton, 1990.

ADULT FICTION; WITH EDGAR JOHNSON, UNDER JOINT PSEUDONYM A. E. JOHNSON

The Secret Gift, Doubleday, 1961.
A Blues I Can Whistle, Four Winds, 1969.

OTHER

Johnson's manuscripts are included in the Kerlan Collection, University of Minnesota.

SIDELIGHTS: Annabell and Edgar Johnson came from very different backgrounds to form their writing partnership, as Annabell recalled in an autobiographical essay included in *Third Book of Junior Authors.* Edgar was born in a coal-mining town in Montana and applied himself to a variety of jobs as a young man. He worked as a railroad section hand, tried his luck at a career as a semi-professional baseball player, and even played the fiddle with an old-time country dance band before embarking upon a career as a ceramic artist and author. Annabell was raised in the more conventional surroundings afforded by St. Louis, Missouri, but was drawn to the excitement of New York City when she was old enough to leave home. She lived a rather bohemian existence while she pursued her dream of becoming a writer, and supported herself by holding jobs in several different publishing houses. Their paths merged during the 1940s when Edgar arrived in New York City to study art. They shared a common love of the history and drama of life in the Old West; and after they married, Annabell Johnson was able to make a commitment to becoming a full-time author. The Johnsons fulfilled their desire to communicate this enthusiasm for the West by writing stories for children who lived in urban areas far removed from the rock-strewn landscapes and the independent spirit of frontier life.

The Johnsons spent twelve years travelling throughout the majestic panorama of the western United States. They stayed in a small camp-trailer, and worked temporary or part-time jobs for enough money to continue their journey. Annabell and Edgar lived close to the land, camping in the desert in the wintertime, and spending their summer months high up in the Rocky Mountains. They sought out little-known facets of history from the places they visited, gathering ideas for stories from old letters lying inside dusty glass display cases in local historical museums, and collecting personal recollections from the old-timers who frequented the coffee-shops, front stoops, and other local gathering places in towns they passed through in their travels. The Johnsons compiled accounts of panning for gold, breaking new trails across the land, and other aspects of life unique to the western mountains. When they had accumulated enough material for a story, the couple retreated to the parklands of the national forests to write. Eventually they would emerge with novels populated by characters from the era of western expansion, ready to catch the imagination of the young reader wishing to relive the excitement of the gold rush or the early days of the fur trade, experience the hardships of a wagon trek along the Oregon and Mormon trails, or be caught up in a battle to unionize the coal mines.

As time passed, the Johnsons focused their writing more toward the present era to help young adults examine and come to terms with the changes in today's world. Their writings dealt with such subjects as E.S.P., terrorism, time travel, and other contemporary topics, while they continued to build stories around the process of self-discovery and ability to come to terms with human nature. In *Finders Keepers,* for example, the plot revolves around two teenagers struggling for survival in the aftermath of a disastrous explosion at a nuclear power plant. *A Memory of Dragons* is the story of an eighteen-year-old boy named Paul who, while intellectually brilliant (he is employed by the defense industry), is nonetheless haunted by vivid memories of what seems to be a previous life, dealing with the aftereffects of the death of an abusive father, and meanwhile is involved with a love interest. Paul is sought by two political rivals and becomes embroiled in an international power struggle during the energy crisis of 1991. "That this is not confusing, but stunningly effective in its pace, action, and intricacy, is a testament to the capability of the authors," asserted a contributor to the *Bulletin of the Center for Children's Books.* The Johnsons' books, consistently well-received by both critics and their young adult readership, are noted for their ability to bring to the reader a vivid sense of time and place through an economy of detail. Whether it be their beloved Old West or a modern location, the Johnsons created believable and colorful characters to inhabit their settings, and main characters with whom their young audience can identify. "There are four major elements in a science fiction story: character, background, conflict, and plot," wrote Ben Bova in a *Los Angeles Times* review of *A Memory of Dragons;* "The Johnsons get high grades in all four."

BIOGRAPHICAL/CRITICAL SOURCES:

BOOKS

Books for Children, 1960-1965, American Library Association, 1966.
Carlson, G. Robert, *Books and the Teen-Age Reader,* Harper, 1967.
Child Study Association of America, *The Children's Bookshelf,* Bantam, 1965.

De Montreville, Doris, and Donna Hill, editors, *Third Book of Junior Authors,* H. W. Wilson, 1972.

Larrick, Nancy, *A Parent's Guide to Children's Reading,* 3rd edition, Doubleday, 1969.

Twentieth-Century Children's Writers, St. James Press, 1989.

PERIODICALS

Book World, October 13, 1968.

Bulletin of the Center for Children's Books, July-August, 1984; November, 1985; February, 1987.

Library Journal, February 1, 1957.

Los Angeles Times, November 8, 1986.

New York Times Book Review, November 9, 1969; May 2, 1971.

Young Reader's Review, June, 1968.

* * *

JOHNSON, Edgar (Raymond) 1912-1990
(A. E. Johnson, joint pseudonym)

PERSONAL: Born October 24, 1912, in Washoe, MT; died December 2, 1990; son of Oscar and Martha Johnson; married Annabell Jones (a writer), September 14, 1949. *Education:* Studied at Billings Polytechnic Institute; graduated from Kansas City Art Institute; further study at New York State College of Ceramics at Alfred University. *Avocational Interests:* Seventeenth-century music, fishing.

ADDRESSES: Home—2925 South Teller, Denver, CO 80227.

CAREER: Ceramic artist and head of ceramics department, Kansas City Art Institute, 1948-49; also model-maker, jeweler and woodcarver, with work exhibited in one-man show in New York City, and included in Museum of Modern Art exhibition of American handcrafts; free-lance writer, mainly in collaboration with wife, Annabell Johnson. Sometime restorer of antique musical instruments for Smithsonian Institution, Washington, D.C.

AWARDS, HONORS: Spring Book Festival Award, 1959, for *The Black Symbol,* and 1960, for *Torrie;* Friends of American Writers Award, 1962, for *The Secret Gift;* Golden Spur Award, Western Writers of America, 1966, for *The Burning Glass;* William Allen White Children's Book Award, 1967, for *The Grizzly.*

WRITINGS:

JUVENILE; WITH WIFE, ANNABELL JOHNSON

The Big Rock Candy, Crowell, 1957.

The Black Symbol, illustrated by Brian Saunders, Harper, 1959.

Torrie, illustrated by Pearl Falconer, Harper, 1960.

The Bearcat, Harper, 1960.

The Rescued Heart, Harper, 1961.

Pickpocket Run, Harper, 1961.

Wilderness Bride, Harper, 1962.

A Golden Touch, Harper, 1963.

The Grizzly, illustrated by Gilbert Riswold, Harper, 1964.

A Peculiar Magic, illustrated by Lynd Ward, Houghton, 1965.

The Burning Glass, Harper, 1966.

Count Me Gone, Simon & Schuster, 1968.

The Last Knife (short stories), Simon & Schuster, 1971.

Finders, Keepers, Four Winds, 1981.

An Alien Music, Four Winds, 1982.

The Danger Quotient, Harper, 1984.

Prisoner of Psi, Atheneum, 1985.

A Memory of Dragons, Atheneum, 1986.

Gamebuster, illustrated by Stephen Marchesi, Dutton, 1990.

ADULT FICTION; WITH ANNABELL JOHNSON, UNDER JOINT PSEUDONYM A. E. JOHNSON

The Secret Gift, Doubleday, 1961.

A Blues I Can Whistle, Four Winds, 1969.

OTHER

Johnson's manuscripts are included in the Kerlan Collection, University of Minnesota.

SIDELIGHTS: Edgar and Annabell Johnson have coauthored many popular works of historical and science-fiction for both young adult and adult readers. For more information, see the "Sidelights" section for Annabell Johnson.

BIOGRAPHICAL/CRITICAL SOURCES:

BOOKS

Books for Children, 1960-1965, American Library Association, 1966.

Carlson, G. Robert, *Books and the Teen-Age Reader,* Harper, 1967.

Child Study Association of America, *The Children's Bookshelf,* Bantam, 1965.

De Montreville, Doris, and Donna Hill, editors, *Third Book of Junior Authors,* H. W. Wilson, 1972.

Larrick, Nancy, *A Parent's Guide to Children's Reading,* 3rd edition, Doubleday, 1969.

Twentieth-Century Children's Writers, St. James Press, 1989.

PERIODICALS

Book World, October 13, 1968.

Bulletin of the Center for Children's Books, July-August, 1984; November, 1985; February, 1987.

Library Journal, February 1, 1957.

Los Angeles Times, November 8, 1986.

New York Times Book Review, November 9, 1969; May 2,
  1971.
Young Reader's Review, June, 1968.

    [Sketch reviewed by wife, Annabell Johnson]

          *   *   *

JUDD, Cyril
  See POHL, Frederik

K

KAHN, Peggy
See KATZ, Bobbi

*   *   *

KATZ, Bobbi 1933-
(Barbara George, Emily George, Gail George,
Peggy Kahn, Della Maison, Don E. Plumme,
Ali Reich)

PERSONAL: Born May 2, 1933, in Newburgh, NY;
daughter of George and Margaret (Kahn) Shapiro; married Harold D. Katz (an optometrist), July 15, 1956 (divorced, 1978); children: Joshua, Lori. *Education:* Goucher College, B.A. (with honors), 1954; also studied at Hebrew University of Jerusalem, 1955-56. *Politics:* Peace and
environmental activist; registered Democrat.

ADDRESSES: Home—65 West 96th St., No. 21H, New
York, NY 10025. *Office*—Random House, 225 Park Ave.
S., New York, NY 10003.

CAREER: Began as a free-lance writer and editor of Middle Eastern affairs, 1954; Department of Welfare, Newburgh, NY, social worker, 1956-58; Headstart, Newburgh, NY, social worker, 1966-69; Greater Newburgh
Arts Council, Newburgh, NY, executive director of
weekly radio program, "Art in Action," 1968-71; Greater
Cornwall School District, Cornwall, NY, writing consultant, 1970-78; free-lance writer and editor of environmental and educational materials, 1977-82; Random House,
New York City, juvenile division in-house writer and editor, 1982—. Mount St. Mary's College, Newburgh, NY,
taught courses in short story writing, 1977-78; has conducted poetry workshops for children, teachers, and librarians.

MEMBER: Authors League of America, American Litto-
ral Society, Union of Concerned Scientists, FAMI, Phi
Beta Kappa.

WRITINGS:

I'll Build My Friend a Mountain, Scholastic Inc., 1972.
Nothing but a Dog, Feminist Press, 1972.
Upside Down and Inside Out: Poems for All Your Pockets,
  Watts, 1973.
The Manifesto and Me—Meg, Watts, 1974.
Rod-and-Reel Trouble, Albert Whitman, 1974.
1,001 Words, Watts, 1975.
Snow Bunny, Albert Whitman, 1976.
Volleyball Jinx, Albert Whitman, 1977.
Poems for Small Friends, Random House, 1989.

EDITOR OF ANTHOLOGIES

Bedtime Bear's Book of Bedtime Poems, Random House,
  1983.
Birthday Bear's Book of Birthday Poems, Random House,
  1983.
A Popple in Your Pocket and Other Funny Poems, Random
  House, 1986.
Ghosts and Goosebumps: Poems to Make You Shiver, Ran-
  dom House, 1991.
Puddle Wonderful: Poems to Welcome Spring, Random
  House, in press.

OTHER

Also creator of numerous other books, mainly based on
licensed characters, for Random House, under own name
and various pseudonyms, including Barbara George,
Emily George, Gail George, Peggy Kahn, Della Maison,
Don E. Plumme, and Ali Reich. Author of educational
materials. Contributor of poetry and articles to anthologies and magazines.

WORK IN PROGRESS: Numerous picture books for Random House; collections of original poetry.

SIDELIGHTS: Bobbi Katz once told *CA:* "I write for children because I hope to join those writers and artists who delight, sensitize, and give hope to children." Katz has reading and speaking competence in French, Spanish, and Hebrew.

* * *

KEENE, Carolyn
   See McFARLANE, Leslie (Charles)

* * *

KEITH, Carlton
   See ROBERTSON, Keith (Carlton)

* * *

KENNEY, Susan (McIlvaine) 1941-

PERSONAL: Born April 28, 1941, in Summit, NJ; daughter of James Morrow (a lawyer and executive) and Virginia (a housewife; maiden name, Tucker) McIlvaine; married Edwin James Kenney, Jr. (a college professor), November 28, 1964; children: one son, one daughter. *Education:* Northwestern University, B.A. (with honors), 1963; Cornell University, M.A., 1964, Ph.D., 1968. *Politics:* Liberal. *Religion:* Protestant.

ADDRESSES: Office—Department of English, Colby College, Waterville, ME 04901. *Agent*—Maxine Groffsky Literary Agency, 2 Fifth Ave, New York, NY 10011.

CAREER: Colby College, Waterville, ME, assistant professor, 1968-82, associate professor, 1982-86, professor of English, 1986—, director of creative writing, 1991—.

MEMBER: Authors Guild, Authors League of America, PEN, Phi Beta Kappa.

AWARDS, HONORS: First prize, O. Henry Awards, 1982, for "Facing Front" (short story); National Endowment for the Arts fellow, 1983-84; New Voice Award, Quality Paperback Book Club, 1985, for *In Another Country.*

WRITINGS:

Garden of Malice (mystery), Scribner, 1983.
In Another Country, Viking, 1984.
Graves in Academe (mystery), Viking, 1985.
Sailing, Viking, 1988.
One Fell Sloop (mystery), Viking, 1990.

Contributor of stories and articles to magazines, including *Boston Globe, Massachusetts Review, Hudson Review, McCall's,* and *Ladies' Home Journal;* reviewer for *New York Times Book Review.*

WORK IN PROGRESS: The Ghost of the Barbizon, a novel/memoir; another mystery, *Groomed for Death.*

SIDELIGHTS: With two awards to her credit, Susan Kenney has emerged as a novelist whose work has been repeatedly well received by critics. Of her 1984 novel *In Another Country,* Avery Rome of the *Philadelphia Inquirer* writes, "Susan Kenney's quiet debut as a novelist may signal the most breathtaking achievement of the literary year." While noting that many first novels tend to be heavily autobiographical, Douglas Hill comments in the *Globe and Mail* that "Kenney makes a fictional work of curious and compelling strength." According to Liz Rosenberg of the *Chicago Tribune,* Kenney's second novel, *Sailing,* is a "profound expression of the goodness of life and the mystery of death. It is a beautiful and scary book." C. D. B. Bryan of the *New York Times Book Review* agrees: "Susan Kenney's *Sailing* is more than remarkable, it's real. One reads it as one read *In Another Country;* with admiration for her, her family, and for the honesty, grace, and understanding with which she writes of scudding the menace and caress of life's towering waves."

In Another Country is a novel consisting of six interlacing stories narrated by a young woman living in a small college town in Vermont. Both wife and mother, Sara Boyd must learn to discard her illusions of what should be and cope with mortality and the illnesses that have touched those close to her: her father's death when she was twelve, her mother's insanity, and her husband's battle with cancer. Kenney's second novel, *Sailing,* is a continuation of the Boyd family saga. Phil Boyd faces a recurrence of the cancer that increasingly threatens his life while Sara can only watch him in his isolation. The solitary act of sailing provides a metaphor for Phil in his attempts to cope with his illness: "He stares at the lighted X-rays, past [his doctor's] pointing finger, beyond the knobs of coral, through the ribs of sunken ships, into the sea of darkness, where the shadows lie."

"Ms. Kenney introduces ghosts into her narrative," writes Christopher Lehmann-Haupt in the *New York Times,* "She narrates the entire novel in the present tense, yet scrambles her chronology so it's hard to distinguish now from then." He goes on to say, "If [Kenney] has returned to familiar territory, she has explored it from new angles. If she has depressed us with the subject of cancer, she has elated us with the courage of its victim. If she has given us ghosts and time-worn plot tricks, she has done so with a light enough touch to make them acceptable and even entertaining."

"Most of the time life doesn't provide very good stories, or art, period," Kenney once told *CA,* "Art makes stories—or pictures or music or sculpture—out of what life has to offer. Realism is realism; whether something really happened or not is irrelevant. If you can make a story seem real, then it seems autobiographical, as though it really happened to the person telling or experiencing the story. That's realism as Joseph Conrad defined it; 'My task which I am trying to achieve is by the power of the written word to make you hear, to make you feel—it is above all, to make you see.' "

Death is a recurrent theme for Kenney, who breaks from writing serious fiction by plotting murder mysteries. "Since [finishing *In Another Country*], I've alternated novels with mysteries, though I usually end up working on one of each at the same time," she told *CA.* "Then I can go back and forth. I have come to think of mysteries as another genre of fiction entirely, descended from the traditional romance (something else I picked up from Joseph Conrad) and therefore distinct from literary realism." Her most recent contribution to the mystery genre, *One Fell Sloop,* takes place on an island off the coast of Maine, and was described by Kenney as "an ingenious locked-room mystery." *Graves in Academe* involves a young English professor who finds herself in the midst of a series of literature-based murders at a small Maine college. Elaine Kendall, writing for the *Los Angeles Times,* comments: "Altogether different in intent, style, tone, and mood from *In Another Country, Graves in Academe* is far-fetched fun, especially for those who still have their dog-eared copies of Norton's anthology handy."

BIOGRAPHICAL/CRITICAL SOURCES:

BOOKS

Kenney, Susan, *Sailing,* Viking, 1988.

PERIODICALS

Chicago Tribune, June 27, 1988.
Globe and Mail (Toronto), October 19, 1985.
Los Angles Times Book Review, September 3, 1985; July 3, 1988, p. 11.
New York Times, February 6, 1985; April 7, 1988, p. 7.
New York Times Book Review, August 5, 1984.
Philadelphia Enquirer, July 1, 1984.
Publishers Weekly, March 22, 1985, p. 18.
Times Literary Supplement, November 2, 1984.
Washington Post Book World, June 13, 1984; April 17, 1988, p. 10.

KERR, M. E.
See MEAKER, Marijane (Agnes)

*   *   *

KESSELMAN, Judi R.
See KESSELMAN-TURKEL, Judi

*   *   *

KESSELMAN-TURKEL, Judi   1934-
   (Judi R. Kesselman, Judi K-Turkel, Pauline Turkel)

PERSONAL: Born January 3, 1934, in Bronx, NY; daughter of Samuel S. and Pauline (Turkel) Rosenthal; married Joseph Kesselman, February 27, 1957 (separated September, 1975); married Franklynn Peterson; children: Joseph Jay, Jeffrey Peter; stepchildren: David Douglass, Kevin Andrew. *Education:* Brooklyn College (now Brooklyn College of the City University of New York), B.A. (cum laude), 1955. *Avocational interests:* Playing piano, travel, rare book collecting.

ADDRESSES: Office—P/K Associates, Inc., 4343 West Beltline Hwy., Madison, WI 53711-3860.

CAREER: Free-lance writer. *Screen Stories,* New York City, story editor, 1956-58; Sterling Publications, New York City, editor, 1959; K.M.R. Publications, New York City, editor, 1961-62; McFadden-Bartell, senior editor, 1962; Dell Publishing Co., New York City, managing editor, 1964; contributing editor to *Pageant,* 1967-68, *Physician's Management,* 1975-79, and *Prime Times,* 1979-84; P/K Associates, Inc., Madison, WI, partner. Instructor in adult communications and writing in Great Neck Public Schools, 1974-76, at the University of Wisconsin Extension, 1976-80, and Rhinelander School of the Arts, 1985—.

MEMBER: Authors Guild, Authors League of America, American Society of Journalists and Authors, National Press Club, Wisconsin Council of Writers (president).

AWARDS, HONORS: Jesse H. Neal Award for editorial achievement, American Business Press Association, 1977; (with Franklynn Peterson) Distinguished Consumer Journalism Award, National Press Club, 1984, 1985, for syndicated columns "The Business Computer" and "Frank and Judi on Computers."

WRITINGS:

WITH FRANKLYNN PETERSON

Good Writing: A Basic College Composition Textbook, F. Watts, 1981.

Test-Taking Strategies, Contemporary Books, 1981.
Study Smarts, Contemporary Books, 1981.
The Homeowner's Book of Lists, Contemporary Books, 1981.
How to Improve Damn Near Everything around Your Home, Prentice-Hall, 1982.
The Author's Handbook, Prentice-Hall, 1982, revised edition, Dodd, 1987.
The Magazine Writer's Handbook, Prentice-Hall, 1982, revised edition, Dodd, 1987.
Research Shortcuts, Contemporary Books, 1982.
The Grammar Crammer: How to Write Perfect Sentences, Contemporary Books, 1982.
Note-Taking Made Easy, Contemporary Books, 1982.
Vocabulary Builder: The Practically Painless Way to a Larger Vocabulary, Contemporary Books, 1982.
Spelling Simplified, Contemporary Books, 1983.
Getting It Down: How to Put Your Ideas on Paper, Contemporary Books, 1983.

Author and syndicator (with Peterson) of newspaper computer columns "The Business Computer" and "Frank and Judi on Computers," 1983—.

UNDER NAME JUDI R. KESSELMAN

Stopping Out: A Guide to Leaving College and Getting Back In, M. Evans, 1976.
(With Franklynn Peterson) *The Do-It-Yourself Custom Van Book,* Regnery, 1977.
(With Peterson and Frank Konishi) *Eat Anything Exercise Diet,* Morrow, 1979.
(With Peterson) *Handbook of Snowmobile Maintenance and Repair,* Dutton, 1979.
(With Peterson) *Vans* (juvenile), Dandelion Press, 1979.
(With Peterson) *I Can Use Tools* (juvenile), Elsevier-Nelson/Dutton, 1981.

OTHER

Contributor to periodicals and newspapers, including *Omni, Fortune, McCall's, New York Times, Playgirl,* and *Popular Mechanics.*

WORK IN PROGRESS: Books on computer use for the general public; a play; a novel; several magazine articles.

SIDELIGHTS: Judi Kesselman-Turkel once told *CA:* "I find that one of the hardest things I must deal with as a writer is frustration: the frustration of preparing what I know is the best book on the subject and seeing it die aborning because the publisher has decided not to publicize it, or has given it the wrong title, or has attempted to sell it in the wrong market; the frustration of having to abandon book projects or turn down magazine assignments that are extremely worthwhile because the publisher or editor can't or won't give enough of an advance or writing fee to enable me to undertake the project and

still pay the bills. Being a full-time free-lance writer is itself a great frustration because publishers and editors won't pay an experienced author any more than the author of a first book or article—a situation that doesn't exist in *any* other field of work. Joining into a writing partnership . . . immeasurably helped me cope with this frustration. In this lonely endeavor, writing, it's a great luxury not to have to slog along entirely alone.'"*

*   *   *

KILODNEY, Crad 1948-

PERSONAL: Born February 13, 1948, in Jamaica, NY. *Education:* University of Michigan, B.S., 1968.

ADDRESSES: Office—1712 Avenue Rd., P.O. Box 54541, North York, Ontario, Canada M5M 4N5.

CAREER: Exposition Press, Smithtown, NY, copywriter, 1970-73; employed as warehouse laborer, salesman, and office worker by Toronto area publishers, 1973-78; writer, 1978—. Creator and owner of publishing imprint, Charnel House, 1979—.

WRITINGS:

SATIRE

Mental Cases, Lowlands Review, 1978.
World under Anaesthesia, Charnel House, 1979.
Gainfully Employed in Limbo, Charnel House, 1980.
Lightning Struck My Dick, Virgo Press, 1980.
Human Secrets, Charnel House, Book 1, 1981, Book 2, 1982.
Sex Slaves of the Astro-Mutants, Charnel House, 1982.
Terminal Ward, Charnel House, 1983.
Pork College, Coach House Press, 1984.
Bang Heads Here, Suffering Bastards, Charnel House, 1984.
The Orange Book, Charnel House, 1984.
The Blue Book, Charnel House, 1985.
The Green Book, Charnel House, 1985.
The Scarlet Book, Charnel House, 1985.
The Yellow Book, Charnel House, 1985.
Cathy, Charnel House, 1985.
Foul Pus from Dead Dogs, Charnel House, 1986.
Incurable Trucks & Speeding Diseases, Charnel House, 1986.
Simple Stories for Idiots, Charnel House, 1986.
Nice Stories for Canadians, Charnel House, 1988.
I Chewed Mrs. Ewing's Raw Guts, Charnel House, 1988.
Excrement, Charnel House, 1988.
Malignant Humors, Black Moss Press, 1988.
Blood-Sucking Monkeys from North Tonawanda, Charnel House, 1989.
Girl on the Subway, Black Moss Press, 1990.

Junior Brain Tumors in Action, Charnel House, 1990.
Putrid Scum, Charnel House, 1991.

EDITOR

Worst Canadian Stories, two volumes, Charnel House, 1987.
The First Charnel House Anthology of Bad Poetry, Charnel House, 1989.

OTHER

Work included in anthologies, including *Canadian Short Fiction Anthology, Volume 2,* Intermedia, 1982; *Pushcart Prize, X,* Pushcart Press, 1985; and *Into the Night Life,* Nightwood Editions, 1986. Contributor to magazines in the United States, Canada, and England. Author of advice column in Canadian magazine *Rustler,* 1978-81.

WORK IN PROGRESS: Collections of stories, for Charnel House.

SIDELIGHTS: Crad Kilodney once told *CA:* "To the best of my knowledge I am the only writer in the world who publishes his own books and sells them on the street as a full-time occupation. I write books to keep myself from committing murder."

BIOGRAPHICAL/CRITICAL SOURCES:

PERIODICALS

Gargoyle, April, 1985.

*   *   *

KING, Joyce
See CHING, Julia (Chia-yi)

*   *   *

KLASS, Sheila Solomon 1927-

PERSONAL: Born November 6, 1927, in New York, NY; daughter of Abraham Louis (a presser) and Virginia (Glatter) Solomon; married Morton Klass (a professor of anthropology), May 2, 1953; children: Perri Elizabeth, David Arnold, Judith Alexandra. *Education:* Brooklyn College (now Brooklyn College of the City University of New York), B.A., 1949; University of Iowa, M.A., 1951, M.F.A., 1953. *Religion:* Jewish.

ADDRESSES: Home—330 Sylvan Ave., Leonia, NJ 07605. *Office*—Department of English, Manhattan Community College of the City University of New York, 199 Chambers St., New York, NY 10007. *Agent*—Joanna Cole, Elaine Markson Literary Agency, Inc., 44 Greenwich Ave., New York, NY 10011.

CAREER: Worked as an aide in a psychopathic hospital, Iowa City, IA, 1949-51; Julia Ward Howe School, New York City, English teacher, 1951-57; Manhattan Community College of the City University of New York, New York City, began as assistant professor, currently professor of English, 1965—. Guest at Yaddo colony, 1974.

MEMBER: International PEN.

AWARDS, HONORS: Bicentennial Prize, Leonia Drama Guild, 1976, for one-act play, *Otherwise It Only Makes One Hundred Ninety-Nine.*

WRITINGS:

Come Back on Monday, Abelard-Schuman, 1960.
Everyone in This House Makes Babies, Doubleday, 1964.
Bahadur Means Hero, Gambit, 1969.
A Perpetual Surprise, Apple-Wood, 1981.
Nobody Knows Me in Miami, Scribner, 1981.
To See My Mother Dance, Scribner, 1981.
Alive and Starting Over, Scribner, 1983.
The Bennington Stitch, Scribner, 1985.
Page Four, Scribner, 1986.
Credit-Card Carole, Scribner, 1987.

Also author of one-act play, *Otherwise It Only Makes One Hundred Ninety-Nine.* Contributor of short stories and humorous articles to *Hadassah, Manhattan Mind, New York Times,* and other publications.

WORK IN PROGRESS: The Marble Princess, a novel.

SIDELIGHTS: Sheila Solomon Klass once told *CA:* "I've been a writer since adolescence and I know it's a unique and chronic madness. I have my first rejection slip from the *New Yorker,* dated October 11, 1948. It reads 'I'm afraid the vote went against the Solomon pieces. We found them a bit too fragmentary, sorry to say.' As a young writer, I was greatly encouraged by this: to be too fragmentary for the *New Yorker* surely meant talent. Perhaps there is some commemorative token they award after . . . years of such a stable, harmonious relationship. I hope so.

"I write because writing is supreme pleasure. Creating a story on paper is a peculiar joy unlike any other. Just the writing itself is the first reward. Later, if a relative or a friend reads the work and admires it, the delight is heightened. Then, if an editor likes it well enough to print it, the delight bursts all boundaries. And if the book is printed and makes money, that is sheer ecstasy. But it is irrelevant to the writing itself. This pleasure in the act of writing makes teaching writing a delightful job. What I'm doing is introducing students to the highest high in the whole world—the high that is achieved by creating new and wonderful works out of their own heads. To my very great pleasure, all three of my children are writers.

"My life and what happens around me, what I hear about and read about—these are the sources that initiate the act of writing. But, almost immediately, imagination takes over and the story acquires its own energy and direction. What *really* happened is not pertinent. It's forgotten. Fiction is not autobiography. It is experience transmuted by the imagination in inexplicable ways. It has its own truth and its own life. I rarely remember after finishing a story or a book what actually happened and what I made up. An idea simply nags and nags—like a child requiring attention—and it doesn't go away until the writing. Then, and only then, there is peace.

"I hope my writing entertains, for while it may instruct the mind, or purge the emotions, or ennoble the spirit, if it doesn't offer diversion I feel it is unsuccessful. I have an attic room in which I write. Silence and seclusion are all that I require, rare treasures not easily come by in a busy household. Early morning is the best time of day for me, very early before the others are up. I've concluded that the longest distance on earth for the writer who is also a mother and a wife is the distance from the kitchen to the typewriter. I'm becoming quite adept as a long-distance runner."

BIOGRAPHICAL/CRITICAL SOURCES:

PERIODICALS

Los Angeles Times, March 19, 1982.
New York Times Book Review, December 11, 1983; October 27, 1985.*

*   *   *

KLEIN, Herbert Sanford 1936-

PERSONAL: Born January 6, 1936, in New York, NY; son of Emil A. and Florence (Friedman) Klein; married, September 3, 1956 (divorced); children: Rachel, Daniel, Jacob. *Education:* University of Chicago, A.B., 1957, M.A., 1959, Ph.D., 1963.

ADDRESSES: Home—21 Claremont Ave., New York, NY 10027. *Office*—Department of History, Columbia University, New York, NY 10027.

CAREER: University of Chicago, Chicago, IL, instructor, 1962-63, assistant professor, 1963-67, associate professor of history, 1967-69; Columbia University, New York City, associate professor, 1969-71, professor of history, 1971—.

MEMBER: Conference on Latin American History.

AWARDS, HONORS: Henry L. and Grace Doherty fellow, Bolivia, 1960-61; Social Science Research Council fellow, Spain, 1964-65 and 1971-72; Ford Foundation fellow, Argentina and Brazil, 1965-67; American Council of

Learned Societies fellow, 1973; Simon F. Guggenheim fellow, 1980-81; Woodrow Wilson Fellow, Smithsonian Institution, 1980-81; senior Fulbright lecturer at Hebrew University, Jerusalem, 1983, Universidad de Sao Paulo, 1986, and Universidad de Buenos Aires, 1988; grants from Fulbright, for research in Bolivia, 1963, National Science Foundation, 1974-76, National Endowment for the Humanities, 1975-77, and Tinker, 1975-77; Department of Education Fulbright-Hayes research fellowship, 1988-89.

WRITINGS:

Slavery in the Americas: A Comparative Study of Cuba and Virginia, University of Chicago Press, 1967.
Parties and Political Change in Bolivia, 1880-1952, Cambridge University Press, 1970.
The Middle Passage: Comparative Studies in the Atlantic Slave Trade, Princeton University Press, 1978.
(With J. Kelley) *Revolution and the Rebirth of Inequality: A Theory Applied to the National Revolution of Bolivia,* University of California Press, 1981.
Bolivia: The Evolution of a Multi-Ethnic Society, Oxford University Press, 1982, revised edition, 1991.
(With J. TePaske) *Royal Treasures of the Spanish Empire in America, 1580-1825,* three volumes, Duke University Press, 1982.
African Slavery in Latin America and the Caribbean, Oxford University Press, 1986.
(Editor with Edmar Bacha) *Social Change in Brazil, 1945-1985, The Incomplete Transformation,* University of New Mexico Press, 1989.
Haciendas and Ayllus: Rural Society in the Bolivian Andes in the 18th and 19th Centuries, Stanford University Press, 1992.

Contributor of numerous articles and reviews to professional journals.

*   *   *

KLEIN, Norma 1938-1989

PERSONAL: Born May 13, 1938, in New York, NY; died following a brief illness, April 25, 1989, in New York, NY; daughter of Emanuel (a psychoanalyst) and Sadie (Frankel) Klein; married Erwin Fleissner (a biochemist), July 27, 1963; children: Jennifer Luise, Katherine Nicole. *Education:* Attended Cornell University, 1956-57; Barnard College, B.A. (cum laude), 1960; Columbia University, M.A., 1963. *Politics:* Democrat.

ADDRESSES: Agent—Elaine Markson, 44 Greenwich Ave., New York, NY 10011.

CAREER: Author of novels, short stories, poetry, and children's fiction. Instructor of fiction at Yale and Wesleyan universities.

MEMBER: P.E.N. (co-chairman of children's book committee), Phi Beta Kappa.

AWARDS, HONORS: Girls Can Be Anything was selected one of Child Study Association of America's Children's Books of the Year, 1973; *Media & Methods* Maxi Award for Paperbacks, 1975, and selected one of New York Public Library's Books for the Teen Age, 1980, both for *Sunshine; Love Is One of the Choices* was selected one of *School Library Journal*'s Best Books of the Year, 1978; O. Henry Award, 1983, for short story "The Wrong Man."

WRITINGS:

YOUNG ADULT NOVELS

Mom, the Wolf Man and Me, Pantheon, 1972.
It's Not What You Expect, Pantheon, 1973.
Confessions of an Only Child, illustrations by Richard Cuffari, Pantheon, 1974.
Taking Sides, Pantheon, 1974.
Coming to Life, Simon & Schuster, 1974.
What It's All About, Dial Press, 1975.
Hiding, Four Winds Press, 1976.
Girls Turn Wives, Simon & Schuster, 1976.
It's Okay if You Don't Love Me, Dial, 1977.
Love Is One of the Choices, Dial, 1978.
Tomboy (sequel to *Confessions of an Only Child*), Four Winds Press, 1978.
Breaking Up, Pantheon, 1980.
A Honey of a Chimp, Pantheon, 1980.
Robbie and the Leap Year Blues, Dial, 1981.
The Queen of the What Ifs, Fawcett, 1982.
Beginner's Love, Dial, 1982.
Bizou, Viking, 1983.
Snapshots, Dial, 1984.
Angel Face, Viking, 1984.
The Cheerleader, Knopf, 1985.
Family Secrets, Dial, 1985.
Give and Take, Viking, 1985.
Going Backwards, Scholastic, 1986.
Older Men, Dial, 1987.
My Life as a Body, Knopf, 1987.
Now That I Know, Bantam, 1988.
No More Saturday Nights, Knopf, 1988.
That's My Baby, Viking, 1988.
Learning How to Fall, 1989.
Just Friends, 1990.

ADULT NOVELS

Give Me One Good Reason, Putnam, 1973.
Domestic Arrangements, M. Evans, 1981.
Wives and Other Women, St. Martin's, 1982.
The Swap, St. Martin's, 1983.
Lovers, Viking, 1984.
American Dreams, Dutton, 1987.

The World as It Is, Dutton, 1989.

NOVELIZATIONS

Sunshine: A Novel (based on a television special written by Carol Sobieski), Holt, 1974.
The Sunshine Years (based on a television series), Dell, 1975.
Sunshine Christmas (based on a screenplay by Sobieski), Futura, 1977.
French Postcards (based on screenplay of the same title), Fawcett, 1979.

BOOKS FOR JUVENILES

Girls Can Be Anything (Junior Literary Guild selection), illustrations by Roy Doty, Dutton, 1973.
If I Had It My Way, illustrations by Ray Cruz, Pantheon, 1974.
Dinosaur's Housewarming Party (Junior Literary Guild selection), illustrations by James Marshall, Crown, 1974.
Naomi in the Middle, illustrations by Leigh Grant, Dial, 1974.
A Train for Jane, illustrations by Miriam Schottland, Feminist Press, 1974.
Red Sky, Blue Trees, illustrations by Pat Grant Porter, Pantheon, 1975.
Visiting Pamela, illustrations by Kay Chorao, Dial, 1979.
Baryshnikov's Nutcracker (adaptation of the "Nutcracker Ballet"), illustrated with photographs by Ken Regan, Christopher Little, and Martha Swope, Putnam, 1983.

OTHER

Love and Other Euphemisms (novella and five short stories), Putnam, 1972.
Sextet in A Minor (novella and thirteen short stories), St. Martin's, 1983.

Work has been anthologized in *Prize Stories: The O. Henry Awards,* 1963, and 1968, and *The Best American Short Stories of 1969,* 1969. Contributor of over sixty short stories to magazines, including *Sewanee Review, Mademoiselle, Cosmopolitan, Prairie Schooner,* and *Denver Quarterly.*

ADAPTATIONS:

Mom, the Wolf Man and Me was recorded on cassette by Caedmon, 1977, and was filmed by Time-Life Productions, 1979; *Confessions of an Only Child* was recorded on cassette by Caedmon, 1977.

SIDELIGHTS: Until her death in 1989, Norma Klein was considered by many critics to be an immensely gifted and skillful writer who was popular with readers of all ages—both young and old. While she garnered a loyal and significant audience for her fiction for adults, Klein was best known for her novels for young adults. In these enormously popular books, Klein attempted to realistically portray contemporary young people as they dealt with such problems as divorce, young love, budding adolescent sexuality, and such social issues as racism, sexism, and contraception. A very prolific author, Klein published on the average of two or three books a year for most of her professional writing career, in addition to over sixty short stories.

Klein began her writing career composing short stories for literary quarterlies. Although she loved writing short stories and felt very suited to this literary genre, Klein found these stories generally difficult to have published. They also had a limited audience. She realized that these vignettes would not reach the number of readers in the way that a novel would. She once explained her dilemma to *CA*: "In the decade from 1960 to 1970, I mainly devoted myself to writing short stories. But I found it was impossible to get a short story collection published without having written a novel. So, in 1970 I wrote a novel, *Pratfalls,* which was finally published with five of my already published short stories [in 1972, under the title *Love and Other Euphemisms.*] I gradually became converted to writing novels and imagine that I will not return to short stories for a long time. It saddens me that there is so little interest in stories in America today, but I've decided not to spend my life fighting it."

It was after the birth of her first daughter that Klein decided to combine her decision to concentrate on writing novels with her new found interest in writing for young people. "I began writing children's books after reading the millionth picture book to my older daughter and figuring I would like to give it a try," Klein revealed to *CA*. "An agent suggested that I would have an easier time getting a novel for eight-to-twelve year olds accepted than a picture book so I wrote one, *Mom, the Wolf Man and Me.* I found I enjoyed writing for children very much, partly perhaps because I got such a warm response to *Mom.*"

Not only was *Mom, the Wolf Man and Me* received warmly and enthusiastically by most reviewers, but the book was one of Klein's most commercially successful, introducing her to a new and larger audience. In *Mom, the Wolf Man and Me* the reader meets Brett, a teenager whose mother never married Brett's father and who is currently living with Theo, a man Brett cares for very much. Brett's mother and Theo are trying to decide whether to get married. Although there is the occasional problem, Brett sees her family's alternate lifestyle as being quite normal and satisfying.

This novel, like many of Klein's works involve out-of-the-mainstream lifestyles and characters that are at times out of the ordinary presented in a sensitive, insightful, and matter-of-fact manner. "The effect of [*Mom, the Wolf Man and Me*] would be totally different if the tone were strident or smart," stated Ethel L. Heins in *Horn Book.* "But the writing is low-keyed, witty, and honest, accurately echoing the spontaneous expression of contemporary children; and the unorthodox characters are warmly human." In a *School Library Journal* review of *Mom, the Wolf Man and Me,* Marilyn R. Singer wrote that "Klein has a fund of right ideas on life and is giving them to just the right age group. Pre-teens are concerned about how they will shape their lives, but they rarely find any clues in the fiction written for them. [In *Mom, the Wolf Man and Me*] they are treated to a commendably honest view of the way some people choose to live."

While many writers for young people tend to focus their writing on either the female or male point of view, Klein wrote with both sexes in mind. While many of her earlier young adult novels, such as *It's Not What You Expect, Confessions of an Only Child,* and *Love Is One of the Choices,* spotlighted strong, spunky girls, other Klein works, such as *Robbie and the Leap Year Blues, Angel Face,* and *Give and Take,* highlighted interesting, sensitive male characters. Reviewers have praised Klein for her ability to create likable, lifelike characters with whom her readers can easily identify.

Writing about Klein's *Mom, the Wolf Man and Me,* Margery Fisher pointed out in *Who's Who in Children's Books: A Treasury of the Familiar Characters of Childhood* that "Norma Klein's crisp, witty, intelligent style indicated that she is primarily interested in character—in the fascinating differences between one human being and another, the surprising effect they can have on one another. To do this through the words of a girl of eleven—brash, abrupt, unintrospective, sometimes naive—is a real achievement." And Dan Wakefield declared in the *New York Times Book Review* that "best of all, Norma Klein avoids the darkest and most dangerous pitfall of an adult writing a dramatic story about adolescents: She is never condescending. One ends the book liking not only the teen-age characters but also the author who had the empathy, understanding and talent to create them."

Whether she reported from the male point of view in *Snapshots,* her story about amateur photographers, Sean and Marc, or stressed the female perspective through Marina's eyes in *Girls Can Be Anything,* Klein was recognized for producing poignant and realistic fiction illuminating contemporary situations and problems. "Klein bends over backwards to shake up stereotypes," noted Gail E. Muirhead in *School Library Journal.* Lucy Rosenthal remarked in *Ms.:* "Pregnancy, outside of marriage or in ambiguous marital circumstances, is a recurrent motif of Klein's writing. Far from being obsessional, it seems to serve the purpose of exploring the problem of a woman's free exercise of options in a changing society. . . . [*Give Me One Good Reason,* for example, presents] the virtues of different life-possibilities and lifestyles, of the kinds of social extensions human beings, free and not-so-free, are making and can make in a changing society. . . . Klein's novel is more life-like than literary, a storyteller's book, not a poet's, the work of a writer engaged more with life and its possibilities than with language and its resources for language's own sake." And a writer for *Booklist* commented that *Mom, the Wolf Man and Me* "is written in a lively modern style and is candid and objective in treatment. . . . Children of conventional background are likely to be fascinated by the uninhibited portrayal of contemporary life."

Although she is known for writing about unconventional characters, out-of-the-mainstream lifestyles, and controversial topics, Klein has been praised for her frankness, sensitivity, and understanding. For instance, Dan Wakefield related in the *New York Times Book Review* that "Norma Klein has a nice sense of what teen-agers today might be feeling about themselves, each other, their bodies and minds, their friends and parents. . . . [She] manages to write in an open, intelligent manner about such potentially ticklish subjects as contraception, pregnancy, racial, religious and regional prejudice [and] mother-daughter jealousy. . . . Despite all this, you never have the sense that you are getting an informational handbook dressed up as a novel." And Betty B. Page reported in a *Library Journal* review of *It's Okay if You Don't Love Me* that in this book as well as other Klein books "the trauma and confusion of the sexual coming-of-age by a liberated young woman is presented with skill and understanding."

While extremely popular with many reviewers and readers, Klein's books also triggered much controversy. At least nine of her books were targeted by groups seeking their removal from library shelves. However, Klein did not seek controversy when she wrote about such topics as teen sexuality and contraception. As she once explained in an interview with the *New York Times:* "I'm not a rebel, trying to stir things up just to be provocative. I'm doing it because I feel like writing about real life."

While most reviewers have noted and appreciated the sensitive and straightforward manner in which Klein handled such topics as divorce, teenage pregnancy, abortion, and lesbianism, a number of them maintain that Klein seemed to be overly tolerant of the circumstances in which she placed her characters. These critics felt that Klein failed to show the entire picture behind the problems. "Her writing leaves out the real complexities of living," Margaret Burns Ferrari declared in *America.* In her review of *Girls Turn Wives,* Ferrari observed that "problems are easily solved, death is quickly sidestepped, affairs are gracefully ended with no one hurt, husbands and wives are charmingly reunited after separations, no one is lonely for long

and kids say the cutest things. Klein writes like a Walt Disney staff writer, which is irritating in a novel that clearly wishes to represent social reality." Joyce Smothers commented in her review of *Love Is One of the Choices* published in *Library Journal:* "With minimal plot and maximal dialogue, the author brings [the two protagonists of *Love Is One of the Choices*] through their respective sexual awakenings and to new realization of their inner—and outer—selves. Klein's characters are reactions against stereotypes. . . . The book moves right along, with many very funny conversations. But the world she has created is a rarefied one, in which everyone is brilliant and/or sophisticated, and there is always time to talk. It's fun to visit, but does anyone really live there?"

On the other side of this debate, Denise P. Donavin related in *Booklist:* "Klein's treatment of . . . troubled, searching individuals is direct, poignant, and affective." Finally, Paul Stuewe also found authentic dialogue coupled with skillful use of the narrative voice two reasons for what he sensed was Klein's strong character presence. Stuewe remarked in *Quill & Quire* that Klein was "particularly skilled at demonstrating character through dialogue as well as description making clever use of her . . . narrator's direct but unsophisticated perceptions of familiar events."

Klein also cultivated respect and popularity as an author of adult fiction. As in her novels for young adults, Klein's adult fiction explored contemporary issues, relationships, and problems. For example, Marilyn Lockhart stated in her *Library Journal* review of Klein's fictional look at three modern women and their lives, *Wives and Other Women:* "As the plot [of *Wives and Other Women*] flashes between 1970 and today, Klein relates the story of three warm, sympathetic characters. . . . Full of insights, realistic dialogue, and warm and human interactions, this is engrossing and lively recommended reading."

In another of her novels aimed at adults, *American Dreams,* Klein wrote about two married couple who grew up together and remained friends for over thirty years. During these years, the couple's friendship continued as they struggled to cope with infidelity, divorce, death, and other problems commonly shared by many modern marriages. Meredith Brucker explained in the *Los Angeles Book Review* that *American Dreams* "is intricately constructed of flash-forward chapters at five-year intervals from each of the four's point of view. Exercising the same skill she used when writing for the young, Norma Klein fleshes out her parental characters with such diverse and sympathetic personals that here they almost steal the interest from the juvenile leads."

However, whether it be in her cleverly structured stories involving feisty adolescents dealing with such issues as divorce, sexuality, teenage pregnancy, or her engaging fiction for adults, readers have found Klein's writings to be an enjoyable journey worth taking. Lucy Rosenthal seemed to sum up the feelings of many of Klein's readers—both young and old—when she suggested in *Ms.* that reading a book written by Klein "is like spending time in the company of an open-minded, tactful, decent, and generous friend."

BIOGRAPHICAL/CRITICAL SOURCES:

BOOKS

Authors and Artists for Young People, Volume 2, Gale, 1989, pp. 139-150.
Children's Literature Review, Volume 2, Gale, 1976.
Contemporary Literary Criticism, Volume 30, Gale, 1984.
Fisher, Margery, *Who's Who in Children's Books: A Treasury of the Familiar Characters of Childhood,* Holt, 1975, p. 54.
Phy, Allene Stuart, *Presenting Norma Klein,* Twayne, 1988.
Something about the Author Autobiography Series, Volume 1, Gale, 1986, pp. 155-168.

PERIODICALS

America, July 10, 1976, p. 18.
Booklist, January 1, 1973, pp. 449-450; August, 1983, p. 1448.
Horn Book, February, 1973, p. 57.
Library Journal, April 15, 1977, p. 948; November 15, 1978, p. 2351; June 1, 1982, p. 1112.
Los Angeles Times, November 5, 1986; December 14, 1988; May 12, 1989.
Los Angeles Times Book Review, December 30, 1984, p. 16; January 27, 1985, p. 3; March 29, 1987, p. 23; June 28, 1987, p. 4.
Ms., January, 1974, pp. 36-37.
New York Times, August 24, 1986, p. 20.
New York Times Book Review, October 15, 1972, pp. 31-33; May 1, 1977, p. 10.
Publishers Weekly, March 9, 1984, p. 106.
Quill and Quire, October, 1981, p. 44.
School Library Journal, December, 1972, pp. 60-61; November, 1974, p. 57.
Washington Post Book World, June 5, 1988, p. 8.

OBITUARIES:

PERIODICALS

New York Times, April 27, 1989.*

KLUGE, P(aul) F(rederick) 1942-

PERSONAL: Born January 24, 1942, in Berkeley Heights, NJ; son of Walter (a machinist) and Maria (Ensslen) Kluge; married Pamela Hollie (a journalist), February 14, 1977. *Education:* Kenyon College, B.A., 1964; University of Chicago, M.A., 1965, Ph.D., 1967.

ADDRESSES: Home—927 Michigan Ave., Evanston, IL 60202. *Agent*—Michael V. Carlisle, William Morris Agency, 1350 Avenue of the Americas, New York, NY 10019.

CAREER: Writer, 1969—. Peace Corps volunteer and then speech writer and political aide in Micronesia, 1960s. Staff reporter for *Wall Street Journal,* 1969, 1970; assistant editor for *Life,* 1970, 1971. Occasional visiting professor at Kenyon College, 1987—.

WRITINGS:

The Day That I Die (novel), Bobbs-Merrill, 1976.
Eddie and the Cruisers (novel), Viking, 1980.
Season for War (novel), Freundlich Books, 1984.
MacArthur's Ghost (novel), Arbor House, 1987.
The Edge of Paradise: America in Micronesia (nonfiction), Random House, 1991.

Contributor to periodicals.

ADAPTATIONS: Eddie and the Cruisers was filmed by Embassy Pictures, 1983; the film *Dog Day Afternoon* was based on a *Life* Magazine article which Kluge co-authored.

WORK IN PROGRESS: A nonfiction account—including teaching experience, memory and reflection, and reportage—of a year in the life of a small college, Kenyon College.

SIDELIGHTS: P. F. Kluge told *CA:* "If I wrote only magazine articles, I would despair. If I confined myself to novels, I would also despair. I do both, and from two negatives, attempt to construct a positive. The differences between fiction and nonfiction—between my novels and everything else I wrote—mattered much more to me [earlier] than they now do. Old distinctions have blurred, for better *and* for worse. It's all writing, and it's always hard. I do the best I can, with the time and talent I have."

BIOGRAPHICAL/CRITICAL SOURCES:

PERIODICALS

Chicago Tribune, April 29, 1991.
Islands Magazine, March/April, 1991.
Los Angeles Times, December 19, 1980; September 23, 1983; December 13, 1987, p. 12; March 27, 1991, p. E6.
New Yorker, July 22, 1991.

New York Times, September 23, 1983; May 5, 1991.
New York Times Book Review, December 30, 1984; May 4, 1991, p. 16.
Washington Post, May 12, 1991.

*   *   *

KNIGHT, Vick R(alph), Jr.   1928-

PERSONAL: Born April 6, 1928, in Lakewood, OH; son of Vick R., Sr. (an advertising executive and composer) and Janice (Higgins) Knight; married Beverly Joyce McKeighan, April 14, 1949 (divorced, 1973); married B. Carolyn Schlee, 1981; children: (first marriage) Stephen Foster, Mary Ann. *Education:* University of Southern California, B.S., 1952; Los Angeles State College of Applied Arts and Sciences (now California State University, Los Angeles), M.A., 1958; Whittier College, graduate study, 1959-61; Long Beach State College (now California State University, Long Beach), graduate study, 1960-61; California State College at Fullerton (now California State University, Fullerton), graduate study, 1961-64; Claremont Graduate School, graduate study, 1963-71; California Coast University, Ed.D., 1991. *Avocational interests:* Herpetology (the study of reptiles and amphibians), Greek history, environment, the films and follies of W. C. Fields.

ADDRESSES: Home—22597 Canyon Lake Dr., S., Canyon Lake, CA 92587.

CAREER: Producer-director of "Here Comes Tom Harmon," radio series for American Broadcasting Co., 1947-50; school teacher and vice-principal in Pico Rivera, CA, 1952-59; school principal in Placentia, CA, 1959-64, assistant superintendent, 1965-71; Pepperdine College (now University), Los Angeles, CA, coordinator of graduate education, 1968-70; National General West, Inc. (real estate investments), Fullerton, CA, vice-president, 1971-74; Children's Hospital of Orange County, Orange, CA, director of development and community relations, 1974-84; Aristan Press, Canyon Lake, CA, editor, 1984—; Lake Elsinore Valley Community Development Co., executive director, 1988—. Educational consultant, Key Records, 1960—; associate director of field services planning, La Verne College, 1970—; chairman of the board of William Claude Fields Foundation, 1972—. *Military service:* U.S. Navy (Armed Forces Radio Service), 1946-48.

MEMBER: International Wine and Food Society, International Association of Business Communicators, American Film Institute, National Society of Fund Raising Executives, American Society of Composers, Authors and Publishers, Society of Children's Book Writers, Authors League, National Association for Hospital Development, National Education Association, National School Public Relations Association, California Teachers Association, Audubon Society, Nature Conservancy, Sierra Club, Western Society of Naturalists, United States Junior Chamber of Commerce (director, 1958-59), California Junior Chamber of Commerce (vice-president, 1957-58), Pico Rivera Junior Chamber of Commerce, Kiwanis (president of Placentia branch, 1960), Friends of the UCI Library (president), Friends of the Canyon Lake Public Library (founding president), Canyon Lake Home Owners Club (president), West Atwood Yacht Club (commodore, 1971-72), Escoffier Society, Blue Key, Cardinal and Gold, W. C. Fields Fan Club of North America (president), International Stuffed Cabbage Appreciation Society, International Platform Association, Turtles International Association, Skull and Dagger, Exhausted Roosters, Los Compadres con Libros, E Clampus Vitus, Anti-Slubberdegulion Society, Phi Sigma Kappa, Alpha Delta Sigma, Theta Nu Epsilon.

AWARDS, HONORS: Named one of California's five outstanding young men, California State Junior Chamber of Commerce, 1959; Distinguished Citizen Award, Whittier College, 1960; Educator of the Year Award, Orange County Press Club, 1970; Author and Book Award, University of California, Irvine, 1973; Outstanding Service Award, Reading Educators Guild of California State University, Fullerton, 1979.

WRITINGS:

(With John E. Moore) *It's Our World,* Charter, 1972.
(With Moore) *It's Our Future,* Charter, 1972.
(With Moore) *It's Our Choice,* Charter, 1972.
(With Larry Harris) *Twilight of the Animal Kingdom,* Ritchie, 1972.
Snakes of Hawaii, Nature Guides of the West, 1972.
Earle the Squirrel, Ritchie, 1974.
The Night the Crayons Talked, Ritchie, 1974.
Send for Haym Salomon!, Borden, 1976.
(With Moore) *Remedial Mathematics Series,* six volumes, Testing and Teaching Institute of America, 1983.
Citizen Soldier: Col. John Sevier, Aristan, 1985.
Heinz-Kirsch Family History, Family History, 1990.

Author of "Nature Notebook," a syndicated newspaper column, 1954-62.

WORK IN PROGRESS: My Word!, a lexicon of favorite words of famous people; *A Tale of Twos,* the story of twins through the ages; *Honk if You're Horny,* a history of bumperstickers; *A Navel Salute,* a history of the omphalos; *Joby and the Wishing Well,* a children's story.

KNIGHT-PATTERSON, W. M.
See KULSKI, Wladyslaw W(szebor)

*   *   *

KOHN, Richard H(enry) 1940-

PERSONAL: Born December 29, 1940, in Chicago, IL; son of Henry L. (an attorney) and Kate H. (a physician; maiden name, Hirschberg) Kohn; married Lynne Holtan (a psychotherapist and clinical social worker), August 15, 1964; children: Abigail, Samuel. *Education:* Harvard University, A.B., 1962; University of Wisconsin—Madison, M.S., 1964, Ph.D., 1968.

ADDRESSES: Office—Department of History, CB 3195, University of North Carolina at Chapel Hill, Chapel Hill, NC 27599-3195.

CAREER: City College of the City University of New York, New York City, assistant professor of history, 1968-71; Rutgers University, New Brunswick, NJ, assistant professor, 1971-75, associate professor, 1975-83, professor of history, 1983-84. Harold Keith Johnson Visiting Professor of Military History at U.S. Army Military History Institute, U.S. Army War College, 1980-81; Department of the Air Force, Washington, DC, chief of Office of Air Force History, 1981-91; University of North Carolina at Chapel Hill, associate professor of history, 1991—.

MEMBER: Organization of American Historians, American Historical Association, Society for Military History, Air Force Historical Foundation.

AWARDS, HONORS: National Endowment for the Humanities bicentennial grant, 1970-71; American Philosophical Society research grant, 1970-71; Binkley-Stephenson Prize for best article from Organization of American Historians, 1973, for an article in the *Journal of American History;* American Council of Learned Societies fellow, 1977-78; certificate of appreciation for patriotic civilian service from the Department of the Army, 1982; President's Award, Air Force Historical Foundation, 1986; decoration for exceptional civilian service from the Department of the Air Force, 1991.

WRITINGS:

Eagle and Sword: The Federalists and the Creation of the Military Establishment in America, 1783-1802, Free Press, 1975.
(Co-editor) *Air Superiority in World War II,* Office of Air Force History, 1983.
(Co-editor) *Air Superiority in World War II and Korea: An Interview with General James Ferguson, General Robert M. Lee, General William Momyer, and Lieutenant*

General Elwood R. Quesada, Office of Air Force History, 1983.
(Co-editor) *Air Interdiction in World War II, Korea, and Vietnam: An Interview with General Earl E. Partridge, General Jacob E. Smart, and General John W. Vogt,* Office of Air Force History, 1986.
(Co-editor) *Strategic Air Warfare: An Interview with General Leon W. Johnson, General Curtis E. LeMay, General David Burchinal, and General Jack J. Catton,* Office of Air Force History, 1988.
(Editor) *The United States Military under the Constitution of the United States, 1789-1989* (originally appeared in *Revue Internationale d'Histoire Militaire,* number 69, 1990), New York University Press, 1991.

Also author of *The United States and Treaties Between the State of New York and the Oneida and Stockbridge Indians, 1795-1847,* Clearwater Publishing. Contributor to *Reconsiderations on the Revolutionary War,* Don Higginbotham, editor, Greenwood Press, 1978.

"THE AMERICAN MILITARY EXPERIENCE" SERIES

Military Laws of the United States from the Civil War through the War Powers Act of 1973: An Original Anthology, Arno, 1979.
Anglo-American Anti-Military Tracts, 1697-1830: An Original Anthology, Arno, 1979.

Also editor of series volumes 1-32, Arno, 1979.

OTHER

Contributor to periodicals, including *William and Mary Quarterly, Journal of American History,* and *American Historical Review.*

WORK IN PROGRESS: Books on how the United States makes and experiences war and the rise of the military establishment in the twentieth century.

SIDELIGHTS: In *Eagle and Sword: The Federalists and the Creation of the Military Establishment in America, 1783-1802* Richard H. Kohn examines the development of the U.S. national army during the last two decades of the eighteenth century. The author discusses the standing army's most active advocates—particularly Alexander Hamilton—and explores the existing domestic conditions that, in many ways, justified the establishment of a national army at that time. One critic, writing in the *New York Review of Books,* commended Kohn's comprehensive scholarship and the "valuable information" he presents on the period. "Kohn's thesis will provoke controversy," the reviewer added; "his research commands attention."

Kohn once told *CA:* "In the years since *Eagle and Sword* was finished, my interests have broadened to include virtually all of American military history. I continue to be fascinated and puzzled by the contradictions in our military past. Our security absorbs an immense amount of our wealth and energy; keys to understanding our predicament, I continue to believe, lie in unraveling our past. . . . My long-term projects include studies on how the United States makes and experiences war, and how the nation came to possess a large military establishment after World War II." More recently he said: "If we are to preserve our own security and fulfill our responsibilities in the world and to future generations, we need to study war and its relationship to society in as broad, and as intensive, terms as we can."

BIOGRAPHICAL/CRITICAL SOURCES:

PERIODICALS

New York Review of Books, October 16, 1975.
New York Times Book Review, November 30, 1975.
Times Literary Supplement, November 26, 1976.

*   *   *

KRAUSE, Pat 1930-

PERSONAL: Born January 26, 1930, in Tuscaloosa, AL; daughter of Allan Walker (a physician) and Florence (a teacher; maiden name, Wilson) Blair; married Frank Krause (an insurance representative), August 7, 1950; children: Judith, Jim, Barbara, Kathy. *Education:* Attended Reliance Business College, 1948-49, and University of Regina, 1970, 1972.

ADDRESSES: Home and office—89 Bell St., Regina, Saskatchewan, Canada S4S 5V2.

CAREER: Mac & Mac Men's Wear, Regina, Saskatchewan, stenographer and bookkeeper, 1949-51; housewife and mother, 1951-65; apartment rental agent in Regina, 1965-70; University of Saskatchewan, Saskatoon, project assistant in continuing medical education, 1970-76; Canadian Broadcasting Corp., Regina, radio writer and commentator, 1976-79; University of Regina, Regina, communications officer, 1979-85; full-time writer and writing workshop instructor, 1985—. Free-lance radio writer and commentator, 1971—. Saskatchewan Summer School of the Arts, director of writing workshops, 1975-80, workshop leader, 1976-82.

MEMBER: Writers' Union of Canada, PEN, Association of Canadian Television and Radio Artists, Saskatchewan Writers Guild.

AWARDS, HONORS: Saskatchewan Arts Board, W. O. Mitchell Bursary, 1975, and grants, 1984 and 1989; story awards, Saskatchewan Writers Guild, 1978, for "*Playboy,*" 1980, for "*Sudden Squalls,*" 1981, for "*Vital Statis-*

tic," and 1983, for "*Put It in Writing: (When You Hate Your Mom Forever)*"; Government of Saskatchewan Department of Culture and Youth Literary Award, 1980, and honorable mention, Saskatchewan Library Association's Canada-wide competition for young adult books, 1981, both for *Freshie;* City of Regina writing grant, 1981; research grant, University of Regina, 1984; honorable mention, *Prism International* fiction contest, 1987.

WRITINGS:

Freshie (juvenile novel), Potlash Publications, 1982.
Best Kept Secrets (short story collection), Coteau Books, 1988.

Work represented in anthologies, including *Sundogs, Saskatchewan Gold, Canadian Children's Annual* (1980), and *More Saskatchewan Gold.*

WORK IN PROGRESS: A novel, *Southern Relations;* short stories.

SIDELIGHTS: Pat Krause told *CA:* "It's never too late or too early to follow your dream of becoming an author. My childhood dream was to be a foreign correspondent complete with rumpled trench coat, Veronica Lake hairdo, and Katharine Hepburn sophistication. I planned to cover the war-torn capitals of Europe with dashing male colleagues, sip goblets of wine in secluded cafes with them, and wave a French cigaret in a long ebony holder to dismiss their accolades for all the Pulitzer Prizes I'd won.

"Instead, I married my high-school sweetheart, and we raised four children, plus other assorted flying, creeping, crawling, defecating, and chewing creatures. Life often resembled living in a war-town environment, but I didn't have time to file any award-winning dispatches.

"Suddenly, it was 1970. The war was over. It was time to recycle my dream. Our eldest daughter, Judith Krause, like many teen-agers, dreamt about becoming a famous poet. So we began the lifelong apprenticeship required to become published writers together by taking a University of Regina night class in creative writing.

"Since then, Judith has published a book of poetry, *What We Bring Home* (Coteau, 1986), and we share a dream of writing bestsellers, receiving top literary awards, selling the movie rights, and becoming rich and famous authors.

"Wide awake, we write as fast as we can."

*   *   *

K-TURKEL, Judi
See KESSELMAN-TURKEL, Judi

KUHLMANN, Susan
    See LOHAFER, Susan

*   *   *

KUHN, Alfred   1914-1981

PERSONAL: Born December 22, 1914, in Reading, PA; died August 19, 1981; son of Alvin Boyd (an author) and Mary G. (Leippe) Kuhn; married Nina de Angeli, October 18, 1941; children: David, Jeffrey, Henry. *Education:* Albright College, B.A., 1935; University of Pennsylvania, M.A., 1941, Ph.D., 1951.

CAREER: University of Pennsylvania, Philadelphia, instructor in industry, 1946-49; University of Cincinnati, Cincinnati, OH, beginning in 1949, began as assistant professor, became David Stinton Professor of Economics and Sociology. Labor arbitrator.

MEMBER: American Economic Association, Industrial Relations Research Association, Society for General Systems Research, American Association of University Professors, American Civil Liberties Union, Academy of Management, Academy of Independent Scholars, Association for Integrative Studies, American Sociological Association, Social Science Education Consortium.

WRITINGS:

Study of Racial Discrimination in Cincinnati, Wilder Foundation, 1952.
Arbitration in Transit: An Evaluation of Wage Criteria, University of Pennsylvania Press, 1952.
Labor: Institutions and Economics, Rinehart, 1956, revised edition, Harcourt, 1967.
The Study of Society: A Unified Approach, Irwin, 1963 (published in England as *The Study of Society: A Multi-Disciplinary Approach,* Tavistock Publications, 1966).
(With Kenneth Boulding and Lawrence Senesh) *System Analysis and Its Use in the Classroom,* Social Science Education Consortium, 1973.
The Logic of Social Systems: A Unified, Deductive, System-Based Approach to Social Science, Jossey-Bass, 1974.
Unified Social Science, Dorsey, 1975.
(With Edward Herman) *Collective Bargaining and Industrial Relations,* Prentice-Hall, 1981.
The Logic of Organization: Social Science Framework for Organizations, Jossey-Bass, 1982.

Contributor of articles on wage theory, systems theory, and philosophy to professional journals.*

    [Death date provided by wife, Mary G. Kuhn]

KUHN, Karl F(rancis)   1939-

PERSONAL: Born October 25, 1939, in Louisville, KY; son of Fred L. (a pharmacist) and Mary Francis (a teacher; maiden name, Walsh) Kuhn; married Mary Sharon Roos, November 24, 1960; children: Karyn, Kimberly, Karl, Jr., Keith, Kevin. *Education:* Bellarmine College, B.A., 1961; University of Kentucky, M.S., 1964, Ph.D., 1973. *Politics:* "Getting more liberal with age." *Religion:* Roman Catholic. *Avocational interests:* "Grandchildren."

ADDRESSES: Home—264 Sunset Ave., Richmond, KY 40475. *Office*—Department of Physics, Eastern Kentucky University, Richmond, KY 40475.

CAREER: Eastern Kentucky University, Richmond, KY, instructor, 1963-68, assistant professor, 1969-72, associate professor and professor of physics, 1973—. Development engineer for Sylvania Electric Co., 1965-66.

MEMBER: American Association of Physics Teachers, Astronomical Society of the Pacific, Kentucky Association of Physics Teachers, Kentucky Association for Progress in Science.

WRITINGS:

Physics for People Who Think They Don't Like Physics, Saunders, 1976.
Basic Physics, John Wiley & Sons, 1979.
Physics in Your World, Saunders, 1980.
Astronomy: A Journey into Science, West Publishing Co., 1989.
In Quest of the Universe, West Publishing Co., 1991.

SIDELIGHTS: Karl F. Kuhn writes: "My primary professional interest is in teaching elementary physics and astronomy. I try not to take myself too seriously, and I hope that this attitude is reflected in my books."

*   *   *

KUITERT, H(arminus) Martinus   1924-

PERSONAL: Born November 11, 1924, in the Netherlands. *Education:* Free University of Amsterdam, Dr. Theol., 1957, Dr. Theol., 1962.

ADDRESSES: Home—Mr. Troelstralaan 45, Amstelveen, Netherlands.

CAREER: Clergyman of Dutch Reformed Church; pastor in South Holland province, 1950-55, and in Amsterdam, 1955-65; Free University of Amsterdam, Amsterdam, Netherlands, associate professor of dogmatics, 1965-66, professor of dogmatics and ethics, 1967—. Member of the National Health Council, 1978—.

WRITINGS:

De mensvormigheid Gods, Kok, 1962.

(Editor with H.A.M. Fiolet) *Uit Tweeen een,* Lemniscaat, 1966.

De spelers en het spel, Amsterdam, Ten Have, 1967, translation published as *Signals from the Bible,* Eerdmans, 1972.

Gott in Menschengestalt, Kaiser, 1967.

(With G. P. Hartvelt) *In de Kring,* Meinema, 1968.

(With Hartvelt) *Waar het op aankomt,* Meinema, 1968.

De realiteit van het geloof, Kok, 1968, translation by Lewis B. Smedes published as *The Reality of Faith,* Eerdmans, 1968.

Verstaat gij wat gij leest?, Kok, 1969, translation published as *Do You Understand What You Read?,* Eerdmans, 1970.

Anders Gezegd, Kok, 1970.

Om em Om, Kok, 1972.

Zonder geloof vaart niemand wel, Ten Have, 1974, translation J. K. Tuinstra published as *The Necessity of Faith,* Eerdmans, 1976.

Wat heet geloven?, Ten Have, 1977.

Een gewenste dood. Euthanasie als godsdienstig en moreel probleem, Ten Have, 1981.

Everything is Politics but Politics is Not Everything, translation by John Bowden, Eerdmans, 1986.*

* * *

KULSKI, Wladyslaw W(szebor) 1903- (W. W. Coole, W. M. Knight-Patterson, Politicus)

PERSONAL: Born July 27, 1903, in Warsaw, Poland; son of Julian (state official) and Antonina (Ostrowski) Kulski; married Antonina Reutt, October 28, 1938. *Education:* Warsaw School of Law, LL.M., 1925; Paris School of Law, LL.D., 1927.

ADDRESSES: Home—1624 Marion Ave., Durham, NC 27705. *Office*—Department of Political Science, Duke University, Durham, NC 27705.

CAREER: Polish Foreign Service, 1928-45, member of staff of League of Nations service at Polish Ministry of Foreign Affairs, 1928-33, secretary, counsellor of Polish Permanent Delegation to League of Nations, 1933-36, head of legal service at Ministry of Foreign Affairs, 1936-40, counsellor, Minister Plenipotentiary at Polish Embassy in London, 1940-45; public lecturer in the U.S., 1946-47; University of Alabama, Tuscaloosa, lecturer in political science, 1947-48, professor of political science, 1948-51; Syracuse University, Syracuse, NY, professor of political science, 1951-63; Duke University, Durham, NC,

James B. Duke Distinguished Professor, 1963-73. Lecturer at Foreign Service Institute, Department of State, U.S. Air University, and Army Strategic Intelligence School.

MEMBER: American Society of International Law, American Political Science Association, American Association for the Slavic Studies, American Association of University Professors.

AWARDS, HONORS: Fulbright research award and John Simon Guggenheim Memorial Foundation research fellowship for research in France, 1961-62; Guggenheim research fellowship, 1969-70.

WRITINGS:

Le Probleme de la Securite Internationale, A. Pedone, 1927.

Wspelczesna Europa Polityczna, Ksiegarnia Powszechna (Warsaw-Krakow), 1939.

The Soviet Regime: Communism in Practice, Syracuse University Press, 1954, 4th edition, 1964.

(Co-author) *Handbuch das Weltkommunismus,* Karl Alber, 1958, English edition published as *Handbook on Communism,* Praeger, 1962.

Peaceful Co-Existence: An Analysis of Soviet Foreign Policy, Regnery, 1959.

(Co-author) *The Ethic of Power,* Harper, 1962.

International Politics in a Revolutionary Age, Lippincott, 1964, 2nd edition, 1968.

(Co-author) *Systems Integrating the International Community,* Van Nostrand, 1964.

DeGaulle and the World: The Foreign Policy of the Fifth French Republic, Syracuse University Press, 1966.

The Soviet Union in World Affairs: A Documented Analysis, 1964-1972, Syracuse University Press, 1973.

Germany and Poland: From War to Peaceful Relations, Syracuse University Press, 1976.

UNDER PSEUDONYM W. W. COOLE

(Editor with M. F. Potter) *Thus Spake Germany,* Harper, 1941, reprint published as *Thus Speaks Germany,* AMS Press, 1990.

(Co-editor) *Anthology of Crime,* Hutchinson, 1945.

UNDER PSEUDONYM W. M. KNIGHT-PATTERSON

Germany from Defeat to Conquest: 1913-1933, Allen & Unwin, 1945.

Contributor of more than twenty articles to professional journals.*

KUNHARDT, Philip B(radish), Jr. 1928-

PERSONAL: Born February 5, 1928, in New York City; son of Philip Bradish (in wool business) and Dorothy (Meserue) Kunhardt; married Katharine Trowbridge; children: Philip III, Peter, Jean, Sandra, Sarah, Michael. *Education:* Princeton University, B.A.

ADDRESSES: Office—Time, Inc., Rockefeller Center, New York, NY 10017. *Agent*—Paul Reynolds, 12 East 42 St., New York, NY 10017.

CAREER: Writer. Worked for Time, Inc.; was managing editor of *Life* magazine.

MEMBER: Century Club.

AWARDS, HONORS: Christopher Book Award, 1971, for *My Father's House.*

WRITINGS:

Twenty Days, Harper, 1965.
My Father's House, Random House, 1971.
Mathew Brady and His World, Time-Life, 1977.
A New Birth of Freedom, Little, Brown, 1983.
Life Smiles Back, Simon & Schuster, 1987.
Life in Camelot: The Kennedy Years, Volume 1, Little, Brown, 1988.
Life Laughs Last, Simon & Schuster, 1989.
The Joy of Life, Little, Brown, 1989.

Also editor of *Life: The First Fifty Years, 1936-1986.*

WORK IN PROGRESS: A book on Abraham Lincoln, for Little, Brown.

SIDELIGHTS: Philip B. Kunhardt once told *CA:* "I have worked for Time, Inc., for twenty-nine years and so my book writing has been done at nights, on weekends, and vacations, or on sabbaticals. Motivation comes from needing the money, getting satisfaction from writing; I never read a book I've written once it's published."

BIOGRAPHICAL/CRITICAL SOURCES:

PERIODICALS

Los Angeles Times Book Review, November 27, 1983.
Tribune Books (Chicago), December 13, 1987.
Washington Post Book World, November 23, 1986.*

* * *

KUNREUTHER, Howard Charles 1938-

PERSONAL: Born November 14, 1938, in New York City; son of Richard and Bobbie (Baskin) Kunreuther; married Sylvia Anne Clifford, May 4, 1968. *Education:* Bates College, A.B., 1959; Massachusetts Institute of

Technology, 1959-63, Ph.D., 1965; Econometric Institute, Rotterdam, Netherlands, graduate study, 1963-64.

ADDRESSES: Home—509 Putnam Rd., Merion, PA 19066. *Office*—Department of Decision Sciences, Wharton School of Finance and Commerce, University of Pennsylvania, Philadelphia, PA 19104.

CAREER: Institute for Defense Analyses, Arlington, VA, economist, 1964-65; University of Chicago, Graduate School of Business, Chicago, IL, assistant professor of applied economics, 1966-72; University of Pennsylvania, Wharton School of Finance and Commerce, Philadelphia, PA, professor of decision sciences, 1973—. Risk Group task leader, International Institute of Applied Systems Analysis, 1980-82.

MEMBER: Institute of Management Sciences, American Economics Association, Phi Beta Kappa.

AWARDS, HONORS: Fulbright fellowship in Netherlands, 1963-64; Elizur Wright Award, American Risk and Insurance Association, 1971; Western Electric Teaching Award, 1980.

WRITINGS:

(With Douglas Dacy) *The Economics of Natural Disaster Disasters: Implications for Federal Policy,* Free Press, 1969.
Recovery from Natural Disasters: Insurance or Federal Aid?, American Enterprise Publications, 1973.
Disaster Insurance Protection: Public Policy Lessons, Wiley, 1978.
Risk Analysis and Decision Practices: The Siting of LEG Facilities in Four Countries, Springer Verlag, 1983.

Contributor to *Management Science* and other professional journals.

WORK IN PROGRESS: Studies of decision-making by individuals with respect to low probability-high loss events.

SIDELIGHTS: Howard Charles Kunreuther's book *The Economics of Natural Disaster Disasters: Implications for Federal Policy* evolved out of a study on the economic problems connected with recovery following the Alaskan earthquake of 1964. His book *Risk Analysis and Decision Practices: The Siting of LEG Facilities in Four Countries* evolved out of his work as risk group task leader for the International Institute of Applied Systems Analysis from 1980 to 1982.*

* * *

KUNZ, Virginia B(rainard) 1921-

PERSONAL: Surname pronounced "Coons"; born October 5, 1921, in Fairmont, MN; daughter of Dudley Shattuck (an educator and writer) and Merl (Anderson) Brainard; married Richard Carl Kunz, April 22, 1950; children: Susan Virginia, David Brainard. *Education:* Attended St. Cloud State College, 1939-40; Iowa State University, B.S., 1943. *Politics:* Republican. *Religion:* Presbyterian.

ADDRESSES: Home—323 Landmark Center, 75 West 5th St., St. Paul, MN 55102.

CAREER: Minneapolis Star and Tribune, Minneapolis, MN, worked as reporter, feature writer, and section editor, 1944-51, 1953-57; Minnesota Association for Retarded Children, state public information director, 1958-62; Ramsey County Historical Society, St. Paul, MN, secretary, 1962-73, executive director, 1973—.

AWARDS, HONORS: Five National Federation of Press Women first place awards; Page One Award of Twin Cities Newspaper Guild, 1950, 1953.

WRITINGS:

Muskets to Missiles: A Military History of Minnesota, Minnesota Statehood Centennial Commission, 1958.
The French in America, Lerner, 1966.
The Germans in America, Lerner, 1966.
(Editor) *Farming in Early Minnesota,* Ramsey County Historical Society, 1968.
(Co-author) *The Collector's Book of Railroadiana,* Hawthorn, 1976.
St. Paul: Saga of an American City, Windsor Publications, 1977.
Minnetonka Yacht Club Centennial, 1882-1982, Minnetonka Yacht Club Sailing School, 1982.
St. Paul: A Modern Renaissance, Windsor Publications, 1986.

Founding editor, *Ramsey County History* (semi-annual publication).*

*   *   *

KUSNICK, Barry A.   1910-

PERSONAL: Born October 3, 1910, in New York City; son of Isaac (a rabbi) and Fanny (Black) Kusnick; married June D. Lee, 1949 (divorced); married Lilyan McNeely (an administrative assistant), July 2, 1966; children: Judith Landy, Janet. *Education:* Attended University of California at Los Angeles. *Politics:* Democrat. *Religion:* None. *Avocational interests:* Piano playing, photography, tennis, music, sailboating.

CAREER: ITT Gilfillian, Los Angeles, CA, senior development engineer, 1947-50; Librascope Inc. Singer, Glendale, CA, senior engineer, 1950-63; Bell & Howell, Pasa-

dena, CA, senior member of technical staff, 1963-64; Houston Fearless Corp., Los Angeles, CA, chief design engineer, 1964; Bell & Howell, Pasadena, CA, senior member of technical staff, 1965-67; ITT Aerospace, San Fernando, CA, senior development engineer, 1967-71; Litton Industries, Beverly Hills, CA, engineer group leader, 1969-71.

MEMBER: Buccaneer Yacht Club.

WRITINGS:

The Complete Boatman, Dial, 1975.
The Boatman's Bible, Dial, 1977.
The Yacht Inventory, Ziff-Davis, 1979.

Contributor to *Boating* magazine.

WORK IN PROGRESS: Maritime Law; An American Family.

*   *   *

KUSPIT, Donald B(urton)   1935-

PERSONAL: Born March 26, 1935, in New York City; son of Morris (a manager) and Celia Kuspit; married Judith Price (a psychologist), 1962. *Education:* Columbia University, B.A., 1955; Yale University, M.A., 1958; University of Frankfurt, Ph.D., 1960; Pennsylvania State University, M.A., 1964; University of Michigan, Ph.D., 1971.

ADDRESSES: Office—Department of Art, State University of New York at Stony Brook, Stony Brook, NY, 11794.

CAREER: University of Frankfurt, Frankfurt, West Germany (now Germany), lecturer in English, 1957-59; Pennsylvania State University, University Park, assistant professor of philosophy, 1960-64; University of Saarland, Saarbruecken, Germany, Fulbright lecturer in philosophy and American studies, 1964-65; University of Windsor, Windsor, Ontario, associate professor of philosophy, 1966-70; University of North Carolina, Chapel Hill, professor of art history, 1970-78; State University of New York at Stony Brook, professor of art and head of department, 1978-83. Guest lecturer at School for Visual Arts, 1976—; A. D. White Professor at Large, Cornell University, 1991—.

MEMBER: American Society of Aesthetics, College Art Association of America.

AWARDS, HONORS: Canada Council fellowship, 1968-69; National Endowment for the Humanities younger humanist fellowship, 1973-74; Guggenheim fellowship, 1977-78.

WRITINGS:

Clement Greenberg, Art Critic, University of Wisconsin Press, 1979.

Leon Golub: Existentialist Activist Painter, Rutgers University Press, 1985, 2nd edition published as *The Existential Activist Painter, The Example of Leon Golub,* 1986.

(With Betty Collings) *Thomas Macaulay: Sculptural Views on Perceptual Ambiguity,* Dayton Art, 1986.

(With Stephen S. High) *Aggression, Subversion, Seduction: Young German Painters,* Portland School Baxter, 1986.

Erich Fischl, Random House, 1987.

(With Bruce McWright) *Constitution: Group Material,* Temple University Gallery, 1987.

Louis Bourgeois, edited by Elisabeth Avedon, Random House, 1988.

The New Subjectivism: Art in the 1980s, UMI Research Press, 1988.

Stephen de Staebler: The Figure, Chronicle Books, 1988.

(Author of introduction) *Fables and Fantasies: From the Collection of Susan Kasen and Robert D. Summer,* Duke, 1988.

The Critic Is Artist: The Intentionality of Art, UMI Research Press, 1988.

Alex Katz: Night Paintings, Abrams, 1991.

(With Janet Kardon) *Robert Kushner,* University of Pennsylvania Contemporary Art, in press.

EDITOR; ALL PUBLISHED BY UMI RESEARCH PRESS

Sandra L. Underwood, *Charles H. Caffin: A Voice for Modernism,* 1983.

Amy C. Simowitz, *Theory of Art in the "Encyclopedie",* 1983.

Misook Song, *Art Theories of Charles Blanc, 1813-1882,* 1984.

Lawrence Alloway, *Network: Art and the Complete Present,* 1984.

Joseph Masheck, *Historical Present: Essays of the 1970s,* 1984.

Robert Pincus-Witten, *Eye to Eye: Twenty Years of Art Criticism,* 1984.

Martin Pops, *Vermeer: Consciousness and the Chamber of Being,* 1984.

Dennis Adrian, *Sight Out of Mind: Essays and Criticism on Art,* 1985.

Nicolas Calas, *Transfigurations: Art Critical Essays on the Modern Period,* 1985.

Susan N. Platt, *Modernism in the 1920s: Interpretations of Modern Art in New York from Expressionism to Constructivism,* 1985.

Patricia Mathews, *Aurier's Symbolist Art Criticism and Theory,* 1986.

Beverly Twitchell, *Cezanne and Formalism in Bloomsbury,* 1986.

Roger Benjamin, *Matisse's "Notes of a Painter": Criticism, Theory, and Context, 1891-1908,* 1986.

Miriam K. Levin, *Republican Art and Ideology in Late Nineteenth-Century France,* 1986.

Peter Plagens, *Moonlight Blues: An Artist's Art Criticism,* 1986.

(And author of foreword) Dore Ashton, *Out of the Whirlwind: Three Decades of Arts Commentary,* 1987.

Matthew L. Rohn, *Visual Dynamics in Jackson Pollock's Abstractions,* 1987.

Kent Hooper, *Ernest Barlach's Literary and Visual Art: The Issue of Multiple Talent,* 1987.

Annette Kahn, *J. K. Huysmans: Novelist, Poet and Art Critic,* 1987.

Lawrence W. Markert, *Arthur Symons: Critic of the Seven Arts,* 1987.

Stewart Buettner, *American Art Theory, 1945-70,* 1988.

Bernard Schultz, *Art and Anatomy in Renaissance Italy,* 1988.

Carol M. Zemel, *The Formation of a Legend: Van Gogh Criticism, 1890-1920,* 1988.

Stephen C. Foster, *The Critics of Abstract Expressionism,* 1988.

Peter Selz, *Art in a Turbulent Era,* 1988.

Jeanne Siegel, *Artword 2: Discourse on the Early '80s,* 1988.

Pincus-Witten, *Postminimalism into Maximalism: American Art, 1966-1986,* 1988.

Arlene Raven, *Feminist Art Criticism: An Anthology,* 1988.

Raven and others, *Crossing Over: Feminism and Art of Social Concern,* 1988.

Michael D. Hall, *Stereoscopic Perspective: Reflections on American Fine and Folk Art,* 1988.

Jo Anna Isaak, *The Ruin of Representation in Modernist Art and Texts,* 1988.

Carol A. Mahsun, *Pop Art Criticism: An Anthology,* 1988.

(Co-editor) Katherine Hoffman, *Collage: Critical Views,* 1989.

Barbara B. Lynes, *O'Keefe, Steiglitz, and the Critics, 1916-1929,* 1989.

(With Raven) *Art in the Public Interest,* 1989.

BIOGRAPHICAL/CRITICAL SOURCES:

PERIODICALS

Los Angeles Times Book Review, May 26, 1985.
New York Times Book Review, February 17, 1980.

KWEIT, Robert W(illiam) 1946-

PERSONAL: Born July 2, 1946, in Long Island City, NY; son of Irving (in business) and Sylvia (in business; maiden name, Greenfield) Kweit; married Mary Grisez, November 26, 1976. *Education:* Syracuse University, A.B., 1967; University of Pennsylvania, M.A., 1968, Ph.D., 1974.

ADDRESSES: Home—3823 Fairview Dr., Grand Forks, ND 58201. *Office*—Department of Political Science, Box 8276, University of North Dakota, Grand Forks, ND 58202.

CAREER: St. Joseph's College, Philadelphia, PA, lecturer in political science, 1971-74; Hamilton College, Clinton, NY, assistant professor of political science, 1974-76; University of North Dakota, Grand Forks, assistant professor, 1976-79, associate professor, 1979-83, professor of political science, 1983—, director of graduate study, 1977-90, chairman of department, 1990—, summer research professor, 1979, 1982, 1988. Member of Grand Forks Planning Commission, 1981—, and Metropolitan Planning Organization, 1982-88. *Military service:* U.S. Army Reserve, 1967-74; became captain.

MEMBER: American Political Science Association, American Society for Public Administration, American Association of University Professors (president of University of North Dakota chapter, 1987-89, North Dakota State conference president, 1988-89, national council president, 1990-93); National Association of Schools of Public Affairs and Administration (principal representative, 1977-81), Association for Retarded Citizens, Midwest Political Science Association, Pi Sigma Alpha.

WRITINGS:

(With wife, Mary Grisez Kweit) *Concepts and Methods for Political Analysis,* Prentice-Hall, 1981.
(With M. G. Kweit) *Implementing Citizen Participation in a Bureaucratic Society: A Contingency Approach,* Praeger, 1981.
(Contributor) Alan Abramowitz and others, editors, *The Life of the Parties: Activists in Presidential Politics,* University of Tennessee Press, 1984.
(Contributor) De Sario and Langton, editor, *Citizen Participation in Public Decision Making,* Greenwood Press, 1987.
(With M.G. Kweit) *People and Politics in Urban America,* Brooks/Cole, 1990.
(With Don Cozzetto and M. G. Kweit) *Public Budgeting: Politics, Institutions, and Processes,* Longman, in press.

Contributor of articles and reviews to political science and public policy journals.

SIDELIGHTS: Robert W. Kweit told *CA:* "Americans tend to have negative attitudes towards bureaucracy and bureaucrats because of inflated and conflicting expectations. Social problems have been transferred to government because the private sector has not been able to solve them. It therefore should not be surprising that the public sector also comes up short. Public bureaucrats are hampered in their quest to solve problems by politicians who take all the credit and shift all the blame. Further, we expect the public sector to be as 'efficient' as the private sector (American steel companies? Lockheed?), yet we also want it to be democratically accountable—which imposes all kinds of roadblocks to efficiency not facing the private sector.

"These problems are exacerbated in urban politics because of Americans' antipathy toward cities. What is needed is a more objective understanding of the bureaucracy and a more realistic appraisal of what government will do. We should accentuate the positive aspects of our cities rather than the negative and work to create urban environments more satisfactory to all.

"What makes studying these concerns more satisfying is that they dove-tail quite nicely with my wife's interest in political behavior and allow us to work together, thus sharing the work-load and emphasizing our individual strengths."

*　　　*　　　*

KYES, Robert L(ange) 1933-

PERSONAL: Born July 8, 1933, in Allegan, MI; son of Walter Morris (a land appraiser) and Antoinette (Lange) Kyes; married Rose-Reiman (a teacher and intern consultant), September 1, 1956 (divorced); children: Anne, Susan. *Education:* University of Michigan, B.A., 1958, Ph.D., 1964; Brown University, A.M., 1959; graduate study, University of Hamburg, 1959-60. *Avocational interests:* Travel, carpentry, nature study.

ADDRESSES: Home—1950 Longshore Dr., Ann Arbor, MI 48105. *Office*—Department of German, University of Michigan, 3144 Modern Languages Building, Ann Arbor, MI 48109.

CAREER: University of Michigan, Ann Arbor, assistant professor, 1964-68, associate professor, 1968-74, professor of Germanic languages, 1974—. Visiting associate professor of German linguistics, University of Colorado, 1968-69. *Military service:* U.S. Navy, 1951-54.

MEMBER: Linguistic Society of America, American Association of Teachers of German, Midwest Modern Language Association, Linguistic Association of Canada and the United States.

AWARDS, HONORS: Rackham faculty grant, University of Michigan, 1972; Distinguished Service Award, University of Michigan, 1966.

WRITINGS:

(With V. C. Hubbs) *German in Review,* Macmillan, 1966.
The Old Low Franconian Psalms and Glosses, University of Michigan Press, 1969.
(Reviser with H. H. Waengler) *Contemporary German,* 2nd edition (Kyes was not associated with the first edition), McGraw-Hill, 1971.

(With T. L. Markey and P. J. Roberge) *German and Its Dialects: A Grammar of Proto-German,* Volume 3, Benjamins, 1977.
Dictionary of the Old Low and Central Franconian Psalms and Glosses, M. Neimeyer (Tubingen), 1983.

Contributor of articles and reviews to *Language, Lingua, Modern Language Journal,* and *Michigan Germanic Studies.*

WORK IN PROGRESS: A *Glossary of Old Netherlandic; Old Netherlandic Phonology; The Old Saxon Heliand Manuscript Monacensis: Text, Notes, and Glossary.*

SIDELIGHTS: Robert L. Kyes writes that his current language project is German syntax.*

L

LAMPTON, Chris
  See LAMPTON, Christopher F.

*   *   *

LAMPTON, Christopher
  See LAMPTON, Christopher F.

*   *   *

LAMPTON, Christopher F.
  (Chris Lampton, Christopher Lampton)

PERSONAL: Education: Received degree in broadcast journalism.

ADDRESSES: Home—Maryland.

CAREER: Writer.

WRITINGS:

FOR YOUNG PEOPLE; UNDER NAME CHRISTOPHER LAMPTON, EXCEPT AS NOTED; PUBLISHED BY F. WATTS

Black Holes and Other Secrets of the Universe, 1980.
Meteorology: An Introduction, 1981.
Fusion: The Eternal Flame, 1982.
Planet Earth, 1982.
The Sun, 1982.
Dinosaurs and the Age of Reptiles, 1983.
DNA and the Creation of New Life, 1983.
Prehistoric Animals, 1983.
Programming in BASIC, 1983.
Space Sciences, illustrations by Anne Canevari Green, 1983.
Computer Languages, 1983.
Advanced BASIC, 1984.
BASIC for Beginners, 1984.

COBOL for Beginners, 1984.
FORTRAN for Beginners, 1984.
The Micro Dictionary, 1984.
Pascal for Beginners, 1984.
PILOT for Beginners, 1984.
Advanced BASIC for Beginners, 1984.
6502 Assembly-Language Programming for Apple, Commodore, and Atari Computers, 1985.
Forth for Beginners, 1985.
Graphics and Animation on the Commodore 64, 1985.
Z80 Assembly-Language: Programming for Radio Shack, Timex Sinclair, Adam, and CP/M Computers, 1985.
Graphics and Animation on the TRS-80: Models I, III, and 4, 1985.
Flying Safe?, 1986.
Graphics and Animation on the Apple II, II Plus, IIe and IIc, 1986.
Graphics and Animation on the Atari: 800, 400, 1200XL, and 600XL, 1986.
How to Create Adventure Games, 1986.
How to Create Computer Games, 1986.
Mass Extinctions: One Theory of Why the Dinosaurs Vanished, 1986.
Astronomy: From Copernicus to the Space Telescope, 1987.
The Space Telescope, 1987.
Star Wars, 1987.
CD-ROMS, 1987.
Endangered Species, 1988.
Rocketry: From Goddard to Space Travel, 1988.
Supernova!, 1988.
(Under name Christopher F. Lampton) *Thomas Alva Edison,* 1988.
Undersea Archaeology, 1988.
Wernher von Braun, 1988.
Stars and Planets: A Useful and Entertaining Tool to Guide Youngsters into the Twenty-First Century, illustrations by Ron Miller, 1988.

New Theories on the Dinosaurs, 1989.
New Theories on the Origins of the Human Race, 1989.
New Theories on the Birth of the Universe, 1989.
Predicting AIDS and Other Epidemics, 1989.
Predicting Nuclear and Other Technological Disasters, 1989.
Gene Technology: Confronting the Issues, 1990.
Telecommunications: From Telegraphs to Modems, 1991.

OTHER; UNDER NAME CHRISTOPHER LAMPTON, EXCEPT AS NOTED

(With David Bischoff) *The Seeker,* Laser Books, 1976.
(Under name Chris Lampton) *Gateway to Limbo* (science fiction novel), Doubleday, 1979.
(Under name Christopher F. Lampton) *Superconductors,* Enslow, 1989.
Bathtubs, Slides, Roller Coaster Rails: Simple Machines That Are Really Inclined Planes, illustrations by Carol Nicklaus, Millbrook, 1991.
Marbles, Roller Skates, Doorknobs: Simple Machines That Are Really Wheels, illustrations by Nicklaus, Millbrook, 1991.
Seesaws, Nutcrackers, Brooms: Simple Machines That Are Really Levers, illustrations by Nicklaus, Millbrook, 1991.
Simple Machines That Are Really Pulleys, Millbrook, 1991.
Blizzard Alert!, Millbrook, 1991.
Earthquake Alert!, Millbrook, 1991.
Forest Fire Alert!, Millbrook, 1991.
Hurricane Alert!, Millbrook, 1991.
Tornado Alert!, Millbrook, 1991.
Volcano Alert!, Millbrook, 1991.
Nintendo Action Games, Millbrook, 1991.
Nintendo Role-Playing Games, Millbrook, 1991.*

*   *   *

LANE, Jerry
   See MARTIN, Patricia Miles

*   *   *

LANEGRAN, David A(ndrew) 1941-

PERSONAL: Born November 27, 1941, in St. Paul, MN; son of Walter B. and Lita E. (Wilson) Lanegran; married Karen Rae Nygren (in women's fashion), September 11, 1964; children: Kimberley Rae, Elizabeth Ann, Eric David, Katherine Jane. *Education:* Macalester College, B.A., 1963; University of Minnesota, M.A., 1967, Ph.D., 1970. *Politics:* Democratic Farmer Labor party. *Religion:* Presbyterian.

ADDRESSES: Home—140 South Wheeler, St. Paul, MN 55105. *Office*—Department of Geography and Urban Studies, Macalester College, St. Paul, MN 55105.

CAREER: Macalester College, St. Paul, MN, assistant professor, 1969-76, associate professor of geography, 1977—. Principal of Lanegran, Richter & Sandeen (consultants). Member of visiting faculty at University of Minnesota, University of California at Berkley, and Pennsylvania State University. General Sevice Foundation, program associate, 1979—; Minnesota Landmarks, managing director, 1980-82, president and chief executive officer, 1988—; Highwind Properties, executive director, 1982-84; St. Paul City Planning Commission, chairman, 1983—; Old Town Restorations, member of board of directors; Grand Avenue Business Association, former member of board of directors. Association of American Geographers, member of board of directors, 1986-89, treasurer, 1988-89; National Council for Geographic Education, member of board of directors, 1990—; Minnesota Alliance for Geographic Education, coordinator; Geographic Education National Implementation Project, member of steering committee. Project director of ten separate research and educational institutes funded by both federal grants and various private foundations.

MEMBER: Association of American Geographers, National Council for Geographic Education.

AWARDS, HONORS: Award of excellence, Minnesota Society of the American Institute of Architects, for contributions to "historical, architectural, and neighborhood awareness"; award for teaching excellence, Burlington-Northern Teachers Federation, 1988; elected to South St. Paul Hall of Excellence, 1989; selected by *Change* magazine as one of the ten outstanding college teachers of geography in the United States.

WRITINGS:

(With Risa Palm) *Invitation to Geography,* McGraw, 1973.
Urban Dynamics in St. Paul, Old Town Restoration Press, 1977.
The Lake District of Minneapolis, Living Historical Museum Press, 1979,
St. Paul Omnibus: A Guide to Historic St. Paul, Old Town Restoration Press, 1979.
(Coauthor) *Legacy of Minneapolis,* Voyager Press, 1983.
(With Judith Martin) *Where We Live: Residential Districts of the Twin Cities,* University of Minnesota Press, 1983.
St. Anthony Park: Portrait of a Community, Minnesota Historical Society, 1987.
The St. Paul Experiment: Initiatives of the Latimer Administration, PED Press, 1989.

WORK IN PROGRESS: An introductory college textbook in human geography.

SIDELIGHTS: David A. Lanegran once told *CA:* "I strive to increase the sense of place among the residents of the twin cities through publications and non-profit renovation and restoration projects."

* * *

LATHAM, Mavis
   See CLARK, Mavis Thorpe

* * *

LAVOND, Paul Dennis
   See POHL, Frederik

* * *

LEA, Joan
   See NEUFELD, John Arthur

* * *

LEBOVICH, William Louis   1948-

PERSONAL: Born February 10, 1948, in Boston, MA; son of Harry and Florence Lebovich; married Karen Sloan (in public relations), June 9, 1974; children: two. *Education:* Brandeis University, B.A. (with honors), 1970; attended New York University School of Law, 1970-71; Boston University, M.A., A.B.D., 1974. *Religion:* Jewish.

ADDRESSES: Office—7302 Summit Ave., Chevy Chase, MD 20815.

CAREER: National Park Service, Washington, DC, architectural historian, 1974—, and photographer, 1988—.

MEMBER: Society of Architectural Historians, local historical societies.

WRITINGS:

(Contributor) Richard Guy Wilson, editor, *AIA Gold Medal,* McGraw, 1983.
America's City Halls, Preservation Press (Washington, DC), 1984.
(Contributor) *Built in USA,* Preservation Press, 1985.
(Compiler) *A Record in Detail: The Architectural Photographs of Jack E. Boucher,* University of Missouri Press, 1988.
(Contributor) John Burns, editor, *Recording Historic Structures,* AIA Press (Washington, DC), 1991.

Design for Dignity, Wiley, in press.

Contributor to magazines, including *Inland Architect, Commonwealth, Nineteenth Century,* and *Art and Australia.*

SIDELIGHTS: "The goal of my writing and research," William Louis Lebovich once told *CA,* "is to provide an integrated view of architecture, showing through a particular building or type of building how architecture reflects and influences economic, political, cultural, as well as artistic factors. No building is independent of the time and society that built it and no building should be written about without discussing the larger context of time and society."

Lebovich more recently added, "With the passage of the Americans with Disabilities Act in July, 1990, the importance of designing barrier-free architecture has received national recognition. . . . *Design for Dignity* is a compilation of accessible design solutions, intending to show designers the best work being done in this field."

* * *

LEPPMANN, Wolfgang Arthur   1922-

PERSONAL: Born July 9, 1922, in Berlin, Germany; son of Franz and Ida (von Riegler) Leppmann; married Theodosia Gudrun Olafson, 1946; children: Hans Christian, Karen Gerda, Erika Margaret. *Education:* McGill University, A.B., 1948, A.M., 1949; Princeton University, Ph.D., 1952. *Avocational interests:* Archeology, travel.

ADDRESSES: Home—2655 Central Blvd., Eugene, OR 97403. *Office*—Department of German, University of Oregon, Eugene, OR 97403.

CAREER: Brown University, Providence, RI, instructor of German, 1951-54; University of Oregon, Eugene, 1954-64, began as assistant professor, became associate professor, professor of German, 1964—, department chairman, 1964-66, 1967-68. Visiting professor of German, Vassar College, 1966-67, University of Toronto, 1968-69, Yale University, 1975, and University of Virginia, 1979. *Military service:* Royal Canadian Artillery, two years; became lieutenant.

MEMBER: Modern Language Association of America, American Association of Teachers of German (former president, North-West chapter), American Association of University Professors, Authors League of America, Archeological Institute of America, Goethe Society, Reform Club (Montreal).

AWARDS, HONORS: Alexander von Humboldt fellow, 1958-59, 1962-63, 1973; Guggenheim Foundation fellow, 1962, 1971-72.

WRITINGS:

The German Image of Goethe, Oxford University Press, 1961.
Pompeii: Eine Stadt in Literatur und Leben, Nymphenburger, 1966, translation published as *Pompeii in Fact and Fiction,* Elek Books, 1968.
Winckelmann, Knopf, 1970.
Rilke: A Life (originally published in Germany, 1981), translated from the German by Russell M. Stockman, Fromm International, 1984.
Gerhart Hauptmann: Leben, Werk und Zeit, Scherz, 1986.

OTHER

Contributor to *Die Zeit* (Hamburg), *Montreal Gazette, Saturday Night,* and scholarly journals, including *Comparative Literature.*

SIDELIGHTS: Writing in his native German, author Wolfgang Leppmann has been noted for his comprehensive biographies of the pre-eminent figures Johann Wolfgang Goethe, Johann Winkelmann, and Ranier Maria Rilke. Acknowledging Leppmann's success in recreating for the reader the setting for Rilke's turbulent life, Melvin Maddocks of *Time* describes *Rilke: A Life* as "the kind of biography such cases require: a solid rather than brilliant account." Writing in the *Los Angeles Times Book Review,* Barbara Tritel comments, "[Leppmann] approaches his task with a doggedness that is a hallmark of German scholarship," and later adds that "Rilke scholars will no doubt appreciate the service Leppmann has rendered."

BIOGRAPHICAL/CRITICAL SOURCES:

PERIODICALS

Los Angeles Times Book Review, October 14, 1984, p. 4.
London Observer, March 21, 1971.
New Yorker, November 28, 1970; October 8, 1984.
New York Review of Books, September 27, 1984, p. 17.
New York Times, June 20, 1984, p. 23.
New York Times Book Review, October 7, 1984, p. 24.
Saturday Review, October 10, 1970.
Time, May 28, 1984, p. 86.*

*   *   *

LEVI, Werner 1912-

PERSONAL: Born March 23, 1912, in Halberstadt, Germany; immigrated to United States, 1940; son of Gustav (a merchant) and Zipora (Petuchowski) Levi; married Ilse Steuermann, July 22, 1936; children: Antonia Judith, Matthew David. *Education:* Attended University of Geneva, 1930, University of Paris, 1930, University of Berlin, 1930-31, University of Heidelberg, 1932, and University

of Frankfurt, 1932-33; University of Fribourg, D.J., 1934; University of Minnesota, M.A., 1943, Ph.D., 1944. *Politics:* Independent. *Religion:* Jewish. *Avocational interests:* Music (violin), carpentry.

ADDRESSES: Home—2400 Sonoma St., Honolulu, Hawaii. *Office*—625 Porteus Hall, 2424 Maile Way, University of Hawaii, Honolulu, Hawaii 96822.

CAREER: University of Minnesota, Minneapolis, instructor, 1944-45, assistant professor, 1945-48, associate professor, 1948-51, professor of political science, 1951-63; University of Hawaii, Honolulu, professor of political science, 1963—, senior specialist at East-West Center, 1967. Visiting professor at University of Melbourne, 1947, University of Marburg, 1948, Delhi University, 1950, and Graduate Institute of International Studies in Geneva, 1958-59. Fulbright professor at Australian National University, 1955, and University of Munich, 1966-67. Carnegie visiting professor at University of Hawaii, 1961. Visiting lecturer at other universities in Denmark, Netherlands, Australia, Malaya, India, Germany, France, and Japan.

AWARDS, HONORS: International essay contest prize, Committee for Economic Development, 1958; American Institute of Indian Studies research fellow in India, 1965; Outstanding Achievement Award, University of Minnesota, 1985; Excellence in Teaching Award, College of Social Science, University of Hawaii.

WRITINGS:

American-Australian Relations, University of Minnesota Press, 1947.
Fundamentals of World Organization, University of Minnesota Press, 1950.
Free India in Asia, University of Minnesota Press, 1952.
Modern China's Foreign Policy, University of Minnesota Press, 1953.
Australia's Outlook on Asia, Michigan State University Press, 1958, reprinted, Greenwood Press, 1979.
The Challenge of World Politics in South and Southeast Asia, Prentice-Hall, 1968.
Religion and Political Development: A Theoretical Analysis, East-West Center, 1968.
The US-USSR-China Triangle, Centre d'etude du Sud-Est Asiatique et de l'Extreme-Orient, 1969.
International Politics: Foundations of the System, University of Minnesota Press, 1974.
Law and Politics in the International Society, Sage Publications, 1976, published as *International Law and International Politics,* 1976.
Contemporary International Law: A Concise Introduction, Westview, 1979, 2nd edition, 1991.
The Coming End of War, Sage Publications, 1981.

From Alms to Liberation: The Catholic Church, the Theologians, Poverty and Politics, Praeger, 1989.

Also author of book chapters. Contributor of numerous articles to periodicals, including *American Political Science Review, Far Eastern Quarterly, Journal of Asian Studies,* and *Political Science Quarterly.*

*   *   *

LEVINE, Philip 1928-

PERSONAL: Born January 10, 1928, in Detroit, MI; son of A. Harry (a businessman) and Esther Gertrude (a bookseller; maiden name, Priscoll) Levine; married Frances Artley (an actress and costumer), July 4, 1954; children: Mark, John, Theodore Henri. *Education:* Wayne University (now Wayne State University), A.B., 1950, A.M., 1954; University of Iowa, M.F.A., 1957. *Politics:* Anarchist. *Religion:* Anarchist.

ADDRESSES: Home—4549 North Van Ness Ave., Fresno, CA 93704. *Office*—Department of English, California State University, Fresno, CA 93710; (autumn) Department of English, Tufts University, Medford, MA 02155.

CAREER: Poet. Worked at "a succession of stupid jobs" in Detroit, MI, during the early 1950s, for companies including Chevy Gear and Axle, Detroit Transmission, and Wyandotte Chemical; University of Iowa, Iowa City, member of faculty, 1955-57; California State University, Fresno, professor of English, 1958—; Tufts University, Medford, MA, professor of English, 1981 —. Elliston Professor of Poetry, University of Cincinnati, 1976; poet-in-residence, National University of Australia, Canberra, summer, 1978; visiting professor of poetry, Columbia University, 1978, 1981, 1984, New York University, 1984 and 1991, and Brown University, 1985; teacher at Squaw Valley Writers Community, Bread Loaf, and Midnight Sun. Has read his poetry at the Library of Congress, Poetry Center of San Francisco, Pasadena Art Gallery, Guggenheim Museum, Princeton University, Massachusetts Institute of Technology, University of Michigan, University of California, Stanford University, Wayne State University, University of Iowa, San Francisco State University, Harvard University, Yale University, Brown University, and other schools. Chair of literature board, National Endowment for the Arts, 1984-85.

AWARDS, HONORS: Stanford University poetry fellowship, 1957; Joseph Henry Jackson Award, San Francisco Foundation, 1961, for manuscript "Berenda Slough and Other Poems" (later published as *On the Edge,* 1963); Chaplebrook Foundation grant, 1969; National Endowment for the Arts grants, 1969, 1970 (refused), 1976, 1981, 1987; named outstanding lecturer, California State University, Fresno, 1971; named outstanding professor, California State University System, 1972; Frank O'Hara Prize, *Poetry,* 1973; National Institute of Arts and Letters grant, 1973; award of merit, American Academy of Arts and Letters, 1974; Frank O'Hara Prize and Levinson Prize, *Poetry,* 1974; Guggenheim fellowships, 1974, 1981; Harriet Monroe Memorial Prize for Poetry, University of Chicago, 1976; Lenore Marshall Award for Best American Book of Poems, 1976, for *The Names of the Lost;* American Book Award for Poetry, 1979, for *Ashes: Poems New and Old;* National Book Critics Circle Prize, 1979, for *Ashes* and *7 Years from Somewhere;* notable book award, American Library Association, 1979, for *7 Years from Somewhere; Selected Poems* nominated for *Los Angeles Times* Book Prize, 1984; Golden Rose Award, New England Poetry Society, 1985; Ruth Lilly Award, Modern Poetry Association and American Council for the Arts, 1987, "in recognition of outstanding achievement"; Elmer Holmes Bobst Award, New York University, 1990, for "a life in poetry"; *Los Angeles Times* Book Prize, and National Book Award for Poetry, both 1991, both for *What Work Is.*

WRITINGS:

POEMS

On the Edge, limited edition, Stone Wall Press, 1961, 2nd edition, 1963.

Silent in America: Vivas for Those Who Failed, limited edition, Shaw Avenue Press (Iowa City), 1965.

Not This Pig, Wesleyan University Press, 1968.

5 Detroits, Unicorn Press, 1970.

Thistles: A Poem Sequence, limited edition, Turret Books (London), 1970.

Pili's Wall, Unicorn Press, 1971, revised edition, 1980.

Red Dust, illustrated with prints by Marcia Mann, Kayak, 1971.

They Feed They Lion, Atheneum, 1972.

1933, Atheneum, 1974.

New Season (pamphlet), Graywolf Press (Port Townsend, WA), 1975.

On the Edge and Over: Poems Old, Lost, and New, Cloud Marauder, 1976.

The Names of the Lost, limited edition, Windhover Press (Iowa City), 1976, 2nd edition, Atheneum, 1976.

7 Years from Somewhere, Atheneum, 1979.

Ashes: Poems New and Old, Atheneum, 1979.

One for the Rose, Atheneum, 1981.

Selected Poems, Atheneum, 1984.

Sweet Will, Atheneum, 1985.

A Walk with Tom Jefferson, Knopf, 1988.

New Selected Poems, Knopf, 1991.

What Work Is, Knopf, 1991.

OTHER

(Editor with Henri Coulette) *Character and Crisis: A Contemporary Reader,* McGraw, 1966.

(Editor and translator with Ernesto Trejo) Jaime Sabines, *Tarumba: The Selected Poems of Jaime Sabines,* Twin Peaks Press, 1979.

Don't Ask (collection of interviews with Levine), University of Michigan Press, 1979.

(Editor with Ada Long, and translator) Gloria Fuertes, *Off the Map: Selected Poems,* Wesleyan University Press, 1984.

(Co-editor with D. Wojahn and B. Henderson) *The Pushcart Prize XI,* Pushcart Press, 1986.

(Editor) John Keats, *The Essential Keats,* Ecco Press, 1987.

Also author of introduction, Dennis Sampson, *Forgiveness,* Milkweed Editions, 1990. Contributor of poems to numerous anthologies, including *Midland,* Random House, 1961; *New Poets of England and America,* Meridian, 1962; *Poet's Choice,* Dial, 1962; *American Poems,* Southern Illinois University Press, 1964; *Naked Poetry,* Bobbs-Merrill, 1969. Contributor of poems to periodicals, including *New Yorker, Poetry, New York Review of Books, Hudson Review, Paris Review,* and *Harper's.* Also narrator of sound recordings, *The Poetry and Voice of Philip Levine,* Caedmon, 1976, and *Hear Me,* Watershed Tapes.

WORK IN PROGRESS: A work of fiction, "for the first time in twenty years," and a book of essays, most of which are already published.

SIDELIGHTS: Poet Philip Levine "is a large, ironic Whitman of the industrial heartland," who, according to Edward Hirsch in *New York Times Book Review,* should be considered "one of our quintessentially urban poets." The son of Russian-Jewish immigrants, Levine was born and raised in industrial Detroit and acquired a political awareness early. As a young boy in the midst of the Great Depression, he listened to his elders discuss the political "isms" and was fascinated by the events of the Spanish Civil War. His heroes were not only those individuals who struggled against fascism and the state but ordinary folks who worked at hopeless jobs simply to stave off poverty. Joan Taylor writes in the *Dictionary of Literary Biography:* "Levine met his enemy in the gray arenas of industrialism, . . . of factory hum and stink, vacant lots, junkyards, and railroad tracks. . . . Levine's hero is the lonely individual who tries and often fails within this big industrial machine."

While working in the auto plants of Detroit during the 1950s, Levine resolved "to find a voice for the voiceless," he told *CA.* "I saw that the people that I was working with . . . were voiceless in a way," he explains in *Detroit Magazine.* "In terms of the literature of the United States they

weren't being heard. Nobody was speaking for them. And as young people will, you know, I took this foolish vow that I would speak for them and that's what my life would be. And sure enough I've gone and done it. Or I've tried anyway. . . . I just hope I have the strength to carry it all the way through." For more than three decades, Levine has spoken for the working men and women of America's industrial cities.

In *Hudson Review,* Vernon Young finds that Levine "has never acknowledged the claim of any society save that of the bluecollar dispossessed, the marginal and crunched for whom he has elected to be the evangelist and spokesman." Herbert Leibowitz, in a *New York Times Book Review* article on Levine's award-winning collection *Ashes: Poems New and Old,* comments: "Levine has returned again and again in his poems to the lives of factory workers trapped by poverty and the drudgery of the assembly line, which breaks the body and scars the spirit." However, the speaker in Levine's poems "is never a blue-collar caricature," argues Richard Tillinghast in his *New York Times Book Review,* "but someone with brains, feelings and a free-wheeling imagination that constantly fights to free him from his prosaic environment."

In addition to concentrating on the working class in his work, Levine has paid tribute to the Spanish anarchist movement of the 1930s, especially in *The Names of the Lost.* According to Leibowitz, "Though he was too young to fight in that war, it embodies for him the historical exemplum: a people's uprising that succeeded, quixotically, for a few rare days in hinting at what a genuine egalitarian society might be." Charles Molesworth explains in *The Fierce Embrace* that Levine connected the Spanish revolutionaries with Detroit's laboring class during a brooding stay in Barcelona: "Both cities are built on the backs of sullen, exploited workers, and the faded revolution in one smolders like the blunting, racist fear in the other." As Leibowitz sums up, "The poet's 'Spanish self,' as he calls it, is kin to his Detroit self. Both bear witness to the visionary ideal destroyed."

Levine's concentration on the negative aspects of working class life has led many critics to describe his work as dark, brooding, and without solace. However, in *Cry of the Human* Ralph J. Mills Jr. notes that a certain resigned acceptance of the harshness of industrial life leads Levine to "an acceptance of pain and the admission that failure, defeat, and imperfection —but not surrender!—are unavoidable." Levine is extremely sensitive to people who feel trapped in their jobs or their lives, and his portraits can't help but convey this feeling of doom. *Time's* Paul Gray, for instance, calls Levine's speakers "guerillas, trapped in an endless battle long after the war is lost." This sense of defeat is particularly strong when the poet recalls scenes from his Detroit childhood, where the grey bulk of unemployment and violence colored his life.

Despite its painful quality, Levine's verse displays a certain joyfulness, a sense of victory-in-defeat, suggests Marie Borroff. Writing in the *Yale Review,* she describes the title poem of *They Feed They Lion* as "a litany celebrating, in rhythms and images of unflagging, piston-like force, the majestic strength of the oppressed, rising equally out of the substances of the poisoned industrial landscape and the intangibles of humiliation." Hirsch finds that while anger and indignation lie at the core of Levine's poetry, his later poems "have developed a softer edge while maintaining their brooding intensity." Mazzocco asserts that Levine is "affectionate in his hate, hard in his compassion," and fully aware of "the twilit other world where the negative and the positive seem to be twins of the same coin, where the poet is both victor and victim, and at times blessed because he is both." And Richard Hugo comments in the *American Poetry Review:* "Levine's poems are important because in them we hear and we care." Though Levine's poems tell of despair, pain, and inadequacy, Hugo feels that they still hold out the hope that we can triumph over sadness through language and song. Because Levine has kept alive in himself "the impulse to sing," Hugo concludes that Levine "is destined to become one of the most celebrated poets of the time."

W. S. Di Piero asserts in *Commonweal* that Levine's consistent desire to trumpet the cause of the common man sometimes "risks a kind of melodrama," which tends to weaken the impact of his verse. In the *New York Times Book Review,* Robert Pinsky says that "it must be admitted that Levine's work is uneven and that its failing is the maudlin, . . . the locking of tone into a flaw or groove, running there without the capacity for modulation of emotion: a single, sustained whine, piercing but not penetrating." Di Piero, however, believes "that in Levine's case this is a flaw of a high order, commensurate with his high ambition." Pinsky qualifies his criticism as well, stating that "Levine has earned and undertaken the hardness of high standards."

Levine's poetry for and about the common man is distinguished by simple diction and a rhythmic narrative style—by what Pinsky calls "the strength of a living syntax." In an *American Poetry Review* appraisal of *Ashes* and *7 Years from Somewhere,* Dave Smith notes that in Levine's poems "the language, the figures of speech, the narrative progressions are never so obscure, so truncated as to forbid less sophisticated readers. Though he takes on the largest subjects of death, love, courage, manhood, loyalty, etc., he brings the mysteries of existence down into the ordinarily inarticulate events and objects of daily life." "Levine's poetic world values reality above all else," Robert D. Spector remarks in the *Saturday Review,* "a reality

that is reinforced by his earthy language, colloquial syntax, and natural rhythms." Molesworth believes that Levine's work reflects the mistrust of language that characterizes the laboring people of whom he writes. Therefore, rather than compressing multiple meanings into individual words and phrases, and balancing their tonal and semantic qualities, as in traditionally conceived poetry, Levine's simple narratives work to reflect the concrete and matter-of-fact speech patterns of working people. Taylor describes this aspect of Levine's work as a concern with what is "*out there*" rather than the more typical "postmodernist concern with words as the process by which one perceives what is out there." Levine himself, in an interview with Calvin Bedient in *Parnassus,* defines his "ideal poem" as one in which "no words are noticed. You look through them into a vision of . . . the people, the place."

Several critics have faulted Levine for the very reliance on narrative descriptions of realistic situations that are his hallmark. Finding Levine to be too realistic, Clayton Eshleman claims in a *Los Angeles Times* review of *Selected Poems* that "the literal perspective admits only a single actor in a single life scene." Because Levine's poetic stance "boils down to: This is what happened to me and this is what I am," Eshleman concludes that more imaginative poetic devices such as association, word play, and ambiguity would be alien in his verse. Helen Vendler thinks that this lack of traditional poetic devices makes Levine "simply a memoir-writer in prose who chops up his reminiscent paragraphs into short lines," and asks in her *New York Review of Books* appraisal of *One for the Rose,* "Is there any compelling reason why it should be called poetry?" This objection to Levine's verse originates in "the primarily narrative nature" of his poems, says Taylor, who concludes that "Levine may now be approaching the solution more closely than ever in his growing concern with his language and his lines as they reflect his poetic vision." Thomas Hackett, in his *Village Voice* review of *A Walk with Tom Jefferson,* argues that, rather than being a weakness, Levine's "strength is the declarative, practically journalistic sentence. He is most visual and precise when he roots his voice in hard, earthy nouns."

Levine has also been criticized, as Leibowitz puts it, for "digging for gold in a nearly exhausted vein." "Some have said he has written the same poem for years, that he lacks variety and vision," Smith comments. "True, his vision is such a relentless denunciation of injustice that he has occasionally engaged in reductive oversimplifications." Smith believes that despite this objection and others, Levine's poetry is "nearly a national treasure." According to Jack Anderson in *Prairie Schooner,* "Levine achieves a calm resolution, . . . one devoid of easy sentimentality and consonant with his flinty perceptions." "When he focuses on the private pains and social ills of others, his best poems oblige us to cry with him," Alan Helms states in the *Partisan Review.*

Levine's ability to craft deeply affecting poems has long been his hallmark, and he is among the few contemporary poets who write convincingly about working people without being condescending. "His poems are personal, love poems, poems of horror, poems about the experiencing of America," Stephen Spender writes in the *New York Review of Books.* And Joyce Carol Oates says in the *American Poetry Review,* "He is one of those poets whose work is so emotionally intense, and yet so controlled, so concentrated, that the accumulative effect of reading a number of his related poems can be shattering." "I really think he is extraordinary," Oates concludes, "a visionary of our dense, troubled mysterious time."

BIOGRAPHICAL/CRITICAL SOURCES:

BOOKS

Buckley, Christopher, *Stranger to Nothing: On the Poetry of Philip Levine,* University of Michigan Press, 1991.

Contemporary Literary Criticism, Gale, Volume 2, 1974, Volume 4, 1975, Volume 5, 1976, Volume 9, 1978, Volume 14, 1980.

Levine, Philip, *Don't Ask,* University of Michigan Press, 1979.

Mills, Ralph J., Jr., *Cry of the Human,* University of Illinois Press, 1975.

Molesworth, Charles, *The Fierce Embrace: A Study of Contemporary American Poetry,* University of Missouri Press, 1979.

Taylor, Joan, *Dictionary of Literary Biography,* Volume 5: *American Poets since World War II,* Gale, 1980.

PERIODICALS

American Poetry Review, November, 1972; May, 1973; March, 1974; May, 1974; May, 1977; November, 1979.

Antioch Review, spring/summer, 1977.

Carleton Miscellany, fall, 1968.

Chicago Tribune Book World, August 5, 1984.

Commonweal, October 12, 1979.

Detroit Magazine, February 26, 1978.

Georgia Review, spring, 1980.

Harper's, January, 1980.

Hudson Review, winter, 1979-80.

Kenyon Review, fall, 1989.

Los Angeles Times, September 10, 1984.

Los Angeles Times Book Review, October 21, 1984.

Nation, February 2, 1980.

New Leader, January 17, 1977; August 13, 1979.

New York Review of Books, April 25, 1968; September 20, 1973; April 3, 1975; December 17, 1981.

New York Times, May 29, 1985.

New York Times Book Review, July 16, 1972; February 20, 1977; October 7, 1979; September 12, 1982; August 5, 1984.

New York Times Magazine, February 3, 1980.

Parnassus, fall/winter, 1972; fall/winter, 1974; fall/winter, 1977; spring/summer, 1978.

Poetry, July, 1972; March, 1975; August, 1977; December, 1980; December, 1989.

Prairie Schooner, winter, 1974.

Saturday Review, June 1, 1968; March 11, 1972; September 7, 1977.

Sewanee Review, spring, 1976.

Shenandoah, summer, 1972.

Time, June 25, 1979.

Times Literary Supplement, September 11, 1981; July 2, 1982.

Village Voice Literary Supplement, May, 1982; July 19, 1988.

Virginia Quarterly Review, autumn, 1972.

Western Humanities Review, autumn, 1972.

Yale Review, autumn, 1972; autumn, 1980.

—*Sketch by Tom Pendergast*

*   *   *

LEVINSON, Riki

PERSONAL: Born in Brooklyn, NY; daughter of Samuel E. (a jewelry designer and cantor) and Anna S. (an insurance broker; maiden name, Blau) Friedberg; married Morton Levinson (an attorney; deceased), March 7, 1944; children: Gerry L. (daughter). *Education:* Cooper Union School of Arts and Sciences, B.A., 1943. *Religion:* Jewish. *Avocational interests:* Natural history, especially animal behavior; architecture, particularly old homes and ancient cultures; the sea.

ADDRESSES: Home—230 East 50th St., Apt. 7A, New York, NY 10022.

CAREER: Free-lance designer, 1945-70; Western Publishing Co., Inc., New York City, design and manufacturing manager of Education Division, 1970-72; E. P. Dutton, New York City, art director, 1972-86, assistant publisher and art director, 1986-87, associate publisher and art director of children's books, 1987-91; consultant art director and editor, 1991—.

MEMBER: American Institute of Graphic Arts, Authors Guild, Authors League of America, Cooper Union Alumni Association.

AWARDS, HONORS: Numerous graphic awards as a free-lance designer and art director; *Watch the Stars Come Out* was named a notable book by the American Library Association, a Children's Editors Choice by *Booklist,* and a *Redbook* Top Ten Picture Book, and received a Parents' Choice Award for literature from the Parents' Choice Foundation, all 1985, and was a "Reading Rainbow" feature on PBS-Television, 1986; *Watch the Stars Come Out*, 1985, *I Go With My Family to Grandma's*, 1986, *DinnieAbbieSister-r-r!*, 1987, and *Our Home Is the Sea*, 1988, were all named Notable Children's Trade Books in the field of social studies by the joint committee of the National Council for the Social Studies and the Children's Book Council; *I Go With My Family to Grandma's* was named one of Child Study Association of America's Children's Books of the Year, 1986, and a Jefferson Cup Award honor book in the Field of U.S. History and Historical Fiction from the Virginia Library Association, 1987; Georgia Children's Book Award nomination, University of Georgia—College of Education, for *DinnieAbbieSister-r-r!*

WRITINGS:

JUVENILE FICTION

Watch the Stars Come Out, illustrated by Diane Goode, Dutton, 1985.
I Go With My Family to Grandma's, illustrated by Goode, 1986.
Touch! Touch!, illustrated by True Kelley, Dutton, 1987.
DinnieAbbieSister-r-r!, illustrated by Helen Cogancherry, Bradbury, 1987.
Our Home Is the Sea, illustrated by Dennis Luzak, Dutton, 1988.
(Reteller) *The Emperor's New Clothes*, illustrated by Robert Byrd, Dutton, 1991.
Me Baby!, illustrated by Marilyn Hafner, Dutton, 1991.

ADAPTATIONS: "Watch the Stars Come Out" (filmstrip with cassette; audiocassette), Miller-Brody, 1986; *I Go with My Family* has also been adapted as a filmstrip.

Watch the Stars Come Out has been translated into Spanish.

WORK IN PROGRESS: Boys Here—Girls There, and *Country Dawn to Dusk*.

SIDELIGHTS: Having grown up in a family with two older brothers and two younger brothers, Riki Levinson once told *CA:* "I write about family. Family is the most important part of my life, and I find it a warm and personal experience to write about it. It is reassuring, to me, that children don't change, no matter when they live." Commenting on *DinnieAbbieSister-r-r!*, *Horn Book* reviewer Nancy Vasilakis asserted that "Warm family scenes, Jewish traditions lovingly evoked, and the sense of a simpler time characterize this quiet, richly-flavored story."

The author enjoyed geometry and creative writing in high school. However, she attended college on an art scholarship, graduated in 1943, and later commented that "Until September of 1983 I had never written a story since high school. One day I told my husband that I had an idea for a story but that I didn't know how to write. And he said, 'Don't worry about writing—just put it down. . . .' When the words and sounds fill my head, and I can't stop myself, I sit down and write."

BIOGRAPHICAL/CRITICAL SOURCES:

BOOKS

Something about the Author, Volume 52, Gale, 1988.

PERIODICALS

Porte, Barbara Ann, review of *DinnieAbbieSister-r-r!, New York Times Book Review,* March 29, 1987, p. 26.
Vasilakis, Nancy, review of *DinnieAbbieSister-r-r!, Horn Book,* July/August 1987, pp. 459-460.

*   *   *

LEWIS, Francine
    See WELLS, Helen

*   *   *

LIGHTNER, Robert P(aul) 1931-

PERSONAL: Born April 4, 1931, in Cleona, PA; son of Ernest A. and Edith (Miller) Lightner; married Pearl Hostetter, July 27, 1952; children: Nancy Kay, Nadine Pearl, Natalie Sue. *Education:* Baptist Bible Seminary, Johnson City, NY, Th.B., 1955; Dallas Theological Seminary, Th.M., 1959, Th.D., 1964; Southern Methodist University, M.L.A., 1972. *Politics:* Republican.

ADDRESSES: Home—2449 Wildoak Cir., Dallas, TX 75528. *Office*—Dallas Theological Seminary, 3909 Swiss Ave., Dallas, TX 75204.

CAREER: Ordained minister of Baptist Church, 1968. Grace Baptist Church, DeQueen, AR, pastor, 1956-57; Baptist Bible Seminary, Johnson City, NY, instructor, 1959-61, assistant professor, 1964-66, associate professor of systematic theology, 1967-68, head of department, 1964-66; Dallas Theological Seminary, Dallas, TX, assistant professor, 1968-74, associate professor, 1974-84, professor of systematic theology, 1984—.

MEMBER: Evangelical Theological Society, Near East Archaeological Society.

WRITINGS:

Neo-Liberalism, Regular Baptist Press, 1959.

Neo-Evangelicalism, Regular Baptist Press, 1959.

The Tongues Tide, Empire State Baptist, 1964.

Speaking in Tongues and Divine Healing, Regular Baptist Press, 1965.

The Savior and the Scriptures, Presbyterian & Reformed Publishing, 1966.

The Death Christ Died: A Case for Unlimited Atonement, Regular Baptist Press, 1967.

Triumph through Tragedy, Baker Press, 1969.

Church Union: A Layman's Guide, Regular Baptist Press, 1971.

The First Fundamental: God, Thomas Nelson, 1973.

Heaven for Those Who Can't Believe, Regular Baptist Press, 1977.

Truth for the Good Life, Accent Books, 1978.

Bible Knowledge Commentary (on *Epistle to the Philippians*), Victor Books, 1983.

Evangelical Theology: A Survey and Review, Baker Book, 1985.

The Last Days Handbook, Thomas Nelson, 1990.

Sin, the Savior & Salvation, Thomas Nelson, 1991.

Also contributor to *Walroord: A Tribute,* Moody, 1982.

*   *   *

LIMB, Sue 1946-
(Sue Porter)

PERSONAL: Born September 12, 1946, in Hitchin, Hertfordshire, England; daughter of Lewis Wilfred (a civil servant) and Margaret Winifred (a teacher) Limb; married Roy Sydney Porter (an historian), August 15, 1970 (divorced September, 1982); married Johannes Nickolaas Maria Vriend (a composer and conductor), March 21, 1984. *Education:* Newnham College, Cambridge, B.A. (with honors), 1968, graduate study, 1968-72.

ADDRESSES: Agent—June Hall, 5th Floor, The Chambers, Chelsea Harbour, Lots Rd., London SW10 0XF, England.

CAREER: St. Ivo School, St. Ives, England, teacher of English and drama, 1974-77; writer, 1977—.

MEMBER: Royal Horticultural Society, Migraine Association, Campaign for Nuclear Disarmament, Amnesty International, Greenpeace.

AWARDS, HONORS: Best children's radio program award, Sony Corp., 1983, for "Big and Little" comedy series.

WRITINGS:

(With Patrick Cordingley) *Captain Oates: Soldier and Explorer* (biography), Batsford, 1982.

Up the Garden Path (comic novel), Bodley Head, 1984.

Love Forty (autobiography), Bantam, 1986.

Love's Labours (novel), Corgi Books, 1989.

Dulcie Domum's Bad Housekeeping, Fourth Estate, 1990.

UNDER NAME SUE PORTER

Action Pack: Situations for Drama, Edward Arnold, 1977.

Problem Page, Edward Arnold, 1980.

Monkey (play; adapted from a Chinese myth), produced in London, 1981.

Play It Again, Edward Arnold, 1984.

OTHER

Also author of comedy series for British Broadcasting Corp. (BBC), including "Big and Little" (for children), 1983, and "The Wordsmiths at Gorsemere: An Everyday Story of Towering Genius," 1985; also author of comedy television series "Up the Garden Path," based on her novel of the same title. Contributor to *Guardian.*

SIDELIGHTS: Sue Limb told *CA:* "We must laugh to stay healthy. Most of my writing is comedy. I'm extremely happy to try to make people laugh. Comedy can contain profound truths about human life, and it can be a political and moral weapon. It demands enormous discipline. Like many comedians, I am rather a solitary creature and, if not exactly misanthropic, I am quite hermit-like.

"My first book, the biography of Captain Oates, grew out of a childhood fascination with Scott's 1913 expedition to the Antarctic and the light it throws on English social history. Assisted by Oates's octogenarian sister, I wrote the book in 1964, when I was eighteen. The manuscript remained unpublished, however, until Major Patrick Cordingley, an officer in Oates's regiment, appeared and proposed he help me with a rewrite. Cordingley provided much invaluable military research, and we rewrote the book together in 1980.

"The comic novel *Up the Garden Path* and my comic series 'The Wordsmiths of Gorsemere' much more closely represent the type of work I am doing now. I find it impossible to resist cracking jokes, however bad they may be. I am also aware that the harder I try to write great literature the more abysmally I fail. My modest aim now is to amuse and perhaps comment sardonically *en passant* upon the more outrageous absurdities of life.

"It is interesting that some people are surprised to find that there are funny women, but it is no surprise to the women. Male publishers, editors, and the male-dominated literary establishment are now eagerly promoting any woman with pretensions toward comedy, in an attempt to make up for centuries of conditioning which only a few brave geniuses (such as Jane Austen) have been defiant enough to ignore. Even Jane Austen apologized for her own incisive intelligence and malicious wit—a sure sign of the depth and pervasiveness of the male prejudice against female satire. At last, things seem to be changing."

BIOGRAPHICAL/CRITICAL SOURCES:

BOOKS

Limb, Sue, *Love Forty* (autobiography), Bantam, 1986.

PERIODICALS

Times, December 8, 1990, p. 25.
Times Literary Supplement, April 13, 1984, p. 396.

* * *

LLOYD EVANS, Barbara 1924-

PERSONAL: Born April 5, 1924, in Malvern, Worcestershire, England; daughter of Ernest Joseph (a civil servant) and Edith Mary (Kings) Bowen; married Gareth Lloyd Evans (a lecturer and writer), August 29, 1949 (died October, 1984); children: Lynette, Jeremy, Martin. *Education:* University of Birmingham, B.A., 1944, M.A., 1946; Oxford University, teaching diploma, 1945.

ADDRESSES: Home—1 Hunts Rd., Stratford-upon-Avon, Warwickshire CV37 7JG, England.

CAREER: University of Birmingham, Birmingham, England, lecturer in English, 1959-76; teacher of English in high school in England, 1960—.

WRITINGS:

(Editor) *Something to Offer: A Selection of Contemporary Prose and Verse,* Blackie & Son, 1968.
(With husband, Gareth Lloyd Evans) *Everyman's Companion to Shakespeare,* Dent, 1978.
(With Lloyd Evans) *Everyman's Companion to the Brontes,* Dent, 1980, published in United States as *The Scribner Companion to the Brontes,* Scribner, 1982.
(Editor) Lloyd Evans, *The Upstart Crow: An Introduction to Shakespeare's Plays,* Dent, 1982.
(Editor) *Plays by Gareth Lloyd Evans,* Dent, 1982.
(Editor with Lloyd Evans) *Plays in Review 1956-80: British Drama and the Critics,* Methuen, 1985.
(Editor) *Five Hundred Years of English Poetry: Chaucer to Arnold,* Peter Bedrick, 1989, published in England as *The Batsford Book of English Poetry: Chaucer to Arnold,* Batsford, 1989.

Also author of the plays *The Three Bears* and *Chirp the Bold Bad Chick,* both broadcast by the British Broadcasting Corp. (BBC). Contributor of stories, poems, and articles to adult and juvenile magazines.

WORK IN PROGRESS: The Poems of Emily Bronte, for Batsford; plays for the BBC; poems; children's stories.

SIDELIGHTS: Barbara Lloyd Evans told *CA:* "At this time of my life, my greatest pleasures are reading and listening to music. I particularly enjoy reading poetry—working on the anthology, *Five Hundred Years of English Poetry,* was great fun and very rewarding, as is my present project (Emily Bronte's poetry)—and, even more, I enjoy, as I always have done, trying to write it. At present the relearning of Latin and my attempts to translate Latin verse into English verse is exercising my wits and patience. I also seek out modern foreign novels (in translation, of course!) as I believe I learn more about other countries from their novels than from the travel books written about them."

* * *

LOHAFER, Susan 1942-
(Susan Kuhlmann)

PERSONAL: Born June 23, 1942, in Goshen, NY. *Education:* Radcliffe College, A.B., 1964; Stanford University, M.A., 1966; New York University, Ph.D., 1970.

ADDRESSES: Office—Department of English, University of Iowa, Iowa City, IO 52240.

CAREER: Ohio State University, Columbus, visiting assistant professor of English, 1972-73; University of Iowa, Iowa City, assistant professor, 1973-77, associate professor, 1977—, professor of English, 1983—.

MEMBER: Modern Language Association of America.

WRITINGS:

(Under name Susan Kuhlmann) *Knave, Fool, and Genius: The Confidence Man as He Appears in Nineteenth-Century American Fiction,* University of North Carolina Press, 1973.
Coming to Terms with the Short Story, Louisiana State University Press, 1983.

Contributor of short stories to literary quarterlies.*

* * *

LOXSMITH, John
See BRUNNER, John (Kilian Houston)

* * *

LUNDWALL, Sam J(errie) 1941-

PERSONAL: Born February 24, 1941, in Stockholm, Sweden; son of Thore (a master mechanic) and Sissi

(Kuehn) Lundwall; married Ingrid Olofsdotter, June 16, 1972; children: Karin Beatrice Christina. *Education:* University of Stockholm, E.E., 1967.

ADDRESSES: Home—Storskogsvaegen 19, S-161 39 Bromma, Sweden. *Office*—Box 17030, S-16117 Bromma, Sweden. *Agent*—Spectrum Literary Agency, 60 East 42nd St., New York, NY 10017.

CAREER: SSTA (Stockholm Technical Night-School), Stockholm, Sweden, electronics engineer, 1956-60; University of Stockholm, Stockholm, professional photographer, 1964-67; Christer Christian Photographic School, Fox Amphoux, France, professional photographer, 1967-68; Swedish Broadcasting Corp., Stockholm, television producer, 1968-69; Askild & Kaernekull Foerlag AB (publishers), Stockholm, editor for science fiction, 1970-73; Delta Foerlags AB (publishers), Bromma, Sweden, president, 1973-80. Judge, John W. Campbell Award, World Science Fiction Convention. Has directed television films; made short animated film based on his song, "Waltz with Karin"; has recorded his own songs for Philips and Knaeppupp recording companies; has appeared on television, radio, and film as singer and artist throughout Scandinavia. *Military service:* Swedish Air Force, 1960-61; electronics engineer.

MEMBER: World Science Fiction Society (president; member of board, European society), Science Fiction Writers of America.

AWARDS, HONORS: "Waltz with Karin" was named Sweden's best short film by the Swedish Film Institute, 1967; Alvar award as Scandinavia's leading science fiction author from Futura (science fiction organization), 1971; Finnish Designer's Award for best book cover, 1971; Harrison Award, 1983; Karel Award, 1990.

WRITINGS:

Bibliografi oever science fiction och fantasy (title means "Bibliography of Science Fiction and Fantasy"), Fiktiva, 1964, revised edition, 1984.
Visor i vaar tid (title means "Songs of Our Times"), Sonora, 1965.
Science Fiction: Fraan begynnelsen till vaara dagar (title means "Science Fiction: From the Beginning to Our Days"), Svergies Radio, 1969.
Alice's World, Ace Books, 1971.
No Time for Heroes, Ace Books, 1971.
Science Fiction: What It's All About, Ace Books, 1971.
Bernhard the Conqueror, DAW Books, 1973.
Den Fantastiska romanen (textbooks on fantastic stories and novels), four volumes, Gummessons Grafiska, 1973-74.
King Kong Blues, DAW Books, 1974.

Bibliografi oever science fiction och fantasy: 1741-1971, Lindqvist, 1974.
What Is Science Fiction?, Meulenhoff, 1974.
Bernhards magiska sommar (title means "Bernhards Magic Summer"), Lindqvist, 1975.
Alltid lady MacBeth (title means "Always Lady Mac-Beth"), Delta, 1975.
Moerkrets furste (title means "The Prince of Darkness"), Delta, 1975.
Mardroemmem (title means "The Nightmare"), Lindqvist, 1976.
Gaest i Frankensteins hus (title means "Guest in the House of Frankenstein"), Delta, 1976.
Utopia-Dystopia, Delta, 1977.
Science fiction pa svenska (title means "Science Fiction in Swedish"), Delta, 1977.
Science Fiction: An Illustrated History, Grosset, 1978.
Faengelsestaden (title means "The Prison City"), Norstedt, 1978.
Flicka i foenster vid vaerldens kant (title means "The Girl in the Window at the Edge of the World"), Norstedt, 1980.
Crash, Norstedt, 1982.
Tiden och Amelie (title means "Time and Amelie"), Fakta & Fantasi, 1985.
Gestalter i sten (title means "Figures in Stone"), Fakta & Fantasi, 1988.
Frukost bland ruinerna (title means "Breakfast among the Ruins"), Fakta & Fantasi, 1988.
Vasja Ambartsurian, Fakta & Fantasi, 1991.

Editor on numerous science fiction anthologies and of collected works of Jules Verne; translator into Swedish of more than 150 novels and of poems by Francois Villon and George Brassens; author, producer, and director of television script from Frank Robinson's *The Hunting Season* and of other television films; author and composer of more than two hundred songs. Contributor of articles to Swedish edition of *Help!* and *Mad.* Contributor of cartoons to Swedish edition of *Popular Photography.* Editor-in-chief of *Jules Verne—Magasinet,* 1972—; editor, *Science Fiction-Serien,* 1973.

WORK IN PROGRESS: Ygor, a novel.

*   *   *

LYNGSTAD, Sverre   1922-

PERSONAL: Born April 30, 1922, in Norway; son of Bernhard Theodor (a farmer) and Anna Lyngstad; married Alexandra Halina Danielewicz, May 15, 1953 (divorced, 1975); children: Karin. *Education:* University of Oslo, B.A. (English), 1943, B.A. (history), 1946; University of Washington, Seattle, M.A., 1949; New York University, Ph.D., 1960.

ADDRESSES: Home—180 Park Row, 5-C, New York, NY 10038. *Office*—Department of Humanities, New Jersey Institute of Technology, 323 Martin Luther King Blvd., Newark, NJ 07102.

CAREER: City College (now City College of the City University of New York), New York City, lecturer in English, 1954-55; Hofstra College (now University), Long Island, NY, instructor in English, 1955-60; Queens College of the City of New York (now Queens College of the City University of New York), Flushing, NY, instructor in English, 1960-62; New Jersey Institute of Technology, Newark, NJ, assistant professor, 1962-65, associate professor, 1965-68, professor, 1968-89, distinguished professor of English, 1989—. Consultant on Scandinavian literature to Grove Press, New York, 1963-68.

MEMBER: International Society for the Study of Time, Modern Language Association of America (executive committee for Scandinavian literature), American Comparative Literature Association, Society for the Advancement of Scandinavian Study, American-Scandinavian Foundation, Ibsen Society of America.

AWARDS, HONORS: Publication grant, Royal Norwegian Consulate General, 1981, for *Norway: Review of National Literatures;* translation fellowship grant, National Endowment for the Arts, 1984; *Choice* Outstanding Academic Book citation, 1985, for *Sigurd Hoel's Fiction;* St. Olav Medal from King Olav V of Norway, 1987; translation grant from Norwegian Cultural Council, 1987, for *Adam's Diary,* and 1990, for *The Troll Circle;* named "Scandinavian of the Month" by *Scandinavian-American Bulletin,* May, 1988; Harlan J. Perlis award for excellence in research, New Jersey Institute of Technology, 1990.

WRITINGS:

(Translator) Sven Hassel, *Comrades of War,* Fawcett, 1963.
(Translator with wife, Alexandra Halina Lyngstad) Lev Tolstoy, *Childhood, Boyhood, and Youth,* Washington Square Press, 1968.
(With A. H. Lyngstad) *Ivan Goncharov,* Twayne, 1972.
(Translator) Erik Krag, *Dostoevsky: The Literary Artist,* Humanities, 1976.
Jonas Lie, Twayne, 1977.
(Editor and contributor) *Norway: Review of National Literatures,* Volume 12, Griffon House, 1983.
Sigurd Hoel's Fiction: Cultural Criticism and Tragic Vision, Greenwood Press, 1984.
(Translator) Knut Faldbakken, *Adam's Diary,* University of Nebraska Press, 1988.

(Translator) Sigurd Hoel, *The Troll Circle,* University of Nebraska Press, 1991.

Contributor to *Approaches to Teaching "A Doll's House,"* edited by Yvonne Shafer, Modern Language Association of America, 1984, *Women Writers of the Seventeenth Century,* edited by Katharina M. Wilson and Frank J. Warnke, University of Georgia Press, 1989, *Encyclopedia of Poetry and Poetics* (revised as *Princeton Encyclopedia of Poetry and Poetics*), *Encyclopedia of World Literature, Princeton Handbook of Poetic Terms, Dictionary of Scandinavian Literature,* and *Twentieth-Century Literary Criticism.* Also translator from the Norwegian of poetry and drama. Has presented papers at professional meetings, and served as a reviewer for publishers, learned journals, and the National Endowment for the Humanities. Contributor to periodicals, including *Alternative Futures, Bitterroot, Edda, International Poetry Review, Moving Out, Newark Review, Scandinavian Review, Scandinavian-American Bulletin, Scandinavica, Scandinavian Studies,* and *Webster Review.*

SIDELIGHTS: Sverre Lyngstad told *CA:* "As an expatriate Norwegian thoroughly acculturated before arrival in the U.S.A., I have always found myself in-between, straddling cultures. If you come from a small country, you feel elated to become part of a more varied and exciting cultural scene; yet the urge to return to your origins, not just for visits to family and friends but—in a richly sensuous phrase from Henry James's *The Sense of the Past*—to 'remount the stream of time, really bathe in its upper and more natural waters' will sooner or later become irresistible. Eventually, wherever you happen to be physically, in your mind you are in two places at once, *there* as well as *here.* In my own case the virtual presence of the past grew so strong that I had no choice but to objectify it, give it some concrete expression. So, instead of doing what an English Ph.D. usually does, I came increasingly to write about and do translations from Norwegian literature. I became a mediator between different language areas and literary cultures."

"While this sounds, uncomfortably, like fate, I have tried to make sense of it through an idea of the Czech writer Milan Kundera, as stated in the *New York Times Book Review:* 'A literature aimed solely at a national readership . . . fails to fulfill its basic function. . . . In our times we must consider a book that is unable to become a part of the world's literature to be non-existent.' If Kundera is right, literary mediation is important indeed. I see my work as critic and translator as a modest effort to help writers on the fringe, geographically and linguistically, become part of world literature, thereby escaping the limbo of non-existence."

BIOGRAPHICAL/CRITICAL SOURCES:

PERIODICALS

New York Times Book Review, January 8, 1978.

M

MABRY, Donald J(oseph) 1941-

PERSONAL: Born April 21, 1941, in Atlanta, GA; son of Jerry Leon and Eunice (Harris) Mabry; married Susan Johnston, July 28, 1962 (divorced, October, 1986); children: Scott Landon, Mark Robert. *Education:* Kenyon College, B.A. (cum laude), 1963; Bowling Green State University, M.Ed., 1964; University of Florida, graduate study, 1965; Syracuse University, Ph.D., 1970.

ADDRESSES: Home—206 Hiwassee Dr., Starkville, MS 39759. *Office*—Drawer AS, College of Arts and Sciences, Mississippi State University, Mississippi State, MS 39762.

CAREER: St. Johns River Junior College, Palatka, FL, member of social science faculty, 1964-67; Mississippi State University, Mississippi State, assistant professor, 1970-74, associate professor, 1974-80, professor of history, 1980—, College of Arts and Sciences, Budget and Research Director, 1991—. University of Kansas, special assistant to the chancellor, 1978-79.

MEMBER: Latin American Studies Association, Conference on Latin American History, Committee on Mexican Studies, Social Science History Association, Southeastern Conference on Latin American Studies.

AWARDS, HONORS: Newberry Library fellow, 1975; American Council on Education fellow for academic administration, 1978-79; Mellon fellow for academic administration, 1978-79; Center for International Security and Strategic Studies, senior fellow, 1981—; Mississippi State University Alumni Award for excellence in teaching, research, and service, 1987.

WRITINGS:

Mexico's Accion Nacional: A Catholic Alternative to Revolution, Syracuse University Press, 1973.

(Contributor) Harold E. Davis and others, editors, *Revolutionaries: Traditionalists and Dictators in Latin America,* Cooper Square, 1973.

(With Robert J. Shafer) *Neighbors—Mexico and the United States: Wetbacks and Oil,* Nelson-Hall, 1981.

The Mexican University and the State: Student Conflicts, 1910-1971, Texas A&M University Press, 1982.

(Editor and contributor) *The Latin American Narcotics Trade and U.S. National Security,* Greenwood Press, 1989.

Contributor to *Encyclopedia Americana Annual,* Grolier, 1973—. Contributor to periodicals, including: *The Americas, Business History Review, History of Education Quarterly, Journal of Inter-American Studies and World Affairs, Journal of Church and State, New Scholar, Sociology, Western Political Quarterly.*

*   *   *

MAESTRO, Betsy C(rippen) 1944-

PERSONAL: Surname is pronounced "Ma-*es*-troh"; born January 5, 1944, in New York, NY; daughter of Harlan R. (a design consultant) and Norma (in education; maiden name, Sherman) Crippen; married second husband, Giulio Maestro (a free-lance writer and book illustrator), December 16, 1972; children: (second marriage) Daniela Marisa, Marco Claudio. *Education:* Southern Connecticut State College, B.S., 1964, M.S., 1970. *Politics:* Democrat. *Avocational interests:* Reading, cooking, photography, travel, art, antiques.

ADDRESSES: Home and office—74 Mile Creek Rd., Old Lyme, CT 06371.

CAREER: Deer Run School, East Haven, CT, kindergarten and first grade teacher, 1964-75; writer, 1975—.

MEMBER: National Education Association, Connecticut Education Association.

AWARDS, HONORS: Fat Polka-Dot Cat and Other Haiku was selected one of Child Study Association of America's Children's Books of the Year, 1976, as was *The Story of the Statue of Liberty,* 1987; *Lambs for Dinner* was selected a Children's Choice by the International Reading Association and the Children's Book Council, 1979; American Library Association Notable Book citation, 1981, for *Traffic: A Book of Opposites,* 1987, for *A More Perfect Union,* and 1991, for *The Discovery of the Americas; Ferryboat* was selected a Notable Children's Trade Book in the Field of Social Studies by the National Council for Social Studies and the Children's Book Council, 1986.

WRITINGS:

JUVENILE PICTURE BOOKS; ALL ILLUSTRATED BY HUSBAND, GIULIO MAESTRO

A Wise Monkey Tale (Junior Literary Guild selection), Crown, 1975.

Where Is My Friend? A Word Concept Book (Junior Literary Guild selection), Crown, 1976.

Fat Polka-Dot Cat and Other Haiku, Dutton, 1976.

In My Boat, Crowell, 1976.

Harriet Goes to the Circus: A Number Concept Book, Crown, 1977.

Busy Day: A Book of Action Words (Junior Literary Guild selection), Crown, 1978.

Lambs for Dinner, Crown, 1978.

On the Go: A Book of Adjectives (Junior Literary Guild selection), Crown, 1979.

Harriet Reads Signs and More Signs: A Word Concept Book (Junior Literary Guild selection), Crown, 1981.

Traffic: A Book of Opposites, Crown, 1981.

The Key to the Kingdom, Harcourt, 1982.

The Guessing Game, Grosset, 1983.

Just Enough Rosie, Grosset, 1983.

(With Ellen DelVecchio) *Big City Port,* Four Winds, 1983.

On the Town: A Book of Clothing Words, Crown, 1983.

Around the Clock with Harriet: A Book about Telling Time, Crown, 1984.

Harriet the Elephant, Crown, 1984.

Harriet at Play, Crown, 1984.

Harriet at School, Crown, 1984.

Harriet at Home, Crown, 1984.

Harriet at Work, Crown, 1984.

Camping Out: A Book of Action Words, Crown, 1984.

Through the Year with Harriet, Crown, 1985.

Ferryboat (Junior Literary Guild selection), Crowell, 1986.

The Story of the Statue of Liberty, Lothrop, 1986.

The Grab-Bag Party, Golden Press, 1986.

The Pandas Take a Vacation, Golden Press, 1986.

The Perfect Picnic, Golden Press, 1987.

The Travels of Freddie and Frannie Frog, Golden Press, 1987.

A More Perfect Union: The Story of Our Constitution, Lothrop, 1987.

Dollars and Cents for Harriet, Crown, 1988.

Taxi: A Book of City Words, Clarion, 1989.

Temperature and You, Lodestar, 1989.

Snow Day, Scholastic, 1989.

Delivery Van: Words for Town and Country, Clarion Books, 1990.

A Sea Full of Sharks, Scholastic, 1990.

Temperature and You, Lodestar, 1990.

The Discovery of the Americas, Lothrop, 1991.

The Discovery of the Americas Activity Book, Lothrop, 1992.

All Aboard Overnight, Clairion, 1992.

How Apples Grow, HarperCollins, 1992.

Bike Trip, HarperCollins, 1992.

Take a Look at Snakes, Scholastic, 1992.

WORK IN PROGRESS: Books about money, leaves, bats, American exploration, government, and religion.

SIDELIGHTS: Betsy C. Maestro, a former kindergarten and first grade teacher, and her husband Giulio Maestro, a former advertising designer, have been creating concept books for young children since 1975. Explaining her approach to writing, Maestro told interviewer Marguerite Feitlowitz: "I concentrate on what a given concept means in the life of a young child. For example, I recently did a book on temperature. What are the ways in which a child thinks about temperature? He may consider it in terms of the weather, what garments to wear, whether to go outdoors. The child may associate 'temperature' with fever and being sick. Our concept books are not intended solely to impart information. Of course they accomplish this aim, but always in a way that is closely allied with children's experiences and emotional life."

Maestro once told *CA:* "When you work on picture books for young children, it is impossible to think of the story or concept separately from the illustration. The two are one. I have been very lucky in that, since Giulio and I work together most of the time, we both have a lot of input in each area and give each other suggestions and advice. I loved books as a child (and still do!) and enjoy sharing the ones I write with all the children we know." The Maestros' books have been praised for their simplicity, clarity, and colorful graphics. Reviewing *On the Town: A Book of Clothing Words,* a *School Library Journal* contributor writes: "Readers familiar with the Maestro style will recognize the fresh, good-natured approach and the resourcefulness which make *On the Town* click."

"Writing for children is much more difficult than most people realize," Maestro told Feitlowitz. "Picture-book authors are often asked, 'Do you plan to write for grownups?' as though that would signify 'graduation' for us. In my opinion, most people who ask the question have a low regard for children. I have no interest in writing for adults. A good children's book is like poetry: you have comparatively few words to work with, and your text must sing. It must work equally well read silently as read aloud. I love the challenge of taking something complicated and expressing it simply. I hope that my books help give children an early love of reading and learning."

BIOGRAPHICAL/CRITICAL SOURCES:

BOOKS

Contemporary Authors New Revision Series, Volume 23, Gale, 1988, pp. 259-260.

Maestro, Betsy C., in an interview with Margarite Feitlowitz, *Something about the Author,* Volume 59, Gale, 1990.

Ward, Martha E., and Dorothy A. Marquardt, *Authors of Books for Young People,* supplement to the second edition, Scarecrow, 1979.

PERIODICALS

Day (New London, CT), November 6, 1986, p. C1.
School Library Journal, November, 1983.

*   *   *

MAESTRO, Giulio 1942-

PERSONAL: Given name is pronounced "*Jool*-yoh," and surname, "Ma-*es*-troh"; born May 6, 1942, in New York, NY; son of Marcello (a writer) and Edna (Ten Eyck) Maestro; married Betsy Crippen (a teacher and writer), December 16, 1972; children: Daniela Marisa, Marco Claudio. *Education:* Cooper Union, B.F.A., 1964; further study in printmaking at Pratt Graphics Center, 1965-68. *Avocational interests:* Reading, painting, woodworking, gardening, making jam, travel.

ADDRESSES: Home and office—74 Mile Creek Rd., Old Lyme, CT 06371.

CAREER: Design Organization, Inc. (advertising design), New York City, assistant to art director, 1965-66; Warren A. Kass Graphics, Inc. (advertising design), New York City, assistant art director, 1966-69; free-lance writer and book illustrator, 1969—. *Exhibitions:* Society of Illustrators Show, New York City, 1968, 1974; American Institute of Graphic Arts, New York, NY, 1974; Art Director's Club, New York, NY, 1978, 1982; Fourteenth Exhibition of Original Pictures of International Children's

Books, Japan, 1979. Works represented in the De Grummond Collection, University of Southern Mississippi, and the Kerlan Collection, University of Minnesota.

AWARDS, HONORS: From Petals to Pinecones was selected one of Child Study Association of America's Children's Books of the Year, 1969, as were *Two Good Friends, Number Ideas through Pictures, Gray Duck Catches a Friend,* and *Milk, Butter and Cheese,* all 1974, *Oil, A Pack of Riddles, The Great Ghost Rescue,* and *Who Said Meow?,* all 1975, *Fat Polka-Dot Cat and Other Haiku,* 1976, *Train Whistles, Razzle-Dazzle Riddles, Space Telescope,* and *Hurricane Watch,* all 1986, and *Sunshine Makes the Seasons,* and *The Story of the Statue of Liberty,* both 1987; *The Tortoise's Tug of War* was included in the American Institute of Graphic Arts Children's Book Show, 1971-72, as was *Three Kittens,* 1973-74; Merit Award from the Art Directors Club of New York, 1978, for *Harriet Goes to the Circus; Harriet Goes to the Circus* was selected a Children's Choice by the International Reading Association and the Children's Book Council, 1978, as were *Lambs for Dinner,* 1979, *Fiddle with a Riddle,* 1980, *Moonkey,* 1982, and *Halloween Howls,* 1984; *Fish Facts and Bird Brains* was selected an outstanding Science Trade Book for Children by the National Science Teachers Association, 1985; *Ferryboat* was selected a Notable Children's Trade Book in the Field of Social Studies by the National Council for Social Studies and the Children's Book Council, 1986.

WRITINGS:

JUVENILE; ALL SELF-ILLUSTRATED

(Reteller) *The Tortoise's Tug of War,* Bradbury, 1971.
The Remarkable Plant in Apartment 4, Bradbury, 1973, published in England as *The Remarkable Plant in Flat No. 4,* Macmillan, 1974.
One More and One Less: A Number Concept Book (Junior Literary Guild selection), Crown, 1974.
Leopard Is Sick, Greenwillow, 1978.
Leopard and the Noisy Monkeys, Greenwillow, 1979.
A Raft of Riddles, Dutton, 1982.
Halloween Howls: Riddles That Are a Scream, Dutton, 1983.
Riddle Romp, Clarion, 1983.
What's a Frank Frank? Tasty Homograph Riddles, Clarion, 1984.
Razzle-Dazzle Riddles, Clarion, 1985.
What's Mite Might? Homophone Riddles to Boost Your Word Power, Clarion, 1986.
Riddle Roundup, Clarion, 1989.
More Halloween Howls, Dutton, 1992.

ILLUSTRATOR; JUVENILE PICTURE BOOKS BY WIFE, BETSY C. MAESTRO

A Wise Monkey Tale (Junior Literary Guild selection), Crown, 1975.

Where Is My Friend? A Word Concept Book (Junior Literary Guild selection), Crown, 1976.

Fat Polka-Dot Cat and Other Haiku, Dutton, 1976.

In My Boat, Crowell, 1976.

Harriet Goes to the Circus: A Number Concept Book, 1977.

Busy Day: A Book of Action Words (Junior Literary Guild selection), Crown, 1978.

Lambs for Dinner, Crown, 1978.

On the Go: A Book of Adjectives (Junior Literary Guild selection), Crown, 1979.

Harriet Reads Signs and More Signs: A Word Concept Book (Junior Literary Guild selection), Crown, 1981.

Traffic: A Book of Opposites (ALA Notable Book), Crown, 1981.

The Key to the Kingdom, Harcourt, 1982.

The Guessing Game, Grosset, 1983.

Just Enough Rosie, Grosset, 1983.

(Ellen DelVecchio, co-author) *Big City Port,* Four Winds, 1983.

On the Town: A Book of Clothing Words, Crown, 1983.

Around the Clock with Harriet: A Book about Telling Time, Crown, 1984.

Harriet the Elephant, Crown, 1984.

Harriet at Play, Crown, 1984.

Harriet at School, Crown, 1984.

Harriet at Home, Crown, 1984.

Harriet at Work, Crown, 1984.

Camping Out: A Book of Action Words, Crown, 1984.

Through the Year with Harriet, Crown, 1985.

Ferryboat (Junior Literary Guild selection),Crowell, 1986.

The Story of the Statue of Liberty, Lothrop, 1986.

The Grab-Bag Party, Golden Press, 1986.

The Pandas Take a Vacation, Golden Press, 1986.

The Perfect Picnic, Golden Press, 1987.

The Travels of Freddie and Frannie Frog, Golden Press, 1987.

A More Perfect Union: The Story of Our Constitution (ALA Notable Book), Lothrop, 1987.

Dollars and Cents for Harriet, Crown, 1988.

(And coauthor) *Taxi: A Book of City Words,* Clarion, 1989.

(And coauthor) *Temperature and You,* Lodestar, 1989.

Snow Day, Scholastic, 1989.

(And coauthor) *Delivery Van: Words for Town and Country,* Clarion Books, 1990.

A Sea Full of Sharks, Scholastic, 1990.

The Discovery of the Americas (ALA Notable Book), Lothrop, 1991.

The Discovery of the Americas Activity Book, Lothrop, 1992.

All Aboard Overnight, Clarion, 1992.

How Apples Grow, HarperCollins, 1992.

Bike Trip, HarperCollins, 1992.

Take a Look at Snakes, Scholastic, 1992.

ILLUSTRATOR; JUVENILE

Joseph J. McCoy, *Swans,* Lothrop, 1967.

Millie McWhirter, *A Magic Morning with Uncle Al,* Collins & World, 1969.

Katherine Cutler, *From Petals to Pinecones: A Nature Art and Craft Book,* Lothrop, 1969.

Rudyard Kipling, *The Beginning of the Armadillos,* St. Martin's, 1970.

Cutler, *Creative Shellcraft,* Lothrop, 1971.

(With others) Richard Shaw, editor, *The Fox Book,* Warner, 1971.

Elyse Sommer, *The Bread Dough Craft Book,* Lothrop, 1972.

Franklyn M. Branley, *The Beginning of the Earth,* Crowell, 1972, revised edition, 1987.

Jo Phillips, *Right Angles: Paper-Folding Geometry,* Crowell, 1972.

E. Sommer, *Designing with Cutouts: The Art of Decoupage,* Lothrop, 1973.

E. Sommer, *Make It with Burlap,* Lothrop, 1973.

(With others) Shaw, editor, *The Cat Book,* Warner, 1973.

Roma Gans, *Millions and Millions of Crystals,* Crowell, 1973.

Mirra Ginsburg, *What Kind of Bird Is That?,* Crown, 1973.

Ginsburg, *Three Kittens* (Junior Literary Guild selection), Crown, 1973.

Vicki Kimmel Artis, *Gray Duck Catches a Friend,* Putnam, 1974.

Tony Johnston, *Fig Tale,* Putnam, 1974.

Judy Delton, *Two Good Friends* (ALA Notable Book; Junior Literary Guild selection), Crown, 1974.

Harry Milgrom, *Egg-Ventures* (Junior Literary Guild selection), Dutton, 1974.

Mannis Charosh, *Number Ideas through Pictures,* Crowell, 1974.

Carolyn Meyer, *Milk, Butter and Cheese: The Story of Dairy Products,* Morrow, 1974.

Sarah Riedman, *Trees Alive,* Lothrop, 1974.

Melvin Berger, *The New Air Book,* Crowell, 1974.

(With others) Shaw, editor, *The Bird Book,* Warner, 1974.

Eva Ibbotson, *The Great Ghost Rescue,* Walck, 1975.

Maria Polushkin, *Who Said Meow?* (Junior Literary Guild selection), Crown, 1975.

William R. Gerler, compiler, *A Pack of Riddles,* Dutton, 1975.

Gans, *Oil: The Buried Treasure,* Crowell, 1975.

John Trivett, *Building Tables on Tables: A Book about Multiplication,* Crowell, 1975.

E. Sommer and Joellen Sommer, *A Patchwork, Applique, and Quilting Primer,* Lothrop, 1975.

(With others) Shaw, editor, *The Mouse Book,* Warner, 1975.

Sigmund Kalina, *How to Make a Dinosaur,* Lothrop, 1976.

Gans, *Caves,* Crowell, 1976.

Berger, *Energy from the Sun,* Crowell, 1976.

Delton, *Two Is Company,* Crown, 1976.

Delton, *Three Friends Find Spring* (Junior Literary Guild selection), Crown, 1977.

Delton, *Penny-Wise, Fun-Foolish,* Crown, 1977.

Isaac Asimov, *Mars, the Red Planet,* Lothrop, 1977.

Eva Barwell, *Make Your Pet a Present,* Lothrop, 1977.

Caroline Anne Levine, *Knockout Knock Knocks,* Dutton, 1978.

Gaile Kay Haines, *Natural and Synthetic Poisons,* Morrow, 1978.

J. Trivett and Daphne Trivett, *Time for Clocks,* Crowell, 1979.

Vicki Cobb, *More Science Experiments You Can Eat,* Lippincott, 1979.

Joanne E. Bernstein, *Fiddle with a Riddle: Write Your Own Riddles* (Junior Literary Guild selection), Dutton, 1979.

Asimov, *Saturn and Beyond,* Lothrop, 1979.

Ruth Lerner Perle and Susan Horowitz, adapters, *Little Red Riding Hood with Benjy and Bubbles,* Holt, 1979.

Perle and Horowitz, adapters, *The Fisherman and His Wife with Benjy and Bubbles,* Holt, 1979.

Perle and Horowitz, adapters, *Rumpelstiltskin with Benjy and Bubbles,* Holt, 1979.

Perle and Horowitz, adapters, *Sleeping Beauty with Benjy and Bubbles,* Holt, 1979.

Ginsburg, *Kitten from One to Ten,* Crown, 1980.

Delton, *Groundhog's Day at the Doctor,* Parents Magazine Press, 1980.

Boris Arnov, *Water: Experiments to Understand It,* Lothrop, 1980.

Andrea G. Zimmerman, *The Riddle Zoo,* Dutton, 1981.

Mike Thaler, *Moonkey,* Harper, 1981.

Marvin Terban, *Eight Ate: A Feast of Homonym Riddles,* Clarion Books, 1982.

Terban, *In a Pickle: And Other Funny Idioms,* Clarion, 1983.

Levine, *The Silly Kid Joke Book,* Dutton, 1983.

Seymour Simon, *Dinosaurs Are the Biggest Animals That Ever Lived: And Other Wrong Ideas You Thought Were True,* Lippincott, 1984.

Branley, *Comets,* Crowell, 1984.

Terban, *I Think I Thought and Other Tricky Verbs,* Clarion, 1984.

Helen Roney Sattler, *Fish Facts and Bird Brains: Animal Intelligence,* Dutton, 1984.

Branley, *Space Telescope: A Voyage into Space Book,* Crowell, 1985.

Branley, *Sunshine Makes the Seasons,* revised edition, Crowell, 1985 (Maestro was not associated with the earlier editions).

Sattler, *Train Whistles: A Language in Code,* revised edition, Lothrop, 1985.

Terban, *Too Hot to Hoot: Funny Palindrome Riddles,* Clarion, 1985.

Branley, *Hurricane Watch,* Crowell, 1986.

Terban, *Your Foot's on My Feet! And Other Tricky Nouns,* Clarion, 1986.

Terban, *Mad as a Wet Hen and Other Funny Idioms,* Clarion, 1987.

Branley, *Rockets and Satellites,* revised edition, Crowell, 1987.

Terban, *Guppies in Tuxedos: Funny Eponyms,* Clarion, 1988.

Branley, *Tornado Alert!,* Crowell, 1988.

Terban, *Superdupers,* Clarion, 1989.

OTHER

Some of Maestro's work has been published in Germany, France, Spain, the Netherlands, England, and Japan.

SIDELIGHTS: Children's book author and illustrator Giulio Maestro once told *CA:* "I was born in New York City and lived in Greenwich Village most of my life. My family owned a house on Charlton Street, and I attended the Little Red School House from kindergarten through grade six. I started drawing and painting before I even went to school." Interviewed by Marguerite Feitlowitz, Maestro stated: "My boyhood idols were Walt Disney and ["Pogo" comic strip cartoonist] Walt Kelly, and I even wrote to the Disney studio and to Kelly personally. The Disney studio sent me illustrative material, and Walt Kelly wrote me a letter personally, saying 'If you really want to do this, you have to draw everyday. You really have to keep at it.' Enclosed was an original drawing as well. A letter from Walt Kelly—it's hard to put into words what a thrill that was for me. It lent weight to all the drawing I was doing."

Among the books illustrated by Maestro are those written by his wife, Betsy C. Maestro. In a statement appearing in *Junior Literary Guild,* Giulio Maestro mentioned some of the attention to detail featured in their concept-book collaborations: "The typeface used in *Busy Day* was chosen for clarity, and the overall format determined in two ways: the fairly small page size allows for a book that is easily managed by small hands; the unobtrusive border on each page confines each word-concept to that page, so that there can be no confusion."

Assessing his own skills, Maestro told Feitlowitz, "First and foremost I'm an illustrator." However, he still enjoys writing humorous works: "I don't fancy myself a great storyteller, but I love words and word play. . . . The riddle books are full of homonyms, puns, and plays-on-words, often fairly sophisticated. They're intended not only to be brainteasers to the reader, but also good ammunition for stumping friends. I'm happy that my publishers didn't attempt to lower the difficulty level of these books. One of my pet peeves is that too often educators and publishers expect too little of kids. The ability to use language effectively has to be nurtured. Young minds should be encouraged to think more complex thoughts and exposed to rich language in reading materials. I hope my word-play books, through humor in text and pictures, help children to take joy in the subtleties of language and word meanings."

BIOGRAPHICAL/CRITICAL SOURCES:

BOOKS

Contemporary Authors New Revision Series, Volume 23, Gale, 1988, pp. 260-261.
Kingman, Lee, and others, compilers, *Illustrators of Children's Books: 1967-1976,* Horn Book, 1978.
Maestro, Giulio, in an interview with Marguerite Feitlowitz, *Something about the Author,* Volume 59, Gale, 1990, pp. 119-128.
Ward, Martha E., and Dorothy A. Marquardt, *Illustrators of Books for Young People,* Scarecrow, 1975.

PERIODICALS

Day (New London, CT), November 6, 1986, p. C1.
Horn Book, April, 1972.
Junior Literary Guild, March, 1978.

*   *   *

MAISON, Della
See KATZ, Bobbi

*   *   *

MALLOWAN, Agatha Christie
See CHRISTIE, Agatha (Mary Clarissa)

*   *   *

MARCH, Carl
See FLEISCHMAN, (Albert) Sid(ney)

*   *   *

MARETH, Glenville
See GILBERT, Willie

MARINER, Scott
See POHL, Frederik

*   *   *

MARTIN, Patricia Miles   1899-1986
(Patricia A. Miles; Jerry Lane, Miska Miles, pseudonyms)

PERSONAL: Born November 14, 1899, in Cherokee, KS; died January 2, 1986, in San Mateo, CA; cremated, ashes scattered at sea; daughter of Thomas J. and Nellie Ada (White) Miles; married Edward Richard Martin (a real estate investor), October 24, 1942 (died, 1979). *Education:* Attended San Mateo College, 1965-66; attended University of Wyoming.

CAREER: Teacher in elementary schools in Denver, CO, and Arminto, WY, for four years during the 1930s. Writer of children's books.

MEMBER: Authors Guild, Authors League of America, Authors and Artists Workshop, Burlingame Writers Club.

AWARDS, HONORS: Children's Spring Book Festival Honor Book Award, 1959, for *The Pointed Brush;* *Mississippi Possum* was on the *New York Times* list of 75 recommended titles, 1965; Commonwealth Club of California Medal, 1971, American Library Association Honor Book Award, Christopher Medal, Woodward Park School Award, and Newbery honor book, all 1972, and Brooklyn Museum-Brooklyn Public Library Art Books for Children Citation, 1973, all for *Annie and the Old One;* New York Academy of Sciences Citation, 1973, for *Wharf Rat.*

WRITINGS:

Sylvester Jones and the Voice in the Forest, Lothrop, 1958.
The Pointed Brush (illustrated by Roger Duvoisin), Lothrop, 1959.
Chandler Chipmunk's Flying Lesson, and Other Stories, Abingdon, 1960.
The Little Brown Hen (illustrated by Harper Johnson), Crowell, 1960.
Suzu and the Bride Doll (illustrated by Kazue Mizumura), Rand McNally, 1960.
Happy Piper and the Goat (illustrated by Kurt Werth; Junior Literary Guild selection), Lothrop, 1960.
Benjie Goes into Business, Putnam, 1961.
The Raccoon and Mrs. McGinnis (illustrated by L. Weisgard), Putnam, 1961.
Show and Tell (illustrated by Tom Hamil), Putnam, 1962.
The Rice Bowl Pet (illustrated by Ezra J. Keats), Crowell, 1962.
The Lucky Little Porcupine (illustrated by L. Smith), Putnam, 1963.

The Birthday Present (illustrated by Margo Locke), Abingdon, 1963.

Little Two and the Peach Tree (illustrated by Joan Berg; Junior Literary Guild selection), Atheneum, 1963.

Calvin and the Cub Scouts (illustrated by T. Hamil), Putnam, 1964.

No, No, Rosina (illustrated by Earl Thollander), Putnam, 1964.

The Greedy One (illustrated by K. Mizumura; Junior Literary Guild selection), Rand McNally, 1964.

The Broomtail Bronc (illustrated by M. Locke), Abingdon, 1965.

Jump, Frog, Jump (illustrated by E. Thollander; Junior Literary Guild selection), Putnam, 1965.

The Bony Pony (illustrated by G. Dines), Putnam, 1965.

Rolling the Cheese (illustrated by Alton Raible), Atheneum, 1966.

The Pumpkin Patch (illustrated by T. Hamil), Putnam, 1966.

Sing, Sailor, Sing (illustrated by G. Booth), Golden Gate, 1966.

Mrs. Crumble and Fire Engine Number 7, Putnam, 1966.

Woody's Big Trouble (illustrated by Paul Galdone), Putnam, 1967.

Dolls from Cheyenne (illustrated by Don Almquist), Putnam, 1967.

Friend of Miguel (illustrated by Genial), Rand McNally, 1967.

Trina's Boxcar (illustrated by Robert L. Jefferson), Abingdon, 1967.

Grandma's Gun (illustrated by Robert Corey), Golden Gate, 1968.

A Long Ago Christmas (illustrated by Albert Orbaan), Putnam, 1968.

Kumi and the Pearl (illustrated by T. Hamil), Putnam, 1968.

One Special Dog (illustrated by Lucy Hawkinson and John Hawkinson; Junior Literary Guild selection), Rand McNally, 1968.

(With Theodore Clymer) *Stanley, the Dog Next Door, and Other Stories,* Ginn, 1969.

The Dog and the Boat Boy (illustrated by E. Thollander), Putnam, 1969.

Indians: The First Americans (nonfiction; illustrated by Robert Frankenberg), Parents Magazine Press, 1970.

The Eskimos: People of Alaska (nonfiction; illustrated by R. Frankenberg), Parents Magazine Press, 1970.

That Cat 1-2-3, Putnam, 1970.

Navajo Pet (illustrated by John Hamberger), Putnam, 1971.

There Goes the Tiger! (illustrated by T. Hamil), Putnam, 1971.

Chicanos: Mexicans in the United States (nonfiction; illustrated by R. Frankenberg), Parents Magazine Press, 1971.

Be Brave, Charlie (illustrated by Bonnie Johnson), Putnam, 1973.

Two Plays about Foolish People (illustrated by Gabriel Lisowski), Putnam, 1973.

(With Clymer) *May I Come In?,* Ginn, 1976.

BIOGRAPHIES

Abraham Lincoln (illustrated by G. Schrotter), Putnam, 1964.

Pocahontas (illustrated by P. Takajian), Putnam, 1964.

John Fitzgerald Kennedy (illustrated by Paul Frame), Putnam, 1965.

Daniel Boone (illustrated by G. Dines), Putnam, 1965.

Jefferson Davis (illustrated by S. Tamen), Putnam, 1966.

Andrew Jackson (illustrated by S. Tamer), Putnam, 1966.

Dolly Madison (illustrated by Unada), Putnam, 1967.

John Marshall (illustrated by S. Tamer), Putnam, 1967.

Jacqueline Kennedy Onassis (illustrated by P. Frame), Putnam, 1969.

James Madison, Putnam, 1970.

Zachary Taylor, Putnam, 1970.

Thomas Alva Edison (illustrated by Fermin Rocker), Putnam, 1971.

UNDER PSEUDONYM MISKA MILES

Kickapoo (illustrated by Wesley Dennis; Junior Literary Guild selection), Atlantic-Little, Brown, 1961.

Dusty and the Fiddlers (illustrated by Erik Blegvad), Atlantic-Little, Brown, 1962.

See a White Horse (illustrated by W. Dennis; Junior Literary Guild selection), Atlantic-Little, Brown, 1963.

Pony in the Schoolhouse (illustrated by E. Blegvad), Atlantic-Little, Brown, 1964.

Mississippi Possum (illustrated by John Schoenherr), Atlantic-Little, Brown, 1965.

Teacher's Pet (illustrated by Fen H. Lasell; Junior Literary Guild selection), Atlantic-Little, Brown, 1966.

Fox and the Fire (illustrated by J. Schoenherr; *Horn Book* honor list; ALA Notable Book), Atlantic-Little, Brown, 1966.

Rabbit Garden (illustrated by J. Schoenherr), Atlantic-Little, Brown, 1967.

The Pieces of Home (illustrated by Victor Ambrus; Junior Literary Guild selection), Atlantic-Little, Brown, 1967.

Uncle Fonzo's Ford (illustrated by Wendy Watson; Junior Literary Guild selection), Atlantic-Little, Brown, 1968.

Nobody's Cat (illustrated by J. Schoenherr; ALA Notable Book), Atlantic-Little, Brown, 1969.

Apricot ABC (illustrated by Peter Parnall), Atlantic-Little, Brown, 1969.

Hoagie's Rifle-Gun (illustrated by J. Schoenherr; Junior Literary Guild selection), Atlantic-Little, Brown, 1970.

Gertrude's Pocket (illustrated by Emily McCully; Junior Literary Guild selection), Atlantic-Little, Brown, 1970.

Eddie's Bear (illustrated by J. Schoenherr), Atlantic-Little, Brown, 1971.

Annie and the Old One (illustrated by P. Parnall; *Horn Book* honor list; ALA Notable Book; Junior Literary Guild selection), Atlantic-Little, Brown, 1971.

Wharf Rat (illustrated by J. Schoenherr), Atlantic-Little, Brown, 1972.

Somebody's Dog (illustrated by J. Schoenherr), Atlantic-Little, Brown, 1973.

Otter in the Cove (illustrated by J. Schoenherr), Atlantic-Little, Brown, 1974.

Tree House Town (illustrated by E. McCully), Atlantic-Little, Brown, 1975.

Swim, Little Duck (illustrated by Jim Arnosky; Junior Literary Guild selection), Atlantic-Little, Brown, 1976.

Aaron's Door (illustrated by Alan E. Cober), Atlantic-Little, Brown, 1976.

Chicken Forgets (illustrated by J. Arnosky), Atlantic-Little, Brown, 1976.

Small Rabbit (illustrated by J. Arnosky), Atlantic-Little, Brown, 1977.

Beaver Moon (illustrated by J. Schoenherr), Atlantic-Little, Brown, 1978.

Noisy Gander (illustrated by Leslie Morrill), Dutton, 1978.

Mouse Six and the Happy Birthday (illustrated by L. Morrill), Dutton, 1978.

Jenny's Cat (illustrated by W. Watson), Dutton, 1979.

This Little Pig (illustrated by L. Morrill), Dutton, 1980.

(With Ted Clymer) *Horse and the Bad Morning* (illustrated by L. Morrill), Dutton, 1982.

UNDER PSEUDONYM JERRY LANE

In the Zoo, Ginn, 1974.
Run!, Ginn, 1974.

OTHER

Martin's manuscripts are housed at the de Grummond Collection of the University of Southern Mississippi and at the Kerlan Collection of the University of Minnesota.

ADAPTATIONS: Annie and the Old One was adapted as a film by Greenhouse Films, 1976, and as a filmstrip with cassette and teacher's guide by Newbery Award Records, 1980.

SIDELIGHTS: Patricia Miles Martin wrote for young people about a variety of different cultures, people, and animals. Her books ranged from fiction to biographies and concerned Eskimoes, Indians, and Asian peoples, as well as those who live in the rural Midwest. Despite the diversity in her work, most of her inspiration came, as Martin once explained, from "the things that are most important to me—children, animals, birds. And the backgrounds that presently hover in my mind are my own—a wonderful Kansas farm, our neighborhood today, and a Navajo reservation."

Martin claimed that she became a writer quite by accident: "One day in 1957 we had a chair that needed upholstering, and I decided to attend a class in upholstery which was given at the College of San Mateo. When I went to enroll, the class was full. I walked by another classroom and looked in the door. There were a few empty desks there. It was a class in creative writing, and there was room for me. I found my desk and sat down to write."

Her first book was published in 1958, and from then on she wrote some one hundred further titles, many of which were chosen as American Library Association Notable Books, Junior Literary Guild selections, and *Horn Book* honor books. "I try to pace my stories," Martin explained. "First, I may write about that Midwest of mine, which takes me on a nice trip backward in time, and then I write about the Orient, which takes me across a sea. *Little Two and the Peach Tree* was written because I wanted to say that a picture is worth ten thousand words."

Martin wrote books in order, she once said, "to pass on to children the values I live by." To do this, she planned her stories very carefully: "Before I start a story, I must have one line—one thought that I consider important enough to share with my readers. Then, having that thought, I know where I'd like to set the story, and whether a boy or girl or an animal will be best suited to tell what I want to tell.

"As an example, I wanted to share this thought with my young readers: in times of emergency, enemies forget enmity. In connection with this particular thought, I traveled to Sonoma, where a devastating fire had swept the forests around the Valley of the Moon, and this area became the setting for *The Fox and the Fire,* in which natural enemies, the fox and the rabbit, travel together to escape the fire."

Martin was careful to make all the details in her books accurate. "I am a meticulous researcher in connection with each story," she explained. "(I write every day, sometimes starting as early as six o'clock in the morning, and work a minimum of six hours a day.) Even though the setting may not be definitely located in the text of the book, it is accurately and definitely located in my mind. The flower that I might mention will be correctly blooming there."

Annie and the Old One, winner of the Christopher Award and a Newbery honor book, tells the story of a young Navajo girl who confronts the imminent death of her grandmother. When her grandmother announces that she will die when Annie's mother finishes the rug she is weaving, Annie works to keep her mother away from her work. The reviewer for the *Washington Post Book World* called *Annie and the Old One* a "simple story" of "gentle restraint." Speaking of the book, Martin said: "I know I couldn't write a good novel. I'm not a person of many words. It's great that I do what I do."

BIOGRAPHICAL/CRITICAL SOURCES:

PERIODICALS

Book World, November 9, 1969.
Christian Science Monitor, May 4, 1967; November 2, 1967.
Detroit News, November 28, 1971.
New York Times Book Review, July 24, 1977; November 13, 1977.
Washington Post Book World, August 11, 1985, p. 13.
Young Readers Review, April, 1966; April, 1967.

* * *

MASON, Ernst
See POHL, Frederik

* * *

MAYNE, William (James Carter) 1928-
(Martin Cobalt, Charles Molin; Dynely James,
a joint pseudonym)

PERSONAL: Born March 16, 1928, in Kingston upon Hull, Yorkshire, England; son of William and Dorothy (Fea) Mayne. *Avocational interests:* Vintage cars, composing music, building on to his Yorkshire cottage.

ADDRESSES: Agent—David Higham Associates Ltd., 5-8 Lower John St., Golden Square, London W1R 4HA, England.

CAREER: Writer of books for children and young people.

AWARDS, HONORS: Carnegie Medal from British Library Association for best children's book of year, 1957, for *A Grass Rope.*

WRITINGS:

Follow the Footprints, illustrated by Shirley Hughes, Oxford University Press, 1953.

The World Upside Down, illustrated by Hughes, Oxford University Press, 1954.
A Swarm in May, illustrated by C. Walter Hodges, Oxford University Press, 1955, Bobbs-Merrill, 1957.
The Member of the Marsh, illustrated by Lynton Lamb, Oxford University Press, 1956.
Choristers' Cake, illustrated by Hodges, Oxford University Press, 1956, Bobbs-Merrill, 1958.
The Blue Boat, illustrated by Geraldine Spence, Oxford University Press, 1957, Dutton, 1960.
A Grass Rope, illustrated by Lamb, Oxford University Press, 1957, Dutton, 1962.
The Long Night, illustrated by D. J. Watkins-Pitchford, Basil Blackwell, 1957.
Underground Alley, illustrated by Marcia Lane Foster, Oxford University Press, 1958, Dutton, 1961.
(With R. D. Caesar, under joint pseudonym Dynely James) *The Gobbling Billy,* Dutton, 1959.
The Thumbstick, illustrated by Tessa Theobald, Oxford University Press, 1959.
Thirteen O'Clock, illustrated by Watkins-Pitchford, Basil Blackwell, 1959.
Over the Horizon; or, Around the World in Fifteen Stories, Duell, Sloan & Pearce, 1960.
The Rolling Season, illustrated by Christopher Brooker, Oxford University Press, 1960.
Cathedral Wednesday, illustrated by Hodges, Oxford University Press, 1960.
The Fishing Party, illustrated by Brooker, Hamish Hamilton, 1960.
Summer Visitors, illustrated by William Stobbs, Oxford University Press, 1961.
The Glass Ball, illustrated by Janet Duchesne, Hamish Hamilton, 1961, Dutton, 1962.
The Changeling, illustrated by Victor Adams, Oxford University Press, 1961, Dutton, 1963.
The Last Bus, illustrated by Margery Gill, Hamish Hamilton, 1962.
The Twelve Dancers, illustrated by Lamb, Hamish Hamilton, 1962.
The Man from the North Pole, illustrated by Prudence Seward, Hamish Hamilton, 1963.
On the Stepping Stones, illustrated by Seward, Hamish Hamilton, 1963.
Words and Music, illustrated by Lamb, Hamish Hamilton, 1963.
A Parcel of Tree, illustrated by Gill, Penguin, 1963.
Plot Night, illustrated by Duchesne, Hamish Hamilton, 1963, Dutton, 1968.
Water Boatman, illustrated by Anne Linton, Hamish Hamilton, 1964.
Sand, illustrated by Gill, Hamish Hamilton, 1964.
A Day without Wind, illustrated by Gill, Dutton, 1964.

Whistling Rufus, illustrated by Raymond Briggs, Hamish Hamilton, 1964, Dutton, 1965.

(Editor with Eleanor Farjeon) *The Hamish Hamilton Book of Kings*, illustrated by Victor Ambrus, Hamish Hamilton, 1964, published as *A Cavalcade of Kings*, Walck, 1965.

The Big Wheel and the Little Wheel, illustrated by Duchesne, Hamish Hamilton, 1965.

No More School, illustrated by Peter Warner, Hamish Hamilton, 1965.

(Editor with Farjeon) *A Cavalcade Queens*, illustrated by Ambrus, Walck, 1965, published in England as *The Hamish Hamilton Book of Queens*, Hamish Hamilton, 1965.

Pig in the Middle, illustrated by Mary Russon, Hamish Hamilton, 1965, Dutton, 1966.

(Under pseudonym Charles Molin) "Dormouse Tales" series, five books, illustrated by Leslie Wood, Hamish Hamilton, 1966.

Rooftops, illustrated by Russon, Hamish Hamilton, 1966.

Earthfasts, Hamish Hamilton, 1966, Dutton, 1967.

The Old Zion, illustrated by Gill, Hamish Hamilton, 1966, Dutton, 1967.

The Battlefield, illustrated by Russon, Dutton, 1967.

The Big Egg, illustrated by Gill, Hamish Hamilton, 1967.

(Compiler) *The Hamish Hamilton Book of Heroes*, illustrated by Krystyna Turska, Hamish Hamilton, 1967, published as *William Mayne's Book of Heroes*, Dutton, 1968.

The Toffee Join, illustrated by Hughes, Hamish Hamilton, 1968.

The Yellow Aeroplane, illustrated by Trevor Stubley, Hamish Hamilton, 1968.

The House on Fairmont, illustrated by Fritz Wegner, Dutton, 1968.

Over the Hills and Far Away, Hamish Hamilton, 1968, published as *The Hill Road*, Dutton, 1969.

(Compiler) *The Hamish Hamilton Book of Giants*, Hamish Hamilton, 1968, published as *William Mayne's Book of Giants*, Dutton, 1969.

Ravensgill, Dutton, 1970.

A Game of Dark, Dutton, 1971.

(Editor) *Ghosts*, Thomas Nelson, 1971.

Royal Harry, Hamish Hamilton, 1971, Dutton, 1972.

The Incline, Dutton, 1972.

Skiffy, illustrated by Nicholas Fisk, Hamish Hamilton, 1972.

(Under pseudonym Martin Cobalt) *The Swallows*, Heinemann, 1972, published as *Pool of Swallows*, Nelson, 1974.

The Jersey Shore, Dutton, 1973.

A Year and a Day, illustrated by Turska, Dutton, 1976.

Party Pants, illustrated by Joanna Stubbs, Knight, 1977.

It, Hamish Hamilton, 1977.

Max's Dream, Hamish Hamilton, 1977, Greenwillow Books, 1978.

While the Bells Ring, illustrated by Janet Rawlins, Hamish Hamilton, 1979.

Salt River Times, illustrated by Elizabeth Honey, Greenwillow Books, 1980.

The Mouse and the Egg, illustrated by Turska, Greenwillow Books, 1981.

The Patchwork Cat, illustrated by Nicola Bayley, Knopf, 1981.

Winter Quarters, J. Cape, 1982.

Skiffy and the Twin Planets, Hamish Hamilton, 1982.

All the King's Men, J. Cape, 1982, Delacorte, 1988.

The Mouldy, illustrated by Bayley, Random House, 1983.

Underground Creatures, Hamish Hamilton, 1983.

A Small Pudding for Wee Gowrie, illustrated by Martin Cottam, Macmillan, 1983.

The Yellow Book of Hob Stories, illustrated by Patrick Benson, Philomel Books, 1984.

The Blue Book of Hob Stories, illustrated by Benson, Putnam, 1984.

The Green Book of Hob Stories, illustrated by Benson, Putnam, 1984.

The Red Book of Hob Stories, illustrated by Benson, Putnam, 1984.

Drift, J. Cape, 1985, Delacorte, 1986.

Kelpie, J. Cape, 1987.

Tiger's Railway, illustrated by Juan Wijngaard, Walker, 1987.

The Blemyahs, illustrated by Wijngaard, Walker, 1987.

Gideon Ahoy!, Viking Kestrel, 1987, Delacorte, 1989.

The Farm that Ran Out of Names, J. Cape, 1989.

Antar and the Eagles, Doubleday, 1990.

"ANIMAL LIBRARY" SERIES

Come, Come to My Corner, Prentice-Hall, 1986.
Corbie, Prentice-Hall, 1986.
Tibber, Prentice-Hall, 1986.
Barnabas Walks, Prentice-Hall, 1986.
Lamb Shenkin, Prentice-Hall, 1987.
A House in Town, Prentice-Hall, 1987.
Leapfrog, Prentice-Hall, 1987.
Mousewing, Prentice-Hall, 1987.

OTHER

Contributor to periodicals. Composer of incidental music for *Holly from the Bongs*, 1965.

SIDELIGHTS: William Mayne is regarded by many to be one of the most important contemporary British authors of books for children and young people. Often described as uniquely gifted and extraordinarily talented, Mayne has written nearly one hundred books since his first book, *Follow the Footprints*, was published in 1953. During his impressive and sustained writing career, Mayne has been successful bridging genre and age groups by writing picture books for the very young and fantasy and mystery books for juveniles. However, Mayne is perhaps best known for his young adult novels. Considered a technically skilled writer and frequently praised for his originality in plot and style, Mayne describes his writing style as that of "an observer." "All I am doing," he explains to *CA*, "is looking at things now and showing them to myself when I was younger."

Although he was twenty-five years old when his first work was published, Mayne became interested in writing when he was about eight years old—just around the time he entered the Choir School at Canterbury on a scholarship. Raised in a family of seven—with three sisters and one brother, Mayne felt writing was one thing that was his alone and that he did not have to share. "I think I knew [writing] would be a good excuse for hiding among my own thoughts, away from the rest of the family," Mayne observes in an essay for *Third Book of Junior Authors*. "I think it is important for everybody to be able to get away from others. It is certainly important for me to be able to, but since I like being with other people too, and want them to know it, what I do when I am alone is think about other times and places, and write books about them. It shows me that when I am in my own withdrawn world I am still in the real one."

While writing was an important part of his life and a great emotional outlet, Mayne did not seriously consider writing as a viable career choice until after he left the Choir School. For several more years, Mayne studied and fine-tuned his writing style and technique until *Follow the Footprints* was accepted for publication.

Follow the Footprints is the tale of two British youngsters, Andrew and Caroline, and their hunt for a hidden treasure amidst the colorful countryside of Cumberland, England. Intrigued by local legends describing a mysterious treasure, the children attempt to track down the precious prize. During their search, the pair is caught up in a web of danger and suspense.

Follow the Footprints possesses three characteristics that can be found in many of Mayne's more well-read and loved stories, including his popular novels for young adult readers. By setting his stories in the countryside of England, incorporating legends and tales into the plot, and creating interesting and believable characters, Mayne writes novels that reviewers such as *Growing Point*'s Margery Fisher describe as "always surprising, new-minted and compelling." A contributor to *Junior Bookshelf* adds that Mayne's writing possesses "a superb sense of atmosphere, brilliant characterization and subtle observation, above all a poet's interest in the commonplaces of everyday life and an awareness of their cosmic significance."

Although a number of his works do contain similar fundamental elements, Mayne's books are by no means carbon copies of each other. A writer for the *Times Literary Supplement* held that "without going outside the familiar convention of seek-and-find adventure in an English country setting, William Mayne has quickly established himself as the most original good writer for children in our immediate time." And Hamish Fotheringham notes in *Junior Bookshelf* that Mayne's "first published story was *Follow the Footprints*, the story of a 'treasure hunt,' a motif which William Mayne had developed with freshness and originality in the majority of his books." Fotheringham goes on to state that "this framework of well described country setting, local legends, excellently drawn pen portraits, sparkling dialogues and a plot rich in incidents is used by the author in his other 'treasure hunt' stories. Framework is hardly the correct term. Variations on a theme would perhaps be a better description, for William Mayne has a poet's ear for the music of language—the sound as well as the sense."

By often locating many of his tales in quaint English country villages similar to his own home in Yorkshire, Mayne is writing about a region he knows well and loves. Mayne has lived his whole life in a part of England that is abundantly colorful and rich in tradition and he has successfully reflected its atmosphere and dialogue in novels such as *The Member of the Marsh*, *Earthfasts*, and *Ravensgill*. In a *Times Literary Supplement* article on Mayne and his work, a writer discusses *Ravensgill*: "As always, [Mayne's] sense of setting and his perception of the interrelation of people and places are remarkable. The action of *Ravensgill* happens against the background of a rural community that is essentially modern but which functions at a leisured pace, in time with the seasons and the subtlest movements of the weather. . . . No one senses and portrays these shifts and changes more accurately than Mr. Mayne." And in a *Junior Bookshelf* review of *The Member of the Marsh*, a critic comments that "Mr. Mayne is a master of the use of setting. . . . He knows the country well and communicates his appreciation of its not-very-obvious charms."

Mayne frequently adapts many of the local legends he heard as a child in his stories to cast a spell of adventure and mystery—a second characteristic frequently appearing in Mayne's books. *Earthfasts*, *A Game of Dark*, *It*, and *The Hill Road* are just a few examples of how Mayne expertly combines old tales and belief in the supernatural with present-day situations to produce an enjoyable mix of fantasy that critics have praised. For instance, in a review of *Earthfasts*, Ivan Sandrof proclaims in the *New York Times Book Review* that "Mayne is a verbal magician, economical of word, startlingly imaginative, who kindles flame with a brisk prod of word and situation quickly said and set. The Merlinesque touch is very real. He has ability to seize the Now and suddenly make it glitter with meaning, mystery, terror. The result is shuddery delight."

In addition to exploring his childhood fascination with fables, myths, and the supernatural, Mayne often inserts his long-standing curiosity with treasure hunts into his fiction. For example, in *A Swarm in May, A Grass Rope, The Thumbstick*, and *Words and Music,* Mayne spins a tale involving a search for treasure that uncovers more than material riches. A writer for *Junior Bookshelf* offers *The Thumbstick* as an good representation of Mayne's unique style of capturing his reader's attention by writing about mysterious and unexplainable happenings taking place during treasure hunts. As the reviewer reports: "*The Thumbstick* is one of Mayne's Yorkshire stories. Like all his books it is a tale of living traditions. It is also about a treasure hunt. Like every one of Mayne's books, too, it is astonishingly unlike every other one."

Marcus Crouch summarizes in *Treasure Seekers and Borrowers: Children's Books in Britain 1900-1960* that Mayne's *A Swarm in May,* "like all his subsequent books, was whole and indivisible; plot, setting, characters, writing, all contributed to the final effect; but the writing was the catalyst. Mayne's prose was a delicate, sensitive instrument, exactly suited to it purpose. The dialogue was exquisitely right, the description (which was never extraneous but always dedicated to forwarding the narrative) was spare and beautiful. . . . Although the theme of a search for treasure was recurrent, each story was strikingly original." Crouch continues to explain that "his stories grow inevitable out of their settings and their characters. . . . In spite of his love of ancient traditions, he is essentially a contemporary writer. He belongs to the post-war world and understands the social phenomena which have developed since 1945. Understanding and a deep unsentimental affection for young people enrich his wise, subtle stories."

A third common element contained in most of Mayne's books is his pattern of showcasing delightful and believable characters and their dialogue. Mayne's genuine love and true understanding of children is apparent in his sensitive and good humored portrayal of his characters, their language, and their universe. Writing about Mayne's talent for accurately recreating a child's world, Ruth Hill Viguers remarks in *A Critical History of Children's Literature* that "to browse through a number of [Mayne's] books at the same time is to realize how many people he has brought to life in print and how complete an individual each one is. The children disagree, sometimes quarrel and weep, but the atmosphere that one remembers in his many stories is good humor. The relationships are affectionate and amusing, the dialogue full of quips and jokes and amiable insults."

Edward Blishen notes in *Good Writers for Young Readers* that "William Mayne's stories are full of . . . pure true comedy of talk among children, of talk between children and adults. . . . And, apart from his purely comic concern with words, William Mayne understands beautifully that language is itself part of the adventure of being alive and that, by misleading or puzzling or illuminating, it can inspire or direct events."

These factors of setting, mysterious intrigue, and sensitive portrayal of characters combine to make Mayne's books for children unique and lovingly personal. "A writer of protean gifts," observes Stephen Fraser in *Five Owls,* "William Mayne consistently lifts the world of children's books to new levels of literary excellence with each new work. He writes in the best storytelling tradition and knows how to keep his listeners' rapt attention with strong images, clean solid language, and momentum built by foreshadowing and cliffhanging chapter endings. He is a master."

A reviewer for *Junior Bookshelf* believes that *A Grass Rope* perfectly highlights Mayne's talent and ability as a writer of fiction for young adults. He stresses in his review of *A Grass Rope:* "Mr. Mayne has infinite resources. First, style. He has the gift of describing everyday things as if he were seeing them for the first time, and he shares this freshness of vision with his readers. . . . He has, too, a fine sense of landscape and of atmosphere. The harsh Pennine country to this story is an essential actor in the drama; one sees it all the time, as one feels the hill mists, and hears the distant rush of water and the barking of foxes. He has a deep understanding of children. No one ever acts or speaks out of character. He is moreover, a fine story-teller, who knows how to set his narrative in motion so that it gains in momentum as it goes. And everything is colored with his characteristic sober humor."

While primarily recognized as a writer for young adults, Mayne has also written numerous picture books that have been very well-received by younger readers. Generally, these books have been described by numerous reviewers as imaginative and amusing stories involving colorful characters. Joan Aiken declares in *Children's Literature in Education* that "when writing for children it is important to be absolutely sure of your own meanings and intentions and to take the utmost pains to convey these to the reader . . . William Mayne is marvelous at this."

The most popular of Mayne's works for children are his books featuring, Hob, a tiny elf-like character that is invisible to adults. It is Hob's job to protect his human family from evil. "Hob lives under the stars," explains Alan Hollinghurst in the *Times Literary Supplement.* "He is about two feet high, middle-aged, balding, Jewish, smokes a pipe and wears green slippers and a fleecy cotton vest and long-johns. He looks like a diminutive version of Mel Brooks, but his role is not to make people laugh: he is a simple, un-ironical person, conscientious and kind, and he survives by doing good."

Delightfully illustrated by Patrick Benson, *The Yellow Book of Hob Stories, The Blue Book of Hob Stories, The Green Book of Hob Stories,* and *The Red Book of Hob Stories* have been described by Susan H. Patron in *School Library Journal* as "original, imaginative and sprightly"—a book with "innate appeal." And John Cech elaborates in the *Washington Post Book World* that "these are wonderful, clever stories, brilliantly illustrated by Patrick Benson in pen and ink with color washes. They're a splendid treat for a spring night's reading—for any night's reading. Like the flowers in the garden, one marvels over them, wishes there were more, and is deeply grateful that there are these to make a bouquet of magic."

However, unlike his picture books for young children, Mayne has not achieved the same level of popularity with his young adult readers as he has received from reviewers. Two primary reasons have been suggested to account for the smaller number of fans of Mayne's young adult novels as opposed to the larger number of reviewers who enjoy and praise his books. One reason can be attributed to Mayne's intricate writing style, which revolves around skillful use of language. The other factor is Mayne's involved and detailed plot or story lines. "The works of William Mayne can usually be relied upon to arouse conflicting opinions in the mind of the adult reader," asserts Lance Salway in *Times Literary Supplement.* "Pretentious, difficult, obscure, complex . . . these are a few of the many adjectives which have been heaped on his recent books, along with other more adulatory. But there can be no doubt at all about his strength as craftsman and innovator, or of his ability to capture the essence of place and character in precise prose."

"Mr. Mayne is not an easy writer, as we know," declares a reviewer for *Junior Bookshelf.* "His love of words, his range of ideas and his interest in psychology, which are the very essence of his art, all act as stumbling-blocks to the young reader. . . . He writes, as he must, to please himself. Will he at the same time please others? Yes, he will delight those who deserve writing of this quality, the children, a minority but not an insignificant one, who can recognize the truth of his observation of boys' behaviour and who can relish the convincing oddity of his adults."

Finally, Natalie Babbitt seems to sum up the thoughts of many admirers of Mayne's talents as a writer when she reflects in the *New York Times Book Review:* "Perhaps it is simply that he cares very much about what he is doing, that instead of being skimmed from the surface, his stories come from very deep in the well. This is a rare thing in

children's fiction and should be celebrated wherever it is found."

BIOGRAPHICAL/CRITICAL SOURCES:

BOOKS

Blishen, Edward, *Good Writers for Young Readers,* Hart-Davis, 1977, pp. 79-85.
Blishen, Edward, *The Thorny Paradise: Writers on Writing for Children,* Kestral Books, 1975, pp. 65-76.
Cameron, Eleanor, *The Green and Burning Tree: On Writing and Enjoyment of Children's Books,* Little, Brown, 1969, pp. 3-136.
Contemporary Literary Criticism, Volume 12, Gale, 1979.
Contemporary Literary Review, Volume 25, Gale, 1991.
Crouch, Marcus, *Treasure Seekers and Borrowers: Children's Books in Britain 1900-1960,* Library Association, 1962, pp. 112-138.
Fisher, Margery, *Intent upon Reading: A Critical Appraisal of Modern Fiction for Children,* Brockhampton Press, 1961, pp. 270-96.
Frank, Eyre, *British Children's Books in the Twentieth Century,* Longman, 1971, revised edition, 1979, pp. 76-156.
Something about the Author Autobiography Series, Volume 11, Gale, 1991.
Third Book of Junior Authors, H. W. Wilson, 1972.
Townsend, John Rowe, *A Sense of Story: Essays on Contemporary Writers for Children,* Lippincott, 1971, pp 130-42.
Viguers, Ruth Hill, *A Critical History of Children's Literature,* Macmillan, 1969, pp. 567-600.

PERIODICALS

Children's Book Review, June, 1971, p. 91; October, 1973, pp. 133-35.
Children's Literature in Education, July, 1970, pp. 48-55; November, 1972, pp. 7-23; May, 1973, pp. 37-8; Volume 20, number 1, 1989.
Five Owls, July-August, 1990, p. 109.
Growing Point, July, 1965, pp. 769-70; May, 1985; May, 1987; November, 1989, p. 5234.
In Review: Canadian Books for Children, winter, 1972, pp. 5-14.
Junior Bookshelf, July, 1956, p. 144; December, 1956, pp. 341-42; July, 1957, pp. 143-44; December, 1957, pp. 318-19; July, 1959, pp. 152-53; October, 1959, pp. 185-89; July, 1963, p. 156.
New York Herald Tribune, April 3, 1960, p. 9.
New York Review of Books, February 18, 1988, pp. 11-13.
New York Times Book Review, May 14, 1967, p. 30; October 10, 1971, p. 8; May 2, 1976, p. 40; September 24, 1989.
School Librarian, March, 1984, pp. 5-12.
School Library Journal, April, 1985, p. 90.

Signal, September, 1975, pp. 107-13; September, 1976, pp. 107-13; May, 1977, p. 76; January, 1979, pp. 9-25.

Times Literary Supplement, November 23, 1956, p. 7; November 24, 1966, p. 1080; November 30, 1967, p. 1140; July 2, 1970, p. 713; October 22, 1971, p. 1319; October 1, 1976, p. 1241; July 23, 1982, p. 788; November 26, 1982, p. 1302; March 30, 1984, p. 338; April 17, 1987, p. 421.

Use of English, autumn, 1978, pp. 99-103.

Washington Post Book World, May 13, 1984, p. 15.*

*   *   *

MAZZOTTA, Giuseppe   1942-

PERSONAL: Born January 1, 1942, in Curinga, Italy; son of Pasquale and Rose Mazzotta; married Carol Carlson, March 2, 1972; children: Rosanna, Antony, Paula. *Education:* University of Toronto, B.A., 1965, M.A., 1966; Cornell University, Ph.D., 1969. *Religion:* Roman Catholic. *Avocational interests:* Theology, literature, basketball, baseball, soccer.

ADDRESSES: Home—152 Waite St., Hamden, CT 06517. *Office*—Department of Italian, Yale University, New Haven, CT 06520.

CAREER: Cornell University, Ithaca, NY, assistant professor, 1969-70; Yale University, New Haven, CT, assistant professor, 1970-72; University of Toronto, Toronto, Ontario, associate professor, 1972-73; Cornell University, associate professor, 1973-78, professor of Romance studies, 1978-83; Yale University, professor of Italian, 1983—.

WRITINGS:

Dante, Poet of the Desert: History and Allegory in the Divine Comedy, Princeton University Press, 1979.

The World at Play: A Study of Boccaccio's Decameron, Princeton University Press, 1985.

(Co-editor) *Magister Regis: Studies in Honor of R. E. Kaske,* Fordham University Press, 1986.

Critical Essays on Dante, G. K. Hall, 1991.

WORK IN PROGRESS: Dante's Vision and the Circle of Knowledge; work on Petrarch's myths.

*   *   *

McCANN, Edson
See POHL, Frederik

McCREIGH, James
See POHL, Frederik

*   *   *

McFARLANE, Leslie (Charles)   1902-1977
(Franklin W. Dixon, James Cody Ferris, Carolyn Keene, Roy Rockwood, house pseudonyms)

PERSONAL: Born October 25, 1902, in Carleton Place, Ontario, Canada; died September 6, 1977, in Whitby, Ontario, Canada; son of John Henry (an elementary school principal) and Rebecca (Barnett) McFarlane; married Amy Ashmore (died, 1955); married Beatrice Greenaway Kenney, 1957; children: (first marriage) Patricia, Brian, Norah. *Education:* Attended schools in Haileybury, Ontario, Canada.

CAREER: Author, screenwriter, producer, and director. Newspaper reporter during the 1910s and 1920s, working for the *Haileyburian,* Haileybury, Ontario, *Cobalt Daily Nugget,* Cobalt, Ontario, *Sudbury Star,* Sudbury, Ontario, *Ottawa Journal,* and *Montreal Herald; Springfield Republican,* Springfield, MA, reporter, 1926; Stratemeyer Syndicate, East Orange, NJ, ghost writer of books for children, 1926-46; National Film Board of Canada, Montreal, Ontario, documentary film producer and director, 1943-57; head of television drama script department for Canadian Broadcasting Corp. (CBC), 1958-60.

AWARDS, HONORS: British Film Academy Award, 1951, for *Royal Journey;* nomination for Academy Award for best one-reel short subject from Academy of Motion Picture Arts and Sciences, 1953, for *Herring Hunt; Liberty* magazine award, 1960's, for best television playwright of the year; award from "Canada Day" festival of Canadian literature, Mohawk College, Hamilton, Ontario, 1977.

WRITINGS:

UNDER PSEUDONYM FRANKLIN W. DIXON; BOOKS IN THE "HARDY BOYS" SERIES

The Tower Treasure, illustrations by Walter S. Rogers, Grosset, 1927, facsimile of original edition, Applewood Books, 1991.

The House on the Cliff, illustrations by Rogers, Grosset, 1927, facsimile of original edition, Applewood Books, 1991.

The Secret of the Old Mill, illustrations by Rogers, Grosset, 1927, facsimile of original edition, Applewood Books, 1991.

The Missing Chums, illustrations by Rogers, Grosset, 1928.

Hunting for Hidden Gold, illustrations by Rogers, Grosset, 1928.

The Shore Road Mystery, illustrations by Rogers, Grosset, 1928.

The Secret of the Caves, illustrations by Rogers, Grosset, 1929.

The Mystery of Cabin Island, illustrations by Rogers, Grosset, 1929.

The Great Airport Mystery, illustrations by Rogers, Grosset, 1930.

What Happened at Midnight, illustrations by Rogers, Grosset, 1932.

While the Clock Ticked, illustrations by J. Clemens Gretter, Grosset, 1932.

The Sinister Sign Post, illustrations by Gretter, Grosset, 1936.

A Figure in Hiding, illustrations by Paul Laune, Grosset, 1937.

The Secret Warning, illustrations by Laune, Grosset, 1938.

The Flickering Torch Mystery, illustrations by Laune, Grosset, 1943.

The Short-Wave Mystery, illustrations by Russell H. Tandy, Grosset, 1945.

The Secret Panel, illustrations by Tandy, Grosset, 1946.

The Phantom Freighter, illustrations by Tandy, Grosset, 1947.

UNDER PSEUDONYM CAROLYN KEENE; BOOKS IN THE "DANA GIRLS" SERIES

By the Light of the Study Lamp, illustrations by Ferdinand E. Warren, Grosset, 1934.

The Secret at Lone Tree Cottage, illustrations by Warren, Grosset, 1934.

In the Shadow of the Tower, illustrations by Warren, Grosset, 1934.

A Three-Cornered Mystery, illustrations by Warren, Grosset, 1935.

UNDER PSEUDONYM ROY ROCKWOOD; BOOKS IN THE "DAVE FEARLESS" SERIES

Dave Fearless Under the Ocean; or, The Treasure of the Lost Submarine, Garden City Publishing Co., 1926.

Dave Fearless in the Black Jungle; or, Lost Among the Cannibals, Garden City Publishing Co., 1926.

Dave Fearless Near the South Pole; or, The Giant Whales of Snow Island, Garden City Publishing Co., 1926.

Dave Fearless Caught by Malay Pirates; or, The Secret of Bamboo Island, Garden City Publishing Co., 1926.

Dave Fearless on the Ship of Mystery; or, The Strange Hermit of Shark Cove, Garden City Publishing Co., 1927.

Dave Fearless on the Lost Brig; or, Abandoned in the Big Hurricane, Garden City Publishing Co., 1927.

Dave Fearless at Whirlpool Point; or, The Mystery of the Water Cave, Garden City Publishing Co., 1927.

BOOKS IN THE "CHECKMATE" SERIES

Agent of the Falcon, Methuen, 1975.

The Dynamite Flynns, Methuen, 1975.

The Mystery of Spider Lake, Methuen, 1975.

Squeeze Play, Methuen, 1975.

Breakaway, Methuen, 1976.

The Snow Hawk, Methuen, 1976.

OTHER

Streets of Shadow (adult novel), Dutton, 1930.

The Murder Tree (adult novel), Dutton, 1931.

(And director) *The Boy Who Stopped Niagara* (film), J. Arthur Rank, 1947.

Royal Journey (documentary film), United Artists, 1951.

Herring Hunt (documentary film), RKO, 1953.

The Last of the Great Picnics (juvenile), illustrations by Lewis Parker, McClelland & Stewart, 1965.

McGonigle Scores!, McClelland & Stewart, 1966.

Fire in the North: A Play Commemorating the Fiftieth Anniversary of the Haileybury Fire (first broadcast on CBC radio as part of the series *The Bush and the Salon,* 1972), Highway Book Shop (Cobalt, Ontario), 1972.

A Kid in Haileybury (autobiography), Highway Book Shop, 1975.

Ghost of the Hardy Boys (autobiography), Methuen/Two Continents Publications, 1976.

Also author, under pseudonym James Cody Ferris, of *The X Bar X Boys with the Border Patrol,* Grosset. Also author, producer, or director of more than fifty films, including *A Friend at the Door,* 1950. Also author of dozens of unpublished radio plays, including *Something to Remember.* Also author of more than seventy plays for television, including *The Eye-Opener Man* and *Pilgrim, Why Do You Come?* Contributor of one hundred novelettes, two hundred short stories, and numerous serials to magazines, including *Maclean's Magazine, Toronto Star Weekly, Argosy, Liberty, Vanity Fair, Canadian Home Journal, Country Gentleman, Adventure, West, Red-Blooded Stories, Mystery Stories, Top Notch, Real Detective, Detective Fiction Weekly, All-Star Detective, Thrilling Sport, Sport Story,* and *Knockout.*

SIDELIGHTS: A writer whose career spanned five decades and whose work included plays, books for adults and children, and film, radio, and television scripts, Leslie McFarlane is best remembered for the books he wrote in the "Hardy Boys" series, the popular mystery/adventure series for boys. McFarlane wrote twenty-one of the early Hardy Boys adventures, including the first eleven volumes, and helped set the tone for the enduring series. Estimated sales of the Hardy Boys books still run at over 2 million copies a year, with a total of over 60 million copies sold throughout the world. The first volume in the series,

The Tower Treasure, written by McFarlane, has sold over 1.5 million copies alone. The Hardy Boys books have been translated into French, Italian, Dutch, Norwegian, Swedish, Danish, and other languages, and the characters have been adapted for television, comic books, and a host of toys and game products. Jonathan Cott, writing in *Esquire,* called the Hardy Boys' series "the most popular boys' books of all time."

In 1926, while working as a reporter for the *Springfield Republican,* McFarlane answered an ad for fiction writers in a journalism trade magazine. The ad was placed by the Stratemeyer Syndicate, a packager of such popular children's series as Nancy Drew, the Bobbsey Twins, and Tom Swift. McFarlane was offered an opportunity to write for the Dave Fearless series—an ongoing saga about a young deep-sea diver and underwater explorer—working from chapter-by-chapter outlines provided by Edward Stratemeyer himself, head of the syndicate. Pay was a straight one hundred dollars per book, no royalties. The books would be published under the Stratemeyer house pseudonym of Roy Rockwood. McFarlane considered the offer. "By working full time for the Stratemeyer Syndicate I could easily whack out four books a month, double my income and get some sleep at night," he explained in his autobiography *Ghost of the Hardy Boys.* McFarlane accepted the offer. His first assignment, *Dave Fearless Under the Ocean,* was written quickly: "I heaved a gusty sigh as the typewriter clattered 'The End' and I pulled the final page from the typewriter. The manuscript, unread, unrevised and uncorrected, went into a large, brown envelope which, in turn, went into the outgoing mail basket. There wasn't even a carbon copy."

McFarlane was soon a regular contributor to Stratemeyer, writing a total of seven books in the Dave Fearless series. McFarlane claimed in *Ghost of the Hardy Boys:* "In the forty-seven years since then, . . . I have never encountered anyone who has ever heard of Dave Fearless. I have never seen a Dave Fearless book in a bookstore, on a paperback rack, on a library shelf or even in any of the dusty caves in obscure shops where old books go when they die. I have never come across any reference to Dave in any book or article. On a shelf in my small library the yellowing volumes I hammered out for Edward Stratemeyer stand as the solid evidence that there actually was a Dave Fearless series. Otherwise I might begin to doubt."

Edward Stratemeyer's next project for McFarlane proved to be more durable than the Dave Fearless books. Inspired by the popularity of mystery novels for adults, particularly the mysteries of S. S. Van Dine, Stratemeyer reasoned that a boys' mystery series featuring two young detectives might do very well. He approached McFarlane with the idea for the Hardy Boys, two brothers named Frank and Joe Hardy who solve mysteries in their hometown of Bay-port. The Hardy Boys books would be published under the Stratemeyer house pseudonym of Franklin W. Dixon. McFarlane recalled in *Ghost of the Hardy Boys:* "Stratemeyer noted that the books would be clothbound and therefore priced a little higher than paperbacks. This in turn would justify a little higher payment for the manuscript—$125 to be exact. He had attached an information sheet for guidance and the plot outline of the initial volume."

McFarlane accepted the assignment. "It seemed to me," he wrote in his autobiography, "that the Hardy Boys deserved something better than the slapdash treatment Dave Fearless had been getting. It was still hack work, no doubt, but did the new series have to be all that hack? There was, after all, the chance to contribute a little style, occasional words of more than two syllables, maybe a little sensory stimuli."

To make the Hardy Boys a cut above the usual Stratemeyer series, McFarlane made sure the books were full of humor, reasoning that young readers would appreciate some laughs. Where the Stratemeyer outline called for an ordinary scene, McFarlane often turned it into a comic scene as well. Characters introduced merely to further one book's plot became in McFarlane's hands enduring favorites whose comic idiosyncracies were appreciated in many subsequent Hardy Boys adventures. The character Aunt Gertrude, for instance, was introduced as a helper to Mrs. Hardy. But she immediately became a comic foil whose constant badgering of the boys was a running joke in many later books. "A school teacher told me a while back," McFarlane recounted in *Ghost of the Hardy Boys,* "that when she asked her class to name their favorite characters in fiction she found Aunt Gertrude right up there with Huckleberry Finn. This caused her no little embarrassment. She had never heard of Aunt Gertrude and didn't care to lose face by asking."

In every book, McFarlane also included scenes of the boys eating food, remembering that when he was a young boy he appreciated food. "Boys are always hungry," as he explained in his autobiography. Whenever the boys were about to go out on a case, Mrs. Hardy got busy making sandwiches for them. And often, in addition to a handsome cash reward, the boys were paid for their crime-solving efforts with a hefty meal as well. In every Hardy Boys adventure Joe and Frank had at least one big feast, each bite of which was lovingly described by McFarlane.

Speaking to David Palmer in *Canadian Children's Literature,* McFarlane commented: "I did take trouble with the writing of [the Hardy Boys books], you know. Many of the writers of boys' books of that time wrote very hastily, and some of them weren't very good writers anyway. Some man who was interviewed said that Stratemeyer hired hacks, drunks and broken-down newspaper men and so on to write them. Well, I think that's a bit of slander, but we weren't all that good, let's say."

Writing in his autobiography, McFarlane explained that he developed a professional attitude towards his work. "The professional attitude was difficult to define," he stated. "If one is willing to accept money for writing a certain kind of material, he should do his best. The young, the uncultured or unsophisticated reader is not to blame for his condition and should not be despised—certainly not by the writer who lives by that reader's nickels and dimes.

"The Dave Fearless outlines had been outrageous fantasies, bordering on burlesque. Viewed in one light, they were comic works. 'The Hardy Boys' were likewise contrived for wish fulfillment but I had learned not to despise them. They had their lowly place in the world of commercial publishing, with its variety of reading matter as infinite as the mind of man. They were written swiftly, but not carelessly. I gave thought to grammar, sentence structure, choice of words, pace, the techniques of suspense, all within the limits of the medium which was in this case mass-produced, assembly-line fiction for boys."

McFarlane went on to write twenty-one volumes of the Hardy Boys mysteries. He told Palmer: "The stories were almost ridiculously easy to write. You hardly seemed to be working at all, you could do them very quickly." In time, however, McFarlane grew tired of the series. "It was drudgery, real drudgery, after a while," he told Palmer. He explained in *Ghost of the Hardy Boys:* "There was no quarrel, no dramatic break with the Syndicate for which I had toiled over a period of twenty years and ground out more than two million words. I merely sent in the manuscript with a note to the effect that I was too busy to take on any further assignments. The Syndicate didn't plead with me to continue. In fact, the Syndicate didn't seem to care much one way or the other. Other spooks were always available." The Hardy Boys have since been written by a score of other writers, all of whom have published under the Stratemeyer house pseudonym Franklin W. Dixon.

McFarlane claimed that he paid no attention to the Hardy Boys' books after he was through writing them. "I never read them," he wrote in his autobiography. "Whenever a new one arrived I might skim through a few pages and then the volume would join its predecessors on a bookcase shelf. Under glass, like a row of embalmed owls, so the dust wouldn't get at them." He had no idea that the Hardy Boys were popular with young readers until his son approached him in the mid-1940s and asked about the books on the shelf. "Did you read them when you were a kid?" his son asked. "Read them? I wrote them," McFarlane re-

plied. His son's astonished awe puzzled him until it was explained that all his son's friends read the Hardy Boys. "You can buy them in Simpson's," his son said. "Next day I went to the department store," McFarlane recalled in his autobiography, "and damned if the lad wasn't right! They *did* have shelves of them. . . . I began to see the Hardy Boys books wherever I went, in small bookstores and large, even in railway depots and corner stores. There seemed to be an epidemic."

Despite the phenomenal success of the Hardy Boys McFarlane received relatively little money for his work. As he explained in his autobiography, however, the low pay did not upset him: "I was not swindled. I accepted the terms of Edward Stratemeyer and the importance of the money was related to my needs. I was free to reject any of the assignments. Writing is not a profession on which one embarks under duress. No one forces anyone to become a writer. No one even asks him. He writes because he enjoys writing, and if he doesn't enjoy it he should get out of the profession. It follows, then, that if he is doing something he enjoys he should not complain if the financial rewards are less than he expected or thinks he deserves."

After leaving the Stratemeyer Syndicate, McFarlane worked for the National Film Board of Canada. During his twelve years with the board, he wrote, directed or produced over fifty documentary films. Later he moved to the Canadian Broadcasting Corp., writing numerous radio scripts and over seventy plays for television. In the 1970s several of his pulp magazine serials from the 1930s— wilderness adventure tales and sports stories—were revamped and issued in book form as part of Methuen's Checkmate series.

Palmer summed up McFarlane as "one of the world's most popular children's authors and a prolific contributor to Canadian popular culture." Writing in the *Dictionary of Literary Biography,* J. Kieran Kealy claimed that the title of McFarlane's autobiography, *Ghost of the Hardy Boys,* "suggests that McFarlane fully realized that, despite a lifetime of writing under his own name, he would be best remembered for the books he ghosted. But he also suggests that one should not underestimate his contributions to these formulaic texts. Moreover, when one compares the rather bland, humorless boys' adventures being published today by a more 'modern' stable of ghostwriters with the original Hardy Boys adventures, one is inclined to agree with McFarlane's own appraisal of the boys' first exploits: 'I thought that I had written a hell of a good book—of its kind. . . .'"

BIOGRAPHICAL/CRITICAL SOURCES:

BOOKS

Billman, Carol, *The Secret of the Stratemeyer Syndicate: Nancy Drew, the Hardy Boys, and the Million Dollar Fiction Factory,* Ungar, 1986.
Dictionary of Literary Biography, Volume 88: *Canadian Writers, 1920-1959, Second Series,* Gale, 1989, pp. 213-215.
Johnson, Deidre, editor and compiler, *Stratemeyer Pseudonyms and Series Books: An Annotated Checklist of Stratemeyer and Stratemeyer Syndicate Publications,* Greenwood Press, 1982.
McFarlane, Leslie, *Ghost of the Hardy Boys,* Methuen/Two Continents Publications, 1976.
Prager, Arthur, *Rascals at Large; or, The Clue in the Old Nostalgia,* Doubleday, 1971.

PERIODICALS

Canadian Children's Literature, Number 11, 1978, pp. 5-19.
Esquire, June, 1986, pp. 225-226.
Rolling Stone, September 9, 1976, pp. 36-40; October 21, 1976, p. 10.
Weekend Magazine, December 15, 1973, pp. 12-15.*

* * *

McGARRITY, Mark 1943-
(Bartholomew Gill)

PERSONAL: Born July 22, 1943, in Holyoke, MA; son of Hugh F. and Cecilia (Gill) McGarrity; married Margaret Wellstood Dull (a photographer), October 10, 1966. *Education:* Brown University, B.A., 1966; Trinity College, Dublin, M.Litt., 1971.

ADDRESSES: Home and office—159 North Shore Rd., Andover, NJ 07821. *Agent*—Robin Rue, Anita Diamant Agency, 310 Madison Ave., New York, NY 10017.

CAREER: Has worked as a speech writer, public relations and annual report writer, and financial reporter. Teacher and free-lance writer, 1969—. Writer in residence, Dover Public Schools, NJ, 1984-85.

AWARDS, HONORS: First prize in critical writing, New Jersey Press Association Competition, 1984; Edgar Award nomination for best novel, Mystery Writers of America, 1989, for *Death of a Joyce Scholar.*

WRITINGS:

Little Augie's Lament (novel), David Grossman, 1973.
Lucky Shuffles (novel), David Grossman, 1973.
A Passing Advantage (novel), Rawson, Wade, 1980.

(Contributor) Dilys Winn, *Murderess Ink,* Workman Publishing, 1980.
Neon Caesar, Pocket Books, 1990.
White Rush/Green Fire, Morrow, 1991.

UNDER PSEUDONYM BARTHOLOMEW GILL; "McGARR" SERIES

McGarr and the Politician's Wife, Scribner, 1976.
McGarr and the Sienese Conspiracy, Scribner, 1977.
McGarr on the Cliffs of Moher, Scribner, 1978.
McGarr and the Dublin Horse Show, Viking, 1980.
McGarr and the P. M. of Belgrave Square, Viking, 1983.
McGarr and the Method of Descartes, Viking, 1984.
McGarr and the Wrath of a Woman Scorned, Viking, 1985.
Death of a Joyce Scholar, Morrow, 1989.
Death of Love, Morrow, 1992.

OTHER

Also contributor to *New Jersey Herald.*

ADAPTATIONS: Neon Caesar was optioned by Paul Monash and is being produced as a television movie; *White Rush/Green Fire* is presently under option by Dustin Hoffman's Punch Productions.

WORK IN PROGRESS: Lake House, a generational novel of an American family, and *Vektor Arabesque,* a techno-thriller.

SIDELIGHTS: Under his pseudonym, Bartholomew Gill, Mark McGarrity is the creator of a well-received addition to the world of international crime and mystery literature—Peter McGarr, chief superintendent of detectives of the Irish police. In the *Washington Post Book World,* Jean M. White assures readers that McGarr "is no imitation. [The author] has created a solid, original character."

As for McGarrity's writing style, Newgate Callendar notes in the *New York Times Book Review* that "everything [in *McGarr and the Sienese Conspiracy*] is nicely relaxed. . . . Yet there is a great deal of tension, and also enough action to satisfy the reader who demands gore. McGarr . . . sort of ambles through everything. . . . There is never any feeling of heavy breathing. Gill paces everything beautifully. *McGarr and the Sienese Conspiracy* is very well plotted, very civilized and very, very good."

In *Death of a Joyce Scholar,* McGarr is faced with a murder of which one suspect says, "You'll have to think Joyce and Beckett and books if you're going to get anywhere with this thing." McGarr reads James Joyce's *Ulysses* to solve the case. Says Margaret Cannon in the *Globe and Mail,* "All of *Ulysses* and, ultimately, all of the intelligence and venality of Joyce's complex Dublin play a role." *Death of a Joyce Scholar,* which earned McGarrity a nomination for the Edgar Award, is praised in another *Wash-*

ington Post Book World review by White who says, "In *The Death of a Joyce Scholar,* the eighth in a series featuring Irish Chief Inspector Peter McGarr, Bartholomew Gill has written a police procedural that defies the limits of its genre. He has taken the format and turned it into a richly textured, intricate novel that examines the Irish psyche as well as a murder. The problems explored are as much human as criminal."

BIOGRAPHICAL/CRITICAL SOURCES:

BOOKS

McGarrity, Mark, *Death of a Joyce Scholar,* Morrow, 1989.

PERIODICALS

Globe and Mail (Toronto), August 8, 1989.
New Republic, June 10, 1978.
New York Times, December 13, 1984.
New York Times Book Review, April 8, 1973; May 1, 1977; February 12, 1978; June 18, 1989; October 6, 1991.
Washington Post Book World, August 20, 1978; June 16, 1989.

*   *   *

McGIVERN, Maureen Daly
See DALY, Maureen

*   *   *

McKENDRICK, Melveena (Christine) 1941-

PERSONAL: Born March 23, 1941, in Glamorgan, Wales; daughter of James Powell (a teacher) and Catherine Letitia Jones; married Neil McKendrick (a historian), March 18, 1968; children: Olivia, Cornelia. *Education:* King's College, London, B.A. (with first class honors), 1963; Girton College, Cambridge, Ph.D., 1967.

ADDRESSES: Home—Howe House, Huntingdon Rd., Cambridge CB3 0LX, England. *Office*—Girton College, Cambridge University, Cambridge CB3 0JG, England.

CAREER: Cambridge University, Girton College, Cambridge, England, fellow, 1967-70, tutor, 1970-74, senior tutor, 1974-81, lecturer in Spanish, 1970—. British Academy, research reader, 1990-92.

WRITINGS:

Ferdinand and Isabella, American Heritage, 1968.
A Concise History of Spain, McGraw, 1972.
Woman and Society in the Spanish Drama of the Golden Age, Cambridge University Press, 1974.
Cervantes, Little, Brown, 1982.

(Contributor) Beth Miller, editor, *Women in Hispanic Literature: Icons and Fallen Idols,* University of California Press, 1983.
Theatre in Spain, 1492-1700, Cambridge University Press, 1989.
(Contributor) J.M. Ruano de la Haza, editor, *El mundo del teatro espanol en su siglo de oro,* Oltowa, 1989.
(Contributor) Diago and Ferrer, editors, *Comedias y comediantes,* Valencia, 1991.
(With A. A. Parker) Hacia Calderon de la Barca, *El magico prodigioso* (annotated edition), Oxford University Press, 1992.

Also contributor to *Calderon: Critical Studies,* edited by J.E. Vatey, 1973, *Feminism and Hispanic Literature,* edited by, Lisa Conde, 1991, *Hacia Calderon,* edited by Hans Flasche, 1991.

Contributor to numerous professional journals.

WORK IN PROGRESS: The Theatre and the Establishment in Seventeenth Century Spain; Calderon's Women.

SIDELIGHTS: Melveena McKendrick's *Cervantes* is described by Alan Cheuse in the *Los Angeles Times Book Review* as a "scrupulously researched and extremely well-written biography of the Spanish master." Cheuse remarks that "documentation of the life of a giant is, as McKendrick impresses upon us, shadowy and not always available. But the portrait she works up of the man, his work, and the age that produced them, belongs on a shelf alongside our favorite studies of Shakespeare and Faulkner." In *Cervantes,* as E.C. Riley comments in the *Times Literary Supplement,* "known facts and uncertainties are handled in a measured and sensible way, and from time to time useful second thoughts are prompted about things often taken for granted." The book's utility as a scholarly work is limited by the fact that a list of source references has been omitted, Riley observes, but, "aside from this deficiency—which will not worry the average reader much—the next British or American biographer of Cervantes will have to work hard to better this one."

BIOGRAPHICAL/CRITICAL SOURCES:

PERIODICALS

Los Angeles Time Book Review, May 31, 1981.
Times Literary Supplement, July 3, 1981.

*   *   *

McOWAN, Rennie 1933-

PERSONAL: Surname is pronounced Mak-*oh*-an; born January 12, 1933, in Stirling, Scotland; son of Robert (a teacher) and Janet (a teacher; maiden name, Ross)

McOwan; married Agnes Mooney (a teacher), August 1, 1959; children: Lesley Clare, Michael, Thomas, Niall. *Politics:* Scottish Nationalist. *Religion:* Roman Catholic.

ADDRESSES: Home and office—7 Williamfield Ave., Stirling FK7 9AH, Scotland.

CAREER: Journalist and feature writer with *Stirling Journal,* Kemsley Newspapers, Scotsman Publications, and the *Evening Dispatch,* 1950-60; National Trust for Scotland, public relations officer, 1961-79; *Evening News,* Edinburgh, Scotland, senior feature writer, 1979-84; freelance writer and broadcaster, 1984—.

MEMBER: National Union of Journalists, Society of Antiquaries of Scotland, Dollar Civic Trust (honorary member).

WRITINGS:

The Man Who Bought Mountains, National Trust for Scotland, 1976.
Tales of Stirling Castle and the Battle of Bannockburn (history), Lang Syne Publishing, 1978.
Tales of Ben and Glen (Ben Nevis), Lang Syne Publishing, 1979.
(Contributor) *Walking in Scotland,* Spur Publications, 1981.
(Contributor) Hamish Brown, editor, *Poetry of the Scottish Hills,* Aberdeen University Press, 1982.
Light on Dumyat (juvenile novel), St. Andrew Press, 1982.
Walks in the Trossachs and the Rob Roy Country, St. Andrew Press, 1983.
The White Stag Adventure (juvenile novel), Richard Drew, 1984.
The Scottish Clans (history), Lang Syne Publishing, 1985.
(Contributor) H. Brown, editor, *Speak to the Hills* (poetry), Aberdeen University Press, 1985.
(Contributor) Ken Wilson and Richard Gilbert, editors, *Wild Walks,* Diadem, 1988.
(With H. Brown, Richard Mearns, and Ward Lock) *Great Walks: Scotland,* Cassell, 1989.
(Contributor) Martin Collins, editor, *Classic Coastal Walks of Britain,* Oxford Illustrated Press, 1990.
The Green Hills (stories of the Ochil Hills), Clackmannan District Library, 1990.
(Contributor) Martin Collins, editor, *On Foot Through History,* Scottish Section, Oxford Illustrated Press, 1991.
Tartans: Facts and Myths, Jarrolds, 1991.

Contributor of poems and articles to magazines, including *Scots Magazine,* and *Leopard,* and to newspapers, including *Glasgow Herald,* and *The Scotsman and Scotland on Sunday.*

ADAPTATIONS: The White Stag Adventure was adapted for radio and broadcast by the British Broadcasting Corp. (BBC), 1984.

WORK IN PROGRESS: A third juvenile novel, and a book about Scottish mountains which have supernatural or "magic" associations.

SIDELIGHTS: Rennie McOwan told *CA:* "I am intensely interested in Scottish politics, history, and conservation issues. I am a mountaineer, and I guide American walking groups in Scotland each summer. I have camped, climbed, and walked in Scotland for thirty years and am a member of outdoor clubs.

"My walking groups want to be taken on pass or glen walks of about ten miles—longer and rugged or shorter and easier, depending on age and fitness of the party—and like being told about the area's history, flora, and fauna. I try to tell them of today's 'face' and then link it to past centuries. They are keen to know how the area functions—jobs, housing, family patterns, and so on. I try to link Scots History with their own. They are nearly all delightful people and I enjoy it very much. I also take some of them to stately homes or historic sites on specific days.

"I also write *en route* commentaries covering the countryside we drive through and deliver the material over a microphone (I do this for Scottish groups too). Sometimes we include visits to islands, which are always very popular.

"I write for the pleasure of self-expression, of trying to pass on to others, however inadequately, the pleasure that areas of activity give me. My love of Scotland and the great need for urgent and sensible conservation policies to be implemented by the government, the spiritual quality of wilderness, and the 'feel' of Scottish history are, I think, shown in my writing. My adventure novel for children, *Light on Dumyat* (pronounced Dum-eye-at, a peak in the Ochil Hills in central Scotland), was chosen by the central region in 1983 as the theme of the primary, or junior, schools conference at Stirling University because it covers adventure, nature lore, history, and conservation.

"I also get immense pleasure from lecturing in schools and to writer's groups on children's literature and creative writing, financed by the Scottish Arts council, and being an occasional guest lecturer in the film and media studies department of Stirling University."

*   *   *

MEAKER, M. J.
See MEAKER, Marijane (Agnes)

MEAKER, Marijane (Agnes) 1927-
(M. J. Meaker; Ann Aldrich, Mary James, M. E. Kerr, Vin Packer, pseudonyms)

PERSONAL: Born May 27, 1927, in Auburn, NY; daughter of Ellis R. (a mayonnaise manufacturer) and Ida T. Meaker. *Education:* University of Missouri, B.A., 1949.

ADDRESSES: Home—12 Deep Six Dr., East Hampton, NY 11937. *Agent*—Julia Fallowfield, McIntosh & Otis, Inc., 475 Fifth Ave., New York, NY 10017.

CAREER: Worked at several jobs, including assistant file clerk for D. P. Dutton (publisher), 1949-50; free-lance writer, 1949—. Volunteer writing teacher at Commercial Manhattan Central High, 1968. Founding member of the Ashawagh Writers' Workshop.

MEMBER: PEN, Authors League of America, Society of Children's Book Writers.

AWARDS, HONORS: American Library Association (ALA) notable book, one of *School Library Journal's* best books of the year, both 1972, and winner of the Media and Methods Maxi Awards, 1974, all for *Dinky Hocker Shoots Smack!; Book World's* Children's Spring Book Festival honor book, one of Child Study Association's Children's books of the year, and one of *New York Times'* outstanding books of the year, all 1973, all for *If I Love You, Am I Trapped Forever?;* one of *School Library Journal's* best books of the year, 1974, for *The Son of Someone Famous;* ALA notable book, one of ALA's best books for young adults, and one of *New York Times'* outstanding books of the year, all 1975, all for *Is That You, Miss Blue?;* one of *School Library Journal's* best books of the year, 1977, for *I'll Love You When You're More Like Me;* Christopher Award, The Christophers, *School Library Journal's* book of the year award, one of *New York Times'* outstanding books of the year, all 1978, and one of New York Public Library's best books for the teen age, 1980 and 1981, all for *Gentlehands;* Golden Kite Award, Society of Children's Book Writers, one of *School Library Journal's* best books of the year, both 1981, and one of New York Public Library's books for the teen age, 1982, all for *Little Little;* one of *School Library Journal's* best books of the year, 1982, for *What I Really Think of You;* one of ALA best books for young adults, 1983, for *Me, Me, Me, Me, Me: Not a Novel;* one of ALA best books for young adults, 1985, for *I Stay Near You;* one of ALA recommended books for the reluctant young adult reader, 1986, and California Young Reader Medal, 1991, both for *Night Kites.*

WRITINGS:

FICTION

(Under name M. J. Meaker) *Hometown,* Doubleday, 1967.
Game of Survival, New American Library, 1968.

Shockproof Sydney Skate, Little, Brown, 1972.
(Under pseudonym Mary James) *Shoebag* (young adult), Scholastic Inc., 1990.

NONFICTION

(Under pseudonym Ann Aldrich) *We Walk Alone,* Gold Medal Books, 1955.
(Under pseudonym Ann Aldrich) *We Too Must Love,* Gold Medal Books, 1958.
(Under pseudonym Ann Aldrich) *Carol, in a Thousand Cities,* Gold Medal Books, 1960.
(Under pseudonym Ann Aldrich) *We Two Won't Last,* Gold Medal Books, 1963.
(Under name M. J. Meaker) *Sudden Endings,* Doubleday, 1964, paperback edition published under pseudonym Vin Packer, Fawcett, 1964.
Take a Lesbian to Lunch, MacFadden-Bartell, 1972.
Me, Me, Me, Me, Me: Not a Novel (autobiography), Harper, 1983.

YOUNG ADULT FICTION; UNDER PSEUDONYM M. E. KERR

Dinky Hocker Shoots Smack!, Harper, 1972.
If I Love You, Am I Trapped Forever?, Harper, 1973.
The Son of Someone Famous, Harper, 1974.
Is That You, Miss Blue?, Harper, 1975.
Love Is a Missing Person, Harper, 1975.
I'll Love You When You're More Like Me, Harper, 1977.
Gentlehands, Harper, 1978.
Little Little, Harper, 1981.
What I Really Think of You, Harper, 1982.
Him She Loves?, Harper, 1984.
I Stay Near You, Harper, 1985.
Night Kites, Harper, 1986.
Fell, Harper, 1987.
Fell Back, Harper, 1989.
Fell Down, Harper, 1991.

Contributor to *Sixteen,* edited by Donald R. Gallo, Delacorte, 1984.

FICTION; UNDER PSEUDONYM VIN PACKER

Dark Intruder, Gold Medal Books, 1952.
Spring Fire, Gold Medal Books, 1952.
Look Back to Love, Gold Medal Books, 1953.
Come Destroy Me, Gold Medal Books, 1954.
Whisper His Sin, Gold Medal Books, 1954.
The Thrill Kids, Gold Medal Books, 1955.
Dark Don't Catch Me, Gold Medal Books, 1956.
The Young and Violent, Gold Medal Books, 1956.
Three-Day Terror, Gold Medal Books, 1957.
The Evil Friendship, Gold Medal Books, 1958.
5:45 to Suburbia, Gold Medal Books, 1958.
The Twisted Ones, Gold Medal Books, 1959.
The Damnation of Adam Blessing, Gold Medal Books, 1961.

The Girl on the Best Seller List, Gold Medal Books, 1961.
Something in the Shadows, Gold Medal Books, 1961.
Intimate Victims, Gold Medal Books, 1962.
Alone at Night, Gold Medal Books, 1963.
The Hare in March, New American Library, 1967.
Don't Rely on Gemini, Delacorte Press, 1969.

ADAPTATIONS: Dinky Hocker Shoots Smack! has been optioned for film, and was broadcast as a television afternoon special by Learning Corporation of America, 1978. *If I Love You Am I Trapped Forever?* has been recorded on audio cassette and released by Random House, 1979.

WORK IN PROGRESS: A second Mary James book, for Scholastic Inc.; a new "Fell" book, for Harper.

SIDELIGHTS: Marijane Meaker explains in an essay for *Something about the Author Autobiography Series* that it was the combination of reading Paul Zindel and teaching writing classes at Commercial Manhattan Central High School that prompted her to try writing for the young adult audience. Until then, Meaker had been spending most of her time writing suspense stories under the pseudonym Vin Packer and nonfiction under her own name and the pseudonym Ann Aldrich. In her autobiographical essay, Meaker discusses the publication of her first young adult novel, *Dinky Hocker Shoots Smack!:* "Since I love pseudonyms," says Meaker, "I decided to call myself M. E. Kerr, a play on my last name, Meaker." When the book was actually successful, Meaker decided to take a second look at the category of young adult fiction. "Miraculously," recalls Meaker in her essay, "as I sat down to make notes for possible future stories, things that happened to me long ago came back clear as a bell, and ringing, and making me smile and shake my head as I realized I had stories in me about *me*—no longer disguised as a homicidal maniac, or a twisted criminal bent on a scam, but as the small-town kid I'd been, so typically American and middle class and yes, vulnerable, but not as tragic and complicated as I used to imagine. So I had a new identity for myself in middle age: M. E. Kerr." And with this new identity, Meaker has created juvenile novels that "are among the most outstanding being published today," writes Mary Kingsbury in *Horn Book,* adding: "For in each of them and with varying degrees of 'credibility and grace,' she attempts to clarify the why of people. Her willingness to confront serious issues coupled with her artistic abilities lifts her novels above the myriad problem-novels that have little to recommend them but their topicality."

According to Kingsbury, Meaker's novels are essentially about love—"its presence and, more commonly, its absence in the lives of her characters." She portrays adolescents who learn that the people they love will, "more often than not, fail to live up to their expectations," says Kingsbury, adding, "In addition to this common theme, the novels share a pattern of elements and literary devices. Each introduces at least one contemporary issue such as mental illness, drug addiction, anti-Semitism, alcoholism, and racism. Each portrays the development of adolescent sexuality, and several offer insight into adult sexuality as well. Adolescents in all the books begin to view their parents more realistically and with greater understanding."

Meaker's first young adult novel, *Dinky Hocker Shoots Smack!,* was inspired by one of her students—an obese young girl named Tiny. In the novel, Meaker tells the story of an overweight girl who goes to extraordinary measures to gain the love and attention of her parents. Dinky "shoots smack," or rather, pretends that she does in order to wrest her too-busy mother away from the junkies Mrs. Hocker is dedicated to rehabilitating. Dinky fights to make people understand that the lack of exterior problems does not necessarily point to the absence of private ones, summarizes Dale Carlson in the *New York Times Book Review.* The character of Dinky Hocker is "likable, credible, distinctive," asserts a *Times Literary Supplement* reviewer. Meaker "has an ear for catching the sound of real people talking and a heart for finding the center of real people's problems," observes Carlson, concluding: "This is a brilliantly funny book that will make you cry. It is full of wit and wisdom and an astonishing immediacy that comes from spare, honest writing."

Another book for young people, *The Son of Someone Famous,* introduces Adam Blessing, a boy whose reaction to his famous diplomat father is to become "a confirmed failure who's been kicked out of more elite schools than he can remember," notes Joyce Alpern in the *Washington Post Book World.* Adam goes to live with his Uncle Charlie in a small Vermont town, where he befriends a local girl who also feels like an outcast; and their relationship and shared escapades give them both a sense of belonging. It is also during this sojourn that Adam discovers that his "perfect" father does not always know what is best. Meaker makes "the familiar point about learning to accept others and ourselves, faults and all," comments Alpern, adding that "she is wise enough to realize that life is more than an extended problem-solving session and adroit enough to entertain." A *Times Literary Supplement* reviewer echoes Alpern, noting that there is "some good, amusing writing throughout" *The Son of Someone Famous,* but concludes that "perhaps finally the impression is of something bright but rather vacuous." And in a second *New York Times Book Review* article, Carlson concurs, calling Meaker "a brilliant writer with an ear for the minute agonies and hilarity of adolescents and their relationship to themselves and each other. But unlike her first novel, *Dinky Hocker Shoots Smack!,* in this, her subject matter is slight and her insights too glib."

In *Is That You, Miss Blue?,* Meaker relates the tale of Miss Blue, a fervently religious woman who teaches at Charles Boarding School. The story is narrated by a fifteen-year-old student named Flanders who observes how intense ridicule and forced isolation—dealt by both students and parents—is prompting Miss Blue to lose her mind. By the novel's end, Flanders comes to protest "the type of exile reserved for those who march to the beat of a different drummer," remarks Alix Nelson in the *New York Times Book Review.* Meaker "has used the familiar microcosm of boarding school to make several points which apply at large," continues Nelson, "and to make them with so much grace, charm, and poignancy that one closes the book with the feeling, 'this is the way life really is.'"

A fourth novel, *Gentlehands,* begins as the familiar story of a lower middle-class boy vying for the attentions of a wealthy young beauty. Sixteen-year-old Buddy Boyle manages to overcome with earnestness, good humor, and good looks, the social and financial gulfs that separate him from his love, Skye Pennington. He even impresses Skye with his charming and wealthy grandfather, a man with whom Buddy becomes increasingly close. Yet this simple story evolves into a nightmare when a visiting investigative reporter exposes Buddy's grandfather as a brutal former Nazi concentration camp guard. By the novel's end, Buddy is just beginning to come to grips with the shattering revelation. *Times Literary Supplement* reviewer Nicholas Tucker finds *Gentlehands* "very readable," but sees the grandfather character as "unconvincing" and the plot turn as "a modish and pretentious note on which to end." Richard Bradford of the *New York Times Book Review* expresses an opposing view, however, maintaining that the story's surprise turn is an arresting exposition of "the paradoxes that exist in the heart of man. . . . If [the author] fails to explain thoroughly the alarming enigma of Frank Trenker's double life, it is only because there is, finally, no explanation possible." Meaker has a "superb" ear for youthful dialogue and a thorough understanding of youthful feelings concludes Bradford.

With *Little Little,* Meaker once again writes "about likeable outcasts," points out Suzanne Freeman in the *Washington Post Book World.* The narrators of *Little Little* are two teenage dwarves, Little Little and Sydney Cinnamon. Mama La Belle, Little Little's mother, has marriage in mind for her daughter, her candidate being a famous midget evangelist named Little Lion. Sydney and Little Lion vie for Little Little's heart, relates Freeman, "and some fairly silly stuff ensues." But even though *Little Little* "is essentially a love story," asserts Marilyn Kaye in the *New York Times Book Review,* "the author gently weaves into the plot the general anguish and specific problems intrinsically bound to a minority world." Many aspects of the dwarves' daily lives are described, points out

Freeman—Meaker "doesn't stoop to tricks. . . . This is a story about courage and tolerance and growing up without growing bigger." *Little Little,* concludes Kaye, provides for the reader "a set of engaging personalities, an unusual perspective, and an entertaining, tender romance that offers both technical strength and a low-key emotional tug."

Meaker's "finger is evidently on the pulse of teenage needs and fears," claims Jennifer Fitzgerald in the *School Library Journal,* "giving her, in . . . *Night Kites,* an especially deft perspective on Erick Rudd's overwhelming emotions: his first experience of sexual passion, bound up with guilt and peer ostracism, since he has fallen in love with his best friend's girlfriend. The usual tensions of family life are skillfully conveyed as parental expectations clash with filial exasperation." Complicating Erick's senior year even more is the discovery that his older brother Pete has AIDS. As Pete moves closer to death, writes Audrey B. Eaglen in the *New York Times Book Review,* Erick comes to terms with his brother's disease, only to lose his girlfriend when she finds out about Pete. "In less sure hands," maintains Eaglen, "this moving and understated examination of the angst of first love and first sex, of the effects of a catastrophic illness on one family, . . . could have been just another problem novel." Meaker has constructed "a fine story, beautifully told, with characters that ring true," concludes Eaglen, and "has simply never been better in her long and lauded career."

Meaker returns to suspense writing, combining it with the element of love, in *Fell,* the first book in a new series. John Fell first meets his girlfriend Keats' next-door neighbor when she fails to show up for the senior prom, states a *Publishers Weekly* contributor. Woodrow Pingree immediately takes an interest in Fell and offers him ten thousand dollars to attend Gardner prep school as his son, Woodrow Pingree, Jr. Another ten thousand will be added if Fell is able to get into an exclusive fraternity known as the Sevens. Fell attends Gardner and is successful in everything he does, until he discovers that the Pingree family has been arrested for selling nuclear secrets. Meaker "has taken a heavy summer romance . . . and used it as a vehicle for her satiric humor," claims a *Horn Book* reviewer. And although Gloria Miklowitz writes in the *Los Angeles Times* that "the plot becomes as complex as a Chinese puzzle," *School Library Journal* contributor Susan L. Locke concludes: "The plot is well constructed and the characterization is superb. . . . [Meaker's] breezy style smacks with vitality and realistic humor." The second book in the series, *Fell Back,* continues the action of the first. One of Fell's classmates, and a fellow member of the Sevens, has committed suicide, explains Jim Naughton in the *Washington Post Book World.* And as Fell investigates the suicide, he becomes involved in another murder, the drug scene, and a love affair. Praising Meaker's style as "breezy, biting and wonderfully observant," Naughton thinks that she "keeps the action moving so quickly the seams in this patchy plot barely show through." Marjorie Lewis, however, points out in the *School Library Journal* that "although this fell short in story, Fell's charm is considerable, and readers will like him and his insecurities."

In addition to fiction, Meaker has also written *Me, Me, Me, Me, Me: Not a Novel,* an autobiographical memoir for young adults that "unveils a deliciously wicked sense of humor," declares *New York Times Book Review* contributor Joyce Milton. In answer to her readers' questions, Meaker "describes with drama, humor, and perception a youth less exotic but no less entertaining and compelling," maintains Nancy C. Hammond in *Horn Book.* Her rebellious teenage years are presented, as are her friends and others who influenced her during this period of her life, points out *Best Sellers* contributor Paul A. Caron. "The author's style and technique are very effective. She presents these autobiographical chapters in such a way that the reader enters into stories without realizing it," continues Caron, adding that Meaker "has written a fascinating, yet timeless look at herself and others, which will not only delight her fans, but will no doubt increase their number."

Naughton considers Meaker "a master of the young adult novel." And in her autobiographical essay, Meaker explains her attraction to this genre: "I love writing, and I particularly love writing for young adults. I know other young adult writers who claim that their books are just slotted into that category, and claim there's no difference between an adult novel and a young adult one . . . I beg to disagree. When I write for young adults I know they're still wrestling with very important problems like winning and losing, not feeling accepted or accepting, prejudice, love—all the things adults ultimately get hardened to, and forgetful of. I know my audience hasn't yet made up their minds about everything, that they're still vulnerable and open to suggestion and able to change their minds . . . Give me that kind of an audience any day!"

BIOGRAPHICAL/CRITICAL SOURCES:

BOOKS

Contemporary Literary Criticism, Gale, Volume 12, 1980, Volume 35, 1985.

Crawford, Elizabeth D., and Doris de Montreville, *Fourth Book of Junior Authors and Illustrators,* H. W. Wilson, 1978.

Donelson, Kenneth L., and Alleen Pace Nilsen, *Literature for Today's Young Adults,* Scott, Foresman, 1980, 2nd edition, 1985.

Kirkpatrick, D. L., editor, *Twentieth-Century Children's Writers,* St. Martin's, 1978.

Meaker, Marijane (under pseudonym M. E. Kerr), essay in *Something about the Author Autobiography Series,* Volume 1, Gale, 1986.

Nilsen, *Presenting M. E. Kerr,* Twayne, 1986.

Rees, David, *Painted Desert, Green Shade: Essays on Contemporary Writers of Fiction for Children and Young Adults,* Horn Book, 1984.

PERIODICALS

Best Sellers, June, 1983; September, 1984.

Chicago Tribune Book World, March 2, 1986.

English Journal, December, 1975; February, 1986.

Horn Book, February, 1973; August, 1975; June, 1977; August, 1983; September/October, 1986; July/August, 1987.

Los Angeles Times, October 25, 1986; August 1, 1987.

New York Post, July 8, 1978.

New York Times Book Review, February 11, 1973; September 16, 1973; April 7, 1974; April 13, 1975; October 19, 1975; April 30, 1978; May 17, 1981; September 12, 1982; May 22, 1983; June 5, 1983; April 13, 1986.

Publishers Weekly, February 24, 1984; May 30, 1986; June 26, 1987; September 29, 1989.

School Library Journal, May, 1986; September, 1986; November, 1986; August, 1987; September, 1989.

Times Literary Supplement, November 23, 1973; September 19, 1975; December 1, 1978.

Voice of Youth Advocates, February, 1985; June, 1986; October, 1987; February, 1991.

Washington Post Book World, May 19, 1974; May 10, 1981; July 11, 1982; April 10, 1983; May 12, 1985; May 11, 1986; June 10, 1990.

*   *   *

MEANS, Florence Crannell   1891-1980

PERSONAL: Born May 15, 1891, in Baldwinsville, NY; died November 19, 1980, in Boulder, CO; daughter of Philip Wendell (a minister, author and educator) and Fannie Eleanor (Grout) Crannell; married Carleton Bell Means (an attorney and businessman), 1912; children: Eleanor Crannell (Mrs. Angus C. Hull). *Education:* Attended Henry Read School of Art, 1910-11, Macpherson College, 1922-29, and University of Denver, 1923-24. *Politics:* Independent. *Religion:* Baptist.

CAREER: Writer. Lecturer, Writer's Conference in the Rocky Mountains, Boulder, CO, 1947-48, and University of Denver Writers' Workshop, 1947-54.

MEMBER: Colorado Authors League, Denver Woman's Press Club, Soroptimist International, Colorado Poetry Society, Delta Kappa Gamma, Zeta Tau Alpha.

AWARDS, HONORS: Child Study Association annual award for character-building book, 1945, and Newbery Honor Book, 1946, both for *The Moved-Outers;* Nancy Bloch Annual Award for a book dealing with intercultural relations, 1957, for *Knock at the Door, Emmy;* churchmanship citation, Central Baptist Seminary, 1962.

WRITINGS:

JUVENILE FICTION

(With Harriet Fullen) *Rafael and Consuelo: Stories and Studies about Mexicans in the United States for Primary Children,* Friendship Press, 1929.
A Candle in the Mist, Houghton, 1931.
Ranch and Ring, Houghton, 1932.
Dusky Day, Houghton, 1933.
A Bowlful of Stars, Houghton, 1934.
Rainbow Bridge, Friendship Press, 1934.
Penny for Luck, Houghton, 1935.
Tangled Waters, Houghton, 1935.
The Singing Wood, Houghton, 1937.
Shattered Windows, Houghton, 1938.
Adella Mary in Old New Mexico, Houghton, 1939.
Across the Fruited Plain, Friendship Press, 1940.
At the End of Nowhere, Houghton, 1940.
All 'round Me Shinin', Baptist Board of Education, c. 1940.
Frankie and Willie Go a Far Piece, Baptist Board of Education, c. 1940.
Some California Poppies and How They Grew, Baptist Board of Education, c. 1940.
Children of the Promise, Friendship Press, 1941.
Whispering Girl, Houghton, 1941.
Shadow over Wide Rain, Houghton, 1942.
Teresita of the Valley, Houghton, 1943.
Peter of the Mesa, Friendship Press, 1944.
Wither the Tribes Go Up, Northern Baptist Convention, 1944.
The Moved-Outers, Houghton, 1945.
Great Day in the Morning, Houghton, 1946.
Assorted Sisters, Houghton, 1947.
The House under the Hill, Houghton, 1949.
(With Carl Means) *The Silver Fleece,* Winston, 1950.
Hetty of the Grande Deluxe, Houghton, 1951.
Alicia, Houghton, 1953.
The Rains Will Come, Houghton, 1954.
Knock at the Door, Emmy, Houghton, 1956.
Reach for a Star, Houghton, 1957.
Borrowed Brother, Houghton, 1958.
Emmy and the Blue Door, Houghton, 1959.
But I Am Sara, Houghton, 1961.
That Girl Andy, Houghton, 1962.
Tolliver, Houghton, 1963.
It Takes All Kinds, Houghton, 1964.
Us Maltbys, Houghton, 1966.

Our Cup Is Broken, Houghton, 1969.
Smith Valley, Houghton, 1973.

OTHER

Tara Finds the Door to Happiness (play), Friendship Press, 1926.
The Black Tents: A Junior Play of Life among the Bedouins of Syria, Friendship Press, 1926.
Pepita's Adventures in Friendship: A Play for Juniors about Mexicans in the United States, Friendship Press, 1929.
(With Frances Somers Riggs) *Children of the Great Spirit: A Course on the American Indian* (juvenile), Friendship Press, 1932.
Carvers' George: A Biography of George Washington Carver (juvenile), Houghton, 1952.
Sagebrush Surgeon (adult biography), Friendship Press, 1955.
Sunlight on the Hopi Mesas: The Story of Abigail E. Johnson (adult biography), Judson Press, 1960.
Biography of Frederick Douglass, Imperial International, 1969.

Also author of pamphlets on American Indian tribes published by the Baptist Missionary Society. A collection of Means' manuscripts is housed at the University of Colorado Library, Boulder.

SIDELIGHTS: Florence Crannell Means was a white woman who wrote young adult books about minorities. "In the 1930s and '40s," Suzanne Rahn explained in *Lion and the Unicorn,* "she made herself a specialist, all but unique, in ethnic children's literature. In books designed mainly for girls in their teens, her attractive heroines were black, Chicano, Hopi, Navajo, Japanese-American." Means' novel *The Moved-Outers,* dealing with the round-up of Japanese-Americans during the Second World War, was a Newbery Honor Book in 1946.

"How did I come to write books?" Means once commented. "For somewhat the same reason the alpinist gives for climbing the mountain: because it's there. The first full-sized [book], *A Candle in the Mist,* was definitely 'there,' in the pioneering of my maternal grandparents, going from settled farming community in Wisconsin to the southwest corner of Minnesota in 1872. All my life I had heard the stories of those adventurous days, from my grandparents when we visited them, from my mother, who was the original of the Janey Eleanor of the book. Already, nearly forty years ago, our young people seemed rootless, and here were roots.

"The books about minority groups have had varied motivation—more than any other the desire to introduce one group of people to another, who otherwise might never know them, and so might regard them with the fear which is bred of lack of knowledge, and which in its turn breeds the hate, the prejudice which I have seen blazing out in destructive force against all Germans, against all Japanese, against all Negroes. This desired 'introduction' meant presenting living characters in a true setting, sympathetically but without sentimentality. And that end could be gained only by studying widely, talking with persons who had intimate acquaintance with the group, and then—going to the group and getting really acquainted with them. So I have spent much time in Carolina Low Country and on its tidal islands and Tuskee; in the southwest among the Hopis and the Navajos, visiting perhaps twenty other tribes in New York, California, Arizona, New Mexico, Oklahoma, to get better understanding of the two tribes I was writing about.

"I spent a little time in a Chinese apartment house in San Francisco, and in a Chinese cannery village on the Sacramento. I visited the Japanese Relocation Center nearest me, in southwestern Colorado. We visited Mexican friends in Denver slums, in the southern part of Colorado, where the Hispano had been influential and respected for nearly two hundred years.

"And why was my aim at the young? Because, I think, an adult reading such a book would accept its message only if he was of the same mind to begin with. But the adolescent, as has been proved by careful research, can be really moved—and changed—by it, if characters are so strong and situations so vital as to force self-identification."

Means acquired her strong beliefs from her father, Philip Wendell Crannell, a minister who served for some twenty-five years as president of Kansas City Theological Seminary. As Siri Andrews wrote in *Horn Book,* "Dr. Crannell was a scholar, a poet and a wit; he was as well a man of absolutely no racial consciousness. His daughter's earliest memories are of the men and women of many races who visited in their home, and to her a mingling of different colors on an equal footing has never seemed strange."

After writing early books about the American Indians, Jews, Mexican-Americans, and blacks, Means turned in 1945 to the plight of the Japanese-Americans. The United States government had ordered the internment of all Japanese-Americans for the duration of the Second World War. Japanese-Americans were taken from their homes and businesses to live in isolated detention camps in semi-prison conditions. Means' novel *The Moved-Outers* focused on the children of these evacuees.

Speaking of *The Moved-Outers,* Andrews noted: "It took courage to write of these people in the midst of war, against a tide of hate which washed over even small children who did not know that they were 'different' from other American children. But Mrs. Means felt that young people must somehow be helped to see what had hap-

pened, how this might affect the innocent victims and to face the possibly tragic results in a peace-time United States. It is a vivid and timely book, with true and detailed descriptions of daily existence in the temporary relocation centers and the monotonous permanent camps, of the lack of privacy, the disillusionment, the physical restrictions. . . . There is no criticism in the book of the decision which caused the evacuation, or the way in which it was carried out—only a description of the humanly tragic results."

Rahn pointed out that since the 1960s, white writers about minorities have been discounted. The prevailing mood among teachers and librarians was to "deny that any white author can depict the black experience with authenticity; logically, this caveat would apply to other minorities as well. . . . Now that we have writers for children who are themselves black, Chicano, American Indian, and Japanese-American, why reconsider [Florence Crannell Means], most of whose books were written forty, even fifty years ago? First, I would say, because her best novels give us insight, comparable to those of a fine historical novel, into black and Navajo experience of the 1930s, and Japanese-American life during World War II. Secondly, because what she did as a writer can still work."

In her private life, Means lived by her principles. She and her husband raised their own daughter, Eleanor, and "adopted" Chinese children in Shanghai, several Japanese-American children, a Spanish-American boy, and children in Burma. In addition, Means claimed to have a Navajo "granddaughter" as well.

BIOGRAPHICAL/CRITICAL SOURCES:

BOOKS

The Junior Book of Authors, 2nd edition, H. W. Wilson, 1951.
Rider, Elizabeth, *The Story behind Modern Books,* Dodd, 1949.
Writing Books for Boys and Girls: A Young Wings Anthology, Junior Literary Guild-Doubleday, 1952.

PERIODICALS

Atlantic, December, 1969, p. 150.
Booklist, October 15, 1969, p. 273; March 1, 1974, p. 737.
Boulder Daily Camera (Boulder, CO), December 18, 1962.
Horn Book, January, 1946, pp. 15-30; April, 1981.
Lion and the Unicorn, April, 1987, pp. 98-115.
New York Times Book Review, August 17, 1969, p. 22.
Publishers Weekly, February 27, 1981, p. 284.
Saturday Review, September 13, 1969, p. 37.*

MERAS, Phyllis 1931-

PERSONAL: Surname is pronounced "*Mer*-a"; born May 10, 1931, in Brooklyn, NY; daughter of Edmond Albert (a teacher) and Leslie (a teacher; maiden name, Ross) Meras; married Thomas Cocroft (an artist), November 3, 1968. *Education:* Wellesley College, B.A., 1953; Columbia University, M.S., 1954; also attended Institut des Hautes Etudes Internationales, Geneva, Switzerland. *Politics:* Democrat. *Religion:* Congregationalist.

ADDRESSES: Home—Music St., West Tisbury, MA. *Office*—*Vineyard Gazette,* Edgartown, MA 02539.

CAREER: Providence Journal, Providence, RI, copy editor and reporter, 1954-57, 1959-61, travel editor, 1976—; *Ladies Home Journal,* Philadelphia, PA, writer, 1958-59; *Weekly Tribune,* Geneva, Switzerland, editor-in-chief, 1961-62; *New York Times,* New York City, reporter and copy editor for travel section, 1962-68; *Vineyard Gazette,* Edgartown, MA, managing editor, 1968-74, contributing editor, 1974—.

AWARDS, HONORS: Exchange fellow, Government of Switzerland, 1957; Pulitzer fellow in critical writing, 1966.

WRITINGS:

First Spring: A Journal of Martha's Vineyard, Chatham Press, 1972.
A Yankee Way with Wood, Houghton, 1975.
Miniatures: How to Make, Use, and Sell Them, Houghton, 1976.
Vacation Crafts, Houghton, 1978.
(With Julianna Turkevich) *Christmas Angels,* Houghton, 1979.
Carry-Out Cuisine, Houghton, 1982.
The Mermaids of Chenonceaux: An Anecdotal Guide to Europe, Congdon & Weed, 1983.
Exploring Rhode Island: A Visitor's Guide to the Ocean State, Providence Journal, 1984.
(With Linda Glick Conway) *The New Carry-Out Cuisine,* Houghton, 1986.
Castles, Keeps, and Leprechauns, Congdon & Weed, 1988.
Eastern Europe: A Traveler's Companion, Houghton, 1991.

SIDELIGHTS: The "great virtue" of Phyllis Meras' *The Mermaids of Chenonceaux: An Anecdotal Guide to Europe,* Peter S. Prescott writes in *Newsweek,* "is its originality—I know of nothing like it." Telling the historical or legendary stories associated with over eight hundred sites in Europe, the book provides the "magic" that tourists search out, according to Carolyn See in the *Los Angeles Times.* "The market for *The Mermaids of Chenonceaux,*" See believes, "is for anyone who (1) is going to Europe, (2) is saving or planning to go to Europe, or (3) regrets never having gone to Europe. . . . This is a book that will be

around long after this year's budget hotels have closed their doors, and this decade's three-star restaurants have had their Michelin epaulets torn away."

BIOGRAPHICAL/CRITICAL SOURCES:

PERIODICALS

Chicago Tribune Book World, December 5, 1982.
Los Angeles Times, January 7, 1983.
Newsweek, June 27, 1983.
Washington Post, November 12, 1986.

*   *   *

MEYER, Linda D(oreen) 1948-

PERSONAL: Born April 2, 1948, in Santa Barbara, CA; daughter of John Floyd (an assistant fire chief) and Dorothy (Baker) Potter; married Lee Meyer (an electrical engineer), September 6, 1969; children: Joshua Scott, Matthew Sean. *Education:* Attended University of California, Santa Barbara, 1966-68; San Jose State University, B.A., 1971. *Politics:* Social Democrat. *Religion:* Born-again Christian.

ADDRESSES: Home—7821 175th St. S.W., Edmonds, WA 98020. *Office*—Chas. Franklin Press, 18409 90th Ave. W., Edmonds, WA 98020.

CAREER: Women's Community Clinic, San Jose, CA, pregnancy counselor, 1973-75; Childbirth Education Association of Snohomish County, WA, cesarean childbirth educator, 1978-81, founding member of board of directors of Cesarean Family; Birthplace, Seattle, WA, baby care instructor, 1979-80. Chas. Franklin Press, Edmonds, WA, president, 1979—.

MEMBER: Pacific Northwest Writer's Conference, Santa Barbara Writer's Conference.

WRITINGS:

The Cesarean (R)evolution: A Handbook for Parents and Childbirth Educators, Chas. Franklin, 1979, 2nd edition, 1981.
(Editor) Gayle C. Baker and Vivian Montey, *Special Delivery: A Book for Kids about Cesarean and Vaginal Birth,* Chas. Franklin, 1981.
(Editor) Barbara Ciaramitaro, *Help for Depressed Mothers,* Chas. Franklin, 1982.
(Editor) Frances S. Dayee, *Private Zone: A Book Teaching Children Sexual Assault Prevention Skills,* Chas. Franklin, 1982.
(With Cynthia L. Duffy) *Responsible Childbirth: How to Give Birth Normally and Avoid a Cesarean Section,* R & E Research Associates, 1984.
Safety Zone: A Book Teaching Child Abduction Prevention Skills, Chas. Franklin, 1984.
I Take Good Care of Me, Chas. Franklin, 1989.

Harriet Tubman: They Called Me Moses, Parenting Press, 1990.

(Editor) John and Roberta Hogan, *Trapped in Kuwait: Countdown to Armageddon,* Chas. Franklin, 1991.

Also editor of "Children's Safety" series.

SIDELIGHTS: Linda D. Meyer once told *CA:* "I began my writing career by accident, not ever intending to be a writer. Now, next to my family, it is the love of my life. With a bachelor's in social psychology, I had eventually intended to get my master's in social work and become a professional counselor, dealing specifically with troubled teenagers. I learned, however, that I could make much more of an impact with my pen. The projects I choose, whether fiction or nonfiction, still usually reflect my background in the fields of counseling and the social sciences. The writer's life can be extremely isolated and, depending on the subjects one chooses, very emotional, but once addicted, you can't get loose. Writing, for a writer, is life itself."

Meyer explained her first venture into writing: "After having my own two children in births by surgery, I became sensitive to the cesarean situation and studied to receive my certification to teach cesarean childbirth classes. In my exposure to the field as mother, student, and instructor, I learned many behind-the-scene things that were not covered elsewhere. Most importantly, I wanted to assure parents that in this age of involved childbirth they needn't relinquish control and responsibility over the birth simply because it may be by surgery. So over the year preceding the start of the book, I kept a sheet of paper on which I would occasionally jot down a subject 'which somebody ought to write about someday.' Then a few weeks before Christmas, 1978, the words started pouring into my head. Inspiration is the only word for it. I was compelled to sit down and write or I couldn't sleep at night.

"Some people wonder how the mother of two preschoolers finds the time and energy to write a book. My secret was that I napped every day with the children. Then I wrote most evenings from eight o'clock when the children went to bed until midnight or 1:00 A.M. The first draft took about five weeks while the second and third each took about two weeks.

"I was tremendously influenced by a fellow childbirth educator and writer, Vicki Walton, whose book *Have It Your Way* was first 'self-published' and then taken over by a big publishing firm. Without her encouragement and guidance, I would never have attempted this project, much less completed it. Having her example to emulate was of inestimable value and impressed on me the importance of a mentor."

MILES, Miska
See MARTIN, Patricia Miles

*   *   *

MILES, Patricia A.
See MARTIN, Patricia Miles

*   *   *

MITCHAM, Carl 1941-

PERSONAL: Born September 20, 1941, in Dallas, TX; married Marylee Daniel Hawley; children: Mark, Jessica, Emilie, Anna. *Education:* University of Colorado, B.A. (summa cum laude), 1967, M.A., 1969; Fordham University, Ph.D., 1988.

ADDRESSES: Office—Science, Technology, Society Program, Pennsylvania State University, University Park, PA 16802.

CAREER: Berea College, Berea, KY, instructor in philosophy, 1970-72; St. Catharine College, St. Catharine, KY, lecturer in philosophy and social science, 1972-82; Polytechnic University, associate professor of humanities, 1982-89, director of Philosophy and Technology Studies Center, 1984-90; Penn State University, associate professor of philosophy and of science, technology, and society, 1989—, director of Science, Technology, Society Program, 1990—. Member of Columbia University Seminar on the History and Philosophy of Science, 1982-88; visiting scholar at University of Puerto Rico, Mayaguez, 1988.

MEMBER: American Catholic Philosophical Association, Society for the History of Technology, Society for Philosophy and Technology (president, 1980-82), Humanities and Technology Association, National Association for Science, Technology, and Society, Society for Social Studies of Science.

AWARDS, HONORS: Abbot Payson Usher Prize from Society for the History of Technology, 1974, for *Bibliography of the Philosophy of Technology;* National Science Foundation-National Endowment for the Humanities grant, 1978-80, for "Bibliography of the Philosophy of Technology: 1975-78"; Kentucky Humanities Council grant, 1981-82, for "Intentional Communities in Central Kentucky"; Exxon Education Foundation grant, 1984-86, for course development in philosophy and technology studies; Distinguished Faculty Award from Polytechnic University Student Council, 1985; grants from Franklin J. Matchette Foundation, American Council of Learned Societies, J. M. Foundation, MacArthur Foundation, New York Council on the Humanities, IBM Corporation, and Goethe House New York.

WRITINGS:

(Editor with Robert Mackey) *Philosophy and Technology: Readings in the Philosophical Problems of Technology,* Free Press, 1972, reprinted with updated bibliography, 1983.

(With Mackey) *Bibliography of the Philosophy of Technology,* University of Chicago Press, 1973, reprinted with index, Books on Demand, 1985.

(Editor with Jim Grote) *Theology and Technology: Essays in Christian Analysis and Exegesis,* University Press of America, 1984.

(Editor with Alois Huning) *Philosophy and Technology II: Information Technology and Computers in Theory and Practice,* D. Reidel, 1985.

Que es la filosofia de la tecnologia? (Spanish version of essay entitled "What Is the Philosophy of Technology?," originally published in *International Philosophical Quarterly,* 1985), Anthropos (Barcelona, Spain), 1989.

(With Margarita Pena, Elena Lugo, and Jim Ward) *El nuevo mundo de la filosofia y la tecnologia,* STS Press (University Park, PA), 1990.

Contributor to books, including *A Guide to the Culture of Science, Technology, and Medicine,* edited by Paul T. Durbin, Free Press, 1980, and with Grote to *Encyclopedia of Bioethics,* 1982. Contributor, sometimes under pseudonyms, of articles, reviews, poems, translations, and stories to scholarly works and periodicals, including *Philosophy Today, Research in Philosophy and Technology, International Philosophical Quarterly, Philosophy and Technology,* and *Colorado Quarterly. Research in Philosophy and Technology* (annual), review and bibliography editor, 1978-85, bibliography editor, 1990—, editor with Grote of Volume 4, 1981, and Volume 6, 1983, member of editorial board, 1986—. Guest editor of special theme issues of *Technology in Society,* 1984, and *Cross Currents,* 1985. Member of editorial board of *Technology in Society,* 1985—, *Research in Technology Studies,* 1986—, *Philosophy and Technology,* 1986—, *Ellul Studies Forum,* 1989—, *Journal of Social and Biological Structures,* 1990—.

WORK IN PROGRESS: *Spanish Philosophy of Technology, Philosophy and Technology, Engineering Ethics throughout the World: Introduction, Documentation, and Bibliography, De Technologia: On How to Begin to Think about Technology in a Philosophical Way.*

*   *   *

MITCHELL, Ken(neth Ronald) 1940-

PERSONAL: Born in Moose Jaw, Saskatchewan, Canada. *Education:* University of Saskatchewan, M.A., 1967.

ADDRESSES: Office—University of Regina, Regina, Saskatchewan, Canada. *Agent*—Bella Pomer Agency, 22 Shallmar Blvd., Toronto, Ontario, Canada M5N 2Z8.

CAREER: University of Regina, Regina, Saskatchewan, professor, 1967—. Participated in Mexico-Canada Writer's Colloquium, 1982.

AWARDS, HONORS: Canada-Scotland exchange fellow, 1979-80; Canadian Authors Association Literary Award (for drama), 1986, for *Gone the Burning Sun.*

WRITINGS:

PLAYS

Heroes (one act), Playwrights Co-op, 1973.
This Train, Playwrights Co-op, 1973.
(With Humphrey and the Dumptrucks) *Cruel Tears* (country opera), Talon Books, 1977.
(With David Liang) *The Great Cultural Revolution* (Chinese opera), Playwrights Canada, 1980.
Chautauqua Girl, Playwrights Canada, 1982.
Gone the Burning Sun, Playwrights Canada, 1982.
The Shipbuilder, Fifth House, 1990.

SCREENPLAYS

Striker, National Film Board of Canada, 1977.
The Hounds of Notre Dame, Fraser Films, 1980.
The Front Line, Canadian Broadcasting Corp., 1985.
M.V.P., Canadian Broadcasting Corp., 1985.

OTHER

Wandering Rafferty (novel), Macmillan, 1972.
The Meadowlark Connection: A Saskatchewan Thriller (adapted from his own radio dramatic serial, *The Meadowlark Caper*), Pile of Bones Publisher, 1975.
(Editor) *Horizon: Writings of the Canadian Prairie,* Oxford University Press, 1977.
Everybody Gets Something Here (stories), Macmillan, 1977.
Davin: The Politician, NeWest Press, 1979.
The Con Man (novel), Talon Books, 1979.
Sinclair Ross: A Reader's Guide (criticism), Coteau Books, 1981.
Ken Mitchell Country, Coteau Books, 1984.
Through the Nan Da Gate (poetry), Thistledown Press, 1986.
Witches and Idiots (poetry), Coteau Books, 1990.

WORK IN PROGRESS: A novel set in Tibet and China.

SIDELIGHTS: Ken Mitchell's writing distinguishes itself through a profound sensitivity to landscape. Mitchell was raised on the Canadian prairie, and the region's empty openness haunts his work. His facility for conveying the emotional quality of frontier life prompted Maggie Siggins of the *Globe and Mail* to assert that his literary production "has become the quintessential portrait of Canadian Prairie life." As a professor, Mitchell promotes the writing and study of deliberately Canadian literature. Mitchell's commitment to Canadian literature is coupled with his immense respect for Chinese culture. He has taught and traveled extensively in China, and continuously strives to find harmony between his occidental inheritance and his eastern fascination. Speaking of China, Mitchell told Siggins: "I think it is the most civilized place in the world. The people are by far the most courteous, the most child-loving and most future-oriented. And in many ways China is the last frontier culturally."

Mitchell balances his passions for Canada and China in *Gone the Burning Sun,* a play based on the life of Dr. Norman Bethune, a Canadian Communist who tended Mao Tse-Tung's troops during the Sino-Japanese War. In the course of his research, Mitchell found that he and the doctor had a common Scottish ancestor. Because of this link, Mitchell became particularly intrigued by Bethune's psychological development among the Chinese. He concluded that "what makes the play work is the effect the country had on Bethune. I really tried to integrate myself with his personality."

BIOGRAPHICAL/CRITICAL SOURCES:

PERIODICALS

Globe and Mail, March 21, 1987.

*   *   *

MOLIN, Charles
    See MAYNE, William (James Carter)

*   *   *

MONJO, F(erdinand) N(icholas, III)   1924-1978

PERSONAL: Born August 28, 1924, in Stamford, CT; died October 9, 1978, in New York, NY; married Louise Elaine Lyczak, 1950; children: three sons and one daughter. *Education:* Columbia University, B.A., 1946.

CAREER: Simon & Schuster, New York City, editor of Golden Books, 1953-58; American Heritage Press, New York City, editor of American Heritage Junior Library, 1958-61; Coward McCann and Geoghegan, New York City, assistant director, 1961-69, vice-president and editorial director of children's books, 1969-78.

AWARDS, HONORS: A memorial fund has been established in Monjo's name at the New York Society Library.

WRITINGS:

Indian Summer, Harper, 1968.

The Drinking Gourd, Harper, 1970.
The One Bad Thing about Father, Harper, 1970.
Pirates in Panama, Simon & Schuster, 1970.
The Jezebel Wolf, Simon & Schuster, 1971.
The Vicksburg Veteran, Simon & Schuster, 1971.
Slater's Mill, Simon & Schuster, 1972.
Rudi and the Distelfink, Windmill Books, 1972.
The Secret of the Sachem's Tree, Coward McCann, 1972.
Poor Richard in France, Holt, 1973.
Me and Willie and Pa: The Story of Abraham Lincoln and His Son Tad, Simon & Schuster, 1973.
Clarence and the Burglar, Coward McCann, 1973.
Grand Papa and Ellen Aroon, Holt, 1974.
The Sea-Beggar's Son, Coward McCann, 1974.
King George's Head Was Made of Lead, Coward McCann, 1974.
Letters to Horseface: Being the Story of Wolfgang Amadeus Mozart's Journey to Italy, 1769-1770, When He Was a Boy of Fourteen, Viking Press, 1975.
Gettysburg: Tad Lincoln's Story, Windmill Books, 1976.
Willie Jasper's Golden Eagle, Doubleday, 1976.
Zenas and the Shaving Mill, Coward McCann, 1976.
The Porcelain Pagoda, Viking Press, 1976.
A Namesake for Nathan: Being an Account of Captain Nathan Hale by His Twelve-Year-Old Sister, Coward McCann, 1977.
The House on Stink Alley: A Story about the Pilgrims in Holland, Holt, 1977.
Prisoners of the Scrambling Dragon, Holt, 1980.

OTHER

(Translator with Nina Ignatowicz) Reiner Zimnik, *The Crane,* Harper, 1970.

SIDELIGHTS: F. N. Monjo wrote historical fiction and nonfiction for young readers. He was inspired to write about history by his family's own colorful past. His father's family emigrated from Spain to become fur merchants who sent ships to Alaska to trade with the Eskimos. His mother's family were from Mississippi and had stories to tell about the Civil War and the days of the plantations. "Listening to stories like these," Monjo stated in *Cricket Magazine,* "brought history alive so vividly for me that I was never able to read it, later, as if it were a mere collection of facts and dates. Hearing my two families discuss the past—often with considerable heat and color—made it clear to me that people like Grant and Lincoln certainly had been flesh and blood creatures. And if this were true, why then, I could begin to imagine that perhaps even such remote creatures as Elizabeth of England or Caesar (or even Sir Edmund Andros) might once have been alive."

After graduating from college, Monjo went on to become an editor with several New York publishing houses. "As an editor," Monjo told *Horn Book,* "I began to realize that most of the fun of history lay in the details that most children's books seemed to omit. So I resolved to try writing some books for young children, limited to incidents or mere glimpses from history, but allowing enough leisure and space to be able to include the details that help so much to bring a scene to life."

Monjo's first historical fiction for children was *Indian Summer,* a story of a pioneer family in Kentucky who fight off an Indian attack. The pioneers, as Trevelyn Jones explained in *School Library Journal,* "battle for their lives and cleverly defeat the Indians. Children are fascinated by the Indian wars and this is an exciting story for the very youngest readers."

Many of Monjo's books were written from a child's point of view in an effort to humanize the historical characters portrayed. "We can—if we insist upon it—overwhelm our six and eight-year-olds with vast, monolithic, unsmiling, profiles," Monjo wrote in *Horn Book.* "I remember, as a child, seeing newsreels of Gutzon Borglum chopping those giant, grim faces of Washington, Lincoln, and Teddy Roosevelt into the Dakota cliffs.

"In a way I'm glad they're there. But, as a child, I couldn't imagine that they represented anyone who had ever been a little boy, or that any one of those men had ever cracked a joke or made a pass or fallen on his face. No. They rose up seven stories tall, just as formidable and as poised and as eternal and as unbelievable as the statues of the Egyptian Pharaohs on the Nile."

Monjo felt such portraits to be forbidding to children. He wanted to create more realistic historical characters. "I decided that I would try to offer some flawed, partial, impressionistic, and irreverent portraits of great Americans to children today," he explained in *Horn Book.* "I wanted these shirt-sleeve miniatures to contain only those details that a young child might be likely to admire and understand. I wanted to be sure to include any jokes and mistakes the great men themselves might have made. I wanted to show their foibles and to present the hero not as a huge, remote icon—but, instead, as an intimate, palpable, fallible surprise."

In *Poor Richard in France,* Monjo wrote a story about Benjamin Franklin told from the viewpoint of his grandson Benny. "Benny's views of events," wrote Carol Chatfield in *School Library Journal,* "is based on a skeleton of facts embellished with humorous touches: e.g., he reports that Franklin wouldn't be surprised to see his face painted on chamber pots in a souvenir shop. . . . On the more serious side, there are excerpts from *Poor Richard's Almanack* and frequent references to Franklin's thoughts on life." Zena Sutherland, writing in *Bulletin of the Center for Children's Books,* found that "Seven-year-old Benny's

comments are lively and humorous, and in a perfectly natural way they give a good bit of information about Franklin and about the rebellion against the British."

Monjo's *Letters to Horseface* related fourteen-year-old Mozart's tour of Italy through fictitious letters home to his sister, nicknamed Horseface. "What Monjo has done," wrote Harold C. Schonberg in the *New York Times Book Review,* "is to reconstruct the trip though young Mozart's mind, and he has done a remarkable job. The letters read as though they actually came from Wolfgang's pen. . . . Anybody reading this little book will get a good idea of how the mind of a musical genius works." A critic for *Publishers Weekly* noted that Monjo "is very good at evoking personalities, times and places. . . . The book is a fascinating glimpse at the travels and triumphs of [Mozart] as he was accompanied by his father on a tour from Salzburg to Milan."

Writing in *Horn Book,* Monjo explained why he wrote historical fiction. "We need to inspire our gifted young people to make an attempt at greatness. We need to make them want to reach out after that splendid, elusive, brass ring known as achievement and make it theirs. Our age is more tawdry than we wish it to be, and we yearn for some heroes and heroines for ourselves and for the future. I have not yet utterly abandoned the Western World. It has produced many men and women who still make my skin prickle. I have not yet abandoned the American experiment, for it has produced large numbers of people whom I wish I might have emulated. That is why I would like my books to arouse young people. To make them understand that all great human beings were once uncertain children, unaware of their powers. I want my books to incite children to dare to do something marvelous. For, if they dare, perhaps they will succeed."

BIOGRAPHICAL/CRITICAL SOURCES:

BOOKS

Children's Literature Review, Volume 2, Gale, 1976, pp. 120-126.

PERIODICALS

Bulletin of the Center for Children's Books, March, 1974, pp. 115-116.
Children's Book Review, October, 1971, p. 163.
Cricket Magazine, September, 1975.
Horn Book, October, 1975.
New York Times Book Review, April 25, 1971, p. 40; November 16, 1975, p. 33.
Publishers Weekly, November 17, 1975, p. 97.
Saturday Review, March 21, 1970, p. 39.
School Library Journal, November, 1968, p. 108; December, 1973, p. 43.*

MONTHAN, Doris Born 1924-

PERSONAL: Surname is pronounced "*Mon*-tan"; born May 26, 1924, in Manitowoc, WI; daughter of Edgar Jacob (a banker) and Linda Sophia (Vogt) Born; married Guy Monthan (a teacher and photographer), September 20, 1952; children: William Edgar. *Education:* Attended University of Arizona, 1943-44, New York University, 1948-49, Columbia University, 1950-51, and Northern Arizona University, 1976, 1982. *Politics:* Democrat. *Religion:* Episcopalian.

ADDRESSES: Home—P.O. Box 1698, Flagstaff, AZ 86002.

CAREER: Tucson Daily Citizen, Tucson, AZ, women's editor, 1944-45; *Women's Wear Daily,* New York City, section editor, 1945-46; University of Arizona, Tucson, writer for Press Bureau and publicist for Artists and Lecture Series, 1946-47; free-lance writer and tutor in Mexico City, Mexico, 1947-48; Brentanno's, New York City, clerk-typist, 1948; Gunther-Jaeckel (women's clothing store), New York City, in publicity and public relations, 1948; *Simplicity Fashion,* New York City, associate editor, 1949-51; Stamps-Conhaim Newspaper Mat Service, Los Angeles, CA, copywriter, 1952; Rexall Drug Co., Los Angeles, copywriter, 1952-53; Crown Sleep Shops, Pasadena, CA, advertising manager, 1953-67; free-lance writer in Pasadena, 1967-68; May Co., Los Angeles, copywriter, 1968; Northland Press, Flagstaff, AZ, editor in chief, 1970-72; Museum of Northern Arizona, Flagstaff, editor of museum notes, 1972-75; free-lance writer and editor, 1975—. Owner of Writing Lab, 1983-85. Member of board of directors of Flagstaff Festival of the Arts, 1971-82; panelist for Arizona Commission on the arts and Assistance League of Flagstaff, 1983-86.

MEMBER: Kappa Kappa Gamma.

AWARDS, HONORS: Best Western Book Award from Rounce and Coffin Club and nonfiction award from Border Regional Library Association, both 1975, for *Art and Indian Individualists;* national alumnae achievement award from Kappa Kappa Gamma, 1984; *The Pueblo Storyteller* was voted one of the "Ten Best Southwest Books of 1986" by Border Regional Library Association, and one of the "Best Books on the Southwest for the Year" by the *Arizona Daily Star,* 1986.

WRITINGS:

The Thief (novel), Putnam, 1961.
(Editor) *Harmsen's Western Americana,* Northland Press, 1971.
(Editor) *Scholder/Indians,* Northland Press, 1972.
(With husband, Guy Monthan) *Art and Indian Individualists,* Northland Press, 1975.
R. C. Gorman: The Lithographs, Northland Press, 1978.

(With G. Monthan) *Nacimientos: Nativity Scenes by Southwest Indians,* Northland Press, 1979, 2nd edition, Avanyu Publishing, 1990.
(With G. Monthan and Barbara Babcock) *The Pueblo Storyteller* (art book), University of Arizona Press, 1986.
R. C. Gorman: A Retrospective, Northland Press, 1990.

Contributor to *American Indian Art.*

WORK IN PROGRESS: Gerald Nailor, Navajo Artist, with Clay Lockett.

SIDELIGHTS: Doris Born Monthan once told *CA:* "Fiction and poetry are my first loves, but the need to make a living has led me into the marketplace. I have done almost every type of writing in my checkered career—news stories and features for newspapers and magazines, advertising and publicity copy on every subject from pharmaceuticals to fashion. I have enjoyed most of the jobs and felt they kept me limber, like the daily practice of a pianist does. I have also had many jobs unrelated to writing, which never appear on my resumes, but for a writer, they are all grist for the mill. I have sat on both sides of the desk, as editor and author. They are very compatible positions and each career can supply helpful insight for the other.

"What later became a chapter in my novel, *The Thief,* began as a short story in the Writing Workshop at Columbia University. The people I met at a guest ranch while working there as a waitress and maid formed the cast of characters (though much-changed and transformed) for the novel, and the guest ranch itself provided the setting. I also wrote a story based on some of the people I met while working at Brentanno's Out of Print Department. It was never published (or even sent out), but I have been thinking of it recently as a play, which I hope to get to soon.

Regarding Indian art and artists in the Southwest: It is interesting to note that of the seventeen artists I wrote about in *Art and Indian Individualists* in the early 1970s, five have died, one is partially disabled by an accident, one is very aged and no longer produces; but of the remaining ten, several are now millionaires, and all of the others are very well off. This affluence could never have occurred, even among the most famous Indian artists, before the 1970s or mid-1970s. Many younger Indian artists in all media are returning to native crafts after careers in business or are selecting them immediately. There is a tremendous revival in pottery, the second oldest craft after basket making, particularly in figurative art.

"I was particularly aware of this while researching *The Pueblo Storyteller* book, a survey of pueblo potters who make Storyteller figures and other figurative art. We have documented 233 potters, ranging in age from eight to eighty-five, who are now engaged in making clay figures and other more traditional pottery, and most of them are making their living from it. Almost all of them have been taught by their mothers or some other family member. There are also three times as many sculptors as there were ten years ago and many new painters and jewelry designers and craftsmen. I believe Southwest Indian art has not yet reached its peak, though many thought it had in the early 1970s. Many young artists are benefiting from art training at the college level—using new material and techniques, and seeking a wider range of expression."

More recently, Monthan added: "Currently I am working on fiction but sadly miss having a writing workshop to attend regularly. Workshops and writing classes have always provided the impetus and discipline I seem to need when writing fiction. I would like to pay tribute to those who have helped me so much in the past: Phyllis A. Whitney's fiction writing class at New York University, John R. Humphreys' workshop at Columbia University, Edna Vann's workshop in Los Angeles, and the writing workshop of the late Zola Helen Ross in Seattle. I wish that all aspiring writers might have the opportunity to work with such gifted and generous mentors."

*　　*　　*

MOORE, Rayburn Sabatzky 1920-

PERSONAL: Born May 26, 1920, in Helena, AR; son of Max Sabatzky (a wholesale grocer) and Sammie Lou (Rayburn) Moore; married Margaret Elizabeth Bear, August 30, 1947; children: Margaret Elizabeth, Robert Rayburn. *Education:* Hendrix College, A.A., 1940; Vanderbilt University, A.B., 1942, M.A., 1947; Duke University, Ph.D., 1956. *Religion:* Presbyterian.

ADDRESSES: Home—106 St. James Dr., Athens, GA 30606. *Office*—Department of English, Park Hall, University of Georgia, Athens, GA 30602.

CAREER: Interstate Grocer Co., Helena, AR, vice-president, 1947-50; Hendrix College, Conway, AR, 1954-59, began as assistant professor, became professor of English; University of Georgia, Athens, associate professor, 1959-65, professor, 1965-90, professor emeritus of English, 1990—, director of graduate studies in English, 1964-69, chairman of American Studies Program, 1968-90, chairman of Division of Language and Literature, 1975-90. *Military service:* U.S. Army, 1942-46; served in Pacific Theater; became captain.

MEMBER: Modern Language Association of America (member of executive committee, General Topics VI, 1972-74), Poe Studies Association, South Atlantic Modern Language Association (member of executive council,

1975-77; member of nominating committee, 1985-87), Southeastern American Studies Association, Southern Historical Association, Society for the Study of Southern Literature (member of executive council, 1968, 1974-80; vice-president, 1981-82; president, 1983-84), Virginia Historical Society, Henry James Society, Philological Association of the Carolinas, Blue Key, Phi Beta Kappa.

WRITINGS:

Constance Fenimore Woolson, Twayne, 1963.
(Editor) Constance Fenimore Woolson, *"For the Major" and Selected Short Stories of Constance Fenimore Woolson,* College & University Press, 1967.
Paul Hamilton Hayne, Twayne, 1972.
(Editor) *A Man of Letters in the Nineteenth-Century South: Selected Letters of Paul Hamilton Hayne,* Louisiana State University Press, 1982.
(Senior editor) *A History of Southern Literature,* Louisiana State University Press, 1985.
(Editor) *Selected Letters of Henry James to Edmund Gosse, 1882-1915,* Louisiana State University Press, 1988.
(Editor) *The Correspondence of Henry James and the House of Macmillan, 1877-1914,* Louisiana State University Press, 1992.

Also contributor to numerous books, including *Notable American Women, 1607-1950,* edited by Edward James and others, two volumes, Harvard University Press, 1971, *Southern Literary Study: Problems and Possibilities,* edited by Louis D. Rubin, Jr., and C. Hugh Holman, University of North Carolina Press, 1975, *A Biographical Guide to Southern Literature,* edited by Rubin and others, Louisiana State University Press, 1979, and several editions of *Dictionary of Literary Biography,* Gale. Also contributor of over one hundred articles and book reviews to scholarly journals.

BIOGRAPHICAL/CRITICAL SOURCES:

PERIODICALS

New York Times Book Review, December 1, 1985.

*　　*　　*

MORE, Caroline
See CONE, Molly Lamken

*　　*　　*

MUNSCH, Robert (Norman) 1945-

PERSONAL: Born June 11, 1945, in Pittsburgh, PA; immigrated to Canada; naturalized citizen, 1983; son of

Thomas John (a lawyer) and Margaret (a homemaker; maiden name, McKeon) Munsch; married Ann Beeler (a university educator), January 22, 1973; children: Julie, Andrew, Tyya. *Education:* Studied for the Roman Catholic priesthood for seven years; Fordham University, B.A. (history), 1969; Boston University, M.A. (anthropology), 1971; Tufts University, M.Ed. (child studies), 1973. *Avocational interests:* Cycling, geology.

ADDRESSES: Home—Guelph, Ontario, Canada; and c/o Writers' Union of Canada, 24 Ryerson Ave., Toronto, Ontario, Canada M5T 2P3.

CAREER: Storyteller and author of books for children. Bay Area Childcare, Coos Bay, OR, teacher, 1973-75; University of Guelph, Guelph, Ontario, head teacher at Family Studies Laboratory Preschool and assistant professor, 1975-84.

MEMBER: Association of Canadian Television and Radio Artists (ACTRA), Canadian Association of Children's Authors, Illustrators, and Performers, Writers Union of Canada.

AWARDS, HONORS: Canada Council grant, 1982; Ruth Schwartz Children's Book Award from Ontario Arts Council, 1985, for *Thomas' Snowsuit;* Juno Award for best Canadian children's record, 1985, for *Murmel, Murmel, Munsch: More Outrageous Stories;* Author of the Year, Canadian Booksellers Association, 1991.

WRITINGS:

FOR CHILDREN

The Mud Puddle, illustrations by Sami Suomalainen, Annick Press, 1979, revised edition, 1982.
The Dark, illustrations by Suomalainen, Annick Press, 1979.
The Paper Bag Princess, illustrations by Michael Martchenko, Annick Press, 1980.
Jonathan Cleaned Up, Then He Heard a Sound; or, Blackberry Subway Jam, illustrations by Martchenko, Annick Press, 1981.
The Boy in the Drawer, illustrations by Martchenko, Annick Press, 1982.
Murmel, Murmel, Murmel, illustrations by Martchenko, Annick Press, 1982.
Angela's Airplane, illustrations by Martchenko, Annick Press, 1983.
David's Father, illustrations by Martchenko, Annick Press, 1983.
The Fire Station, illustrations by Martchenko, Annick Press, 1983.
Mortimer, illustrations by Martchenko, Annick Press, 1983.
Millicent and the Wind, illustrations by Suzanne Duranceau, Annick Press, 1984.

Thomas' Snowsuit, illustrations by Martchenko, Annick Press, 1985.
50 Below Zero, illustrations by Martchenko, Annick Press, 1985.
I Have to Go, illustrations by Martchenko, Annick Press, 1986.
Love You Forever, illustrations by Sheila McGraw, Firefly Books, 1986.
Moira's Birthday, illustrations by Martchenko, Firefly Books, 1987.
A Promise Is a Promise, illustrations by Vladyana Krykorka, Annick Press, 1988.
Pigs, illustrations by Martchenko, Annick Press, 1989.
Giant; or, Waiting for the Thursday Boat, illustrations by Gilles Tibo, Annick Press, 1989.
Something Good, illustrations by Martchenko, Annick Press, 1990.
Good Families Don't, illustrations by Alan Daniel, Doubleday, 1990.
Show and Tell, illustrations by Martchenko, Annick Press, 1991.

RECORDINGS

Munsch: Favourite Stories (contains published and unpublished works), narrated by Munsch, Kids' Records (Toronto), 1983.
Murmel, Murmel, Munsch: More Outrageous Stories, narrated by Munsch, Kid's Records, 1985.
Love You Forever, Kid's Records, 1987.

OTHER

Contributor of articles to periodicals, including *Journal of the Canadian Association for Young Children.* Munsch's works have been translated into nine languages, including Spanish, French, German, and Swedish.

ADAPTATIONS: Jonathan Cleaned Up, Then He Heard a Sound; or, Blackberry Subway Jam was made into an animated film and released by the National Film Board of Canada, 1984; some of Munsch's stories have been adapted for film and released as filmstrip and tape combinations by the Society for Visual Education.

SIDELIGHTS: Whether it is in front of a small audience of children at a day-care center or a large concert hall filled with parents and their kids, Robert Munsch has delighted both young and old since the early 1970s with his performances of original stories for the young. Now a best-selling author in Canada, Munsch has written down his best stories in a number of well-received books and has also recorded several of his favorites tales. Using a combination of humor, repetition, and appealing child characters, his "work shows a mastery of the form of the picture book as a small dramatic script," says *Horn Book* contributor Sarah Ellis. "His picture books work well with a single child or a beginning reader, but their great delight is discovered in reading them aloud to groups."

The path Munsch took toward becoming a storyteller was far from direct. At first, he had planned to become a Roman Catholic priest; toward that end he studied seven years with the idea that he would eventually be an anthropological missionary. But, Munsch writes in *Canadian Children's Literature,* "I . . . made the mistake of taking a part-time job in a day-care centre. I liked the kids better than anthropology. Maybe that was because I came from a family of nine children. I went through a series of jobs with young children (day-care, infant day-care, nursery school and an orphanage). Along the way I picked up a degree in childhood education."

In his work with children, Munsch discovered that he had a natural gift for entertaining them with stories he made up as he told them. His first improvised story, *Mortimer,* originally started out as a song accompanied by Munsch and his audience rattling containers filled with corn. The song goes like this: "Clang, clang, rattle bing bang/Gonna make my noise all day./Clang, clang, rattle bing bang,/ Gonna make my noise all day." The story is about a little boy who refuses to go to sleep despite the efforts of his entire family, his neighbors, and even the police to make him go to bed. In the end he falls asleep out of pure exhaustion.

Munsch did not write down *Mortimer* for some time. Instead, other day-care workers heard about and memorized the story so that they could tell it to their own children. It was not until Munsch took a job at the University of Guelph that he was urged by the director of his department to try and publish his writing. Munsch had a hard time writing *Mortimer* until he realized that he should write as if he were recording one of his performances. This made his writing sound more spontaneous and fun to read out loud. Munsch required a lot of feedback from his young audience, too. Only the tales that the children requested to hear many times were, he felt, good enough to publish. "I figured out once that the stories the children kept requesting came to two percent of my total output," he says.

Mailing his stories to several different publishers, two of his submissions, *The Mud Puddle* and *The Dark,* were accepted by Annick Press and published in 1979. *Mortimer* was not published until four years later. "Munsch's stories are mainly of contemporary, urban, domestic life, with a large dash of extravagant fantasy," Ellis observes. "They reflect a jaunty belief in the power of children. His protagonists, reminiscent of those of Marie Hall Ets, are strong, confident, and full of initiative."

The Mud Puddle and *The Dark* show how children "are concerned about darkness, loss of security, and monsters," says Carol Anne Wien in a *Canadian Children's Literature*

article. "Munsch understands this. In each of his books he personifies one such concern. Once the problem is visible, it can, of course, be tackled." In *The Mud Puddle* a little girl fights off a bothersome mud puddle that keeps getting her dirty by dumping soapy water on it; the same little girl defeats a horrible monster that grows by eating shadows in *The Dark.* Another plucky Munsch hero saves his father in *50 Below Zero* when the father sleepwalks outside during a cold winter night.

Some of Munsch's characters are spunky children who stubbornly refuse to do what is expected of them. Sometimes they defy their parents, as in *Mortimer* or *Thomas' Snowsuit,* in which Thomas resists wearing an ugly brown snowsuit, or *I Have to Go!,* in which Andrew will not "go pee" before his family leaves for a long trip. Other Munsch characters challenge authorities even more frustrating than parents, as is the case in *Jonathan Cleaned Up, Then He Heard a Sound; or, Blackberry Subway Jam.* In this story, Jonathan has to fight City Hall to get the bureaucrats to remove a subway station from his living room. Jonathan is told by officials that the computer directed city planners to put the station there, and the computer, of course, is never wrong. But there are ways around such problems, and Jonathan discovers a solution by bribing an official with several cases of homemade blackberry jam.

Munsch likes to throw in words like "pee" and "underwear" in stories like *I Have to Go!* because they titillate his young audiences. *Quill and Quire* reviewer Ann Vanderhoof describes one as-yet-unpublished book, "The Fart," as the most extreme example of how far Munsch will go. "The Fart" tells how "Jule Ann finds a great big purple, green and yellow fart lying on her bed. . . . 'The kids go absolutely bananas [about this story],' Munsch says. The parents? 'Eighty per cent think it's really neat; the other twenty per cent ask "How could you?"' He describes his stories as middle-of-the-road taboo. 'Farts are perfect: you're not supposed to talk about them, but they're not very threatening. If you tell stories about sex, for example, young children find that too threatening.' "

Other Munsch stories challenge different conventions. In *The Paper Bag Princess,* a gently feminist tale, Princess Elizabeth saves Prince Ronald from a dragon only to hear the ungrateful prince complain that she looks messy. Elizabeth decides he is a "bum" and refuses to marry him. Some critics have complained about this ending, calling it sexist. In another *Canadian Children's Literature* review, for example, Wien expresses that this "resolution in the story has a negative impact on boys; thus, it is sexist." Other critics, however, believe that Munsch offers a delightful twist to the traditional Prince-rescues-Princess story. *Canadian Children's Literature* reviewer Joan McGrath, for one, writes: "Munsch's celebrated *Paper Bag*

Princess is . . . becoming a cult-heroine for the skipping-rope set."

Munsch usually spends up to three years retelling and revising his stories in front of audiences before he writes them down, but with *Jonathan Cleaned Up* he began writing down some stories—or parts of them—without performing them first. Another change in Munsch's books is, as Ellis remarks, a movement "toward a more classic picture-book style." More recent books like *Millicent and the Wind* and *Love You Forever*—Munsch's most successful book, which has sold over four million copies—are more "ambitiously produced" and, as Gwyneth Evans observes in *Canadian Children's Literature, Millicent and the Wind* is "more gentle, evocative, and poetic than [Munsch's] previous books." *Millicent and the Wind* is about a lonely girl who finds a new friend when the wind carries a child to Milicent's isolated mountain home. *Love You Forever,* the tale of one mother's unending love for her son, is also "quieter and more introspective" than earlier books, according to Andre Gagnon in *CM: Canadian Materials for Schools and Libraries.* However, the author returns to more rollicking, humorous stories with books like *Moira's Birthday,* in which Moira invites her whole school to her house for a party, much to her parents' dismay.

Despite the success of Munsch's books, he has continued to do what he does best: tell stories in front of live audiences. For awhile Munsch performed in front of crowds as large as three thousand people. But in 1987, when his schedule became too hectic, he went back to being a storyteller for day-care centers, libraries, and schools, usually working for free; he also teaches workshops for adults and teenagers on how to be a storyteller. Much to the dismay of teachers and librarians, who have tried booking him in advance, Munsch does his free storytellings with little or no advance notice, often simply showing up at the front door and asking to tell stories.

BIOGRAPHICAL/CRITICAL SOURCES:

BOOKS

McDonough, Irma, editor, *Profiles 2,* Canadian Library Association, 1982.

PERIODICALS

Books in Canada, October, 1981; December, 1981; August/September, 1982; December, 1982; May, 1983; December, 1983; November, 1985.
Canadian Children's Literature, Numbers 15 and 16, 1980, pp. 115-119; Number 22, 1981, pp. 56-61; Number 30, 1983, pp. 88-91; Numbers 39 and 40, 1985, pp. 125-130; Number 43, 1986, pp. 22-25.
CM: Canadian Materials for Schools and Libraries, March, 1987, pp. 78-79.
Globe and Mail (Toronto), November 5, 1983; January 24, 1987.
Horn Book, May/June, 1985, pp. 342-345.
In Review, February, 1980; April, 1981; October, 1981; February, 1982.
Maclean's, December 13, 1982; December 9, 1985.
Quill & Quire, February, 1981; May, 1982, p. 37; June, 1982; May, 1983; August, 1983; November, 1984; December, 1985; April, 1986.
Sun (Vancouver), December 3, 1983.

—*Sketch by Kevin S. Hile*

N

NACHMAN, Gerald 1938-

PERSONAL: Born January 13, 1938, in Oakland, CA; son of Leonard Calvert (a salesman and actor) and Isabel (Weil) Nachman; married Mary Campbell McGeachy, September 3, 1966 (divorced, 1979). *Education:* Merritt College, A.A., 1958; San Jose State University, B.A., 1960. *Politics:* Independent. *Religion:* Jewish.

ADDRESSES: Home—281 Juanita Way, San Francisco, CA 94127. *Office—San Francisco Chronicle,* 150 Fourth St., San Francisco, CA 94103.

CAREER: San Jose Mercury, San Jose, CA, humor columnist and television critic, 1960-63; *New York Post,* New York City, feature writer, 1964-66; *Oakland Tribune,* Oakland, CA, drama and film critic and columnist, 1966-71; *New York Daily News,* New York City, feature writer and television critic, 1972-73, syndicated humor columnist, 1973-79; *San Francisco Chronicle,* San Francisco, CA, theater critic and columnist, 1979—. Adjunct professor of journalism, New York University, spring, 1976. Member of Pulitzer Prize jury to select best play, 1991-92.

AWARDS, HONORS: Page One Award, New York Newspaper Guild, 1965, for humor piece in *New York Post;* feature-writing award, Associated Press, 1974, for series "The Party-Goers"; Deems Taylor Award, American Society of Composers, Authors and Publishers (ASCAP), for critical writing on lyricists.

WRITINGS:

Playing House, Doubleday, 1977.
Out on a Whim: Some Very Close Brushes with Life (collection), Doubleday, 1983.
The Fragile Bachelor, Ten Speed Press, 1989.

Also author of *The Portable Nachman,* 1960, and co-author of satirical musical revue *Quirks,* 1979. Contributor to books, including *Snooze,* Workman Publishing, 1988. Past author of twice-weekly humor column, "The Single Life," syndicated by Universal Press Syndicate. Contributor of articles to periodicals, including *Esquire, Newsweek, New York Times, Cosmopolitan, Penthouse, Saturday Review,* and *TheaterWeek.*

SIDELIGHTS: Reviewing Gerald Nachman's collection *Out on a Whim: Some Very Close Brushes with Life,* Anatole Broyard of the *New York Times* compares the author to a man walking down a street observing everything around him. "He strolls not only along the street," notes Broyard, "but through the whole of our urban culture as well. And as he does, he throws out his comments, like a man feeding breadcrumbs to pigeons." Nachman tells how to speed-read in body language and offers suggestions for improving television (have Alistair Cooke do introductions to such shows as *Love Boat*); he also studies the relative talking styles of men and women and explains how they developed. Broyard describes the resulting book as "a witty and civilized introduction to the situation comedy we call life."

BIOGRAPHICAL/CRITICAL SOURCES:

PERIODICALS

Newsweek, June 9, 1975.
New York Times, March 7. 1983.
Time, August 23, 1976.

* * *

NESS, Evaline (Michelow) 1911-1986

PERSONAL: Born April 24, 1911, in Union City, OH; died of a heart attack, August 12, 1986, in Kingston, NY;

daughter of Albert and Myrtle Woods (Carter) Michelow; married commercial artist named Mac (divorced); married Eliot Ness (public safety director; former treasury agent), 1938 (divorced, 1946); married Arnold A. Bayard (mechanical engineer), 1959. *Education:* Attended Ball State Teachers College, 1931-32, Chicago Art Institute, 1933-35, Corcoran Gallery of Art, Washington, DC, 1943-45, and Accademia de Belle Arti, Rome, Italy, 1951-52. *Avocational interests:* Cricket, tennis, chess, music.

ADDRESSES: Home—303 Cocoanut Row, Palm Beach, FL 33480.

CAREER: Artist, tapestry designer, illustrator and author of children's books. Teacher of children's art classes, Corcoran School of Art, Washington, DC, 1943-45, and Parsons School of Design, New York City, 1959-60; fashion illustrator at Saks Fifth Avenue, New York City, 1946-49; magazine and advertising illustrator, 1946-49.

AWARDS, HONORS: First prize for painting, Corcoran Art Gallery, Washington, DC; American Library Association (ALA) Notable Book, 1958, for *The Sherwood Ring;* ALA Notable Book and *Horn Book* honor list citation, both 1962, for *Thistle and Thyme: Tales from Scotland; Horn Book* honor list citation, 1963, for *The Princess and the Lion;* Caldecott Honor Book and *Horn Book* honor list citation, both 1963, for *All in the Morning Early;* Caldecott Honor Book and *Horn Book* honor list citation, both 1964, for *A Pocketful of Cricket;* Caldecott Honor Book and ALA Notable Book, both 1965, for *Tom Tit Tot: An English Folk Tale; Horn Book* honor list citation, 1966, for *Sam, Bangs and Moonshine; Horn Book* honor list citation, 1967, for *Mr. Miacca: An English Folk Tale;* Caldecott Medal, 1967, for *Sam, Bangs and Moonshine;* Hans Christian Andersen award nomination, 1972; ALA Notable Book and *Horn Book* honor list citation, both 1972, both for *Old Mother Hubbard and Her Dog.*

WRITINGS:

ALL SELF-ILLUSTRATED

Josefina February, Scribner, 1963.
A Gift for Sula Sula, Scribner, 1963.
Exactly Alike, Scribner, 1964.
Pavo and the Princess, Scribner, 1964.
A Double Discovery, Scribner, 1965.
Sam, Bangs, and Moonshine, Holt, 1966.
Long, Broad, and Quickeye (adapted from Andrew Lang's version of the Bohemian fairy tale), Scribner, 1969.
The Girl and the Goatherd; or, This and That and Thus and So, Dutton, 1970.
Do You Have the Time, Lydia?, Dutton, 1971.
Yeck Eck, Dutton, 1974.
Marcella's Guardian Angel, Holiday House, 1979.

Fierce the Lion, Holiday House, 1980.

ILLUSTRATOR

Mary J. Gibbons, *Story of Ophelia,* Doubleday, 1954.
Charlton Ogburn, *The Bridge,* Houghton, 1957.
Elizabeth Pope, *The Sherwood Ring,* Houghton, 1958.
Elizabeth Coatsworth, *Lonely Maria,* Pantheon, 1960.
Maurice Osborne, Jr., *Ondine, the Story of a Bird Who Was Different,* Houghton, 1960.
Mary B. Miller, *Listen—The Birds; Poems,* Pantheon, 1961.
Barbara Robinson, *Across from Indian Shore,* Lothrop, 1962.
Julia Cunningham, *Macaroon,* Pantheon, 1962.
Sorche Nic Leodhas, *Thistle and Thyme: Tales and Legends from Scotland,* Holt, 1962.
Helen E. Buckley, *Where Did Josie Go?,* Lothrop, 1962.
S. N. Leodhas, *All in the Morning Early,* Holt, 1963.
Eve Merriam, *Funny Town,* Crowell-Collier, 1963.
E. Coatsworth, *The Princess and the Lion,* Pantheon, 1963.
H. E. Buckley, *Some Cheese for Charles,* Pantheon, 1964.
J. Cunningham, *Candle Tales,* Pantheon, 1964.
H. E. Buckley, *Josie and the Snow,* Lothrop, 1964.
Rebecca Caudill, *A Pocketful of Cricket,* Holt, 1964.
Lloyd Alexander, *Coll and His White Pig,* Holt, 1965.
Virginia Haviland, *Tom Tit Tot: An English Folk Tale,* edited by Joseph Jacobs, Scribner, 1965.
V. Haviland, *Favorite Fairy Tales Told in Italy,* Little, Brown, 1965.
Sylvia Cassedy, *Pierino and the Bell,* Doubleday, 1966.
H. E. Buckley, *Josie's Buttercup,* Lothrop, 1967.
Mr. Miacca: An English Folk Tale, edited by J. Jacobs, Holt, 1967.
L. Alexander, *The Truthful Harp,* Holt, 1967.
S. N. Leodhas, *Kellyburn Braes,* Holt, 1968.
Maxine Kumin and Anne Sexton, *Joey and the Birthday Present,* McGraw, 1969.
S. N. Leodhas, *A Scottish Songbook,* Holt, 1969.
Lucille Clifton, *Some of the Days of Everett Anderson,* Holt, 1970.
L. Clifton, *Everett Anderson's Christmas Coming,* Holt, 1971.
H. E. Buckley, *Too Many Crackers,* Lothrop, 1971.
Sarah Catherine Martin, *Old Mother Hubbard and Her Dog,* Holt, 1972.
L. Clifton, *Don't You Remember?,* Dutton, 1973.
Algernon David Black, *The Woman of the Wood: A Tale from Old Russia,* Holt, 1973.
Margaret Wise Brown, *The Steamroller, A Fantasy,* Walker, 1974.
M. Kumin and A. Sexton, *A Wizard's Tears,* McGraw, 1975.

Nathan Zimelman, *The Lives of My Cat Alfred* (Junior Literary Guild selection), Dutton, 1976.

Walter de la Mare, *The Warmint,* Scribner, 1976.

The Devil's Bridge (legend), retold by Charles Scribner, Jr., McGraw, 1978.

M. Kumin, *What Color Is Caesar?,* McGraw, 1978.

Steven Kroll, *The Hand-Me-Down Doll,* Holiday House, 1983.

DESIGNER AND ILLUSTRATOR

American Colonial Paper House: To Cut Out and Color, Scribner, 1975.

Paper Palace: To Cut Out and Color, Scribner, 1976.

Four Rooms from the Metropolitan Museum: To Cut Out and Color, Scribner, 1978.

A Victorian Paper House: To Cut Out and Color, Scribner, 1978.

A Shaker Paper House: To Cut Out and Color, Scribner, 1979.

OTHER

Editor, *Amelia Mixed the Mustard, and Other Poems,* Scribner, 1975.

Ness' manuscripts are collected at the Kerlan Collection of the University of Minnesota in Minneapolis, at the de-Grummond Collection at the University of Southern Mississippi in Hattiesburg, at the Free Library of Philadelphia, and at the Iowa City Public Library.

SIDELIGHTS: Evaline Ness, author and prize-winning illustrator of books for children, grew up cutting out pictures from magazines to illustrate her older sister's stories about knights and rescued princesses. Her artistic aptitude went unrecognized in school; and upon graduation, she attended Ball State Teachers College in Muncie, Indiana, to study library science. When an English assignment offered the choice of writing a paper or illustrating King Arthur's Court, though, Ness resumed her fledgling art career. "I illustrated . . . in full color," recalled Ness in an essay in *Something about the Author Autobiography Series.* "My series of paintings were hung on the wall for a whole week!" Rather than return to Muncie for a second year of college, Ness enrolled in the fine arts department at the Chicago Art Institute, where she studied for two years. While in Chicago, she also ventured into fashion drawing art and magazine illustration. Marriage ensued, including one to former U.S. treasury agent Eliot Ness, whose exploits during prohibition served as the basis for the television series *The Untouchables.* Ness pursued additional study at the Corcoran School of Art in Washington, D.C., the Accademia de Belle Arti in Rome, and the Art Students League in New York City before an editor at Houghton Mifflin persuaded her to illustrate a children's book—an event that altered her career. "During the months of work

on the book, I realized the same kind of peace and enjoyment that comes when I paint for myself," she indicated in her acceptance speech for the Caldecott Medal—reprinted in *Horn Book*—adding, "After that I accepted almost every manuscript sent to me by publishers. Each one was a new exciting experience."

Throughout her career, Ness employed a variety of illustrating techniques, including "woodcut, serigraphy, rubber-roller . . ., scratching through black paint on acetate, ink splattering, and sometimes just spitting," she said in her acceptance speech. And her skillful illustrations have been praised widely for their freshness. According to Philip A. Sadler in the *Dictionary of Literary Biography,* "Ness received her greatest recognition for her work done between 1963 and 1967." Her illustrations for Sorche Nic Leodhas' *All in the Morning Early,* Rebecca Caudill's *A Pocketful of Cricket,* and Virginia Haviland's *Tom Tit Tot: An English Folk Tale,* were runners-up in the Caldecott Medal competition; and her own *Sam, Bangs, & Moonshine* won the medal in 1967.

Sam, Bangs, & Moonshine is about a fisherman's daughter who has trouble distinguishing between fantasy and reality. "One day when I was looking through a portfolio in which I keep drawings I make for no reason at all, I found one of a ragged, displaced-person little girl who was quietly ecstatic over a starfish . . .," related Ness in her acceptance speech, adding that "the shabby misplaced child of my drawing became Sam, who told lies. And what else could she be except a fisherman's daughter, with all those drawings of boats handy? . . . I really cannot tell you *how* I wrote the story. All I know is that I sat at the typewriter for four days and nothing happened. On the fifth day it struck." Praising the "unusually creative story," Evelyn Geller and Eric Moon note in *School Library Journal* that Ness presents the element of fantasy with realism and sympathy. John Gruen agreed, indicating in the *Washington Post Book World* that Ness "handles an overly fanciful tale with a good deal of down-to-earth realism." And in the words of Bernard J. Lonsdale and Helen K. Mackintosh in their *Children Experience Literature,* the book "is a tribute to the writing and illustrating genius of Evaline Ness."

"Evaline Ness was, in my opinion, the most brilliant and original illustrator of children's books in America in recent times," stated Betty Boegehold in *Twentieth-Century Children's Writers,* adding that "Ness's words speak for themselves; their poetry, their clarity, their honesty well match her subtle but straightforward portraits of children. . . . Ness gave us, in both words and pictures, children as they really are—beautiful, straight, and honest, involved in the pleasures and problems of life." And Sadler, who believed that Ness "rightfully earned her place among the most outstanding illustrators of books for children," remarked that "her illustrations . . . will enrich the lives of children for generations to come, and adults who know and love books for children will treasure her highly individualistic contributions to the art of children's literature."

BIOGRAPHICAL/CRITICAL SOURCES:

BOOKS

Children's Literature Review, Volume 6, Gale, 1984.

de Montreville, Doris, and Elizabeth D. Crawford, *Fourth Book of Junior Authors and Illustrators*, Wilson, 1978.

Dictionary of Literary Biography, Volume 61: *American Writers for Children since 1960: Poets, Illustrators, and Nonfiction Authors*, Gale, 1987.

Hopkins, Lee Bennett, *Books Are By People*, Citation Press, 1969.

Kingman, Lee, and others, *Illustrators of Children's Books: 1957-1966*, Horn Book, 1968.

Klemin, Diana, *The Art of Art for Children's Books*, Clarkson Potter, 1966.

Lanes, Selma G., *Down the Rabbit Hole*, Atheneum, 1971.

Lonsdale, Bernard J., and Helen K. Mackintosh, *Children Experience Literature*, Random House, 1973, p. 248.

Something about the Author Autobiography Series, Volume 1, Gale, 1986.

Twentieth-Century Children's Writers, 3rd edition, St. James Press, 1989.

Ward, Martha E., and Dorothy A. Marquardt, *Authors of Books for Young People*, 2nd edition, Scarecrow, 1971.

PERIODICALS

America, December 6, 1975.

American Artist, January, 1956, pp. 29-33; June, 1967, pp. 32-37.

Horn Book, August, 1967, pp. 438-43.

National Observer, August 4, 1969.

New York Times Book Review, May 9, 1965; October 25, 1970; May 4, 1975; April 8, 1979.

Saturday Review, May 31, 1975.

School Library Journal, October, 1966, p. 218.

Theatre Crafts, September, 1978.

Times Literary Supplement, April 2, 1971; October 22, 1971; November 3, 1972; April 6, 1973.

Village Voice, December 16, 1974.

Washington Post Book World, October 30, 1966, p. 5; May 4, 1969; November 8, 1970; December 8, 1974.*

NEUFELD, John (Arthur) 1938-
(Joan Lea)

PERSONAL: Born December 14, 1938, in Chicago, IL; son of Leonard Carl (a manufacturer) and Rhoda (Padway) Neufeld. *Education:* Yale University, B.A., 1960.

ADDRESSES: Home—1015 N. Kings Rd., No. 316, Los Angeles, CA 90069. *Agent*—Arthur Pine, 1780 Broadway, New York, NY 10019.

CAREER: Editor, teacher, television scriptwriter, and author. Harcourt, Brace, and World, New York City, advertising copy writer; Franklin Watts, Inc., publicist.

AWARDS, HONORS: Notable Book Award, American Library Association, for both *Edgar Allan* and *Lisa, Bright and Dark*.

WRITINGS:

Edgar Allan, S. G. Phillips, 1968.
Lisa, Bright and Dark, S. G. Phillips, 1969.
Touching, S. G. Phillips, 1970.
Sleep Two, Three, Four!, Harper, 1971.
You Think I'd Go around Making These Things Up?, Random House, 1973.
For the Wrong Reasons, Norton, 1973.
Freddy's Book, Random House, 1973.
Sunday Father, New American Library, 1975.
(Under pseudonym Joan Lea) *Trading Up*, Atheneum, 1975.
The Fun of It, Putnam, 1977.
A Small Civil War, Fawcett/Ballantine, 1982.
Sharelle, New American Library, 1983.
Rolling the Stone, New American Library, 1984.
Family Fortunes, Atheneum, 1988.

TELEPLAYS

Lisa, Bright and Dark (*Hallmark Hall of Fame* presentation), NBC-TV, 1973.
You Lie So Deep, My Love, ABC-TV, 1975.

Also author of *Death Sentence*, ABC-TV.

ADAPTATIONS: Edgar Allan, Freddy's Book, For All the Wrong Reasons, The Fun of It, A Small Civil War, and *Sharelle* have all been optioned for television.

SIDELIGHTS: In both his books for young people and adults, John Neufeld tackles difficult issues with insight, humor, and strongly realized characters. Whether writing about mental illness, political oppression, prejudice, or teen pregnancy, Neufeld strives for accuracy and honesty. Many of his works feature young protagonists whose perceptiveness and capability are in sharp contrast to the general ineffectiveness of the adults around them. "I hadn't planned to write for children, or young adults," Neufeld admitted in an essay for *Something about the Author Auto-*

biography Series (SAAS). "The things that interest me are ideas and problems that face us all, but which we often face first when we're young. If writing about how imaginary young people meet and overcome certain problems helps real young people when *they* meet the same problems, then I was doing something useful as well as fun."

Neufeld's early interest in books was fostered by his mother, a former English teacher who encouraged her three children to read many types of literature. Neufeld told *SAAS:* "I was encouraged to read anything I could find in our house. There were worlds to choose. Classics; current best-sellers; series adventures suitable for boys; collections of plays (Ibsen, Coward, Maugham, Shaw); children's books." While still in junior high school, Neufeld began to write stories modeled on those he read in magazines such as the *Saturday Evening Post.* None of the stories sold, however, and Neufeld soon became too busy with other things to write for pleasure.

After college, Neufeld went on an extended tour of England. Upon his return, he was drafted into the Army for a six-month tour of duty at Fort Leonard, Missouri. "I was assigned (no doubt only on the basis of my Yale diploma) to teach English to men who were to become clerk-typists for the Army. I liked the Army. (I seemed to have liked just about everything in those days). I liked the food; I liked the people who served with me . . . and I was proud as hell to have weathered basic training as well as I did," Neufeld related in his essay.

Upon his release from the Army, Neufeld began to think seriously about his future plans. "It was time to grow up," he disclosed, "I had to find a job somewhere, doing something." Because he loved reading and writing, Neufeld decided that publishing was a good career choice. He spent three months looking for a job in New York and Boston. Eventually, Neufeld found work as an advertising copy editor for a publishing firm; he later moved on to publicity and promotion. When not at work, Neufeld wrote television dramas (all unproduced), one-act plays, and a "terrible novel." He wrote in *SAAS:* "I was not unhappy. I *was* writing. I enjoyed it. I now know I was practicing, learning, copying, editing, and exploring. Of course I had no assurance that all this would . . . make me any better than I had been, but I had hope."

Neufeld's first novel, *Edgar Allan,* was inspired by a true story. "An editor for a small California publishing house . . . had a story she thought I could write and write well," he noted. "She told me the bare bones story of a family that had adopted a black child and, because of community pressures and their own fears, gave him up." While interested in the story, Neufeld did not want to use newspaper accounts. "I wanted the story to be my own. . . . I wanted to concentrate on the children in the family, the

white children, and I wanted complete freedom to make them whatever I could," he wrote in *SAAS.*

Critical response to *Edgar Allan* was generally favorable. Richard Horchler, writing in the *New York Times Book Review,* called the novel "a serious work of art . . . about what it means to be human." He added: "Better than easy answers, *Edgar Allan* offers an experience in the growth of compassion and understanding." "This book about a family on trial is one to save and share and perhaps to discuss; certainly its reflection of reality will be noted and praised by the young people who read it," lauded Jean C. Thompson in *School Library Journal.* And Virginia Haviland praised the novel in *Horn Book,* noting that "issues and relationships more complex than those commonly found in literature for young readers are presented in depth and with conviction."

Neufeld followed *Edgar Allan* with a number of novels that dealt with complex themes and situations. *Lisa, Bright and Dark* chronicled a young woman's descent into madness and her friends' desperate attempts to help her. *Touching* examined the effects of a debilitating disease on a family, while *Sleep Two, Three, Four!* explored a fictional United States where fear becomes a very real part of everyday life. As with *Edgar Allan,* critics praised the author's ability to handle difficult issues. *Lisa, Bright and Dark* was called "superior to most junior novels" by Sada Fretz of *School Library Journal.* In a review of *Touching* for *English Journal,* John W. Connor spoke of Neufeld as "a careful writer. Every word, every nuance in this tale builds to the final page of the novel." Connor restated this point of view in a later review of *Sleep Two, Three, Four!* for *English Journal:* "Neufeld's masterful use of language to build suspense enhances the reading. The author rarely wastes his words."

Neufeld has also written books that appeal to an older audience, such as *For All the Wrong Reasons, Trading Up,* and *Family Fortunes.* In these books, as in Neufeld's young adult titles, the emphasis is on realistic characterization and complex themes. Part of Neufeld's success lies in his understanding of his audience. He told *SAAS:* "Praise and encouragement are very important to any young person facing an obstacle of any sort. But learning to understand the *similarities* between you and other people is desperately important. Its what can pull you down if you let it (it needn't) but it's also what can make your work, as a writer, understandable and enjoyable. . . . It's what we all have in common—our humanity, our joys, our disappointments."

BIOGRAPHICAL/CRITICAL SOURCES:

BOOKS

Something about the Author Autobiography Series, Volume 3, Gale, 1986, pp. 175-87.

PERIODICALS

English Journal, December, 1970, pp. 1303-04; February, 1972, pp. 305-306.
Horn Book, April, 1969, p. 172.
Los Angeles Times Book Review, December 13, 1987, p. 11.
New York Times Book Review, November 3, 1968, p. 33.
School Library Journal, December, 1968, p. 47; February, 1970, p. 90.
Times Literary Supplement, July 15, 1977; January 25, 1980.
Washington Post Book World, August 21, 1983.*

* * *

NEVILLE, Emily Cheney 1919-

PERSONAL: Born December 28, 1919, in Manchester, CT; daughter of Howell (an economist) and Anne (Bunce) Cheney; married Glenn Neville (a newspaperman with Hearst Corp.), December 18, 1948 (died June 1, 1965); children: Emily Tam, Glenn H., Dessie, Marcy Ann, Alec. *Education:* Bryn Mawr College, A.B., 1940; Albany Law School, J.D., 1976. *Politics:* Democrat. *Religion:* United Church of Christ. *Avocational interests:* Travel, reading, animals.

ADDRESSES: Home—Keene Valley, NY 12943.

CAREER: New York Daily News, New York City, office girl, 1941; *New York Daily Mirror,* New York City, reporter, 1941-43; currently in private law practice. Writer for young people. Active in Essex County, NY, "End Domestic Violence," Mountain and Valley In-Home Services; Mental Hygiene Association, Keene Valley Congregational Church and New York Conference United Church of Christ, and Keene Valley Library.

AWARDS, HONORS: John Newbery Medal, 1964, for *It's Like This, Cat;* Jane Addams Children's Book Award, 1966, for *Berries Goodman.*

WRITINGS:

It's Like This, Cat, illustrated by Emil Weiss, Harper, 1963.
Berries Goodman, Harper, 1965.
The Seventeenth-Street Gang, illustrated by Emily McCully, Harper, 1966.
Traveler from a Small Kingdom, illustrated by George Mocniak, Harper, 1968.

Fogarty, Harper, 1969.
Garden of Broken Glass, Delacorte, 1975.
The Bridge, illustrated by Ronald Himler, Harper, 1988.
The China Year, Harper, 1991.

ADAPTATIONS: It's Like This, Cat is available in a large print edition, on record and tape, and also on a video, made by American School Publishers, Newbery Productions.

SIDELIGHTS: Emily Cheney Neville is best known for *It's Like This, Cat,* her first novel, which was awarded the Newbery in 1964. It was one of the first books directed specifically at young adults to feature a contemporary, urban setting, and it is praised by critics for its insightful depiction of the feelings of a boy towards his family, friends and everyday life. Neville told *Contemporary Authors (CA):* "My writing is probably an outgrowth of my childhood in a large, clannish New England family, mingled with my own quite different experiences raising five children in New York City."

"I grew up in a very close-knit large family," Neville tells *Something about the Author (SATA),* "played and went to school exclusively with my cousins until I was 11." The youngest of seven children, Neville was born "on the Cheney place in South Manchester, Connecticut," she explains in her *Something about the Author Autobiography Series (SAAS)* entry. "The Place was like a golf course—green, mowed, fragrant or snow covered, and laced with curving red-dirt roads connecting a dozen or more Cheney houses. Father and Mother built theirs about 1899, soon after their marriage. Father had seven brother, four sisters, and eleven first cousins, most of them living on the Place in Manchester, and many working for the family Cheney Silk Mills."

Neville lost her mother to pneumonia in 1931. She was sent with her sister to their summer home through the summer vacations, and developed her own methods of coping with solitude. "With no radio, TV, or other playmates," she tells *SATA,* "I read a great deal, and always liked the idea of trying to write stories myself. They were the usual kind of childhood and schoolgirl efforts, on up to the high school and college literary magazine and newspaper reports." In high school, she writes in *SAAS,* "I saw myself in print: two stories in the school magazine, one a fable about a camel, and the other about a girl who visited her strange old uncle. The girl in the story, who had gone out on a date, was sketched satirically, and the sympathetic character was the old man, immersed in his work and the thoughts inside his head."

At 16, Neville left home to attend Bryn Mawr College, where she majored in economics and history. "College for me, in 1936," she writes in her *SAAS* entry, "was definitely a step into a bigger and freer world than the Cheney

Place. . . . At last, I was living with a bunch of people my own age, with minimal adult interference, and on the whole I loved it." "After college," Neville continues in *SATA,* "I went to work as an errand girl for the *New York Daily News,* then to the *New York Mirror.*" At the *Mirror* she began as a copygirl, but as World War II progressed and more men were drafted into the army, she progressed to writing a daily column, "Only Human." It was also while working at the *Mirror* that she met Glenn Neville, her future husband. They were married in 1948, and Neville settled down to raise their five children.

"I started writing regularly about 1961," Neville remembers in her *SAAS* entry, "when my youngest child started school. Before that I had made erratic attempts at a story or an essay, but nothing was published. Fooling around one day on a cranky old typewriter with sticking keys and no return lever, I started being a boy arguing with his father. . . . I had never written in the first person before, and it was fun, wonderfully freeing, just to *be* someone else, finally to *be* a boy in a way that came naturally, in writing. That experiment grew into a story, 'Cat and I,' which was published in the *Sunday Mirror.*"

It's Like This, Cat is the story of a young boy and his cat and their life together in New York City. Neville tells *SATA* that *It's Like This, Cat* describes a childhood essentially different from her own. She says, "I thought how many boy-and-dog sagas had been written, and figured a boy-and-cat theme would be a change and would lend itself readily to light treatment in a big-city setting." "The day I signed the contract and knew it was actually going to be a book was the big day of my life," she continues in *SAAS.* "Getting published is the difference between writing and being an author." *It's Like This, Cat* won the Newbery Award for excellence in children's literature in 1964. In their study *Children and Books,* May Hill Arbuthnot and Zena Henderson call it "impressive both for its lightly humorous, easy style and the fidelity with which it portrays a fourteen-year-old boy."

"The years between forty and forty-five were probably the most satisfactory years of my life," Neville remembers in her *SAAS* essay. "I had work I enjoyed and knew how to do; after that work, children to work or play with; food to cook and a husband to come home at night. . . . [But] those easy days ended with Glenn's second stroke and death in June of 1965." The trauma marked a major break in Neville's life. "As an adult I hadn't really made decisions or thought who I was—certainly I never consciously planned to be a mother or a wife," she continues. "Things had happened and carried me along. Now, without Glenn, I wasn't at all sure who I was, what I liked, or what I wanted to do."

Gradually Neville lost her taste for writing. She published another four books between 1965 and 1970, but, she explains in *SAAS,* "a book I started, in about 1969, ground to a halt." Searching for something else to do with her life, she states, "it occurred to me that Dave's father in *Cat* was a lawyer, that my own father had had to leave law school because of illness, and that my hero in *Fogarty* was a law-school dropout. Personally I hadn't thought of law school right after college, because I emphatically wanted no more schools right then. But what about now?" Neville received her law degree in 1976 and has spent many of the intervening years in private practice.

"Practicing law and writing books," Neville told *CA* in 1981, "almost requires two heads. I hope to get back to writing a book again, but it will be about children and animals and parents, how they talk and why they do what they do with each other. There's no 'bottom line' in my books, while the law is overwhelmingly concerned with just that—the result." Neville's next book, *The Bridge,* was published in 1988. It provides a vivid picture, full of technical details, of the construction of a new bridge leading to the driveway of a young boy's house. "I realize there's no way I can live alone in a little rural village," Neville concludes in her *SAAS* essay, "and have enough stirring in my head to write about. . . . My identity as a person is still growing, as whose isn't."

BIOGRAPHICAL/CRITICAL SOURCES:

BOOKS

Arbuthnot, May Hill, and Zena Henderson, *Children and Books,* 4th edition, Scott, Foresman, 1972.
Contemporary Literary Criticism, Volume 12, Gale, 1980.
de Montreville, Doris, and Donna Hill, editors, *Third Book of Junior Authors,* H. W. Wilson, 1972.
Kingston, Carolyn T., *The Tragic Mode in Children's Literature,* Teachers College Press, 1974.
Meigs, Cornelia, editor, *A Critical History of Children's Literature,* revised edition, Macmillan, 1969.
Something about the Author, Volume 1, Gale, 1971.
Something about the Author Autobiography Series, Volume 2, Gale, 1986, pp. 157-73.

PERIODICALS

Book World, May 5, 1968.
Christian Science Monitor, May 9, 1963.
Horn Book, August, 1964, pp. 405-08.
National Observer, August 22, 1968.
New York Times Book Review, May 12, 1963; April 25, 1965; November 6, 1966; January 11, 1970; June 15, 1975; February 19, 1989.
Saturday Review, November 12, 1966; November 8, 1969.

NICHOLS, Peter
See YOUD, (Christopher) Samuel

*   *   *

NICHOLS, (Joanna) Ruth 1948-

PERSONAL: Born March 4, 1948, in Toronto, Ontario, Canada; daughter of Edward Morris and Ruby (Smith) Nichols; married William Norman Houston, September 21, 1974. *Education:* University of British Columbia, B.A., 1969; McMaster University, M.A., 1974, Ph.D., 1977. *Politics:* None. *Religion:* None.

CAREER: Writer. Carleton University, Ottawa, Ontario, lecturer, 1974.

AWARDS, HONORS: Woodrow Wilson fellowship, 1969-70; Canada Council fellowship, 1971-74; Canadian Association of Children's Librarians bronze medal, 1973, for *The Marrow of the World;* Shankar's International Literary Contest for Children grand prize.

WRITINGS:

Ceremony of Innocence (novel), Faber, 1969.
A Walk Out of the World (juvenile), illustrations by Trina Schart Hyman, Harcourt, 1969.
The Marrow of the World (juvenile), illustrations by Hyman, Atheneum, 1972.
A Comparison of Three Group Reading Tests in Surveying the Attainment of First Year Secondary Children (booklet), Centre for the Teaching of Reading, 1975.
Song of the Pearl (juvenile), Atheneum, 1976.
The Left-Handed Spirit (juvenile), Atheneum, 1978.
The Burning of the Rose (historical novel), Headline, 1990.
What Dangers Deep (historical novel), Headline, 1992.

SIDELIGHTS: Ruth Nichol's juvenile novels are fantasies in which "imaginative force is achieved," Gwyneth Evans writers in *Canadian Children's Literature,* "by an essentially symbolic use of landscape . . . the terrain reflects the moral and spiritual condition of its inhabitants, or of the questors passing through it." Nichols once told *CA* that "the *meaning* of experience" is the motivation for her writing. "In other times this would have been a religious quest. It remains so even after the disintegration of Christianity which I think we are witnessing. In my novels it leads me to ask what sources of hope and self-affirmation can be found in everyday experience." Evans concludes that Nichols' "expressionist technique whereby the landscape becomes a projection of the state of mind of her protagonists, embodying all the doubt and despair of those divided natures, makes her fantasies darkly compelling."

With *The Burning of the Rose,* Nichols tries her hand at writing a historical novel set in the latter half of the fif-

teenth century. The heroine of the novel, Claire Tarleton, is an orphan rescued and raised by aristocratic parents when her parents are killed by the plague. Through Claire's adventures we see the vivid world of Renaissance Europe, from the 100 Year's War to the banker Cosimo de Medici. Nancy Wigston, writing in the *Globe & Mail,* contends that "it is to author Nichols' credit that her story—and there is lots of plot here—rises above the predictable and lifts the curtain of history so dazzlingly, and so often." Wigston also believes that Claire "could, given time, make a most creditable ancestor for a Gloria Steinem or even a Margaret Atwood."

BIOGRAPHICAL/CRITICAL SOURCES:

PERIODICALS

Canadian Children's Literature, No. 15, 1980.
Christian Science Monitor, May 1, 1969.
Commonweal, May 23, 1969; November 10, 1978.
Globe & Mail (Toronto), March 17, 1990.
New York Times Book Review, May 18, 1969.
Observer, November 9, 1969.
Quill and Quire, June, 1982.
Saturday Night, January, 1973.
Times (London), February 14, 1991, p. 24.
Times Literary Supplement, October 23, 1969.
Washington Post Book World, May 4, 1969; November 12, 1978.

*   *   *

NYSTROM, Carolyn 1940-

PERSONAL: Born May 22, 1940, in West Union, OH; daughter of Wilbur N. (a factory worker) and Ada (a homemaker; maiden name, Musser) Abbott; married J. Roger Nystrom (a teacher), August 26, 1961; children: Sheri, Lori, Randy, Craig. *Education:* Wheaton College, B.A., 1962. *Politics:* Independent. *Religion:* Evangelical Presbyterian.

ADDRESSES: Home—38 West 566 Sunset, St. Charles, IL 60174. *Office*—c/o Curtis Bruce Agency, 3015 Evergreen Dr., Plover, WI 54467.

CAREER: Ohio Soldiers' and Sailors' Orphans' Home, Xenia, part-time houseparent and playground supervisor, 1958-62; teacher of second grade at public elementary schools in Glendale Heights, IL, 1962-67, and Elmhurst, IL, 1970-73; foster parent in St. Charles, IL, 1973-75; writer, 1974—.

AWARDS, HONORS: Gold Medallion Book Award for Best Children's Book of the Year, Christian Booksellers Association, 1982, for *What Happens When We Die?;* Children's Book of the Year Award, Christian Booksellers Convention (Europe), 1987, for *Mike's Lonely Summer.*

WRITINGS:

Forgive Me If I'm Frayed around the Edges, Moody, 1977 (published in England as *Fostering No Illusions,* Scripture Union, 1979).

(With Margaret Fromer) *A Woman's Workshop on James,* Zondervan, 1980.

A Woman's Workshop on Romans, Zondervan, 1981, published as *Workshop on Romans,* 1991.

A Woman's Workshop on David and His Psalms, Zondervan, 1982, published as *Workshop on David and His Psalms,* 1989.

New Life: A Woman's Workshop on Salvation, Zondervan, 1983, revised edition published as *Basic Beliefs: A Woman's Workshop on the Christian Faith,* 1986, published as *Workshop on the Christian Faith,* 1989.

Characters and Kings, Part I: A Woman's Workshop on Israel under the Kings, Zondervan, 1985.

(With Fromer) *People in Turmoil: A Woman's Workshop on I Corinthians,* Zondervan, 1985, published as *Workshop on First Corinthians,* 1991.

Characters and Kings, Part II: A Woman's Workshop in the History of Israel, Zondervan, 1985.

Behold Your Christ: A Woman's Workshop, Zondervan, 1986.

Who Is Jesus? A Woman's Workshop on the Gospel of Mark, Zondervan, 1987, published as *Workshop on Mark,* 1989.

Workshop on the Gospel of John, Zondervan, 1989.

Compass for a Dark Road: Letters of Peter and Jude, Inter-Varsity Press, 1991.

Borning Chamber, Inter-Varsity Press, 1992.

Loving God, Inter-Varsity Press, 1992.

Living in the World, Inter-Varsity Press, 1992.

Finding Contentment, Inter-Varsity Press, 1992.

Loving Each Other, Inter-Varsity Press, 1992.

JUVENILES

I Learn about the Bible, Creation House, 1977.

Angels and Me, Creation House, 1978.

Mark: God on the Move (teen workbook with teacher's guide), Harold Shaw, 1978.

Acts: Church on the Move (teen workbook with teacher's guide), Harold Shaw, 1979.

(With Fromer) *Acts: Missions Accomplished* (teen workbook with teacher's guide), Harold Shaw, 1979.

Romans: Christianity on Trial (teen workbook with teacher's guide), Harold Shaw, 1980.

Who Is God?, Moody, 1980.

Who Is Jesus?, Moody, 1980.

The Holy Spirit in Me, Moody, 1980.

What Is Prayer?, Moody, 1980.

Lord, I Want to Have a Quiet Time (teen devotional journal), Christian Herald, 1981, revised edition, Harold Shaw, 1984, revised edition published as *Meeting with God,* 1991.

Why Do I Do Things Wrong?, Moody, 1981.

What Is a Christian?, Moody, 1981.

What Is the Church?, Moody, 1981.

What Happens When We Die?, Moody, 1981.

What Is the Bible?, Moody, 1982.

Growing Jesus' Way, Moody, 1982.

(With Fromer) *James: Roadmap for Down-to-Earth Christians* (teen workbook with teacher's guide), Harold Shaw, 1982.

Jesus Is No Secret, Moody, 1983.

Before I Was Born, Crossway Books, 1985.

Salvation, Harold Shaw, 1985.

At the Starting Line: Beginning New Life (student workbook and teacher's guide), Harold Shaw, 1985.

Mike's Lonely Summer, Lion Publishing, 1986.

(With Matthew Floding) *Relationships: Face to Face* (student workbook and teacher's guide), Harold Shaw, 1986.

Mario's Big Question: Where Do I Belong?, Lion Publishing, 1987.

(With Floding) *Who Am I?: A Look in the Mirror* (student workbook and teacher's guide), Harold Shaw, 1987.

Jenny and Grandpa: What Is It Like to Be Old?, Lion Publishing, 1988.

(With Floding) *Sexuality: God's Good Idea* (student workbook and teacher's guide), Harold Shaw, 1988.

The Trouble with Josh: What Is It Like to Be Different?, Lion Publishing, 1989.

Emma Says Goodby, Lion Publishing, 1990.

I Learn to Trust God, Moody, 1990.

I Learn to Tell the Truth, Moody, 1990.

I Learn to Obey Rules, Moody, 1990.

I Learn to Love My Enemies, Moody, 1990.

The Lark Who Had No Song (picture book), Lion Publishing, 1991.

OTHER

Many of Nystrom's books have been translated into other languages, including Chinese, Japanese, Malay, Finnish, German, Spanish, Norwegian, Afrikaans, and Swedish.

WORK IN PROGRESS: An eight-volume series of study guides designed to help people mature in Christian character, for Inter-Varsity Press; "I keep thinking about a novel."

SIDELIGHTS: Carolyn Nystrom told *CA:* "I think that the Bible, if it is worth anything at all, is relevant to all of life. Therefore, I write books that will help people, not to study *about* the Bible, but to study the Bible itself. I hope that as people begin to see what the Bible says and to understand its interwoven meanings their lives will take on a richer expression of oneness with their creator.

"I couldn't write so much if it weren't for my husband, a teacher, who takes over the reins of the household as soon as school is out in June. He cooks, cleans, does laundry, chauffeurs the children, and takes phone messages, as well as doing the usual husbandly jobs of mowing the lawn and repairing the cars. I, on the other hand, leave at seven o'clock in the morning, work out with aerobic dancing for an hour, then retire to a quiet, air-conditioned office with a windowless door and no phone. I return home at six o'clock to find supper on the table—a luxury afforded few working women.

"About half of my writing for the year is accomplished during those ten weeks of summer. In the fall, my husband and I switch jobs again; I become a fulltime homemaker and write only when time is available—about ten to twenty hours per week.

"Some of my children's books touch controversial areas, such as death and sex. I want my books on these subjects to represent the best possible research and craftsmanship. At the same time, I want to speak from a biblical perspective. In writing *What Happens When We Die?*, for example, I studied what many educational psychologists had to say about what worries children and what things a child can comprehend about death at different stages of development. I also studied textbooks of systematic theology, as well as the Bible, to understand what theologians hold as inherent to the Christian view of death.

"Similarly, in writing the sex education book *Before I Was Born,* I read all the children's sex education books in the library, dating back to the 1920s. I also studied the friction points between biblical teaching and current mores. I wanted to create a book for the five- to nine-year-old age group that would not blush at specific sexual information but would present sexuality as one of God's loving gifts to be enjoyed within the context of marriage. My book shows frontal nudity, a couple in bed, and childbirth without cover-ups. But it also speaks of thoughtfully selecting a marriage partner, and it contains a wedding scene with a simple explanation of the marriage vows. I find that many parents want just this kind of help in telling their children the facts of life."

Nystrom adds: "Recently, I completed the 'Lion Care' series. This series helps children face some of the difficulties in their lives: divorce, adoption, learning disabilities, aging grandparents, terminal illness. Once again, I chose to research carefully—then face the issue head on. A girl stands by her aunt's bedside while she dies; a boy believes that nobody loves him because he can't learn, and he can't sit still. But I also try to provide hope and help in these troubled scenes. I want my writing to prod and comfort—at the same time."

O

OKIMOTO, Jean Davies 1942-

PERSONAL: Born December 14, 1942, in Cleveland, OH; daughter of Norman Hugh (in business) and Edith (Williams) Davies; married Peter C. Kirkman, August 26, 1961 (divorced, 1971); married Joseph T. Okimoto (a psychiatrist), May 19, 1973; children: (first marriage) Katherine, Amy; (second marriage) Stephen, Dylan. *Education:* Attended DePauw University, 1960-63, and University of Washington, Seattle, 1971-72; Antioch College, M.A., 1977. *Avocational interests:* Swimming, sailing, painting.

ADDRESSES: Office—2700 East Madison, Seattle, WA 98112. *Agent*—Ruth Cohen, P.O. Box 7626, Menlo Park, CA 94025.

CAREER: High school teacher of remedial reading in Seattle, WA, 1972-73; University of Washington, Seattle, editorial consultant in child psychiatry, 1973-74; Mount Baker Youth Service Bureau, Seattle, assistant to director, 1974-75; private practice of psychotherapy in Seattle, 1975—. Seattle Public Schools, volunteer tutor, 1969; Franklin Area School Council, chairman, 1970; Mount Baker Youth Service Bureau, chairman, 1973. Creator and chairperson of Mayor's Reading Awards.

MEMBER: American Personnel and Guidance Association, PEN, Authors Guild, Authors League of America, Pacific Northwest Writers' Conference, Seattle Freelancers.

AWARDS, HONORS: Washington State Governor's Writers' Award, 1982, for *It's Just Too Much;* American Library Association Best Book for Young Adults and International Reading Association Choice Book, both 1987, both for *Jason's Women.*

WRITINGS:

My Mother Is Not Married to My Father (children's novel), Putnam, 1979.
It's Just Too Much (children's novel), Putnam, 1980.
Norman Schnurman, Average Person (children's novel), Putnam, 1982.
Who Did It, Jenny Lake? (young adult novel), Putnam, 1983.
Jason's Women, Atlantic Monthly Press, 1986.
Boomerang Kids, Little, Brown, 1987.
Blumpoe the Grumpoe Meets Arnold the Cat, Little, Brown, 1990.
Take a Chance, Gramps!, Little, Brown, 1990.
Molly By Any Other Name, Scholastic, 1990.
Hum It Again, Jeremy (one-act play), published in *Center Stage,* edited by Don Gallo, Harper, 1990.

Contributor of short stories to books, including *Visions,* edited by Gallo, Delacorte, 1988; and *Connections,* edited by Gallo, Delacorte, 1989.

WORK IN PROGRESS: A screenplay based on *Jason's Women.*

SIDELIGHTS: Jean Davies Okimoto once wrote: "I had my first newspaper when I was in the sixth grade. It lasted for three issues, until it was censored by my mother, and it folded.

"In my other life (first marriage) I was an Air Force officer's wife. I wrote satire and funny articles for the Officers' Wives Club magazine, which the general's wife did not think were funny. My husband was almost kicked out of the Air Force because of my writing. I will write a novel about this someday. Revenge is an important motivation in my career.

"I coached a thirteen-year-old-girls' soccer team for two years. We lost most of our games but we had a great time.

I would tell them that it didn't matter if they won or lost but how they played the game. I think they would have preferred winning. I love soccer, the Seattle Sonics and Seattle Seahawks. The only spectator sports I don't like are car racing, boxing, and bull-fighting.

"I think the world is sad and funny. Being a psychotherapist probably influences my writing. I am interested in writing about family relationships, although I might write a very commercial and somewhat disgusting book someday to make money."

BIOGRAPHICAL/CRITICAL SOURCES:

PERIODICALS

Seattle Times, November 15, 1981.

*   *   *

OLSEN, Ib Spang 1921-
(Padre Detine, a joint pseudonym)

PERSONAL: Born June 11, 1921, in Copenhagen, Denmark; son of Ole Christian (a gardener) and Soffu (Nielsen) Olsen; married Grete Geisler, May 3, 1947 (divorced, 1960); married Nulle Oeigaard (an artist), September 8, 1962; children: (first marriage) Tune, Tine; (second marriage) Martin, Lasse. Education: Blaagaards Seminarium, teacher training, 1939-43; Royal Danish Academy of Art, study of graphic art, 1945-49. Politics: Democratic Socialist.

ADDRESSES: Home—Slotsparken 64, Bagsvaerd 2880, Denmark. Agent—International Children's Book Service, Kildeskovsvej 21, Gentofte 2820, Denmark.

CAREER: Illustrator of Sunday magazine supplements for Danish newspapers, 1942; schoolteacher in Denmark, 1952-60; full-time writer and illustrator, 1960—. Has also designed murals for schools, posters, and ceramic pieces. Began work in Danish television, 1964, with numerous animated programs for young people to his credit.

AWARDS, HONORS: Danish Ministry of Culture Award for best illustrated children's book of the year, 1962, for Drengen i maanen, 1963, for Regnen and Blaesten, 1964, for Boernerim, and 1966, for Mosekonens bryg; Danish Society for Bookcraft's honor list of year's outstanding books, 1964, for Kiosken paa torvet, 1968, for Lars Peter's cykel, 1969, for Hokus Pokus og andre boernerim, 1971, for Roegen; Illustrator's Prize, Organization for Friends of Books, 1966; International Board on Books for Young People honors list, 1966, runner-up for Hans Christian Andersen medal, 1968, 1970, Hans Christian Andersen Medal, 1972; Hendrixen Medal for outstanding bookcraft, 1967, for Halfdans abc; diploma, Bratislava Biennial,

1967: honorable mention, Association of Authors of Juvenile Literature in Finland, 1971, for Lars Peter's cykel; Storm Petersen Legatet, 1971, for body of work; Danish Book Craft Society Prize, 1976.

WRITINGS:

SELF-ILLUSTRATED CHILDREN'S BOOKS

Det lille lokomotiv, G. E. C. Gad, 1956, translation by Virginia Allen Jensen published as The Little Locomotive, Coward, 1976, published in England as The Little Shunting Engine, World's Work, 1976.

Mosekonens bryg, Kunst og Kultur, 1957, translation by Jensen published as The Marsh Crone's Brew, Abingdon, 1960.

Boernene paa vejen, Gjellerups, 1958.

Bedstemors vaegtaeppe, Kunst og Kultur, 1958.

(With Torben Brostroem) Boern: Det foerste aar i ord og tegninger (verse), Hasselbalch, 1962.

Drengen i maanen, Gyldendal, 1962, translation by Jensen published as The Boy in the Moon, Abingdon, 1963, Parents' Magazine, 1971.

Blaesten, Gyldendal, 1963.

Regnen, Gyldendal, 1963.

Kiosken paa torvet, Gyldendal, 1964.

Kattehuset, Gyldendal, 1968, translation by Jensen published as Cat Alley, Coward, 1971.

Hvordan vi fik vores naboer, Gyldendal, 1969.

Marie-hoenen, Gyldendal, 1969.

Where is Martin?, translation by Jensen, Angus & Robertson, 1969.

Roegen, Gyldendal, 1970, translation by Jensen published as Smoke, Coward, 1972.

Pjer Brumme: Historier om en lille bjoern, Gyldendal, 1971.

Folkene paa vejen, Gyldendal, 1972.

(Adaptor) Vilhelm Bergsoe, Nissen fra timsgaard, Gyldendal, 1973, translation by Jensen published as The Nisse from Timsgaard, Coward, 1974.

(With Martin Hansen) I Kristoffers spor, Gyldendal, 1973.

Gamle fru glad, Gyldendal, 1974.

24 breve til nissen, Rhodos, 1975.

Min tjeneste hos bjergmanden, Boernenes Boghandel, 1975.

Thors rejse til Udgaard, Gyldendal, 1975.

(With Lennart Hellsing) Old Mother Hubbard and Her Dog, translated by Jensen, Coward, 1976.

Thors rejse til hymer, Gyldendal, 1977.

Thor og hammeren, Gyldendal, 1978.

Lille dreng paa oesterbro, Gyldendal, 1980.

Kanonfotografen: Som man raber i skoven (plays), Schonberg, 1983.

Allan alene, Gyldendal, 1988.

ILLUSTRATOR

Prinsessen paa Glasbjerget (folk tales), J. H. Schultz, 1946.

Ester Nagel, compiler, *Danske folkeeventyr,* Kunst og Kultur, 1950.

Frank Jaeger, *Hverdaghistorier,* Wivel, 1951.

Jaeger, *Tune, det foerste aar,* H. Branner, 1951.

Fem smaa troldeboern, Danske, 1952.

Nissen flytter med, Gyldendal, 1955.

Abrikosia, Hoest & Soen, 1958.

Virginia Allen Jensen, *Lars Peter's Birthday,* Abington, 1959.

Jakob Johannes Bech Nygaard, *Tobias tryllemus,* Martins, 1961, translation by Edith Joan McCormick published as *Tobias, the Magic Mouse,* Harcourt, 1968.

Halfdan Wedel Rasmussen, *Boernerim,* Schoenberg, 1964.

Hans Christian Andersen, *Digte,* edited by Bo Groenbech, Danske Arnkrone, 1966.

Morten poulsens urtehave, Hoest & Soen, 1967.

Rasmussen, *Halfdans abc,* Illustrations-forlaget, 1967.

Molbohistorier, Schoenberg, 1967.

Rasmussen, *Den lille fraekke Frederik og andre boernerim,* Branner & Korch, 1967.

Jensen, *Lars Peters cykel,* Gyldendal, 1968, published as *Lars Peter's Bicycle,* Angus & Robertson, 1970.

Lise Soerensen, *Da lyset gik ud,* Gyldendal, 1968.

Rasmussen, *Hokus pokus og andre boernerim,* Schoenberg, 1969, translation published as *Hocus Pocus,* Angus & Robertson, 1973.

Ole Restrup, *Odin og Tor,* G. E. C. Gad, 1969.

Kjeld Elfelt, *Aesop: 50 fabler,* Schoenberg, 1970.

Rasmussen, *Otte digte om snaps,* Udgiveren, 1970.

Rasmussen, *Noget om Nanette,* Schoenberg, 1972.

The Thirteen Clocks, Sigvaldi, 1973.

Joergen Lorenzen, *Danske folkeviser: Et hundrede udvalgte danske viser,* G. E. C. 1974.

Cecil Boedker, *Barnet i sivkurven,* P. Haase og Soens, 1975.

Boedker, *Da jorden forsvandt,* P. Haase og Soens, 1975.

Boedker, *Den udgalgte,* Danske Bibelselskab, 1977.

Ebbe Klovedal Reich, *De forste: 30 fortaellinger om Danmarks fodsel* (first of three volumes of Medieval Danish folksongs), Vindrose, 1981.

Reich, *Ploven og de to svaerd: 30 fortaelinger fra Danmarks unge dage* (second of three volumes of Medieval Danish folksongs), Vindrose, 1982.

Reich, *Den baerende magt; 30 fortaelinger om Danmarks syv-otte yngst slaegtled* (third of three volumes of Medieval Danish folksongs), Vindrose, 1983.

Designer of numerous book-jackets; illustrator of Danish language editions of works by Herman Melville, Geoffrey Chaucer, and Mark Twain; animator of films for Danish Television including: *Hvad bliver det naeste?, Taarnuret, Vitaminerne, Den store krage, Nikolai, Stregen der loeb henad,* and *Stregen der loeb opad.* Original illustrations for four books were given by the author to the Kerlan Collection, University of Minnesota.

OTHER

(With Erik E. Frederiksen under joint pseudonym Padre Detine) *En Sydamerikaner i Nordsjaelland* (humorous tales), privately printed, 1960.

Om direkte kopl, Grafodan, c. 1971.

(With Gunnar Jakobsen) *Ib Spang Olsens bogarbejder 1944-1981: En bibliografi,* Schonberg, 1982.

Magasinet, Hjemmets sondag og jeg, Fremad, 1984.

Ib Spang Olsen's books have been published in his native Denmark, England, the Faroe Islands, Finland, Germany, Greenland, Holland, Japan, Norway, South Africa, Sweden, the United States, and Wales.

SIDELIGHTS: Ib Spang Olsen began his prolific career primarily as an illustrator of books for adults. It was only after his own children were born and he found himself pressed for numerous bedside stories that he turned his efforts towards writing and illustrating literature for a younger audience. "The child seems close, and is, nevertheless, a stranger," he said in his 1972 Hans Christian Andersen Medal acceptance speech given before the International Board on Books for Young People. "The child exists in another world. He doesn't tell us about it, and we have forgotten how it was for us when we lived in that world. We can try to put ourselves in his place; we can remember a little, and we try to sense the rest. We employ what we call *fantasy,* but we don't know how much of his fantasy seems like common sense to the child. And when we adults think that a child is being very imaginative, perhaps the child is trying to arrive at a reasonable explanation for something that is puzzling him."

Juxtaposing the real and the imaginary is a recurrent theme in many of Olsen's works for children, as in his popular book *Where is Martin?.* In this story, Laura follows her small brother Martin from the everyday world of their modern, sterile apartment building into quite another dimension, full of children and magic, where all the rules suddenly change, the uncommon is commonplace, and where strange cats abound. "This is a book of dreams and a dream of a book," writes a reviewer in the *Times Literary Supplement,* "Ib Spang Olsen has peered deeply into the looking-glass." Olsen composes his prose to reflect the mythic context of his stories, by adopting a more poetic, musical quality than exists in normal speaking or reading language. In accounting for a modern child's unique perception of reality, he attempts to downplay the nostalgic quality resulting from memories of his own childhood. Olsen sees this as a difficulty in writing responsibly for children, because to be truthful to his young audience, he can only create stories based upon personal recollections and experiences.

The humorous and energetic pictures accompanying the texts of his stories also reflect Olsen's ability to objectively draw upon his own "child within" in recreating that "other world" within the pages of his books. All of the illustrations are created using the "direct-copy" method, which entails drawing directly onto the copy-film. A separate film is created for each of the four colors used in each single illustration, and the films are not combined until the printing process, thereby making the finished book the original artwork. The lithographic quality of the resulting illustration reflects Olsen's interest in classic graphic techniques, and his desire to retain the hand of the artist within an era of large presses and modern printing technology.

BIOGRAPHICAL/CRITICAL SOURCES:

BOOKS

Kingman, Lee, and others, compilers, *Illustrators of Children's Books: 1957-1966,* Horn Book, 1968.

PERIODICALS

Bookbird, Volume 19, 1972.
Booklist, November 15, 1972, p. 302; May 15, 1976, p. 1338.
Horn Book, April, 1972, p. 138; August, 1972. p. 364; August, 1976, p. 388; February, 1978, p. 36.
Times Literary Supplement, October 16, 1969, p. 1200; October 22, 1971, p. 1325; April 28, 1972, p. 488.
Top of the News, January, 1973; June, 1973.

*   *   *

OPPENHEIMER, Joan L(etson) 1925-

PERSONAL: Born January 25, 1925, in Ellendale, ND; daughter of Maurice Devillo (a teacher) and Lola (Jones) Letson; married Robert Gridley, April 10, 1943 (divorced, 1953); married Elwyn S. Oppenheimer, June 19, 1953; children: (first marriage) Donald B., Jeffrey L.; (second marriage) Debra L. *Education:* Attended Northwestern University, 1944, and Southwestern College, 1966-70. *Politics:* Democrat. *Religion:* Protestant.

ADDRESSES: Home—1663 Mills St., Chula Vista, CA 91913. *Agent*—Bobbe Siegel, 41 West 53rd St., New York, NY 10024.

CAREER: First National Bank, Chicago, IL, clerk, 1942-43; Federal Bureau of Investigation (FBI), Chicago, stenographer, 1943-45; U.S. Gauge Co., Chicago, secretary, 1945; Lever Brothers, Chicago, secretary, 1946; Rohr Corp., secretary, 1952-53; Southwestern College, Chula Vista, CA, instructor in creative writing, 1977-84;

University of California, San Diego, La Jolla, CA, instructor in creative writing, 1982-88; private workshop instructor, 1988—. Workshop leader at the Santa Barbara Writers Conference.

MEMBER: Mystery Writers of America.

WRITINGS:

JUVENILE BOOKS

The Coming Down Time, Transition Press, 1969.
Run for Your Luck, Hawthorn, 1971.
The Nobody Road, Scholastic Inc., 1974.
On the Outside, Looking In, Scholastic Inc., 1975.
Francesca, Baby, Scholastic Inc., 1976.
The Lost Summer, Scholastic Inc., 1977.
It Isn't Easy Being a Teenaged Millionaire, Scholastic Inc., 1978.
Walk beside Me, Be My Friend, Scholastic Inc., 1978.
One Step Apart, Tempo Books, 1978.
No Laughing Matter, Tempo Books, 1978.
The Voices of Julie, Scholastic Inc., 1979.
Which Mother Is Mine?, Bantam, 1980.
Working on It, Harcourt, 1980.
Gardine versus Hanover, Harper, 1982.
Second Chance, Scholastic Inc., 1982.
The Missing Sunrise, Scholastic Inc., 1983.
Stepsisters, Archway, 1983.
A Clown Like Me, Harper, 1985.
Toughing It Out, Silhouette, 1987.

ADULT MYSTERY NOVELS

Rattlesnakes and Roses, Perseverance Press, 1987.
Trouble at Gabourys, Walker, 1987.
Cornelia, Reinvented, Mysterious Press, 1992.

OTHER

Contributor to anthologies, including *Today's Stories from "Seventeen,"* Macmillan, 1971; *Short Story Scene,* Globe, 1974; *Dreamstalkers,* Economy Co., 1975; and *Oceans and Orbits,* Laidlaw Brothers, 1977. Also contributor to popular magazines, including *Redbook, Woman's Day, Seventeen, Ingenue, Boy's Life,* and *Alfred Hitchcock Mystery Magazine.*

ADAPTATIONS: Francesca, Baby, It Isn't Easy Being a Teenaged Millionaire, and *Which Mother is Mine?* have each been adapted for television and broadcast as an *ABC Afterschool Special.*

SIDELIGHTS: Joan L. Oppenheimer once told *CA:* "I began writing for young people [ages 10 to 18] because it is a group facing so many serious problems in today's world. I felt strongly that a young reader might be interested in a fictional character facing a problem, learning to cope and perhaps gaining some insight into possible solutions.

"Whenever I can, I go to the young people involved with the problems I cover in fiction (drugs, alcohol, broken homes, foster homes, etc.) and get their own views. This can cover anything from family to friends to school to the way they see the world today. When I have enough material to live comfortably in a teenaged mind for several months, I am ready to write the book already in rough outline.

"The feedback from these books has been tremendous. My young readers seem to appreciate honesty in the handling of problems they are already familiar with. They develop a greater understanding of these problems and of others who struggle with them—and they write to tell me so. In my opinion, these letters are one of the greatest rewards in writing for young people."

Oppenheimer is especially pleased with the reaction to *Francesca, Baby.* The story of two young girls and their alcoholic mother, it is being distributed as an educational tool by Walt Disney Productions. "It is marvelous to know that it can help children cope with this tremendous problem," Oppenheimer commented. "And it obviously helps children understand others who are less fortunate than they in such home situations. I am, therefore, a writer who frequently weeps over her fan mail!"

Oppenheimer recently added: "I feel particularly fortunate to be writing now in a fourth genre: short stories for adults, short stories for teens, books for teens and, presently, mysteries for adults. I have loved mysteries ever since I discovered them, not yet in my teens—I read EVERYTHING as a child. For five years now, I've been writing mysteries for adults. I truly feel I'm one of the luckiest writers I know."

BIOGRAPHICAL/CRITICAL SOURCES:

PERIODICALS

Philadelphia Inquirer, January 9, 1972.
Star News (National City, CA), August 21, 1969.

*   *   *

OWEN, Jack 1929-
(Jack Dykes)

PERSONAL: Born June 21, 1929, in Yorkshire, England.

ADDRESSES: Home—46 Kingsway, Cottingham, North Humberside, HU16 5BB, England. *Agent*—Richard Gollner, Radala & Associates, 17 Avenue Mansions, Finchley Rd., London NW3 7AX, England.

CAREER: Commissioners of Customs and Excise, London, England, customs and excise officer, 1951—. *Military service:* British Army, 1947-49.

WRITINGS:

UNDER PSEUDONYM JACK DYKES

The Taste of Yesterday (novel), Dent, 1969.
Pig in the Middle (novel), Dent, 1971.
Harpoon to Kill (novel), Dent, 1972.
Smuggling on the Yorkshire Coast (nonfiction), Dalesman Publishing, 1978.
Palm Beach: An Irreverent Guide, Old Book Shop Publications, 1986.

WORK IN PROGRESS: The Whaler's Graveyard, a book about England's last Arctic whaler; *Roll, Alabama, Roll!,* a novel about the Confederacy's British gunboat.

SIDELIGHTS: Jack Owen once told *CA:* "Writing is damned hard work. I wish I knew why I do it."*

*   *   *

OWEN, Roger C(orey) 1928-

PERSONAL: Born September 14, 1928, in Port Arthur, TX; son of Richard B. and Evelyn (Corey) Owen; married Suzanne Martinez, 1951; children: five. *Education:* Michigan State University, B.A., 1953; University of Arizona, M.A., 1957; University of California, Los Angeles, Ph.D., 1962.

ADDRESSES: Home—25 Duck Pond Rd., Glen Cove, NY 11542. *Office*—Department of Anthropology, Queens College of the City University of New York, Flushing, NY 11367.

CAREER: University of California, Los Angeles, field director of Paipai Interdisciplinary Research Project, 1958-59; University of California, Santa Barbara, instructor, 1959-61, assistant professor, 1961-64, associate professor of anthropology, 1964-67; Queens College of the City University of New York, Flushing, NY, professor of anthropology, 1967—. Visiting professor at Fundacao Escola de Sociologia e Politica, 1964-65; visiting lecturer at University of Arizona, summers, 1968 and 1974, Sweetbriar College, 1972, University of California, Irvine, 1972, and Widener College, 1975. Consultant to National Science Foundation, General Motors, Educational Associates, Inc., Department of Health, Education and Welfare, and Wenner-Gren Foundation.

MEMBER: American Anthropological Association (fellow), American Association for the Advancement of Science, Current Anthropology (associate), American Ethnological Society (member of council, 1966-69), Southwestern Anthropological Association (president, 1963-64), Sigma Xi.

AWARDS, HONORS: Grants from Licensed Beverages Industries, Inc., 1964-66, National Science Foundation, 1966-67, and Holt, Rhinehart & Winston, 1969-71.

WRITINGS:

(Editor with others) *The North American Indians: A Sourcebook,* Macmillan, 1967.
(Contributor) Walter Buckley, editor, *Readings in Modern Systems Research for the Behavioral Scientist,* Aldine, 1968.
Inquiring about Cultures, with databook and teacher's guide, Holt, 1972, revised edition published as *Inquiring about Cultures: Anthropology and Sociology,* 1976.
(Contributor) Talal Asad, editor, *Anthropology and the Colonial Encounter,* Humanities, 1979.
Studies in the Economic and Social History of Palestine in the Nineteenth and Twentieth Centuries, Southern Illinois University Press, 1982.
The Middle East in the World Economy, Routledge, Chapman & Hall, 1987.

Also contributor to *Handbook of Middle American Indians* and *Encyclopedia of Indians of the Americas.* Contributor of more than thirty articles and reviews to anthropology journals.

WORK IN PROGRESS: *The Anthropology of Native North America,* for Macmillan.*

*   *   *

OWENS, Richard Meredith   1944-

PERSONAL: Born January 11, 1944; son of Gilbert Meredith and Charlotte (Vainder) Owens. *Education:* Attended Johns Hopkins University.

ADDRESSES: Home—40 Helen Lane, Mill Valley, CA 94941.

CAREER: Works in advertising, marketing and design.

AWARDS, HONORS: Best promotion of year award, *Advertising Age,* 1974, for Levi's Denim Art Contest.

WRITINGS:

American Denim, Abrams, 1975.
The Professional Singer's Guide to New York, AIMS, 1983.
Towards a Career in Europe, AIMS, 1983.

Also author of *How to Decorate Your Levi's,* Simon & Schuster.

WORK IN PROGRESS: *The Art of Batik; Jerome Wallace: The Batik Man of Kauai.*

OXTOBY, Willard Gurdon   1933-

PERSONAL: Surname is accented on first syllable; born July 29, 1933, in Kentfield, CA; son of Gurdon Corning and Mirian Burrell (White) Oxtoby; married Layla Jurji, September 27, 1958 (deceased, June 17, 1980); children: David Merrill, Susan Elizabeth. *Education:* Stanford University, B.A., 1955; post-graduate study, American School of Oriental Research, Jerusalem, 1958-60; Princeton University, M.A., 1961, Ph.D., 1962; Harvard University, postdoctoral study, 1964-66. *Religion:* United Presbyterian Church in the U.S.A.

ADDRESSES: Home—2 Gordon Rd., Willowdale, Toronto, Ontario M2P 1E1, Canada. *Office*—Trinity College, University of Toronto, Toronto, Ontario M5S 1H8, Canada.

CAREER: McGill University, Montreal, Quebec, lecturer, 1960-63, assistant professor of Old Testament, 1963-64; Harvard University, Cambridge, MA, teaching fellow in world religions, 1965-66; Yale University, New Haven, CT, associate professor of religious studies, 1971—, director, Centre for Religious Studies, 1976—. Visiting professor of Near Eastern languages, University of Michigan, 1964.

MEMBER: Canadian Society for the Study of Religion, American Society for the Study of Religion (secretary, 1969-75), American Academy of Religion, American Oriental Society, Society for Values in Higher Education.

WRITINGS:

Some Inscriptions on the Safaitic Bedouin, American Oriental Society, 1968.
Ancient Iran and Zoroastrianism in Festschriften: An Index, Council on the Study of Religion (Waterloo, Ontario), 1973.
(Editor) *Religious Diversity: Essays by Wilfred Cantwell Smith,* Harper, 1976.
(Co-author) *Justice and Reconciliation in the Arab-Israeli Conflict: A Christian Perspective,* Friendship Press, 1979.
The Meaning of Other Faiths, Westminster John Knox, 1983.

Editor, "Studies in Religion," American Academy of Religion monograph series, 1968-70; member of editorial board, *Soundings* (publication of Society for Religion in Higher Education), 1968-71.*

*   *   *

OZINGA, James Richard   1932-

PERSONAL: Born March 6, 1932, in Grand Rapids, MI; son of James (a pattern maker) and Esther Ruth (Van

Houten) Ozinga; married Suzanne Willard (a hospital vice-president), December 31, 1959; children: James Michael, Kurt Stephen, Karen Sue. *Education:* Calvin College, B.A., 1956; Calvin Seminary, B.D., 1959; graduate study at University of Michigan, 1959-60; Western Michigan University, A.B., 1962, M.A., 1964; Michigan State University, Ph.D., 1968. *Avocational interests:* Reading mysteries.

ADDRESSES: Home—62 Bellarmine, Rochester, MI 48309. *Office*—Department of Political Science, Oakland University, Rochester, MI 48063.

CAREER: Oakland University, Rochester, MI, assistant professor, 1967-73, associate professor, 1973-84, professor of political science, 1984—. *Military service:* U.S. Air Force, 1951-53; became sergeant.

MEMBER: International Society for Systems Research, Michigan Association of Environmental Professionals, American Association for the Advancement of Science.

WRITINGS:

Communism: A Tarnished Promise, C. E. Merrill, 1975.
Prodigal Human, McFarland, 1985.
Communism: The Story of Its Idea and Its Implementation, Prentice-Hall, 1987, 2nd edition, 1991.
The Rapacki Plan: The Nineteen-Fifty-Seven Proposal to Denuclearize Central Europe, and An Analysis of Its Rejection, McFarland, 1989.
(With John Lowenhardt and Eric von Ree) *The Rise and Fall of the Soviet Politburo,* St. Martin's Press, 1992.

Also contributor to political science journals.

P

PACKER, J(ames) I(nnell) 1926-

PERSONAL: Born July 22, 1926, in Twyning, Gloucestershire, England; son of James Percy (a clerk) and Dorothy (Harris) Packer; married Ethel Mullett; children: Ruth, Naomi, Martin. *Education:* Corpus Christi College, Oxford, B.A., 1948, M.A. and D.Phil., both 1954; also attended Wycliffe Hall, Oxford, 1949-52. *Politics:* "Eclectic." *Religion:* Anglican. *Avocational interests:* Music (Western classical and early American jazz), cricket, railroads.

ADDRESSES: Office—Regent College, 5800 University Blvd., Vancouver, British Columbia, Canada V6T 2E4.

CAREER: Anglican clergyman; assistant curate in Birmingham, England, 1952-54; Tyndale Hall, Bristol, England, tutor, 1955-61; Latimer House, Oxford, England, librarian, 1961-64, warden, 1964-69; Tyndale Hall, principal, 1970-71; Trinity College, Bristol, associate principal, 1971-79; Regent College, Vancouver, British Columbia, professor of historical and systematic theology, 1979—. Visiting professor at Westminster Theological Seminary, 1968; adjunct professor, Gordon-Conwell Seminary, 1975-88.

WRITINGS:

"Fundamentalism" and the Word of God, Eerdmans, 1958.
(Translator and editor with O. R. Johnston) *Luther's Bondage of the Will,* Revell, 1958.
Evangelism and the Sovereignty of God, Inter-Varsity Press, 1961.
God Has Spoken, Westminster, 1965, 2nd edition, Inter-Varsity Press, 1980.
(With A. M. Stibbs) *The Spirit within You,* Hodder & Stoughton, 1967.
Knowing God, Inter-Varsity Press, 1973.

I Want to Be a Christian, Tyndale House, 1977.
Knowing Man, Cornerstone Press, 1979.
Beyond the Battle for the Bible, Cornerstone Press, 1980.
God's Words, Inter-Varsity Press, 1982.
Keep in Step with the Spirit, Revell, 1984.
(With Thomas Howard) *Christianity: The True Humanism,* Word Books, 1985.
Your Father Loves You, Harold Shaw, 1986.
Hot Tub Religion, Tyndale House, 1987.
A Quest for Godliness: The Puritan Vision of the Christian Life, Crossway, 1990.

Senior editor, *Christianity Today,* 1985—.

Knowing God has been published in fourteen languages.

WORK IN PROGRESS: Research on biblical, historical, and systematic theology.

*   *   *

PACKER, Vin
See MEAKER, Marijane (Agnes)

*   *   *

PARISH, James Robert 1944-

PERSONAL: Born April 21, 1944, in Cambridge, MA; son of Fred A. (an allergist) and Ann Lois (Magilavy) Parish. *Education:* University of Pennsylvania, B.A., 1964, LL.B., 1967. *Religion:* Jewish.

ADDRESSES: Home—4338 Gentry Avenue, No. 1, Studio City, CA 91604.

CAREER: Admitted to the bar of New York State, 1968; Cape Playhouse, Dennis, MA, publicist and properties manager, 1961-64; Entertainment Copyright Research Co., Inc., New York City, director, 1967-68; *Variety,* New York City, reporter, 1968-69; *Motion Picture Daily,* New York City, reporter, 1969; Harold Rand & Co., Inc. (publicity firm), New York City, entertainment publicist, 1969-70; free-lance writer, 1970—. Founder of Entertainment Copyright Research Co., Inc., and JRP Media Inc.

MEMBER: Kate Smith U.S.A. Friends' Club, Phi Beta Kappa.

WRITINGS:

The American Movies: The History, Films, Awards; A Pictorial Encyclopedia, Galahad Books, 1969.

The American Movies Reference Book: The Sound Era, Prentice-Hall, 1969.

Movie Greats: The Players, Directors, Producers, Garland Books, 1969.

(With Alan G. Barbour and Alvin H. Marill) *Errol Flynn,* Cinefax, 1969.

(Compiler with Barbour and Marill) *Karloff,* Cinefax, 1969.

(With Paul Michael) *The Emmy Awards: A Pictorial History,* Crown, 1970.

The Fox Girls, Arlington House, 1971.

(Editor) *The Great Movie Series,* A. S. Barnes, 1971.

(With Marill) *The Cinema of Edward G. Robinson,* A. S. Barnes, 1972.

The Paramount Pretties, Arlington House, 1972.

The Slapstick Queens, A. S. Barnes, 1973.

Actors' Television Credits: 1950-1972 (also see below), Scarecrow, 1973, Supplement 1 (to 1976; with Mark Trost), 1978, Supplement 2 (1977-1981; with Vincent Terrace), 1982, Supplement 3 (1982-1985; with Terrace), 1986, revised edition (with Terrace) published as *The Complete Actors' Television Credits, 1948-1988,* Scarecrow, Volume 1: *Actors,* 1989, Volume 2: *Actresses,* 1990.

(With Ronald L. Bowers) *The MGM Stock Company: The Golden Era,* Arlington House, 1973.

Good Dames, A. S. Barnes, 1973.

(With Michael R. Pitts) *The Great Spy Pictures,* Scarecrow, 1974.

The RKO Gals, Arlington House, 1974.

(With Steven Whitney) *The George Raft File: The Unauthorized Biography* Drake, 1974.

(With Whitney) *Vincent Price Unmasked,* Drake, 1974.

Hollywood's Great Love Teams, Arlington House, 1974.

(With Pitts) *Film Directors: A Guide to Their American Films,* Scarecrow, 1974.

(With Don E. Stanke) *The Glamour Girls,* Arlington House, 1975.

The Elvis Presley Scrapbook, Ballantine, 1975.

Great Movie Heroes, Harper & Row, 1975.

(With Stanke) *The Debonairs,* Arlington House, 1975.

(With Jack Ano) *Liza!: An Unauthorized Biography,* Pocket Books, 1975, published in England as *Liza: Her Cinderella Nightmare,* W. H. Allen, 1975.

(With Pitts) *The Great Gangster Pictures,* Scarecrow, 1976.

(With Pitts) *The Great Western Pictures,* Scarecrow, 1976.

(With Lennard DeCarl) *Hollywood Players: The Forties,* Arlington House, 1976.

(With William T. Leonard) *Hollywood Players: The Thirties,* Arlington House, 1976.

The Tough Guys, Arlington House, 1976.

Great Child Stars, Ace Books, 1976.

Great Western Stars, Ace Books, 1976.

(With Stanke) *The Swashbucklers,* Arlington House, 1976.

(With Kingsley Canham) *Film Directors Guide: Western Europe,* Scarecrow, 1976.

The Jeanette MacDonald Story, Mason/Charter, 1976.

(With Pitts) *The Great Science Fiction Pictures,* Scarecrow, 1977.

(With Stanke and Pitts) *The All-Americans,* Arlington House, 1977.

(With Canham) *Film Actors Guide: Western Europe,* Scarecrow, 1977.

(With Stanke) *The Leading Ladies,* Arlington House, 1977.

Hollywood Character Actors, Arlington House, 1978.

The Hollywood Beauties, Arlington House, 1978.

(With Pitts) *Hollywood on Hollywood,* Scarecrow, 1978.

(With Leonard) *The Funsters,* Arlington House, 1979.

(With Stanke) *The Forties Gals,* Arlington House, 1980.

(With Mank) *The Hollywood Reliables,* Arlington House, 1980.

(With Mank and Richard Picchiarini) *The Best of MGM: The Golden Years (1928-59),* Arlington House, 1981.

(With Pitts) *The Great Spy Pictures II,* Scarecrow, 1986.

(With Pitts) *The Great Gangster Pictures II,* Scarecrow, 1987.

(With Pitts) *The Great Western Pictures II,* Scarecrow, 1988.

(With George H. Hill) *Black Action Films: Plots, Critiques, Casts, and Credits for 235 Theatrical and Made-for-Television Releases,* McFarland, 1989.

(With Pitts) *Hollywood Songsters,* Garland, 1990.

(With Pitts) *The Great Science Fiction Pictures II,* Scarecrow, 1990.

The Great Detective Pictures, Scarecrow, 1990.

The Great Combat Pictures: Twentieth-Century Warfare on the Screen, Scarecrow, 1990.

The Great Cop Pictures, Scarecrow, 1990.

Prison Pictures from Hollywood: Plots, Critiques, Casts, and Credits for 293 Theatrical and Made-for-Television Releases, McFarland, 1991.

Hollywood's Great Musicals, Scarecrow, 1991.

Hollywood Baby Boomers, Garland, 1991.
Prostitution in Hollywood Films, McFarland, 1991.
The Hollywood Death Book, Pioneer Paperbacks, 1992.

Also a contributor to newspapers and entertainment papers, and a series editor for various publishers of performing arts books.

BIOGRAPHICAL/CRITICAL SOURCES:

PERIODICALS

Los Angeles Times Book Review, May 10, 1981.

*   *   *

PARK, Jordan
See POHL, Frederik

*   *   *

PAVORD, Anna 1940-

PERSONAL: Born September 20, 1940, in Abergavenny, Wales; daughter of Arthur (a headmaster) and Christabel (a teacher; maiden name, Lewis) Pavord; married Trevor Ware (in marketing), June 18, 1966; children: Oenone, Vanessa, Tilly. *Education:* University of Leicester, B.A. (with honors), 1962. *Politics:* None. *Religion:* Pantheist. *Avocational interests:* "I read Evelyn Waugh for pleasure, J. S. Mill for my soul. I walk with my husband and study landscape history and architecture."

ADDRESSES: Home—Old Rectory, Puncknowle, Dorchester, Dorset, England. *Office—Observer,* 8 St. Andrews Hill, London EC4V 5JA, England. *Agent*—Caradoc King, A. P. Watt & Co., 20 John St., London WC1R 4HL, England.

CAREER: Lintas Ltd. (advertising agency), London, England, copywriter, 1962-63; BBC-TV, London, director, 1963-69; free-lance journalist, author and broadcaster, 1969—.

WRITINGS:

Growing Things (juvenile gardening book), Macmillan, 1982.
Foliage, Pavilion, 1990.
The Flowering Year, Chatto & Windus, 1991.

Contributor to newspapers and writer/presenter of a ten part television series entitled *Flowering Passions,* Channel 4 TV, 1991.

SIDELIGHTS: Anna Pavord once told *CA:* "I write to keep our seventeenth-century house standing, a thirteenth-century dovecote in repair, my garden from becoming an impenetrable jungle, and my children educated."

PAYNE, Leanne 1932-

PERSONAL: Given name is pronounced "Lee-*ann*"; born June 26, 1932, in Omaha, NE; daughter of Robert Hugh (a pharmacist) and Forrest (Williamson) Mabrey; divorced, 1952; children: Deborah Payne Bostrom. *Education:* Wheaton College, B.A. (with honors), 1971, M.A. (with high honors), 1974; University of Arkansas, M.Ed., 1973. *Religion:* Episcopalian.

ADDRESSES: Home—Milwaukee, WI. *Office*—Pastoral Care Ministries, Inc., P.O. Box 17702, Milwaukee, WI 53217.

CAREER: Veterans Administration Hospital, Little Rock, AR, clerk and requirements analyst, 1957-63; Wheaton College, Wheaton, IL, member of student personnel staff, 1965-68, special instructor in English, 1973-76, pastoral counselor, 1976-78, lecturer and missioner, 1978—; Pastoral Care Ministries, Inc., Milwaukee, WI, founder and president, 1982—. Member of faculty at Creighton University; research fellow at Yale University Divinity School; mission leader at Episcopal, evangelical, and nondenominational churches; seminar speaker; lecturer at pastoral care retreats in the United States and abroad.

MEMBER: Lambda Iota Tau.

WRITINGS:

Real Presence: The Holy Spirit in the Works of C. S. Lewis, Crossway, 1979.
The Broken Image: Restoring Personal Wholeness through Healing Prayer, Crossway, 1981.
The Healing of the Homosexual, Crossway, 1984.
Crisis in Masculinity, Crossway, 1985.
The Healing Presence, Crossway, 1989.
Restoring the Christian Soul through Healing Prayer, Crossway, 1991.

WORK IN PROGRESS: Gnosticism; Virtues and Vices; and *Christian Healing.*

SIDELIGHTS: Leanne Payne wrote: "Like Agnes Sanford, Catherine Marshall, and most who have written and ministered in the area of prayer for healing, I found the healing presence of Christ when in drastic need of healing for myself. I came to understand and especially to emphasize the indwelling presence of Christ and the need to 'practice this presence' in the healing of persons. As I passed this understanding on to others, I saw them as dramatically healed as I had been. Later, taking up theological studies, I looked for theologians, philosophers, and Christian writers whose intellectual systems were large enough to contain the realities that I had experienced within the Christian faith. In C. S. Lewis I found such a mind and heart, and out of my study of him came *Real Presence.*

"*Real Presence* contains the theology that is present not only in the mind of C. S. Lewis, but in that of 'mere' Christians of all time; it is best expounded in the apostles Paul and John. This is the theology which explains my experience of healing, and is inherent in my books on prayer for healing. I have written specifically on prayer for the healing of sexual neuroses (rather than on healing of depression and so on) because the need for healing and understanding of how to pray for healing in this area is so very great. I hope to turn my attention to prayer for healing of other problems in future writing."

* * *

PENNINGTON, M. (Robert John) Basil 1931-

PERSONAL: Born July 28, 1931, in Brooklyn, NY; son of Dale J. (an engineer) and Helene J. Pennington. *Education:* Cathedral College of the Immaculate Conception, 1951; Pontifical University of St. Thomas Aquinas, S.T.L. (cum laude), 1959; Pontifical University of the Gregorianum, J.C.B. (summa cum laude), 1962, J.C.L. (summa cum laude), 1963; graduate study at Pontifical University of St. Thomas Aquinas and Benedictine International College of St. Anselm.

ADDRESSES: Office—School of Theology, St. Joseph's Abbey, Spencer, MA 01562.

CAREER: Entered Order of Cistercians of the Strict Observance (OCSO), 1951, ordained Roman Catholic priest, 1957; St. Joseph's Abbey, Spencer, MA, professor of moral theology, 1959-61, professor of theology and church law, 1963—, pastoral counselor at Retreat House, 1959-61, 1963—, librarian at Institute of Monastic Studies, 1960-61, lecturer at institute, 1971-72, assistant director of novices, summer, 1962, and vocation director, 1978-81. Head of Monastic Council on Church Law, 1964—; member of Commission of Law, Order of Cistercians of the Strict Observance, 1969—; head of Interreligious Monastic Colloquium, 1977; member of advisory board, est, 1979-81, Center for Contemplative Studies, 1979—, North American Board for East-West Relations, 1984—, and Lilly Foundation, 1988—; member of board of directors, John Paul II Center for Prayer and Study for Peace and Food for the Poor; Mastery Foundation, chairperson; member of Ecumenical Institute of Spirituality and Academie Nationale de Reims. Cistercian Publications, founding editor, 1968-73, chairperson, 1973-76. Organizer and director of ecumenical conferences and symposia; guest lecturer at conferences, institutes, and universities all over the world; consultant to Second Vatican Council.

MEMBER: Studies in Formative Spirituality (international board of consultants), Canon Law Society of America, Catholic Theological Society of America, Association of Cistercian Scholars.

AWARDS, HONORS: Pope John Paul II award from National Vocation Directors Conference, 1985.

WRITINGS:

(In Latin) *Propositum monasticum de Codice iuris canonici recognoscendo* (title means "Monastic Proposal for the Renewal of the Code of Canon Law"), St. Joseph's Abbey, 1966.
Daily We Touch Him: Practical Religious Experiences, Doubleday, 1977.
O Holy Mountain: Diary of a Visit to Mount Athos, Doubleday, 1978.
(With Sergius Bolshakoff) *In Search of True Wisdom: Visits to Spiritual Fathers,* Doubleday, 1979.
Centering Prayer, Doubleday, 1980.
Jubilee, Paulist Press, 1981.
Challenges in Prayer, Michael Glazier, 1982.
Monastic Journey to India, Seabury, 1982.
A Place Apart, Doubleday, 1983.
Called, New Thinking on Christian Vocation, Seabury, 1983.
Monastery, Harper, 1983.
Last of the Fathers, St. Bede's Publications, 1983.
The Eucharist, Yesterday and Today, Crossroads, 1984.
In the Footsteps of Peter, Doubleday, 1985.
Manual of Life, Paulist Press, 1985.
Pocketbook of Prayers, Doubleday, 1986.
Prayertimes: Morning-Midday-Evening, Doubleday, 1987.
Breaking Bread: The Table Talk of Jesus, Winston, 1987.
Thomas Merton, Brother Monk: The Quest for True Freedom, Harper, 1988.
Mary Today, Doubleday, 1988.
Retreat with Thomas Merton, Amity House, 1988.
Living Our Priesthood Today, Our Sunday Visitor, 1988.
Through the Year with the Saints, Doubleday, 1988.
Centered Living, Doubleday, 1988.
Long on the Journey, Our Sunday Visitor, 1989.
The Way Back Home, Paulist Press, 1990.
Call to the Center, Doubleday, 1990.
Monastic Life, St. Bede's, 1990.
The Monastic Way, Crossroad, 1990.
Praying By Hand, Harper Collins, 1991.
Light from the Cloister, Paulist Press, 1991.
Way of the Cistercians, Liturgical Press, 1991.

EDITOR AND AUTHOR OF INTRODUCTIONS AND NOTES

The Cistercian Spirit: A Symposium in Memory of Thomas Merton, Cistercian Publications, 1969.

Thomas Merton, *The Climate of Monastic Prayer,* Cistercian Publications, 1969.

William of St. Thierry, *Exposition on the Song of Songs,* Cistercian Publications, 1970.

Guerric of Igny, *Liturgical Sermons I,* Cistercian Publications, 1971.

Guerric of Igny, *Liturgical Sermons II,* Cistercian Publications, 1971.

William of St. Thierry, *On Contemplating God, Prayer, Meditations,* Cistercian Publications, 1971.

Rule and Life: An Interdisciplinary Symposium, Cistercian Publications, 1971.

Bernard of Clairvaux, *On the Song of Songs I,* Cistercian Publications, 1971.

Aelred of Rievaulx, *Treatise, Pastoral Prayer,* Cistercian Publications, 1971.

William of St. Thierry, *The Golden Epistle: A Letter to the Brethren at Mont Dieu,* Cistercian Publications, 1971.

(Also contributor) *Contemplative Community: An Interdisciplinary Symposium,* Cistercian Publications, 1972.

Bernard of Clairvaux: Studies Presented to Dom Jean Leclercq, Cistercian Publications, 1973.

One Yet Two: Monastic Tradition East and West, Cistercian Publications, 1976.

Bernard of Clairvaux, *Five Books on Consideration: Advice to a Pope,* Cistercian Publications, 1976.

Bernard of Clairvaux, *On the Song of Songs II,* Cistercian Publications, 1976.

Prayer and Liberation, Alba House, 1976.

Saint Bernard of Clairvaux: Studies Commemorating the Eighth Centenary of His Canonization, Cistercian Publications, 1977.

(Also contributor) *Finding Grace at the Center,* St. Bede's Publications, 1978.

(Editor) *The Last of the Fathers: The Cistercian Fathers of the Twelfth Century* (essay collection), St. Bede's Publications, 1983.

Getting It All Together, Michael Glazier, 1984.

Towards an Integrated Humanity, Cistercian Publications, 1989.

The Living Testament, Harper, 1989.

OTHER

Syndicated writer for National Catholic News Service. Contributor of nearly six hundred articles and reviews to theology and law journals. Member of board of editors of *Citeaux,* 1968—, *Monastic Studies,* 1971—, *Studies in Medieval Culture,* 1972—, and *Studies in Formative Spirituality,* 1980—; consulting editor of *Way of Prayer,* 1982—, and *The Priest,* 1984—.

SIDELIGHTS: M. Basil Pennington once wrote *CA:* "My main interest is to help as many people as I can to come to experience how much God loves them, so that their lives can be fuller and happier in a union of love with him. I am also deeply concerned about the union of the churches and all religions as a basis for a world spirituality that will undergird true fraternal collaboration in the social, political, and economic spheres."

* * *

PERCY, Charles Henry
    See SMITH, Dorothy Gladys

* * *

PETERSON, Franklynn   1938-

PERSONAL: Born May 25, 1938, in Phillips, WI; son of Don C. (a mill worker) and Frances (Watson) Peterson; married second wife Judi Kesselman-Turkel; children: (first marriage) Alicia, David Douglass, Kevin Andrew. *Education:* University of Wisconsin—Madison, B.S., 1960.

ADDRESSES: Office—P/K Associates, Inc., 4343 West Beltline Hwy., Madison, WI 53711-3860.

CAREER: Writer, 1960—; P/K Associates, Inc., Madison, WI, president. Member of Brooklyn Congress of Racial Equality (CORE), 1963-66.

MEMBER: Authors Guild, Authors League of America, American Society of Journalists and Authors (vice-president, 1974-75; co-chairman of Midwest Nonfiction Writers Conference, 1978-82), Wisconsin Academy of Sciences, Arts and Letters.

AWARDS, HONORS: Brotherhood in Media Award, National Conference of Christians and Jews, 1968, for article "Flunk Dick and Jane"; journalism award, American Optometric Association, 1971, for article "New Eye Care Techniques"; Jesse H. Neal Award, American Business Press Association, 1977, for interview series "PhoneScan"; (with Judi Kesselman-Turkel) Distinguished Consumer Journalism Award, National Press Club, 1984, 1985, for syndicated columns "The Business Computer" and "Frank and Judi on Computers."

WRITINGS:

Handbook of Lawnmower Repair, Emerson, 1973, revised edition, Emerson & Hawthorn, 1978.

The Build-It-Yourself Furniture Catalog, Prentice-Hall, 1976.

How to Fix Damn Near Everything, Prentice-Hall, 1977.

Children's Toys You Can Build Yourself, Prentice-Hall, 1978.

(With Judi R. Kesselman and Frank Konishi) *Eat Anything Exercise Diet,* Morrow, 1979.

WITH JUDI R. KESSELMAN

The Do-It-Yourself Custom Van Book, Regnery, 1977.
Vans (juvenile), Dandelion Press, 1979.
Handbook of Snowmobile Maintenance and Repair, Dutton, 1979.
I Can Use Tools (juvenile), Elsevier-Nelson/Dutton, 1981.

WITH JUDI KESSELMAN-TURKEL

Good Writing: A Basic College Composition Textbook, F. Watts, 1981.
Test-Taking Strategies, Contemporary Books, 1981.
Study Smarts, Contemporary Books, 1981.
The Homeowner's Book of Lists, Contemporary Books, 1981.
How to Improve Damn Near Everything around Your Home, Prentice-Hall, 1982.
Research Shortcuts, Contemporary Books, 1982.
The Author's Handbook, Prentice-Hall, 1982, revised edition, Dodd, 1987.
Note-Taking Made Easy, Contemporary Books, 1982.
Vocabulary Builder: The Practically Painless Way to a Larger Vocabulary, Contemporary Books, 1982.
The Grammar Crammer: How to Write Perfect Sentences, Contemporary Books, 1982.
The Magazine Writer's Handbook, Prentice-Hall, 1982, revised edition, Dodd, 1987.
Getting It Down: How to Put Your Ideas on Paper, Contemporary Books, 1983.
Spelling Simplified, Contemporary Books, 1983.

Author and syndicator (with Kesselman-Turkel) of newspaper computer columns "The Business Computer" and "Frank and Judi on Computers," 1983—.

OTHER

Contributor to periodicals and newspapers, including *Ramparts, Science and Mechanics, Holiday Inn, Writer's Digest, Popular Science, Omni, Fortune,* and *Parade.* Editor of newsletters of Brooklyn Congress of Racial Equality, 1964-66, and American Society of Journalists and Authors, 1974-75. Editor of CPA Mirve Report, 1987.

SIDELIGHTS: Franklynn Peterson once told *CA:* "The field of serious, professional writing died in the early 1980s when books and literature became commodities, managed not by professional commodities brokers—who would have realized the value of having products of substance to market—but by editors and publishers who dabble in literature, dabble in business, dabble in aristocratic living, and in general seem unwilling or unqualified to bring a professional, living return on an author's work. I have, therefore, abandoned the full-time professional writing of books and magazine articles and now devote my time to managing P/K Associates, which syndicates my computer column and publishes other periodicals."

BIOGRAPHICAL/CRITICAL SOURCES:

PERIODICALS

Editor and Publisher, September 19, 1987.
Madison Capitol Times, September 26, 1983.
Milwaukee Journal, October 1, 1978.
New York Times Book Review, August 14, 1977.*

*   *   *

PETTIT, Philip   1945-

PERSONAL: Born December 20, 1945, in Ballinasloe, Ireland; son of Michael Anthony (a company director) and Bridget Christina Pettit; married Eileen Theresa McNally (a social worker), July 1, 1978. *Education:* National University of Ireland, B.A., 1966, M.A., 1967; Queen's University, Belfast, Ph.D., 1970. *Politics:* "Liberal Left."

ADDRESSES: Home—46 Southwell St., Weetangera, Canberra, ACT 2614, Australia. *Office*—Research School of Social Sciences, Australian National University, Canberra, ACT 2601, Australia.

CAREER: National University of Ireland, University College, Dublin, lecturer in philosophy, 1968-72, and 1975-77; Cambridge University, Trinity Hall, Cambridge, England, fellow in philosophy, 1972-75; University of Bradford, Bradford, England, professor of philosophy, 1977-83; Australian National University, Institute of Advanced Studies, Canberra, professorial fellow, 1983—, professor, 1989—.

MEMBER: Mind Association, Australian Philosophy Association, Australian Political Science Association.

AWARDS, HONORS: Australian Academy of Social Sciences fellow, 1987; Australian Academy of Humanities fellow, 1988.

WRITINGS:

On the Idea of Phenomenology, Humanities, 1969.
(Editor) *The Gentle Revolution,* Scepter (Dublin), 1969.
The Concept of Structuralism, University of California Press, 1975, revised edition, 1977.
(Editor with Christopher Hookway) *Action and Interpretation,* Cambridge University Press, 1978.
Judging Justice, Routledge & Kegan Paul, 1980.
(With Graham MacDonald) *Semantics and Social Science,* Routledge & Kegan Paul, 1981.
(Editor with John McDowell) *Subject, Thought and Context,* Oxford University Press, 1986.

(Editor with Alan Hamlin) *The Good Polity*, Blackwell, 1989.
(Editor) *Contemporary Political Theory*, Macmillan, 1990.
(With John Braithwaite) *Not Just Deserts*, Oxford University Press, 1990.
(With Chandran Kukathas) *Rawls*, Stanford University Press, 1990.
The Common Mind, Oxford University Press, 1992.

WORK IN PROGRESS: Research on the shaping of our concepts of the common world (with Peter Menzies), on causality and explanation (with Frank Johnson), on free will and responsibility (with Michael Smith), and on institutional design (with Geoffrey Brennan).

SIDELIGHTS: Philip Pettit once told *CA:* "My philosophical outlook is that of a soft naturalist. I am a naturalist in rejecting the idea that the human being is set apart metaphysically from the rest of nature, say, by the possession of a non-physical mind. I am a soft naturalist in holding that there is substance still in the traditional marks of human distinctiveness: in rationality, freedom, creativity, moral insight, and so on."

*   *   *

PHILLPOTTS, (Mary) Adelaide Eden 1896-
(Mary Adelaide Eden Ross)

PERSONAL: Born April 23, 1896, in Ealing, England; daughter of Eden (an author) and Emily (Topham) Phillpotts; married Nicholas Ross (an artist), 1951 (died July 28, 1967). *Education:* Attended Bedford College, London, 1921-22. *Politics:* Labour. *Religion:* "Humanism." *Avocational interests:* Human relationships, art, nature, travel.

ADDRESSES: Home—Trelana, Poughill, Bude, Cornwall, England. *Agent*—Hughes Massie Ltd., 31 Southampton Row, London WC1B 4HL, England.

CAREER: Writer, 1916—. Women's Service Bureau, London, England, secretary, 1917-18; G. K. Ogden, Cambridge, England, secretary, 1918; worked in Red Cross hospitals, 1914-16.

WRITINGS:

NOVELS

The Friend, Heinemann, 1923.
Lodgers in London, Butterworth & Co., 1925, Little, Brown, 1926.
Tomek the Sculptor, Little, Brown, 1927.
A Marriage, Butterworth & Co., 1928.
The Atoning Years, Butterworth & Co., 1929.
Yellow Sands (novelization of the play of the same title; also see below), Chapman & Hall, 1930.
The Youth of Jacob Ackner, Benn, 1931.

The Founder of Shandon, Benn, 1932.
The Growing World, Hutchinson, 1934.
Onward Journey, Hutchinson, 1936.
Broken Allegiance, Hutchinson, 1937.
What's Happened to Rankin?, Rich & Cowan, 1939.
The Round of Life, Rich & Cowan, 1940.
Laugh with Me (based on the play of the same title; also see below), Rich & Cowan, 1941.
Our Little Town, Rich & Cowan, 1942.
From Jane to John, Rich & Cowan, 1943.
The Adventurers, Rich & Cowan, 1944.
The Lodestar, Rich & Cowan, 1946.
The Fosterling, Rich & Cowan, 1949.
Stubborn Earth, Rich & Cowan, 1951.
Village Love, State Mutual Book, 1988.

Also author of *The Gallant Heart*, 1940, and *The Beacon of Memory*, 1990.

PLAYS

Arachne (in verse), Palmer & Hayward, 1920.
Camillus and the Schoolmaster (in verse; one-act), Gowans & Gray, 1923.
Savitri the Faithful (in verse; one-act), Gowans & Gray, 1923.
Akhnaton (in prose and verse), Butterworth & Co., 1926.
(With father, Eden Phillpotts) *Yellow Sands* (three-act comedy; first produced in London at Haymarket Theatre, 1926), Duckworth, 1926.
(With E. Phillpotts) *The Good Old Days* (three-act comedy), Duckworth, 1932.

Also author of play, *Laugh with Me*, 1938.

EDITOR

Letters from John Cooper Powys to Nicholas Ross, Bertramrota, 1971.
A Wild Flower Wreath (autobiography), privately printed, 1974.

OTHER

Illyrion and Other Poems, Palmer & Hayward, 1916.
Man: A Fable, Constable, 1922.
A Song of Man (poems), Linden Press, 1959.
Panorama of the World (travel book), R. Hale, 1969.
Reverie: An Autobiography, R. Hale, 1981.

Also author of writings under name Mary Adelaide Eden Ross.

SIDELIGHTS: Adelaide Eden Phillpotts once told *CA* that her father's encouragement was important to her career, and she advises all aspiring writers simply to write. Phillpotts added: "I have lived through three wars in which this land has engaged. I have worked for peace, with little hope for the future so long as arms trading goes on between nations."

* * *

PIGGOTT, (Alan) Derek 1923-

PERSONAL: Born December 27, 1923, in Chadwell Heath, England. *Education:* Attended Sutton County (England) grammar school.

ADDRESSES: Office—Lasham Gliding Centre, near Alton, Hampshire, England. *Agent*— A.P. Watt Ltd., 26/28 Bedford Row, London WC1R 4HL, England.

CAREER: Lasham Gliding Centre, near Alton, England, chief flying instructor, 1954-89. Lecturer on film flying, gliding, and soaring, with lecture tours in the United States, the Netherlands, and Australia. Stunt pilot for films, including *Those Magnificent Men and Their Flying Machines, Blue Max, Darling Lilli, Red Baron, Villa Rides,* and *Skywards.* Test pilot for gliders and light aircraft; instructor training specialist. *Military service:* Royal Air Force, pilot and instructor, 1942-45.

AWARDS, HONORS: Queen's Commendation; Member of the Order of the British Empire.

WRITINGS:

Gliding: A Handbook on Soaring Flight, A. & C. Black, 1958, 6th edition, 1990.
Beginning Gliding, A. & C. Black, 1975.
Understanding Gliding, A. & C. Black, 1977.
Delta Papa: A Life of Flying (autobiography), Pelham, 1977.
Going Solo, A. & C. Black, 1978.
Understanding Flying Weather, A. & C. Black, 1988.
Derek Piggott on Gliding, A. & C. Black, 1990.
Gliding Safely, A. & C. Black, 1991.

Also author of scripts for a cassette series on gliding and soaring.

BIOGRAPHICAL/CRITICAL SOURCES:

BOOKS

Piggott, Derek, *Delta Papa: A Life of Flying* (autobiography), Pelham, 1977.

* * *

PITT, David C(harles) 1938-

PERSONAL: Born August 15, 1938, in Wellington, New Zealand; son of Maurice Simeon (a teacher) and Elizabeth (Hyams) Pitt; married Carol Haigh, February 13, 1959; children: Jerome Manuel, Sara Elizabeth, Devra Simone, Joshua Dan, Danielle Chana, Joseph Joel, Lisa Monique. *Education:* University of New Zealand, B.A., 1961; Oxford University, B.Litt., 1963, D.Phil., 1965, M.Litt., 1980. *Avocational interests:* Mountains, boating, viticulture, travel.

ADDRESSES: Home—1265 La Cure, Geneva, Switzerland. *Office*—Institut International de Recherches pour la Paix, 34 Boulevard du Pont D'Arve, Geneva, 1205, Switzerland.

CAREER: University of Victoria, Victoria, British Columbia, assistant professor of anthropology and sociology, 1966-67; University of Waikato, Hamilton, New Zealand, professor of sociology and head of department, 1968-71; University of Auckland, Auckland, New Zealand, professor of sociology, head of department, and chairman of European Studies Committee, 1971-79; Institut International de Recherches pour la Paix, Geneva, Switzerland, charge de recherches and member of the Executive Council, 1982—. Visiting professor, University of Bern, 1985-86. Consultant to International Labor Organization, 1968-70, to UNESCO, 1970-71, to United Nations Center for Development Planning (New York), 1972-75, to UNESCAP (Bangkok), 1972-79, to International Union for the Conservation of Nature (Switzerland), 1976—, to World Health Organization, 1979-83 and 1986-90, to Food and Agricultural Organization, 1983-84, to United Nations Environmental Programme, 1983—, to Commonwealth Agricultural Bureau (Oxford), 1988—, and to Bellerive Foundation (Geneva), 1988—.

MEMBER: International Sociological Association (member of council, 1970-78), Royal Anthropological Institute, International Union of Anthropological and Ethnological Sciences.

WRITINGS:

Tradition and Economic Progress in Samoa: A Case Study in the Role of Traditional Social Institutions in Economic Development, Clarendon Press, 1970.
Historical Documents in Anthropology and Sociology, Holt, 1972.
(With C. Macpherson) *Emerging Pluralism,* Longman, 1975.
Social Dynamics of Development, Pergamon, 1976.
(Editor) *Development from Below: Anthropologists and Development Situations,* Aldine, 1976.
(Editor) *Social Class in New Zealand,* Longman, 1977.
(Editor) *Child Labour: A Threat to Health and Development,* World Health Organization, 1981.
(Editor) *Children and War,* Institut International de Recherches Pour la Paix a Geneve, 1983.
Culture and Conservation, Croom Helm, 1984.

(Editor) *The Nature of United Nations Bureaucracies,* Croom Helm, 1985.

Rethinking Population, Environment and Development, Geographisches Institut, Universitat Bern, 1986.

(Editor) *Nuclear Free Zones,* Croom Helm, 1987.

(Editor) *New Ideas in Environmental Education,* Croom Helm, 1988.

(Editor) *Deforestation: Social Dynamics in Watersheds and Mountain Ecosystems,* Routledge, 1988.

(Editor) *The Future of the Environment,* Routledge, 1988.

(Editor) *The Anthropology of War and Peace,* Bergin and Garvey, 1989.

(With Sten Nilsson) *Mountain Worlds in Danger,* Earthscan, 1991.

Contributor to professional journals.

WORK IN PROGRESS: Writing on the sociology of economic development, ethnic relations, social stratification, peace studies, rural society, health, population, and the environment (mountains, climate change).

*   *   *

PIXLEY, Jorge V. 1937-

PERSONAL: Born March 29, 1937, in Chicago, IL; son of John Stage (a physician) and Phebe (Rice) Pixley; married Janyce Irene Babcock, June 14, 1958; children: Rebecca Ray, Kevin Vail, Mark Christian. *Education:* Attended Wheaton College, 1955-56; Kalamazoo College, B.A., 1958; University of Chicago, M.A., 1962, Ph.D., 1968.

ADDRESSES: Office—Seminario Teologico Bautista, Apartado 2555, Managua, Nicaragua.

CAREER: Baptist clergyman, ordained in 1963; Evangelical Seminary of Puerto Rico, Rio Piedras, professor of Old Testament, 1963-75; Seminario Bautista de Mexico, San Jeronimo, professor of Old Testament, 1975-85; Seminario Teologico Bautista, Managua, Nicaragua, professor, 1985—. Visiting professor at Evangelical Faculty of Theology, Buenos Aires, 1969-70.

MEMBER: Society of Biblical Literature, Sociedad Argentina de Profesores de Sagrada Escritura.—

WRITINGS:

Pluralismo de tradiciones en la religion biblica, Editorial La Aurora (Buenos Aires), 1971.

Reino de Dios, Editorial La Aurora, 1977, translation by Donald D. Walsh as *God's Kingdom: A Guide for Biblical Study,* Orbis Books, 1981.

(Editor) *Praxis cristiana y produccion teologica,* Ediciones Sigueme, 1979.

El libro de Job: Comentario biblico latino-americano, Ediciones Seminario Biblico Latinoamericano, 1982.

Exodo: Una lectura evangelica y popular, Casa Unida de Publicaciones, 1983, translation by Robert R. Barr as *On Exodus: A Liberation Perspective,* Orbis Books, 1987.

Biblia y liberacion de los pobres; ensayos exegeticos, Centro Antonio Montessinos (Mexico), 1986.

La Mujer en la construccion de la iglesia, DEI (Costa Rica), 1986.

(With Clodovis Boff) *Opcion por los pobres,* Paulinas (Madrid, Spain), 1986, translation by Pual Burns as *The Bible, the Church, and the Poor,* Orbis Books, 1989.

Hacia una fe evangelical Latinoamericanista, Departamento Ecumenico de Investigaciones (Costa Rica), 1988.

Also author of *Historia sagrada, historia popular; historia de Israel, 1220 a.C. a 135 d.C.* Contributor to *Lutheran Quarterly, Revista Biblica, Process Studies, Servir, Christus, Taller de Teologia, Cauvernos de Teologia,* and numerous other periodicals.

WORK IN PROGRESS: Research on a history of Baptists in Nicaragua.

SIDELIGHTS: Jorge V. Pixley once told *CA* that his "literary activity has been almost entirely in Spanish, and much of it is only intelligible within the Latin American context in which I have lived most of my life."

*   *   *

PLUMME, Don E.
See KATZ, Bobbi

*   *   *

POHL, Frederik 1919-
(Elton V. Andrews, Paul Fleur, Warren F. Howard, Ernst Mason, James McCreigh, Donald Stacy; S. D. Gottesman, Lee Gregor, Cyril Judd, Paul Dennis Lavond, Scott Mariner, Edson McCann, Jordan Park, Charles Satterfield, Dirk Wilson, joint pseudonyms)

PERSONAL: Born November 26, 1919, in New York, NY; son of Fred George (a salesman) and Anna Jane (Mason) Pohl; married Doris Baumgardt, 1940 (divorced, 1944); married Dorothy LesTina, August, 1945 (divorced, 1947); married Judith Merril, 1948 (divorced, 1952); married Carol M. Ulf Stanton, September 15, 1952 (divorced, 1983); married Elizabeth Anne Hall (a professor of English), July, 1984; children: Ann (Mrs. Walter Weary),

Karen (Mrs. Robert Dixon), Frederik III (deceased), Frederik IV, Kathy. *Education:* Attended public schools in Brooklyn, NY, "dropped out in senior year." *Politics:* Democrat. *Religion:* Unitarian.

ADDRESSES: Home and office—Palatine, IL.

CAREER: Writer. Popular Publications, New York City, editor, 1939-43; Popular Science Publishing Co., New York City, editor in book department and assistant circulation manager, 1946-49; literary agent, 1946-53; freelance writer 1953-60; *Galaxy* Magazine, New York City, editor, 1961-69; Ace Books, New York City, executive editor, 1971-72; Bantam Books, New York City, science fiction editor, 1973-79. Staff lecturer, American Management Association, 1966-69; cultural exchange lecturer in science fiction for U.S. Department of State in Yugoslavia, Romania, and the Soviet Union, 1974; also lecturer at more than two hundred colleges in the United States, Canada, and abroad; represented United States at international literary conferences in England, Italy, Brazil, Canada, and Japan. Has appeared on more than four hundred radio and television programs in nine countries. County committeeman, Democratic Party, Monmouth City, NJ, 1956-69; trustee, The Harbour School, Red Bank, NJ, 1972-75, and First Unitarian Church of Monmouth City, 1973-75. *Military service:* U.S. Army Air Forces, 1943-45; received seven battle stars.

MEMBER: Science Fiction Writers of America (president, 1974-76), Authors Guild (Midwest area representative; member of council, 1975—), British Interplanetary Society (fellow), American Astronautical Society, World SF (president, 1980-82), American Association for the Advancement of Science (fellow), World Future Society, American Civil Liberties Union (trustee, Monmouth County, NJ, 1968-71), New York Academy of Sciences.

AWARDS, HONORS: Edward E. Smith Award, 1966; Hugo Award, World Science Fiction Convention, 1966, 1967, and 1968, for best editor, 1974, for short story, "The Meeting," 1978, for best novel, *Gateway,* and 1986, for story "Fermi and Frost"; H. G. Wells Award, 1975; Nebula Award, Science Fiction Writers of America, 1977, for best novel, *Man Plus,* and 1978, for best novel, *Gateway;* John W. Campbell Award, Center for the Study of Science Fiction, 1978, for *Gateway,* and 1986, for *The Years of the City;* American Book Award, 1979, for *JEM;* Popular Culture Association annual award, 1982; guest of honor at science fiction convention in Katowice, Poland, 1987.

WRITINGS:

(Under pseudonym James McCreigh) *Danger Moon,* American Science Fiction (Sydney), 1953.
(With Lester del Rey under joint pseudonym Edson McCann) *Preferred Risk,* Simon & Schuster, 1955.

Alternating Currents (short stories), Ballantine, 1956.
(Under pseudonym Donald Stacy) *The God of Channel 1,* Ballantine, 1956.
(With Walter Lasly) *Turn the Tigers Loose,* Ballantine, 1956.
Edge of the City (novel based on screenplay by Robert Alan Aurthur), Ballantine, 1957.
Slave Ship, Ballantine, 1957.
Tomorrow Times Seven: Science Fiction Stories, Ballantine, 1959.
The Man Who Ate the World, Ballantine, 1960.
Drunkard's Walk, Ballantine, 1960.
(Under pseudonym Ernst Mason) *Tiberius,* Ballantine, 1960.
Turn Left at Thursday: Three Novelettes and Three Stories, Ballantine, 1961.
The Abominable Earthman, Ballantine, 1963.
The Case against Tomorrow: Science Fiction Short Stories, Ballantine, 1965.
A Plague of Pythons, Ballantine, 1965.
The Frederik Pohl Omnibus, Gollancz, 1966.
Digits and Dastards, Ballantine, 1966.
The Age of the Pussyfoot, Ballantine, 1969.
Day Million (short stories), Ballantine, 1970.
Practical Politics, 1972 (nonfiction), Ballantine, 1971.
The Gold at the Starbow's End, Ballantine, 1972.
(With Carol Pohl) *Jupiter,* Ballantine, 1973.
The Best of Frederik Pohl, introduction by Lester del Rey, Doubleday, 1975.
The Early Pohl, Doubleday, 1976.
Man Plus, Random House, 1976.
Gateway, St. Martin's, 1977.
The Way the Future Was: A Memoir, Ballantine, 1978.
JEM, St. Martin's, 1979.
Beyond the Blue Event Horizon, Ballantine, 1980.
Syzygy, Bantam, 1981.
The Cool War, Ballantine, 1981.
Planets Three, Berkley, 1982.
Bipohl, Two Novels: Drunkard's Walk and The Age of the Pussyfoot, Ballantine, 1982.
Starburst, Ballantine, 1982.
Starbow, Ballantine, 1982.
(Author of introduction) *New Visions: A Collection of Modern Science Fiction Art,* Doubleday, 1982.
Midas World, St. Martin's, 1983.
Heechee Rendezvous, Ballantine, 1984.
The Years of the City, Simon & Schuster, 1984.
The Merchant's War, St. Martin's, 1984.
Pohlstars, Ballantine, 1984.
Black Star Rising, Ballantine, 1985.
The Coming of the Quantum Cats, Bantam, 1986.
Chernobyl, Bantam, 1987.
The Annals of the Heechee, Ballantine, 1988.
Narabdela Ltd., Del Rey, 1988.

The Day the Martians Came, St. Martin's, 1988.
Homegoing, Del Rey, 1989.
The Gateway Trip, Del Rey, 1990.
The World at the End of Time, Ballantine, 1990.
Outnumbering the Dead, Century, 1991.

Contributor, sometimes under pseudonyms, to *Galaxy, Worlds of Fantasy, Science Fiction Quarterly, Rogue, Impulse, Astonishing, Imagination, If, Beyond, Playboy, Infinity,* and other magazines.

WITH CYRIL M. KORNBLUTH

(Under joint pseudonym Cyril Judd) *Gunner Cade,* Simon & Schuster, 1952.
(Under joint pseudonym Cyril Judd) *Outpost Mars,* Abelard Press, 1952.
The Space Merchants, Ballantine, 1953, 2nd edition, 1981.
Search the Sky, Ballantine, 1954.
Gladiator-at-Law, Ballantine, 1955.
A Town Is Drowning, Ballantine, 1955.
Presidential Year, Ballantine, 1956.
(Under joint pseudonym Jordan Park) *Sorority House,* Lion Press, 1956.
(Under joint pseudonym Jordan Park) *The Man of Cold Rages,* Pyramid Publications, 1958.
Wolfbane, Ballantine, 1959, reprinted, Garland Publishing, 1975.
The Wonder Effect, Ballantine, 1962.
Our Best: The Best of Frederik Pohl and C. M. Kornbluth, Baen Books, 1987.

WITH JACK WILLIAMSON

Undersea Quest, Gnome Press, 1954.
Undersea Fleet, Gnome Press, 1956.
Undersea City, Gnome Press, 1958.
The Reefs of Space (also see below), Ballantine, 1964.
Starchild (also see below), Ballantine, 1965.
Rogue Star (also see below), Ballantine, 1969.
Farthest Star: The Saga of Cuckoo, Ballantine, 1975.
The Starchild Trilogy: The Reefs of Space, Starchild, and Rogue Star, Paperback Library, 1977.
Wall around a Star, Ballantine, 1983.
Land's End, St. Martin's, 1988.

EDITOR

Beyond the End of Time, Permabooks, 1952.
Star Science Fiction Stories, Ballantine, 1953.
Star Short Novels, Ballantine, 1954.
Assignment in Tomorrow: An Anthology, Hanover House, 1954.
Star of Stars, Doubleday, 1960.
The Expert Dreamer, Doubleday, 1962.
Time Waits for Winthrop, Doubleday, 1962.
The Best Science Fiction from "Worlds of If" Magazine, Galaxy Publishing Corp., 1964.

The Seventh Galaxy Reader, Doubleday, 1964.
Star Fourteen, Whiting & Wheaton, 1966.
The If Reader of Science Fiction, Doubleday, 1966.
The Tenth Galaxy Reader, Doubleday, 1967, published as *Door to Anywhere,* Modern Literary Editions, 1967.
The Eleventh Galaxy Reader, Doubleday, 1969.
Nightmare Age, Ballantine, 1970.
Best Science Fiction for 1972, Ace Books, 1973.
(With Carol Pohl) *Science Fiction: The Great Years,* Ace Books, 1973.
The Science Fiction Roll of Honor, Random House, 1975.
Science Fiction Discoveries, Bantam, 1976.
Science Fiction of the Forties, Avon, 1978.
Galaxy Magazine: Thirty Years of Innovative Science Fiction, Playboy Press, 1980.
Nebula Winners Fourteen, Harper, 1980.
(Co-editor) *The Great Science Fiction Series,* Harper, 1980.
(With son, Frederik Pohl IV) *Science Fiction: Studies in Film,* Ace Books, 1981.
Yesterday's Tomorrows: Favorite Stories from Forty Years as a Science Fiction Editor, Berkley, 1982.
(With wife, Elizabeth Anne Hill) *Tales from the Planet Earth,* St. Martin's, 1986.
(With others) *Worlds of If: A Retrospective Anthology,* Bluejay Books, 1986.

SIDELIGHTS: "Like all the other great men in SF," writes Algis Budrys in the *Magazine of Fantasy and Science Fiction,* "Frederik Pohl is idiosyncratic, essentially self-made, and brilliant. Unlike many of the others, he has an extremely broad range of interests and education." As both an author and editor Pohl has been, Robert Scholes and Eric S. Rabkin assert in *Science Fiction: History, Science, Vision,* "One of the few men to make a genuine impact on the science fiction field."

In the 1950s, Pohl wrote a number of influential books with the late C. M. Kornbluth in which they "pioneered and excelled in a completely new kind of science fiction," writes Charles Platt in *Dream Makers: The Uncommon People Who Write Science Fiction.* "They invented and played with 'Sociological SF'—alternate futures here on Earth, exaggerating and satirizing real-life social forces and trends." The best of these collaborations was *The Space Merchants,* a satirical look at a world ruled by advertising; the book was inspired by Pohl's own short stint in an advertising agency. In this world, "exploitation of resources, pollution of environment, and overpopulation are all rampant," Scholes and Rabkin point out, "while the advertisers use every device of behavior control including addictive substances in the products. The beauty of [the book] is that it manages to be absurd and at the same time frighteningly close to the way that many people actually think. The lightness of touch and consistency of imagination make it a true classic of science fiction." "This novel is the single work most mentioned when Pohl's fiction is discussed," Stephen H. Goldman of the *Dictionary of Literary Biography* explains. "It is on every critic's list of science fiction classics and has never been out of print since its first appearance. While Pohl and Kornbluth produced other highly readable novels *The Space Merchants* remains their single greatest achievement." The book has been translated into over fifteen languages, including Japanese, Hebrew, Serbo-Croatian, Dutch, and Latvian.

As editor of *Galaxy* and later with Bantam Books, Pohl was a strong supporter of the 'new wave' writers in science fiction—writers who borrowed literary techniques from mainstream literature to use in their science fiction, while eliminating what they saw as the genre's cliches. Ironically, Pohl came under fire from some of these writers for being too conservative. "I published the majority of 'new-wave' writers," Pohl told Platt. "It wasn't the stories I objected to, it was the snottiness of the proponents. . . . The thing that the 'new wave' did that I treasure was to shake up old dinosaurs, like Isaac [Asimov], and for that matter me . . . , and show them that you do not really have to construct a story according to the 1930s pulp or Hollywood standards."

Some of the new wave's influence can be seen in Pohl's prize-winning novel *Gateway,* the story of the discovery of an ancient spaceport of the Heechee, a long-dead civilization. Each spaceship found at the port is operable, but so highly advanced that the propulsion system and the destination for which it is programmed are incomprehensible to humans. A few brave adventurers dare to travel in the ships in a kind of lottery system. "Occasionally," writes Goldman, "one of the Heechee ships lands at a site that is filled with undiscovered artifacts, and the human riders share in the financial rewards these discoveries can bring." At other times, the adventurers never return, or return dead. The story, Mark Rose of the *New Republic* finds, "conveys a vivid sense of the pathos and absurdity of human ignorance in attempting to exploit a barely understood universe." Patrick Parrinder of the *Times Literary Supplement* agrees: "The novel is remarkable for its portrayal of human explorers rushing into space in a mood of abject fear and greed, in machines they cannot understand or control."

The story of the spaceport and its hazardous explorations is interspersed with seriocomic scenes involving a guilt-ridden adventurer—an adventurer who made a fortune during a trip on which he was forced to abandon the woman he loves—and his computer psychoanalyst. "Pohl's touch is always light and sure," Rose comments, "and, indeed parts of the novel are extremely funny." Goldman notes that in *Gateway* "Pohl has finally balanced the demands of an imaginative world and the presentation

of a highly complex character. . . . This balance has led to his most successful novel thus far." In *Gateway,* Roz Kaveney of *Books and Bookmen* believes, Pohl "successfully combined wit and humanity in a novel of character. [The result is] a highly competent, darkly witty entertainment." Other critics found the computer psychoanalyst a particularly believable character. "What makes this book so intriguing," Peter Ackroyd of *Spectator* writes, "is not its occasional satire and consistent good humor, but the fact that Pohl has managed to convey the insistent presence of the non-human, a presence which may indeed haunt our future."

Pohl's next novel, *JEM,* also won critical praise. Set in the near future when the Earth has been divided into three camps—People, Fuel, and Food—the novel tells the story of three bands of human colonists on another planet. When there is a war and a resulting social breakdown on Earth, the colony is suddenly independent and "must then find a way to reconcile its divisions, both among the colonists and between the colonists and the three excellently depicted native sapient species, if it is to survive," writes Tom Easton of the *Magazine of Fantasy and Science Fiction.* Gerald Jonas of the *New York Times Book Review* compares *JEM* to *The Space Merchants* because "*JEM* is also social satire—but without the humor." "It is essentially a political allegory," Alex de Jonge of Spectator observes, "describing the struggle between the world's three blocs . . . each attempting to colonize a planet."

The colonization of Jem repeats some mistakes made on Earth. "With systematic, undeviating logic," writes Budrys, "Pohl depicts the consequent rape of Jem. As each of the expeditions struggles to do its best, there are moments of hope, and moments of triumph. But they are all no more than peaks on a downhill slope. The ending of it all is so genuinely sad that one realizes abruptly how rarely SF evokes pure sorrow, and how profound Pohl's vision was in conceiving of this story." Russell Lord of the *Christian Science Monitor* found it is Pohl's "basically poetic imagination that elevates this novel to a high position among the author's works."

Joseph McClellan of the *Washington Post Book World* offers an insight into what has made Pohl's writing among the best in the science fiction field. "Pohl's work," McClellan writes, "offers science fiction at its best: basic human problems . . . woven deftly into an intricate plot; pure adventure happening to believable (if not deeply drawn) characters in surroundings almost beyond the borders of imagination; and at the end, when other questions have been laid to rest, the posing of a new question as unfathomable as time and space themselves."

Although his work as a science fiction writer has brought him an international reputation, Pohl has also played a large role in science fiction publishing, having served stints as the editor of *Galaxy* magazine, and as editor with the paperback publishing firms of Ballantine, Ace Books, and Bantam. In these positions, he has helped to develop new talent in the genre and publish daring or experimental work by more experienced writers. Among the books Pohl has brought into print are Joanna Russ's *The Female Man,* a controversial feminist novel, and Samuel Delany's *Dhalgren,* a novel which had been seeking a publisher for many years before Pohl took a chance on it. *Dhalgren* went on to sell over one million copies.

Writing in the *Contemporary Authors Autobiography Series,* Pohl remembers: "When I was ten years old my wildest ambition was to be a successful science fiction writer. I thought it would be a worthwhile and satisfying and even glamorous way to live . . . and, do you know?, it is!"

BIOGRAPHICAL/CRITICAL SOURCES:

BOOKS

Aldiss, Brian, *Billion Year Spree: The History of Science Fiction,* Doubleday, 1973.
Amis, Kingsley, *New Maps of Hell: A Survey of Science Fiction,* Harcourt, 1960.
Carter, Paul A., *The Creation of Tomorrow: Fifty Years of Magazine Science Fiction,* Columbia University Press, 1977.
Contemporary Authors Autobiography Series, Volume 1, Gale, 1984.
Contemporary Literary Criticism, Volume 18, Gale, 1981.
Dictionary of Literary Biography, Volume 8: *Twentieth Century American Science Fiction Writers,* Gale, 1981.
Platt, Charles, *Dream Makers: The Uncommon People Who Write Science Fiction,* Berkley, 1980.
Pohl, Frederik, *The Way the Future Was: Memoir,* Ballantine, 1978.
Scholes, Robert and Eric S. Rabkin, *Science Fiction: History, Science, Vision,* Oxford University Press, 1977.
Walker, Paul, *Speaking of Science Fiction: The Paul Walker Interviews,* Luna Press, 1978.

PERIODICALS

Analog, February, 1977; January, 1979; December, 1979; May, 1980.
Books and Bookmen, November, 1979.
Christian Science Monitor, June 20, 1979.
Los Angeles Times, December 11, 1986.
Magazine of Fantasy and Science Fiction, March, 1978; September, 1979.
New Republic, November 26, 1977.
New Statesman, April 15, 1977.
New York Times, September 7, 1983.

New York Times Book Review, March 27, 1977; May 20, 1979; November 15, 1987; April 24, 1988; July 2, 1989.
Publishers Weekly, July 31, 1978.
Spectator, January 28, 1978.
Times (London), November 24, 1983; August 8, 1985; January 16, 1988; January 17, 1991.
Times Literary Supplement, January 14, 1977; January 27, 1978; May 14, 1983.
Tribune Books (Chicago), March 15, 1987; August 16, 1987; August 21, 1988; July 15, 1990; December 30, 1990.
Washington Post, October 4, 1987.
Washington Post Book World, March 14, 1980; November 23, 1980; July 25, 1982; February 28, 1988; April 30, 1989.

*   *   *

POLITICUS
See KULSKI, Wladyslaw W(szebor)

*   *   *

POLLAND, Madeleine A(ngela Cahill)   1918-
(Frances Adrian)

PERSONAL: Born May 31, 1918, in Kinsale, County Cork, Ireland; daughter of Patrick Richard (a civil servant) and Christina (Culkin) Cahill; married Arthur Joseph Polland (an accountant), June 10, 1946 (died, October, 1987); children: Charlotte Frances, Fergus Adrian. *Politics:* Conservative. *Religion:* Roman Catholic. *Avocational interests:* Lawn bowls, travel, museums, art.

ADDRESSES: Home—Edificio Hercules 634, Avenida Gamonal, Arroyo de la Miel, Malaga, Spain.

CAREER: Letchworth Public Library, Letchworth, England, assistant librarian, 1938-42; writer, 1958—. Guest speaker, New York Public Library Children's Book Fair, 1968. *Military service:* Women's Auxiliary Air Force, ground-controlled interception division of radar, 1942-45.

AWARDS, HONORS: New York Herald Tribune Honor Book, 1961, for *Children of the Red King,* and 1962, for *Beorn the Proud.*

WRITINGS:

JUVENILE NOVELS

Children of the Red King, Constable, 1960, Holt, 1961.
The Town across the Water, Constable, 1961, Holt, 1963.
Beorn the Proud, Constable, 1961, Holt, 1962.
Fingal's Quest, Doubleday, 1961.
The White Twilight, Constable, 1962, Holt, 1965.

Chuiraquimba and the Black Robes, Doubleday, 1962.
The City of the Golden House, Doubleday, 1963.
The Queen's Blessing, Constable, 1963, Holt, 1964.
Flame Over Tara, Doubleday, 1964.
Mission to Cathay, Doubleday, 1965.
Queen without Crown, Constable, 1965, Holt, 1966.
Deirdre, Doubleday, 1967.
To Tell My People, Hutchinson, 1968.
Stranger in the Hills, Doubleday, 1968.
Alhambra, Doubleday, 1970.
To Kill a King, Holt, 1971.
A Family Affair, Hutchinson, 1971.
Daughter of the Sea, Doubleday, 1972, published in England as *Daughter to Poseidon,* Hutchinson, 1972.
Prince of the Double Axe, Abelard-Schuman, 1976.

ADULT NOVELS

Thicker Than Water, Holt, 1966.
Minutes of a Murder, Holt, 1967, published in England as *The Little Spot of Bother,* Hutchinson, 1967.
Random Army, Hutchinson, 1969, published as *Shattered Summer,* Doubleday, 1970.
Package to Spain, Walker, 1971.
(Under pseudonym Frances Adrian) *Double Shadow,* Fawcett, 1978.
All Their Kingdoms, Delacorte, 1981.
The Heart Speaks Many Ways, Delacorte, 1982.
No Price Too High, Delacorte, 1984.
As It Was in the Beginning, Piatkus, 1987.
Rich Man's Flowers, Piatkus, 1990.

SIDELIGHTS: Madeleine A. Polland writes novels based on events and people in European, especially Irish, history. "My sense of history," she explains in her article for the *Something About the Author Autobiography Series* (*SAAS*), "has always been an important aspect of my writing: my consciousness of the feet that have walked before mine, and the fact that no matter how early the period, all those concerned were still *people.* Like ourselves."

To make her historical novels as realistic as possible, Polland has often visited the actual places she writes about, and walked the paths the historical people of her stories walked. Except for two stories set in China and Paraguay, she writes in her *SAAS* article, "I had the pleasure of walking through the settings for myself, in Ireland, Scotland, Denmark, England, and Spain, always in the company of some, if not all, of my family."

Polland has claimed that on several occasions she has felt odd sensations when visiting an historical site, sensations which gave her a brief vision of earlier times. Writing in *Horn Book,* she tells of visiting Sussex in southern England and suddenly feeling afraid: "I was shivering with a dreadful terror that was certainly not my own, nor could I gain any peace until I left the spot and gone away." Only

later did she discover that the early Roman invaders had passed through that part of England and the fear she felt was akin to the fear that the early natives must have felt on confronting the Roman soldiers. In *To Tell My People* Polland writes of that time, and she has her character Lumna feel "the onslaught of terror at the first manifestations of a civilization she had never dreamed of. The same terror that I myself knew in the same spot."

Sometimes Polland draws on her own experience to create her fiction. As a little girl, she remembers the Irish civil war and the turmoil of that period, especially the time when her home town was burned to the ground. In *City of the Golden House,* a story set in ancient Rome, Polland drew on her memories to write of the burning of Rome. She explains in *Horn Book:* "I needed to re-create all the horror and terror of the fire of Rome during the reign of Emperor Nero. . . . I knew quite clearly that although I was writing of the fire of Rome, it was the burning of [my home town of] Kinsale which I recounted: a haunting from my childhood."

Polland's insistence that people of times long past are essentially the same as the people of today has allowed her to create realistic characters in all of her historical fiction. The realism of her characters adds to the realism of her settings as well. A reviewer for *Horn Book* finds that in *The White Twilight* Polland "has told an absorbing story with an unusual historical setting and individual, well-realized characters. The beautiful writing and the strong feeling of place make the story rich and rewarding." A reviewer for *Junior Bookshelf* praises the realistic emotions of *Prince of the Double Axe:* "Death is shown as a kindly end to old age and suffering, fear as natural as loyalty and courage. Altogether, a sensitive and well-told story."

Since the late 1960s, Polland has lived on the Mediterranean coast of Spain, where she and her late husband retired. Speaking of her adopted country in her *SAAS* article, Polland writes: "They say of this coast that if you want to, on Christmas Day you can swim in the morning in the sea, ski through the afternoon in the mountains, and still be home for your Christmas dinner. A lovely life."

BIOGRAPHICAL/CRITICAL SOURCES:

BOOKS

de Montreville, Dorris, and Donna Hill, editors, *Third Book of Junior Authors,* H. W. Wilson, 1972.
Something About the Author Autobiography Series, Volume 8, Gale, 1989, pp. 227-242.

PERIODICALS

Best Sellers, March 15, 1971; April, 1979; October, 1982.
Books and Bookmen, January, 1973.
British Book News, April, 1987; May, 1987.

Bulletin of the Center for Children's Books, October, 1973.
Christian Science Monitor, November 12, 1970.
Commonweal, May 21, 1971.
Horn Book, June, 1965; June, 1966; August, 1967; April, 1968, pp. 147-150; October, 1968; October, 1970; December, 1970; June, 1971.
Junior Bookshelf, February, 1977.
Library Journal, October 15, 1970.
New York Times Book Review, May 9, 1965; July 18, 1965; July 9, 1967; October 27, 1968; February 6, 1972.
Publishers Weekly, February, 1973.
Punch, April 12, 1967.
Saturday Review, July 17, 1965; July 24, 1965.
Spectator, December 5, 1970.
Times Literary Supplement, May 25, 1967; July 27, 1967; November 30, 1967; October 3, 1968; June 26, 1969; October 30, 1970; April 2, 1971; May 14, 1971; December 8, 1972.

*　　*　　*

PORTER, Sue
See LIMB, Sue

*　　*　　*

POST, Jonathan F(rench) S(cott) 1947-

PERSONAL: Born May 11, 1947, in Rochester, NY; son of Frederick W. (a lawyer) and Margaret S. (a teacher) Post; married Susan L. Gallick (a scholar), 1975; children, Jessica, Frederick. *Education:* Amherst College, A.B., 1970; University of Rochester, Ph.D., 1975.

ADDRESSES: Home—9431 Bianca Ave., Northridge, CA 91325. *Office*—Department of English, 15 Rolfe, University of California, 405 Hilgard Ave., Los Angeles, CA 90024.

CAREER: Yale University, New Haven, CT, assistant professor of English, 1975-80; University of California, Los Angeles, associate professor of English, 1980—.

AWARDS, HONORS: Folger Shakespeare Library fellow, 1974; National Endowment for the Humanities fellow, 1979-80; Guggenheim fellow, 1984-85.

WRITINGS:

Henry Vaughan: The Unfolding Vision, Princeton University Press, 1982.
Sir Thomas Browne, G. K. Hall, 1987.

Contributor to literature journals. Editor, *George Herbert Journal,* Volume VII, numbers 1 and 2, 1983.

WORK IN PROGRESS: Researching and writing a book on seventeenth-century poetry for *The Routledge History of English Poetry.*

SIDELIGHTS: Jonathan F. S. Post told *CA:* "I wrote a book on Henry Vaughan because I was moved by the combination of regional vision, religious belief, and political pressures, all of which come together to produce some extraordinary poetry, poetry different from that of his mentor, George Herbert, but very satisfying in its own right. Why does one put these thoughts on paper? First for sheer survival, to continue to be able to afford the luxury of reading and teaching poetry; then for less explicit but probably more important reasons: to try to understand what an author is doing, something that always escapes me in the lecture hall but, when I'm lucky, returns to me late at night or in the quiet moments during the day. It can, of course, never be finally captured, and probably for that reason, I keep up the quest of putting pen to paper."

Post adds, "I wrote a second book, this time on Sir Thomas Browne, in part because I could never fully escape from his haunting prose rhythms, which I encountered as an undergraduate, and this was a way at least to fix my thinking about them; in part because of a continued interest I have in the slightly less canonical English authors of the seventeenth century; and in part because I find the greatest pleasure of reading for me still lies in attempting to imagine how others write, and Browne presents a particularly interesting and challenging case since, as Lamb noted, it is as a writer of 'beautiful obliquities' that Browne is most haunting."

BIOGRAPHICAL/CRITICAL SOURCES:

PERIODICALS

Virginia Quarterly Review, summer, 1983.

*　　*　　*

PRICE, (Edward) Reynolds 1933-

PERSONAL: Born February 1, 1933, in Macon, NC; son of William Solomon and Elizabeth (Rodwell) Price. *Education:* Duke University, A.B. (summa cum laude), 1955; Merton College, Oxford, B. Litt., 1958.

ADDRESSES: Home—4813 Duke Station, Durham, NC 27706. *Office*—Department of English, Duke University, Durham, NC 27706. *Agent*—Harriet Wasserman, Literary Agency, Inc., 137 East 36th St., New York, NY 10016.

CAREER: Duke University, Durham, NC, instructor, 1958-61, assistant professor, 1961-68, associate professor, 1968-72, professor of English, 1972-77, James B. Duke

Professor of English, 1977—, acting chairman, 1983. Writer-in-residence at University of North Carolina at Chapel Hill, spring, 1965, University of Kansas, 1967, 1969, 1980, and University of North Carolina at Greensboro, 1971; Glasgow Professor, Washington and Lee University, 1971; faculty member, Salzberg Seminar, Salzberg, Austria, 1977. National Endowment for the Arts, Literature Advisory Panel, member, 1973-77, chairman, 1977.

MEMBER: American Academy and Institute of Arts and Letters, Phi Beta Kappa, Phi Delta Theta.

AWARDS, HONORS: Angier Duke Scholar, 1955; Rhodes Scholar, 1955-58; William Faulkner Foundation Award (notable first novel), and Sir Walter Raleigh Award, both 1962, for *A Long and Happy Life;* Guggenheim fellow, 1964-65; National Association of Independent Schools Award, 1964; National Endowment for the Arts fellow, 1967-68; National Institute of Arts and Letters Award, 1971; Bellamann Foundation Award, 1972; Lillian Smith Award, 1976, for *Surrender the Earth;* Sir Walter Raleigh Award, 1976, 1981, 1984, 1986; North Carolina Award, 1977; National Book Award nomination (translation), 1979, for *A Palpable God;* Roanoke-Chowan Poetry Award, 1982; National Book Critics Circle Award (best work of fiction), 1986, for *Kate Vaiden;* Elmer H. Bobst Award, 1988; Fund for New American Plays grant, 1989, for *New Music;* D. Litt., St. Andrew's Presbyterian College and Wake Forest University.

WRITINGS:

NOVELS

A Long and Happy Life, Atheneum, 1962.
A Generous Man, Atheneum, 1966.
Love and Work, Atheneum, 1968.
The Surface of Earth, Atheneum, 1975.
The Source of Light, Atheneum, 1981.
Mustian: Two Novels and A Story, Atheneum, 1983.
Kate Vaiden, Atheneum, 1986.
The Laws of Ice, Atheneum, 1986.
Good Hearts, Atheneum, 1988.
The Tongues of Angels, Atheneum, 1990.

PLAYS

Early Dark: A Play (three-act play; adapted from *A Long and Happy Life;* first produced Off-Broadway at the WPA Theater, April, 1978), Atheneum, 1977.
New Music (trilogy; contains *August Snow, Night Dance,* and *Better Days;* produced in Cleveland, OH, November, 1989), Atheneum, 1990.

POETRY

Late Warnings: Four Poems, Albondocani, 1968.
Lessons Learned: Seven Poems, Albondocani, 1977.

Nine Mysteries: Four Joyful, Four Sorrowful, One Glorious, Palaemon Press, 1979.
The Laws of Ice, Atheneum, 1985.
The Use of Fire, Atheneum, 1990.

OTHER

The Names and Faces of Heroes (stories), Atheneum, 1963.
(Contributor) *The Arts and the Public,* University of Chicago Press, 1967.
Permanent Errors (short stories and a novella), Atheneum, 1970.
(Author of introduction) Henry James, *The Wings of the Dove,* C. E. Merrill, 1970.
Things Themselves: Essays and Scenes, Atheneum, 1972.
Presence and Absence: Versions from the Bible (limited edition; originally published as a pamphlet by the Friends of Duke University Library), Bruccoli Clark, 1973.
(Contributor) *Symbolism and Modern Literature: Studies in Honor of Wallace Fowlie,* Duke University Press, 1978.
A Palpable God: Thirty Stories Translated from the Bible with an Essay on the Origins and Life of Narrative, Atheneum, 1978.
A Final Letter, Sylvester & Orphanos, 1980.
The Annual Heron (limited edition), Albondocani, 1980.
Country Mouse, City Mouse, North Carolina Wesleyan College Press, 1981.
Vital Provisions, Atheneum, 1982.
Private Contentment, Atheneum, 1984.
House Snake, Lord John, 1986.
The Chapel, Duke University, Duke University Press, 1986.
A Common Room: New and Selected Essays, 1954-1987, Atheneum, 1988.
Real Copies, North Carolina Wesleyan College Press, 1988.
Clear Pictures: First Loves, First Guides (memoir), Atheneum, 1989.
The Foreseeable Future: Three Long Stories, Atheneum, 1990.

Also author of *Oracles: Six Versions from the Bible* (limited edition), Friends of the Duke University Library. Contributor of poetry, reviews, and articles to numerous magazines and newspapers, including *Time, Harper's, Saturday Review,* and *Washington Post.* Editor, *The Archive,* 1954-55; advisory editor, *Shenandoah,* 1964—.

Price's books have been translated into over sixteen languages, including French, German, and Italian.

SIDELIGHTS: Reynolds Price wears many hats—novelist, short story writer, poet, playwright, essayist, teacher—but he is perhaps best known for his works that feature the backroads and valleys of his native North Carolina. While Price dislikes the "southern writer" label, he nevertheless acknowledges the influence of venerable southern authors such as Eudora Welty. "One of the things [Welty] showed me as a writer was that the kinds of people I had grown up with were the kind of people one could write marvelous fiction about," he told the *Washington Post*. By concentrating on those aspects of the rural South that he was most familiar with, Price created a body of work noted for both its unique sense of place and off-beat cast of characters. A bout with cancer of the spinal cord left Price paralyzed from the waist down in 1984; while the experience changed Price's physical world, it also led to one of the most fertile periods of his career (including the publication of his much-acclaimed novel *Kate Vaiden*). Price explained his prolific output to the *Washington Post* by saying: "I don't write with a conscious sense of the hangman at my door, of my own mortality. But I am a tremendously driven person, and I have gotten more so since sitting down. Words just come out of me the way my beard comes out. Who could stop it?"

Price was born in Macon, North Carolina. His father was a traveling salesman who stayed close to home, while his mother was an "eccentric rogue" whose individuality left a large mark on her young son. Early on, Price found he had an aptitude for writing. His skill eventually won him a scholarship to Duke University and, after graduation, a Rhodes Scholarship for study at Oxford University. After his return from England, Price accepted a teaching position at Duke University, where his students included Anne Tyler and Josephine Humphries. Price never left North Carolina, preferring instead to remain where he felt most comfortable: near his students in a house filled with memorabilia he affectionately refers to as "a *lotta* stuff."

Price received a great deal of praise for his first novel, *A Long and Happy Life*. Primarily the story of country girl Rosacoke Mustain, *A Long and Happy Life* was especially lauded for its sense of style and strong characterizations. Richard Sullivan noted that "there's not a wasted word. The characters . . . all jump with vitality," while Gene Baro termed Price's observations "vivid and acute." Baro added that Price "passes that ultimate test of a novelist: he has the ability to create a character that is memorable." Interestingly, many critics compared the stylistic and thematic concerns of *A Long and Happy Life* to those found in Price's highly praised 1986 novel, *Kate Vaiden*. According to Michael Spector of the *Washington Post*, Price was surprised by the association. Price told Spector: "My God, [*A Long and Happy Life*] is such an old book now in my life I no longer feel like the person who wrote it. I don't happen to feel by any means that it was the best book I ever wrote, or even the best before *Kate Vaiden*."

Much of the praise given to both *A Long and Happy Life* and *Kate Vaiden* related to Price's strong characterizations of women. According to Elaine Kendall of the *Los Angeles Times Book Review*, "*A Long and Happy Life* belonged almost entirely to the heroine of Rosacoke Mustain, and each of the novels and stories following that stunning debut have been enlightened by unforgettable female protagonists. *Kate Vaiden* is the ultimate extension of Price's thesis, a first-person-singular novel written as the autobiography of a woman coming of age in the South during the Depression and war years." "At once tender and frightening, lyrical and dramatic, this novel is the product of a storyteller working at the height of his artistic powers," Michiko Kakutani likewise extolled in the *New York Times*. Price maintained that in focussing on characters like Kate, he was attempting to debunk the idea that "a man cannot 'understand' a woman and vice versa." By giving his female and male characters complex personas and motivations, Price created what he described for Kendall as "a contained look at a human hero," a character who is as much everywoman as everyman.

Carefully drawn characters constitute just one hallmark of Price's work. In novels such as *The Surface of the Earth* and *The Source of Light*, Price explored the boundaries of narrative, especially those that exist between written and spoken language. "Basically, all my novels and short stories are invented, with little pieces of actual, observed reality and dialogue. The speech of my characters often comes from natives of eastern North Carolina, which is my home country," Price told Herbert Mitgang of the *New York Times*. Price's use of language was heavily influenced by the Southern oral tradition. This tradition of tale-telling, with its heavy emphasis on history and drama, offered a wealth of thematic concepts for Price. He told Elizabeth Venant of the *Los Angeles Times Book Review* that "as long as there remains anything that's recognizably Southern—this strange society with a tremendously powerful black presence in it, its very strong connections with some sort of Christianity, a major heritage as an agrarian society, a slave-owning past, a tragic war fought and lost on the premises—as long as there's any kind of continuing memory of that, then I think literature will continue to rise from it."

Price drew on his memories of growing up in this "strange society" in order to write *Clear Pictures: First Loves, First Guides*. Begun during a particularly painful period in Price's convalescence from cancer treatments, *Clear Pictures* covers the first twenty-one years of the author's life. In his memoir, Price spends a great deal of time discussing the influence of his parents, especially his mother Elizabeth (who, he admits, was in many ways the model for Kate Vaiden). Price also recreates, in great detail, the small towns that formed the backdrop of his youth:

Macon, Asheboro, and Warrenton. *Clear Pictures* met with an enthusiastic reception from critics, many of whom were impressed by Price's ability to depict the past in vibrant detail. Jonathan Kirsch of the *Los Angeles Times Book Review* remarked that Price "has returned to the secret world of his own childhood, a place where others have found a threatening and dangerous darkness, but Price discovered only the purest light. To be sure, he found suffering and terror and even death, and he describes them in sometimes heartbreaking detail, but *Clear Pictures* still glows with that bright, healing light." "Remarkable for its Proustian detail," noted Genevieve Stuttaford of *Publishers Weekly.* "This lucid biography portrays a mind learning to trust and reach out to the world."

In recent years, Price has been encouraged by the return of many aspiring young writers to their Southern roots. While some of these authors find inspiration in the fast pace of urban areas like Atlanta, others are rediscovering the story-telling tradition so closely identified with Southern culture. Price has also derived great pleasure from his students, many of whom maintain contact with the author long after they leave school. When teaching his writing course, Price completes the same writing tasks that he assigns his students. "I discovered earlier that I couldn't offer only one story for discussion, because the students were afraid of insulting the teacher," Price related to *Publishers Weekly.* He added: "But if I do all the fairly elementary exercises required right from the beginning, that gives the students a truer sense that I'm in the same canoe as they are. They give me a quiet, fresh pair of glasses." According to Mitgang, while Price does not actively encourage or dissuade his students from adopting writing as a career, he nevertheless strives to be "honest, especially on the mechanics of writing," believing that one should "never tell a young poet all his faults."

Since the onslaught of his cancer, Price has drawn much of his own inspiration from a past made clearer by self-hypnosis. First prescribed as an analgesic for the pain of Price's illness, the self-hypnosis opened a floodgate of memories. "The sensation was so powerful that I felt as if I'd whiffed a potent drug," Price wrote in *Clear Pictures.* "As I began to feel the gathered force of so much past, I turned to write a story I'd planned but never begun." Price also used these memories when writing *The Tongues of Angels,* a novel about a precocious young boy's turbulent stay at summer camp. On one level a very basic look at camp life, *The Tongues of Angels* also contains discussions heavily grounded in philosophic thought. Many of Price's friends were moved by the book, especially those who had attended summer camp themselves. Price expressed his surprise at this development to John Blades of the *Chicago Tribune:* "I hadn't realized what a nerve I was touching. It seems that most of my friends, certainly those who are middle-aged, have strong and pleasant memories of their weeks, sometimes years, at summer camp. And they look back with a lot of fondness on the goofy but loveable institution that summer camp was in those days."

Price has been careful not to let his illness and the restrictions it imposes upon him impede either his life or his work. A basically happy man who claims "I think I am programmed to laugh every five minutes," Price has also resisted the urge to reveal the secrets of his recovery. "I don't feel ready yet to say, 'Look at me. Didn't I go through this wonderfully?,' " he told Venant. "I don't want to give the devil ideas. 'Oh you think you have gotten through this wonderfully, do you? Well then try this.' " Above all, Price has remained primarily concerned with the quality of his work. As he told Ruth Pollock Coughlin of the *Detroit News,* "If I aim at whatever time is left to my faculties, it may be the oldest aim of all: to go on being a picture-maker." Price added that in writing works like *Clear Pictures,* he was "trying one more time to make a thing I've tried since childhood—at least a room of tall clear pictures that look like the world and are mainly worth watching."

CA INTERVIEW

CA interviewed Reynolds Price by telephone on January 18, 1991, at his home near Durham, North Carolina.

CA: You've had both the discipline and the good fortune to explore your world in several forms: novels, short stories, poetry, essays, memoir, plays. Is there something to say, starting out, about the benefits and maybe the difficulties of examining your material in these different ways?

PRICE: Apart from the normal difficulties of trying to do anything well, I don't think any particular form or genre has presented more difficult problems than another. Obviously the novel requires much the most sustained application of energy. Certainly in the beginning of my career I found it considerably easier to write shorter things— poems, essays, short stories. But I think the longer I've continued to write the novel, the more I have felt that it has gone from being a difficult kind of application to being a job that has the joys of steady work that I feel good about.

I've enjoyed working in the different forms. One of the real problems in having a "literary career" is that, if you go on doing it for as long as I have, which is since I was twenty-one years old, part of what you're trying to do is keep yourself interested. And even more important than that, you're keeping yourself alert. You're trying continually to discover ways to clean your spectacles so that you can go on watching the world with a depth and freshness that anyone past the age of thirty-five knows are difficult to maintain.

CA: You might have become an artist, like the first-person narrator of your 1990 novel The Tongues of Angels, *but before you were out of high school you came to feel your painting skills were insufficient for a career, as you said in the 1989 memoir* Clear Pictures. *Do you think some part of your experience in painting and drawing has helped you as a writer?*

PRICE: I think it has, tremendously. I think it trained my powers of witness, if you will. I talked in *Clear Pictures* about the fact that both my parents were especially watchful people, my mother perhaps most of all. That may well have come from the fact that she was an orphan. Both her parents had died when she was young, and she had to grow up in someone else's family. Though it was in fact the family of her loving sister, she was still a bit of an outrider, an outlaw, in her childhood. And I think outlaws and the excluded of the world do very much tend to be the keen watchers of the world. They'd better be. I think perhaps the years I spent drawing and painting intensified what was probably a kind of acquired bent from my mother.

CA: Do you still draw and paint?

PRICE: I have spasms of it. I haven't done anything now for several years. I might pick up an occasional pad and sketch, but nothing sustained. I had my first spinal surgery in 1984, and as a result of the surgery and the radiation I was unable to write for four or five months. During that period I did a tremendous amount of drawing. Once it all ended, after about a year, it became clear to me that part of what I was apparently doing was repeating the whole pattern of my beginning to be involved in writing, which was to start out with the painting and drawing and somehow let that segue into another form of mimesis, another form of portraying the visible world. What I'd been working on before the surgery was *Kate Vaiden*. Afterwards, the book broke down completely on me, and it was four or five months before I could get back to work on it. Painting turned out to be the bridge that got me across the ravine.

CA: Do you feel your illness changed the course of that book in any way?

PRICE: I suspect that it did. Strangely enough, I had literally written the last sentence of Part One of the three parts of the book the day that I went into the hospital. So I had come to a natural stopping point in the story. That was both good and difficult. The difficulty was in making a leap from Part One to Part Two. I think if I had stopped in the middle of a scene, I might have been able to pick it up immediately and write the answer that the other character gives to what had just been said. But I had to get her across the gap between Part One and Part Two, and I couldn't do it for a long time. Once I did start, the novel moved with tremendous rapidity for me. I think I must have recommenced around December of '84 or January of '85, and I had finished by June.

I don't think there can be any doubt that there were changes in the book that are attributable to the events that I had gone through in recent months, but because I never plan novels in fine detail, I couldn't say how I might have veered off an original plan. I never had a detailed outline. I had only a general knowledge that Kate would discover her lost son at the end of the book and that we would leave the novel with the thought that she was trying to make contact, but we wouldn't know what the nature of that contact would be. Otherwise the details invented themselves. So perhaps a detail such as Kate's discovering that she has cancer may well be directly a result of my own surgery. I certainly didn't feel driven to put in something about cancer because I'd just had it. But who knows? It very likely turned up for that reason.

CA: I was fascinated to read after I read the novel that your mother had been the inspiration for Kate.

PRICE: She was. Again, the events of the novel have almost no resemblance to the events of my mother's life. And Kate's a lot younger than my mother: My mother was born in 1905. But the atmosphere of Kate, of this person who's undergone an awful domestic tragedy early in her life, was the atmosphere of my mother's life. Her mother died when my mother was five, and her father died when she was fourteen.

CA: Like so many of your characters, Kate is someone the outsider might not take a second look at, the "ordinary" person whom you always show not to be ordinary.

PRICE: That's something I've consciously wanted to do from the beginning of my career. I think it's partly because I came from a family in which people were gentle and civilized but not highly literate. Only one or two members of either side of my family ever attended the university. So all my life I've felt a desire to make those generally inarticulate people articulate in fiction.

CA: Many readers knew you first as the author of A Long and Happy Life, *which told the early story of Rosacoke Mustian and Wesley Beavers. Rosacoke had first surfaced, though, in a story you wrote in 1955, "A Chain of Love." Mustians appeared in other books and stories, and Rosa and Wesley reappeared in 1988 in* Good Hearts. *What kept you interested in the family over a span of more than thirty years?*

PRICE: It would be hard to say. As I said in the preface in the book called *Mustian,* which brings together the existing Mustian stories up to 1983, they started when I was a senior in college and had to produce a short story for a creative writing class. I came up then with this story about Rosacoke, which I talked a good deal about in that preface. I simply can't say why.

In the winter of 1964, after the very appalling weeks and months that surrounded the assassination of John Kennedy, I was trying to write the novel that ultimately became *The Surface of Earth,* but it seemed too depressing and too difficult for me to focus on at such a low ebb in our national life. I suddenly found myself thinking about a kind of rural comedy, and the character of Rosacoke's brother Milo came to hand as the most available character to be the center of this story. *A Generous Man* fairly quickly built itself around the character of Milo, though of course it backdated him to his early teens, earlier than *A Long and Happy Life.*

If you had asked me about the Mustians a year after I finished *A Generous Man,* I probably would have said, I'm sure I'm through with the Mustians. But in the early '70s I thought maybe I should look at them again. I made some notes and then I thought, No, that's it; let's leave them alone. So I got down to about 1985 or 1986, right after I'd finished *Kate Vaiden,* and I thought I was going to write a novel in the male first person, a novel that, though it would have no direct connection with the plot or the characters of *Kate Vaiden,* would be a sort of male companion to the female point of view in Kate. But I couldn't write it. It wasn't ready to happen in 1986. Then all of a sudden I found myself thinking about the possibility that Wesley was going to run away from home and leave Rosa alone and that a disaster would happen to her. The next thing I knew, I was writing what turned out to be *Good Hearts.* There's very little conscious planning in the way my books come to me. They just arrive, and I try to have the sense to get them down.

CA: Do you think Wesley and Rosa might come back?

PRICE: I'm not going to say no this time! But I have absolutely no plans or ideas for that. If they come back, they'll come knocking at the door in their own time.

CA: At one time you expressed strong feelings for The Surface of Earth *and* The Source of Light, *both of which failed to get widespread critical acceptance at the time they were published. Do you think those books will get another look from at least academic critics because of the publicity your more recent work has gotten?*

PRICE: They do get a lot of attention; I'm always being sent articles that people have written about them. I think

it's impossible to calculate what further attention they'll get. As for how I feel about them, those books constitute a single long novel which comes in two parts, and those nearly thousand pages of fiction certainly constitute to this point the largest attempt that I've made. And large doesn't mean the greatest number of pages; it means the most sustained attempt to look at the most of human life, the largest piece of time and character. In that sense I have a special fondness for the books. But there's really nothing I've written that I'm ashamed of or wish I could make disappear. I certainly don't go back and reread my own work. Not that I think it's bad, but it's sort of like going back and looking at old photographs of one's self and thinking, Oh, look at my haircut!—which of course I thought was wonderful at the time. I'm not a narcissist about my own work, but I'm glad I wrote it all.

CA: The hypnosis therapy you undertook to help you control pain gave you the heightened memory of childhood experiences that was part of the impetus to write the memoir Clear Pictures. *Does that kind of recall continue to happen?*

PRICE: No, not in the same way. After I had that series of what I call hypnosis lessons at Duke Hospital, memory was coming back in a kind of tumble that was abnormal for me. I've always had what I thought was a good memory, but that was a fairly phenomenal adventure for just those few months. In fact, the first great rush of memory I got as a result of the hypnosis was the material that became *The Tongues of Angels.* It was a lot of memory about my working as a camp counselor in the mountains of North Carolina when I was twenty years old; that all started flooding back over me in great detail. Then I began to make notes for those memories; I thought, Someday I'll write a book based on that summer of mine in the mountains near Asheville. But memories about my family and the towns in which I grew up were tumbling in simultaneously. For whatever unknown reason, I began writing the family memories first. Once *Clear Pictures* was finished, I turned back and got out my notes about old Camp Sequoia and began working on what became *The Tongues of Angels.*

CA: That book was the second novel you'd written in the first-person voice, Kate Vaiden *having been the first. How did you make that choice in the two novels, and what significance might be attached to its coming late in the sequence of your work?*

PRICE: I had done an occasional short story in the first person, and in my second volume of stories, *Permanent Errors,* there was a novella in the male first person. I'm trying to finish a novel now which is also in the male first person, and it may be the result of this hope that I've had to write a companion novel to *Kate.* I think I was a bit allergic to the first person early in my career. I was always quoting to my students something that Hemingway had said, which was that anybody can write a novel in the first person. I sort of know what he meant: If you have the normal novelist's gift for mimicry, you can just say, I am this person, and start talking as that person. In many ways that's easier than saying he or she did so-and-so. But why I've had this explosion of three first-person novels in recent years I couldn't say. I've enjoyed it tremendously, but I wouldn't hesitate to write a third-person novel tomorrow. In fact I have been writing a lot of short stories the last couple of years, and most of those are third-person stories.

CA: What accounts for the increase in short stories?

PRICE: For the first time in my life, I've made myself a member of my short-story class. I teach a senior graduate class in short-story writing, and this semester I'm teaching a long-story class. I've made myself a contributing member: I do the assignments when the students do, and that's resulted in my coming up with the first new batch of stories I've had since 1970, when my second volume of stories was published. I put my stories out on the table and urge the students to be as honest with the teacher as he is with them. Of course, they probably aren't quite as candid as they ought to be, but with a little encouragement, they dig in pretty well.

CA: The titles of your 1985 poetry collection, The Laws of Ice, *and your 1990 one,* The Use of Fire, *make me think of Robert Frost's poem "Fire and Ice." Would you talk about how those opposites figure in your titles and in the collections?*

PRICE: I haven't counted, but I think the majority of the poems in *The Laws of Ice* come after the cancer surgery I had in the summer of '84. The title poem is very much about the experience of being totally ambushed at a particular moment in one's life by an enemy so enormous that even if one survives, one is going to become a new person as a result of that encounter. The laws of ice are the laws of death and affliction to which we are all subject from the moment we're born. *The Use of Fire* contains a great many poems which are based in the second and third surgeries I had and the wonderful period of recovery I've had since the fall of '86, when the most recent surgery occurred. There's a kind of spaciousness and relaxation and a sort of serene retrospection in *The Use of Fire* which I don't feel in *The Laws of Ice* at all. There's literal fire and ice then—literal terror and great warmth.

CA: Being sensitive to the frustration and real damage book reviewers can cause writers, how do you approach doing reviews and criticism of other people's work?

PRICE: In the very beginning of my career, I wrote one or two snooty reviews of the "I could do better than this"

sort. But I think I very quickly realized that just wasn't worth doing, that there were plenty of people out there who were ready to take care of the "beat 'em up in the alley" detail, and I decided that since my time and energy were limited anyway, I wasn't going to review books that I didn't already know I liked. Since then, whenever anyone has asked me to review a book, I've always said that I would look at it and give them a quick answer, but I wouldn't do it sight unseen because I don't feel any necessity to beat up on people's writing.

There was one book I reviewed years ago, a book of short stories for children that I profoundly felt should be kept out of the hands of children. They were stories very much about violence and sexual abuse, and it seemed to me that for the age group they were being aimed at, they were a very bad idea. But that's the only case I can think of when I've written a review saying, "Do not buy this book—or at least, do not give it to your child." Other than that I've reviewed books that I knew in principle I was going to like and that I wanted to praise. I think the whole premise of book reviewing is so unexamined. A mediocre novel is not at all likely to damage the world or to damage anyone else's soul. At the very most it might set their pocketbook back fifteen or twenty dollars. I never have understood the passion that highly negative reviewers like to take in their line about movies and books. To be a professional reviewer seems very strange, in any case.

CA: You've taught for most of your adult life. What's made it worth the doing?

PRICE: I worked out a wonderful relationship in 1963 whereby I teach one semester a year. For the last few years that's been the spring semester. I teach two courses; I teach two days a week and usually come in part of another day for conferences. Since college terms have gotten so short, I'm really teaching under four months a year. I put most of my energy during that four months into the teaching. It's been sort of like crop rotation: teaching four months, writing for eight, then teaching four. But since I've now made myself a member of the short-story class, I continue writing during my teaching semesters.

I get a tremendous sense of reward from the students I work with. I generally teach the poetry of Milton, and I have about forty-five people in that class. In the writing class, ideally I have about twelve—this semester I have fifteen, which is a little bit larger than I wanted, but there were that many good people. I wanted to be a teacher as far back as I wanted to be a writer, and I know that my wanting to be a teacher was a result of my having such disciplined and demanding teachers in my childhood. I came along in the last great age of the old-maid schoolteacher, and I was tremendously responsive to those women. It's one of my great joys now that I'm still in touch with some of them.

CA: It's widely felt that students don't come to college with the background in reading that students used to bring to college—back in the days of those old-maid schoolteachers. How do you deal with that in teaching?

PRICE: I was an undergraduate at Duke from 1951 to 1955, and partly I try to remind myself that among my own contemporaries there were lots of boys who'd never read the daily paper, much less Tolstoy. So we may be looking back at the past with much too rosy spectacles. But there's very little one can do for the student who's eighteen or twenty-one and comes in saying he's never read anything. You can hand him basic lists of whatever books you think are indispensable for whatever kind of work he hopes to do—and I've known the rare students who have actually taken off a couple of years and worked at a pizza restaurant or whatever to read their way through the books they'd never read.

But it is unfortunate if people don't read those books while they're young. I know the reading I did before I was sixteen or so sank into me in a way that nothing ever has since—partly, I guess, because our minds aren't nearly as full of stuff when we're children as they are later. Our files get so crowded as we get older. I'm really thrilled that, sort of by accident, I read *Anna Karenina* when I was fourteen or fifteen, and *Madame Bovary*. I can see now what great books they are, but they don't take the top of my head off the way they did when I first read them. I remember the moment in which I finished the scene of Emma Bovary's death, and it was as though a tornado had hit the house. Now I read it and I think it's a very great novel, I'm glad it exists, but I'm not swept off to Kansas on my bicycle.

CA: North Carolina seems an uncommonly fertile and nurturing ground for writers. Do you have any thoughts on why this is so?

PRICE: I think with all its woes and with all its insistence on sending Jesse Helms to the Senate, North Carolina has a gentler brand of Southern life than most of the deeper Southern states. It's a more welcoming place. It's more prepared to tolerate the kinds of people that writers generally are—prickly customers, gadflies on the hide of society. But I think we owe the present bonanza of fine novelists and poets and dramatists to the existence of wonderful universities and colleges in the state; that's the ultimate reason. There's the nexus of Duke and Chapel Hill and North Carolina State all within twenty miles of one another. And a great many of the people who went to those universities have decided to continue to live here because it is such a good place.

CA: Unlike some major writers born in the South, you stayed in the South, without a rebellion or an apology. For people who haven't read what you've written on the subject, would you talk about that choice and how you think it has affected your writing?

PRICE: In my childhood and adolescence, aside from a few bad experiences with my childish contemporaries, I had a very good experience in the South. I wasn't aware that I was in the South; I was aware that I was in a loving family in towns that I mostly liked. So I never felt, "Oh my God, get me out of Dixie" and caught the Silver Meteor to streak out of Raleigh to Penn Station, which a lot of my contemporaries and slightly older people did. I will, though, have to be honest and say that my return to the South after I'd spent three years in graduate school in England was fortuitous. I'd been in my last year at Oxford thinking I had to try to get a job from three or four thousand miles away, and I suddenly got a letter from Duke, my alma mater, asking if I'd accept a three-year contract to come back and teach freshman English. It seemed the easiest way on earth to solve the problem of getting a job from that far away. So I came back in 1958 and began teaching at Duke. One thing led to another, the way it can do in life, and I've simply stayed here because it turned out that I never wanted to go anywhere else. I don't know what would have happened if I'd been offered a good job at Swarthmore. Or at Dartmouth—I might have wound up living in New England. I had not passionately planted my banner on Southern soil and said, "I proclaim this my homeland forevermore." But that's the way it turned out, and I have no regrets, far from it.

CA: Are there movies under way now from any of the novels?

PRICE: Movies in my career have been under way forever. *A Long and Happy Life* was sold to the movies about ten minutes after it was published. Now it's had literally about a dozen movie options on it. *Kate Vaiden* seems very close to becoming a film, and a very fine artist has bought *The Tongues of Angels*, which is presently having a screenplay written—not by me. I hope that's going to be done. I did one television play on request for American Playhouse, a play called "Private Contentment," which they produced beautifully. That was very satisfying. But so far I've had no feature films. I'd love to see one. I've loved movies since I was old enough to be carried into them, and I'd be delighted to see what someone would make of a book of mine. I hope I'll get to eventually.

CA: You mentioned earlier the novel that you're working on now. Do you have plans beyond that, or long-range goals for your writing?

PRICE: No. I just want to keep doing more of the same. I have a book of three long stories coming out this spring from Atheneum. It's called *The Foreseeable Future*. And I've just had *New Music* published, a trilogy of plays produced last year in Cleveland. They cover over forty years in the life of a family. And I'm about to finish this new novel. That's what's on my plate at the moment, and I don't have specific plans for anything else. But that doesn't worry me, because I almost never have plans from one book to the next.

BIOGRAPHICAL/CRITICAL SOURCES:

BOOKS

Contemporary Literary Criticism, Volume 3, Gale, 1975, Volume 6, 1976, Volume 13, 1980, Volume 43, 1987, Volume 50, 1988.
Dictionary of Literary Biography, Volume 2: *American Novelists since World War II,* Gale, 1978.

PERIODICALS

Chicago Tribune, May 11, 1990.
Detroit News, July 17, 1989.
Globe and Mail (Toronto), July 2, 1988.
Los Angeles Times Book Review, July 10, 1986; January 3, 1988; May 22, 1988; August 3, 1989.
New York Times, June 24, 1986; January 4, 1987; June 26, 1989; August 26, 1989; November 4, 1989.
New York Times Book Review, May 8, 1988; June 4, 1989; May 13, 1990.
Publishers Weekly, March 13, 1987; April 21, 1989; December 15, 1989; January 24, 1991.
Times (London), February 5, 1987.
Washington Post, September 7, 1986; January 13, 1987.
Washington Post Book World, February 14, 1988; April 10, 1988; May 6, 1990.*

—Sketch by Elizabeth A. Des Chenes

—Interview by Jean W. Ross

* * *

PRICE, Steven D(avid)   1940-

PERSONAL: Born April 17, 1940, in Brooklyn, NY; son of Martin and Rose (Myiofis) Price; married Jenene C. Levy, August 18, 1968 (divorced, 1972); married Anne London Wolf (a travel agent), October 29, 1978. *Educa-*tion: University of Rochester, B.A., 1962; Yale University, LL.B., 1965.

ADDRESSES: Home and office—510 East 85th St., New York, NY 10028.

CAREER: Lawyer, subsidiary rights director, and editor in publishing field, New York City, 1965-71; free-lance writer, 1971-78; International Management Group, New York City, literary agent, 1978-80; writer, 1980—; in public relations, 1990—.

MEMBER: International Alliance of Equestrian Journalists, American Horse Shows Association.

WRITINGS:

Teaching Riding at Summer Camps, Stephen Greene Press, 1971.
Panorama of American Horses, Westover Publishing, 1972.
Get a Horse!: Basics of Backyard Horsekeeping, Viking, 1974.
Practical Guide to Owning Your Own Horse, Wilshire, 1974.
Take Me Home, Praeger, 1974.
(With William J. Goode) *The Second-Time-Single Man's Survival Handbook,* Praeger, 1974.
Horseback Vacation Guide, Stephen Greene Press, 1975.
Old as the Hills: The Story of Bluegrass Music, Viking, 1976.
(With Anthony D'Ambrosio, Jr.) *Schooling to Show: Basics of Hunter-Jumper Training,* Viking, 1976.
(Editor with others) *The Whole Horse Catalog,* Simon & Schuster, 1977, revised edition, 1985.
(With Joy Slater) *Riding's a Joy,* Doubleday, 1982.
(With Alix Coleman) *All the King's Horses: The Story of the Budweiser Clydesdales,* Penguin Books, 1983.
(With Charles Kauffman) *Riding for a Fall,* Tor Books, 1988.
The Polo Primer: A Guide for Players and Spectators, Viking, 1988.

SIDELIGHTS: Steven D. Price told *CA:* "Literary aspirations notwithstanding, specialization is essential if the nonfiction writer is to survive financially. In my case, books and articles about horses in general have been narrowed to hunter-jumper subjects. Such focusing permits greater depth and the development of a reputation."

Q

QUINE, W. V.
See QUINE, Willard Van Orman

*   *   *

QUINE, Willard V.
See QUINE, Willard Van Orman

*   *   *

QUINE, Willard Van Orman 1908-
(Willard V. Quine, W. V. Quine)

PERSONAL: Born June 25, 1908, in Akron, OH; son of Cloyd Robert and Harriet (Van Orman) Quine; married, 1948; wife's name, Marjorie; children: Elizabeth Quine Roberts, Norma, Douglas, Margaret Quine McGovern. *Education:* Oberlin College, A.B., 1930; Harvard University, A.M., 1931, Ph.D., 1932; Oxford University, M.A., 1953.

ADDRESSES: Home—38 Chestnut St., Boston, MA 02108. *Office*—Department of Philosophy, Harvard University, Cambridge, MA 02138.

CAREER: Harvard University, Cambridge, MA, Sheldon Traveling Fellow to Vienna, Austria, Prague, Czechoslovakia, and Warsaw, Poland, 1932-33, junior fellow, Society of Fellows, 1933-36, instructor, 1936-41, associate professor, 1941-48, professor of philosophy, 1948-56, Pierce Professor of Philosophy, 1956-78, Pierce Professor of Philosophy emeritus, 1978—. Visiting professor, University of San Paulo, 1942, Tokyo University, 1959, Rockefeller University, 1968, and College of France, 1969; Eastman Visiting Professor, Oxford University, 1953-54; Hagerstrom Lecturer, Uppsala University, 1973. Member, Insti-

tute for Advanced Study, 1956-57. Consultant, Rand Corp., 1949.

MEMBER: Institut International de Philosophie, American Academy of Arts and Sciences, National Academy of Sciences, American Philosophical Society, American Philosophical Association (president of Eastern Division, 1957), Institut de France, Association for Symbolic Logic (president, 1953-56), British Academy, Norwegian Academy.

AWARDS, HONORS: Litt.D., Oberlin College, 1955, University of Akron, 1965, Washington University, 1966, Temple University, 1970, Oxford University, 1970, Cambridge University, 1978, and Ripon College, 1983; doctorat, University of Lille, 1956, University of Uppsala, 1980, University of Berne, 1982, and University of Granada, 1986; L.L.D., Ohio State University, 1957, and Harvard University, 1979; Center for Advanced Study in the Behavioral Sciences fellow, 1958-59; Center for Advanced Studies fellow, Wesleyan University, 1965; L.H.D., University of Chicago, 1967, Syracuse University, 1981, and Adelphi University, 1988; Nicholas M. Butler Gold Medal, Columbia University, 1970; Sir Henry Saville fellow, Merton College, Oxford University, 1973-74.

WRITINGS:

A System of Logistic, Harvard University Press, 1934.

(Under name Willard V. Quine) *Mathematical Logic,* Norton, 1940, revised edition, Harvard University Press, 1951.

(Under name W. V. Quine) *Elementary Logic,* Ginn, 1941, revised edition, Harvard University Press, 1981.

O Sentido da Nova Logica, Martins, 1944.

(Under name W. V. Quine) *Methods of Logic,* Holt, 1950, 4th edition, Harvard University Press, 1982.

(Under name Willard V. Quine) *From a Logical Point of View: Nine Logico-Philosophical Essays,* Harvard University Press, 1953, 2nd revised edition, 1961.

(Under name Willard V. Quine) *Word and Object,* M.I.T. Press, 1960.

(Under name Willard V. Quine) *Set Theory and Its Logic,* Harvard University Press, 1963, revised edition, 1969.

(Under name W. V. Quine) *The Ways of Paradox and Other Essays,* Random House, 1966, revised and enlarged edition, Harvard University Press, 1976.

Selected Logic Papers, Random House, 1966.

(Under name Willard V. Quine) *Ontological Relativity and Other Essays,* Columbia University Press, 1969.

(With J. S. Ullian; under name W. V. Quine) *The Web of Belief,* Random House, 1970, 2nd edition, 1978.

(Under name W. V. Quine) *Philosophy of Logic,* Prentice-Hall, 1970, 2nd edition, Harvard University Press, 1986.

(Under name Willard V. Quine) *Algebraic Logic and Predicate Functors,* Irvington, 1971.

The Roots of Reference, Open Court, 1973.

(Under name W. V. Quine) *Theories and Things,* Harvard University Press, 1981.

The Time of My Life (autobiographical), M.I.T. Press, 1985.

(Under name W. V. Quine) *Quiddities: An Intermittently Philosophical Dictionary,* Harvard University Press, 1987.

La Scienza e i Dati di Senso, Armando, 1988.

Pursuit of Truth, Harvard University Press, 1990.

The Logic of Sequences, Garland Publishing, 1991.

(With Rudolf Carnap; under name Willard V. Quine) *Dear Carnap, Dear Van: The Quine-Carnap Correspondence and Related Work,* University of California Press, 1991.

Contributor of articles to mathematics and philosophy journals. Consulting editor, *Journal of Symbolic Logic,* 1936-52. Quine's books have been translated into eleven foreign languages.

SIDELIGHTS: Willard Van Orman Quine, a specialist in symbolic logic who began as a mathematical logician and in later books explores semantics, epistemology, and metaphysics, has achieved high esteem in the field of philosophy. Anthony Quinton characterizes Quine in the London *Times* as "one of the most admired and discussed of philosophers in the English-speaking world." John Gross notes in the *New York Times* that Quine "has won a world reputation for his work on logic; those in a position to judge have often described him as one of the greatest of living philosophers." A *Times Literary Supplement* reviewer observes: "The death of Bertrand Russell has deprived the philosophical world of its greatest contemporary figure. Of those who remain perhaps no one has a

higher professional reputation than the American philosopher, Willard Van Orman Quine." Yet Quine himself, who taught logic at Harvard University for over forty years, does not consider logic of paramount importance. As he explained to a *New York Times* interviewer: "I think this would be an awful world if everyone made a point of trying to be logical and acted according to his conclusions. There's so much chance of error along the way. And it's conceivable that there are some illusions without which people would be less happy."

BIOGRAPHICAL/CRITICAL SOURCES:

BOOKS

Quine, Willard Van Orman, *The Time of My Life* (autobiographical), M.I.T. Press, 1985.

Quine, Willard Van Orman, and Rudolf Carnap, *Dear Carnap, Dear Van: The Quine-Carnap Correspondence and Related Work,* University of California Press, 1991.

PERIODICALS

Los Angeles Times Book Review, October 4, 1987.
New York Times, November 9, 1969; September 29, 1987.
Times (London), April 14, 1990.
Times Literary Supplement, October 9, 1970; November 19, 1987; August 10, 1990.

*   *   *

QUINN, Niall 1943-

PERSONAL: Born May 29, 1943, in Dublin, Ireland. *Education:* Attended secondary school in Dublin, Ireland. *Religion:* None.

ADDRESSES: Home—98 Ardilaun, Portmarnock, County Dublin, Ireland.

CAREER: Writer.

AWARDS, HONORS: First prize for literature from Irish Arts Council, 1981, for *Voyovic and Other Stories.*

WRITINGS:

Rejection (one-act play), produced in London, England at Act Inn Theatre, 1972.

Voyovic and Other Stories, Wolfhound Press, 1980, new edition, 1983; published in the United States as *Brigitte: A Novella and Stories,* Braziller, 1981.

Cafe Cong (novel), Wolfhound Press, 1983.

Stolen Air, Dufour, 1989.

(Editor with Peter Jenner) *Disorders of Movement: Clinical, Pharmacological and Physiological Aspects,* Academic Press, 1990.

SIDELIGHTS: When *CA* asked Niall Quinn about his early years and schooling, he answered: "Many and varied were these daylight prisons veiled by the name of school and staffed without exception by thick-headed drill sergeants in mufti. And these rattlers of rote I endured from my sixth to my sixteenth year. Since then I have been assiduously pursuing the 'holy curiosity of inquiry' and this, alone, is education."

He continued: "I've been on and off a seaman, never on for more than four months, and over the years I've managed to sail under the flags of Britain, Holland, Germany, Norway, Italy, Greece, Panama, Liberia, and Singapore. Between times I worked in Scotland Yard (as a dishwasher); also in countless factories and storehouses, and once as a tax inspector for Her Majesty's Government."

When asked about his motivation for writing, Quinn replied: "Somewhere in the thesaurus, 'motivation' collides with 'excuse.' The writing impulse is, of course, simply that: the urge to write. Regressions from there fragment the truth that the whole of the writing impulse is greater than the sum of the parts, however interesting and curious these may be. But the natural urge to find and express symmetry—in science or art—plays a large part. The circumstances of a writer are always internal—literature has been written in prisons and in mansions, and all places between."

BIOGRAPHICAL/CRITICAL SOURCES:

PERIODICALS

Irish Times, November 17, 1981.
Times Literary Supplement, January 16, 1981.*

R

RAINTREE, Lee
See SELLERS, Con(nie Leslie, Jr.)

* * *

RASH, Nancy 1940-
(Mary Harrison)

PERSONAL: Born November 19, 1940, in Louisville, KY; daughter of Dillman Atkinson (a financial consultant) and Nancy (Batson) Rash; married Remo Fabbri, Jr. (a physician), June 27, 1962 (divorced, 1983); married Frank M. Turner (a university professor/administrator), July 29, 1984; children:(first marriage) Gian Dillman Rash Fabbri. *Education:* Radcliffe College, B.A., 1962 (magna cum laude); Bryn Mawr College, M.A., 1965, Ph.D. 1971. *Politics:* Independent. *Religion:* Episcopalian. *Avocational interests:* history.

ADDRESSES: Home—35 Hillhouse Ave., New Haven, CT, 06511. *Office*—Department of Art History, Connecticut College, 270 Mohegan Ave., New London, CT, 06320.

CAREER: Connecticut College, New London, assistant professor, 1972-76, associate professor, 1976-80, professor of art history and chairperson of department, 1980—, Lucy C. McDonnel chairperson, 1991. Visiting lecturer at Yale University, 1975.

MEMBER: International Center for Medieval Art, College Art Association, Renaissance Society of America, Association of Historians of American Art, Medieval Academy, Phi Beta Kappa.

WRITINGS:

(Under pseudonym Mary Harrison) *Infertility: A Couple's Guide to Causes and Treatments,* Houghton, 1977.
The Painting and Politics of George Caleb Bingham, Yale University Press, 1991.

Contributor to magazines, including *Good Housekeeping* (under pseudonym Mary Harrison), *Journal of the Warburg and Courtauld Institutes, Numismatic Chronicle,* and *Gesta.*

WORK IN PROGRESS: Research on art during the American Civil War.

SIDELIGHTS: Nancy Rash once told *CA:* "Personal experiences and the lack of such a book led me to write *Infertility,* and the letters I have received demonstrate how many people needed help and sympathy. The medical community has also voiced an interest in using this book for patients. My other two areas of interest are history and the history of art, professionally motivated but personally satisfying." Ms. Rash has more recently commented: "Recapturing the past became easier, as I worked on *The Painting and Politics of George Caleb Bingham,* because of the letters he and his friends left, and the daily accounts, in newspapers, of life in central Missouri in the mid-19th century."

* * *

RASKIN, Ellen 1928-1984

PERSONAL: Born March 13, 1928, in Milwaukee, WI; died August 8, 1984, of complications from connective-tissue disease, in New York, NY; daughter of Sol and Margaret (Goldfisch) Raskin; married Dennis Flanagan (editor of *Scientific American*), August 1, 1960; children: (first marriage) Susan Metcalf. *Education:* Attended University of Wisconsin, 1945-49. *Avocational interests:* Book collecting, gardening.

CAREER: Commercial illustrator and designer, New York City, beginning 1950; author and illustrator of children's books, 1966-1984. Instructor in illustration at Pratt

Institute, 1963, Syracuse University, 1976; guest lecturer at University of Berkeley, 1969, 1972, and 1977. *Exhibitions*— Group shows: American Institute of Graphic Arts, 50 Years of Graphic Arts in American show, 1966; Biennale of Illustrations, Bratislava, Czechoslovakia, 1969; Biennale of Applied Graphic Art, Brno, Czechoslovakia, 1972; Contemporary American Illustrators of Children's Books, 1974-75.

MEMBER: American Institute of Graphic Arts, Asia Society, Authors Guild, Authors League of America.

AWARDS, HONORS: Distinctive Merit Award, 1958, Silver Medal, 1959, both from Art Directors Clubs; *New York Herald Tribune* Spring Book Festival Award (best picture book), 1966, for *Nothing Ever Happens on My Block; Songs of Innocence* was included in American Institute of Graphic Arts exhibit of 50 best books of the year, 1966; *Spectacles* was named one of the best illustrated children's books by *New York Times Book Review,* 1968; Children's Book Council chose *The Mysterious Disappearance of Leon (I Mean Noel),* 1972, *Who, Said Sue, Said Whoo?,* 1974, and *Figgs & Phantoms,* 1975, for the Children's Book Showcase; *Boston Globe-Horn Book* Honor, 1973, for *Who, Said Sue, Said Whoo?; Figgs & Phantoms* was chosen for the American Institute of Graphic Arts Children's Book Show, 1973-74, and as a Newbery honor book, 1975; Edgar Allan Poe Special Award, Mystery Writers of America, 1975, for *The Tattooed Potato and Other Clues; Boston Globe-Horn Book* Best Fiction Award, 1978, Newbery Medal, 1979, and American Book Award nomination, all for *The Westing Game;* an Ellen Raskin Lecture Symposium has been established in Milwaukee.

WRITINGS:

ALL SELF-ILLUSTRATED

Nothing Ever Happens on My Block (ALA Notable Book), Atheneum, 1966.
(Composer of music and illustrator) William Blake, *Songs of Innocence,* two volumes, Doubleday, 1966.
Silly Songs and Sad (poetry), Crowell, 1967.
Spectacles (ALA Notable Book), Atheneum, 1968.
Ghost in a Four-Room Apartment (Junior Literary Guild selection), Atheneum, 1969.
And It Rained (ALA Notable Book), Atheneum, 1969.
(Adapter) Christina Rosetti, *Goblin Market,* Dutton, 1970.
A & THE; or, William T. C. Baumgarten Comes to Town, Atheneum, 1970.
The World's Greatest Freak Show, Atheneum, 1971.
The Mysterious Disappearance of Leon (I Mean Noel) (Junior Literary Guild selection; ALA Notable Book), Dutton, 1972.
Franklin Stein (ALA Notable Book), Atheneum, 1972.

Moe Q. McGlutch, He Smokes Too Much, Parents Magazine Press, 1973.
Who, Said Sue, Said Whoo? (poetry; ALA Notable Book), Atheneum, 1973.
Moose, Goose and Little Nobody (ALA Notable Book), Parents Magazine Press, 1974.
Figgs & Phantoms (ALA Notable Book), Dutton, 1974.
The Tattooed Potato and Other Clues (ALA Notable Book), Dutton, 1975.
Twenty-two, Twenty-three, Atheneum, 1976.
The Westing Game, Dutton, 1978.

ILLUSTRATOR

Claire H. Bishop, editor, *Happy Christmas: Tales for Boys and Girls,* Frederick Ungar, 1956.
Dylan Thomas, *A Child's Christmas in Wales,* New Directions, 1959.
Ruth Krauss, *Mama I Wish I Was Snow, Child You'd Be Very Cold,* Atheneum, 1962.
Edgar Allan Poe, *Poems of Edgar Allan Poe,* edited by Dwight Macdonald, Crowell, 1965.
Aileen Fisher and Olive Rabe, *We Dickensons,* Atheneum, 1965.
Louis Untermeyer, editor, *Paths of Poetry: Twenty-five Poets and Their Poems,* Delacorte, 1966.
Molly Cone, *The Jewish Sabbath,* Crowell, 1966.
Arthur G. Razzell and K. G. Watts, *Probability,* Doubleday, 1967.
Robert Herrick, *Poems of Robert Herrick,* edited by Winfield T. Scott, Crowell, 1967.
D. H. Lawrence, *D. H. Lawrence: Poems Selected for Young People,* edited by William Cole, Viking, 1967.
Vera Cleaver and Bill Cleaver, *Ellen Grae,* Lippincott, 1967.
A. G. Razzell and K. G. Watts, *This Is Four: The Idea of a Number,* Doubleday, 1967.
V. Cleaver and B. Cleaver, *Lady Ellen Grae,* Lippincott, 1968.
Nancy Larrick, editor, *Piping Down the Valleys Wild: Poetry for the Young of All Ages,* Delacorte, 1968.
A. Fisher and O. Rabe, *We Alcotts,* Atheneum, 1968.
A. G. Razzell and K. G. Watts, *Symmetry,* Doubleday, 1968.
Susan Bartlett, *Books: A Book to Begin On,* Holt, 1968.
Suzanne Stark Morrow, *Inatuk's Friend* (Junior Literary Guild selection), Atlantic-Little, Brown, 1968.
Renee K. Weiss, editor, *A Paper Zoo: A Collection of Animal Poems by Modern American Poets,* Macmillan, 1968.
Rebecca Caudill, *Come Along!,* Holt, 1969.
A. G. Razzell and K. G. Watts, *Circles and Curves,* Doubleday, 1969.

Sara Brewton and John E. Brewton, editors, *Shrieks at Midnight: Macabre Poems, Eerie and Humorous,* Crowell, 1969.

A. G. Razzell and K. G. Watts, *Three and the Shape of Three,* Doubleday, 1969.

Alan Gardner, *Elidor,* Walck, 1970.

OTHER

Also designer of over one thousand book jackets.

Collections of Raskin's papers are housed at the Milwaukee Public Library, at the Kerlan Collection, University of Minnesota, and at the Children's Cooperative Book Center, University of Wisconsin, Madison.

SIDELIGHTS: Ellen Raskin was known as an illustrator of children's picture books and as a writer of mystery novels for older children. In both roles, she won critical and popular acclaim. In her picture books, according to Marilyn H. Karrenbrock in the *Dictionary of Literary Biography,* Raskin was "an inveterate puzzlemaker, a trickster, a razzle-dazzle-sleight-of-hand artist." This talent for puzzle-making served Raskin well in her novels, as well, in which she combined wildly preposterous plots with solid mysteries.

Speaking to Jim Roginski in *Behind the Covers: Interviews with Authors and Illustrators of Books for Children and Young Adults,* Raskin explained how she wrote a book: "I always write five times as much as I have to and then cut and cut, and make everything readable. The most important thing for me are the first few words, the first line to catch the reader. You can always start over again. I do. I write too much as it is. And, before you ask, I never know the ending. If I do know the ending by the second draft, I don't want to write the book. The ending is my reward for doing that book. So maybe on the fourth draft when I type out the ending I love it! I always have happy endings, too, because I write children's books and I do them specifically for children. And I never make fun of people. I'm very sensitive to that. Perhaps because I was made fun of as a child by other children; or perhaps because I love my characters too much."

Figgs & Phantoms is one of Raskin's most popular mysteries and an example of her creative approach. Focusing on a family of onetime vaudeville performers, the book features characters with names like Mona Lisa Newton, Florence Italy Figg, and Sissie Figg Newton. Truman the Human Pretzel can bend himself into any shape; the brothers Romulus the Walking Encyclopedia and Remus the Talking Adding Machine can answer any question; and Newt Newton is the town's worst used car salesman, trading plain-colored Cadillacs for shiny Edsels. Word play, eccentric twists of plot, and typographical jokes abound. Manyof the jokes concern the rare book business

(Florence Italy Newton is a bookdealer) and allusions are made to a score of books and authors. As Alice Bach noted in the *New York Times Book Review:* "Underneath the swagger and intricacies of a mystery salted with book-lined clues the author has written an elegant romance, extended a Victorian bouquet to all bibliophiles."

More importantly, *Figgs & Phantoms* tells a serious story of a young girl coming to grips with the death of a beloved relative. Young Mona Figg follows her deceased Uncle Flo into the afterworld and in so doing, learns of her own need to live life to the fullest capacity. "Readers may find the book a mystery, or an allegory, or a philosophical story—or possibly a spoof on all three," Ethel L. Heins wrote in *Horn Book.* A critic for *Kirkus Reviews* found some flaws in the story: "The zanniness here seems more often forced than inspired. . . . Still a juvenile novel—however unstrung—that takes such farcical liberties with death, grief and readers' expectations is rare enough to rate a hearing, and the Figgs—all mask and gesture though they are—do come up with a few show-stopping lines."

The Newbery Medal-winning *The Westing Game* "brought a glowing close to a fine career," as Karrenbrock noted. Telling the story of a quirky will left by wealthy industrialist Samuel Westing (who lived in "Westing House"), the book gathers together a group of oddly-assorted characters who must, to inherit a fortune, play "the Westing game"—a game with apparently different rules for each player. The game may also uncover the identity of Samuel Westing's killer. Disguises, shifting identities, and the confusing nature of the puzzle game provide Turtle Wexler, the book's 13-year-old protagonist, with plenty to investigate. "Raskin," wrote Denise M. Wilms in *Booklist,* "is an arch storyteller here, cagily dropping clues and embellishing her intricate plot with the seriocomic foibles of an eminently eccentric cast."

Raskin explained in *Horn Book* how she wrote *The Westing Game:* "I sat down at the typewriter with no wish of an idea, just the urge to write another children's book. . . . It is 1976, the Bicentennial year. My story will have a historical background; its locale, the place I know best: Milwaukee. . . . Recalling that Amy Kellman's daughter asked for a puzzle-mystery, I decide that the format of my historical treatise will be a puzzle-mystery (whatever that is). I type out the words of 'America the Beautiful' and cut them apart. Meanwhile on television . . . come reports of the death of an infamous millionaire. Anyone who can spell *Howard Hughes* is forging a will. . . . Now I have Lake Michigan, a jumbled 'America the Beautiful,' the first draft of a very strange will, and a dead millionaire—a fine beginning for a puzzle-mystery."

Critics enjoyed the book's puzzle-mystery. Georgess McHargue in the *New York Times Book Review* found the book to be trickier than the ordinary mystery novel. "This is not a book for the easily confused, the unsophisticated, or the purist mystery fan," McHague wrote, "but it's great fun for those who enjoy illusion, word play or sleight of hand and don't mind a small rustle of paper in the background." Similarly, Sid Fleischman wrote in the *Washington Post Book World* that "here the terrain is lush with puns and other word play, with comic shribbery and broadleafed notions. . . . [Raskin] piles mystery upon mystery. . . . Her literary choreography is bouncy, complex and full of surprises."

In her Newbery Medal acceptance speech, Raskin clarified that *The Westing Game* had won the award, not her. "It is the book that is the important thing, not who I am or how I did it, but the book. Not me, the book. I fear for the book in this age of inflated personalities, in which the public's appetite for an insight into the lives of the famous has been whetted by publicity-puffers and profit-pushers into an insatiable hunger for gossip. I worry that who-the-writer-is has become of more interest than what-the-writer-writes. I am concerned that this dangerous distortion may twist its way into children's literature.

"I do understand the attempt to introduce books to children through their authors, and in my travels I have seen it done effectively and well. I salute all efforts to encourage reading. But an author is not a performer; meeting an author is not a substitute for reading a book. It is the book that lives, not the author."

BIOGRAPHICAL/CRITICAL SOURCES:

BOOKS

Bader, Barbara, *American Picture Books from Noah's Ark to the Beast Within,* Macmillan, 1976.
Children's Literature Review, Gale, Volume 1, 1976, Volume 12, 1987.
Dictionary of Literary Biography, Volume 52: *American Writers for Children since 1960: Fiction,* Gale, 1986, pp.314-325.
Roginski, Jim, *Behind the Covers: Interviews with Authors and Illustrators of Books for Children and Young Adults,* Libraries Unlimited, 1985, pp. 167-176.

PERIODICALS

Booklist, June 1, 1978.
Horn Book, October, 1974, pp. 138-139; August, 1979, pp. 385-391.
Kirkus Reviews, April 15, 1974, pp. 425-426.
New York Times Book Review, May 4, 1975, pp. 34-35; June 25, 1978, pp. 36-37.
Washington Post Book World, June 11, 1978, p. E4.

OBITUARIES:

PERIODICALS

New York Times, August 10, 1984.
Publishers Weekly, August 31, 1984.
School Library Journal, September, 1984.*

*   *   *

REICH, Ali
   See KATZ, Bobbi

*   *   *

REID, William H(oward)   1945-

PERSONAL: Born April 10, 1945, in Dallas, TX; son of Howard Clinton (a psychiatrist) and Lucile (an artist; maiden name, Lattanner) Reid. *Education:* University of Minnesota, B.A., 1966, M.D., 1970; University of California, Berkeley, M.P.H., 1975.

ADDRESSES: Office—P.O. Box 49817, Austin, TX 78765.

CAREER: University of Nebraska, Omaha, clinical research psychiatrist in Medical Center and Nebraska Psychiatric Institute, 1977-86; Colonial Hills Hospital, San Antonio, TX, medical director, 1986-89; University of Texas, Austin, professor of psychiatry, director of Texas department of Mental Health and Mental Retardation, 1989—. Northwestern University, lecturer, 1978-82; Rush Medical College, Chicago, visiting associate professor, 1979-82. Consultant in forensic psychiatry. *Military service:* U.S. Army, Medical Corps, chief of mental hygiene, 1971-73.

MEMBER: American Medical Association, American Psychiatric Association, American Public Health Association, American Academy of Psychiatry and the Law (president, 1988-89).

WRITINGS:

(Editor) *Mathematical Problems in the Geophysical Sciences I: Geophysical Fluid Dynamics,* American Mathematical Society, 1971.
(Editor) *Mathematical Problems in the Geophysical Sciences II: Inverse Problems, Dynamo Theory and Tides,* American Mathematical Society, 1971.
(Editor) *The Psychopath: A Comprehensive Study of Antisocial Disorders and Behavior,* Brunner, 1978.
Psychiatry for the House Officer, Brunner, 1979.
Basic Intensive Psychotherapy, Brunner, 1980.
(Editor) *Treatment of Antisocial Syndromes,* Van Nostrand, 1981.

(Coeditor) *Terrorism: Interdisciplinary Perspectives,* American Psychiatric Association, 1983.

Treatment of the DSM-III Psychiatric Disorders, Brunner, 1983, revised edition published as *The Treatment of Psychiatric Disorders: Revised for the DSM-III-R,* 1988.

(Coeditor) *Assaults within Psychiatric Facilities,* Grune, 1983.

(Coeditor) *Unmasking the Psychopath: Antisocial Personality and Related Syndromes,* Norton, 1986.

(With Michael G. Wise) *DSM-III-R Training Guide: For Use with the American Psychiatric Association's Diagnostic and Statistical Manual of Mental Disorders,* Brunner, 1989.

Also contributor of thirty chapters to professional books and more than seventy articles to medical journals; composer of twenty-five musical compositions. Editor of *Public Medicine,* 1990—; member of editorial boards of six professional journals.

WORK IN PROGRESS: With D. Reid, *Tech to Exec: A Guide for Professionals Who Want to Be Executives;* a third edition of *The Treatment of Psychiatric Disorders,* for Brunner; with Michael G. Wise, *Training Guide for DSM-IV,* for Brunner.

SIDELIGHTS: William H. Reid asked *CA,* "What's with all this nonfiction? Why won't anyone ask me to write a good *novel?*" Reid, a psychiatrist as well as an author, examines various aspects of mental illness, including psychopathy and antisocial syndromes.

*   *   *

REILLY, Patrick   1932-

PERSONAL: Born January 1, 1932, in Glasgow, Scotland; son of Edward (an insulator) and Catherine (Cassidy) Reilly; married Rose Fitzpatrick, March 3, 1957; children: Edward, Joseph, Patricia, James, Roseanne, Annemarie. *Education:* Glasgow University, M.A. (first-class honors), 1961; Pembroke College, Oxford, B.Litt., 1963. *Politics:* Labour. *Religion:* Roman Catholic.

ADDRESSES: Home—7 Arundel Dr., Bishopbriggs, Glasgow G64 3JF, Scotland. *Office*—Department of English, University of Glasgow, Glasgow G12 8QQ, Scotland.

CAREER: Writer. *Military service:* British Army, 1950-52; became sergeant.

MEMBER: Catholic Education Commission for Scotland, Newman Society.

WRITINGS:

Jonathan Swift: The Brave Desponder, Southern Illinois University Press, 1982.

George Orwell: The Age's Adversary, Macmillan, 1985.

(Contributor) Ken Simpson, editor, *Henry Fielding: Justice Observed,* Vision Press, 1985.

The Literature of Guilt: From "Gulliver" to Golding, Macmillan, 1988.

Nineteen Eighty-Four: Past, Present, and Future, Twayne's Masterwork Studies, 1989.

Tom Jones: Adventure and Providence, Twayne's Masterwork Series, 1991.

Lord of the Flies: Fathers and Sons, Twayne's Masterwork Studies, 1992.

WORK IN PROGRESS: A book on James Joyce; a book on the English Novel from Hardy to the Second World War; articles on Charles Dickens, James Joyce, George Eliot, Anthony Burgess, and Thomas More, and on education and religion.

SIDELIGHTS: According to *Times Literary Supplement* reviewer F.S.L. Lyons, Patrick Reilly presents an "informative and frequently illuminating" study in *Jonathan Swift: The Brave Desponder.* The critic observed that Reilly presents a picture of the English satirist with which some scholars would violently disagree; the author "places Swift firmly in a seventeenth-century rather than in an eighteenth-century context," Lyons wrote, "and sees him as essentially a backward-looking man." "One senses that in this brilliant and provocative book the stimulation of just such counter-currents is an important part of the author's aim," added the critic.

BIOGRAPHICAL/CRITICAL SOURCES:

PERIODICALS

Times Literary Supplement, October 15, 1982.

*   *   *

RIEDMAN, Sarah R(egal)   1902-

PERSONAL: Born April 20, 1902, in Kishiniev, Rumania; became U.S. citizen, 1918; daughter of Benjamin and Hilda (Gdansky) Regal; married Maurice F. Riedman, June 26, 1921; married second husband, Elton T. Gustafson, December 8, 1953 (died, 1969); children: (first marriage) Olin, Eric. *Education:* Hunter College (now Hunter College of the City University of New York), B.A., 1926; New York University, M.S., 1928; Columbia University, Ph.D., 1935.

ADDRESSES: Home—7 Palmetto Way, Jensen Beach, FL 33457.

CAREER: Hunter College (now Hunter College of the City University of New York), New York City, instructor,

1926-30; Brooklyn College (now Brooklyn College of the City University of New York), Brooklyn, 1930-52, began as instructor, became assistant professor of biology; freelance scientific writer, 1952-58; Hoffmann-LaRoche, Inc., Nutley, NJ, director of medical literature, 1958-67, consultant, 1967—. Lecturer on science for young people.

MEMBER: American Association for Advancement of Science, Authors League, Authors Guild of America, American Medical Writers Association (fellow), New York Academy of Sciences, Sigma Xi.

WRITINGS:

How Man Discovered His Body, Young World Books, 1947, revised edition, Abelard, 1966.
The Physiology of Work and Play, Dryden, 1950.
Water for People, H. Schuman, 1951, revised edition, Abelard, 1961.
Grass, Our Greatest Crop, Thomas Nelson, 1952.
Your Blood and You, H. Shuman, 1952, revised edition published as *Your Blood and You: The Story of Circulation,* Abelard, 1963.
(With Albert Schatz) *The Story of Microbes,* Harper, 1952.
Food for People, Abelard, 1954, 2nd revised edition, 1976.
The World through Your Senses, Abelard, 1954, revised edition, 1962.
Let's Take a Trip to a Skyscraper, Abelard, 1955.
Let's Take a Trip to a Fishery, Abelard, 1956.
Our Hormones and How They Work, Abelard, 1956, revised edition published as *Hormones: How They Work,* 1973.
Antoine Lavoisier: Scientist and Citizen, Thomas Nelson, 1957, revised edition, Abelard, 1967.
Men and Women behind the Atom, Abelard, 1959.
Let's Take a Trip to a Cement Plant, Abelard, 1959.
Charles Darwin, Holt, 1959.
Shots without Guns: The Story of Vaccination, Rand McNally, 1960, published as *The Story of Vaccination,* Bailey Bros. & Swinfen, 1974.
Trailblazer of American Science, Rand McNally, 1961.
Masters of the Scalpel, Rand McNally, 1962.
World Provider: The Story of Grass, Abelard, 1962.
Naming Living Things: The Grouping of Plants and Animals, Rand McNally, 1963.
(With husband, Elton T. Gustafson) *Portraits of Nobel Laureates in Medicine and Physiology,* Abelard, 1963.
Clang, Clang: The Story of Trolleys, Rand McNally, 1964.
(With Clarence C. Green) *Benjamin Rush: Physician, Patriot, Founding Father,* Abelard, 1964.
(With Charles H. Carter) *Drugs in Neurospastic Disorders,* C. C Thomas, 1965.
(With E. T. Gustafson) *Home Is the Sea: For Whales,* Rand McNally, 1966.
(Editor) Suzanne Loebl, *Fighting the Unseen: The Story of Viruses,* Abelard, 1967.

(Editor) Loebl, *Exploring the Mind,* Abelard, 1968.
((With Gustafson) *Focus on Sharks,* Abelard, 1969.
(Editor) Matt Warner, *Your World—Your Survival,* Abelard, 1970.
Heart, Western Publishing, 1974.
Trees Alive, Lothrop, 1974.
(With Ross Witham) *Turtles: Extinction, or Survival?,* Abelard, 1974.
How Wildlife Survives Natural Disasters, McKay, 1977.
Sharks, F. Watts, 1977.
Allergies, F. Watts, 1978.
Gardening without Soil, F. Watts, 1978.
Have You Ever Seen a Shell Walking?, McKay, 1978.
Spiders, F. Watts, 1979.
Diabetes, F. Watts, 1980.
Odd Habitats of Land Animals, McKay, 1980.
Biological Clocks, Crowell, 1982.
The Good Looks Skin Book, Messner, 1983.

Also contributor to *World Encyclopedia, Book of Knowledge, Basic Everyday Encyclopedia,* and to magazines.

WORK IN PROGRESS: (With Dr. Neg Tsai) *Psychiatry in China;* and *The Ends of the World, Poles Apart,* a book about the Antarctic and Arctic regions.*

* * *

RIGA, Peter J(ohn) 1933-

PERSONAL: Born October 29, 1933, in Buffalo, NY; son of John and Margaret (Cannito) Riga. *Education:* Catholic University of Louvain, Ph.D., 1954, S.T.D., 1958; Catholic University of Washington, M.S., 1962; University of San Francisco, J.D., 1977; University of California, Berkeley, J.S.D., 1980. *Religion:* Roman Catholic.

ADDRESSES: Home—8927 Gaylord Dr., No. 143, Houston, TX 77024. *Office*—Notre Dame University, Notre Dame, IN 46556.

CAREER: Ordained to Catholic priesthood, Louvain, Belgium, 1958; St. John Vianney Seminary, East Aurora, NY, professor of dogmatic theology, 1961, librarian, 1962; Notre Dame University, Notre Dame, IN, professor of theology, 1965—.

MEMBER: Theological Society of America, Catholic Philosophical Association, American Library Association, Catholic Library Association, Catholic Council on Civil Liberties.

WRITINGS:

Sin and Penance, Bruce, 1962.
Catholic Thought and Crisis, Bruce, 1963.
Peace on Earth: A Commentary, Herder & Herder, 1963.

A Guide to Pacem in Terris for Students, Paulist Press, 1964.

John XXIII and the City of Man, Newman, 1966.

The Church Renewed, Sheed, 1966.

The Church and Revolution, Bruce, 1967.

The Church Made Relevant, Fides, 1967.

Be Sons of Your Father, Alba, 1969.

Death of the American Republic, Associated Press, 1980.

Right to Die or Right to Live?, Associated Faculty Press, 1981.

Human Rights as Human and Christian Realities, Associated Faculty Press, 1982.

WORK IN PROGRESS: Interest in Theology; Gratia Christi, Grace and the Christian; Catholic Social Thought; Law, Jurisprudence, and the History of Law.*

*   *   *

RIGGS, John R(aymond) 1945-

PERSONAL: Born February 27, 1945, in Beech Grove, IN; son of Samuel H. (a chemical engineer) and Lucille (a bookkeeper; maiden name, Ruff) Riggs; married Cynthia Perkins, September 2, 1967 (divorced, 1976); married Carole Gossett, July 1, 1988; children: (first marriage) Heidi Ann, Shawn Justin; (second marriage) Flint Anderson, Susan Anderson. *Education:* Indiana University—Bloomington, B.S., 1967, M.A., 1968; University of Michigan, graduate study, 1970-71.

ADDRESSES: Home and office—Rt. 2, Box 320, Greencastle, IN 46135.

CAREER: Teacher of English and athletic coach at schools in Greencastle, IN, 1968-75; quality control night foreman at factory in Greencastle, 1975-78; DePauw University, Greencastle, crew chief for river research, 1979—, archives researcher, 1983—; high school football coach, 1983-88; writer. Member of board of directors of Oakala Lake Corp., 1975-76, 1989-91; member of Madison Township Volunteer Fireman.

WRITINGS:

MYSTERY NOVELS

The Last Laugh, Dembner, 1984.

Let Sleeping Dogs Lie, Dembner, 1985.

The Glory Hound, Dembner, 1986, published as *Hunting Ground,* Jove, 1992.

Haunt of the Nightingale, Dembner, 1988.

Wolf in Sheep's Clothing, Dembner, 1989.

One Man's Poison, Dembner, 1991.

Dead Letter, Barricade-Dembner, 1992.

OTHER

Also author of other novels, a musical, and song lyrics.

Four of Riggs's novels have been published in Japan.

SIDELIGHTS: John R. Riggs told *CA:* "I did not choose writing. It chose me. I started my first novel in the summer of 1972 while I was still teaching. Since then I've written at least fifteen unpublished novels, one unpublished musical, and lyrics for more than one hundred songs. At the same time I worked at anything, including carpentry, splitting wood, hunting, and trapping.

"I plan to continue writing as long as there is hope for publication (perhaps even if not). I did not know in the beginning how hard it would be to get a novel published. I might never have started, though I have since decided there is nothing else I want to do, no other way I would rather live.

"To write is to live free—free to fail, free to hope and dream, free to wander wherever my mind leads me. It's the freedom of childhood, with all its aches and pains, rejections and humiliations, and glorious possibilities that always seem to run one step ahead of me. It's the feeling that this day belongs to me and no one else. And no matter how tired or discouraged or frustrated I become, I have no one to blame except myself. There's something satisfying in that—and magical.

"My mysteries are set in the mythical town of Oakalla, Wisconsin, which is based on my hometown of Mulberry, Indiana, and is (I hope) a good representative of small-town America. My protagonist is Garth Ryland, editor and publisher of the *Oakalla Reporter.* Garth is a man of principle, but is also wryly aware of his own fallibility. He is a self-proclaimed 'duck' (a plodder rather than a prancer), a dogged seeker of truth, and while a romantic at heart, a realist in the face of life.

"Garth's search for the answers that puzzle him are in many ways my search for the answers that puzzle me. Why do we commit crimes against each other? What motivates each and every one of us to do good or to do evil or to fall somewhere in between? Why do some triumph where others fail? Is it luck, the cut of the cards, circumstance, or something born within us that drives us to both greatness and despair?

"More than anything else Garth finds that we are each unique, each with our own stories to tell, and that simple descriptions are usually inadequate for even the 'simplest' among us. And it is his interactions with the varied and colorful characters that live in Oakalla that are the heart of my mysteries."

BIOGRAPHICAL/CRITICAL SOURCES:

PERIODICALS

Tribune Books (Chicago), July 3, 1988, p. 4.

RIORDAN, Michael 1946-

PERSONAL: Born December 3, 1946, in Springfield, MA; son of Edward John (a postal clerk) and Evelyn (a secretary; maiden name, Hnizdo) Riordan; married Linda Michelle Goodman (an artist), April 8, 1979. *Education:* Massachusetts Institute of Technology, S.B., 1968, Ph.D., 1973.

ADDRESSES: Home—P.O. Box 130, La Honda, CA 94020. *Office*—Cheshire Books, 514 Bryant St., Palo Alto, CA 94301.

CAREER: Massachusetts Institute of Technology, Cambridge, postdoctoral research associate in physics, 1973-75; Cheshire Books, Palo Alto, CA, editor and publisher, 1976—. Instructor at Cabrillo College, 1978-80. Research Scientist, University of Rochester, 1985-87.

MEMBER: International Solar Energy Society, American Association for the Advancement of Science, American Physical Science Society, Northern California Solar Energy Association (member of board of directors, 1980-81; vice-president, 1982), Sigma Xi.

WRITINGS:

(With Bruce Anderson) *The Solar Home Book,* Brick House, 1976.
(Editor with Tom Gage and Richard Merrill) *Energy Primer,* Delta Books, 1978.
(Editor) *The Day after Midnight: The Effects of Nuclear War,* Cheshire Books, 1982.
The Hunting of the Quark, Simon & Schuster, 1986.
(With Anderson) *The New Solar Home Book,* Brick House, 1987.
(With David N. Schramm) *The Shadows of Creation: Dark Matter and the Structure of the Universe,* W. H. Freeman & Co., 1991.

Contributor to *Technology Review* and *New Scientist.*

SIDELIGHTS: Michael Riordan commented: "From my experience in high-energy physics, I have derived an intense interest in bringing the discoveries of modern science and technology to an educated lay audience. I am particularly concerned that the philosophical underpinnings and assumptions behind modern science be made explicit in my works."

BIOGRAPHICAL/CRITICAL SOURCES:

PERIODICALS

Los Angeles Times Book Review, October 31, 1982.
New York Times Book Review, October 31, 1982; September 27, 1987; March 31, 1991.*

ROBACKER, Earl Francis 1904-

PERSONAL: Born April 11, 1904, in Panther, PA; son of Francis A. and Anna C. (Huguenin) Robacker; married Ada Fenner, March 16, 1929. *Education:* East Stroudsburg State College, B.S., 1928; New York University, M.A., 1931, Ph.D., 1941.

ADDRESSES: Home—White Plains, NY 10605.

CAREER: Public school teacher of English in South Sterling, PA, 1922-24, and Easton, PA, 1926-28; White Plains Public Schools, White Plains, NY, teacher of English, 1928-59, division director of decentralized high school, 1960-68. Lecturer at New York University, 1945-49. Historical consultant to National Park Service, 1970-74.

AWARDS, HONORS: Historic Schaefferstown citation for distinguished service, 1972; with wife, Ada Robacker, Incentive Award for distinguished service from National Park Service, 1973; with Ada Robacker, silver loving cup from Kurztown Folk Festival, 1974, for twenty-five years of service; distinguished alumnus award, East Stroudsburg State College, 1980.

WRITINGS:

Pennsylvania German Literature, University of Pennsylvania Press, 1942.
Pennsylvania Dutch Stuff, University of Pennsylvania Press, 1944.
(With wife, Ada F. Robacker) *Pennsylvania German Cooky Cutters and Cookies* (monograph), Plymouth Meeting, 1946.
Touch of the Dutchland, A. S. Barnes, 1965, reissued as *Arts of the Pennsylvania Dutch,* 1968.
Old Stuff in Up-Country Pennsylvania, A. S. Barnes, 1973.
(With Ada Robacker) *Spatterware and Sponge: Hardy Perennials of Ceramics,* A. S. Barnes, 1978.

Contributor to *Antiques,* newspapers, and other journals. Antiques editor of *Pennsylvania Folklife Quarterly,* 1954.

WORK IN PROGRESS: What to Read about the Pennsylvania Dutch; A Selective, Annotated Summary, 1930-1980, Associated University Presses, 1982.

SIDELIGHTS: Earl Francis Robacker has a reading knowledge of Pennsylvania Dutch dialects.*

*   *   *

ROBARDS, Sherman M(arshall) 1939-

PERSONAL: Born October 7, 1939, in New York City; son of Sidney M. (a business executive) and C. Louise (Sherman) Robards; married Susan Lee Hayes, January

14, 1962 (divorced, 1981); children: John M., Jeffrey S. *Education:* Hamilton College, B.A., 1961.

ADDRESSES: Office—*New York Times,* 229 West 43rd St., New York, NY 10036.

CAREER: New York Herald Tribune, New York City, assistant financial editor, 1963-66; *Fortune,* New York City, associate editor, 1966-67; *New York Times,* New York City, staff writer, 1967-73, wine columnist, 1979—. Commentator on *The Topic Is Wine,* WQXR Radio, New York City, 1972—. Lecturer on wine.

MEMBER: International Wine and Food Society, Confrerie des Chevaliers du Tastevin (officier-commandeur), Commanderie de Bordeaux (governor), Compagnons de Beaujolais, Confrerie St. Etienne.

WRITINGS:

Wine Cellar Journal, Quadrangle, 1974.
New York Times Book of Wine, Quadrangle, 1976.
California Wine Album, Workman, 1981.
A Votre Sante, Bantam, 1982.

Contributor to wine journals.*

*   *   *

ROBERTSON, Heather Margaret 1942-

PERSONAL: Born March 19, 1942, in Winnipeg, Manitoba, Canada; daughter of Harry (a teacher) and Margaret (Duncan) Robertson; married David Hildebrandt, May 16, 1968 (divorced, 1974); married Andrew Marshall (a broadcaster and publisher), July 11, 1975; children: (second marriage) Aaron. *Education:* University of Manitoba, B.A., 1963; Columbia University, M.A., 1964. *Religion:* None.

ADDRESSES: Home—175 Sherwood Ave., Toronto, Ontario, Canada M4P 2A9. *Agent*—Bella Pomer, 22 Shallmar Ave., Toronto, Ontario, Canada.

CAREER: Winnipeg Tribune, Winnipeg, Manitoba, reporter and critic, 1964-66; Canadian Broadcasting Corp., Winnipeg, radio producer and television story editor in public affairs, 1968-71; *Maclean's* magazine, television critic and feature writer, 1971-75; free-lance writer, 1971—.

MEMBER: Association of Canadian Radio and Television Artists, Writers' Union of Canada.

AWARDS, HONORS: Woodrow Wilson fellow, 1963-64; first novel award, *Books in Canada,* 1983, for *Willie: A Romance;* fiction prize, Canadian Authors' Association, 1984, for *Willie: A Romance;* talking book of the year, Canadian National Institute for the Blind, 1984; second prize

for best fiction book of the year, Periodical Marketers of Canada, 1984.

WRITINGS:

Reservations Are for Indians, James Lorimer, 1970.
Grass Roots, James Lorimer, 1973.
Salt of the Earth, James Lorimer, 1974.
A Terrible Beauty: The Art of Canada at War, James Lorimer, 1977.
The Flying Bandit, James Lorimer, 1981.
Willie: A Romance (fiction), James Lorimer, 1983.
(Editor) *A Gentleman Adventurer: The Arctic Diaries of Richard Bonnycastle,* Lester, Orpen & Dennys, 1984.
(Editor) Charles Boulton, *I Fought Riel,* James Lorimer, 1985.
Lily: A Rhapsody in Red (fiction), James Lorimer, 1986.
Igor: A Novel of Intrigue (fiction), James Lorimer, 1989.
More Than a Rose: Prime Ministers, Wives and Other Women, Seal, 1991.

Contributor to Canadian magazines; contributor to anthologies, including *Her Own Woman,* Macmillan, 1975; *Canadian Newspapers: The Inside Story,* Hurtig, 1980; and *From the Country: Writings about Rural Canada,* Camden House, 1991; columnist for the *Canadian Forum.*

SIDELIGHTS: Heather Margaret Robertson once commented, "I am fascinated by the literary potential of real people and real events, the attempt to render the raw material of specific human experience into words which not only capture its truth but reveal its meaning. I like to explore the boundaries between journalism and fiction, the point at which a real human being becomes a 'character' in a book."

BIOGRAPHICAL/CRITICAL SOURCES:

PERIODICALS

Christian Science Monitor, January 19, 1985.
Globe and Mail (Toronto), October 5, 1991, p. C10.

*   *   *

ROBERTSON, Keith (Carlton) 1914-1991 (Carlton Keith)

PERSONAL: Born May 9, 1914, in Dows, IA; died September 23, 1991, in Hopewell, NJ; son of Myron Clifford (a merchant) and Harriet (Hughes) Robertson; married Elisabeth Hexter (a bookseller), November 2, 1946; children: Christina Harriet, Hope Elisabeth, Jeffry Keith. *Education:* U.S. Naval Academy, B.S., 1937. *Politics:* Republican. *Religion:* Protestant.

ADDRESSES: Home—P.O. Box 398, Booknoll Farm, Hopewell, NJ 08525. *Agent*—c/o Viking Press, 40 West 23rd St., New York, NY 10010.

CAREER: Refrigeration engineer, 1937-41; employee of publishing firm, 1945-47; free-lance writer, 1947-58; Bay Ridge Specialty Co., Inc. (ceramics manufacturer), Trenton, NJ, president, 1958-69; writer, 1969—. Trustee, Hopewell Museum. *Military service:* U.S. Navy, radioman on battleship, 1931-33; officer, on destroyers, 1941-45; now Captain, U.S. Naval Reserve.

AWARDS, HONORS: Spring Book Festival award, 1956, for *The Pilgrim Goose;* William Allen White Award, 1961, for *Henry Reed, Inc.;* William Allen White Award, 1969, Pacific Northwest Library Association's "Young Reader's Choice" award, 1969, and Nene award, 1970, all for *Henry Reed's Baby Sitting Service;* New Jersey Institute of Technology awards, both 1969, for *New Jersey* and *The Money Machine.*

WRITINGS:

FOR CHILDREN; FICTION

Ticktock and Jim, illustrated by Wesley Dennis, Winston, 1948, published as *Watch for a Pony,* Heinemann, 1949.
Ticktock and Jim, Deputy Sheriffs, illustrated by Everett Stahl, Winston, 1949.
The Dog Next Door, illustrated by Morgan Dennis, Viking, 1950.
The Missing Brother, illustrated by Rafaello Busoni, Viking, 1950.
The Lonesome Sorrel, illustrated by Taylor Oughton, Winston, 1952.
The Mystery of Burnt Hill, illustrated by Busoni, Viking, 1952.
Mascot of the Melroy, illustrated by Jack Weaver, Viking, 1953.
Outlaws of the Sourland, illustrated by Isami Kashiwagi, Viking, 1953.
Three Stuffed Owls, illustrated by Weaver, Viking, 1954.
Ice to India, illustrated by Weaver, Viking, 1955.
The Phantom Rider, illustrated by Weaver, Viking, 1955.
The Pilgrim Goose, illustrated by Erick Berry, Viking, 1956.
The Pinto Deer, illustrated by Kashiwagi, Viking, 1956.
The Crow and the Castle, illustrated by Robert Grenier, Viking, 1957.
Henry Reed, Inc., illustrated by Robert McCloskey, Viking, 1958.
If Wishes Were Horses, illustrated by Paul Kennedy, Harper, 1958.
Henry Reed's Journey, illustrated by McCloskey, Viking, 1963.
Henry Reed's Baby-Sitting Service, illustrated by McCloskey, Viking, 1966.
The Year of the Jeep, illustrated by W. T. Mars, Viking, 1968.

The Money Machine, illustrated by George Porter, Viking, 1969.
Henry Reed's Big Show, illustrated by McCloskey, Viking, 1970.
In Search of a Sandhill Crane, illustrated by Richard Cuffari, Viking, 1973.
Tales of Myrtle the Turtle, illustrated by Peter Parnall, Viking, 1974.
Henry Reed's Think Tank, Viking Kestrel, 1986.

FOR ADULTS; UNDER PSEUDONYM, CARLTON KEITH

The Diamond-Studded Typewriter, Macmillan, 1958, published as *A Gem of a Murder,* Dell, 1959.
Missing, Presumed Dead, Doubleday, 1961.
Rich Uncle, Doubleday, 1963.
The Hiding Place, Doubleday, 1965.
The Crayfish Dinner, Doubleday, 1966, published as *The Elusive Epicure,* Hale, 1966.
A Taste of Sangria, Doubleday, 1968, published as *The Missing Book-Keeper,* Hale, 1969.

OTHER

The Wreck of the Saginaw, illustrated by Jack Weaver, Viking, 1954.
The Navy: From Civilian to Sailor, illustrated by Charles Geer, Viking, 1958.
New Jersey, McCann, 1969.

Robertson's manuscripts are included in the May Massee Collection, Emporia State University, Kansas.

WORK IN PROGRESS: A mystery story for adults and a book for children.

SIDELIGHTS: Keith Robertson's children's books describe "the mythical middle-America upon which nostalgia for a golden past is built," says Joan McGrath in *Twentieth-Century Children's Writers.* In such books as the award-winning *Henry Reed, Inc.* and *Henry Reed's Baby-Sitting Service,* Robertson relates the adventures of Henry Reed, an all-American boy who somehow manages to get himself into—and out of—some of the stickiest jams since Tom Sawyer floated down the Mississippi. Similarly, his other children's books share with the Henry Reed stories a focus on intelligent, mischievous boys who get involved in complicated situations. In all of these books, which are aimed at a ten- to fifteen-year-old audience, the main characters are portrayed as wholesome, harmless boys who have great fun exploring the world around them. Robertson also writes mystery novels for adults that employ the same kind of fast-paced, action-packed plots as his children's books.

Robertson was born in Dows, Iowa, in 1914, but his father's wanderlust led the family all over the Midwest; they eventually lived in Minnesota, Kansas, Wisconsin, Oklahoma, Missouri, and Iowa. Robertson's first book, *Ticktock and Jim,* described his life growing up on a farm in Missouri. Robertson says: "I started writing when I was a boy in school. Oddly, people will encourage a boy if he says he wants to be a doctor, engineer, or scientist but will tell him he is being impractical if he says he wants to write books. For this and various other reasons, I abandoned my ambition to become a writer for some years."

Upon graduating from high school, Robertson was unsure of what he wanted to do with his life, so he joined the U.S. Navy and spent two years at sea as a radioman. Robertson went straight from sea to school, getting a degree from the U.S. Naval Academy. But four years after graduation, with World War II heating up, he was called back to service. Even though he was an officer, Robertson remembers long stretches of boredom at sea punctuated by brief periods of excitement, according to an autobiographical sketch in *More Junior Authors.* Looking out over the calm sea from the deck of his ship, he made up his mind to become a writer, and after the war ended he was able to make that dream come true.

"My first book for young people was largely an accident," Robertson comments. After returning from the war, "I was selling books for a firm which specialized in children's books," he continues. "Naturally I read a number and decided to try one myself. Once I had one in print I was hooked." He quit his job, and soon he and his wife, Elisabeth, moved to a small farm in New Jersey. Elisabeth decided to open a used book store, and books soon filled all areas of the house. His three children loved animals, so the barns were filled with horses, sheep, goats, rabbits, geese, chickens, dogs and cats. Amidst this chaos Robertson wrote many of his books for children, which were often set in the semi-rural area in which he lived. Robertson notes that his children "provided [him] with many of the incidents and ideas for [his] books. They have never been in any sense characters in any of them, however."

Robertson has developed an interesting technique for writing his books: "For some time I have been dictating my books on tape. I find this works well if one can dictate uninterruptedly. It is particularly good for conversation. However, one tends to be too verbose and the first version needs to be cut considerably." Robertson has vowed that he will continue to write for children, because "the letters an author gets from young readers are enough to make his labors eminently worthwhile and enjoyable."

BIOGRAPHICAL/CRITICAL SOURCES:

BOOKS

Fuller, Muriel, editor, *More Junior Authors,* H. W. Wilson, 1963, pp. 171-172.

McGrath, Joan, essay on Keith Robertson, *Twentieth-Century Children's Writers,* 3rd edition, St. James Press, 1989, pp. 832-833.

PERIODICALS

Horn Book, April, 1971.
Library Journal, June 15, 1968; January 15, 1970; January 15, 1971.
New York Times Book Review, July 28, 1968.
School Library Journal, February, 1978.*

*   *   *

ROBINSON, Jeffrey 1945-

PERSONAL: Born October 19, 1945, in Long Beach, NY; son of S. Jesse and Jessie (Roth) Robinson; married Aline Benayoun, 1985; children: Joshua Seth. *Education:* Temple University, B.S., 1967.

ADDRESSES: Home—39 Montagu Square, London W1H 1TJ, England. *Agent*—Leslie Gardner, Artellus Ltd., 235 East 79th St., New York, NY 10021.

CAREER: Writer for television, radio, magazines, and newspapers, 1962—. *Military service:* U.S. Air Force, 1967-71; became captain.

MEMBER: International PEN.

WRITINGS:

Bette Davis: Her Stage and Film Career, Proteus, 1982.
Teamwork: Comedy Teams in the Movies, Proteus, 1983.
The Risk Takers: Portraits of Money, Ego, and Power, Allen & Unwin, 1985.
Pietrov and Other Games (novel), New English Library, 1985, published as *The Pietrov Game,* Pocket Books, 1987.
Minus Millionaires; or, How to Blow a Fortune, Unwin-Hyman, 1987.
The Ginger Jar (novel), New English Library, 1987, Pocket Books, in press.
Yamani: The Inside Story of the Man Who Ran OPEC (biography), Simon & Schuster, 1987.
Rainier & Grace, Atlantic Monthly, 1989.

Contributor of more than six hundred articles and stories to American and British periodicals.

WORK IN PROGRESS: Naked Chic, a nonfiction book, and *Witch Hazel Crude,* a novel.

SIDELIGHTS: Jeffrey Robinson once told *CA* that he lived from 1971 to 1982 in southern France, where he supported himself by writing magazine features and short stories. He then moved to England to concentrate on writing books. One of these books, *The Risk Takers,* is a study of some of Britain's most controversial businessmen. The author makes no attempt in this work to whitewash the activities which led these figures to financial success, and he includes a wide variety of personalities in his seventeen commentaries. Many of his subjects have been scrutinized by national regulatory agencies or the police and castigated by the press. According to *Times Literary Supplement* reviewer J. H. C. Leach, Robinson "makes some pleasingly astringent comments on his risk-takers, whom he is far from viewing with starry eyes." *The Risk Takers* was a British best seller in 1985 partly because, as Leach emphasized, Robinson "has clearly been at pains to get his facts right."

In some of his subsequent books, the author has also taken a look at other wealthy, influential personalities. *Minus Millionaires; or, How to Blow a Fortune* is the off-beat sequel to the *Risk Takers*. Looking at the flip side of the coin, Robinson studies the foibles and follies of men and women who have squandered fortunes. *Yamani: The Inside Story of the Man Who Ran OPEC* tells about Saudi Arabia's former oil minister who for two dozen years was one of the most powerful men on earth. Related Robinson, "Zaki Yamani emerges with charm, intelligence, and world-class charisma. Often pictured as the man who blackmailed the West with the oil embargo in 1973 and the spectacular price rises of 1979, both his successes and his failures lay in the wonderful contradiction of his being a Harvard smoothy, a political moderate, and just an old fashioned Bedouin camel trader."

BIOGRAPHICAL/CRITICAL SOURCES:

PERIODICALS

Globe and Mail (Toronto), April 22, 1989.
Irish Independent (Dublin), September 24, 1985; September 26, 1985.
Lloyds List, August 17, 1985; July 12, 1986.
Los Angeles Times, March 29, 1988.
Punch, December 11, 1985; September 24, 1986.
Sunday Times (London), June 29, 1986.
Sunday Tribune (Dublin), September 29, 1985.
Times Literary Supplement, September 6, 1985.
Today, July 17, 1986.
Wall Street Journal, August 27, 1985.
Washington Post Book World, July 2, 1989.*

*   *   *

ROCKWOOD, Roy
   See McFARLANE, Leslie (Charles)

RODDENBERRY, Eugene Wesley   1921-1991
   (Gene Roddenberry)

PERSONAL: Professional name, Gene Roddenberry; born August 19, 1921, in El Paso, TX; died of a heart attack, October 24, 1991, in Los Angeles, CA; son of Eugene Edward (a master sergeant in U.S. Army) and Carolyn Glen (Goleman) Roddenberry; married Eileen Anita Rexroat, June 20, 1942 (divorced July, 1969); married Majel Barrett (an actress), August 6, 1969; children: (first marriage) Darleen Roddenberry, Dawn Alison R. Compton; (second marriage) Eugene Wesley, Jr. *Education:* Los Angeles City College, A.A., 1941; attended University of California, Los Angeles, University of Miami, and Columbia University. *Politics:* Democrat.

ADDRESSES: Home—Los Angeles, CA. *Office*—c/o Paramount Pictures, 5555 Melrose Ave., Hollywood, CA 90038. *Agent*—Leonard Maizlish, 10573 Pico Blvd., Suite 246, Los Angeles, CA 90064.

CAREER: Pan American Airways, pilot, 1945-49; Los Angeles Police Department, Los Angeles, CA, 1949-53, began as police officer, became sergeant; creator, producer, and writer of television programs and motion pictures, 1953—. President of Norway Productions, Inc. *Military service:* U.S. Army Air Forces, 1941-45; became second lieutenant; received Distinguished Flying Cross and Air Medal.

MEMBER: Writers Guild of America, West (past member of executive council), Science Fiction Writers of America, World Future Society, Academy of Television Arts and Sciences (former member of board of governors), American Civil Liberties Union, Caucus for Producers, Writers, and Directors, National Space Society (board of directors), Planetary Society, L-5 Society, Academy of Science Fiction, Fantasy, and Horror Films, Los Angeles Police Band Associates (board of directors), Explorers Club (New York City), Bel Air Country Club, La Costa Country Club.

AWARDS, HONORS: Writers Guild of America Award for best teleplay of the year, 1958, for "Helen of Abiginian," an episode of *Have Gun Will Travel;* Golden Reel awards from Film Council of America, 1962, for *The Lieutenant,* and 1966, for *Star Trek;* special award from Twenty-fourth World Science Fair Convention, 1966, for *Star Trek;* Hugo Award for best dramatic presentation from World Science Fiction Convention, 1967, for "The Menagerie," and 1968, for "The City on the Edge of Forever," both episodes of *Star Trek;* Brotherhood Award from National Association for the Advancement of Colored People (NAACP), 1967; Gold Medal from *Photoplay* for most popular television show, 1968, for *Star Trek;* special plaque from Twenty-sixth World Science Fiction Convention, 1968, for *Star Trek;* Image Award from the

NAACP, 1969, for *Star Trek;* Emmy Award for Children's Entertainment Series from the Academy of Television Arts and Sciences, 1975, for animated series *Star Trek;* Freedom Through Knowledge Award from National Space Club, 1979, for lifetime achievement; American Freedom Award from the National Space Club, 1980, for lifetime achievement; Star on Hollywood Walk of Fame, 1985; three Emmy Awards and the Peabody Award, all 1987, all for *Star Trek: The Next Generation;* Jack Benny Memorial Award from the March of Dimes, 1990, for lifetime achievement; commendation from Civil Aeronautics Board for rescue efforts for 1948 Pan Am airlines crash. D.H.L. from Emerson College, 1973; D.Litt. from Union College, 1977; D.Sc. from Clarkson College, 1981.

WRITINGS:

(With Stephen E. Whitfield) *The Making of "Star Trek,"* Ballantine, 1968.

The Questor Tapes (based on the pilot; also see below), adapted by D. C. Fontana, Ballantine, 1974.

Star Trek: The Motion Picture, Simon & Schuster, 1979.

(With Susan Sackett) *The Making of "Star Trek: The Motion Picture,"* Simon & Schuster, 1980.

(With Sackett) *"Star Trek": The First Twenty-five Years,* Pocket Books, 1991.

Author of over eighty scripts for television programs, including *Goodyear-TV Playhouse, The Kaiser Aluminum Hour, Chevron Theatre, Four Star Playhouse, Dragnet, Jane Wyman Presents, Naked City,* and *Have Gun Will Travel.* Contributor of articles to aeronautical magazines. Contributor of poetry to *Embers* and *New York Times.* Poems included in anthologies.

TELEVISION; CREATOR, WRITER, AND PRODUCER

The Lieutenant, National Broadcasting Co. (NBC), 1960-61.

Star Trek (series), NBC, 1966-69.

Genesis II (pilot), Columbia Broadcasting System (CBS), 1973.

Planet Earth (pilot), American Broadcasting Co. (ABC), 1974.

The Questor Tapes (pilot), NBC, 1974.

Spectre (pilot), NBC, 1977.

TELEVISION; CREATOR AND EXECUTIVE PRODUCER

Star Trek: The Next Generation (syndicated series), 1987—.

MOTION PICTURES; CREATOR, WRITER, AND PRODUCER

Pretty Maids All in a Row, Metro-Goldwyn-Mayer, (MGM), 1970.

Star Trek: The Motion Picture, Paramount, 1979.

MOTION PICTURES; EXECUTIVE CONSULTANT

Star Trek II: The Wrath of Khan, Paramount, 1982.

Star Trek III: The Search for Spock, Paramount, 1984.

Star Trek IV: The Voyage Home, Paramount, 1986.

Star Trek V: The Final Frontier, Paramount, 1989.

Star Trek VI: The Undiscovered Country, Paramount, 1991.

ADAPTATIONS: The original seventy-nine episodes of the *Star Trek* television series have been presented on videocassette by Paramount Home Video, and numerous episodes made available on RCA VideoDiscs. NBC-TV broadcasted an original animated series based on the *Star Trek* television series from September 8, 1973 to August 30, 1975. The first five *Star Trek* motion pictures have been made available on videocassette by Paramount Home Video.

SIDELIGHTS: When Gene Roddenberry launched the television series *Star Trek* on September 8, 1966, he had no way of knowing that it would become one of the largest popular phenomenons of the late twentieth century. When the series celebrated its twenty-fifth anniversary in 1991, there was more to celebrate than just the original seventy-nine episodes: there were five movies, a second thriving television series, *Star Trek: The Next Generation,* one hundred novels, and nearly half a billion dollars in merchandising sales. Roddenberry, who told *Starlog*'s Ian Spelling that he made *Star Trek* because he thought "science fiction hadn't been done well on television," had been the unifying force behind *Star Trek* from the very beginning.

Star Trek had a shaky start after its 1966 debut, never rising higher than fiftieth in the Neilsen ratings and battling constant threats of cancellation. But the support of its audience and science fiction writers prevented studio executives from canceling the series. In time Roddenberry and *Star Trek* acquired a following of loyal fans—known as Trekkies—who started over three hundred fifty fan clubs whose members attend over four hundred annual conventions and publish more than five hundred *Star Trek* fanzines, small-circulation periodicals dedicated to every aspect of the show. Reruns of the seventy-nine original episodes have been syndicated by 114 stations in the United States and in 131 foreign markets, and *Star Trek*'s rerun audience of ten million fans expanded seventy-seven percent between 1977 and 1979. Prompted by the continued success of the series, Paramount Pictures began producing several *Star Trek* movies starring the original television series cast. According to reviewers, Roddenberry's brain child—whether a motion picture or a television series—captures its audience's fancy by being entertaining, by appealing to its viewers' emotional needs, by establishing a standard of credibility, and by presenting likable characters.

At first Roddenberry drew people to *Star Trek* by providing something for everyone. William Shatner, star of the series, observed that the show presented action, adventure, and villains for children, philosophical concepts for adults, science for technology buffs, and even psychedelia for hippies. Steve Simels, expressing a common critical viewpoint in *Stereo Review,* stated that "the damned thing was more consistently entertaining, on the most basic level, than any other American TV action series before or since."

People also enjoy *Star Trek* because, like all science fiction, it provides a means of escaping from the ordinary. As the Apollo space missions expanded the imagination of the American television audience, people were increasingly intrigued by the possibilities of extraterrestrial life forms. David Gerrold observed in *The World of "Star Trek"* that "instead of merely a world, *Star Trek* made its fans aware of a whole galaxy, a universe, made them realize that Earth was merely one speck of matter in a tiny corner of space and time." *Star Trek*'s mission "to explore strange new worlds, to seek out new life and new civilizations, to boldly go where no man has gone before" appeals to the escapist in every individual.

Though setting an adventure-drama series in outer space was not an innovation in television programming, a number of observers held that Roddenberry handled the idea more effectively than his predecessors. Gerrold offered this analogy: "*Star Trek* wasn't the first place the concept of man exploring the galaxy appeared—but then again, Shakespeare wasn't the first writer to deal with Troilus and Cressida. Shakespeare just did it a little bit better. And so did Roddenberry." Gerrold emphasized that the series established a high level of quality for later science fiction programs. He believed that *Star Trek* was "one of the finest television formats ever conceived." Likewise, syndicated columnist Gary Deeb calculated that—on a scale of one to ten—*Star Trek* is a nine as well as "one of the best programs ever produced by television."

Television's filming techniques and technological advances in special effects made science fiction presentations increasingly realistic and appealing during the 1960s. Additionally, the U.S. space program stimulated interest in the sci-fi genre because people related more to space exploration. In Isaac Asimov's opinion, *Star Trek* signified television's effort to acquire a broad-based audience for a science fiction series, reported Desmond Ryan in the *Detroit News Magazine.*

Roddenberry gave *Star Trek* a format similar to that of *Wagon Train,* a weekly television program about pioneers traveling westward armed with existing American myths.

Although the western frontier was once regarded as the final frontier, the idea of people carrying American myths into the unknown persisted, observed William Blake Tyrrell in the *Journal of Popular Culture. Star Trek* premiered during the 1960s when American myths were being challenged, contended Ryan, and the program explored the issue of alienation from religion, morality, and government. In the process, some critics believe, *Star Trek* appealed to the viewers' emotional needs and revived their self-esteem as a nation.

Roddenberry told a *Penthouse* interviewer: "I think that the purpose of all writing is to reach people and say something you believe in and think is important. . . . [W]ith fiction and drama and a certain amount of adventure you reach them easier and you reach more of them and you can infiltrate your messages into them." One of the clearest messages that Roddenberry tried to get across was that humans needed to be more tolerant of diversity, to open their mind to experiencing different cultures. Gerrold argues that *Star Trek* was special because "Once in a while [the crew] would come up against a culture that might be just a little more compassionate, or a little more aware, or a little more *alive.*" *Newsweek* reviewer Charles Leerhsen thinks that the audience appreciates these "lessons in liberalism" in the same way they appreciate the lessons provided by television shows such as *The Honeymooners* and *All in the Family.*

Tyrrell remarked that "*Star Trek* is a product of the dreams and nightmares of the 60's. It came to those who needed the confidence and triumph of the American past while fearing a present that foreboded the disappearance of the American way." In the 1970s, when Watergate and the trauma of Vietnam continued to challenge many of America's fundamental beliefs, *Star Trek* appeared in syndicated reruns around the country and gained increasing popularity among viewers who longed for old-fashioned heroes and a release from the disillusionment of current events. *Newsweek*'s Jack Kroll, for instance, believed that "the idolizing of *Star Trek* may be a nostalgia for the image of the self-confident, generous but ready-to-fight America."

In addition to fortifying its audience's confidence as a nation, *Star Trek* conveys messages of belonging and diversity in facing the future. Roddenberry showed that humans can indeed survive in the universe even though there are complex and often dangerous creatures. Roddenberry told *Starlog:* "If there was one theme in all of *Star Trek* it was that the glory of our universe is its infinite combinations of diversity. That all beauty comes out of its diversity. What a terrible, boring world it would be if everyone agreed with everyone else." According to *"Star Trek" Lives!,* the series maintains that "we can learn to live together as human beings, as intelligent beings even when we are not 'human,' and we can learn to cherish our diversity and not destroy each other." Roddenberry further explained in the *Detroit News Magazine* that the series "didn't say be tolerant, be a good guy. We said be civilized. Welcome diversity because it's exciting."

Star Trek possesses a spiritual quality, too. It has been compared to a religious journey of spiritual transcendence, for it attempts to reconcile spiritual values and civilization. As Betsy Caprio noted in *"Star Trek": Good News in Modern Images*, *Star Trek*'s audience sees "that there is a journey to take, a quest that will bring meaning to their lives."

Most importantly, people like *Star Trek* because it is believable. Roddenberry wanted to create a science fiction story about real people and the human condition. He worked for credibility, realizing that "people aren't going to stop eating or sleeping or getting dressed in a few hundred years. We're trying to imagine, based on what we know today, what they'll most likely be eating or wearing or thinking." To achieve this, he presented plots and characters to which the audience could relate.

Though set in the twenty-third century, each episode is a morality play concerning twentieth-century attitudes, Gerrold commented. And Karin Blair observed in *Meaning in "Star Trek"* that "the great enterprise at stake is dramatizing our own encounters with the unknown and hence the alien within ourselves, as well as the alien beyond." For Blair and for many other critics, contemporary man is the leading figure in *Star Trek* because viewers identify the program's episodes as stories about themselves. Gerrold held this to be *Star Trek*'s greatest strength. "Imagine a story where the hero does everything that he believes to be correct—and the audience identifies with him totally in his actions because they believe them to be correct too," he instructed. "Imagine that he is ultimately wrong in some of his decisions—when (and if) he learns better, then so will the audience."

Star Trek's characters are especially easy to relate to because "they are representative of the American Sphere of Influence today," Gerrold noted, adding that the characters' "attitudes, their manner of speaking, their ways of reacting, even their ways of making love, are all contemporary." Plus the crew operates from believable motives and human concerns. For example, viewers recognized Mr. Spock, the science officer, as an alienated individual. Spock is half human and half Vulcan, a race which prides itself on being absolutely logical and unencumbered by emotions. Spock does not have a place in either the human or the Vulcan world, but he does belong in terms of the *Enterprise*'s society. Here he knows what is expected of him, and he responds accordingly.

In general, Spock behaves like a Vulcan and subjugates his personal feelings and ambitions to reason and his sense of duty, but he is not actually emotionless as "The Naked Time" revealed. In this episode, a disease which eliminates emotional defenses spreads through the Enterprise. Spock simply isolates himself from the rest of the crew and cries. By the fourth *Star Trek* movie it becomes even more clear that Spock can experience emotion, and the fact that he has hid those emotions because of his pride makes the character even more human. Blair agreed that "although half-human, perhaps because half-human, Spock is consummately humane." He is not like his human peers, but he stays aboard the Enterprise because the crew needs him. He influences and changes those around him, who affect Spock in the same manner. And Spock becomes more human over time in spite of his alien nature.

The *Enterprise*'s doctor, on the other hand, acts as a mother image on the ship, according to Blair. "Bones" McCoy genuinely cares for people as individuals. He is a mixture of Ben Casey, the medieval Good Physician, and the biblical Good Samaritan. Viewers see the conflict of an emotional person in a rational profession in McCoy. Blair observed that he is "a personality characterized by emotion and intuition, a professional commitment to caring for the physical and emotional health of others, a personal commitment to the inherited notions of self-sacrificing love and guilt."

In Blair's estimation, McCoy represents traditional values, including compassion, and Spock symbolizes a passage to the future paved with reason. They appear to dislike each other, but their outward incompatibility comes from the shock of seeing themselves in each other. As representations of two extremes, McCoy and Spock define their captain's internal struggle with compassion and reason. Captain Kirk—the balance of McCoy and Spock—is the perfect man for the future, Blair maintained: well-rounded, vigorous, intelligent, capable, sensitive, and in control of his emotions.

These characters proved to be immensely popular, particularly Spock. He enjoyed overwhelming popular support, so much so that Gerrold claimed that "the network, and a good many fans, would have been just as happy if the show had been called *The Mr. Spock Hour*." Other cast members were also very popular. Uhura, the communications officer, shows women to be responsible and valuable. Scotty, the chief engineer, is a man of action; the helmsman Sulu obediently carries out orders, and the Russian Chekov symbolizes future generations. The popularity of these characters was illustrated when the first *Star Trek* movie appeared nearly ten years after the television series suspended production. "Do you realize this is the first motion picture to come along where all the characters are already set with the public?" James Doohan, *Star Trek*'s

Scotty, asked Steve Hoffman in a *Cincinnati Enquirer* interview. "The fans are going to go and see all their friends up on the screen, the same friends they have seen for 12 and 13 years."

The fans' devotion has been rewarded by several *Star Trek* movies, which have had box office and video grosses exceeding half a billion dollars. In many ways the movies follow the same familiar format of the original television series: the crew of the Enterprise is called upon to deal with a problem somewhere in the galaxy, and in the course of solving the problem they learn more about themselves and each other. Though each of the movies has been successful at the box office, they have received mixed reviews. Some critics hailed the improvement in special effects that make the movies so exciting, while others thought that the enhanced technology had de-emphasized the characters that most fans went to the movies to see. Almost every critic noted the increasing age of the crew members, and Peter Travers, reviewing *Star Trek V: The Final Frontier* for *Rolling Stone,* commented that "what could have been a heartfelt valedictory to the troops in the September of their light-years becomes instead a losing battle to keep gray hairs, crow's-feet and unsightly bulges at bay."

Roddenberry was involved with each of the movies, acting as writer and producer for *Star Trek: The Motion Picture,* and as executive consultant for *Star Trek II: The Wrath of Khan, Star Trek III: The Search for Spock, Star Trek IV: The Voyage Home, Star Trek V: The Final Frontier* and *Star Trek VI: The Undiscovered Country.* He recalled in *Variety:* "I invented the term 'executive story consultant,' and set the rules: That they have to show me everything they do . . . from the first lines [through] all the rewrites and the dailies." By making sure that the crew did not kill foreign life forms arbitrarily and by ensuring that the characters behaved consistently with their long past, Roddenberry was able to maintain a continuity that makes the *Star Trek* movies far more than just sequels exploiting an audience's desire to see the characters yet again.

In October, 1987, buoyed by the successes of the movies, Roddenberry created and became executive producer for a new television series, *Star Trek: The Next Generation.* This program, set seventy-eight years after the final *Star Trek* episode, operates with an entirely new set of characters, but the show's premise remains the same. Bill Turque, writing in *Newsweek,* said "*The Next Generation* carries the heart of the old, campy *Star Trek:* cheesy uniforms, dialogue laced with Aquarian hokum, silly aliens and the endearingly naive vision of a future in which humanity survives to explore the stars."

Though viewers find much in the new series familiar, Turque remarked: "There's little New Frontier-style meddling with cultures that worship computers or adapt Na-

zism as a way of life. Instead, *The Next Generation* is tinged with an '80s sobriety and an ambivalence about the use of power. 'These are not the '60s and the issues are not that simple,' says Roddenberry. 'Now we write shows with maybe not a clear-cut answer.' " However, *Rolling Stone* reviewer Benjamin Svetkey thought that "if anything, the new *Star Trek* is even more like a civics lesson from your high-school librarian."

Perhaps the biggest challenge in creating the new show was coming up with a new set of characters. Svetkey argued that the biggest success has been Captain Kirk's replacement, Jean-Luc Picard: "Played by the British actor Patrick Stewart, the *Enterprise*'s new commander is older than William Shatner's swashbuckling James Kirk—and considerably more complex." Roddenberry did not try to replace Mr. Spock—a difficult task—but instead gathered a crew that comes from all over the galaxy, including an android named Data and a Klingon named Worf.

Initially the show met with resistance from Trekkies who couldn't imagine the show without Spock, Bones, Sulu, and Uhura. But consistently strong scripts and quality acting eventually won over a large audience, and in 1991 *Star Trek: The Next Generation* was, according to the *Detroit News,* "the most-watched dramatic program on TV, and the highest-rated weekly syndicated series in the country." Roddenberry told *Penthouse* that "like it or not, television is literature" and "literature—usually fiction—is responsible for more changes in public opinion than news articles or sermons." Roddenberry has certainly had a huge influence on public opinion, for his programs have turned science fiction from an outcast into a mainstay of the entertainment business. Judging from the wide audience that has consistently watched both the television series and the movies, science fiction Roddenberry-style will continue to attract fans well into the twenty-third-century world of Roddenberry's creation.

BIOGRAPHICAL/CRITICAL SOURCES:

BOOKS

Blair, Karin, *Meaning in "Star Trek,"* Anima Books, 1976.

Caprio, Betsy, *"Star Trek": Good News in Modern Images,* Sheed, Andrews & McMeel, 1978.

Contemporary Literary Criticism, Volume 17, Gale, 1981.

Gerrold, David, *The World of "Star Trek,"* Ballantine, 1972.

Lichtenberg, Jacqueline, Sondra Marshak, and Joan Winston, *"Star Trek" Lives!,* Bantam, 1975.

PERIODICALS

Best of Starlog, Volume 2, 1981.

Christian Century, January 16, 1980; August 18-25, 1982.

Cincinnati Enquirer, December 16, 1979.

Detroit News, September 26, 1991.
Detroit News Magazine, December 9, 1979.
Journal of Popular Culture, spring, 1977; fall, 1979.
Maclean's, June 14, 1982.
Nation, August 21-28, 1982.
New Republic, December 29, 1979.
Newsweek, January 29, 1968; December 19, 1979; December 22, 1986; June 19, 1989; October 22, 1990.
New York, December 24, 1979; June 21, 1982; June 19, 1989.
New Yorker, December 17, 1979; June 28, 1982.
New York Times, October 15, 1967; August 25, 1968; February 18, 1969; June 4, 1969; January 21, 1979; November 23, 1979; December 8, 1979; January 14, 1980; October 9, 1980; December 23, 1981; May 23, 1982; June 4, 1982; June 8, 1982; June 27, 1982; July 4, 1982; September 8, 1982.
Popular Science, December, 1967.
Progressive, March, 1980.
Rolling Stone, July 22, 1982; September 2, 1982; December 3, 1987; July 13-27, 1989.
Saturday Evening Post, May, 1979.
Saturday Review, June 17, 1967; February 2, 1980.
School Library Journal, May, 1980.
Science Digest, December, 1979.
Science Fiction and Fantasy Book Review, December 9, 1979.
Show Business, May 9, 1970.
Starlog, January, 1983; July, 1986; November, 1986.
Stereo Review, March, 1980.
Time, January 15, 1979; December 17, 1979; June 7, 1982; June 26, 1989.
USA Today, September, 1982.
Variety, December 17, 1986.
Voice of Youth Advocates, April, 1980; August, 1980.
Washington Post Book World, January 27, 1980.

*   *   *

RODDENBERRY, Gene
See RODDENBERRY, Eugene Wesley

*   *   *

ROMPKEY, Ronald (George) 1943-

PERSONAL: Born February 10, 1943, in St. John's, Newfoundland, Canada; son of William H., Sr., and Margaret (Fudge) Rompkey; married Noreen Golfman (a university professor), August 5, 1983. *Education:* Memorial University of Newfoundland, B.A., 1965, B.Ed., 1966, M.A., 1968; King's College, London, Ph.D., 1972.

ADDRESSES: Office—Department of English Language and Literature, Memorial University of Newfoundland, St. John's, Newfoundland, Canada A1C 5S7.

CAREER: University of Alberta, Edmonton, lecturer in English, 1976-77, 1979-82; University of Saskatchewan, Saskatoon, assistant professor of English, 1977-79; University of Lethbridge, Lethbridge, Alberta, assistant professor of English, 1982-83; University of Maine at Orono, visiting professor of English, 1983-84; Memorial University of Newfoundland, St. John's, assistant professor, 1984-86, associate professor of English, 1986—. Honorary *aide de camp* to Governor-General of Canada, 1984-88, to Lieutenant-Governor of Newfoundland, 1986-91. *Military service:* Canadian Naval Reserve, 1961—, commander, Naval Control of Shipping Organization, Newfoundland, 1988—; commanding officer of HMCS *Cabot,* 1984—; present rank, commander.

MEMBER: Association of Canadian University Teachers of English, Writers' Union of Canada, American Society for Eighteenth-Century Studies, Modern Language Association of America, Royal Society of Arts (fellow), Royal Historical Society (fellow).

WRITINGS:

(Editor and author of introduction) *Expeditions of Honour: The Journal of John Salusbury in Halifax, Nova Scotia, 1749-1753,* University of Delaware Press, 1982.
Soame Jenyns, Twayne, 1984.
Grenfell of Labrador: A Biography, University of Toronto Press, 1991.
(Editor and author of introduction) Elliott Merrick, *The Long Crossing and Other Labrador Tales,* University of Main Press, in press.

SIDELIGHTS: Ronald Rompkey once told *CA:* "My writing is concerned with the life and literature of the eighteenth century, particularly the activities surrounding the life of Samuel Johnson. In *Expeditions of Honour,* I first set out to establish biographical details for John Salusbury (1707-1762), the father of Mrs. Hester Thrale (later Piozzi), close friend and biographer of Johnson. I then wanted to publish Salusbury's observations about the founding of Halifax, Nova Scotia, since they are the only private, unofficial observations of these events known.

"In the case of *Soame Jenyns,* I was interested in setting straight the life of an individual with a long political career in England and a considerable publication record. Even though Jenyns wrote poetry as well as prose works on politics, economics, and religion, his reputation had been determined by a crushing review—written by Johnson and published in the *Literary Magazine*—of his tract *A Free Inquiry Into the Nature and Origin of Evil* (1757). My intention was to show that this event overshadowed much of what he accomplished as a writer and a public figure."

Rompkey more recently added: "In my biography of Sir Wilfred Grenfell, I am attempting to change the perception of Grenfell as a heroic doctor and missionary and to concentrate on his role as social reformer in Newfoundland and Labrador."

*   *   *

ROSS, Mary Adelaide Eden
See PHILLPOTTS, (Mary) Adelaide Eden

*   *   *

RUBIN, Lillian B(reslow)   1924-

PERSONAL: Born January 13, 1924, in Philadelphia, PA; daughter of Sol and Rae (Vinin) Breslow; married Seymour Katz, March 6, 1943 (divorced); married Henry M. Rubin (a writer), March 4, 1962; children: Marcy. *Education:* University of California, Berkeley, B.A. (with great distinction), 1967, M.A., 1968, Ph.D., 1971; postdoctoral study, 1971-72. *Religion:* Jewish.

ADDRESSES: Home and office—823 Craft Ave., El Cerrito, CA 94530. *Agent*—Rhoda Weyr, William Morris Agency, 1350 Avenue of the Americas, New York, NY 10019.

CAREER: University of California, Cowell Memorial Hospital, Berkeley, research sociologist, 1971-72; Wright Institute, Berkeley, CA, professor of sociology and psychology, 1972-76; licensed marriage, family, and child counselor in private practice, 1972—; writer, 1972—. Senior research associate, Institute for Scientific Analysis, 1972—; consultant to National Center for the Prevention and Control of Rape, 1976-77; senior research associate, Institute for the Study of Social Change, University of California, Berkeley, 1977—. Lecturer at Mills College, 1973; visiting professor at University of California, Berkeley, 1979.

MEMBER: American Sociological Association, Society for the Study of Social Problems, Sociologists for Women in Society, Society for the Psychological Study of Social Issues, National Council on Family Relations, California Association of Marriage and Family Counselors, Phi Beta Kappa.

AWARDS, HONORS: National Institute of Mental Health grants, 1974-76, 1976-79, and 1979-82; Copeland fellow, Amherst College, 1977.

WRITINGS:

Busing & Backlash: White against White in an Urban School District, University of California Press, 1972.
Worlds of Pain: Life in the Working-Class Family, Basic Books, 1976.
Women of a Certain Age: The Midlife Search for Self, Harper, 1979.
Intimate Strangers: Men and Women Together, Harper, 1983.
Just Friends: The Role of Friendship in Our Lives, Harper, 1985.
Quiet Rage: Bernie Goetz in a Time of Madness, Farrar, Straus, 1986.
Erotic Wars: What Happened to the Sexual Revolution?, Farrar, Straus, 1990.

CONTRIBUTOR

Norene Harris and others, editors, *The Integration of American Schools,* Allyn & Bacon, 1975.
Arlene S. Skolnick and Jerome H. Skolnick, editors, *Family in Transition,* 2nd edition, Little, Brown, 1977.
Martha Kirkpatrick, editor, *Women's Sexuality,* Plenum, 1979.
Lynne A. Bond and James C. Rosen, editors, *Primary Prevention of Psychopathology,* Volume 4: *Promoting Competence and Coping during Adulthood,* University Press of New England, 1979.

OTHER

Contributor of numerous papers to professional journals.

SIDELIGHTS: Lillian B. Rubin is a social psychologist and writer who embarked on her career in mid-life. Rubin's books offer perspectives on such modern sociological issues as integration of public schools, the plight of the blue collar worker, and the sometimes strained relations between men and women. In her works, the author draws upon in-depth interviews to reach conclusions not only about individuals but also about American society at large. *Ms.* magazine reviewer Barbara Garson notes that Rubin's books are often "sophisticated and moving expressions of sadness, loneliness, and anger." The critic continues: "Rubin's footnotes show that she is very well grounded in the method and literature of the social sciences. It is with high courage that she departs from her training and takes the risk, particularly great for a woman, of being labeled 'unscientific.' She does so in order to present a fuller—almost novelistic—picture of the world she knows from her own background."

Rubin told *CA:* "All my works reflect my own life." She was born in Philadelphia and was brought up in a one-parent, working-class family. She herself married young and followed so-called traditional paths for a woman until the mid-1960s, when she became active in political and social causes. She was just under forty when she entered the University of California, Berkeley, as a candidate for a Bachelor's degree. By the time she turned fifty, Rubin had earned a Ph.D. in sociology, was a licensed marriage and family counselor, and was a research associate at the Institute for Scientific Analysis in San Francisco.

Rubin's first book, *Busing and Backlash: White against White in a California School District,* was published in 1972. The work details the difficulties experienced by the Richmond Unified School District when a busing policy was proposed in 1968. In the *Progressive,* David E. Gillespie writes: "Ms. Rubin set out in two and a half years of research to learn *why* the whites of the Richmond Unified School District in the San Francisco Bay area acted as they did in 1968 to 1971 on the busing issue. A finding larger than the real trauma over busing soon began to emerge." Rubin's work was praised for its empathy toward those whites opposed to busing, even though she favored the practice herself. Gillespie concludes: "This is a book that for the most part will hold the interest of all Americans concerned more than casually with the unification of our people in something other than name."

In her next book the author turned to another pressing national problem—discontent in the working-class. *Worlds of Pain: Life in the Working-Class Family* is based on fifty lengthy interviews with white, working-class couples with an emphasis on the particular strains and conflicts in their lives. Although some critics have faulted Rubin for the selectivity of her sample, most agree that the work illuminates some distinct problems associated with a blue collar lifestyle. "Rubin does well in documenting the current desperate state of family life for many Americans," claims Kathleen McCourt in the *American Journal of Sociology.* ". . . Rubin has added significantly to literature on the family and the working class." *Society* contributor Gerald Handel deems *Worlds of Pain* "both clearly drawn and heartfelt, the work of an observer who has also been a participant. There are many keenly noted details and perceptive comments." The critic adds: "It says something for the power and accuracy of qualitative methods that this study conducted by a woman of working-class origins confirms so many findings of earlier studies conducted by researchers—men and women—of middle-class background."

Perhaps the best known of Rubin's books is *Women of a Certain Age: The Midlife Search for Self.* Once again the author bases her study on in-depth interviews with 160 women aged thirty-five to fifty-four, women who have faced a variety of daunting transitions in middle age. *Progressive* correspondent Ann Morrissett Davidon writes that the book "is lean and the message clear: Women must and will find their own identities." Davidon notes, however, that *Women of a Certain Age* is not "one more exhor-

tation of the 'me decade' urging women to grab for themselves, indulge themselves, pamper themselves. It is rather an encouragement for midlife women to do the hard work of overcoming their fears and anger, to emerge into a world that needs their skills and strengths too long confined exclusively to the home or in self-effacing 'volunteerism.'" *Contemporary Sociology* contributor Rose Laub Coser likewise observes that Rubin "writes with fervor and gives us a gripping story. She understands her respondents not only because she has the ability to uncover what is latent but because she feels free to call on her own experiences to help her understand her material."

Rubin has continued to publish books that confront social issues from a personal, psychological perspective. In *Quiet Rage: Bernie Goetz in a Time of Madness,* she explores the motives that led the infamous "subway vigilante" to shoot four black teenagers in New York City. *Just Friends: The Role of Friendship in Our Lives* documents the difficulties encountered by close friends in a society that tends to consign friendship to an ancillary role, and *Erotic Wars: What Happened to the Sexual Revolution?* documents American sexuality in an aging but "liberated" population. In the *Village Voice,* Wendy Kaminer maintains that Rubin's books depart from standard self-help treatises because they are more thoughtful and scholarly, with less resort to easy answers and advice. Rubin, concludes the reviewer, "has a talent for talking about relationships and psychoanalytic theories without resorting to psychobabble." A *New York Times Book Review* correspondent notes that Rubin's work "does not offer answers . . . but it raises serious questions about traditional assumptions, thus marking a way to answers."

Rubin told *CA:* "I came to writing late in life, after I entered college as a freshman at age 39. My first paper, written for a freshman English course, earned me a C—a situation my perfectionist soul determined to remedy as quickly as possible. My early writing endeavors soon earned better grades, but remained a painful and difficult task until I found the courage to speak in a voice that was mine about issues that had some deep personal meaning to me. We all have protective ways of presenting self to the world—ways we long ago learned would bring the approbation we need. But to be artistically successful, a writer must dare to put out the true self and risk the judgments that will inevitably come. For any of us, there's probably nothing more difficult; for a writer, there's also nothing more rewarding."

BIOGRAPHICAL/CRITICAL SOURCES:

BOOKS

Contemporary Issues Criticism, Volume 2, Gale, 1984.

PERIODICALS

American Journal of Sociology, November, 1977.
Contemporary Psychology, October, 1977; March, 1980.
Contemporary Sociology, September, 1973; March, 1978; May, 1981.
Los Angeles Times, September 25, 1986; January 22, 1987.
Ms., November, 1977, pp. 43-4.
New Republic, August 15, 1983.
New York Review of Books, April 23, 1987.
New York Times, September 29, 1986.
New York Times Book Review, November 4, 1979; September 15, 1985.
Progressive, November, 1972; December, 1979.
Social Science Quarterly, March, 1974.
Society, September-October, 1977.
Village Voice, November 5, 1985; September 18, 1990.
Washington Post, October 19, 1979; June 7, 1983; October 18, 1986.
Washington Post Book World, September 1, 1985; August 19, 1990.*

—*Sketch by Anne Janette Johnson*

* * *

RUKEYSER, William Simon 1939-

PERSONAL: Born June 8, 1939, in New York City; son of Merryle Stanley and Berenice (Simon) Rukeyser; married Elisabeth Mary Garnett, November 21, 1963; children: Lisa Ellen, James William. *Education:* Princeton University, A.B., 1961; additional study, Christ's College, Cambridge, 1962-63.

ADDRESSES: Home—1509 Rudder Ln., Knoxville, TN 37919. *Office*—Whittle Communications, 505 Market St., Knoxville, TN 37902.

CAREER/WRITINGS: Wall Street Journal, New York City, copyreader, 1961-62, staff reporter in Europe, 1963-67; *Fortune* magazine, New York City, associate editor, 1967-71, member of board of editors, 1971-72, managing editor, 1980-86; Time, Inc., director of international business development, 1986-88; *Money* magazine, New York City, managing editor, 1972-80; Whittle Communications, Knoxville, TN, editor-in-chief, and executive vice-president, 1988-91, chairman and chief executive officer of Whittle Books, 1991—. Commentator, *Good Morning America,* ABC-TV, 1978-85, CBS Radio Stations News Service, 1979-86. Director, Knoxville Symphony Orchestra and Knoxville Museum of Art.

MEMBER: Union County (NJ) Medical Society (member of judges committee, 1977-80), National Mental Health Association (co-chairman of capital campaign committee, 1984-85).

RUSHFORD, Patricia H(elen) 1943-

PERSONAL: Born December 4, 1943, in Rugby, ND; daughter of Hjalmar and Dagny (a homemaker; maiden name, Olsen) Anderson; married Ronald G. Rushford (a self-employed investor), 1963; children: David W., Caryl E. *Education:* Clark College, Vancouver, WA, A.A.S., 1972; Western Evangelical Seminary, Portland, OR, M.A., 1991. *Religion:* Christian.

ADDRESSES: Home and office—3600 Edgewood Dr., Vancouver, WA 98661.

CAREER: Registered nurse, 1972; author, speaker, 1980—; counselor, 1991—.

MEMBER: Pacific Northwest Writers, Oregon Christian Writers Association.

AWARDS, HONORS: Writer of the Year Award from Mount Hermon Christian Writer's Conference, 1983; Writer of the Year Award in Christian Parenting from Warner Pacific Writer's Conference, 1984, for *Have You Hugged Your Teenager Today?* and *The Care and Feeding of Sick Kids.*

WRITINGS:

Have You Hugged Your Teenager Today?, Fleming Revell, 1982.
The Care and Feeding of Sick Kids, Ronald N. Haynes, 1983, revised as *Caring for Your Sick Child,* Fleming Revell, 1983.
The Help, Hope, and Cope Book for People with Aging Parents, Fleming Revell, 1985.
Kristen's Choice (young adult novel), Augsburg, 1986.
What Kids Need Most in a Mom, Fleming Revell, 1986.
(With Jean Lush) *The Emotional Phases of a Woman's Life,* Fleming Revell, 1987.
Love Is a Many Splintered Thing, Fleming Revell, 1990.
Lost in the Money Maze: Finding Your Way Through, Aglow Publications, in press.

Contributing editor of *PRN* (newsletter of Nurses for Laughter), and *Christian Parenting Today.*

WORK IN PROGRESS: The Humpty Dumpty Syndrome: Putting Yourself Back Together Again, for Revell; *Putting Your Child Back Together Again: Healing for the Broken Child.*

SIDELIGHTS: "I began my writing career in 1980," Patricia H. Rushford told *CA.* "With each new book I write, I think, 'There. I've run out of words. I've no more ideas.' Then I think, '*I'm* going to take a break.' But it never happens. Words keep coming. Ideas flow like a hundred waterfalls, pooling into different streams. So I write, and write, and write. And I love every minute of it."

Along with her work as an author, Rushford speaks on topics including parenting, women's issues, money management, aging, and marriage and relationships. A registered nurse with an M.A. in Christian counseling, Rushford conducts workshops and retreat programs across the United States.

Rushford has appeared on radio and television talk shows in the United States and Canada, including "AM Northwest," "Prime Time America," and "Focus on the Family."

*   *   *

RYE, Anthony
   See YOUD, (Christopher) Samuel

S

SACHS, Michael L(eo) 1951-

PERSONAL: Born September 7, 1951, in New York, NY; son of George (a company president) and Eva (an artist) Sachs; married Fay Ades (a public health nutritionist), August 22, 1981. *Education:* Union College, Schenectady, NY, B.S. (cum laude), 1973; Hollins College, M.A., 1975; Florida State University, Ph.D., 1980; Loyola College, M.S., 1989. *Politics:* Democrat. *Religion:* Jewish. *Avocational interests:* Exercising, going to movies, reading.

ADDRESSES: Home—804 Elkins Ave., Elkins Park, PA 19117. *Office*—Department of Physical Education, 048-00, Temple University, Philadelphia, PA 19122.

CAREER: Universite du Quebec a Trois-Rivieres, assistant professor of sport psychology, 1980-83; University of Maryland at Baltimore, research project coordinator, department of pediatrics, 1983-89; Temple University, Philadelphia, PA, associate professor, 1989—. F. A. Davis Company, Philadelphia, sports medicine advisory board member, 1984-90; consultant to numerous organizations.

MEMBER: International Society of Sport Psychology, North American Society for the Psychology of Sport and Physical Activity, North American Society for the Sociology of Sport, American Psychological Association, American Association on Mental Retardation, American Alliance for Health, Physical Education, Recreation, and Dance, Association for the Advancement of Applied Sport Psychology (fellow; executive board member; health psychology committee chairperson, 1985-88; president, 1990-92), Society for the Advancement of Social Psychology, Running Psychologists, Pennsylvania Association for Health, Physical Education, Recreation, and Dance, Maryland Psychological Association (fellow; member of board of educational affairs, 1988-89), Psi Chi, Phi Epsilon Kappa (Florida State University chapter vice president, 1976-77; president, 1977-78), Phi Kappa Phi.

AWARDS, HONORS: Certificate of Merit, Florida Association for Health, Physical Education, and Recreation, 1976, 1977; outstanding dissertation award, Sport Psychology Academy of the National Association for Sport and Physical Education, 1981.

WRITINGS:

(Associate editor and contributor) *Psychology of Running,* Human Kinetics, 1981.
(Editor with Gary W. Buffone, and contributor) *Running as Therapy: An Integrated Approach,* University of Nebraska Press, 1984.
(Editor with Kevin L. Burke) *Directory of Graduate Programs in Applied Sport Psychology,* Association for the Advancement of Applied Sport Psychology, 1986, 2nd edition, 1989.

Also contributor to books, including *The Exercising Adult,* edited by Robert C. Cantu, Collamore, 1982; *Sports Medicine, Sports Sciences: Bridging the Gap,* edited by Cantu and William J. Gillespie, Collamore, 1982; *Mental Training for Coaches and Athletes,* edited by Terry Orlick, John T. Partington, and John H. Salmela, Coaching Association of Canada, 1982; *Sport in Perspective,* edited by Partington, Orlick, and Salmela, Coaching Association of Canada, 1982; *Psychological Foundations of Sport and Exercise,* edited by John M. Silva and Robert Weinberg, Human Kinetics, 1984; *Exercise and Mental Health,* edited by William P. Morgan and Stephen E. Goldston, Hemisphere Publishing, 1987; *Psychology of Sports, Exercise, and Fitness: Social and Personal Issues,* edited by L. Diamant, Hemisphere Publishing, 1991; and *Handbook on Research in Sport Psychology,* edited by R. N. Singer, M. Murphey, and L. K. Tennant, Macmillan, in press.

Also editor of a sport psychology column for the newsletter of the Society for the Advancement of Social Psychology, 1978-86; editor of the newsletter of Running Psychologists, 1979-83; official bibliographer of Running Psychologists, 1979-86; editor of the *Sport Sociology Academy Newsletter,* 1980-82; coeditor of the *Bulletin of the Canadian Society for Psychomotor Learning and Sport Psychology,* 1982-83; contributing editor to Division 47 newsletter of Running Psychologists, 1988-1990; contributor of more than thirty articles and reviews to physical education journals and sports magazines, including *Journal of Sport Behavior, Journal of Physical Education and Recreation, Runner's World,* and *Racing South;* editorial advisory board member of *Wellness Perspectives: Research, Theory and Practice* (formerly *Wellness Perspectives*), 1984—; editorial board member of *Journal of Applied Sport Psychology,* 1988—.

WORK IN PROGRESS: Research on psychology of running, particularly addiction to running, the "runner's high," and cognitive strategies used during running.

SIDELIGHTS: Michael L. Sachs once told *CA:* "My interests in exercise [and] sport psychology in general, and the use of running in particular, date back to 1973, when I discovered that I could integrate my academic interests in psychology with my participant interest in sports. I started reading and doing research in the area, and went on to get my Ph.D. in the field. I began running in 1975, and I have enjoyed it ever since. It has proven to be effective for me, as well as for many other individuals, in coping with stress and enhancing the quality of life (and perhaps the quantity as well).

"The field of exercise psychology offers many exciting avenues, in teaching, research, and practice, and anyone interested in integrating psychology with exercise and sport should be encouraged to pursue his or her interests. At the very least, one finds many personal rewards from regular participation in sport and physical activity."

*   *   *

SAINT-JACQUES, Bernard 1928-

PERSONAL: Born April 26, 1928, in Montreal, Quebec, Canada; son of Albert and Germaine (Lefebvre) Saint-Jacques; married Marguerite Fauquenoy (a professor), April 3, 1967. *Education:* Montreal University, B.A., 1949, Licence, 1954; Sophia University, M.A., 1962; Georgetown University, M.A., 1964; University of Paris, Doctorate, 1966.

ADDRESSES: Office—Department of Linguistics, University of British Columbia, Vancouver, British Columbia, Canada V6T 1W5, and Aichi Shukutoku University, Katahira, Nagakute, Nagakute-cho, Aichi-gun, Aichi 480-11, Japan (April-June and October-December).

CAREER: University of British Columbia, Vancouver, assistant professor, 1967-69, associate professor, 1969-78, professor of linguistics and Asian studies, 1978-90; Aichi Shukutoku University, Aichi, Japan, professor of linguistics and Asian studies, 1990—.

MEMBER: Linguistic Society of America, Linguistic Society of Japan.

WRITINGS:

Analyse structurale de la syntaxe du japonais moderne, Librairie C. Klincksieck, 1966, translation by author published as *Structural Analysis of Modern Japanese,* University of British Columbia Press, 1971.
Aspects sociolinguistiques du bilinguisme Canadien, International Center for Research on Bilingualism, 1976.
(Editor, with Howard Giles) *Language and Ethnic Interaction,* Pergamon, 1979.
(Editor, with Matsuo Soga) *Japanese Studies in Canada,* Carleton University, 1985.

Contributor to books, including *The Individual, Language and Society in Canada,* edited by W. H. Coons and others, Canada Council, 1977; *Aspects of Bilingualism,* edited by Michel Paradis, Hornbeam Press, 1978; *The Languages of Canada,* edited by J. K. Chambers, Didier, 1979; *Options Nouvelles en didactique du francais langue etrangere,* Didier, 1982; *The Canadian Encyclopedia,* Hurtig, 1985; *Royal Society of Canada,* Ottawa, 1986; *Atipa Revisite ou les itineraires de Parepou,* edited by M. Fauquenoy, L'Harmattan (Paris), 1989; and *Langue et Identite,* edited by N. Corbett, Les Presses de L'Universite Laval (Quebec), 1990. Also contributor to periodicals, including *Pacific Affairs, La Linguistique, General Linguistics, Foundations of Language, Bulletin de la Societe de linguistique de Paris, Language, Journal of Language and Social Psychology, Canadian Journal of Linguistics, Journal of Asian Studies, Visible Language,* and *Word.*

WORK IN PROGRESS: The use of languages in Japan, written in Japanese; recent changes in Japanese culture and society; conditions of successful trade with Japan.

*   *   *

SAMELSON, William 1928-

PERSONAL: Born September 21, 1928, in Sosnowiec, Poland; son of Harry and Balbina (Stibel) Samelson; married Rosa Salinas (a ballet dancer), August 22, 1954; children: James, Regina Faye, Henry, Morris. *Education:* University of Heidelberg, B.S., 1948; Western Reserve University (now Case Western Reserve University), B.A., 1950; Kent State University, M.A., 1954; University of Illinois, additional study, 1954-55; University of Texas, Ph.D., 1960.

Avocational interests: Playing tennis, running several miles every day.

ADDRESSES: Office—Trinity University, 715 Stadium Drive, San Antonio, TX 78284.

CAREER: San Antonio College, San Antonio, TX, professor of foreign languages, 1956—, Piper Professor, 1982—; Trinity University, San Antonio, adjunct professor, 1985—. *Military service:* U.S. Army, 1951-53.

MEMBER: American Teachers Association, Modern Language Association of America, Authors Guild, Authors League of America.

WRITINGS:

Gerhart Herrmann Mostar: A Critical Profile, Mouton, 1966.
(Editor) *Der Sinn des Lesens* (anthology), Odyssey, 1968.
All Lie in Wait (novel), Prentice-Hall, 1969.
The Sephardi Heritage: Romances and Songs of The Sephardim (monograph), Valentine, Mitchell, 1972.
English as a Second Language (textbook), Reston, *Phase One: Let's Converse,* 1973, 2nd edition, 1980, *Phase Two: Let's Read,* 1974, 2nd edition, 1982, *Phase Three: Let's Write,* 1975, 2nd edition, 1982, *Phase Four: Let's Continue,* 1979, *Phase Zero Plus,* 1981.
One Bridge to Life (novel), Clark Davis, 1989.
El Legado Sefaradi, Encuadernacior Progresso, 1990.

Contributor of short stories to magazines, including a series in *Jewish Forum.*

WORK IN PROGRESS: Between Two Worlds, a novel.

SIDELIGHTS: William Samelson once explained to *CA* that his writing has been motivated for the most part by World War II experiences (*All Lie in Wait* is a war book). He speaks German, French, Yiddish, Spanish, Russian, Polish, and Hebrew.

BIOGRAPHICAL/CRITICAL SOURCES:

PERIODICALS

Reconstructionist, May 23, 1969.

*   *   *

SAMUEL, Alan E(douard) 1932-

PERSONAL: Born July 24, 1932, in Queens, NY; son of Edgar Aaron and Hortense (Kesner) Samuel; married Doris Lichtenthal, June 10, 1953 (divorced, 1964); married Deborah Hobson, June 13, 1964 (divorced, 1973); married Valerie Stevens, February 15, 1975; children: (first marriage) Deborah Joan, Jean Carol, Katharine Ann, Elizabeth Rose; (second marriage) Alexandra Whit-

ney; (third marriage) Fraser, Roderick John, Kristen Ellen Jessica, Marion Catherine. *Education:* Hamilton College, B.A., 1953; Yale University, M.A., 1957, Ph.D., 1959.

ADDRESSES: Home—36 Glencairn Ave., Toronto, Ontario, Canada M4R 1M5.

CAREER: Yale University, New Haven, CT, instructor, 1959-63, assistant professor of classics, 1963-66; University of Toronto, University College, Toronto, Ontario, associate professor, 1966-67, professor of ancient history, 1967—. *Military service:* U.S. Naval Reserve, 1953-56; became lieutenant.

MEMBER: Comite Internationale de Papyrologie, American Philological Association (former director), Archeological Institute of America, American Society of Papyrologists (secretary-treasurer, 1968; president, 1973).

AWARDS, HONORS: Guggenhiem fellow, 1983-84.

WRITINGS:

Ptolemaic Chronology, Beck (Munich), 1962.
Alexander's Royal Journals, Historia, 1965.
The Mycenaeans in History, Prentice-Hall, 1966.
(With John F. Oates and C. Bradford Welles) *Yale Papyri in the Beinecke Rare Book and Manuscript Library,* American Society of Papyrologists, 1967.
(With W. Keith Hastings) *Death and Taxes: Ostraka in the Royal Ontario Museum,* A.M. Hakkert, 1971.
Greek and Roman Chronology: Calendars and Years in Classical Antiquity, Beck, 1972.
(With R.S. Bagnall) *Ostraka in the Royal Ontario Museum II,* Samuel Stevens, 1976.
Treasures of Canada, Samuel Stevens, 1980.
From Athens to Alexandria: Hellenism and Social Goals in Ptolemaic Egypt, Studia Hellenistica (Louvain), 1983.
The Promise of the West: The Greek World, Rome, and Judaism, Routledge, 1988.
The Shifting Sands of History, Publications of the Association of Ancient Historians, 1989.
(Contributor) *Hellenistic History and Culture,* University of California Press, 1992.

Contributor of articles to professional journals.

*   *   *

SATTERFIELD, Charles
See POHL, Frederik

SAWYER, Ruth 1880-1970

PERSONAL: Born August 5, 1880, in Boston, MA; died June 3, 1970; daughter of Francis Milton (an importer) and Ethelinda J. (Smith) Sawyer; married Albert C. Durand (a doctor), June 4, 1911; children: David, Margaret (Mrs. Robert McCloskey). *Education:* Columbia University, B.S., 1904. *Religion:* Unitarian.

CAREER: Short story writer and author of books for children. New York *Sun,* New York City, feature writer in Ireland, 1905, and 1907. Storyteller for the New York Lecture Bureau, beginning 1908, and started the first storytelling program for children at the New York Public Library.

AWARDS, HONORS: Newbery Medal, American Library Association, 1937, and Lewis Carroll Shelf Award, 1964, both for *Roller Skates;* Caldecott Medal, 1945, for *The Christmas Anna Angel* (illustrated by Kate Seredy), and 1954, for *Journey Cake, Ho!* (illustrated by Robert McCloskey); Regina Medal, Catholic Library Association, 1965; Laura Ingalls Wilder Medal, American Library Association, 1965, for her "substantial and lasting contribution to literature for children."

WRITINGS:

JUVENILES

A Child's Year-Book, illustrated by the author, Harper, 1917.
The Tale of the Enchanted Bunnies, Harper, 1923.
Tono Antonio, illustrated by F. Luis Mora, Viking Press, 1934.
Picture Tales from Spain, illustrated by Carlos Sanchez, F. A. Stokes, 1936.
Roller Skates, illustrated by Valenti Angelo, Viking Press, 1936, reprinted, Peter Smith, 1988.
The Year of Jubilo, illustrated by Edward Shenton, Viking Press, 1940, reprinted, 1970, (published in England as *Lucinda's Year of Jubilo,* Bodley Head, 1965).
The Least One, illustrated by Leo Politi, Viking Press, 1941.
Old Con and Patrick, illustrated by Cathal O'Toole, Viking Press, 1946.
The Little Red Horse, illustrated by Jay Hyde Barnum, Viking Press, 1950.
The Gold of Bernardino, privately printed, 1952.
Journey Cake, Ho!, illustrated by Robert McCloskey, Viking Press, 1953, reprinted, Puffin Books, 1978.
A Cottage for Betsy, illustrated by Vera Bock, Harper, 1954.
The Enchanted Schoolhouse, illustrated by Hugh Tory, Viking Press, 1956.

(With Emmy Molles) *Dietrich of Berne and the Dwarf-King Laurin: Hero Tales of the Austrian Tirol,* illustrated by Frederick Chapman, Viking Press, 1963.
Daddles: The Story of a Plain Hound-Dog, illustrated by Robert Frankenberg, Little, Brown, 1964.
My Spain: A Story-Teller's Year of Collecting, Viking Press, 1967.

CHRISTMAS STORIES

This Way to Christmas, Harper, 1916, revised edition, 1970, new edition illustrated by Maginal Wright Barney, Harper, 1924.
The Long Christmas, illustrated by V. Angelo, Viking Press, 1941, reprinted, 1966.
The Christmas Anna Angel, illustrated by Kate Seredy, Viking Press, 1944.
This Is the Christmas: A Serbian Folk Tale, Horn Book, 1945.
Maggie Rose: Her Birthday Christmas, illustrated by Maurice Sendak, Harper, 1952.
The Year of the Christmas Dragon, illustrated by Hugh Tory, Viking Press, 1960.
Joy to the World: Christmas Legends, illustrated by Trina S. Hyman, Little, Brown, 1966.

ADULT BOOKS

The Primrose Ring, Harper, 1915.
Seven Miles to Arden, Harper, 1916.
Herself, Himself, and Myself, Harper, 1917.
Doctor Danny (stories), illustrated by J. Scott Williams, Harper, 1918.
Leerie, illustrated by Clinton Balmer, Harper, 1920.
The Silver Sixpence, illustrated by James H. Crank, Harper, 1921.
Gladiola Murphy, Harper, 1923.
Four Ducks on a Pond, Harper, 1928.
Folkhouse: The Autobiography of a Home, illustrated by Allan McNab, D. Appleton, 1932.
The Luck of the Road, Appleton-Century, 1934.
Gallant: The Story of Storm Veblen (published serially as *Hillmen's Gold*), Appleton-Century, 1936.

RECORDINGS

Ruth Sawyer: Storyteller, 1965.

OTHER

The Sidhe of Ben-Mor: An Irish Folk Play, Badger, 1910.
The Awakening, first produced in New York City, 1918.
The Way of the Storyteller, Macmillan, 1942, revised edition, Viking Press, 1977.
How to Tell a Story, F. E. Compton, 1962.

Contributor of over 200 articles, stories, poems, and serials to periodicals, including *Atlantic Monthly, Horn Book,* and *Outlook.* The College of Sainte Catherine Library, St. Paul, MN, owns a collection of Sawyer's manuscripts.

ADAPTATIONS: The Primrose Ring was filmed by Lasky Feature Play Co., 1917; the story "Christmas Apple," published in *This Way to Christmas,* was adapted for the stage as a two-scene play by Margaret D. Williams and published by Samuel French, 1939; *Journey Cake, Ho!* was adapted as a filmstrip, with sound and picture-cued text booklet, by Weston Woods Studios, 1967.

SIDELIGHTS: Ruth Sawyer was known as a teller of folktales, which she collected from around the world, and as a writer of stories about children from other cultures. Among her most popular books are the Caldecott Medal-winning *The Christmas Anna Angel,* about a Hungarian girl who yearns for a traditional Christmas celebration, and the Newbery Medal-winning *Roller Skates,* the story of a young girl who explores New York City.

As a child, Sawyer developed a love for stories from her Irish nurse, Johanna, who told her stories at bedtime. The nurse also gave Ruth a love for Irish folklore, an interest which later led her to study and collect folklore from around the world. At Columbia University, Sawyer majored in folklore and storytelling and after graduation, she worked for the New York Public Lecture Bureau, telling stories twice a week at different locations around the city. She also worked as a correspondent in Ireland for the *New York Sun* newspaper.

Many of Sawyer's books were inspired by folktales, especially those from Spain. Her *Picture Tales from Spain* was based on a trip she made to that country and on the stories she was told by the people she met. Another story from Spain was *Tono Antonio,* based on a young boy Sawyer met on this journey. The Spanish stories of Washington Irving had enthralled Sawyer when she was a girl, giving her a desire to visit Spain. "It may seem a far cry," she explained in *Horn Book,* "from a Maine farmhouse in mid-summer fog to Granada in winter splendor. In years it spans half a lifetime. But for the child lying stomach down beside the hearth, lost in *The Tales of the Alhambra* and *The Conquest of Granada,* Washington Irving laid a starry trail across the ocean and those years."

One of Sawyer's most popular books was *Roller Skates,* the story of one year in the life of Lucinda, a young girl who is permitted to roller-skate wherever she pleases in New York City. In the course of her travels throughout the city, she meets and befriends people from all sorts of backgrounds, in the process learning something about the importance of individual freedom. In her Newbery Award acceptance speech, Sawyer explained: "If this book has any point at all it lies in that fact of freedom for every child, in his own way, that he, too, may catch the music of the spheres. . . . A free child is a happy child; and

there is nothing more lovely; even a disagreeable child ceases to be disagreeable and is liked."

Roller Skates stirred a controversy when it first appeared because it dealt frankly with death. As Elizabeth Segel noted in *Horn Book,* "By confronting a sordid murder and the death of a tiny child, rather than the more easily accepted deaths of a pet or an aged grandparent, and by integrating these experiences with other aspects of Lucinda's year of discovery and growth, the book, in fact, deals more fully and frankly with the child's experience of death than do many of the books turned out these days."

Yet, most critics focus on the book's primary message of freedom. "Yes, Lucinda lives," Segel wrote, "and her vitality makes *Roller Skates* still readable and engaging. Depicted as neither a typical child nor an object-lesson heroine, Lucinda embodies a freedom as liberating to children's books as her year of roller-skating was to her own life."

Sawyer won a Caldcott Medal for the book *Journey Cake, Ho!,* a story derived from folktales of the American South. When a young boy must go on a search for a new home, he is given a "journey cake" to eat along the way. But the cake falls out of his pack and rolls away, and the boy's frantic efforts to retrieve the cake form the story. "Where did *Journey Cake, Ho!* have its start?," Sawyer asked in an article for *Young Wings.* "It began a hundred years ago in the mountains of Kentucky, North Carolina, and Tennessee. The people told the story. They sang it. They laughed over it. But the story I have written is different from any versions I have heard, but the bare bones are the same. And I like it."

A large part of Sawyer's work are Christmas stories, many of them based on traditional or folk tales from around the world. *This Way to Christmas* features Sawyer's son David as the main character. When his parents are away, David's Irish caretakers tell Christmas stories to entertain him. These ten stories make up *This Way to Christmas.* Included is one of Sawyer's personal favorites, "The Voyage of the Wee Red Cap," a story she heard from an elderly tinker while visiting Ireland. When she returned to New York, Anne Carroll Moore invited her to tell the story to a group of children at the New York Public Library. "I shall always remember the faces of the American-born Irish boys who came over from a nearby parochial school," Sawyer recalled in *Horn Book.* "I shall always remember Miss Moore's lighting of candles; and the Christmas wishes that came out of that first library story hour. Those candles have never gone out for me; they still burn and always will."

The Long Christmas, dedicated to Sawyer's daughter, is a collection of thirteen holiday stories, one for each day from St. Thomas's Day to Candlemas. It contains, according to Jacqueline Overton in *Horn Book,* "Legends from many countries, ancient and modern, gentle and serious, joyous and gay, and she prefaced them with some of the traditional things that have gone into the keeping of Christmas: The good food, 'gay and of infinite variety,' the lighting, the bedecking, the festivity." Writing of *The Long Christmas* in *Horn Book,* Beryl Robinson remarked: "I return to this book yearly in anticipation of the Christmas season, rereading every tale, choosing those that will be a part of the year's festival."

Sawyer's *The Christmas Anna Angel* was inspired by a real-life experience of her Hungarian friend, Anna Kester. Anna recalled one Christmas in Hungary when she was a little girl and there was a food shortage. Despite the lack of flour and other baking essentials, Anna wanted to have a traditional Christmas cake to hang on the tree. Her desire becomes reality when she dreams of a Christmas angel and an angel appears. "Anna Kester's faithful memory, Ruth Sawyer's warm telling of the story of *The Christmas Anna Angel* and Kate Seredy's lovely pictures have worked their magic," Jacqueline Overton wrote in *Horn Book.* The book won Sawyer a Caldecott Medal in 1954.

Speaking in *Horn Book,* Sawyer once stated: "So often I have heard a sharp criticism from a parent when she has found a shabby, dog-eared book on the library shelf. How shortsighted is such a parent! I rejoice over every one I find. It speaks more eloquently than all the good reviews how much beloved that book has been."

BIOGRAPHICAL/CRITICAL SOURCES:

BOOKS

Dictionary of Literary Biography, Volume 22: *American Writers for Children, 1900-1960,* Gale, 1983.
Haviland, Virginia, *Ruth Sawyer,* Walck, 1965.

PERIODICALS

Bulletin of the New York Public Library, November-December, 1956, pp. 593-598.
Horn Book, January, 1936, pp. 34-38; July 1937, pp. 251-256; November-December, 1944, pp. 447-460; October, 1965, pp. 474-480; August, 1979, pp. 454-458.
Young Wings, December, 1953.*

*   *   *

SAXON, A(rthur) H(artley)   1935-

PERSONAL: Born March 24, 1935, in Pittsburgh, PA; son of Arthur Fred (an engineer) and Gladys (Hartley) Saxon; married Gail Mildred Larson (a nurse), September 13, 1957; children: Jonathan, Eric. *Education:* University of Pittsburgh, B.A. (summa cum laude), 1956; Columbia University, M.A., 1961; Yale University, Ph.D., 1966; Southern Connecticut State University, M.L.S., 1988. *Politics:* Independent. *Avocational interests:* Science, sailing, and photography.

ADDRESSES: Home—166 Orchard Hill Dr., Fairfield, CT 06430.

CAREER: Hospital for Special Surgery, New York City, chief chemist and research consultant, 1963-64; West Haven Veterans Hospital, West Haven, CT, chief of blood bank, 1964-66; University of Pittsburgh, Pittsburgh, PA, assistant professor, department of speech and theater and department of English, 1966-69; University of Connecticut, Storrs, associate professor, department of theater, 1969-71; City University of New York, New York City, associate professor of theatre at City College and at Graduate School and University Center, 1971-76; writer and lecturer, 1976—. Visiting associate professor of theatre, Temple University, 1978-81; visiting professor of American studies, Yale University, 1981; visiting professor of communications, Chapman College, 1983. Consultant to Barnum Museum, Bridgeport, CT, Peabody Museum of Natural History at Yale University, and the Bridgeport and Westport, CT, public libraries. *Military service:* U.S. Army, 1958-60.

MEMBER: Authors Guild, Authors League of America, British Society for Theatre Research, Club du Cirque (lifetime honorary member), Phi Beta Kappa.

AWARDS, HONORS: Fellowships from the Woodrow Wilson Foundation and the National Institutes of Health; Ford Foundation grant for research in Europe, 1967; Guggenheim Foundation fellow, 1971, 1982; American Council of Learned Societies fellow, 1978; American Philosophical Society grant, 1980; Barnum Festival Society medal, 1980; presented with the key to Bridgeport, CT, 1983, for various contributions to the city; Barnard Hewitt Award, American Society for Theatre Research, 1990, for outstanding research in theatre history.

WRITINGS:

Enter Foot and Horse: A History of Hippodrama in England and France, Yale University Press, 1968.
The Life and Art of Andrew Ducrow and the Romantic Age of the English Circus, Archon Books, 1978.
(Editor) *The Autobiography of Mrs. Tom Thumb,* Archon Books, 1979.
(Editor) *Selected Letters of P. T. Barnum,* Columbia University Press, 1983.
P. T. Barnum: The Legend and the Man, Columbia University Press, 1989.

Contributor to *Encyclopedia of the Horse,* edited by C. E. G. Hope and G. N. Jackson, Viking, 1973, and *Le Grand Livre du Cirque,* edited by Monica J. Renevey, Edito-

Service, 1977. Founder and first general editor of "Archon Books on Popular Entertainments" series, 1977-80. Contributor to *Encyclopaedia Britannica* and to theatre and circus journals. American editor, *Theatre Research/ Recherches Theatrales,* 1970-73; American reviewer of circuses for *Le Cirque dans l'Univers* (Paris); member of advisory board, *London Stage, 1800-1900,* beginning 1973.

ADAPTATIONS: P. T. Barnum: The Legend and the Man was recorded for the "Talking Books" program of the National Library Service for the Blind and Handicapped in 1990.

WORK IN PROGRESS: Editing *Barnumiana: A Select, Annotated Bibliography of Works by or Relating to P. T. Barnum,* and *The Memoirs of Joseph T. McCaddon, Including a Biography of His Famous Brother-in-Law James A. Bailey.*

SIDELIGHTS: In *Selected Letters of P. T. Barnum* and *P. T. Barnum: The Legend and the Man,* A. H. Saxon has done much to revive the reputation of America's most famous circus master. Saxon, a noted authority on the circus who is also a working biochemist, spent nearly twenty years collecting information for his Barnum books, which attempt to correct the many myths and misunderstandings about the man who was considered one of the nineteenth century's great con men. The collection of over 300 letters, carefully edited by Saxon, shows the private side of a man who relentlessly promoted his public career in a frequently revised autobiography, which misled people into believing he was a crass huckster. In the biography, Saxon's objective was to show the "antagonism between the Barnum of popular imagination and Barnum as he really was or wished to be," writes Ricky Jay in the *Los Angeles Times Book Review. Wall Street Journal* reviewer Dave Shifleet calls the book "a brave work of literary rehabilitation," and Hugh Brogan, writing in the *Times Literary Supplement,* claims that Saxon "not only settles most of the questions surrounding Barnum's career: he also paints the great showman's achievements in plain, bright colours and makes them wholly intelligible." Robert S. Pelton, curator of the Barnum Museum in Bridgeport, Connecticut, told Randall Beach in a *New York Times* review that this biography "will be the definitive study of Barnum for at least a generation."

BIOGRAPHICAL/CRITICAL SOURCES:

PERIODICALS

Los Angeles Times Book Review, September 17, 1989, p. 1.
New York Times, September 9, 1990.
New York Times Book Review, June 5, 1983; January 21, 1990, p. 21.

Times Literary Supplement, April 29, 1983; November 17-23, 1989, p. 1262.
Wall Street Journal, May 17, 1990.
World's Fair (London), July 13, 1990.

* * *

SCHROEDER, Andreas (Peter) 1946-

PERSONAL: Born November 26, 1946, in Hoheneggelsen, Germany; son of Ernst (a carpenter) and Ruth (an organist; maiden name, Bartel) Schroeder; married Sharon Elizabeth Brown (in business management); children: Sabrina Anne, Vanessa. *Education:* University of British Columbia, B.A., 1969, M.A., 1971. *Politics:* New Democrat. *Religion:* Mennonite.

ADDRESSES: Home—P.O. Box 3127, Mission, British Columbia, Canada V2V 4J3.

CAREER: Prism International, Vancouver, British Columbia, editorial assistant, 1968-69; *Contemporary Literature in Translation,* Vancouver, founding editor, 1969-79; free-lance writer, 1979—. Member of faculty at University of Victoria, 1975-77; writer-in-residence at the Regina Public Library, 1980-81, University of Winnipeg, 1983-84, Fraser Valley Public Library, 1985, and the University of British Columbia, 1985-87. Member of board of directors of British Columbia Film Co-op, 1970-71; founder and chairman of Public Lending Right Commission of Canada, 1985-88. Hosted *Synapse,* a weekly literary television show.

MEMBER: International PEN, Writers Union of Canada (chairman, 1976-77), League of Canadian Poets, Canadian Periodical Publishers Association, Periodical Writers Association.

AWARDS, HONORS: Canada Council grants, 1968, 1971, 1973, 1975, 1979, 1984, 1986; Gordon Woodward Memorial Award, University of British Columbia, 1969, for short story, "The Past People"; script prize, National Film Board, 1971, for *The Late Man;* finalist, Governor-General's Award (nonfiction), 1977, for *Shaking It Rough: A Prison Memoir;* finalist, Sealbooks First Novel Award, 1983; Investigative Journalism Award, Canadian Association of Journalists, 1991.

WRITINGS:

The Ozone Minotaur (poems), Sono Nis Press, 1969.
(Translator with Michael Bullock) *The Stage and Creative Arts,* New York Graphic Society, 1969.
(Editor with Joel Michael Yates) *Contemporary Poetry of British Columbia,* Sono Nis Press, Volume 1, 1970, Volume 2, 1972.
File of Uncertainties (poems), Sono Nis Press, 1971.

(With David Frith) *uniVerse* (concrete poems), MassAge Press, 1971.

The Late Man (stories), Sono Nis Press, 1972.

(Editor with Rudy Wiebe) *Stories from Pacific and Arctic Canada,* Macmillan, 1974.

(Translator) *Collected Stories of Ilse Aichinger,* Sono Nis Press, 1974.

Shaking It Rough: A Prison Memoir, Doubleday, 1976.

(Editor) *Words from Inside* (anthology), Prison Arts Foundation, 1978.

Toccata in "D" (novel), Oolichan Press, 1985.

Dust-Ship Glory, Doubleday, 1986.

(Translator) Christoph Meckel, *In the Land of Umbramauts,* Nordic Press, 1986.

The Mennonites: A History of Their Lives in Canada, Douglas & McIntyre, 1990.

(With Jack Thiessen) *The Eleventh Commandment* (stories; based on Schroeder's translation from the Mennonite Low-German), Thistledown Press, 1990.

Carved in Wood: The History of Mission, B.C. 1862-1992, D. W. Friesen, 1991.

SCREENPLAYS

The Plastic Mile, Ruvinsky Productions, 1969.

(And director) *Immobile,* MassAge Productions, 1969.

(And director) *The Pub,* MassAge Productions, 1970.

(And director) *The Late Man,* Odyssey Films, 1973.

OTHER

Author of weekly column in *Vancouver Province,* 1968-73. Editor of *Poetry Canada,* 1970-71; literary critic for *Vancouver Province-Pacific Press,* 1970-73; member of editorial board of *Canadian Fiction,* 1971—, and *Grain,* 1989—.

WORK IN PROGRESS: Eating My Father's Island, a collection of short fiction.

SIDELIGHTS: Andreas Schroeder told *CA:* "If youth is the time to try everything out, and middle age the time to straighten out the resulting chaos (Francois de La Rochefoucault), then I have probably reached middle age. Several decades ago I was frantically writing in every genre invented and a few besides, producing radio documentaries (CBC Ideas), directing films (*The Late Man, The Pub, Immobile*), founding and editing magazines (*Contemporary Literature in Translation, Canadian Fiction, Words from Inside*), writing weekly literary columns (*Vancouver Province*), teaching creative writing (University of British Columbia, University of Victoria, etc.) and hosting a weekly literary television show (*Synapse*). I raced motorcycles, parachuted out of small airplanes, lived with a Bedouin tribe in Baalbek (Lebanon) and served as chairman of the Writers Union of Canada (1976-77).

"Today, I concentrate mostly on writing. The motorcycle rusts, the parachute moulders; it's just me and my word processor. Occasionally I forget myself and commit cultural politics (i.e. founding chairman of the Public Lending Right Commission, 1985-88), but then I come back to my senses and return to writing once more. The pursuit of writing seems to require the longest apprenticeship in the world. Maybe that should bother me, but it doesn't.

"I was born to a Mennonite family in West Germany in 1946. We immigrated to Canada in 1951. We were headed for a small town in British Columbia called Mission, which struck my religious parents as portentous. But when we got there we discovered it was merely the station nearest to Abbotsford, where my parents ended up spending two years hoeing corn and beans by hand to pay for their overseas passage. Twenty years later, having forgotten the story, I searched for a mountaintop site to build on and found one in Mission—which is where I, Sharon and our two daughters Sabrina and Vanessa have settled down. I suppose it's true: I've never liked unfinished business."

BIOGRAPHICAL/CRITICAL SOURCES:

BOOKS

Dictionary of Literary Biography, Volume 53: *Canadian Writers since 1960,* Gale, 1986.

Twigg, Alan, *Strong Voices,* Harbor Publishing, 1990.

PERIODICALS

Best Sellers, June, 1977.

Canadian Fiction, 1977.

Saturday Night, October, 1976.

*   *   *

SCHUERER, Ernst 1933-

PERSONAL: Born September 13, 1933, in Germany; naturalized U.S. citizen, 1961; son of Josef (a craftsman) and Hermine (Ahlbrink) Schuerer; married Margarete Richter, June 20, 1964; children: Frank, Norbert, Anne. *Education:* University of Texas, B.A., 1960; Yale University, M.A., 1962, Ph.D., 1965. *Politics:* Democratic. *Avocational interests:* "Philosophy, archeology, traveling and travel literature. Exploration. History."

ADDRESSES: Home—705 East Foster Ave., State College, PA 16801. *Office*—Department of German, Pennsylvania State University, S-323 Burrowes Bldg., University Park, PA 16802.

CAREER: Yale University, New Haven, CT, instructor, 1965-67, assistant professor, 1967-70, associate professor of German, 1970-73, director of undergraduate studies,

1971-73; University of Florida, Gainesville, professor of German, 1973-78, chairman of department, 1977-78; Pennsylvania State University, University Park, professor of German, 1978—, head of department, 1978-1991.

MEMBER: International Association for German Philology and Literature, International Brecht Society, Modern Languages Association of America, American Association of Teachers of German, American Comparative Literature Association, American Association of Teachers of Foreign Languages, Kafka Society of America, Society for Exile Students, Phi Beta Kappa.

AWARDS, HONORS: Woodrow Wilson fellowship, 1960-61; Morse fellowship, Yale University, 1968-69; Alexander von Humboldt fellowship, 1973; American Council of Learned Societies travel grant, 1980; German Academic Exchange Service fellowship, 1984; National Certificate of Merit, Goethe Institute/ American Association of Teachers of German, 1985; Honorary member Phi Sigma Jota, International Foriegn Language Honor Society, 1987; Institute for the Arts and Humanistic Studies fellowship, 1991.

WRITINGS:

(Editor) *Lebendige Form,* Wilhelm Fink, 1970.
Georg Kaiser, Twayne, 1971.
Georg Kaiser und Bertolt Brecht, Atheneum, 1971.
Georg Kaiser: Nebeneinander, Reclam (Stuttgart), 1978.
Carl Sternheim: Tabula rasa, Reclam, 1978.
Ernst Toller: Hoppla, wir leben!, Reclam, 1980.
Reinhard Sorge: Der Bettler, Reclam, 1985.
(Editor) *B.Traven: Life and Work,* Pennsylvania State University Press, 1987.

CONTRIBUTOR

Horst Denkler, editor, *Gedichte der "Menschheitsdaemmerung,"* Wihelm fink, 1971.
Manfred Durzak, editor, *Die deutsche Exilliteratur 1933-1945,* Reclam, 1973.
Wolfgang Rothe, editor, *Die deutsch Literatur der Weimarer Republik,* 1974.
Dietrich Papenfuss and Jurgen Soering, editors, *Rezeption der deutschen Gegenwarts-literatur in Ausland,* Kohlhammer (Stuttgart), 1976.
Holger A. Pausch and Ernest Reinhold, editors, *Georg Kaiser Symposium,* Agora (Berlin), 1980.
Armin Arnold, editor, *Georg Kaiser,* Klett (Stuttgart), 1980.
John M. Spalek and Robert F. Bell, editors, *Exile: The Writer's Experience,* University of North Carolina Press, 1982.
Klaus Siebenhaar and Herman Haarmann, editors, *Preis der Vernunft,* Medusa (Berlin/Vienna), 1982.
Jost Hermand, editor, *Zu Ernst Toller: Drama and Engagement,* Klett, 1982.

Paul Michael Luetzeler, *Brochs "Verzauberung,"* Suhrkamp (Frankfurt), 1983.
Roland Jost and Hansgeorg Schimdt-Bergmann, editors, *Im Dialog mit der Moderne,* Atheneum, 1986.
Franz Jung, *Werk in Einzelausgaben,* Nautilus, 1986.
Michael Kessler and Paul M. Lutzeler (editors) *Herman Broch: Das dichterische Werk,* Stauffenburg, 1987.
Palmer Museum of Art, editor, *Emil Nolde: Works from American Collections,* Pennsylvania University Press, 1988.

Contributor to professional journals, including *Monatshefte, Books Abroad, Journal of English and German Philology, German Studies, German Quarterly, Modern Austrian Literature, Colloquia Germanica,* and *Germanic Review.*

WORK IN PROGRESS: Edition of articles on Franz Jung. Articles on Georg Kaiser.

SIDELIGHTS: Ernst Schuerer told *CA:* "Reading and writing are as essential to a full life as eating and sleeping. They open us up and make us aware of new and unknown worlds."

* * *

SCHUR, Norman W(arren) 1907-

PERSONAL: Born October 7, 1907, in Boston, MA; son of Isaac H. (a banker) and Martha (Reinherz) Schur; married Marjorie Tas, December 31, 1941; children: Joanna (Mrs. Eric Weber), Warren Michael, Moira (Mrs. Kevin J. Craw), Geoffrey Emile. *Education:* Harvard College, A.B. (summa cum laude), 1926; Columbia University, J.D., 1930; attended University of Rome and Sorbonne. *Politics:* "Honesty." *Religion:* "No preference."

ADDRESSES: Home—37 Davis Hill Rd., Weston, CT 06883 (November to April); Gun Green Farm, Water Lane, Hawkhurst, Kent TN18 5DE, England (May to October).

CAREER: Attorney. Proskauer, Rose & Paskus, New York City, associate, 1930-33; private practice of law, 1933-50; partner of law firms in New York City, Simons, Schur & Straus, 1950-53, Diamond, Schur, Perl & Sewel, 1953-56, Schur & Perl, 1956-58, and Schur, Rubin & Montgomery, 1960-65; counsel to Bernton, Hoeniger, Freitag & Abbey, New York City, and King & Plotkin, Stamford, CT, both 1965-74; private practice of law, 1973—. Former consultant on American law and taxation in England.

MEMBER: Wig and Pen Club (London), Marylebone Cricket Club (London), Kent County Cricket Club (Canterbury, England), Middlesex County Cricket Club (London), Hawkhurst Cricket Club (Hawkhurst, England), Phi Beta Kappa.

AWARDS, HONORS: Franklin Medal and Derby Medal, Boston Latin School, 1923; Sheldon Fellowship, Harvard University, 1926.

WRITINGS:

British Self-Taught: With Comments in American, Macmillan, 1972, revised edition published as *English English: A Descriptive Dictionary,* Verbatim, 1980.
1000 Most Important Words, Ballantine, 1982.
Practical English: 1000 Most Effective Words, Ballantine, 1983.
1000 Most Challenging Words, Ballantine, 1987.
British English: A to Zed, Facts on File, 1987.
A Dictionary of Challenging Words, Penguin, 1989.
1000 Most Obscure Words, Facts on File, 1990.

WORK IN PROGRESS: A memoir.

SIDELIGHTS: Norman W. Schur has been a word buff from his earliest years. "Language," he maintained in *Westport News,* is "a living breathing, expanding and contracting thing, changing all the time." While living in England, Schur was struck by the sometimes baffling differences between British and American English. His notes on the subject led to his first book, *British Self-Taught.* Revised some years later and republished as *English English,* the book received favorable reviews from both British and American critics.

In addition to word choice, notes Leonard Feather in the *Los Angeles Times,* "subtle differences of punctuation, syntax, spelling, and pronunciation and the uses of prepositions are examined." The social and political dimensions of language are also discussed, "sometimes briefly, occasionally in long, fascinating essays." Feather calls the "splendidly researched, wittily written" book "as much entertainment as education, especially for those of us who have lived both in the United Kingdom and the United States." Although British critic E.S. Turner suggests in a *Times Literary Supplement* review that the differences in the two varieties of English may be somewhat exaggerated by Schur, he praises the book as "informative, discursive, idiosyncratic, amused and amusing."

BIOGRAPHICAL/CRITICAL SOURCES:

PERIODICALS

Los Angeles Times, April 5, 1981.
Times Literary Supplement, March 20, 1981.
Westport News, February 4, 1981.

* * *

SCHWAB, George 1931-

PERSONAL: Born November 25, 1931; son of Arkady (a medical doctor) and Klara (Jacobson) Schwab; married

Eleonora Storch, February 27, 1965; children: Clarence Boris, Claude Arkady, Solan Bernhard. *Education:* City College (now City College of the City University of New York), B.A., 1954; Columbia University, M.A., 1955, Ph.D., 1968. *Avocational interests:* Art collecting (primarily contemporary French, German, and American abstract art, Yugoslavian naive art, and stage designs by Russian and French artists).

ADDRESSES: Home—140 Riverside Dr., New York, NY 10024. *Office*—Department of History, City College of the City University of New York, 138th St. and Convent Ave., New York, NY 10031; and Graduate School and University Center, City University of New York, 33 West 42nd St., New York, NY 10036.

CAREER: Columbia University, New York City, lecturer in political science, 1959; City College of the City University of New York, New York City, lecturer, 1960-68, assistant professor, 1968-72, associate professor, 1973-80, professor of history, 1980—; City University of New York, Graduate School and University Center, New York City, editor of *American Foreign Policy Newsletter,* 1976—, senior vice-president of National Committee of American Foreign Policy, 1985—.

MEMBER: International Platform Association, American Historical Association, American Political Science Association, Phi Alpha Theta.

AWARDS, HONORS: City University of New York Research Foundation grants, 1970, 1972, 1981-82, and 1989-90; Volkswagen Foundation grant, 1978; Earhart Foundation award, 1989.

WRITINGS:

Dayez: Beyond Abstract Art, L'Edition d'Art H. Piazza (Paris), 1967.
The Challenge of the Exception: An Introduction to the Political Ideas of Carl Schmitt between 1921 and 1936, Duncker & Humblot (Berlin), 1970, 2nd edition, Greenwood Press, 1989.
(Translator and author of introduction and notes) Carl Schmitt, *The Concept of the Political,* Rutgers University Press, 1976.
(Editor) *Eurocommunism: The Ideological and Political-Theoretical Foundations,* Greenwood Press, 1981.
(Editor with Henry Friedlander, and contributor) *Detente in Historical Perspective,* 2nd edition, Irvington, 1981.
(Editor and contributor) *Ideology and Foreign Policy: A Global Perspective,* Irvington, 1981.
(Editor and contributor) *United States Foreign Policy at the Crossroads,* Greenwood Press, 1982.
(Translator and author of introduction and notes) Schmitt, *Political Theology,* M.I.T. Press, 1985.

(With Jean Lescure) *Dayez,* Collection Terre des Peintres (Paris), 1991.

Contributor to books, including *Epirrhosis,* Duncker & Humblot, 1968; *Germany in World Politics,* Cyrco Press, 1979; *Muted Voices,* Philosophical Library, 1987; and *Elie Wiesel: Between Memory and Hope,* New York University Press, 1990. Contributor to *Encyclopedia Judaica.* Editor of series "Global Perspectives in History and Politics," Greenwood Press, 1981—. Contributor to periodicals, including *Orbis, TELOS, Interpretation,* and *Canadian Journal of Political and Social Theory.*

SIDELIGHTS: George Schwab told *CA:* "To be a recognized author in the English-speaking world is an accomplishment. To see my works in foreign languages is thrilling."

*   *   *

SCOTT, Roney
See GAULT, William Campbell

*   *   *

SELDEN, George
See THOMPSON, George Selden

*   *   *

SELLERS, Con(nie Leslie, Jr.) 1922-
(Robert Crane, Lee Raintree, and 95 other pseudonyms)

PERSONAL: Born March 1, 1922, in Shubuta, MS; son of Connie Leslie (a handyman) and Vivian May (Menasco) Sellers; married Mary Frances Raineri (a writer and rancher), June 16, 1943; children: Leonard L., Shannon E. *Education:* Attended Monterey Peninsula College (army language school), 1957-58. *Politics:* "Hard-nosed independent." *Religion:* Protestant. *Avocational interests:* Morgan horses, Simmental cattle, casting model soldiers.

ADDRESSES: Home—Bella Maria Ranch, Wilderville, OR 97543. *Office*—The Korea Connection, Literary/ Film Productions, Box 276, Wilderville, OR 97543. *Agent*—Jane Rotrosen Berkey, 226 East 32nd St., New York, NY 10016.

CAREER: Writer and rancher. Worked variously as archery instructor, sign painter, news deliverer, and printer's devil; instructor in writing at Rogue Community College. *Military service:* U.S. Army, 1940-56; earned more than

forty awards, including French Croix de Guerre with Palm, Bronze Star, Combat Infantry Badge with Star, and Purple Heart.

MEMBER: Southern Oregon Writers Club.

AWARDS, HONORS: Awards from magazines for short stories; Gold Medal for best fiction based on fact, *West Coast Review of Books,* 1980, for *The Last Flower.*

WRITINGS:

F.S.C.: The Shocking Story of a Probable America, Novel Books, 1963.
Too Late the Hero, Pyramid Books, 1970.
(With Sherry Caldwell) *A Horse's Astrologer,* Cordovan Corp., 1973.
(Under pseudonym Lee Raintree, with others) *Dallas* (novel adapted from the television series), Dell, 1978.
(With Anthony Wilson) *Bed of Strangers,* Dell, 1978.
Marilee, Pocket Books, 1978.
Sweet Caroline, Pocket Books, 1979.
The Last Flower, Pocket Books, 1979.
Since You've Been Gone, Jove Books, 1980.
Keepers of the House, Pocket Books, 1983.
This Promised Earth, Bantam, 1985.
The Black Magnolia, Bantam, 1986.
Trouble in Mind, Bantam, 1986.
Mansei!, Bantam, 1987.
Those Frightened Years, Bantam, 1988.
Brothers in Battle, Pocket Books, 1989.
"Men at Arms" series, four books, Pocket Books, 1991-1992.

Also author of *Private World.* Author under several pseudonyms, including Robert Crane, of series of war novels for Pyramid Books, including *Born of Battle: Sergeant Corbin's War, The Sergeant and the Queen,* and *Where Have All the Soldiers Gone?;* also author of numerous other books under pseudonyms. Contributor to periodicals.

WORK IN PROGRESS: Fiction.

SIDELIGHTS: Con Sellers told *CA:* "Motivation? After general discharge from the army for alcoholism, I was thirty-five years old with a wife and two sons, dead broke and in debt. With some ten years of army PR behind me, writing seemed my only out. I went to school under the GI bill, mostly to learn how to think as a civilian. If I couldn't make it free-lance, I'd go back to newspapers.

"I have achieved what I'd hoped through writing novels—a good living, freedom, and the ability to tell a good story. My working habits are sloppy now. Once I thought if anyone couldn't turn out ten pages a day, he was in the wrong business. Age and health (and perhaps success) slowed that. I usually work from one to five or six p.m., and if I'm tight against a deadline, back at night."

"The purpose behind any book? Doing a good job, selling it, help some reader to laugh or cry. I suppose I put a good deal more into *This Promised Earth,* because much of it concerned my own family. *Dallas* alone was in fourteen languages; some of the others went to the United Kingdom (I believe, a different language), Portugal, Sweden, Finland, etc. As for adaptations, it seems I do things backward. I do the tie-ins, as with *Dallas* and *Too Late the Hero,* a movie with Cliff Robertson and Michael Caine.

"I give advice to aspiring writers every week for four hours at my local college, where I pay my dues to society. Since I'm a full-time writer who teaches, and not a teacher who sometimes writes, the class is a success. We have *sold* twenty-nine novels so far, for front money ranging from $500 to $300,000; a two book package offer of $250,000. Over the years, this class has become a living thing, almost self-starting. Students come back over and over, even those who sell, because everyone gets too close to his own work and needs criticism. I would advise any beginner to study the market and write for it. Writing a book, then wondering where to send it—two strikes on you and the third coming up, if you don't know how to do a detailed outline.

"Certainly, I've been influenced by other writers, since I began reading on my own at about age seven. But it's amazing how many of those I once thought wonderful are now terrible. I can read few writers now, because of bad mechanics and bad editing. The novels I consider good, I try to learn from—a better technique, a better way of handling dialogue. Contemporary writers—God, how lucky some of them are, to be published at all; some are magnificent. Of late, I am beginning to think that women are better novelists. I wrote the second mash note of my life to Judith Guest. But writing worth, as beauty, is in the eye of the beholder. What I think is great, others may not like at all. My opinion of the current literary scene? It doesn't matter; I write what my editors/agents want, in general. Of course, the characters and basic premise are mine, a major point: write from *character,* because all stories are about people.

"The most important step in my career was finding my agent, Jane Rotrosen Berkey. Until she took me in hand, I had never gotten more than $3,000 advance; now we talk $100,000. Lucking out with *good* editors (and where do they find the others?), like Linda Grey and Kate Miciak of Bantam, and Ann Patty and Paul McCarthy of Pocket, was another major break. Am I 'commercial?' Damned right; I leave art to artists—who usually sell insurance or pump gas for a living."

BIOGRAPHICAL/CRITICAL SOURCES:

PERIODICALS

Daily Courier (Grants Pass, OR), January 20-28, 1979.
Illinois Valley News (Cave Junction, OR), January 18, 1979.
Mail Tribune (Medford, OR), 1980.

*   *   *

SHERBURNE, Zoa (Morin) 1912-

PERSONAL: Born September 30, 1912, in Seattle, WA; daughter of Thomas Joseph and Zoa (Webber) Morin; married Herbert Newton Sherburne, June 5, 1935 (deceased); children: Mrs. Marie Brumble, Mrs. Norene Purdue, Mrs. Zoey Holte, Herbert Jr., Thomas, Philip, Anne, Robert. *Education:* Attended parochial schools in Seattle, WA. *Avocational interests:* bowling, dancing, civic activities, public speaking about writing.

ADDRESSES: Home—2401 North East Blakeley, Seattle, WA 98105. *Agent*—Ann Elmo Agency Inc., 52 Vanderbilt Ave., New York, NY 10017.

CAREER: Writer. Cornish School of Allied Arts, Seattle, WA, teacher of short story writing, 1957; lecturer.

MEMBER: National League of American Penwomen (second vice-president, Seattle national branch), Seattle Freelance Writers (president, 1954), Phi Delta Nu (president, 1950).

AWARDS, HONORS: Woman of Achievement award, Theta Sigma Phi Matrix, 1950; Woman of the Year, Phi Delta Nu, 1951; Best Book for Young People award, Child Study Association, 1959, for *Jennifer;* Henry Broderick Award, 1960; Governor's Writers' Day Award, 1967.

WRITINGS:

Shadow of a Star, Hurst & Blacklett, 1959.
Journey out of Darkness, Hurst & Blacklett, 1961.

FOR YOUNG ADULTS

Almost April, Morrow, 1956.
The High White Wall, Morrow, 1957.
Princess in Denim, Morrow, 1958.
Jennifer, Morrow, 1959.
Evening Star, Morrow, 1960.
Ballerina on Skates, Morrow, 1961.
Girl in the Shadows, Morrow, 1963.
Stranger in the House, Morrow, 1963.
River at Her Feet, Morrow, 1965.
Girl in the Mirror, Morrow, 1966.
Too Bad about the Haines Girl, Morrow, 1967.
The Girl Who Knew Tomorrow, Morrow, 1970.

Leslie, Morrow, 1972.
Why Have the Birds Stopped Singing?, Morrow, 1974.

OTHER

Also contributor of over three hundred short stories and articles, and numerous verses, to periodicals.

ADAPTATIONS: Stranger in the House was adapted for television as a film entitled *Memories Never Die,* starring Lindsey Wagner, which was first broadcast by Columbia Broadcast System, Inc. (CBS-TV) in December, 1982.

SIDELIGHTS: Zoa Sherburne began her career as a young adult novelist after she had been married for several years and had three children at home, but her enthusiasm for writing has been with her since childhood. She grew up in Seattle, Washington, and was one of four daughters. Searching for a means to establish an individual identity among all the girls in her family, she decided to become a writer.

Sherburne's first success at authorship occurred when she was about ten years old. She composed a Mother's Day poem that she read aloud and which, as she remembers, brought tears to her mother's eyes. Several years later, while in the sixth grade, she wrote her first play which was produced by her schoolmates. The positive feedback she received for her efforts inspired her return to writing several years later after a chance occurrence. While listening to the radio one afternoon, she heard the announcement of a national poetry contest and decided to compose a poem of the required twenty-five lines. Sherburne sent in her entry and was rewarded for her efforts by winning a cash prize. She used the prize money to enroll in a local writing school. "My husband thought it was a great idea and even consented to baby-sit while I attended an evening class in commercial writing," she recalled. "This led to a brief but rewarding career in short story [publication] . . . I found that I really loved to write and I met many editors who were happy to encourage me." The advent of television led to a drop-off in the periodical market demand for short stories, so Sherburne tried her hand at novel writing and found that she enjoyed it equally as much.

Throughout her career as a young adult novelist, Sherburne has dealt with many subjects of a timely nature. The young protagonists within her books have had to deal with such things as alcoholic parents, mental illness, racial prejudice, and compulsive eating disorders. In *The Girl Who Knew Tomorrow,* the main character, Angie, is created with the capacity for "second sight," and the book's story line involves the problems that her uniqueness cause both Angie and her family. Throughout her work, Sherburne shows herself consistently able to handle even the most difficult of topics with sensitivity and realism. For example, in her novel *Too Bad about the Haines Girl* she tackles

the problem of teenage pregnancy. Melinda Haines is a high school student who discovers that she is pregnant in her senior year. The story line revolves around the choices Melinda faces while coping with her situation, and the consequences she must bear in choosing to keep her child, necessitating a confrontation with both her boyfriend and her family. A critic in *Saturday Review* noted that while the book's plot was not unique, from the available "[books] for teenage girls that [focus] on the problem of the young unwed mother, this is one of the best to date"; and Irene Hunt of the *New York Times Book Review* commented: "Mrs. Sherburne hews to the line with the integrity of a skilled writer."

Although not noted for highly imaginative subplots, Sherburne's books have had great appeal among their teenage audience, which can identify with the element of strong family support that she interjects throughout her stories. While grounding her fiction in optimistic realism, Sherburne flavors some of her novels with historical or Gothic elements. *Why Have the Birds Stopped Singing?* is not only a story of a young girl coping with complications that epilepsy brings to her life, but also "an entertaining time travel adventure," according to a *Booklist* reviewer, who commended the book for its "well-drawn historical setting and unbroken line of tension."

Sherburne has continued to write almost exclusively for teenage girls of junior high school age. "I wrote problem stories because I felt that there were too many boy-next-door books for young girls, and the young girls I knew had more serious things to cope with," she once commented. "They had brothers and sisters who had problems, they fell in and out of love with the wrong boys, they were gay and sad and sometimes tragic and more often very funny. They rebelled, and they made mistakes, and sometimes they were sorry and sometimes not. In short, they were the girls who eventually became the characters in my books and I felt that I knew them as well as I know the palm of my hand."

BIOGRAPHICAL/CRITICAL SOURCES:

PERIODICALS

Booklist, July 1, 1974, p. 1202.
Christian Science Monitor, May 4, 1967.
Library Journal, December 15, 1970, p. 4368; January 15, 1973, p. 270; May 15, 1974, p. 1488.
New York Times Book Review, November 6, 1966, p. 20; March 5, 1967, p. 30.
Saturday Review, March 18, 1967.
Young Readers' Review, May, 1967.

SHERRY, John E(rnest) H(orwath) 1932-

PERSONAL: Born March 17, 1932, in New York, NY; son of John H. (a professor of law and an attorney) and Margaret (Horwath) Sherry; married Margaret Louise Singer, September 16, 1961 (died March 24, 1987); married Eleanor A. Fullerton, January 6, 1991; children: (first marriage) John II, Suzanne Cover, Douglas Marshall. *Education:* Yale University, B.A., 1954; Columbia University, J.D., 1959; New York University, LL.M., 1968. *Politics:* Independent. *Religion:* Protestant.

ADDRESSES: Home—1026 Hanshaw Rd., Ithaca, NY 14850. *Office*—School of Hotel Administration, Cornell University, Ithaca, NY 14853.

CAREER: Admitted to the Bar of New York State, 1962, and U.S. Supreme Court and State of Ohio, both 1967. Clerk to U.S. District Court judge, New York City, 1959-60; Baker, Nelson, Williams & Mitchell (law firm), New York City, associate, 1960-61; attorney-at-law, New York City, beginning 1962; confidential clerk to judge in New York State Court of Claims, 1963-65; John H. Sherry (law firm), New York City, associate, 1965-67; University of Akron, Akron, OH, assistant professor of law and director of clinical programs, 1967-70; California State University, San Diego (now University of San Diego), associate professor of law, 1970-72; Cornell University, Ithaca, NY, associate professor, 1972-81, professor of law, 1982—, graduate faculty representative, 1987-90. U.S. Department of State, member of Advisory Committee on Hotelkeepers' Liability, 1973—, diplomatic representative, 1978. Instructor of international tourism and travel law, Hangzhou University, People's Republic of China, 1983. Elected honorary president, International Forum of Travel and Tourism Advocates, 1983; external collaborator on Study for World Tourism Organization. Consultant to Sales Managers Association, 1974-75, and to American Hotel and Motel Association. *Military service:* U.S. Army, 1955-57, served in Korea; became first lieutenant. U.S. Army, 1961-62, Fort Bragg; became captain, 1965.

WRITINGS:

(With father, John H. Sherry) *The Laws of Innkeepers: For Hotels, Motels, Restaurants, and Clubs,* Cornell University Press, 1972, 2nd revised edition, 1981, published with *Supplement,* 1985, 3rd edition (sole author), 1992.

Hotel and Motel Law: Instructors Guide and Student Manual, Educational Institute of the American Hotel and Motel Association, 1976.

Legal Aspects of Foodservice Management, National Institute for the Foodservice Industry/N. C. Brown, 1984.

(With Jordan L. Paust and Robert D. Upp) *Business Law,* 4th edition, West Publishing, 1984.

Contributor to *International Uniform Law in Practice,* Oceana, 1989. Author of column "The Innside of the Law," in *Cornell Hotel and Restaurant Administration Quarterly.* Contributor to various law reviews.

WORK IN PROGRESS: Legal Aspects of Tourism and Travel Abroad, for Cornell University Press; a new text for *Business Law; International Travel and Tourism Law.*

SIDELIGHTS: John E. H. Sherry told *CA:* "Since graduation from law school, I have practiced in the hospitality field with my father when not engaged in teaching activities. My father and uncles have made their careers in this industry, particularly in the areas of hotel accounting and law, and this provided me with strong motivation and interest in developing legal texts as industry guides and as research vehicles for future scholarship. My current work with the State Department has reinforced this objective, and I have had the opportunity to meet with government and industry representatives throughout the world toward that end. My overall aim is to provide both the travel consumer and the industry executive with a balanced, objective view of the current state of the law and to point up future problem areas, with the ultimate objective of establishing a uniform international set of rules for innkeepers akin to the Warsaw Convention for air carriers.

"I spent the spring semester and summer of 1983 teaching international tourism and travel law to university students and professionals at Hangzhou University, People's Republic of China, as well as in Hong Kong, Japan, and Hawaii. In November of 1983, I was elected honorary president of the International Forum of Travel and Tourism Advocates, a new body headquartered in Jerusalem, Israel, to foster better world understanding and exchange of law-related matters. I am presently an external collaborator preparing a study of security and legal protection of tourists for the World Tourism Organization. During my forthcoming sabbatical leave in 1993, I hope to complete my *International Travel and Tourism Law* manuscript and intensify my professional activities in that area.

"All of these endeavors suggest a growing sensitivity to and understanding of the role of law in the promotion of global tourism and travel."

*   *   *

SHINGLETON, John D.

PERSONAL: Education—Michigan State University, B.A., 1948. *Avocational interests:* Sports (especially tennis).

ADDRESSES: Office—Office of Placement Services, Michigan State University, East Lansing, MI 48824.

CAREER: Wyandotte Chemical Corp., lathe operator; Ford Motor Co., Dearborn, MI, accountant; Detroit Edison Co., Detroit, MI, personnel interviewer; Michigan State University, East Lansing, served as assistant director of personnel, assistant director of placement, administrative officer of engineering project in Madras and Poona, India, assistant to secretary of board of trustees, director of placement, 1963—, acting director of intercollegiate athletics, 1975-76, member of university development council, and as member of board of trustees. Member of board of governors of College Placement Council; member of College-Industry Personnel Group. Member of Lansing Tri-County Area Manpower Planning Council, Michigan Department of Education *ad hoc* committee on placement, and board of directors of Michigan governor's Executive Corps. Guest on television programs, including the *Today Show*. Member of board of governors of National Fresh Water Fishing Hall of Fame. *Military service:* U.S. Army Air Forces, pilot.

MEMBER: Association for School, College, and University Staffing, Great Lakes Association for School, College, and University Staffing, Michigan College Placement Association, Michigan College and University Placement Association.

WRITINGS:

(With Phil Frank) *The Trout, the Whole Trout, and Nothing but the Trout,* Winchester Press, 1974.
(Co-author) *How to Increase Your Net Value,* Winchester Press, 1975.
College to Career: Finding Yourself in the Job Market, McGraw, 1977.
(With Patrick Scheetz) *Recruiting Trends, 1981-1982,* Placement Services, Michigan State University, 1981.
Career Planning in 1990's, Garrett Park Press, 1991.
Interviewing in Your Senior Year, NTC Publishing Group, 1992.

Also co-author of *Which Niche?,* 1969. Contributor to magazines, including *Parade, Business World, Michigan Challenge, Graduate,* and *American Youth.* Columnist for the *Detroit Free Press,* 1984-88.

WORK IN PROGRESS: A book on mid-career change, for Career Publishing.

*   *   *

SIEGEL, Marcia B. 1932-

PERSONAL: Born September 17, 1932, in New York, NY; daughter of Abraham (a journalist) and Lillian (Straus) Bernstein. *Education:* Connecticut College, B.A., 1954.

ADDRESSES: Home—244 West 72 Street, New York, NY, 10023. Agent—Spieler Agency, 154 West 57th Street, Room 135, New York, NY 10019.

CAREER: *Eagle-Tribune,* Lawrence, MA, reporter, 1959-61; *Metal Center News* (magazine), New York City, editorial assistant, 1961; Connecticut College, Office of Press Relations, New London, assistant, 1962-63; Clark Center for the Performing Arts, New York City, registrar, 1963-64; Library of Recorded Masterpieces, New York City, office manager, 1964-66; *Dance Scope* (magazine), founder/editor, 1964-66; *Arts in Society* (magazine), New York City, dance consultant, 1967-76; *Hudson Review,* dance critic and contributing editor, 1971—; *Soho Weekly News,* dance critic, 1974-82; New York University, associate professor of performance studies, 1983—. Director and member of faculty, West Coast Institute for Dance Criticism at California State University and Long Beach and Mills College, 1972-75, and Texas Institute for Dance Criticism, 1976-78. Visiting teacher and lecturer of dance criticism at workshops and seminars in Israel, England, the United States, and throughout Europe; visiting teacher and critic at Ohio State University, 1973, University of Wisconsin—Madison, 1975-76, Sarah Lawrence College, 1977-79, New York University, 1979, Walker Art Center, Minneapolis, MN, 1980, University of Iowa Writer's Workshop, 1980-81, Manhattanville College, 1982. Guest teacher, Copenhagen University, Finish Theatre Academy (Helsinki), both 1991. Association of American Dance Companies, board of directors, 1966-69; Dance Critics Association, board of directors, 1978-80; Laban Institute of Movement Studies, advisory council.

MEMBER: Phi Beta Kappa.

AWARDS, HONORS: Guggenheim Memorial fellowship, 1974-75; Japan Foundation fellowship, 1978; Ingram Merrill foundation grant, 1982, for completion of *Days on Earth: The Dance of Doris Humphrey:* challenge grant, New York University Humanities Council for Curriculum Development, 1985; discretionary grant, Asian Cultural Council, 1989, for travel in Indonesia.

WRITINGS:

At the Vanishing Point, Saturday Review Press, 1972.
Please Run on the Playground, Connecticut Commission on the Arts, 1975.
Watching the Dance Go By, Houghton, 1977.
The Shapes of Change: Images of American Dance, Houghton, 1979.
Then—The Early Years of Modern Dance (play), first produced in Salt Lake City, UT, at Repertory Dance Theatre, 1980.
Days on Earth: The Dance of Doris Humphrey, Yale University Press, 1987.

The Tail of the Dragon: New Dance, 1976-1982, Duke University Press, 1991.

Editor of *Dancer's Notes*, 1969, and *Nik: A Documentary*, Dance Perspectives Foundation, 1971. Contributor of articles and reviews to a variety of journals, including *Art in Society, American Poetry Review, American Theatre, Ballet News, Ballet International, Ballet Review, Dance, Dance Ink, Dance Research Journal, The Dial, Harpers, Kenyon Review, New York, New York Press, T.D.R., Time Out,* and *U. S. Information Agency,* and to the *Washington Post* and other newspapers.

SIDELIGHTS: "A critic of dance is in some ways a self-appointed historian," writes Marcia B. Siegel in *The Shapes of Change: Images of American Dance.* In this study of the growth of distinctively American choreography spanning the past seventy-five years, Ms. Siegel balances her role as noted dance critic with that of historian to provide a valuable record of dance literature. "[She] goes beyond the usual kind of historical reassessment that every reputable scholar must attempt," writes Dale Harris in the *New York Times Book Review.* Harris later adds, "By tracking down . . . as many of the works by major creators of the last half century as survive, and by describing them at some length and in a manner that combines accuracy and imagination, she has enriched our knowledge of the past."

BIOGRAPHICAL/CRITICAL SOURCES:

BOOKS

The Shapes of Change: Images of American Dance, Houghton, 1979.

PERIODICALS

Los Angeles Times Book Review, December 29, 1985, p. 4.
New York Times, April 22, 1977, p. C-25.
New York Times Book Review, July 1, 1979, p. 9; January 18, 1981, p. 35; February 28, 1988, p. 24.
Washington Post Book World, June 30, 1979, p. 2; January 18, 1981, p. 8.

*   *   *

SMART, Carol 1948-

PERSONAL: Born December 20, 1948, in London, England; daughter of Ernest (a hotel proprietor) and Vera (Armsden) Pinnock; married Barry Smart (a lecturer in sociology), September 22, 1972 (divorced, 1980). *Education:* Portsmouth Polytechnic, B.A. (with honors), 1972; University of Sheffield, M.A., 1974, Ph.D., 1984.

ADDRESSES: Office—Department of Social Policy and Sociology, University of Leeds, West Yorkshire, England.

CAREER: Social worker, 1972-73; Sheffield University, Sheffield, England, postgraduate tutor in sociology, 1973-74; Trent Polytechnic, Nottingham, England, lecturer in sociology, 1974-78; Sheffield University, Social Science Research Council, research fellow, 1979-82; Institute of Psychiatry, London, England, research sociologist, 1982-84; National Council for One Parent Families, London, Director, 1984-85; University of Warwick, senior lecturer in sociology, 1985-91; University of Leeds, Leeds, England, professor of sociology, 1991—.

MEMBER: British Sociological Association, Association of University Teachers.

WRITINGS:

Women, Crime, and Criminology: A Feminist Critique, Routledge & Kegan Paul, 1976.
(Editor with Barry Smart) *Women, Sexuality, and Social Control,* Routledge & Kegan Paul, 1977.
The Ties That Bind, Routledge & Kegan Paul, 1984.
(Editor with Julia Brophy) *Women in Law,* Routledge & Kegan Paul, 1985.
Feminism and the Power of Law, Routledge & Kegan Paul, 1989.
(Editor with Selma Sevenhuijsen) *Child Custody and the Politics of Gender,* Routledge & Kegan Paul, 1989.
(Editor) *Regulating Womanhood: Historical Essays on Marriage, Motherhood and Sexuality,* Routledge & Kegan Paul, 1991.

Editor, *International Journal of the Sociology of Law,* 1987-91; editor, *Social and Legal Studies,* 1991—. Contributor to periodicals, including *Feminist Review* and *Journal of Law and Society.*

WORK IN PROGRESS: Feminist theory as it relates to the body; research on child custody after divorce; aspects of feminist legal theory.

SIDELIGHTS: Carol Smart told *CA:* "I wrote *Women, Crime, and Criminology: A Feminist Critique* as a consequence of being a feminist in a master's course in criminology. I realised very quickly that there was little adequate material on women and crime and felt that the whole area needed to be reappraised. I am particularly concerned about the sexist treatment of women in the criminal process (e.g. prostitutes and rape victims) and intend to do more research in this area."

Smart later added: "I have been writing in the field of women and law for over a decade. Much of my work has been concerned with the application of feminist ideas to legal policy. Recently, I have become more interested in theoretical issues of feminist thought."

SMITH, Dodie
 See SMITH, Dorothy Gladys

*   *   *

SMITH, Dorothy Gladys 1896-1990
 (Dodie Smith; pseudonyms: C. L. Anthony,
 Charles Henry Percy)

PERSONAL: Born May 3, 1896, in Whitefield, Lancashire, England; died November 24, 1990; daughter of Ernest Walter and Ella (Furber) Smith; married Alec Macbeth Beesley, 1939 (died, 1987). *Education:* Attended Manchester School and St. Paul's Girls' School, London; studied for the stage at Royal Academy of Dramatic Art, London. *Avocational interests:* Reading, music, dogs, donkeys.

ADDRESSES: Home—The Barretts, Finchingfield, Essex, England.

CAREER: Actress, 1915-22; Heal & Son (furnishing company), London, England, buyer, 1923-32; full-time writer, 1932-90.

WRITINGS:

PLAYS; UNDER PSEUDONYM C. L. ANTHONY

British Talent, first produced in London at Three Arts Club, 1924.
Autumn Crocus (three-act comedy; first produced in London at Lyric Theatre, April 6, 1931; produced on Broadway at Morosco Theatre, November, 1932; also see below), Samuel French, 1931.
Service (three-act comedy; first produced in London at Wyndham's Theatre, October 12, 1932; also see below), Gollancz, 1932, acting edition, Samuel French, 1937.
Touch Wood (three-act comedy; first produced in London at Theatre Royal, Haymarket, May 16, 1934; also see below), Samuel French, 1934.

PLAYS; UNDER NAME DODIE SMITH

Call It a Day (three-act comedy; first produced in London at Globe Theatre, October 30, 1935; produced at Morosco Theatre, 1936), Samuel French, 1936, acting edition, 1937.
Bonnet over the Windmill (three-act comedy; first produced in London at New Theatre, September 8, 1937), Heinemann, 1937.
(And co-director) *Dear Octopus* (three-act comedy; first produced in London at Queen's Theatre, September 14, 1938; produced on Broadway at Broadhurst Theatre, 1939; revived at Theatre Royal, Haymarket,

1967), Heinemann, 1938, acting edition, Samuel French, 1939.
Autumn Crocus, Service, and Touch Wood: Three Plays, Heinemann, 1939.
Lovers and Friends (three-act comedy; first produced on Broadway at Plymouth Theatre, November 29, 1943), Samuel French, 1944.
Letter from Paris (three-act comedy adapted from Henry James's novel, *The Reverberator;* first produced in London at Aldwych Theatre, October 10, 1952), Heinemann, 1954.
I Capture the Castle (two-act romantic comedy adapted by the author from her novel of the same title; first produced at Aldwych Theatre, March 4, 1954; also see below), Samuel French, 1952.
These People, Those Books (three-act comedy), first produced in Leeds at Grand Theatre, 1958.
Amateur Means Lover (three-act comedy; first produced in Liverpool at Liverpool Playhouse, 1961), Samuel French, 1962.

NOVELS; UNDER NAME DODIE SMITH

I Capture the Castle, Atlantic/Little, Brown, 1948.
The New Moon with the Old, Atlantic/Little, Brown, 1963.
The Town in Bloom, Atlantic/Little, Brown, 1965.
It Ends with Revelations, Atlantic/Little, Brown, 1967.
A Tale of Two Families, Walker, 1970.
The Girl from the Candle-lit Bath, W. H. Allen, 1978.

FOR CHILDREN; UNDER NAME DODIE SMITH

The Hundred and One Dalmatians, illustrations by Janet Grahame-Johnstone and Anne Grahame-Johnstone, Heinemann, 1956, Viking, 1957, reprinted with illustrations by Michael Dooling, Viking/Puffin Books, 1989.
The Starlight Barking: More about the Hundred and One Dalmatians, illustrations by J. Grahame-Johnstone and A. Grahame-Johnstone, Heinemann, 1967, Simon & Schuster, 1968.
The Midnight Kittens, illustrations by J. Grahame-Johnstone and A. Grahame-Johnstone, W. H. Allen, 1978.

AUTOBIOGRAPHIES; UNDER NAME DODIE SMITH

Look Back with Love: A Manchester Childhood, Heinemann, 1974.
Look Back with Mixed Feelings, W. H. Allen, 1978.
Look Back with Astonishment, W. H. Allen, 1979.
Look Back with Gratitude, Muller Blond and White, 1985.

SCREENPLAYS

(With Frank Partos) *The Uninvited* (adapted from the novel by Dorothy Macardle), Paramount, 1944.

(With Lesser Samuels) *Darling, How Could You!* (adapted from *Alice-Sit-by-the-Fire* by James M. Barrie), Paramount, 1951.

Also author of screenplay "Schoolgirl Rebels" (under pseudonym Charles Henry Percy), 1915.

ADAPTATIONS: Autumn Crocus was filmed in England, 1934; *Call It a Day* was made into a movie by Warner Brothers, 1937; *Service* was filmed by Metro-Goldwyn-Mayer in 1944 as *Looking Forward; Dear Octopus* was also filmed in England, 1945; *The Hundred and One Dalmatians* was filmed by Walt Disney Productions as *One Hundred and One Dalmatians,* 1961.

SIDELIGHTS: Often remembered as the author of *The Hundred and One Dalmatians,* the children's story that Walt Disney Studios filmed as the animated *One Hundred and One Dalmatians,* Dorothy Gladys Smith was primarily an author of works for adults, including plays, novels, and several autobiographical works. Smith, better known by the name Dodie Smith, first gained recognition as a playwright, going by the name of C. L. Anthony until 1935, when she began to write under her own name. Her plays are generally light comedies about middle-class life that earned enough popular and critical praise in their time for *Dictionary of Literary Biography* contributor Martha Hadsel to deem Smith "one of the few successful women dramatists in England and American during the first half of the twentieth century."

Smith credited her early family life as the greatest factor in determining her future career. "When I was eighteen months old," Smith once told *CA,* "my father died, and after that my mother and I lived with her family—my grandparents, three uncles and two aunts—in an old house with a garden sloping towards the Manchester Ship Canal. It was a stimulating household. Both my mother and grandmother wrote and composed. Almost everyone sang and played some musical instrument (we owned three pianos, a violin, a mandolin, a guitar and a banjo) and one uncle, an admirable amateur actor, was often to be heard rehearsing, preferably with me on hand to give him his cues. Although I had been taken to theatres long before I could read, it was this hearing of my uncle's parts which really aroused my interest in acting and in playwriting; the cues I gave got longer and longer and, by the age of nine, I had written a forty-page play. When I read this aloud to my mother she fell asleep—to awake and say apologetically, 'But darling, it was so dull.' "

Her mother's reaction did not discourage Smith in any way. Nevertheless, her original plan was to become an actress and not a playwright. After studying at the Royal Academy of Art, she performed professionally with some of her fellow students before becoming a member of the Portsmouth Repertory Theatre. During World War I,

Smith went to France to help entertain the soldiers there, and she also played a role in a Zurich performance of John Galsworthy's *Pigeon.* But in 1923 the young actress decided to leave the theater and work as a buyer for Heal and Son, a furniture company where she was employed for the next eight years.

Then, in 1931, Smith sold her play *Autumn Crocus* to one of her former stage directors. Although she had written a screenplay and a stage play before, *Autumn Crocus* was the work that turned her career around. The "romantic comedy brought Smith immediate success because of its winning combination of an Alpine setting, humor, music, and a love story," according to Hadsel. The next two plays that Smith published under the C. L. Anthony pseudonym, *Service* and *Touch Wood,* were also critically acclaimed, and Hadsel notes that some reviewers even compared *Touch Wood* to the work of the famous nineteenth-century Norwegian dramatist, Henrik Ibsen.

Call It a Day was the first play Smith wrote under her own name, as well as her most financially rewarding work. It ran for almost two hundred performances in New York City and had over five hundred performances in London. "By this time," related Hadsel, "she had purchased The Barretts, a cottage near the village of Finchingfield, Essex, and had made writing her full-time occupation." Traveling to the United States in 1938 to help with a New York City production of her *Dear Octopus,* Smith decided to remain in America, where she married her business manager, Alec Macbeth Beesley. During the next fifteen years she lived mostly in California and did some writing for Paramount Studios. It was while she was living in Pennsylvania, however, that she published her first—and most popular—novel, *I Capture the Castle.*

After returning to England, Smith continued to write plays and novels, but she also began writing stories for children, including *The Hundred and One Dalmatians* and its sequel, *The Starlight Barking: More about the Hundred and One Dalmatians.* The owner of a number of pet dalmatians herself, it is not surprising that Smith chose to make her main characters—Pongo, Missis Pongo, and their myriad puppies—dalmatians, and the adventures they have while foiling the plans of the evil furrier's wife, Cruella de Vil, have entertained many young readers. The last years of Smith's life were spent working on her autobiography, the four volumes of which, entitled *Look Back with Love: A Manchester Childhood, Look Back with Mixed Feelings, Look Back with Astonishment,* and *Look Back with Gratitude,* relate her experiences from childhood to the years she spent in the United States.

Although some critics have at times complained about what they considered Smith's "superficiality" in her work, Hadsel noted that her characters have appealed to audiences because they are "close enough to reality that . . . [people] feel comfortably at home with them, yet they are imaginative enough that her audience could find refreshment." Having made a successful career for herself as a writer in several genres, Smith nevertheless once revealed to *CA:* "I consider myself a lightweight author, but God knows I approach my work with as much seriousness as if it were Holy Writ."

BIOGRAPHICAL/CRITICAL SOURCES:

BOOKS

Dictionary of Literary Biography, Volume 10: *Modern British Dramatists, 1900-1945,* Gale, 1982, pp. 158-162.

OBITUARIES:

PERIODICALS

Times (London), November 27, 1990.*

—*Sketch by Kevin S. Hile*

*   *   *

SNYDER, Bernadette McCarver   1930-

PERSONAL: Born December 6, 1930, in Long Island, NY; daughter of William C. (in private business) and Hazel (a housewife; maiden name, Davids) McCarver; married John William Snyder (in U.S. Civil Service), September 28, 1963; children: Matthew Joseph. *Education:* Attended private school in Nashville, TN. *Religion:* Roman Catholic.

ADDRESSES: Home and office—1201 Cheverly Ct., St. Louis, MO 63146.

CAREER: Speight Agency, Nashville, TN, advertising copywriter, 1950s; Gardner Advertising, St. Louis, MO, advertising copywriter, 1960s; homemaker and free-lance writer, 1965-77; Liguori Publications, Liguori, MO, director of special advertising, 1977-85; free-lance writer, 1986—.

MEMBER: International Platform Association.

WRITINGS:

Hoorays and Hosannas: An Everyday-Anyday Book of Family Ideas and Activities, Ave Maria Press, 1980.
Graham Crackers, Galoshes, and God: Laughs from Everyday Life, Prayers for Everyday Problems, Liguori Publications, 1982.
Dear God, I Have This Terrible Problem: A Housewife's Secret Letters, Liguori Publications, 1983.
(With sister, Hazelmai McCarver Terry) *Decorations for Forty-Four Parish Celebrations,* Twenty-Third Publications, 1983.

The Kitchen Sink Prayer Book, Liguori Publications, 1984.
Everyday Prayers for Everyday People, Our Sunday Visitor, 1984.
Heavenly Hash (collected columns), Our Sunday Visitor, 1985.
MORE Graham Crackers, Galoshes and God, Liguori Publications, 1985.
Merry Mary Meditations, Liguori Publications, 1987.
(With Terry) *Decorating for Sundays and Holy Days,* Twenty-Third Publications, Cycle C: *Themes, Homily Suggestions, Activities,* 1988, Cycle A, 1989, Cycle B, 1990.
365 Fun Facts for Catholic Kids: Inspiring Ideas, Saintly Surprises, Non-Trivial Tidbits, Liguori Publications, 1989.
150 Fun Facts Found in the Bible—for Kids of All Ages, Liguori Publications, 1990.
The Fun Facts Dictionary: A World of Weird, Wonderful Words, Liguori Publications, 1991.
That's Life, Liguori Publications, 1991.

Also author of "A Mother's Meditation," a weekly column in *Our Sunday Visitor.*

SIDELIGHTS: Bernadette McCarver Snyder once told *CA:* "I always wanted to become a writer—and I'm still trying to 'become' one. I started writing in school and continued taking writing classes and collecting rejection slips for several years but got sidetracked when I started getting paid real money for writing television commercials and other advertising. When I married and 'retired' to raise a family, I thought I'd have more time for writing—but actually had less than ever. However, I continued doing free-lance advertising and did sell some humor articles.

"I never thought I would have the stick-to-itiveness to write a whole book but in 1977, I started working in the advertising department of a publisher of religious books. As I worked with others' manuscripts, I thought 'why not?' And since I had had success writing humor articles, I thought 'why not a humorous religious book?' My first book was accepted by the second publisher I sent it to—and after that, the company where I was working noticed I was an 'author' and published my next one. Now I have actually had a publisher ask me to write a book for them—a nice contrast to my collection of rejection slips!

"There aren't too many religious humor books on the market so maybe that's why mine have sold well. But I think of God as a good friend, rather than a judge sitting on a cloud watching to see if I make a mistake—and I don't think he minds my laughing about and rejoicing in all the funny and delightful things in his world. In fact, I think he often laughs along with me—because he's the one who gave me the crazy kind of mind that would associate God with such things as graham crackers, goulash, galoshes, heavenly hash, and kitchen sinks!"

*   *   *

SOLO, Robert A(lexander) 1916-

PERSONAL: Born August 2, 1916, in Philadelphia, PA; son of Louis (a merchant) and Rebecca (Muchnick) Solo; married Carolyn Shaw Bell, June, 1942 (divorced, 1949); married Roselyn Starr (a university teacher), August, 1958; children: (first marriage) Tova. *Education:* Harvard University, B.S. (magna cum laude), 1938; American University, M.A., 1941; Cornell University, Ph.D., 1953; also attended London School of Economics and Political Science. *Politics:* "Democratic Left." *Religion:* Jewish.

ADDRESSES: Office—Department of Economics, Michigan State University, East Lansing, MI 48823.

CAREER: Economist in U.S. Government agencies, Washington, DC, 1939-41; WCAU-Television (Columbia Broadcasting System affiliate), Philadelphia, PA, writer and script chief, 1948-49; Rutgers University, New Brunswick, NJ, instructor, 1952-54, assistant professor of economics, 1954-55; McGill University, Montreal, Quebec, visiting lecturer in economics, 1955-56; City College (now City College of the City University of New York), New York, NY, assistant professor of economics, 1956-59; Economic Development Administration of Commonwealth of Puerto Rico, San Juan, consultant, 1959-61; National Planning Association, Washington, DC, project director, 1961-63; Organization for Economic Cooperation and Development, Paris, France, consultant to directorate of scientific affairs, 1963-64; Sorbonne, University of Paris, Paris, France, lecturer in economics, 1964-65; National Academy of Sciences and National Research Council, Washington, DC, special associate to foreign secretary, 1965; Princeton University, Princeton, NJ, senior research economist, 1965-66; Michigan State University, East Lansing, professor of economics and management, 1966-68, professor of economics, 1969-81, professor emeritus, 1981—, director of Institute of International Business and Economic Development Studies, 1966-68. Visiting lecturer, University of Michigan, summer, 1955; professeur associe, University of Paris, 1971; Fulbright lecturer, University of Grenoble, 1972-73. Consultant to U.S. Senate subcommittee on patents, trademarks, and copyrights, 1956-58, to National Aeronautics and Space Administration (NASA), 1965-67, and to National Conference Board, 1970-72. *Military service:* U.S. Navy, 1941-46.

WRITINGS:

Industrial Capacity in the United States, Office of Price Administration and Civilian Supply, 1941.

(With Georges Agadjanian) *La Vallee des ombres* (novel), Editions de la Maison Francaise, 1941.

(Editor and contributor) *Economics and the Public Interest,* Rutgers University Press, 1955.

Synthetic Rubber: A Case Study in Technological Development under Government Direction, U.S. Government Printing Office (for U.S. Senate Committee on the Judiciary), 1959.

Essai sur l'Amerique, Editions de la Diaspora Francaise, 1960.

Journal, Editions de la Diaspora Francaise, 1961.

Economic Organizations and Social Systems, Bobbs-Merrill, 1967.

(Editor with Everett Rogers, and contributor) *Inducing Technological Advance in Economic Growth and Development,* Michigan State University Press, 1973.

The Political Authority and the Market System, South-Western, 1974.

Organizing Science for Technology Transfer in Economic Development, Michigan State University Press, 1975.

Across the High Technology Threshold: The Case of Synthetic Rubber, Norwood Editions, 1980.

(Editor with Charles Anderson, and contributor) *Value Judgements and Income Distribution,* Praeger, 1981.

The Positive State, South-Western, 1982.

The Philosophy of Science, and Economics, Macmillan, 1991.

Opportunity Knocks: American Economic Policy after Gorbachev, M.E. Sharpe, 1991.

Contributor to books, including *The Economics of Technological Change,* edited by Nathan Rosenberg, Penguin, 1971; *Frontiers of Social Thought,* edited by Martin Pfaff, North-Holland Publishing, 1975; *Grants and Exchange,* edited by Pfaff, North-Holland Publishing, 1976; *The Economy as a System of Power,* edited by Warren Samuels, Transaction Books, 1979; *Contemporary Economists in Perspective,* edited by Spiegel and Samuels, JAI Press, 1984; *American Economic Policy,* edited by Alperovitz and Skurski, University of Notre Dame Press, 1984; *An International Political Economy,* edited by Hollist and Tullis, Westview Press, 1985; *Energy Resources Development,* edited by Ender and Kim, Quorm Books, 1987; and *Current Issues in Microeconomics,* edited by Hey, Macmillan, 1989. Also contributor to *America's World Role for the Next Twenty-five Years,* proceedings of a professional conference in Taiwan, 1976. Contributor of about one hundred articles and reviews to economics journals and other publications, including *Saturday Review, Technology and Culture, Current, Looking Ahead, Challenge, Canadian Bar Review, Journal of Philosophy,* and *Social Science.*

WORK IN PROGRESS: Andre Francois-Poncet's Third Reich (with wife, Roselyn Solo), a panoramic vision of the extraordinary man who served as Ambassador of France in Berlin and Rome; *Everyman's Michel Foucault,* review, explanation and clarification of the works of the late great French philosopher.

SIDELIGHTS: In a *Science* review, Kenneth E. Boulding calls Robert A. Solo's *Economic Organizations and Social Systems* "an important work, a milestone on the long and difficult road toward the development of an adequate theory of the dynamics of the world social system." He notes that although the book is somewhat uneven in style "with some long, textbookish passages of rather dull though usually accurate and insightful analysis of social systems," these are interspersed with "passages that are on fire with intellectual and humane passion, and historical vignettes which are masterpieces of condensation and insight with not a word wasted." Boulding concludes that "if this is a work of insight rather than of science it is because of the absence of an adequate system of social instrumentation. . . . The cognitive theory of social change, which Solo is propounding, will remain in the realm of insight until we develop an adequate information system for what might be called a mass cognitive structure. This we do not now have, and in its absence we have to rely on illustration rather than demonstration."

Solo once told *CA:* "I sometimes wonder why many who are so beautifully articulate verbally cannot write effectively. I think it has something to do with the need for an audience. Writing is a kind of talking to yourself, listening to yourself, evaluating yourself by yourself, a solitary business in a way, not for the one geared into and needing the active interplay of conversation and the immediacy of discourse. Before the writer is the dreamer, and for both there is a closed world, a space of rich solitude, for them a haven and the vital source."

BIOGRAPHICAL/CRITICAL SOURCES:

PERIODICALS

Science, September, 1967.

*   *   *

SOUTH, Clark
See SWAIN, Dwight V(reeland)

*   *   *

STACY, Donald
See POHL, Frederik

STAINES, Trevor
See BRUNNER, John (Kilian Houston)

*   *   *

STEINER, Paul

PERSONAL: Born in Germany; son of Otto (a banker) and Bertha (Sulmann) Steiner. *Education:* New York University, B.S., 1947. *Avocational interests:* Collecting stamps and ancient relics, art.

ADDRESSES: Home—161 West 54th St., Suite 402, New York, NY 10019.

CAREER: Coronet, New York City, features editor, 1947-53, humor editor, 1963; North American Newspaper Alliance, New York City, columnist and feature writer, 1958-80; Women's News Service, New York City, correspondent, 1959-74; Bell-McClure Syndicate's Pop Scene Service, New York City, feature writer and interviewer, 1967-80; correspondent for *New York Post,* 1977-79, 1981-82, *National Enquirer,* 1977—, *New York,* 1978—, *National Star,* 1978—, *Us,* 1978-80, *Globe,* 1979—, *People,* 1980—, *New York Daily News,* 1980—, *Prevue,* 1983-86, Reuters news service, 1984—, Copley Press Inc., 1984—, *USA Today,* 1984—, and *Manhattan,* 1985-86. *Military service:* U.S. Army, served during World War II.

MEMBER: Alpha Delta Sigma, Psi Chi Omega, Alpha Epsilon Pi.

AWARDS, HONORS: Beaux Arts awards, 1968, for satire, 1969, for press, 1970, for columns, and 1991, for book author; International Press Award, John King Productions, 1981; World Culture prize, Centro Studi e Ricetche Dell Nazione, Italy, 1985.

WRITINGS:

Israel Laughs: A Collection of Humor from the Jewish State, Bloch, 1950.
Women and Children First, Bantam, 1955.
Bedtime Laughs, Lion Press, 1956.
Bottoms Up, edited by Charles Preston, Dell, 1957.
Bedside Bachelor, Lion Press, 1957.
Useless Information: How to Know More and More about Less and Less, Citadel, 1959.
How to Be Offensive to Practically Everybody, Citadel, 1960.
Sex after Six, Hillman, 1961.
More Useless Information, Citadel, 1962.
Useless Facts of History, Abelard, 1964.
175 Little Known Facts about John F. Kennedy, Citadel, 1964.
Useless Facts about Women, Abelard, 1965.

(Editor) Adlai E. Stevenson, *The Stevenson Wit and Wisdom,* Pyramid, 1965.

1001 Tips for Teens, Pyramid, 1967.

Presidential Oddities, Manor, 1976.

Author of columns, *Jewish Herald,* 1988—, "Theatre Chat" in *Theatre Week,* 1988—, "Steiner's Stage" in *Call-Back,* 1989—, "Trifles" in *Big Apple News,* 1990—, "Theatre Talk" in *Dramatics,* 1991—, and *Playbill,* "New York Quickies" in *Showbiz,* 1991—, and *Cable TV World,* "Working Rules" and "Picket Lines" in *Partners,* "New York Pro and Con" in *Promenade,* "The Wheel of Fortune" in *Fate,* "Israel Laughs" in *American Zionist,* "Where in the World" in *Travel Weekly,* "Places to Go" in *Signature,* "Musically Speaking" in *ASCAP Today,* "Notes and Quotes" in *Escapade,* "Raw and Recent" in *Caper,* "Odds and Ends" in *True Love,* "Artistic Notions" in *ArtSpeak,* "Extra Special" in *Murray Hill News,* "Sunday's People" for *New York Daily News* (Sunday edition), "Wits at the Wheel" in *Car Pages,* and "Trivia I.Q." for Columbia Features Syndicate. Contributor of features, quizzes and short humor to *This Week, TV Guide, Redbook, Show Business Illustrated, Reader's Digest, New York Times Magazine, Pageant, Argosy, Maclean's, Teen World, Cavalier, Variety, Critic's Guide, Bravo, Military Life, Cat Fancy, Dog Fancy, Entertainment West, Wall Street Journal, Gem, Newsday, Queens Tribune, Omni, Metropolitan Home, Linn's Stamp News* and other magazines and newspapers. Contributing editor to *ArtSpeak,* 1979—, *Jewish Journal,* 1984—, *Broadway,* 1985—, *Models and Talent,* 1985—, and to *Metro Jewish Life, Singles, Critique, New York Entertainer,* and *TGIF Entertainment.*

SIDELIGHTS: Paul Steiner once wrote: "I've always preferred short pieces to long ones—concentrating on the unusual, the humorous, the unknown or little-known facts. When I started out there was mostly a demand for unusual incidents; now there is a demand for celebrity news. . . . There are thousands of fine editors and writers—I'm talking about nonfiction—who can write superbly and with correct grammar and punctuation. But there are mighty few who have a knack for the light touch, the bizarre. I agree with Adlai E. Stevenson's dictum: 'It's easy to make people cry, but very hard to make them laugh.' I'm grateful to the editors who have appreciated my enthusiasm for and furthered my search for material that amuses and entertains. Without them I'd be sculpting in snow or engraving soap bubbles, as people wiser than I have said."

*   *   *

STETTNER, Irving   1922-

PERSONAL: Born November 7, 1922, in Brooklyn, NY; son of Morris (a carpenter) and Nettie (Falk) Stettner;

children: Mona. *Education:* Attended Columbia University, 1946-47. *Politics:* None. *Religion:* None.

ADDRESSES: Home—129 Second Ave., No. 19, New York, NY 10003.

CAREER: Has worked variously as a farmer, free-lance writer, painter, door-to-door salesman, seaman, cafe sketch artist, watercolorist, and carpenter. Work has been exhibited at thirteen one-man shows in New York, France, and Japan. *Military service:* U.S. Army, Signal Corps, 1942-45.

WRITINGS:

On the Second Avenue Patrol: Selected Poems, Home Planet Publications, 1976.

Anna: A Bicentennial Poem, Amphora Press, 1977.

Jo Ann in the White House (one-act play; first produced in New York City at Theatre Genesis, 1978), X Press Press, 1977.

Hurrah!: Selected Poems, Downtown Poets Press, 1979.

Footloose, Gonfolan Press, 1981.

Thumbing Down to Rivera, Writers Unlimited, 1986.

Beggars in Paradise, Writers Unlimited, 1991.

Self-Portrait: Twelve Poems for the Road, Sun Dog Press, 1991.

Contributor of poems to more than thirty-five magazines in the United States and abroad, including Greece, Italy, Poland, and France. Editor of *Stroker.*

WORK IN PROGRESS: An autobiographical novel.

SIDELIGHTS: Irving Stettner told *CA:* "I write basically for self-expression. Always a little surprised when I hear someone say they like what I've written. My big influences are Walt Whitman, Arthur Rimbaud, Henry Miller, John Cowper Powys. I live in New York but detest it; have to go every two years to France a month or so, just to feel like a human being. Meanwhile feel little rapport with the current American literary scene. Only U.S. writers I read are Tommy Trantino and William Joyce."

*   *   *

STEWART, John   1933-

PERSONAL: Born January 24, 1933, in Trinidad; son of Ernest (a musician) and Irene (Holder) Stewart; married Belva Scott, April 12, 1960 (divorced, 1968); married Sandra MacDonald (an executive program developer), June 7, 1969; children: Malcolm, Jabali, Laini. *Education:* California State University, Los Angeles, B.A., 1960; Stanford University, M.A., 1965; University of Iowa, M.F.A., 1966; University of California, Los Angeles, Ph.D, 1973.

ADDRESSES: Office—Afro-American Studies Program, University of California, Davis, CA 95616.

CAREER: California State University, Fresno, 1966-72, began as assistant professor, became associate professor of English; University of Illinois at Urbana-Champaign, 1972-84, began as assistant professor, became associate professor of English; Ohio State University, Columbus, professor of English and anthropology, 1984-91; University of California, Davis, director of Afro-American Studies program, 1991—.

AWARDS, HONORS: Winifred Holtby Memorial Award, Royal Society of Literature, 1972; National Education Association Creative Writing Award, 1978; award from Institute for Advanced Study, 1979-80; award from Illinois Arts Council, 1984.

WRITINGS:

Last Cool Days, Deutch, 1970.
Curving Road, University of Illinois Press, 1975.
Drinkers, Drummers and Decent Folk, State University of New York Press, 1989.
(With Bessie Jones) *For the Ancestors,* University of Illinois Press, 1983.

Contributor to books, including *Chant of Saints,* edited by Michael S. Harper and Robert Stepto, University of Illinois Press, 1979; *Best West Indian Short Stories,* edited by Kenneth Ramchand, Nelson & Sons, 1981; *The Anthropology of Experience,* edited by Ed Bruner and Victor Turner, University of Illinois Press, 1985; *Literature and Anthropology,* edited by Dennis and Aycock, Texas Tech Press, 1989; *Faber Book of Contemporary Caribbean Short Stories,* edited by Mervyn Morris, Faber & Faber, 1990.

WORK IN PROGRESS: Research on ethnography of Caribbean societies.

* * *

SUTCLIFF, Rosemary 1920-

PERSONAL: Born December 14, 1920, in East Clanden, Surrey, England; daughter of George Ernest (an officer in the Royal Navy) and Nessie Elizabeth (Lawton) Sutcliff. *Education:* Educated privately and at Bideford School of Art, 1935-39. *Politics:* "Vaguely Conservative." *Religion:* Unorthodox Church of England. *Avocational interests:* Archaeology, anthropology, primitive religion, making collages and costume jewelry.

ADDRESSES: Home—Swallowshaw, Walberton, Arundel, West Sussex BN18 0PQ, England.

CAREER: Writer, 1945—.

MEMBER: PEN, National Book League, Society of Authors, Royal Society of Miniature Painters.

AWARDS, HONORS: Carnegie Medal commendation, 1955, and American Library Association (ALA) Notable Book, both for *The Eagle of the Ninth;* Carnegie Medal commendation, *New York Herald Tribune's* Children's Spring Book Festival honor book, both 1957, and ALA Notable Book, all for *The Shield Ring;* Carnegie Medal commendation, and *New York Herald Tribune's* Children's Spring Book Festival honor book, both 1958, both for *The Silver Branch;* Carnegie Medal commendation, 1959, Hans Christian Andersen Award honor book, 1959, International Board on Books for Young People honor list, 1960, Highly Commended Author, 1974, and ALA Notable Book, all for *Warrior Scarlet;* Carnegie Medal, 1960, and ALA Notable Book, both for *The Lantern Bearers;* ALA Notable Book, 1960, for *Knight's Fee; New York Herald Tribune's* Children's Spring Book Festival Award, 1962, ALA Notable Book, and *Horn Book* honor list, all for *Dawn Wind;* ALA Notable Book, and *Horn Book* honor list, both 1962, both for *Beowulf;* ALA Notable Book, and *Horn Book* honor list, both 1963, both for *The Hound of Ulster;* ALA Notable Book, *Horn Book* honor list, both 1965, and Children's Literature Association Phoenix Award, 1985, all for *The Mark of the Horse Lord; Horn Book* honor list, 1967, for *The High Deeds of Finn MacCool;* Lewis Carroll Shelf Award, 1971, ALA Notable Book, and *Horn Book* honor list, all for *The Witch's Brat; Boston Globe-Horn Book* Award for outstanding text, Carnegie Medal runner-up, both 1972, ALA Notable Book, and *Horn Book* honor list, all for *Tristan and Iseult; Heather, Oak, and Olive: Three Stories* was selected one of Child Study Association's "Children's Books of the Year," 1972, and *The Capricorn Bracelet* was selected, 1973; Officer, Order of the British Empire, 1975; *Boston Globe-Horn Book* honor book for fiction, 1977, and *Horn Book* honor list, both for *Blood Feud; Children's Book Bulletin* Other Award, 1978, for *Song for a Dark Queen; Horn Book* honor list, 1978, for *Sun Horse, Sun Moon;* Children's Rights Workshop Award, 1978; ALA Notable Book, 1982, for *The Road to Camlann: The Death of King Arthur;* Royal Society of Literature fellow, 1982; Commander, Order of the British Empire, 1992.

WRITINGS:

Lady in Waiting (novel), Hodder & Stoughton, 1956, Coward, 1957.
The Rider of the White Horse (novel), Hodder & Stoughton, 1959, abridged edition, Penguin, 1964, published in the United States as *Rider on a White Horse,* Coward, 1960.
Rudyard Kipling, Bodley Head, 1960, Walck, 1961, bound with *Arthur Ransome,* by Hugh Shelley, and *Walter de la Mare,* by Leonard Clark, Bodley Head, 1968.

Sword at Sunset (novel; Literary Guild selection), illustrated by John Vernon Lord, Coward, 1963, abridged edition, Longmans, 1967.

The Flowers of Adonis (novel), Hodder & Stoughton, 1969, Coward, 1970.

Blood and Sand, Hodder & Stoughton, 1987.

"ROMAN BRITAIN" TRILOGY

The Eagle of the Ninth (also see below), illustrated by C. Walter Hodges, Oxford University Press, 1954, Walck, 1961.

The Silver Branch (also see below), illustrated by Charles Keeping, Oxford University Press, 1957, Walck, 1959.

The Lantern Bearers (also see below), illustrated by Keeping, Walck, 1959, revised edition, Oxford University Press, 1965.

Three Legions: A Trilogy (contains *The Eagle of the Ninth, The Silver Branch,* and *The Lantern Bearers*), Oxford University Press, 1980.

"ARTHURIAN KNIGHTS" TRILOGY

The Light beyond the Forest: The Quest for the Holy Grail, illustrated by Shirley Felts, Bodley Head, 1979, Dutton, 1980.

The Sword and the Circle: King Arthur and the Knights of the Round Table, illustrated by Felts, Dutton, 1981.

The Road to Camlann: The Death of King Arthur, illustrated by Felts, Bodley Head, 1981, Dutton Children's Books, 1982.

CHILDREN'S BOOKS

The Chronicles of Robin Hood, illustrated by C. Walter Hodges, Walck, 1950.

The Queen Elizabeth Story, illustrated by Hodges, Walck, 1950.

The Armourer's House, illustrated by Hodges, Walck, 1951.

Brother Dusty-Feet, illustrated by Hodges, Walck, 1952.

Simon, illustrated by Richard Kennedy, Walck, 1953.

Outcast, illustrated by Kennedy, Walck, 1955.

The Shield Ring, illustrated by Hodges, Walck, 1956.

Warrior Scarlet, illustrated by Charles Keeping, Walck, 1958, 2nd edition, 1966.

The Bridge-Builders, Blackwell, 1959.

Knight's Fee, illustrated by Keeping, Walck, 1960.

Houses and History, illustrated by William Stobbs, Batsford, 1960, Putnam, 1965.

Dawn Wind, illustrated by Keeping, Oxford University Press, 1961, Walck, 1962.

Dragon Slayer, illustrated by Keeping, Bodley Head, 1961, published as *Beowulf,* Dutton, 1962, published as *Dragon Slayer: The Story of Beowulf,* Macmillan, 1980.

The Hound of Ulster, illustrated by Victor Ambrus, Dutton, 1963.

Heroes and History, illustrated by Keeping, Putnam, 1965.

A Saxon Settler, illustrated by John Lawrence, Oxford University Press, 1965.

The Mark of the Horse Lord, illustrated by Keeping, Walck, 1965.

The High Deeds of Finn MacCool, illustrated by Michael Charlton, Dutton, 1967.

The Chief's Daughter (also see below), illustrated by Ambrus, Hamish Hamilton, 1967.

A Circlet of Oak Leaves (also see below), illustrated by Ambrus, Hamish Hamilton, 1968.

The Witch's Brat, illustrated by Richard Lebenson, Walck, 1970, illustrated by Robert Micklewright, Oxford University Press, 1970.

Tristan and Iseult, illustrated by Ambrus, Dutton, 1971.

The Truce of the Games, illustrated by Ambrus, Hamish Hamilton, 1971.

Heather, Oak, and Olive: Three Stories (contains *The Chief's Daughter, A Circlet of Oak Leaves,* and "A Crown of Wild Olive"), illustrated by Ambrus, Dutton, 1972.

The Capricorn Bracelet (based on BBC scripts for a series on Roman Scotland), illustrated by Richard Cuffari, Walck, 1973, illustrated by Keeping, Oxford University Press, 1973.

The Changeling, illustrated by Ambrus, Hamish Hamilton, 1974.

(With Margaret Lyford-Pike) *We Lived in Drumfyvie,* Blackie, 1975.

Blood Feud, illustrated by Keeping, Oxford University Press, 1976, Dutton, 1977.

Shifting Sands, illustrated by Laszlo Acs, Hamish Hamilton, 1977.

Sun Horse, Moon Horse, illustrated by Shirley Felts, Bodley Head, 1977, Dutton, 1978.

(Editor with Monica Dickens) *Is Anyone There?,* Penguin, 1978.

Song for a Dark Queen, Pelham Books, 1978, Crowell, 1979.

Frontier Wolf, Oxford University Press, 1980.

Eagle's Egg, illustrated by Ambrus, Hamish Hamilton, 1981.

Bonnie Dundee, Bodley Head, 1983, Dutton, 1984.

Flame-Coloured Taffeta, Oxford University Press, 1985, published in the United States as *Flame-Colored Taffeta,* Farrar, Straus, 1986.

The Roundabout Horse, illustrated by Alan Marks, Hamilton Children's, 1986.

The Best of Rosemary Sutcliff, Chancellor, 1987, Peter Bedrick, 1989.

Little Hound Found, Hamilton Children's, 1989.

A Little Dog Like You, illustrated by Jane Johnson, Simon & Schuster, 1990.
The Shining Company, Farrar, Straus, 1990.

OTHER

Blue Remembered Hills: A Recollection (autobiography), Bodley Head, 1983, Morrow, 1984.
Mary Bedell (play), produced in Chichester, 1986.

Also co-author with Stephen Weeks of a screenplay, *Ghost Story,* 1975, and author of radio scripts for BBC Scotland. *Dragon Slayer, the Story of Beowulf* has also been recorded onto audio cassette (read by Sean Barrett), G. K. Hall Audio, 1986. A collection of Sutcliff's manuscripts is housed at the Kerlan Collection, University of Minnesota.

ADAPTATIONS: Song for a Dark Queen was adapted for stage by Nigel Bryant, Heinemann, 1984.

SIDELIGHTS: "For Rosemary Sutcliff the past is not something to be taken down from the shelf and dusted. It comes out of her pages alive and breathing and now," maintains John Rowe Townsend in his *A Sense of Story: Essays on Contemporary Writers.* A Carnegie Medal-winning author, Sutcliff is essentially a storyteller, bringing history to life through her heroes, the atmospheres she creates, and the sense of continuity found in her works. She presents the history of England through the experiences of virtuous young men and women who overcome many difficulties despite their personal and physical limitations. Sutcliff also explores history through her many retellings of old legends or stories, such as those of King Arthur and the Knights of the Round Table and Beowulf. In these works, she presents well-known heroes, often adding a new dimension to their tales. "Most critics," contend May Hill Arbuthnot and Zena Sutherland in their *Children and Books,* "would say that at the present time the greatest writer of historical fiction for children and youth is unquestionably Rosemary Sutcliff."

Sutcliff's "Roman Britain" trilogy begins with *The Eagle of the Ninth,* which concerns a young Roman centurion and his first few years spent in second-century Britain. Marcus Aquila is about to begin what he hopes will be a lengthy and magnificent military career and is at the same time resolved to find his father, who mysteriously disappeared on his way to battle with the Ninth Legion ten years earlier. *The Eagle of the Ninth* "is one of the few good stories" covering the period of Roman rule in Britain, maintains Ruth M. McEvoy in *Junior Libraries.* And a *Booklist* contributor concludes that the realistic background and characters make this a novel that "will reward appreciative readers."

The Silver Branch, the second book in the "Roman Britain" trilogy, takes place during the latter part of the third century and tells the story of Justin, a junior surgeon who

has just arrived from Albion, and his centurion kinsman Flavius. The two young men are aware of the political turmoil around them, and when the emperor is killed, they are forced into hiding, eventually realizing that the hope of a unified Britain is at risk. "All the characters . . . are entirely credible," remarks Lavinia R. Davis in the *New York Times Book Review,* adding that the meticulous details "create a brilliant background for a vigorous and unusually moving narrative." And in a *Horn Book* review, Virginia Haviland recommends the novel for those young people on their way "to becoming discriminating readers of adult historical fiction."

"*The Lantern Bearers* is the most closely-woven novel of the trilogy," claims Margaret Meek in her *Rosemary Sutcliff,* adding that "in it the hero bears within himself the conflict of dark and light, the burden of his time and of himself." In this final book, Sutcliff presents the decline of Roman Britain through the character of Aquila, who deserts in order to remain in Britain when the last of the Romans pull out. "The characterizations are vivid, varied and convincing," maintains Margaret Sherwood Libby in the *New York Herald Tribune Book Review,* and "the plot, both interesting and plausible, has its significance heightened by the recurring symbolism of light in dark days." Meek recognizes this theme of light and dark in all three of the books: "The conflict of the light and dark is the stuff of legend in all ages. . . . Sutcliff's artistry is a blend of this realization in her own terms and an instructive personal identification with problems which beset the young, problems of identity, of self-realization."

The medieval stories of King Arthur and the Knights of the Round Table are the subjects of Sutcliff's "Arthurian Knights" trilogy. *The Light beyond the Forest: The Quest for the Holy Grail* deals with the mystical search that Bors, Perceval, Galahad, and Lancelot conduct in an attempt to liberate the Wasteland from a religious curse. Although Donald K. Fry, writing in *School Library Journal,* finds Sutcliff's retelling to be "sentimental and overexplained," a *Horn Book* contributor asserts that "a few archaic words unobtrusively add color to a narrative noteworthy for the grace and clarity of its prose." *The Sword and the Circle: King Arthur and the Knights of the Round Table* brings together thirteen Arthurian stories that are clarified by the allusions to the movements of other characters such as Merlin, Morgan le Fay, and Sir Lancelot, writes a *Horn Book* contributor. "As in her other retellings," continues the contributor, Sutcliff "is constantly sensitive to the pageantry of color and rejoices in echoing the sounds and scents of nature." And Ann Evans declares in a *Times Literary Supplement* review that the collection "stands far above" any other. The final book in the trilogy, *The Road to Camlann: The Death of King Arthur,* centers on Mordred's destruction of the round table, Lancelot's love of Guenevere, and the wars and the final battle, ending with

Lancelot's death. Sutcliff is able to relate the penetrating sadness of the story, Marcus Crouch points out in a *Junior Bookshelf* review: "Here young readers and their parents may be assured, is the best of a great and lasting story matched with the best of one of this age's great writers." Sutcliff's trilogy stands as "a valiant attempt to bring the often tragic, violent and sensual tales within the compass of children's understanding without cutting the heart from them," concludes *Times Educational Supplement* contributor Neil Philip.

With *Warrior Scarlet* and *Dawn Wind,* Sutcliff continues her tales of the making of Britain through two new young heroes. The story of the Bronze Age in England is told in *Warrior Scarlet* by focusing on a boy and his coming to manhood. In this heroic age, explains Meek, Drem must kill a wolf in single combat in order to hunt with the men, and if he fails, he is an outcast and must keep sheep with the Little Dark People. "Sutcliff has widened her range to cover the hinterland of history and realized," continues Meek, "with the clarity we have come to expect, every aspect of the people of the Bronze Age, from hunting spears and cooking pots to king-making and burial customs, from childhood to old age. The book is coloured throughout with sunset bronze." *Warrior Scarlet,* concludes a *Times Literary Supplement* reviewer, provides a strong "emotional experience" and "is outstanding among children's books of any kind."

Chronologically, *Dawn Wind* follows *The Lantern Bearers,* for it deals with sixth-century Britain at the time of the invasion of the Saxons. The fourteen-year-old British hero, Owain, is the only survivor of a brutal battle with the Saxons that demolished his people. In the destroyed city, the only life Owain finds is Regina, a lost and half-starved girl. The two are bound by misery, then by mutual respect, and when Regina becomes ill Owain takes her to a Saxon settlement. The Saxons take care of Regina but sell Owain into slavery, and eleven years later he comes back for her. "So life is not snuffed out by the night," conclude Arbuthnot and Sutherland. "Sutcliff gives children and youth historical fiction that builds courage and faith that life will go on and is well worth the struggle."

As she did in her Arthurian trilogy, Sutcliff takes on other tales and retells them in such works as *Beowulf, The Hound of Ulster, The High Deeds of Finn MacCool,* and *Tristan and Iseult.* "The well-read will revel" in the splendid language and in "the generous use of historical detail" found in *Beowulf,* asserts Mary Louise Hector in the *New York Times Book Review.* In *The Hound of Ulster,* Sutcliff tells the early Irish story of Cuchulain, the Champion of Ulster. Using various techniques, Sutcliff interprets the seasoned tales, notes *Book Week* contributor Margaret Sherwood Libby, achieving the sensation of increasing excitement. "Rarely are young readers confronted with such

exultant joy, such fierce hatred and such stark tragedy," adds Libby. *The High Deeds of Finn MacCool* also retells an Irish legend—that of the famous captain of the *Fianna* and his many adventures. Sutcliff's "style is flowingly beautiful," describes a *Times Literary Supplement* reviewer. And Paul Heins states in *Horn Book* that the stories are told in such a way that they "fairly cry out for listeners." The famous Celtic love story of Tristan and Iseult is narrated in Sutcliff's work of the same title. *Tristan and Iseult* "moves along with epic cadence and grandeur" asserts Heins; and a *Times Literary Supplement* contributor maintains that the narrative is "superbly managed."

With *Blood and Sand,* Sutcliff recounts the history of a different time and place than those found in her previous novels. The protagonist is Thomas Keith, a Scottish soldier who is captured by Turkish forces during the Napoleonic Wars. Persuaded to join the viceroy's army, Thomas trains in desert combat and eventually commands a troop of calvary in a long campaign to free the holy cities. During the campaign, he gets married, acts as the governor of Medina, and develops a close friendship with the viceroy's son. "Loyalty and friendship" hold Sutcliff's historically based account together, explains a *Publishers Weekly* reviewer, concluding that *Blood and Sand* is "a memorable, sensitively rendered story."

Flame-Coloured Taffeta leaves the deserts and the battle fields behind, returning to England and the Sussex Downs, between Chichester and the sea. Twelve-year-old Damaris Crocker of Carthagena Farm and Peter Ballard from the vicarage know the woods near their home very well, and it is here that they find Tom, a wounded messenger for the lost cause of the Jacobite court, explains Joanna Motion in the *Times Literary Supplement.* The two children are not concerned with the rights and wrongs of the situation, but feel they must protect and help the wounded man. Many adventures ensue, including a fox hunt, a midnight rescue of Tom, and an exciting escape through the woods. "A beautifully written and intricately woven tale, this novel should appeal to any lover of historical fiction," claims *Voice of Youth Advocates* contributor Ellen Gullick. Motion concludes that *Flame-Coloured Taffeta* "succeeds as an enjoyable, soundly-crafted short novel where no whisker of plot or detail of character is wasted. And the sense of history under the lanes, the past seeped into the landscape, as Damaris looks out to sea from her farm house built of wrecked Armada timbers, will be familiar and satisfying to Sutcliff's many admirers."

The setting of *The Shining Company* will also be familiar to many of the author's admirers. "Fans of Sutcliff's historical fiction will welcome her return to the post-Roman British setting of some of her finest novels as she tells a stirring tale," points out *School Library Journal* contributor Christine Behrmann. The story is told by Prosper, who joins Prince Gorthyn as a shield-bearer when the prince enlists in a company formed to unite the British kingdoms against the Saxon threat. Much of the story, relates Behrmann, is concerned with the coming together of men from diverse parts of Britain, combining under a common cause. "Sutcliff has called all of her considerable talents into play here," says Behrmann, adding that readers who are willing to succumb to Sutcliff's "hypnotic language will be drawn into a truly splendid adventure."

Like her novels for young adults, Sutcliff's adult novels also delve into history. *Sword at Sunset* is a retelling of the legend of King Arthur that blends "legend, historical scholarship and masterfully humane storytelling to illuminate the misty and romantic era that preceded the Dark Ages," remarks a Chicago *Tribune Books* reviewer. Sutcliff has placed Arthur outside the legends, imbuing him with more believability, according to Robert Payne in the *New York Times Book Review*. "This time," writes Payne, "he is a living presence who moves in a brilliantly lit and fantastic landscape only remotely connected with ancient England." Reflecting on the novel's craftsmanship, Payne concludes: "Sutcliff is a spellbinder. While we read, we believe everything she says. She has hammered out a style that rises and falls like the waves of the sea." Another adult novel, *The Flowers of Adonis,* is the story of Alkibiades, a fifth-century B.C. Athenian general and statesman. "The story of irrepressible Alkibiades, the godlike Athenian general of Peloponnesian War fame, is told most effectively through the first-person reminiscences of a cast of characters," explains a *Horn Book* reviewer. An arrogant and ambitious man, Alkibiades was both loved and hated, and his dream of creating an Athenian empire made him commander of the fleet. *The Flowers of Adonis,* remarks a *Publishers Weekly* contributor, "is a work of high literary quality" that is written with a "deep love of the era and a scholar's knowledge." And Stephen J. Laut concludes in *Best Sellers:* "The story of this incredible, glamorous hero is told with great faithfulness to the sources. . . . If historical novels are your thing, by all means read this one."

After spending most of her time writing about the history of others, Sutcliff recounts her own history in *Blue Remembered Hills: A Recollection.* She describes her isolated childhood caused by a severe case of rheumatoid arthritis, her father's career as a naval officer, and her mother's obsessive personality. A storyteller, Sutcliff's mother became overprotective during her daughter's illness, refusing any outside help and expecting unlimited love and loyalty in return; she believed Sutcliff should desire no other companions. Sutcliff also discusses her training in miniature painting and the fact that she had no inclination for it. "Told with robust candour and fond photographic memory for detail, especially for outdoor places and gar-

dens, it is an engrossing record of close family relationships, and also of quite unusually adverse conditions not so much overcome as cheerfully ignored and set on one side," observes Joan Aiken in the *Times Educational Supplement*. "Youthful addicts of . . . Sutcliff's books will obviously wish to read this record of her childhood—which is why, presumably, the present memoir stops at the point where childhood ends. But the book is not written *for* children, it is related wholly from an adult standpoint, and with such honesty and vivacity that one can only hope the second instalment of the story—dealing with how . . . Sutcliff's major works conceived and came into being—will not be too far behind," concludes Aiken.

These major works have been described by Sheila A. Egoff in her *Thursday's Child: Trends and Patterns in Contemporary Children's Literature* as "a virtually perfect mesh of history and fiction." Sutcliff "seems to work from no recipe for mixing fact and imagination and thus, like fantasy, which it also resembles in its magic qualities, her writing defies neat categorization." Similarly, Philip contends that "to call the books historical novels is to limit them disgracefully." Sutcliff "does not bring 'history' to the reader," continues Philip, "but involves the reader in the past—not just for the duration of a book, but for ever. She can animate the past, bring it to life inside the reader in a most personal and lasting way." Sutcliff immerses herself and the reader in the time period that she is relating, and "her method of settling on the felt details that remain in the mind, driven along the nerves of the hero, is even more convincing than the historian's account," upholds Meek. "Sutcliff's name," declares Evans, "will be remembered and revered long after others have been forgotten."

BIOGRAPHICAL/CRITICAL SOURCES:

BOOKS

Arbuthnot, May Hill, and Zena Sutherland, *Children and Books,* Scott, Foresman, 1972.

Butts, Dennis, editor, *Good Writers for Young Readers,* Hart-Davis Educational, 1977.

Cameron, Helen, *The Green and Burning Tree: On the Writing and Enjoyment of Children's Books,* Little, Brown, 1969.

Children's Literature Review, Volume 1, Gale, 1976.

Contemporary Literary Criticism, Volume 26, Gale, 1983.

Crouch, Marcus, *Treasure Seekers and Borrowers: Children's Books in Britain 1900-1960,* Library Association, 1962.

Crouch, *The Nesbit Tradition: The Children's Novel in England 1945-1970,* Benn, 1972.

Egoff, Sheila A., *Thursday's Child: Trends and Patterns in Contemporary Children's Literature,* American Library Association, 1981.

Field, Elinor Whitney, editor, *Horn Book Reflections: On Children's Books and Reading, Selected from Eighteen Years of The Horn Book Magazine—1949-1966,* Horn Book, 1969.

Georgiou, Constantine, *Children and Their Literature,* Prentice-Hall, 1969.

Green, Roger Lancelyn, *Tellers of Tales: British Authors of Children's Books from 1800 to 1964,* Kaye & Ward, 1965.

Meek, Margaret, *Rosemary Sutcliff,* Walck, 1962.

Townsend, John Rowe, *A Sense of Story: Essays on Contemporary Writing for Children,* Lippincott, 1971.

Townsend, *Written for Children: An Outline of English Language Children's Literature,* Lippincott, 1974.

PERIODICALS

Best Sellers, February 15, 1970.

Booklist, February 1, 1955.

Book Week, March 15, 1964.

Horn Book, June, 1958; February, 1968; April, 1970; December, 1971; August, 1980; February, 1982.

Junior Bookshelf, December, 1981.

Junior Libraries, January, 1955.

New Statesman, October 2, 1954; November 16, 1957; November 12, 1960.

New Yorker, October 22, 1984.

New York Herald Tribune Book Review, February 14, 1960.

New York Times Book Review, October 26, 1952; January 9, 1955; March 17, 1957; June 29, 1958; January 4, 1959; April 22, 1962; November 11, 1962; May 26, 1963; May 3, 1964; November 7, 1965; January 30, 1966; February 15, 1970; September 30, 1973; April 5, 1987.

Observer, February 6, 1983.

Publishers Weekly, December 1, 1969; November 1, 1971; January 7, 1983; October 6, 1989; June 8, 1990.

Saturday Review, May 11, 1957; November 1, 1958; November 12, 1960.

School Library Journal, August, 1980; July, 1990.

Times (London), January 26, 1983; June 9, 1990.

Times Educational Supplement, October 23, 1981; February 19, 1982; January 14, 1983; January 13, 1984.

Times Literary Supplement, November 27, 1953; November 19, 1954; November 21, 1958; December 4, 1959; November 25, 1960; June 14, 1963; June 17, 1965; December 9, 1965; May 25, 1967; October 30, 1970; July 2, 1971; September 28, 1973; April 4, 1975; December 10, 1976; July 15, 1977; December 2, 1977; July 7, 1978; November 21, 1980; March 27, 1981; April 22, 1983; September 30, 1983; September 19, 1986.

Tribune Books (Chicago), March 8, 1987.

Voice of Youth Advocates, February, 1987.

Washington Post Book World, November 5, 1967; September 9, 1990.

—*Sketch by Susan M. Reicha*

* * *

SWAIN, Dwight V(reeland) 1915-
(Nick Carter, John Cleve, Clark South)

PERSONAL: Born November 17, 1915, in Rochester, MI; son of John Edgar (a railroad telegrapher) and Florence (Vreeland) Swain; married Margaret Simpson (a musician and college teacher), August 6, 1942 (divorced, 1968); married Joye Raechel Boulton (an interpreter, teacher, and writer), February 12, 1969; children: Thomas McCray, Rocio Raechel, Antonia, Ronald. *Education:* Jackson Junior College, A.A., 1935; University of Michigan, B.A., 1937; University of Oklahoma, M.A., 1954. *Politics:* Democrat.

ADDRESSES: Home and office—1304 McKinley Ave., Norman, OK 73072.

CAREER: Part-time free-lance writer, 1934-41, 1948-71; member of editorial staffs of daily and weekly newspapers in Michigan, Pennsylvania, California, and Oklahoma, and of *Flying* (magazine), 1937-41; full-time free-lance writer, 1942, 1946-48, 1971—; University of Oklahoma, Norman, script writer for University Motion Picture Unit, 1949-65, professor of journalism, 1952-74, professor emeritus, 1974—. *Eagle Magazine,* field reporter on Central American guerrilla activities, 1983-84. National Cowboy Hall of Fame and Western Heritage Center, member of awards committee, 1960-71; BHS Productions, Inc., vice-president, 1961-71; Palmer Writers' School, creator of "Fact and Fiction" writing course, 1965, member of national advisory board, 1966-74. *Military service:* U.S. Army, 1942-46.

MEMBER: World Science Fiction Association, American Medical Writers Association (honorary member), Mystery Writers of America, Science Fiction Writers of America, Southwest Mystery Writers of America, Oklahoma Writers Federation (honorary member).

AWARDS, HONORS: Honorary Lieutenant Governor, Oklahoma, 1970; "Okie" award, Oklahoma Writers Federation, 1977; professional writing award, University of Oklahoma, 1979; Focus on Oklahoma Award, Oklahoma Film and Television Producers Association, 1980, for animated film, *Guy with an Itch;* recognized for "outstanding achievement in, and contribution to, the motion picture and television industry," Oklahoma International Film Festival, 1982; Governor's Arts in Education Award, 1984; Guest of Honor, Pulpcon 20, 1991; inducted into Oklahoma Professional Writers Hall of Fame as Grand Master, 1991.

WRITINGS:

The Transposed Man, Ace Books, 1955.

Tricks and Techniques of the Selling Writer, Doubleday, 1965, revised edition published as *Techniques of the Selling Writer,* University of Oklahoma Press, 1974.

Film Scriptwriting: A Practical Manual, Hastings House, 1976, 2nd edition, with wife Joye R. Swain, Focal Press, 1988.

(Under name Nick Carter) *The Pemex Chart,* Charter Books, 1979.

Scripting for Video and Audiovisual Media, Focal Press, 1981, revised edition published as *Scripting for the New AV Technologies,* 1991.

(With J. Swain) *Dimensions* (three-part television miniseries), KOKH-TV, 1982.

(Under name John Cleve) *The Planet Poisoner,* Berkley Books, 1984.

(Author of foreword, afterword, and biography) Jack London, *The Call of the Wild,* Aerie Books, 1986.

(Author of foreward, afterward and biography) Jack London, *White Fang,* Aerie Books, 1988.

Creating Characters: How to Build Story People, Writer's Digest Books, 1990.

Monster, Pinnacle Books, 1991.

Author and co-producer of feature film *Stark Fear,* 1963; author of animated film *Guy with an Itch;* author of radio scripts, brochures, pamphlets, and other materials; scriptwriter for over fifty informational films for the University of Oklahoma Motion Picture Unit and independent producers, and of audiovisual materials for the U.S. Postal Service and private businesses. Contributor to books, including *Every Page Perfect,* by Mary Lynn and Georgia E. McKinney, Sandia, 1987; *The Writer's Digest Handbook of Short Story Writing,* Writer's Digest Books, 1988. Author of "Pulp" (column) for *Mystery Scene* (magazine), 1989—; contributor of articles, reviews, short fiction, and fifty magazine novels to national periodicals, including *Amazing Stories, Braniff Place, Business Screen, Eagle Magazine, Fantastic Adventures, Giant Western, Imagination, Imaginative Tales, Labor Today, Mammoth Detective, Mike Shayne Mystery Magazine, Specialty Salesman, True, The Writer,* and *Writer's Digest,* with some early work published under the pseudonym Clark South.

SIDELIGHTS: "I sometimes envy those writers who live within the confines of well-organized careers," Dwight V. Swain once told *CA.* "Though for twenty years I used half-time teaching as a security blanket, my own tendency too often has been to grab the angle that intrigued me at the moment, or to find myself stuck with the one economic necessity dictated. So I've worked jobs ranging from crop tramp and ordinary seaman to expert witness (in pornography trials) to communications consultant, and written on topics ranging from the great auto industry sitdown strikes of the thirties and the Polish Air Force in World War II to the hydrofracturing of oil wells and how to promote the welfare of bobwhite quail.

"The projects that have made me the most money—instructional/technical things—often have left me less than inspired, while my agent wouldn't even handle my favorite novel *Monster.* But my dissatisfactions are muted by the fact that in recent years my weird way of life and a wife cooperative far beyond the call of duty have afforded me five years' residence in Mexico, six months in Costa Rica, and briefer pauses in spots ranging from revolutionary Nicaragua to Marrakesh, Morocco—plus actual acquaintance with a considerable number of those fascinating people writers traditionally are supposed to meet."

Swain more recently commented, "My current satisfactions include my library (which, at ten thousand volumes, has become a delightful albatross too large to permit me to change residences permanently); my word processor—an electronic wonder which gives the old line, 'Write on!,' new meaning, and the fact that calls still come from places as far apart as Canada's maritime provinces and the hinterlands of Mexico to doctor film scripts and conduct writing workshops."

T

TARLOCK, A(nthony) Dan 1940-

PERSONAL: Born June 2, 1940, in Oakland, CA; son of Anthony James (an economist) and Fay (a writer and editor; maiden name, Ollerton) Tarlock; married Vivien Cecily Gross (a lawyer), April 5, 1977; children: Robert Gross, Katherine Gross, Marc Gross. *Education:* Stanford University, A.B., 1962, LL.B., 1965.

ADDRESSES: Home—230 Dempster, Evanston, IL 60202. *Office*—Chicago-Kent College of Law, Chicago, IL 60691.

CAREER: Indiana University, Bloomington, assistant professor, 1968-70, associate professor, 1970-72, professor of law, 1972-80; Chicago-Kent College of Law, Chicago, IL, professor of law, 1981—. Visiting professor at University of Pennsylvania, 1974-75, University of Utah, 1978, and University of Chicago, 1979; Raymond A. Rice Distinguished Visiting Professor of Law, University of Kansas, 1985. President of Bloomington City Planning Commission, 1972-73.

WRITINGS:

(With C. J. Meyers) *Water Resource Management,* Foundation Press, 1971, 2nd edition, 1980, 3rd edition, with J. Corbridge and D. Getches, 1988.
(With Meyers) *Selected Legal and Economic Aspects of Environmental Protection,* Foundation Press, 1971.
(With John Hanks and Eva Hanks) *Environmental Law and Policy,* West Publishing, 1974.
(With Hanks and Hanks) *Land Use Controls,* Little, Brown, 1981.
(With F. A. Anderson and D. R. Mandelker) *Environmental Protection: Law and Policy,* Little, Brown, 1984, 2nd edition, 1990.
Law of Water Rights and Resources, Clark Board Co., 1988.

WORK IN PROGRESS: Water Transfers in the West: Equity, Efficiency, and the Environment, report of National Academy Committee, 1992.

SIDELIGHTS: A. Dan Tarlock once told *CA:* "A major personal and professional interest of mine is the history and development of the Far West, and a good deal of my professional work centers on the appropriate legal structure to accommodate western resource use conflicts. My major interest concerns the regulation of all types of natural resources development: land, air, and water. I am especially interested in the history of the development of private exploitation regimes, such as the law of western water rights, and the tension between these systems and the persistent demand that the right to develop and use resources must now be shared among private owners, 'interested' neighbors, and the state itself. Much of my professional interest centers on the origins and contemporary manifestation of these conflicts in the Far West as well as in similar parts of the world."

*   *   *

TAVARD, George H(enry) 1922-

PERSONAL: Born February 6, 1922, in Nancy, France; son of Henri Ernest and Marguerite (Wasser) Tavard. *Education:* Major Seminary, B. Scholastic Philosophy, 1942; Facultes Catholiques, S.T.D., 1949.

ADDRESSES: Home—330 Market St., Brighton, MA 02135.

CAREER: Ordained Roman Catholic priest of Assumptionist Order, 1947; Capenor House, Surrey, England, lecturer, 1948-50; *Documentation Catholique,* Paris, France, assistant editor, 1950-51; Assumption College, Worcester, MA, lecturer, 1958-59; Mount Mercy College (now Carlow College), Pittsburgh, PA, chairman, department of theology, 1960-67; Pennsylvania State University, State College, professor, 1967-69; Methodist Theological School, Ohio, Delaware, professor, 1970-89, professor emeritus, 1989—. Expert, Second Vatican Council; Catholic observer/consultant to Consultation on Church Union.

MEMBER: Catholic Theological Society of America, Catholic Historical Association, Society for Reformation Research, Delta Epsilon Sigma.

WRITINGS:

The Catholic Approach to Protestantism, Harper, 1955.
The Church, the Layman, and the Modern World, Macmillan, 1959.
Protestantism, Hawthorn, 1959.
Protestant Hopes and the Catholic Responsibility, Fides, 1960, revised edition, 1964.
Two Centuries of Ecumenism, Fides, 1960.
Holy Writ or Holy Church, Harper, 1960.
Paul Tillich and the Christian Message, Scribner, 1962.
Quest for Catholicity: The Development of High Church Anglicanism, Herder, 1964.
The Church Tomorrow, Herder, 1965.
Woman in Christian Tradition, University of Notre Dame Press, 1973.
The Inner Life, Paulist/Newman, 1976.
A Way of Love, Orbis, 1977.
Song for Avalokita (poems), Dorrance, 1979.
La Septieme Vague (poems), Editions St. Germain des Pres (Paris), 1980.
Le Silence d'une Demi-heure, Editions St. Germain des Pres, 1980.
The Vision of the Trinity, University Press of America, 1981.
Images of the Christ, University Press of America, 1982.
Justification: An Ecumenical Study, Fortress, 1983.
A Theology for Ministry, Michael Glazier, 1983.
Sentiers de la Demeure, Editions St. Germain des Pres, 1984.
Poetry and Contemplation in St. John of the Cross, Ohio University Press, 1988.
Juana Ines de la Cruz and the Theology of Beauty, University of Notre Dame Press, 1991.

*   *   *

TAYLOR, Charles D(oonan) 1938-
(David Charles)

PERSONAL: Born October 20, 1938, in Hartford, CT; son of Jack D. (a financier) and Ruth (a teacher; maiden name, Hunter) Taylor; married Georgeanne L. Laitala (a

teacher), July 24, 1965; children: Jack M. T., Bennett Hunter. *Education:* Middlebury College, B.A., 1960.

ADDRESSES: Home—Manchester, MA 01944.

CAREER: Addison-Wesley Publishing Co., Reading, MA, salesman and editor, 1965-71; Book Production Services, Inc., Danvers, MA, president and treasurer, 1971-78; Books and Production East, Inc., Manchester, MA, packager and agent, 1979-83; writer. *Military service:* U.S. Naval Reserve, 1961-64; became lieutenant junior grade.

MEMBER: Authors Guild, Authors League of America, U.S. Naval Institute, Navy League of the United States.

WRITINGS:

Show of Force, St. Martin's, 1980.
The Sunset Patriots, Jove, 1982.
First Salvo, Jove, 1984.
Choke Point, Jove, 1985.
Silent Hunter, Jove, 1986.
Counter Strike, Jove, 1987.
(Under pseudonym David Charles) *Shadows of Vengeance,* Tor, 1988.
Warship, Jove, 1989.
Boomer, Pocket Books, 1990.
Deep Sting, Pocket Books, 1991.

WORK IN PROGRESS: Sightings, a suspense novel based in the Pacific Rim.

SIDELIGHTS: Charles D. Taylor told *CA:* "Many people have claimed that the sudden and radical changes in the world order will damage the potential of suspense/spy/action-adventure novels. On the contrary, there has never been a greater challenge to the democratic order, the rights of the individual, or the abilities of those of us who write in this genre. Nor has there ever been more opportunity for both established and aspiring novelists."

*   *   *

TAYLOR, John Russell 1935-

PERSONAL: Born June 19, 1935, in Dover, Kent, England; son of Arthur Russell and Kathleen (Picker) Taylor. *Education:* Jesus College, Cambridge University, B.A., 1956; Courtauld Institute of Art, London, England, research on art nouveau book illustration, 1956-58.

ADDRESSES: Home—11 Hollytree Close, Inner Park Rd., London SW19, England. *Office*—*The Times,* 1 Pennington Street, London E1, England. *Agent*—A. D. Peters, 10 Buckingham St., London WC2, England.

CAREER: Times Educational Supplement, London, England, sub-editor, 1959-60; *Times Literary Supplement,*

London, editorial assistant, 1961-63; *The Times,* London, entertainment correspondent, 1959-63, film critic, 1963-73, art critic, 1978—. Lecturer on film at Tufts University, 1970-71; professor of cinema at the University of Southern California, 1972-78.

MEMBER: Film and Television Press Guild (London), Critics Circle (London), Society of Cinematologists (New York).

WRITINGS:

Joseph L. Mankiewicz: An Index to His Work, British Film Institute, 1960.
The Angry Theatre; New British Drama, Hill & Wang, 1962, revised and expanded edition, 1969, published in England as *Anger and After: A Guide to the New British Drama,* Methuen, 1962, revised edition, Penguin, 1963, 2nd revised edition, Methuen, 1969.
Anatomy of a Television Play; An Inquiry into the Production of Two ABC Armchair Theatre Plays: "The Rose Affair" by Alun Owen, and "Afternoon of a Nymph" by Robert Muller, Weidenfeld & Nicolson, 1962.
Cinema Eye, Cinema Ear: Some Key Filmmakers of the Sixties, Hill & Wang, 1964.
(Editor and author of introduction) *John Arden: Three Plays,* Penguin, 1965.
(Editor and author of introduction) *New English Dramatists 8,* Penguin, 1966.
The Penguin Dictionary of the Theatre, Penguin, 1966, revised edition, 1970, 2nd revised edition published as *A Dictionary of the Theatre,* 1976.
The Art Nouveau Book in Britain, Methuen, 1966, MIT Press, 1967.
The Rise and Fall of the Well-Made Play, Hill & Wang, 1967.
Preston Sturges, Secker & Warburg, 1967.
(Editor) *John Osborne: "Look Back in Anger"; A Casebook,* Macmillan, 1968, Aurora Publishers, 1970.
(With Brian Brooke) *The Art Dealers,* Scribner, 1969.
Harold Pinter, edited by Ian Scott-Kilvert, Longman for the British Council and the National Book League, 1969.
(With Arthur Jackson) *The Hollywood Musical,* McGraw-Hill, 1971.
The Second Wave: British Drama for the Seventies, Hill & Wang, 1971, revised edition, Eyre Methuen, 1978.
(Editor) Graham Greene, *The Pleasure-Dome: The Collected Film Criticism, 1935-40,* Secker & Warburg, 1972, Oxford University Press, 1980.
(Editor) Greene, *Graham Greene on Film,* Simon & Schuster, 1973.
David Storey, edited by Scott-Kilvert, Longman for the British Council, 1974.
Peter Shaffer, edited by Scott-Kilvert, Longman for the British Council, 1974.

Directors and Directions: Cinema for the Seventies, Hill & Wang, 1975.
Hitch: The Life and Times of Alfred Hitchcock, Pantheon Books, 1978, published in England as *Hitch: The Life and Work of Alfred Hitchcock,* Faber, 1978.
(With Hugh Hunt and Kenneth Richards) *The Revels History of Drama in English,* Volume 7: *1880 to the Present Day,* edited by Clifford Leech and T. W. Craik, Methuen, 1978.
Impressionism, Hennerwood Publications, 1981.
Strangers in Paradise: The Hollywood Emigres, 1933-1950, Holt, 1983.
Ingrid Bergman, photographs from the Kobal collection, St. Martin's, 1983.
Alec Guinness: A Celebration, Little, Brown, 1984.
Vivien Leigh, Elm Tree, 1984.
(With John Kobal) *Portraits of the British Cinema: 60 Glorious Years, 1925-1985,* photographs from the Kobal collection, Aurum Press, 1985, Salem House, 1986.
Orson Welles: A Celebration, Little, Brown, 1986.
Edward Wolfe, Trefoil Books for Odette Gilbert Gallery, 1986.
Meninsky, Redcliffe Press, 1990.
Art for Sale, Barrie & Jenkins, 1990.
Impressionist Dreams: The Artists and the World They Painted, Barrie & Jenkins, 1990.

Also author of the introduction for *50 Superstars,* edited by John Kobal, Hamlyn, 1974. Contributor to *Shakespeare: A Celebration,* Penguin, 1964; also contributor to periodicals. Editor of *Films and Filming,* 1983-90.

SIDELIGHTS: John Russell Taylor, best known for his film and art reviews for the London *Times,* has been called an "impartial critic" by a *Times Literary Supplement* reviewer; and in 1967, a *Drama* contributor referred to him as "possibly the best cinema reviewer writing in [England], immensely well informed, objective, sane and mostly uninfluenced by current intellectual foibles." Taylor continues to examine the topics of his reviews—the theatre, the film world, and the art world—in his books; and major Hollywood personalities, such as Alfred Hitchcock, are among the many subjects discussed.

Eliot Fremont-Smith maintains in *Village Voice* that Hitchcock's "sense of fun, lust for the macabre, psychological daring, technical innovation, exacting orderliness, authority with actors, rubber face, and long brilliant career" make him "the most immediately fascinating of directors." The "comprehensive" *Hitch: The Life and Times of Alfred Hitchcock,* continues Fremont-Smith, "serves him and us superbly." Focusing mainly on Hitchcock's career, "Taylor has written a very useful book about a professional at work," observes *New York Times Book Review* contributor Nora Sayre. However, comparing Taylor's work with Francois Truffaut's book-length interview with

Hitchcock, Christopher Lehmann-Haupt of the *New York Times* finds that "almost all of the vast detail concerning the films that appears in Taylor's book is also present in Truffaut's." And, "in short," concludes Lehmann-Haupt, "Taylor's biography is necessary only to demonstrate that such a book is not really necessary." Fremont-Smith, though, claims: "Taylor deals with everything—the Catholic upbringing, the early silent films, the frustrations with Korda and Selznick, the transplant to Hollywood, the private life, . . . the uncertain periods in his career, the constant experimentation, and the triumphs. . . . The writing is clear, the subject nifty, the book admiring but not fawning. And you come out happy."

Strangers in Paradise: The Hollywood Emigres 1933-1950 deals with the refugees from Nazi Germany and other parts of Europe who flocked to Hollywood during the 1930s and 1940s, explains a *Publishers Weekly* contributor. "From oceans of research the author distils a fresh essence, a detailed study on the flight to Hollywood, from their culturally fettering homelands, of Europe's film makers, and what happened to those who flew," comments Basil Boothroyd in the London *Times*. In addition to the filmmakers, Taylor also discusses refugee artists, writers, and intellectuals, prompting S. S. Prawer to claim in the *Times Literary Supplement*: "One cannot help feeling that Taylor has cast his net too wide; that he would have done better to confine himself to emigres connected with the film-world." Jonathan Yardley, though, writes in the *Washington Post* that "Taylor tells this story gracefully and engagingly, and he has many perceptive observations to make." And the *Publishers Weekly* contributor concludes that *Strangers in Paradise* is an "enjoyable, well-researched story," adding that "by turns funny and sad, this is a book that is consistently interesting."

BIOGRAPHICAL/CRITICAL SOURCES:

PERIODICALS

Drama, winter, 1967.
Los Angeles Times Book Review, May 15, 1983; March 11, 1984; February 24, 1985.
Newsweek, December 16, 1985.
New York Times, November 28, 1978.
New York Times Book Review, November 19, 1978; July 10, 1983.
Publishers Weekly, February 4, 1983.
Time, June 20, 1983.
Times (London), March 3, 1978.
Times Literary Supplement, December 14, 1967; March 11, 1983; December 7, 1984; November 28, 1986.
Village Voice, October 9, 1978.
Washington Post, January 5, 1978; April 13, 1983.
Washington Post Book World, July 8, 1984.*

TEMKO, Florence

PERSONAL: Married second husband, Henry Petzal; children: (first marriage) Joan, Ronald, Stephen. *Education:* Attended Wycombe Abbey, London School of Economics and Political Science, and New School for Social Research.

ADDRESSES: Home and office—5050 La Jolla Blvd. P-C, San Diego, CA 92109.

CAREER: Free-lance writer. Workshop and seminar presenter at Metropolitan Museum of Art, University of California San Diego, Boston Library, Chicago Library, and San Francisco Library. Former assistant to the director at Berkshire Museum, Pittsfield, MA.

MEMBER: American Society of Journalists and Authors, Authors League of America, Authors Guild, National League of American Pen Women, American Craftsman, Artist-Craftsmen of New York.

WRITINGS:

Kirigami: The Creative Art of Papercutting, Platt, 1962.
Party Fun with Origami, Platt, 1963.
Paperfolding to Begin With, Bobbs-Merrill, 1968.
Papercutting, Doubleday, 1973.
Feltcraft, Doubleday, 1974.
Paper: Folded, Cut, Sculpted, Macmillan, 1974.
Paper Capers, Scholastic Book Services, 1974.
Self-Stick Craft, Doubleday, 1975.
Decoupage Crafts, Doubleday, 1976.
Folk Crafts for World Friendship, Doubleday, 1976.
The Big Felt Burger and 27 Other Craft Projects to Relish, Doubleday, 1977.
The Magic of Kirigami, Japan Publications, 1978.
Paperworks, Bobbs-Merrill, 1979.
Let's Take a Trip, Milton Bradley Co., 1982.
Chinese Papercuts, China Books, 1982.
Elementary Art Games and Puzzles, Prentice-Hall, 1983.
New Knitting, HP Publishing, 1984.
Paper Pandas and Jumping Frogs, China Books, 1986.
Paper Tricks, Scholastic, 1988.
Paper Jewelry, Heian International, 1990.
Paper Tricks II, Scholastic, 1990.
Scary Things, Willowisp Press, 1991.
Origami for Beginners, Tuttle, 1991.
Made with Paper, Dragon's World/Paper Tiger Books, 1991.
Multi-Cultural Crafts for World Friendship, China Books, 1992.

Contributor to books, including *National Camp Directors Guide,* 1974; *The Golden Happy Birthday Book,* Golden Press, 1976; *Tools of the Writers Trade,* HarperCollins, 1990; and *The Favorites,* Institute of Children's Literature, 1991. Also contributor to magazines and newspapers, including *Grade Teacher, Faces, Sky, Instructor, Yarn Market, New York Times,* and *Boston Globe.* Author of weekly column, "Things to Make," in *Berkshire Eagle* and other newspapers.

WORK IN PROGRESS: Masterworks of Origami, 1993.

SIDELIGHTS: Florence Temko told *CA:* "Years ago I could not have imagined in my wildest dreams that I would become a published writer. I always enjoyed designing gifts and decorations for birthdays and holidays for relatives and friends. I especially enjoyed origami and other paper arts. As a result I was often asked to conduct workshops and seminars in schools, universities and museums. Participants suggested I put my ideas into a book, but when I approached publishers they were not enthusiastic. Finally, after about fifteen tries, my first book did make it and once you are in print, it is easier to do it again. An editor discovered that I had a special talent for presenting clear instructions that readers could follow easily. Her support gave me confidence to find my 'voice' as a writer specializing on the subject of crafts. Besides almost thirty books I have written a weekly 'How to' column for newspapers for five years, have contributed to many national magazines and have appeared on television in the U.S. and other countries. Who would have thought!"

*   *   *

TESSLER, Mark A(rnold) 1941-

PERSONAL: Born July 25, 1941, in Youngstown, OH; son of Sidney L. and Louise (Kirtz) Tessler; married Patricia Mayerson, June 12, 1966; children: Joelle. *Education:* Attended Hebrew University, Jerusalem, Israel, 1961-62; Case Western Reserve University, B.A., 1963; University of Tunis, certificate, 1965; Northwestern University, Ph.D., 1969; also attended Institute of World Affairs, Salisbury, CT.

ADDRESSES: Home—4671 North Woodburn, Milwaukee, WI 53211. *Office*—Department of Political Science, University of Wisconsin, Milwaukee, WI 53211.

CAREER: University of Wisconsin-Milwaukee, instructor, 1968-69, assistant professor, 1969-74, associate professor, 1974-76, professor of political science, 1976—, chairperson of department, 1976-79. Director of political research laboratory, 1970-71, director graduate studies, 1973-76, director of international relations major, with responsibility for undergraduate student majors, 1986—. Research associate in sociology, University of Tunis, 1972-73, and in political science, Hebrew University of Jerusalem, 1982; faculty associate reporting on Middle East and North Africa, Universities Field Staff International, 1979-88; lecturing and consulting, United States Informa-

tion Agency, Sudan and Mauritania, 1984, Senegal, 1988, and Quatar, Jordan, and Israel, 1991. Participant in numerous research projects on Middle East and African development; international lecturer and/or consultant on research methods and development studies in these regions at various institutions, including the National Universities of Rwanda, Zaire, and Ivory Coast. Director, Wisconsin Universities United Nations Summer Seminars, 1969, 1970, and 1975, Institute of World Affairs Summer Institute, 1971, and University Wisconsin-Milwaukee/Marquette University Center for International Studies, 1991—. Board of directors, Institute of Maghribi Studies, 1984-86 and 1987-90, and Tangier American Legation Museum Society, 1989—; selection committee, Social Science Research Counsel, 1976-80; chair, Council for International Exchange of Scholars, 1985-88. Proposal and manuscript referee for granting agencies, publishers, and professional journals, including National Science Foundation, Ford Foundation, Princeton University Press, *American Political Science Review,* and *Comparative Politics.*

MEMBER: American Political Science Association, African Studies Association, Middle East Studies Associations, Association for Israel Studies (vice-president, 1987-89; president, 1989-91).

AWARDS, HONORS: Grants from Social Science Research Council, 1972-73, American Philosophical Society, 1972 and 1974, International Communication Agency, 1978-79, National Endowment for the Humanities, 1979, Ford Foundation and Rockefeller Foundation, both 1983, American Institute of Magribi Studies, 1989-1990, United States Information Agency, 1982-92, United States Department of Education, 1991-92; Fulbright awards, 1976 and 1980.

WRITINGS:

(Editor and contributor) *A New Look at the Middle East,* Institute of World Affairs, University of Wisconsin-Milwaukee, 1971.

(Editor with William O'Barr and David Spain, and contributor) *Survey Research in Africa: Its Applications and Limits,* Northwestern University Press, 1973.

(With O'Barr and Spain) *Tradition and Identity in Changing Africa,* Harper, 1973.

(Editor with Naiem Sherbiny, and contributor) *Arab Oil: Impact on the Arab Countries and Global Implications,* Praeger, 1976.

(Co-author) *Political Elites in Arab North Africa,* Longman, 1982.

(Co-author) *The Evaluation and Application of Survey Research in the Arab World,* Westview, 1987.

(Co-author) *Israel, Egypt and the Palestinians: From Camp David to Intifada,* Indiana University Press, 1989.

A History of the Israeli-Palestinian Conflict, Indiana University Press, 1992.

CONTRIBUTOR

Russell Stone and John Simmons, editors, *Change in Tunisia: Essays in the Social Sciences,* State University of New York Press, 1976.

James Allman, editor, *Women's Status and Fertility in the Muslim World,* Praeger, 1978.

Women in the Muslim World, Harvard University Press, 1978.

R. D. McLaurin, editor, *The Political Role of Minorities in the Middle East,* Praeger, 1979.

R. Wirsing, editor, *The Protection of Minorities,* Pergamon, 1980.

Georgina Ashworth, editor, *World Minorities,* Volume III, Minority Rights Group, 1980.

Charles Keyes, editor, *Ethnic Change,* University of Washington Press, 1981.

David Gould and Jacques Katuala, editors, *Development Administration Modules for Francophone Africa,* National Association of Schools of Public Affairs and Administration, 1981.

Tawfic Farrah, editor, *Political Behavior in the Arab States,* Westview, 1983.

Louis Kamel Meleika, editor, *Readings in Social Psychology in the Arab World,* Volume III, Egyptian National Organization of the Book, 1984.

David Long and Bernard Reich, editors, *The Government and Politics of the Middle East and North Africa,* Westview Press, 1986.

I. W. Zartman, editor, *The Political Economy of Morocco,* Praeger, 1987.

Israeli Policies in the Occupied Territories, League of Arab States, 1988.

Author of numerous reports and monographs for Universities Field Staff International. Contributor of articles and reviews to periodicals, including *New Republic, World Affairs, Journal of Social Psychology, Social Science Quarterly,* and *Christian Science Monitor.*

*   *   *

THOMPSON, George Selden 1929-1989
(George Selden)

PERSONAL: Born May 14, 1929, in Hartford, CT; died of complications from a gastrointestinal hemorrhage, December 5, 1989, in New York, NY; son of Hartwell Green (a doctor) and Sigrid (Johnson) Thompson. *Education:* Yale University, B.A., 1951. *Politics:* Independent. *Religion:* Independent. *Avocational interests:* Archaeology, music.

ADDRESSES: c/o Farrar, Straus, & Giroux, Inc., 19 Union Sq. W., New York, NY 10003.

CAREER: Writer of children's fiction, biographies, plays, and screenplays.

AWARDS, HONORS: Fulbright scholarship to Italy, 1951-52; Newbery Honor Book citation, 1961, and Lewis Carroll Shelf Award, 1963, both for *The Cricket in Times Square;* Christopher Book Award, 1969, for *Tucker's Countryside;* William Allen White Children's Book Award, 1978, for *Harry Cat's Pet Puppy.*

WRITINGS:

FOR CHILDREN; UNDER NAME GEORGE SELDEN

The Dog That Could Swim under Water: Memoirs of a Springer Spaniel, illustrated by Morgan Dennis, Viking, 1956.

The Garden under the Sea, illustrated by Garry MacKenzie, Viking, 1957, published as *Oscar Lobster's Fair Exchange,* illustrated by Peter Lippman, Harper, 1966.

The Cricket in Times Square, illustrated by Garth Williams, Farrar, Straus, 1960.

I See What I See!, illustrated by Robert Galster, Farrar, Straus, 1962.

The Mice, the Monks and the Christmas Tree, illustrated by Jan Balet, Macmillan, 1963.

Heinrich Schliemann, Discoverer of Buried Treasure (biography), illustrated by Lorence Bjorklund, Macmillan, 1964.

Sir Arthur Evans, Discoverer of Knossos (biography), illustrated by Lee Ames, Macmillan, 1964.

Sparrow Socks, illustrated by Lippman, Harper, 1965.

The Children's Story (play; based on the novel by James Clavell), Dramatists Play Service, 1966.

The Dunkard, illustrated by Lippman, Harper, 1968.

Tucker's Countryside, illustrated by Williams, Farrar, Straus, 1969.

The Genie of Sutton Place (adapted from his television play of the same title, written with Kenneth Hever, produced by Westinghouse "Studio One"; also see below), Farrar, Straus, 1973.

Harry Cat's Pet Puppy, illustrated by Williams, Farrar, Straus, 1974.

Chester Cricket's Pigeon Ride, illustrated by Williams, Farrar, Straus, 1981.

Irma and Jerry, illustrated by Leslie H. Morrill, Avon, 1982.

Chester Cricket's New Home, illustrated by Williams, Farrar, Straus, 1983.

Harry Kitten and Tucker Mouse, illustrated by Williams, Farrar, Straus, 1985.

The Old Meadow, illustrated by Williams, Farrar, Straus, 1987.

Also author of unproduced film script based on the television play, "The Genie of Sutton Place," for Spoleto Productions.

ADAPTATIONS: The Cricket in Times Square was produced as a dramatized recording by Miller-Brody Productions in 1972, and was produced as an animated television show by the American Broadcasting Company (ABC) in 1973. Disney Studios holds an option on *The Genie of Sutton Place.*

SIDELIGHTS: With the debut of the beloved characters Harry Cat, Tucker Mouse, and Chester Cricket in his 1960 story, *The Cricket in Times Square,* George Selden Thompson created a trio of animal friends who have delighted readers for decades. Before his death in 1989, Thompson—who wrote under the name George Selden—offered readers six more books following their adventures, including *Tucker's Countryside, Harry Cat's Pet Puppy, Chester Cricket's Pigeon Ride, Chester Cricket's New Home, Harry Kitten and Tucker Mouse,* and *The Old Meadow. Dictionary of Literary Biography* contributor Lesley S. Potts explained the appeal of Selden's animal friends: "Their all-too-human concerns and the give-and-take of their relationships lend complete credibility to the whimsical notion that a cat, a mouse, and a cricket could be the truest of friends. . . . Selden's clear and simple writing style provides insight into human frailties such as snobbery, greed, possessiveness, prejudice, ignorance, and vanity in a gently probing, yet affectionate, manner, without resorting to sentimentality."

"Like Chester Cricket," related Lee Bennett Hopkins in his *More Books by More People,* "George Selden was born in Connecticut—Hartford—and grew up there." As a child the author developed a love of nature, archaeology, and music. "I didn't have a particularly artistic home," Selden commented, "but I realized early that I wanted to be a writer. Both my brother and I had plenty of exposure to music, especially opera, through my mother. And it was my father, a doctor, who read a lot. I never had any idea that one day I'd write for children. I always liked children's literature, even as an adult." As a student at Yale University, Selden wrote for the literary magazine and was a member of the Elizabethan Club. He later won a Fulbright scholarship and went to Perugia and Rome, Italy, where he studied Latin and Greek.

When Selden returned to the United States after a year abroad it was with the determination to become a published writer. He decided to give himself three years to see whether he could make it in his chosen profession. "I started out as a playwright . . . ," Selden once told *CA,* "but I wasn't having too much success with my plays. A friend of mine who was employed at Viking at the time suggested that I write a children's book. I did and it was published, although I've disowned it now; it was the first one and I really don't like it too much. I'd always been interested in the field, but that got me *practically* interested. I began to think that I might be able to do something in it myself, and that's how I started." Although Potts similarly believed that Selden's first book, *The Dog That Could Swim under Water: Memoirs of a Springer Spaniel,* is not his best, the critic pointed out that its "theme of friends helping friends was to become a familiar one, more fully developed, in Selden's subsequent books. . . . [It also] shows the beginnings of a breezy, warm, and humorous style of writing."

Selden followed *The Dog That Could Swim under Water* with what Potts called "a prototype" for his later books, *The Garden under the Sea,* later reprinted as *Oscar Lobster's Fair Exchange,* which uses animal characters to satirize human behavior. Selden got the idea for his story from his stays at his family's summer house on Long Island Sound, where his familiarity with the coastal setting added believability to the book's narration. The story is about how Oscar organizes his friends to take human belongings from the shore of Long Island Sound as a response to vacationers who have been "stealing" rocks and shells from the beach; the sea creatures' adventures offer plenty of opportunities for humor and witty dialogue. Critics praised *The Garden under the Sea* for, as one *Virginia Kirkus' Service* reviewer wrote, "Selden's knowledge of the sea, and his ear for a humorous, salty tale."

Just as Selden was inspired to write *The Garden under the Sea* by his walks along the Long Island Sound beaches, the subways of New York City inspired him to write *The Cricket in Times Square.* One late night Selden was in the Times Square subway station when he heard the unexpected sound of a cricket's chirp, which reminded him of his former home in Connecticut. Immediately, a story rushed into his mind about a cricket who, like him, found himself in the hustle and bustle of New York City and was homesick for the countryside. To help the lost cricket, Selden invented a streetwise, materialistic mouse and a soft-spoken, kindly cat, and Chester, Tucker, and Harry were born.

In their first adventure, Chester accidentally arrives in Times Square after he sneaks into a picnic basket containing one of his favorite foods, liverwurst. Befriended by Harry and Tucker, who have taken up residence in a drainpipe, and a boy named Mario Bellini, Chester is discovered to possess a remarkable gift for music. Learning a wide variety of popular and classical tunes by listening to the radio, Chester—with the help of Harry and Tucker—saves the financially troubled newsstand that belongs to Mario's family by putting on a grand performance that makes Chester and the Bellinis famous. After saving the newsstand, however, Chester's homesickness gets the better of him and he returns to Connecticut.

The Cricket in Times Square is a unique work because, as Potts reported, it was "the first time . . . an animal fantasy was located entirely in the big city." More importantly, critics praised the book for its well-drawn plot and lively characterization. One *New York Herald Tribune Book Review* critic pointed out that the author's earlier books "had the same excellent writing and original imaginative twist but they lacked the unified plot we have in [*The Cricket in Times Square*]. This is absolutely grand fun for anyone." And *Spectator* reviewer Benny Green called the book a "rare commodity, a children's book with subtle, vigorous and credible characterisations." Today, as Hopkins noted, *The Cricket in Times Square* is considered "a modern classic in children's literature."

Although Selden received many requests from readers for him to write a sequel to *The Cricket in Times Square,* he did not sit down to create a new adventure about these characters for almost a decade because he wanted to wait until another idea struck him that he felt would be worthy of Chester and his friends. Instead, he went on to write other works, such as two biographies and several more children's stories featuring new characters. His biographies, *Heinrich Schliemann, Discoverer of Buried Treasure* and *Sir Arthur Evans, Discoverer of Knossos,* were done by Selden because of his interest in archaeology. Schliemann was a pioneer in the science of archaeology and discoverer of ancient Troy, and Evans discovered the remains of the Minoan civilization.

Like the author's earlier fiction, stories such as *Sparrow Socks, The Dunkard,* and *The Genie of Sutton Place* contain the usual Selden touches of satire and a focus on the importance of friendship. *The Dunkard* is a satirical picture book that spoofs the idea of show-and-tell days at school; *Sparrow Socks* relates how a group of sparrows help save a Scottish sock factory in gratitude for the socks that young Angus McFee has knitted them. In a somewhat more complex tale, Selden uses some of his knowledge of archaeology in *The Genie of Sutton Place* to add some realism to the story of how Tim enlists the help of a genie to prevent his aunt from taking his beloved dog Sam away. None of these books, however, have achieved the same amount of popularity as the Cricket stories. Even Selden's *Irma and Jerry,* a book with a premise—it involves a Connecticut animal (a dog this time) that ventures into New York City—that resembles that of *The Cricket in Times Square,* was not nearly as successful.

Selden's favorite book about his well-known trio was the first sequel to *The Cricket in Times Square, Tucker's Countryside.* This was partly because it has to do with a subject that was very close to his heart: the conservation of nature. In this adventure, Harry and Tucker travel to Chester's home in a Connecticut meadow to save it from a building project. After *Tucker's Countryside,* Selden alternated the next five books of the series between Chester's home in the Old Meadow and Tucker's and Harry's New York City neighborhood. The books were generally well received by critics. For example, Margery Fisher praised *Harry Cat's Pet Puppy* in her *Growing Point* review for being "warm-hearted without being sentimental and full of a zippy dialogue." Only *Chester Cricket's Pigeon Ride* drew much negative response, largely because Selden adopted a picture book format in this case. Reviewers complained about the "slightness of the story line," as Potts reported. But Potts defended that "within its limitations as a pictorial essay, it succeeds very well."

Two years after the publication of his last Chester Cricket tale, *The Old Meadow,* Selden passed away in New York City. Though many will remember him for the Cricket stories, all of Selden's books share the same distinctive theme of friendship. "Implicit in Selden's friendship theme," observed Potts, "is the importance of understanding and caring between people of different backgrounds, beliefs, and temperaments. Whether the characters involved in a story are as incongruous as a cat, a mouse, and a cricket or a boy, a dog-turned-man, and an Arabian genie, their differences are minimized and their common bond of humanity is stressed." Because of a shared concern for friendship and humanity, said Potts, Selden's stories "have been linked to the works of [*Charlotte's Web* author] E. B. White and Kenneth Graham," who wrote *The Wind in the Willows.* Like these writers, the critic declared, Selden has "assured him[self] a lasting place in children's literature."

For an earlier published interview, see *Contemporary Authors New Revision Series,* Volume 21, Gale, 1987.

BIOGRAPHICAL/CRITICAL SOURCES:

BOOKS

Blount, Margery, *Animal Land: The Creatures of Children's Fiction,* Morrow, 1975, pp. 131-151.
Contemporary Literary Criticism, Volume 8, Gale, 1985, pp. 195-203.
Dictionary of Literary Biography, Volume 52: *American Writers for Children since 1960: Fiction,* Gale, 1986, pp. 325-333.
Hopkins, Lee Bennett, *More Books by More People,* Citation Press, 1974, pp. 304-307.

PERIODICALS

Bulletin of the Center for Children's Books, February, 1984; February, 1987; January, 1988.
Children's Book Review, June, 1971, p. 92.
Christian Science Monitor, October 3, 1973.

Growing Point, April, 1978, p. 3291; March, 1984, p. 4213.

Horn Book, August, 1969; August, 1973, pp. 382-383; October, 1974.

Junior Bookshelf, June, 1971, p. 187; August, 1978, p. 195; February, 1984, p. 29.

Kirkus Reviews, December 15, 1974, p. 1305; September 15, 1981, p. 1161.

National Observer, June 9, 1969, p. 23.

New York Herald Tribune Book Review, November 13, 1960, p. 5.

New York Times Book Review, September 20, 1964, p. 26; June 24, 1973, p. 8; March 13, 1983, p. 29; January 22, 1984, p. 24.

Reading Teacher, February, 1976, p. 511.

School Librarian and School Library Review, July, 1965, p. 249.

School Library Journal, September, 1969, p. 161; November, 1982, p. 104.

Spectator, April 16, 1977, pp. 26-27.

Times Literary Supplement, April 7, 1978; July 23, 1982.

Virginia Kirkus' Service, January 15, 1956, pp. 43-44; January 15, 1957, pp. 37-38; August 1, 1962, p. 682; October 1, 1965, pp. 1035-1036.

Washington Post Book World, August 9, 1981, p. 9.

Young Readers Review, December, 1965.

OBITUARIES:

PERIODICALS

Los Angeles Times, December 10, 1989.

New York Times, December 6, 1989.

School Library Journal, January, 1990, p. 18.*

—*Sketch by Kevin S. Hile*

*   *   *

TIPPETTE, Giles 1934-

PERSONAL: Born August 25, 1934, in Texas; son of O. B. and Mary Grace (Harpster) Tippette; married Mildred Ann Mebane, 1956 (divorced, 1975); married Betsyanne Wright Pool, 1981; children: (first marriage) Shanna, Lisa. *Education:* Sam Houston University, B.S., 1959. *Politics:* "Distrust all politics and politicians." *Religion:* No formal.

ADDRESSES: Home—Corpus Christi, TX. *Agent*—Owen Laster, William Morris Agency, 1350 Avenue of the Americas, New York, NY 10019.

CAREER: Writer. Has held a variety of jobs, including rodeo contestant, diamond courier, and gold miner in Mexico.

MEMBER: Authors Guild, Authors League of America.

WRITINGS:

The Bank Robber (novel), Macmillan, 1970, published as *The Spikes Gang,* Pocket Books, 1971.

The Trojan Cow (novel), Macmillan, 1971.

The Brave Man (nonfiction), Macmillan, 1972.

Saturday's Children (nonfiction), Macmillan, 1973.

Austin Davis (novel), Dell, 1975.

The Sunshine Killers (novel), Dell, 1975.

The Survivalist (novel), Macmillan, 1975.

The Mercenaries, Delacorte, 1976.

Wilson's Gold, Dell, 1980.

Wilson's Luck, Dell, 1980.

Wilson's Choice, Dell, 1981.

Wilson's Revenge, Dell, 1981.

Wilson's Woman, Dell, 1982.

The Texas Bank Robbing Company, Dell, 1982.

Hard Luck Money, Dell, 1982.

Wilson Young on the Run, Dell, 1983.

China Blue, Dell, 1984.

Bad News (novel), Berkley Publishing, 1989.

Donkey Baseball and Other Sporting Delights (nonfiction), Taylor Publishing (Dallas), 1989.

Cross Fire (novel), Berkley Publishing, 1990.

I'll Try Anything Once: Misadventures of a Sports Guy (nonfiction), Taylor Publishing, 1991.

Hard Rock (novel), Berkley Publishing, 1991.

Jailbreak (novel), Berkley Publishing, 1991.

Sixkiller (novel), Berkley Publishing, 1992.

Also author of manuscript, "Man of Ice." Contributor to magazines, including *Argosy, Esquire, Newsweek, Sports Illustrated, Texas Monthly,* and *Time.*

ADAPTATIONS: Two of Giles Tippette's novels, *Austin Davis* and *The Bank Robber,* have been made into movies. His manuscript "Man of Ice" was adapted for a television movie, "Target Risk."

WORK IN PROGRESS: An untitled work of fiction.

*   *   *

TITON, Jeff Todd 1943-

PERSONAL: Born December 8, 1943, in Jersey City, NJ; son of Milton and Edith Titon; married Paula Protze, July 16, 1966; children: Emily. *Education:* Amherst College, B.A., 1965; University of Minnesota, M.A., 1967, Ph.D., 1971.

ADDRESSES: Home—202 Armington St., Cranston, RI 02905. *Office*—Department of Music, Brown University, Providence, RI 02912.

CAREER: Lazy Bill Lucas Blues Band, Minneapolis, MN, guitarist, 1969-71; Tufts University, Medford, MA, assistant professor, 1971-77, associate professor of English and music, 1977-86; Brown University, Providence, RI, professor of Music, 1986—. Indiana University, visiting assistant professor of folklore, 1977; Carleton College, visiting professor of American studies, 1985; Berea College, visiting professor of Appalachian studies, 1990.

MEMBER: American Studies Association, American Folklore Society, Society for Ethnomusicology (member of council, 1977-80, 1984—; president, Northeast chapter, 1982-84).

AWARDS, HONORS: National Endowment for the Humanities fellow, 1977-78, 1986; Deems Taylor Award, American Society of Composers, Authors, and Publishers, 1977, for *Early Downhome Blues: A Musical and Cultural Analysis.*

WRITINGS:

Early Downhome Blues: A Musical and Cultural Analysis, University of Illinois Press, 1977.
Downhome Blues Lyrics, G. K. Hall, 1981, 2nd edition, University of Illinois Press, 1990.
Powerhouse for God (recording), University of North Carolina Press, 1982.
Worlds of Music, Schirmer Books, 1984, 2nd edition, 1991.
Powerhouse for God, University of Texas Press, 1988.
Powerhouse for God (screenplay adapted from book of same title), Documentary Educational Resources, 1989.
Give Me This Mountain, University of Illinois Press, 1989.

Editor of *Ethnomusicology,* 1990—. Contributor to other folklore and ethnomusicology publications.

WORK IN PROGRESS: Editing and contributing to North American volume of *Garland Encyclopedia of World Music;* researching the nature of knowledge about music.

*   *   *

TREVOR, William
  See COX, William Trevor

*   *   *

TROY, Nancy J. 1952-

PERSONAL: Born December 27, 1952, in New York, NY; daughter of William B. (a business executive) and Joanne (Joslin) Troy; married Wim de Wit. *Education:* Wesleyan University, B.A. (magna cum laude), 1974; Yale University, M.A., 1976, Ph.D., 1979.

ADDRESSES: Home—701 Washington Ave., Wilmette, IL 60091. *Office*—Department of Art History, Northwestern University, Evanston, IL 60208.

CAREER: Johns Hopkins University, Baltimore, MD, assistant professor of history of art, 1979-83; Northwestern University, Evanston, IL, assistant professor, 1983-85, associate professor of art history, 1985—, chairperson of department, 1990—. Solomon R. Guggenheim Museum, curatorial coordinator and special consultant, 1974; National Gallery of Art, assistant to curator of French paintings, summer, 1975; Yale University, research assistant, 1975, guest curator at Art Gallery, 1979. Member of Maryland Council on the Arts, 1981-82; Baltimore Museum of Art, member of committee on collections and fine arts accessions committee, both 1979-82. Art examiner and reviewer for numerous colleges, universities, and grant programs. Has chaired symposia, delivered numerous lectures, and sat on panels for symposia, seminars, conferences, and exhibitions. Consultant to Art Institute of Chicago and Walter Art Center.

MEMBER: College Art Association of America, Society of Architectural Historians (secretary of Chicago chapter, 1984-85).

AWARDS, HONORS: Kress Foundation travel grants, 1976, 1977; Fulbright-Hays fellow in the Netherlands, 1977-78, 1978; American Council of Learned Societies fellow, 1981, 1982-83, grant-in-aid, 1991; National Endowment for the Humanities fellow, 1982-83; Graham Foundation for Advanced Studies in the Fine Arts grants, 1982, for photographs, 1989, for *Modernism and the Decorative Arts in France: Art Nouveau to Le Corbusier;* Lilly Endowment fellow, 1984-85; American Philosophical Society grant, 1986; Institute for Advanced Study, School of Historical Studies, fellow, 1987; Getty Center for the History of Art and the Humanities senior scholar, 1989-90.

WRITINGS:

Mondrian and Neo-Plasticism in America (exhibition catalogue), Yale University Art Gallery, 1979.
The De Stilj Environment, MIT Press, 1983.
Modernism and the Decorative Arts in France: Art Nouveau to Le Corbusier, Yale University Press, 1991.

Contributor to books, including *The Hudson River School: Nineteenth-Century American Landscapes in the Wadsworth Atheneum,* edited by Theodore Stebbins, Wadsworth Atheneum, 1976; *De Stilj, 1917-1931: Visions of Utopia,* edited by Mildred Friedman, Abbeville Press, 1982; and *The Historical Image: Essays on Art and Culture in France, 1750-1950,* Yale University Press, 1992. Contributor to art and museum journals, including *Art Bulletin, Archithese, Arts Magazine, Studies in Art History, Yale University Art Gallery Bulletin, Design Book Review,* and

Journal of the Society of Architectural Historians. Contributing editor, *Design Issues,* 1984-88.

WORK IN PROGRESS: A book, *Couture and Culture: Fashion and the Marketing of Modernism.*

BIOGRAPHICAL/CRITICAL SOURCES:

PERIODICALS

Chicago Tribune, September 15, 1991, section 10, p. 15.

*   *   *

TRUE, Michael (D.) 1933-

PERSONAL: Born November 8, 1933, in Oklahoma City, OK; son of Guy Herbert and Agnes (Murphy) True; married Mary Patricia Delaney, April 20, 1958; children: Mary, Michael, John, Christopher, Elizabeth, Anne. *Education:* University of Oklahoma, B.A., 1955; University of Minnesota, M.A., 1957; Duke University, Ph.D., 1964; postdoctoral study at Harvard University, 1967-68, Columbia University, 1976-77, and University of Wisconsin, 1989. *Religion:* Roman Catholic.

ADDRESSES: Home—4 Westland St., Worcester, MA 01602. *Office*—Department of English, Assumption College, Worcester, MA 01615-0005.

CAREER: Remington Rand Univac, St. Paul, MN, technical writer, 1958-59; Duke University, Durham, NC, lecturer in English, 1960-61; North Carolina College at Durham (now North Carolina Central University), lecturer in English, 1961; Indiana State University, Terre Haute, assistant professor of English, 1961-65; Assumption College, Worcester, MA, assistant professor, 1965-67, associate professor, 1967-74, professor of English, 1974—, chairman of department, 1974-76, 1988. Visiting professor, Clark University, 1967-80, and Nanjing University, People's Republic of China, 1984-85, 1989; Sheffer Visiting Professor of Religion, Colorado College, 1988, 1990. Consultant in nonfiction writing, Upper Midwest Writer's Conference, 1973, 1975, 1977-78, 1979-80, 1982; consultant to University of Central Arkansas Writers Conference, 1976-77; consultant to European Council of International Schools in London, 1979, in Brussels, 1980, in The Hague, 1981, and in Geneva, 1982. *Military service:* U.S. Army, 1957-58.

MEMBER: International Peace Research Association, American Studies Association, National Council of Teachers of English (director, 1973-78), New England College English Association (director, 1965-69, 1975-79; president, 1980-81), Civil Liberties Union of Massachusetts.

AWARDS, HONORS: National Endowment for the Humanities fellow at Columbia University, 1976-77; F.

Andre Favat Award from Massachusetts Council of Teachers of English, 1980.

WRITINGS:

Should the Catholic College Survive? and Other Impertinent Questions, Assumption Student Press, 1971.
Worcester Poets, with Notes toward a Literary History, Worcester County Poetry Association, 1972.
Poets in the Schools: A Handbook, National Council of Teachers of English, 1976.
Homemade Social Justice, Fides/Claretian, 1982.
Justice-Seekers, Peacemakers: Thirty-two Portraits in Courage, XXIII Publications, 1985.
Worcester Area Writers, 1680-1980, Worcester Public Library, 1987.
(Editor) *Daniel Berrigan: Poetry, Drama, Prose,* Orbis Books, 1988.
Ordinary People: Family Life and Global Values, Orbis Books, 1991.

Contributor to books, including *Contemporary Poets,* edited by James Vinson, St. Martin's, 1975, 4th edition, 1985, *Three Mountains Press Poetry Anthology, 1975,* edited by Denis Carbonneau, Three Mountains Press, 1976, *American Writers,* Scribner, 1979, and *War or Peace? The Search for New Answers,* Orbis Books, 1981. Also contributor to numerous periodicals, including *Commonweal, Progressive, New Republic, Cross-Currents, Bulletin of the New York Public Library, Ms.,* and *Harvard Divinity Bulletin.*

WORK IN PROGRESS: The Nonviolent Tradition and American Literature, for Syracuse University Press, and a series of portraits of nonviolent activists from around the world.

SIDELIGHTS: Michael True once wrote *CA:* "I want to write good, clear prose, like George Orwell's, about literature and survival. I am deeply concerned about various threats to the moral imagination posed by injustice and nuclear armaments in our time; and especially after teaching in China for a year, I am convinced that twentieth-century art and literature in America speak directly to these issues."

*   *   *

TUAN, Yi-Fu 1930-

PERSONAL: Born December 5, 1930, in Tientsin, China; came to the United States in 1951, naturalized citizen, 1973; son of Mao-Lan (a diplomat) and Lui Kung (Tao) Tuan. *Education:* Oxford University, B.A., 1951, M.A., 1955; University of California, Berkeley, Ph.D., 1957.

ADDRESSES: Office—Department of Geography, University of Wisconsin, Madison, WI 53706.

CAREER: Indiana University at Bloomington, instructor in geography, 1956-58; University of Chicago, Chicago, IL, research fellow in statistics, 1958-59; University of New Mexico, Albuquerque, 1959-65, began as assistant professor, became associate professor of geography; University of Toronto, Toronto, Ontario, associate professor of geography, 1966-68; University of Minnesota, Minneapolis, professor of geography, 1968-84; University of Wisconsin—Madison, professor of geography, 1984—. Visiting instructor, Oxford University, 1966, and University of Hawaii, 1973; Australian National University, Morrison Lecturer, 1975; University of California, Davis, distinguished visiting professor, 1975-76; Vilas Research Professor, 1985; guest lecturer at colleges and universities.

MEMBER: American Association for the Advancement of Science (fellow), Association of American Geographers, Association for Asian Studies, American Geographical Society, Association for the Study of Man-Environment Relations.

AWARDS, HONORS: Guggenheim fellowship, 1967-68; "meritorious contribution to geography" award, Association of American Geographers, 1973; Fulbright-Hays senior scholarship, 1975; Cullum Geographical Medal, American Geographical Society, 1987.

WRITINGS:

Pediments in Southeastern Arizona, University of California Press, 1959.
The Hydrologic Cycle and the Wisdom of God: A Theme in Geoteleology, University of Toronto Press, 1968.
China, Aldine, 1970.
Man and Nature, Association of American Geographers, 1971.
Topophilia, Prentice-Hall, 1974.
Space and Place: The Perspective of Experience, University of Minnesota Press, 1977.
Landscapes of Fear, Pantheon, 1980.
Segmented Worlds and Self: Group Life and Individual Consciousness, University of Minnesota Press, 1982.
Dominance and Affection: The Making of Pets, Yale University Press, 1984.
The Good Life, University of Wisconsin Press, 1986.
Morality and Imagination: Paradoxes of Progress, University of Wisconsin Press, 1989.

Contributor to geography journals.

WORK IN PROGRESS: Research into the good life, imagination, and the real.

SIDELIGHTS: "By his own confession [Yi-Fu Tuan] is as much a psychologist as a geographer, concerned above all with the way human beings respond to their physical environment," observes Paul Robinson in the *New York Times Book Review.* In *Landscapes of Fear* Tuan explores the influence of fear on stages of individual and historical development, concluding it a constant in human nature. Each age in history had its specific fears, notes Tuan, citing disease and natural disaster in earlier times, nuclear holocaust and overpopulation today. The author maintains that the quest to conquer fear has led humans to manufacture fences, cities, legends, myths, and even philosophical systems. According to Jack Sullivan in the *Washington Post Book World,* Tuan believes that "people can adapt to almost anything and that anxiety itself can be a positive force: it can drive us to security but also to adventure; it can signal an openness to the reality that life is change."

Though Christopher Lehmann-Haupt describes Tuan's conclusion in *Landscapes of Fear* as "an extremely arresting one," he writes in the *New York Times* that the point disappears amidst disorganization and aimless form: "The . . . trouble with Professor Tuan's book is that he offers his evidence before he explains what he is driving at. . . . He explores childhood fear, fear of nature, fear in the medieval world, the city and the countryside, fear of nature, disease, witches and ghosts, before he at long last frames his provocative thesis." Jonathan Raban expresses a similar viewpoint in the *New York Times Book Review,* claiming that Tuan's book "turns out to be a thorough-going disappointment—a series of blundering and inconclusive skirmishes with a fascinating subject."

Graham Hough asserts in the *Times Literary Supplement* that in *Landscapes of Fear* Tuan "casts his net too wide," yet he generally praises the work: "Tuan writes crisply and vividly, his reading is diverse and extensive, and he assembles an array of historical and anthropological bric-a-brac, beliefs, anecdotes, and reports of research that never fail to interest." Sullivan, too, comments on the strength of Tuan's prose, stating "[*Landscapes of Fear*] has a special force and eloquence . . . because of [his] avoidance of academese and his gift for imagery."

BIOGRAPHICAL/CRITICAL SOURCES:

PERIODICALS

New York Times, January 2, 1980.
New York Times Book Review, January 27, 1980; February 10, 1985; March 16, 1986, p. 17; June 25, 1989, p. 29.
Times Literary Supplement, September 26, 1980.
Washington Post Book World, February 10, 1980.

*   *   *

TURKEL, Pauline
   See KESSELMAN-TURKEL, Judi

U

UDELL, Jon G(erald) 1935-

PERSONAL: Born June 22, 1935, in Columbus, WI; son of Roy Grant and Jessie (Foster) Udell; married Susan Smykla, May 16, 1960; children: Jon G., Jr., Roy Steven, Susan E., Bruce F., Alan J., Kenneth G. *Education:* University of Wisconsin, B.B.A., 1957, M.B.A., 1958, Ph.D., 1961; University of California, Berkeley, postdoctoral study, summer, 1963. *Politics:* Independent. *Religion:* Presbyterian.

ADDRESSES: Home—5210 Barton Rd., Madison, WI 53711. *Office*—Graduate School of Business, University of Wisconsin, Madison, WI 53706.

CAREER: University of Wisconsin—Madison, instructor, 1959-61, assistant professor, 1961-65, associate professor, 1965-68, professor of business, 1968—, Irwin Maier Professor of Business, 1976—, assistant director of Bureau of Business Research and Service, 1959-63, associate director, 1963-66, director, 1967-74. Cornell University, visiting associate professor, 1966-67. Federal Home Loan Bank of Chicago, chairman of board, 1982-89, public interest director, 1973-80, 1982-89. Member of board of directors, United Banks of Wisconsin, 1975-85, Research Products Corp., Wisconsin Energy Corp., Wisconsin Electric Power Co., Versa Technologies, Inc., Wisconsin Youth Symphony Orchestras, and Association of Private Enterprise Education.

Service to State of Wisconsin includes director of State Chamber of Commerce, member of governor's council for economic development, chairman of governor's conference on mergers and acquisitions, co-chairman of governor's executive conference on marketing and research and development, member of governor's committee on commerce and industry, member, vice-president, and president of consumer advisory council of Department of Agriculture, chairman of economic mission for the seventies, and trustee and vice-president of Wonderful Wisconsin Foundation. Member of various local committees and organizations in Madison. Corporate member and adviser, Man-Environment Communications Center; technical adviser to advisory committee of Project Sanguine; member of advisory committee, Educational Satellite Telecommunications Center. Consultant to American Newspaper Publishers Association, Wisconsin Builders Association, and Mosinee Paper Co.

MEMBER: American Marketing Association, Phi Beta Kappa, Beta Gamma Sigma, Phi Kappa Phi, Phi Eta Sigma, Rotary International.

AWARDS, HONORS: Citations from the governor of Wisconsin, 1970, for contributions to the state's economic development, and 1971, for service to the state; Sidney S. Goldish Award, International Newspaper Promotion Association, for contribution to newspaper research; Marketer of the Year Award, Wisconsin Chapter of American Marketing Association, 1976; Robert A. Jerred Distinguished Service Award, University of Wisconsin, 1986; Paul Harris Fellow, Rotary International, 1989; Presidential Award, Wisconsin Builders Association, 1989, for outstanding contributions to the shelter industry, 1989.

WRITINGS:

Tabulation of Retail Trade Survey Questionnaires, University of Wisconsin, 1959.

The Second Midwest Newsprint Survey, Bureau of Business Research and Service, University of Wisconsin, and Inland Daily Press Association, 1960.

An Analysis of Midwest Newsprint Consumption, University of Wisconsin and Inland Daily Press Association, 1961.

A New Analysis of Midwest Newsprint Supply and Demand, University of Wisconsin and Inland Daily Press Association, 1962.

A Model of Non-Price Competitive Strategy, Bureau of Business Research and Service, University of Wisconsin, 1963.

An Analysis of National and Regional Newsprint Trends, American Newspaper Publishers Association, 1964.

The Economic Future of the Newspaper Business, American Newspaper Publishers Association, 1965.

1975 U.S. Newsprint Consumption: An Economic Analysis of Consumption Trends with Projections for the Next Decade, American Newspaper Publishers Association, 1965.

The Growth of Newsprint Consumption by United States Newspapers, American Newspaper Publishers Association, 1966.

The Growth of Newspapers and Newsprint Consumption in the Midwest, Inland Daily Press Association, 1967.

(With William Strang) *Consumer Attitudes and Shopping Behavior in the South Wood County Area: An Attempt to Develop New Methodology for Retail Trade Analysis,* University of Wisconsin, 1967.

Newsprint Consumption in the United States: 1956-1966, and the Current Outlook, American Newspaper Publishers Association, 1967.

(With Strang and Gene Gohlke) *Wisconsin's Economy in 1975: Wisconsin's Economic Growth since World War II and Projections for 1975,* Bureau of Business Research and Service, University of Wisconsin, and University of Wisconsin Foundation, 1968.

U.S. Newspaper Growth and Newsprint Consumption, American Newspaper Publishers Association, 1968.

Social and Economic Consequences of the Merger Movement in Wisconsin, Division of Economic Development, State of Wisconsin, 1969.

Economic Growth and Newsprint Consumption of Midwest Newspapers Projected through 1975, Inland Daily Press Association, 1969.

U.S. Newsprint Consumption and Economic Growth, 1958-1968, and the Current Outlook, American Newspaper Publishers Association, 1969.

(Editor with Linda Kohl, and contributor) *Marketing and Research and Development,* Division of Economic Development, State of Wisconsin, 1970.

(With Strang, William P. Glade, and James E. Littlefield) *Marketing in a Developing Nation,* Heath, 1970.

Future Newsprint Demand: 1970-1980, American Newspaper Publishers Association, 1970.

(With Strang) *Perceptions of Wisconsin: A Study of the Strengths and Weaknesses of Wisconsin as Seen by Manufacturing Executives,* Journal Co. and Bureau of Business Research and Service, University of Wisconsin, 1972.

(With Strang) *Importance of Location Decision Factors as Seen by Southeastern Wisconsin Industry,* Journal Co. and Bureau of Business Research and Service, University of Wisconsin, 1972.

Taxation and Changes of Residency, Journal Co. and Bureau of Business Research and Service, University of Wisconsin, 1972.

(With Strang) *Importance of Location Decision Factors as Seen by Wisconsin Manufacturers in a Sixty-Five County Area,* Journal Co. and Bureau of Business Research and Service, University of Wisconsin, 1972.

Research and Development in Wisconsin Industry: An Analysis of Current Programs and Future Research and Development Needs of Wisconsin Manufacturers, Bureau of Business Research and Service, University of Wisconsin, 1972.

Perceptions of Wisconsin: The State as Seen by the Leaders of Organized Labor, Journal Co. and Bureau of Business Research and Service, University of Wisconsin, 1972.

The State as Seen by Rank and File Delegates to the American Federation of Labor-Congress of Industrial Organizations Biennial Convention, Journal Co. and Bureau of Business Research and Service, University of Wisconsin, 1972.

Successful Marketing Strategies in American Industry, Mimir Publishers, 1972.

The Economic Impact of Man-Made Lakes on Area Businesses, Bureau of Business Research and Service, University of Wisconsin, 1973.

Expenditures and Perceptions of Property Owners at Lakes Sherwood and Camelot, Bureau of Business Research and Service, University of Wisconsin, 1973.

The Supply and Demand for Newsprint in the United States, 1962-1973, American Newspaper Publishers Association, 1974.

The U.S. Economy and Newspaper Growth, American Newspaper Publishers Association, 1974.

Dynamics of U.S. Daily Newspapers and Newsprint Consumption, American Newspaper Publishers Association, 1976.

U.S. Economic Growth and Newsprint Consumption, American Newspaper Publishers Association, 1977.

(With Strang and E. Lauck Parke) *Skilled Labor in the Milwaukee Area: The Supply, Education, Problems and Opportunities,* Graduate School of Business, University of Wisconsin—Madison, 1977.

The Impact of Recent Legislation on Wisconsin Manufacturers and Employment Growth, Graduate School of Business, University of Wisconsin—Madison, 1977.

The Economics of the American Newspaper, Hastings House, 1978.

Future Newspaper and Newsprint Growth: 1977-1985, American Newspaper Publishers Association, 1978.

Rockford, Illinois (five economic studies), Rock Valley College, 1978.

Executive Evaluations of National Tax Proposals, Wisconsin Association of Manufacturers and Commerce, 1978.

Toward Economic Development in Illinois through Better Understanding and Cooperation by Industry, Labor, Government and Education, Community College Board of the State of Illinois, 1978.

Wisconsin's Taxation of Capital Gains: Fair? Progressive? Competitive?, Public Expenditure Survey of Wisconsin, 1979.

The Daily Newspaper: Where It Stands Today, International Circulation Managers Association, 1979.

Newsprint and Its Economic Utilisation, INCA-FIEJ Research Association, 1979.

Prognosis of Future Developments in North America, INCA-FIEJ Research Association, 1979.

U.S. Newspapers and Newsprint as a New Decade Begins, American Newspaper Publishers Association, 1980.

(With William M. Babcock, Jr.) *Death Taxes in Wisconsin,* Public Expenditure Research Foundation, 1980.

Inflation, Competition, and Future Survival, U.S. Government Printing Office, 1980.

(With Gene R. Laczniak) *Marketing in an Age of Change,* Wiley, 1981, international edition published as *Marketing in an Age of Change: International Edition,* 1982.

(With Louis M. Rohlmeier, Jr., and Laird B. Anderson) *Reporting on Business and the Economy,* Prentice-Hall, 1981.

The Future of the U.S. Newspapers and Newsprint Consumption, 1980-1985, American Newspaper Publishers Association, 1981.

U.S. Newspapers and Newsprint Consumption: Decade of the Seventies and the Future, American Newspaper Publishers Association, 1982.

(With Charles S. Taylor) *Kenaf-Newsprint System: General Feasibility Study,* American Newspaper Publishers Association, 1982.

The Outlook for U.S. Newspapers and Newsprint Consumption, 1983-1990, American Newspaper Publishers Association, 1983.

Wisconsin's Business Climate as Seen by Manufacturing Executives, Graduate School of Business, University of Wisconsin—Madison, 1985.

An Economic Analysis of U.S. Newspaper Growth and Newsprint Consumption with Projections for 1995, American Newspaper Publishers Association, 1986.

Report on Engineering Education in Wisconsin, Phase I: Wisconsin Industrial Leaders' Perception, Wisconsin Society of Professional Engineers, 1986.

The Future of the U.S. Economy as Envisioned by Leaders in American Industry, Graduate School of Business, University of Wisconsin—Madison, 1987.

The Growth of Newspapers and the U.S. Economic and Newsprint Outlook for 1988, American Newspaper Publishers Association, 1987.

The Growth and Outlook for U.S. Newspapers and Newsprint Consumption, American Newspaper Publishers Association, 1988.

An Economic Appraisal of U.S. Newspapers and Newsprint Consumption, American Newspaper Publishers Association, 1989.

U.S. Newspapers and Newsprint Consumption in the New Decade, American Newspaper Publishers Association, 1991.

A Profile of Wisconsin's Homebuilding Industry, School of Business, University of Wisconsin—Madison, 1991.

Quality of Business Life in Wisconsin, School of Business, University of Wisconsin—Madison, 1991.

Also author of research reports. Contributor to books, including *Markets and Marketing in Developing Economies,* edited by Reed Mayer and Stanley C. Hollander, Irwin, 1968; and *The Newspaper in Satellite's Age,* [Rome], 1987; contributor to conference reports and proceedings. Contributor of over one hundred twenty articles to professional journals, including *Journal of Marketing, Management Science, Journalism Quarterly, Mergers and Acquisitions,* and *Administrative Science Quarterly.* Member of editorial board, *Journal of Private Enterprise* and *Media Economics.*

SIDELIGHTS: Jon G. Udell told *CA:* "Research, objectively and carefully executed, can produce knowledge. However, that knowledge must be disseminated to others if society is to see the light and benefit from its illumination. That is why writing and publication are so essential to the advancement of mankind."

* * *

URQUHART, Colin   1940-

PERSONAL: Born January 26, 1940, in Twickenham, England; son of Kenneth Hector (an architect) and Lilian Rosida (Batten) Urquhart; married Caroline Josephine May (a housewife and author), October 24, 1964; children: Claire, Clive Ross, Andrea. *Education:* King's College, London, associate, 1963.

ADDRESSES: Office—Kingdom Faith Ministries, Roffey Pl., Crawley Rd., Faygate, Horsham, West Sussex RH12 4SA, England. *Agent*—Edward England Books, Crowton House, The Broadway, Crowborough, East Sussex TN6 1AB, England.

CAREER: Ordained Anglican priest, 1963; Anglican curate in Cheshunt, England, 1963-67; priest in charge of Anglican church in Letchworth, England, 1967-70; vicar of Anglican church in Luton, England, 1970-76; Kingdom Faith Ministries (formerly Bethany Fellowship), Horsham, West Sussex, England, director, 1976—.

WRITINGS:

When the Spirit Comes (autobiography), Hodder & Stoughton, 1974, Bethany Fellowship (U.S.), 1975.
My Father Is the Gardener, Hodder & Stoughton, 1977.
Anything You Ask, Hodder & Stoughton, 1978.
In Christ Jesus, Hodder & Stoughton, 1981.
Faith for the Future (autobiography), Hodder & Stoughton, 1982.
Holy Fire, Hodder & Stoughton, 1984.
The Positive Kingdom, Hodder & Stoughton, 1985.
Receive Your Healing, Hodder & Stoughton, 1986.
Listen and Live, Hodder & Stoughton, 1987.
Personal Victory, Hodder & Stoughton, 1988.
"My Dear Child . . . ," Hodder & Stoughton, 1990, Creation House, 1991.
The Faith Dynamic, Kingdom Faith Ministries, 1990.
Our Rich Inheritance, Kingdom Faith Ministries, 1991.
Revival Is Coming, Kingdom Faith Ministries, 1991.

Contributor to Christian magazines.

WORK IN PROGRESS: Work on *"My Dear Son . . . ,"* a sequel to *"My Dear Child . . . "*; preparation for "Direct Counselling" material for Biblical counselling and healing.

SIDELIGHTS: Colin Urquhart described his work to *CA* as "the teaching of the Bible in the power of the Holy Spirit, and ministry to individuals within the corporate church in his power. I am concerned with evangelism and revival."

He added: "My writing began out of an experience of revival in the church where I was pastor and in the movement of the Holy Spirit that brought many to new life, the empowering of the Holy Spirit and to healing in the name of Jesus. My present ministry has been an extension of the local ministry traveling to many nations encouraging renewal and revival. Each of the books that has been written has come out of personal experience of the word being lived out in practice. Most are simple biblical expositions but related very much for everyday life and to how it is possible for us to live according to the Word and in the power of the Holy Spirit.

"There has always been a ready market for the books here because of the extent of the ministry in this country and beyond. This is a great responsibility but it is also a tremendous opportunity. There are so many today who are discovering the experience of the Holy Spirit but without their lives getting deeply rooted in the word of God. They need to know how to live victoriously, overcoming all the difficulties of the world, the flesh, and the devil. So each

of the books is written very much from a faith perspective, that Jesus means us to take his promises seriously.

"We are able to do the same things as he has done and greater things still. We are to anticipate that God will answer our prayers of faith, doing as he promised, anything we ask in the name of Jesus. Obviously such promises can only be fulfilled in the power of the Holy Spirit. Therefore it is important for every Christian to know a true baptism in the Holy Spirit where the life and power of God's spirit is released throughout their whole being."

BIOGRAPHICAL/CRITICAL SOURCES:

BOOKS

Urquhart, Caroline, *His God, My God,* Hodder & Stoughton, 1983.
Urquhart, Colin, *When the Spirit Comes* (autobiography), Hodder & Stoughton, 1974, Bethany Fellowship (U.S.), 1975.
Urquhart, Colin, *Faith for the Future* (autobiography), Hodder & Stoughton, 1982.

*   *   *

UTLEE, (J.) Maarten   1949-

PERSONAL: Born January 13, 1949, in Utrecht, Netherlands; came to the United States in 1953, naturalized citizen, 1959; son of A. J. Utlee (a chemist) and A. L. Wilkinson (a teacher). *Education:* Reed College, B.A., 1969; Johns Hopkins University, M.A., 1972, Ph.D., 1975. *Avocational interests:* Collecting old books and maps, listening to string quartets.

ADDRESSES: Home—14 Allingham Ct., Haverstock Hill, London NW3, England. *Office*—Department of History, University of Alabama, Box 1936, Tuscaloosa, AL 35487.

CAREER: Stanford University, Stanford, CA, lecturer in undergraduate studies, 1974-75; Hobart and William Smith Colleges, Geneva, NY, assistant professor of history, 1975-78; Davidson College, Davidson, NC, visiting assistant professor of history and humanities, 1979-80; University of Alabama, Tuscaloosa, assistant professor of history, 1980-83, associate professor, 1983-88, director of Alabama Oxford Program, 1982 and 1983. Director, M.A. Program in Military History, Maxwell A.F.B., 1986.

MEMBER: American Catholic Historical Association, Historians of Early Modern Europe.

AWARDS, HONORS: National Endowment for Humanities fellow at University of North Carolina, 1978-79; Newberry Library fellow, 1980.

WRITINGS:

The Abbey of St. Germaine des Pres in the Seventeenth Century, Yale University Press, 1981.
Adapting to Conditions: War and Society in the Eighteenth Century, University of Alabama Press, 1986.
(Translator) Pierre Goubert, *The Course of French History,* F. Watts, 1988.

Contributor to history journals.

WORK IN PROGRESS: Letters and the Republic of Letters, 1680-1720, a long-term study of international scholarly communication; *Sir Hans Sloane, Scientist,* an intellectual biography.

SIDELIGHTS: Maarten Utlee told *CA:* "My European background has been of great value in historical research and writing. I am fluent in Dutch and French, and can read other European languages. I believe that young historians should make every effort to read documents from archives, and to this end I try to visit Europe as often as possible.

"My graduate studies at Johns Hopkins were directed by Orest Ranum, a good friend and model for a generation of French historians. Ranum was able to balance my independent tendencies with the requirements of established historiographical tradition. He encouraged me to do my research in France on less well-known subjects.

"My study of St. Germaine des Pres, a powerful Benedictine monastery in Paris, came about when my explorations in archives revealed extensive *series* of documents: accounts, minutes of the chapter, chronicles of memorable events. Monastic life had received little attention from French historians in recent years, but the sources were there for the *Annales*-school history, that is, one emphasizing social and economic trends. I took notes for most of 1971 and 1972, then moved to Leuven, Belgium, where I lived in a Franciscan monastery and enrolled as an independent researcher at the university. Writing and various part-time jobs occupied me from 1973 to 1975. Since then I have held a series of short-term positions at campuses around the country—and I have fortunately been able to survive. After years of traveling, it is a relief to settle in a larger institution and to see my research efforts appreciated.

"Many historical works are autobiographical, and mine certainly contain autobiographical elements. I have written about monastic scholars and businessmen in my first book and studied the social mobility of eighteenth-century bourgeois. The longer study of international scholarly communication naturally grew out of earlier work, an interest in European culture as a whole, and a faith in the community of scholars. It's a pleasure to know that my students and readers include many people who are *not* professional historians. Two of my volumes have been selected by book clubs, reaching a larger public."*

V

VALI, Ferenc Albert 1905-1984

PERSONAL: Born May 25, 1905, in Budapest, Hungary; died of cancer, November 19, 1984, in Leeds, MA; came to the United States in 1957; naturalized citizen; son of Martin and Elza (Philipp) Vali; married Rose Nagel (an artist), March 22, 1949. *Education:* University of Budapest, Doctor Juris, 1927; London School of Economics and Political Science, Ph.D., 1932; Academy of International Law, The Hague, Netherlands, diploma, 1932.

CAREER: Member of Hungarian Bar, 1932-43, 1946-47; attorney in Budapest, Hungary, 1932-43; University of Budapest, Budapest, professional lecturer, Faculty of Law and Political Science, 1935-43, professor, 1946-49; University of Istanbul, Istanbul, Turkey, visiting professor, 1943-46; adviser on international law to Hungarian Ministry of Finance, 1947-49; legal adviser to Hungarian branch office of International Business Machines Corporation (IBM), 1949-51; Harvard University, Center for International Affairs, Cambridge, MA, research associate, 1958-61; University of Massachusetts—Amherst, professor of political science, 1961-75, professor emeritus, 1975-84. Visiting professor of international law, Cornell Law School, spring, 1959, and Florida International University, Miami.

MEMBER: American Political Science Association, American Society of International Law, American Academy of Political and Social Science.

AWARDS, HONORS: Rockefeller Foundation fellow, 1957-58; LL.D., Wayne State University, 1962.

WRITINGS:

The Clause of Public Order, University of Budapest Press, 1928.
Die Deutsch-Oesterreichische Zollunion, Manz, 1932.

Servitudes of International Law: A Study of Rights in Foreign Territory, P. S. King & Son, 1933, 2nd edition, Stevens & Son, 1958.
Rift and Revolt in Hungary, Harvard University Press, 1961.
The Quest for a United Germany, Johns Hopkins Press, 1967.
Bridge across the Bosporus: The Foreign Policy of Turkey, Johns Hopkins Press, 1971.
The Turkish Straits and NATO, Hoover Institution Press, 1972.
Politics of the Indian Ocean Region: The Balances of Power, Free Press, 1976.
A Scholar's Odyssey (autobiography), edited by Karl W. Ryavec, Iowa State University Press, 1990.

Also author of *Black Nightshade,* a book about his prison experience. Contributor to books on communism and international relations, including *The Communist States at the Crossroads between Moscow and Peking,* edited by Adam Bromke, Praeger, 1965, and *The Communist States in Disarray,* University of Minnesota Press, 1972. Contributor of articles on international law and international relations to American, Hungarian, and British journals.

SIDELIGHTS: Arrested by the Hungarian Security Police with his wife, Rose, in August, 1951, Ferenc Albert Vali was convicted of high treason for espionage and sentenced to fifteen years in prison. He was provisionally released in October, 1956. After the first successful days of the Revolution, in which Hungary sought to break free from the Soviet-controlled Warsaw Pact, Vali was recalled to the University of Budapest and participated in an attempt to reorganize the Hungarian Ministry of Foreign Affairs. After the downfall of the Revolution in November, the Valis decided to leave the country in order to avoid reimprisonment.

At the Center for International Affairs at Harvard University, Vali worked with Henry Kissinger and Zbigniew Brzezinski. He made numerous research trips, and he once told *CA* that "the most outstanding among them was a journey around the periphery of the Indian Ocean." In 1977 Vali was invited by the Australian National University at Canberra to work on a project concerning the strategic problems of the Indian Ocean. His *Servitudes of International Law: A Study of Rights in Foreign Territory* is an internationally-used textbook.

BIOGRAPHICAL/CRITICAL SOURCES:

BOOKS

Vali, Ferenc, *A Scholar's Odyssey,* edited by Karl A. Ryavec, Iowa State University Press, 1990.

OBITUARIES:

PERIODICALS

Chicago Tribune, November 23, 1984.
New York Times, November 20, 1984.
Washington Times, November 26, 1984.*

*   *   *

VERRAL, Charles Spain   1904-1990
(George L. Eaton)

PERSONAL: Born November 7, 1904, in Highfield, Ontario, Canada; died of complications from lung cancer, April 1, 1990, in New York, NY; son of George William and Kate E. (Peacocke) Verral; married Jean Mithoefer, March 19, 1932; children: Charles Spain, Jr. *Education:* Attended Upper Canada College, 1919-23, and Ontario College of Art, 1923-26. *Religion:* Episcopalian. *Avocational interests:* Amateur magician, cartooning, tennis.

ADDRESSES: Home and office—79 Jane St., New York, NY 10014.

CAREER: Free-lance commercial artist, New York City, 1927-30; Clayton Publications, New York City, editor, 1930-33, art director, 1933-35; free-lance writer, New York City, 1935-60; writer-editor, Golden Press, 1960-61, biography editor, *Harper Encyclopedia of Science,* 1961-62; Reader's Digest Association, New York City, editor-writer for General Books, 1962-74; free-lance writer and editor, 1974-90.

MEMBER: Mystery Writers of America, Authors Guild, Authors League of America, Arts and Letters Club (Toronto).

WRITINGS:

Captain of the Ice, Crowell, 1953.
Champion of the Court, Crowell, 1954.

Men of Flight: Conquest of the Air, Aladdin Books, 1954.
The King of the Diamond, Crowell, 1955.
Mighty Men of Baseball, Aladdin Books, 1955.
High Danger, Sterling, 1955.
The Wonderful World Series, Crowell, 1956.
Walt Disney's "The Great Locomotive Chase," Simon & Schuster, 1956.
Annie Oakley, Sharpshooter, Simon & Schuster, 1957.
Lassie and the Daring Rescue, Simon & Schuster, 1957.
Brave Eagle, Simon & Schuster, 1957.
Broken Arrow, Simon & Schuster, 1957.
The Lone Ranger and Tonto, Simon & Schuster, 1957.
Rin-Tin-Tin and the Outlaw, Simon & Schuster, 1957.
(Editor) Sir Arthur Conan Doyle, *Sherlock Holmes* (abridged edition), illustrated by Tom Gill, Simon & Schuster, 1957.
Lassie and Her Day in the Sun, Simon & Schuster, 1958.
Cheyenne, Simon & Schuster, 1958.
Walt Disney's "Andy Burnett," Simon & Schuster, 1958.
Play Ball, Simon & Schuster, 1958.
Zorro, Simon & Schuster, 1958.
Smoky the Bear, Simon & Schuster, 1958.
Rin-Tin-Tin and the Hidden Treasure, Simon & Schuster, 1959.
Zorro and the Secret Plan, Simon & Schuster, 1959.
Walt Disney's "The Shaggy Dog," Simon & Schuster, 1959.
The Winning Quarterback, Crowell, 1960.
The Case of the Missing Message, Golden Press, 1960.
Smoky the Bear and His Animal Friends, Golden Press, 1960.
The Flying Car, Golden Press, 1961.
Jets, Prentice-Hall, 1962.
Go! The Story of Outer Space, Prentice-Hall, 1962.
Robert Goddard: Father of the Space Age, Prentice-Hall, 1963.
Babe Ruth: Sultan of Swat, Garrard, 1976.
Casey Stengal: Baseball's Great Manager, Garrard, 1978.
Popeye Goes Fishing, Grosset & Dunlap, 1980.
Popeye and the Haunted House, Grosset & Dunlap, 1980.
Popeye Climbs a Mountain, Grosset & Dunlap, 1980.

Coauthor, under pseudonym George L. Eaton, of the "Bill Barnes" series for *Air Trails,* 1934-43; also author of scripts for "Mandrake the Magician" radio series, 1940-41; continuity writer for *Hap Hooper* comic strip, United Features Syndicate, 1941-47. Contributor to a variety of Reader's Digest Association publications, including *Great World Atlas,* 1963, *These United States,* 1968, *Great Events of the 20th Century,* 1975, and *Champions of Sports,* 1984. Contributor of articles and short stories to numerous magazines and anthologies.

SIDELIGHTS: Charles Spain Verral once told *CA:* "The often-asked question, 'What started you writing?,' is an easy one for me to answer by saying: Being read to as a child. I was the youngest of seven children—I had five sisters and one brother, two years older. We all grew up in a small town in Ontario, Canada, where the winters were long and severe—and totally wonderful. Once the snows came to bury the streets in those early 1900 years, nothing moved on wheels in our town until spring.

"It was the habit for the family on many winter nights to gather around the warmth of the fireplace while my mother read to us. There was no television then, of course, no radio and the nearest motion picture theaters were in Toronto, many miles away. My mother was born in Limerick, Ireland, and she loved to read aloud. She was exceptionally gifted at it, never a stumble, never a mispronunciation, always with a lilt. In another time, another age, she could have been an accomplished actress. She gave the characters in her readings such distinctive speech patterns that they came vividly alive. Often her readings were from her beloved Charles Dickens, but her range was wide—Rudyard Kipling, Mark Twain, Alexander Dumas and many other greats, together with the then-modern books such as *The Broad Highway*. My father, a successful businessman and involved in politics, joined the family circle whenever he could, listening in silent contentment.

"Being the youngest, I was exposed to books that were of interest to my older sisters and, I suppose, considered today to be beyond my understanding and liking. Which was not true. The first book I remember was *Lorna Doone*. Even now I can recall the delicious terror I felt as a young John Rudd crouched at the side of the road in the blackness of night while the band of murderous Doone outlaws galloped past across the moors.

"The reading aloud didn't stop with these family gatherings as far as my brother and I were concerned. Practically every night in our very young years after we were tucked in bed, we were read to by my oldest sister. These were different kinds of stories—tales of derring-do, of knights, of exploration and high adventure by Robert Louis Stevenson, by Walter Scott, by George Alfred Henty, by Conan Doyle, by Jules Verne, and the rest of that noble company.

"Living in Canada as we did gave our family access to a wealth of books and magazines from England as well as those from the United States. How could I ever forget those early *Wizard of Oz* books by L. Frank Baum or the stories in that gem of a magazine, *St. Nicholas?* Yet, of all the publications, perhaps the ones that most influenced me as a writer were a series of volumes from England, entitled *Chums* and *The Boys Own Annual*. Both were weekly publications but they came to my brother and to me each Christmas bound in great thick annual volumes of some one thousand pages each. These pages were crammed with exciting stories of high adventure and hilarious humor,

too, and all well-illustrated. It took a full year at least to get through these mammoth books before another Christmas and another set arrived.

"The stories in *Chums* and *Boys Own* were, in a sense, not dissimilar to the pulp fiction of much later years. And it was to these action-filled pulp magazines that I sold my first stories in my middle twenties. On my shelf over my typewriter today is a row of volumes of *Chums* and *Boys Own*. They are very old, yellowing, sagging through their bindings, yet each one is to me an Aladdin's lamp that will never go out."

OBITUARIES:

PERIODICALS

New York Times, April 3, 1990.*

*   *   *

VEZHINOV, Pavel
   See GOUGOV, Nikola Delchev

*   *   *

VOIGT, Cynthia   1942-

PERSONAL: Born February 25, 1942, in Boston, MA; daughter of Frederick C. (a corporate executive) and Elise (Keeney) Irving; married first husband, September, 1964 (divorced, 1972); married Walter Voigt (a teacher), August 30, 1974; children: (first marriage) Jessica; (second marriage) Peter. *Education:* Smith College, B.A., 1963; graduate study at St. Michael's College (now College of Santa Fe). *Politics:* Independent.

ADDRESSES: Home—Deer Isle, ME. *Office*—c/o Atheneum, 866 Third Ave., New York, NY 10022.

CAREER: J. Walter Thompson Advertising Agency, New York City, secretary, 1964; teacher of English at high school in Glen Burnie, MD, 1965-67; The Key School, Annapolis, MD, teacher of English, 1968-69, department chairman, 1971-79, part-time teacher and department chairman, 1981-88; author of books for young readers, 1981—.

AWARDS, HONORS: Notable Children's Trade Book in the Field of Social Studies, National Council for Social Studies/Children's Book Council, *New York Times* Outstanding Books citation, and American Book Award nomination, all 1981, all for *Homecoming;* American Library Association (ALA) Best Young Adult Books citation, 1982, for *Tell Me If the Lovers Are Losers,* and 1983, for

A Solitary Blue; Newbery Medal, ALA, and *Boston Globe-Horn Book* Honor Book citation, both 1983, and ALA Notable Book citation, all for *Dicey's Song;* Parents' Choice Award, 1983, Newbery Honor Book, and *Boston Globe-Horn Book* Honor Book citation, both 1984, all for *A Solitary Blue;* Edgar Allan Poe Award for best juvenile mystery, Mystery Writers of America, 1984, for *The Callender Papers;* Child Study Association of America's Children's Books of the Year citation, 1987, for *Come a Stranger;* Silver Pencil Award (Holland), 1988, and Deutscher Jugend Literatur Preis (Germany), 1989, both for *The Runner;* California Young Readers' Medal, 1990, for *Izzy, Willy-Nilly.*

WRITINGS:

Homecoming, Atheneum, 1981.
Tell Me If the Lovers Are Losers, Atheneum, 1982.
Dicey's Song, Atheneum, 1982.
The Callender Papers, Atheneum, 1983.
A Solitary Blue, Atheneum, 1983.
Building Blocks, Atheneum, 1984.
The Runner, Atheneum, 1985.
Jackaroo, Atheneum, 1985.
Izzy, Willy-Nilly, Atheneum, 1986.
Come a Stranger, Atheneum, 1986.
Stories about Rosie, illustrated by Dennis Kendrick, Atheneum, 1986.
Sons from Afar, Atheneum, 1987.
Tree by Leaf, Atheneum, 1988.
Seventeen against the Dealer, Atheneum, 1989.
On Fortune's Wheel, Macmillan, 1990.
Tillerman Saga (omnibus volume), Fawcett, 1990.
The Vandemark Mummy, Atheneum, 1991.
Orfe, Atheneum, 1992.
David and Jonathan, Scholastic, Inc., 1992.

ADAPTATIONS: Dicey's Song was made into a filmstrip-cassette set by Guidance Associates, 1986.

SIDELIGHTS: "Cynthia Voigt depicts adolescents with dignity and compassion in her impressive novels," Sylvia Patterson Iskander remarks in *Twentieth-Century Children's Writers.* Her characters "generally possess a streak of independence or self-reliance enabling them to succeed, not only in tangible endeavors, but also . . . in creating bonds of friendship and family ties despite serious hardships." Voigt is perhaps best known for her "Tillerman" novels, including the Newbery winner *Dicey's Song* and Honor Book *A Solitary Blue,* which trace three generations of a Maryland family. Besides contemporary novels such as the Tillerman books and the popular *Izzy, Willy-Nilly,* Voigt's work also includes the gothic mystery *The Callender Papers,* the fantasies *Jackaroo* and *On Fortune's Wheel,* and a time-travel story, *Building Blocks.* But whatever her subject, Voigt can be counted on to produce well-written narratives "that are impossible to put down," as a *Kirkus Reviews* critic says, "not because of breathtaking plots but because her characters so involve the reader in their inner lives."

"I decided in the ninth grade that I wanted to become a writer," Voigt once remarked. "At first, I wrote mostly short stories and poetry. I didn't even know the word 'submission' then, let alone the subtler vagaries of publishing." While at Smith College, Voigt took creative writing classes "but [I] considered them real bombs. Clearly what I was submitting didn't catch anyone's eye." Searching for a means to support herself after graduation, Voigt moved to New York where she found a place with an advertising agency. After she married her first husband in 1964, Voigt moved with him to New Mexico, where she again sought work. Secretarial jobs being hard to find, the author decided to qualify for a teaching job. "I vowed I would never teach when I left Smith," Voigt related, "and yet, the minute I walked into a classroom, I loved it."

Voigt continued to teach after her divorce, when she and her daughter moved back east to Maryland. As part of preparing lesson plans, Voigt searched the local library for books her fifth-graders could read and write about. After finding as many as thirty interesting books at one time, the author revealed, "I realized one could tell stories which had the shape of real books—novels—for kids the age of my students. I began to get ideas for young adult novels and juvenile books. . . . I felt I had suddenly discovered and was exploring a new country." The author elaborated in an interview with Jean W. Ross for *Contemporary Authors New Revision Series* (*CANR*): "Even before I'd thought of writing for that market, it struck me that that was where the reading I most consistently enjoyed was going on."

Although Voigt had found a field that suited her, it still took her some time to get her first book published. "What I didn't realize was that you send things to more than one place," Voigt told Ross. "I figured that if they were good enough, then everybody would know it; and if somebody said no, that meant they weren't good enough." Eventually Atheneum accepted *Homecoming,* which follows four children who are abandoned by their mother in a supermarket parking lot. The story of how Dicey, the eldest sister, leads the family to their grandmother's home in Maryland was published in 1981 to generally positive critical reviews.

Ruth M. Stein of *Language Arts,* for instance, calls *Homecoming* "rich in character development, sensitive to atmosphere, and woven from many lives, the threads of which the author never loses sight." "A story of this calibre involves the reader in both heart and mind," *Junior Bookshelf* reviewer E. Colwell similarly comments. While some parts of the novel may be overlong, the critic continues, "the characters are so convincing in their faults and virtues and their humanity that this is forgotten." *New York Times Book Review* contributor Kathleen Leverich concurs, noting that "despite flaws," *Homecoming* "is a glowing book" that "makes for an enthralling journey to a gratifying end."

Voigt's Newbery-winner *Dicey's Song* continues the story of the Tillermans as they, and especially teenage Dicey, adjust to a new life with their grandmother. "In spite of its carefully circumscribed rural setting, *Dicey's Song* is rich with themes and harmonies, even verities," Alice Digilio of the *Washington Post Book World* writes. "Loyalty and love, 'reaching out' as Gram says, are the qualities Voigt writes about here with grace and wit." "The vividness of Dicey is striking," *Booklist* writer Denise M. Wilms comments; "Voigt has plumbed and probed her character inside out to fashion a memorable protagonist. Unlike most sequels," the critic continues, "this outdoes its predecessor by being more fully realized and consequently more resonant." "It is good to be able to concur wholeheartedly with those who chose *Dicey's Song* for the 1983 Newbery Award," M. Hobbs of *Junior Bookshelf* says. "It is well-written, thoughtful, imaginative and haunting."

"As I wrote about Jeff in Dicey's story, where he had a certain purpose to serve," the author remarked in *Language Arts*, "I found myself thinking about his particular story, what had happened to him, how he had come to be where he was, and who he was. That story wanted telling." Jeff's story, of how he comes to terms with his mother's abandonment and his father's reserved nature, is the basis for Voigt's next book, *A Solitary Blue*. Voigt presents the Tillermans and some of the events from *Dicey's Song* from an outsider's point of view; but like *Dicey's Song*, "the story is full-bodied and carefully drawn," Wilms writes in *Booklist*. Paul Janezco observes in *Voice of Youth Advocates* that the novel has some flaws that "seem to cloud the central issues"; nonetheless, he admits, the novel "is a strong, sensitive, and well written portrayal of the relationship between love and risk." With "an emotional depth that is compelling," Wilms concludes, *A Solitary Blue* "is richly resonant—perhaps the best Voigt venture yet."

Other Tillerman books also approach the family from different points of view. *The Runner* shows Dicey's uncle "Bullet" as a distant, sometimes arrogant teenager who learns to overcome his prejudice and trust others. "Voigt sails *The Runner* through some heavy seas, but always with a steady hand," Digilio comments. "She's never preachy, her story never contrived for didactic purpose." And in *Come a Stranger*, Dicey's friend Mina takes center stage; although Mina is black, "Voigt is not interested in writing a 'message' novel," Meg Wolitzer states in the *Los Angeles Times*. "Instead, she gives us a real character searching to figure out what it means to be different." Although the Tillerman books now number over half a dozen, there has been no decrease in quality, according to *Los Angeles Times* critic Mitzi Myers. "Few sequels are as rich as the original story, but Voigt succeeds because she is filling out a canvas, not just repeating a plot. Although each book is satisfying in itself," the critic concludes, "the cumulative weight of the whole series gives the body of her work remarkable depth."

Voigt's other works possess the same virtues as her Tillerman books; "these novels have shown her deft hand with plot and character, and in *Jackaroo* she carries these skills into new territory in a fine strong fantasy," Patty Campbell comments in *Wilson Library Bulletin*. *Izzy, Willy-Nilly* recounts a young girl's adjustment to the amputation of her leg; "baldly stated, the plot sounds syrupy," Campbell writes in another review, but "in Voigt's skillful hands, the story is spare and clean, with compassion but no sentimentality." And in *Tree by Leaf*, which takes place shortly after World War I, "the author distinguishes her work from other young-adult novels of the 'coping' genre" by having the protagonist Clothilde interact with a mysterious "Voice" that permits her "to express her doubts and fears and, most important, to reach her own conclusions," Dulcie Leimbach summarizes in the *New York Times Book Review*. In this period piece, the critic concludes, Voigt "once again . . . has written a novel that her young adolescent audience will appreciate and remember."

"I don't know why I write for young people," Voigt revealed to Ross. "I think of myself, as a matter of fact, as someone who writes for people who like to read. I don't want to label myself; that's what it is. And my books seem to have a fairly broad readership." One reason for this, according to Marilyn Kaye, is that "Voigt has a nice way with language, blunt, taut and precise," as the critic writes in the *New York Times Book Review*. "She uses small but powerful images that rise above the ordinary yet still remain within the grasp of a juvenile audience." Another appealing feature of Voigt's work is that she "never takes sides in the war of generations," Digilio explains. "Instead she promotes understanding between adults and children, and she values the efforts of children, as well as those of adults, to appreciate the other's point of view." "Captivating stories, richly drawn characters with all the idiosyncrasies of real people and a fine-tuned understanding of the complexity and importance of family relationships—these qualities make her books unusually rewarding for adults and teens alike," Ann Martin-Leff concludes in *New Directions for Women*.

Although Voigt's work has earned her critical praise and prestigious awards, she still considers the publication of *Homecoming* "the most important award I've won," she once commented. The author explained: "After years of working on my own, I was suddenly encouraged and accepted by others. Awards are external, they happen after the real work has been done. They are presents, and while they are intensely satisfying they do not give me the same kind of pleasure as being in the middle of a work that is going well."

For an earlier published interview, see entry in *Contemporary Authors New Revision Series,* Volume 18.

BIOGRAPHICAL/CRITICAL SOURCES:

BOOKS

Children's Literature Review, Volume 13, Gale, 1987.
Contemporary Literary Criticism, Volume 30, Gale, 1984.
Twentieth-Century Children's Writers, 3rd edition, St. James Press, 1989, pp. 1004-1005.

PERIODICALS

Booklist, September 1, 1982, pp. 49-50; September 1, 1983, p. 92.
Children's Literature in Education, spring, 1985, pp. 45-52.
Christian Science Monitor, May 13, 1983, p. B2; November 1, 1985, p. B1.
Horn Book, August, 1983, pp. 410-413.
Junior Bookshelf, June, 1984, pp. 146-147.
Kirkus Reviews, June 1, 1986, p. 872.
Language Arts, January, 1982, pp. 55-56; December, 1985, pp. 876-80.
Los Angeles Times, November 22, 1986; January 30, 1988.
New Directions for Women, May-June, 1985, p. 20.
New York Times Book Review, May 10, 1981, p. 38; May 16, 1982, p. 28; March 6, 1983, p. 30; August 14, 1983, p. 29; November 27, 1983, pp. 34-35; June 12, 1988, p. 35.
School Library Journal, November, 1983, pp. 33-37.
Times Literary Supplement, May 9, 1986, p. 514; July 24, 1987, p. 804; September 18-24, 1987, p. 1028; May 6-12, 1988, p. 513; April 7-13, 1989, p. 378.
Voice of Youth Advocates, April, 1984, p. 36.
Washington Post Book World, February 13, 1983, pp. 8-9; June 10, 1984, pp. 6-7; November 10, 1985, p. 17; May 11, 1986, pp. 17, 22; September 14, 1986, p. 11; April 10, 1988, p. 12.
Wilson Library Bulletin, March, 1986, pp. 50-51; November, 1986, p. 49.

—*Sketch by Diane Telgen*

VOZNESENSKY, Andrei (Andreievich) 1933-

PERSONAL: Born May 12, 1933, in Moscow, U.S.S.R. (now Russia); son of Andrei (an engineer and professor) and Antonina (a teacher; maiden name, Pastuschichina) Voznesensky; married Zoya Boguslavskaya (an author and literary critic); children: Leonid. *Education:* Received degree from Institute of Architecture (Moscow), 1957.

ADDRESSES: Home—Kotelnicheskaya, nab. 1/15, Block W, Apt. 62, Moscow, Russia. *Agent*—c/o Soviet Writers Union, Ulitsa Vorovskogo, 52, Moscow, Russia.

CAREER: Poet.

MEMBER: International PEN (vice-president, Russian branch), Soviet Writers Union, American Academy of Arts and Letters, Bayerische Kunst Akademie, French Academy Merime.

AWARDS, HONORS: Nomination for Lenin Prize in literature, 1966, for *Antimiry* ("Anti-worlds"); nomination for Books Abroad/Neustadt International Prize for literature, 1975; State Literature Prize, 1978, for *Vitrazhnykh del master;* International award for distinguished achievement in poetry, 1978, for *Nostalgia for the Present.*

WRITINGS:

IN ENGLISH

Selected Poems, translated and introduction by Anselm Hollo, Grove, 1964.
Antimiry, [Moscow], 1964, translation by W. H. Auden, Richard Wilbur, Stanley Kunitz, William Jay Smith, and others published as *Antiworlds,* Basic Books, 1966, enlarged edition published as *Antiworlds and the Fifth Ace,* text in English and Russian, 1967.
Voznesensky: Selected Poems, translation and introduction by Herbert Marshall, Hill & Wang, 1966 (published in England as *Selected Poems,* Methuen, 1966).
Dogalypse (translations from San Francisco poetry reading), City Lights, 1972.
Little Woods: Recent Poems by Andrei Voznesensky (includes poems from *Ten'zvuka;* also see below), translated by Geoffrey Dutton and Igor Mezbakov-Koriakin, introduction by Yevgeny Yevtushenko translated by Eleanor Jacka, Sun Books (Melbourne), 1972.
Avos, translation by Kunitz and others published as *Story Under Full Sail,* Doubleday, 1974.
Nostalgia for the Present, translated by Wilbur, Smith, Lawrence Ferlinghetti, Robert Bly, Allen Ginsberg, and others, forewords by Edward Kennedy and Arthur Miller, Doubleday, 1978.
An Arrow in the Wall: Selected Poetry and Prose, edited and translated by William Jay Smith and Frank D. Reeve, Holt, 1987.

(With others) *Chagall Discovered: From Russian and Private Collections,* H. L. Levin, 1988.

OTHER

Mozaika (title means "Mosaic"), [Vladimir], 1960.

Parabola, [Moscow], 1960.

Pishetsya kak lyubitsya (title means "I Write as I Love"), text in Russian and Italian, Feltrinelli (Milan), 1962.

Treugol'naya grusha (title means "The Triangular Pear"), [Moscow], 1962.

Menya pugayutformalizmom, Flegon Press, 1963.

Akhillesovo serdtse (title means "An Achilles Heart"), [Moscow], 1966.

Moi lybovnyi dnevnik (title means "My Diary of Love"), Flegon Press, 1966.

Stikhi, [Moscow], 1967.

Ten'zvuka (title means "The Shadow of Sound"), [Moscow], 1970.

Vzglyad (title means "The Glance"), [Moscow], 1972.

Vypustiptitsu! (title means "Let the Bird Free"), [Moscow], 1974.

Dubovyi list violonchel'nyi (title means "Violincello Oak Leaf "), [Moscow], 1975.

Vitrazhnykh del master (title means "The Stained Glass Panel Master"), [Moscow], 1976.

Soblazn (title means "Temptation"), [Moscow], 1978.

Also author of *The Eternal Flesh,* 1978, *Andrey Polisadov,* 1980, and, with others, of *Metropol* (poetry and prose), 1979.

SIDELIGHTS: "The name of Voznesensky in Soviet poetry often becomes the centre of heated discussion," observed Vladimir Ognev. "The young poet leaves nobody indifferent. Widely differing estimations are given to his poetry-some call him a daring innovator, others a cold rhymester." Regardless of the more critical views of his work, Voznesensky warmed the hearts of his followers—and heated the tempers of Soviet officials—during his rise to international prominence in the 1960s. His swift, uncluttered, and often bold verse differed radically from the restricted poetry the Soviet Union had known in the Stalin years; and Russian audiences responded enthusiastically to the young poet's work. Though often compared to the verse of Yevgeny Yevtushenko, Voznesensky's poetry is considered more complex and more intellectual than that of his peer. The public acclaim he enjoyed early in the 1960s dwindled considerably at the end of the decade, largely because of recurrent Soviet crack-downs on authors who failed to promote the country's cause.

As a child, Voznesensky was introduced to Russia's great literary tradition by his mother, who surrounded him with books by great authors—Blok, Dostoevsky, Pasternak—and read poetry to him as well. Voznesensky experimented a bit with writing when he was young, but devoted himself mainly to painting and drawing. After receiving his degree from the Moscow Architectural Institute, however, his interest in architecture dropped. "Architecture was burned out in me," he recollected. "I became a poet." Some of his poems appeared in magazines at that time and two years later, in 1960, he published his first book, *Mosaika.*

Despite having a tremendously rich Russian poetic tradition to follow, "the only poet who influenced me," Voznesensky once declared, "was Pasternak, who was my god, my father, and for a long time, my university." Strangely, however, Voznesensky feels no similarity between his own poetry and that of his mentor. As a teenager he had sent some of his poems to Pasternak, who consequently invited Voznesensky to visit. The poems were obvious Pasternak imitations. Later, though, Voznesensky sent some of his post-graduate poems to Pasternak, revealing an entirely different poet. "Yes, this is no longer Pasternak," an admiring Pasternak reportedly said. "This is Voznesensky, a poet in his own right." The compliment encouraged Voznesensky: "I felt I had finally made it." In the 1980s, Voznesensky participated in the drive to reinstate Pasternak into the Soviet Writers Union, giving the writer official status in the Soviet Union for the first time since 1958.

Several factors contributed to Voznesensky's "meteoric" rise from a developing poet to one of the Soviet Union's most prominent literary figures. To begin with, poetry is Russia's "national art," contends Voznesensky. This natural interest in poetry combined with a Soviet generation which had "finally achieved sufficient material well-being to afford an interest in spiritual and philosophical matters," reported Peter Young. Thus, when artists like Yevtushenko and Voznesensky began giving poetry readings, these "semipolitical acts," wrote *Newsweek,* "gave voice to the dissatisfaction and exuberance of Soviet youth and created a huge audience" for poetry. By American standards, the audiences were stupendous. Typical crowds for readings by Yevtushenko and Voznesensky numbered more than fourteen thousand. Enthusiasm for the printed word matched the enthusiasm for the spoken. Voznesensky's *Akhillesovo serdtse* ("An Achilles Heart"), for example, had a printing of 100,000 to meet public demand for more than a half-million orders. Such statistics alone support Stanley Kunitz's contention that "the Russian appetite for poetry is simply enormous." Even today, reports say, Voznesensky's new books sell out within hours of publication.

The popularity of Yevtushenko and Voznesensky brought inevitable comparisons between the two. As Olga Carlisle pointed out, while "Voznesensky's popularity among young Russians is second only to Yevtushenko's . . . [and] he often rates first with the connoisseurs. His verse is full of youthfulness and talent—youth is his main theme as it is Yevtushenko's; in Voznesensky, however, it is never coquettish." David Burg offered another comparison between the two poets: "Voznesensky, a friend and initially a protege of Yevtushenko's, is a poet of an entirely different type. Being more bookish and more clearly conscious of his literary forbears, Voznesensky perpetuates (probably consciously) one specific trend in Russian poetry—the school of futurism, represented by Khlebnikov and Mayakovsky, Tsvetayeva, and Pasternak." According to Robin Milner-Gulland, however, their shared significance overshadows their differences: "Yevtushenko and Voznesensky: their work is certainly different enough," he declared. "The one rhetorical, the other cerebral; but their melodious names are inseparable, used (not only in the West but in their own country) to typify modern Russian poetry."

For a poet with such a popular audience, Voznesensky can be surprisingly complex; but he has continually defended himself against those who feel he is unnecessarily oblique. "The poet is not the one to supply the answers for mankind," he once contended. "All he can do is pose the questions. And if the poems are complicated, why then so is life. The problem of the poet as a human being is not to become standardized, [but] to be individual, and in this effort the poet provides the reader with the material and way of thinking to achieve it."

To Soviet government officials and heads of the Soviet Writers Union, Voznesensky was somewhat more of an individual than they would have liked: many times during his career he has been at the center of controversy. Charges of obscurantism were among the several hurled at Voznesensky in the early 1960s. One especially noteworthy denunciation took place in 1963, when Nikita Khrushchev reprimanded Voznesensky and other Western-oriented intellectuals, accusing them of straying from the paths of "Soviet realism." Attacks continued in 1965 when the government-controlled Communist youth newspaper accused him of obscurity of content and experimenting with complicated poetic forms. Three years later the Soviet press again stood against him, including Voznesensky in a group of "so-called intellectuals [who] continue to display ideological immaturity," reported the *Washington Post.* By 1969, government suppression had erased Voznesensky's name from Soviet literary journals. And, early in 1979, Voznesensky and several other writers were chastised for their roles in the publication of *Metropol,* a new literary magazine which challenged the government's strict control of the arts.

One much publicized incident involving Soviet restrictions occurred in 1967, when a New York City reading had to be canceled. Two days before the scheduled reading, rumors that Voznesensky had been the target of attempts to contain him were confirmed when he wired an uncharacteristically terse message, "Can't come." The powerful and conservative Soviet Writers Union apparently objected to Voznesensky's pro-American attitudes and his refusal to propagate Soviet politics during a previous American tour. (Voznesensky has always avoided political discussions on his U.S. visits.) At first, messages from Moscow said Voznesensky was sick; later reports revealed that his passport had been sent to the U.S. Embassy with a request for a visa. But renewed hope for Voznesensky's appearance faded when the poet himself phoned New York and canceled his visit. One of the program's participants, Stanley Kunitz, remained unconvinced by the Writers Union's apparent change of heart. "This was a ruse to get off the hook," he charged. "It's very clear what they did. We are not fooled by the last minute reversal [by the Soviet authorities]." Voznesensky himself attacked the Writers Union in a letter addressed to the Communist party newspaper, *Pravda.* "Clearly," he wrote, "the leadership of the union does not regard writers as human beings. This lying, prevarication and knocking people's heads together is standard practice." *Pravda* refused to publish the letter; weeks later it appeared in the *New York Times.*

Despite his conflicts with Soviet authorities, Voznesensky maintains an intense love for his own country. In one poem, for example, "he exalted the ancient idea that it is Russia's mission to save the world from darkness," reported the *New York Times.* Voznesensky has also admired the United States and, particularly, Robert Kennedy. The poet and the senator met together in 1967 and discussed, among other topics, the youth of their respective countries. After Kennedy's death, Voznesensky published a poem paying tribute to his assassinated friend.

Besides earning the attention of U.S. audiences, Voznesensky has become a favorite of several distinguished U.S. literary figures. Among the poets who have translated his work into English are Kunitz, Richard Wilbur, William Jay Smith, Robert Bly, W. H. Auden, Allen Ginsberg, and Lawrence Ferlinghetti. In his introduction to *Nostalgia for the Present,* playwright Arthur Miller assessed Voznesensky's efforts: "He has tried to speak, in these poems, as though he alone had a tongue, as though he alone had learned the news of today and tomorrow, as though the space taken up by his poem were precious and must not be used by counterfeit words." Another Voznesensky admirer, Auden, once gave these reasons for appreciating the poet: "As a fellow maker, I am struck first and foremost by his craftmanship. . . . Obvious, too, at a glance is the wide range of subject matter by which Mr. Voznesensky is imaginatively excited . . . and the variety of tones, elegiac, rebellious, etc., he can command. Lastly, every word he writes, even when he is criticizing, reveals a profound love for his native land and its traditions."

One particular theme in Voznesensky's work is that of the individual lost in a technological society. In his review of *Antiworlds,* Graham Martin noted "Voznesensky's main bogy is 'the cyclotron,' symbol of all the dehumanising pressures in the modern world, and in 'Oza,' a long difficult poem, he deploys all his satiric force against 'the scientist,' damn his eyes." Similarly, M. L. Rosenthal found in Voznesensky "a satirist . . . who is against the computerization of the soul." As Auden pointed out, however, Voznesensky's focus can vary considerably. Miller Williams explained: "Voznesensky is an exciting writer who bangs and tumbles through his poems, knocking over icons and knocking down walls, talking with curiosity, anguish, and joy—in sharp and startling metaphor—about love and technology, science and art, the self and the soul and Andrei Voznesensky and people." Another admirer, A. Alvarez, praised Voznesensky, too, for "whatever direct, passionate thrust launches them [his poems in *Antiworlds*], they curve obliquely and brilliantly through layer after layer of experience before they land again."

Translations have been a difficulty with reviewers of Voznesensky's work, especially in some of the earlier volumes. Anselm Hollo's translations in *Selected Poems* (1964), for example, disappointed Gibbons Ruark. Voznesensky's "work is clearly superior to Yevtushenko's," Ruark wrote in comparing the two poets. "Unfortunately, his excellence seldom shows through Anselm Hollo's translations." Critics agreed that Herbert Marshall's translations in *Voznesensky: Selected Poems* surpassed Hollo's. "The volume of selections by Herbert Marshall is, on the whole, an improvement over Anselm Hollo," wrote the *Hudson Review.* "But it is still an awkward and in places a careless performance." Other translations of Voznesensky's work have received considerably more praise. M. L. Rosenthal compared the translations in *Antiworlds* to those of Marshall and concluded: "We are better off with the seven translators of . . . [*Antiworlds*]. They adapt themselves, often superbly, to his temperament. They help us, through purely poetic means as well as through their attempt to render his sense both literally and connotatively, to feel his compassion, his pain, his hilarity, his buffoonery, his delicacy and calculated coarseness." Meanwhile, Alvarez offered this unequivocal praise for *Antiworlds:* "The translations . . . are immaculate; they simply couldn't have been better done." *Nostalgia for the Present* also featured seven translators, but according to Stefan Kanfer "they are not of equal worth. . . . The best work is the least obtrusive: working with Voznesensky's supple and difficult lines, Max Hayward, Vera Durham and William Jay Smith have given the Russian, both man and language, a new voice."

Voznesensky himself has spoken with a new voice in his later poetry. He has become more introspective, his poems more complex. He explained some changes to William Jay Smith while on his 1977 U.S. reading tour: "When I came before, I was like a rock and roll star. I read poems like 'Goya' and 'Moscow Bells' that were perhaps more dramatic than my recent work. My new poems are more delicate maybe, but I was happy that my audiences liked them too." Voznesensky also detected a change in U.S. audiences, finding them more serious and more conservative than in the past, prompting Smith to wonder if "the poet himself was more mature, probing farther beneath the surface in his search for reality. If so, he had in the process of maturing lost none of the exuberance, humor, and vitality that make him one of the world's finest poets as well as one of the most enjoyable."

BIOGRAPHICAL/CRITICAL SOURCES:

BOOKS

Carlisle, Olga, *Voices in the Snow,* Random, 1962.
Carlisle, Olga, *Poets on Street Corners,* Random, 1969.
Contemporary Literary Criticism, Gale, Volume 1, 1973; Volume 15, 1980; Volume 57, 1990.
Voznesensky, Andrei, *Nostalgia for the Present,* Doubleday, 1978.

PERIODICALS

Atlantic, July, 1966.
Christian Science Monitor, April 7, 1966; June 30, 1967; November 13, 1978.
Encounter, July, 1968.
Hudson Review, spring, 1967; autumn, 1968.
Life, April 1, 1966.
Listener, September 7, 1967.
London Magazine, June, 1967.
Los Angeles Times, January 8, 1984; April 8, 1987.
Los Angeles Times Book Review, March 29, 1987.
Nation, November 11, 1968.
New Republic, July 1, 1967; November 18, 1972.
Newsweek, May 15, 1967; July 3, 1967; August 21, 1967.
New Yorker, August 26, 1967.
New York Review of Books, April 14, 1966.
New York Times, August 23, 1965; August 29, 1965; March 24, 1966; March 26, 1966; June 19, 1966; April 1, 1967; April 22, 1967; May 6, 1967; June 19, 1967; June 20, 1967; June 21, 1967; June 22, 1967; August 3, 1967; August 11, 1967; September 7, 1967; June 17, 1968; June 20, 1968; May 27, 1969; May 22, 1978; June 9, 1985; June 18, 1985; October 20, 1986; February 24, 1987; March 16, 1987; June 2, 1987; April 25, 1988.
New York Times Biographical Edition, October 21, 1971.
New York Times Book Review, May 14, 1967; April 16, 1972; December 17, 1978; July 8, 1979; March 29, 1987.
New York Times Magazine, August 20, 1967.

Observer Review, July 9, 1967.

Partisan Review, winter, 1968.

Poetry, April, 1967; November, 1967.

Problems of Communism, September-October, 1962.

Saturday Review, February 4, 1978.

Shenandoah, winter, 1968.

Spectator, July 5, 1966.

Time, August 16, 1967; March 9, 1970; May 18, 1970; January 15, 1979.

Times Literary Supplement, November 2, 1967; November 27, 1970; October 11, 1974.

Vogue, February 1, 1972.

Washington Post, June 15, 1968; February 25, 1969; February 4, 1979; May 9, 1987; May 17, 1987.

Washington Post Book World, June 14, 1987.*

W

WALLEY, David G. 1945-

PERSONAL: Born March 18, 1945, in Plainfield, NJ; son of Miron Monroe (a Lawyer) and Sylvia (Silot) Walley. *Education:* Rutgers University, B.A., 1967; Hofstra University, graduate study, 1967-68. *Politics:* "Wary." *Religion:* "Uncommitted." *Avocational interests:* Photography, electronic music, carpentry and house restoration, Fortean phenomena.

ADDRESSES: Home—Witzend Manor, 62 New Ashford Rd., Williamstown, MA 01267-3073.

CAREER: Music critic, book and arts reviewer, editor, lecturer, and media consultant. Has written for *Jazz and Pop, Zygote, Woodstock Times, Changes, East Village Other, New York Ace, Los Angeles Free Press,* and other periodicals. Williams College, Williamstown, MA, visiting professor in American studies and sociology; Pine Cobble School, Williamstown, writer in residence.

WRITINGS:

(Contributor) Jonathan Eisen, editor, *The Age of Rock 2,* Random House, 1970.
(Contributor) T. Becker, editor, *Government Lawlessness in America,* Oxford University Press, 1971.
No Commercial Potential: The Saga of Frank Zappa and the Mothers of Invention, Dutton, 1972, revised edition published as *No Commercial Potential: Frank Zappa Then and Now,* 1980.
Nothing in Moderation, Drake, 1975, published as *The Ernie Kovacs Phile,* Bolder Books, 1978.
Exhibit A (screenplay), Zanatas Productions, 1976.

WORK IN PROGRESS: Being There and Not, for St. Martin's; *Eventual Time,* for Bantam.

SIDELIGHTS: David G. Walley once told *CA* that he saw himself as a "cultural historian" who has "written on two essential cultural figures from two different ages, [Frank] Zappa and [Ernie] Kovacs." More recently he said: "I still consider myself a cultural historian, but my focus is no longer exclusively in music and art. Cultural accidents like the sixties don't always happen the same way twice, nor would I want them to. Quite obviously the time is near when all the inter-dependent computer/communication systems worldwide will have one glorious chaotic belch and things will get sorted out anew. There is no need to frantically seek new cultural referents and guideposts since they will appear quite suddenly and surprisingly of their own accord.

"I have been reading Roman histories—Livy, Tacitus, Seutonious, as well as the satirists and poets, Juvenal, Horace. Why? Because it always pays to keep up with the latest mystery trends since people have always been pretty much the same and politics changes little. The perspective is invaluable, you know.

"If any of you out there are actually reading this entry, I'm talking to you! Consciousness is where it's at. Remember it's the change which keeps writers on their toes; it's the change and how [one] adapts and grows with it."

* * *

WALVIN, James 1942-

PERSONAL: Born February 1, 1942, in Manchester, England; son of James (an engineer) and Emma (Wood) Walvin. *Education:* University of Keele, B.A. (with first-class honors), 1964; McMaster University, M.A. (with first-class honors), 1965; University of York, Ph.D., 1970.

ADDRESSES: Office—Department of History, University of York, York, England.

CAREER: University of York, York, England, began as faculty member in department of history, became provost.

AWARDS, HONORS: Martin Luther King, Jr. Memorial Prize, 1974, for *Black and White: The Negro and English Society, 1555-1945.*

WRITINGS:

(With M. J. Craton) *A Jamaican Plantation,* University of Toronto Press, 1970.

The Black Presence: A Documentary of the Negro in Britain, Orbach & Chambers, 1971, Schocken, 1972.

Black and White: The Negro and English Society, 1555-1945, Allen Lane, 1972.

The People's Game: A Social History of British Football, Allen Lane, 1975.

(Editor with Craton) *Slavery, Abolition and Emancipation,* Longman, 1976.

Beside the Seaside: A Social History of the Popular Seaside Holiday, Allen Lane, 1978.

Leisure and Society, 1830-1950, Longman, 1978.

(Editor with Eltis) *Abolition of the Atlantic Slave Trade,* University of Wisconsin Press, 1981.

A Child's World: A Social History of English Childhood, 1800-1914, Penguin Books, 1982.

(Editor) *Slavery and British Society, 1776-1848,* Macmillan, 1982.

(With Edward Royle) *English Radicals and Reformers, 1760-1848,* University of Kentucky Press, 1982.

Slavery and Slave Trade: An Illustrated History, University of Mississippi, 1983.

Black Personalities: Africans in Britain in the Era of Slavery, Louisiana State University Press, 1983.

(Editor with John Walton) *Leisure in Britain since 1800,* Manchester University Press, 1983.

Passage to Britain: Immigration in History and Politics, Penguin Books, 1984.

English Urban Life, 1776-1851, Hutchinson, 1984.

(Editor with C. Emsley) *Peasants, Artisans and Proletarians,* Croom Helm, 1985.

Football and the Decline of Britain, Macmillan, 1986.

England, Slaves and Freedom, 1776-1838, University of Mississippi Press, 1986.

Victorian Values, University of Georgia Press, 1987.

(Editor with J. A. Mangan) *Manliness and Morality,* Manchester University Press, 1987.

Victorian Values was published to accompany the British television documentary of the same name.

SIDELIGHTS: A history of the rise and fall of British radicalism, *English Radicals and Reformers, 760-1848,* which James Walvin co-authored with Edward Royle, closely examines the tendencies of this political movement, its promotion of a free and widespread press, and the accompanying attitude that government required constant monitoring in order to minimize its abuses. I. J. Prothero finds in the *Times Literary Supplement* that the book's "value is as a very serviceable and succinct survey of recent historical scholarship, commented on and used in a common-sense way from the vantage point of broad familiarity with the politics of the period."

BIOGRAPHICAL/CRITICAL SOURCES:

PERIODICALS

Times (London), April 8, 1987.
Times Literary Supplement, January 23, 1983.

*   *   *

WARD, (John Stephen) Keith   1938-

PERSONAL: Born August 22, 1938, in Hexham, Northumberland, England; son of John (a director) and Evelyn (Simpson) Ward; married Marian Trotman (a teacher), June 22, 1963; children: Fiona Caroline, Alun James Kendall. *Education:* University of Wales, B.A., 1962; Linacre College, Oxford, B.Litt., 1967.

ADDRESSES: Office—Christ Church, Oxford, OX1 1DP, England.

CAREER: University of Glasgow, Glasgow, Scotland, lecturer in logic, 1964-66, lecturer in moral philosophy, 1966-69; University of St. Andrews, St. Andrews, Scotland, lecturer in moral philosophy, 1969-71; University of London, King's College, London, England, lecturer in philosophy of religion, 1971-74; Cambridge University, Trinity Hall, Cambridge, England, dean, 1974-82; University of London, King's College, professor of moral theology, 1982-86, professor of philosophy of religion, 1986-91; University of Oxford, Oxford, England, Regius Professor of Divinity, 1991—. *Military service:* Royal Air Force, 1956-58; served in Strategic Air Command.

WRITINGS:

Fifty Key Words in Philosophy, John Knox, 1969.
Ethics and Christianity, Humanities, 1970.
The Development of Kant's View of Ethics, Basil Blackwell, 1972.
The Concept God, St. Martin's, 1975.
The Christian Way, S.P.C.K., 1976.
The Divine Image: The Foundations of Christian Morality, S.P.C.K., 1976.
Rational Theology and the Creativity of God, Pilgrim Press, 1982.
Holding Fast to God, S.P.C.K., 1983.
The Living God, S.P.C.K., 1984.
Images of Eternity, Darton, Longman, Todd, 1988.
The Rule of Love, Darton, Longman, and Todd, 1989.
Divine Action, Collins, 1990.

A Vision to Pursue, SCM Publications, 1991.

Contributor of articles to academic journals.

BIOGRAPHICAL/CRITICAL SOURCES:

PERIODICALS

Times Literary Supplement, October 23, 1970; September 3, 1982; April 7, 1988.

*   *   *

WEBBER, Robert (Eugene) 1933-

PERSONAL: Born November 27, 1933, in Stouchburg, PA; married Joanne Lindsell; children: John, Alexandra, Stefany, Jeremy. *Education:* Bob Jones University, B.A., 1956; Reformed Episcopal Seminary, B.D., 1959; Covenant Theological Seminary, Th.M., 1960; Concordia Theological Seminary, Th.D., 1969. *Religion:* Episcopal.

ADDRESSES: Office—Department of Theology, Wheaton College, Wheaton, IL 60187.

CAREER: Covenant College, Dade County, GA, instructor in religion, 1960-65; Covenant Theological Seminary, St. Louis, MO, assistant professor of church history, 1965-68; Wheaton College, Wheaton, IL, associate professor, 1968-80, professor of theology, 1980—. Editor-in-chief, Creation House, 1972—.

WRITINGS:

How to Choose a Christian College, Creation House, 1973.
Common Roots: A Call to Evangelical Maturity, Zondervan, 1978.
(Editor with Donald Bloesch) *The Orthodox Evangelicals,* Thomas Nelson, 1978.
The Secular Saint: A Case for Evangelical Social Responsibility, Zondervan, 1979.
God Still Speaks: A Biblical View of Christian Communication, Thomas Nelson, 1980.
Worship Old and New, Zondervan, 1982.
Secular Humanism: Threat and Challenge, Zondervan, 1982.
Evangelicals on the Canterbury Trail, Word, Inc., 1985.
Worship Is a Verb, Word, Inc., 1985, 2nd edition, Abbott-Martyn Press, 1991.
Church and World: Antitheses, Paradox, or Transformation, Zondervan, 1985.
Celebrating Our Faith: Evangelism through Worship, Harper, 1985.
The Book of Family Worship, Thomas Nelson, 1985.
I Believe, Zondervan, 1986.
What Christians Believe, Zondervan, 1989.
Workshop on Worship, Zondervan, 1990.
Signs of Wonder: The Healing Power of Worship for Seekers and Believers, Abbott-Martyn Press, 1991.

WORK IN PROGRESS: The Topical Encyclopedia of Christian Worship, seven volumes, for Abbott-Martyn Press.

SIDELIGHTS: Robert Webber told *CA:* "I write to learn. You might say it is my project or continuing education." Webber's *Common Roots* has been translated into Korean and *The Secular Saint* into Chinese.

*   *   *

WEBER, C(larence) A(dam) 1903-

PERSONAL: Born May 2, 1903, in Winfield, KS; son of William J. (a minister) and Pearl L. (a university professor; maiden name, Hunter) Weber; married Mary E. Beaty, August 7, 1925 (died August 17, 1987); children: Betty Lois (Mrs. Charles A. Dewey), Jane Ellen (Mrs. Don V. Ruck). *Education:* Illinois College, A.B., 1924; University of Illinois, M.A., 1929; Northwestern University, Ph.D., 1943. *Religion:* Methodist. *Avocational interests:* Fishing, boating, photography.

ADDRESSES: Home—110 Whitney Commons, 1204 Whitney Ave., Hamden, CT 06517.

CAREER: Oakland Township High School, Oakland, IL, head of math department, and coach, 1925-28; superintendent of public schools in Hume, Galva, and Cicero, IL, 1928-44; University of Connecticut, Storrs, associate professor, 1945-46, professor of education, 1950-66, professor emeritus, 1967—, dean of Fort Trumbull branch, 1946-50, dean of School of Education, 1960-61, chairman of department of school administration, 1966. Corporator of Windham Memorial Hospital, Willimantic, CT, 1966—.

MEMBER: National Education Association, American Association of School Administrators, National Retired Teachers Association, Smithsonian Institution, Rotary International (district governor, 1965-66), Masons, Sigma Pi, Phi Delta Kappa.

AWARDS, HONORS: Distinguished Service Award, Illinois College, 1988; Athletic Hall of Fame, Illinois College, 1991.

WRITINGS:

Personnel Problems of School Administrators, McGraw, 1954.
Fundamentals of Educational Leadership, McGraw, 1955.
Industrial Leadership, Chilton, 1959.
Leadership in Personnel Management in Public Schools, Warren Green, 1970.
Roots of Rebellion, Warren Green, 1971.
What the People Ought to Know about School Administration, Interstate, 1971.
(With Jean Poull) *Songs of the Cajean,* Vantage, 1979.

Diamonds in the Driveway, Vantage, 1979.
Double Trouble: The Autobiography of C. A. Weber, Maverick, 1980.
(With Poull) *Let's Cut the Cost of College Education*, Interstate, 1981.

Also author of *Organization and Administration of Public Education in Connecticut*, 1951, *Welcome to the Rotary Club*, 1971, and *Mary E. Weber: A Biography*, 1977. Contributor to numerous education journals.

WORK IN PROGRESS: Volume II of autobiography, *Double Trouble.*

BIOGRAPHICAL/CRITICAL SOURCES:

BOOKS

Weber, C. A., *Double Trouble: The Autobiography of C. A. Weber*, Maverick, 1980.

*   *   *

WEINRICH, A(nna) K(atharina) H(ildegard) 1933-
(Sister Mary Aquina)

PERSONAL: Born November 4, 1933, in Wuppertal, Germany; daughter of Leo (a teacher) and Anny (Cohnen) Weinrich. *Education:* University of Zimbabwe, B.A., 1959; University of Manchester, M.A., 1962, Ph.D., 1965; C. G. Jung Institute, Zurich, Switzerland, diploma in analytical psychology, 1986; International Society for Sandplay Therapy, London, diploma in sandplay therapy, 1989.

ADDRESSES: Home—115 Dunfield Rd., London SE6 3RD, England.

CAREER: Religious training in the Dominican Order, 1954-56. School of Social Work, Salisbury, Rhodesia (now Zimbabwe), lecturer in social anthropology, 1965-66; University of Zimbabwe (now University of Zimbabwe), Salisbury, lecturer, 1966-71, senior lecturer in social anthropology, 1972-75; United Nations Social, Educational, and Cultural Organization (UNESCO), Paris, researcher, 1975-77; University of Dar-es-Salaam, Dar-es-Salaam, Tanzania, associate professor of sociology, 1977-80; government of Zimbabwe, member of the Commission of Inquiry into Incomes, Prices and Conditions of Service, 1980-81, member of the First Delimitation Commission for Common Roll Constituencies, 1981, and senior research officer in the parliament, 1981-82. Also lecturer at Internationale Gessellschaft fuer Arztliche Psychotherapie, and Jungian analyst in private practice in London.

MEMBER: Dominican Order, International Association for Analytical Psychology, International Society for Sand-

play Therapy, Association of Graduate Analytical Psychologists, Independent Group of Analytical Psychologists, Analytical Psychology Club, Guild of Pastoral Psychology.

WRITINGS:

Chiefs and Councils in Rhodesia: Transition from Patriarchal to Bureaucratic Power, University of South Carolina Press, 1971.
Rhodesia: The Ousting of the Tangwena, International Defense and Aid Fund for Southern Africa, 1972.
Black and White Elites in Rural Rhodesia, Rowman and Littlefield, 1973.
African Farmers in Rhodesia: Old and New Peasant Communities in Karangaland, Oxford University Press, 1975.
Cold Comfort Farm Society: A Christian Commune in Rhodesia, Old Umtali Methodist Mission Press, 1975.
Mucheke: Race, Status, and Politics in a Rhodesian Community, Holmes & Meier, 1976.
The Tonga People on the Southern Shore of Lake Kariba, Mambo Press (Rhodesia), 1977.
(Translator, with Ilse Fischer) Harald Vocke, *The Lebanese War: Its Origins and Political Dimensions*, C. Hurst, 1978.
Women and Racial Discrimination in Rhodesia, UNESCO (Paris), 1979.
African Marriage in Zimbabwe and the Impact of Christianity, Holmes McDougall, 1982.
Der Kelch und die Schlange, Walter Verlag (Switzerland), 1989, translation published as *The Chalice and the Snake*, Sigo Press, 1991.
Journeys of Self-Discovery, Sigo Press, 1991.

Contributor of chapters to numerous books. Contributor, sometimes under the name of Sister Mary Aquina, of over fifty articles to social studies journals and journals of analytical psychology.

WORK IN PROGRESS: An autobiography.

SIDELIGHTS: A. K. H. Weinrich told *CA:* "When I started my writing career in Africa in 1971, I was impelled to share with others my discoveries of African society, a society so grossly misunderstood by the white people among whom I lived. During the liberation struggle of Zimbabwe, when members of the Central Committee of the Zimbabwe African National Union (ZANU) were in preventive detention, one of them smuggled a note out to me on which he had written: 'Your writings are the only writings by a white person with which we Africans can totally identify ourselves.' This was for me the greatest praise and more important than any published reviews which I received.

"Now, some twenty years later, I am still writing, but now I am writing from an inner urge. Whereas in former years I felt like an explorer of the outer world, now I am exploring the inner world of myself and of my patients, walking with them among the archetypes of their dreams, helping them to understand the sources of their suffering and enabling them to find their road towards personal happiness."

*   *   *

WELLERSHOFF, Dieter   1925-

PERSONAL: Born November 3, 1925, in Neuss, Germany; son of Walter and Claere (Weber) Wellershoff; married Maria von Thadden, May 16, 1952; children: Irene, Gerald, Marianne. *Education:* Gymnasium Grevenbroich, diploma, 1946; University of Bonn, D.Phil., 1952.

ADDRESSES: Home—Mainzer Strasse 45, Cologne, Germany 5000.

CAREER: Deutsche Studentenzeitung, Bonn, West Germany (now Germany), editor, 1953-56; Verlag Kiepenheuer & Witsch (publisher), Cologne, West Germany, reader, 1959-81. Honorary professor, University of Bonn, 1989. *Military service:* German Army, 1943-45.

MEMBER: International PEN, Academy of Science and Literature (Mainz), Wissenschaftskolleg Berlin.

AWARDS, HONORS: Hoerspielpreis der Kriegsblinden, 1961; Kritikerpreis, 1971; Heinrich-Boell-Preis der Stadt Koeln, 1988.

WRITINGS:

IN ENGLISH TRANSLATION

Ein schoener Tag (novel), Kiepenheuer & Witsch, 1969, translation by Dorothea Oppenheimer published as *A Beautiful Day,* Harper, 1971.

Der Sieger nimmt alles, Kiepenheuer & Witsch, 1983, translation by Paul Knight published as *Winner Takes All,* Carcanet, 1986.

IN GERMAN

Gottfried Benn: Phaenotyp dieser Stunde (title means "Gottfried Benn: Phenotype of This Hour"), Kiepenheuer & Witsch, 1958.

(Editor) Gottfried Benn, *Gesammelte Werke* (title means "Collected Works"), four volumes, Limes, 1958-62.

Am ungenauen Ort (two radio plays; title means "At an Uncertain Place"), Limes, 1960.

Anni Nabels Boxschau (title means "Anni Nabels' Box-Show"), Kiepenheuer & Witsch, 1962.

Der Gleichgueltige: Versuche ueber Hemingway, Camus, Benn, und Beckett (literary criticism; title means "The Indifferent: Essays on Hemingway, Camus, Benn, and Beckett"), Kiepenheuer & Witsch, 1963.

Die Bittgaenger [und] Die Schatten (two radio plays; title means "The Supple Cat [and] Shadows"), Reclam, 1968.

Die Schattengrenze (novel; title means "The Edge of the Shadow"), Kiepenheuer & Witsch, 1969.

Literatur und Veraenderung: Versuche zu einer Metakritik der Literatur (title means "Literature and Change: Essays on a Metacritic of Literature"), Kiepenheuer & Witsch, 1969.

Das Schreien der Katze im Sack (radio plays; title means "Cry of the Cat in the Bag"), Kiepenheuer & Witsch, 1970.

Einladung an alle (novel; title means "Invitation to Everyone"), Kiepenheuer & Witsch, 1972.

Literatur und Lustprinzip (essays; title means "Literature and the Pleasure Principle"), Kiepenheuer & Witsch, 1973.

Doppelt belichtetes Seestueck und andere Texte (title means "Double Exposed Seascape and Other Texts"), Kiepenheuer & Witsch, 1974.

Die Aufloesung des Kunstbegriffs (title means "The Dissolution of the Art Concept"), Suhrkamp, 1976.

Die Schoenheit des Schimpansen (novel; title means "The Beauty of the Chimpanzee"), Kiepenheuer & Witsch, 1977.

Die Wahrheit der Literatur (lectures), Fink Verlag, 1980.

Die Sirene (novel), Kiepenheuer & Witsch, 1980.

Die Arbeit des Lebens (autobiographical work), Kiepenheuer & Witsch, 1985.

Die Koerper und die Traeume (stories), Kiepenheuer & Witsch, 1986.

Der Roman und die Erfahrbarkeit der Welt (essays), Kiepenheuer & Witsch, 1988.

Pan und die Engel: Ansichten von Koeln, Kiepenheuer & Witsch, 1990.

Blick auf einen fernen Berg, Kiepenheuer & Witsch, 1991.

Also author of television plays including *Eskalation,* 1976, *Gluecksucher* (title means "Happiness Hunter"), 1977, *Freiheiten der Langeweile* (title means "Freedoms of Boredom"), 1978, and *Phantasten,* 1979; author of movie script for *Gluecksucher,* 1979.

WORK IN PROGRESS: Narratives, essays, television motion pictures.

SIDELIGHTS: Once affiliated with a major German publishing house, Dieter Wellershoff is credited with bringing together German "new novelists" to form the Koelner Schule. In addition, he has won renown as a radio playwright and as a new novelist himself.

Wellershoff once commented: "For me to write means to renew the perception of life, to free it from prejudice and conformist and schematic points of view. That is why crisis experiences and light as well as violent emotions in a usual situation especially attract me. In periods of instability, in the situation of loss of orientation are the chances of renewal. My books reckon with curious and fearless readers, who are interested in the human being and are ready to follow extreme developments to their end."

Wellershoff once described himself as a realist. "Reality, however, is never a durable possession," he said. "It escapes, it must always be explored and be questioned again. This is an endless task. And, in contrast with science, literature does not impart knowledge, but experiences. Experiences are ardent knowledge. They encroach upon existence and set themselves in motion."

BIOGRAPHICAL/CRITICAL SOURCES:

BOOKS

Durzak, M., H. Steinecke, and K. Bullivant, editors, *Dieter Wellershoff, Studien zu seinem Werk,* Kiepenheuer & Witsch, 1990.
Helmreich, Hans, *Dieter Wellershoff,* C. H. Beck, 1982.
Hinton, R., editor, *Der Schriftsteller Dieter Wellershoff,* Kiepenheuer & Witsch, 1976.
Wellershoff, Dieter, *Die Arbeit des Lebens,* Kiepenheuer & Witsch, 1985.

PERIODICALS

Books Abroad, spring, 1970; autumn, 1970.
New York Times Book Review, January 4, 1987.

*   *   *

WELLS, Helen   1910-1986
(Francine Lewis)

PERSONAL: Name legally changed; born March 29, 1910, in Danville, IL; died suddenly, February 10, 1986; buried in Danville, IL; daughter of Henry M. and Henrietta (Basch) Weinstock; married, June 7, 1984. *Education:* New York University, B.S. (with honors), 1934; Programming and Systems Institute, New York, diploma, 1969; New York University, School of Continuing Education, student, 1962-77. *Politics:* Democrat. *Religion:* Jewish. *Avocational interests:* Electronic data processing, piano.

ADDRESSES: Agent—McIntosh & Otis, Inc., 475 5th Ave., New York, NY 10017.

CAREER: Full-time professional writer. Institute of Children's Literature, Redding Ridge, CT, instructor, 1976-78. Four-year volunteer escorting Latin-American visitors to U.S., Rockefeller Institute of Inter-American Affairs.

MEMBER: Authors Guild, Author's League of America, Mystery Writers of America (member of board of directors, 1970-78, 1984-86; national secretary, 1973-75; membership chairman, 1985-86), National Writers Union, Women's National Book Association, Writers' Roundtable, National Arts Club.

AWARDS, HONORS: Gottheil Medal, Temple Emanu-El; Recipient of $1000 prize for a short story during the late 1930s; the 1986 Juvenile Series Writers Conference, Corning, NY, was dedicated to the memory of Helen Wells.

WRITINGS:

The Girl in the White Coat, Messner, 1953.
Escape By Night: A Story of the Underground Railroad, Winston, 1953.
A Flair for People, Messner, 1955.
Adam Gimbel, Pioneer Trader, McKay, 1955.
Introducing Patti Lewis, Home Economist, Messner, 1956.
A City for Jean, Funk, 1956.
Barnum, Showman of America, McKay, 1957.
Doctor Betty, Messner, 1969.
(Contributor) Lucy Freeman, *Crime Writers on Their Art,* Ungar, 1982.

Also author of *Occupation, Murder,* 1984.

"CHERRY AMES" SERIES

Cherry Ames, Student Nurse, Grosset, 1943.
. . . , *Army Nurse,* Grosset, 1944.
. . . , *Chief Nurse,* Grosset, 1944.
. . . , *Senior Nurse,* Grosset, 1944.
. . . , *Private Duty Nurse,* Grosset, 1945.
. . . , *Flight Nurse,* Grosset, 1945.
. . . , *Veteran's Nurse,* Grosset, 1946.
. . . , *Visiting Nurse,* Grosset, 1947.
. . . , *Cruise Nurse,* Grosset, 1948.
. . . , *Boarding School Nurse,* Grosset, 1955.
. . . , *Department Store Nurse,* Grosset, 1956.
. . . , *Camp Nurse,* Grosset, 1957.
Cherry Ames' Book of First Aid and Home Nursing, Grosset, 1959.
. . . *at Hilton Hospital,* Grosset, 1959.
. . . , *Island Nurse,* Grosset, 1960.
. . . , *Rural Nurse,* Grosset, 1960.
. . . , *Staff Nurse,* Grosset, 1962.
. . . , *Companion Nurse,* Grosset, 1964.
. . . , *Jungle Nurse,* Grosset, 1965.
Mystery in the Doctor's Office, Grosset, 1966.
Ski Nurse Mystery, Grosset, 1968.
Mystery of Rogue's Cave, Grosset, 1972.

Also author of *Cherry Ames Christmas Annual* (short stories).

"VICKI BARR" SERIES

Silver Wings for Vicki, Grosset, 1947.
Vicki Finds the Answer, Grosset, 1948.
The Hidden Valley Mystery, Grosset, 1949.
Peril over the Airport, Grosset, 1953.
The Search for the Missing Twin, Grosset, 1954.
The Ghost at the Waterfall, Grosset, 1956.
The Clue of the Golden Coin, Grosset, 1958.
The Silver Ring Mystery, Grosset, 1960.
The Clue of the Carved Ruby, Grosset, 1961.
The Mystery of Flight 908, Grosset, 1962.
The Brass Idol Mystery, Grosset, 1964.

"POLLY FRENCH" SERIES; UNDER PSEUDONYM FRANCINE LEWIS

Polly French of Whitford High, A. Whitman, 1952.
. . . Finds Out, A. Whitman, 1953.
. . . Takes Charge, A. Whitman, 1954.
. . . and the Surprising Stranger, A. Whitman, 1955.

OTHER

Also author of radio shows and short stories for adults. Editor, *The Arch* (New York University literary magazine), 1929-30. The "Cherry Ames" and "Vicki Barr" series have also been published in numerous countries, including Canada, Britain, Norway, Sweden, Denmark, Finland, Iceland, Japan, France, Italy, Holland, and Bolivia. Books, manuscripts, and papers are kept at Florida State University.

ADAPTATIONS: Several plays based on Wells's stories have been broadcast on radio and television.

WORK IN PROGRESS: Wells was working on *Birthmark,* a mystery novel for adults begun in 1983.

SIDELIGHTS: Helen Wells, an American children's author who also wrote under the name Francine Lewis, is best known for her books about nurses and nursing (the "Cherry Ames" series) and the "Vicki Barr" mystery series.

Robert Wells, Helen's brother, told *Something about the Author* interviewer Marguerite Feitlowitz about his life with his sister in Danville, Illinois, where they were born. "We were born in the very house where our mother and all her siblings were born. Danville is pretty much the town that Cherry Ames lived in. It was a big, comfortable, old-fashioned kind of house with lots of space surrounding it and a yard full of fruit trees. As soon as she was big enough, Helen learned to climb trees, and in the summer would bring a cushion up with her, settle into a comfortable branch, and spend the afternoon reading. She was always reading and writing; writing was as natural to her as breathing."

Robert recalled that during World War I, he would dress up in an old soldier suit so that Helen and her friend could pretend they were Red Cross nurses caring for a wounded man. Helen learned to play piano from her mother, who was the best pianist in Danville. "Our father was born and raised in Vienna, the youngest son in a large, wealthy family," he said. "His mother died when he was small, and his father remarried. He was told by his father that he would never be obliged to work, that he would become a gentleman scholar instead. In spirit, our father remained a gentleman scholar. However, as our grandfather died when our father was nine and the relatives took all the money, he did indeed have to work. He came to the States and eventually became associated with National Cash Register. When Helen was about seven, Dad was offered a New York territory. He was very keen on this, for though he liked Danville, he wanted us to have broader educational and cultural opportunities.

"My sister loved New York from the moment we arrived. She was an honor student and skipped a couple of grades, as I recall. She won the Gottheil Medal from Temple Emanu-El, where she was confirmed. My sister also took piano lessons from a wonderful English woman who had a studio at Carnegie Hall. Every year there was an ambitious recital in which my sister and mother were frequently featured playing duets. Helen was always given the more brilliant part. These recitals were big, splendid occasions—they spent months preparing, and it showed."

The family returned to Danville to visit relatives including their uncle, who was an important influence on Helen. "Our uncle taught us to appreciate America," he said. "Dad's influence was decidedly European and Jewish (both our parents were Jews, and we were raised with a consciousness of that tradition), whereas our uncle's ancestors fought for the States during the American Revolution. He was a direct descendant of George Washington's mother."

When Helen graduated from high school at age sixteen, she was not allowed to leave for college. Instead she attended Columbia University extension courses and the Art Students League. When eighteen, she went to New York University and graduated with honors, having studied philosophy, psychology, and sociology. She was the first woman to edit the campus literary magazine, *The Arch.*

In 1934, she became a social worker. "Her supervisor was stunned by a hair-raising vivid report of a slum family Helen had written, and recognized immediately that she was a writer," her brother recalled. "She introduced her to an editor, who helped my sister break into magazine writing. But Helen kept her job as a social worker for four or five more years. Although she took her job very seriously—this was the Depression and times were hard for all of us—her primary interest was writing. She spent whatever free time she had at her desk, creating, imagining." Wells once wrote, "A course in playwriting taught me a very great deal about how to construct a story. I never expect to write a play for theatre—but it is no accident that my stories 'play,' and several have been dramatized on radio and television." Short stories by Wells were acclaimed as well as popular. Her brother recalled, "One year, one of her short stories won a thousand-dollar prize—a fortune in those days. She and her best friend had a wonderful time with the money, with no regrets."

During this time she also wrote a novel. Her brother said it was "a very ambitious novel about social issues and their process of resolution—a fictionalized account of the late Depression. She was exploring the ways in which young people responded to existing problems and tried to generate solutions. I don't know if she ever tried to publish that book. She threw most of it away, which I think was a great shame, because even now, parts of it come back to me, and very powerfully."

Wells spent many hours in hospitals talking to nurses getting background information for her Cherry Ames books. When she needed information for the series, she traveled to hospitals that offered special care. Her keen eye for detail also enhanced the quality of her books. Her brother said, "She saw so much more than the rest of us. Her descriptions of a leaf, a dress, an opera, a bird, were incredibly passionate and detailed. She experienced things very deeply, and then made a gift of those experiences."

In 1958, Wells started traveling widely, making one major trip each year. She visited Mexico, Brazil, Guatemala, Portugal, Russia, Germany, Hungary, Austria, Greece, Egypt, Israel, England, Scandinavia, and Italy. She made a number of trips to Spain, where her father's grandmother was born. She also toured the United States and particularly enjoyed the states of the Pacific Northwest.

"Helen had great style, gave resplendent parties, and had lots of friends. She subscribed to the Metropolitan Opera and the Philharmonic," her brother said. She also loved to attend plays, sometimes accompanied by her brother, who liked her descriptions of performances afterward better than the actual shows.

Wells taught children's literature writing at the Institute of Children's Literature, was active in the Mystery Writers of America, and was a friend to many writers. One of those friends remembers Wells as a very lovely, generous, and gentle person with strong emotions who worked with great energy to establish a writers' union.

The Cherry Ames books and Vicki Barr mysteries brought Wells fan mail that was delivered by the pound. They are valuable collectors items now. Her brother, who wanted them to be available to the public, arranged for them to be kept with the author's manuscripts and other papers at Florida State University.

BIOGRAPHICAL/CRITICAL SOURCES:

BOOKS

Ward, Martha E., and Dorothy A. Marquardt, editors, *Authors of Books for Young People,* 2nd edition, Scarecrow, 1971.
Wells, Robert, in an interview with Marguerite Feitlowitz, in *Something about the Author,* Volume 49, Gale, pp. 201-204.

PERIODICALS

Best Sellers, November 1, 1969, p. 308.
Kirkus Reviews, September 15, 1969, p. 1010.
Library Journal, November 15, 1969, p. 4303.

OBITUARIES:

PERIODICALS

New York Times, February 13, 1986.*

*   *   *

WELLS, Merle William 1918-

PERSONAL: Born December 1, 1918, in Lethbridge, Alberta, Canada; U.S. citizen born abroad; came to United States in 1930; son of Norman Danby (a farmer) and Minnie Muir (a teacher; maiden name, Huckett) Wells. *Education:* Boise Junior College (now Boise State University), A.A., 1939; College of Idaho, A.B., 1941; University of California, Berkeley, M.A., 1947, Ph.D., 1950. *Religion:* Presbyterian.

ADDRESSES: Home—200 North Third, #701, Boise, ID 83702. *Office*—Idaho State Historical Society, 610 North Julia Davis Dr., Boise, ID 83702.

CAREER: College of Idaho, Caldwell, instructor in history, 1942-46; Alliance College, Cambridge Springs, PA, associate professor of history, 1950-58; Idaho State Historical Society, Boise, historian and archivist, 1959-86. State of Idaho, Boise, archivist, 1952-86, historic preservation officer, 1968-86. College of Idaho, visiting professor, 1959; Boise State University, lecturer, 1963—. Idaho State Employees Credit Union, director, 1964-67, treasurer, 1966-67; Idaho Farm Workers' Services, Inc., director, 1965-68, president, 1968—; National Conference of State Historic Preservation Officers, director, 1976-81, chairman of Western states council on geographic names,

1982-83. Member of board of directors, Sawtooth Interpretative Association, 1972—, and of history department, General Assembly of the United Presbyterian Church, 1978-84; member of general board, Idaho Council of Churches, 1966-75. Member, National Migrant Advisory Council, National Council of Churches, 1964-67, Idaho State Commission on the Arts and Humanities, 1966-67, Idaho State Bicentennial Commission, 1971-76, and National Trust for Historic Preservation.

MEMBER: American Historical Association, Society of American Archivists (fellow), National Association of State Archives and Records Administrators, American Association for State and Local History (member of council, 1973-77), American Association of University Professors, Western History Association (member of council, 1973-76), Pacific Northwest Library Association, Idaho Zoological Society (vice-president, 1982-84; member of board of directors, 1984—), Idaho Library Association.

AWARDS, HONORS: L.H.D., College of Idaho, 1981, University of Idaho, 1990.

WRITINGS:

(With Merrill D. Beal) *History of Idaho,* Lewis Historical Publishing, 1959.
Rush to Idaho, Idaho Bureau of Mines and Geology, 1961.
Gold Camps and Silver Cities, Idaho Bureau of Mines and Geology, 1964.
Idaho: A Student's Guide to Localized History, Teacher's College Press, Columbia University, 1965.
A Short History of Idaho, Idaho State Historical Society, 1974.
(With Harry H. Caldwell) *Economic and Ecological History Support Study for a Case Study of Federal Expenditures on a Water and Related Land Resource Project, Boise Project, Idaho and Oregon,* Idaho Water Resources Research Institute, University of Idaho, 1974.
Idaho: An Illustrated History, Idaho State Historical Society, 1976.
Anti-Mormonism in Idaho, 1872-1892, Brigham Young University Press, 1978.
An Atlas of Idaho Territory, Idaho State Historical Society, 1978.
(Author of introduction) Brigham D. Madsen, *The Lemhi: Sacajawea's People,* Caxton Printers, 1979.
(Author of introduction) Madsen, *The Northern Shoshoni,* Caxton Printers, 1980.
Boise: An Illustrated History, Windsor Publications, 1982.
(Contributor) *Geology of Northwest Utah, Southern Idaho and Northeast Nevada,* Utah Geological Association, 1984.
Idaho: Gem of the Mountains, Windsor Publications, 1985.

Lewis and Clark in Idaho, Lewis and Clark Heritage Foundation, Idaho Chapter, 1990.

Contributor to *Encyclopaedia Britannica, American Oxford Encyclopedia, World Book Encyclopedia,* and *Crowell-Collier Encyclopedia.* Contributor of about fifty articles to history journals. Former editor, *Idaho Yesterdays;* member of editorial board, *Pacific Northwest Quarterly.*

WORK IN PROGRESS: Northwest labor history, mining history in Idaho, gold and silver in U.S. history, and Pacific Northwest political history and public administration, church history, and Snake Country exploration.

SIDELIGHTS: Merle William Wells told *CA:* "My primary career objective has been to gain increased cooperation among academic and historical agency historians. While on academic leave, I spent more than two years in independent practice as a consulting historian more than a decade before such a venture became at all common. When historic preservation offered career opportunities for a greater variety of historical disciplines, I promoted increased cooperation nationally as well as locally, among historians, archaeologists, and architectural historians. My recent concern, shared by other state historic preservation officers with academic experience, has been to develop superior historic contexts for preservation planning. Most of my publications have been designed to accomplish these goals.

"My primary interest in historical interpretation comes from teaching logic and philosophy as well as history. This approach has led me to avoid letting traditional preconceptions (and misconceptions) obscure an understanding of interesting events of the past. I am not inclined toward historical revision, but generally approach subjects that have been neglected—or misunderstood through lack of basic research. To a great extent, my attitude towards historical investigation derives from early exposure to comparative history as a fourth generation Canadian, as well as third generation in the United States. Most of my research has been concentrated on complex subjects that have resisted simple analysis and have required close attention over a long period of time. My investigation of Idaho's anti-Mormons took most of forty years and still is subject to revision. So are most of my other specialties."

Wells adds: "My Boise State University and University of Idaho faculty affiliations have enabled me to assist graduate students and other investigators to contribute to Northwest history literature. Since 1986, my time, however, has been devoted primarily to my own publication projects, which focus upon improved interpretation of regional history.

"With expansion of interest in National Park Service sites in Idaho and in National Historic Trails (primarily Lewis and Clark, California, Oregon, and Nez Perce), I have been active in developing material for publication upon those subjects. All of them are important for integrating Idaho and Pacific Northwest history into a national context. My concern for recent Pacific Northwest history governs most of my current activity. Opportunities for useful studies have almost no limits, so I try to stimulate interest in contemporary history to meet pressing needs of our time."

*   *   *

WESTIN, Richard A(xel) 1945-

PERSONAL: Born July 8, 1945, in London, England; came to the United States, 1952; son of Gosta Victor (a diplomat) and Muriel Yalden (a veterinarian; maiden name, Thomson) Westin; married Elizabeth J. Cook (an optometrist), June 13, 1981; children: Monica Jean, Charles William. *Education:* Columbia University, B.A., 1967, M.B.A., 1968; University of Pennsylvania, J.D., 1972.

ADDRESSES: Home—3764 Ingold, Houston, TX 77005. *Office*—Law Center, University of Houston, Houston, TX 77004.

CAREER: Dewey, Ballantine, Bushby, Palmer & Wood (law firm), New York City, associate, 1972-75; Vermont Life Insurance Co., Montpelier, tax counsel, 1975-79; Illinois Institute of Technology, Chicago-Kent College of Law, Chicago, associate professor of law, 1979-83; University of Tennessee, Knoxville, associate professor of law, 1983-84; University of Houston, Houston, TX, professor of law, 1984—. Director of Millenium Leasing Corp. Former consultant to World Bank and United Nations.

MEMBER: American Bar Association (leader of Task Force on Liquidation and Reincorporation), Vermont Bar Association, California Bar Association.

WRITINGS:

Middle Income Tax Planning and Shelters, McGraw, 1982.
(With Alan H. Neff) *Tax, Attacks, and Counterattacks: Your Indispensable Guide to Long-Range Tax Strategy,* Harcourt, 1983.
Casebook: Federal Income Taxation of Domestic Natural Resources, John Marshall Press, 1987.
Natural Resource Taxation: Timber, Oil and Gas, and Minerals, PLI, 1987.
Federal Tax Planning, 3 volumes, Shepards'/McGraw, 1990.
(With K. Keeling) *Treatise: Tax Methods and Periods,* Callaghan, 1991.

(With Gaines and others) *Taxation for Environmental Protection,* Quorum, 1991.

Also author of *Cases and Materials on Exempt Organizations.* Contributor to law journals.

WORK IN PROGRESS: Research for a book on environmental taxation of natural resources.

SIDELIGHTS: Richard A. Westin told *CA:* "Alan Neff and I decided to write a joint book in which we could bowdlerize the rather severe material written for and published by Shepards'/McGraw-Hill. The book wound up being a good product in that it really does tell people how to *think* about tax planning in the most general terms, after which annual variations in the details of tax planning become comprehensible. Unfortunately, while the book enjoyed fine reviews, its sales were modest—evidently because the public wants the boldest and most venal formats, it seems. Alan Neff has since tried his hand, with some success, at writing a mystery thriller. I am writing a technical book on the taxation of natural resources."

*   *   *

WESTMACOTT, Mary
See CHRISTIE, Agatha (Mary Clarissa)

*   *   *

WHITE, E(lwyn) B(rooks) 1899-1985

PERSONAL: Born July 11, 1899, in Mount Vernon, NY; died after suffering from Alzheimer's disease, October 1, 1985, in North Brooklin, ME; son of Samuel Tilly (a piano manufacturer) and Jessie (Hart) White; married Katharine Sergeant Angell (a *New Yorker* editor), November 13, 1929 (died, July 20, 1977); children: Joel McCoun; stepchildren: Nancy Angell Stableford, Roger Angell. *Education:* Cornell University, A.B., 1921.

ADDRESSES: Home—North Brooklin, ME 04661. *Office*—*New Yorker,* 20 West 43rd St., New York, NY 10036.

CAREER: Reporter with United Press and the American Legion News Service, 1921; *Seattle Times,* Seattle, WA, reporter, 1922-23; copywriter with Frank Seaman, Inc., and Newmark, Inc., New York City, 1924-25; *New Yorker,* New York City, writer and contributing editor, beginning 1926. *Military service:* U.S. Army, 1918.

MEMBER: National Institute of Arts and Letters, American Academy of Arts and Sciences (fellow), American Academy of Arts and Letters, Phi Beta Kappa, Phi Gamma Delta.

AWARDS, HONORS: Limited Editions Club gold medal, 1945, for "a work most likely to attain the stature of a classic," for *One Man's Meat;* Litt.D., Dartmouth College, University of Maine, and Yale University, all 1948, Bowdoin College, 1950, Hamilton College, 1952, and Harvard University, 1954; Newbery Honor Book, 1953, Lewis Carroll Shelf Award, 1958, George C. Stone Center for Children's Books Recognition of Merit Award, 1970, and the New England Round Table of Children's Libraries Award, 1973, all for *Charlotte's Web;* Page One Award, New York Newspaper Guild, 1954, and National Association of Independent Schools Award, 1955, both for *The Second Tree from the Corner;* L.H.D., Colby College, 1954.

National Institute of Arts and Letters gold medal, 1960, for his contribution to literature; Presidential Medal of Freedom, 1963; Laura Ingalls Wilder Award, American Library Association, 1970, for "a lasting contribution to children's literature"; National Medal for Literature, National Institute of Arts and Letters, 1971; *The Trumpet of the Swan* was nominated for a National Book Award, 1971, was included on the International Board on Books for Young People Honor List, 1972, and received the Children's Book Award from the William Allen White Library at Emporia State University, 1973, the Sequoyah Children's Book Award from the Oklahoma Library Association, 1973, the Sue Hefley Award from the Louisiana Association of School Librarians, 1974, and the Young Hoosier Award from the Indiana School Librarians Association, 1975; Pulitzer Prize special citation, 1978, for the body of his work.

WRITINGS:

The Lady Is Cold (poems), Harper, 1929.
(With James Thurber) *Is Sex Necessary?; or, Why You Feel the Way You Do,* Harper, 1929, reprinted, Queens House, 1977.
(Author of introduction) James Thurber, *The Owl in the Attic,* Harper, 1931.
(Editor) *Ho-Hum: Newsbreaks from the "New Yorker,"* Farrar & Rinehart, 1931.
(Editor) *Another Ho-Hum: More Newsbreaks from the "New Yorker,"* Farrar & Rinehart, 1932.
Alice through the Cellophane (pamphlet), John Day, 1933.
Every Day Is Saturday, Harper, 1934.
Farewell to Model T, Putnam, 1936.
The Fox of Peapack and Other Poems, Harper, 1938.
Quo Vadimus?; or, The Case for the Bicycle, Harper, 1939.
(Editor with wife, Katharine Sergeant White, and author of introduction) *A Subtreasury of American Humor,* Coward, 1941, reprinted, Capricorn Books, 1962.
One Man's Meat (also see below; essays previously published in *Harper's*), Harper, 1942, enlarged edition, 1944, reprinted with new introduction, 1982.

(Author of introduction) Roy E. Jones, *A Basic Chicken Guide for the Small Flock Owner,* Morrow, 1944.
World Government and Peace: Selected Notes and Comment, 1943-1945, F. R. Publishing, 1945.
Stuart Little (also see below; juvenile), Harper, 1945.
The Wild Flag: Editorials from the "New Yorker" on Federal World Government and Other Matters, Houghton, 1946.
Here Is New York, Harper, 1949.
(Author of introduction) Don Marquis, *the lives and times of archy and mehitabel,* Doubleday, 1950.
Charlotte's Web (also see below; juvenile), Harper, 1952.
The Second Tree from the Corner, Harper, 1954, new edition, with new introduction, 1984.
(Editorial supervisor and contributor) William Strunk, Jr., *The Elements of Style,* Macmillan, 2nd edition (White not associated with previous edition), 1959, 3rd edition, 1979.
The Points of My Compass: Letters from the East, the West, the North, the South, Harper, 1962.
An E. B. White Reader, edited by William W. Watt and Robert W. Bradford, Harper, 1966.
Topics: Our New Countryman at the U.N. (pamphlet), Congressional Press, 1968.
The Trumpet of the Swan (also see below; juvenile), Harper, 1970.
E. B. White Boxed Set (contains *Charlotte's Web, Stuart Little,* and *The Trumpet of the Swan*), Harper, 1975.
Letters of E. B. White, edited by Dorothy Lobrano Guth, Harper, 1976.
Essays of E. B. White, Harper, 1977.
(Editor) K. S. White, *Onward and Upward in the Garden,* Farrar, Straus, 1979.
Poems and Sketches of E. B. White, Harper, 1981.
(With others) *A Gift from Maine,* Guy Gannett, 1984.
Writings from the New Yorker, 1925-1976, edited by Rebecca M. Dale, Harper, 1990.

Author of column, "One Man's Meat," *Harper's,* 1938-43. Contributor to periodicals.

RECORDINGS

Stuart Little, Dell, 1973.
Charlotte's Web (narrated by White), RCA, 1976.

ADAPTATIONS: Stuart Little was filmed for television by the National Broadcasting Company in 1966; *Charlotte's Web* was adapted as an animated film by Paramount in 1972 and adapted as a filmstrip by Stephen Bosustow Productions, 1974, and by Films Incorporated, 1976; the short story "the Family That Dwelt Apart" was adapted as an animated film by Learning Corporation of America in 1974.

SIDELIGHTS: Few writers have achieved recognition in as many fields as did E. B. White. He was regarded as one of the finest essayists of the twentieth century; he was the author of two classics of children's literature, *Charlotte's Web* and *Stuart Little;* and his extensive contributions to the *New Yorker* were instrumental in making that magazine a success.

White began his writing career in 1921 after graduating from Cornell University, where he served as editor of the school newspaper. He worked for a time as a reporter with two news services in New York City, then drove a Model T cross country with his friend Howard Cushman. "When they ran out of money," the late James Thurber recounted in an article for the *Saturday Review of Literature,* "they played for their supper—and their gasoline—on a fascinating musical instrument that White had made out of some pieces of wire and an old shoe or something." Ending up in Seattle, White took a job as a reporter for the *Seattle Times.* He lasted less than a year. White explained in *The Points of My Compass: Letters from the East, the West, the North, the South:* "As a newspaper reporter I was almost useless." He worked for a short time as a mess boy on a ship bound for Alaska but soon returned to New York, where he spent two years as an advertising copywriter.

It was while working as a copywriter that White began to submit short pieces to the fledgling *New Yorker* magazine, barely a few months old at the time. Editor Harold Ross "was so taken by the pieces White submitted to *The New Yorker,*" John Ciardi wrote in the *Washington Post Book World,* "that he hired White to write the 'Talk of the Town' section with which the magazine still opens." Both Ross and Katharine Angell, the magazine's literary editor who later became White's wife, found White's style ideal for the *New Yorker.* They "were not slow to perceive that here were the perfect eye and ear, the authentic voice and accent for their struggling magazine," Thurber stated. Over the next forty years, White contributed poems, essays, sketches, stories, and even photo captions to the *New Yorker.* He wrote the "Talk of the Town" section for eleven years. For many years, too, he wrote the "Newsbreak" fillers, short items taken from magazines and newspapers and reprinted with a humorous comment. White, Thurber explained, "had a hand in everything: he even painted a cover and wrote a few advertisements."

Russell Maloney, in an article for the *Saturday Review of Literature,* credited White with "setting *The New Yorker's* editorial style" in his "Talk of the Town" section. This style, Maloney went on, is "modest, sly, elliptical, allusive, prim, slightly countrified, wistful, and (God help us) whimsical." Thurber credited White with changing the *New Yorker.* "It is not too much to say that . . . White was the most valuable person on the magazine," Thurber wrote. "His delicate tinkering with the works of *The New Yorker* caused it to move with a new ease and grace." An-

other "one of E. B. White's great contributions to *The New Yorker,*" Maloney believed, "was his insistence, against almost overwhelming opposition, that Thurber was a funny artist whose pictures should appear in the magazine." Thurber had long been a staff writer for the *New Yorker,* having attained the position after White arranged an interview for him. To amuse his co-workers, Thurber sketched humorous cartoons at the office. White urged him to submit these cartoons to the magazine, but Thurber had little faith in them and refused to try. One day White collected some of Thurber's pencil drawings from his wastebasket, inked them in, and submitted them to the *New Yorker's* art editor. They were accepted. Thurber went on to become a very popular cartoonist as well as writer.

In 1929 White collaborated with Thurber on *Is Sex Necessary?; or, Why You Feel the Way You Do,* a spoof of sex manuals. The book made "both White and Thurber well known," according to Edward C. Sampson in the *Dictionary of Literary Biography.* The two authors, Sampson explained, "parody the serious writers on the subject, making light of complexities, taking a mock-serious attitude toward the obvious, delighting in reducing the case-history technique to an absurdity, and making fun of those writers who proceeded by definition." They expound on such crucial topics as "Osculatory Justification," "Schmalhausen Trouble" (when couples live in small apartments), and "The Nature of the American Male: A Study of Pedestalism." Will Cuppy of the *New York Herald Tribune Book Review* called *Is Sex Necessary?* "a minor classic—and one uses the term 'minor' only because it is gorgeously funny and not quite ponderous enough to be major. Let's compromise and just call it a classic." Thurber's drawings, turned out in a few hours, illustrate the book, which has gone through more than twenty-five printings since it first appeared. White's share of the royalties enabled him to marry Katharine Angell on November 13, 1929.

Over the years, it has been White's essays for the *New Yorker*—many of which are collected in 1977's *Essays of E. B. White*—that have done the most to build his literary reputation. White's essays are personal and informal, seem to happen upon their subject as they ramble along, and have a gentle humor about them. New York City, where the *New Yorker* has its offices, and the Maine countryside, where White owned a farm, are the two most common settings. White often began with a small incident in his own life and then extrapolated larger implications from it. One of his first pieces for the *New Yorker,* for example, was a recounting of an accident at a Manhattan restaurant in which a glass of buttermilk was spilled on his suit. The waitress, White related, "was a little girl, so I let her blot me. In my ear she whispered a million apologies, hopelessly garbled, infinitely forlorn. And I whispered that the suit was four years old, and that I hated dark clothes anyway. One has, in life, so few chances to lie heroically." In other pieces, Christopher Lehmann-Haupt of the *New York Times* noted, White has arrived "at the subject of disarmament by way of Mary Martin's furniture, or at the prospects of American democracy by the route of a dachshund named Fred." This idea is echoed by the late Joseph Wood Krutch, writing in the *Saturday Review,* who maintained that White is "generally concerned less with the Queen than with the little mouse under her chair." William Howarth of the *Washington Post Book World* argued that, for White, "connecting small moments to big issues is a literary impulse." Howarth went on to say that White "can capture moments of rare evanescence —a small tree, second from the corner and backlit by the sun, 'each gilt-edged leaf perfectly drunk with excellence and delicacy.' "

In all of his essays, White's style was clear, personal, and unaffected. It is, Louis Hasley wrote in the *Connecticut Review,* "transparent and unobtrusive. With him, more than with most writers, the style is the man: careful, steady, sure, resourceful, concrete without flourish, capable of fun and even surrealistic fancy, and as often as not, expressing a deadly seriousness that may be richly compounded with humor." Similarly, Webster Schott wrote in the *New Republic* that "White has such a subtly-developed literary technique it's almost impossible to know when the words are running the writing, when Mr. White's head is in command, or when the central nervous system has taken over to pick up subliminal signals. That's style for you: marriage of idea, language, sensibility."

Although White's essays cover a wide range of topics— from observations of nature to the problems of city living and from political commentary to literary parody—they invariably display a gentle humor. White saw humor as a necessary counterbalance to everyday life. As he stated in his introduction to *A Subtreasury of American Humor,* "there is a deep vein of melancholy running through everyone's life and . . . a humorist, perhaps more sensible of it than some others, compensates for it actively and positively." In the early days of his career, White was, Sampson wrote, "considered to be primarily a humorist." An example of White's humor can be found in one of the essays collected in *One Man's Meat* in which White speaks of his dog. "For a number of years," he wrote, "I have been agreeably encumbered by a very large and dissolute dachshund named Fred. Of all the dogs whom I have served I've never known one who understood so much of what I say or held it in such deep contempt. When I address Fred I never have to raise either my voice or my hopes. He even disobeys me when I instruct him in something that he wants to do. And when I answer his peremptory scratch at the door and hold the door open for him

to walk through, he stops in the middle and lights a cigarette, just to hold me up."

When White turned his attention to political matters, he often focused on the arms race and the tensions between the world's nations. His approach to politics was typically oblique. In one essay published in *The Second Tree from the Corner,* for example, White tells of participating in a routine air raid drill in his office building. As his elevator passes the thirteenth floor on its way to the basement, he notices that it is numbered "14." Nuclear scientists had successfully looked "into the core of the sun," White observed, "but it might have been a good idea if they had waited to do that until the rest of us could look the number 13 square in the face. Such is the true nature of our peculiar dilemma." White was known as a forceful advocate of world government, which he recommended for democratic nations only, and as a defender of individual privacy.

A concern for the environment, inspired by Henry David Thoreau's *Walden,* was also evident in White's life and work. White described Thoreau, in one of the essays collected in *The Points of My Compass,* as being the companion and chider for the "fellows who hate compromise and have compromised, fellows who love wildness and have lived tamely," and as the man "who long ago gave corroboration to impulses they perceived were right and issued warnings against things they instinctively knew to be their enemies." In common with Thoreau, White was skeptical about the benefits of material progress and suspected that perhaps what has been left behind is more valuable than what has replaced it. He is, Hasley commented, "a cautious critic of progress, fearing the loss of the precious sense for basic things." Following the example of Thoreau, who lived close to the land, White in 1934 bought a salt water farm in North Brooklin, Maine. He and his wife moved there permanently in 1938 and took to raising geese, chickens, and sheep. The essays collected in *One Man's Meat,* originally written as monthly columns for *Harper's* magazine, are set on White's farm and chronicle his daily life in the country.

Most critics praise White for his work as an essayist. Lehmann-Haupt called him "an essayist's essayist," while Hasley labeled White "our best living personal essayist." Writing in the *New York Times,* Irwin Edman remarked that "White is the finest essayist in the United States. He says wise things gracefully; he is the master of an idiom at once exact and suggestive, distinguished yet familiar." White is, Sampson concluded, "generally recognized as one of the best essayists of the twentieth century."

Although White's essays have won him overwhelming critical acclaim, he was more popularly known as the author of *Charlotte's Web* and *Stuart Little,* two classics of

American children's literature. White wrote only three books for children in all, but many observers rank him with such notables in the field of children's literature as Lewis Carroll, the author of *Alice in Wonderland.* Sampson acknowledged that *Charlotte's Web* "may well turn out to be the longest remembered of his works." "What makes White's three books outstanding," Sampson continued, "is that he has written them in the classical tradition of children's stories. . . . What the child [learns from White's books]—and what children learn from the other fine children's books—is a great deal about loyalty, honesty, love, sadness, and happiness."

Inspired by a vivid dream, White began in 1939 to write a children's story about a small, mouse-like character. Whenever one of his eighteen nieces and nephews wanted to be told a story, White improvised new adventures for his hero, whom he named Stuart Little. In 1945, he gathered these adventures together into a book-length manuscript which he sent to Harper & Row for consideration. Children's book editor Ursula Nordstrom found it "marvelously well-written, and funny, and touching," she recalled in an article for the *New York Times Book Review,* and accepted *Stuart Little* for publication.

White worked closely with artist Garth Williams on the illustrations for the book. Williams brought his drawings to Nordstrom's office in New York, she mailed them to White in Maine, and White wrote down his suggestions and ideas and mailed them back to her with the drawings. In this way the illustrations for *Stuart Little* were completed to the satisfaction of both author and artist. Williams's illustrations, John Gillespie and Diana Lembo wrote in *Introducing Books: A Guide for the Middle Grades,* "complement the text beautifully."

Publication of *Stuart Little* met with opposition from Anne Carroll Moore, head of children's literature at the New York Public Library and the most influential person in juvenile publishing at the time. After reading the book in galleys, Moore thought it "was nonaffirmative, inconclusive, unfit for children, and she felt that it would harm its author if published," Nordstrom related. Nonetheless, Harper went ahead with publication, convinced that *Stuart Little* showed merit. "It is unnerving," Nordstrom quoted White as saying, "to be told you're bad for children; but I detected in Miss Moore's letter an assumption that there are rules governing the writing of juvenile literature. . . . And this I was not sure of. I had followed my instincts in writing about Stuart, and following one's instincts seemed to be the way a writer should operate."

The book tells the story of the Little family's second child, Stuart, who happens to be two inches tall and looks like a mouse, although the Littles themselves are normal-sized and human. Because of his modest stature and adventur-

ous nature, Stuart finds himself in a series of wild situations: he is hoisted aloft by a window shade, attacked by a housecat, dropped into a bathtub drain to retrieve a lost ring, and even put into a piano to free some stuck keys. Stuart's "somewhat random adventures show him to be brave, ingenious, enterprising, and of romantic inclination," Peter M. Neumeyer wrote in the *Dictionary of Literary Biography.* Neumeyer also believed that White "has imaginatively extrapolated [Stuart's adventures] with all the ingenuity of Jonathan Swift plotting Gulliver's stay in Lilliput."

When Stuart's newfound love Margalo, a bird, flies away to escape the Littles' housecat, Stuart follows. The remainder of the book concerns his unsuccessful quest for her. "Like any knight errant," Neumeyer wrote, "Stuart is tempted and distracted during this pursuit." These distractions include wooing a girl during a canoe ride and teaching a class of fifth-graders when their regular teacher is sick. But the book ends with Stuart driving away in his toy car, continuing his search for Margalo. Calling *Stuart Little* "a lively and, at times, tender book that is a delight to both the imagination and the emotions," Gillespie and Lembo nevertheless found that "the rather inconclusive ending has somewhat marred its appeal for a few readers." Speaking of the book's ending in his *Letters of E. B. White,* White revealed: "Quite a number of children have written me to ask about Stuart. They want to know whether he got back home and whether he found Margalo. They are good questions, but I did not answer them in the book because, in a way, Stuart's journey symbolizes the continuing journey that everybody takes—in search of what is perfect and unattainable. This is perhaps too elusive an idea to put into a book for children, but I put it in anyway." John Rowe Townsend, in his *Written for Children: An Outline of English Language Children's Literature,* mused that "perhaps the ending is right; Stuart's is a quest for freedom and beauty, and such a quest is never completed."

Several reviewers believed that *Stuart Little* has the same wide appeal as do the classics of children's literature. Writing in the *Saturday Review of Literature,* R. C. Benet believed that readers of all ages will enjoy the book. "The exact number of years of the reader," he stated, "won't matter here any more than it does with 'Alice,' 'The Wind in the Willows,' some of [A. A.] Milne, or indeed the work of Walt Disney, who created that other popular mouse." The *Springfield Republican* critic agreed, finding that "readers of [Ernest] Hemingway as well as six-year-olds will find the book worth their while, much as grown-up readers of 'Alice in Wonderland' . . . find that classic. 'Stuart Little,' indeed, is in the school of 'Alice,' though by no means an imitation." It is a "memorable *Wanderjahr* for children," Timothy Foote wrote in *Time,* "loaded with longing and nostalgia." Foote went on to note that *Stuart Little* "still sells and sells." On its way to becoming "one of the classics of American children's literature," as Neumeyer described it, *Stuart Little* has sold more than two million copies in English and has been translated into twenty other languages.

White's next children's book, *Charlotte's Web,* was published in 1952. Without fanfare, or even a previous mention that he was working on another children's book, White dropped by his publisher's office with the manuscript. He took Nordstrom by surprise. "He gave me the only copy in existence of 'Charlotte's Web,'" she remembered, "got back on the elevator and left." Nordstrom read only a few chapters before deciding to publish the book. "I couldn't believe that it was so good!" she commented.

Called by Roger Sale in his *Fairy Tales and After: From Snow White to E. B. White* "probably *the* classic American children's book of the last thirty years," *Charlotte's Web* is set on a farm much like the one White owned in Maine. The story "seems to have developed," Neumeyer observed, "directly and exclusively out of White's joy in his own rural existence." White explained to Lee Bennett Hopkins in *More Books by More People:* "I like animals and my barn is a very pleasant place to be. . . . One day when I was on my way to feed the pig, I began feeling sorry for the pig because, like most pigs, he was doomed to die. This made me sad. So I started thinking of ways to save a pig's life. I had been watching a big, gray spider at her work and was impressed by how clever she was at weaving. Gradually I worked the spider into the story, . . . a story of friendship and salvation on a farm." Sale noted that White has referred to *Charlotte's Web* as a "hymn to the barn." "It is the word 'hymn,'" Sale wrote, "and the sense of celebration and praise, that is important here. . . . The essential celebration is of the beautiful things change brings or can bring."

Charlotte's Web tells the story of Wilbur, a small pig destined for slaughter, who is saved by his friend Charlotte, a spider, when she weaves the words "Some Pig" into a web above Wilbur's pen. People who see this miraculous message are so impressed by it that Wilbur is spared and even put on display at the local fair. But during their stay at the fair, Charlotte dies. In the final lines of the book, Wilbur remembers her as being "in a class by herself. It is not often that someone comes along who is a true friend and a good writer. Charlotte was both." David Rees, writing in *The Marble in the Water: Essays on Contemporary Writers of Fiction for Children and Young Adults,* called *Charlotte's Web* "the one great modern classic about death." Speaking of the book's closing lines, Rees believed them to be "comforting, not depressing. White is telling the child that he is allowed to mourn; that he is allowed

to remember with a certain sadness." "The profound themes of selfless love and acceptance of death are found in this story," Gillespie and Lembo wrote, "and are significantly although delicately explored."

Charlotte's death is shown to be a natural part of the cycle of existence. It is "made bearable," Townsend believed, "by the continuance of life through her offspring." Rees pointed out that immediately following the passage about Charlotte's death comes another passage about the birth of her children and of small animals on the farm. White's idea "that death is an inevitable and necessary part of the whole scheme of things," Rees stated, "is made acceptable by the emphasis he puts, after Charlotte dies, on the joy and happiness of birth." Townsend, too, saw that "the passage of seasons, the round of nature, are unobtrusively indicated" throughout the story.

One indication of this cycle is to be found in the passage of the young girl Fern from childhood. Fern was responsible for saving Wilbur when he was the runt of the litter. She later nursed him until he reached a healthy size, and she visited him in his barn as well. But as she grows older, Fern is less attentive to Wilbur and the other animals. Her attention instead centers on the upcoming fair and a certain boy who will be there. Fern begins the book as one of the central characters, but ends by being only peripheral to the story. "Fern has begun the saving of Wilbur," Townsend noted, "but by the end she has forgotten him; that is life, too. Childhood ends."

Charlotte's Web is written in a style that reminded Neumeyer of "an eighteenth-century definition of poetry: 'proper words in proper places'—the *mot juste.*" This quality is also noted by Eleanor Cameron in her study *The Green and Burning Bush: On the Writing and Enjoyment of Children's Books.* "The artistry of [*Charlotte's Web*]," Cameron wrote, "lies not at all in the use of unusual words but, as in all of Mr. White's prose for adults and children alike, in the way he combines words, creates intimations." In *A Critical History of Children's Literature,* Ruth Hill Viguers argued that the story of *Charlotte's Web* is thin and nonsensical, but that White, partly through his style, manages to overcome this weakness. "Mr. White has triumphed," Viguers stated. "The style and wit of his writing, his wisdom and his remembrance of a child's rapt concern with the things he loves strengthened the slender thread of story."

Critical evaluation of *Charlotte's Web* places it among the very best of its genre. It is "outstanding among post-war American children's fiction," Townsend believed. "As a piece of work," Eudora Welty wrote in the *New York Times,* "[*Charlotte's Web*] is just about perfect, and just about magical in the way it is done." The reviewer for the *Chicago Sunday Tribune* judged *Charlotte's Web* to be a "rare story of a beautiful friendship," as well as "witty and wise, lively and tender." Since its initial publication in 1952, *Charlotte's Web* has become a classic of American children's literature and has sold well over three million copies. Among books for children, Neumeyer summed up, *Charlotte's Web* "must surely be one of the most widely read and best beloved of this century."

It wasn't until 1970 that White published his next children's book, *The Trumpet of the Swan*. It has much in common with his earlier efforts. As in *Stuart Little* and *Charlotte's Web*, the characters in *The Trumpet of the Swan* are animals who participate in the human world and overcome great obstacles to achieve their desires. And like the previous two books, *The Trumpet of the Swan* grew out of an experience in White's own life. His fascination with the trumpeter swans at the Philadelphia Zoo, initiated by a story in the *New York Times*, led White to tell the story of Louis, a voiceless trumpeter swan. Because he cannot speak, his human friend Sam Beaver takes Louis to school with him to learn to read and write. Thereafter, Louis carries a chalkboard and chalk with him to write out his messages. His father, wanting him to be able to communicate with other swans as well, steals a trumpet for him to play. Soon Louis's trumpet playing leads to nightclub work and to a meeting with Serena, a female swan with whom he falls in love.

Writing in the *New York Times Book Review*, John Updike expressed his opinion that *The Trumpet of the Swan* joins *Stuart Little* and *Charlotte's Web* "on the shelf of classics." Although it differs from the previous books, Updike found that *Trumpet* "has superior qualities of its own; it is the most spacious and serene of the three, the one most imbued with the author's sense of the precious instinctual heritage represented by wild nature, . . . yet [the book] does not lack the inimitable tone of the two earlier works—the simplicity that never condescends, the straight and earnest telling that happens upon, rather than veers into, comedy." Neumeyer believed that although it does not compare favorably with *Stuart Little* and *Charlotte's Web*, *The Trumpet of the Swan* "is adventurous, imaginative, and it has some touching moments."

White told Justin Wintle and Emma Fisher in *The Pied Pipers: Interviews with the Influential Creators of Children's Literature* the difference he saw between writing for children and writing for adults. "In my experience, the only difference (save for a very slight modification of vocabulary) is in one's state of mind," he explained. "Children are a wonderful audience—they are so eager, so receptive, so quick. I have great respect for their powers of observation and reasoning. But like any good writer, I write to amuse myself, not some imaginary audience."

Critical evaluations of White's career show that although he may have written only to amuse himself, he had in the

process entertained many others as well. Hasley defined White as "a kind of national housekeeper and caretaker. He has gone on steadily and quietly, looking around and ahead, poking into public and domestic corners, . . . and hardly any literate American has not benefited from his humor, his nonsense, his creativity, and his engaging wisdom." Calling him "the humble, kindly senior guru of delicate American humor," Jay Scriba of the *Milwaukee Journal* pointed out that White, "a master wordsmith, . . . is probably in more college literary anthologies than any other" writer. "The pleasures of reading White's prose," Jonathan Yardley wrote in the *Washington Post*, "are many and great." Speaking of *One Man's Meat*, a collection of magazine columns, Yardley saw White as "one of the few writers of this or any other century who has succeeded in transforming the ephemera of journalism into something that demands to be called literature." Edward Hoagland, writing in the *New York Times Book Review*, mused that "there are times, reading an E. B. White book of essays, when you think he must be the most likable man of letters alive. This is as it should be in a collection of personal pieces; and if you are some kind of writer yourself, you probably want to imitate him."

Upon receiving the National Medal for Literature in 1971, White wrote an article for *Publishers Weekly* in which he thanked the National Institute of Arts and Letters for the award. In this article he defines the role of the writer. "I have always felt," White stated, "that the first duty of a writer was to ascend—to make flights, carrying others along if he could manage it. To do this takes courage. . . . Today, with so much of earth damaged and endangered, with so much of life dispiriting or joyless, a writer's courage can easily fail him. I feel this daily. . . . But despair is not good—for the writer, for anyone. Only hope can carry us aloft. . . . Only hope, and a certain faith. . . . This faith is a writer's faith, for writing itself is an act of faith, nothing else. And it must be the writer, above all others, who keeps it alive—choked with laughter, or with pain."

BIOGRAPHICAL/CRITICAL SOURCES:

BOOKS

Anderson, A. J., *E. B. White: A Bibliography*, Scarecrow, 1978.
Authors in the News, Volume 2, Gale, 1976.
Benet, Laura, *Famous English and American Essayists*, Dodd, 1966.
Cameron, Eleanor, *The Green and Burning Bush: On the Writing and Enjoyment of Children's Books*, Atlantic-Little, Brown, 1969.
Children's Literature Review, Volume 1, Gale, 1976.

Contemporary Literary Criticism, Gale, Volume 10, 1979, Volume 34, 1985, Volume 39, 1986.

Dictionary of Literary Biography, Gale, Volume 11: *American Humorists, 1800-1950,* Part 2, 1982, Volume 22: *American Writers for Children, 1900-1960,* 1983.

Elledge, Scott, *E. B. White: A Biography,* Norton, 1984.

Fadiman, Clifton, *Party of One,* World Publishing, 1955.

Georgiou, Constantine, *Children and Their Literature,* Prentice-Hall, 1969.

Gillespie, John and Diana Lembo, *Introducing Books: A Guide for the Middle Grades,* Bowker, 1970.

Gillespie, John and Diana Lembo, *Juniorplots: A Book Talk Manual for Teachers and Librarians,* Bowker, 1967.

Hall, Katherine Romans, *E. B. White: A Bibliographic Catalogue of Printed Materials in the Department of Rare Books, Cornell University Library,* Garland Publishing, 1979.

Hoffmann, Miriam and Eva Samuels, editors, *Authors and Illustrators of Children's Books: Writings on Their Lives and Works,* Bowker, 1972.

Hopkins, Lee Bennett, *More Books by More People,* Citation, 1974.

Kramer, Dale, *Ross and the "New Yorker,"* Doubleday, 1951.

Lanes, Selma G., *Down the Rabbit Hole: Adventures and Misadventures in the Realm of Children's Literature,* Atheneum, 1972.

Meigs, Cornelia, editor, *A Critical History of Children's Literature,* revised edition, Macmillan, 1969.

Rees, David, *The Marble in the Water: Essays on Contemporary Writers of Fiction for Children and Young Adults,* Horn Book, 1980.

Rogers, Barbara J., *E. B. White,* Scribner, 1979.

Sale, Roger, *Fairy Tales and After: From Snow White to E. B. White,* Harvard University Press, 1978.

Sampson, Edward C., *E. B. White,* Twayne, 1974.

Smith, James Steel, *A Critical Approach to Children's Literature,* McGraw, 1967.

Thurber, James, *The Years with Ross,* Little, Brown, 1959.

Townsend, John Rowe, *Written for Children: An Outline of English Language Children's Literature,* revised edition, Lippincott, 1974.

Unger, Leonard, editor, *American Writers: A Collection of Literary Biographies,* Volume 4, Scribner, 1974.

Van Gelder, Robert, *Writers and Writing,* Scribner, 1946.

White, E. B., *Charlotte's Web,* Harper, 1952.

White, E. B., *Letters of E. B. White,* edited by Dorothy Lobrano Guth, Harper, 1976.

White, E. B., *One Man's Meat,* Harper, 1942, enlarged edition, 1944, reprinted, 1982.

White, E. B., *The Points of My Compass: Letters from the East, the West, the North, the South,* Harper, 1962.

White, E. B., *The Second Tree from the Corner,* Harper, 1954, reprinted, 1984.

White, E. B. and Katharine Sergeant White, editors, *A Subtreasury of American Humor,* Coward, 1941, reprinted, Capricorn Books, 1962.

Wintle, Justin and Emma Fisher, *The Pied Pipers: Interviews with the Influential Creators of Children's Literature,* Paddington Press, 1975.

Yates, Norris W., *American Humorists,* Iowa State University Press, 1964.

PERIODICALS

Chicago Sunday Tribune, November 16, 1952; October 21, 1962.

Chicago Tribune, November 2, 1990.

Children's Literature in Education, May, 1973.

College English, April, 1946; December, 1961.

Connecticut Review, October, 1971.

Los Angeles Times Book Review, August 22, 1982.

Milwaukee Journal, October 13, 1975.

Nation, August 14, 1929.

National Review, June 10, 1977.

New Republic, February 15, 1954; November 24, 1962.

New York Herald Tribune Book Review, May 26, 1929; December 28, 1929; January 17, 1954; October 21, 1962.

New York Review of Books, October 27, 1977.

New York Times, October 7, 1934; October 28, 1945; October 19, 1952; January 17, 1954; July 11, 1969; January 23, 1970; November 17, 1976; September 19, 1977; November 20, 1981; October 27, 1985; February 11, 1986; December 19, 1990.

New York Times Book Review, October 28, 1962; May 24, 1970; June 28, 1970; May 12, 1974; November 8, 1981.

Publishers Weekly, December 6, 1971; December 13, 1976.

Saturday Review, January 30, 1954; November 24, 1962; June 27, 1970.

Saturday Review of Literature, December 7, 1929; October 27, 1934; October 15, 1938; December 8, 1945; August 30, 1947.

Springfield Republican, October 21, 1945.

Time, December 20, 1976; January 25, 1982.

Washington Post, December 1, 1982.

Washington Post Book World, November 8, 1981; October 14, 1984.

Wilson Library Bulletin, February, 1972.

OBITUARIES:

PERIODICALS

Chicago Tribune, October 2, 1985.
Detroit Free Press, October 2, 1985.
Detroit News, October 2, 1985.

Los Angeles Times, October 2, 1985.
New American Weekly, October 28, 1985.
Newsday, October 2, 1985.
Newsweek, October 14, 1985.
New York Times, October 2, 1985.
Publishers Weekly, October 11, 1985.
School Library Journal, November, 1985.
Time, October 14, 1985.
Times (London), October 3, 1985.
Washington Post, October 2, 1985.*

[Sketch reviewed by son, Joel McCoun White]

* * *

WHITE, T(erence) H(anbury) 1906-1964
(James Aston)

PERSONAL: Born May 29, 1906, in Bombay, India; came to England, 1911; suffered an acute coronary after an American speaking tour and died at sea on board the *S.S. Exeter,* January 17, 1964; son of Garrick Hanbury (a policeman) and Constance Edith Southcote (Aston) White. *Education:* Attended Cheltonham College, 1920-24; Queens' College, Cambridge, B.A. (first class honors), 1928.

CAREER: Teacher at preparatory school in England, 1930-32; head of Department of English, Stowe School, Buckinghamshire, 1932-36. Writer residing in Ireland, 1939-46, Jersey, Channel Islands, 1946-47, and Alderney, Channel Islands, 1947-64.

MEMBER: British Falconer's Club.

WRITINGS:

Loved Helen and Other Poems, Chatto & Windus, 1929.
The Green Bay Tree; or, The Wicked Man Touches Wood (verses), Heffer, 1929.
(With Ronald McNair Scott) *Dead Mr. Nixon,* Cassell, 1931.
(Under pseudonym James Aston) *They Winter Abroad: A Novel,* Viking, 1932, reprinted under author's real name, Chatto & Windus, 1969.
(Under pseudonym James Aston) *First Lesson: A Novel,* Chatto & Windus, 1932, Knopf, 1933.
Darkness at Pemberley, Gollancz, 1932, Century, 1933.
Farewell Victoria, Collins, 1933, H. Smith & R. Hans, 1934, new edition, Putnam, 1960.
Earth Stopped; or, Mr. Marx's Sporting Tour, Collins, 1934.
Gone to Ground: A Novel, Collins, 1935.
Song through Space and Other Poems, Lincoln-Williams, 1935.
England Have My Bones (memoir), Macmillan, 1936, Putnam, 1982.

Burke's Steerage; or, The Amateur Gentleman's Introduction to Noble Sports and Pastimes, Collins, 1938.
The Sword in the Stone (Book-of-the-Month Club selection; also see below), Collins, 1938, Putnam, 1939.
The Witch in the Wood, Putnam, 1939, published as *The Queen of Air and Darkness* (also see below), 1958.
The Ill-Made Knight (also see below), Putnam, 1940.
Mistress Masham's Repose (Book-of-the-Month Club selection), illustrated by Fritz Eichenberg, Putnam, 1946.
The Elephant and the Kangaroo, Putnam, 1947.
The Age of Scandal: An Excursion through a Minor Period, Putnam, 1950.
The Goshawk, J. Cape, 1951, Putnam, 1952, new edition, Longman, 1973.
The Scandalmonger, Putnam, 1952.
(Editor and translator) *The Book of Beasts: A Translation from a Latin Bestiary of the 12th Century,* Putnam, 1954.
The Master: An Adventure Story, Putnam, 1957.
The Once and Future King (contains *The Sword in the Stone, The Queen of Air and Darkness, The Ill-Made Knight,* and *The Candle in the Wind*), Putnam, 1958, new edition, 1967.
The Godstone and the Blackymor, illustrated by Edward Ardizzone, Putnam, 1959.
America at Last: The American Journal of T. H. White, Putnam, 1965.
The White/Garnett Letters, edited by David Garnett, Viking, 1968.
The Book of Merlyn: The Unpublished Conclusion to The Once and Future King, University of Texas Press, 1977.
A Joy Proposed (verses), Rota, 1980.
The Maharajah and Other Stories, Putnam, 1981.
Letters to a Friend: The Correspondence between T. H. White and L. J. Potts, selected and edited by Francois Gallix, Putnam, 1982.

Also author of the periodical *Terence White's Verse-Reel,* beginning 1939.

ADAPTATIONS: The Once and Future King formed the basis for Alan Jay Lerner's and Frederick Loewe's musical play *Camelot,* first produced at the Majestic Theater, New York City, in 1960. It starred Richard Burton, Julie Andrews, Robert Goulet, and Roddy McDowell. *Camelot* was made into a motion picture in 1967 by Warner Bros., starring Richard Harris, Vanessa Redgrave, and Franco Nero. Walt Disney Productions released *The Sword in the Stone* as an animated feature under the same title in 1963.

SIDELIGHTS: T. H. White first gained popularity for his nonfiction works about the countryside of the United Kingdom, but he is best known today for his fantastic fiction. In his tetralogy *The Once and Future King*—called by Lin Carter in *Imaginary Worlds* "one of the most brilliant fantasy novels in literature"—he made the legends of King Arthur accessible for the twentieth century. *Mistress Masham's Repose* places a colony of Lilliputians (from *Gulliver's Travels*) on an English estate. *The Master: An Adventure Story* tells of two children held prisoner on an island and has been compared with the adventure stories of Robert Louis Stevenson. "The character of the author himself—headstrong, eccentric, humorous, and kind," declared a critic for the *Chicago Sunday Tribune,* "is so woven into his descriptions of people and places that it does not seem as though he was merely describing them for you, but had brought you there. He has the priceless gift of being able suddenly to look at something upside down and make you see it in the same way."

White had an extremely unhappy childhood. His parents were a quarrelsome couple who divorced when White was fourteen. They had married hastily, and found only later that they were not at all compatible. "There was a great deal of shooting in the air in those days," Sylvia Townsend Warner quotes White as saying in her biography *T. H. White.* "I am told that my father and mother were to be found wrestling with a pistol, one on either side of my cot, each claiming that he or she was going to shoot the other, and himself or herself, but in any case, beginning with me." White's aunt is quoted in the same source, saying, "My sister-in-law was of an extremely jealous nature and if the little boy showed affection for his father, climbing on his lap or asking if he could go out with him, she at once tried to provide some counter-action."

Around 1912, White was sent to his maternal grandparents' home, where he lived happily for six years. In 1920, however, his parents divorced. "This meant that my home and education collapsed about my ears," White explained in Warner's book; "and ever since I have been arming myself against disaster." In September of that year he was sent to Cheltenham College, a boys' school intended in part for training army officers. He discovered new miseries at the school; discipline was enforced along Army lines, by certain upperclass students called "Prefects," and White described his housemaster—a teacher residing in the boys' boarding-house—as "sadistic." "Throughout his life," Warner writes in her introduction to *The Book of Merlyn,* "White was subject to fears: fears from without—a menacing, psychopathic mother, the prefects at Cheltenham College 'rattling their canes,' poverty, tuberculosis, public opinion; fears from within—fear of being afraid, of being a failure, of being trapped." "His life was a running battle with these fears," Warner continues, "which he fought with courage, levity, sardonic wit, and industry. He was never without a project, never tired of learning, and had a high opinion of his capacities."

The trauma of these childhood years left White with a sense of inferiority that compelled him to excel. "This is why I learn," he explained years later in Warner's biography. "Now, believe it or not, I can shoot with a bow and arrow, so when the next atomic bomb is dropped, poor old White will be hopping about in a suit of skins shooting caribou or something with a bow and arrow." "Compensating for my sense of inferiority, my sense of danger, my sense of disaster," he went on, "I had to learn to paint even, and not only to paint—oils, art and all that sort of thing—but to build and mix concrete and to be a carpenter and to saw and screw and put in a nail without bending it. Not only did I have to be physically good at things, I had to excel with my head as well as with my body and hands. I had to get first-class honours with distinction at the University. I had to be a scholar. I had to learn medieval Latin shorthand so as to translate bestiaries."

White entered Queens' College, Cambridge, after leaving Cheltenham. His life there proved much happier; he became a favorite of his professors. His tutor, L. J. Potts, became a life-long friend and correspondent, one of the few people in whom White could confide. When he was stricken with tuberculosis in his second year, the professors formed a convalescent fund to send him to Italy to recuperate—where he composed his first novel, *They Winter Abroad*—and, after he graduated, they helped him win an appointment as head of the Department of English at Stowe School. "It was a position of authority under an enlightened headmaster who allowed him ample rope," Warner writes in her introduction to *The Book of Merlyn.* "He learned to fly, in order to come to terms with a fear of falling from high places, and to think rather better of the human race by meeting farm laborers at the local inn."

Soon, however, White tired of the teaching and sought a way to leave the profession. In 1936 he compiled *England Have My Bones,* a book made up of bits and pieces of his fishing, hunting, and flying experiences; the book became a national bestseller, and provided him with enough income to abandon teaching permanently. It was while living in a gamekeeper's cottage near Stowe that White rediscovered Thomas Malory's *Morte d'Arthur,* the fifteenth-century account of "The Matter of Britain"—the legends and tales surrounding the figure of King Arthur. "Do you remember I once wrote a thesis on the Morte d'Arthur?" White wrote in a letter that is cited in Warner's book. "Naturally I did not read Malory when writing the thesis on him, but one night last autumn I got desperate among my books and picked him up in lack of anything else. Then I was thrilled and astonished to find (a) that the thing was a perfect tragedy, with a beginning, a middle, and an end implicit in the beginning, and (b) that the characters were real people with recognizable reactions which could be forecast. Anyway, I somehow started writing a book. It is not a satire. Indeed, I am afraid it is rather warm-hearted—mainly about birds and beasts. It seems impossible to determine whether it is for grown-ups or children. It is more or less a kind of wish-fulfillment of the things I should like to have happened to me when I was a boy."

The book, which White described to his friend as "a preface to Malory," was an account of Arthur's youth. White called the volume *The Sword in the Stone,* and the book itself tells of the young man's training for his future role as king. The young Arthur (familiarly called Wart) is being raised in a quiet backwoods English castle by Sir Ector, his guardian, along with Sir Ector's son Kay. The two young men take lessons from the magician Merlyn, a schoolmasterish type holding very progressive ideas about education and politics because he lives backwards through time. Many of the lessons Merlyn reserves especially for Wart have to do with animals and the important ideas he can learn from them. Through Merlyn's tutelage, Wart learns about courage, perseverance, the use of strength and the abuse of power, and he gains a perspective on his relationship to the rest of the animal kingdom which prepares him for his future as king of England.

White finished *The Sword in the Stone* in 1938. It was published in England and in America, where it was chosen as a Book-of-the-Month Club selection. White immediately began work on the sequel, *The Witch in the Wood* (later published as *The Queen of Air and Darkness*), which sets the stage for the tragedy of Arthur's life and death. "The whole Arthurian story is a regular greek doom, comparable to that of Orestes," the author wrote in his diary (quoted in Warner's introduction to *The Book of Merlyn*). The book shows Arthur beginning to put Merlyn's teaching to use, introducing in England the rule of Law instead of oppression. Among his chief opponents, however, were the kings of the North, the Gaels—including Lot of Orkney, the husband of Arthur's half-sister Morgause. In White's retelling of the story, Arthur is seduced by Morgause after he defeats Lot and the other Gaels in battle. The end result was Mordred. This, states White at the end of *The Queen of Air and Darkness,* "is why Sir Thomas Malory called his very long book the *Death* of Arthur. . . . It deals with the reasons why the young man came to grief at the end. It is the tragedy, the Aristotelian and comprehensive tragedy, of sin coming home to roost. That is why we have to take note of the parentage of Arthur's son Mordred, and to remember, when the time comes, that the king had slept with his own sister. He did not know he was doing so, and perhaps it may have been due to her, but it seems, in tragedy, that innocence is not enough."

The Ill-Made Knight followed *The Queen of Air and Darkness.* It tells of the search for the Holy Grail, and how Arthur's Table became scattered because of it. Arthur is less evident in this story than he had been in the first two; instead, Sir Lancelot is the main focus of the book. White first presents him as a child prodigy, raised to become the best knight in the world both physically and spiritually. He then relates how Lancelot came to Camelot, and how he became the foremost knight of Arthur's Round Table. White shows Lancelot as a distinctly human figure, regarding himself as ugly and disfigured, but trained to demand the best of himself and prone to regard himself as a failure whenever he falls below his own expectations. "There is no easy-going writing in *The Ill-Made Knight,*" states Warner in her introduction to *The Book of Merlyn,* "where the Doom tightens on Arthur and Lancelot is compelled to be instrumental in it by his love for Guenever."

The Candle in the Wind forms the fourth volume of *The Once and Future King.* It was never published separately, and only appeared in the collection with edited versions of the first three books. It traces the years of Arthur's long defeat: Mordred plots to undo the king's accomplishments, using the affair between Lancelot and Guenever as a lever. Slowly Arthur is forced to bring war against his friend, a strife that is ended only when Mordred, with his band of Nazi-like Threshers, attempts to seize power in England. The book ends with Arthur facing Mordred's army across Salisbury plain, stripped of everything except the hope that his dream might live on.

The Candle in the Wind was the last book White wrote that was based on Malory's work, but White realized that it was not the end of his own version of the story. On November 14th, 1940, he wrote (cited in Warner's introduction), "Pendragon can still be saved, and elevated into a superb success, by altering the last past of Book 4, and taking Arthur back to his animals." In a letter to L. J. Potts dated December 6, 1940, which Warner cites in her introduction, he explained that *The Candle in the Wind* "will end on the night before the last battle, with Arthur absolutely wretched. And after that I am going to add a new 5th volume, in which Arthur rejoins Merlyn underground. . . . You see, I have suddenly discovered that (1) the central theme of Morte d'Arthur is to find an antidote to war, (2) that the best way to examine the politics of man is to observe him, with Aristotle, as a political animal." Since the final volume would feature the reappearance of Arthur's teacher, it would be called *The Book of Merlyn.* White concluded, "I shall have the marvelous opportunity of bringing the wheel full circle, and ending on an animal note like the one I began on. This will turn my completed epic into a perfect fruit, 'rounded off and bright and done.' "

Unfortunately, World War II played havoc with White's plan. By the time he completed *The Candle in the Wind* and *The Book of Merlyn,* England was at war and suffering from paper shortages. White's English publisher balked at the idea of producing such a long, expensive work. "After prolonged negotiations," Warner writes in her introduction, ". . . the fivefold *Once and Future King* was laid by." *The Book of Merlyn* was not published with the other four books in 1957; it did not appear until 1977, fifteen years after White's death, when the University of Texas Press discovered the manuscript among some of White's papers. However, it disappointed some readers because of White's determination to prove his thesis: "the book," declares Warner in her introduction, "clatters on like a factory with analysis, proof and counterproof, exhortation, demonstration, explanation, historical examples, parables from nature—even the hedgehog talks too much."

In the years between the publication of *The Ill-Made Knight* and *The Once and Future King* White completed several other children's books, including *Mistress Masham's Repose* and *The Master*. Although these are respected works—Donald Barr, in the *New York Times Book Review,* calls *The Master* "one of the most beguiling and yet one of the most straightforward of Mr. White's tales"—they have not attracted the same popularity or critical attention as has *The Once and Future King*. "Even on the most superficial level," writes Erwin D. Canham in the *Christian Science Monitor,* " . . . it is a masterpiece." "It is Britain's traditional saga, much more than myth . . . ," he continues, "and at a still deeper level, it is the struggle of human living for good and against sin, with the temporary triumph of tragedy but the eternal invincibility of good. Arthur is also 'the Future King.' His meaning, along the pathway of humanseeking, promises that man's birthright is never destroyed." "All this, and infinitely more," Canham concludes, "is woven together with literary genius, archaelogical authority, and a freshness which is as bright as the dawn of history and the memories we associate with a golden age."

White himself was undergoing personal problems by the time the war ended; although he had lived in Ireland for nearly six years, he was still regarded by the locals as a foreigner and a possible spy, and in 1946 he was asked to leave. He settled in the Channel Islands and continued to write. White's greatest popularity came some years later, with the opening of the Broadway musical *Camelot* in 1960. He wrote, in a passage quoted in Warner's biography, "The reviews of the musical have been mixed, but it will survive under its own power. I have pretended to everybody that I am perfectly satisfied with this new version of my book, as it is a corporate effort which involves many people, some of whom I love, and it is up to me to put a shoulder to the wheel. . . . Julie [Andrews] is as always enchanting beyond words and Richard Burton, who plays Arthur, is a great Shakespearian actor from the Old Vic.

I have been totally accepted by every member of the cast and every stage hand—even by Lerner and Loewe themselves—and spend every performance crawling over every corner of the theatre to find out how the wheels go round." A U.S. lecture followed in 1963-64, and it was on his return from this that White died. His epitaph calls him an "author who from a troubled heart delighted others loving and praising this life."

BIOGRAPHICAL/CRITICAL SOURCES:

BOOKS

Carter, Lin, *Imaginary Worlds: The Art of Fantasy,* Ballantine Books, 1973.
Contemporary Literary Criticism, Volume 30, Gale, 1984.
Crane, John K., *T. H. White,* Twayne, 1974.
Warner, Sylvia Townsend, *T. H. White: A Biography,* Viking, 1967.
Warner, Sylvia Townsend, author of introduction, *The Book of Merlyn* by T. H. White, University of Texas Press, 1977, pp. ix-xxvi.
White, T. H., *The Once and Future King* (contains *The Sword in the Stone, The Queen of Air and Darkness, The Ill-Made Knight,* and *The Candle in the Wind*), Putnam, 1958, new edition, 1967.
White, T. H., *America at Last: The American Journal of T. H. White,* Putnam, 1965.
White, T. H., *The White/Garnett Letters,* edited by David Garnett, Viking, 1968.

PERIODICALS

Chicago Sunday Tribune, July 5, 1959.
Christian Science Monitor, August 28, 1958, p. 11.
Horn Book, October, 1981, pp. 565-70.
New York Herald Tribune, March 24, 1957.
New York Times Book Review, March 24, 1957, pp. 4, 24.
San Francisco Chronicle, March 23, 1952.
Times Literary Supplement, April 25, 1958.

OBITUARIES:

PERIODICALS

Illustrated London News, January 25, 1964.
Newsweek, January 27, 1964.
New York Times, January 18, 1964.
Publishers Weekly, January 27, 1964.*

—*Sketch by Kenneth R. Shepherd*

*   *   *

WILK, Max 1920-

PERSONAL: Born July 30, 1920, in New York, NY; son of Jacob and Eva (Zalk) Wilk; married Barbara Balensweig, 1949; children: David, Richard, Mary Frances. *Education:* Yale University, B.A., 1941.

ADDRESSES: Home—29 Surf Rd., Westport, CT.

CAREER: Formerly worked in several capacities for Columbia Broadcasting System-Television (CBS-TV), New York City; free-lance writer, 1948—. Dramaturge at Eugene O'Neill Theatre Conference, Waterford, CT, 1980-91. *Military service:* U.S. Army.

MEMBER: Century Association and Yale Club (both New York City).

AWARDS, HONORS: Emmy, Peabody, and Writers Guild of America East awards for scripts; Deems Taylor Award for best book on American popular music, American Society of Composers, Authors and Publishers, 1974, for *They're Playing Our Song.*

WRITINGS:

Don't Raise the Bridge, Lower the River, Macmillan, 1960.
Rich Is Better, Macmillan, 1962.
Help! Help! Help!; or, Atrocity Stories from All Over, Macmillan, 1963.
The Beard, Simon & Schuster, 1965.
One of Our Brains Is Draining, Norton, 1967.
The Yellow Submarine, New American Library, 1968.
A Dirty Mind Never Sleeps, Norton, 1969.
My Masterpiece, Norton, 1970.
The Wit and Wisdom of Hollywood, Atheneum, 1971.
They're Playing Our Song, Atheneum, 1973, reprinted, Moyer Bell, 1990.
Memory Lane, Studio International (London), 1973, Ballantine, 1974.
Eliminate the Middleman, Norton, 1974.
Every Day's a Matinee, Norton, 1975.
The Kissinger Noodles; or, Westward Mr. Ho, Norton, 1976.
The Golden Age of Television, Delacorte, 1977, published as *The Golden Age of Television: Notes from the Survivors,* Moyer Bell, 1989.
The Moving Picture Boys, Norton, 1978.
Get Out and Get Under, Norton, 1981.
(With Audrey Wood) *Represented by Audrey Wood,* Doubleday, 1983.
A Tough Act to Follow, Norton, 1985.
(With Harold Sack) *American Treasure Hunt: The Legacy of Israel Sack,* Little, Brown, 1986.
And Did You Once See Sidney Plain?: A Random Memoir of S. J. Perelman, Norton, 1986.
Beautiful Morning: The History of "Oklahoma!", Grove, 1992.

Also author of screenplays and numerous television scripts and adaptations. Contributor to periodicals.

WORK IN PROGRESS: Mr. Williams and Miss Wood, a play.

BIOGRAPHICAL/CRITICAL SOURCES:

PERIODICALS

Best Sellers, May 15, 1969; October 1, 1970.
Books and Bookmen, May, 1968; July, 1974; May, 1975.
Chicago Sunday Tribune, April 3, 1960.
Cue, August 14, 1971.
Life, July 30, 1971.
Los Angeles Times, August 29, 1986.
New Yorker, March 12, 1960; November 6, 1978.
New York Herald Tribune Books, April 1, 1962.
New York Times Book Review, February 28, 1960; March 10, 1968; March 24, 1974; February 9, 1986; September 7, 1986; January 3, 1988.
San Francisco Chronicle, May 13, 1962.
Saturday Review, March 19, 1960.
Time, April 14, 1986.
Variety, July 14, 1971.
Vogue, September 1, 1971.

*   *   *

WILNER, Eleanor   1937-

PERSONAL: Born July 29, 1937, in Cleveland, Ohio; daughter of Bernard Everett (a lawyer) and Gertrude (an artist; maiden name, Sherby) Rand; married Robert Weinberg (a professor of physics); children: Trudy. *Education:* Goucher College, B.A., 1959; Johns Hopkins University, M.A., 1964, Ph.D., 1973.

ADDRESSES: Home—324 South 12th St., Philadelphia, PA 19107.

CAREER: Baltimore News American, Baltimore, MD, reporter, 1959-60; WFBR Radio, Baltimore, feature writer, 1961-62; Maryland State Commission on the Aging, consultant, 1962-63; Morgan State University, Baltimore, instructor in English, 1964-69; Goucher College, Towson, MD, instructor, 1971-73, assistant professor, 1977-78, lecturer in English, beginning 1978; *American Poetry Review,* Philadelphia, PA, editor, 1975-77; Temple University, Philadelphia, associate professor in Tokyo, Japan, 1984-86; University of Iowa, Iowa City, poet-in-residence, fall, 1987; University of Chicago, Chicago, IL, poet-in-residence, spring, 1987, 1990; MFA Program for Writers, Warren Wilson College, Swannanoa, NC, faculty, 1989—.

MEMBER: Phi Betta Kappa.

AWARDS, HONORS: Manuscript award, Writers Conference at University of Colorado, 1970, for poetry; creative writing grant, National Endowment for the Arts,

1976-77; Juniper Prize, University of Massachusetts Press, 1979, for *Maya;* literature grant, Pennsylvania Council on the Arts, 1985; Pennbook/Philadelphia Award for literary excellence, 1990; MacArthur Foundation fellow, 1991.

WRITINGS:

Gathering the Winds: Visionary Imagination and Radical Transformation of Self and Society, Johns Hopkins University Press, 1975.
Maya (poems), University of Massachusetts Press, 1979.
Shekhinah, University of Chicago Press, 1984.
Sarah's Choice (poems), University of Chicago Press, 1989.

Contributor to anthologies, including *Best Poems of 1976: Borestone Mountain Poetry Awards,* Pacific Books, 1977; *Four Contemporary Poets,* La Vida Press, 1984; and *The Best American Poetry, 1990,* Scribners and Macmillan/ Collier, 1990. Also contributor of poems, criticism, and reviews to literary journals.

SIDELIGHTS: Eleanor Wilner has been active in civil rights and peace movements.

BIOGRAPHICAL/CRITICAL SOURCES:

PERIODICALS

Times Literary Supplement, May 31, 1991, p. 11.

* * *

WILSON, Dirk
   See POHL, Frederik

* * *

WOOD, Allen W(illiam) 1942-

PERSONAL: Born October 26, 1942, in Seattle, WA; son of Forrest Elmer (a supervisor at Boeing Aircraft Co.) and Alleen (Blumberg) Wood; married Rega Clark, June 20, 1965; children: Henry Engelsberg, Stephen Frederick. *Education:* Reed College, B.A., 1964; Yale University, M.A., 1966, Ph.D., 1968.

ADDRESSES: Home—206 University Ave., Ithaca, NY 14850. *Office*—Department of Philosophy, 218 Goldwin Smith Hall, Cornell University, Ithaca, NY 14853.

CAREER: Cornell University, Ithaca, NY, assistant professor, 1968-73, associate professor, 1973-80, professor of philosophy, 1980—. Visiting assistant professor, University of Michigan, 1973; visiting professor, University of California at San Diego, 1986.

AWARDS, HONORS: Cornell Society for Humanities summer fellowship, 1970; Guggenheim fellowship, 1983, for *Hegel's Moral Philosophy.*

WRITINGS:

Kant's Moral Religion, Cornell University Press, 1970.
Kant's Rational Theology, Cornell University Press, 1978.
(Translator with Gertrude M. Clark) Immanuel Kant, *Lectures on Philosophical Theology,* Cornell University Press, 1978.
Karl Marx, Routledge & Kegan Paul, 1981.
(Editor) *Self and Nature in Kant's Philosophy,* Cornell University Press, 1984.
Hegel's Ethical Thought, Cambridge University Press, 1990.
(Editor) Georg Wilhelm Friedrich Hegel, *Elements of the Philosophy of Right,* translated by H. B. Nisbet, Cambridge Univeristy Press, 1991.

WORK IN PROGRESS: Working on *Kant's Moral Theory* and a new translation of Immanuel Kant's *Critique of Pure Reason.*

BIOGRAPHICAL/CRITICAL SOURCES:

PERIODICALS

Times Literary Supplement, June 19, 1991.

* * *

WOODCOTT, Keith
   See BRUNNER, John (Kilian Houston)

* * *

WORCHEL, Stephen 1946-

PERSONAL: Born February 27, 1946, in Washington, DC; son of Philip (a professor) and Libby (Goldberg) Worchel; married Frances Ferris; children: Leah Marie, Jessica Anne, Elise Rachel, Hannah Nicole. *Education:* University of Texas at Austin, B.A. (with honors), 1967; Duke University, Ph.D., 1971. *Avocational interests:* Farming (raising livestock and horses), international travel (Greece, Southeast Asia, Mexico).

ADDRESSES: Home—College Station, TX. *Office*—Department of Psychology, Texas A&M University, College Station, TX 77843.

CAREER: Duke University, Durham, NC, instructor in psychology, 1969-71; University of North Carolina at Chapel Hill, assistant professor of psychology, 1971-74; University of Virginia, Charlottesville, associate professor, 1974-78, professor of psychology, 1978-83; Texas

A&M University, College Station, professor of psychology and head of department, 1983—. Summer lecturer, Chulalongkorn University, 1969; visiting assistant professor, North Carolina Central University, spring, 1971; visiting lecturer, Fort Bragg, 1971-73; visiting scholar, Fudan University, Shanghai, China. Research assistant for Stimulmatics, Inc., 1967; trainee with U.S. Public Health Service, 1967-68; research associate at Institute of Research in Social Science. Member of board of trustees, Jung Education Center, Houston, TX; member of board, International Center for Social Justice, Utrecht, Netherlands. Chairperson of professional meetings.

MEMBER: International Society of Political Psychology, International Society for Research in Conflict, European Association of Experimental Social Psychology, American Psychological Association (fellow), Society of Experimental Social Psychology, Eastern Psychological Association, Southeastern Psychological Association, Southwestern Psychological Association, Phi Beta Delta.

AWARDS, HONORS: National Science Foundation grants, 1973-75, 1977-80; Wilson Gee Foundation grant, 1976; Fulbright fellow in Greece, 1979-80; National Institute of Mental Health research grant, 1980-84; Advanced Research Projects grant, 1988-91.

WRITINGS:

(With Joel Cooper) *Understanding Social Psychology,* Dorsey, 1976, 3rd edition, 1983, 5th edition also with George Goethals, Brooks/Cole, 1991.

(Editor with William G. Austin and contributor) *The Social Psychology of Intergroup Relations,* Brooks/Cole, 1979.

(With Peter Sheras) *Clinical Psychology: A Social Psychological Approach,* Van Nostrand, 1979.

(With Goethals) *The Psychology of Individual Adjustment,* Random House, 1981.

(With Wayne Shebilske) *Psychology: Principles and Applications,* Prentice-Hall, 1983, 4th edition, 1992.

(With Goethals) *Adjustment: Pathways to Personal Growth,* Prentice-Hall, 1985, 2nd edition, 1989.

(With Austin) *The Psychology of Intergroup Relations,* 2nd edition, Nelson-Hall, 1985.

(With Jeff Simpson and Wendy Wood) *Group Process and Productivity,* Sage Publications, in press.

(With Simpson) *Conflict between People and Peoples,* Nelson-Hall, in press.

CONTRIBUTOR

Lawrence Wrightsman and J. C. Brighan, editors, *Contemporary Issues in Social Psychology,* Brooks/Cole, 1973.

Samuel Himmelfarb and A. H. Eagly, editors, *Readings in Attitude Change,* Wiley, 1974.

J. H. Harvey, W. J. Ikes, and R. F. Kidd, editors, *New Directions in Attribution Research,* Lawrence Erlbaum, 1977.

Andrew Baum and Yakov Epstein, editors, *Human Response to Crowding,* Lawrence Erlbaum, 1978.

Ervin Staub, Daniel Bar-Tal, Jerzy Karylowski, and Janusz Reykowski, editors, *Development and Maintenance of Prosocial Behavior,* Plenum, 1984.

G. Stricker and R. Kiesner, editors, *The Implications of Nonclinical Research for Clinical Practice,* Plenum, 1985.

Karen Duffy, John Grosh, and Paul Olezak, editors, *Issues in Community Mediation,* Guilford, 1991.

Angelica Mucchi-Faina and Serge Moscorici, editors, *Minority Influence,* Nelson-Hall, in press.

OTHER

Author of scripts for training films for Virginia prison personnel. Editor of psychology series for Van Nostrand, 1977-78; series editor for Nelson-Hall, 1983—. Contributor of more than seventy articles to psychology journals. Associate editor, *Personality and Social Psychology Bulletin,* 1977-81; advisory editor, *Psychological Abstracts,* 1976-83; consulting editor, *Journal of Personality and Social Psychology,* 1977-81; member of editorial board, *Environmental Psychology and Nonverbal Behavior,* 1976-79, and *Basic and Applied Social Psychology,* 1983—.

SIDELIGHTS: Stephen Worchel told *CA:* "My major interest is in writing psychology books that illustrate the relevance of the field to the readers. As the world becomes increasingly complex, individuals experience greater difficulties in developing meaningful interpersonal relationships. The psychological study of human relations should provide some useful guidelines.

"I am also deeply concerned about the rifts caused by intergroup and international conflict. My writing and research is aimed at helping me better understand the causes of this conflict and how constructive solutions can be developed. In addition to writing, my academic interests include research and teaching in social and environmental psychology."

*　　*　　*

WRIGHT, Charles Alan 1927-

PERSONAL: Born September 3, 1927, in Philadelphia, PA; son of Charles A. (a public relations representative) and Helen (McCormack) Wright; married Mary Joan Herriott, July 8, 1950 (divorced, 1955); married Eleanor Custis Broyles, December 17, 1955; children: (first marriage) Charles Edward; (second marriage) Henrietta, Cecily; (stepchildren) Eleanor Clarke, Margot Clarke. *Edu-*

cation: Wesleyan University, A.B., 1947; Yale University, LL.B., 1949. *Politics:* Republican. *Religion:* Episcopalian.*Avocational interests:* Reading and reviewing mystery novels, fishing, railroads, coaching intramural football.

ADDRESSES: Home—5304 Western Hills Drive, Austin, TX 78731. *Office*—School of Law, The University of Texas at Austin, 727 East 26th Street, Austin, TX 78705.

CAREER: Admitted to the Bar of Minnesota, 1951, Texas, 1959, and the U.S. Supreme Court, 1957. University of Minnesota, Minneapolis, assistant professor, 1950-53, associate professor of law, 1953-55; University of Texas, Austin, associate professor, 1955-58, professor of law, 1958-65, Charles T. McCormick Professor of Law, 1965-80, William B. Bates Chair for the Administration of Justice, 1980—, Hayden W. Head Regents Chair, 1990-91. University of Pennsylvania, visiting professor, 1959-60; Harvard University, visiting professor, 1964-65; Yale University, visiting professor, 1968-69; Wolfson College (England), visiting fellow, 1984; Cambridge University, Arthur Goodhart Professor in Legal Science, 1990-91. Alabama Commission for Judicial Reform, consultant, 1955-56; Counsel for President of the United States, consultant, 1973; Supreme Court Historical Society Yearbook, member of board of editors, 1987—. Capitol Broadcasting Association, member of board of trustees, 1966—, chairman, 1969-90; Austin Symphony Orchestra Society, member of board of directors, 1966—, executive committee, 1966-70, 1972-83, 1986—; Austin Choral Union, member of board of trustees, 1984—; Commission on the Bicentennial of the United States Constitution, member, 1985—; Austin Lyric Opera, member of board of trustees, 1986—. St. Stephen's Episcopal School, member of board of trustees, 1962-66; St. Andrew's Episcopal School, member of board of trustees, 1971-74, 1977-80, 1981-84, chairman, 1973-74, 1979-80; Church of the Good Shepherd, member of vestry, 1970-74, 1981-84, senior warden, 1973-74; National Collegiate Athletic Association, member of committee on infractions, 1973-83, chairman, 1978-83, member of select committee on athletic problems and concerns in higher education, 1982-83.

MEMBER: American Bar Association, American Law Institute (council, 1969—; second vice-president 1987-88; first vice-president, 1988—), Institute of Judicial Administration, American Judiacure Society, American Bar Foundation (life fellow), Standing Committee on Rules of Practice and Procedure of the Judicial Conference of the United States, Fourth Circuit Judicial Conference, Philosophical Society of Texas, Austin Country Club, Barton Creek Country Club, Headliners Club, Metropolitan Club, Ridge Harbor Yacht Club, Tarry House, The Century Association, Yale Club of New York City.

AWARDS, HONORS: Student Bar Association Teaching Excellence Award, 1980; fellow, American Academy of Arts and Sciences, 1984; honorary fellow, Wolfson College (England), 1986; fellows research award, Fellows of the American Bar Foundation, 1989.

WRITINGS:

Wright's Minnesota Rules, Callaghan, 1954.
Cases on Remedies, West Publishing, 1955.
(Editor) Barron and Holtzoff, *Federal Practice and Procedures,* seven volumes, West Publishing, 1958-61.
(With C. T. McCormick and J. H. Chadbourn) *Cases on Federal Courts,* Foundation Press, 4th edition, 1962, 8th edition, 1988.
Handbook of the Law of Federal Courts, West Publishing, 1963, 4th edition, 1983.
(With H. M. Reasoner) *Procedure: The Handmaid of Justice,* West Publishing, 1965.
Federal Practice and Procedure, West Publishing, Volumes 1-3: *Criminal,* 1969, 2nd edition, 1982; (with A. R. Miller) Volumes 4-12: *Civil,* 1969-73, (with Miller and M. K. Kane), 2nd edition, 1983-90; (with Miller and E. H. Cooper) Volumes 13-20: *Jurisdiction,* 1975-82, 2nd edition, 1984-88; (with K. W. Graham and V. J. Gold) Volumes 21-24: *Evidence,* 1977-89; (with Gold) Volume 27: *Evidence,* 1990.
(With R. H. Field and P. J. Mishkin) *American Law Institute Study of the Division of Jurisdiction Between State and Federal Courts,* American Law Institute, 1969.
Ships, Footballs, and Other Diversions, privately printed, 1972.

*   *   *

WUNDER, John Remley 1945-

PERSONAL: Born January 7, 1945, in Vinton, IA; son of Arnold Henry and Mary (Remley) Wunder; married Susan Anderson (a teacher), September 6, 1969; children: Amanda Jaye, Nell Caroline. *Education:* University of Iowa, B.A., 1967, J.D. and M.A., both 1970; University of Washington, Seattle, Ph.D., 1974. *Politics:* Democrat.

ADDRESSES: Home—4208 65th St., Lubbock, TX 79413. *Office*—Department of History, Texas Tech University, Lubbock, TX 79409.

CAREER: University of Washington, Seattle, instructor in history, 1974; Lewis and Clark College, Portland, OR, visiting assistant professor of history, 1974; Case Western Reserve University, Cleveland, OH, assistant professor of history, 1974-78; Texas Tech University, Lubbock, associate professor of history and law, 1978—. Visiting associate professor at Columbia University, 1976.

WRITINGS:

Inferior Courts, Superior Justice: Justices of the Peace of the Northwest Frontier, 1853-1889, Greenwood Press, 1979.

(Editor) *At Home on the Range: Essays on the History of Western Social and Domestic Life,* Greenwood Press, 1985.

(Editor) *Working the Range: Essays on the History of Western Land Management and the Environment,* Greenwood Press, 1985.

(Editor) *Historian of the American Frontier: A Bio-Bibliographical Sourcebook,* Greenwood Press, 1988.

The Kiowa: Great Plains, Chelsea House, 1989.

WORK IN PROGRESS: Editing *Hopi: Contemporary Challenges,* with Edna Glenn; *No More Treaties: The Resolution of 1871.*

SIDELIGHTS: John Remley Wunder once told *CA:* "My recent research concerns American Indians and law in a historical perspective that will hopefully provide information for use in solving contemporary problems. The primary focus of my academic writing has been in the area of Western United States social legal history. My first book on justices of the peace in the Pacific Northwest concerned some basic questions: what was the quality of justice at the grassroots level on the American frontier, who were the justices of the peace, and how violent was the American frontier? My research led me to conclude that justices of the peace did dispense a relatively high quality of justice; that the economic and social elite held these desirable offices; and that because of these factors, violence on the American frontier, at least intracultural violence, was minimal. This research led me to consider intracultural legal themes, particularly in respect to the Chinese and Native American. I have written several articles on Chinese and American frontier law, and I am writing a book on the dissolution of the treaty-making power of the United States and American Indians and the jurisprudential impact this has had on these relationships.

"Contemporary Indian challenges are the subject of two edited collections as well as of my treaties research. Much of the challenge involves the vital question of sovereignty—who has it and how much. One of the most interesting and crucial developments for Native Americans today revolves around the American Indian Religious Freedom Act of 1978 and its implementation. This act in its interpretation could mean for Native Americans today what the Declaration of Independence meant to white Americas over two hundred years ago. Properly implemented, Indians will at last be free to control their own environment and their own lives—away from non-Indian interference. Let us hope that this curious melding of the First Amendment and Fourteenth Amendment will occur."

BIOGRAPHICAL/CRITICAL SOURCES:

PERIODICALS

American Historical Review, February, 1980.*

*　　　*　　　*

WYATT, Jane
See BRADBURY, Bianca (Ryley)

*　　　*　　　*

WYLIE, Francis E(rnest) 1905-
(Jeff Wylie)

PERSONAL: Born April 25, 1905, in Bloomfield, IN; son of William Henry (a clergyman) and Maude (Stout) Wylie; married Elizabeth Johnson, April 8, 1929; children: David A., Richard M. *Education:* Indiana University, A.B., 1928; also attended DePauw University, 1924-25, and University of Grenoble, 1926-27. *Politics:* Independent. *Religion:* Independent. *Avocational interests:* Natural history, conservation.

ADDRESSES: Home—2 Merrill St., Hingham, MA 02043. *Agent*—Boston Literary Agency, P.O. Box 1472, Manchester, MA 01944.

CAREER: Louisville Herald-Post, Louisville, KY, reporter and editor, 1928-36; *Louisville Courier-Journal,* Louisville, reporter and editor, 1937-44; Time, Inc., Boston, MA, chief of News Bureau, 1944-54; Massachusetts Institute of Technology, Cambridge, MA, director of public relations, 1955-70; Boston University, Boston, special assistant, 1971-72; Massachusetts Institute of Technology, consultant, 1973-74; writer, 1974—.

WRITINGS:

M.I.T. in Perspective, Little, Brown, 1976.

Tides and the Pull of the Moon, Stephen Greene Press, 1979.

Contributor to magazines and newspapers, sometimes under pseudonym Jeff Wylie. Member of editorial board of *Finance,* 1971-76.

WORK IN PROGRESS: The Old and New Colony, history of Boston's South Shore; research.

SIDELIGHTS: Francis E. Wylie told *CA,* "Given a choice, would writers rather have their words in cuneiform on clay tablets, readable after 5,000 years, or in hieroglyphs on stone, or on parchment, beautifully illuminated by medieval monks, or on high sulphite paper, which soon begins to crumble? Aside from the fact that everyone prefers to be alive and since few can hope for literary immortality, most of us are content with perishable pulp and, in a communications age, the opportunity to reach an audience."

*   *   *

WYLIE, Jeff
    See WYLIE, Francis E(rnest)

Y

YOUD, (Christopher) Samuel 1922-
(John Christopher, Hilary Ford, William Godfrey, Peter Graaf, Peter Nichols, Anthony Rye)

PERSONAL: Born April 16, 1922, in Knowsley, Lancashire, England; married Joyce Fairbairn, October 23, 1946 (marriage ended); married Jessica Valerie Ball, December 24, 1980; children: (first marriage) Nicholas, Rose, Elizabeth, Sheila, Margret. *Education:* Attended Peter Symonds School, Winchester, England. *Politics:* Tory Radical.

ADDRESSES: Home—One Whitefriars, Rye, East Sussex TN31 7LE, England; and c/o Society of Authors, 84 Drayton Gardens, London SW10 9SB, England.

CAREER: Free-lance writer, 1946-48; worked in and eventually headed the Industrial Diamond Information Bureau of the Diamond Corporation, 1949-58; full-time writer, 1958—. *Military service:* British Army, Royal Signals, 1941-46.

AWARDS, HONORS: Rockefeller Foundation grant, 1946-48; International Fantasy Award runner-up, 1957, for *The Death of Grass;* American Library Association Notable Book award, c. 1967, for *The White Mountains;* Guardian Award runner-up, 1969, George G. Stone Center for Children's Books Recognition of Merit Award, 1977, both for *The Tripods Trilogy;* Christopher Award, 1970, Guardian Award for children's fiction, 1971, both for *The Guardians;* German Children's Book Prize, 1976, for *Die Waechter* (German translation of *The Guardians*); Parents' Choice Award from Parents' Choice Foundation, 1983, for *New Found Land.*

WRITINGS:

ADULT NOVELS

The Winter Swan, Dobson, 1949.
Babel Itself, Cassell, 1951.
Brave Conquerors, Cassell, 1952.
Crown and Anchor, Cassell, 1953.
A Palace of Strangers, Cassell, 1954.
The Opportunist, Harper, 1955, published in England as *Holly Ash,* Cassell, 1955.
The Choice, Simon & Schuster, 1961, published in England as *The Burning Bird,* Longmans, Green, 1964.
Messages of Love, Simon & Schuster, 1961.
The Summers at Accorn, Longmans, Green, 1963.

UNDER PSEUDONYM JOHN CHRISTOPHER; FOR CHILDREN

The Tripods Trilogy, Macmillan, Book 1: *The White Mountains,* illustrated by John Raynes, 1967, Book 2: *The City of Gold and Lead,* 1967, Book 3: *The Pool of Fire,* 1968, all published in 2nd edition, Collier, 1988.
The Lotus Caves, Macmillan, 1969.
The Guardians, Macmillan, 1970.
The Sword Trilogy, Macmillan, Book 1: *The Prince in Waiting,* 1970, Book 2: *Beyond the Burning Lands,* 1971, Book 3: *The Sword of the Spirits,* 1972, all published in 2nd edition, Collier, 1989.
In the Beginning (structural readers edition; also see below), illustrated by Clyde Pearson, Longmans, Green, 1972.
Dom and Va (expanded from *In the Beginning*), Macmillan, 1973.
Wild Jack, Macmillan, 1974.
Empty World, Hamish Hamilton, 1977, Dutton, 1978.
The Fireball Trilogy, Dutton, Book 1: *Fireball,* 1981, Book 2: *New Found Land,* 1983, Book 3: *Dragon Dance,* 1986.

When the Tripods Came, Dutton, 1988.

The Twenty-second Century (short stories), Grayson, 1954, Lancer, 1962.

The Year of the Comet, M. Joseph, 1955, published as *Planet in Peril,* Avon, 1959.

No Blade of Grass, Simon & Schuster, 1956, published in England as *The Death of Grass,* M. Joseph, 1956.

The Caves of Night, Eyre & Spottiswoode, 1958, Simon & Schuster, 1959.

A Scent of White Poppies, Simon & Schuster, 1959.

The White Voyage, Simon & Schuster, 1960, published in England as *The Long Voyage,* Eyre & Spottiswoode, 1960.

The Long Winter, Simon & Schuster, 1962, published in England as *The World in Winter,* Eyre & Spottiswoode, 1962.

Sweeney's Island, Simon & Schuster, 1964, published in England as *Cloud on Silver,* Hodder & Stoughton, 1964.

The Possessors, Simon & Schuster, 1965.

A Wrinkle in the Skin, Hodder & Stoughton, 1965, published as *The Ragged Edge,* Simon & Schuster, 1966.

The Little People, Simon & Schuster, 1967.

Pendulum, Simon & Schuster, 1968.

Felix Walking (novel), Simon & Schuster, 1958.

Felix Running (novel), Eyre & Spottiswoode, 1959.

Bella on the Roof (novel), Longmans, Green, 1965.

A Figure in Grey (juvenile), World's Work, 1973.

Sarnia (novel), Doubleday, 1974.

Castle Malindine (novel), Hamish Hamilton, 1975, Harper, 1976.

A Bride for Bedivere (novel), Hamish Hamilton, 1976, Harper, 1977.

Malleson at Melbourne, Museum Press, 1956.

The Friendly Game, M. Joseph, 1957.

Give the Devil His Due, Mill, 1957, published in England as *Dust and the Curious Boy,* M. Joseph, 1957.

Daughter Fair, Ives Washburn, 1958.

The Sapphire Conference, Ives Washburn, 1959.

The Gull's Kiss, P. Davies, 1962.

Patchwork of Death (novel), Holt, 1965.

Giant's Arrow (novel), Gollancz, 1956, published under name Samuel Youd under same title, Simon & Schuster, 1960.

Contributor to various anthologies and of articles and short stories to periodicals, including *Astounding Stories, Esquire, Cricket, Playboy, Ellery Queen, New Worlds, Fantasy and Science Fiction, Galaxy,* and *Encounter.*

ADAPTATIONS: No Blade of Grass was made into a film produced and directed by Cornell Wilde, c. 1970; *The Tripods Trilogy* was made into two television series produced by Richard Bates and broadcast by the British Broadcasting Corp. and the Public Broadcasting Service; *The Caves of Night* has been made into a film by Wilde; *The Guardians* (a six-part serial) and *Empty World* (a ninety minute teleplay) have been adapted for German television. Many of Youd's books have been published in Braille and as talking books.

SIDELIGHTS: An author of novels for both children and adults under several pseudonyms, Samuel Youd has been most highly acclaimed for the science fiction novels he has written under the pseudonym John Christopher. Among these are three trilogies for children, *The Tripods Trilogy, The Sword Trilogy,* and *The Fireball Trilogy,* the award-winning *The Guardians,* and a book for adults, *No Blade of Grass,* which was runner-up for the International Fantasy Award behind J. R. R. Tolkien's *The Lord of the Rings.* Although many of his books are set in the future, Youd tells *Children's Literature in Education* interviewer John Gough, "I don't now like being classified as a science fiction writer because I regard science fiction as having strayed from extrapolation into error: there seems to me no credible means of exploring beyond the solar system; and the solar system, of course, we now know to be barren and uninteresting." The author's books instead reveal an interest in the past, the future societies he portrays often resembling those of medieval times; he is also more concerned with characterization than with speculations about the future.

"I have been involved with writing since my early teens, in the thirties," Youd writes in his *Something about the Author Autobiography* (*SAAS*) entry. "Prior to [World War II], I published an amateur magazine (*The Fantast*) and wrote pieces—verse, articles, fiction—for it and similar magazines. In the first winter of the war I had my first short story published professionally, in *Lilliput,* and wrote part of a novel, fairly heavily derived from the fiction of Aldous Huxley which I then intensely admired." He later submitted his unfinished novel for consideration for the Atlantic Awards in Literature, funded by the Rockefeller

Foundation, hoping to win a grant worth 250 pounds. But the award committee asked Youd if he could submit something that he had written more recently; so the author sent them the first chapters of what would later become *The Winter Swan* and won the grant.

From that point on, Youd considered himself a serious writer. Finding a steady job to support himself, he began writing short stories for science fiction magazines like *Galaxy* and *Astounding*. He wrote his science fiction stories under a pseudonym so that he could associate his real name with his other novels. With the 1950s came the "Golden Age of Science Fiction," an opportune time for Youd to come out with his story collection, *The Twenty-second Century*. This book later led to the novel *The Year of the Comet,* which was based on some of the ideas in his short stories.

By this time Youd had become a father. His growing family, he realized, could not be adequately supported by a job that he says in *SAAS* was "poorly paid and had no prospects." So the author "began to write with increasing urgency, working in the evenings and through weekends." He wrote everything from science fiction to comedies to thrillers to mainstream novels, "using a different pen name for each genre, regarding it as only fair that a reader should know what he might reasonably expect under a particular label." His first great success came with the publication of *No Blade of Grass,* which was later bought for movie production by Metro-Goldwyn-Mayer. From then until the late 1960s, Youd wrote science fiction and mainstream novels. "This was the point at which another publisher suggested I try my hand at writing for children. What he wanted was science fiction, on which the small reputation I possessed was founded. But during the preceding years I had tired of this . . . : the past interested me more. I wondered if it might be possible to blend his requirement with my inclination."

Youd came up with the idea of writing about a future world in which society had become as primitive as that of the Middle Ages after some great calamity. The calamity he chose for *The Tripods Trilogy,* which includes *The White Mountains, The City of Gold and Lead, The Pool of Fire,* and a more recent sequel, *When the Tripods Came,* was the staple science fiction idea of an alien invasion in which the aliens take control of the human race by controlling people's minds. To keep humans even more firmly under their control, the aliens impose on their subjects a feudal system modelled after medieval Europe. In Youd's other trilogies—*The Sword Trilogy,* which includes *The Prince in Waiting, Beyond the Burning Lands,* and *The Sword of the Spirits,* and *The Fireball Trilogy,* which includes *Fireball, New Found Land,* and *Dragon Dance*—the author uses similar settings that resemble the past. Natural disasters cause society to regress into the Dark

Ages in *The Sword Trilogy,* while in *The Fireball Trilogy* Youd uses the device of a parallel reality to take his characters to a world where the Roman Empire rules Europe, Aztecs have extended their rule into North America, and China is ruled by warlords and a form of magic.

A recurring theme in several of Youd's novels is, as John Rowe Townsend puts it in his *A Sense of Story: Essays on Contemporary Writers for Children,* "the question of freedom and authority: painful freedom and comfortable submission to authority." In *The Tripods Trilogy,* for example, while people are made servants of the aliens, "it is a happy servitude," according to Hugh Crago and Maureen Crago in *Children's Book Review.* "The struggle for freedom succeeds, but the new world government breaks down in its own inner conflicts." Similarly, the alien plant that takes control of a moon colony in *The Lotus Caves* and the aliens in *The Guardians*—who take over the Earth with a form of surgical mind control similar to that in *The Tripods Trilogy*—also offer an easy, subservient way of life. Yet Youd's characters struggle to win their freedom even if it means loss of security. About this theme Youd tells Gough that "freedom of thought is perhaps the greatest good, and needs to be fought for and sacrificed for. I suppose it's something of a reverse of the conventional Eden story: the apple which tempts my characters is one that will remove the knowledge of good and evil. As to free will versus determinism, . . . I have an instinctive belief in free will probably because I feel that a life excluding that belief would not be worth living."

Some critics of Youd's writing have become frustrated with his science fiction stories because they do not emphasize science and technology very much. The author recalls in his *SAAS* essay how the television adaptation of his *Tripods* trilogy was criticized by respected science fiction writer Brian Aldiss: "He was scathing of what he termed 'backwards looking science fiction,' and especially scathing about the Tripods themselves. 'They don't even,' he observed with crushing contempt, 'have infra-red. . . .' (This, incidentally, is an interesting example of the way in which science fiction's preoccupation with technology builds in obsolescence: infra-red vision is an accepted part of the scene today, but was not when I wrote the books in the sixties.)" Youd agrees that speculating about advanced technology is not one of his main considerations. "I am more concerned with what happens inside the individual than what happens to society as a whole," he states.

Over the years, Youd has has published more than fifty adult and children's books. Of his stories for the young, he says in Townsend's book: "What I have learned is that writing for children is at least as exacting and concentration-demanding as writing for adults. But one can add another word: stimulating. It is the form of writing which I can now least imagine giving up."

BIOGRAPHICAL/CRITICAL SOURCES:

BOOKS

Amis, Kingsley, *New Maps of Hell: A Survey of Science Fiction,* Harcourt, 1960.

Arbuthnot, May Hill, and Zena Sutherland, *Children and Books,* 4th edition, Scott, Foresman, 1972, p. 260.

Children's Literature Review, Volume 2, Gale, 1976.

Crouch, Marcus, *The Nesbit Tradition: The Children's Novel in England, 1945-1970,* Benn, 1972, pp. 51-52.

Fisher, Margery, *Who's Who in Children's Books: A Treasury of the Familiar Characters of Childhood,* Holt, 1975, pp. 306, 309.

Moskowitz, Samuel, *Seekers of Tomorrow: Masters of Modern Science Fiction,* World Publishing, 1966.

Something about the Author Autobiography Series, Volume 6, Gale, 1988, pp. 297-312.

Townsend, John Rowe, *A Sense of Story: Essays on Contemporary Writers for Children,* Lippincott, 1971, pp. 48-55.

Townsend, John Rowe, *Written for Children: An Outline of English-Language Children's Literature,* Lippincott, 1974, pp. 215-216.

PERIODICALS

Books and Bookmen, February, 1965.
Books for Keeps, July, 1981, pp. 14-15.
Bulletin of the Center for Children's Books, December, 1967, p. 57; February, 1972, p. 88; July/August, 1973, p. 168; May, 1986.
Chicago Tribune, July 1, 1962.
Children's Book Review, February, 1971, pp. 18-19; June, 1971, pp. 77-79; September, 1971, pp. 122-123; September, 1972, p. 113; December, 1973, pp. 176-177; winter, 1974-75, p. 150.
Children's Literature in Education, summer, 1984, pp. 93-102.
Christian Science Monitor, November 7, 1968.
Fantastic Universe, June, 1958.
Horn Book, December, 1969, pp. 673, 675; December, 1971, p. 619; August, 1974, p. 375.
Junior Bookshelf, February, 1968, p. 59; February, 1971, pp. 51-52; December, 1973, p. 402; February, 1975, p. 58.
Kirkus Reviews, March 15, 1973, p. 324; August 1, 1974, pp. 803-804.
Saturday Evening Post, April 27, 1957.
School Librarian, June, 1971, p. 155.
School Library Journal, September, 1968, p. 131.
Signal, January, 1971, pp. 18-23.
Space Voyager, June-July, 1984, pp. 52-54.
Times (London), May 25, 1967.
Times Literary Supplement, April 16, 1970, p. 417; December 11, 1970, p. 1460; July 2, 1971, p. 767.
The Writer, June, 1966; November, 1968.

—*Sketch by Kevin S. Hile*

Z

ZALEZNIK, Abraham 1924-

PERSONAL: Born January 30, 1924, in Philadelphia, PA; married wife Elizabeth (a director of special education); children: Dori, Ira. *Education:* Alma College, A.B., 1945; Harvard University, M.B.A., 1947, D.C.S., 1951; postdoctoral study at Boston Psychoanalytic Society and Institute, 1960-65.

ADDRESSES: Home—151 Follen Rd., Lexington, MA 02173. *Office*—Harvard Business School, Harvard University, Soldiers Field, Boston, MA 02163.

CAREER: Harvard University, Harvard Business School, Boston, MA, instructor, 1948-51, assistant professor, 1951-56, associate professor, 1956-61, professor, 1961-67, Cahners-Rabb Professor of social psychology of management, 1967—. Director of Purity Supreme Supermarkets, Park Electrochemical Corp., Madico Inc., Evans Products Co., Pueblo International, Inc., Gaulin Corp. Trustee, Beth Israel Hospital, Boston. *Military service:* U.S. Navy, 1942-46.

MEMBER: American Psychoanalytic Association, American Sociological Society, Boston Psychoanalytic Society and Institute.

WRITINGS:

(With David Moment) *The Dynamics of Interpersonal Behavior,* Wiley, 1964.
(With R. C. Hodgson and D. J. Levinson) *The Executive Role Constellation,* Division of Research, Harvard Business School, 1965.
Human Dilemmas of Leadership, Harper, 1966.
(With G. Dalton and L. B. Barnes) *The Distribution of Authority in Formal Organizations,* Division of Research, Harvard Business School, 1968.
(With others) *Orientation and Conflict in Career,* Harvard Business School, 1970.

(With Manfred F. R. Kets de Vries) *Power and the Corporate Mind,* Houghton, 1975.
The Managerial Mystique, Edward Burlingame/Harper, 1989.

Contributor of articles to *Harvard Business Review, Behavioral Science, Bulletin of the Menninger Clinic,* and other journals in his field.

WORK IN PROGRESS: Communicating with Business Audiences; research on decision-making and the psychology of the self, on organizations in crisis, and on psychic disequilibria and social change.

BIOGRAPHICAL/CRITICAL SOURCES:

PERIODICALS

New York Times Books Review, June 18, 1989; May 20, 1990.*

*   *   *

ZARETSKY, Eli 1940-

PERSONAL: Born February 29, 1940, in Brooklyn, NY; son of David (a hairdresser) and Pauline (Silverman) Zaretsky; divorced; children: Natasha. *Education:* University of Michigan, B.A., 1960; Brooklyn College of the City University of New York, M.A., 1963; University of Maryland, Ph.D., 1978.

ADDRESSES: Home—279 Mangels St., San Francisco, CA 94131. *Office*—2728 Durant, Berkeley, CA 94704.

CAREER: Wells College, Aurora, NY, instructor in history, 1967-69; *Socialist Review,* Oakland, CA, managing editor, 1969-76; San Francisco State University, San Francisco, CA, instructor in history, 1978; Duke University, Durham, NC, fellow of Institute for the Study of the Family and the State, Institute for Policy Sciences, 1978—. Instructor at the Pentagon, summer, 1967, Andrews Air Force Base, summer, 1968, and University of California, Berkeley, 1973-74; lecturer at various colleges and universities.

AWARDS, HONORS: Committee for Research on Women (fellow), American Council of Learned Societies (fellow), National Endowment for the Humanities grant.

WRITINGS:

Capitalism, the Family, and Personal Life, Harper, 1976, revised edition, 1986.
(Editor) *The Polish Peasant in Europe and America,* University of Illinois, 1984.

Contributor of more than forty articles and translations to magazines, including *Insurgent Sociologist, New Left Review,* and *Journal of Psychohistory.* Associate editor of *Psychohistory Review.*

WORK IN PROGRESS: A history of psychoanalysis; a book on the state and the family.*

*   *   *

ZAYAS-BAZAN, Eduardo 1935-

PERSONAL: Born November 17, 1935, in Camaguey, Cuba; son of Manuel Eduardo (a longshoreman) and Aida Loret de Mola de Zayas-Bazan; married Elena Pedroso (a teacher), December 12, 1959; children: Eddy, Elena. *Education:* Attended University of Havana, 1953-56; Universidad Nacional Jose Marti, J.D., 1958; Kansas State Teachers College, M.S., 1966. *Religion:* Roman Catholic.

ADDRESSES: Home—1419 Meadowbrook Dr., Johnson City, TN 37601. *Office*—Department of Foreign Languages, East Tennessee State University, Johnson City, TN 37601.

CAREER: Swimming instructor in Camaguey, Cuba, 1958-59; insurance broker and attorney in Camaguey, 1959-60; prisoner in Cuba, 1961-62; U.S. Cuban Refugee Assistance Program, Miami, FL, social worker, 1962-64; high school Spanish teacher in Plattsmouth, NE, 1964-65, and Topeka, KS, 1965-66; Appalachian State University, Boone, NC, instructor in Spanish, 1966-68; East Tennessee State University, Johnson City, assistant professor, 1968-73, associate professor of Spanish and chairman of department of languages, 1973-79, chairman of department of foreign languages, 1979—, director of three summer-abroad programs in Spain and Mexico. President of Sister Cities International, Johnson City, 1972-77.

MEMBER: American Association of Teachers of Spanish and Portuguese, Association of Departments of Foreign Languages, Modern Language Association, Tennessee Foreign Language Teaching Association, Tennessee Foreign Language Teaching Association (president, 1980-81), Sigma Delta Pi.

AWARDS, HONORS: East Tennessee State University Distinguished Faculty Award, 1978.

WRITINGS:

(Editor with Anthony G. Lozano) *Del amor a la revolucion: An Intermediate Spanish American Reader* (title means "From Love to Revolution"), Norton, 1975.
(Editor with M. Laurentino Suarez) *Selected Proceedings of the 27th Annual Mountain Interstate Foreign Language Conference,* Research Council of East Tennessee State University, 1978.
(Editor with Laurentino Suarez) *De aqui y de alla: Estampas del mundo Hispanico* (title means "From Here and There"), Heath, 1980.
(Translator) *Secret Report on Cuban Revolution,* Transaction, 1981.
(With Gaston J. Fernandez) *Que me Cuenta: Temas de hoy de Siempre,* Heath, 1983.
(With Fernandez) *Asi Somos,* Heath, 1990.

Also translator of *On Divine Predicates,* Kazi Publications. Contributor to *Hispania, Paris Review, Fitzgerald-Hemingway Annual,* and *Tennessee Teacher.*

WORK IN PROGRESS: A historical novel on Cuba.

*   *   *

ZEITLIN, Irving M. 1928-

PERSONAL: Born October 19, 1928, in Detroit, MI; son of Albert and Rose Zeitlin; married Esther Ann Levine (an artist), August 15, 1950; children: Ruth, Michael, Beth, Jeremy. *Education:* Wayne State University, B.A., 1958, M.A., 1961; Princeton University, M.A., 1963, Ph.D., 1964.

ADDRESSES: Home—439 Sumach St., Toronto, Ontario, Canada. *Office*—Department of Sociology, University of Toronto, Toronto, Ontario Canada M5T 1PG.

CAREER: Indiana University, Bloomington, IN, assistant professor, 1965-68, associate professor of sociology, 1968-70; Washington University, St. Louis, MO, professor of sociology, 1970-72, chairman of department, 1971-72; University of Toronto, Toronto, Ontario, professor of sociology and chairman of department, 1972—.

MEMBER: American Sociological Association, Canadian Sociology and Anthropology Association.

AWARDS, HONORS: National Science Foundation postdoctoral fellow, 1964-65.

WRITINGS:

Marxism: A Re-Examination, Van Nostrand, 1967.

Ideology and the Development of Sociological Theory, Prentice-Hall, 1968, 4th edition, 1990.

Liberty, Equality, and Revolution in Alexis de Tocqueville, Little, Brown, 1971.

Capitalism and Imperialism: An Introduction to Neo-Marxian Concepts, Markham, 1972.

Rethinking Sociology: A Critique of Contemporary Theory, Prentice-Hall, 1973.

The Social Condition of Humanity, Oxford University Press, 1981, 2nd edition, 1984, new edition with R. J. Brym, (Canada), 1991.

Ancient Judaism: Biblical Criticism from Max Weber to the Present, Basil Blackwell, 1985.

Jesus and the Judaism of His Time, Basil Blackwell/Polity Press, 1989.

Plato's Vision, Prentice-Hall/Simon & Schuster, in press.

Contributor to *Journal of World History, Cahiers de l'Isea,* and other journals.

*   *   *

ZERBE, Jerome (B.) 1904-1988

PERSONAL: Born July 24, 1904, in Euclid, OH; died after a long illness, August 19, 1988, in New York City; son of Jerome Brainard (president of Ohio & Pennsylvania Coal Co.) and Susan (Eichelberger) Zerbe. *Education:* Yale University, Ph.B., 1928; studied portrait painting in Paris, France, 1928-31.

CAREER: Art editor of *Parade* (a weekly), Cleveland, OH, 1931-33; moved on to New York and invented a job for himself—the society photographer specializing in the personal candid camera; *Town and Country,* New York City, photographer, 1933-88, society editor, 1949-74; feature writer for *Sunday Mirror,* 1945-58. Publicist in his early days in New York City for the Rainbow Room and later, for another fashionable haunt, El Morocco; host at the Brazillian Pavillion at the New York World's Fair, 1939, and the Italian Pavillion, 1940 (departed when Italy declared war on France but hosted a party at his apartment for all the waiters and their wives to show personal friendliness); sometime columnist for *New York Journal American;* weekly columnist for *San Francisco Chronicle* and, in season, for *Palm Beach Illustrated,* 1967-88. Appeared in the film *House of the Seven Gables,* 1968-1970. Photographs displayed in several showings, 1926 and 1929. *Military service:* U.S. Naval Reserve, chief photographer's mate, 1942-45; served on Admiral Nimitz's staff in Honolulu and Guam, on Vice Admiral McCain's staff in the China Sea and off the Philippines, and aboard the

"U.S.S. Essex" during the first Tokyo strike and two Iwo Jima landings; landed on Okinawa and Japan with with Marine forces; received Bronze Star, and Presidential Unit and Navy Unit citations.

WRITINGS:

People on Parade (photo book), introduction by Lucius Beebe, Kemp, 1934.

El Morocco's Family Album (photo book), introduction by Beebe, privately printed, 1937.

Les Pavillons (photo book), text by Cyril Connolly, Macmillan, 1962.

The Art of Social Climbing, Doubleday, 1965.

Happy Times (photos of celebrities), text by Brendan Gill, Harcourt, 1973.

Pavilions of Europe, Walker & Co., 1976.

Small Castles and Pavilions of Europe, Walker & Co., 1976.

Photographs have appeared in other books, including cookbooks, and in national magazines.

SIDELIGHTS: Jerome Zerbe's first pavilion photo book was the result, he said, of "a long time dream of my youth to do a book on those enchanting little mansions de plaisance in and around Paris." Zerbe never married, was devoted to his neices and nephews, and entertained frequently. His photos of celebrities enjoying New York City nightlife helped to make the El Morocco nightclub one of the best-known clubs in the world. Though he liked to capture famous figures in casual moments, they appreciated that he refrained from publishing indiscreet or unflattering portraits.

During World War II he trained in Washington, D.C., which he called a "ghastly place," and then was sent to San Francisco, which he called "sheer heaven, without a cent." As chief photographer's mate in the U.S. Navy and later as Admiral Nimitz's personal photographer, he chronicled the defeat of Japan. One of his favorite photographs was a candid shot he took of General Wainwright shortly after the landings in Japan. He recalled that the General was only a few hours from the concentration camp: "Oh, how he savored the drink made for him!"

OBITUARIES:

PERIODICALS

Chicago Tribune, August 25, 1988.
New York Times, August 23, 1988.*

*   *   *

ZIMMERMAN, Joseph Francis 1928-

PERSONAL: Born June 29, 1928, in Keene, NH; son of John Joseph (a sporting goods dealer) and May (Gallagher) Zimmerman; married Margaret B. Brennan, August 2, 1958; children: Deirdre Ann. *Education:* University of New Hampshire, B.A., 1950; Syracuse University, M.A., 1951, Ph.D., 1954. *Politics:* Independent. *Religion:* Roman Catholic.

ADDRESSES: Home—82 Greenock Rd., Delmar, NY 12054. *Office*—Graduate School of Public Affairs, State University of New York, Albany, NY 12222.

CAREER: Worcester Polytechnic Institute, Worcester, MA, instructor, 1954-55, assistant professor, 1955-57, associate professor, 1957-62, professor of government, 1962-65; State University of New York at Albany, Graduate School of Public Affairs, professor of political science, 1965—, chairman of department of political science, 1973-74, director of Local Government Studies Center, 1965-68. Lecturer in government, Clark University, Worcester, 1956-65. Staff director, New York State Joint Legislative Committee on Mass Transportation, 1967-68; research director, New York State Joint Legislative Committee on Transportation, 1968-73, New York State Select Legislative Committee on Transportation, 1974-76, New York State Senate Committee on Transportation, 1976-82, and Legislative Commission on Critical Transportation Problems, 1982—. Corporator, Visiting Nurse Association, 1960-65; director, Lincoln Neighborhood Center, 1960-65; chairman, Albany County Citizens Charter Commission, 1976-78. Consultant, Massachusetts Department of Commerce, Massachusetts Commission on Atomic Energy, United States Railway Association, city of Houston, New York State Association of Towns, and others. *Military service:* U.S. Air Force, 1951-53; became first lieutenant.

MEMBER: American Political Science Association, Academy of Political Science, National Municipal League, American Academy of Political and Social Science, American Society for Public Administration, Public Personnel Association, American Planning and Civic Association, New England Political Science Association, Worcester Association of Historians and Political Scientists.

AWARDS, HONORS: Choice award, American Association of Research and University Libraries, 1984, for *State-Local Relations: A Partnership Approach.*

WRITINGS:

State and Local Government, Barnes & Noble, 1962, 3rd edition, 1978.

Readings in State and Local Government, Holt, 1964.

(Contributing editor) *Dictionary of Political Science,* Philosophical Library, 1964.

The Massachusetts Town Meeting: A Tenacious Institution, State University of New York at Albany, 1967.

(Editor) *Government of the Metropolis,* Holt, 1968.

Subnational Politics, Holt, 1970.

The Federated City: Community Control in Large Cities, St. Martin's, 1972.

Pragmatic Federalism: The Reassignment of Functional Responsibility, U.S. Advisory Commission on Intergovernmental Relations, 1976.

(With Frank W. Prescott) *The Politics of the Veto of Legislation in New York,* University Press of America, 1980.

The Government and Politics of New York State, New York University Press, 1981.

Measuring Local Discretionary Authority, Advisory Commission on Intergovernmental Relations, 1981.

(With daughter, Deirdre A. Zimmerman) *The Politics of Subnational Governance,* University Press of America, 1983, 2nd edition, 1991.

State-Local Relations: A Partnership Approach, Praeger, 1983.

Participatory Democracy: Populism Revived, Praeger, 1986.

Federal Preemption: The Silent Revolution, Iowa State University Press, 1991.

(With Wilma Rule) *United States Electoral Systems: Their Impact on Women and Minorities,* Greenwood Press, 1992.

Contemporary American Federalism: The Growth of National Power, Leicester University Press, 1992.

Contributor to books, including *Encyclopedia Britannica.* Also contributor of articles to educational, civic, and finance journals and to *Worcester Telegram.* Editor, *Metropolitan Area Annual, Metropolitan Area Digest, Metropolitan Surveys,* and *Metropolitan Viewpoints,* 1965-68.